Exploring American Histories

VALUE EDITION

D1571888

VALUE EDITION

Exploring American Histories

A SURVEY

Fourth Edition

Nancy A. Hewitt
Rutgers University

Steven F. Lawson
Rutgers University

bedford/st.martin's
Macmillan Learning

Boston | New York

To Mary and Charles Takacs, Florence and Hiram Hewitt, Sarah and Abraham Parker, Lena and Ben Lawson, Irene and Robert Hewitt, and Ceil and Murray Lawson who made our American Histories possible.

Vice President: Leasa Burton
Program Director: Erika Gutierrez
Senior Program Manager: William J. Lombardo;
Director of Content Development: Jane Knetzger
Senior Development Editor: Leah R. Strauss
Assistant Editor: Julia Bell
Director of Media Editorial: Adam Whitehurst
Media Editor: Mollie Chandler
Marketing Manager: Melissa Rodriguez
Senior Director, Content Management Enhancement: Tracey Kuehn
Senior Managing Editor: Michael Granger
Executive Content Project Manager: Gregory Erb
Assistant Content Project Manager: Esther Saks
Workflow Project Manager: Lisa McDowell
Production Supervisors: Robin Besofsky, Robert Cherry
Director of Design, Content Management: Diana Blume
Interior Design: Jerilyn DiCarlo
Cover Design: William Boardman
Cartographer: Mapping Specialists, Ltd.
Text Permissions Editor: Michael McCarty
Text Permissions Researcher: Elaine Kosta, Lumina Datamatics
Photo Permissions Editor: Christine Buese
Photo Researcher: Naomi Kornhauser, Cheryl DuBois, Lumina Datamatics
Director of Digital Production: Keri deManigold
Media Project Manager: Michelle Camisa
Editorial Services: Lumina Datamatics, Inc.
Copyeditor: Harold Johnson
Indexer: Michael Ferreira
Composition: Lumina Datamatics, Inc.
Cover Art: Private Collection, Waterhouse & Dodd, London, UK/Bridgeman Images
Printing and Binding: LSC Communications

Library of Congress Control Number: 2021930839

ISBN: 978-1-319-24450-7 (Combined Edition)
ISBN: 978-1-319-33130-6 (Volume 1)
ISBN: 978-1-319-33133-7 (Volume 2)

Printed in the United States of America.
1 2 3 4 5 6   26 25 24 23 22 21

ACKNOWLEDGMENTS
Acknowledgments and copyrights appear on the same page as the text and art selections they cover; these acknowledgments and copyrights constitute an extension of the copyright page.

For information, write: Bedford/St. Martin's, 75 Arlington Street, Boston, MA 02116

Preface

We are delighted to publish the fourth edition of *Exploring American Histories,* Value Edition. This Value Edition offers the unabridged narrative of the comprehensive edition with its signature emphasis on the diverse histories of the United States in a two-color, trade-sized format. With each edition, our central focus has been to provide a U.S. history survey text that represents a rich assortment of American perspectives. The new edition is available now for the first time in **Achieve**, Macmillan Learning's innovative new learning platform. Whenever an instructor assigns **Achieve**, students have access to all the resources of the comprehensive text (*Exploring American Histories: A Survey with Sources*), including its special features and its primary and secondary sources.

Engage Your Students with Achieve

Exploring American Histories, Fourth Edition, is available in a variety of print and digital formats, with Achieve offering the greatest value. Built with instructors and students in mind, **Achieve** includes the full-color e-book of the comprehensive version (*Exploring American Histories: A Survey with Sources*), gradebook, **Learning-Curve** adaptive quizzing, assessment tools, insights and reporting, and integration options. Whenever an instructor assigns **Achieve** (with the option of bundling the print book at a low cost), students have access to all the resources of *Exploring American Histories: A Survey with Sources*, including its unique collection of source features that appear in every chapter.

 The Right Balance between Narrative and Primary Sources. Inspired by our own teaching, we wanted to create a textbook that would provide everything we would want to use in class, in one place. Many texts include some primary sources, but we found the balance between narrative (too much) and primary sources (too few) didn't suit our courses. We crafted the narrative to make room to include more primary sources and integrate them to help students make the necessary connections that spur them to think critically. *Exploring American Histories* is comprehensive in the essentials of American history, but with a carefully selected amount of detail that is more in tune with what instructors can realistically expect their students to comprehend. Achieve for *Exploring American Histories* offers a format which provides just the right balance between narrative and primary sources, along with consistent pedagogy that helps students analyze primary-source material.

 Building-Blocks Approach to Analyzing Sources. We know that students in the introductory survey course often need help in developing the ability to think critically about primary sources. In the fourth edition, we continue to promote historical thinking skills by providing a consistent pedagogical framework for analyzing sources. In each chapter in Achieve, our building-blocks approach ensures that students can progress from working with a single source (Guided Primary Source Analysis), to comparing paired sources (Comparative Primary Source Analysis), to tackling a set of sources from varied perspectives (Primary Source Project). In this way, students can increase their confidence and skills in analyzing primary sources. Students also have the chance to evaluate how historians use primary sources to construct their own interpretations (Comparative Secondary Source Analysis). In Achieve, each one of these features includes a short quiz as part of this wrap-around pedagogy.

Progression in Primary Source Work. Each chapter in Achieve contains seven to eight substantial, featured primary sources—both written and visual—with unique pedagogy aimed at helping students make connections between the sources and the text's major themes. Each source is clearly cross-referenced within the text so that students can connect the source to the narrative text. We also underscore the importance of primary sources by opening each chapter in Achieve with a **Window to the Past**—a facsimile of some portion of a primary source that appears in the chapter. To help students make connections between the narrative and sources, we embed **Explore** prompts at key junctures in the narrative that describe what the sources illuminate. Such integration is designed to help students make a firm connection between the narrative of history and the evidence upon which it is built.

- In Achieve, each chapter begins with a **Guided Primary Source Analysis** of a textual or visual source, with a headnote offering historical context and questions in the margins to help students consider a specific phrase or feature and analyze the source as a whole. These targeted questions are intended to guide students in reading and understanding a primary source. A **Put It in Context** question prompts students to consider the source in terms of the broad themes of the chapter. A multiple-choice quiz in Achieve for this and the following source features gauges students' understanding of the assignment.

- Next, each chapter in Achieve contains a **Comparative Primary Source Analysis**, a paired set of primary sources that show contrasting or complementary perspectives on a particular issue. This feature marks a step up in difficulty from the previous Guided Primary Source Analysis by asking students to analyze sources through their similarities and differences. These primary sources are introduced by a single headnote and are followed by **Interpret the Evidence** and **Put It in Context** questions that prompt students to analyze and compare the items and place them in a larger historical framework.

- At the end of every chapter in Achieve, a **Primary Source Project** provides the capstone of our integrated primary-sources approach. Each Primary Source Project brings together four or five sources focused on a critical issue central to that chapter. It is introduced by a brief overview and ends with **Interpret the Evidence** and **Put It in Context** questions that ask students to draw conclusions based on what they have learned in the chapter and read or seen in the sources.

An Introduction to Secondary Sources. In addition to the primary source features in each chapter, we extend the building-block approach by offering two scholars' perspectives on a significant topic related to the chapter. The **Comparative Secondary Source Analysis** feature in Achieve includes a brief introduction and **Examine the Sources** and **Put It in Context** questions, which ask students to compare two secondary sources and identify how they reflect the primary sources and narrative of the textbook. For example, for the early republic, chapter 7 provides selections on partisanship in the 1800 election by Eric Burns and John Ferling. Chapter 11, on the expansion of slavery, contrasts a view of enslaved family life offered by Robert Fogelman and Stanley Engerman with one by Deborah Gray White. With respect to the Progressive Era, chapter 19 offers divergent excerpts on reform in the South by C. Vann Woodward and Glenda Elizabeth Gilmore. Chapter 23 on World War II compares a selection on FDR and the Holocaust by David Wyman with that of Richard Breitman and Allan J. Lichtman. These selections demonstrate how historical scholarship, built upon the analysis of primary sources, can generate different interpretations of the same topic. They reinforce the idea that history changes over time, and help students to get a glimpse into the debates among historians.

Variety of Perspectives. We have selected sources that provide multiple perspectives on important issues, including both well-known sources and those that are less familiar. In all time periods, some groups of Americans are far better represented in primary sources than others. Those who were wealthy, well educated, and politically powerful, produced and preserved many primary sources about their lives, and their voices are well represented in this textbook. We have provided sources by Native Americans, enslaved Africans, free blacks, racial and ethnic minorities, immigrants, rural residents, working people, women, and young people. The lives of those who left few primary sources of their own can often be illuminated by carefully reading sources written by elites to see what information they yield about less well-documented groups. The questions that we ask about these sources are intended to help students read between the lines or see beyond the main image to uncover new meanings. Firsthand accounts include paintings, illustrations, sermons, speeches, letters, diaries, newspaper articles, political cartoons, advertisements, and photographs.

We challenge students to consider diverse viewpoints. For example, in chapter 5, students read contradictory testimony and examine an engraving to analyze the events that became known as the Boston Massacre. In chapter 12, they compare the views on the Fugitive Slave Law of a black abolitionist and the president of the United States. In chapter 18, students have to reconcile two very different views by a Chinese immigrant and a Supreme Court justice concerning the status of Chinese Americans in the late nineteenth century. In chapter 28, we ask readers to reconsider the depiction of the 1980s as a conservative decade in light of widespread protests challenging President Reagan's military build-up against the Soviet Union.

Comparing Biographies

We believe that the most appealing entry to the past starts with individuals and how people in their daily lives connect to larger political, economic, cultural, and international developments. Each chapter opens with **Comparing American Histories**, a pair of biographies that showcase individuals who experienced and influenced events in a particular period, and then returns to them throughout the chapter to strengthen the connections and highlight their place in the larger picture. These biographies cover both well-known Americans — such as Daniel Shays, Frederick Douglass, Andrew Carnegie, and Eleanor Roosevelt — and those who never gained fame or fortune — such as the Cherokee chief John Ross, activist Amy

Post, labor organizer Luisa Moreno, and World War II internee Fred Korematsu. Introducing such a broad range of biographical subjects illuminates the many ways that individuals shaped and were shaped by historical events. This strategy also makes visible throughout the text the intersections where history from the top down meets history from the bottom up, and the relationships between social and political histories and economic, cultural, and diplomatic developments.

New Content and Updates to the Narrative

We have engaged the most recent scholarship to ensure the most useful and accurate textbook. In addition to more expansive attention to regional, racial, and ethnic diversity, we have updated our approach to a number of other historical developments, such as systemic racism, pandemics, and the development of capitalist systems in various periods. We continue to pay significant attention to African Americans and women and to expand coverage on the histories of Native Americans, Mexican Americans, Latino Americans, and Asian Americans throughout the book in the narrative and sources.

Expanded Coverage of Diversity. We have made updates in each chapter, many of them focused on providing even greater representation of diverse peoples. In chapter 3, for example, the coverage of Native Americans has been amplified and more names of specific tribes are included to highlight the variety and number of Native American nations. Chapter 6 has been reorganized in order to expand coverage of multi-ethnic, multiracial forces fighting on both sides in the Revolution and to highlight the role and fate of various Native American nations. In chapter 9, there is a fuller discussion of Denmark Vesey and his planned rebellion, and more on anti-black violence in the North. Chapter 10 has been revised to highlight more black people as pioneers of the Antislavery Movement, and the section on women's roles has been reorganized to emphasize black women and interracial efforts. Chapter 13 includes new material on Mexican Americans and Tejanos; enslaved blacks as contraband/refugees; and women as nurses, doctors and soldiers. Chapter 21 includes new coverage of the Tulsa Race Massacre of 1921; the Osage Indians in Oklahoma and the murders to steal their oil rights; and the League of United Latin American Citizens (LULAC), which formed in 1929. Chapter 25 includes coverage of an important case affecting Mexican Americans, *Hernandez v. Texas (1954);* and also new coverage on systemic racism in the North. Chapter 26 includes coverage of Mexican American activist, Rejes Tijerna, and also the 1968 Bilingual Education Act.

New Biographies. We have continued to diversify the biographies offered in the chapter-opening **Comparing American Histories.** Accordingly, in Volume 1 we introduce 4 new individuals. These include Powhatan, leader of the largest native confederacy in the mid-Atlantic region (chapter 2); Pontiac, head of a pan-tribal alliance to force the British out of their territory (chapter 5); Elizabeth (Mum Bett) Freeman, whose freedom suit contributed to Massachusetts ending slavery during the American Revolution (chapter 6); and José Antonio Menchaca, a Tejano military leader who fought for Texas independence (chapter 11). In Volume 2 we now include Pauli Murray, the African American civil rights activist and feminist (chapter 27); Demetria Martinez, the Mexican American writer and immigrant advocate (chapter 28); and Alicia Garza, the African American community organizer and co-founder of Black Lives Matter (chapter 29).

New Primary Source Projects. Volume 1 and Volume 2 each contain two new primary source projects in Achieve. Chapter 9 offers a project on Cherokee engagement with white society and the chapter 12 project now focuses on the debates over secession. Chapter 19 provides a project on women's suffrage and the ratification of the nineteenth amendment, and chapter 20 includes a project on the 1918 influenza pandemic

Adjustments to Chapter Organization. The major organizational change in Volume 1 is the movement of the secession debates and the beginning of the Civil War from chapter 13 to chapter 12. This allows for extended discussions in chapter 13 of American Indians, Mexican Americans, African Americans, and women during the Civil War, and of black refugees who used the chaos of war to claim their independence.

In Volume 2, we have added material on the extremely divisive 2020 presidential election and Joseph Biden's victory over Donald Trump in the final chapter. Chapter 29 covers the COVID-19 pandemic; the police killings of George Floyd and Breonna Taylor and the nationwide protests they inspired; the collapse of the U.S. economy caused by the pandemic; the January 6, 2021 insurrection at the Capitol; and the subsequent second impeachment of Trump. These events are still unfolding and we intend to provide a framework to help students understand these controversial issues as they evolve.

New Maps and Figures. In Volume 1, we added maps on tribal locations of native peoples at the time of European contact (chapter 1) and revised maps to clarify the role of Native Americans in the American Revolution (chapter 6). We also added a table on migration to the Americas that illustrates the movement of Europeans as well as the forced migration of Africans (chapter 4). In Volume 2, we have added a table on World War I casualties by country (chapter 20); a table on nuclear warheads in the United States, Soviet Union, and United Kingdom, 1945–1960 (chapter 24); a revised table on immigrant growth by home region, 1981–2010 (chapter 28); and a new map on U.S. intervention in Central America and the Caribbean, 1954–1989 (chapter 28). In Achieve, every chapter includes a Map Quiz related to one of the chapter maps that helps students build their geographic literacy skills. We have also changed about one-quarter of the illustrations from the previous edition.

Achieve: Helping Instructors Teach with Digital Resources

Exploring American Histories is now available for the first time in **Achieve**, Macmillan Learning's new complete course platform, which provides access to the narrative as well as a wealth of primary sources and other features, along with assessments and robust insights and reports at the ready, all in one accessible and affordably priced product. Achieve also includes a downloadable e-book for reading offline. Whenever an instructor assigns **Achieve**, students have access to all the resources of the comprehensive print text (*Exploring American Histories: A Survey with Sources*), including its special features and its primary and secondary sources.

Helping Students Understand the Narrative. Like the print book, each chapter in the **Achieve e-book** includes the following elements to help students make sense of their reading: **Learning Objectives** in the chapter openers prepare students to read the chapter with clear goals in mind; **chapter conclusions** summarize the chapters to help students identify main developments; **Review & Relate** questions help students focus on main themes and concepts presented in each major section of the chapter; **key terms** in boldface highlight important content. All terms are explained in the narrative as well as defined in a glossary at the end of the book; and the **Chapter Review** lets students review key terms, important concepts, and notable events.

Adaptive Learning with LearningCurve. Achieve offers access to **LearningCurve**, an online adaptive learning tool that helps students actively rehearse what they have read and achieve a deeper understanding and retention of the material. With this adaptive quizzing, students accumulate points toward a target score as they go, giving the interaction a game-like feel. Feedback for incorrect responses explains why the answer is incorrect and directs students back to the text to review before they attempt to answer the question again. The end result is a better understanding of the key elements of the text. Instructors who assign LearningCurve report that their students come to class prepared for discussion and enjoy using it. In addition, LearningCurve's reporting feature allows instructors to quickly diagnose which concepts students are struggling with so they can adjust lectures and activities accordingly.

Nurturing Skill Development. Further opportunities for skill development are available through the special activities provided in **Achieve**, many of which are available for the first time with the fourth edition of *Exploring American Histories*. These easy-to-use assignments include new **chronology exercises**, new **reflection activities** that invite students to reflect on what they have read in each chapter, **instructor activity guides** that instructors can use for either remote or in-person collaborative learning, **source and feature quizzes**, **research and writing tutorials with quizzes**, and more. Achieve is a rich asset for instructors who want to support students however they encounter them, whether teaching in a face-to-face, hybrid, or fully remote setting. *Exploring American Histories* combines an engaging narrative with a rich set of digital and print features available in Achieve that promote the comprehension of content, active learning, and skill development. (To learn more about the benefits of LearningCurve, Achieve, and the different versions to package with these digital tools, see the Versions and Supplements section on page xvii.)

Companion Primary Source Reader. For instructors who value even more options, a **companion primary source reader** is available in Achieve and as a printed text. **Thinking through Sources for Exploring American Histories in Achieve** provides an additional primary source project for each chapter along with activities. These activities supply self-graded exercises that help students not only understand the sources but also think critically about them. First, a short **quiz after each source** offers students the opportunity to check their understanding of materials that often derive from quite distant times and places. Some questions focus on audience, purpose, point of view, limitations, or context, while others challenge students to draw conclusions about the source or to compare one source with another. And a **Draw Conclusions from the Evidence activity** challenges students to assess whether a specific piece of evidence drawn from the sources supports or challenges a stated conclusion. Collectively these assignments create an active learning environment where reading with a purpose is reinforced by immediate feedback and support. This feedback for each rejoinder creates an active learning environment where students are rewarded for reaching the correct answer through their own process of investigation. **Achieve** is thus a rich asset for instructors who want to support students in all settings, from traditional lectures to "flipped" classrooms. *Exploring American Histories* seeks to promote active learning in various ways.

Teaching with Primary Sources. We understand that the instructor's role is crucial in teaching students how to analyze primary-source materials and develop interpretations. Instructors can use the primary sources available in Achieve in many different ways—as in-class discussion prompts, for take-home writing assignments, and as the basis for exam questions—and also in different combinations with primary sources throughout or across chapters being compared and contrasted with one another.

- **The Instructor's Manual.** The Instructor's Manual for *Exploring American Histories* (available in Achieve) provides a wealth of creative suggestions for using the primary source program effectively. We have written a section, entitled **"Teaching American Histories with Primary Sources,"** which provides ideas and resources for both new and experienced faculty. It offers basic guidelines for teaching students how to analyze sources critically and suggests ways to integrate selected primary sources into lectures, discussions, small group projects, and writing assignments. We also suggest ideas for linking in-text primary sources with the opening biographies, maps, and illustrations in a particular chapter and for using the **Primary Source Projects** to help students understand the entangled histories of the diverse groups that comprise North America and the United States. (See the Versions and Supplements section on page xvii for more information on all the available instructor resources.)

- **Guide to Analyzing Primary and Secondary Sources.** This checklist at the start of the Achieve e-book gives students a quick and efficient lesson on how to read and analyze sources and what kinds of questions to ask in understanding them. We know that many students find primary sources intimidating. Eighteenth and nineteenth century sources contain spellings and language often difficult for modern students to comprehend. Yet, students also have difficulty with contemporary primary sources because in the digital age of Facebook and Twitter they are exposed to information in tiny fragments and without proper verification. Thus, the checklist will guide students in how to approach sources from any era and what to look for in exploring them.

Acknowledgments

We wish to thank the talented scholars and teachers who were kind enough to give their time and knowledge to help us with our revision, as well as those who provided advice in preparation for previous editions. Historians who provided special insight for the fourth edition include the following:

Jonathan Atkins, *Berry College;* Joseph Cullon, *Worcester State University;* Nancy Duke, *Daytona State College;* Jared Eberle, *Oklahoma State University-Stillwater;* Gary Edwards, *Arkansas State University-Main Campus;* Keona Ervin, *University of Missouri-Columbia;* Gabrielle Everett, *Jefferson College;* Roger Flynn, *Anderson University;* Melissa Franson, *SUNY College at New Paltz;* Portia Hopkins, *Lee College;* Richard Hughes, *Illinois State*

University; Tracy K'Meyer, *University of Louisville;* Daniel Kotzin, *Medaille College;* Stephanie Laffer, *University of West Georgia;* Florence Lemoine, *Cosumnes River College;* Alexander Marriott, *Alvin Community College;* Jim McIntyre, *Moraine Valley Community College;* Robert Parkinson, *Binghamton University–SUNY;* Donald Seals, *Kilgore College;* Sean Trundle, *University of Nebraska-Lincoln;* Trey Welborn, *Georgia College & State University;* and Adrienne Winans, *Utah Valley University.*

We are also grateful to those who provided ideas and suggestions for previous editions:

Rob Alderson, *Perimeter College at Georgia State University;* Benjamin Allen, *South Texas College;* Daniel Allen, *Trinity Valley Community College;* Leann Almquist, *Middle Georgia State University;* Christine Anderson, *Xavier University;* Uzoamaka Melissa C. Anyiwo, *Curry College;* Rebecca Arnfeld, *California State University, Sacramento;* David Arnold, *Columbia Basin College;* Brian Alnutt, *Northampton Community College;* Anthony A. Ball, *Housatonic Community College;* Terry A. Barnhart, *Eastern Illinois University;* John Belohlavek, *University of South Florida;* Edwin Benson, *North Harford High School;* Paul Berk, *Christian Brothers University;* Deborah L. Blackwell, *Texas A&M International University;* Jeff Bloodworth, *Gannon University;* Carl Bon Tempo, *University at Albany–SUNY;* Thomas Born, *Blinn College;* Margaret Bramlett, *St. Andrews Episcopal High School;* Martha Jane Brazy, *University of South Alabama;* Lauren K. Bristow, *Collin College;* Tsekani Browne, *Duquesne University;* Jon L. Brudvig, *Dickinson State University;* Richard Buckelew, *Bethune-Cookman University;* Timothy Buckner, *Troy University;* Dave Bush, *Shasta College;* Monica Butler, *Seminole State College of Florida;* Barbara Calluori, *Montclair State University;* Julia Schiavone Camacho, *The University of Texas at El Paso;* Jacqueline Campbell, *Francis Marion University;* Amy Canfield, *Lewis-Clark State College;* Michael Cangemi, *Binghamton University;* Roger Carpenter, *University of Louisiana, Monroe;* Dominic Carrillo, *Grossmont College;* Mark R. Cheathem, *Cumberland University;* Keith Chu, *Bergen Community College;* Laurel A. Clark, *University of Hartford;* Myles L. Clowers, *San Diego City College;* Remalian Cocar, *Georgia Gwinnett College;* Lori Coleman, *Tunxis Community College;* Wilbert E. Corprew, *SUNY Broome;* Hamilton Cravens, *Iowa State University;* Audrey Crawford, *Houston Community College;* Vanessa Crispin-Peralta, *Moorpark College;* John Crum, *University of Delaware;* David Cullen, *Collin College;* Gregory K. Culver, *Austin Peay State University;* Alex G. Cummins, *St. Johns River State College;* Robert Chris Davis, *Lone Star College–Kingwood;* Susanne Deberry-Cole, *Morgan State University;* Julian J. DelGaudio, *Long Beach City College;* Patricia Norred Derr, *Kutztown University;* Thomas Devine, *California State University, Northridge;* Tom Dicke, *Missouri State University;* Andy Digh, *Mercer University;* Gary Donato, *Massachusetts Bay Community College;* John Donoghue, *Loyola University Chicago;* Timothy Draper, *Waubonsee Community College;* David Dzurec, *University of Scranton;* Susan Eckelmann, *University of Tennessee, Chattanooga;* George Edgar, *Modesto Junior College;* Keith Edgerton, *Montana State University Billings;* Taulby Edmondson, *Virginia Tech;* Ashton Ellett, *University of Georgia;* Blake Ellis, *Lone Star College;* Christine Erickson, *Indiana University–Purdue University Fort Wayne;* Keona K. Ervin, *University of Missouri;* Todd Estes, *Oakland University;* Gabrielle Everett,

Jefferson College; Julie Fairchild, *Sinclair Community College;* Robert Glen Findley, *Odessa College;* Randy Finley, *Georgia Perimeter College;* Tiffany Fink, *Hardin-Simmons University;* Kirsten Fischer, *University of Minnesota;* Michelle Fishman-Cross, *College of Staten Island;* Roger Flynn, *TriCounty Technical College;* Jeffrey Forret, *Lamar University;* Jonathan Foster, *Great Basin College;* Kristen Foster, *Marquette University;* Sarah Franklin, *University of North Alabama;* Michael Frawley, *University of Texas of the Permian Basin;* Susan Freeman, *Western Michigan University;* Nancy Gabin, *Purdue University;* Kevin Gannon, *Grand View University;* Benton Gates, *Indiana University–Purdue University Fort Wayne;* Bruce Geelhoed, *Ball State University;* Mark Gelfand, *Boston College;* Robert Genter, *Nassau Community College;* Jason George, *The Bryn Mawr School;* Judith A. Giesberg, *Villanova University;* Dana Goodrich, *Northwest Vista College;* Sherry Ann Gray, *Mid-South Community College;* Chad Gregory, *Tri-County Technical College;* Patrick Griffin, *University of Notre Dame;* Audrey Grounds, *University of South Florida;* Abbie Grubb, *San Jacinto College –South;* Kenneth Grubb, *Wharton County Junior College;* Larry Grubbs, *Georgia State University;* Aaron Gulyas, *Mott Community College;* Scott Gurman, *Northern Illinois University;* Melanie Gustafson, *University of Vermont;* Ashley Haines, *Mt. San Antonio College;* Dennis Halpin, *Virginia Tech;* Hunter Hampton, *University of Missouri;* Tona Hangen, *Worcester State University;* Brian Hart, *Del Mar College;* Paul Hart, *Texas State University;* Paul Harvey, *University of Colorado Colorado Springs;* Stephen Henderson, *William Penn University;* Kimberly Hernandez, *University of Wisconsin-Milwaukee;* Lacey A. Holley-McCann, *Columbia State Community College;* Woody Holton, *University of Richmond;* Vilja Hulden, *University of Arizona;* Creed Hyatt, *Lehigh Carbon Community College;* Colette A. Hyman, *Winona State University;* Brenda Jackson-Abernathy, *Belmont University;* Joe Jaynes, *Collin College;* Troy R. Johnson, *California State University, Long Beach;* Shelli Jordan-Zirkle, *Shoreline Community College;* Stephen Katz, *Community College of Philadelphia;* Lesley Kauffman, *San Jacinto College-Central;* Jennifer Kelly, *The University of Texas at Austin;* Kelly Kennington, *Auburn University;* Andrew E. Kersten, *University of Wisconsin–Green Bay;* Tina M. Kibbe, *Lamar University;* Melanie Kiechle, *Virginia Tech;* Janilyn M. Kocher, *Richland Community College;* Don Knox, *Wayland Baptist University;* Max Krochmal, *Duke University;* Peggy Lambert, *Lone Star College;* Stephanie Lamphere, *Sierra College;* Jennifer R. Lang, *Delgado Community College;* Todd Laugen, *Metropolitan State University of Denver;* Carolyn J. Lawes, *Old Dominion University;* John Leazer, *Carthage College;* Marianne Leeper, *Trinity Valley Community College;* Alan Lehmann, *Blinn College–Brenham;* John S. Leiby, *Paradise Valley Community College;* Leslie Leighton, *Georgia State University;* Mitchell Lerner, *The Ohio State University;* Carole N. Lester, *University of Texas at Dallas;* Amanda Littauer, *Northern Illinois University;* Matthew Loayza, *Minnesota State University, Mankato;* Gabriel J. Loiacono, *University of Wisconsin Oshkosh;* Carmen Lopez, *Miami Dade College;* Robert Lyle, *University of North Georgia;* John F. Lyons, *Joliet Junior College;* Lorie Maltby, *Henderson Community College;* Christopher Manning, *Loyola University Chicago;* Amani Marshall, *Georgia State University;* Phil Martin, *San Jacinto College–South;* David Mason, *Georgia Gwinnett College;* Marty D. Matthews, *North Carolina State University;* Eric Mayer, *Victor Valley College;* Suzanne K. McCormack, *Community College of Rhode Island;* David McDaniel, *Marquette*

University; J. Kent McGaughy, *Houston Community College, Northwest;* Alan McPherson, *Howard University;* Sarah Hand Meacham, *Virginia Commonwealth University;* Jason Mead, *Johnson University;* Brian Craig Miller, *Emporia State University;* Robert Miller, *California State University, San Marcos;* Brett Mizelle, *California State University, Long Beach;* Mark Moser, *The University of North Carolina at Greensboro;* Ricky Moser, *Kilgore College;* Jennifer Murray, *Coastal Carolina University;* Peter C. Murray, *Methodist University;* Steven E. Nash, *East Tennessee State University;* Chris Newman, *Elgin Community College;* David Noon, *University of Alaska Southeast;* Richard H. Owens, *West Liberty University;* Alison Parker, *College at Brockport, SUNY;* Craig Pascoe, *Georgia College;* David J. Peavler, *Towson University;* Linda Pelon, *McLennan Community College;* Laura A. Perry, *University of Memphis;* Wesley Phelps, *University of St. Thomas;* Jamie Pietruska, *Rutgers University;* Sandra Piseno, *Clayton State University;* Merline Pitre, *Texas Southern University;* Eunice G. Pollack, *University of North Texas;* Kimberly Porter, *University of North Dakota;* Cynthia Prescott, *University of North Dakota;* Gene Preuss, *University of Houston;* Sandra Pryor, *Old Dominion University;* Rhonda Ragsdale, *Lone Star College;* Ray Rast, *Gonzaga University;* Michaela Reaves, *California Lutheran University;* Peggy Renner, *Glendale Community College;* Steven D. Reschly, *Truman State University;* Barney J. Rickman, *Valdosta State University;* Pamela Riney-Kehrberg, *Iowa State University;* Paul Ringel, *High Point University;* Jason Ripper, *Everett Community College;* Timothy Roberts, *Western Illinois University;* Glenn Robins, *Georgia Southwestern State University;* Alicia E. Rodriquez, *California State University, Bakersfield;* Mark Roehrs, *Lincoln Land Community College;* Patricia Roessner, *Marple Newtown High School;* John G. Roush, *St. Petersburg College;* James Russell, *St. Thomas Aquinas College;* Eric Schlereth, *The University of Texas at Dallas;* Gregory L. Schneider, *Emporia State University;* Debra Schultz, *Kingsborough Community College, CUNY;* Ronald Schultz, *University of Wyoming;* Stanley K. Schultz, *University of Wisconsin–Madison;* Scott Seagle, *University of Tennessee at Chattanooga;* Donald Seals, *Kilgore College;* Sharon Shackelford, *Erie Community College;* Donald R. Shaffer, *American Public University System;* Gregory Shealy, *Saint John's River State College;* Cathy Hoult Shewring, *Montgomery County Community College;* Jill Silos-Rooney, *Massachusetts Bay Community College;* David J. Silverman, *The George Washington University;* Beth Slutsky, *California State University, Sacramento;* Andrea Smalley, *Northern Illinois University;* Karen Smith, *Emporia State University;* Molly Smith, *Friends School of Baltimore;* Suzie Smith, *Trinity Valley Community College;* Troy Smith, *Tennessee Tech University;* David L. Snead, *Liberty University;* David Snyder, *Delaware Valley College;* David Soll, *University of Wisconsin–Eau Claire;* Gary Sprayberry, *Columbus State University;* Jodie Steeley, *Merced College;* Bethany Stollar, *Tennessee State University;* Bryan E. Stone, *Del Mar College;* Jason Stratton, *Bakersfield College;* Emily Straus, *SUNY Fredonia;* Kristen Streater, *Collin College;* Joseph Stromberg, *San Jacinto College–Central;* Jean Stuntz, *West Texas A&M University;* Sarah Swedberg, *Colorado Mesa University;* Nikki M. Taylor, *University of Cincinnati;* Heather Ann Thompson, *Temple University;* Timothy Thurber, *Virginia Commonwealth University;* Christopher Thrasher, *Calhoun Community College;* T. J. Tomlin, *University of Northern Colorado;* Jeffrey Trask, *Georgia State University;* Laura Trauth, *Community College of Baltimore County–Essex;* Russell M. Tremayne, *College of Southern Idaho;* Laura Tuennerman-Kaplan, *California University of Pennsylvania;*

Linda Upham-Bornstein, *Plymouth State University;* Mark VanDriel, *University of South Carolina;* Kevin Vanzant, *Tennessee State University;* Ramon C. Veloso, *Palomar College;* Morgan Veraluz, *Tennessee State University;* Vincent Vinikas, *The University of Arkansas at Little Rock;* David Voelker, *University of Wisconsin–Green Bay;* Melissa Walker, *Converse College;* William Wantland, *Mount Vernon Nazarene University;* Ed Wehrle, *Eastern Illinois University;* David Weiland, *Collin College;* Eddie Weller, *San Jacinto College-South;* Shane West, *Lone Star College-Greenspoint Center;* Geoffrey West, *San Diego Mesa College;* Kenneth B. White, *Modesto Junior College;* Matt White, *Paris Junior College;* Anne Will, *Skagit Valley College;* John P. Williams, *Collin College;* Zachery R. Williams, *University of Akron;* Gregory Wilson, *University of Akron;* Kurt Windisch, *University of Georgia;* Jonathan Wlasiuk, *The Ohio State University;* Timothy Wright *Shoreline Community College;* Timothy L. Wood, *Southwest Baptist University;* Nancy Beck Young, *University of Houston;* Maria Cristina Zaccarini, *Adelphi University;* Nancy Zens, *Central Oregon Community College;* and Jean Hansen Zuckweiler, *University of Northern Colorado*

We want to thank Bob and Sharon Constantine and Richard and Bobbie Sirmons for their good company and sustenance during the pandemic and other critical events of 2020. In addition a number of scholars generously answered our questions for this fourth edition and provided research critical to our latest revisions: Catherine Brekus, Lisa Brooks, Ellen Hartigan-O'Connor, April Haynes, Maeve Kane, William Link, Tiya Miles, Theda Perdue, Manisha Sinha, Amy Murrell Taylor, Kevin Vrevich, and Brenda Withington. We also appreciate the help the following scholars, archivists, and students gave us in providing the information we needed at critical points in the writing of earlier editions of this text: Lori Birrell, Julia Bowes, Leslie Brown, Andrew Buchanan, Gillian Carroll, Susan J. Carroll, Jacqueline Castledine, Derek Chang, Paul Clemens, Dorothy Sue Cobble, Jane Coleman-Harbison, Alison Cronk, Kayo Denda, Elisabeth Eittreim, David Foglesong, Phyllis Hunter, Tera Hunter, Molly Inabinett, Kenneth Kvamme, William Link, James Livingston, Julia Livingston, Justin Lorts, Melissa Mead, Gilda Morales, Andrew Preston, Vicki L. Ruiz, Julia Sandy-Bailey, Susan Schrepfer, Bonnie Smith, Melissa Stein, Margaret Sumner, Camilla Townsend, Jessica Unger, Anne Valk, and Melinda Wallington. We also want to thank Rob Heinrich and Julia Sandy for their work in compiling the primary source projects for the first edition of the companion source reader, *Thinking through Sources: Exploring American Histories.*

We would particularly like to applaud the many hardworking and creative people at Bedford/St. Martin's (Macmillan Learning) who guided us through the labyrinthine process of writing this fourth edition. No one was more important to us than Leah Strauss, our editor with a keen eye and a light touch, and William Lombardo, senior executive program manager, who has seen us through all four editions. They were joined by an excellent team at Macmillan, including Erika Gutierrez, senior program director; Gregory Erb, executive content project manager; Julia Bell, assistant editor; Mollie Chandler, media editor; Stephanie Sosa, associate editor; and Melissa Rodriguez, senior marketing manager. We thank cover designer, William Boardman, and Naomi Kornhauser for image research for which we are grateful. We will always remain thankful to Sara Wise and Patricia Rossi for their advice about and enthusiasm for a primary source-based American History textbook and to Joan

Feinberg, who had the vision that guided us through every page of this book. Thanks as well to Michael Rosenberg whose enthusiasm inspired us to keep thinking anew about the past. Finally, we would like to express our gratitude to our friends and family who have encouraged us through every edition and have even read the book without it being assigned.

Nancy A. Hewitt and Steven F. Lawson

Versions and Supplements

Adopters of *Exploring American Histories* and their students have access to abundant digital and print resources and tools, including documents, assessment and presentation materials, the acclaimed *Bedford Series in History and Culture* volumes, and much more. *Exploring American Histories* is now available for the first time in Achieve, Macmillan Learning's new complete course platform, which provides access to the narrative as well as a wealth of primary sources and other features, along with assessments and robust insights and reports at the ready, all in one affordably priced product. Achieve also includes a downloadable e-book for reading offline. See the following text for more information, visit the book's catalog site at macmillanlearning.com, or contact your local Macmillan Learning sales representative.

Get the Right Version and Volume for Your Class—Digital, Print, and Value Options.

Whether it's a digital course platform, e-book, print book, value option, or package combining digital and print products, *Exploring American Histories* is available in a variety of volumes and formats so you can choose what works best for your course. The **comprehensive *Exploring American Histories*** includes a full-color art and map program and a rich set of features and primary and secondary sources. Digital options for the comprehensive version include the full course platform of Achieve for *Exploring American Histories* (see below for the description of Achieve's benefits), as well as e-books. The comprehensive version is also available in print in three volume options. For great value in a streamlined product, ***Exploring American Histories*, Value Edition**, offers the unabridged narrative and selected two-color art and maps—without special features or primary or secondary sources—at a steep discount. The Value Edition is available in e-book format, as well as print, in three volume options, with loose-leaf format available for the least expensive price option. For the best value, purchase Achieve on its own or package it with the print version of your choice for a small add-on cost. *Exploring American Histories* is available in the following volume configurations:

- **Combined Volume** (Chapters 1–29). Available in Achieve (1- and 2-term subscriptions), e-books, and print volumes for the comprehensive and Value editions.
- **Volume 1: To 1877** (Chapters 1–14). Available in Achieve (1- and 2-term subscriptions), e-books, and print volumes for the comprehensive and Value editions, including loose-leaf format for the Value editions.
- **Volume 2: Since 1865** (Chapters 14–29). Available in Achieve (1- and 2-term subscriptions), e-books, and print volumes for the comprehensive and Value editions, including loose-leaf format for the Value editions.

As noted below, any of these volumes can be packaged with additional titles for a discount. To get ISBNs for discount packages, visit **macmillanlearning.com** or contact your Macmillan Learning sales representative.

Achieve Assign Achieve—A Comprehensive Course Platform with E-book, Skill-Building Assessments, and Analytics for Instructors

Affordably priced, intuitive, and easy to use, Achieve is a breakthrough solution for building students' skills and confidence in history courses. Achieve for *Exploring American Histories* includes the rich resources and skill-building content of the e-books for the complete comprehensive text and companion reader, *Thinking through Sources for Exploring American Histories*, alongside a robust set of summative and formative assessments—many autograded—that help students build confidence in their mastery of the material, reflect on their learning, and build critical, higher-level thinking skills. Achieve for *Exploring American Histories* includes LearningCurve adaptive quizzing that—when assigned—helps ensure that students do the reading before class; autograded exercises that teach students how to build a thesis and support an argument; quizzes that check student comprehension of primary sources and boxed features; chapter summative quizzes that test student knowledge after they've completed the reading; tutorials with quizzing that build skills such as working with primary sources and avoiding plagiarism; assignable chapter reflection questions that encourage students to engage with their learning; active reading activities that help students read actively for key concepts; class activity guides that can be used in synchronous and asynchronous courses; and iClicker polling questions that engage students during class. These features, plus additional primary source documents, map quizzes, customizable test banks, and detailed reports on student progress make Achieve an invaluable asset for any instructor.

Achieve easily integrates with course management systems, and with fast ways to build assignments and organize content, it lets teachers build the courses they want to teach while holding students accountable. For more information, or to arrange a demo or class test, contact us at **historymktg@macmillan.com**.

LearningCurve Assign LearningCurve So Your Students Come to Class Prepared

Students using Achieve receive access to LearningCurve for *Exploring American Histories*. Assigning LearningCurve in place of reading quizzes is easy for instructors, and the reporting features help instructors track overall class trends and spot topics that are giving students trouble so they can adjust their lectures and class activities. This online learning tool is popular with students because it was designed to help them rehearse content at their own pace in a nonthreatening, game-like environment. The feedback for wrong answers provides instructional coaching and sends students back to the book for review. Students answer as many questions as necessary to reach a target score, with repeated chances to revisit material they haven't mastered. When LearningCurve is assigned, students come to class better prepared.

▷ iClicker iClicker Student App, Active Learning Simplified

The iClicker student app offers simple, flexible tools to help you give students a voice and facilitate active learning in the classroom. Students can participate with the devices they already bring to class using our iClicker student mobile app (which works with smart phones, tablets, or laptops). We've now integrated iClicker with Macmillan's Achieve to make it easier than ever to synchronize grades and promote engagement—both in and out of class. iClicker can be used synchronously through its polling feature, or asynchronously for assignments. To learn more, talk to your Macmillan Learning sales representative or visit us at **www.iclicker.com**.

Take Advantage of Instructor Resources

Bedford/St. Martin's has developed a rich array of teaching resources for this book and for this course. They range from lecture and presentation materials and assessment tools to course management options. Most can be found in Achieve or can be downloaded or ordered at **macmillanlearning.com**.

Instructor's Resource Manual. The Instructor's Resource Manual offers both experienced and first-time instructors tools for presenting textbook material in engaging ways. It includes content learning objectives, annotated chapter outlines, and strategies for teaching with the textbook, plus suggestions on how to get the most out of LearningCurve, and a survival guide for first-time teaching assistants.

Guide to Changing Editions. Designed to facilitate an instructor's transition from the previous edition of *Exploring American Histories* to the new edition, this guide presents an overview of major changes across the book and of changes in each chapter.

Online Test Bank. The test bank includes a mix of fresh, carefully crafted multiple-choice, short-answer, and essay questions for each chapter. Some of the multiple-choice questions feature a map as the prompt. All questions appear in easy-to-use test bank software that allows instructors to add, edit, re-sequence, filter by question type, and print questions and answers. Instructors can also export questions into a variety of course management systems.

The Bedford Lecture Kit: Lecture Outlines, Maps, and Images. Look good and save time with *The Bedford Lecture Kit*. This resource includes fully customizable multimedia presentations built around chapter outlines that are embedded with maps, figures, and images from the textbook and are supplemented by more detailed instructor notes on key points and concepts.

Print, Digital, and Custom Options for More Choice and Value

For information on packages and discounts up to 50%, visit **macmillanlearning.com**, or contact your local Macmillan Learning sales representative.

Thinking through Sources for Exploring American Histories, **Third Edition.** This companion reader provides an additional primary source project with four to five written and visual sources focused on a central topic to accompany each chapter of *Exploring American Histories*. To aid students in approaching and interpreting the sources, the project for each chapter contains an introduction, document headnotes, and questions for discussion. This companion reader is an exceptional value for students and offers plenty of assignment options for instructors, and is included in Achieve with autograded quizzes for each source. *Thinking through Sources for Exploring American Histories* is also available on its own as a downloadable e-book.

Bedford Document Collections. These affordable, brief document projects provide five to seven primary sources, an introduction, historical background, and other pedagogical features. Each curated project—designed for use in a single class period and written by a historian about a favorite topic—poses a historical question and guides students through analysis of the sources. Examples include "What Caused the Civil War?"; "The California Gold Rush: A Trans-Pacific Phenomenon"; and "War Stories: Black Soldiers and the Long Civil Rights Movement." These primary source projects are available in a low-cost, easy-to-use digital format or can be combined with other course materials in Bedford Select to create an affordable, personalized print product. For more information on using Bedford Select to customize your course materials with these and other resources, **visit macmillanlearning.com/bedfordselect**.

Bedford Tutorials for History. Designed to provide resources relevant to individual courses, this collection of over a dozen brief units, each 16 pages long and loaded with examples, guides students through basic skills such as using historical evidence effectively, working with primary sources, taking effective notes, avoiding plagiarism and citing sources, and more. For more information, visit **macmillanlearning.com/historytutorials**.

The Bedford Series in History and Culture. Now available in low-cost e-books as well as print volumes, the more than 100 titles in this highly praised series combine first-rate scholarship, historical narrative, and important primary documents for undergraduate courses. Each title is brief, inexpensive, and focused on a specific topic or period. Recent titles in the series include: *The Chinese Exclusion Act and Angel Island: A Brief History with Documents*, by Judy Yung; *The Life of P.T. Barnum, Written by Himself, with Related Documents*, edited with an introduction by Stephen Mihm; and *The California Gold Rush: A Brief History with Documents*, by Andrew C. Isenberg. For a complete list of titles, **visit macmillanlearning.com**. Package discounts are available.

Trade Books. History titles published by sister companies Hill and Wang; Farrar, Straus and Giroux; Henry Holt and Company; St. Martin's Press; Picador; and Palgrave Macmillan are available at a 50% discount when packaged with Bedford/St. Martin's textbooks. For more information, **visit macmillanlearning.com/tradeup**.

A Pocket Guide to Writing in History. Available in a low-cost e-book as well as in print and updated to reflect changes made in the 2017 Chicago Manual of Style revision, this portable and affordable reference tool by Mary Lynn Rampolla provides reading, writing, and research advice useful to students in all history courses. Concise yet comprehensive advice on approaching typical history assignments, developing critical reading skills, writing effective history papers, conducting research, using and documenting sources, and avoiding plagiarism — enhanced with practical tips and examples throughout — has made this slim reference a best-seller. Deep discounts are available when bundled with a survey textbook.

A Student's Guide to History. Available in a low-cost e-book as well as in print and updated to reflect changes made in the 2017 Chicago Manual of Style revision, this complete guide to success in any history course provides the practical help students need to be successful. In addition to introducing students to the nature of the discipline, author Jules Benjamin teaches a wide range of skills from preparing for exams to approaching common writing assignments, and explains the research and documentation process with plentiful examples. Deep discounts are available when bundled with a survey textbook.

Brief Contents

1 Mapping Global Frontiers to 1590 1

2 Colonization and Conflicts 1580–1680 28

3 Colonial America amid Global Change 1680–1754 55

4 Religious Strife and Social Upheavals 1680–1754 83

5 War and Empire 1754–1774 110

6 The American Revolution 1775–1783 135

7 Forging a New Nation 1783–1800 162

8 The Early Republic 1790–1820 189

9 Defending and Redefining the Nation 1809–1832 216

10 Social and Cultural Ferment in the North 1820–1850 244

11 Slavery Expands South and West 1830–1850 272

12 Imperial Ambitions and Sectional Crises 1842–1861 300

13 Civil War 1861–1865 325

14 Emancipation and Reconstruction 1863–1877 349

15 The West 1865–1896 373

16 Industrial America 1877–1900 400

17 Workers and Farmers in the Age of Organization 1877–1900 427

18 Cities, Immigrants, and the Nation 1880–1914 451

19 Progressivism and the Search for Order 1900–1917 474

20 Empire, Wars, and Pandemic 1898–1919 501

21 The Twenties 1919–1929 528

22 Depression, Dissent, and the New Deal 1929–1940 555

23 World War II 1933–1945 581

24 The Opening of the Cold War 1945–1961 608

25 Troubled Innocence 1945–1961 633

26 Liberalism and Its Challengers 1960–1973 660

27 The Swing toward Conservatism 1968–1980 689

28 The Triumph of Conservatism, the End of the Cold War,
and the Rise of the New World Order 1980–1992 714

29 The Challenges of a Globalized World 1993 to the present 741

Contents

Preface   v

Versions and Supplements   xvii

Maps, Figures, and Tables   xxxviii

CHAPTER 1

Mapping Global Frontiers to 1590   1

Comparing American Histories   1
  Malintzin and Martin Waldseemüller

Native Peoples in the Americas   3
  Native Peoples Develop Diverse Cultures   3   •   The Aztecs, the Maya, and the
  Incas   5   •   Native Cultures to the North   6

Europe Expands Its Reach   9
  The Mediterranean World   9   •   Portugal Pursues Long-Distance
  Trade   10   •   European Encounters with West Africa   11

Worlds Collide   13
  Europeans Cross the Atlantic   13   •   Europeans Explore the
  Americas   14   •   Mapmaking and Printing   16   •   The Columbian
  Exchange   17

Europeans Make Claims to North America   19
  Spaniards Conquer Indian Empires   19   •   Spanish Adventurers Head
  North   21   •   Europeans Compete in North America   22   •   Spain Seeks
  Dominion in Europe and the Americas   23

Conclusion: A Transformed America   25   •   Chapter Review   26

CHAPTER 2

Colonization and Conflicts 1580–1680   28

Comparing American Histories   28
  Powhatan and Anne Hutchinson

Religious, Economic, and Imperial Transformations   30
  The Protestant Reformation   30   •   Spain's Global Empire
  Declines   31   •   France Enters the Race for Empire   33   •   The Dutch Expand
  into North America   35

The English Seek an Empire   37
  The English Establish Jamestown   37   •   Tobacco Fuels Growth
  in Virginia   38   •   Expansion, Rebellion, and the Emergence of
  Slavery   40   •   The English Compete for West Indies Possessions   43

Pilgrims and Puritans Settle New England 45
Pilgrims Arrive in Massachusetts 45 • The Puritan Migration 46 • The Puritan Worldview 47 • Dissenters Challenge Puritan Authority 48 • Wars in Old and New England 49

Conclusion: European Empires in North America 51 • Chapter Review 52

CHAPTER 3

Colonial America amid Global Change 1680–1754 55

Comparing American Histories 55
William Moraley Jr. and Eliza Lucas

Europeans Expand Their Claims 57
English Colonies Grow and Multiply 57 • The Pueblo Revolt and Spain's Fragile Empire 59 • France Seeks Land and Control 60

European Wars and American Consequences 62
Colonial Conflicts and Indian Alliances 62 • Indians Resist European Encroachment 63 • Conflicts on the Southern Frontier 66

The Benefits and Costs of Empire 67
Colonial Traders Join Global Networks 67 • Imperial Policies Focus on Profits 68 • The Atlantic Slave Trade 70 • Seaport Cities and Consumer Cultures 71

Labor in North America 73
Finding Work in the Colonies 73 • Coping with Economic Distress 74 • Rural Americans Face Changing Conditions 75 • Slavery Takes Hold in the South 77 • Africans Resist Their Enslavement 79

Conclusion: Changing Fortunes in British North America 80 • Chapter Review 81

CHAPTER 4

Religious Strife and Social Upheavals 1680–1754 83

Comparing American Histories 83
Gilbert Tennent and Sarah Grosvenor

An Ungodly Society? 85
The Rise of Religious Anxieties 85 • Cries of Witchcraft 86

Family and Household Dynamics 87
Women's Changing Status 87 • Working Families 88 • Reproduction and Women's Roles 89 • The Limits of Patriarchal Order 90

Diversity and Competition in Colonial Society 93
Population Growth and Economic Competition 93 • Increasing Diversity 95 • Expansion and Conflict 96

Religious Awakenings 99
The Roots of the Great Awakening 99 • An Outburst of
Revivals 101 • Religious Dissension 101

Political Awakenings 103
Changing Political Relations 103 • Dissent and Protest 104 • Transforming
Urban Politics 106

Conclusion: A Divided Society 108 • Chapter Review 108

CHAPTER 5

War and Empire 1754–1774 110

Comparing American Histories 110
George Washington and Pontiac

Imperial Conflicts and Indian Wars, 1754–1763 112
The Opening Battles 112 • A Shift to Global War 114 • The Costs of
Victory 115 • Battles and Boundaries on the Frontier 116 • Conflicts over
Land and Labor Escalate 119

Postwar British Policies and Colonial Unity 120
Common Grievances 120 • Forging Ties across the Colonies 121 • Great
Britain Seeks Greater Control 122

Resistance to Britain Intensifies 123
The Stamp Act Inspires Coordinated Resistance 123 • The Townshend
Act 126 • The Boston Massacre 127 • Continuing Conflicts at
Home 128 • Tea and Widening Resistance 129 • The Continental Congress
and Colonial Unity 131

Conclusion: Liberty within Empire 132 • Chapter Review 133

CHAPTER 6

The American Revolution 1775–1783 135

Comparing American Histories 135
Thomas Paine and Elizabeth Freeman

The Question of Independence 137
Armed Conflict Erupts 137 • Building a Continental Army 139 • Reasons
for Caution and for Action 140 • Declaring Independence 140

Choosing Sides 141
Recruiting Supporters 142 • Choosing Neutrality 143 • Committing to
Independence 143

Fighting for Independence, 1776–1777 144
British Troops Gain Early Victories 145 • Patriots Prevail in New
Jersey 145 • A Critical Year of Warfare 146 • Patriots Gain Critical
Assistance 148 • Surviving on the Home Front 149

Governing in Revolutionary Times 149

Colonies Become States 150 • Patriots Divide over Slavery 150 • France Allies with the Patriots 151 • Raising Armies and Funds 152 • Indians and Patriots Battle for Land 152 • Conflicts Escalate on the Frontier 153

Winning the War and the Peace, 1778–1783 155

War Rages in the South 155 • An Uncertain Peace 157 • A Surprising Victory 158

Conclusion: Legacies of the Revolution 159 • **Chapter Review** 160

CHAPTER 7

Forging a New Nation 1783–1800 162

Comparing American Histories 162

Daniel Shays and Alexander Hamilton

Financial, Frontier, and Foreign Problems 164

Continental Officers Threaten Confederation 164 • Indians, Land, and the Northwest Ordinance 164 • Depression and Debt 167

On the Political Margins 168

Separating Church and State 168 • African Americans Struggle for Rights 168 • Women Seek Wider Roles 170 • Indebted Farmers Fuel Political Crises 170

Reframing the American Government 171

The Constitutional Convention of 1787 172 • Americans Battle over Ratification 174 • Organizing the Federal Government 175 • Hamilton Forges an Economic Agenda 176

Years of Crisis, 1792–1796 178

Foreign Trade and Foreign Wars 178 • Disease and Dissent 180 • Further Conflicts on the Frontier 181

The First Party System 183

The Adams Presidency 183 • The Election of 1800 185

Conclusion: A Young Nation Comes of Age 186 • **Chapter Review** 187

CHAPTER 8

The Early Republic 1790–1820 189

Comparing American Histories 189

Parker Cleaveland and Sacagawea

The Dilemmas of National Identity 191

Education for a New Nation 191 • Literary and Cultural Developments 193 • Religious Renewal 194 • The Racial Limits of "American" Culture 195 • A New Capital for a New Nation 197

Extending Federal Power 199

A New Administration Faces Challenges 199 • The Louisiana Purchase and Indian Societies 200 • The Supreme Court Extends Its Reach 201 • Democratic-Republicans Expand Federal Powers 203

Remaking America's Economic Character 204
Native Lands and American Migrations 204 • Technology Reshapes Agriculture and Industry 208 • Transforming Domestic Production 209 • Technology, Cotton, and Slaves 210

**Conclusion: New Identities and New Challenges 213 •
Chapter Review 214**

CHAPTER 9

Defending and Redefining the Nation 1809–1832 216

Comparing American Histories 216
Dolley Madison and John Ross

Conflicts at Home and Abroad 218
Tensions at Sea and on the Frontier 218 • War with Britain and Its Indian Allies 219

National Expansion and Regional Economies 222
Governments Fuel Economic Growth 223 • Americans Expand the Nation's Borders 225 • Regional Economic Development 226

Economic and Political Crises 228
The Panic of 1819 228 • Slavery in Missouri 229

The Expansion and Limits of American Democracy 231
Expanding Voting Rights 231 • Racist Restrictions and Racial Violence 233 • Political Realignments 234 • The Presidential Election of 1828 235

Jacksonian Politics in Action 237
A Democratic Spirit? 237 • Confrontations over Tariffs and the Bank 238 • Contesting Indian Removal 239

**Conclusion: The Nation Faces New Challenges 240 •
Chapter Review 242**

CHAPTER 10

Social and Cultural Ferment in the North 1820–1850 244

Comparing American Histories 244
Charles Grandison Finney and Amy Kirby Post

The Market Revolution 246
Creating an Urban Landscape 246 • The Lure of Urban Life 247 • The Roots of Urban Disorder 249 • The New Middle Class 250

The Rise of Industry 252
Factory Towns and Women Workers 252 • The Decline of Craft Work and Workingmen's Responses 253 • The Panic of 1837 254

Saving the Nation from Sin 255
The Second Great Awakening 255 • New Visions of Faith and Reform 256 • Transcendentalism 257

Organizing for Change   259
Varieties of Reform   259   •   The Problem of Poverty   260   •   The Temperance Movement   261   •   Utopian Communities   261

Abolitionism Expands and Divides   263
The Beginnings of the Antislavery Movement   263   •   Abolition Gains Ground and Enemies   265   •   Abolitionism and Women's Rights   266   •   The Rise of Antislavery Parties   268

Conclusion: From the North to the Nation   269   •   Chapter Review   270

CHAPTER 11
Slavery Expands South and West 1830–1850   272

Comparing American Histories   272
José Antonio Menchaca and Solomon Northup

Planters Expand the Slave System   274
A Plantation Society Develops in the South   275   •   Urban Life in the Slave South   276   •   The Consequences of Slavery's Expansion   276

Slave Society and Culture   278
Enslaved Labor Fuels the Economy   279   •   Developing an African American Culture   280   •   Resistance and Rebellion   281

Planters Tighten Control   282
Harsher Treatment for Southern Blacks   282   •   White Southerners without Slaves   283   •   Planters Seek to Unify Southern Whites   284

Democrats Face Political and Economic Crises   285
The Battle for Texas   285   •   Indians Resist Removal   287   •   Van Buren and the Panic of 1837   290   •   The Whigs Win the White House   291

The National Government Looks to the West   291
Expanding to Oregon and Texas   292   •   Pursuing War with Mexico   293   •   Debates over Slavery Intensify   295

Conclusion: Geographical Expansion and Political Division   296   •   Chapter Review   298

CHAPTER 12
Imperial Ambitions and Sectional Crises 1842–1861   300

Comparing American Histories   300
John C. Frémont and Dred Scott

Claiming the West   302
Traveling the Overland Trail   302   •   The Gold Rush   303   •   A Crowded Land   304

Expansion and the Politics of Slavery   307
California and the Compromise of 1850   307   •   The Fugitive Slave Act Inspires Northern Protest   308   •   Pierce Encourages U.S. Expansion   310

Sectional Crises Intensify   311
Popularizing Antislavery Sentiment   312   •   The Kansas-Nebraska Act Stirs Dissent   312   •   Bleeding Kansas and the Election of 1856   314   •   The *Dred Scott* Decision   316

From Sectional Crisis to Southern Secession   316
Cortina's War and John Brown's Raid   317   •   The Election of 1860   319   •   From Secession to War   319

Conclusion: A Nation Divided   322   •   Chapter Review   323

CHAPTER 13

Civil War 1861–1865   325

Comparing American Histories   325
Frederick Douglass and Rose O'Neal Greenhow

The Nation at War, 1861–1862   327
Both Sides Prepare for War   327   •   Wartime Roles of African Americans, Indians, and Mexican Americans   329   •   Union Politicians Consider Emancipation   332

War Transforms the North and the South   333
Life and Death on the Battlefield   334   •   The Northern Economy Expands   335   •   Urbanization and Industrialization in the South   335   •   Women Aid the War Effort   336   •   Dissent and Protest in the Midst of War   338

The Tide of War Turns, 1863–1865   340
Key Victories for the Union   340   •   African Americans Contribute to Victory   342   •   The Final Battles of a Hard War   343   •   The War Comes to an End   345

Conclusion: An Uncertain Future   346   •   Chapter Review   347

CHAPTER 14

Emancipation and Reconstruction 1863–1877   349

Comparing American Histories   349
Jefferson Franklin Long and Andrew Johnson

Emancipation   351
African Americans Embrace Freedom   351   •   Reuniting Families Torn Apart by Slavery   352   •   Freedom to Learn   354   •   Freedom to Worship and the Leadership Role of Black Churches   354

National Reconstruction   355
Abraham Lincoln Plans for Reunification   355   •   Andrew Johnson and Presidential Reconstruction   356   •   Johnson and Congressional Resistance   358   •   Congressional Reconstruction   360   •   The Struggle for Universal Suffrage   361

Remaking the South   363
Whites Reconstruct the South   363   •   Black Political Participation and Economic
Opportunities   364   •   White Resistance to Congressional Reconstruction   366

The Unraveling of Reconstruction   367
The Republican Retreat   367   •   Congressional and Judicial
Retreat   368   •   The Presidential Compromise of 1876   369

Conclusion: The Legacies of Reconstruction   370   •   Chapter Review   371

CHAPTER 15

The West 1865–1896   373

Comparing American Histories   373
Annie Oakley and Geronimo

Opening the West   375
The Great Plains   376   •   Federal Policy and Foreign Investment   376

Indians and Resistance to Expansion   378
Indian Civilizations   378   •   Federal Policy toward Indians before
1870   380   •   Reconstruction and Indians   381   •   Indian
Defeat   382   •   Reforming Indian Policy   383   •   Indian Assimilation and
Resistance   384

The Mining and Lumber Industries   385
The Business of Mining   386   •   Life in the Mining Towns   386   •   The Lumber
Boom   387

The Cattle Industry and Commercial Farming   388
The Life of the Cowboy   388   •   The Rise of Commercial
Ranching   389   •   Commercial Farming   389   •   Women
Homesteaders   392   •   Farming on the Great Plains   392

Diversity in the Far West   394
Mormons   394   •   Californios and Mexican Americans   395   •   The
Chinese   396

Conclusion: The Ambiguous Legacy of the West   397   •
Chapter Review   398

CHAPTER 16

Industrial America 1877–1900   400

Comparing American Histories   400
Andrew Carnegie and John Sherman

America Industrializes   402
The New Industrial Economy   402   •   Innovation and
Inventions   404   •   Building a New South   405   •   Industrial
Consolidation   406   •   The Growth of Corporations   409

Laissez-Faire, Social Darwinism, and Their Critics   410
The Doctrines of Success   411   •   Challenges to Laissez-Faire   413

Society and Culture in the Gilded Age 414

Wealthy and Middle-Class Leisure-Time Pursuits 414 • Changing Gender
Roles 416 • Black America and Jim Crow 418

National Politics in the Era of Industrialization 420

The Weak Presidency 420 • Congressional Inefficiency 421 • The Business
of Politics 422 • An Energized and Entertained Electorate 422

Conclusion: Industrial America 424 • Chapter Review 425

CHAPTER 17

**Workers and Farmers in the Age of Organization
1877–1900 427**

Comparing American Histories 427

John McLuckie and Mary Elizabeth Lease

Working People Organize 429

The Industrialization of Labor 429 • Organizing Unions 433 • Clashes
between Workers and Owners 435 • Working-Class Leisure in Industrial
America 438

Farmers Organize 441

Farmers Unite 441 • Populists Rise Up 443

The Depression of the 1890s 444

Depression Politics 444 • Political Realignment in the Election of
1896 445 • The Decline of the Populists 447

Conclusion: A Passion for Organization 448 • Chapter Review 449

CHAPTER 18

Cities, Immigrants, and the Nation 1880–1914 451

Comparing American Histories 451

Beryl Lassin and Maria Vik Takacs

A New Wave of Immigrants 453

Immigrants Arrive from Many Lands 453 • Creating Immigrant
Communities 456 • Hostility toward Recent Immigrants 458 •
The Assimilation Dilemma 460

Becoming an Urban Nation 461

The New Industrial City 461 • Expand Upward and Outward 465 •
How the Other Half Lived 466

Urban Politics at the Turn of the Century 468

Political Machines and City Bosses 469 • Urban Reformers 471

Conclusion: A Nation of Cities 472 • Chapter Review 473

CHAPTER 19

Progressivism and the Search for Order 1900–1917   474

Comparing American Histories   474
Gifford Pinchot and Geneva Stratton-Porter

The Roots of Progressivism   476
Progressive Origins 476 • Muckrakers 477

Humanitarian and Social Justice Reform   477
Female Progressives and the Poor 477 • Fighting for Women's
Suffrage 479 • Progressivism and African Americans 482 • Progressivism
and Indians 484

Morality and Social Control   485
Prohibition 485 • Prostitution, Narcotics, and Juvenile
Delinquency 485 • Birth Control 486 • Immigration Restriction 487

Good Government Progressivism   488
Municipal and State Reform 488 • Conservation and Preservation of the
Environment 489

Presidential Progressivism   491
Theodore Roosevelt and the Square Deal 491 • Taft Retreats from
Progressivism 494 • The Election of 1912 494 • Woodrow Wilson and the
New Freedom Agenda 495

Conclusion: The Progressive Legacy   497 • Chapter Review   499

CHAPTER 20

Empire, Wars, and Pandemic 1898–1919   501

Comparing American Histories   501
Alfred Thayer Mahan and José Martí

The Awakening of Imperialism   503
The Economics of Expansion 503 • Cultural Justifications for
Imperialism 504 • Gender and Empire 505

The War with Spain   506
Revolution in Cuba 506 • The War of 1898 507 • The Pacification of
Cuba 508 • The Philippine War 509

Extending U.S. Imperialism, 1899–1913   511
Theodore Roosevelt and "Big Stick" Diplomacy 511 • Opening the Door in
China 512

Wilson and American Foreign Policy, 1912–1917   513
Diplomacy and War 513 • Making the World Safe for Democracy 515

Fighting the War at Home   518
Government by Commission 519 • Winning Hearts and Minds 520 •
1918–1919 Influenza Pandemic 522 • Waging Peace 523 • The Failure of
Ratification 524

Conclusion: A U.S. Empire   525 • Chapter Review   526

CHAPTER 21

The Twenties 1919–1929   528

Comparing American Histories   528
David Curtis (D. C.) Stephenson and Ossian Sweet

Social Turmoil   530
The Red Scare, 1919–1920   530   •   Racial Violence in the Postwar Era   532

Prosperity, Consumption, and Growth   533
Government Promotion of the Economy   534   •   Americans Become
Consumers   535   •   Urbanization   537   •   Perilous Prosperity   538

Challenges to Social Conventions   540
Breaking with the Old Morality   540   •   The Harlem
Renaissance   541   •   Marcus Garvey and Black Nationalism   542

Culture Wars   544
Prohibition   544   •   Nativists versus Immigrants   544   •   Resurrection of the
Ku Klux Klan   547   •   Fundamentalism versus Modernism   548

Politics and the Fading of Prosperity   549
The Battle for the Soul of the Democratic Party   549   •   Lingering
Progressivism   551   •   Financial Crash   551

Conclusion: The Transitional Twenties   552   •   **Chapter Review**   553

CHAPTER 22

Depression, Dissent, and the New Deal 1929–1940   555

Comparing American Histories   555
Eleanor Roosevelt and Luisa Moreno

The Great Depression   557
Hoover Faces the Depression   557   •   Hoovervilles and Dust
Storms   559   •   Challenges for Racial Minorities   560   •   Families under
Strain   562   •   Organized Protest   563

The New Deal   565
Roosevelt Restores Confidence   565   •   Steps toward Recovery   566   •   Direct
Assistance and Relief   568   •   New Deal Critics   569

The New Deal Moves to the Left   571
Expanding Relief Measures   571   •   Establishing Social
Security   572   •   Organized Labor Strikes Back   573   •   A Half Deal for Racial
Minorities   574   •   Decline of the New Deal   576

Conclusion: New Deal Liberalism   578   •   **Chapter Review**   579

CHAPTER 23

World War II 1933–1945   581

Comparing American Histories   581
J. Robert Oppenheimer and Fred Korematsu

The Road toward War   583
The Growing Crisis in Europe 583 • The Challenge to
Isolationism 584 • The United States Enters the War 586

The Home-Front Economy   587
Managing the Wartime Economy 587 • New Opportunities for
Women 590 • Everyday Life on the Home Front 590

Fighting for Equality at Home   592
The Origins of the Civil Rights Movement 592 • Struggles for Mexican
Americans 593 • American Indians 594 • The Ordeal of Japanese
Americans 594

Global War   597
War in Europe 597 • War in the Pacific 599 • Ending the
War 600 • Evidence of the Holocaust 602

Conclusion: The Impact of World War II   605 • Chapter Review   606

CHAPTER 24

The Opening of the Cold War 1945–1961   608

Comparing American Histories   608
George Frost Kennan and Julius and Ethel Rosenberg

The Origins of the Cold War, 1945–1947   610
Mutual Misunderstandings 610 • The Truman Doctrine 612 • The
Marshall Plan and Economic Containment 613

The Cold War Hardens, 1948–1953   614
Military Containment 614 • The Korean War 616 • The Korean War and
the Imperial Presidency 618

Combating Communism at Home, 1945–1954   620
Loyalty and the Second Red Scare 620 • McCarthyism 622

The Cold War Expands, 1953–1961   624
Nuclear Weapons and Containment 624 • Decolonization 627 •
Interventions in the Middle East, Latin America, and Africa 627 • Early
Intervention in Vietnam, 1954–1960 629

Conclusion: The Cold War and Anticommunism   630 •
Chapter Review   631

CHAPTER 25

Troubled Innocence 1945–1961   633

Comparing American Histories   633
Alan Freed and Grace Metalious

Peacetime Transition and the Boom Years   635
Peacetime Challenges, 1945–1948   635   •   Economic Conversion and Labor
Discontent   635   •   Truman, the New Deal Coalition, and the Election of
1948   636   •   Economic Boom   637   •   Baby Boom   637   •   Changes in Living
Patterns   639

The Culture of the 1950s   641
The Rise of Television   641   •   Wild Ones on the Big Screen   642   •   The
Influence of Teenage Culture   643   •   The Lives of Women   644   •   Religious
Revival   644   •   Beats and Other Nonconformists   645

The Growth of the Civil Rights Movement   646
The Rise of the Southern Civil Rights Movement   646   •   School Segregation
and the Supreme Court   647   •   The Montgomery Bus Boycott   648   •   White
Resistance to Desegregation   649   •   The Sit-Ins   650   •   Civil Rights Struggles
in the North   650   •   Civil Rights Struggles in the West   652

Domestic Politics in the Eisenhower Era   653
Modern Republicanism   654   •   The Election of 1960   655

Conclusion: Postwar Politics and Culture   657   •   Chapter Review   658

CHAPTER 26

Liberalism and Its Challengers 1960–1973   660

Comparing American Histories   660
Earl Warren and Bayard Rustin

The Politics of Liberalism   661
Kennedy's New Frontier   662   •   Kennedy, the Cold War, and Cuba   662

The Civil Rights Movement Intensifies, 1961–1968   664
Freedom Rides   664   •   Kennedy Supports Civil Rights   665   •   Freedom
Summer and Voting Rights   666   •   Civil Rights and Black Power   669

Federal Efforts toward Social Reform, 1964–1968   671
The Great Society   671   •   The Warren Court   672

The Vietnam War, 1961–1969   674
Kennedy's Intervention in South Vietnam   674   •   Johnson Escalates the War in
Vietnam   674

Challenges to the Liberal Establishment   677
The New Left   678   •   The Counterculture   679   •   Liberation
Movements   680   •   The Revival of Conservatism   684

Conclusion: Liberalism and Its Discontents   686   •   Chapter Review   687

CHAPTER 27

The Swing toward Conservatism 1968–1980   689

Comparing American Histories   689
   Louise Day Hicks and Pauli Murray

Nixon: War and Diplomacy, 1969–1974   691
   The Election of 1968 691 • The Failure of Vietnamization 692 • The Cold
   War Thaws 693 • Crisis in the Middle East and at Home 694

Nixon and Politics, 1969–1974   695
   Pragmatic Conservatism 695 • The Nixon Landslide and Watergate Scandal,
   1972–1974 695

The Presidency of Jimmy Carter, 1976–1980   698
   Jimmy Carter and the Limits of Affluence 698 • The Perils of
   Détente 701 • Challenges in the Middle East 702

The Persistence of Liberalism in the 1970s   703
   Popular Culture 703 • Women's Movement 704 •
   Environmentalism 705 • Racial Struggles Continue 706 •
   Mexican Americans Challenge Discrimination 708

The New Right Rises   709
   Tax Revolt 709 • Neoconservatism 709 • Christian Conservatism 710

Conclusion: The Swing toward Conservatism 711 • Chapter Review 712

CHAPTER 28

The Triumph of Conservatism, the End of the Cold War, and the Rise of the New World Order 1980–1992   714

Comparing American Histories   714
   George Pratt Shultz and Demetria Martinez

The Reagan Revolution   716
   Reagan and Reaganomics 716 • The Implementation of Social
   Conservatism 720

Reagan and the End of the Cold War, 1981–1988   721
   "The Evil Empire" 722 • Human Rights and the Fight against
   Communism 722 • Fighting International Terrorism 725 • The Nuclear
   Freeze Movement 726 • The Road to Nuclear De-escalation 728

The Presidency of George H. W. Bush, 1989–1993   729
   "Kinder and Gentler" Conservatism 729 • The Breakup of the Soviet
   Union 730 • Globalization and the New World Order 732 • Managing
   Conflict after the Cold War 735 • The 1992 Election 737

Conclusion: Conservative Ascendancy and the End of the Cold War 738 •
Chapter Review 739

CHAPTER 29

The Challenges of a Globalized World 1993 to the present   741

Comparing American Histories   741
William Henry (Bill) Gates III and Alicia Garza

Transforming American Society   743
The Computer Revolution   743   •   The Changing American Population   744

Political Polarization and Globalization in the Clinton Years   745
Politics during the Clinton Administration   746   •   Global Challenges   747

The Presidency of George W. Bush   749
Bush and Compassionate Conservatism   749   •   The Iraq War   750   •   Bush's
Second Term   753

The Challenges Faced by President Barack Obama   753
The Great Recession   754   •   Obama and the Great Recession   754   •   The
2010 Revolt against Obama   756   •   Obama's Second Term   757   •   Latinos
and Immigration   757   •   Asian Americans   758   •   African
Americans and Systemic Racism   759   •   The Native American Struggle
Continued   760   •   Obama and the World   760

The Presidency of Donald Trump   762
The 2016 Election   762   •   The Trump Presidency   764   •   Pandemic, Protests,
and Politics   766

Conclusion: Technology, Terror, and Pandemic in a Global Society   768   •
Chapter Review   770

Appendix

The Declaration of Independence   A-1

The Articles of Confederation and Perpetual Union   A-4

The Constitution of the United States   A-9

Amendments to the Constitution
(including six unratified amendments)   A-16

Admission of States to the Union   A-24

Presidents of the United States   A-25

Glossary   G-1

Index   I-1

Maps, Figures, and Tables

Maps

Chapter 1

MAP 1.1 The Settling of the Americas   4

MAP 1.2 Native American Peoples, c. 500–1500 C.E.   8

MAP 1.3 European Explorations in the Americas, 1492–1536   15

MAP 1.4 The Columbian Exchange, Sixteenth Century   18

MAP 1.5 Spanish Explorations in North America, 1528–1542   22

Chapter 2

MAP 2.1 Approximate Tribal Locations at First Contact with Europeans   34

MAP 2.2 The Growth of English Settlement in the Chesapeake, c. 1650   40

MAP 2.3 West Indies and Carolina in the Seventeenth Century   44

Chapter 3

MAP 3.1 European Empires and Indian Nations in North America, 1715–1750   64

MAP 3.2 North Atlantic Trade in the Eighteenth Century   68

MAP 3.3 Ethnic and Racial Diversity in British North America, 1750   76

Chapter 4

MAP 4.1 Frontier Settlements and Indian Towns in Pennsylvania, 1700–1740   96

MAP 4.2 Religious Diversity in 1750   102

Chapter 5

MAP 5.1 The French and Indian War, 1754–1763   115

MAP 5.2 British Conflicts with Indians, 1758–1763, and the Proclamation Line   117

Chapter 6

MAP 6.1 The War in the North, 1775–1778   147

MAP 6.2 The War in the West and the South, 1777–1782   154

Chapter 7

MAP 7.1 Cessions of Western Land, 1782–1802   166

MAP 7.2 American Indians in the Ohio River Valley, c. 1785–1795   182

Chapter 8

MAP 8.1 Lewis and Clark and Zebulon Pike Expeditions, 1804–1807   202

MAP 8.2 Indian Land Cessions, 1790–1820   205

Chapter 9

MAP 9.1 The War of 1812 220

MAP 9.2 Roads and Canals to 1837 224

MAP 9.3 The Missouri Compromise and Westward Expansion, 1820s 230

Chapter 10

MAP 10.1 Religious Movements in the Burned-Over District, 1831–1848 256

MAP 10.2 The Underground Railroad, c. 1850 264

Chapter 11

MAP 11.1 The Spread of Slavery and Cotton, 1820–1860 278

MAP 11.2 Indian Removals and Relocations, 1820s–1840s 288

MAP 11.3 The Mexican-American War, 1846–1848 294

Chapter 12

MAP 12.1 Western Trails and Indian Nations, c. 1850 305

MAP 12.2 Kansas-Nebraska Territory 314

MAP 12.3 The Election of 1860 320

MAP 12.4 The Original Confederacy 321

Chapter 13

MAP 13.1 Early Civil War Battles, 1861–1862 331

MAP 13.2 Battles of Gettysburg and Vicksburg, 1863 341

Chapter 14

MAP 14.1 Reconstruction in the South 361

MAP 14.2 The Election of 1876 370

Chapter 15

MAP 15.1 The American West, 1860–1900 375

MAP 15.2 The Indian Frontier, 1870 379

Chapter 16

MAP 16.1 The New South, 1900 407

MAP 16.2 Black Disfranchisement in the South, 1889–1908 419

Chapter 17

MAP 17.1 The Great Railroad Strike 436

MAP 17.2 The Election of 1896 446

Chapter 18

MAP 18.1 Immigrants in the U.S., 1910 455

Chapter 19

MAP 19.1 Women's Suffrage 480

MAP 19.2 National Parks and Forests 490

Chapter 20

MAP 20.1   The War of 1898   510

MAP 20.2   European Alliances, 1914   517

Chapter 21

MAP 21.1   The Shift from Rural to Urban Population, 1920–1930   538

MAP 21.2   The Election of 1924   550

Chapter 22

MAP 22.1   The Dust Bowl   560

Chapter 23

MAP 23.1   World War II in Europe, 1941–1945   598

MAP 23.2   World War II in the Pacific, 1941–1945   600

Chapter 24

MAP 24.1   The Cold War in Europe, 1945–1955   616

MAP 24.2   The Korean War, 1950–1953   619

Chapter 25

MAP 25.1   Lunch Counter Sit-Ins, February–April 1960   651

MAP 25.2   The Election of 1960   656

Chapter 26

MAP 26.1   The Bay of Pigs Invasion, 1961   663

MAP 26.2   The Vietnam War, 1968   677

Chapter 27

MAP 27.1   The Election of 1968   692

MAP 27.2   The Sun and Rust Belts   700

Chapter 28

MAP 28.1   The Election of 1980   717

MAP 28.2   The United States in Central America and the Caribbean, 1954–1989   724

MAP 28.3   The United States in the Middle East, 1978–1991   726

MAP 28.4   The Fall of Communism in Eastern Europe and the Soviet Union, 1989–1991   732

Chapter 29

MAP 29.1   The Breakup of Yugoslavia, 1991–2008   749

MAP 29.2   The Middle East, 2000–2017   761

Figures and Tables

TABLE 3.1 English Colonies Established in North America, 1607–1750 59

FIGURE 3.1 The Slave Trade in Numbers, 1501–1866 71

FIGURE 3.2 Indentured Servants and Slaves in Six Maryland Counties, 1662–1717 73

TABLE 4.1 Sex Ratios in the White Population for Selected Colonies, 1624–1755 88

TABLE 4.2 Sexual Coercion Cases Downgraded in Chester County, Pennsylvania, 1731–1739 92

FIGURE 4.1 Transatlantic Migrations, 1500–1640 & 1641–1750 94

TABLE 7.1 Votes of State-Ratifying Conventions 175

TABLE 8.1 Prices at George Davenport's Trading Post, Rock Island, Illinois, c. 1820 207

TABLE 8.2 Growth of Cotton Production in the United States, 1790–1830 212

FIGURE 9.1 The Elections of 1824 and 1828 236

FIGURE 10.1 Immigration to the United States, 1820–1860 248

FIGURE 13.1 Economies of the North and South, 1860 328

FIGURE 15.1 British Foreign Investment in the United States, 1876 377

FIGURE 16.1 Expansion of the Railroad System, 1870–1900 403

TABLE 16.1 An Age of Organizations, 1876–1896 415

FIGURE 17.1 Union Membership, 1870–1900 434

TABLE 18.1 Percentage of Immigrant Departures versus Arrivals, 1875–1914 456

TABLE 18.2 Percentage Rural and Urban Population in U.S., 1880–1910 462

TABLE 19.1 National Progressive Legislation 493

FIGURE 20.1 U.S. Exports and Imports, 1870–1910 504

TABLE 20.1 World War I Casualties Percentage of Deaths in Mobilized Forces in World War I by Country 518

FIGURE 21.1 Production of Consumer Goods, 1921 and 1929 535

FIGURE 21.2 Income Inequality, 1923–1929 539

FIGURE 22.1 Unemployment, 1920–1945 558

FIGURE 22.2 Farm Foreclosures, 1932–1942 564

TABLE 22.1 Major New Deal Measures, 1933–1938 572

FIGURE 23.1 Real Gross Domestic Product of the Great Powers, 1938–1945 588

TABLE 24.1 Nuclear Warheads, United States, Soviet Union, United Kingdom, 1945–1960 626

FIGURE 25.1 Economic Growth, 1945–1965 638

FIGURE 25.2 The Baby Boom, 1946–1964 639

FIGURE 26.1 Black Voter Registration in the South, 1947–1976 668

TABLE 26.1 Major Great Society Measures, 1964–1968 673

FIGURE 27.1 Global Per Capita Energy Consumption 699

FIGURE 27.2 United States Unemployment Rate and Inflation Rate (the "Misery Index") 700

FIGURE 28.1 Immigrant Arrivals to the United States, 1960–2000 721

FIGURE 29.1 Immigrant Growth by Home Region, 1981–2010 745

FIGURE 29.2 Wealth Inequality (Capital Income), 2011 755

About the Cover Image

Street Scene, New Orleans, **by Andre Mantelet-Martel (born 1876)** In this oil painting, the French-born artist Andre Mantelet-Martel captures the uniqueness and diversity of New Orleans in the nineteenth century. Founded by the French, taken over by the Spanish, and then returned to French control, New Orleans and the Louisiana Territory were bought by the United States under President Thomas Jefferson in 1803. Near the mouth of the Mississippi River, New Orleans has been a major port city throughout American history. Spanish, French, Anglo, Native American, and African inhabitants of the city created a rich cultural mixture unparalleled in the nation. The birthplace of jazz and Mardi Gras, New Orleans has also played important roles in the War of 1812, the sale and distribution of enslaved labor, the Civil War, Reconstruction, and the civil rights movement. Mantelet-Martel's painting depicts the diversity of residents walking through one of the city's plazas.

Private Collection, Waterhouse & Dodd, London, UK/Bridgeman Images

Exploring American Histories

VALUE EDITION

1

Mapping Global Frontiers

to 1590

LEARNING OBJECTIVES

After reading this chapter you will be able to:

- Describe the diverse societies that populated the Americas prior to European exploration.

- Explain the reasons for European exploration and expansion, and compare the impact of this expansion on Europe and Africa.

- Evaluate the reasons for Europeans' success in reaching the Americas, and compare the impact of the Columbian exchange on American Indians, Africans, and Europeans.

- Analyze how the Spanish created an empire in the Americas, and describe the impact of Spain's empire building on Indian empires and European nations.

COMPARING AMERICAN HISTORIES

In 1519 a young Indian woman named **Malintzin** was thrust into the center of dramatic events that transformed not only her world but also the world at large. As a young girl, Malintzin, whose birth name is lost to history, lived in the rural area of Coatzacoalcos on the frontier between the expanding kingdom of the Mexica and the declining Mayan states of the Yucatán peninsula. Raised in a noble household, Malintzin was fluent in Nahuatl, the language of the Mexica.

In 1515 or 1516, when she was between the ages of eight and twelve, Malintzin was taken by or given to Mexica merchants, perhaps as a peace offering to stave off military attacks. She then entered a well-established trade in slaves, consisting mostly of women and girls, who were sent eastward to work in the expanding cotton fields or the households of their

1

owners. She may also have been forced into a sexual relationship with a landowner. Whatever her situation, Malintzin learned the Mayan language during her captivity.

In 1517 Mayan villagers sighted Spanish adventurers along local rivers and drove them off. But in 1519 the Spaniards returned. The Maya's lightweight armor made of dense layers of cotton, cloth, and leather and their wooden arrows were no match for the invaders' steel swords, guns, and horses. Forced to surrender, the Maya offered the Spaniards food, gold, and twenty enslaved women, including Malintzin. The Spanish leader, Hernán Cortés, baptized the enslaved women and assigned each of them Christian names, although the women did not consent to this ritual. Cortés then divided the women among his senior officers, giving Malintzin to the highest-ranking noble.

Already fluent in Nahuatl and Mayan, Malintzin soon learned Spanish. Within a matter of months, she became the Spaniards' chief translator. As Cortés moved into territories ruled by the Mexica (whom the Spaniards called Aztecs), his success depended on his ability to understand Aztec ways of thinking and to convince subjugated groups to fight against their despotic rulers. Malintzin thus accompanied Cortés at every step, including his triumphant conquest of the Aztec capital in the fall of 1521.

At the same time that Malintzin played a key role in the conquest of the Aztecs, **Martin Waldseemüller** sought to map the frontiers along which these conflicts erupted. Born in present-day Germany in the early 1470s, Waldseemüller enrolled at the University of Fribourg in 1490, where he probably studied theology. He would gain fame, however, as a cartographer, or mapmaker.

In 1507 Waldseemüller and Mathias Ringmann, working at a scholarly religious institute in St. Dié in northern France, produced a map of the world, a small globe, and a Latin translation of the four voyages of the Italian explorer Amerigo Vespucci. The map and the globe, entitled *Universalis Cosmographia*, depict the "known" world as well as the "new" worlds recently discovered by European explorers. The latter include an elongated territory labeled *America*, set between the continents of Africa and Asia. It was named in honor of Amerigo Vespucci, who first recognized that the lands Columbus reached were part of a separate continent. The map, covering some 36 square feet, offered a view of the world never before attempted.

In 1516 Waldseemüller produced an updated map of the world, the *Carta Marina*. Apparently in response to challenges regarding Vespucci's role in discovering new territories, he substituted the term *Terra Incognita* ("unknown land") for the region he had earlier labeled America. But the 1507 map had already circulated widely, and *America* became part of the European lexicon.

A COMPARISON OF THE PERSONAL HISTORIES of Malintzin and Martin Waldseemüller highlights the profound consequences of contact between the peoples of Europe and those of the Americas. The Mexica, or Aztec, and the Spanish were most affected during this period, but France and England would soon also seek footholds in the Americas. For millennia, travel and communication between the two sides of the Atlantic had been extremely limited. Then, in the sixteenth century—and despite significant obstacles—animals, plants, goods, ideas, and people began circulating between Europe and what became known as America. Malintzin and Waldseemüller, in their very different ways, helped map the frontiers of this global society and contributed to the dramatic transformations that followed.

Native Peoples in the Americas

The first people in the Americas almost certainly arrived as migrants from northeast Asia, but the timing of such migrations remains in doubt. They likely began at least 25,000 years ago. It is also difficult to estimate the population of the Americas before contact with Europeans. Estimates range from 37 million to 100 million. It is clear, however, that the vast majority of people lived within a few hundred miles of the equator, and the smallest number—perhaps 4 to 7 million—lived in present-day North America. By the fifteenth century, like other regions of the world, the Americas were home to diverse societies, ranging from coastal fishing villages to nomadic hunter-gatherers to settled horticulturalists to city-centered empires.

Native Peoples Develop Diverse Cultures

The settlement of the Americas was encouraged by the growth of glaciers on the North American continent between about 38,000 and 14,000 B.C.E. This development led to a dramatic drop in sea levels and created a land bridge in the Bering Strait, between present-day Siberia and Alaska, called **Beringia**. The first migrations may have occurred about 20,000 to 25,000 years ago, during a warming trend when melting glaciers retreated from large areas of land. During the warming trend, some settlers probably traveled from the northeastern region of the Asian Steppe (southern Siberia) to Beringia, following herds of mammoths, musk oxen, and woolly rhinoceroses. Then, 15,000 to 20,000 years ago, descendants of some of these settlers followed coastal pathways and the Pacific shore line, taking advantage of the rich maritime resources. These coastal journeys may help explain how Asiatic migrants peopled vast areas of South America in just a few thousand years. As immense expanses of ice returned to many regions some 13,000 years ago, the routes that migrants could follow shifted and forced many groups to push inland or further south.

Whether over land or sea, those moving inland had to skirt melting glaciers to find better hunting grounds and more abundant plant life. When the mammoths and other large game disappeared from large areas about 10,000 years ago, people became more dependent on smaller game, fish, roots, berries, and other plant foods to survive. At the same time, new groups of migrants headed east from Beringia. These included Inuit and Aleut peoples who arrived in present-day Alaska thousands of years after more southern areas had been settled (Map 1.1).

Between 8000 and 2000 B.C.E., some communities in the Americas began establishing agricultural systems that encouraged more stable settlements and population

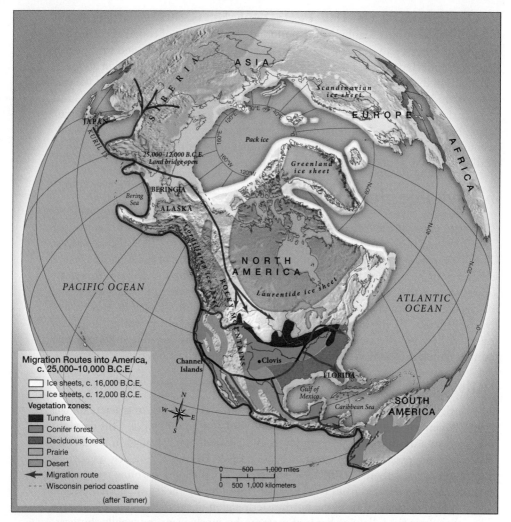

MAP 1.1 The Settling of the Americas

Beginning about 25,000 B.C.E., Asian peoples likely migrated to America across a land bridge after expanding glaciers lowered sea levels. Others probably followed the coastline in boats. As glaciers retreated over several centuries, they opened corridors along which people migrated, leaving traces in archaeological sites in present-day Wisconsin, New Mexico, Florida, Central America, and Chile.

growth. **Horticulture**—a form of agriculture in which people work small plots of land with simple tools—became highly developed in the area of present-day Mexico. There men and women developed improved strains of maize (or Indian corn). They also cultivated protein-rich beans, squash, tomatoes, potatoes, and manioc (a root vegetable, also known as cassava or yucca root). The combination of beans, squash, and corn offered an especially nutritious diet while maintaining the fertility of the soil. Moreover, high yields produced surplus food that could be stored or traded to neighboring communities.

By 500 C.E., complex societies, rooted in intensive agriculture, began to thrive in the equatorial region. Between 500 and 1500 C.E., the spread of maize cultivation northward into the present-day American Southwest and beyond fostered economic developments that necessitated irrigation and led to the diversification of native societies. Small bands of hunters and gatherers continued to thrive in deserts and forests while impressive civilizations arose on swamplands and grasslands, and in the mountains.

The Aztecs, the Maya, and the Incas

Three significant civilizations emerged by the early sixteenth century: Aztec and Mayan societies in the equatorial region and Inca society along the Pacific coast in present-day Peru. Technologically advanced and with knowledge of mathematics and astronomy, these societies were characterized by vast mineral wealth, large urban centers, highly ritualized religions, and complex political systems. Unlike their counterparts in Europe, Asia, and Africa, they did not develop the wheel to aid in transportation, nor did they have steel tools and weapons. Since most of their commerce was carried out over land or along rivers and coastlines, they did not build large boats. They also lacked horses, which had disappeared from the region thousands of years earlier. Still, the Aztecs, Maya, and Incas established grand cities and civilizations.

Around 1325 C.E., the **Aztecs**, who called themselves Mexica, built their capital, Tenochtitlán, on the site of present-day Mexico City. Seminomadic warriors who invaded and then settled the region, the Aztecs drew on local residents' knowledge of irrigation and cultivation and adopted their written language. Aztec commoners, who tilled communally owned lands, were ruled over by priests and nobles. The nobles formed a warrior class and owned vast estates on which they employed both serfs and slaves captured from non-Aztec communities in the region. Priests promised fertility—for the land and its people—but demanded human sacrifices, including thousands of men and women from captured tribes. To sustain their society, Aztecs extended their trade networks, offering pottery, cloth, and leather goods in exchange for textiles and obsidian to make sharp-edged tools and weapons. As Malintzin's story illustrates, enslaved women were an important component of this trade.

When Malintzin was sold to a Mayan village by Aztec merchants, she was being traded from one grand civilization to another. The **Maya** slowly settled the Yucatán peninsula and the rain forests of present-day Guatemala between roughly 900 B.C.E. and 300 C.E. They established large cities that were home to skilled artisans and developed elaborate systems for irrigation and water storage. Farmers worked the fields and labored to build huge stone temples and palaces for rulers who claimed to be descended from the gods. Learned men developed mathematical calculations, astronomical systems, hieroglyphic writing, and a calendar.

Yet the Mayan civilization began to decline around 800 C.E. An economic crisis, likely the result of drought and exacerbated by heavy taxation, probably drove peasant families into the interior. While many towns and religious sites were abandoned, some communities survived the crisis and reemerged as thriving city-states. By the early sixteenth century, they were trading with the Aztecs.

The **Incas** developed an equally impressive civilization in the Andes Mountains along the Pacific coast. The Inca empire, like the Aztec empire, was built on the accomplishments of earlier societies. At the height of their power, in the fifteenth century, the Incas controlled some 16 million people spread over 350,000 square miles. They constructed an expansive system of roads and garrisons to ensure the flow of food, trade goods, and soldiers from their capital at Cuzco through the surrounding mountains and valleys.

The key to Inca success was the cultivation of fertile mountain valleys. Cuzco, some eleven thousand feet above sea level, lay in the center of the Inca empire, with the Huaylas and Titicaca valleys on either side. Here residents cultivated potatoes and other crops on terraces watered by an elaborate irrigation system. Miners dug gold and silver from the mountains, and artisans crafted the metals into jewelry and decorative items. Thousands of laborers constructed elaborate palaces and temples. And like the Aztec priests, Inca priests sacrificed humans to the gods to stave off natural disasters and military defeat.

Native Cultures to the North

To the north of these grand civilizations, smaller societies with less elaborate cultures thrived. In present-day Arizona and New Mexico, the Mogollon and Hohokam established communities around 500 C.E. The Mogollon were expert potters, while the Hohokam, migrating north from Mexico, developed extensive irrigation systems. Farther north, in present-day Utah and Colorado, the ancient Pueblo people built adobe and masonry homes cut into cliffs around 750 C.E. After migrating south and constructing large buildings that included administrative offices, religious centers, and craft shops, the Pueblo returned to their cliff dwellings in the 1100s for

Female Figurine, Peru, c. 1430–1532 This figurine made of gold depicts a Mamacona, who was similar to a nun in Incan society. Daughters of the nobility or young women of exceptional beauty lived in temple sanctuaries and dedicated themselves to the sun god, Inti. They served the Inca people and priests. The multicolored woolen robe and gold pin indicate this woman's special status. Werner Forman/Universal Images Group/Getty Images

protection from invaders. There, drought eventually caused them to disperse into smaller groups.

Farther north on the plains that stretched from present-day Colorado into Canada, hunting societies developed around herds of bison. A weighted spear-throwing device, called an *atlatl*, allowed hunters to capture smaller game, while nets, hooks, and snares allowed them to catch birds, fish, and small animals. Societies in the Great Plains as well as the Great Basin (between the Rockies and the Sierra Nevada) generally remained small and widely scattered. Given the arid conditions in these regions, communities needed a large expanse of territory as they followed migrating animals or seasonal plant sources. Here the adoption of the bow and arrow, in about 500 C.E., proved the most significant technological development.

Other native societies, like the Mandan, settled along rivers in the heart of the continent (present-day North and South Dakota). The rich soil along the banks fostered farming, while forests and plains attracted diverse animals for hunting. Around 1250 C.E., however, an extended drought forced these settlements to contract, and competition for resources increased among Mandan villages and with other native groups in the region.

Hunting-gathering societies also emerged along the Pacific coast, where the abundance of fish, small game, and plant life provided the resources to develop permanent settlements. The Chumash Indians, near present-day Santa Barbara, California, harvested resources from the land and the ocean. Women gathered acorns and pine nuts, while men fished and hunted. The Chumash, whose villages sometimes held a thousand inhabitants, participated in regional exchange networks up and down the coast.

Even larger societies with more elaborate social, religious, and political systems developed near the Mississippi River. A group that came to be called the **Hopewell people** established a thriving culture there in the early centuries C.E. The river and its surrounding lands provided fertile fields and easy access to distant communities. Centered in present-day southern Ohio and western Illinois, the Hopewell constructed towns of four to six thousand people. Artifacts from their burial sites reflect extensive trading networks that stretched from the Missouri River to Lake Superior, and from the Rocky Mountains to the Appalachian region and Florida.

Beginning around 500 C.E., the Hopewell culture gave birth to larger and more complex societies that flourished in the Mississippi River valley and to the south and east. As bows and arrows spread into the region, people hunted more game in the thick forests. But Mississippian groups also learned to cultivate corn. By providing a staple crop, corn allowed the population to expand dramatically. More complex political and religious systems developed in which elite rulers gained greater control over the labor of farmers and hunters. Mississippian peoples created massive earthworks sculpted in the shape of serpents, birds, and other creatures. Some earthen sculptures stood higher than 70 feet and stretched longer than 1,300 feet. Mississippians also constructed huge temple mounds that could cover nearly 16 acres.

By about 1100 C.E., the Cahokia people established the largest Mississippian settlement, near present-day St. Louis, which may have housed ten to thirty thousand inhabitants (Map 1.2). Powerful chieftains extended trade networks from the Great Lakes to the Gulf of Mexico, conquered smaller villages, and created a centralized government. Shells from the Atlantic coast, copper from the Great Lakes, buffalo

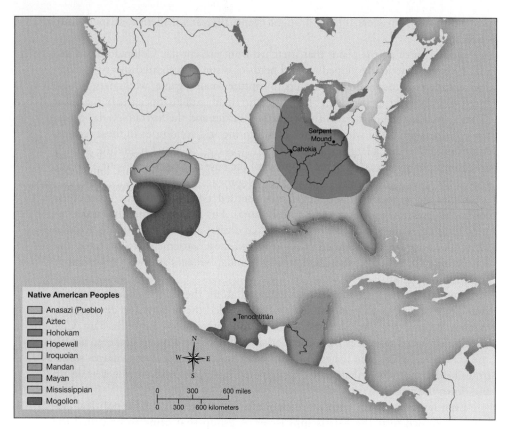

MAP 1.2   Native American Peoples, c. 500–1500 c.e.
Many distinct cultures developed in the Americas in the ten centuries before 1500. Some societies, like the Mississippians, developed extensive trade networks over land or along rivers and coastlines. Societies in the same region often learned from those who preceded them, such as the Aztec from the Maya, but other groups battled over scarce resources.

hides from the Great Plains, and other items found at Cahokian sites provide evidence of a trade network that extended across large parts of North America. By the 1200s, however, deforestation, drought, and perhaps disease, affected the Cahokian people, as did overhunting. Many settlements dispersed. After 1400, political turmoil and increased warfare among native peoples joined with environmental changes to ensure the decline of Mississippian culture.

REVIEW & RELATE

- Compare and contrast the Aztecs, Incas, and Maya. What similarities and differences do you note?
- How did the societies of North America differ from those of the equatorial zone and the Andes?

Europe Expands Its Reach

The complex societies that emerged in the Americas were made possible by an agricultural revolution that included the establishment of crop systems, the domestication of animals, and the development of tools. This agricultural revolution, spurred by the end of the Wisconsin glaciation, transformed eastern North America in the 1100s and 1200s C.E. Even more dramatic developments had occurred centuries earlier — between 4000 and 3000 B.C.E — in the Fertile Crescent of the Middle East and in China. Increased productivity there ensured population growth and allowed attention to science, trade, politics, religion, and the arts. Over millennia, knowledge from these civilizations made its way into Europe. At the height of the Roman Empire in the early centuries C.E., dense global trade networks connected the peoples of Europe, Africa, and Asia. With the decline of Roman power in western Europe, those connections broke down, but commercial ties continued to thrive among diverse peoples surrounding the Mediterranean Sea. Portuguese explorers, denied access to that rich Mediterranean world by the politics of the period, instead sought trade routes along the coast of Africa. Increased trade with African kingdoms by Portugal and other European societies included the purchase of slaves. This lucrative and devastating commerce would expand dramatically as European nations colonized the Americas.

The Mediterranean World

Beginning in the seventh century Islam proved one of the most dynamic cultural, political, and military forces in the world. By the ninth century, Islamic (also known as Muslim) regimes created an Arab empire that controlled most of southwest Asia and North Africa and conquered parts of the Iberian peninsula in Europe. In the eleventh and twelfth centuries, Catholic leaders launched several military and religious campaigns to reclaim Jerusalem and other sites associated with Jesus for the Church. Later known as the **Crusades**, these campaigns largely failed, but they enhanced the roles of Italian merchants, who profited from both outfitting Crusaders and opening new trade routes to the East. Moreover, these campaigns inspired explorers and adventurers throughout Europe.

In the Middle East, inhabitants had managed to survive droughts and other ecological crises and sustain productive economic systems. In the Mediterranean world, this productivity depended on technological advances in irrigation and navigation and a vast network of slave-trading centers and enslaved laborers. It was the productivity of agriculture — developed centuries earlier than in Europe or America — that allowed societies along the southern Mediterranean, in northern Africa, and in southwest Asia to excel in astronomy, mathematics, architecture, and the arts.

Medieval European states proved far less adept at staving off human and environmental disasters. Besieged by drought and disease as well as wars and peasant rebellions, rulers across the continent expended most of their resources on trying to sustain their population and protect their borders. In the 1340s, as Europeans began to trade with various regions of Asia, flea-infested rats carried the bubonic plague and other epidemic diseases on board ships and into European seaports. From the 1340s to the early fifteenth century, the bubonic plague — later called the **Black Death** — periodically ravaged European cities and towns. The initial **pandemic** — a deadly disease that covers a wide geographic area—spread across Europe between 1346 and 1350, killing about 36 million people, half of Europe's population. A century-long war between France and England added to the death and destruction.

By the early fifteenth century, the plague had retreated from much of Europe, and the climate had improved. Only then were European peoples able to benefit significantly from the riches of the East. Smaller populations led to an improved standard of living. Then rising birthrates and increased productivity, beginning in Italian city-states, fueled a resurgence of trade with other parts of the world. The profits from agriculture and commerce allowed the wealthy and powerful to begin investing in the arts and luxury goods. Indeed, a cultural **Renaissance** (from the French word for "rebirth") flourished in the Italian city-states and then spread to France, Spain, the Low Countries, and central Europe.

This cultural rebirth went hand in hand with political unification as more powerful rulers extended their control over smaller city-states and principalities. A vibrant and religiously tolerant culture had existed in Muslim Spain from the eighth to the tenth century, but that was followed by a long period of persecution of Christians. When Christians began reconquering Spain after 1200, Muslims and Jews alike became targets. Then in 1469, the marriage of Isabella of Castile and Ferdinand II of Aragon sealed the unification of Christian Spain. By 1492 their combined forces expelled the last Muslim conquerors from the Iberian peninsula. Promoting Catholicism to create a more unified national identity, Isabella and Ferdinand launched an Inquisition against supposed heretics and executed or expelled some 200,000 Jews as well. Despite the brutality of the reconquest and the Inquisition, Catholic Spain had the wealth and military power to forge its own trade networks with North Africa, India, and other Asian lands.

Yet Italy controlled the most important routes through the Mediterranean, so leaders in Spain and neighboring Portugal sought alternate paths to riches. Their efforts were aided by explorers, missionaries, and merchants who traveled to Morocco, Turkey, India, and other distant lands. They brought back trade goods and knowledge of astronomy, shipbuilding, mapmaking, and navigation that allowed Iberians to venture farther south along the Atlantic coast of Africa and, eventually, west into the uncharted Atlantic Ocean.

Portugal Pursues Long-Distance Trade

Cut off from the Mediterranean by Italian city-states and Muslim rulers in North Africa, Portugal looked toward the Atlantic. Although a tiny nation, Portugal benefited from the leadership of its young prince, Henry, who launched explorations of the African coast in the 1420s, hoping to find a passage to India via the Atlantic Ocean. Prince Henry—known as Henry the Navigator—gathered information from astronomers, geographers, mapmakers, and craftsmen in the Arab world and recruited Italian cartographers and navigators along with Portuguese scholars, sailors, and captains. He then launched a systematic campaign of exploration, observation, shipbuilding, and long-distance trade that revolutionized Europe and shaped developments in Africa and the Americas.

Prince Henry and his colleagues developed ships known as caravels—vessels with narrow hulls and triangular sails that were especially effective for navigating the coast of West Africa. His staff also created state-of-the-art maritime charts, maps, and astronomical tables; perfected navigational instruments; and mastered the complex wind and sea currents along the African coast. Soon Portugal was trading in gold, ivory, and slaves from West Africa.

In 1482 Portugal built Elmina Castle, a trading post and fort on the Gold Coast (present-day Ghana). Further expeditions were launched from the castle; five years later, a fleet led by Bartolomeu Dias rounded the Cape of Good Hope, on the southernmost tip of Africa. This feat demonstrated the possibility of sailing directly from the Atlantic to the Indian Ocean. Vasco da Gama followed this route to India in 1497, returning to Portugal in 1499, his ships laden with valuable cinnamon and pepper.

By the early sixteenth century, Portuguese traders had wrested control of the India trade from Arab fleets. They established fortified trading posts at key locations on the Indian Ocean and extended their expeditions to Indonesia, China, and Japan. Within a decade, the Portuguese had become the leaders in international trade. Spain, England, France, and the Netherlands competed for a share of this newfound wealth by developing long-distance markets that brought spices, ivory, silks, cotton cloth, and other luxury goods to Europe.

With expanding populations and greater agricultural productivity, European nations developed more efficient systems of taxation, built larger military forces, and adapted gunpowder to new kinds of weapons. The surge in population provided the men to labor on merchant vessels, staff forts, and protect trade routes. More people began to settle in cities, which grew into important commercial centers. Slowly, a form of capitalism based on market exchange, private ownership, and capital accumulation and reinvestment developed across much of Europe.

European Encounters with West Africa

Enslaved Africans were among the most lucrative commodity traded by European merchants. Slavery had been practiced in Europe, America, Africa, and other parts of the world for centuries. The enslaved were often captives of war or individuals sold in payment for deaths or injuries to conquering enemies. In some places, including Roman society, slavery was inheritable. In others, such as Anglo-Saxon England, slaves were sometimes sold along with the land they had worked. In other areas, enslaved men and women retained some legal rights and bondage was not passed on to their children. With the advent of European participation in the African slave trade and increased African demand for European goods, the system of bondage changed. The scale of the trade expanded significantly, transforming Europe and Africa and eventually the Americas.

In the fifteenth century, Europeans were most familiar with North Africa, a region deeply influenced by Islam and characterized by large kingdoms, well-developed cities, and an extensive network of trading centers. In northeast Africa, including Egypt, city-states flourished, with ties to India, the Middle East, and China. In northwest Africa, Timbuktu linked North Africa to empires south of the Great Desert as well as to Europe. Here African slaves labored for wealthier Africans in a system of bound labor long familiar to Europeans.

As trade with western Africa increased, however, Europeans came into contact with communities that lived by hunting and subsistence agriculture. This unleashed

African Salt Cellar This ivory salt cellar was carved in the fifteenth or sixteenth century in Sierra Leone, on the West African coast and was made for sale to Portuguese traders. The artisan depicted traditional geometric designs and African reptiles but clothed the four male and four female African figures in items of European dress. Werner Forman Archive/Bridgeman Images

conflict among Africans even within the same kingdom. In 1526, Mvemba A Nzinga, king of the Kongo, wrote to the king of Portugal, John III, complaining "that many of our people, keenly desirous as they are of the wares and things of your Kingdoms, . . . seize many of our people," including freedmen and noblemen, "and take them to be sold to the white men." To stop this illegal commerce, Nzinga asked that Portuguese men entering the Kongo immediately inform noblemen and court officials and comply with existing rules of trade. Nzinga's request was ignored.

By the mid-sixteenth century, European nations established competing forts along the African coast from the Gold Coast and Senegambia in the north to the Bight of Biafra and West Central Africa in the south. Increasingly, the enslaved Africans shipped from these forts came from communities that had been raided or conquered by more powerful groups. They arrived at the coast exhausted, hungry, dirty, and with few clothes. They worshipped gods unfamiliar to Europeans, and their cultural customs and social practices seemed strange and primitive. Over time, the image of the West African slave came to dominate European visions of the entire continent.

As traders from Portugal, Spain, Holland, and England brought back more enslaved Africans, negative depictions took deeper hold. Woodcuts and prints circulated in Europe in which half-naked Africans appeared more like apes than humans while biblical stories reinforced notions of Africans as inherently inferior. In the Bible, Ham had sinned against his father, Noah. Noah then cursed Ham's son Canaan to a life of slavery. Increasingly, European Christians considered Africans the "sons of Ham," infidels assigned by God to a life of bondage. This self-serving idea was used to justify the enslavement of black men, women, and children.

Of course, these distorted images of West Africans did not reflect the diverse peoples and societies that made their home in the area's tropical rain forests, plains, and savannas. Still, as the slave trade expanded in the sixteenth and seventeenth centuries, it destabilized large areas of western and central Africa, with smaller societies decimated by raids and even larger kingdoms damaged by the extensive commerce in human beings.

Some Africans, particularly rulers of the most powerful African kingdoms, were active participants in the slave trade. For instance, because women were more highly valued by Muslim traders in North Africa and Asia, African traders steered women to these profitable markets. At the same time, African societies organized along matrilineal lines—where goods and political power passed through the mother's line—tried to protect women against enslavement. Other groups sought to limit the sale of men.

Ultimately, men, women, and children were captured by African as well as Portuguese, Spanish, Dutch, and English traders. Europeans did not institute a system of perpetual slavery, in which enslavement was inherited from one generation to the next. Instead, Africans formed another class of bound labor, alongside peasants, indentured servants, criminals, and apprentices. Few distinctions among bound laborers were based on race. Wealthy Englishmen, for instance, viewed both African and Irish laborers as ignorant and unruly heathens. However, as Europeans began to conquer and colonize the Americas and demands for labor increased dramatically, ideas about race and slavery would change significantly.

REVIEW & RELATE	• How and why did Europeans expand their connections with Africa and the Middle East in the fifteenth century? • How did early European encounters with West Africans influence Europeans' ideas about African peoples and reshape existing systems of slavery?

Worlds Collide

In the 1520s and 1530s, Spain and Portugal chartered traders to ship enslaved Africans to the Caribbean, Brazil, Mexico, and Peru. The success of this trade relied heavily on the efforts of European cartographers, who used information from explorers and adventurers to map these areas. The maps illustrate the growing connections among Europe, Africa, and the Americas even as they also reflect the continued dominance of the Mediterranean region, the Middle East, India, and China in European visions of the world. Yet that world was changing rapidly as Europeans introduced guns, horses, and new diseases to the Americas and came in contact with previously unknown flora and fauna. The resulting exchange of plants, animals, and germs transformed the two continents as well as the wider world.

Europeans Cross the Atlantic

The first Europeans to discover lands in the western Atlantic were Norsemen. In the late tenth century, Scandinavian seafarers led by Erik the Red reached Greenland. Sailing still farther west, Erik's son Leif led a party that discovered an area in North

America that they called Vinland, near the Gulf of St. Lawrence. The Norse established a small settlement there around 1000 C.E., and people from Greenland continued to visit Vinland for centuries. By 1450, however, the Greenland settlements had disappeared.

Nearly a half century after Norse settlers abandoned Greenland, a Genoese navigator named Christopher Columbus visited the Spanish court of Ferdinand and Isabella and proposed an **Enterprise of the Indies**. Portuguese explorers used this name for the region that included present-day South Asia and Southeast Asia and surrounding islands. Because Italian city-states controlled the Mediterranean and Portugal dominated the routes around Africa, Spain sought a third path to the rich Eastern trade. Columbus claimed he could find it by sailing west across the Atlantic to Japan, China, or the Indies themselves.

Columbus's 1492 proposal was timely. Having just expelled the last Muslims and Jews from Granada and imposed Catholic orthodoxy on a now-unified nation, the Spanish monarchs sought to expand their empire. After winning Queen Isabella's support, the Genoese captain headed off in three small ships with ninety men. They stopped briefly at the Canary Islands and then headed due west on September 6, 1492.

Columbus had calculated the distance to Japan, which he judged the nearest island, based on Ptolemy's division of the world into 360 degrees of north-south lines of longitude. But in making his calculations, Columbus made a number of errors that led him to believe that it was possible to sail from Spain to Asia in about a month. The miscalculations nearly led to mutiny, but disaster was averted when a lookout finally spotted a small island on October 12. Columbus named the island San Salvador and made contact with local residents, whom he named Indians in the belief that he had found East Indies islands near Japan or China. Columbus was impressed with their warm welcome and considered the gold jewelry Indians wore as a sign of great riches in the region.

Columbus and his crew were welcomed as heroes when they returned to Spain in March 1493. Their discovery of islands seemingly unclaimed by any known power led the pope to confer Spanish sovereignty over all lands already claimed or to be claimed 100 leagues west of the Cape Verde Islands. A protest by Portugal soon led to a treaty that moved the line 270 leagues farther west, granting Portugal control of territory that became Brazil and Spain control of the rest of what became known as South America.

Europeans Explore the Americas

Columbus made three more voyages to the Caribbean to claim land for Spain and sought to convince those who accompanied him to build houses, plant crops, and cut logs for forts. But the men had come for gold, and when the Indians stopped trading willingly, the Spaniards used force to claim their riches. Columbus sought to impose a more rigid discipline but failed. On his final voyage, he introduced a system of *encomienda*, by which leading men received land and the labor of all Indians residing on it. By the time of Columbus's death in 1506, the islands he had discovered were dissolving into chaos as traders and adventurers fought with Indians and one another over the spoils of conquest. By then, no one believed that Columbus had discovered a route to China, but few people understood the revolutionary importance of the lands he had found.

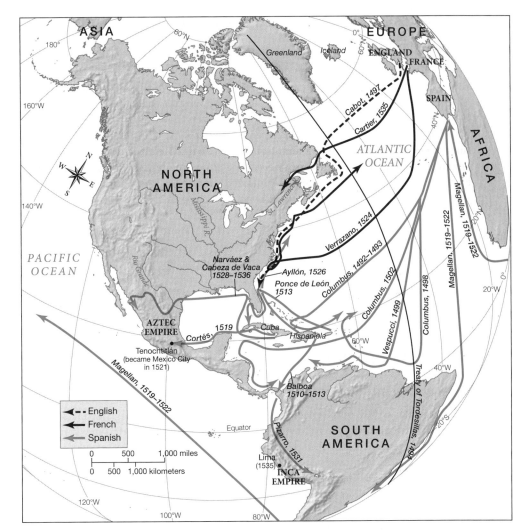

MAP 1.3   **European Explorations in the Americas, 1492–1536**
Early explorers, funded by Spain, sought trade routes to Asia or gold, silver, and other riches
in the Americas. The success of these voyages encouraged adventurous Spaniards to travel
throughout the West Indies, South America, and regions immediately to the north. It also
inspired the first expeditions by the French and the English in North America.

      Nonetheless, Columbus's voyages inspired others to head across the Atlantic (Map
1.3). In 1497 another Genoese navigator, John Cabot (or Caboto), sailing under the
English flag, reached an island off Cape Breton in the North Atlantic, where he discovered good cod fishing but met no local inhabitants. He continued down the Atlantic
coast, at one point being able to see Cuba to the east according to Cabot's son Sebastian.
Over the next several years, John and Sebastian made more trips to North America.
Although England failed to follow up on their discoveries, in 1500, a Spanish mapmaker
showed British flags planted along the Atlantic coast as far south as present-day Florida.

More important at the time, Portuguese and Spanish mariners continued to explore the western edges of the Caribbean. Amerigo Vespucci, a Florentine merchant, joined one such voyage in 1499. It was Vespucci's account of his journey that led Martin Waldseemüller to identify the new continent he charted on his 1507 *Universalis Cosmographia* as "America." Meanwhile, Spanish explorers subdued tribes like the Arawak and Taino in the Caribbean and headed toward the mainland. In 1513 Vasco Nuñez de Balboa traveled across the Isthmus of Darien (now Panama) and became the first known European to see the Pacific Ocean. That same year, the Spanish explorer Juan Ponce de León explored a peninsula that he named Florida and claimed it for Spain. Although British explorers had earlier claimed the territory, it was Spain that erected the first forts there, and they maintained control for 250 years.

Ferdinand Magellan launched an even more impressive expedition in August 1519 when he, with the support of Charles V of Spain, sought a passageway through South America to Asia. In October 1520, after fifteen months of struggle and travail, his crew discovered a strait at the southernmost tip of South America that connected the Atlantic and Pacific Oceans. Ill with scurvy and near starvation, the crew reached Guam and then the Philippines in March 1521. Magellan died there a month later, but one of his five ships and eighteen of the original crew finally made it back to Seville in September 1522, having successfully circumnavigated the globe. Despite the enormous loss of life and equipment, Magellan's lone ship was loaded with valuable spices and detailed information for cartographers, and his venture allowed Spain to claim the Philippine Islands.

Mapmaking and Printing

Waldseemüller's 1507 map reflected the expanding contacts among Europe, Africa, and the Americas. Over the following decades, cartographers charted newly discovered islands, traced coastlines and bays, and situated each new piece of data in relation to lands already known.

The dissemination of geographical knowledge was greatly facilitated by advances in information technology. The Chinese had developed a form of printing with wood blocks in the tenth century, and woodcut pictures appeared in Europe in the fifteenth century. In the 1440s, German craftsmen invented a form of movable metal type in which each letter was created in a separate mold. This allowed printers to rearrange the type for each page and create multiple copies of a single manuscript more quickly and more cheaply than ever before. Between 1452 and 1455, Johannes Gutenberg, a German goldsmith, printed some 180 copies of the Bible with movable type. Although this was not the first book printed using the new system, Gutenberg's Bible marked a revolutionary change in the production and circulation of written texts.

Innovations in printing helped publicize Portuguese and Spanish explorations, the travels of European adventurers, and the atlases created by Waldseemüller and other cartographers. Italian craftsmen contributed by manufacturing paper that was thinner and cheaper than traditional vellum and parchment. Books were still expensive, and they could be read only by the small minority of Europeans who were literate. Still, mechanical printing rapidly increased the speed with which knowledge was circulated. The enhanced ability to exchange ideas encouraged their expression and ensured the flow of information among scholars and rulers across Europe.

The peoples of the Americas had their own ways of charting land, waterways, and boundary lines and of circulating information. The Maya, for instance, developed a system of glyphs—images that represented prefixes, suffixes, numbers, people, or words. Scribes carved glyphs into large flat stones, or *stela*, providing local residents with histories of important events. In settled farming villages, this system communicated information to a large portion of the population. But it could not serve, as printed pages did, to disseminate ideas more widely. Similarly, the extant maps created by the Maya, Aztecs, and other native groups tended to focus on specific locales. Still, we know that these groups traded across long distances, so they must have had some means of tracing rivers, mountains, and villages beyond their own communities.

The Columbian Exchange

The Spaniards were aided in their conquest of the Americas by germs as well as maps, guns, and horses. Because native peoples in the Western Hemisphere had had almost no contact with the rest of the world for millennia, they lacked immunity to most germs carried by Europeans. A series of pandemics caused by measles, typhus, smallpox, and other diseases decimated communities throughout the hemisphere. Disease and warfare first eradicated the Arawak and Taino on Hispaniola, wiping out some 300,000 people. In the Inca empire, the population plummeted from about 9 million in 1530 to less than half a million by 1630. Among the Aztecs, the Maya, and their neighbors, the population collapsed from some 40 million people around 1500 to about 3 million a century and a half later. The germs spread northward as well, leading to pandemics among the Pueblo peoples of the Southwest and the Mississippian cultures of the Southeast.

These demographic disasters—far more devastating than the bubonic plague in Europe—were part of what historians call the **Columbian exchange**. This exchange also involved animals, plants, and seeds and affected Africa and Asia as well as Europe and the Americas. The transfer of flora and fauna and the spread of diseases transformed the economies and environments of all four continents. Initially, the catastrophic decline in Indian populations ensured the victory of Spain and other European powers over American populations. Africans' partial immunity to malaria and yellow fever then made them attractive to Europeans seeking laborers for Caribbean islands after the native population was decimated. At the same time, African coconuts and bananas were traded to Europe, while European traders provided their African counterparts with iron and pigs. Asia also participated in the exchange, introducing both Europe and Africa to sugar, rice, tea, and highly coveted spices.

America, in turn, provided Europeans with high-yielding, nutrient-rich foods like maize and potatoes, as well as new indulgences like tobacco and cacao. The East Indies had the perfect climate for producing sugar, an enormously profitable trade item. After discovering that sugar could be produced on Caribbean islands, the region became known as the West Indies. When mixed with cacao, sugar created an addictive drink known as chocolate.

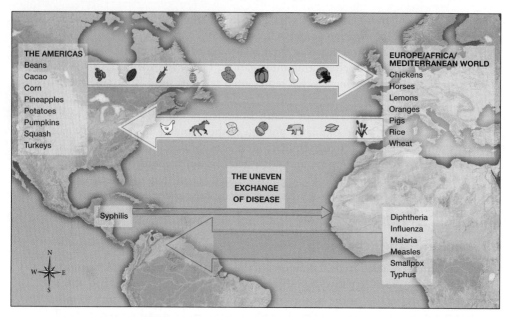

MAP 1.4   The Columbian Exchange, Sixteenth Century

When Europeans made contact with Africa and the Americas, they initiated an exchange of plants, animals, and germs that transformed all three continents. The contact among these previously isolated ecosystems caused dramatic transformations in food, labor, and mortality. American crops changed eating habits across Europe, while diseases devastated native populations even as foreign grains and domesticated animals thrived in the Americas.

In exchange for products that America offered to Europe and Africa, these continents sent rice, wheat, rye, lemons, and oranges as well as horses, cattle, pigs, chickens, and honeybees to the Western Hemisphere (Map 1.4). The grain crops transformed the American landscape, particularly in North America, where wheat became a major food source. Cattle and pigs, meanwhile, changed native diets, while horses inspired new methods of farming, transportation, and warfare throughout the Americas.

The Columbian exchange benefited Europe far more than the Americas. Initially, it also benefited Africa, providing new crops with high yields and rich nutrients. Ultimately, however, the spread of sugar and rice to the West Indies and European cravings for tobacco and cacao increased the demand for labor, which could not be met by the declining population of Indians. This situation ensured the expansion of the African slave trade to the Americas. The consequences of the Columbian exchange were thus monumental for the peoples of all three continents.

REVIEW & RELATE	• What were the short-term consequences in both Europe and the Americas of Columbus's voyages?
	• How did the Columbian exchange transform both the Americas and Europe?

Europeans Make Claims to North America

With the help of native translators, warriors, and laborers, Spanish soldiers called **conquistadors** conquered some of the richest and most populous lands in South America in the early sixteenth century. The conquered Inca and Aztec empires produced vast quantities of gold and silver, making Spain the treasure-house of Europe and ensuring its dominance on the continent for several decades. Some Spaniards headed north, hoping to find gold in the southern regions of North America or develop new routes to Asia. Following Spain's successes, rulers of other European nations began to fund expeditions to North America. France and England both launched efforts to claim colonies in the Americas. However, they failed to find the riches Spain had acquired. By the late sixteenth century, Spanish supremacy in the Americas and the wealth acquired there transformed the European economy. But conquest also raised critical questions about Spanish responsibilities to God and humanity.

Spaniards Conquer Indian Empires

Although rulers in Spain supposedly set the agenda for American ventures, it was difficult to control the campaigns of their emissaries at such a distance. The Spanish crown held the power to grant successful leaders vast amounts of land and Indian labor via the encomienda system. But the leaders themselves then divided up their prizes to reward those who served under them, giving them in effect an authority that they sometimes lacked in law. This dynamic helped make Cortés's conquest of the Aztecs possible.

Diego de Velásquez, the Spanish governor of Cuba, granted Cortés the right to explore and trade along the coast of South America. He gave him no authority, however, to attack native peoples in the region or claim land for himself. But seeing the possibility for gaining great riches, Cortés forged alliances with local rulers willing to join the attack against the Aztec chief, Montezuma. From the perspective of local Indian communities, Cortés's presence offered an opportunity to strike back against the brutal Aztec regime.

Despite their assumption of cultural superiority, many Spaniards who accompanied Cortés were astonished by Aztec cities, canals, and temples, which rivaled those in Europe. Seeing these architectural wonders may have given some soldiers pause about trying to conquer the Indian kingdom. But when Montezuma presented Cortés with large quantities of precious objects, including gold-encrusted jewelry, as a peace offering, he alerted Spaniards to the vast wealth awaiting them in the Aztec capital. When Cortés and his men marched to Tenochtitlán in 1519, Montezuma was indecisive in his response. After an early effort to ambush the Spaniards failed, the Aztec leader allowed Cortés to march his men into the capital city, where they took Montezuma hostage. In response, Aztec warriors attacked the Spaniards, but Cortés and his men managed to fight their way out of Tenochtitlán. They suffered heavy losses and might have been crushed by their Aztec foes but for the alliances forged with native groups in the surrounding area. Given time to regroup, the remaining Spanish soldiers and their allies attacked the Aztecs with superior steel weapons, horses, and trained dogs and gained a final victory.

An Inca with Smallpox Baltasar Jaime Martínez Compañón served as the bishop of Trujillo, Peru in the 1780s. He created a nine-volume codex for King Charles IV of Spain, which included 1,411 watercolor paintings tracing the history of native communities. This picture from Volume II shows an indigenous woman with smallpox isolated in a small hut. Album/Art Resource, NY

The Spanish victory was also aided by the germs that soldiers carried with them. Smallpox swept through Tenochtitlán in 1521, killing thousands and leaving Montezuma's army severely weakened. This human catastrophe as much as military resources and strategies allowed Cortés to conquer the capital that year. He then claimed the entire region as New Spain, assigned soldiers to construct the new capital of Mexico City, and asserted Spanish authority over the native groups that had allied with him.

As news of Cortés's victory spread, other Spanish conquistadors sought gold and glory in the Americas. Most important, in 1524 Francisco Pizarro conquered the vast Inca empire in present-day Peru. Once again, the Spaniards were aided by the spread of European diseases and smaller tribes' hatred of Inca rule. This victory ensured Spanish access to vast supplies of silver in Potosí (in present-day Bolivia) and the surrounding mountains. It also ensured the spread of enslaved African labor from plantation agriculture to mining. Spain was now in control of the most densely populated regions of South America, which also contained the greatest mineral wealth. Still, the diversity of populations in these regions — wealthy Spanish *encomenderos*, much poorer Spanish soldiers, Indians, and Africans — concerned authorities. In response, the Spanish developed a caste system that defined the status of these diverse populations and ensured that Spaniards remained at the top of the hierarchy even as wealthy landowners distinguished themselves from their poorer countrymen. In one decade, life for Aztecs and other Indians as well as the Spanish changed dramatically.

Spanish Adventurers Head North

In 1526, a company of Spanish women and men traveled from the West Indies as far north as the Santee River in present-day South Carolina. They planned to settle in the region and then search for gold and other valuables. The effort failed, but two years later Pánfilo de Narváez—one of the survivors—led four hundred soldiers from Cuba to Florida's Tampa Bay. Seeking precious metals, the party instead confronted hunger, disease, and hostile Indians. The ragtag group continued to journey along the Gulf coast, until only four men, led by Álvar Núñez Cabeza de Vaca, made their way from Galveston Bay back to Mexico City. In both cases, native peoples effectively defended their political sovereignty, economic prosperity, and religious beliefs.

A decade later, in 1539, a survivor of Narváez's ill-fated venture—a North African named Esteban—led a party of Spaniards from Mexico back north. Lured by tales of Seven Golden Cities, the party instead encountered Zuñi Indians, who attacked the Spaniards and killed Esteban. Still, the men who returned to Mexico passed on stories of large and wealthy cities. Hoping to find fame and fortune, Francisco Vásquez de Coronado launched a grand expedition northward in 1540. Angered when they failed to discover fabulous wealth, Coronado and his men terrorized the region, burning towns, killing residents, and stealing goods before returning to Mexico.

Hernando de Soto headed another effort to find wealth in North America. An experienced conquistador, de Soto received royal authority in 1539 to explore Florida. That spring he established a village near Tampa Bay with more than six hundred Spanish, Indian, and African men, and a few women. A few months later, de Soto and the bulk of his company traveled up the west Florida coast with Juan Ortiz, a member of the Narváez expedition and an especially useful guide and interpreter. That winter, the expedition traveled into present-day Georgia and the Carolinas in an unsuccessful search for riches (Map 1.5).

On their return trip, de Soto's men engaged in a brutal battle with local Indians led by Chief Tuskaloosa. Although the Spaniards claimed victory, they lost a significant number of men and horses and most of their equipment. Fearing that word of the disaster would reach Spain, de Soto steered his men away from supply ships in the Gulf of Mexico and headed back north. The group traveled into present-day Tennessee, then turned west, and in May 1541 became the first Europeans to report seeing the vast Mississippi River. Crossing it, they journeyed on into Arkansas, Oklahoma, and Texas. By the winter of 1542, the expedition had lost more men and supplies to Indians, and de Soto had died. The remaining members finally returned to Spanish territory the next summer.

The lengthy journey of de Soto and his men brought European diseases into new areas, leading to epidemics and the depopulation of once-substantial native communities. At the same time, the Spaniards left horses and pigs behind, creating new sources of transportation and food for native peoples. Although most Spaniards considered de Soto's journey a failure, the Spanish crown claimed vast new territories. Two decades later, in 1565, Pedro Menéndez de Avilés established a mission settlement on the northeast coast of Florida, named St. Augustine. It became the first permanent European settlement in North America. Still, unlike the conquest of central

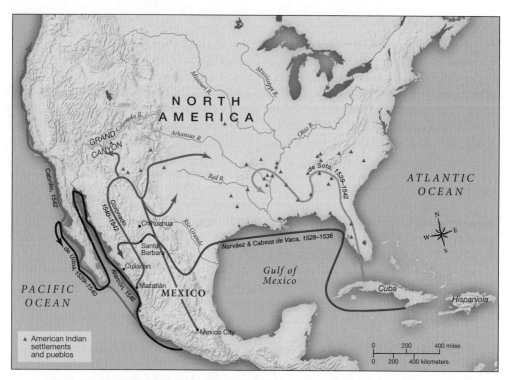

MAP 1.5   Spanish Explorations in North America, 1528–1542
Spanish explorers in North America hoped to find gold and other treasures. Instead, they encountered difficult terrain and native peoples hostile to Spanish intruders. Many Spaniards died on these expeditions, and they failed to discover new sources of wealth. But they laid the foundations for Spanish settlements in Florida, northern Mexico, and California while devastating local Indian populations.

and South America, the colonization of North America forced Spaniards to accept some of the native people's political and economic systems, religious beliefs, and even gender roles. When they refused to do so, open rebellions often resulted.

Europeans Compete in North America

Spain's early ventures in North America helped inspire French and English explorers to establish their own footholds on the continent. The French entered the race for empire in 1524, when an Italian navigator named Giovanni da Verrazano led a French company along the coast of North America. Landing initially near Cape Fear on the Carolina coast, the expedition headed north, sailing into what would become New York harbor. Verrazano then continued north, claiming lands all along the coast for France.

A decade later, in 1534, the Frenchman Jacques Cartier sailed to the Gulf of St. Lawrence. In two subsequent expeditions, Cartier pushed deeper into the territory known as Canada. Although he failed to discover precious metals or the elusive passage to the Pacific Ocean, he did trade for furs with local Indians. Cartier also inspired a French nobleman, the Sieur de Roberval, and several hundred followers to attempt a permanent settlement at Quebec in 1542. But the project was abandoned within a year because of harsh weather, disease, and high mortality.

English interest in North America was ignited by Spanish and French challenges to claims John Cabot had made along the Atlantic coast in the 1490s. To secure these rights, the English needed to colonize the disputed lands. Since the English crown did not have funds to support settlement, the earliest ventures were financed by minor noblemen who hoped to gain both wealth and the crown's favor. The earliest of these, in Newfoundland and Maine, failed.

The most promising effort to secure an English foothold was organized by Sir Walter Raleigh. Claiming all the land north of Florida for England, Raleigh called the vast territory Virginia (after Elizabeth I, "the Virgin Queen"). In 1585 Raleigh sent a group of soldiers to found a colony on Roanoke Island, off the coast of present-day North Carolina. The colony would establish England's claims and allow English sailors stationed there to seize Spanish ships laden with valuables. This venture lasted less than a year. In 1587 Raleigh tried again, sending a group of 117 men, women, and children to Roanoke. However, when supply ships came to fortify the settlement in 1590, the settlers had all disappeared, their fate unknown.

By 1590, then, nearly a century after Columbus's initial voyage, only Spain had established permanent colonies in the Americas, mostly in the West Indies, Mexico, and South America. The French and the English, despite numerous efforts, had not sustained a single ongoing settlement by the end of the sixteenth century. Yet neither nation gave up hope of benefiting from the wealth of the Americas.

Spain Seeks Dominion in Europe and the Americas

The continued desire of European nations to gain colonies in the Americas resulted from the enormous wealth garnered by Spanish conquests. That wealth transformed economies throughout Europe. Between 1500 and 1650, Spanish ships carried home more than 180 tons of gold and 16,000 tons of silver from Mexico and Potosí. About one-fifth of this amount was taken by the Spanish crown for taxes; the rest was dispersed among supporters of the expeditions; family and friends of those who conquered lands, gained *encomiendas*, or participated in trade; and soldiers and sailors who returned from America. The money was spent mainly on luxury goods imported from the Americas, Asia, or other European nations. Very little of this wealth was invested in improving conditions at home. Indeed, the rapid infusion of gold and silver fueled inflation, making it harder for ordinary people to afford the necessities of life.

In one area, however, employment for the poor expanded rapidly. Spain's King Philip II (r. 1556–1598) used American gold and silver to fund a variety of military campaigns, ensuring an endless demand for soldiers and sailors. The king, a devout Catholic, claimed to be doing God's work as Spain conquered Italy and Portugal, including the latter's colonies in Africa, and tightened its grip on the Netherlands, which had been acquired by Spain through marriage in the early sixteenth century.

Despite the obvious material benefits, the Spaniards were not blind to the enormous human costs of colonization, and the conquest of the Americas inspired heated debates within Spain. Catholic leaders believed that the conversion of native peoples to Christianity was critical to Spanish success in the Americas. However, most royal officials and colonial agents viewed the extraction of precious metals as far more important. They argued that cheap labor was essential to creating wealth. Yet brutal conditions led to the death of huge numbers of Indians, which made it nearly impossible to convert others to Catholicism.

By 1550, tales of the widespread torture and enslavement of Indians convinced the Spanish king Carlos V (r. 1519–1556) to gather a group of theologians, jurists, and philosophers at Valladolid to discuss the moral and legal implications of conquest. Bartolomé de Las Casas took a leading role in defending the rights of Indians. A former conquistador and Dominican friar, Las Casas had spent many years preaching to Indians in America. "And so what man of sound mind," he asked, "will approve a war against men who are harmless, ignorant, gentle, temperate, unarmed, and destitute of every human defense?" Las Casas argued that even if Spain defeated the Indians, the souls of those killed would be lost to God, while among the survivors "hatred and loathing of the Christian religion" would prevail. He even suggested replacing Indian labor with African labor, apparently less concerned with the souls of black people.

Juan Ginés de Sepúlveda, the royal historian, attacked Las Casas's arguments. Although he had never set foot in America, he read reports of cannibalism and other violations of "natural law" among native peoples. Since the Indians were savages, the civilized Spaniards were obligated to "destroy barbarism and educate these people to a more humane and virtuous life." If they refused such help, Spanish rule "can be imposed upon them by force of arms." Although Ginés de Sepúlveda spoke for the majority at Valladolid, Las Casas and his supporters continued to press their case as Spain expanded its reach into North America.

At the same time, American riches increasingly flowed beyond Spain's borders. The Netherlands was a key beneficiary of this wealth, becoming a center for Spanish shipbuilding and trade. Still, the Dutch were never completely under Spanish control, and they traded gold, silver, and other items to France, England, and other European nations. Goods also followed older routes across the Mediterranean to the Ottoman empire, where traders could make huge profits on exotic items from the Americas. Thus, while some Europeans suffered under Spanish power, others benefited from the riches brought to the continent. By the late sixteenth century, the desire for a greater share of those riches revitalized imperial dreams among the French and English as well as the Dutch.

REVIEW & RELATE	• What motivated the Spanish to conquer and colonize the Americas? • What were the consequences in Europe of Spain's acquisition of an American empire?

Conclusion: A Transformed America

For centuries, Asian peoples migrated to the Americas by land and sea. They developed an astonishing array of cultures and societies, from small hunting-and-gathering bands to complex empires. In the fourteenth and fifteenth centuries, extensive commercial and political networks existed among the Mississippians, the Aztecs, and the Incas, although only the latter two continued to thrive by the late 1400s. In southern Europe, too, during the fifteenth century, economic, cultural, and political advances fueled interest in long-distance trade and exploration. Italy and Portugal led these efforts, but their monopoly of trade routes across the Mediterranean and around Africa to Asia forced Spain to look west in hopes of gaining access to China and the Indies. In doing so, the Spanish unexpectedly came into contact with the Americas.

When Spanish explorers happened upon Caribbean islands and the nearby mainland, they created contacts between populations that would be dramatically transformed in a matter of decades. While native residents of the Americas were sometimes eager to trade with the newcomers and to form alliances against their traditional enemies, they fought against those they considered invaders. Yet some of the most significant invaders—plants, pigs, and especially germs—were impossible to defend against. Even Europeans seeking peaceful relations with native inhabitants or bent on conversion rather than conquest brought diseases that devastated local populations, and plants and animals that transformed their landscape, diet, and traditional ways of life.

Waldseemüller died in 1521 or 1522, so he did not see the most dramatic changes that his remarkably accurate maps inspired. Malintzin, however, experienced those changes firsthand. She watched as disease ravaged rural villages and the capital city of Tenochtitlán. She encountered horses, pigs, attack dogs, and other European animals. She ate the foods and wore the clothes that her Spanish captors provided. In 1522, Malintzin gave birth to Cortés's son; two years later, she served as interpreter when he ventured north to conquer more territory. In 1526 or 1527, however, she married a Spanish soldier, Juan Jaramillo, settled in Mexico City, and bore two more children. As more and more Spaniards, including the first women, settled in New Spain, Malintzin realized that her children would grow up in a world very different from the one in which she was raised.

From 1490 to 1590, the most dramatic and devastating changes for native peoples occurred in Mexico, the West Indies, Central America, and South America. Events there presaged what would happen throughout the Americas. As Spanish conquistadors ventured into Florida and the Gulf Coast and French and English explorers sought to gain footholds along the Atlantic seaboard, they carried sufficient germs, seeds, and animals to transform native societies even before Europeans established permanent settlements in North America.

In the century to come, contacts and conflicts between native peoples and Europeans would escalate as France, England, and the Netherlands joined Spain in colonizing North America. Conflicts among European nations and among Indian nations also multiplied as they struggled to control land, labor, and trade. Moreover, as Indian populations died out in some regions and fended off conquest in others, Europeans turned increasingly to the trade in Africans to provide the labor to produce enormously profitable items like sugar, coffee, and tobacco.

Chapter 1 Review

KEY TERMS

Beringia, 3
horticulture, 4
Aztecs, 5
Maya, 5
Incas, 5
Hopewell people, 7
Crusades, 9

Black Death, 9
pandemic, 9
Renaissance, 10
Enterprise of the Indies, 14
encomienda, 14
Columbian exchange, 17
conquistadors, 19

REVIEW & RELATE

1. Compare and contrast the Aztecs, Incas, and Maya. What similarities and differences do you note?
2. How did the societies of North America differ from those of the equatorial zone and the Andes?
3. How and why did Europeans expand their connections with Africa and the Middle East in the fifteenth century?
4. How did early European encounters with West Africans influence Europeans' ideas about African peoples and reshape existing systems of slavery?
5. What were the short-term consequences in both Europe and the Americas of Columbus's voyages?
6. How did the Columbian exchange transform both the Americas and Europe?
7. What motivated the Spanish to conquer and colonize the Americas?
8. What were the consequences in Europe of Spain's acquisition of an American empire?

TIMELINE OF EVENTS

25,000–13,000 B.C.E.	• First northeast Asians migrate to the Americas
900 B.C.E.–300 C.E.	• Maya settle Yucatán peninsula
500 C.E.	• Mogollon and Hohokam settle in southwestern North America; spread of maize cultivation northward begins
500–1400	• Mississippian peoples establish complex cultures
800	• Mayan civilization begins to decline
1000	• Norse settle in North America
1325	• Aztecs build Tenochtitlán

1340s	• Black Death (bubonic plague) in Europe
1400–1500	• Inca empire reaches its height
1440s	• Portuguese begin to trade along the coast of West Africa
1452–1455	• Johannes Gutenberg prints Bibles using movable type
1469	• Unification of Spain
1487	• Bartolomeu Dias rounds the Cape of Good Hope
1492	• Spain expels Muslim conquerors and Jews Christopher Columbus's first voyage to the Americas
1497	• Vasco da Gama sails to India
1507	• Martin Waldseemüller and Mathias Ringmann publish *Universalis Cosmographia*
1519	• Malintzin captured by Spaniards
1519–1521	• Hernán Cortés conquers the Aztecs
1519–1522	• Ferdinand Magellan's fleet circumnavigates the globe
1524	• Francisco Pizarro conquers the Incas
1587	• English settle Roanoke Island

2

Colonization and Conflicts

1580–1680

LEARNING OBJECTIVES

After reading this chapter you will be able to:

- Discuss the impact of the Reformation and Counter-Reformation and the emerging Atlantic economy on European nations and their goals in the American colonies.

- Evaluate the ways that European demands for land and trade, upheavals among indentured servants, and the emergence of slavery transformed the lives of Indians and colonists in diverse regions of North America.

- Analyze the influence of Puritanism on New England's development and how religious and political upheavals in England fueled Puritan expansion and conflicts with Indians in that region.

COMPARING AMERICAN HISTORIES

A boy named Wahunsenacawh was born in the 1540s to a powerful family of Algonquian-speaking Indians in the Middle Atlantic region west of Chesepiooc (Chesapeake) Bay. As an adult, he inherited leadership of a group of four to six Algonquian-speaking tribes. By the early 1600s, through diplomacy and force, Wahunsenacawh expanded this confederacy to about thirty tribes comprising some 12,000–15,000 inhabitants. Now called **Powhatan**, meaning the chief of chiefs, he lived at Werowocomoco, an ancient Indian site along the York River.

In April 1607, a boatload of 104 Englishmen led by Captain John Smith arrived in Chesapeake Bay and founded a settlement south of the York River. They named it Jamestown in honor of King James I and claimed the land for England. When news of their arrival reached Powhatan, the powerful chief likely hoped that this small community of light-skinned men might bring goods to trade.

When Powhatan's younger brother discovered Smith and two of his Jamestown comrades in the chief's territory that December, he brought them to Powhatan. While Smith was eventually released, his two comrades were executed. Powhatan likely performed an adoption ceremony for Smith to bring him and the English settlement under Powhatan's authority. In a typical ceremony, Powhatan would send one of his daughters—in this case, twelve-year-old Pocahontas—to indicate that the captive was spared. Captain Smith, who had just seen two comrades slain, did not understand the meaning of the ceremony or why he was spared. Anticipating further violence, he returned to Jamestown and urged residents to build fortifications for security.

The following fall, colonists elected Smith president of the Jamestown council. He insisted that colonists must intimidate the Indians and labor on farms and fortifications daily. Many colonists were opposed or ill-prepared to undertake such labors. Instead, hungry colonists demanded or seized corn from Indian villages. This mystified Powhatan: "What will it availe you to take that by force [which] you might quickly have by love, or destroy them that provide you food?"

Dissatisfied with Smith, the Virginia Company imposed a new set of leaders in 1609. When the situation deteriorated further, Powhatan again had to consider how to deal with what he likely viewed as ungrateful newcomers.

While the Virginia Company contemplated its economic interests, other Englishmen and women contemplated their souls. Critics of the Church of England formed a number of dissenting congregations in the early seventeenth century, part of a Protestant Reformation that swept across Europe. The Virginia Company benefited from this upheaval by offering legal charters to private investors, including dissenting Pilgrims in 1620. Other dissenters, including Puritans in 1630, gained royal charters from the English government.

Anne Hutchinson, a forty-five-year-old wife and mother, joined the Puritan migration. Born in Lincolnshire, England, in 1591, Anne was well educated when she married William Hutchinson, a merchant, in 1612. The Hutchinsons and their children began attending Puritan sermons, and in 1634 they followed the Reverend John Cotton to Massachusetts Bay.

Anne Hutchinson was well-versed in the Bible, and Reverend Cotton urged her to hold prayer meetings in her home for pregnant and nursing women who did not attend regular services. Hutchinson, like Cotton, preached that individuals must rely solely on God's grace rather than a saintly life or good works to ensure salvation. Many Puritan ministers had come to oppose this position, but Hutchinson did not retreat.

Her intransigence shocked Puritan leaders, who were embroiled in a deadly war with the powerful Pequot nation. In August 1637, with Hutchinson's following expanding, Puritan leaders condemned her meetings.

Refusing to recant her views, Hutchinson was put on trial that November. She mounted a vigorous defense, but the Puritan judges convicted her of heresy and banished her from Massachusetts Bay. Hutchinson's family, and dozens of followers moved to the recently established colony of Rhode Island. Although safe from her critics, she would eventually succumb to an Indian attack.

COMPARING THE AMERICAN HISTORIES of Powhatan and Anne Hutchinson illustrates the complex relationships between Indians and English settlers as well as among colonists themselves. Because silver and gold were not found north of Mexico, English, French, and Dutch colonists depended on farming, fishing, and trade as their entrée to the growing Atlantic economy. These efforts required either negotiating with Indians or taking their lands. Although Indian confederacies and communities in northern regions were smaller than the Maya and Inca Empires, they resisted European dominion for much longer. This necessitated ever-shifting alliances between European colonizers and Indian nations. The resulting conflicts dramatically transformed the lives of American Indians and European colonists between 1580 and 1680.

Religious, Economic, and Imperial Transformations

The Puritans were part of a relatively new religious movement known as **Protestantism** that had emerged around 1520. Protestants challenged Catholic policies and practices but did not form a single church of their own. Instead, they formed distinct denominations in various regions of Europe. Catholics sought to counter their claims by revitalizing their faith, reasserting control, and converting Indians in lands they claimed in North America. These religious conflicts shaped developments across North America. So, too, did the search for commercial success as France, the Netherlands, and England sought a foothold in North America. Whether seeking conversions, land, trading partners, or military allies, Europeans were forced to negotiate with or conquer diverse Indian nations and confederacies, each of which had its own economic and military interests to consider.

The Protestant Reformation

Critiques of the Catholic Church multiplied in the early sixteenth century, driven by papal involvement in conflicts among monarchs and corruption among church officials. But the most vocal critics focused on immorality, ignorance, and absenteeism among clergy. These anticlerical views appeared in popular songs and printed images as well as in learned texts by theologians such as Martin Luther.

Luther, a professor of theology in Germany, believed that faith alone led to salvation, which could be granted only by God. He challenged the Catholic Church's claim that individuals could achieve salvation by buying indulgences, which were documents that absolved the buyer of sin. The church profited enormously from these sales, but they suggested that God's grace could be purchased. In 1517 Luther wrote an extended argument against indulgences and sent it to the local bishop. His writings soon gained a wider audience.

Luther's followers, who protested Catholic practices, became known as Protestants. His teachings circulated widely through sermons and printed texts, and his claim that ordinary people should read and reflect on the Scriptures appealed to the literate middle classes. Meanwhile his attacks on indulgences and corruption attracted those who resented the church's wealth and priests' indifference to their flocks. In Switzerland, John Calvin developed a version of Protestantism in which civil magistrates and reformed ministers ruled over a Christian society. Calvin argued that God had decided at the beginning of time who was saved and who was damned. Calvin's idea, known as predestination, energized Protestants who understood salvation as a gift from an all-knowing God in which the "works" of sinful humans played no part.

The Protestant Reformation quickly spread through central and northern Europe. English rulers, too, came under the influence of Protestantism in the 1530s, although for different reasons. When the pope refused to annul the marriage of King Henry VIII (r. 1509–1547) and Catherine of Aragon, Henry denounced papal authority and established the **Church of England**, or Anglicanism, with himself as "defender of the faith." Despite the king's conversion to Protestantism, the Church of England retained many Catholic practices.

In countries like Spain and France with strong central governments and powerful ties to the Catholic Church, a strong Catholic Counter-Reformation largely quashed Protestantism. Yet, Catholic leaders also initiated reforms to counter their critics. In 1545 Pope Paul II called together a commission of cardinals, known as the Council of Trent (1545–1563), which founded new seminaries to train priests and returned monastic orders to their spiritual foundations. Both Protestant and Catholic leaders urged followers to spread their faith across the Atlantic, and religious minorities sought a safe haven there.

Just as important, political struggles erupted between Catholic and Protestant rulers in Europe, inspiring more people to migrate to North America. Many were attracted by economic opportunities while others were forced to labor on their behalf. Together, these migrants fueled an expanding Atlantic economy built on fish, furs, sugar, and increasingly slavery.

Spain's Global Empire Declines

As religious conflicts escalated in Europe, Spaniards in America continued to push north in hopes of expanding their empire. The nature of Spanish expansion, however, changed. As a result of the Council of Trent and the Catholic Counter-Reformation, Spain increasingly emphasized its religious mission. Thus Spanish authorities decided in 1573 that missionaries rather than soldiers should direct new settlements. Franciscan priests began founding missions on the margins of Pueblo villages north of Mexico. They named the area Nuevo México (New Mexico), and many learned Indian languages. In the following decades, some twenty thousand Pueblo women and men converted to Catholicism. However, many still retained traditional beliefs and practices, which missionaries tried, unsuccessfully, to eradicate through flogging and other punishments.

At the same time, Franciscans tried to force the Pueblo people to adopt European ways. They insisted that men rather than women farm the land and that Indians

San Esteban del Rey Mission   Opened in 1644 after fourteen years of construction, this Spanish mission in present-day New Mexico provided instruction in Christianity and Hispanic customs for the Acoma (Pueblo) people. To this end, Spanish missionaries prohibited traditional Pueblo practices such as performing dances and wearing masks. The mission was one of the few to survive Pueblo revolts in the late seventeenth century. age fotostock/Superstock

speak, cook, and dress like Spaniards. Missionaries also largely ignored Spanish laws intended to protect Indians from coerced labor, demanding that Pueblos build churches, provide the missions with food, and carry their goods to market. Wealthy landowners who followed the missionaries into New Mexico also demanded tribute in the form of goods and labor.

In 1598 Juan de Oñate, from a wealthy mining family, established a trading post and fort in the upper Rio Grande valley. The 500 soldiers who accompanied him seized corn and clothing from Pueblo villages and murdered or raped those who resisted. Indians at the Acoma pueblo confronted these soldiers, and eleven Spaniards were killed. The Spanish retaliated, slaughtering 500 men and 300 women and children. Fearing reprisals, most Spaniards withdrew from the region.

In 1610 Spaniards returned, founded Santa Fe, and established a network of missions and estates owned by *encomenderos*, Spanish elites granted land and the right to exploit Indian labor. This time the Pueblo people largely accepted the new situation. While they feared military reprisals if they challenged Spanish authorities, they also sought Spanish protection following a period of drought, disease, and raids by Apache and Navajo tribes. Yet their faith in the Franciscans' spiritual power faded when conditions did not improve. Although Spain maintained a firm hold on

Florida and its colonies in the West Indies, it focused most of its efforts in the West, allowing other European powers to expand into eastern North America.

France Enters the Race for Empire

In the late sixteenth century, French, Dutch, and English investors became increasingly interested in gaining a foothold in North America. First, however, they had to break Catholic Spain's grip on the Atlantic world. The Protestant Reformation helped shape the alliances that shattered Spain's American monopoly. As head of the Church of England, Queen Elizabeth I (King Henry VIII's daughter, r. 1558–1603) sought closer political and commercial ties with Protestant nations like the Netherlands. The queen also assented to, and benefited from, raids on Spanish ships by Francis Drake and other privateers. In 1588 King Philip II of Spain (r. 1556–1598) decided to punish England for these attacks and its intervention in the Netherlands. He sent a massive armada to spearhead the invasion of England. However, the English, aided by Dutch ships and lucky weather conditions, defeated the armada and ensured that the two nations could compete for riches and colonies in North America.

Although French rulers shared Spain's Catholic faith, they, too, were rivals and sought greater access to North American colonies. Once in North America, the French adopted attitudes and policies that differed significantly from those of Spain. This was due in part to their interest in trade rather than conquest. The French had profited from fishing the North Atlantic since the mid-sixteenth century, but their efforts to establish settlements in Newfoundland and Nova Scotia met with fierce Indian resistance. Gradually French traders established relations with local Indians, exchanging iron kettles and other European goods for valuable beaver skins.

By the early seventeenth century, France's King Henry IV (r. 1589–1610) sought to profit more directly from the North American trade. With the Edict of Nantes (1598), the king ended decades of religious wars by granting political rights and limited toleration to French Protestants, known as Huguenots, many of whom had sought refuge in North America. He then focused on developing the lucrative Atlantic trade in fish and furs. Samuel de Champlain, sponsored by a French fur-trading company, founded that nation's first permanent settlement in North America in 1608 at Quebec. Accompanied by several dozen men, Champlain joined a Huron raid on the Iroquois, who resided south of the Great Lakes. By using guns, the French helped ensure a Huron victory and a powerful ally for the French. But the battle also fueled lasting bitterness among the Iroquois.

Trade relations flourished between the French and their Indian allies. Both became part of the flourishing **Atlantic economy**, in which traders and colonists in the Americas exchanged European goods with Indian nations, which in turn provided those European countries with fish, furs, and other increasingly valuable items. The commercial character of the French venture was made clear by the relatively few French men and even fewer women who settled in North America. Government policies discouraged mass migration as did reports of short growing seasons and severe winters. Cardinal Richelieu, the king's chief minister, urged priests and nuns to migrate to New France but barred further emigration by Protestant Huguenots. Thus into the 1630s, French settlements in North America consisted largely of fishermen, fur traders, and Catholic missionaries. Fur traders were critical to sustaining French land claims and warding off encroachment by the English, whose villages radiated out from Massachusetts Bay. The French journeyed throughout eastern Canada, aided by the Huron tribe, and established a fortified trading post at Montreal in 1643. Over the next three decades, the French pushed farther west, feeding Europe's growing market for beaver skins. However, as they extended the fur trade beyond the St. Lawrence River valley, they left their Huron allies behind.

As the Dutch entered the fur trade via forts along the Hudson River, Iroquois in that region sought to keep the Huron from trading their high-quality furs to the Dutch (Map 2.1). With guns supplied by Dutch merchants, the Iroquois led a series of assaults on Huron villages. In this way, they also secured captives to restore their population, which was decimated by disease.

MAP 2.1   Approximate Tribal Locations at First Contact with Europeans
Maps of early European colonies in North America often highlight the locations of Spanish, French, Dutch, and English settlements. However, it was the complex network of native communities, with their pre-existing patterns of settlement, migration, trade, and conflict, which profoundly shaped how these European colonies developed.

As they ventured west, some Frenchmen took Indian wives, who were skilled at tanning and drying animal pelts and provided companionship and kinship ties to powerful native leaders. Despite Catholic criticism of these marriages, they strengthened commercial relations and fostered French alliances with the Ojibwe and Dakota nations in the Great Lakes region. These alliances, in turn, created a middle ground in which economic and cultural exchanges led to a remarkable degree of mutual adaptation. The mixed-race children of French men and Indian women, known as **metis**, became translators, guides, and traders themselves. French traders also benefited from Indian technology, especially canoes, while natives adopted iron cooking pots and European cloth.

Still, France could only capitalize on its North American colonies by maintaining profits from the fur trade. In moving ever westward, French traders carried European diseases into new areas, intensified warfare among native groups, and stretched their small population of settlers ever thinner. However fragile their empire, French explorers, traders, and priests extended their reach beyond the Great Lakes and by 1681 moved southward along the Mississippi to a territory they named Louisiana in honor of King Louis XIV (r. 1643–1715).

The conflicts between commerce and conversion in Spanish America were far less severe in New France. French traders relied on Indian allies, and some French Jesuit priests also sought to build on native beliefs and learn Indians' languages and customs. Although Catholics assumed that their own religious beliefs and cultural values were superior to those of the Indians, many sought to engage native inhabitants on their own terms. Thus one French Jesuit employed the Huron belief that "our souls have desires which are inborn and concealed" to explain Christian doctrines of sin and salvation to potential converts. Still, missionaries—like traders—carried deadly germs, and Catholics sought conversion, not mutual adaptation. While many Indian nations benefited from their alliances with the French in the short term, the long-term costs proved devastating.

The Dutch Expand into North America

The Protestant Dutch had no interest in bringing religion to Indians in America. From the beginning, their goals were almost purely economic. As Spain's shipbuilding center, the Netherlands had benefited from the wealth pouring in from South America, and an affluent merchant class emerged. However, the Dutch also embraced Calvinism and sought to separate themselves from Catholic Spain. In 1581 the Netherlands declared independence from King Philip II (r. 1556–1598). Although Spain refused to recognize the new status for several decades, by 1600 the Netherlands was both a Protestant haven and the trading hub of Europe. Indeed, the Dutch East India Company controlled trade routes to much of Asia and parts of Africa.

With technology and skills developed under Spanish control, the Dutch became central to the Atlantic economy as well. In 1609 they established a fur-trading center on the Hudson River in present-day New York, which was part of what became known as the middle colonies. The small number of Dutch traders developed friendly relations with important Mohawk and Munsee communities, which were linked respectively to Iroquois and Algonquian allies. Dutch authorities recognized Indian sovereignty and insisted land be purchased rather than taken from local Indians. In 1614, the trading post was moved south to Fort Orange, near present-day

Albany. The Dutch fur trade also benefitted England and Russia, where artisans created beaver hats from the raw skins shipped to Amsterdam.

In 1624, to fend off French and English raids on ships sent downriver from Fort Orange, the Dutch established New Amsterdam on Manhattan Island, which they purchased from the Lenape Indians. The new settlement was organized by the Dutch West India Company, which was chartered three years earlier. New Amsterdam attracted a diverse community of traders, fishermen, artisans, and farmers. It was noted for its religious toleration as well as the independence of its female colonists. Dutch wives, unlike other European women, retained their separate legal status after marriage. Husbands and wives shared property, and widows often inherited businesses as well as domestic goods. Indeed, Dutch trading networks were rooted in networks of kin and community that stretched east, south, and west from Amsterdam to Cape Town, Java, Guyana, New Amsterdam, and beyond. By the 1630s, the Dutch would play a major role in the Atlantic slave trade, eventually transporting more than half a million enslaved Africans to the Americas.

Early Dutch settlers in New Netherland developed peaceful relations with the Mohawk and Munsee, who also rooted their trade networks in kin and community relations. However, by the 1630s, as colonists established farms along the Hudson River and Long Island, amid large communities of Algonquian Indians, tensions escalated. Then, in 1639, Governor Willem Kieft demanded an annual tribute in wampum or grain. Local Algonquians resisted, raiding Dutch farms on the frontier and killing at least two colonists. Raids and killings continued on both sides. In 1643, Kieft launched a surprise attack on an Indian encampment on Manhattan Island, murdering eighty people, mostly women and children. Outraged Algonquians burned and looted homes north of the city, killed livestock, and murdered settlers. For two decades, sporadic warfare continued. The Algonquians suffered some 1,000 deaths compared to 200 settlers.

Amid these devastating conflicts, the Dutch continued to trade for furs with Mohawks along the upper Hudson River. This powerful tribe had the backing of the even more powerful Iroquois Confederacy. The confederacy's ties to Indians farther west allowed the Mohawk to provide beaver skins to Dutch traders long after beavers died out in the Hudson valley. Still, the Mohawk people did not deceive themselves. As one chief proclaimed in 1659, "The Dutch say we are brothers and that we are joined together with chains, but that lasts only so long as we have beavers."

Meanwhile reports of atrocities by Indians and the Dutch circulated in the Netherlands, damaging New Amsterdam's reputation and slowing migration. A series of wars with their former ally England further weakened Dutch power in America. In 1664, England sent a naval convoy to take New Amsterdam. Exhausted by decades of unrelenting conflict, the Dutch surrendered to the English without a fight.

REVIEW & RELATE

- How did the Protestant Reformation and Catholic Counter-Reformation shape the course of European expansion in the Americas?
- How did the French and Dutch colonies in North America differ from the Spanish empire to the south, and how were these differences shaped by Indian nations?

The English Seek an Empire

The English, like the French and the Dutch, entered the race for an American empire well after the Spanish. England did not have a permanent settlement in the Americas until the founding of **Jamestown** at the mouth of Chesapeake Bay in 1607. In the 1620s, the English established settlements in the West Indies, which quickly became the economic engine of English colonization. Expansion into these areas demanded new modes of labor to ensure a return on investment. Large numbers of indentured servants crossed the Atlantic and enslaved Indians labored throughout the English colonies, while growing numbers of Africans were forced onto ships for sale in the Americas. Meanwhile, the rapid expansion of English settlement increased military conflicts with Indian nations and fueled tensions among settlers.

The English Establish Jamestown

England's success in colonizing North America depended in part on a new economic model in which investors purchased shares in joint-stock companies that could raise large amounts of money quickly. If the venture succeeded, investors shared the profits. If they failed, no investor suffered the whole loss. In 1606 a group of London merchants formed the Virginia Company, and King James I granted them the right to settle a vast area of North America, from present-day New York to North Carolina.

Some of the men that the Virginia Company recruited as colonists were gentlemen who hoped to get rich through the discovery of precious metals. They also recruited skilled artisans and laborers to launch the settlement, many of whom hoped to gain wealth and status. A few men who planned to stay for an extended period brought their wives, which was almost unheard of among the Spanish and French. Arriving on the coast of North America in April 1607, the colonists established Jamestown along a river, a site they chose mainly for its easy defense knowing that it lay within territory controlled by a large confederation of Indians. Although bothered by the settlement's mosquito-infested environment, the colonists focused their energies on constructing buildings, producing food, and searching for gold and silver.

The Englishmen quickly made contact with the Indian chief Powhatan, who presided over a confederation of some thirty tribes, which surrounded the small Jamestown settlement. The **Powhatan Confederacy** was powerful, and for the first two years English settlers depended on its generosity to survive. While a severe drought between 1606 and 1612 caused a shortage of food among both Indians and the English, the problem was exacerbated in Jamestown by some colonists' refusal to engage in manual labor. Moreover, the nearby water was tainted by salt from the ocean and diseases festered in the low-lying area, killing more than half of the original settlers.

Powhatan assisted the settlers in hopes they would provide him with English cloth, iron hatchets, and even guns. His capture and subsequent release of John Smith in 1607 suggests his interest in trading with the newcomers even as he sought to subordinate them. But leaders like Captain Smith considered Powhatan and his warriors a threat rather than an asset. When unable to feed themselves that first year, Jamestown residents raided Indian villages for corn and other food, making

Powhatan increasingly wary. The settlers' decision to construct a fort only bolstered the Indians' concern.

Meanwhile the Virginia Company devised a plan to stave off the collapse of its colony. It started selling seven-year joint-stock options to raise funds and recruited new settlers to produce staple crops, glassware, or other items for export. Interested individuals who could not afford to invest cash could sign an indenture for service in Virginia. After seven years, these indentured servants would gain their freedom and receive a hundred acres of land. In June 1609, a new contingent of colonists attracted by this plan—five hundred men and a hundred women—sailed for Jamestown.

The new arrivals, however, had not brought enough supplies to sustain the colony through the winter. Powhatan did offer some aid, but Indians, too, suffered shortages that winter. A "starving time" settled on Jamestown. By the spring of 1610, seven of every eight settlers who had arrived in Jamestown since 1607 were dead.

That June, the sixty survivors decided to abandon the colony and sail for home. They were surprised to meet three English ships in the harbor loaded with supplies and three hundred more settlers. Emboldened by fresh supplies and an enlarged population, Jamestown's new leaders adopted an aggressive military posture, attacking native villages, burning crops, killing many Indians, and taking others captive. They believed that such brutality would convince neighboring tribes to obey English demands for food and labor.

Tobacco Fuels Growth in Virginia

It was not military aggression, however, but the discovery of a viable cash crop that saved the English colony. Orinoco tobacco, grown in the West Indies and South America, sold well in England and Europe. Virginia colonist John Rolfe began to experiment with its growth in 1612, just as the drought lifted. Production of the leaf soared as eager English investors poured seeds, supplies, and labor into Jamestown. Exports multiplied rapidly, from 2,000 pounds in 1615 to 40,000 pounds five years later and an incredible 1.5 million pounds by 1629.

However, tobacco cultivation exacerbated tensions between colonists and Indians. As production increased, prices declined. Farmers could increase their profits only by obtaining more land and more laborers. In response, the Virginia Company offered land to indentured laborers who spent seven years clearing new fields and creating more plantations. Yet in most cases, the Powhatan Confederacy already claimed the land granted to these would-be colonists.

Despite growing conflicts over land, Powhatan tried one last time to create an alliance between his confederacy and the English settlers. Perhaps he was encouraged by the return of rain and hoped that increased productivity would ease relations with the English. In 1614, he allowed his daughter Pocahontas, who had spent considerable time in Jamestown, to marry John Rolfe, forging the kind of familial bond that created alliances between Indian tribes. Pocahontas converted to Christianity and two years later traveled to England with Rolfe and their infant son. While there, however, she fell ill and died in 1617. The next year, Powhatan died, and his younger brother Opechancanough took over as chief. Rolfe and his son returned to Virginia, but relations between colonists and the confederacy once again deteriorated.

Scene on an American Tobacco Plantation   Pomet, physician to the French King Louis XIV included this engraving in his *A Compleat History of Drugs*, published in London in 1725. It shows a tobacco plant on the right as enslaved men, women, and children process the leaves on the left.
Photo12/Universal Images Group via Getty Images

The English crown made clear its intentions in 1619 by granting Virginia colonists the right to establish a local governing body, the **House of Burgesses**. Its members could make laws and levy taxes, although the English governor or the company council in London held veto power. The Virginia Company also resolved to recruit more female settlers as a way to increase the colony's population. More young women and men arrived as **indentured servants**, working in the fields and homes of more affluent Englishmen for a set period of time in exchange for passage to America. Also in 1619, an English ship carried the first boatload of twenty Africans to Jamestown. They were bound as indentured servants to farmers desperate for labor.

Although the English colony still hugged the Atlantic coast, its geographical expansion and enhanced political authority increased conflict with native inhabitants. In March 1622, after repeated English incursions on land cleared and farmed by Indians, Chief Opechancanough launched a surprise attack that killed nearly a third of the colonists. In retaliation, Englishmen assaulted native villages, killed inhabitants, burned cornfields, and sold Indian captives into slavery.

The English proclaimed victory in 1623, but hostilities continued for nearly a decade. The very next year, King James asserted his authority over the colony by annulling the Virginia Company charter. He appointed the governor and a small advisory council, required that legislation passed by the House of Burgesses be ratified by the Privy Council, and demanded that property owners pay taxes to support the Church of England. These regulations became the model for royal colonies throughout North America.

Still, royal proclamations could not halt Indian opposition. In 1644, the Powhatan Confederacy launched a second uprising against the English, killing hundreds of colonists. After two years of bitter warfare, Chief Opechancanough was finally captured and then killed. With the English population now too large to eradicate, the remaining members of the Confederacy either moved to new areas or submitted to English authority.

Expansion, Rebellion, and the Emergence of Slavery

By the 1630s, despite continued conflicts with Indians, Virginia was well on its way to commercial success. The most successful tobacco planters acquired growing numbers of indentured servants, including some Africans as well as thousands of English and Irish immigrants. Between 1640 and 1670, some 40,000 to 50,000 of these servants and immigrants settled in Virginia and neighboring Maryland (Map 2.2). Maryland was founded in 1632 when King Charles I, the successor to James I, granted most of the territory north of Chesapeake Bay to Cecilius Calvert and appointed him Lord Baltimore. Calvert was among the minority of English who remained a Catholic,

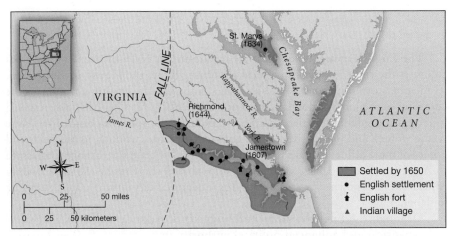

MAP 2.2   The Growth of English Settlement in the Chesapeake, c. 1650
With the success of tobacco, English plantations and forts spread along the James River and north to St. Mary's. By 1650 most Chesapeake Indian tribes had been vanquished or forced to move north and west. The fall line, which marked the limit of navigable waterways, kept English settlements close to the Atlantic coast but also ensured easy shipment of goods.

A Susquehannock Warrior   John Smith published a remarkably accurate map of Virginia in 1612. It included major geographical features and the names of some 200 Indian towns. Smith placed a sketch of a Susquehannock warrior in the upper right-hand corner; at his feet, Smith noted that the Susquehannock were "a Gyant-like people." This map was widely used for seven decades. Beinecke Rare Book and Manuscript Library, Yale University

and he planned to create Maryland as a refuge for his persecuted co-worshippers. Appointing his brother Leonard Calvert as governor, he carefully recruited the first colonists, including artisans and farmers (mainly Protestant) as well as wealthy merchants and aristocrats (mostly Catholic). When conflict festered between the Catholic elite and the Protestant majority, Governor Calvert convinced the Maryland assembly to pass an Act of Religious Toleration in 1649, granting religious freedom to all Christians.

Taken together, Maryland and Virginia formed the Chesapeake region of the English empire—a crucial engine of the Atlantic economy. Both colonies relied on tobacco to produce the wealth that fueled their growth, and both introduced African labor to complement the supply of white indentured servants. Still, neither colony initially developed a legal code of slavery. From 1650 on, however, improved economic conditions in England meant fewer English men and women were willing to gamble on a better life in North America. Even though the number of African laborers remained small until late in the century, colonial leaders increased their control over that population. Most importantly, in 1660 the House of Burgesses passed an act that allowed black laborers to be enslaved and in 1662 defined slavery as an inherited status passed on from mothers to children. Maryland followed suit two years later.

The march toward full-blown racial slavery had begun in Barbados, which established the model that Chesapeake authorities followed. The booming sugar industry on the island spurred the development of plantation slavery, and both proved critical to the Atlantic economy. In 1660 blacks in Barbados formed a majority of the population. Twenty years later, there were seventeen enslaved

Africans for every white indentured servant on Barbados. The growth of slavery on the island depended almost wholly on imports from Africa since enslaved persons there died faster than they could reproduce themselves. In the context of high death rates, brutal working conditions, and massive imports, Barbados systematized its slave code, defining enslaved Africans as chattel — that is, as mere property more akin to livestock than to human beings.

While enslaved Africans would become, in time, a crucial component of the Chesapeake labor force, indentured servants made up the majority of bound workers in Virginia and Maryland for most of the seventeenth century. They, too, labored under harsh conditions and severe punishments, including beating, whipping, and branding, for a variety of infractions. Some white servants made common cause with black laborers who worked side by side with them on tobacco plantations. They ran away together, stole goods from their masters, and planned uprisings and rebellions.

By the 1660s and 1670s, the population of indentured servants who had become free formed a growing and increasingly unhappy class. Most were struggling economically, working as common laborers or tenants on large estates. Meanwhile, those who claimed land on the frontier were confronted by hostile Indians like the Susquehannock. Virginia governor Sir William Berkeley, who levied taxes to support nine forts along the frontier, had little patience with the complaints of these colonists. His priorities were securing sufficient labor for wealthy tobacco planters and maintaining the profitable deerskin trade with the Algonquian Indians. Frontier settlers' call for an aggressive Indian policy would hurt both.

Impatient frontiersmen refused to accept Berkeley's stance, and in late 1675, attacked Indians in the region. Unlike colonial leaders back east, frontier settlers generally considered all Indians hostile. Thus, rather than attacking only the Susquehannock, they also assaulted Indians allied with the English. Moreover, when local Virginia militiamen surrounded a Susquehannock village, they ignored pleas for peace and murdered five chiefs. Susquehannock warriors retaliated with raids on frontier farms. Amid this open warfare, Governor Berkeley still refused to send troops, and disgruntled farmers sought the leadership of Nathaniel Bacon. Bacon came from a wealthy family and was related to Berkeley by marriage. Yet he defied the governor's authority and called up an army to attack Indians across the colony. **Bacon's Rebellion** had begun. Frontier farmers formed an important part of Bacon's coalition; but affluent planters who had been left out of Berkeley's inner circle also joined Bacon in hopes of gaining access to power and profits. Even many bound laborers, black and white, assumed that anyone who opposed the governor was on their side.

In the summer of 1676, Governor Berkeley declared Bacon guilty of treason. Rather than waiting to be captured, Bacon led his army toward Jamestown. Berkeley then arranged a hastily called election to undercut the rebellion. Even though Berkeley rescinded the right of men without property to vote, Bacon's supporters won control of the House of Burgesses, and Bacon won new adherents. These included "news wives," lower-class women who spread information about oppressive conditions to aid the rebels. As Bacon's army marched across Virginia, his men plundered the plantations of Berkeley and his supporters.

In September they reached Jamestown after the governor and his administration fled across Chesapeake Bay. The rebels burned the capital to the ground, victory seemingly theirs.

Only a month later, however, Bacon died of dysentery, and the movement he formed unraveled. Governor Berkeley quickly reclaimed power. He hanged twenty-three rebel leaders and incited his followers to plunder the estates of planters who had supported Bacon. But he could not undo the damage to Indian relations on the Virginia frontier. Bacon's army had killed or enslaved hundreds of once-friendly Indians and left behind a tragic and bitter legacy.

Another important consequence of the rebellion was that wealthy planters and investors realized the depth of frustration among poor whites willing to make common cause with their black counterparts. Having regained power, white planters worked to crush any such interracial alliance. Virginia legislators began to improve the conditions and rights of poor white settlers while imposing new restrictions on blacks. In 1672, in an effort to meet the growing demand for labor in the West Indies and the Chesapeake, King Charles II chartered the Royal African Company to carry enslaved Africans to North America.

Enslaved Indians from Virginia were also being shipped to the West Indies. That trade, which began in the mid-1600s, resulted from tribes like the Westos raiding other Indian communities and exchanging captives to the English for guns. By the 1660s, the Westos used their guns to prey on Indians further south who were still using bows and arrows. They sold these enslaved Indians to English traders in Charles Town, a thriving port in South Carolina. In 1682, Westos themselves were sold into slavery after being defeated by Shawnee Indians working for other Carolina traders.

The English Compete for West Indies Possessions

While tobacco held great promise in Virginia, investors were eager to find other lucrative exports to increase profits via the Atlantic economy. Some turned their sights on the West Indies. In the 1620s, the English developed permanent settlements on St. Christopher, Barbados, and Nevis (Map 2.3). English migrants settled in especially large numbers in Barbados and brought in white indentured servants, many Irish and Scotch, to cultivate tobacco and cotton and raise livestock.

In the 1630s, falling tobacco prices resulted in economic stagnation on Barbados. By that time, however, a few planters were considering another avenue to wealth: sugarcane. English and European consumers absorbed as much sugar as the market could provide, but producing sugar was difficult, expensive, and labor-intensive. In addition, the sugar that was sent from America needed further refinement in Europe before being sold to consumers. The Dutch had built the best refineries in Europe, but their small West Indies colonies could not supply sufficient raw material. By 1640 they formed a partnership with English planters, offering them the knowledge and financing to cultivate sugar on Barbados, which would be refined in the Netherlands. That decision reshaped the economic and political landscape of North America and intensified competition for labor.

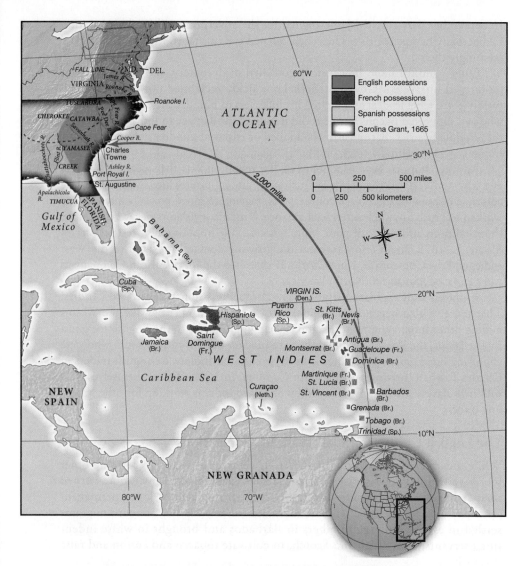

MAP 2.3   West Indies and Carolina in the Seventeenth Century
Beginning in the 1630s, sugar cultivation transformed West Indies colonies. The British consumed sugar in large quantities, ensuring the economic success of Barbados and its neighbors and a vast increase in the enslaved population. In the 1660s, Barbados planters obtained a charter for Carolina and sent many early settlers—white planters and merchants as well as enslaved laborers—to this mainland colony.

REVIEW & RELATE
- How did the Virginia colony and the Powhatan Confederacy evolve between 1607 and the 1670s?
- How did the growth of English colonies on the mainland and in the West Indies shape conflicts in Virginia and demands for labor throughout North America?

Pilgrims and Puritans Settle New England

Five years after John Smith left Jamestown for England, he set out to map the Atlantic coast. In 1616, he published a tract that emphasized the similarity of the climate and terrain in the north Atlantic to the British Isles, and called the area New England. Smith argued that commercial success there would depend on recruiting settlers with the necessary skills and offering them land and a say in the colony's management.

The religious dissenters who settled the region in the 1620s and 1630s embraced Smith's ideas. Because they planned to establish permanent settlements, their ships brought merchants, farmers, and artisans accompanied by wives and children. **Pilgrims** (also known as Separatists) landed on the Massachusetts coast in 1620 and established a settlement at Plymouth. Their goal was to found a religious community wholly separate from the Anglican Church. The Puritans, who hoped to purify rather than separate from the Church of England, arrived a decade later and developed their own colony in Massachusetts Bay. Yet the land the English dissenters claimed was home to diverse native communities, including the Pequot, Wampanoag, Massachusetts, and Narragansett. Over decades, these Indian nations had developed diplomatic strategies to minimize, though not eliminate, conflicts in the region. As English settlements grew, colonists, too, faced questions about how best to deal with the Indian communities that surrounded them.

Pilgrims Arrive in Massachusetts

The Pilgrims sought to form a separate church and community in a land untainted by Catholicism, Anglicanism, or European cosmopolitanism. Armed with a charter from the Virginia Company, thirty-five Pilgrims from Leiden in the Netherlands joined several dozen from England and set sail on the *Mayflower* in September 1620.

Battered by storms, the ship veered off course, landing at Cape Cod in present-day Massachusetts in early December. Before leaving the ship, the settlers, led by William Bradford, signed a pact to form a "civill body politick." This **Mayflower Compact**, which was the first written constitution adopted in North America, followed the Separatist model of a self-governing religious congregation.

After several forays along the coast, the Pilgrims located an uninhabited village surrounded by cornfields where they established their new home, Plymouth. Uncertain of native intentions, the Pilgrims were unsettled by sightings of Indians. They did not realize that a smallpox epidemic brought by English fishermen or European sailors had ravaged the area between 1616 and 1619, killing a large percentage of the local Indian population. Initially, fevers and other diseases proved deadly to the settlers as well. By the spring of 1621, only half of the original Pilgrims remained alive.

Desperate to find food, the survivors were stunned when two English-speaking Indians — Samoset (Abenaki) and Squanto (Patuxet) — appeared at Plymouth that March. Both had been captured as young boys by European explorers. Squanto showed them how to plant corn and where to fish. He also served as an interpreter and intermediary for Pilgrims, who negotiated a fragile peace with Massasoit, chief of the Wampanoag tribe. Although concerned by the power of English guns, Massasoit hoped to create an alliance that would assist him against his traditional native enemies. With Wampanoag assistance, the surviving Pilgrims soon regained their health.

In summer 1621, reinforcements arrived from England, and the next year the Pilgrims received a charter granting them rights to Plymouth Plantation and a degree of self-government. Although some Pilgrims hoped to convert the Indians, other leaders favored a more aggressive stance. One Indian nation, the Massachusetts, posed an especially serious threat. In 1623 Captain Miles Standish led an attack on its main village after kidnapping and killing the chief and his younger brother. Standish's strategy, though controversial, ensured that Massasoit, the colonists' Wampanoag ally, was now the most powerful chief in the region.

The Puritan Migration

A new group of dissenters, the **Puritans**, was also making plans to develop an American settlement. Puritans believed that their country's church and government had grown corrupt and was being chastened by an all-powerful God. During the early seventeenth century, the English population boomed but harvests failed, leading to famine, crime, unemployment, and inflation. The enclosure movement, in which landlords fenced in fields and hired a few laborers and tenants to replace a large number of peasant farmers, increased the number of landless vagrants. At the same time, the English cloth industry nearly collapsed under the weight of competition from abroad. In the Puritans' view, these problems were divine punishments for the nation's sins.

The Puritans envisioned New England as a safe haven from God's wrath. In 1623, affluent Puritans had received a royal charter for the Massachusetts Bay Company. Under Puritan lawyer John Winthrop's leadership, they made plans for their own North American colony. Unlike Pilgrims, Puritans believed that England and the Anglican Church could be redeemed. By prospering spiritually and materially in America, they could establish a model "City upon a Hill" that would inspire reform among residents of the mother country.

The Puritans who arrived in North America in 1630 were better supplied, more prosperous, and more numerous than both the Plymouth and Jamestown pioneers. The Puritans, who sailed on seventeen ships, included ministers, merchants, craftsmen, and farmers. Many arrived with their entire families. The community benefited from being well supplied and including substantial numbers of women who provided critical domestic and farm labor and ensured a high birthrate.

The first Puritan settlers arrived north of Plymouth in 1630 and named their community Boston, after the port city in England from which they had departed. Once established, they relocated the Massachusetts Bay Company's capital and records to New England, thereby converting their commercial charter into the founding document of a self-governing colony. They instituted a new kind of polity in which adult male church members participated in the election of a governor, deputy governor, and legislature. Although the Puritans suffered a difficult first winter, they quickly recovered and soon cultivated sufficient crops to feed themselves and a steady stream of new migrants. During the 1630s, some eighteen thousand Puritans migrated to New England. Even without a cash crop like tobacco or sugar, their colony flourished.

Eager to take advantage of abundant land in the area, the close-knit community spread quickly beyond its original boundaries. Most Puritans sought friendly relations with local Indians, especially the Massachusetts, but this did not stop their expansion into native lands. As new settlements ringed the original at Boston, the legislature established townships with governing bodies that supported a local church and school. By the time the migration of Puritans slowed around 1640, Massachusetts Bay had become a thriving commercial center. They shipped codfish, lumber, grain, pork, and cheese to England in exchange for manufactured goods and to the West Indies for rum and molasses. This trade, along with a relatively healthy climate, and a fairly equal ratio of women to men, ensured a stable and prosperous colony.

The Puritans and Pilgrims also benefited from the smallpox epidemic of 1633–1634. Plymouth Governor William Bradford reported a mortality rate of 95 percent in some native villages, including the Pequot. This powerful tribe, located at the mouth of the Connecticut River, controlled the regional trade in wampum—strings of shells used in intertribal trade and diplomacy. Bradford considered the fact that the English were spared when the Pequot were not as the "marvelous goodnes and providens of God."

While Puritans were pleased that more land was now available for settlement, some sought to convert their Indian neighbors to Christianity. Puritan missionaries taught Indian pupils how to read the Bible, and a few exceptional students attended Harvard College, founded in 1636. Wawaus, a Nipmuck convert, was apprenticed to a printer and given the name James Printer. He eventually worked the first printing press in America, which was installed at the Harvard Indian College. In an effort to wean converts from their traditional customs and beliefs, missionary John Eliot created "praying towns," where Christian Indians could live among others who shared their faith. They were also protected from English settlers seeking to exploit them. As with other native converts, most "praying Indians" continued to embrace traditional rituals and beliefs alongside Christian practices.

The Puritan Worldview

Opposed to the lavish rituals and rigid hierarchy of the Church of England and believing that few Anglicans truly felt the grace of God, Puritans set out to establish a simpler form of worship. They focused on their inner lives and on the purity of their church and community. Puritans followed Calvin, believing in an all-knowing God whose true Word was presented in the Bible. The biblically sanctioned church was a congregation formed by a group of believers who made a covenant with God. Only a small minority of people, known as Saints, were granted God's grace.

Whether one was a Saint and thereby saved was predetermined by and known only to God. Still, some Puritans believed that the chosen were likely to lead a saintly life. Visible signs included a passionate response to the preaching of God's Word, a sense of doubt and despair over one's soul, and that wonderful sense of reassurance that came with God's "saving grace." God's hand in the world appeared in nature as well. Comets and eclipses, as well as epidemics, were considered "remarkable providences."

Shared religious beliefs helped forge a unified community where faith guided civil as well as spiritual decisions. While ministers were discouraged from holding political office, political leaders were devout Puritans who were expected to promote a godly society. Leaders and most followers believed in a hierarchical society. In determining who got land and how much, Puritan leaders assured that wealthier families would continue to thrive. These men also served as judge and jury for those accused of crimes or sins. Their leadership was largely successful, yet almost from the beginning, some Puritans challenged fundamental aspects of religious teachings and, in the process, the community itself.

Dissenters Challenge Puritan Authority

In the early 1630s, Roger Williams, a Salem minister, criticized Puritan leaders for not being sufficiently pure in their rejection of the Church of England and the English monarchy. Embracing separatist views, he moved to Plymouth, but soon criticized their relation to the Church of England as well. He also attacked the king and the royal charter, convinced that colonists should only gain land in New England through legitimate purchase from the various Indian tribes. Returning to Salem in 1633, Williams soon set off a conflict between Salem and the General Court over whether he should be allowed to preach given his claims about the church, the king, and the charter. In October 1635, the General Court finally banished Williams from Massachusetts Bay because of his "diverse, new and dangerous ideas." He moved south with a dozen followers, eventually buying land from the Narragansetts and establishing the community of Providence in an area beyond the bounds of the royal charter. He forged an alliance with the Narragansett, the most powerful nation in the region, that lasted forty years. Williams and his followers insisted on "liberty of conscience" and a clear separation of church and state. Thus, unlike Massachusetts Bay, Providence welcomed Quakers and Jews to the community and also became home to the first Baptist church in America.

A year after Williams's departure, Anne Hutchinson was accused of sedition, or trying to overthrow the government by challenging colonial leaders. She was put on trial in November 1637. An eloquent orator, Hutchinson ultimately claimed that her authority to challenge Puritan leaders came from "an immediate revelation" from God, "the voice of his own spirit to my soul." Since Puritans believed that God spoke only through the intermediary of properly appointed male ministers, her claim was condemned as heretical.

Hutchinson was seen as a threat not only because of her religious beliefs but also because she was a woman. The Reverend Hugh Peter, for example, reprimanded her at trial: "You have stept out of your place, you have rather bine a Husband than a Wife and a preacher than a Hearer; and a Magistrate than a Subject." Many considered her challenge to Puritan authority more serious because she also challenged traditional gender hierarchies. Once banished, Hutchinson and her followers joined Williams's Rhode Island colony.

Wars in Old and New England

Alongside confrontations with Anne Hutchinson and Roger Williams, Puritans faced threats from their Indian neighbors. The Pequot nation had been allies of the English for several years but increasingly protested colonists' continued expansion into their territory. Some Puritans feared they "would cause all the Indians in the country to join to root out all the English." With the Pequot weakened by smallpox, English leaders used the death of two Englishmen in 1636 to justify a military expedition against them. The Narragansett, who were rivals of the Pequot, allied with the English in the **Pequot War**. After months of bloody conflict, the English and their Indian allies launched a brutal attack on a palisaded Pequot village in May 1637 that left some four hundred men, women, and children dead. At the Treaty of Hartford in 1638, the English stripped the decimated tribe of their sovereignty and their name.

Puritans in England were soon engaged in armed conflict as well, against other Englishmen. Differences over religion, taxation, and royal authority had strained relations between Protestants in Parliament and the crown for decades, as James I (r. 1603–1625) and his son Charles I (r. 1625–1649) sought to consolidate their own power at Parliament's expense. In 1642 the relationship between Parliament and King Charles I broke down completely, and the country descended into civil war. Puritan Oliver Cromwell emerged as the leader of the Protestant parliamentary forces, and after several years of fighting, he claimed victory. Charles I was executed, Parliament established a republican commonwealth, and bishops and elaborate rituals were banished from the Church of England. Cromwell ruled England as a military dictator until his death in 1658. By then, much of England had tired of religious conflict and Puritan rule, so Charles I's son, Charles II (r. 1660–1685), was invited to return from exile on the continent and restore the monarchy and the Church of England. In 1660, when Charles II acceded to the throne, the Puritans recognized that their only hope for building a godly republic lay in North America.

During the civil war of the 1640s, English settlements had grown rapidly as a result of both natural increase and migration. Taking control of more and more native lands, English communities stretched from Connecticut through Massachusetts and Rhode Island and north to Maine. Colonial governments began establishing fortified towns along their northern frontier to serve as a buffer between the French and Indians, on one side, and southern English towns, including Boston, on the other. Despite their military purpose, the towns were settled by families. Male inhabitants worked on the town's defenses and served in local militias. However, when fighting erupted, women also took up arms, and all residents were at risk of being wounded, killed, or captured.

The English king and Parliament, embroiled in war at home, paid little attention to events in North America, allowing these New England colonies to develop with little oversight. In 1664, after the restoration of the monarchy, the English wrested control of New Amsterdam from the Dutch and renamed it New York. A decade later, the English could claim dominance—in population, trade, and politics—over other European powers vying for empires along the northern Atlantic coast.

The spread of English control was still contested, however, by diverse Indian groups. In 1651, Plymouth leaders tried to force the elderly Wampanoag chief Massasoit, their long-time ally, to grant them lands along the Ktetit (later Taunton) River.

He refused, declaring that only Weetamoo, his kinswoman and the "Squa Sachem" of that region, could authorize such a grant. Weetamoo, like Anne Hutchison, challenged English assumptions about gender roles and refused to bow to the will of English authorities. She married Massasoit's son, Wamsutta, and became sister-in-law to Metacom, another Wampanoag leader. But she still retained power over the territory she brought to this family alliance.

Numbers, however, were on the side of the English. Only 15,000 to 16,000 native people remained in New England by 1670, a loss of some 80 percent over fifty years. Meanwhile the English population reached more than 50,000. In 1671 the English at Plymouth demanded that the Wampanoag, who had been their allies since the 1620s, surrender their guns and be ruled by English law. Instead, many Indians hid their weapons and, over the next several years, raided frontier farms and killed some settlers. English authorities responded by hanging three Wampanoag men, and tightening their frontier defenses.

In 1662, Metacom, called King Philip by the English, became chief of the Wampanoag. Initially, he continued friendly relations with Puritans. But their efforts to continually expand into Wampanoag and other Indian territories angered him. By 1675, he argued that Europeans must be forced out of the region if Indians were to survive. As conflicts erupted between Indians and colonists that fall, Metacom and his party took refuge with the widowed Weetamoo. The English insisted that Metacom/ King Philip had initiated the war but were convinced they could win an easy victory. Nonetheless, the General Court declared that residents of fortified towns—women and men—must not flee but remain "for the defence of such places." Metacom's forces allied with Nipmucks and smaller groups of other Algonquian-speaking communities, attacking fortified towns and outlying villages. They also launched assaults on Plymouth and Providence and marched within twenty miles of Boston. While the Narragansett had declared their neutrality early in the war, they offered sanctuary to noncombatants from warring tribes. As a result, their long-time English allies declared war on them in November 1675.

As the conflict continued into 1676, it became increasingly brutal. That February, Wampanoag attacked the town of Lancaster and took captives, including Mary Rowlandson and her children. They then marched into the Great Swamp, where Indians fled to regroup, and Rowlandson was assigned to work for Weetamoo. The English meanwhile allied with remnants of the Pequot along with Mohawks and Mohegans. Metacom and the Wampanoag pushed west, hoping to ally with more powerful tribes like the Mohawk. Instead the Mohawk attacked the Wampanoag while English, Pequot, and Mohegan forces ambushed the Narragansett and attacked enemy villages, killing hundreds of Indians and selling hundreds more into slavery in the West Indies.

Attacks on colonial towns and Indian villages continued into 1676. That August, English troops finally killed Metacom, but the war continued. The remaining Wampanoag, Narragansett, and Nipmuck moved north and west, seeking aid from other Indians as they ran short of men, guns, and food. Finally, the Treaty of Casco Bay ended the war in April 1678.

While some 1,000 English settlers were killed and dozens were taken captive during the war, Indian losses were even more catastrophic. Food shortages and disease combined with military deaths to kill at least 4,000 men, women, and children, about a quarter of the remaining Indian population of New England. Indian power in southern New England collapsed as survivors moved north and gradually intermarried with tribes allied with the French. After the carnage spilled into New York, Iroquois leaders and colonists met at Albany in 1677 to salvage their lucrative fur trade. Forming an alliance to forestall future conflicts, they ensured that furs and land would continue to define the complex relations between Indians and Europeans across the northern colonies.

REVIEW & RELATE

- How did Puritan religious views shape New England's development?
- Why did conflict between New England settlers and the region's Indians escalate over the course of the seventeenth century and with what consequences?

Conclusion: European Empires in North America

When Powhatan died in 1618, English, French and Dutch efforts to colonize North America had barely begun. Over the next seventy years, those efforts would look very different from the Spanish conquest they initially hoped to replicate. Powhatan's efforts to bring Jamestown under his control or into a productive alliance collapsed because English success required permanent settlement, abundant land, and sufficient laborers. Alliances with Indians were important for French, Dutch, and English colonists along the Atlantic coast. But they were constantly undermined by European expansion and the need for cheap labor. Success in the burgeoning Atlantic economy—whether through tobacco, sugar, or furs and whether led by commercial interests or religious dissenters—depended as importantly on economic ties and political alliances (or conflicts) back home. Success also often required that European women and men rethink their economic and social roles, adapting to conditions in North America.

European colonists found different ways to prosper in Virginia, Canada, New England, and New Amsterdam, but they still faced daunting choices. Most important, should they create alliances with local Indians for sustenance and trade, or should they seek to dominate them and take what they needed? John Smith, Miles Standish, and many other colonial leaders supported an aggressive policy, much like that of Spain. However, some Europeans in New England, New Amsterdam, and Canada advocated a less violent approach. Many French Jesuit priests and Puritans like Roger Williams focused on the spiritual and material benefits of conversion. Far more argued that building alliances was the most effective means of advancing trade and gaining land, furs, and other goods valued by Europeans. Conflicts over religious beliefs and government support for frontier settlers also created divisions among

European settlers. The banishment of Anne Hutchinson from Massachusetts Bay in 1636 and the response to Bacon's Rebellion in Virginia in 1676 revealed the lengths to which colonial leaders would go to protect their power and authority.

Such internal divisions were often intertwined with or overwhelmed by conflicts with Indians. Although English, Dutch, and French colonists profited from trade relations and military alliances with Indian nations, conflicts and wars repeatedly erupted along the Atlantic Coast. European settlers fought the Powhatan Confederacy in the 1620s and 1640s, the Pequot in the 1630s, Algonquian-speaking tribes in New Netherland in the 1640s, and the Susquehannock in Virginia and the Wampanoag and Narragansett in New England in the 1670s. While the French did not go to war with their Huron allies, they left them to fight alone against the Iroquois when the fur trade moved west. The exhaustion of furs along the Atlantic coast increased the vulnerability of other Indian communities as well. Devastated by European- borne diseases and without valuable items to trade, their very survival was at stake. Indians in New Amsterdam as well as New England resisted the many losses they suffered, often with violence. Anne Hutchinson and her six youngest children had moved to the outer reaches of New Netherland in 1642 after the death of her husband. A year later, she and five of her children were killed by Indians in response to Governor William Kieft's slaughter of peaceful Indians in the region.

As European settlements expanded beyond the Atlantic coast in the late seventeenth century, their prosperity continued to depend on trade goods and land that were often in Indian hands. At the same time, a growing demand for labor led wealthier settlers to seek an increased supply of indentured servants from Europe and enslaved workers from Africa. Over the next half century, relations between settlers and Indians, between wealthy and poor settlers, between whites and blacks, and among European nations vying for empires would grow even more complicated and conflicted.

Chapter 2 Review

KEY TERMS

Protestantism, 30
Church of England, 31
Atlantic economy, 33
metis, 35
Jamestown, 37
Powhatan Confederacy, 37
House of Burgesses, 39

indentured servants, 39
Bacon's Rebellion, 42
Pilgrims, 45
Mayflower Compact, 45
Puritans, 46
Pequot War, 49

REVIEW & RELATE

1. How did the Protestant Reformation and Catholic Counter-Reformation shape the course of European expansion in the Americas?

2. How did the French and Dutch colonies in North America differ from the Spanish empire to the south, and how were these differences shaped by Indian nations?

3. How did the Virginia colony and the Powhatan Confederacy evolve between 1607 and the 1670s?

4. How did the growth of the English colonies on the mainland and in the West Indies shape conflicts in Virginia and demands for labor throughout North America?

5. How did Puritan religious views shape New England's development?

6. Why did conflict between New England settlers and the region's Indians escalate over the course of the seventeenth century and with what consequences?

TIMELINE OF EVENTS

1517	• Protestant Reformation begins
1530s	• England breaks with the Roman Catholic Church
1545–1563	• Council of Trent
1598	• Acoma pueblo uprising, Edict of Nantes
1607	• Jamestown founded
1608	• French settle in Quebec
1609	• Dutch settle on the Hudson River
1612–1614	• Tobacco cultivation begins in Virginia
1619	• First Africans arrive in Virginia
1620	• Pilgrims found Plymouth settlement
1622	• Powhatan Confederacy attack Virginia colonists
1624	• Dutch establish New Amsterdam
1630	• Puritans found Massachusetts Bay colony
1632	• Maryland founded
1635	• Roger Williams moves to Rhode Island

1636–1637	• Pequot War
1637	• Anne Hutchinson banished from Massachusetts Bay colony
1642–1649	• English civil war
1643–1645	• Governor Kieft's war against Indians in New Netherland
1644	• War between Powhatan Confederacy and Virginia colonists
1660	• Monarchy restored in England
1660–1664	• Virginia and Maryland establish lifelong, inherited slavery
1664	• Dutch surrender New Amsterdam to the English
1675–1676	• King Philip's War

3

Colonial America amid Global Change

1680–1754

LEARNING OBJECTIVES

After reading this chapter you will be able to:

- Compare the development of Spanish, French, and English colonies from the late sixteenth to the mid-seventeenth century.

- Analyze the effects of European wars on relations among different groups of European colonists and among diverse Indian nations.

- Examine how the American colonies became part of a global trading network.

- Describe the changing character of labor in the English colonies, including the expansion of African and Indian slavery.

COMPARING AMERICAN HISTORIES

In 1729, at age thirty, **William Moraley Jr.** signed an indenture to serve a five-year term as a "bound servant" in the "American Plantations." This was not what his parents had imagined for him. The son of a journeyman watchmaker, Moraley received a good education and was offered a clerkship with a London lawyer. But Moraley preferred London's pleasures to legal training. At age nineteen, out of money, he was forced to return home and become an apprentice watchmaker for his father. Moraley made a poor apprentice, and in 1725, his father rewrote his will, leaving him just 20 shillings. When Moraley's father died unexpectedly, his more generous widow gave her son 20 pounds. Moraley headed back to London in 1728.

Times were hard in London, and Moraley failed to find work. After being imprisoned for debt, he sold his labor for five years in return for passage to America. Arriving in the colonies in December 1729, William was indentured to Isaac Pearson, a Quaker clockmaker and goldsmith in Burlington, New Jersey. Preferring to live in a large city like Philadelphia, he ran away but was soon captured. Most runaway servants had their contracts extended, but Moraley did not. For the next three years, he worked for Pearson alongside another indentured servant and an enslaved boy. Pearson allowed William to travel the countryside fixing clocks and watches, and the servant observed the far worse conditions of enslaved workers. Perhaps having recouped his investment, Pearson released Moraley from his contract two years early.

Moraley spent the next twenty months traveling the northern colonies, but found no steady employment. Hounded by creditors, he returned to England, penniless and unemployed. In 1743, hoping to cash in on popular interest in adventure tales, he published an account of his travels. In the book, entitled *The Infortunate, the Voyage and Adventures of William Moraley, an Indentured Servant*, he offered a poor man's view of eighteenth-century North America. Like so much else in Moraley's life, the book was not a success.

In 1738, while Moraley was trying to carve out a career as a writer, sixteen-year-old **Eliza Lucas**, the eldest daughter of Colonel George Lucas, arrived at Wappoo, her father's estate near Charleston, South Carolina. Eliza was born on Antigua, in the West Indies, where her father served with the British army and owned a sugar plantation worked by enslaved laborers. The move to the Carolinas was necessitated by her mother's ill health, but it created an unusual opportunity for Eliza. When Colonel Lucas was called back to Antigua in May 1739, he left Eliza in charge of his estate.

For the next five years, Eliza Lucas managed Wappoo and two other Carolina plantations owned by her father. Rising each day at 5 a.m., she checked on the fields and the enslaved laborers who worked them, balanced the books, nursed her mother, taught her younger sister to read, and wrote to her younger brothers at school in England. Eliza improved the value of her family's estates by experimenting with new crops. With her father's enthusiastic support, she cultivated indigo, a plant used for making textile dyes. Her success, however, ensured the expansion of the estate's enslaved labor force.

Eliza Lucas was soon encouraging neighboring planters to follow her lead. With financial aid from the colonial legislature and Parliament, indigo became a profitable export from South Carolina, second only to rice. One of the neighbors she befriended was Charles Pinckney, whom she would later marry, adding her enslaved laborers and landholdings to his.

COMPARING THE AMERICAN HISTORIES of William Moraley and Eliza Lucas illuminates profound shifts in the global economy. Labor and goods from the Atlantic economy now became fully integrated into trade networks from Europe to Asia and Africa. Between 1680 and 1750, indentured servants, enslaved Africans and Indians, planters, soldiers, merchants, and artisans traveled along these new trade networks. So, too, did sugar, rum, tobacco, indigo, cloth, and a host of other items. As England, France, and Spain expanded their empires, colonists developed new crops for export and increased the demand for manufactured goods from elsewhere. Yet the vibrant, increasingly global economy was fraught with peril. Economic crises, the uncertainties of maritime navigation, and outbreaks of war caused constant disruptions. For some Europeans, the opportunities offered by colonization outweighed the dangers; for others, fortune was less kind, and the results were disappointing, even disastrous. Enslaved Africans faced even more devastating circumstances as slavery and the slave trade expanded exponentially. So, too, did many Indians caught between expanding European settlements and powerful native adversaries.

Europeans Expand Their Claims

Beginning with the restoration of the monarchy in 1660, English kings began granting North American land and commercial rights to men who were loyal to the crown. France and Spain also expanded their empires in North America, and all three frequently came into conflict with each other in the late seventeenth and early eighteenth centuries. At the same time, American Indians challenged European efforts to displace them from their homelands while also attempting to establish new communities beyond colonists' reach.

English Colonies Grow and Multiply

Shortly after Charles II (r. 1660–1685) was restored to the English throne, Connecticut and Rhode Island requested and received royal charters that granted them some local authority. These charters could be changed only with the agreement of both parties, and Connecticut and Rhode Island maintained this local autonomy throughout the colonial period. In other colonies, however, Charles II asserted his authority by rewarding loyal supporters with land grants and commercial rights, which could more easily be changed or revoked than royal charters could. He also appointed his supporters to the newly formed Lords of Trade and Plantations, which advised the English Privy Council on policies in the far-flung English empire. He was even more generous with his brother James, the Duke of York. Charles II granted him control over all the lands between the Delaware and Connecticut Rivers, once known as New Netherland, but now known as New York. He then conveyed the adjacent lands to investors who established the colonies of East and West Jersey. Finally, Charles II repaid debts to Admiral Sir William Penn by granting his son huge tracts of land in the Middle Atlantic region. Six years later, William Penn Jr. left the Church of England and joined the Society of Friends, or Quakers. This radical Protestant sect was severely persecuted in England, so the twenty-two-year-old Penn turned his holdings into a Quaker refuge named Pennsylvania.

Between 1660 and 1685, York, Penn, and other English gentlemen were established as the overseers of a string of **proprietary colonies** from Carolina to New York. Although Charles II could have intruded into the government of these colonies, he rarely did. Instead, local conditions and the proprietor's vision largely dictated what was possible. Most proprietors envisioned the creation of a manorial system in their colony, one in which they and other gentry presided over workers producing goods for export. In practice, however, a range of relationships emerged between property owners and workers. For instance, small farmers and laborers in northern Carolina rose up and forced proprietors there to offer land at reasonable prices and a semblance of self-government. In the southern part of Carolina, however, English planters with West Indies connections dominated. They created a mainland version of Barbados by introducing enslaved Africans as laborers, carving out plantations, and trading with the West Indies.

William Penn provided a more progressive model of colonial rule. He established friendly relations with the local Lenni-Lenape Indians and drew up a Frame of Government in 1681 that recognized religious freedom for all Christians. It also allowed all property-owning men to vote and hold office. Under Penn's leadership, Pennsylvania attracted thousands of middling farm families, most of them Quakers, as well as artisans and merchants.

Charles II's death in 1685 marked an abrupt shift in crown-colony relations. His successor, James II (r. 1685–1688), instituted a more authoritarian regime both at home and abroad. He consolidated the colonies in the Northeast and established tighter controls. His royal officials banned town meetings, challenged land titles granted under the original colonial charters, and imposed new taxes. Fortunately for the colonists, the Catholic James II alienated his subjects in England as well as in the colonies, inspiring a bloodless coup in 1688, the so-called **Glorious Revolution**. His Protestant daughter Mary (r. 1689–1694) and her husband, William of Orange (r. 1689–1702), then ascended the throne, introducing more democratic systems of governance in England and the colonies. Two years later, John Locke, a physician and philosopher, wrote a widely circulated treatise supporting the initiatives of William and Mary by insisting that government depended on the consent of the governed.

Eager to restore political order and create a commercially profitable empire, William and Mary established the new colony of Massachusetts (which included Plymouth, Massachusetts Bay, and Maine) and restored town meetings and an elected assembly. But the 1692 charter also granted the English crown the right to appoint a royal governor and officials to enforce customs regulations. It ensured religious freedom to members of the Church of England and allowed all male property owners (not just Puritans) to be elected to the assembly. In Maryland, too, the crown imposed a royal governor and replaced the Catholic Church with the Church of England as the established religion. And in New York, wealthy English merchants won the backing of the newly appointed royal governor, who instituted a representative assembly and supported a merchant-dominated Board of Aldermen. In 1696, William consolidated various bodies related to policies in England's far-flung plantations into the Lord Commissioners for Trade and Plantations, known as the Board of Trade. Taken as a whole, William and Mary's policies instituted a partnership between England and colonial elites by allowing colonists to retain long-standing local governmental institutions while also asserting royal authority to appoint governors and ensure the influence of the Church of England (Table 3.1).

TABLE 3.1		ENGLISH COLONIES ESTABLISHED IN NORTH AMERICA, 1607–1750		
Colony	Date	Original Colony Type	Religion	Status in 1750
Virginia	1624	Royal	Church of England	Royal
Massachusetts	1630	Charter	Congregationalist	Royal with charter
Maryland	1632	Proprietary	Catholic	Royal
Connecticut	1662	Charter	Congregationalist	Charter
Rhode Island	1663	Charter	No established church	Charter
Carolina	1663	Proprietary	Church of England	
North	1691	Proprietary		Royal
South	1691	Proprietary		Royal
New Jersey	1664	Proprietary	Church of England	Royal
New York	1664	Proprietary	Church of England	Royal
Pennsylvania	1681	Proprietary	Quaker	Proprietary
Delaware	1704	Proprietary	Lutheran/Quaker	Proprietary
Georgia	1732	Charter	Church of England	(Royal 1752)
New Hampshire (separated from Massachusetts)	1691	Royal	Congregationalist	Royal

In the early eighteenth century, England's North American colonies took the form that they would retain until the revolution in 1776. In 1702 East and West Jersey united into the colony of New Jersey. Delaware separated from Pennsylvania in 1704. By 1710 North Carolina became fully independent of South Carolina. Finally, in 1732, the colony of Georgia was chartered as a buffer between Spanish Florida and the plantations of South Carolina. At the same time, settlers pushed back the frontier in all directions.

The Pueblo Revolt and Spain's Fragile Empire

Meanwhile Spain's forces in North America were spread dangerously thin. In Florida, Indians resisted the spread of Spanish cattle ranching in the 1670s. Some moved their settlements north to the Carolina border, wooed by the English who eagerly exchanged European goods for deerskins. The efforts of the English to interfere with Spanish-Indian trade networks fueled growing tensions along this Anglo-Spanish frontier. To the west, in New Mexico, open conflict erupted between Spanish and Pueblo peoples when war broke out in Europe in 1702. Tensions between Spanish missionaries and *encomenderos* and the Pueblo nation had simmered for decades (see "Spain's Global Empire Declines" in chapter 2). Relations worsened in the 1670s when a drought led to famine in the area and brought a revival of Indian rituals that the Spaniards considered heretical and threatening. Meanwhile, Spanish forces were failing to protect the Pueblos against devastating raids by Apache and Navajo warriors, while Catholic prayers failed to stop Pueblo deaths in a 1671 epidemic.

When some Pueblos returned to their traditional priests, Spanish officials hanged three Indian leaders for idolatry and whipped and incarcerated forty-three others. Among those punished was Popé, a militant Pueblo. Upon his release, Popé began planning a broad-based revolt. On August 10, 1680, seventeen thousand Pueblo Indians initiated a coordinated assault on numerous Spanish missions and forts. They destroyed buildings and farms, burned crops and houses, and smeared excrement on Christian altars. The Spaniards retreated to Mexico without launching any significant counterattack.

Still, the Spaniards reconquered parts of New Mexico in the 1690s, aided by growing internal conflict among the Pueblos and raids by the Apache. The governor general of New Spain worked hard to subdue the province and in 1696 crushed the rebels and opened new lands for settlement. Meanwhile Franciscan missionaries improved relations with the Pueblos by allowing them to retain more indigenous practices.

Yet despite the Spanish reconquest, in the long run the **Pueblo revolt** limited Spanish expansion by strengthening other indigenous peoples in the region. In the aftermath of the revolt, some Pueblo refugees moved north and taught the Navajo how to grow corn, raise sheep, and ride horses. Through the Navajo, the Ute, Shoshone, and Comanche peoples also gained access to horses. By the 1730s, the Comanches launched mounted bison hunts as well as raids on other Indian nations. At Taos, they traded Indian captives into slavery for more horses and guns. Thus the Pueblo provided other Indian nations with the means to support larger populations, wider commercial networks, and more warriors. These nations continued to contest Spanish rule.

At the same time, Spain sought to reinforce its claims to Texas (named after the Tejas Indians) in response to French settlements in the lower Mississippi valley. In the early eighteenth century, Spanish missions and forts appeared along the route from San Juan Batista to the border of present-day Louisiana. Although small and scattered, these outposts were meant to ensure Spain's claim to Texas. But the presence of large and powerful Indian nations, including the Caddo and the Apache, forced Spanish residents to accept many native customs in order to maintain their presence in the region.

France Seeks Land and Control

Louis XIV of France (r. 1643–1715) claimed absolute power derived from what he believed was his divine right to rule. One of his missions was to extend the boundaries of France's North American colonies. Still, French efforts were focused more on exploration and trade than on settlement. In 1682 French adventurers and their Indian allies journeyed from the *Pays d'en Haut*, the Upper Country surrounding the Great Lakes, down the Mississippi River. Led by the French explorer René-Robert Cavelier, Sieur de La Salle, the party traveled to the Gulf of Mexico and claimed all the land drained by the river's tributaries for France. The new territory of Louisiana promised great wealth, but its development stalled when La Salle failed in his attempt to establish a colony.

Ambush of the Villasur Expedition, c. 1720   An unknown artist painted this battle scene on buffalo hide. In 1720, Spanish soldiers and Pueblo warriors tried to expel the French from the lower Mississippi River valley. Instead, French soldiers and their Indian allies ambushed the expedition and killed forty-five men. Two of the dead, Spanish Father Juan Minguez and Pueblo leader Joseph Naranjo, are shown here in the center. MPI/Archive Photos/Getty Images

Still eager for a southern outlet for furs, the French did not give up. After several more attempts at colonization in the early eighteenth century, French settlers maintained a toehold along Louisiana's Gulf coast. Most important, Pierre LeMoyne d'Iberville and his brother established forts at Biloxi and Mobile bays, where they traded with local Choctaw Indians. They recruited settlers from Canada and France, and these two small outposts survived despite conflicts among settlers, pressure from the English and the Spanish, a wave of epidemics, and a lack of supplies from France. Nevertheless, Louisiana counted only three hundred French settlers by 1715.

Continuing to promote commercial relations with diverse Indian nations, the French built a string of missions and forts along the upper Mississippi and Illinois Rivers. The most important of these, Kaskaskia (just south of Cahokia), developed into a multicultural community of Indian farmers and artisans, French fur traders, and Jesuit missionaries. These outposts in the continent's interior allowed France to challenge both English and Spanish claims to North America. In addition, extensive trade with a range of Indian nations ensured that French power was far greater than the small number of French settlers suggests.

REVIEW & RELATE

- What role did the crown play in the expansion of the English North American colonies in the second half of the seventeenth century?
- How did the development of the Spanish and French colonies in the late seventeenth century differ from that of the English colonies?

European Wars and American Consequences

The importance of the Atlantic economy in the late seventeenth and early eighteenth centuries ensured that developments in Europe would reshape American colonies. From 1689 until 1713, Europe was in an almost constant state of war, with continental conflicts spilling over into colonial possessions in North America. The result was increased tensions between colonists of different nationalities and diverse Indian nations as well as between Indians and colonists and between colonists and their home countries.

Colonial Conflicts and Indian Alliances

France was at the center of much of the European warfare of the period. Louis XIV hoped to expand France's borders and gain supremacy in Europe. To this end, he built a powerful professional army under state authority. Having gained victories in the Spanish Netherlands, Flanders, Strasbourg, and Lorraine, the French army seemed invincible.

Between 1689 and 1697, France and England fought their first sustained war in North America, **King William's War**. The war began over conflicting French and English interests on the European continent, but it soon spread to the American frontier when English and Iroquois forces attacked French and Huron settlements around Montreal and northern New York.

Although neither side had gained significant territory when peace was declared in 1697, the war had important consequences. Many colonists serving in the English army died of battle wounds, smallpox, and inadequate rations. Those who survived resented their treatment and the unnecessary deaths of so many comrades. The Iroquois fared even worse. Their fur trade was devastated, and hundreds of Mohawks and Oneidas were forced to flee from France's Huron, Ottawa, Ojibwe, and Potawatomi allies along the eastern Great Lakes. Moreover, "French Indians" and Iroquois continued to attack each other for years after the peace settlement. Finally, in 1701, the Iroquois agreed to end their raids and remain neutral in all future European conflicts. Wary of further European entanglements, Iroquois leaders focused on rebuilding their tattered confederacy.

Taking advantage of French military success, Antoine Laumet de La Mothe, Sieur de Cadillac, founded Fort Pontchartrain du Detroit in 1701 on a strategic strait on the Detroit River that joined the Great Lakes and linked the St. Lawrence and Mississippi Rivers. Established at what was then the western point of European settlement, Cadillac envisioned a post that would consolidate French control of the fur trade by forestalling England's advance into the region and reinforcing France's trade relations with Indian nations to the East and the West. Detroit consolidated France's eastern and western fur-trading networks and provided a longer growing season for settlers than Montreal or Quebec.

Still, neither the peace treaty of 1701 nor the establishment of Fort Detroit could end European battles over North America's lands and resources. Indeed, as Indian agents and traders from the various colonial powers learned Indian languages, negotiated with diverse tribes, intermarried with or converted Indian families, and joined in Indian rituals, it became impossible to disentangle European conflicts from North American economic and political networks.

A second protracted conflict, known as the **War of the Spanish Succession** (1702–1713) or Queen Anne's War, had even more devastating effects on North America. The conflict erupted in Europe when Charles II of Spain (r. 1665–1700) died without an heir, launching a contest for the Spanish kingdom and its colonies. France and Spain squared off against England, the Netherlands, Austria, and Prussia. In North America, however, it was England and her Indian allies that faced France, Spain, and their Indian allies. Each European nation sought to gain additional territory, while Indians hoped to increase the value of their alliances.

After more than a decade of savage fighting, Queen Anne's War ended in 1713 with the Treaty of Utrecht, which sought to secure a prolonged peace by balancing the interests of the great powers in Europe and their colonial possessions. By then, England had consolidated power at home by incorporating Scotland into Great Britain through the 1707 Act of Union. In 1713, a weakened France surrendered Newfoundland, Nova Scotia, and the Hudson Bay Territory to England, while Spain granted England control of St. Kitts in the West Indies, Gibraltar, and Minorca as well as the right to sell African slaves in its American colonies. Europeans' Indian allies did not participate in these negotiations, though those who fought with the English benefitted from that nation's expansion into new North American markets. Still, neither the treaty nor Britain's consolidation forestalled further conflict. Indeed, Spain, France, and Britain all strengthened fortifications along their North American borders (Map 3.1).

Indians Resist European Encroachment

The seemingly ceaseless European conflicts in North America put incredible pressure on Indian peoples to choose sides. It was increasingly difficult for native peoples in colonized areas to remain autonomous, yet Indian nations were not simply pawns of European powers. Some actively sought European allies against their native enemies, and nearly all desired European trade goods like cloth, guns, and horses. The most powerful confederacies, like the Iroquois in New York and the Choctaw in the lower Mississippi River valley, played one European power off another. This became more difficult as the French and Spanish lost ground to the English in North America.

Moreover, as colonial expansion and trade led to war, the power of young male warriors increased in many tribes. In societies like the Cherokee and Iroquois, in which older women had long held significant economic and political authority, this change threatened traditional gender and generational relations. In addition, struggles among English, French, and Spanish forces both reinforced conflicts among Indian peoples that existed before European settlement and created new ones.

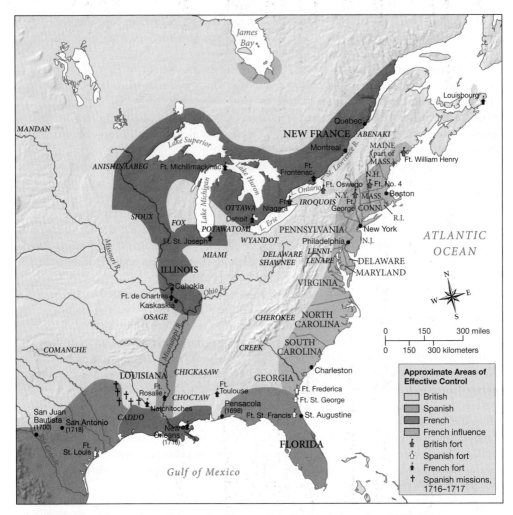

MAP 3.1   European Empires and Indian Nations in North America, 1715–1750
European nations competed with one another and with numerous Indian nations for control of vast areas of North America. Although wars continually reshaped areas under European and Indian control, this map shows the general outlines of the empires claimed by each European nation, the key forts established to maintain those claims, and the major Indian nations in each area.

The trade in guns was especially significant in escalating conflicts among tribes in the Southeast during the late seventeenth century. By that period, the most precious commodity Indians in the region had to trade were Indian captives sold as slaves. Indians had always taken captives in war, but some of those captives had been adopted into the victorious nation. Now, however, war was almost constant in many areas, and captives were more valuable when sold as slaves to Europeans. The English in Carolina encouraged the Westo and later the Savannah nation to raid tribes in Spanish Florida, exchanging their captives for guns. The Chickasaws ranged further west, raiding tribes across the Mississippi River and then force-marching their captives to Charleston for sale. As slave raiding spread across the Anglo-Spanish borders, more peaceful tribes were forced to acquire guns for self-protection. In addition, many Indian nations were forced off traditional lands by slave-raiding Indian foes. Some of these displaced groups merged to form new tribes, like the Yamasee in the Southeast.

Indian slave traders both intensified the violence among native peoples and spread European diseases further west. The Great Southeastern Smallpox epidemic that raged from 1696 to 1700 erupted first among European colonists and enslaved Africans but then swept through Indian communities across the Southeast and west to the Mississippi valley. It devastated Indian societies that had been displaced and weakened by warfare and slave raiding and created crises even for those, like the Yamasee, who had sustained their alliance with the English by enslaving other Indians.

The vicious cycle of guns and enslavement convinced some southern Indians to develop a pan-Indian alliance in the 1710s similar to that forged by New England Indians in the 1670s (see "Wars in Old and New England" in chapter 2). First, a group of Tuscarora warriors, hoping to gain support from other tribes, launched an attack on North Carolina settlements in September 1711. In the **Tuscarora War** that followed, South Carolina colonists came to the aid of their North Carolina countrymen and persuaded the Yamasee, Catawba, and Cherokee nations to join forces against the Tuscarora. Meanwhile political leaders in North Carolina convinced a competing group of Tuscarora to ally with the colonists. By 1713 the war was largely over, and in 1715 the Tuscarora signed a peace treaty and forfeited their lands. Many then migrated north and were accepted as the sixth nation of the Iroquois Confederacy.

The end of the Tuscarora War did not mean peace, however. The Yamasee people remained deeply in debt to British merchants as the trade in deerskins and slaves moved west. Yet they were no longer able to secure sufficient captives to meet colonists' demands. The Yamasee also needed to adopt more captives as their own population shrank from disease and war. In turn, British colonists in South Carolina imported more African slaves to meet their need for labor. As the situation deteriorated, the Yamasee secured allies among the Creek and Cherokee and in 1715 launched an all-out effort to force the British out. For the next two years, this Yamasee-led coalition warred against the South Carolina militia. The British gained victory in the **Yamasee War** only after the Cherokee switched their allegiance to the colonists in early 1716. The final Indian nations withdrew from the conflict in 1717, and a fragile peace followed.

While the Yamasee War did not oust the British, it transformed the political landscape of native North America. In its aftermath, the Creek and Catawba tribes emerged as powerful new confederations, the Cherokee became the major trading partner of the British, and the Yamasee nation was seriously weakened. Moreover, as the Cherokee allied with the British, the Creek and the Caddo tribes strengthened their alliance with the French.

Despite the British victory, colonists on the Carolina frontier faced raids on their settlements for decades to come. In the 1720s and 1730s, settlers in the Middle Atlantic colonies also experienced fierce resistance to their westward expansion. And attacks on New Englanders along the Canadian frontier periodically disrupted settlement there. Still, many Indian tribes were pushed out of their homelands. As they resettled in new regions, they alternately allied and fought with native peoples already living there. At the same time, the trade in Indian slaves expanded in the west as the French and the Spanish competed for economic partners and military allies.

Conflicts on the Southern Frontier

Indians were not the only people to have their world shaken by war. By 1720 years of warfare and upheaval had transformed the mind-set of many colonists. Although most considered themselves loyal British subjects, many believed that British proprietors remained largely unconcerned with the colonies' welfare. Others resented the British army's treatment of colonial militia and Parliament's unwillingness to aid settlers against Indian attacks. Moreover, the growing numbers of settlers who arrived from other parts of Europe had little investment in British authority.

The impact of Britain's ongoing conflicts with Spain during the 1730s and 1740s illustrates this development. Following the Yamasee War, South Carolina became a royal colony, and its profitable rice and indigo plantations spread southward. Then, in 1732, Parliament established Georgia (named after King George II, r. 1727–1760) on lands north of Florida as a buffer between Carolina colonists and their longtime Spanish foes.

Spanish authorities were furious at this expansion of British territorial claims. Thus in August 1739, a Spanish naval ship captured an English ship captain who was trading illegally in the Spanish West Indies and severed his ear. In response, Great Britain attacked St. Augustine and Cartagena (in present-day Colombia), but its troops were repulsed. In 1742 Spain sent troops into Georgia, but the colonial militia pushed back the attack. By then, the American war had become part of a more general European conflict. Once again France and Spain joined forces while Great Britain supported Germany in Europe. When the war ended in 1748, Britain had ensured the future of Georgia and reaffirmed its military superiority. Once again, however, victory cost the lives of many colonial settlers and soldiers, and some colonists began to wonder whether their interests and those of the British government were truly the same.

Once again, Indians were caught up in these ongoing disputes among Europeans. While both French and Spanish forces attacked the British along the Atlantic coast, they sought to outflank each other in the lower Mississippi River valley and Texas. With the French relying on Caddo, Choctaw, and other Indian allies for trade goods and defense, the Spaniards needed to expand their alliances beyond those with the Tejas. In 1749, Spaniards agreed to stop kidnapping and enslaving Apache women and children and, instead, negotiated peace with that powerful Indian nation.

The British meanwhile became increasingly dependent on a variety of European immigrants to defend colonial frontiers against the French, Spaniards, and Indians. Certainly many Anglo-Americans moved westward as coastal areas became overcrowded, but frontier regions also attracted immigrants from Scotland and Germany who sought refuge and economic opportunity in the colonies. Many headed to the western regions of Virginia and Carolina and to Georgia in the 1730s and 1740s. Meanwhile, South Carolina officials recruited Swiss, German, and French Huguenot as well as Scots-Irish immigrants in the 1740s. Small communities of Jews settled in Charleston as well. Gradually many of these immigrants moved south into Georgia, seeking more and cheaper land. Thus when Spanish, French, or Indian forces attacked the British colonial frontier, they were as likely to face Scots-Irish and German immigrants as Englishmen.

REVIEW & RELATE	• How did the European wars of the late seventeenth and early eighteenth centuries impact relations between colonists and England? • How were Indian alliances and conflicts, with other Indians and with European nations, shaped by the trade in slaves and guns and by wars between European powers?

The Benefits and Costs of Empire

The combined forces of global trade and international warfare altered the political and economic calculations of imperial powers. This was especially true for British North America, where colonists settled as families and created towns that provided key markets for Britain's commercial expansion. Over the course of the eighteenth century, British colonists became increasingly avid consumers of products from North America and around the world. Meanwhile the king and Parliament sought greater control over these far-flung commercial networks.

Colonial Traders Join Global Networks

In the late seventeenth and early eighteenth centuries, trade became truly global. Not only did goods from China, India, the Middle East, Africa, and North America gain currency in England and the rest of Europe, but the tastes of European consumers also helped shape which goods were produced in other parts of the world. For instance, by the early eighteenth century the Chinese were making porcelain teapots and bowls specifically for the English market. The trade in cloth, tea, tobacco, and sugar was similarly influenced by European tastes. The exploitation of enslaved African laborers contributed significantly to this global commerce. They were a crucial item of trade in their own right, and their labor in the Americas ensured steady supplies of sugar, rice, tobacco, and indigo for the world market.

By the early eighteenth century, both the volume and the diversity of goods multiplied. Silk, calico, porcelain, olive oil, wine, and other items were carried from Asia to Europe and the American colonies, while cod, mackerel, shingles, pine boards, barrel staves, rum, sugar, rice, indigo, and tobacco filled ships from America. A healthy trade also grew up within North America as New England fishermen, New York and Charleston merchants, and Caribbean planters met one another's needs. Salted cod and mackerel flowed to the Caribbean, and rum, molasses, and enslaved laborers flowed back to the mainland. This commerce required ships, barrels, docks, warehouses, and wharves, all of which ensured a lively trade in lumber, tar, pitch, and rosin (Map 3.2).

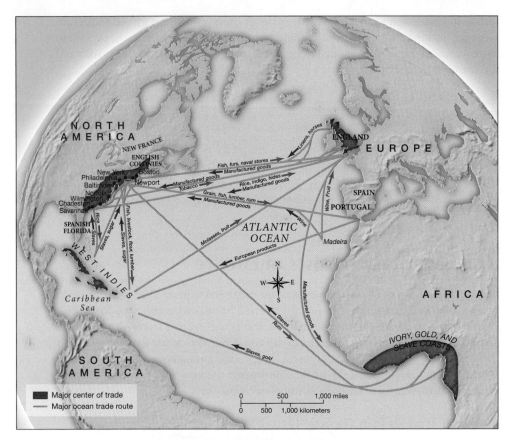

MAP 3.2   North Atlantic Trade in the Eighteenth Century
North Atlantic trade provided various parts of the British empire with raw materials, manufactured goods, and labor. Many ships traveled between only two regions because they were equipped to carry particular kinds of goods—slaves, grains, or manufactured goods. Ultimately, however, people and goods were exchanged among four key points: the West Indies, mainland North America, West Africa, and Great Britain.

The flow of information was critical to the flow of goods and credit. By the early eighteenth century, coffeehouses flourished in port cities around the Atlantic, providing access to the latest news. Merchants, ship captains, and traders met in person to discuss new ventures and to keep apprised of recent developments. British and American periodicals reported on parliamentary legislation, commodity prices in India and Great Britain, the state of trading houses in China, the outbreak of disease in foreign ports, and stock ventures in London. Still, these markets were volatile. In 1720 shares in the British South Seas Company, which had risen to astronomical heights, collapsed. Thousands of investors, including William Moraley's father, lost a great deal of money.

Imperial Policies Focus on Profits

European sovereigns worked to ensure that this international trade and their colonial possessions benefited their own European treasuries. In the late seventeenth century, both Louis XIV and his English rivals embraced a system known as **mercantilism**, which centered on the maintenance of a favorable balance of trade, with more gold and silver flowing into the home country than flowed out. In France, finance minister Jean-Baptiste Colbert honed the system. Beginning in the 1660s, he taxed foreign imports while removing all barriers to trade within French territories. Colonies provided valuable raw materials that could be used to produce manufactured items for sale to foreign nations and to colonists.

While France's mercantile system was limited by the size of its empire, England benefited more fully from such policies. The English crown had access to a far wider array of natural resources from which to manufacture goods and a larger market for these products. Beginning in 1660, Parliament passed a series of **Navigation Acts** that required merchants to conduct trade with the colonies only in English-owned ships. In addition, certain items imported from foreign ports had to be carried in English ships or in ships with predominantly English crews. Finally, a list of "enumerated articles"—including tobacco, cotton, sugar, and indigo—had to be shipped from the colonies to England before being re-exported to foreign ports. Thus the crown benefited directly or indirectly from nearly all commerce conducted by its colonies. But colonies, too, often benefited as when Parliament subsidized the development of indigo in South Carolina.

In 1663 Parliament expanded its imperial reach through additional Navigation Acts, which required that goods sent from Europe to English colonies also pass through British ports. And a decade later, ship captains had to pay a duty or post bond before carrying enumerated articles between colonial ports. These acts ensured not only greater British control over shipping but also additional revenue for the

East Prospect of the City of Philadelphia c. 1778   This view of Philadelphia from New Jersey was originally published as a sepia-toned engraving in London Magazine in 1761. The colored engraving was published in 1778 to highlight the bustling commercial activity in the city, which became the seat of the federal government that July. From The New York Public Library, https://digitalcollections.nypl.org/items/ 510d47d9-7ac4-a3d9-e040-e00a18064a99

crown as captains paid duties in the West Indies, mainland North American, and British ports. Beginning in 1673, England sent customs officials to the colonies to enforce the various parliamentary acts. By 1680, with a consolidated Board of Trade coordinating business with the colonies, London, Bristol, and Liverpool all thrived as barrels of sugar and tobacco and stacks of deer and beaver skins were unloaded at their docks and bolts of dyed cloth and cases of metal tools and guns were put on board for the return voyage. As mechanization and manufacturing expanded in England, Parliament sought to keep the profits at home by quashing nascent industries in the colonies. It thus prohibited the sale of products such as American-made textiles (1699), hats (1732), and iron goods (1750). In addition, Parliament worked to restrict trade among the North American colonies, especially between those on the mainland and in the West Indies.

Despite the increasing regulation, American colonists could own British ships and transport goods produced in the colonies. Indeed, by the mid-eighteenth century, North American merchants oversaw 75 percent of the trade in manufactures sent from Bristol and London to the colonies and 95 percent of the trade with the West Indies. Ironically, then, a system established to benefit Great Britain ended up creating a mercantile elite in British North America. Most of those merchants traded in goods, but some traded in human cargo.

The Atlantic Slave Trade

Parliament chartered the Royal African Company in 1672 as Britain expanded its role in the Atlantic slave trade. Between 1700 and 1808, some 3 million captive Africans were carried on British and Anglo-American ships, about 40 percent of the total of those sold in the Americas in this period (Figure 3.1). Probably half a million Africans died on the voyage across the Atlantic. Huge numbers also died in Africa, while being marched to the coast or held in forts waiting to be forced aboard ships. Yet despite this astounding death rate, the slave trade yielded enormous profits and had far-reaching consequences: The Africans whom British traders bought and sold transformed labor systems in the colonies, fueled international trade, and enriched merchants, planters, and their families and communities.

European traders worked closely with African merchants to gain their human cargo, trading muskets, metalware, and linen for men, women, and children. Originally many of those sold into slavery were captives of war. But by the time British and Anglo-American merchants became central to this notorious trade, their contacts in Africa were procuring labor in any way they could. Over time, African traders moved farther inland to fill the demand, devastating large areas of West Africa, particularly the Congo-Angola region, which supplied some 40 percent of all Atlantic slaves.

The trip across the Atlantic, known as the **Middle Passage**, was a brutal and often deadly experience for Africans. Exhausted and undernourished by the time they boarded the large oceangoing vessels, the captives were placed in dark and crowded holds. Most had been poked and prodded by slave traders, and some had been branded to ensure that a trader received the exact individuals he had purchased. Once in the hold, they might wait for weeks before the ship finally set sail. By that time, the foul-smelling and crowded hold became a nightmare of disease and despair. There was never sufficient food or fresh water for the captives, and women

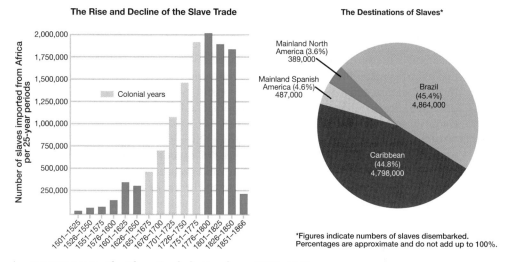

FIGURE 3.1 The Slave Trade in Numbers, 1501–1866

Extraordinary numbers of Africans were shipped as slaves to other parts of the world from the sixteenth to the nineteenth century. The slave trade transformed mainland North America, Brazil, and the West Indies. What broad patterns about the African slave trade can you infer from this data? Source: Estimates Database. 2009. Voyages: Trans-Atlantic Slave Trade Database, http://www.slavevoyages.org/tast /assessment/estimates.faces. Accessed June 15, 2010.

especially were subject to sexual abuse by crew members. Many captives could not communicate with each other since they spoke different languages, and none of them knew exactly where they were going or what would happen when they arrived.

Those who survived the voyage were likely to find themselves in the slave markets of Barbados or Jamaica, where they were put on display for potential buyers. Once purchased, the enslaved workers went through a period of seasoning as they regained their strength, became accustomed to their new environment, and learned commands in a new language. Some did not survive seasoning, falling prey to malnutrition and disease or committing suicide. Others adapted to the new circumstances and adopted enough European or British ways to carry on even as they sought means to resist the shocking and oppressive conditions.

Seaport Cities and Consumer Cultures

The same trade in human cargo that brought misery to millions of Africans provided traders, investors, and plantation owners with huge profits that helped turn America's Atlantic seaport cities into centers of culture and consumption. Charleston was one of the main ports receiving African slaves in the early 1700s, and Eliza Lucas was impressed with its prosperous character. Arriving in 1738, she noted that "the Metropolis is a neat pretty place. The inhabitants [are] polite and live in a very gentile [genteel] manner." North American seaports, with their elegant homes, fine shops, and lively social seasons, did capture the most dynamic aspects of colonial life. Although cities like New York, Boston, Philadelphia, Baltimore, and Charleston contained less than 10 percent of the colonial population, they served as focal points of economic, political, social, and cultural activity.

Affluent urban families created a consumer revolution in North America. Changing patterns of consumption challenged traditional definitions of status. Less tied to birth and family pedigree, status in the colonies became more closely linked to financial success and a genteel lifestyle. Successful men of humble origin, even those of Dutch, Scottish, French, and Jewish heritage, might join the British-dominated colonial gentry.

Of those who made this leap in the early eighteenth century, Benjamin Franklin was the most notable. Franklin was apprenticed to his brother, a printer, an occupation that matched his interest in books, reading, and politics. At age sixteen, Benjamin published (anonymously) his first essays in his brother's paper, the *New England Courant*. Two years later, a family dispute led Benjamin to try his luck in New York and then Philadelphia. His fortunes were fragile, but unlike William Moraley Jr., he combined hard work with a quick wit, good luck, and political connections, which together led to success. In 1729 Franklin purchased the *Pennsylvania Gazette* and became the colony's official printer.

While Franklin worried about the concentration of wealth in too few hands, most colonial elites in the early eighteenth century happily displayed their profits. Leading merchants in Boston, Salem, New York, and Philadelphia emulated British styles and built fine homes that had separate rooms for sleeping, eating, and entertaining guests. Mercantile elites also redesigned the urban landscape, donating money for brick churches and stately town halls. They constructed new roads, wharves, and warehouses to facilitate trade, and they invested in bowling greens and public gardens.

The spread of international commerce created a lively cultural life in thriving colonial cities. The colonial elite replicated British fashions, including elaborate tea rituals. In Boston, the wives of merchants served fine teas imported from East Asia in cups and saucers from China while decorated bowls held sugar from the West Indies. However, the emergence of a colonial aristocracy also revealed growing inequality. Wealthy urban merchants and professionals lived alongside a middling group of artisans and shopkeepers and a growing class of unskilled laborers, widows, orphans, the elderly, the disabled, and the unemployed. In seaport cities, enslaved laborers might live in their owners' homes or be relegated to separate and impoverished communities. In New York City, which boasted the second largest slave market in the mainland colonies in the 1710s, blacks were regularly buried outside the city limits. The frequent wars of the late seventeenth and early eighteenth centuries contributed to these economic and social divisions by boosting the profits of merchants, shipbuilders, and artisans. They temporarily improved the wages of seamen as well. But in their aftermath, rising prices, falling wages, and a lack of jobs led to the concentration of wealth in fewer hands.

REVIEW & RELATE

- What place did North American colonists occupy in the eighteenth-century global trade network?
- How and with what success did the British government maintain control over the colonial economy and ensure that it served Britain's economic and political interests?

Labor in North America

What brought the poor and the wealthy together was the demand for labor. Labor was sorely needed in the colonies, but this did not make it easy to find steady, high-paying employment. Many would-be laborers had few skills and faced fierce competition from other workers for limited, seasonal labor. Moreover, a majority of European immigrants and nearly all Africans arrived in America with significant limits on their freedom.

Finding Work in the Colonies

The lack of demand for free laborers was rooted in many employers' preference for indentured servants, apprentices, or others who came cheap and were bound by contract. Some employed criminals or purchased enslaved workers, who would provide years of service for a set price. Free laborers who sought a decent wage and steady employment needed to match their desire to work with skills that were in demand.

When William Moraley ended his indenture and sought work, he discovered that far fewer colonists than Englishmen owned timepieces, leaving him without a useful trade. So he tramped the countryside, selling his labor when he could, but found no consistent employment. Thousands of other men and women, most without Moraley's education or skills, also found themselves at the mercy of unrelenting economic forces.

Many poor men and women found jobs building homes, loading ships, or spinning yarn. But they were usually employed for only a few months a year. The rest of the time they scrounged for bread and beer, begged in the streets, or stole what they needed. Most lived in ramshackle buildings filled with cramped and unsanitary rooms. Children born into such squalid circumstances were lucky to survive their first year. Those raised in seaport cities might earn a few pence running errands for captains or sailors, but they would never have access to the bounteous goods unloaded at the docks.

By the mid-eighteenth century, older systems of labor, like indentured servitude, began to decline in many areas. In some parts of the North and across the South, white servants were gradually replaced by enslaved Africans (Figure 3.2). At the same time, farm families who could not usefully employ all their children bound out sons and daughters to more prosperous neighbors. Apprentices, too, competed for

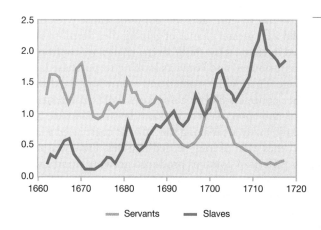

Servants ----- Slaves ▬▬▬

FIGURE 3.2 Indentured Servants and Slaves in Six Maryland Counties, 1662–1717 This chart illustrates a dramatic shift in the Chesapeake labor force between 1662 and 1717. Although based on a study of estate inventories from six Maryland counties, what does the trend shown here suggest about the larger transition in the use of white indentured servants and black slaves on Chesapeake farms? Based on Gloria L. Main, Tobacco Colony: Life in Early Maryland, 1650–1720 (Princeton: Princeton University Press, 1982), 26.

positions. Unlike most servants, apprentices contracted to learn a trade. They trained under the supervision of a craftsman, who gained cheap labor by promising to teach a young man (and most apprentices were men) his trade. But master craftsmen limited the number of apprentices they accepted to maintain the value of their skills.

Another category of laborers emerged in the 1720s. A population explosion in Europe and the rising price of wheat and other items convinced many people to seek passage to America. Shipping agents offered them loans for their passage that were repaid when the immigrants found a colonial employer who would redeem (that is, repay) the agents. In turn, these **redemptioners**, who often traveled with families, labored for the employer for a set number of years. The redemption system was popular in the Middle Atlantic colonies, especially among German immigrants who hoped to establish farms on the Pennsylvania frontier. While many succeeded, their circumstances could be extremely difficult.

Large numbers of convicts, too, entered the British colonies in the eighteenth century. Jailers in charge of Britain's overcrowded prisons offered inmates the option of transportation to the colonies. Hundreds were thus bound out each year to American employers. The combination of indentured servants, redemptioners, apprentices, and convicts ensured that as late as 1750 the majority of white workers—men and women—in the British colonies were bound to some sort of contract.

Some white workers also competed with slaves, especially in the northern colonies. Africans and African Americans formed only a small percentage of the northern population, just 5 percent from Pennsylvania to New Hampshire in 1750. In the colony of New York, however, blacks formed about 14 percent of inhabitants. While some enslaved blacks worked on agricultural estates in the Hudson River valley and New Jersey, even more labored as household servants, dockworkers, seamen, and blacksmiths in New York City alongside British colonists and European immigrants. In addition, some British **enslavers** in the West Indies moved to the mainland and brought their African workers with them. Isaac Royall, for example, traded enslaved Africans as well as sugar and rum from his plantation in Antigua. After surviving a hurricane, smallpox epidemic, and slave revolt on the island, he moved to an estate on the Mystic River in Massachusetts in 1737 with his family and twenty-seven enslaved laborers.

Coping with Economic Distress

Some white workers who were bound by contracts felt common cause with their black counterparts. But whites had a far greater chance of gaining their freedom even before slavery was fully entrenched in colonial law. Still, several challenges confronted white servants, apprentices, redemptioners, and convicts looking to purchase land, open a shop, or earn a decent wage. First, white women and men who gained their freedom from indentures or other contracts had to compete for jobs with a steady supply of redemptioners, convicts, and apprentices as well as other free laborers. Second, by the early eighteenth century, many areas along the Atlantic coast faced a land shortage that threatened the fortunes even of long-settled families. Finally, a population boom in Britain's North American colonies produced growing numbers of young people seeking land and employment. Thus many free laborers migrated from town to town and from country to city seeking work. They hoped to find farmers who needed extra hands for planting and harvesting, ship captains and contractors who would hire them to load or unload cargo or assist in the construction of homes and churches, or wealthy families who needed cooks, laundresses, or nursemaids.

Seasonal and temporary demands for labor created a corps of transient workers. Many New England towns developed systems to "warn out" those who were not official residents. Modeled after the British system, warning-out was meant to ensure that strangers did not become public dependents. Still, being warned did not mean immediate removal. Sometimes transients were simply warned that they were not eligible for poor relief. At other times, constables returned them to an earlier place of residence. In many ways, warning-out served as an early registration system, allowing authorities to encourage the flow of labor, keep residents under surveillance, and protect the town's coffers. But it rarely aided those in need of work.

Residents who were eligible for public assistance might be given food and clothing or boarded with a local family. Many towns began appointing Overseers of the Poor to deal with the growing problem of poverty. By 1750 every seaport city had constructed an almshouse that sheltered white residents without other means of support. In 1723 the Bridewell prison was added to Boston Almshouse, built in 1696. A workhouse was opened on the same site in 1739 to employ the "able-bodied" poor in hopes that profits from it would help fund the almshouse and prison. Still, these efforts at relief fell far short of the need, especially in hard economic times.

Rural Americans Face Changing Conditions

While seaport cities and larger towns fostered a growing cohort of individuals who lived outside traditional households, families remained the central unit of economic organization in rural areas, where the vast majority of Americans lived. Yet farm households, too, had been drawn into the Atlantic economy and the increasingly global circulation of goods and people.

In areas along the Atlantic coast, rural families became part of commercial networks in a variety of ways. Towns and cities needed large supplies of vegetables, meat, butter, barley, wheat, and yarn. Farm families sold these goods and bought sugar, tea, and other imported items that diversified their diet. Few rural families purchased ornamental or luxury items, but cloth or cheese bought in town saved hours of labor at home. Just as important, coastal communities like Salem, Massachusetts and Wilmington, Delaware that were once largely rural became thriving commercial centers in the late seventeenth century.

In New England, the land available for farming shrank as the population soared. In the original Puritan colonies, the population rose from 100,000 in 1700 to 400,000 in 1750. Many parents were no longer able to provide their children with sufficient land for profitable farms. The result was increased migration to the frontier, where families were more dependent on their own labor and a small circle of neighbors. And even this option was not accessible to all. Before 1700, servants who survived their indenture had a good chance of securing land, but by the mid-eighteenth century only two of every ten were likely to become landowners.

In the Middle Atlantic region, the population surged from 50,000 in 1700 to 250,000 in 1750. The increase was due in part to the rapid rise in wheat prices, which leaped by more than 50 percent in Europe. Hoping to take advantage of

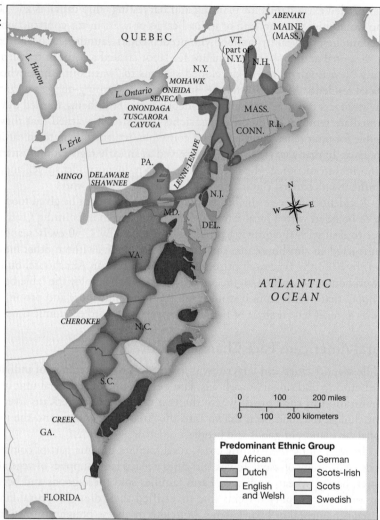

MAP 3.3 Ethnic and Racial Diversity in British North America, 1750 By 1750 British North America was a far more diverse region than it had been fifty years earlier. In 1700 the English dominated most regions, while the Dutch controlled towns and estates in the Hudson River valley. By 1750, however, growing numbers of African Americans, German and Scots-Irish immigrants, and smaller communities of other ethnic groups predominated in various regions.

Predominant Ethnic Group

- African
- Dutch
- English and Welsh
- German
- Scots-Irish
- Scots
- Swedish

this boon, Anglo-Americans, Germans, Scots-Irish, and other immigrants flooded into the region in the early eighteenth century. By the 1740s, German families had created self-contained communities in western Pennsylvania, New York's Mohawk River valley, and the Shenandoah Valley of Virginia. They worshipped in German churches, read German newspapers, and preserved German traditions. Meanwhile Scots-Irish immigrants established churches and communities in New Jersey, central Pennsylvania, and western Maryland and Virginia (Map 3.3).

Further south, immigrants could acquire land more easily, but their chances for economic autonomy were increasingly influenced by the spread of slavery. As hundreds and then thousands of Africans were imported into the Carolinas in the 1720s and 1730s, economic and political power became more entrenched in the hands of planters and merchants. Increasingly, they controlled the markets, wrote the laws, and set the terms by which white as well as black families lived. Farms along inland waterways and on the frontier were crucial in providing food and other items for urban residents and for planters with large labor forces. But farm families increasingly depended on commercial and planter elites to set the prices and market their goods. Those outside this market economy subsisted largely on what they could grow or exchange with neighbors. In addition, as slave raiding increased among Indians, now equipped with guns, many frontier settlements were caught in the crosshairs of wars among native peoples and with English and Spanish communities.

Slavery Takes Hold in the South

The rise of African slavery reshaped the South in numerous ways. A major shift from white indentured servants to black slaves began in Virginia after 1676 and soon spread across the Chesapeake (see Figure 3.2). The Carolinas, meanwhile, developed as a slave society from the start. That is, the Carolinas were not just a society that included enslaved labor, but one in which slavery shaped the political and social as well as the economic structure of the colony. Enslaved workers allowed for the expanded cultivation of cash crops like tobacco, rice, and indigo, which promised high profits for planters as well as merchants. But these developments also made southern enslavers more dependent on the global market and limited opportunities for poorer whites and all blacks. Enslavers' need for more and more land also ensured that Indians and many whites were pushed farther west, sparking more conflicts along the frontier.

In the 1660s, as tobacco cultivation spread across the Chesapeake, the Virginia Assembly had passed a series of laws that defined slavery as a distinct status based on

Sale of Slaves in Charleston, South Carolina Henry Laurens, one of the major slave traders in Charleston, formed a partnership with two other men to import enslaved Africans to North America. This ad focuses on the health of the 250 Africans they are offering for sale, half of whom have developed immunity to smallpox. Being from the Rice Coast, they were also likely skilled in cultivating rice. Library of Congress, Prints and Photographs Division [LC-USZ62-10293]

racial identity and passed to future generations. The enactment of these **slave laws** was driven largely by the growing need for labor, which neither enslaved Indians nor indentured servants could fill. Modeling their laws on statutes passed earlier in Barbados, political leaders ensured that Africans and their descendants would spend their entire lives laboring for white owners. Slavery became a status inherited through the mother, which could not be changed by converting to Christianity. And enslavers were granted the right to kill enslaved workers who resisted their authority. In 1680 the Virginia Assembly made it illegal for "any negro or other slave to carry or arme himself with any club, staffe, gunn, sword, or any other weapon of defence or offence." Nor could the enslaved leave their enslaver's premises without a certificate of permission. Increasingly harsh laws in Virginia and Maryland coincided with a rise in the number of Africans imported to the colonies. The rate of importation also ensured the decline of the free black population in the Chesapeake. In 1668 one-third of all Africans and African Americans in Virginia and Maryland were still free, but the numbers dwindled year by year. Once the Royal African Company started supplying the Chesapeake with slaves directly from Africa in the 1680s, the pace of change quickened. By 1750, 150,000 blacks resided in the Chesapeake, and only about 5 percent remained free.

Direct importation from Africa had other negative consequences on the lives of the enslaved. Far more men than women were imported, skewing the sex ratio in a population that was just beginning to form families and communities. Enslaved women, like men, performed heavy field work, and few bore more than one or two children. When these conditions, along with brutal work regimens, sparked resistance by the enslaved, fearful whites imposed even stricter regulations, further distinguishing between white indentured servants and enslaved blacks.

While slavery in the Carolinas was influenced by developments in the Chesapeake, it was shaped even more directly by practices in the British West Indies. Many wealthy families from Barbados, Antigua, and other sugar islands—including that of Colonel Lucas—established plantations in the Carolinas. At first, they brought enslaved laborers from the West Indies to oversee cattle and pigs and assist in the slaughter of livestock and curing of meat for shipment back to the West Indies. Some of the enslaved grew rice, using techniques learned in West Africa, to supplement their diet. Their owners soon realized that rice might prove very profitable. Although not widely eaten in Europe, rice could provide cheap and nutritious food for sailors, orphans, convicts, and peasants. Relying initially on Africans' knowledge, enslavers began cultivating rice for export. (See Map 2.2 in chapter 2.)

The need for African rice-growing skills and the fear of attacks by Spaniards and Indians led Carolina owners to grant the enslaved rights unheard of in the Chesapeake or the West Indies. Initially enslaved laborers were allowed to carry guns and serve in the militia. For those who nonetheless ran for freedom, Spanish and Indian territories offered refuge. Still, most stayed, depending for support on bonds they had developed in the West Indies. The frequent absence of owners also offered enslaved Carolinians greater autonomy.

Yet as rice cultivation expanded from the 1690s through the early 1700s, slavery in the Carolinas turned more brutal. The Assembly, which included large numbers of enslavers, enacted harsher and harsher slave codes to ensure control of the growing labor force. No longer could the enslaved carry guns, join militias, meet in groups, or travel without a pass. At the same time, the increase in the direct importation of enslaved Africans skewed gender balances and disrupted older community networks. New military patrols by whites enforced laws and labor practices. Some plantations along the Carolina coast turned into virtual labor camps, where thousands of mostly enslaved men worked under harsh conditions with no hope of improvement.

By 1720 blacks outnumbered whites in the Carolinas, and fears of slave rebellions inspired South Carolina officials to impose even harsher laws and more brutal enforcement measures. When Eliza Lucas developed indigo as a cash crop alongside rice in the 1740s, the demand for slave labor increased further. Although far fewer enslaved laborers—about 40,000 by 1750—resided in South Carolina than in the Chesapeake, they constituted more than 60 percent of the colony's total population.

Africans Resist Their Enslavement

Enslaved laborers in British North America resisted their subjugation in a variety of ways. Similar to Indians, they sought to retain customs, foods, belief systems, and languages from their homelands. They tried to incorporate work patterns passed down from one generation to the next into new environments. They challenged masters and overseers by refusing to work, breaking tools, feigning illness, and other means of disputing whites' authority. Some ran for freedom, others fought back in the face of punishment, and still others used arson, poison, or other means to defy owners. A few planned revolts.

However, the consequences for resisting were severe, from whipping, mutilation, and branding to summary execution. Fearful of rebellion, whites often punished people falsely accused of planning revolts. Yet some enslaved workers did plot insurrections against their owners or whites in general. Indeed, northern as well as southern colonies lived with the threat of slave rebellion. In New York City in 1712, several dozen enslaved Africans and Indians set fire to a building. When whites rushed to the scene, the insurgents attacked them with clubs, pistols, axes, and staves, killing eight and injuring many more. The rebels were soon defeated by the militia, however. Authorities executed eighteen insurgents, burning several at the stake as a warning to others. Six of those imprisoned committed suicide. In 1741 a series of suspicious fires in the city led to accusations against a white couple who owned an alehouse where free and enslaved blacks gathered to drink. To protect herself from prosecution, an Irish indentured servant testified that she had overheard discussions of an elaborate plot involving black and white conspirators. Frightened of any hint that poor whites and blacks might make common cause, authorities immediately arrested suspects and eventually executed 34 people, including 4 whites. They also banished 72 blacks from the city. Among those executed was Cuffee, an enslaved laborer who claimed that "a great many people have too much, and others too little."

The most serious slave revolt, however, erupted in South Carolina, just a few miles from Wappoo, the Lucas plantation. A group of recently imported Africans led the **Stono rebellion** in 1739. On Sunday, September 9, a group of enslaved men stole weapons from a country store and killed the owners. They then marched south, along the Stono River, beating drums and recruiting others to join them. Torching plantations and killing whites along the route, they had gathered more than fifty insurgents when armed whites overtook them. In the ensuing battle, dozens of rebels died. The militia, along with Indians hired to assist them, killed another twenty over the next two days and then captured a group of forty, who were executed without trial.

This revolt reverberated widely in a colony where enslaved blacks outnumbered whites nearly two to one, direct importation from Africa was at an all-time high, and Spanish authorities in Florida promised freedom to enslaved runaways. In 1738 the Spanish governor formed a black militia company, and he allowed thirty-eight fugitive families to settle north of St. Augustine and build Fort Mose for their protection. When warfare erupted between Spain and Britain over commercial rivalries in 1739, enslaved Carolinians may have seen their chance to gain freedom en masse. But as with other rebellions, this one failed, and the price of failure was death.

REVIEW & RELATE	• What were the sources of economic and social inequality in North America in the early eighteenth century? • How did the laws and conditions under which poor black and white workers lived during the late seventeenth and early eighteenth centuries differ?

Conclusion: Changing Fortunes in British North America

Global commerce, international wars, and immigration reshaped the economy and geography of North America between 1680 and 1750. Many colonists and some Indians thrived as international trade boomed. In seaport cites, a consumer revolution transformed daily life, fueling the emergence of a colonial elite and the demand for skilled artisans. Others found greater opportunities by pushing inland and establishing farms and communities along new frontiers. But many people failed to benefit from these changes. Indians continued to be dispossessed of their land as white settlers pushed west. As European populations increased, the spread of lethal diseases and nearly constant warfare dealt heavy blows to native communities. To survive, more powerful Indian tribes enslaved more captives from weaker ones to exchange for guns from colonists. At the same time, many indentured servants found it impossible to obtain land or decent wages after they gained their independence. Moving to the frontier in hopes of finding unsettled land, they too became caught up in cycles of war and disease. Still, even if white servants and unskilled workers struggled, they had the benefit of freedom. Black workers were increasingly forced into slavery, with the shrinking percentage of free blacks suffering from intensifying discrimination against the race as a whole. The consequences of international trade and imperial conflicts only widened the gap between economically successful whites, poor whites, weakened Indians, and enslaved blacks.

Increased mechanization and the growth of manufacturing in England contributed to the differences among these Americans. After failing to find an economic foothold in the colonies, indentured servant William Moraley Jr. returned to

England where he made and repaired cheap watches, which were now being turned out in large numbers. Other indentured servants remained in the colonies once free but found it increasingly difficult to obtain land or a living wage. In northern cities and across the South, they increasingly competed with enslaved blacks. These same changes had far more positive effects for some colonists. The mechanization of cloth production in England demanded vast amounts of raw material from the English countryside and the colonies. It ensured, for example, the profitability of indigo. This crop benefited South Carolina planters like Eliza Lucas and—after her marriage in 1744—her husband, Charles Pinckney, a successful planter himself. Still, profits from indigo and other crops could be gained only through enslaving hundreds of laborers and expanding further into Indian territories.

Eliza Pinckney's sons became important leaders in South Carolina, and despite their English education and the benefits they gained through British trade, both developed a strong belief in the rights of the colonies to control their own destinies. Like many American colonists, they were spurred by the consumer revolution, geographical expansion, growing ethnic diversity, and conflicts with Indian and European enemies to develop a mind-set that differed significantly from their counterparts in England. Yet this turn away from the religious and political beliefs that had sustained colonists for generations soon spurred a series of revivals that initially reinforced the importance of faith but ultimately challenged the authority of traditional institutions.

Chapter 3 Review

KEY TERMS

proprietary colonies, 58
Glorious Revolution, 58
Pueblo revolt, 60
King William's War, 62
War of the Spanish Succession, 63
Tuscarora War, 65
Yamasee War, 65

mercantilism, 68
Navigation Acts, 69
Middle Passage, 70
redemptioners, 74
enslavers, 74
slave laws, 78
Stono rebellion, 79

REVIEW & RELATE

1. What role did the crown play in the expansion of the English North American colonies in the second half of the seventeenth century?
2. How did the development of the Spanish and French colonies in the late seventeenth century differ from that of the English colonies?
3. How did the European wars of the late seventeenth and early eighteenth centuries impact relations between colonists and England?

4. How were Indian alliances and conflicts, with other Indians and with European nations, shaped by the trade in slaves and guns and by wars between European powers?

5. What place did North American colonists occupy in the eighteenth-century global trade network?

6. How and with what success did the British government maintain control over the colonial economy and ensure that it served Britain's economic and political interests?

7. What were the sources of economic and social inequality in North America in the early eighteenth century?

8. How did the laws and conditions under which poor black and white workers lived during the late seventeenth and early eighteenth centuries differ?

TIMELINE OF EVENTS

1660	• Monarchy restored in England
1660–1673	• Navigation Acts
1660–1685	• Charles II grants North American proprietorships
1672	• Royal African Company chartered
1680	• Pueblo revolt
1688	• Glorious Revolution
1689–1697	• King William's War
1691–1710	• North Carolina separates from South Carolina
1692	• Colony of Massachusetts established
1700–1750	• New England colonial population quadruples
	• Middle Atlantic colonial population quintuples
1700–1808	• British ships carry 3 million enslaved African to the Americas
1702	• East and West Jersey unite into New Jersey
1702–1713	• War of the Spanish Succession
1704	• Delaware separates from Pennsylvania
1711–1713	• Tuscarora War
1715–1717	• Yamasee War
1732	• Colony of Georgia established
1739	• Stono rebellion
1749	• Spanish settlers in Texas make peace with the Apache

4

Religious Strife and Social Upheavals

1680–1754

LEARNING OBJECTIVES

After reading this chapter you will be able to:

- Explain the relationships among religious, economic, and political tensions and accusations of witchcraft.
- Describe family dynamics, particularly between husbands and wives, and how they changed over time and differed by class and region.
- Understand the ways that economic development, increasing diversity, and continued expansion fueled conflicts among various groups in the early eighteenth century.
- Explain the emergence of the Great Awakening and identify its critics and legacies.
- Describe how the Great Awakening shaped political developments in the 1730s and 1740s.

COMPARING AMERICAN HISTORIES

The son of a Scots-Irish clergyman, **Gilbert Tennent** was born in Vinecash, Ireland, in 1703 and at age fifteen moved with his family to Philadelphia. After receiving an M.A. from Yale College in 1725, Gilbert was ordained a Presbyterian minister in New Brunswick, New Jersey, with little indication of the significant role he would play in a denominational schism.

Tennent entered the ministry at a critical moment, when leaders of a number of denominations had become convinced that the colonies were descending into spiritual apathy. Tennent dedicated himself to sparking a rebirth of Christian commitment, and by the mid-1730s he had gained fame as a revival preacher. At the end of the decade, Tennent journeyed through the middle colonies with Englishman George Whitefield, an Anglican

83

preacher known for igniting powerful revivals. In the fall of 1740, following the death of his wife, Tennent launched his own evangelical "awakenings."

Revivals inspired thousands of religious conversions across denominations, but they also fueled conflicts within established churches. Presbyterians in Britain and America disagreed about whether only those who had had a powerful, personal conversion experience were qualified to be ministers. Tennent made his opinion clear by denouncing unconverted ministers in his sermons, a position that led to his expulsion from the Presbyterian Church in 1741. But many local churches sought converted preachers, and four years later a group of ejected pastors formed a rival synod that trained its own evangelical ministers.

While ministers debated the proper means of saving sinners, ordinary women and men searched their souls. In Pomfret, Connecticut, **Sarah Grosvenor** certainly feared for hers in the summer of 1742 when the unmarried nineteen-year-old realized she was pregnant. Her situation was complicated by her status in the community. She was the daughter of Leicester Grosvenor, an important landowner, town official, and member of the Congregational Church.

The pew next to Sarah and her family was occupied by Nathaniel Sessions and his sons, including the twenty-six-year-old Amasa, who had impregnated Sarah. Many other young women became pregnant out of wedlock in the 1740s, but families accepted the fact as long as the couple married before the child was born. However, Amasa refused to marry Sarah and suggested instead that she have an abortion.

Although Sarah was reluctant to follow this path, Amasa insisted. When herbs traditionally used to induce a miscarriage failed, Amasa introduced Sarah to John Hallowell, a doctor who claimed he could remove the fetus with forceps. After admitting her agonizing situation to her older sister Zerviah and her cousin Hannah, Sarah allowed Hallowell to proceed. He finally induced a miscarriage, but Sarah soon grew feverish, suffered convulsions, and died ten days later.

Apparently Sarah's and Amasa's parents were unaware of the events leading to her demise. Then in 1745, a powerful religious revival swept through the region, and Zerviah and Hannah suffered great spiritual anguish. It is likely they confessed their part in the affair since that year officials brought charges against Amasa Sessions and John Hallowell for Sarah's death. At the men's trial, Zerviah and Hannah testified about their roles and those of Sessions and Hallowell. There was to be no earthly justice, however. Hallowell was found guilty but escaped punishment by fleeing to Rhode Island. Sessions was acquitted and remained in Pomfret, where he married and became a prosperous farmer.

COMPARING THE AMERICAN HISTORIES of Gilbert Tennent and Sarah Grosvenor reveals the power of the religious forces — later called the Great Awakening — that swept through the colonies in the early eighteenth century. Those forces are best understood in the context of larger social, economic, and political changes. By the early eighteenth century, many young people became more independent of their parents and developed tighter bonds with siblings, cousins, and neighbors their own age. Towns and cities developed clearer hierarchies by class and status, which could protect wealthier individuals from being punished for their misdeeds. A double standard of sexual behavior became more entrenched as well, with women subject to greater scrutiny than men for their sexual behavior. These changes occurred as more German and Scots-Irish immigrants brought their own familial ideals and religious beliefs to the colonies. As they pushed settlement westward, they confronted Indians and former servants who were also hoping to find peace and economic opportunity in those areas. Amid these transformations, most young women managed to avoid the fate of Sarah Grosvenor. Still, pastors like Gilbert Tennent feared precisely such consequences if the colonies — growing ever larger and more diverse — did not reclaim their religious foundations.

An Ungodly Society?

As American colonists became more engaged in international and domestic commerce, spiritual commitments appeared to wane. In New England, Congregational ministers condemned the apparent triumph of worldly ambition over religiosity. Nonetheless, some ministers saw economic success as a reward for godly behavior even as they worried that wealth and power opened the door to sin. In the late seventeenth century, these anxieties deepened when accusations of witchcraft erupted across southern New England.

The Rise of Religious Anxieties

In 1686 the Puritan minister Samuel Sewell railed against the behavior of Boston mercantile elites. Citing examples of their depravity in his diary, including drunkenness and cursing, he claimed that such "high-handed wickedness has hardly been heard of before." Sewell was outraged as well by popular practices such as donning powdered wigs in place of God-given hair, wearing scarlet and gold jackets rather than simple black cloth, and offering toasts rather than prayers.

While Sewell spoke for many Puritans concerned with the consequences of commercial success, other religious leaders tried to meld old and new. The Reverend Cotton Mather complained that many colonists showed greater interest in the latest fashions than in the state of their souls. Yet he was attracted by the luxuries available to colonists and hoped to make his own son "a more finished Gentleman." Mather was also fascinated by new scientific endeavors and supported inoculations for smallpox, which others viewed as challenging God's power.

Certainly news of the Glorious Revolution in England (1688) offered Puritans hope of regaining their customary authority (see "English Colonies Grow and Multiply" in chapter 3). But the outbreak of King William's War in 1689 quickly ended any notion of an easy return to peace and prosperity. Instead, continued conflicts at home and abroad and renewed fears of Indian attacks on rural settlements heightened colonists' sense that Satan was at work in the region. Soon, accusations of witchcraft joined outcries against other forms of ungodly behavior.

Cries of Witchcraft

Belief in witchcraft had been widespread in Europe and England for centuries. It was part of a general belief in supernatural causes for events that could not otherwise be explained — severe storms, an eclipse, a rash of deaths among livestock. When a community began to suspect witchcraft, they often pointed to individuals who challenged cultural norms. Women who were quarrelsome, eccentric, poor, or simply too independent were easy to imagine as cavorting with evil spirits and invisible demons.

Witchcraft accusations tended to be most common in times of change and uncertainty. Over the course of the seventeenth century, colonists had begun to spread into new areas seeking more land and greater economic opportunities. But expansion brought with it confrontations with Indians, exposure to new dangers, and greater vulnerability to a harsh environment. As the stress of expansion mounted, witchcraft accusations emerged. Some 160 individuals, mostly women, were accused of witchcraft in Massachusetts and Connecticut and 15 were put to death between 1647 and 1691. Many of the accused were poor, childless, or disgruntled women, but widows who inherited property also came under suspicion, especially if they fought for control against male relatives and neighbors.

The social and economic complexities of witchcraft accusations are well illustrated by the most famous American witch-hunt, the Salem witch trials of the early 1690s. In 1692 residents of Salem, Massachusetts confronted conflicts between long-settled farmers and newer mercantile families, political uncertainties following the Glorious Revolution in England, ongoing threats from Indians, and quarrels over the choice of a new minister. These tensions were brought to a head when the Reverend Samuel Parris's daughter and niece learned voodoo lore and exotic dances from the household's West Indian slave, Tituba. The daughters and servants of neighboring families also became entranced by Tituba's tales and began to tell fortunes, speak in gibberish, and contort their bodies into painful positions. When the girls were questioned about their strange behavior, they pointed not only to Tituba but also to other people in the community. They first accused an elderly female pauper and a homeless widow of bewitching them, but later singled out respectable churchwomen as well as a minister, a wealthy merchant, and a four-year-old child.

Within weeks, more than one hundred individuals, 80 percent of them women, stood accused of witchcraft. Governor William Phips established a special court to handle the cases, over which the Reverend Samuel Sewell presided. Twenty-seven of the accused came to trial, and twenty were found guilty based on testimony from the girls and on spectral evidence, that is, evidence that came to the girls in dreams or visions. In court, the young accusers writhed, shook, and cried out in pain as spirits of the accused, invisible to everyone else, pinched, choked, and bit them. Based on such evidence, nineteen people were hanged, and one was pressed to death with stones.

But when accusations reached into prominent Salem and Boston families, Governor Phips ended the proceedings and released the remaining suspects. In the following months, leading ministers and colonial officials condemned the use of spectral evidence, and some young accusers recanted their testimony.

The Salem trials illuminate far more than beliefs in witchcraft. The trials pitted the daughters and servants of prosperous farmers against the wives and widows of recently arrived merchants. The accusers included young women like nineteen-year-old Mercy Lewis, who was bound out as a servant when her parents were killed by Indians. Fear of attack from hostile Indians, hostile officials in England, or hostile neighbors fostered anxieties in Salem, as it did in many colonial communities. Other anxieties also haunted the accusers. A shortage of land led many New England men to seek their fortune farther west, leaving young women with fewer opportunities to marry. Battles over inheritance forestalled marriages as well. Thomas Putnam Jr., who housed three of the accusers, was in the midst of such a battle. It left his three sisters — the accusers' aunts — in limbo as they awaited legacies that could enhance their marriage prospects. As young women in Salem forged tight bonds in the face of such uncertainties, they turned their anger not against men, but instead against older women, including respectable "goodwives" like Abigail Faulkner.

| REVIEW & RELATE | • What factors led to rising tensions within colonial communities in the early 1700s? |
| | • How did social, economic, and political tensions contribute to an increase in accusations of witchcraft? |

Family and Household Dynamics

Concerns about marriage, property, and inheritance were not limited to Salem or to New England. As the American colonies became more populous and the numbers of women and men more balanced, husbands sought greater control over the behavior of household members while the legal and economic rewards available to most women declined. Yet some women improved their situation by wielding their skills as midwives, brewers, or even plantation managers to benefit themselves and their families.

Women's Changing Status

In most early American colonies, the scarcity of women and workers ensured that many white women gained economic and legal leverage. In the first decades of settlement in the Chesapeake, where women were in especially short supply and mortality was high, young women who arrived as indentured servants and completed their term might marry older men of property. If the husbands died first, widows often took control of the estate and passed on the property to their children. Even in New England, where the numbers of men and women were more balanced from the beginning, the crucial labor of wives in the early decades of settlement was sometimes recognized by their control of family property after a husband's death.

TABLE 4.1	SEX RATIOS IN THE WHITE POPULATION FOR SELECTED COLONIES, 1624–1755		
Date	Colony	White Male Population	White Female Population	Females per 100 Males
1624–1625	Virginia	873	222	25
1660	Maryland	c. 600	c. 190	32
1704	Maryland	11,026	7,136	65
1698	New York	5,066	4,677	92
1726	New Jersey	15,737	14,124	90
1755	Rhode Island	17,860	17,979	101

By the late seventeenth century, however, as the sex ratio in the Chesapeake evened out, white women lost the opportunity to marry "above their class" (see Table 4.1). And across the colonies, more widows lost control of family estates. Even though women still performed vital labor, the spread of indentured servitude and slavery lessened the recognition of wives' contributions, while in urban areas the rise of commerce highlighted their role as consumers rather than producers. As a result, most wives and daughters of English colonists were assigned primarily domestic roles. They also found their legal and economic rights restricted to those accorded their female counterparts in Great Britain.

According to English common law, a wife's status was defined as *feme covert*, which meant that she was legally covered over by (or hidden behind) her husband. The husband controlled his wife's labor, the house in which she lived, the property she brought into the marriage, and any wages she earned. He was also the legal guardian of their children, and through the instrument of his will could continue to control the household after his death.

With the growth and diversity of colonial towns and cities, the **patriarchal family**— a model in which fathers held absolute authority over wives, children, and servants—came to be seen as a crucial bulwark against disorder. Families with wealth were especially eager to control the behavior of their sons and daughters as the parents sought to build social, commercial, and political alliances. The refusal of Amasa Sessions to marry Sarah Grosvenor, for instance, may have resulted from his father's expectation of a better match.

Working Families

Still, for most colonial women and men, daily rounds of labor shaped their lives more powerfully than legal statutes or inheritance rights. Husbands and wives depended on each other to support the family. By the early eighteenth century, many colonial writers promoted the idea of marriage as a partnership, even if the wife remained the junior partner.

This concept of marriage as a partnership took practical form in communities across the colonies. In towns, the wives of artisans often learned aspects of their husband's craft and assisted their husbands in a variety of ways. Given the overlap between homes and workplaces in the eighteenth century, women often cared for apprentices, journeymen, and laborers as well as their own children. Husbands meanwhile labored alongside their subordinates and represented their families' interests to the larger community. Both spouses were expected to provide models of godliness and to encourage prayer and regular church attendance among household members.

On farms, where the vast majority of colonists lived, women and men played crucial if distinct roles. In general, wives and daughters labored inside the home as well as in the surrounding yard with its kitchen garden, milk house, chicken coop, dairy, or washhouse. Husbands and sons worked the fields, kept the livestock, and managed the orchards. Many families supplemented their own labor with that of servants, slaves, or hired field hands. And surplus crops and manufactured goods such as cloth or sausage were exchanged with neighbors or sold at market, creating an economic network of small producers.

Indeed, by the late seventeenth and early eighteenth centuries, many farm families in long-settled areas participated in a household mode of production. Men lent each other tools and draft animals and shared grazing land, while women gathered to spin, sew, and quilt. Individuals with special skills like midwifery or blacksmithing assisted neighbors, adding farm produce or credit to the family ledger. One woman's cheese might be bartered for another woman's jam. A family that owned the necessary equipment might brew neighbors' barley and malt into beer, while a family with a loom would turn yarn into cloth. The system of exchange, managed largely through barter, allowed individual households to function even as they became more specialized in what they produced. Whatever cash was obtained could be used to buy sugar, tea, and other imported goods.

Reproduction and Women's Roles

Maintaining a farm required the work of both women and men, which made marriage an economic as well as a social and religious institution. In the early eighteenth century, more than 90 percent of white women married. By 1700 a New England

Harvest Scene Mary Woodhull was born on Long Island in 1743 and created this colorful needlepoint sampler sometime before her marriage to Amos Underhill. Such decorative samplers were often hung in the family parlor to illustrate the young woman's ideals and skills to prospective husbands. Interestingly here, both the woman and the man are holding scythes used to cut the grain. Granger

wife who married at age twenty and survived to forty-five bore an average of eight children, most of whom lived to adulthood. In the Chesapeake, mortality rates remained higher and the sex ratio still favored men. It thus took another generation for white women in that region to come close to the reproductive rates of their northern counterparts.

Harsh conditions of labor and poor nutrition and health care ensured that fertility rates among enslaved Africans and African Americans remained much lower than those among whites in the early eighteenth century. And fewer infants survived to adulthood. It was not until the 1740s that the majority of enslaved laborers were born in the colonies rather than imported. By then, some southern enslavers, especially those owning larger estates, began to realize that encouraging reproduction made good economic sense. Still, enslaved women, most of whom worked in the fields, gained only minimal relief from their labors during pregnancy.

Colonial mothers who were free combined childbearing and child rearing with a great deal of other work. While some affluent families could afford wet nurses and nannies, most women fended for themselves or hired temporary help for particular tasks. In rural areas, mothers with babies on hip and children under foot hauled water, fed chickens, collected eggs, picked vegetables, prepared meals, spun thread, and manufactured soap and candles. Children were at constant risk of disease and injury, but were spared the overcrowding, the raw sewage, and the foul water that marked ever-growing cities.

Infants were the most vulnerable to disease, and parents were relieved when their children passed their first birthdays. Colonists feared the deaths of mothers as well. In 1700 roughly one out of thirty births ended in the mother's death. Women who bore six to eight children thus faced death on a regular basis. One minister urged pregnant women to prepare their souls, "For ought you know your Death has entered into you."

When a mother died while her children were still young, her husband was likely to remarry soon afterward in order to maintain the family and his farm or business. Even though fathers held legal guardianship over their children, there was little doubt that child rearing, especially for young children, was women's work. Many husbands acknowledged this role, prayed for their wives while in labor, and sought to ease their domestic burdens near the end of a pregnancy. But some women gained little help or protection from their husbands.

The Limits of Patriarchal Order

While most white families accepted the idea of female subordination in return for patriarchal protection, there were signs of change in the early eighteenth century. Sermons against fornication; ads for runaway spouses, servants, and slaves; reports of domestic violence; poems about domineering wives; petitions for divorce; and legal suits charging rape, seduction, or breach of contract make clear that ideals of patriarchal authority did not always match the reality. It is impossible to quantify the frequency with which women contested their subordination, but a variety of evidence points to increasing tensions around issues of control — by husbands over wives, fathers over children, and men over women.

Women's claims about men's misbehavior were often demeaned as gossip, but gossip could be an important weapon for those who had little chance of legal redress. In colonial communities, credit and trust were central to networks of exchange, so damaging a man's reputation could be a serious matter. Still, gossip was not as powerful as legal sanctions. Thus some women who bore illegitimate children, suffered physical and sexual abuse, or were left penniless by a husband who drank might seek assistance from the courts.

Divorce was as rare in the colonies as it was in England. In New England, colonial law allowed for divorce, but few were granted and almost none to women before 1750. In other colonies, divorce could be obtained only by an act of the colonial assembly and was therefore confined to the wealthy and powerful. If a divorce was granted, the wife usually received an allowance for food and clothing. Yet without independent financial resources, she nearly always had to live with relatives. Custody of any children was awarded to fathers who had the economic means to support them, although infants or young girls might be assigned to live with the mother. A quicker and cheaper means of ending an unsatisfactory marriage was to abandon one's spouse. Again wives were at a disadvantage since they had few means to support themselves or their children. Colonial divorce petitions citing desertion and newspaper ads for runaway spouses suggest that it was husbands who fled in at least two-thirds of such cases.

In the rare instances when women did obtain a divorce, they had to bring multiple charges against their husbands. Domestic violence, adultery, or abandonment alone was insufficient to gain redress. Indeed, ministers and relatives were likely to counsel abused wives to change their behavior or suffer in silence. Even evidence of brutal assaults on a wife rarely led to legal redress because physical punishment was widely accepted and husbands had the legal right to "correct" their wives and children.

Single women also faced barriers in seeking legal redress. By the late seventeenth century, church and civil courts in New England gave up on coercing sexually active couples to marry. Judges, however, continued to hear complaints of seduction or breach of contract brought by the fathers of single women who were pregnant but unmarried. Had Sarah Grosvenor survived the abortion, her family could have sued Amasa Sessions on the grounds that he gained "carnal knowledge" of her through "promises of marriage." If the plaintiffs won, the result was no longer marriage, however, but financial support for the child. In 1730 in Concord, Massachusetts, Susanna Holding sued a farmer, Joseph Bright, whom she accused of fathering her illegitimate child. When Bright protested his innocence, Holding found townsmen to testify that the farmer, "in his courting of her . . . had designed to make her his Wife." In this case, the abandoned mother mobilized members of the community, including men, to uphold popular understandings of patriarchal responsibilities. Without such support, women were less likely to win their cases.

Women who were raped faced even greater legal obstacles than those who were seduced and abandoned. In most colonies, rape was a capital crime, punishable by death, and all-male juries were reluctant to find men guilty. Unlikely to win and fearing humiliation in court, few women charged men with rape. Yet more did so than the records might show since judges and justices of the peace sometimes downgraded rape charges to simple assault or fornication, that is, sex outside of marriage (Table 4.2).

TABLE 4.2		SEXUAL COERCION CASES DOWNGRADED IN CHESTER COUNTY, PENNSYLVANIA, 1731–1739	
Date	Defendant/Victim	Charge on Indictment in Testimony	Charge in Docket
1731	Lawrence MacGinnis/Alice Yarnal	Assault with attempt to rape	None
1731	Thomas Culling/Martha Claypool	Assault with attempt to rape	Assault
1734	Abraham Richardson/Mary Smith	Attempted rape	Assault
1734	Thomas Beckett/Mindwell Fulfourd	Theft (testimony of attempted rape)	Theft
1734	Unknown/Christeen Pauper	(Fornication charge against Christeen)	None
1735	Daniel Patterson/Hannah Tanner	Violent assault to ravish	Assault
1736	James White/Hannah McCradle	Attempted rape/adultery	Assault
1737	Robert Mills/Catherine Parry	Rape	None
1738	John West/Isabella Gibson	Attempt to ravish/assault	Fornication
1739	Thomas Halladay/Mary Mouks	Assault with intent to ravish	None

Source: Sharon Block, *Rape and Sexual Power in Early America* (Chapel Hill: University of North Carolina Press). Data from Chester County Quarter Sessions Docket Books and File Papers, 1730–1739.

Young white women had the best chance of gaining support and redress for seduction or rape if they confided in their parents or other elders. But by the mid-eighteenth century, young people were seeking more control over their sexual behavior and marriage prospects. Certain behaviors — sons settling in towns distant from their parents, younger daughters marrying before their older sisters, and single women finding themselves pregnant — increased noticeably. In part, these trends were natural consequences of colonial growth and mobility. The bonds that once held families and communities together began to loosen. But in the process, young women's chances of protecting themselves against errant and abusive men diminished. Just as important, even when they faced desperate situations, young women like Sarah Grosvenor increasingly turned to sisters and friends for help rather than fathers or ministers.

Poor women, especially those who labored as servants, had even fewer options. Servants faced tremendous obstacles in obtaining legal independence from masters or mistresses who beat or sexually assaulted them. Colonial judges and juries generally refused to declare a man who was wealthy enough to support servants guilty of criminal acts against them. Moreover, poor women generally and servants in particular were regularly depicted as lusty and immoral, making it unlikely that they would gain the sympathy of white judges or juries. Enslaved workers faced many of the same obstacles and had even less hope of prevailing against brutal owners. Thus for most servants and slaves, running away was their sole hope for escaping abuse. However, if they were caught, their situation would likely worsen. Even poor whites who lived independently had little chance of addressing issues of domestic violence, seduction, or rape through the courts.

REVIEW & RELATE	• Why and how did the legal and economic circumstances of colonial women decline between 1650 and 1750? How did the circumstances of black and white women compare? • How did patriarchal ideals of family and community shape life and work in colonial America? What happened when men failed to live up to those ideals?

Diversity and Competition in Colonial Society

As the English colonies in North America expanded, divisions increased between established families living in long-settled regions — whether on rural farmsteads or in urban homesteads — and the growing population of women and men with few resources. Although most white colonists still hoped to own their own land and establish themselves as farmers, artisans, or shopkeepers, fewer were likely to succeed than in the past. By 1760 half of all white men in North America owned no property. This growing class cleavage was accompanied by increasing racial, national, and religious diversity, which fostered greater economic competition and social conflict.

Population Growth and Economic Competition

After 1700, the population grew rapidly across the colonies. In 1700 about 250,000 people lived in England's North American colonies. By 1725 that number had doubled, and fifty years later it reached 2.5 million. Much of the increase was due to natural reproduction, but in addition nearly 250,000 immigrants and enslaved Africans arrived in the colonies between 1700 and 1750.

Because more women and children arrived than in earlier decades, higher birthrates and a more youthful population resulted. At the same time, most white colonists in North America enjoyed a better diet than their counterparts in Europe and had access to more abundant natural resources. In the eighteenth century, these colonists began living longer, with more adults surviving to watch their children and grandchildren grow up.

However, as the population soared, the chance for individuals to obtain land or start a business of their own diminished. Those white men and women who had established businesses early generally expanded to meet new needs, making it more difficult for others to compete. The vast majority who planned to make their living from the land found the soil exhausted in long-settled regions. As white colonists sought to carve out farms on the frontier, they found themselves facing forests and swamps or areas already claimed by Indian, French, or Spanish residents. While

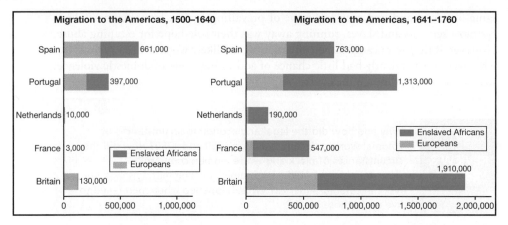

FIGURE 4.1 Transatlantic Migrations, 1500–1640 & 1641–1750 This figure charts the changing population of the Americas from 1500 to 1760. By recording the changing population of various European migrants as well as that of enslaved Africans, the figure reveals the centrality of slavery to the development of the Americas. Which European nation imported the largest number of enslaved Africans in each period, and which European nation held the greatest percentage of enslaved Africans relative to their population?

Source of Data: Stanley L. Engerman and Kenneth L. Sokoloff, "Factor Endowments, Institutions, and Differential Paths of Growth Among New World Economies: A View from Economic Historians of the United States," in *How Latin America Fell Behind: Economic Histories of Brazil and Mexico, 1800–1914*, ed. Stephen Haber (Stanford University Press, 1997, 264).

owning land did not automatically lead to prosperity, most individuals who were landless could only find work as tenant farmers, laborers, or in other unskilled occupations. In the South Carolina backcountry, a visitor in the mid-eighteenth century noted that many white residents "have nought but a Gourd to drink out of, nor a Plate, Knive or Spoon, a Glass, Cup, or anything."

In prosperous parts of the Middle Atlantic colonies like Pennsylvania, many white landless laborers abandoned rural life and searched for urban opportunities. They moved to Philadelphia or other towns and cities in the region, seeking jobs as dockworkers, street vendors, or servants, or as apprentices in one of the skilled trades. But newcomers found the job market flooded with poor whites and free and enslaved blacks. The chances for significant advancement over their lifetime were growing slim (Figure 4.1).

In the South, too, divisions between rich and poor became more pronounced in the early decades of the eighteenth century. Tobacco was the most valuable product in the Chesapeake, and the largest tobacco planters, who owned the most enslaved workers, lived in relative luxury. Although they did not build the kind of fancy plantation homesteads that would appear in the mid-nineteenth century, they benefitted enormously from the thriving Atlantic economy. Planters developed mercantile contacts—including among slave traders—in seaport cities on the Atlantic coast and in the Caribbean. They also imported luxury goods from Europe and began deploying some of their enslaved women as domestic workers to relieve wives and daughters of the strain of household labor.

Even small farmers could purchase and maintain a farm and profit from the tobacco trade. In 1750 two-thirds of white families farmed their own land in Virginia, a larger percentage than in northern colonies. An even higher percentage did so in the Carolinas. Yet small farmers became increasingly dependent on large landowners, who controlled markets, political authority, and the courts. Many artisans, too, depended on wealthy planters for their livelihood, either working for them directly or for the shipping companies and merchants that relied on plantation orders. And the growing number of tenant farmers relied completely on large landowners for their sustenance.

Some southerners fared far worse. One-fifth of all white southerners owned little more than the clothes on their backs in the mid-eighteenth century. At the same time, free blacks in the South found their opportunities for landownership and economic independence increasingly curtailed, while enslaved blacks had little hope of gaining their freedom and held no property of their own.

Increasing Diversity

Population growth and economic divisions were accompanied by increased diversity in the North American colonies. Indentured servants arrived from Ireland, Scotland, and Germany as well as England. Africans were imported in growing numbers and entered a more highly structured system of slavery, whether laboring on southern farms, on northern estates, or in seaport cities. In addition, free families and redemptioners from Ireland, Scotland, the German states, and Sweden came in ever-larger numbers and developed their own communities and cultural institutions. More colonists had also spent time in the Caribbean before settling on the mainland. And the frontiers of British North America were filled with American Indians and French and Spanish settlers.

As the booming population demanded more land, colonists pushed westward to find territory that either was not claimed by others or could be purchased. At the beginning of the eighteenth century, German and Scots-Irish immigrants joined Anglo-American settlers in rural areas of New Jersey, Pennsylvania, and Delaware. In Pennsylvania, many immigrants settled along the Schuylkill and Susquehanna Rivers amid Iroquois, Algonquian, and Siouan towns and negotiated with Indians to obtain farmland. At the same time, Delaware and Shawnee groups, who were pushed out of New Jersey and the Ohio valley by pressure from settlers there, also moved into this region. They negotiated with colonists, the colonial government, and other Indian groups to establish their own towns. All along the Pennsylvania frontier, the lines between Indian and immigrant settlements blurred. Still, many communities prospered in the region, with white settlers exchanging European and colonial trade goods with Indians to gain access to their orchards, waterways, and lands (Map 4.1).

In the 1720s and 1730s, however, Scots-Irish settlers flooded into Pennsylvania when bad harvests and high rents caused them to flee oppressive conditions back home. The new immigrants overwhelmed native communities that had welcomed earlier settlers. The death of William Penn in 1718 exacerbated the situation as his sons and closest advisers struggled to gain control over the colony. Indians were increasingly pushed to the margins as growing numbers of European settlers crowded the frontier.

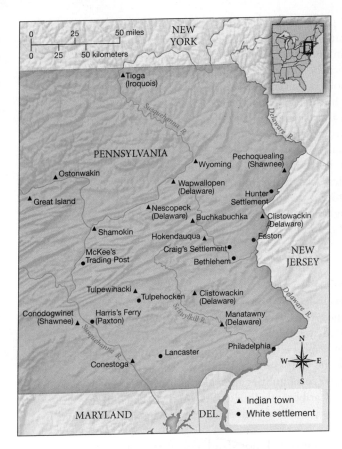

MAP 4.1 **Frontier Settlements and Indian Towns in Pennsylvania, 1700–1740** German and Scots-Irish immigrants to Pennsylvania mingled with Indian settlements in the early eighteenth century as Delaware and Shawnee groups were pushed west from New Jersey. In the 1720s and 1730s, however, European migration escalated dramatically in the fertile river valleys. In response, once-independent Indian tribes joined the Delaware and Shawnee nations to strengthen their position against the influx of colonists. From *At the Crossroads: Indians & Empires on a Mid-Atlantic Frontier, 1700–1763* by Jane T. Merritt, Published for the Omohundro Institute of Early American History and Culture. Copyright © 2003 by the University of North Carolina Press. Used by permission of the publisher. www.uncpress.unc.edu.

Expansion and Conflict

As more and more colonists sought economic opportunities on the frontier, conflicts erupted between earlier British and newer immigrant settlers as well as among immigrant groups. In Pennsylvania, Dutch, Scots-Irish, and German colonists took each other to court, sued land surveyors, and even burned down cabins built by their immigrant foes. For longtime British settlers, such acts only reinforced their sense that recent immigrants were a threat to their society. In 1728 James Logan, William Penn's longtime secretary, complained that the "Palatines [Germans] crowd in upon us and the Irish yet faster." For Logan, these difficulties were exacerbated by what he considered the "idle," "worthless," and "indigent" habits of Scots-Irish and other recent arrivals.

Anglo-Americans hardly set high standards themselves, especially when negotiating with Indians. Even in Pennsylvania, where William Penn had established a reputation for relatively fair dealing, the desire for Indian land led to dishonesty and trickery. Conflicts among Indian nations aided colonial leaders in prying territory from them. Hoping to assert their authority over the independent-minded Delaware Indians, Iroquois chiefs insisted that they held rights to much of the Pennsylvania

Lappawinsa 1757 Lappawinsa was a Delaware chief who signed the Walking Purchase Treaty in 1737. The signers did not know that colonial surveyors had marked the best route and hired runners to "walk off" the territory. Gustavus Hesselius, who migrated from Sweden to Philadelphia in 1711, painted six portraits of native chiefs. They were considered among the most realistic for this period. DEA Picture Library/Getty Images

territory and therefore must be the ones to negotiate with colonial officials. Those colonial authorities, however, produced a questionable treaty supposedly drafted by Penn in 1686 that allowed them to claim large portions of the contested territory. James Logan "discovered" a copy of this treaty, which allowed the English to control an area that could be walked off in a day and a half. Seeking to maintain control of at least some territory, the Iroquois finally agreed to this **Walking Purchase**. The sachems of the far smaller Delaware tribe were then pressured into letting Pennsylvania officials walk off the boundaries. By the time the Delaware acquiesced in the fall of 1737, Pennsylvania surveyors had already marked off the "shortest and best course," which allowed them to extend the boundaries by at least thirty miles beyond those set in the original, and questionable, treaty.

The rapid expansion of the colonial population ensured that conflicts between Indian and colonial leaders over land rights would continue. Meanwhile migrants and immigrants on the frontier increasingly claimed land simply by taking control of it, building houses, and planting crops regardless of Indian claims. This led to conflicts with diverse Indian communities, with English officials who demanded legal contracts and deeds, and among immigrants who settled in the same area.

These conflicts contrasted with developments around the Great Lakes where French traders and Algonquian inhabitants forged military and economic alliances. In this region, which the French called *Pays d'en Haut* (upper country), French colonists and Indians sought diplomatic solutions to problems to protect mutually beneficial trade relations. These relationships also helped fend off challenges from other European and indigenous groups.

Some religiously minded immigrants also worked to improve relations with Indians in Pennsylvania, at least temporarily. The tone had been set by William Penn's Quakers, who generally accepted Indian land claims and tried to pursue honest and fair negotiations. German Moravians who settled in eastern Pennsylvania in the 1740s also developed good relations with area tribes. On Pennsylvania's western frontier, Scots-Irish Presbyterians established alliances with Delaware and Shawnee groups. These alliances, however, were rooted less in religious principles than in the hope of profiting from the fur trade as Indians sought new commercial partners when their French allies became too demanding.

Still, by the mid-eighteenth century, tensions escalated between English and French officials in the region and intensified among various immigrant and religious communities and with Indian communities. The distinct religious traditions and the dramatically different visions of Indian-settler relations drawn from these traditions also sharpened boundaries within and between colonial communities. German Moravians and Scots-Irish Presbyterians in Pennsylvania established churches and schools separate from their Quaker neighbors, while Puritan New Englanders remained suspicious of Quakers as well as other Protestant sects. Moravians and other German sects also flourished in Georgia and the Carolinas, and nearly all sought to isolate themselves from the influences of other groups.

Some religious groups were isolated as much by force as by choice. While most early Irish immigrants were Protestant, by the early eighteenth century more Irish Catholics began to arrive. Then in 1745 some forty thousand Scots who had supported the Catholic monarchs in England prior to the Glorious Revolution were shipped to the Carolinas after a failed rebellion. Even long-settled Catholics, like those in Maryland, were looked on with suspicion by many Protestants. Although only a few hundred Jewish families resided in the colonies by 1750, they too were seen as outsiders. Still, they formed small but enduring communities in a number of seaport cities, where they established synagogues and developed a variety of mercantile ventures.

Africans brought new ideas and practices to North America as well. Transported by force to an unknown land, they may have found religious faith particularly important. Enslaved blacks included some Catholics from regions long held by the Portuguese and a few thousand Muslims, but many Africans initially embraced religious beliefs that were largely unknown to their Anglo-American masters.

As religious affiliations in the colonies multiplied, they reinforced existing concerns about spiritual decline and exacerbated cleavages rooted in nationality, class, and race. These developments heightened concerns among many well-established families over the future of British culture and institutions in North America.

| REVIEW & RELATE | • How and why did economic inequality in the colonies increase in the first half of the eighteenth century?
• How did population growth and increasing diversity contribute to conflict among and anxieties about the various groups inhabiting British North America? |

Religious Awakenings

Whether rooted in fears that worldly concerns were overshadowing spiritual devotion or that growing religious diversity was undermining the power of the church, many Protestant ministers lamented the state of faith in eighteenth-century America. Church leaders in Britain and the rest of Europe shared their fears. Ministers eager to address this crisis of faith—identified in the colonies as **New Light clergy**—worked together to reenergize the faithful and were initially welcomed, or at least tolerated, by more traditional **Old Light clergy**. But by the 1740s, fears that the passionate New Light clergy had gone too far led to a backlash.

The Roots of the Great Awakening

By the eighteenth century, the **Enlightenment**, a European cultural movement that emphasized rational and scientific thinking over traditional religion and superstition, had taken root in the colonies, particularly among elites. The development of a lively print culture spread the ideas of Enlightenment thinkers like the English philosopher John Locke, the German intellectual Immanuel Kant, and the French writer Voltaire across the Atlantic. These thinkers argued that through reason humans could discover the laws that governed the universe and thereby improve society. Benjamin Franklin, a leading printer in Philadelphia, was one of the foremost advocates of Enlightenment ideas in the colonies. His experiments with electricity reflected his faith in rational thought, and his publication of the *Pennsylvania Gazette* and *Poor Richard's Almanac* spread such ideas throughout the colonies in the 1720s and 1730s.

As more colonists were influenced by Enlightenment thought, they became more accepting of religious diversity, which had spread as settlers from diverse countries and denominations arrived in the English colonies. At the same time, Enlightenment ideas could undermine the religious vitality of the colonies. Many Enlightenment thinkers believed in a Christian God but rejected the revelations and rituals that defined traditional church practices and challenged ministerial claims that God was directly engaged in the daily workings of the world.

There were, however, countervailing forces. The German **Pietists** in particular challenged Enlightenment ideas that had influenced many Congregational and Anglican leaders in Europe. Pietists decried the power of established churches and urged individuals to follow their hearts rather than their heads in spiritual matters. Persecuted in Germany, Pietists migrated to Great Britain and North America, where their ideas influenced Scots-Irish Presbyterians and members of the Church of England. John Wesley, the founder of Methodism and a professor of theology at Oxford University, taught Pietist ideas to his students, including George Whitefield. Like the German Pietists, Whitefield considered the North American colonies a perfect venue for restoring intensity and emotion to religious worship.

Some colonists had begun rethinking their religious commitments before Whitefield or the Pietists arrived. By 1700 both laymen and ministers voiced growing concern with the state of colonial religion. Preachers educated in England or at colonial colleges like Harvard and William and Mary often emphasized learned discourse over passion. At the same time, there were too few clergy to meet the demands of the rapidly growing population in North America. In many rural areas, residents grew discouraged at the lack of ministerial attention. Meanwhile urban churches increasingly reflected the class divisions of the larger society, with wealthier members paying substantial rents to seat their families in the front pews. Farmers and shopkeepers rented the cheaper pews in the middle of the church, while the poorest congregants sat on free benches at the very back or in the gallery. Educated clergy might impress the richest parishioners with their learned sermons, but they did little to move the spirits of the congregation at large.

Still, this fear of religious declension was rooted almost solely in the behaviors of white men. While some colonial ministers sought to Christianize Indians, they never considered Indians' own forms of spiritual worship as an indication of religiosity. Nor did they include African Americans in their estimates of colonial piety. Perhaps more surprisingly, white women's religious devotion was considered problematic. In 1692, the Boston minister Cotton Mather declared, "there are fare more godly women in the world than godly men." As the witchcraft trials unfolded, he estimated that women comprised 75 to 80 percent of many Boston area congregations. He saw this as cause for concern, not rejoicing.

Concerns about the declining importance of religion, at least among men, continued into the eighteenth century even as denominations and churches multiplied. In 1719 the Reverend Theodorus Frelinghuysen, a Dutch Reformed minister in New Jersey, sought to reclaim religious enthusiasm by emphasizing parishioners' emotional investment in Christ. The Reverend William Tennent, the father of Gilbert Tennent, arrived in neighboring Pennsylvania with his family about the same time. He despaired that Presbyterian ministers were too few in number to reach the growing population and, like Frelinghuysen, feared that their approach was too didactic. Tennent soon established his own one-room academy to train his sons and other young men for the ministry. Though disparaged by Presbyterian authorities, the school attracted devout students.

Jonathan Edwards, a Congregational minister in Northampton, Massachusetts, joined Enlightenment ideas with religious fervor. A brilliant scholar who studied natural philosophy and science as well as theology, Edwards viewed the natural world as powerful evidence of God's design. He came to view the idea that God elected some individuals for salvation and others for damnation as a source of mystical joy. Although Edwards wrote erudite books and essays, he proclaimed that "our people do not so much need to have their heads stored [with knowledge] as to have their hearts touched." From 1733 to 1735, his sermons on God's absolute sovereignty over man initiated a revival in Northampton that reached hundreds of parishioners.

A few years earlier, Gilbert Tennent had begun urging his flock in New Brunswick, New Jersey to embrace "a true living faith in Jesus Christ." He took his lead from Frelinghuysen, who viewed conversion as a three-step process: Individuals must be convinced of their sinful nature, experience a spiritual rebirth, and then behave piously as evidence of their conversion. Tennent embraced these measures, believing they could lance the "boil" of an unsaved heart and apply the "balsam" of grace and righteousness. Then in 1739 Tennent met Whitefield, who launched a wave of revivals that revitalized and transformed religion across the colonies.

An Outburst of Revivals

Whitefield was perfectly situated to extend the series of revivals that scholars later called the **Great Awakening**. Gifted with a powerful voice, he understood that the expanding networks of communication and travel—developed to promote commerce—could also be used to promote religion. Advertising in newspapers and broadsides and traveling by ship, coach, and horseback, Whitefield made seven trips to the North American colonies beginning in 1738. He reached audiences from Georgia to New England to the Pennsylvania backcountry and inspired ministers in the colonies to expand upon his efforts.

In 1739 Whitefield launched a fifteen-month preaching tour that reached tens of thousands of colonists. Like Edwards, Frelinghuysen, and Tennent, he asked individuals to invest less in material goods and more in spiritual devotion. If they admitted their depraved and sinful state and truly repented, God would hear their prayers. Whitefield danced across the platform, shouted and raged, and gestured dramatically, drawing huge crowds everywhere he went. He attracted 20,000 women and men to individual events, at a time when the entire city of Boston counted just 17,000 residents.

New Light ministers carried on Whitefield's work throughout the 1740s, honing their methods and appeal. Less concerned with denominational affiliation than with core beliefs, they denounced urbane and educated clergy, used extemporaneous oratorical styles and outdoor venues to attract crowds, and invited colonists from all walks of life to build a common Christian community. Some became itinerant preachers, preferring to carry their message throughout the colonies than be constrained by a single church (Map 4.2).

New Light clergy appealed to large numbers of women and also brought young people to religion by the thousands. In addition, thousands of colonists, especially men, who were already church members were "born again," recommitting themselves to their faith. Poor women and men who felt little connection to preaching when they sat on the back benches eagerly joined the crowds at outdoor revivals, where they could stand as close to the pulpit as a rich merchant.

Religious Dissension

Initially, the Great Awakening drew support from large numbers of ministers because it increased religious enthusiasm and church attendance throughout the colonies. After decades of competition from secular concerns, religion once again took center stage. But the early embrace by Old Light clergy diminished as revivals spread farther afield, as critiques of educated clergy became more pointed, and as worshippers left established congregations for new churches. A growing number of ministers and other colonial leaders began to fear that revivalists were providing poor whites, free blacks, women, and even the enslaved with compelling critiques of those in power. By 1742, some Old Light ministers and colonial officials began openly critiquing evangelical revivalists.

Itinerant preachers in the South seemed especially threatening as they invited blacks and whites to attend revivals together and proclaimed their equality before God. Although New Light clergy rarely attacked slavery directly, they implicitly challenged racial hierarchies. In the North, too, revivalists attracted African

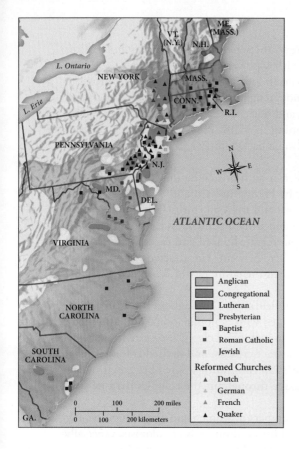

MAP 4.2   Religious Diversity in 1750

Despite the universal appeal of Whitefield and other New Light ministers, religious diversity had increased by 1750. Baptist churches multiplied in New England, where Congregationalists long held sway, while Presbyterian and Lutheran churches spread across the South where Anglicanism was the established church. Non-evangelical houses of worship, such as Quaker meeting houses and Jewish synagogues, also gradually increased in number.

Americans and Indians by emphasizing communal singing and emotional expressions of the spirit, which echoed traditional African and indigenous practices.

Increasingly, Old Light ministers and local officials questioned New Light techniques and influences. One of the most radical New Light preachers, James Davenport, attracted huge crowds when he preached in Boston in the early 1740s. Drawing thousands of colonists to Boston Common day after day, Davenport declared that the people "should drink rat poison rather than listen to corrupt, unconverted clergy." Boston officials finally called a grand jury into session to silence him "on the charge of having said that Boston's ministers were leading the people blindfold to hell."

Even some New Light ministers, including Tennent, considered Davenport extreme. Yet revivals continued throughout the 1740s and beyond. Although they lessened in intensity in many areas, local revivals continued through the 1760s. In Newport, Rhode Island, for instance, Sarah Osborn led a series of revivals in 1766–1767. Osborn was a poor woman with little formal education who had experienced early widowhood, the death of her only son, a second marriage to a widower with three sons, and chronic struggles with depression and disease. She underwent a dramatic conversion in 1742, but her second husband soon suffered a breakdown and the family declared bankruptcy a year later. Osborn then took up teaching while writing a memoir focused on her struggles to follow God's path. In the 1760s, when no evangelical preacher could be found to minister to local residents, Osborn opened her home for prayer and contemplation. Although the central tenets of revivalist preaching—criticisms of educated clergy, itinerancy, and extemporaneous preaching—worked against the movement's institutionalization, it provided space for individual converts to take up the work in their own way. The Great Awakening thus echoed across the colonies into the 1770s, its influence felt in attitudes and practices as well as in churches and meetings.

For example, when, in 1750, King George II (r. 1727–1760) threatened to appoint an Anglican bishop for the North American colonies, many North American ministers, both Old Light and New, resisted the appointment. Most colonists had become used to religious diversity and toleration, at least for Protestants, and had little desire to add church officials to the existing hierarchies of colonial authorities. In various ways, revivalists also highlighted the democratic tendencies in the Bible, particularly in the New Testament. Even as they proclaimed God's wrath against sinners, they also preached that a lack of wealth and power did not diminish a person in God's eyes. And revivalists honed a style of passionate and popular preaching that would shape American religion as well as politics for centuries to come. This mode of communication had immediate application as colonists mobilized to resist what they saw as tyrannical actions by colonial officials and others in authority.

REVIEW & RELATE	• What was the relationship between the Enlightenment and the religious revivals of the early eighteenth century? • What was the immediate impact of the Great Awakening, and what were its legacies for American religious and social life?

Political Awakenings

The effects of eighteenth-century religious awakenings rippled out from churches and revivals to influence social and political relations. New Light clergy allowed colonists to view their resistance to traditional authorities as part of their effort to create a better and more just world. Experiences of self-government, Enlightenment ideas, and protests against perceived corruption in the imperial system also led some colonists to question the right of those in power to impose their will on the community as a whole.

Changing Political Relations

The settlements of the seventeenth century could be regulated with a small number of officials, and in most colonies male settlers agreed on who should rule. However, with geographical expansion, population growth, and commercial development, colonial officials—whether appointed by the crown or selected by local residents—found themselves confronted with a more complex, and more contentious, situation. In New England, most colonies developed participatory town meetings that elected members to their colonial legislatures. In the South, wealthy planters exercised greater authority locally and colony-wide, but they still embraced ideals of self-governance and political liberty.

Throughout the British American colonies, officials were usually educated men who held property and had family ties to other colonial elites. Although ultimate political authority — or sovereignty — rested with the king and Parliament, local officials made many decisions because the king and Parliament were too distant to regulate daily life. Another factor that weakened the power of royal officials was the tradition of town meetings and representative bodies, like the Virginia House of Burgesses, that gave colonists a stake in their own governance. Officials in England and the colonies assumed that most people would defer to those in authority, and they minimized resistance by holding public elections in which freemen cast ballots by voice vote. Not surprisingly, those with wealth and power continued to win office.

Still, evidence from throughout the colonial period indicates that deference to authority was not always sufficient to maintain order. Roger Williams and Anne Hutchinson, Bacon's Rebellion, King Philip's War, the Stono rebellion, the Salem witchcraft trials, and the radical preaching of James Davenport make clear that not everyone willingly supported their supposed superiors. These episodes of dissent and protest were widely scattered across time and place. But as the ideas disseminated by New Light clergy and Enlightenment thinkers converged with changing political relations, resistance to established authority became more frequent and more collective.

Dissent and Protest

Local protests against colonial authorities had a long history. Some settlers challenged colonial leaders' repeated demands for more men and higher taxes to support New England's almost continuous wars against Indians. From the 1670s on, women petitioned authorities for tax relief as well as their men folks' "relief from service." In 1706, five wives of poor fisherman in Marblehead, Massachusetts opposed "with force and arms" colonial officials who sought to confiscate their property for non-payment of taxes. As war raged on, refugees flooded eastern towns and colonists faced injury, capture, or death. By the 1730s, many families insisted they had paid enough when officials repeated their calls for men and money, which led to new rounds of protests.

The issues and methods of protest varied, but collectively they indicate a growing sense of political and economic autonomy among North American colonists. Some protests focused on royal officials like governors and Royal Navy captains; others focused on local authorities, merchants, or large landowners. Whatever the target of resistance, colonists demonstrated their belief that they had rights worth protecting, even against those who held legitimate authority.

Access to reasonably priced food, especially bread, inspired numerous riots. During the 1730s, the price of bread — a critical staple in colonial diets — rose despite falling wheat prices and a recession in seaport cities. Bread rioters attacked grain warehouses, bakeries, and shops, demanding more bread at lower prices. In New England, such uprisings were often led by women, who were responsible for putting bread on the table. When grievances involved domestic or consumer issues, women insisted they had the right to be heard. That idea was reinforced by evangelical clergy's insistence on one's moral obligations to society.

View of Main Street, Boston   Boston's broad Main Street, which ran from the Town Hall to the South Church, was used by laborers, merchants, political leaders, and soldiers. This scene was engraved by the German artist Franz Xavier Habermann, who specialized in scenes of North American cities. The buildings and clothing reflect a European view of Boston's commerce and affluence in the mid-eighteenth century. © RMN-Grand Palais/Art Resource, NY

Public markets also sparked collective protests. In 1737, for instance, Boston officials decided to construct a public market and charge fees to farmers who sold their goods there. Small farmers, who were used to selling produce from the roadside for free, clashed with officials and with larger merchants over the venture. Many Boston residents supported the protesters because the market fees would lessen competition and raise prices. Initially, residents petitioned city officials. When they received no response, opponents demolished the market building and stalls in the middle of the night. Local authorities could find no witnesses to the crime.

Access to land was also a critical issue for colonists. Beginning in the 1740s, protests erupted on estates in New Jersey and along the Hudson River in New York over the leasing policies of landlords as well as the amount of land controlled by speculators. Here, again, tenants and squatters petitioned colonial officials, received no response, and then took collective action. They formed associations, targeted specific landlords, and then burned barns, attacked livestock, and emptied houses and farm buildings of furniture and tools. Embracing Enlightenment ideas of "natural law," they also established regional committees to hear grievances and formed "popular" militia companies and courts to mete out justice to recalcitrant land owners. When landlords and colonial officials called out local militia to arrest the perpetrators, they failed to consider that militia members were often the same poor men whose protests they ignored.

In seaport cities, a frequent source of conflict was the **impressment** of colonial men who were forcibly drafted into service in the Royal Navy. Viewed as a sign of the corrupt practices of imperial authorities, the challenge to impressment energized diverse groups of colonists. Sailors, dockworkers, and men drinking at taverns along the shore, black and white, feared being pressed into military service. Colonial officials, worried about labor shortages, petitioned the British government to stop impressment. Still, it was working men who faced the navy's high mortality rates, bad food, rampant disease, and harsh discipline who fought back against both British and colonial authorities. In 1747 in Boston, a general impressment effort led to three days of rioting. An observer noted that "Negros, servants, and hundreds of seamen seized a naval lieutenant, assaulted a sheriff, and put his deputy in stocks, surrounded the governor's house, and stormed the Town House (city hall)." Such riots did not end the system of impressment, but they showed that many colonists now refused to be deprived of what they considered their natural rights.

The religious upheavals and economic uncertainties of the 1730s and 1740s led colonists to challenge officials with greater frequency than in earlier decades. They justified their actions in evangelical or Enlightenment terms. Most protests also accentuated class lines as small farmers and craftsmen, their wives, and poor whites and free blacks fought against merchants, landowners, and local officials. However, the resistance to impressment proved that colonists could mobilize across economic differences when British policies affected diverse groups.

Transforming Urban Politics

The development of cross-class alliances in the 1730s and 1740s was also visible in the more formal arena of colonial politics. Beginning in the 1730s, some affluent political leaders in cities like New York and Philadelphia began to seek support from a wider constituency. In most cases, conflicts among elites led to these appeals to the "popular" will. In 1731, for instance, a new royal charter confirmed New York City's existence as a "corporation" and stipulated the rights of freemen (residents who could vote in local elections after paying a small fee) and freeholders (individuals, whether residents or not, who held property worth £40 and could vote on that basis). A large number of artisans, shopkeepers, and laborers acquired the necessary means to vote, and shopkeepers and master craftsmen now sat alongside wealthier men on the Common Council. Yet most laboring men did not participate actively in elections until 1733, when local elites led by Lewis Morris sought to mobilize the mass of voters against royal officials, like Governor William Cosby, appointed in London.

Morris, a wealthy man and a judge, joined other colonial elites in believing that the royal officials recently appointed to govern New York were tied to ministerial corruption in England. As chief justice of the provincial court, Morris ruled against Governor Cosby in a suit the new governor brought against his predecessor. Cosby then suspended Morris from office. In the aftermath, Morris and his supporters took his case to the people, who were suffering from a serious economic depression. The Morrisites launched an opposition newspaper, published by apprentice printer John Peter Zenger, to mobilize artisans, shopkeepers, and laborers around an agenda to stimulate the economy and elect men supportive of workers to the city's common council.

In his *New-York Weekly Journal,* Zenger leaped into the political fray, accusing Governor Cosby and his cronies of corruption, incompetence, election fraud, and tyranny. The vitriolic attacks led to Zenger's indictment for seditious libel and his imprisonment in November 1734. At the time, libel related only to whether published material undermined government authority, not whether it was true or false. But Zenger's lead attorney, Andrew Hamilton of Philadelphia, argued that truth must be recognized as a defense against charges of libel. Appealing to a jury of Zenger's peers, Hamilton proclaimed, "It is not the cause of a poor printer, nor of New York alone, which you are now trying. . . . It is the best cause. It is the cause of liberty." In response, jurors ignored the law as written and acquitted Zenger.

Although the decision in the Zenger case did not lead to a change in British libel laws, it did signal the willingness of colonial juries to side with fellow colonists against king and Parliament in at least some situations. Building on their success, Morris and his followers continued to gain popular support. In 1737 his son, Lewis Morris Jr., was appointed speaker of the new Assembly, and the Assembly appointed Zenger as its official printer. But soon the group fell into disarray when royal officials offered political prizes to a few of their leaders. Indeed, the elder Morris accepted appointment as royal governor of New Jersey, after which he switched allegiances and became an advocate of executive authority. Nonetheless, the political movement he led had aroused ordinary freemen to participate in elections, and newspapers and pamphlets increasingly attacked corrupt officials and threats to the rightful liberties of British colonists.

Even as freemen gained a greater voice in urban politics, they could challenge the power of colonial leaders only when the elite were divided. Moreover, the rewards they gained sometimes served to reinforce class divisions. Thus many city workers benefited when the elder Morris used his influence to ensure the building of the city's first permanent almshouse in 1736. The two-year project employed large numbers of artisans and laborers in a period of economic contraction. Once built, however, the almshouse became a symbol of the growing gap between rich and poor. Its existence was also used by future city councils as a justification to eliminate other forms of relief, leaving the poor in worse shape than before.

The rising inequality of wealth was especially apparent in the largest cities of British North America — New York, Philadelphia, Boston, and Charleston — but economic distinctions were also growing in smaller cities and towns. As the price of some goods, such as sugar and tobacco, fell in the 1750s, more colonists were able to afford them. At the same time, however, the expansion of transatlantic trade ensured that wealthier colonists had growing access to silver plates, clocks, tea services, bed and table linens, and other luxury goods. With British exporters extending more credit to colonial merchants and affluent white consumers, the division between rich and poor became increasingly visible to colonists of all backgrounds.

| REVIEW & RELATE | • How did ordinary colonists, both men and women, black and white, express their political opinions and preferences in the first half of the eighteenth century?
• How did politics bring colonists together across economic lines in the first half of the eighteenth century? When did politics highlight and reinforce class divisions? |

Conclusion: A Divided Society

By 1754 religious and political awakenings had transformed colonists' sense of their relation to spiritual and secular authorities. Both Gilbert Tennent and Sarah Grosvenor were caught up in these transitions. As a man and a minister, however, Tennent had far more power to control his destiny than did Grosvenor. While wives and daughters in elite families benefited from their wealth and position, they were also constrained by the strictures of the patriarchal family. Women who were poor, indentured, or enslaved were forced into the greatest dependency on male employers and civic officials. Even women in farm and artisanal families depended on loving husbands and fathers to offset the strictures of patriarchal authority. While few colonists conceived of themselves as part of a united body politic, women probably identified most deeply with their family, town, or church. Still, in certain circumstances, such as ongoing colonial wars, women insisted on their right to protect their households by resisting colonial authorities. Nonetheless, women and men thought of themselves as English, or Scots-Irish, or German, rather than more broadly American. At best, they claimed identity as residents of Massachusetts, New Jersey, or South Carolina rather than British North America.

Between the 1680s and the 1750s, the diversity and divisions among colonists increased as class, racial, religious, and regional differences multiplied across the colonies. Immigrants from Germany, Ireland, and Scotland created their own communities; religious awakenings led to cleavages among Protestants and between them and other religious groups; and economic inequality deepened in seacoast cities. At the same time, conflicts between Indians and settlers intensified along the frontier as growing numbers of enslaved Africans reshaped economic and social relations in the urban North and the rural South.

By midcentury, the colonies as a whole had been transformed in significant ways. Religious leaders gained renewed respect, colonial assemblies wrested more autonomy from royal hands, freemen participated more avidly in political contests, printers and lawyers insisted on the rights and liberties of colonists, and local communities defended those rights in a variety of ways. When military conflicts brought British officials into more direct contact with their colonial subjects in the following decade, they sought to check these trends, with dramatic consequences.

Chapter 4 Review

KEY TERMS

patriarchal family, 88
Walking Purchase, 97
New Light clergy, 99
Old Light clergy, 99

Enlightenment, 99
Pietists, 99
Great Awakening, 101
impressment, 105

REVIEW & RELATE

1. What factors led to rising tensions within colonial communities in the early 1700s?
2. How did social, economic, and political tensions contribute to an increase in accusations of witchcraft?
3. Why and how did the legal and economic circumstances of colonial women decline between 1650 and 1750?
4. How did patriarchal ideals of family and community shape life and work in colonial America? What happened when men failed to live up to those ideals?
5. How and why did economic inequality in the colonies increase in the first half of the eighteenth century?
6. How did population growth and increasing diversity contribute to conflict among and anxieties about the various groups inhabiting British North America?
7. What was the relationship between the Enlightenment and the religious revivals of the early eighteenth century?
8. What was the immediate impact of the Great Awakening, and what were its legacies for American religious and social life?
9. How did ordinary colonists, both men and women, black and white, express their political opinions and preferences in the first half of the eighteenth century?
10. How did politics bring colonists together across economic lines in the first half of the eighteenth century? When did politics highlight and reinforce class divisions?

TIMELINE OF EVENTS

1688	• Glorious Revolution
1692	• Salem witch trials
1700–1750	• 250,000 immigrants and enslaved Africans arrive in the colonies
1700–1775	• Population of British North America grows from 250,000 to 2.5 million
1720–1740	• Influx of Scots-Irish to Pennsylvania
1734	• John Peter Zenger acquitted of libel
1737	• Iroquois and Delaware acquiesce to Walking Purchase
	• Protest against public market in Boston
1739	• George Whitefield launches preaching tour of the colonies
1745	• 40,000 Scottish Catholics shipped to the Carolinas after failed rebellion
1747	• Rioting in Boston against impressment
1750	• Colonists resist appointment of an Anglican bishop for North America

5

War and Empire

1754–1774

COMPARING AMERICAN HISTORIES

Praised as the father of the United States, **George Washington** remained a loyal British subject for forty-three years. He was born in 1732 to a prosperous farm family in eastern Virginia. When his father died in 1743, George became the ward of his half-brother Lawrence, who took control of the family's Mount Vernon estate. Lawrence's father-in-law, William Fairfax, was an agent for one of the chief proprietors of the colony. When George was sixteen, William hired him to help survey land on Virginia's western frontier.

As a surveyor, George journeyed west and came into contact with Indians, friendly and hostile, as well as colonists seeking land. He began investing in western properties, but when Lawrence Washington died in 1752, George suddenly became head of a large estate. He gradually expanded Mount Vernon's boundaries and its enslaved workforce, increasing its profitability.

At the same time, Washington was appointed Lieutenant Colonel in the Virginia militia. In Fall 1753 Virginia's governor sent him to warn the French against encroaching on British territory in the Ohio River valley. The French commander rebuffed Washington and, within six months, gained control of a British post in western Pennsylvania and named it Fort Duquesne. With help from Indians hostile to the French, Washington led a surprise attack on Fort Duquesne in May 1754. The governors of Virginia and North Carolina responded by providing more troops to the newly promoted Colonel Washington. However, the French responded with a much larger force and compelled Washington to surrender.

Washington's fortunes improved when he married the wealthy widow Martha Dandridge Custis in 1759. Now with even more land to defend, Washington supported efforts to extend Britain's North American empire westward to create a buffer against European and Indian foes.

Like Washington, **Pontiac** gained fame as a warrior. However, he fought on the side of the French. He was born between 1712 and 1725 near Lake Erie to parents of mixed native lineage. Around 1723, his family settled in an Ottawa village near the French Fort Detroit. By 1747, Pontiac had become an Ottawa war chief and fought alongside other Indians and the French to defeat British-backed Hurons in the Ohio valley. Then in 1760, British troops defeated French forces at Quebec, essentially ending French control in the region, leaving their native allies without European support.

The next year, General Jeffrey Amherst assumed control of colonial Indian policy as British troops took over French forts and built new ones on native lands. When British colonists pushed further into the Great Lakes/ Ohio valley region, Delaware prophet Neolin urged native people to reject European goods and return to traditional ways. His support grew when France ignored the rights of its Indian allies by ceding its North American lands to Britain in the Peace of Paris in February 1763. That spring, Pontiac held war councils, urging participants from neighboring tribes to join the Ottawa in an attack on Fort Detroit.

Nine hundred warriors from six tribes laid siege to the fort, and Pontiac quickly rose from a local war chief to a regional spokesman for native rights. Indigenous leaders throughout the region organized attacks on other British forts between 1763 and 1766. Initially this decentralized alliance was powerful enough to keep the British from gaining control over the lands France granted them in the Peace of Paris.

COMPARING THE AMERICAN HISTORIES of Washington and Pontiac reveals the challenges faced by colonists and native peoples in the mid-eighteenth century. North America offered many white colonists greater opportunities for advancement than they could achieve back home, but as the colonial population swelled, discord intensified. Conflicts between white settlers and Indian communities, especially in frontier regions, were nearly continuous through the 1760s. As European wars spilled across the Atlantic and colonial wars entangled European rivals, religious, economic, and political strife intensified with momentous consequences. Still, at least through 1774, as colonists in British North America sought to defeat or pacify Indian nations, they negotiated with colonial and parliamentary authorities over policies they viewed as unfair or abusive.

Imperial Conflicts and Indian Wars, 1754–1763

The war that erupted in the Ohio valley in 1754 sparked an enormous shift in political and economic relations in colonial North America. What began as a small-scale, regional conflict expanded into a brutal and lengthy global war. Known as the French and Indian War in North America and as the Seven Years' War in Great Britain and Europe, the extended conflict led to a dramatic expansion of British territory in North America and to increasing demands from American colonists for more control over their own lives.

The Opening Battles

July 1754 marked a critical point in colonial and Indian relations in British North America. Even before the British learned of Washington's defeat in the Ohio valley, they sought to protect the colonies against further threats from the French and their Indian allies. The British were especially interested in cementing an alliance with the powerful Iroquois Confederacy, composed of six northeastern tribes. In June, officials had invited a delegation from the confederacy to a July meeting with colonial representatives at Albany, New York. Benjamin Franklin had a different view of the meeting. He drew up a Plan of Union that would establish a council of representatives from the various colonial assemblies to debate issues of frontier defense, trade, and territorial expansion. Their deliberations would be overseen by a president-general appointed by the British crown. Despite the proposed council's involvement in Indian affairs, Franklin excluded Iroquois or other Indian representatives from his plan.

Although the **Albany Congress** created stronger bonds among a small circle of colonial leaders, it failed to establish a firmer alliance with the Iroquois or resolve problems of colonial governance. The Mohawk warrior and sachem Hendrick Peters Theyanoguin, a member of the Iroquois Confederacy, urged British representatives at the Congress to take forceful action against their common enemies. However, by the time his views were reported in the British press, Iroquois representatives angered by their exclusion from Franklin's plan broke off talks with the British. The Plan of Union was also rejected by colonial delegates, who were unwilling to give up any of their autonomy in military, trade, and political matters to some centralized assembly.

Join or Die Benjamin Franklin created the first political cartoon in American history to accompany an editorial he wrote in the Pennsylvania Gazette in 1754. Franklin's cartoon urged the mainland British colonies to unite politically during the French and Indian War. Legend had it that a snake could come back to life if its severed sections were attached before dusk. Library of Congress, LC-USZC4-5315

Meanwhile royal officials worried that the debates in Albany might force the crown's hand in dealing with the French and their Indian allies.

If war was going to erupt between the British and the French, the Iroquois could not afford to have the outcome decided by imperial powers alone. Indeed, for most Indians, contests among European nations for land and power offered them the best chance of survival in the eighteenth century. They gained leverage as long as opposing imperial powers needed their trade goods and their military and political support. Their leverage would be far more limited if one European nation controlled most of North America.

Still, Indian tribes adopted different strategies. The Delaware, Miami, Ottawa, and Shawnee nations, for example, allied themselves with the French, hoping that a French victory would stop British colonists from invading their settlements in the Ohio River valley. Members of the Iroquois Confederacy, on the other hand, tried to play one power against the other, hoping to win concessions from the British in return for their military support. The Creek, Choctaw, and Cherokee nations also sought to perpetuate the existing stalemate among European powers by bargaining alternately with the British in Georgia and the Carolinas, the French in Louisiana, and the Spaniards in Florida. Faced with incursions into their lands, some Indian tribes, like the Abenaki in northern New England, launched preemptive attacks on colonial settlements.

The British government soon decided to send additional troops to defend its American colonies against attacks from Indians and intrusions from the French. General Edward Braddock arrived with two regiments in 1755, seeking to expel the French from Fort Duquesne. At the same time, colonial militia units were sent to battle the French and their Indian allies along the New York and New England frontiers. Colonel Washington joined Braddock as his personal aide-de-camp. Within months, however, Braddock's forces were ambushed, bludgeoned by French and Indian forces, and Braddock was killed.

Other British forces fared little better during the next three years. Despite having far fewer colonists in North America than the British, the French had established extensive trade networks that helped them gain support from numerous Indian nations in a protracted war. Alternating guerrilla tactics with conventional warfare, the French captured several important forts, built a new one on Lake Champlain, and moved troops deep into British territory. The ineffectiveness of the British and colonial armies also encouraged Indian tribes along the New England and Appalachian frontiers to reclaim land from colonists. Bloody raids devastated many outlying settlements, leading to the death and capture of hundreds of Britain's colonial subjects.

A Shift to Global War

Whereas earlier wars had originated in Europe and spread to American colonies, French victories in North America inspired their European foes to contest British imperial claims elsewhere in the world. In 1756 France and Great Britain officially declared war against each other. Eventually Austria, Russia, Sweden, most of the German states, and Spain allied with France, while Portugal and Prussia sided with Great Britain. Naval warfare erupted in the Mediterranean Sea and the Atlantic and Indian Oceans. Battles were also fought in Europe, the West Indies, India, and the Philippines. By the end of 1757, Britain and its allies had been defeated in nearly every part of the globe. The war appeared to be nearing its end, with France in control.

However, in summer 1757, William Pitt took charge of the British war effort. He poured soldiers and arms into North America along with young and ambitious officers like Henry Bouquet. His strategy energized colonial and British forces, while Prussian forces held the line in Europe. By the summer of 1758, the tide began to turn. In July, British generals recaptured the fort at Louisburg on Cape Breton Island, a key to France's defense of Canada. Then British troops with Bouquet and Washington's aid seized Fort Duquesne, which was renamed Fort Pitt. Other British forces captured Fort Frontenac along the St. Lawrence River, while Prussia defeated France and its allies in Europe and Britain gained key victories in India (Map 5.1). In 1759 General Jeffrey Amherst recaptured Forts Ticonderoga and Crown Point on Lake Champlain while General James Wolfe attacked a much larger French force in Quebec. Despite heavy casualties, including Wolfe himself, the British won Quebec and control of Canada.

Cherokee warriors had allied with British forces to defeat France at Pennsylvania's Fort Duquesne in 1758. The alliance was sealed in part by Britain building Fort Loudon, its first fort west of the Appalachian Mountains, as a base for trade and military protection for native allies. Initially, relations were cordial, and some soldiers stationed there married Cherokee women. However, after Virginia settlers attacked Cherokee warriors returning south from Pennsylvania, some Cherokee retaliated. The situation escalated with the Cherokee hoping to drive colonists out of their hunting grounds. Attacks continued on both sides, and open warfare erupted in 1759. During this Anglo-Cherokee War, Cherokee warriors laid siege to Fort Loudon. However, the Cherokee wives of British soldiers smuggled in food, and their authority over households and agriculture made it impossible to stop the effort. Fort Loudon finally did fall, but by then a smallpox epidemic weakened Cherokee forces. General Jeffrey Amherst then sent 2,800 troops to invade Cherokee territory and end the conflict. British and Scottish soldiers along with colonial militias and their Indian allies sacked fifteen Cherokee villages; killed men, women, and children; and burned acres of fields. A peace agreement was finally signed in fall 1761.

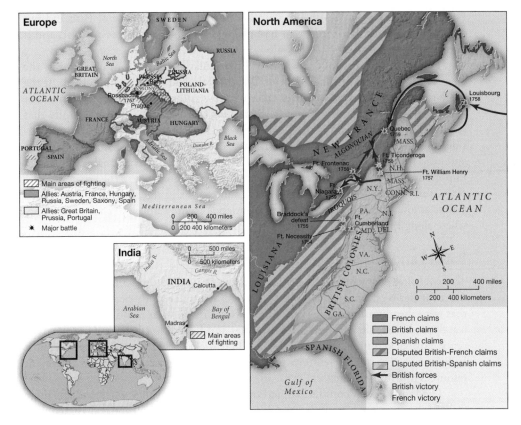

MAP 5.1   **The French and Indian War, 1754–1763**
Clashes between colonial militia units and French and Indian forces erupted in North America in 1754. The conflict helped launch a wider war that engulfed Europe as well as the West Indies and India. In the aftermath of this first global war, Britain gained control of present-day Canada and India, but France retained its West Indies colonies.

The Costs of Victory

Despite Wolfe's victory in 1760 and the end of the Cherokee threat the following year, the war dragged on in North America, Europe, India, and the West Indies until 1763. By then, however, King George III had tired of Pitt's grand strategy and dismissed him. He then opened peace negotiations with France and agreed to give up a number of conquered territories in order to finalize the **Peace of Paris** in 1763. Other countries were ready to negotiate as well. To regain control of Cuba and the Philippines, Spain ceded Florida to Great Britain. While France was expelled from North America, it rewarded Spanish support by granting Spain Louisiana and all French lands west of the Mississippi River. Despite these concessions, the British empire reigned supreme, regaining control of India as well as North America east of the Mississippi, all of Canada, and a number of Caribbean islands.

The wars that erupted between 1754 and 1763 reshaped European empires, transformed patterns of global trade, and initially seemed to tighten bonds between

North American residents and the mother country. Yet the Peace of Paris did not resolve many of the problems that had plagued the colonies before the war, and it created new ones as well.

The incredible cost of the war raised particularly difficult problems. Over the course of the war, the national debt of Great Britain had more than doubled. At the same time, as the North American colonies grew and conflicts erupted along their frontiers, the costs of administering them increased fivefold. With an empire that stretched around the globe, the British crown and Parliament were forced to consider how to pay off war debts, raise funds to administer their far-flung territories, and keep sufficient currency in circulation for expanding international trade. Just as important, the Peace of Paris ignored the claims of Indian tribes to the territories that France and Spain turned over to Great Britain. Nor did the treaty settle contested claims among the colonies themselves over lands in the Ohio River valley and elsewhere along British North America's new frontiers.

Battles and Boundaries on the Frontier

The sweeping character of the British victory encouraged thousands of colonists to move farther west, into lands once controlled by France. This exacerbated tensions that were already rising on the southern and western frontiers of British North America. Sporadic assaults on native communities and frontier settlements continued for years. For backcountry settlers, these conflicts fueled resentments not only against Indians but also against eastern political leaders who rarely provided sufficient resources for frontier defense.

The most serious conflict erupted in the Ohio River valley when Indians there realized the consequences of British victories. When the British captured French forts along the Great Lakes and in the Ohio valley in 1760, they immediately antagonized local Indian groups by hunting and fishing on tribal lands and depriving villages of much-needed food. British traders also defrauded Indians on numerous occasions and General Amherst stopped traditional obligations of gift giving, reduced the value of beaver skins, and refused to provide native traders with guns or ammunition.

The harsh realities of the British regime led some Indians to seek a return to ways of life that preceded the arrival of white men. A Delaware visionary named Neolin preached that Indians had been corrupted by contact with Europeans and urged them to purify themselves by returning to their ancient traditions, abandoning white ways, and reclaiming their lands. Neolin was a prophet, not a warrior, but his message inspired others, including the Ottawa leader Pontiac.

In early 1763, news arrived that France was about to cede all of its North American lands to Britain and Spain without any effort to protect the territory of its former Indian allies. Pontiac then convened a council of more than four hundred Ottawa, Ojibwe, and Huron leaders near Fort Detroit. Drawing on Neolin's vision, he proclaimed, "It is important my brothers, that we should exterminate from our land this nation [Britain], whose only object is our death. . . . we can no longer supply our wants the way we were accustomed to do with our Fathers the French." Having mobilized a half dozen tribes, Pontiac laid siege to Fort Detroit in May 1763. Soon some eighteen Indian nations, including the Chippewa, were attacking British frontier outposts and white settlements along the Great Lakes, Virginia, and Pennsylvania frontier (Map 5.2).

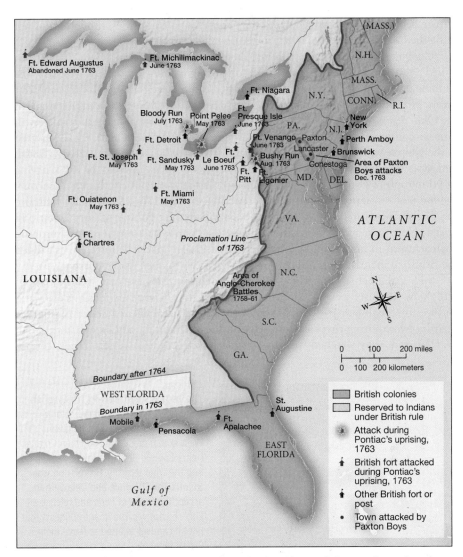

MAP 5.2   British Conflicts with Indians, 1758–1763, and the Proclamation Line
The entrance of British troops into former French territory in the Ohio River valley following the French and Indian War fueled conflicts with Indian nations. Colonists in Pennsylvania and the Carolinas also battled with Indians, including tribes who were allies or remained neutral during the war. Parliament established the Proclamation Line to limit westward expansion and thereby diminish such hostilities.

Accounts of Pontiac's rebellion sparked outrage among settlers and British troops. Many colonists did not distinguish between friendly and hostile Indians. In December 1763, a group of men from Paxton Creek, Pennsylvania raided families of peaceful, Christian Conestoga Indians near Lancaster, killing thirty. Protests from eastern colonists infuriated the Paxton Boys, who then marched on Philadelphia demanding protection from "savages" on the frontier. Benjamin Franklin negotiated a truce between the Paxton Boys and the Pennsylvania authorities, though it did not settle the fundamental issues over protection of western settlers.

Convinced that it could not endure these costly frontier clashes, the British crown issued a proclamation in October 1763 forbidding colonial settlement west of a line running down the Appalachian Mountains to create a buffer between Indians and colonists. Nonetheless, Parliament ordered Colonel Bouquet to subdue hostile Indians in the Ohio region the next year, and battles between British troops and tribes allied with Pontiac continued across the Great Lakes region. While diverse native leaders, such as the Chippewa chief Minavavana, initiated attacks on scattered British forts, British emissaries focused their diplomatic efforts solely on Pontiac. In October 1763, having failed to capture Fort Detroit, Pontiac moved further west but continued to encourage militant resistance to the British occupation. In July 1766, Sir William Johnson, the British Superintendent of Indian Affairs, finally met Pontiac at Fort Ontario in upstate New York, and formally ended hostilities. Pontiac had sought to end European encroachment in his region, but the widespread Indian attacks he inspired instead led the British to increase their military presence in order to quell native uprisings.

Still, Parliament's establishment of the **Proclamation Line of 1763** did temporarily slow colonists' westward movement. However, it heightened tensions over land and wealth. Small farmers, backcountry settlers, and squatters had hoped to improve their lot by acquiring rich farmlands won in the long and bloody French and Indian War. Instead, they watched wealthy speculators claim these western lands, certain

The Indians Delivering Up English Captives, 1766 This hand-colored engraving was based on a Benjamin West sketch made in 1764 when Colonel Henry Bouquet led an army of 1,500 men into the Ohio territory. His mission was to force the Shawnee and Delaware to accept the Peace of Paris and release all English captives. The image suggests that not all captives wanted to leave their Indian families. Library of Congress, Prints and Photographs Division [LC-USZC2-1595]

that the Proclamation was merely "a temporary expedient to quiet the Minds of the Indians." George Washington alone acquired tens of thousands of acres west of the Proclamation Line, land that was once home to native tribes.

Conflicts over Land and Labor Escalate

Conflicts among colonists and with Britain were not confined to frontier regions. Land riots directed against the leasing policies of landlords and the greed of speculators had plagued New York's Hudson valley and New Jersey before the war, and these struggles continued into the 1760s. New clashes also occurred in the Carolinas as settlers stood up to landlords and government officials.

While the French and Indian War raged, the owners of large estates along the Hudson River raised rents and reduced the rights of tenants. In the early eighteenth century, the titles to some of these estates were challenged by small landowners and tenants, but even where legitimate titles existed, tenants declared a moral right to own the land they had long farmed. The manors and estates of the Hudson valley, they claimed, were more appropriate to a feudal government than to an enlightened empire.

Farmers in neighboring New Hampshire were drawn into battles over land when the king's Privy Council in London decided in 1764 that the Green Mountains belonged to New York rather than New Hampshire. Landlords along the Hudson River hoped to expand eastward into this region, but the farmers already living there claimed they had bought the land in good faith and deserved to keep it. The farmers launched guerrilla warfare against New York authorities and large landowners as well as against New York farmers who claimed land that New Hampshire families had cleared and settled. These Green Mountain Boys, led by Ethan Allen, refused to recognize New York authorities as legitimate and established their own local governments and popular courts.

Inspired by the Green Mountain Boys as well as uprisings in New Jersey, tenants in the Hudson valley banded together in 1765 and 1766. Under the leadership of Irish immigrant William Prendergast, a group of tenants calling themselves Levellers refused to pay rent and instead claimed freehold title to the land they farmed. New York tenants petitioned the colonial assembly and sought redress in a variety of ways. But landowners refused to negotiate, and Prendergast concluded that "there was no law for poor men." All of these groups developed visible, well-organized networks of supporters, targeted specific landlords, sought redress first through colonial courts and assemblies, and then established popular militias and other institutions to govern themselves and to challenge those in authority. Although led by men, such community protests required the support of women as well, who took on extra household and agricultural duties while their husbands and sons built resistance movements.

REVIEW & RELATE

- How did the French and Indian War and the subsequent peace treaty affect relations among Britain, American Indian nations, and American colonies?
- How did the French and Indian War and the increasing power of large landowners contribute to conflict between average colonists and colonial elites?

Postwar British Policies and Colonial Unity

Even as ordinary colonists challenged the authority of economic and political elites, colonial leaders tried to persuade the disaffected to turn their anger against royal authorities in Britain. By highlighting colonists' rights as British subjects, local traditions of self-rule, and Enlightenment ideas, these leaders slowly gained support. Some of them even joined earlier opponents in arguing for the rights of the individual. The imposition of new British policies in the decade following the French and Indian War, from 1764 to 1774, was equally important in nurturing common grievances and uniting colonists across regional and economic differences. For instance, the Proclamation Line of 1763 eventually inspired widespread dissent as poor farmers, large landowners, and speculators sought to expand westward. A second policy, impressment, by which the Royal Navy forced young colonial men into military service, also aroused anger across regions and classes. At the same time, the Great Awakening provided colonists with shared ideas about moral principles and new techniques for mass communication. Finally, Britain's efforts to repay its war debts by taxing colonists and its plan to continue quartering troops in North America led colonists to forge intercolonial protest movements.

Common Grievances

Like the Proclamation Line, which denied all colonists the right to settle beyond the Appalachian Mountains, the policy of impressment affected port city residents of all classes. Impressment had been employed by the British during the extended wars of the eighteenth century to procure seamen. While plucking poor men from ports throughout the British Empire, the Royal Navy faced growing resistance to this practice in the American colonies from merchants and common folk alike. Because many free black men worked in jobs tied to the sea, they, too, joined impressment protests.

Seamen and dockworkers had good reason to fight off impressment agents. Men in the Royal Navy faced low wages, bad food, harsh punishment, rampant disease, and high mortality. As the practice escalated with each new war, the efforts of British naval officers and impressment agents to capture new "recruits" met violent resistance, especially in the North American colonies where several hundred men might be impressed at one time. In such circumstances, whole communities joined in the battle.

In the aftermath of the French and Indian War, serious impressment riots erupted in Boston, New York City, and Newport, Rhode Island. Increasingly, poor colonial seamen and dockworkers—white and black—made common cause with the owners of merchant ships and mercantile houses who depended on their labor. Colonial officials—mayors, governors, and customs agents—were caught in the middle. Some upheld the Royal Navy's right of impressment; others tried to placate both naval officers and local residents; and still others resisted what they saw as an oppressive imposition on the rights of colonists. Both those who resisted British authority and those who sought a compromise had to gain the support of the lower and middling classes to succeed.

Employers and politicians who opposed impressment gained an important advantage if they could direct the anger of colonists away from themselves and toward British policies. The decision of British officials to continue quartering troops in the colonies gave local leaders another opportunity to join forces with ordinary colonists. Colonial towns and cities were required to quarter (that is, house and support) British troops even after the Peace of Paris was signed. Some were housed in individual homes, adding to the burdens of housewives who were forced to provide soldiers' food, laundry, and other necessities. While the troops were intended to protect the colonies, they also provided reinforcements for impressment agents and surveillance over other illegal activities like smuggling and domestic manufacturing. Thus a range of issues and policies began to bind colonists together through common grievances against the British Parliament.

Forging Ties across the Colonies

The ties forged between poorer and wealthier colonists over issues of westward expansion, impressment, and quartering grew stronger in the 1760s, but they tended to be localized in seaport cities or in specific areas of the frontier. Creating bonds across the colonies required considerably more effort in a period when communication and transportation beyond local areas were limited. Means had to be found to disseminate information and create a sense of common purpose if the colonists were going to persuade Parliament to take their complaints seriously. One important model for such intercolonial communication was the Great Awakening.

By the 1750s, the Great Awakening was marked more by dissension than by unity as new denominations continued to split off from traditional churches. For example, in the Sandy Creek region of North Carolina, radical Protestants formed the Separate Baptists, who proclaimed a message of absolute spiritual equality. From the late 1750s through the 1770s, Separate Baptists converted thousands of small farmers and farmwives, poor whites, and enslaved women and men and established churches throughout Virginia, Georgia, and the Carolinas.

Like Separate Baptists, Methodists, Dunkards, Moravians, and Quakers also offered southern residents religious experiences that highlighted spiritual equality. Some dissenting preachers invited slaves and free blacks to attend their services alongside white farm families and laborers. Slaveholders and other elite southerners considered such practices outrageous and a challenge to the political as well as the social order.

Most women and men who converted to Separate Baptism, Methodism, or other forms of radical Protestantism did not link their religious conversion directly to politics. But as more and more ordinary colonists and colonial leaders voiced their anger at offensive British policies, evangelical techniques used to rouse the masses to salvation became important for mobilizing colonists to protest. Still, colonial leaders, especially in areas with large enslaved populations, did not imagine Africans and African Americans as part of their audience.

Even though the Great Awakening had spent its religious passion in most parts of North America by the 1760s, the techniques of mass communication and critiques of opulence and corruption it initiated provided emotional and practical ways of forging ties among widely dispersed colonists. Many evangelical preachers had condemned the lavish lifestyles of colonial elites and the spiritual corruption of local officials. Now in the context of conflicts with Great Britain, colonial leaders used such rhetoric to paint Parliament and British officials as aristocrats with little faith and less compassion.

The public sermons and mass gatherings used during the Great Awakening to inspire loyalty to a greater moral cause could now be translated into forms applicable to political protest. The efforts of Great Britain to assert greater control over its North American colonies provided colonial dissidents an opportunity to test out these new ways to forge intercolonial ties.

Great Britain Seeks Greater Control

Until the French and Indian War, British officials and their colonial subjects coexisted in relative harmony. Economic growth led Britain to ignore much of the smuggling and domestic manufacturing that took place in the colonies, since such activities did not significantly disrupt Britain's mercantile policies (see "Imperial Policies Focus on Profits" in chapter 3). Similarly, although the king and Parliament held ultimate political sovereignty, or final authority, over the American colonies, it was easier to allow some local control over political decisions, given the communication challenges created by distance.

This pattern of **benign** (or "salutary") **neglect** led some American colonists to view themselves as more independent of British control than they really were. Many colonists came to see smuggling, domestic manufacturing, and local self-governance as rights rather than privileges. Thus when British officials decided to assert greater control, many colonists protested.

To King George III and to Parliament, asserting control over the colonies was both right and necessary. In 1763 King George appointed George Grenville to lead the British government. As Prime Minister and Chancellor of the Exchequer, Grenville faced an economic depression in England, rebellious farmers opposed to a new tax on domestic cider, and growing numbers of unemployed soldiers returning from the war. He believed that regaining political and economic control in the American colonies could help resolve these crises at home.

Eighteenth-century wars, especially the French and Indian War, cost a fortune. British subjects in England paid taxes to help offset the nation's debts, even though few of them benefited as directly from the British victory as did their counterparts in the American colonies. The colonies would cost the British treasury more if the crown could not control colonists' movement into Indian territories, limit smuggling and domestic manufacturing, and house British troops in the colonies cheaply.

To reassert control, Parliament launched a three-pronged program. First, it sought stricter enforcement of existing laws and reorganized the Board of Trade to centralize policies and ensure their implementation. The **Navigation Acts**, which prohibited smuggling, established guidelines for legal commerce, and set duties on trade items, were the most important laws to be enforced. Second, Parliament extended wartime policies into peacetime. For example, the Quartering Act of 1765 ensured that British troops would remain in the colonies to enforce imperial policies.

Colonial governments were expected to support them by allowing them to use vacant buildings or extra rooms in colonial homes and providing them with food and supplies.

The third part of Grenville's colonial program was the most important. It called for the passage of new laws to raise funds and reestablish the sovereignty of British rule. The first revenue act passed by Parliament was the American Duties Act of 1764, known as the **Sugar Act**. It imposed an **import duty**, or tax, on sugar, coffee, wines, and other luxury items. The act actually reduced the import tax on foreign molasses, which was regularly smuggled into the colonies from the West Indies, but insisted that the duty be collected. The crackdown on smuggling increased the power of customs officers and Britain established the first vice-admiralty courts in North America to ensure that the Sugar Act raised money for the crown. That same year, Parliament passed the Currency Act, which prohibited colonial assemblies from printing paper money or bills of credit. Taken together, these provisions meant that colonists would pay more money into the British treasury even as the supply of money (and illegal goods) diminished in North America.

Some colonial leaders protested the Sugar Act through speeches, pamphlets, and petitions, and Massachusetts established a **committee of correspondence** to circulate concerns to leaders in other colonies. However, dissent remained disorganized and ineffective. Nonetheless, the passage of the Sugar and Currency Acts caused anxiety among many colonists, which was heightened by passage of the Quartering Act the next year. Colonial responses to these developments marked the first steps in an escalating conflict between British officials and their colonial subjects.

REVIEW & RELATE

- Why did British policymakers believe they were justified in seeking to gain greater control over Britain's North American colonies?
- How did Britain's postwar policies help to expand and unify protests across the colonies?

Resistance to Britain Intensifies

Over the next decade, between 1764 and 1774, the British Parliament sought to extend its political and economic control over the American colonies, and colonists periodically resisted. With each instance of resistance, Parliament demanded further submission to royal authority. With each demand for submission, colonists responded with greater assertions of their rights and autonomy. Still, no one imagined that a revolution was in the making.

The Stamp Act Inspires Coordinated Resistance

Grenville decided next to impose a stamp tax on the colonies similar to that long used in England. The stamp tax required that a revenue stamp be affixed to all transactions involving paper items, from newspapers and contracts to playing cards and diplomas. Grenville announced his plans in 1764, a full year before Parliament enacted the **Stamp Act** in the spring of 1765. The tax was to be collected by colonists appointed for the purpose, and the money was to be spent at the direction of Parliament for "defending, protecting and securing the colonies." To the British government, the Stamp Act seemed completely fair. After all, Englishmen paid on average 26 shillings in tax annually, while Bostonians averaged just 1 shilling. Moreover, the act was purposely written to benefit the American colonies.

The colonists viewed it in a more threatening light. The Stamp Act differed from earlier parliamentary laws in three important ways. First, by the time of its passage, the colonies were experiencing rising unemployment, falling wages, and a downturn in trade. All of these developments were exacerbated by the Sugar, Currency, and Quartering Acts passed by Parliament the previous year. Second, critics viewed the Stamp Act as an attempt to control the *internal* affairs of the colonies. It was not an indirect tax on trade, paid by importers and exporters, but a direct tax on daily business. Third, such a direct intervention in the economic affairs of the colonies unleashed the concerns of both local officials and ordinary residents that Parliament was taxing colonists who had no representation in its debates and decisions.

By announcing the Stamp Act a year before its passage, Grenville allowed colonists plenty of time to organize their opposition. In New York City, Boston, and other cities, merchants, traders, artisans, and their wives and daughters formed groups dedicated to the repeal of the Stamp Act. Soon Sons of Liberty, Daughters of Liberty, Sons of Neptune, Vox Populi, and similar organizations emerged to challenge the imposition of the Stamp Act. Even before the act was implemented, angry mobs throughout the colonies attacked stamp distributors. Some were beaten, others tarred and feathered, and all were forced to take an oath never to sell British stamps.

Colonists lodged more formal protests with the British government as well. The Virginia House of Burgesses, led by Patrick Henry, acted first. It passed five resolutions, which it sent to Parliament, denouncing taxation without representation. The Virginia Resolves were reprinted in many colonial newspapers and repeated by orators to eager audiences in Massachusetts and elsewhere. At the same time, the Massachusetts House adopted a circular letter—a written protest circulated to the other colonial assemblies—calling for a congress to be held in New York City in October 1765 to consider the threat posed by the Stamp Act.

In the meantime, popular protests multiplied. The protests turned violent in Boston, where **Sons of Liberty** leaders like Samuel Adams, a Harvard graduate and town official, organized mass demonstrations. Adams modeled his oratory on that of itinerant preachers, but with a political twist. Other activists used more visual means of inspiring their audiences. At dawn on August 14, 1765, the Boston Sons of Liberty hung an effigy of stamp distributor Andrew Oliver on a tree and called for his resignation. A mock funeral procession, joined by farmers, artisans, apprentices, and the poor, marched to Boston Common. The crowd, led by shoemaker and French and Indian War veteran Ebenezer Mackintosh, carried the fake corpse to the Boston stamp office and destroyed the building. Demonstrators saved pieces of lumber, "stamped" them, and set them on fire outside Oliver's house. Oliver, wisely, had already left town.

Oliver's brother-in-law, Lieutenant Governor Thomas Hutchinson, arrived at the scene and tried to quiet the crowd, but he only angered them further. They soon destroyed Oliver's stable house, coach, and carriage, which the crowd saw as signs of aristocratic opulence.

The battle against the Stamp Act unfolded across the colonies with riots, beatings, and resignations reported from Newport, Rhode Island, to New Brunswick, New Jersey, to Charles Town (later Charleston), South Carolina. On November 1, 1765, when the Stamp Act officially took effect, not a single stamp agent remained in his post in the colonies.

Protesters carefully chose their targets: stamp agents, sheriffs, judges, and colonial officials. Even when violence erupted, it remained focused, with most crowds destroying stamps and stamp offices first and then turning to the private property of Stamp Act supporters. These protests made a mockery of notions of deference toward British rule. But they also revealed growing autonomy on the part of middling- and working-class colonists who attacked men of wealth and power, sometimes choosing artisans rather than wealthier men as their leaders. However, this was not primarily a class conflict because many wealthier colonists made common cause with artisans, small farmers, and the poor. Indeed, colonial elites considered themselves the leaders, inspiring popular uprisings through the power of their political arguments and oratorical skills. Still, they refused to support actions they considered too radical.

It was these more affluent protesters who dominated the Stamp Act Congress that met in New York City in October 1765. It brought together twenty-seven delegates from nine colonies. The delegates petitioned Parliament to repeal the Stamp Act, arguing that taxation without representation was tyranny. Delegates then urged colonists to boycott British goods and refuse to pay the stamp tax. Yet they also proclaimed their loyalty to king and country.

The question of representation became a mainstay of colonial protests. Whereas the British accepted the notion of "virtual representation," by which members of Parliament gave voice to the views of particular classes and interests, the North American colonies had developed a system of representation based on locality. According to colonial leaders, only members of Parliament elected by colonists could represent their interests.

Even as delegates at the Stamp Act Congress declared themselves loyal, if disaffected, British subjects, they participated in the process of developing a common identity in the American colonies. Christopher Gadsden of South Carolina expressed the feeling most directly. "We should stand upon the broad common ground of natural rights," he argued. "There should be no New England man, no New-Yorker, known on the continent, but all of us Americans."

Eventually the British Parliament was forced to respond to colonial protests and even more to rising complaints from English merchants and traders whose business had been damaged by colonists' boycott. Parliament repealed the Stamp Act in March 1766, and King George III granted his approval a month later. Victorious colonists looked forward to a new and better relationship between themselves and the British government.

From the colonists' perspective, the crisis triggered by the Stamp Act demonstrated the limits of parliamentary control. Colonists had organized effectively and forced Parliament to repeal the hated legislation. Protests had erupted across the colonies and attracted support from a wide range of colonists. Individual leaders, like Patrick Henry of Virginia and Samuel Adams of Massachusetts, became more widely known through their fiery oratory and their success in appealing to the masses. The Stamp Act agitation also demonstrated the growing influence of ordinary citizens who led parades and demonstrations and joined in attacks on stamp agents and the homes of British officials. The protests also revealed the growing power of the written word and printed images in disseminating ideas among colonists. Broadsides, political cartoons, handbills, newspapers, and pamphlets circulated widely, reinforcing discussions and proclamations at taverns, rallies, demonstrations, and more formal political assemblies.

For all the success of the Stamp Act protests, American colonists still could not imagine in 1765 that protest would ever lead to open revolt against British sovereignty. More well-to-do colonists were concerned that a revolution against British authority might fuel a dual revolution in which small farmers, tenants, servants, white and enslaved, laborers, and even women would rise up against their political and economic superiors in the colonies. Even most middling- and working-class protesters believed that the best solution to the colonies' problems was to gain greater economic and political rights within the British Empire, not to break from it.

The Townshend Act

The repeal of the Stamp Act in March 1766 led directly to Parliament's passage of the Declaratory Act. That act declared that Parliament had the authority to pass any law "to bind the colonies and peoples of North America" closer to Britain. No new tax or policy was established; Parliament simply wanted to proclaim Great Britain's political supremacy in the aftermath of the successful stamp tax protests.

Following this direct assertion of British sovereignty, relative harmony prevailed in the colonies for more than a year. Then in June 1767, Charles Townshend, the new chancellor of the Exchequer, rose to power in England. He persuaded Parliament to return to the model offered by the earlier Sugar Act. The **Townshend Act**, like the Sugar Act, instituted an import tax on a range of items sent to the colonies, including glass, lead, paint, paper, and tea.

Now, however, even an indirect tax led to immediate protests and calls for a boycott of taxed items. In February 1768, Samuel Adams wrote a circular letter reminding colonists of the importance of the boycott, and the Massachusetts Assembly disseminated it to other colonial assemblies. In response, Parliament posted two more British army regiments in Boston and New York City to enforce the law. Angry colonists did not retreat when confronted by this show of military force. Instead, a group of outspoken colonial leaders demanded that colonists refuse to import goods of any kind from Britain.

John Dickinson, a prominent Pennsylvania attorney and Quaker, had published a critique of the Stamp Act, which was sent to Britain as the first protest against Parliament's efforts to tax the colonists. In 1767 and 1768, he wrote a series of letters attacking the Townshend Act, presenting himself as an ordinary colonist by using the pen name "A Farmer." Dickinson argued that any duty on goods was a tax and insisted, "Those who are taxed without their own consent, given by themselves, or their representatives, are slaves. We are taxed without our own consent given by ourselves, or our representatives. We are therefore — I speak it with grief — I speak it with indignation — we are slaves." Only a boycott could demonstrate colonists' insistence on their rights as British subjects.

More than previous efforts to resist British authority, this boycott depended on the support of women, who were generally in charge of the day-to-day purchase of household items. Wives and mothers were expected to boycott a wide array of British goods, while single women and widows who supported themselves as shopkeepers were expected to refrain from selling British goods. Women were also called upon to provide substitutes for boycotted items. Thus, mothers and daughters produced homespun clothing, brewed herbal teas, and expanded their gardens.

Despite the hardships, many colonial women embraced the boycott. As twenty-two-year-old Charity Clarke wrote to a friend in England, "If you English folks won't give us the liberty we ask . . . I will try to gather a number of ladies armed with spinning wheels [along with men] who shall learn to weave & keep sheep, and will retire beyond the reach of arbitrary power." Other women also organized spinning bees in which dozens of participants produced yards of homespun cloth, the wearing of which symbolized female commitment to the cause.

Refusing to drink tea offered women another way to protest parliamentary taxation. In February 1770, more than "300 Mistresses of Families, in which number the Ladies of the Highest Rank and Influence," signed a petition in Boston and pledged to abstain from drinking tea. Dozens of women from less prosperous families signed their own boycott agreement.

The Boston Massacre

Boston women's refusal to drink tea and their participation in spinning bees were part of a highly publicized effort to make their city the center of opposition to the Townshend Act. Printed propaganda, broadsides, demonstrations, and rallies announced to the world that Bostonians rejected Parliament's right to impose its will, or at least its taxes, on the American colonies. Angry over Parliament's policies, Boston men also considered the soldiers, who moonlighted for extra pay, as economic competitors. Throughout the winter of 1769–1770, boys and young men reacted by harassing the growing number of British soldiers stationed in the city.

On the evening of March 5, 1770, young men began throwing snowballs at the lone soldier guarding the Boston Customs House. An angry crowd began milling about was joined by a group of sailors led by Crispus Attucks, an ex-slave of mixed African and Indian ancestry. The guard called for help, and Captain Thomas Preston arrived at the scene with seven British soldiers. He appealed to the "gentlemen" present to disperse the crowd. Instead, the harangues of the crowd continued, and snowballs, stones, and other projectiles flew in greater numbers. Then a gun fired, and soon more shooting erupted. Eleven men in the crowd were hit, and four were "killed on the Spot," including Attucks.

Despite confusion about who, if anyone, gave the order to fire, colonists expressed outrage at the shooting of men on the streets of Boston. Samuel Adams and other Sons of Liberty recognized the incredible potential for anti-British propaganda. Adams organized a mass funeral for those killed, and thousands watched the caskets being paraded through the city. Newspaper editors and broadsides printed by the Sons of Liberty labeled the shooting a "massacre." But when the accused soldiers were tried in Boston for the so-called **Boston Massacre**, the jury acquitted six of the eight of any crime. Still, ordinary colonists as well as colonial leaders were growing more convinced that British rule had become tyrannical and that such tyranny must be opposed.

To ensure that colonists throughout North America learned about the Boston Massacre, committees of correspondence formed once again to spread the news. These committees became important pipelines for sending information about plans and protests across the colonies. They also circulated an engraving by Bostonian Paul Revere that suggested the soldiers purposely shot at a peaceful crowd.

Parliament was already considering the repeal of the Townshend duties, and in the aftermath of the shootings, public pressure increased to do so. Merchants in England and North America insisted that parliamentary policies had resulted in economic losses on both sides of the Atlantic. In response, Parliament repealed all of the Townshend duties except the one on tea, which it retained to demonstrate its political authority to tax the colonies.

Continuing Conflicts at Home

As colonists in Boston and other seaport cities rallied to protest British taxation, other residents of the thirteen colonies continued to challenge authorities closer to home. In the same years as the Stamp Act and Townshend Act protests, tenants in New Jersey and the Hudson valley continued their campaign for economic justice. So, too, did a group called the **Regulators** in central North Carolina. Its leaders included Hermon Husband, a Separatist Baptist, who wrote pamphlets and helped organize the Sandy Creek Association in 1766 to assist poorer farmers and squatters in the region. Conflicts escalated when the North Carolina Assembly, dominated by the eastern slaveholding elite, approved a measure in 1768 to build a stately mansion for Governor Tryon with public funds. Outraged frontier farmers withheld their taxes, took over courthouses, and harassed corrupt local officials. While Governor Tryon claimed that Parliament abused its power in taxing the colonies, he did not recognize such abuses in his own colony. Instead, he increasingly viewed the Regulators as traitors. In spring 1771, he recruited a thousand militiamen to quell what he considered open rebellion on the Carolina frontier. The Regulators amassed two thousand farmers to defend themselves, although Husband, a pacifist, was not among them. But when twenty Regulators were killed and more than a hundred wounded at the Battle of Alamance Creek in May 1771, he surely knew many of the fallen. Six of the defeated Regulators were hanged a month later. Many local residents harbored deep resentments against colonial officials for what they viewed as the slaughter of honest, hardworking men.

Resentments against colonial leaders were not confined to North Carolina. An independent Regulator movement emerged in South Carolina in 1767. Far more effective than their North Carolina counterparts, South Carolina Regulators seized control of the western regions of the colony, took up arms, and established their own system of frontier justice. In 1769 the South Carolina Assembly negotiated a settlement with the Regulators, establishing new parishes in the colony's interior that ensured greater representation for frontier areas and extending colonial political institutions, such as courts and sheriffs, to the region.

Tea and Widening Resistance

For a brief period after the Boston Massacre, conflicts within the colonies generally overshadowed protests against British policies. During this period, the tea tax was collected, the increased funds ensured that British officials in the colonies were less dependent on local assemblies to carry out their duties, and general prosperity seemed to lessen the antagonism between colonists and royal authorities. In May 1773, however, all that changed. That month Parliament passed a new act that granted the revered but financially struggling East India Company a monopoly on shipping and selling tea in the colonies. Although this did not add any new tax or raise the price of tea, it did fuel a new round of protests.

Samuel Adams, Patrick Henry, Christopher Gadsden, and other radicals had continued to view the tea tax as an illegal imposition on colonists and refused to pay it as a matter of principle. They had established committees of correspondence to keep up the pressure for a colony-wide boycott, and Adams published and circulated "Rights of the Colonies," a pamphlet that listed a range of grievances against British policies. Their concerns became the basis for a new round of protests when Parliament, many of whose members invested in the East India Company, granted its monopoly. By eliminating colonial merchants from the profits to be made on tea and implementing a monopoly for a single favored company, Parliament pushed merchants into joining with radicals to demand redress.

Committees of correspondence quickly organized another colony-wide boycott. In some cities, like Charleston, South Carolina, tea was unloaded from East India Company ships but never sold. In others, like New York, the ships were turned back at the port. Only in Boston, however, did violence erupt as ships loaded with tea sat anchored in the harbor. On the night of December 16, 1773, the Sons of Liberty organized a "tea party." After a massive rally against British policy, a group of about fifty men disguised as Indians boarded the British ships and dumped forty-five tons of tea into the sea.

Although hundreds of spectators knew who had boarded the ship, witnesses refused to provide names or other information to British investigators. The Boston Tea Party was a direct challenge to British authority and resulted in large-scale destruction of valuable property.

Parliament responded immediately with a show of force. The **Coercive Acts**, passed in 1774, closed the port of Boston until residents paid for the tea, moved Massachusetts court cases against royal officials back to England, and revoked the colony's charter in order to strengthen the authority of royal officials and weaken that of the colonial assembly. The British government also approved a new Quartering Act, which forced Boston residents to accommodate more soldiers in their homes or build more barracks.

The royal government passed the Coercive Acts to punish Massachusetts and to discourage similar protests in other colonies. Instead, the legislation, which colonists called the **Intolerable Acts**, spurred a militant reaction. Committees of correspondence spread news of the fate of Boston and of Massachusetts. Colonial

Virtual Representation, 1775 This print shows an English lord threatening to shoot a colonist while a Parliament member declares, "I give you that man's money for my use." The American responds, "I will not be robbed." Meanwhile, Britannia heads into "The pit prepared for others"; Boston burns in the background; and a French monk prays with Quebec behind him. Such cartoons were widely used to arouse anti-British sentiments. Library of Congress, 3a053113

leaders, who increasingly identified themselves as patriots, soon formed committees of safety — armed groups of colonists who gathered weapons and munitions and vowed to protect themselves against British encroachments on their rights and institutions. Other colonies sent support, both political and material, to Massachusetts and instituted a wider boycott of British goods. In Edenton, North Carolina, a group of women published a proclamation stating their allegiance to the cause of liberty by refusing to serve or drink British tea. The statement received widespread attention in the American and British press, some laudatory and some satirical.

At the same time, a group of patriots meeting in Williamsburg, Virginia in the spring of 1774 called for colonies to send representatives to a **Continental Congress** to meet in Philadelphia the following September. Delegates planned to discuss how to recalibrate relations between the North American colonies and Great Britain.

By passing the Coercive Acts, Parliament had hoped to dampen long-smoldering conflicts with the colonies. Instead, they flared even brighter, with radical leaders committing themselves to the use of violence, moderate merchants and shopkeepers making common cause with radicals, and ordinary women and men embracing a boycott of all British goods.

The Continental Congress and Colonial Unity

When the Continental Congress convened in Philadelphia in September 1774, fifty-six delegates represented every colony but Georgia. Many of these men—and they were all men—had met before. Some had worked together in the Stamp Act Congress in 1765; others had joined forces in the intervening years on committees of correspondence or in petitions to Parliament. Still, the representatives disagreed on many issues. Some were radicals like Samuel Adams, Patrick Henry, and Christopher Gadsden. Others held moderate views, including George Washington and John Dickinson of Pennsylvania. And a few, like John Jay of New York, voiced more conservative positions.

Despite their differences, all the delegates agreed that the colonies must resist further parliamentary encroachments on their liberties. They talked not of independence but rather of reestablishing the freedoms that colonists had enjoyed in an earlier period. Washington voiced the sentiments of many. Although opposed to the idea of independence, he echoed John Locke by refusing to submit "to the loss of those valuable rights and privileges, which are essential to the happiness of every free State, and without which life, liberty, and property are rendered totally insecure."

To demonstrate their unified resistance to the Coercive Acts, delegates called on colonists to continue the boycott of British goods and to end all colonial exports to Great Britain. Committees were established in all of the colonies to coordinate and enforce these actions. Delegates also insisted that Americans were "entitled to a free and exclusive power of legislation in their several provincial legislatures." By 1774 a growing number of colonists supported these measures and the ideas on which they were based.

The delegates at the Continental Congress could not address all the colonists' grievances, and most had no interest in challenging race, class, or gender relations within the colonies themselves. Nonetheless, it was a significant event because the congress drew power away from individual colonies and local organizations and placed the emphasis instead on colony-wide plans and actions. To some extent, the delegates also shifted leadership of the protests away from militant artisans, like Ebenezer Mackintosh, and put planning back in the hands of men of wealth and standing, including radicals like Samuel Adams. Moreover, even as they denounced Parliament, many representatives felt a special loyalty to the king and sought his intervention to rectify relations between the mother country and the colonies.

REVIEW & RELATE	• How and why did colonial resistance to British policies escalate in the decade following the conclusion of the French and Indian War? • How did internal social and economic divisions shape the colonial response to British policies?

Conclusion: Liberty within Empire

From the Sugar Act in 1764 to the Continental Congress in 1774, colonists reacted strongly to parliamentary efforts to impose greater control over the colonies. Their protests grew increasingly effective as colonists developed organizations, systems of communication, and arguments to buttress their position. Residents of seacoast cities like Boston and New York City developed especially visible and effective challenges, in large part because they generally had the most to lose if Britain implemented new economic, military, and legislative policies.

In frontier areas, such as the Hudson valley, the southern backcountry, and the Great Lakes region, complaints against British tyranny vied with those against colonial land speculators and officials throughout the 1760s and 1770s. Still, few of the white agitators questioned the right of white colonists to claim Indian lands or enslave African labor. While frontier settlers railed against British and colonial officials who limited their access to land and failed to protect them from Indians, most would rather make common cause with wealthy critics of Great Britain than with neighboring native tribes.

One other tie bound the colonists together in 1774. No matter how radical the rhetoric, the aim continued to be resistance to particular policies and greater liberty within the British Empire, not independence from it. Moreover, despite some colonists' opposition to certain parliamentary acts, many others supported British policies. Indeed, the majority of colonists did not participate in protest activities. Most small farmers and backcountry settlers were far removed from urban centers of protest, while poor families in seaport cities who purchased few items to begin with had little interest in boycotts of British goods. Finally, some colonists hesitated to consider open revolt against British rule for fear of a revolution from below. The activities of land rioters, Regulators, evangelical preachers, female petitioners, African American converts to Christianity, and native communities on the frontier reminded well-established settlers that the colonies harbored their own tensions and conflicts.

The fates of Pontiac and George Washington suggest the uncertainties that plagued the British colonies and individuals residing there. It is not clear whether Indians in the Great Lakes region heard about colonists' rejection of the Stamp Act or their growing resistance to British policies. If Pontiac had, he may have supported the British. By 1766, Pontiac was accused of becoming arrogant, believing the power he gained with British authorities gave him greater importance among his own people. Former Ottawa supporters forced him to flee their village in 1768. He resettled further west and told British officials that he was no longer recognized as a chief. The following year, a Peoria warrior killed Pontiac to avenge Pontiac's earlier assault on his uncle. The Peoria band council had approved the assassination. However, Pontiac still loomed large among white settlers, and in the early nineteenth century, officials in Michigan and Illinois named cities in his honor.

Even before Pontiac's death, George Washington had shifted his focus from the frontier conflicts against the French to colonial resistance to British authority. In 1774, he attended the Continental Congress. He then took command of the volunteer militia companies in the colonies and chaired the committee on safety in his home county. Although still opposed to rebellion, he was nonetheless preparing for it. Washington likely agreed with the great British parliamentarian Edmund Burke who, on hearing of events in the American colonies, lamented, "Clouds, indeed, and darkness, rest upon the future." Despite Washington's early failures against French forces in Pennsylvania, he would lead colonists through the darkness and ensure his place in the history of a burgeoning nation.

Chapter 5 Review

KEY TERMS

Albany Congress, 112
Peace of Paris, 115
Proclamation Line of 1763, 118
benign neglect, 122
Navigation Acts, 122
Sugar Act, 123
import duty, 123
committee of correspondence, 123

Stamp Act, 124
Sons of Liberty, 124
Townshend Act, 126
Boston Massacre, 128
Regulators, 128
Coercive Acts (Intolerable Acts), 129
Continental Congress, 130

REVIEW & RELATE

1. How did the French and Indian War and the subsequent peace treaty affect relations among Britain, American Indian nations, and American colonies?
2. How did the French and Indian War and the increasing power of large landowners contribute to conflict between average colonists and colonial elites?
3. Why did British policymakers believe they were justified in seeking to gain greater control over Britain's North American colonies?
4. How did Britain's postwar policies help to expand and unify protests among colonists?
5. How and why did colonial resistance to British policies escalate in the decade following the conclusion of the French and Indian War?
6. How did internal social and economic divisions shape the colonial response to British policies?

TIMELINE OF EVENTS

1754–1763	• French and Indian War (Seven Year's War)
1754	• George Washington attacks Fort Duquesne
	• Albany Congress convenes
1757	• William Pitt takes charge of British war effort
1759–1761	• Anglo-Cherokee War

May 1763	• Pontiac launches pan-Indian revolt
June 1763	• Peace of Paris
October 1763	• Proclamation Line of 1763 established
December 1763	• Paxton Boys attack Conestoga Indians
1764	• Green Mountain Boys resist New York authorities
	• Sugar Act passed
1765	• Stamp Act passed
	• Stamp Act Congress convenes
1766	• Pontiac signs peace treaty with British
	• Stamp Act repealed and Declaratory Act passed
1767	• Townshend Act passed
1770	• Boston Massacre
1771	• Battle of Alamance Creek, North Carolina
1773	• Boston Tea Party
1774	• Coercive Acts passed
	• Continental Congress convenes

6

The American Revolution

1775–1783

COMPARING AMERICAN HISTORIES

One of the foremost pamphleteers of the patriot cause, **Thomas Paine** was born in 1737 in England, where his parents trained him as a corset maker. Eventually he left home and found work as a seaman, a teacher, and a tax collector. He drank heavily and beat both his wives. Yet he also taught working-class children to read and pushed the British government to improve the working conditions and pay of tax collectors. In 1772 Paine was fired from his government job, but a pamphlet he wrote had caught the eye of Benjamin Franklin, who persuaded him to try his luck in the colonies.

135

Arriving in Philadelphia in November 1774 at age thirty-seven, Paine secured a job on the *Pennsylvania Magazine*. The newcomer quickly gained in-depth political knowledge of the intensifying conflicts between the colonies and Great Britain. He also gained patrons for his political tracts among Philadelphia's economic and political elite. When armed conflict with British troops erupted in April 1775, colonial debates over whether to declare independence intensified. Pamphlets were a popular means of influencing these debates, and Paine wrote one entitled *Common Sense* to tip the balance in favor of independence.

Published in January 1776, *Common Sense* proved an instant success. It provided a rationale for independence and an emotional plea for creating a new democratic republic. Paine urged colonists to separate from England and establish a political structure that would ensure liberty and equality for all Americans. "A government of our own is our natural right," he concluded. " 'Tis time to part."

When *Common Sense* was published, an enslaved woman known as Bett was working for the Ashleys in Sheffield, Massachusetts. She was born to enslaved parents around 1742 in Claverack, New York, on the estate of Peiter Hogeboom. When Hogeboom's daughter Hannah married John Ashley, around 1750, the young Bett was given to them as a wedding present. Bett worked for the Ashleys for the next thirty years. Sometime in the late 1760s or early 1770s, the Ashleys allowed Bett to marry, and she gave birth to a daughter, Little Bett. By the 1770s, "Mum" Bett had gained skills as a nurse and midwife.

John Ashley, a wealthy lawyer and landowner, had fought in the French and Indian War. As conflicts between Britain and the colonies escalated, he joined the patriot cause. In January 1773, eleven patriots, including lawyer Theodore Sedgwick, met at his home. They drew up a series of resolutions known as the Sheffield Resolves that decried British tyranny and demanded individual rights. They were printed in the colonies and sent to Parliament. When war erupted in spring 1775, Colonel Ashley was too old to serve, but Bett's husband, whose name is unknown, joined the local militia. He was apparently killed in the war.

In 1780, Hannah Ashley tried to hit one of the enslaved workers, perhaps Little Bett, and Mum Bett intervened. She received a severe blow from a heated shovel and readily showed the scar as evidence of Ashley's brutal treatment. That same year, Mum Bett heard the newly ratified Massachusetts Constitution read aloud. It included the proposition that "All men are born free and equal, and have certain natural, essential, and unalienable rights." Soon after, Mum Bett contacted Theodore Sedgwick, whose antislavery sentiments were well-known, and asked his help in suing for her freedom. Her case and that of another Ashley slave named Brom led the county court to rule that "there can be no such thing as perpetual servitude of a rational creature." Mum Bett took the name **Elizabeth Freeman** and moved to the home of Theodore Sedgwick, where she was respected and paid for her work.

COMPARING THE AMERICAN HISTORIES of Thomas Paine and Elizabeth Freeman demonstrates how the American Revolution transformed individual lives as well as the life of the nation. Paine had failed financially and personally in England but gained fame in the colonies through his skills as a patriot pamphleteer. Freeman was born into slavery, taken from her parents, and forced to watch as her daughter was abused. Then the claims of patriots led to her freedom. While the American Revolution offered opportunities for both Paine and Freeman, most Americans had to choose sides long before it was clear whether the colonists could defeat Great Britain. Moreover, the lengthy war (1775–1783) took a toll on families and communities across the thirteen colonies. Moreover, even with English converts like Paine and homegrown supporters like Freeman, the patriots would need foreign allies to achieve victory. And battlefield victory could not ensure political stability in the new nation.

The Question of Independence

The Continental Congress that met to protest the Coercive Acts adjourned in October 1774, but delegates reconvened in May 1775. During the intervening months, patriot leaders honed their arguments for resisting British tyranny, and committees of correspondence circulated the latest news. While some patriots began advocating resistance in the strongest terms, the eruption of armed clashes between British soldiers and local farmers created the greatest push for independence. It also led the Continental Congress to establish the Continental Army in June 1775. A year later, in July 1776, the congress declared independence.

Armed Conflict Erupts

As debates over independence intensified, patriots along the Atlantic coast expanded their efforts. The Sons of Liberty and other patriot groups spread propaganda against the British, gathered and stored weapons, and organized and trained local militia companies. In addition to boycotting British goods, female patriots manufactured bandages and bullets. Some northern colonists freed enslaved African Americans who agreed to enlist in the militia. Others kept close watch on the movements of British troops.

On April 18, 1775, Boston patriots observed British movement in the harbor. British soldiers were headed to Lexington, intending to confiscate guns and ammunition hidden there and in neighboring Concord and perhaps arrest patriot leaders. To warn his fellow patriots, Paul Revere raced to Lexington on horseback but was stopped on the road to Concord by the British. By that time, however, a network of riders was spreading the alarm and alerted Concord residents of the impending danger.

Early in the morning of April 19, the first shots rang out on the village green of Lexington. After a brief exchange between British soldiers and local militiamen—known as minutemen for the speed with which they assembled—eight colonists lay dead. The British troops then marched on Concord, where they burned colonial supplies. By then, patriots in nearby towns had been alerted. Borrowing guerrilla tactics from native peoples, colonists hid behind trees, walls, and barns and battered the British soldiers as they marched back to Boston, killing 73 and wounding 200.

Word of the conflict traveled quickly. Outraged Bostonians attacked British troops and forced them to retreat to ships in the harbor. The victory was short-lived, however, and the British soon regained control of Boston. But colonial forces entrenched themselves on hills just north of the city. Then in May, Ethan Allen and his Green Mountain Boys joined militias from Connecticut and Massachusetts to capture the British garrison at Fort Ticonderoga, New York. The battle for North America had begun.

When the **Second Continental Congress** convened in Philadelphia on May 10, 1775, the most critical question for delegates like Pennsylvania patriot John Dickinson was how to ensure time for discussion and negotiation. Armed conflict had erupted, but should, or must, revolution follow? Other delegates, including Patrick Henry, insisted that independence was the only appropriate response to armed attacks on colonial residents.

The Battle of Bunker Hill On June 16, 1775, 2,500 British infantry sought to dislodge 1,500 patriot volunteers from Breeds Hill, 600 yards below Charlestown's strategic Bunker Hill. Although the British managed to root out the patriots during a third assault, more than a thousand British soldiers were wounded or killed. British General Thomas Gage lost his command, and the Royal Army no longer seemed invincible. akg-images

Just over a month later, on June 16, British forces under General Sir William Howe attacked patriot fortifications on Breed's Hill and Bunker Hill, north of Boston. The British won the **Battle of Bunker Hill** when patriots ran out of ammunition. But the redcoats — so called because of their bright red uniforms — suffered twice as many casualties as the patriots. The victory allowed the British to maintain control of Boston for nine more months, but the heavy losses emboldened patriot militiamen. Both armies were also fighting smallpox. Howe used the time in Boston to inoculate British troops against the disease, an effective but dangerous cure since some percentage of those inoculated were likely to die.

Building a Continental Army

The Battle of Bunker Hill convinced the Continental Congress to establish an army for the defense of the colonies. They appointed forty-three-year-old George Washington as commander in chief, and he headed to Massachusetts to take command of militia companies already engaged in battle. Since the congress had not yet proclaimed itself a national government, Washington depended largely on the willingness of local militias to accept his command and of individual colonies to supply soldiers, arms, and ammunition. Throughout the summer of 1775, Washington wrote numerous letters to patriot political leaders detailing the army's urgent need for men and supplies. He also sought to remove incompetent officers and improve order among the troops.

As he worked to forge a disciplined army, Washington and his officers developed a twofold military strategy. They sought to drive the British out of Boston and to secure the colonies from attack by British forces and their Indian allies in New York and Canada. In November 1775, American troops under General Richard Montgomery captured Montreal. However, the difficult trek in cold weather and the spread of smallpox decimated the patriot reinforcements led by General Benedict Arnold, and American troops failed to dislodge the British from Quebec.

Smallpox continued to threaten the patriot cause. The Continental Congress refused to let troops be inoculated, fearing the loss of too many men. Still, huge numbers were dying across the north, including Major General John Thomas, Commander of the Continental Army in Quebec. John Adams claimed, "The smallpox is ten times more terrible than Britons, Canadians and Indians, together." In fact, native people died at a higher rate than any other group. By mid-July 1776, an estimated three thousand men of the Northern Army were sick, most with smallpox. Eventually the epidemic eased, but it returned in different regions throughout the revolution.

Despite the disastrous outcome of the Canadian invasion, the Continental Army secured important victories in the winter of 1775–1776. On May 10, 1775, a small force of Green Mountain Boys from Vermont, led by Ethan Allen and Benedict Arnold, captured the small British garrison at Fort Ticonderoga. General Henry Knox later retrieved forty-three cannons captured at the fort to improve Washington's position outside Boston. In March 1776, with the cannons positioned on Dorchester Heights, Washington bombarded the British and drove them from Boston. Eventually the British retreated to Nova Scotia.

Reasons for Caution and for Action

When the British retreated from Boston, the war had already spread into Virginia. In spring 1775, local militias forced Lord Dunmore, Virginia's royal governor, to take refuge on British ships in Norfolk harbor. Dunmore encouraged white servants and enslaved blacks to join him there. Hundreds of black men fought with British troops when the governor led his army back into Virginia in November 1775. After the Battle of Great Bridge, Dunmore reclaimed the governor's mansion and issued an official proclamation that declared "all indent[ur]ed Servants, Negroes or others (appertaining to Rebels)" to be free if they were "able and willing to bear Arms" for the British.

Dunmore's Proclamation, offering freedom to enslaved men who fought for the crown, reinforced earlier challenges to social hierarchies. During the 1760s, Baptist preachers repudiated class and racial distinctions and, even in the South, invited poor whites and enslaved blacks to their services. By 1775, 15 percent of whites in Virginia and hundreds of African Americans had joined Baptist churches. In England itself, a group of radicals drew on anti-authoritarian ideas developed during the English Civil War (1642–1651) to criticize British rule over its expanding empire. Through pamphlets and newspapers, their ideas circulated widely in the colonies. In addition, Enlightenment thinkers generally emphasized individual talent over inherited privilege, a view reinforced by the success of a man like Thomas Paine.

Still, many delegates at the Continental Congress, which included large planters, successful merchants, and professional men, hesitated to act. They held out hope for a negotiated settlement that would increase the colonies' political liberty without disrupting social and economic hierarchies. However, the king and Parliament refused to compromise in any way with the rebellious colonies. Instead, in December 1775, the king prohibited any negotiation or trade with the colonies, increasing the leverage of radicals who argued independence was a necessity. The January 1776 publication of Thomas Paine's *Common Sense* bolstered their case. Paine wielded both biblical references and Enlightenment ideas in his best-selling pamphlet. It impressed patriot leaders as well as ordinary farmers and artisans, who debated his ideas at taverns and coffeehouses.

By the spring of 1776, a growing number of patriots believed that independence was necessary. Colonies began to take control of their legislatures and instruct their delegates to the Continental Congress to support independence. Meanwhile, the congress requested economic and military assistance from France. And in May, the congress advised colonies that had not yet done so to establish independent governments.

Still, many colonists opposed the idea of breaking free from Britain. Charles Inglis, the rector at Trinity Church in New York City, insisted that "limited monarchy is the form of government which is most favorable to liberty."

Declaring Independence

As colonists argued back and forth, Richard Henry Lee of Virginia introduced a motion to the Continental Congress in early June 1776 declaring that "these United Colonies are, and of right ought to be, Free and Independent States." A heated debate followed with Lee and John Adams arguing passionately for independence.

Eventually, even more cautious delegates, like Robert Livingston of New York, were convinced. Livingston concluded that "they should yield to the torrent if they hoped to direct it." He then joined Adams, Thomas Jefferson, Benjamin Franklin, and Roger Sherman on a committee to draft a formal statement justifying independence.

Thirty-three-year-old Jefferson took the lead in preparing the declaration, building on ideas expressed by Paine, Adams, and Lee. He also drew on language used in dozens of "declarations" written by town meetings, county officials, and colonial assemblies. The earliest, the 1773 Sheffield Resolves, proclaimed that "Mankind in a state of nature are equal, free, and independent of each other, and have a right to the undisturbed enjoyment of their lives, their liberty and property." These words are echoed in the most famous line of the Declaration of Independence: "We hold these truths to be self-evident, that all men are created equal, that they are endowed by their Creator with certain unalienable Rights, that among these are Life, Liberty and the pursuit of Happiness." Jefferson was also inspired by the Virginia Declaration of Rights drafted by George Mason in May 1776. This and several similar documents insisted on religious freedom, a right that many colonists viewed as evidence of their being uniquely blessed with liberty. Another central principle was the contract theory of government, proposed by the seventeenth-century British philosopher John Locke. Locke argued that sovereignty resided in the people, who submitted voluntarily to laws and authorities in exchange for protection of their life, liberty, and property. The people could reconstitute or overthrow a government that abused its powers. Jefferson summarized this argument and then listed the abuses and crimes perpetrated by King George III against the colonies, which justified the patriots' decision to break their contract with British authorities.

Once prepared, the **Declaration of Independence** was debated and revised. In the final version, all references to slavery were removed. But delegates agreed to list among the abuses suffered by the colonies the fact that the king "excited domestic insurrections amongst us," referring to the threat posed by Dunmore's Proclamation. On July 2, 1776, delegates from twelve colonies approved the Declaration, with only New York abstaining. Independence was publicly proclaimed on July 4 when the Declaration was published as a broadside to be circulated throughout the colonies.

REVIEW & RELATE	• What challenges did Washington face after accepting command of the Continental Army? • How and why did proponents of independence prevail in the debates that led to the Declaration of Independence?

Choosing Sides

Perhaps half of American colonists actively supported the patriots, and a fifth actively supported the British. The rest tried to stay neutral or were largely indifferent unless the war came to their doorstep. Both patriots and loyalists included men and women from all classes and regions. African Americans and Indians also provided critical support to both sides, hoping to improve their status in the revolution's aftermath.

Recruiting Supporters

Men who took up arms against the British before independence was declared and the women who supported them clearly demonstrated their commitment to the patriot cause. In some colonies, patriots organized local committees, courts, and assemblies to assume governance should British officials lose their authority. White servants and enslaved blacks in Virginia who fled to British ships or marched with Lord Dunmore made their loyalties known as well. Some native tribes, too, declared their allegiance early in the conflict. In May 1775, Colonel Guy Johnson, the new British superintendent for Indian affairs, sought refuge in Canada. He was accompanied by 120 British loyalists and 90 Mohawk warriors led by their mission-educated chief, Joseph Brant (Thayendanegea), and his sister Mary (Konwatsi'tsiaienni), a Mohawk diplomat.

The Continental Congress recognized the importance of native allies to the outcome of any colonial war. It appointed commissioners from the "United Colonies" to meet with representatives of the Iroquois Confederacy in August 1775. While Brant's Mohawk warriors were already committed to the British, some Oneida Indians, influenced by missionaries and patriot sympathizers, wanted to support the colonies. Others, however, urged neutrality, at least for the moment.

Once independence was declared, there was far more pressure to choose sides. The stance of political and military leaders and soldiers was clear. But to win against Great Britain required the support of a large portion of the civilian population as well. As battle lines shifted back and forth across New England, the Middle Atlantic region, and the South, civilians caught up in the fighting were faced with difficult decisions.

Many colonists who remained loyal to the king found safe haven in cities like New York, Newport, and Charleston, which remained under British control throughout much of the war. **Loyalist** men were welcomed by the British army. Still, colonists who made their loyalist sympathies clear risked a good deal. When British troops were forced out of cities or towns they had temporarily occupied, loyalist women and men faced harsh reprisals. Patriots had no qualms about invading the homes and businesses of loyalists and destroying or confiscating property.

Many loyalists were members of the economic and political elite. Others came from ordinary backgrounds. Many tenants, small farmers, and enslaved workers joined the loyalist cause in defiance of landlords, speculators, and wealthy planters. Many poorer loyalists lived in the Hudson valley, their sympathy for the British heightened by the patriot commitments of the powerful men who controlled the region. When the fighting moved into the Carolinas, members of a group called the Regulators—poor frontier farmers who challenged the domination of patriot leaders among the eastern elite—also supported the British.

Perhaps most important, the majority of Indian nations ultimately sided with the British. The Mohawk, Seneca, and Cayuga nations in the North and the Cherokee and Creek nations in the South were among Great Britain's leading allies. Although British efforts to limit colonial migration, such as the Proclamation Line of 1763, had failed, most native leaders still believed that a British victory offered the only hope of ending further encroachments on their territory.

Choosing Neutrality

Early in the war, many tribes followed the Iroquois in proclaiming their neutrality. This included the Delaware and Shawnee in the Ohio River valley and the Oneida in Connecticut. The Oneida's chief warriors declared that the English and patriots were "*two brothers of one blood. We are unwilling to join on either side in such a contest.*" But patriots often refused to accept Indian neutrality. Indeed, colonial troops killed the Shawnee chief Cornstalk under a flag of truce in 1777, leading that nation to ally, finally, with the British.

Colonists who sought to remain neutral during the war also faced hostility. Some 80,000 Quakers, Mennonites, Amish, Shakers, and Moravians considered war immoral and embraced neutrality. These men refused to bear arms, hire substitutes, or pay taxes to new state governments. The largest number of religious pacifists lived in Pennsylvania. Despite Quakerism's deep roots there, pacifists were treated as suspect by both patriots and loyalists.

In June 1778, Pennsylvania authorities jailed nine Mennonite farmers who refused to take an oath of allegiance to the revolutionary government. Their worldly goods were sold by the state, leaving their wives and children destitute. Quakers were routinely fined and imprisoned for refusing to support the patriot cause and harassed by British authorities in the areas they controlled. At the same time, Quaker meetings regularly disciplined members who offered aid to either side. Philadelphia Quakers disowned Betsy Ross after she married a non-Quaker who fought with the patriots and then sewed flags herself for the Continental Army and Navy.

Committing to Independence

After July 4, 1776, the decision to support independence took on new meaning. If the United States failed to win the war, all those who actively supported the cause could be considered traitors. The families of Continental soldiers faced especially difficult decisions as the conflict spread and soldiers moved farther and farther from home. Men too old or too young to fight proved their patriotism by gathering arms and ammunition and patrolling local communities.

Some female patriots accompanied their husbands, fiancés, or brothers as camp followers, cooking, washing clothes, nursing, and providing other services for soldiers. Most patriot women remained at home, however, and demonstrated their commitment by raising funds, gathering information, and, perhaps most importantly, sending clothes, bedding, and medicine to soldiers at the front. The Continental Army was desperately short of supplies from the beginning of the war. Northern women were urged to increase cloth production, while southern women were asked to harvest crops for hungry troops. The response was overwhelming. Women in Hartford, Connecticut produced 1,000 coats and vests and 1,600 shirts in 1776 alone. Across the colonies, women collected clothing door-to-door and opened their homes to sick and wounded soldiers.

Some African American women also became ardent patriots. Phillis Wheatley of Boston, whose owners taught her to read and write, published a collection of poems in 1776 and sent a copy to General Washington. She urged readers to recognize Africans as children of God. Rewarded with freedom by her master, Wheatley was

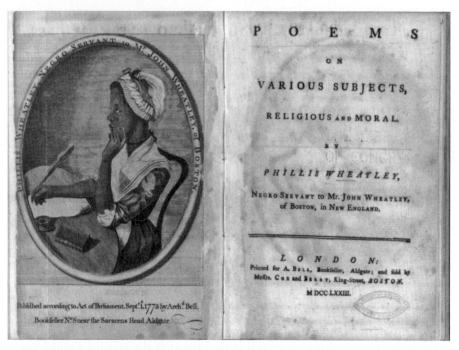

Phillis Wheatley This portrait of Phillis Wheatley appears facing the title page of her book of poems, printed in London in 1773. It was painted by another Boston slave, Scipio Moorhead. Phillis Wheatley converted to Christianity and sided with the patriots in the Revolution. She won her freedom but never gained sufficient support to publish another book of poems. Library of Congress, Prints and Photographs Division [LC-USZ62-56850]

among a small number of blacks who actively supported the patriot cause. Still, the vast majority of blacks were enslaved. While some escaped and joined the British in hopes of gaining their freedom, most were not free to choose sides.

REVIEW & RELATE	• How did colonists choose sides during the Revolutionary War? What factors influenced their decisions? • Why would some Indian tribes try to stay neutral during the conflict? Why did most of those who chose sides support the British?

Fighting for Independence, 1776–1777

After July 4, 1776, battles between British and colonial troops intensified, but it was not until December that the patriots celebrated a major military victory. The rebellion faced a formidable set of challenges. Over the course of the eighteenth century, Great Britain had developed the world's most powerful military force, including a huge navy. Moreover, once independence was declared, the colonists lost their main trading partner and had to find ways to sustain their economy while funding a war. To succeed, the patriots needed support from men and women on the home front as well as the battlefront and assistance from Europeans experienced in fighting the British. It took two years for the patriots and the Continental Army to gain traction against British forces.

British Troops Gain Early Victories

In the summer of 1776, when General Washington tried to lead his army out of Boston to confront British troops set to invade New York City, many soldiers deserted and returned home. They believed that New York men should defend New York. Among the soldiers who remained with Washington, many were landless laborers whose wives and sisters followed the troops as their only means of support. Although Washington tried to rid the army of these camp followers, a few hundred women continued to travel with the troops, providing critical services to ordinary soldiers. Ultimately, Washington arrived in New York with 19,000 men, many of whom were poorly armed and poorly trained, and some of whom were coerced into service by local committees of safety. Camp followers nursed, washed, and cooked for these men.

Throughout the summer, British ships sailed into New York harbor or anchored off the coast of Long Island. General Howe, hoping to overwhelm the colonists, ordered 10,000 troops to march into the city in the weeks immediately after the Declaration of Independence was signed. Still, the Continental Congress rejected Howe's offer of peace and a royal pardon.

So Howe prepared to take control of New York City by force and then march up the Hudson valley, isolating New York and New England from the rest of the rebellious colonies. He was aided by some 8,000 Hessian mercenaries (Germans being paid to fight for the British). On August 27, 1776, British forces clashed with a far smaller contingent of Continentals on Long Island. More than 1,500 patriots were killed, wounded, or taken prisoner in the fierce fighting.

In September, British troops occupied Manhattan. A raging fire, thought but never proved to be arson, destroyed or damaged nearly a quarter of Manhattan's 4,000 buildings, briefly halting their advance. Meanwhile, Washington and his men continued to retreat.

By November, the British had captured Fort Lee in New Jersey and attacked the Continental Army at Fort Washington, north of New York City. Washington then led his weary troops and camp followers into Pennsylvania, while the Continental Congress, fearing a British attack on Philadelphia, fled to Baltimore.

Although General Howe might have ended the patriot threat right then by an aggressive campaign, he wanted to wear down the Continental Army and force the colonies to sue for peace. Washington did not have the troops or arms to launch a major assault, and he hoped that the British would accept American independence once they saw the enormous effort it would take to defeat the colonies. So the war continued.

Patriots Prevail in New Jersey

The Continental Army did not gain a single military victory between July and December 1776. Fortunately for Washington, Howe followed the European tradition of waiting out the winter months and returning to combat after the spring thaw.

This gave the patriots the opportunity to regroup, repair weapons and wagons, and recruit soldiers. Yet Washington was reluctant to face the cold and discomfort of winter with troops discouraged by repeated defeats and retreats.

Camped in eastern Pennsylvania, Washington learned that Hessian troops had been sent to occupy the city of Trenton, New Jersey, just across the Delaware River. On Christmas Eve, Washington attacked Trenton in an icy rain, and the Continentals quickly routed the surprised Hessians. They then marched on Princeton and defeated regular British troops on January 3, 1777. The British army soon retreated from New Jersey, settling back into New York City, and the Continental Congress returned to Philadelphia. By mid-January 1777, it seemed clear to both sides that the conflict would be harder, more costly, and more deadly than anyone had imagined.

Then smallpox once again spread through the Continental Army. When quarantining troops proved insufficient, Washington insisted on inoculating his men. He did so with speed and secrecy while the winter provided a break from fighting. Fortunately, only one percent of his troops died as a result of inoculation.

A Critical Year of Warfare

The British army emerged from winter camp in spring 1777. Its regular army units, American loyalists, Indian allies, Hessians, and naval men-of-war were concentrated largely in New York City and Canada. The Continental forces, numbering fewer than 5,000 men, were then entrenched near Morristown, New Jersey, and Washington feared that an aggressive British assault might succeed.

Meanwhile, the Continental Congress in Philadelphia feared that the British would seek to capture the city and split the United States in two. General Howe did indeed plan on capturing Philadelphia, hoping to force a patriot surrender. Although Washington's force was too small to defeat Howe's army, it delayed his advance by guerrilla attacks and skirmishes. En route, Howe learned that he was expected to reinforce General John Burgoyne's soldiers, who were advancing south from Canada. Instead he continued to Philadelphia and captured it in September 1777 after Burgoyne and his 7,200 troops had regained control of Fort Ticonderoga in July. Burgoyne continued south, but by late July his forces had to stop until supplies from Canada and reinforcements from Howe and General Barry St. Leger reached them.

St. Leger was marching his British troops east through New York State, and Joseph Brant and his sister Molly Brant were gathering a force of Mohawk, Seneca, and Cayuga warriors to support them. But on August 6, they suffered a stunning defeat. In the **Battle of Oriskany** in New York, a band of German American farmers led by General Nicholas Herkimer held off the British advance, allowing Continental General Arnold to reach nearby Fort Stanwix with reinforcements. On August 23, the British troops and their native allies retreated to Canada (Map 6.1).

When General Howe's reinforcements also did not materialize, Burgoyne faced a brutal onslaught in northern New York. In September patriot forces defeated the British at Freeman's Farm, with the British suffering twice the casualties of the Continentals. Fighting intensified in early October, when Burgoyne lost a second battle at Freeman's Farm. Ten days later, he surrendered his remaining army of 5,800 men to General Gates at nearby Saratoga, New York.

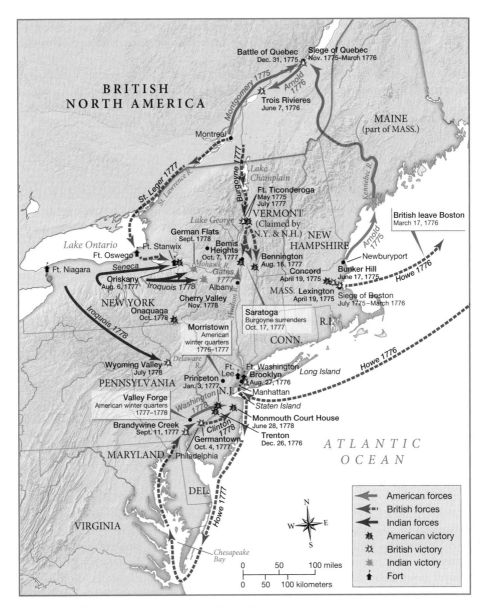

MAP 6.1　The War in the North, 1775–1778
After early battles in Massachusetts, patriots invaded Canada but failed to capture Quebec. The British captured New York City in 1776 and Philadelphia in 1777. New Jersey remained a battle zone. As British forces headed into New York State, they were joined by Iroquois. Although patriots defeated the combined force at Saratoga, battles continued throughout central New York and Pennsylvania.

The Continental Army's victory in the **Battle of Saratoga** stunned the British. It undercut the significance of Howe's victory at Philadelphia and indicated the general's misunderstanding of the nature of the war he was fighting. Meanwhile, the patriot victory energized Washington and his troops as they dug in at Valley Forge for another long winter. It also gave Benjamin Franklin, the Continental Congress envoy to Paris, greater leverage for convincing French officials to support American independence.

Patriots Gain Critical Assistance

Despite significant Continental victories in the fall of 1777, the following winter proved especially difficult. The quarters at **Valley Forge** were again marked by bitter cold, poor food, inadequate clothing, and scarce supplies. A French volunteer arrived to see "a few militia men, poorly clad, and for the most part without shoes; many of them badly armed." Many recent recruits were also poorly trained. Critical assistance arrived with Baron Friedrich von Steuben, a Prussian officer recruited by Benjamin Franklin, who took charge of drilling soldiers. Other officers experienced in European warfare also joined the patriot cause that winter: the Marquis de Lafayette of France, Johann Baron de Kalb of Bavaria, and Thaddeus Kosciusko and Casimir Count Pulaski, both of Poland. The Continental Army continued to be plagued by problems of recruitment, discipline, wages, and supplies. But the contributions of foreign volunteers, along with the leadership of Washington and his officers, sustained the military effort.

Patriots on the home front were also plagued by problems in 1777–1778. Families living in battlefield areas were especially vulnerable to the shifting fortunes of war. When British troops captured Philadelphia in fall 1777, a British officer commandeered the home of Elizabeth Drinker, a Quaker matron. An angry Drinker reported that the officer moved in with "3 Horses 2 Cows 2 Sheep and 3 Turkeys." Women who lived far from the conflict were isolated from such intrusions but were forced to fend for themselves with husbands at the front. Meanwhile, wives of patriot leaders, anxious to end the conflict, formed voluntary societies, like the Ladies Association of Philadelphia led by Esther De Berdt Reed, to provide critical resources for the army.

While most women worked tirelessly on the home front, some continued to cast their fate with the army. Camp followers provided critical services to the military throughout the revolution and suffered, as the troops did, from scarce supplies and harsh weather. Some women also served as spies and couriers for British or Continental forces. Lydia Darragh, a wealthy Philadelphian, eavesdropped on conversations among the British officers who occupied her home and carried detailed reports to Washington hidden in the folds of her dress. Deborah Champion, the daughter of a high-ranking officer in the Continental Army, traveled from Connecticut to Boston to deliver secret messages from her father to George Washington. Accompanied by Aristarchus, an enslaved household laborer, Champion was stopped by British soldiers on several occasions but her mission was never discovered. Others, like Nancy Hart Morgan of Georgia, took more direct action. She lulled half a dozen British soldiers into a sense of security at dinner, hid their guns, and shot two before neighbors came to hang the rest.

Some patriot women took up arms on the battlefield. Margaret Corbin accompanied her husband to the front lines. When her husband was killed at Fort Washington in November 1776, Corbin took his place loading and firing cannons. In addition, a small number of women disguised themselves as men and enlisted as soldiers. Deborah Sampson, an indentured servant in Massachusetts, knew male servants who were recruited into the Continental Army. Late in the war, she disguised herself as a man and enlisted as Robert Shurtliff in a Massachusetts regiment. Sampson served for more than a year, benefitting from lax standards of hygiene and her muscular frame. When a doctor discovered that "Robert" was a woman, Sampson was honorably discharged.

Surviving on the Home Front

Whether black or white, enslaved or free, women and children faced hardship, uncertainty, loneliness, and fear as a result of the war. Even those who did not directly engage enemy troops took on enormous burdens during the conflict. Farm wives plowed and planted and carried on their domestic duties as well. In cities, women worked ceaselessly to find sufficient food, wood, candles, and cloth to maintain themselves and their children.

As the war intensified, Continental and British forces slaughtered cattle and hogs for food, stole corn and other crops or burned them to keep the enemy from obtaining supplies, looted houses and shops, and kidnapped or liberated enslaved laborers and free servants. Some home invasions turned savage. Both patriot and loyalist papers in New York, Philadelphia, and Charleston reported cases of rape.

In these desperate circumstances, many women asserted themselves in order to survive. When merchants hoarded goods in order to make greater profits from rising prices, housewives raided stores and warehouses and took the supplies they needed. Others learned as much as they could about family finances and submitted claims to local officials when their houses, farms, or businesses were damaged or looted. Growing numbers of women banded together to assist one another, help more impoverished families, and supply troops with badly needed clothes, food, bandages, and bullets.

REVIEW & RELATE	• How did the patriot forces fare in 1776? How and why did the tide of war turn in 1777? • What role did colonial women and foreign men play in the conflict in the early years of the war?

Governing in Revolutionary Times

Amid the constant upheavals of war, patriot leaders established new governments. At the national level, responsibilities ranged from coordinating and funding military operations to developing diplomatic relations with foreign countries and Indian nations. At the state level, constitutions had to be drafted and approved, laws enforced, and military needs assessed and met. Whether state or national, new governments had to assure their followers that they were not simply replacing old forms of oppression with new ones. Yet few states moved to eliminate the most oppressive institution in the nation, slavery.

Colonies Become States

For most of the war, the Continental Congress acted in lieu of a national government while the delegates worked to devise a more permanent structure. The congress depended mainly on states for funds and manpower. In 1777, delegates drafted the **Articles of Confederation**, creating a central government with limited powers. They submitted the Articles to the states for approval, and eight of the thirteen states had ratified the plan by mid-1778. Still, nearly three more years passed before the last state, Maryland, approved the Articles.

Without a formal central government, state governments played crucial roles throughout the war. Even before the Continental Congress declared American independence, some colonies had forced royal officials to flee and established new state governments. Some states abided by the regulations in their colonial charters or by English common law. Others created new governments based on a written constitution.

These constitutions reflected the opposition to centralized power fueled by the struggle against British tyranny. In Pennsylvania, patriots developed one of the most democratic constitutions. The governor was replaced by an executive council. The legislature consisted of a single house elected by popular vote. Legislators could only serve for four in any seven years to discourage the formation of a political aristocracy. Although Pennsylvania's constitution was among the most radical, all states limited centralized power in some way.

Most states adopted Virginia's model and included in their constitutions a bill of rights that ensured citizens freedom of the press, freedom of elections, speedy trials by one's peers, humane punishments, and the right to form militias. Some states also insisted on people's freedom of speech and assembly, the right to petition and to bear arms, and equal protection of the laws. The New Jersey constitution of 1776 enfranchised all free inhabitants who met the property qualifications, thereby allowing some single and widowed women and free blacks to vote. However, most new state constitutions allowed only white men with property to vote, and nearly all granted significant power to the legislative branch, where white men of property dominated.

Patriots Divide over Slavery

Although state constitutions were revolutionary in many respects, few of them addressed the issue of slavery. Only Vermont abolished slavery in its 1777 constitution. Legislators in Pennsylvania approved a gradual abolition law by which slaves born after 1780 could claim their freedom at age twenty-eight. In Massachusetts, Mum Bett and Brom successfully sued for their freedom in county court in 1781. Another enslaved laborer sued for his freedom shortly afterward. Quock Walker was promised his freedom at age 21. However, his master died and his widow's second husband, Nathaniel Jennison, refused to release Walker, who fled to a nearby farm. Jennison retrieved Walker and beat him severely. After a series of court cases, the Massachusetts Supreme Court, citing Bett and Brom's case, ruled in 1783 that slavery conflicted with the state constitution. Although the state legislature never abolished slavery in Massachusetts, the institution had died out in the state by 1790.

In southern states like Virginia, the Carolinas, and Georgia, life for enslaved people grew increasingly harsh during the war. Because British forces promised freedom to blacks who fought with them, slave owners and patriot armies in the South did everything possible to ensure that African Americans did not make it behind British lines. When the British retreated, some generals, like Lord Dunmore and Sir Henry Clinton, took black volunteers with them. But thousands more were left behind to fend for themselves.

Nonetheless, the American Revolution dealt a blow to human bondage. For many blacks, Revolutionary ideals required the end of slavery. Northern free black communities grew rapidly during the war, especially in seaport cities. In the South, too, thousands of the formerly enslaved gained freedom, either by joining the British army or by fleeing in the midst of battlefield chaos. As many as one-quarter of South Carolina's enslaved women and men had emancipated themselves by the end of the Revolution. Yet as the Continental Congress worked toward developing a framework for a national government, few delegates considered abolishing slavery immediately throughout the country. Instead, some hoped to limit enslavement and slave trading in ways that would lead to its ultimate demise.

France Allies with the Patriots

In the midst of war, the Continental Congress considered an alliance with France far more critical to success than abolishing slavery. France's long rivalry with Britain made it a likely ally, and the French government had secretly provided funds to the patriots early in the war. In December 1776, the Continental Congress sent Benjamin Franklin to Paris to serve as its unofficial liaison. Franklin was enormously successful, securing supplies and becoming a favorite among the French aristocracy and ordinary citizens alike. Individual French officers, such as Marquis de Lafayette, arrived in North America, helped train Continental troops, and led them into battle.

The French were initially unwilling to forge a formal compact with the upstart patriots. Only after their victory at Saratoga in October 1777 did King Louis XVI agree to an alliance. The following February, the French approved trading rights between the United States and all French possessions. France then recognized the United States as an independent nation, relinquished French territorial claims on mainland North America, and sent troops to reinforce the Continental Army. In return, the United States promised to defend French holdings in the Caribbean. A year later, Spain allied itself with France to protect its own North American holdings.

British leaders responded by declaring war on France. Yet doing so ensured that military conflicts would spread well beyond North America and military expenditures would skyrocket. French forces attacked British outposts in Gibraltar, the Bay of Bengal, Senegal in West Africa, and Grenada in the West Indies. At the same time, the French supplied the United States with military officers, weapons, funds, and critical naval support.

Faced with this new alliance, Britain's prime minister, Lord North (1771–1782), decided to concentrate British forces in New York City. This tactic forced the British army to abandon Philadelphia in summer 1778. For the remainder of the war, New York City provided the sole British stronghold in the North, serving as a supply center and prisoner-of-war camp.

Raising Armies and Funds

The French alliance did create one unintended problem for the Continental Army. When Americans heard that France was sending troops, fewer men volunteered for military service. Local officials had the authority to draft men into the army or to accept substitutes for draftees. In the late 1770s, some draftees forced enslaved men to take their place; others hired landless laborers, the handicapped, or the mentally unfit as substitutes.

As the war spread south and west in 1778–1779, Continental forces were stretched thin, and enlistments faltered further. Soldiers faced injury, disease, and shortages of food and ammunition. They also risked capture by the British, one of the worst fates to befall a Continental. Considered traitors by the British, most captives were held on ships in New York harbor. They faced filthy accommodations, a horrid stench, inadequate water, and widespread disease and abuse. Altogether, between 8,000 and 11,000 patriots died in British prisons in New York—more than died in battle.

Even if the British had allowed the Continental Congress to aid prisoners, it could do little, given the financial problems it faced. With no authority to impose taxes on American citizens, the congress had to borrow money from wealthy patriots, accept loans from France and the Netherlands, and print money of its own—some $200 million by 1780. However, money printed by the states was used far more widely than were Continental dollars. "Continentals" depreciated so quickly that by late 1780 it took one hundred continentals to buy one silver dollar's worth of goods. In 1779, with the cost of goods skyrocketing, housewives, sailors, and artisans in Philadelphia and other cities attacked merchants who were hoarding goods, forcing officials to distribute food to the poor.

The congress finally improved its financial standing slightly by using a $6 million loan from France to back certificates issued to wealthy patriots. Meanwhile states raised money through taxes to provide funds for government operations, backing for its paper money, and other expenses. Most residents found such taxes particularly burdensome given wartime inflation, and even the most patriotic began to protest their inevitable increase. Thus the financial status of the new nation remained precarious.

Indians and Patriots Battle for Land

Although the congress sought alliances with additional Indian nations, colonists' desire to control native lands counteracted such efforts. Most Indian nations had long-standing complaints against colonists who intruded on their lands, and many patriot leaders made it clear that victory would mean further expansion into Indian territories. Indeed some native peoples viewed the patriots' war more as an imperial conquest than a political revolution. In addition, both the British and patriots recruited increasingly diverse fighting forces as the war continued.

In the late 1770s, British forces and their Indian allies fought bitter battles against patriot militias and Continental forces all along the New York and Pennsylvania frontier. The August 1777 battle of Oriskany, which led to the surrender of British General Burgoyne to Continental forces in October, revealed the increasingly multiethnic and multiracial character of the war. German American farmers fought for the patriots alongside Oneida Indians and Anglo-American soldiers against

British soldiers aided by Hessian (that is, German) mercenaries and Mohawk Indians. With members of the Iroquois Confederacy — Oneida and Mohawk — fighting against each other, the confederacy itself became a victim of the revolution.

For nearly three years, patriots and their Indian allies battled British and tribal forces throughout the Mohawk River valley. The British side destroyed patriot settlements, ruined crops, killed civilians, and took women and children captive. Patriots retaliated against the village of Mohawk chief Joseph Brant, killing men, women, and children. In turn, Brant called on his warriors "to defend their Lands and Liberty against the Rebels," who sought to become "sole Masters of this Continent." When Mohawk warriors attacked the village of Cherry Valley, they killed twice as many civilians as soldiers. In May 1779, as retaliatory attacks continued throughout the region, Washington ordered General John Sullivan to undertake the "total destruction and devastation" of Iroquois villages. Mary Jemison, an Irish immigrant captured by Indians in 1755, recalled, "they destroyed every article of the food kind that they could lay their hands on. A part of our corn they burnt, and threw the remainder into the river. They burnt our houses, killed what few cattle and horses they could find, destroyed our fruit trees, and left nothing but the bare soil and timber." The assaults eventually forced thousands of Indians, sick and starving, to flee to British-controlled Fort Niagara.

Patriots and native tribes also battled along the Pennsylvania frontier, where militia leaders' refusal to differentiate between allies and enemies escalated conflicts. Delaware and Shawnee chiefs had pledged support to the patriots, but in fall 1778, patriot forces killed two Shawnee chiefs. Despite apologies from the Continental Congress, another Delaware chief died two months later, also likely killed by militia. Indians allied with patriots viewed such acts as a war of extermination and some changed sides.

By March 1782, the escalating violence bled into the Ohio River valley when one hundred sixty Pennsylvania militiamen attacked a Moravian Mission at Gnadenhutten. Claiming they were seeking revenge for attacks on their frontier settlements, the patriots killed and scalped ninety-six Delaware Indians as they kneeled in prayer. The patriots then piled the victims' bodies in mission buildings before burning the entire community to the ground. Both the Moravians and their Indian converts were pacifists, but they had aided the patriots as guides and spies. Although some patriot leaders condemned the attack, the soldiers were never punished. The massacre caused outrage among their Indian allies.

Conflicts Escalate on the Frontier

In present-day Tennessee, Cherokee who sided with the British became targets of patriot troops. Six thousand patriot soldiers laid waste to thirty-six native villages in 1778. They claimed it was in retaliation for the killing of white intruders along the Watauga River by a renegade Cherokee warrior. Cherokee and Shawnee warriors then attacked Fort Boonesborough, which Daniel Boone had established in 1775 in present-day Kentucky. In July 1778, patriot leader George Rogers Clark led Kentucky militiamen and Canadian volunteers sympathetic to the patriots in attacks on the British fort at Kaskaskia on the Mississippi River. Meanwhile the British, hoping to extend their frontier, established Fort Vincennes on the Ohio River. In a surprise February attack, Clark's troops — strengthened by French soldiers — sought to capture the fort. To convince the British commander to surrender, Clark's men toma-hawked four Indian captives to death in view of British forces. Once Fort Vincennes surrendered, colonists from Virginia began pouring into the region.

Intent on keeping their control of the northern frontier, the British commander at Fort Michilimackinac on Lake Huron recruited Sioux, Chippewa, and Sauk war-riors to attack Spanish forces along the Mississippi, while soldiers at Fort Detroit armed Ottawa, Fox, and Miami warriors to assault American settlers flooding into the Ohio River valley. Clark tried to capture Fort Detroit, but failed. However, Span-ish troops defeated British-allied Indian forces at St. Louis, increasing patriot control in the region (Map 6.2).

As British soldiers, patriots, and native tribes engaged in increasingly brutal bat-tles on the western frontier, Connecticut, Georgia, New York, Massachusetts, and Virginia claimed they already controlled large portions of the region. The states hoped to use these lands to reward soldiers and expand their settlements. However, those claims were challenged by other states, like Maryland, whose boundaries were

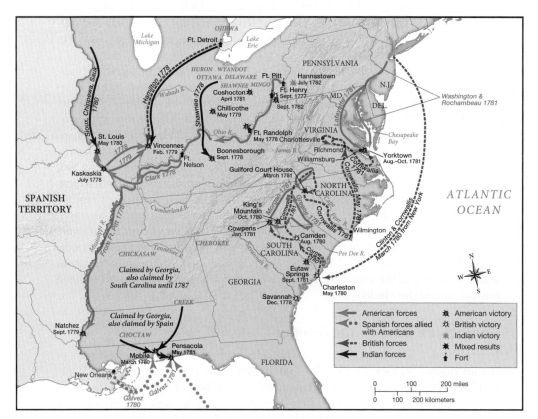

MAP 6.2   The War in the West and the South, 1777–1782
Between 1780 and 1781, major battles between Continental and British troops took place in Virginia and the Carolinas, and the British general Cornwallis finally surrendered at Yorktown, Virginia in October 1781. But patriot forces also battled British troops and their Indian allies from 1777 to 1782 in the Ohio River valley, the lower Mississippi River, and the Gulf coast.

fixed. They argued that if such lands were "wrested from the common enemy by the blood and treasure of the thirteen States," they should be considered "common property," to be parcelled out by Congress. After lengthy debate, New York State finally ceded its western claims to the Continental Congress in 1780, and federal officials assumed that the remaining states would follow suit.

Even this achievement was dampened by an outbreak of "break-bone fever" in August 1780 in Philadelphia, home to the Continental Congress. It affected young and old, women and men, blacks and whites. Severe pains in the head, back, and limbs accompanied a high fever. The famed physician Benjamin Rush, who treated a thousand Philadelphians between August and October, noted that in some cases the disease produced hemorrhagic symptoms, leading occasionally to death. Many who recovered suffered physical and mental weakness for an extended period. When the fever abated in October, the outcome of the revolution was still uncertain.

By March 1781, with land disputes settled among the rebellious states, the outcome looked more hopeful. When Maryland ratified the Articles of Confederation, a new national government was finally formed, unifying the rebellious states just as it appeared they would gain their independence. Still, the congress's guarantee that western lands would be "disposed of for the common benefit of the United States" made clear the imperial intentions of the Confederation government and ensured continued conflicts with native peoples.

REVIEW & RELATE

- What values and concerns shaped state governments during the Revolutionary War?
- What issues and challenges did American Indian tribes face as the Continental Army and Continental Congress fought for independence from the British?

Winning the War and the Peace, 1778–1783

From 1778 to 1781, the revolutionary battlefront moved south as well as west. The king, who believed that southern colonists' sympathies were more loyalist than patriot, insisted on pursuing a southern strategy. The patriots' eventual victory rested on a combination of superb strategy, their French and Spanish allies, and the continued support of affluent men and women. Still, even after the surrender of Britain's army in October 1781, the war dragged on while peace terms were negotiated. The celebrations following the signing of a peace treaty were themselves tempered by protests among Continental soldiers demanding back pay and by the realization of the new nation's looming challenges.

War Rages in the South

While war raged along the frontier, British troops sought to regain control of southern states from Georgia to Virginia. They captured Savannah, Georgia in 1778 and soon extended their control over the entire state. When General Clinton was called north later that year, he left the southern campaign in the hands of Lord Charles Cornwallis.

In May 1780, General Cornwallis reclaimed Charleston, South Carolina. He then evicted patriots from the city, purged them from the state government, gained military control of the state, and imposed loyalty oaths on all Carolinians able to fight. To aid his efforts, local loyalists organized militias to battle patriots in the interior. Banastre Tarleton led one especially vicious company of loyalists who slaughtered civilians and murdered many who surrendered. In retaliation, patriot planter Thomas Sumter organized 800 men who showed a similar disregard for regular army procedures, raiding largely defenseless loyalist settlements near Hanging Rock, South Carolina in August 1780.

As retaliatory violence erupted in the interior of South Carolina, General Gates marched his Continental troops south to join 2,000 militiamen from Virginia and North Carolina. But his troops were exhausted and short of food, and on August 16 Cornwallis won a smashing victory against the combined patriot forces at Camden, South Carolina (see Map 6.2). Soon after news of Gates's defeat reached General Washington, he heard that Benedict Arnold, commander at West Point, had defected to the British.

Suddenly, British chances for victory seemed more hopeful. Cornwallis was in control of Georgia and South Carolina, and local loyalists were eager to gain control of the southern countryside. Meanwhile Continental soldiers in the North mutinied in early 1780 over enlistment terms and pay. Despite patriot victories along the Ohio and Mississippi rivers, patriot morale back east was low, funds were scarce, and civilians were growing weary of the war.

Yet somehow the patriots prevailed. A combination of luck, strong leadership, frontier militia, and French support turned the tide. In October 1780, when Continental hopes looked especially bleak, a group of 800 frontier sharpshooters routed loyalist troops at King's Mountain in South Carolina. The victory kept Cornwallis from advancing into North Carolina and gave the Continentals a chance to regroup.

Shortly after the battle at King's Mountain, Washington sent General Nathanael Greene to replace Gates as head of southern operations. Taking advice from local militia leaders like Daniel Morgan and Francis Marion, Greene divided his limited force into even smaller units. Marion and Morgan each led 300 Continental soldiers into the South Carolina backcountry, picking up hundreds of local militiamen along the way. At the village of Cowpens, Morgan inflicted a devastating defeat on Tarleton's much larger force.

Despite their victory, Continental forces were spread thin and retreated in order to regroup. Cornwallis, enraged at the patriot victory, pursued these Continental forces, but his troops had outrun their cannons, and Greene circled back and attacked them at Guilford Court House. Although Cornwallis eventually forced the far smaller Continental company to withdraw from the battlefield, British troops suffered enormous losses. In August 1781, frustrated at the ease with which patriot forces still found local support in the South, he hunkered down in Yorktown on the Virginia coast and waited for reinforcements from New York.

Washington now coordinated strategy with his French allies. Comte de Rochambeau marched 5,000 troops south from Rhode Island to Virginia as General Lafayette led his troops south along Virginia's eastern shore. At the same time, French naval ships headed north from the West Indies. One unit cut off a British fleet trying to resupply Cornwallis by sea. Another joined up with American privateers to bombard Cornwallis's forces.

By mid-October, British supplies had run out, and it was clear that reinforcements would not be forthcoming. On October 19, 1781, the British army admitted defeat.

An Uncertain Peace

The Continental Army had managed the impossible. It had defeated the British army and won the colonies' independence. Yet even with the surrender after the **Battle of Yorktown**, the war continued in fits and starts. Peace negotiations in Paris dragged on as French, Spanish, British, and American representatives sought to settle a host of issues. Meanwhile, British forces challenged Continental troops in and around New York City.

Some Continental soldiers continued to fight, but others focused on the long-festering issue of overdue wages. When the congress decided in June 1783 to discharge the remaining troops without providing back pay, a near mutiny erupted in Pennsylvania. Nearly three hundred soldiers marched on the congress in Philadelphia, and Washington sent troops to put down the mutiny. Bloodshed was avoided when the Pennsylvania soldiers agreed to accept half pay and certificates for the remainder. Still, the issue of back pay would continue to plague the nation.

Meanwhile patriot representatives in Paris—Benjamin Franklin, John Adams, and John Jay—continued to negotiate peace terms. Rising antiwar sentiment on the British home front forced the government's hand. But the Comte de Vergennes, the French foreign minister, opposed the Americans' republican principles and refused to consider the American delegates as his political equals. Given the importance of the French to the American victory, the congress had instructed its delegates to defer to French wishes. This blocked the American representatives from signing a separate peace with the British.

Eventually, however, U.S. delegates finalized a treaty that secured substantial benefits for the young nation. The United States gained control of all lands south of Canada and north of Louisiana and Florida stretching to the Mississippi River. In addition, the treaty recognized the United States to be "free Sovereign and independent states." Spain signed a separate treaty with Great Britain in which it regained control of Florida. Once again, despite their role in the war, none of the Indian nations that occupied the lands under negotiation were consulted.

When the **Treaty (Peace) of Paris** was finally signed on September 2, 1783, thousands of British troops and their supporters left the colonies for Canada, the West Indies, or England. British soldiers on the western frontier were supposed to be withdrawn at the same time, but they remained for many years and continued to foment hostilities between Indians in the region and U.S. settlers along the frontier.

The evacuation of the British also entailed the exodus of thousands of African Americans who had fought against the patriots. At the end of the war, British officials granted certificates of manumission (freedom) to more than 1,300 men, 900 women, and 700 children. Most of these freed blacks settled in Nova Scotia, where they received small allotments of land from the British. Still, they generally lacked the resources to make such homesteads profitable in the cold climate. Despite these obstacles, some created a small Afro-Canadian community in Nova Scotia, while others migrated to areas considered more hospitable to black residents, such as Sierra Leone.

"Evacuation Day" and Washington's Triumphal Entry into New York City, November 25, 1783   Masses of Americans turned out to cheer General Washington and his officers as they retook control of New York City following the Peace of Paris. This 1879 print was likely made from an earlier painting. It highlights the joy felt by men, women, and children whose hopes for the new United States replaced their dismay at the long years of war and British occupation.   Library of Congress, LC-DIG-pga-02468

A Surprising Victory

Americans had managed to defeat one of the most powerful military forces in the world. That victory resulted from the convergence of many circumstances. Certainly Americans benefited from fighting on their own soil. Their knowledge of the land and its resources as well as earlier experiences fighting against Indians and the French helped prepare them for battles against the British.

Just as important, British troops and officers were far removed from centers of decision making and supplies. Even supplies housed in Canada could not be easily transported the relatively short distance into New York. British commanders were often hesitant to make decisions independently, but awaiting instructions from England proved costly on several occasions, especially since strategists in London often had little sense of conditions in America.

Both sides depended on outsiders for assistance, but here, too, Americans gained the advantage. The British army relied heavily on German mercenaries, Indian allies, and freed blacks to bolster its regular troops. In victory, such "foreign" forces were relatively reliable, but in defeat, many of them chose to look out for their own interests. The patriots failed to secure permanent alliances with the largest indigenous tribes and in the late 1770s lost native support. Instead, the patriots fought alongside French and Spanish armies well prepared to challenge British troops and motivated to gain advantages for France and Spain if Britain was defeated.

Perhaps most important, a British victory was nearly impossible without conquering the American colonies one by one. Because a large percentage of colonists supported the patriot cause, British troops had to contend not only with Continental soldiers but also with an aroused citizenry fighting for its independence.

REVIEW & RELATE	• How and why did the Americans win the Revolutionary War? • What uncertainties and challenges did the new nation face in the immediate aftermath of victory?

Conclusion: Legacies of the Revolution

After the approval of the Declaration of Independence, Thomas Hutchinson, the British official who had gained fame during the Stamp Act upheavals in Boston, charged that patriot leaders had "sought independence from the beginning." But the gradual and almost reluctant move from resistance to revolution in the American colonies suggests otherwise. When faced with threats from British troops, a sufficient number of colonists took up arms to create the reality of war, and this surge of hostilities finally gave the advantage to those urging independence.

The victory over Great Britain won that independence but left the United States confronting difficult problems. Most soldiers simply wanted to return home and reestablish their former lives. But the government's inability to pay back wages and the huge debt the nation owed to private citizens and state and foreign governments ensured difficult economic times ahead. These problems affected American Indians and African Americans as well as whites. Using western lands to reward officers and soldiers who had not received full pay intensified conflicts along the new nation's western frontier. Warfare between settlers and Indians west of the Appalachian Mountains continued for decades. At the same time, slave owners seeking more fertile fields also expanded into the trans-Appalachian region. By 1800 they had carried tens of thousands of enslaved blacks into Kentucky, Tennessee, and the Mississippi Territory. Separated from families back east, enslaved men and women on the frontier engaged in backbreaking labor without the support or camaraderie of the communities left behind.

Although faced with far better opportunities than enslaved laborers, many white soldiers still found the adjustment to postwar life difficult. As former soldiers struggled to reestablish farms and businesses and pay off debts accrued while fighting for independence, many received no compensation for their wartime service until the early 1800s.

Political leaders tried to address the concerns of former soldiers and ordinary citizens while they developed a new government. Within a few years of achieving independence, financial distress among small farmers and tensions with Indians on the western frontier intensified concerns about the ability of the confederation government to secure order and prosperity. While some patriots demanded a new political compact to strengthen the national government, others feared replicating British tyranny.

In the decade following the Revolution, leading patriots engaged in heated disagreements over the best means to unify and stabilize the United States. However, key leaders like Thomas Jefferson, Benjamin Franklin, and John Adams were living abroad as ambassadors, strengthening U.S. ties to Britain and France. In 1787 Thomas Paine, too, left for England, where he wrote pamphlets supporting the French Revolution. He eventually moved to France, but his radical political ideas led to his imprisonment there, and he returned to the United States upon his release. Even here, however, Paine was maligned for his attacks on organized religion and private property. Thus he played no part in the intense debates about how to secure the political future of the United States. Elizabeth Freeman followed political debates among patriots in the Sedgwick home, where she continued her work as a housekeeper and caretaker for the children. In 1808, she retired to a house near her daughter's home in Stockbridge and spent time with her grandchildren. When she died in 1829, her contribution to the end of slavery in Massachusetts was clear, but so too was its expansion across much of the nation.

Chapter 6 Review

KEY TERMS

Second Continental Congress, 138
Battle of Bunker Hill, 139
Dunmore's Proclamation, 140
Common Sense, 140
Declaration of Independence, 141
loyalist, 142
Battle of Oriskany, 146

Battle of Saratoga, 148
Valley Forge, 148
Articles of Confederation, 150
Battle of Yorktown, 157
Treaty (Peace) of Paris, 157

REVIEW & RELATE

1. What challenges did Washington face after accepting the command of the Continental Army?
2. How and why did proponents of independence prevail in the debates that led to the Declaration of Independence?
3. How did colonists choose sides during the Revolutionary War? What factors influenced their decisions?
4. Why would some Indian tribes try to stay neutral during the conflict? Why did most of those who chose sides support the British?
5. How did the patriot forces fare in 1776? How and why did the tide of war turn in 1777?
6. What role did colonial women and foreign men play in the conflict in the early years of the war?

7. What values and concerns shaped state governments during the Revolutionary War?

8. What issues and challenges did American Indian tribes face as the Continental Army and Continental Congress fought for independence from the British?

9. How and why did the Americans win the Revolutionary War?

10. What uncertainties and challenges did the new nation face in the immediate aftermath of victory?

TIMELINE OF EVENTS

April 19, 1775	• Battles of Lexington and Concord
June 1775	• Continental Congress establishes Continental Army
June 16, 1775	• Battle of Bunker Hill
August 1775	• Representatives of Continental Congress and Iroquois Confederacy meet
November 1775	• Lord Dunmore issues his proclamation
January 1776	• Thomas Paine publishes *Common Sense*
June 1776	• Smallpox ravages Continental Army
July 4, 1776	• Continental Congress publicly declares independence
July to mid-December 1776	• British forces defeat Continental Army
December 1776–	• Patriot victories at Trenton and
January 1777	• Princeton
October 1777	• Patriot victory at Saratoga
Winter 1777–1778	• Continental Army encamps at Valley Forge
1778	• Articles of Confederation ratified by eight states
February 1778	• France declares alliance with the United States
1780	• "Mum Bett" (Elizabeth Freeman) sues for freedom
1778–1781	• British and allies battle patriots and allies along the western frontier and the South
March 1781	• Articles of Confederation ratified
October 19, 1781	• British surrender at Yorktown, Virginia
September 2, 1783	• Treaty (Peace) of Paris

7

Forging a New Nation

1783–1800

LEARNING OBJECTIVES

After reading this chapter you will be able to:

- Analyze the major threats to the new nation after the Revolution.
- Explain which groups of Americans were marginalized in this period and how they responded to the changes that occurred.
- Describe the chief debates over the Constitution and its ratification.
- Evaluate the ways that the young nation's economic policies affected its relations with European nations abroad and on the U.S. frontier and fostered partisanship in politics.
- Describe how the presidency of John Adams exacerbated differences between Federalists and Democratic-Republicans and led to Thomas Jefferson's election in 1800.

COMPARING AMERICAN HISTORIES

One of six children born to Irish parents in Hopkinton, Massachusetts, **Daniel Shays** received little formal education. In 1772, age twenty-five, he married, had a child, and settled into farming. But in April 1775, he, his father, and his brother raced toward Concord to meet the British forces. By June, he was among the patriots defending Bunker Hill.

After distinguished service in the Continental Army, Shays purchased a farm in Pelham, Massachusetts in 1780 and hoped to return to a normal life. Instead, economic turmoil roiled the region and the nation. Many farmers had fallen into debt while fighting for independence. They returned to an economic recession and increased taxes as state governments labored to repay wealthy creditors and fund their portion of the federal budget. In western Massachusetts, many farmers faced eviction. Shays kept his farm and represented his town at county conventions that petitioned the state government for economic relief. However, the legislature largely ignored the farmers' concerns.

In 1786, angered by the state's failure to act, armed groups of farmers attacked courthouses throughout western Massachusetts. Although a reluctant leader, Shays headed the largest band of more than a thousand farmer-soldiers.

The uprising, known as Shays's Rebellion, alarmed many state and national leaders who feared such insurgencies might emerge elsewhere. Among those outraged by the rebels was **Alexander Hamilton**, a young New York politician. Hamilton was born illegitimate and impoverished in the British West Indies. Orphaned at eleven, he was apprenticed to a firm of merchants that sent him to the American colonies. There Hamilton was drawn into the activities of radical patriots and joined the Continental Army as a colonel in 1776. He had some success as captain of an artillery company before General George Washington invited him to serve as one of his aides.

During the war, Hamilton fell in love with Elizabeth Schuyler, who came from a wealthy New York family. They married in December 1780. After the war, Hamilton used military and marital contacts to establish himself as a lawyer and financier in New York City. In 1786, Hamilton was elected to the New York State legislature, where he focused on improving the state's finances, and served as a delegate to a convention on interstate commerce held in Annapolis, Maryland. Hamilton and several other delegates advocated a stronger central government. They pushed through a resolution calling for a second convention "to render the constitution of the Federal Government adequate to the exigencies of the Union."

Although the initial response to the call was lukewarm, the eruption of Shays's Rebellion and the government's financial problems soon convinced many political leaders that change was necessary. Although Hamilton played only a small role in the 1787 convention in Philadelphia, he worked tirelessly for ratification of the Constitution drafted there. When the new federal government was established in 1789, Hamilton became the nation's first secretary of the treasury.

COMPARING AMERICAN HISTORIES of Daniel Shays and Alexander Hamilton demonstrates that while patriots came together to win the Revolutionary War, they did not share a common vision of the new nation. Despite the suppression of Shays's Rebellion, the grievances that fueled the uprising persisted. Americans differed significantly over how best to resolve them. By 1787, demand for a stronger central government led to the ratification of a new U.S. Constitution. Hamilton played a leading role in advocating and establishing the new government, particularly by seeking to stabilize and strengthen the national economy. While many political and economic elites applauded his efforts, other national leaders and many ordinary citizens opposed them. These differences, exacerbated by foreign and frontier crises, eventually led to the development of competing political parties and the first contested presidential election in American history.

Financial, Frontier, and Foreign Problems

The United States faced serious financial instability in its formative years. The situation was so desperate that Continental Army officers threatened to march on the confederation congress if they did not receive their pay. Other issues also threatened the emerging nation. Conflicts between settlers and Indian tribes in western areas forced the confederation government to attend more closely to its frontier territories. Meanwhile, Spain closed the port of New Orleans to U.S. trade as individual states struggled to regulate domestic and foreign commerce. Off the coast of North Africa, Barbary pirates attacked U.S. merchant ships. Diplomatic relations with European powers were crucial, but they were hampered by America's outstanding war debts and the relative weakness of the confederation government.

Continental Officers Threaten Confederation

As the American Revolution ground to an end, issues of military pay sparked conflict. Uprisings by ordinary soldiers were common but successfully put down. Complaints from Continental officers, however, posed a greater problem. In 1780 they had extracted a promise from the Continental Congress for half pay for life but had received no compensation since. In December 1782, officers encamped at Newburgh, New York, awaiting a peace treaty, petitioned the confederation government for back pay for themselves and their soldiers, again with no success. By March 1783, most soldiers had returned home without pay, but some five hundred officers remained at Newburgh. Many confederation leaders were sympathetic to the officers' plight and hoped to use pressure from this formidable group to enhance the powers of the congress.

Alexander Hamilton had been pressing state governments to grant the confederation congress a new duty of 5 percent on imported goods, thereby providing the federal government with an independent source of revenue. Perhaps threats of an uprising by officers could convince states like New York to agree to the collection of this import duty. Quietly encouraged by political supporters, dissident officers circulated veiled threats of a military takeover. However, on March 15 the officers were confronted by General George Washington. In an emotional speech, he urged them to respect civilian control of the government. Most officers quickly retreated from their "infamous propositions." At the same time, congressional leaders promised the officers full pay for five years. However, lacking sufficient funds, they could provide only "commutation certificates," promising future payment.

Indians, Land, and the Northwest Ordinance

One anonymous petitioner at Newburgh suggested that the officers move as a group to "some unsettled country" and let the confederation fend for itself. In reality, no such unsettled country existed beyond the thirteen states. Numerous indigenous nations and growing numbers of American settlers claimed control of western lands. In 1784 some two hundred leaders from the Iroquois, Shawnee, Creek, Cherokee, and other nations gathered in St. Louis, where they complained to the Spanish governor that the Americans were "extending themselves like a plague of locusts."

Despite the continued presence of British and Spanish troops in the Ohio River valley, the United States hoped to convince Indian nations that it controlled the territory. In October 1784, U.S. commissioners met with Iroquois delegates at Fort Stanwix, New York and demanded land cessions in western New York and the Ohio valley. When the Seneca chief Cornplanter and other leaders refused, the commissioners insisted that "you are a subdued people" and must submit. An exchange of gifts and captives taken during the Revolution finally ensured the deal. Iroquois leaders not at the meeting disavowed the **Treaty of Fort Stanwix**. But the confederation government insisted it was legal, and New York State began surveying and selling the land. With a similar mix of negotiation and coercion, U.S. commissioners signed treaties at Fort McIntosh, Pennsylvania (1785), and Fort Finney, Ohio (1786), claiming lands held by the Wyandots, Delawares, Shawnees, and others.

As eastern Indians were increasingly pushed into the Ohio River valley, they crowded onto lands already claimed by other native peoples. Initially, these migrations increased conflict among Indians, but eventually some leaders used this forced intimacy to launch pan-Indian movements against further American encroachment on their land.

Indians and U.S. political leaders did share one concern: the vast numbers of squatters, mainly white men and women, living on land to which they had no legal claim. In fall 1784 George Washington traveled west to survey nearly thirty thousand acres of territory he had been granted as a reward for military service. He found much of it occupied by squatters who refused to acknowledge his ownership. Such flaunting of property rights deepened his concerns about the fragility of the confederation government.

The confederation congress was less concerned about individual property rights and more with the refusal of Virginia and Massachusetts to cede the western lands they claimed to federal control. Mistakenly believing that the issue was largely settled once New York ceded her lands, the congress spent another five years—until 1785—negotiating with Virginia and Massachusetts officials before the two states finally relinquished their claims north of the Ohio River (Map 7.1).

To regulate this vast territory, Thomas Jefferson drafted the **Northwest Ordinance** in 1785. It provided that the territory be surveyed and divided into adjoining townships. He hoped to carve nine small states out of the region to enhance the representation of western farmers and to ensure the continued dominance of agrarian views in the national government. The congress revised his proposal, however, stipulating that only three to five states be created from the vast territory and thereby limiting the future clout of western settlers in the federal government.

The population of the territory grew rapidly, with speculators buying up huge tracts of land and selling smaller parcels to eager settlers. In response, congressional leaders modified the Northwest Ordinance in 1787, clarifying the process by which territories could become states. The congress appointed territorial officials and guaranteed residents the basic rights of U.S. citizens. After a territory's population reached 5,000, residents could choose an assembly, but the territorial governor retained the

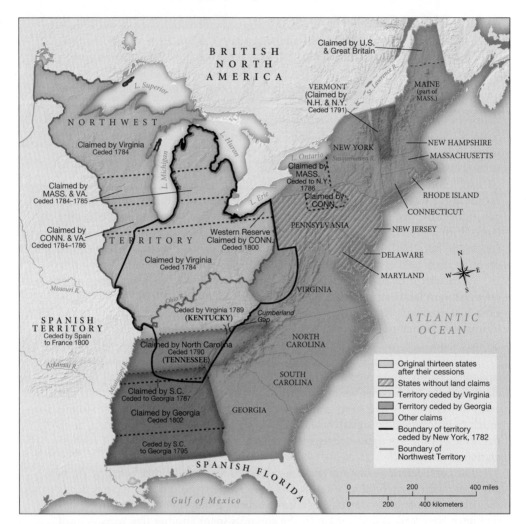

MAP 7.1   Cessions of Western Land, 1782–1802
Beginning under the Articles of Confederation, political leaders sought to resolve competing state claims to western territory based on colonial charters. The confederation congress and then the U.S. Congress gradually persuaded states to cede their lands and create a "national domain," though without taking into account native land claims. Part of this domain was organized as the Northwest Territory.

power to veto legislation. When a prospective state reached a population of 60,000, it could apply for admission to the United States. Thus the congress established an orderly system by which territories became states in the Union.

In a very limited way, the 1787 ordinance also addressed racial concerns in the region. It encouraged fair treatment of Indian nations but did not include any means of enforcing such treatment and failed to resolve tribal land claims. It also abolished slavery throughout the Northwest Territory but mandated the return of any enslaved workers fleeing their owners in other states to forestall a flood of fugitives.

The 1787 legislation did not address territory south of the Ohio River. As American settlers streamed into areas that became Kentucky and Tennessee, they confronted Creek, Choctaw, and Chickasaw tribes, well supplied with weapons by Spanish traders, as well as Cherokee who had sided with the British during the Revolution. The resulting conflicts in the region were largely ignored by the national government for the next quarter century.

Depression and Debt

Disputes over western lands were deeply intertwined with the economic difficulties that plagued the new nation. Victory in the Revolution was followed by years of economic depression and mushrooming debt. While the war fueled the demand for domestic goods and ensured high employment, both the demand and the jobs declined in peacetime. International trade was also slow to recover from a decade of disruption. Meanwhile the nation was saddled with a huge war debt. Individuals, the states, and the federal government all viewed western lands as a solution to their problems despite the fact that no government held secure title to these territories. Farm families could start over on "unclaimed" land; states could distribute land in lieu of cash to veterans or creditors; and congress could sell land to fund its debts. Even if authorities had gained clear titles, there was never enough land to meet these competing needs.

Some national leaders, including Hamilton, focused on other ways of repaying the war debt. Fearing that wealthy creditors would lose faith in a nation that could not repay its debts, they urged states to grant the federal government a percentage of import duties as a way to increase its revenue. But states had their own problems. Legislators in Massachusetts and other states passed hard-money laws that required debts to be repaid in gold or silver rather than in paper currency. Affluent creditors favored these measures to ensure repayment in full. But small farmers, including veterans, who had borrowed paper money during the war, now had to repay those loans in hard currency as the money supply shrank. Taxes, too, were rising as states sought to cover the interest on wartime bonds held by wealthy investors.

Failures of American diplomacy weakened the nation's economy further. In 1783 the British Parliament denied the United States the right to trade with the British West Indies. The following year, Spain, seeking leverage over disputed western territories, prohibited U.S. ships from accessing the port of New Orleans. Spain and Great Britain also threatened U.S. sovereignty by conspiring with American citizens on the frontier and promising them protection from Indians. At the same time, British troops remained in forts on America's western frontier and urged native allies to harass settlers there.

REVIEW & RELATE

- What challenges did the new nation face in the immediate aftermath of the Revolutionary War?
- How did farmers, financial leaders, foreign nations, and Indians react to government efforts to address challenges after the Revolution?

On the Political Margins

A young nation, the United States was forced to the political margins in international affairs. At the same time, some groups within the nation were marginalized as well. Small farmers suffered in the postwar period, but they were not alone. Church leaders who had enjoyed government support in the colonial period now had to compete for members and funds. African Americans, whose hopes for freedom had been raised by the Revolution, continued to fight for an end to enslavement and full-fledged citizenship. Many women also faced challenges as they sought to enhance their role in the nation.

Separating Church and State

Government support of churches ended in most states with the establishment of the United States. Anglican churches had long benefited from British support and taxed residents to support their ministry during the Revolution. But in 1786, the Virginia Assembly approved the Statute of Religious Freedom, which made church attendance and support voluntary. Many other states followed Virginia's lead and removed government support for established churches.

Churches that had dominated the various colonies now faced greater competition. Especially in frontier areas, Baptists and Methodists, the latter of which broke off from the Anglican Church in 1784, gained thousands of converts. The Society of Friends, or Quakers, and the Presbyterians also gained new adherents, while Catholics and Jews experienced greater tolerance than in the colonial era. This diversity ensured that no single religious voice or perspective dominated the new nation. Instead, denominations competed for members, money, and political influence.

Some Protestant churches were also challenged from within by free blacks who sought a greater role in church governance. In 1794 Richard Allen, who had been born enslaved, led a small group of Philadelphia blacks in founding the first African American church in the United States. Initially, this African Methodist Episcopal Church remained within the larger Methodist fold. By the early 1800s, however, Allen's church served as the basis for the first independent black denomination.

African Americans Struggle for Rights

It was no accident that the first independent black church was founded in Philadelphia, which attracted large numbers of free blacks after Pennsylvania adopted a gradual emancipation law in 1780. Although the northern states with the largest enslaved populations — New York and New Jersey — did not pass such laws until 1799 and 1804, respectively, the free black population increased throughout the region.

Many free blacks were migrants from the South, where tens of thousands of enslaved women and men gained their freedom during or immediately following the Revolution. Only a few slave owners took Revolutionary ideals to heart and emancipated their slaves following the war. Others emancipated slaves in their wills, but family members did not always carry out those wishes. In addition, a few states prohibited the importation of slaves from Africa immediately following the Revolution. Still, the enslaved population continued to grow rapidly, and southern legislators made it increasingly difficult for owners to free their slaves and for free blacks to remain in the region.

Richard Allen Born enslaved in Delaware in 1760, Richard Allen purchased his freedom from his master and moved to Philadelphia. This pastel and chalk drawing by an unknown artist shows Allen, a gifted preacher and community leader, in 1784. A decade later, when the white-led Methodist Church began segregating its congregation, Allen founded the African Methodist Episcopal Church, the first independent black church in the United States. The Granger Collection, New York

The limits on emancipation in the South nurtured the growth of free black communities in the North, especially in seaport cities like Philadelphia, New York, and New Bedford. Most African Americans focused on finding jobs, supporting families, and securing the freedom of enslaved relatives. Others, like Richard Allen, sought to establish churches, schools, and voluntary societies and to claim a political voice. Black women and men also established fraternal, literary, and educational societies, calling for the abolition of slavery and civil and political rights for free blacks.

Some northern states, such as New Jersey, granted property-owning blacks the right to vote. Others, such as Pennsylvania, did not specifically exclude them. Yet this was largely because the number of African Americans enfranchised remained small. Small numbers of white women and men aided blacks in their struggles. The Society of Friends, the only religious denomination to oppose slavery in the colonial period, became more outspoken in the 1780s and 1790s. Many Friends, also known as Quakers, withdrew from the slave trade and freed their enslaved workers. Quaker Anthony Benezet, a writer and educator, advocated tirelessly for the abolition of slavery and directed a school for blacks founded by the Society of Friends. Patriot leader and Quaker John Dickinson conditionally manumitted (that is, freed) several dozen enslaved workers on his Delaware farm in 1777. Still, because of a state law that required a bond be paid for each individual freed, Dickinson did not free the last of his enslaved laborers until 1786. A year earlier, a group of wealthy white men organized the New York Manumission Society, which promoted the gradual abolition of slavery in the state. However half of the thirty members held slaves or were involved in the slave trade, including Alexander Hamilton who bought and sold enslaved blacks for his father-in-law. Although these men were more outspoken on the issue of slavery than most whites, their gradualist approach failed to slow the growth of slavery in the wider nation.

Women Seek Wider Roles

Quaker women as well as men testified against slavery in the 1780s, writing statements on the topic in the Society's separate women's meetings. Although few other women experienced such spiritual autonomy, many gained a greater sense of economic and political independence during the Revolution.

Abigail Adams had written her husband John in 1776, "[I]f perticuliar care and attention is not paid to the Laidies we are determined to foment a Rebelion." While she and other elite women sought a more public voice, only New Jersey granted women—property-owning single women or widows—the right to vote. The vast majority of women could only shape political decisions by influencing their male relatives and friends. Fortunately, many leaders of the early Republic viewed wives and mothers as necessary to the development of a strong nation. In 1787 Dr. Benjamin Rush, in his *Essay on Female Education*, developed a concept that historians later labeled **republican motherhood**. He claimed that women could best shape political ideas and relations by "instructing their sons in principles of liberty and government." To prepare young women for this role, Rush suggested educating them in literature, music, composition, geography, history, and bookkeeping.

Judith Sargent Murray offered a more radical approach, arguing that "girls should be enabled to procure for themselves the necessaries of life; independence should be placed within their grasp." A few American women in the late eighteenth century did receive broad educations. Some ran successful businesses; wrote plays, poems, and histories; and established urban salons where women and men discussed the issues of the day. In 1789 Massachusetts became the first state to institute free elementary education for all children, and female academies also multiplied in this period. While schooling for affluent girls was often focused on preparing them for domesticity, the daughters of artisans and farmers learned practical skills, including writing and basic math, to assist in the family enterprise.

While women's influence was praised in the post-Revolutionary era, states rarely expanded women's rights. All states limited women's economic autonomy, although a few allowed married women to enter into business. Divorce was also legalized in many states but was still available only to the wealthy and well connected. Meanwhile women were excluded from juries, legal training, and, with rare exceptions, voting rights.

African American and Indian women lived under much more severe constraints. Most black women were enslaved, and those who were free could usually find jobs only as domestic servants or agricultural workers. Among indigenous nations, years of warfare enhanced men's role as warriors and diplomats while limiting women's political influence. U.S. government officials and Protestant missionaries encouraged native peoples to embrace gender roles that mirrored those of Anglo-American culture, further diminishing women's authority. Moreover, women forced to move west with their tribes lost traditional authority tied to their control of land.

Indebted Farmers Fuel Political Crises

Unlike blacks, Indians, and women, white farmers and workingmen actively sought to expand their political role in the new nation. Under constitutions written during the Revolution, most state governments broadened the electorate, allowing men with less property (or in rare cases no property) to vote and hold office. They also increased representation from western areas of the state.

Still, the economic interests of small farmers and workers diverged sharply from those of wealthy merchants and large landowners. As conflicts between debtors and creditors escalated between 1783 and 1787, state governments came down firmly on the side of the wealthy. But indebted farmers did not give up. They voted, petitioned, and protested to gain more favorable policies. When that failed, debt-ridden farmers in New Hampshire marched on the state capital in September 1786, demanding reform. Cavalry units confronted them and quickly seized and imprisoned the leaders.

Assaults on national authority worried many political leaders far more than farmers' uprisings. The continued efforts of Great Britain and Spain to undercut U.S. sovereignty and ongoing struggles with Indian nations posed especially serious threats. When James Madison and Alexander Hamilton attended the 1785 convention in Annapolis to address problems related to interstate commerce, they discovered that their concerns about the weakness of the confederation were shared by many large landowners, planters, and merchants. Despite these concerns, state legislatures were reluctant to give up the powers conferred on them under the Articles of Confederation.

Still, it was **Shays's Rebellion**, an armed uprising of indebted farmers in western Massachusetts in 1786–1787, that crystallized patriot fears about the limits of the confederation model. In January 1787, a thousand farmer-soldiers led by Daniel Shays headed to the federal arsenal at Springfield, Massachusetts to seize guns and ammunition. While the farmers fought hard, they were routed by state militia and pursued by governor James Bowdoin's army. Many rebel leaders were captured; others, including Shays, escaped to Vermont and New York. Four were convicted and two were hanged before Bowdoin granted amnesty to the others in hopes of avoiding further conflict.

Still the message was clear to many political leaders. On December 26, 1786, Washington had written Henry Knox to express his concerns about the rebellion and upheavals along the frontier: "If the powers [of the central government] are inadequate, amend or alter them; but do not let us sink into the lowest states of humiliation and contempt." Hamilton agreed, claiming that Shays's Rebellion "marked almost the last stage of national humiliation."

REVIEW & RELATE	• How did America's experience of the Revolutionary War change the lives of African Americans and women? • What do uprisings by farmers and debtors tell us about social and economic divisions in the early Republic?

Reframing the American Government

The delegates who met in Philadelphia in May 1787 did not agree on the best way to reform the government. Some delegates, like James Monroe of Virginia, hoped to strengthen the existing government by amending the Articles of Confederation.

Others joined with Madison and Hamilton, who argued for a new governmental structure. Once representatives agreed to draft a new constitution, they still disagreed over questions of representation, the powers of state and national governments, and the limits of popular democracy. Significant compromises had to be reached on these issues to frame a new Constitution.

Other issues arose once the Constitution was ratified and George Washington was inaugurated as president. The government needed to be organized and staffed. A system for levying, collecting, and distributing funds had to be put in place. Diplomatic relations with foreign powers and indigenous nations needed to be reestablished. A bill of rights, demanded by many state ratifying conventions, had to be drafted and approved. Finally, both proponents and opponents of the Constitution had to be convinced that this new government could respond to the varied needs of its citizens.

The Constitutional Convention of 1787

The fifty-five delegates who attended the Philadelphia convention were composed of white, educated men of property. Two-thirds were lawyers, and half had been Continental Army officers. While only eight had signed the Declaration of Independence eleven years earlier, a majority had served in the confederation congress and seven as governors during the confederation period. The elite status of the delegates and the absence of many leading patriots raised concern among those who saw the convention as a threat to the rights of states and of citizens. Indeed, Patrick Henry refused to serve as a delegate, Rhode Island sent no representatives, and some delegates left the meeting in frustration or refused to sign the Constitution that the convention finally proposed. The leaders who hammered out the compromises and wrote and revised the Constitution were those who feared the fragility of the existing confederation. Not wanting to alarm the public, delegates agreed to meet in secret until they had hammered out a new framework of government.

On May 25, the convention opened, and delegates quickly turned to the key question: Revise the Articles of Confederation or draft an entirely new document? The majority of men came to Philadelphia with the intention of amending the Articles. However, a core group who sought a more powerful central government had met before the convention and drafted a plan to replace the Articles. This **Virginia Plan** proposed a strong centralized state, including a bicameral (two-house) legislature in which representation was to be based on population. Members of the two houses would select the national executive and the national judiciary, and would settle disputes between states. Although most delegates opposed the Virginia Plan, it launched discussions in which strengthening the central government was assumed to be the goal.

Discussions of the Virginia Plan raised another issue that nearly paralyzed the convention: the question of representation. Heated debates pitted large states against small states, even though political interests were not necessarily determined by size. Yet delegates held on to size as the critical issue in determining representation. In mid-June, William Patterson introduced the **New Jersey Plan**, which highlighted the needs of smaller states. In this plan, Congress would consist of only one house, with each state having equal representation.

With few signs of compromise, the convention finally appointed a special committee to hammer out the problem of representation. Their report broke the log-jam. Members of the House of Representatives were to be elected by voters in each state; members of the Senate would be appointed by state legislatures. Representation in the House would be determined by population — counted every ten years in a national census — while in the Senate, each state, regardless of size, would have equal representation. While the Senate had more authority than the House in many areas, only the House could introduce funding bills.

Included within this compromise was one of the few direct considerations of slavery at the Philadelphia convention. With little apparent debate, the committee decided that representation in the House of Representatives was to be based on an enumeration of the entire free population and three-fifths of "all other persons," that is, enslaved persons. If delegates had moral scruples about this **three-fifths compromise**, most found them outweighed by the urgency of settling the troublesome question of representation.

Still, slavery was on the minds of delegates. In the same week that the Philadelphia convention tacitly accepted the institution of slavery, the confederation congress in New York City outlawed slavery in the Northwest Territory. News of that decision likely inspired representatives from Georgia and South Carolina to insist that the Constitution protect the slave trade, at least for the immediate future. Delegates in Philadelphia agreed that the importation of slaves would not be interfered with for twenty years. Another provision guaranteed the return of enslaved fugitives to their owners. At the same time, northern delegates insisted that the three-fifths formula be used in assessing taxation as well as representation, ensuring that the South paid for the increased size of its congressional delegation with increased taxes.

Two other issues provoked considerable debate in the following weeks. All delegates supported federalism, a system in which states and the central government shared power, but they disagreed over the balance of power between them. They also disagreed over the degree of popular participation in selecting national leaders. The new Constitution increased the powers of the central government significantly. For instance, Congress would now have the right to raise revenue by levying and collecting taxes and tariffs and coining money; raise armies; regulate interstate commerce; settle disputes between the states; establish uniform rules for the naturalization of immigrants; and make treaties with foreign nations and Indian tribes. But Congress could veto state laws only when those laws challenged "the supreme law of the land," and states retained all rights that were not specifically granted to the federal government.

One of the important powers retained by the states was the right to determine who was eligible to vote even as the Constitution regulated the influence eligible voters would have in national elections. Members of the House of Representatives were to be elected directly by popular vote for two-year terms. Senators — two from each state — were to be selected by state legislatures for a term of six years. Selection of the president was even further removed from voters. The president would be selected by an Electoral College, and state legislatures would decide how to choose its members. Finally, the federal judicial system was to be wholly removed from popular influence. Justices on the Supreme Court were to be appointed by the president and approved by the Senate. Once approved, they served for life to protect their judgments from the pressure of popular opinion. In addition, the Constitution created a separation of powers between these three branches — legislative, executive, and judicial — that limited the authority of each.

When the final debates concluded, only thirty-nine of the original delegates agreed to sign the document. They also agreed that approval by nine states, rather than all thirteen, would make the Constitution the law of the land. Some delegates sought formal reassurance that the powers granted the federal government would not be abused and urged inclusion of a bill of rights, like the Virginia Declaration of Rights. But weary men eager to finish their business voted down the proposal. On September 17, 1787, the Constitution was approved and sent to the states for ratification.

Americans Battle over Ratification

The confederation congress sent the document to state legislatures and asked them to call conventions to consider ratification. These conventions could not modify the document, but only accept or reject it. Thousands of copies of the Constitution also circulated in newspapers and as broadsides. Pamphleteers, civic leaders, and ministers proclaimed their opinions publicly while ordinary citizens in homes, shops, and taverns debated the wisdom of establishing a stronger central government.

Fairly quickly, two sides emerged. The **Federalists**, who supported ratification, came mainly from urban and commercial backgrounds and lived in towns and cities along the Atlantic coast. They considered a stronger central government essential to the economic and political stability of the nation. Their opponents were generally more rural, less wealthy, and more likely to live in interior or frontier regions. Labeled **Antifederalists**, they opposed increasing the powers of the central government.

The pro-Constitution position was presented in a series of editorials that appeared in New York newspapers in 1787 to 1788 and published collectively as *The Federalist Papers*. The authors James Madison, John Jay, and Alexander Hamilton articulated broad principles embraced by supporters of the Constitution. Alexander Hamilton wrote two essays on impeachment, a system devised in medieval England that allowed Parliament to remove a King's ministers, judges, or other officials for "high Crimes and Misdemeanors." The most important essay, however, was *Federalist* No. 10 in which Madison countered the common wisdom that small units of government were most effective in representing the interests of their citizens and avoiding factionalism. He argued that in large units, groups with competing interests had to collaborate and compromise, providing the surest check on the "tyranny of the majority."

Still, Antifederalists worried that a large and powerful central government could lead to tyranny. Small farmers claimed that a strong congress filled with merchants, lawyers, and planters was likely to place the interests of creditors above those of ordinary (and indebted) Americans. Even some wealthy patriots, like Mercy Otis Warren of Boston, feared that the Constitution would empower a few individuals who cared little for the "true interests of the people." And the absence of a bill of rights concerned many Americans.

Federalists worked in each state to soften their critics by persuasive arguments, flattering hospitality, and the promise of a bill of rights once the Constitution was ratified. The quick ratification of the Constitution by Delaware, Pennsylvania, New Jersey, Georgia, and Connecticut by January 1788 strengthened the Federalist position. Federalists also gained the support of influential newspapers based in eastern cities and tied to commercial interests.

Still, the contest in many states was heated. In Massachusetts, Antifederalists, including leaders of Shays's Rebellion, gained the majority among convention delegates. Federalists worked hard to overcome the objections of their opponents, even drafting a preliminary bill of rights. On February 6, Massachusetts delegates voted 187 to 168 in favor of ratification. Maryland and South Carolina followed in April and May. A month later, New Hampshire Federalists won a close vote, making it the ninth state to ratify the Constitution.

However, two of the most populous and powerful states — New York and Virginia — had not yet ratified. Passionate debates erupted in both ratifying conventions, and Federalists decided it was prudent to wait until these states acted before declaring victory. After promising that a bill of rights would be added quickly, Virginia Federalists finally won the day by a few votes. A month later, New York, too, approved the Constitution by a narrow margin. The divided nature of the votes, and the fact that two states (North Carolina and Rhode Island) had still not ratified, meant that the new government would have to prove itself quickly (Table 7.1).

Organizing the Federal Government

Most political leaders hoped that the partisanship of the ratification battle would fade away with the Constitution approved. The Electoral College's unanimous decision to name George Washington the first president and John Adams as vice president helped calm the political turmoil. The two took office in April 1789, launching the new government.

TABLE 7.1	VOTES OF STATE-RATIFYING CONVENTIONS		
State	Date	For	Against
Delaware	December 1787	30	0
Pennsylvania	December 1787	46	23
New Jersey	December 1787	38	0
Georgia	January 1788	26	0
Connecticut	January 1788	128	40
Massachusetts	February 1788	187	168
Maryland	April 1788	63	11
South Carolina	May 1788	149	73
New Hampshire	June 1788	57	47
Virginia	June 1788	89	79
New York	July 1788	30	27
North Carolina	November 1788	194	77
Rhode Island	May 1790	34	32

To bring order to his administration, Washington appointed well-known leaders to head three departments — State, War, and Treasury. Thomas Jefferson was named secretary of state; Henry Knox, secretary of war; and Alexander Hamilton, secretary of the treasury. He also appointed Samuel Osgood, a New York merchant and politician whose home became Washington's residence in the city, as Postmaster General. The president then selected Edmund Randolph to serve as his attorney general, the first step toward establishing a Department of Justice.

Congress, meanwhile, worked to establish a judicial system. The Constitution called for a Supreme Court but provided no specific guidelines. The Judiciary Act of 1789 established a Supreme Court composed of six justices along with thirteen district courts and three circuit courts to hear cases appealed from the states. Congress also quickly produced a bill of rights. Representative James Madison gathered more than two hundred resolutions passed by state ratifying conventions and honed them down to twelve amendments, which Congress approved and submitted to the states for ratification. In 1791 ten of the amendments were ratified, and these became the **Bill of Rights**. It guaranteed the rights of individuals and states in the face of a powerful central government, including freedom of speech, the press, and religion as well as the right to bear arms, petition the government, and be tried by a jury.

Hamilton Forges an Economic Agenda

The new government's leaders recognized that without a stable economy, the best political structure could falter. Thus Hamilton's appointment as secretary of the treasury was especially significant. In formulating his economic policy, Hamilton's main goal was to establish the nation's credit. Paying down the debt and establishing a national bank would strengthen the United States in the eyes of the world and tie wealthy Americans more firmly to the federal government.

Hamilton advocated funding the national debt at face value and assuming the remaining state debts as part of the national debt. To pay for this policy, he planned to raise revenue through government bonds and new taxes. Hamilton also called for the establishment of a central bank to carry out the financial operations of the United States. In three major reports to Congress — on public credit and a national bank in 1790 and on manufactures in 1791 — he laid out a system of state-assisted economic development.

Hamilton's proposal to repay at face value the millions of dollars in securities issued by the confederation was particularly controversial. Thousands of soldiers, farmers, and shopkeepers had been paid with these securities during the war; but needing money in its aftermath, most sold them to speculators for a fraction of their value. These speculators would make enormous profits if the securities were paid off at face value. One of the policy's most ardent critics, Patrick Henry, claimed that Hamilton's policy was intended "to erect, and concentrate, and perpetuate a large monied interest" that would prove "fatal to the existence of American liberty." Despite such passionate opponents, Hamilton gained the support of Washington and other key Federalists.

The federal government's assumption of the remaining state war debts also faced fierce opposition, especially from southern states like Virginia that had already paid off their debt. Hamilton again won his case, though this time only by agreeing to

Society of Pewterers Silk Banner Workingmen in New York City created this painted silk banner. Pewter is a tin alloy used to make inexpensive utensils and kitchenware, which were increasingly popular in the late eighteenth century. Pewterers carried this banner in the July 23, 1788, parade celebrating the ratification of the U.S. Constitution. They thereby proclaimed the place of artisans in the new nation. © Collection of the New-York Historical Society, USA/Bridgeman Images

"redeem" (that is, reimburse) states that had repaid their debts. In addition, Hamilton and his supporters had to agree to move the nation's capital from Philadelphia to a more central location along the Potomac River.

Funding the national debt, assuming the remaining state debts, and redeeming state debts already paid would cost $75.6 million (about $1.5 billion today). But Hamilton believed maintaining some debt was useful. He thus proposed establishing a Bank of the United States, funded by $10 million in stock to be sold to private stockholders and the national government. The bank would serve as a repository for federal revenues and grant loans and sell bills of credit to merchants and investors, thereby creating a permanent national debt. This, he argued, would bind investors to the United States, turning the national debt into a "national blessing."

Not everyone agreed. Jefferson and Madison argued vehemently against the Bank of the United States, noting that there was no constitutional sanction for a federal bank. Hamilton fought back, arguing that Congress had the right to make "all Laws which shall be necessary and proper" for carrying out the provisions of the Constitution. Once again, he prevailed. Congress chartered the bank for a period of twenty years, and Washington signed the legislation into law.

The final piece of Hamilton's plan focused on raising revenue. Congress quickly agreed to pass tariffs on a range of imported goods, which generated some $4 million to $5 million annually. Some congressmen viewed these tariffs as a way to protect new industries in the United States, from furniture to shoes. An excise tax, paid by the producer or seller rather than the consumer, was placed on a variety of goods, notably whiskey. It generated another $1 million each year.

Hamilton's financial policies proved enormously successful in stabilizing the American economy, repaying outstanding debts, and tying men of wealth to the new government. The federal bank effectively collected and distributed the nation's resources. Commerce flourished, revenues rose, and confidence revived among foreign and domestic investors. And while the United States remained an agricultural nation, Hamilton's 1791 "Report on the Subject of Manufactures" foreshadowed the growing significance of industry, which gradually lessened U.S. dependence on European nations.

REVIEW & RELATE	• What issues attracted the most intense debate during the drafting and ratification of the Constitution? Why? • How did Hamilton's policies stabilize the national economy, and why did they nonetheless arouse opposition?

Years of Crisis, 1792–1796

By 1792 Hamilton had succeeded in implementing his plan for U.S. economic development. Yet as Washington began his second term in the spring of 1793, signs of strain appeared throughout the nation. The French Revolution posed challenges to foreign trade and diplomacy. Migration to the frontier increased, which intensified conflicts between Indians and white settlers and increased hostilities between the United States and Great Britain. Yellow fever swept through Philadelphia and other cities, causing fear and disrupting political and economic life. Finally, the excise tax on whiskey fueled armed protests among frontier farmers. This cluster of crises split the Federalists into warring factions during Washington's second term.

Foreign Trade and Foreign Wars

Jefferson and Madison led the opposition to Hamilton's policies. Their supporters were mainly southern Federalists who envisioned the country's future rooted in agriculture, not the commerce and industry supported by Hamilton and his allies. Jefferson agreed with the Scottish economist Adam Smith that an international division of labor could best provide for the world's people. Americans could supply Europe with food and raw materials in exchange for manufactured goods. When wars in Europe, including a revolution in France, disrupted European agriculture in the 1790s, Jefferson's views were reinforced.

Although trade with Europe remained the most important source of goods and wealth for the United States, some merchants expanded into other parts of the globe.

In the mid-1780s, the first American ships reached China, where they traded ginseng root and sea otter pelts for silk, tea, and chinaware. Still, events in Europe had a far greater impact on the United States at the time than those in the Pacific world.

The French Revolution (1789–1799) was especially significant for U.S. politics. The ideals of freedom of speech, assembly, and religion declared in America's Declaration of Independence resonated with French men and women who opposed the tyrannical rule of their King, Louis XVI. The resulting uprising disrupted French agriculture, increasing demand for American wheat, while the efforts of French revolutionaries to institute an egalitarian republic gained support from many Americans. The followers of Jefferson and Madison formed Republican societies, and members adopted the French term *citizen* when addressing each other. At the same time, the importance of workers and farmers among France's revolutionary forces reinforced critiques of the "monied power" that drove Federalist policies.

In late 1792, as French revolutionary leaders began executing thousands of their opponents in the Reign of Terror, wealthy Federalists grew more anxious. The beheading of King Louis XVI horrified them, as did the revolution's condemnation of Christianity. Some members of Republican societies also criticized the brutal turn of the revolution. When France declared war against Prussia, Austria, and finally Great Britain, U.S. merchants worried about the impact on trade. In response, President Washington proclaimed U.S. neutrality in April 1793, prohibiting Americans from providing support or war materials to any belligerent nations — including France or Great Britain.

While the Neutrality Proclamation limited the shipment of certain items to Europe, Americans simultaneously increased trade with colonies in the British and French West Indies. Indeed, U.S. ships captured much of the lucrative sugar trade. At the same time, farmers in the Chesapeake and Middle Atlantic regions filled the growing demand for wheat in Europe, causing their profits to climb.

Yet these benefits did not bring about a political reconciliation. Although Jefferson condemned the French Reign of Terror, he protested the Neutrality Proclamation by resigning his cabinet post. Tensions escalated when the French envoy to the United States, Edmond Genêt, sought to enlist Americans in the European war. Republican clubs poured out to hear him speak and donated generously to the French cause. The British also ignored U.S. neutrality. The Royal Navy stopped U.S. ships carrying French sugar and seized more than 250 vessels. At the same time, Britain supplied Indians in the Ohio River valley with guns and encouraged them to raid U.S. settlements.

President Washington sent John Jay to England to resolve concerns over trade with the British West Indies, compensation for seized American ships, the continued British occupation of frontier forts, and southerners' ongoing demands for reimbursement for slaves evacuated by the British during the Revolution. Jay returned from England in 1794 with a treaty, but it was widely criticized in Congress and the popular press. While securing limited U.S. trading rights in the West Indies, it failed to address British reimbursement for captured cargoes or enslaved workers and granted Britain eighteen months to leave frontier forts. It also demanded that U.S. planters repay British firms for debts accrued during the Revolution. While the **Jay Treaty** was eventually ratified, it remained a source of contention among Federalists.

Disease and Dissent

Despite these foreign crises, it was the effect of Federalist policies on the American frontier that crystallized opposing factions. The ability of the government to respond to these crises was slowed by outbreak of yellow fever in Philadelphia, the nation's capital. In August 1793, yellow fever erupted in Philadelphia, ultimately killing some 5,000 of the city's 50,000 residents. Another 20,000 people fled the city, although nearby towns began refusing entry to these refugees, and cities such as Baltimore and New York established quarantines against Philadelphia residents and goods. The Federal Congress's summer adjournment was extended through November, and officials decided it was not even safe for President Washington to meet with his cabinet officers. Philadelphia's local leaders organized a separate "fever hospital" for those taken ill since the existing hospital did not take infectious cases. Richard Allen and Absalom Jones offered assistance from the Free African Society, assuming — as white doctors did — that blacks had immunity from this fever, much like many did from malaria. However, African Americans died at the same rate as whites, many infected while volunteering as nurses or to bury corpses. Doctors did not yet know that mosquitos carried the fever. So Dr. Benjamin Rush and his colleagues depended on isolating patients and disinfecting houses, streets, wharves, and shops to slow the spread. Residents were urged to wear masks soaked in vinegar and camphor when they were out in public. The custom of shaking hands was avoided. Among federal employees, only those at the post office and the Treasury Department continued to work through the epidemic.

Yellow fever declined in early November with colder weather, but returned to Philadelphia and appeared in New York City, Baltimore, and other port cities throughout the 1790s. When the president and Congress returned to Philadelphia, some must have feared that remnants of the disease were still lurking in the area. However, they had critical issues to address.

In the early 1790s, from Maine to Georgia, Republican societies founded to support the French Revolution demanded the removal of British and Spanish troops from frontier areas, while frontier farmers lashed out at enforcement of the so-called whiskey tax. Many farmers on the frontier grew corn and turned it into whiskey to make it easier to transport and more profitable to sell. The whiskey tax hurt these farmers, hundreds of whom petitioned the federal government for relief.

Western Pennsylvania farmers were particularly incensed and rallied in 1792 and 1793 to protest the tax and those who enforced it. Former North Carolina Regulator Hermon Husband was one of the most outspoken critics of the new excise tax. Adopting tactics from Stamp Act protests and Shays's Rebellion, farmers blocked roads, burned sheriffs in effigy, marched on courthouses, and assaulted tax collectors. The government's failure to respond only fueled the rebels' anger. By 1794 all-out rebellion had erupted.

Washington, Hamilton, and their supporters worried that the rebellion could spread and that it might encourage Indians to rise up as well. Since Spanish and British soldiers were eager to foment trouble along the frontier, the **Whiskey Rebellion** might spark their intervention. Federalists also suspected that pro-French immigrants from Scotland and Ireland helped fuel the growing insurgency.

Unlike 1786, however, when the federal government had no power to intervene in Shays's Rebellion, Washington now federalized militias from four states, calling up nearly thirteen thousand soldiers to quash the uprising. The army that marched into western Pennsylvania in September 1794 vastly outnumbered the "whiskey rebels" and easily suppressed the uprising. Having gained victory, the federal government prosecuted only two of the leaders, who were convicted but later pardoned by Washington.

President Washington proved that the Constitution provided the necessary powers to put down internal threats. Yet in doing so, the administration horrified many Americans who viewed the force used against the farmers as excessive. Jefferson and Madison voiced this outrage from within the Federalist government. The Revolutionary generation had managed to compromise on many issues, from representation and slavery to the balance between federal and state authority. But now Hamilton's economic policies had led to a frontier uprising, and Washington had used a federal army to crush popular dissent. The Federalists were on the verge of open warfare among themselves.

Further Conflicts on the Frontier

In one area, Federalists shared a common concern: the continued threats to U.S. sovereignty by native, British, and Spanish forces. In 1790 Congress had passed the Indian Trade and Intercourse Act to regulate race relations on the frontier and to ensure fair and equitable dealings. However, the act was widely ignored. Moreover, the government failed to stem the flood of settlers into the Ohio and Mississippi River valleys. That decision proved costly.

In 1790 Little Turtle, a war chief of the Miami nation, gathered a large force of Shawnee, Delaware, Ottawa, Chippewa, Sauk, Fox, and other Indians. This pan-Indian alliance successfully attacked federal troops in the Ohio valley that fall. A year later, the allied Indian warriors defeated a large force under General Arthur St. Clair (Map 7.2). The stunning defeat shocked Americans. In the meantime, Spanish authorities negotiated with Creeks and Cherokees to attack U.S. settlements on the southern frontier.

Washington decided to deal with problems in the Northwest Territory first, sending 2,000 men under the command of General Anthony Wayne into the Ohio frontier. In August 1794, Wayne's forces attacked 1,500 to 2,000 Indians gathered at a British fort. In the Battle of Fallen Timbers, the pan-Indian warriors, led by Little Turtle, suffered a bitter defeat. A year later, the warring tribes in the Northwest Territory signed the **Treaty of Greenville**, granting the United States vast tracts of land.

Amid this turmoil, in November 1794, John Jay signed his controversial treaty with Great Britain. With Britain agreeing to withdraw its forces from the U.S. frontier by 1796, the treaty may have helped persuade indigenous nations to accept U.S. peace terms at Greenville. Nonetheless, the Jay Treaty's requirement that Americans make "full and complete compensation" to British firms for Revolutionary War debts without the British compensating U.S. merchants or enslavers for their losses nearly led Congress to reject it. In June 1795, however, the Senate finally approved

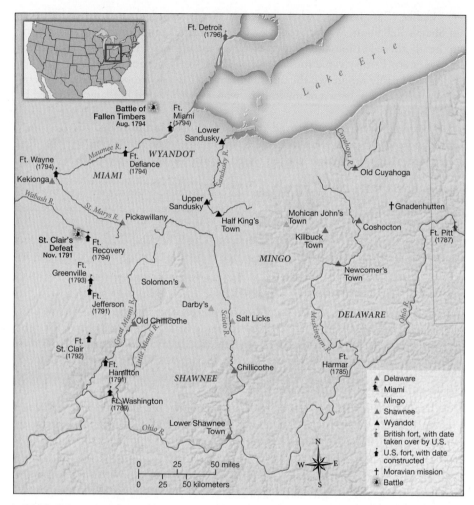

MAP 7.2   American Indians in the Ohio River Valley, c. 1785–1795

Until the mid-eighteenth century, despite conflicts, Indian tribes in the Ohio River valley forged trade and diplomatic relations with various colonial powers. But once the United States established the Northwest Territory in 1785, conflicts between Indians and U.S. settlers and soldiers escalated dramatically. As tribes created pan-Indian alliances, the United States constructed numerous forts in the region.

the treaty without a vote to spare. Before Jay's controversial treaty took effect, Spain agreed to negotiate an end to hostilities on the southern frontier of the United States. Envoy Thomas Pinckney negotiated that treaty, which recognized the thirty-first parallel as the boundary between U.S. and Spanish territory in the South and opened the Mississippi River and the port of New Orleans to U.S. shipping. Many Federalists, especially from the West and South, who opposed the Jay Treaty supported the **Pinckney Treaty**, which was ratified in 1796.

REVIEW & RELATE	• How did events overseas shape domestic American politics and frontier policy in the 1790s? • What common concerns underlay the Whiskey Rebellion and Shays's Rebellion? How did the U.S. government deal differently with each?

The First Party System

In September 1796, when President Washington decided not to run again, he offered a Farewell Address in which he warned against the "spirit of party." "It agitates the community with ill-founded jealousies and false alarms," he claimed, and "kindles the animosity of one part against another." By then, however, Jefferson, Madison, and other opponents of Hamilton's economic policies, Washington's assault on the whiskey rebels, and Jay's Treaty had already formed a distinct party. They called themselves **Democratic-Republicans** and supported Jefferson for president. The Electoral College, hoping to bring the warring sides together, chose Federalist John Adams as president and Thomas Jefferson as vice president. The two disagreed fundamentally on a wide range of issues, and events soon heightened these divisions. Foreign crises once again fueled political antagonisms, and in this charged atmosphere, Federalists in Congress passed two acts in 1798 relating to aliens (immigrants) and to sedition (activities that promote civil disorder). Instead of resolving tensions, however, these laws exacerbated opposition to Federalist rule. By 1800, partisan differences had crystallized, and the Democratic-Republicans threatened to oust the Federalists from power.

The Adams Presidency

The election of 1796 was the first to be contested by candidates identified with opposing parties. Federalists supported John Adams for president and Thomas Pinckney for vice president. The Democratic-Republicans chose Thomas Jefferson and Aaron Burr of New York to represent their interests. When the Electoral College was established, political parties did not exist and, in fact, were seen as promoting conflict. Thus electors were asked to choose the best individuals to serve, regardless of their views. In 1796 they picked Adams for president and Jefferson for vice president, perhaps hoping to lessen partisan divisions by forcing men of different views to compromise. Instead, the effects of an administration divided against itself were nearly disastrous, and opposing interests became more thoroughly entrenched.

Adams and Jefferson had disagreed on almost every major policy issue during Washington's administration. Not surprisingly, the new president rarely took advice from his vice president. At the same time, Adams retained most of Washington's appointees, who often sought advice from Hamilton, undercutting Adams's authority. Worse still, the new president had poor political instincts and faced numerous challenges.

At first, foreign disputes enhanced the authority of the Adams administration. The Federalists remained pro-British, and French seizures of U.S. ships threatened to provoke war. In 1798 Adams tried to negotiate compensation for the losses suffered by merchants. When an American delegation arrived in Paris, however, three French agents demanded a bribe to initiate talks.

Adams made public secret correspondence from the French agents, whose names were listed only as X, Y, and Z. Americans, including Democratic-Republicans, expressed outrage at this French insult to U.S. integrity, which became known as the **XYZ affair**. Congress quickly approved an embargo act that prohibited trade with France and permitted privateering against French ships. For the next two years, the United States fought an undeclared war with France.

Despite praise for his handling of the XYZ affair, Adams feared dissent from opponents at home and abroad. Consequently, the Federalist majority in Congress passed a series of security acts in 1798. The Alien Act allowed the president to order the imprisonment or deportation of noncitizens and was directed primarily at Irish and Scottish dissenters who criticized the government's pro-British policies. Congress also approved the Naturalization Act, which raised the residency requirement for citizenship from five to fourteen years. Finally, Federalists pushed through the Sedition Act, which outlawed "false, scandalous, or malicious statements against

Matthew Lyon and Roger Griswold This political cartoon depicts a fight on the floor of the House of Representatives in February 1798 between Representatives Matthew Lyon of Vermont, a Democratic-Republican brandishing tongs, and Roger Griswold of Connecticut, a Federalist waving a cane. A newspaper editor and a critic of the Alien and Sedition Acts, Lyon was later convicted of sedition but won reelection while in jail. Library of Congress, Prints and Photographs Division [LC-DIG-ppmsca-31832]

President or Congress." In the following months, nearly two dozen Democratic-Republican editors and legislators were arrested for sedition, and some were fined and imprisoned.

Democratic-Republicans were infuriated by the **Alien and Sedition Acts**. They considered the attack on immigrants an attempt to limit the votes of farmers, artisans, and frontiersmen, who formed the core of their supporters. The Sedition Act threatened Democratic-Republican critics of Federalist policies and the First Amendment's guarantee of free speech. Jefferson and Madison encouraged states to pass resolutions that would counter this violation of the Bill of Rights. Using language drafted by the two Democratic-Republican leaders, legislators passed the **Virginia and Kentucky Resolutions**, which declared the Alien and Sedition Acts "void and of no force." They protested against the "alarming infractions of the Constitution," particularly the freedom of speech that "has been justly deemed, the only effectual guardian of every other right." Virginia even claimed that states had a right to nullify any powers exercised by the federal government that were not explicitly granted to it.

Although the Alien and Sedition Acts curbed dissent in the short run, they reinforced popular concerns about the power wielded by the Federalists. Combined with the ongoing war with France, continuing disputes over taxes, and relentless partisan denunciations in the press, these acts set the stage for the presidential election of 1800.

The Election of 1800

By 1800 Adams had negotiated a peaceful settlement of U.S. conflicts with France, considering it one of the greatest achievements of his administration. However, other Federalists, including Hamilton, disagreed and continued to seek open warfare and an all-out victory. Thus the Federalists faced the election of 1800 deeply divided. Democratic-Republicans meanwhile united behind Jefferson and portrayed the Federalists as the "new British" tyrants.

For the first time, congressional caucuses selected candidates for each party. The Federalists agreed on Adams and Charles Cotesworth Pinckney of South Carolina. The Democratic-Republicans again chose Jefferson and Burr as their candidates. The campaign was marked by bitter accusations and denunciations.

In the first highly contested presidential election, the different methods states used to record voters' preferences gained more attention. Only five states determined members of the Electoral College by popular vote. In the rest, state legislatures appointed electors. Created at a time when political parties were considered injurious to good government, the Electoral College was not prepared for the situation it faced in January 1801. Federalist and Democratic-Republican caucuses nominated one candidate for president and one for vice president on party tickets. As a result, Jefferson and Burr received exactly the same number of Electoral College votes, and the House of Representatives then had to break the tie. There Burr sought to gain the presidency with the help of Federalist representatives ardently opposed to Jefferson. But Alexander Hamilton stepped in and warned against Burr's leadership. This helped Jefferson emerge victorious, but it also inflamed animosity between Burr and Hamilton that eventually led to the 1804 duel in which Burr killed Hamilton.

President Jefferson labeled his election a revolution achieved not "by the sword" but by "the suffrage of the people." The election of 1800 was hardly a popular revolution, given the restrictions on suffrage and the methods of selecting the Electoral College. Still, between 1796 and 1800, partisan factions had been transformed into opposing parties, and the United States had managed a peaceful transition from one party to another.

REVIEW & RELATE	• What were the main issues dividing the Federalists and the Democratic-Republicans? • What do the Alien and Sedition Acts and the election of 1800 tell us about political partisanship in late-eighteenth-century America?

Conclusion: A Young Nation Comes of Age

In the 1780s and 1790s, the United States faced numerous obstacles to securing its place as a nation. Financial hardship, massive debts, hostile Indians, and European diplomacy had to be addressed by a federal government that, under the Articles of Confederation, was relatively weak. By 1787 concerns about national security, fueled by rebellious farmers and frontier conflicts, persuaded some political leaders to advocate a new governmental structure. While it required numerous compromises among groups with competing ideas and interests, the Constitution was drafted and, after a fierce battle in several states, ratified.

With the federal government's power strengthened, George Washington took office as the first American president. His administration sought to enhance U.S. power at home and abroad. Secretary of the treasury Alexander Hamilton proposed a series of measures to stabilize the American economy, pay off Revolutionary War debts, and promote trade and industry. However, these policies also aroused opposition, with leaders like Jefferson and Madison and ordinary farmers and frontiersmen questioning the benefits of Hamilton's economic priorities. Differences over the French Revolution also led to heated debates, while the imposition of an excise tax on whiskey fueled open rebellion on the Pennsylvania frontier. Although a majority of Federalists supported Hamilton and an alliance with Britain, they faced growing opposition from those who advocated agrarian ideals and supported the French Revolution.

Conflicts among Federalists drew many Americans into debates over government programs, but large groups remained marginalized or excluded from the political system. Indians, African Americans, and women had little voice in policies that directly affected them. Even white workingmen and farmers found it difficult to influence political priorities and turned to petitions, protests, and even armed uprisings to demonstrate their views.

By 1796, Jefferson and Madison, who led the opposition among Federalists, had formed a separate political party, the Democratic-Republicans. They considered passage of the Alien and Sedition Acts as a direct attack on their supporters, and in 1800 wrested control of Congress and the presidency from the Federalists. Still, this peaceful transition in power boded well for the young United States.

Despite political setbacks, the Federalist legacy remained powerful. Hamilton's policies continued to shape national economic growth, and Federalists retained political power in the Northeast for decades. Meanwhile the benefits that small farmers and frontiersmen like Daniel Shays hoped to gain under Democratic-Republican rule proved largely elusive. Marginalized Americans, including Indians and African Americans, also gained little from the transition to Democratic-Republican leadership. Indeed, the growth of slavery and U.S. westward expansion created greater burdens for these groups.

Yet the Democratic-Republican Party would not be seriously challenged for national power until 1824, giving it nearly a quarter century to implement its vision of the United States. Members of this heterogeneous party would now have to learn to compromise with each other if they were going to achieve their goal of limited federal power in an agrarian republic.

Chapter 7 Review

KEY TERMS

Treaty of Fort Stanwix, 165
Northwest Ordinance, 165
republican motherhood, 170
Shays's Rebellion, 171
Virginia Plan, 172
New Jersey Plan, 172
three-fifths compromise, 173
Federalists, 174
Antifederalists, 174
Bill of Rights, 176

Jay Treaty, 179
Whiskey Rebellion, 180
Treaty of Greenville, 181
Pinckney Treaty, 182
Democratic-Republicans, 183
XYZ affair, 184
Alien and Sedition Acts, 185
Virginia and Kentucky
   Resolutions, 185

REVIEW & RELATE

1. What challenges did the new nation face in the immediate aftermath of the Revolutionary War?
2. How did farmers, financial leaders, foreign nations, and Indians react to government efforts to address challenges after the Revolution?
3. How did America's experience of the Revolutionary War change the lives of African Americans and women?
4. What do uprisings by farmers and debtors tell us about social and economic divisions in the early Republic?
5. What issues attracted the most intense debate during the drafting and ratification of the Constitution? Why?

6. How did Hamilton's policies stabilize the national economy, and why did they nonetheless arouse opposition?

7. How did events overseas shape domestic American politics and frontier policy in the 1790s?

8. What common concerns underlay the Whiskey Rebellion and Shays's Rebellion? How did the U.S. government deal differently with each?

9. What were the main issues dividing the Federalists and the Democratic-Republicans?

10. What do the Alien and Sedition Acts and the election of 1800 tell us about political partisanship in late-eighteenth-century America?

TIMELINE OF EVENTS

1783	• Continental Army officers threaten to mutiny
1784	• Treaty of Fort Stanwix
1785	• Northwest Ordinance passed
	• Annapolis Convention
1786–1787	• Shays's Rebellion
1787	• Constitutional Convention in Philadelphia
	• Northwest Ordinance revised
1788	• U.S. Constitution ratified
1789	• Alexander Hamilton named secretary of the treasury
	• Judiciary Act of 1789 passed
1789–1799	• French Revolution
1790–1794	• Little Turtle leads pan-Indian alliance in the Ohio valley
1791	• Bill of Rights ratified
1793	• Neutrality Proclamation
	• Yellow fever epidemic paralyzes Philadelphia
1794	• Whiskey Rebellion
	• African Methodist Episcopal Church founded
1796	• Jay Treaty and Pinckney Treaty ratified
	• Democratic-Republican Party established
1798	• Alien and Sedition Acts passed
1800	• Election of Thomas Jefferson as president

8

The Early Republic

1790–1820

LEARNING OBJECTIVES

After reading this chapter you will be able to:

- Analyze the ways that social and cultural leaders worked to craft an American identity and how that was complicated by racial, ethnic, and class differences.

- Interpret how the Democratic-Republican ideal of limiting federal power was transformed by international events, westward expansion, and Supreme Court rulings between 1800 and 1808.

- Explain the ways that technology reshaped the American economy and the lives of distinct groups of Americans.

COMPARING AMERICAN HISTORIES

When **Parker Cleaveland** graduated from Harvard University in 1799, his parents expected him to pursue a career in medicine, law, or the ministry. Instead, he turned to teaching. In 1805 Cleaveland secured a position in Brunswick, Maine, as professor of mathematics and natural philosophy at Bowdoin College. A year later, he married Martha Bush. Over the next twenty years, the Cleavelands raised eight children on the Maine frontier, entertained visiting scholars, corresponded with families at other colleges, and boarded dozens of students. While Parker taught the students math and science, Martha trained them in manners and morals. The Cleavelands also served as a model of new ideals of companionate marriage, in which husbands and wives shared interests and affection.

Professor Cleaveland believed in using scientific research to benefit society. When Brunswick workers asked him to identify local rocks, Parker began studying geology and chemistry. In 1816 he published his *Elementary*

189

Treatise on Mineralogy and Geology, providing a basic text for students and interested adults. He also lectured throughout New England, displaying mineral samples and performing chemical experiments.

The Cleavelands viewed the Bowdoin College community as a laboratory in which distinctly American values and ideas could be developed and sustained. So, too, did the residents of other college towns. Although less than 1 percent of men in the United States attended universities at the time, frontier colleges were considered important vehicles for bringing virtue—especially service for the public good—to the far reaches of the early republic. Yet several of these colleges were constructed with the aid of enslaved labor, and all were built on land bought or confiscated from Indians.

The purchase of the Louisiana Territory by President Thomas Jefferson in 1803 marked a new American frontier and ensured further encroachments on native lands. The territory covered 828,000 square miles and stretched from the Mississippi River to the Rocky Mountains and from New Orleans to present-day Montana. The area was home to tens of thousands of indigenous inhabitants.

Three years before the Louisiana Purchase, a Hidatsa raiding party swept into a Shoshone village in the Rocky Mountains and seized captives, including a girl about twelve years old. The girl, **Sacagawea**, and her fellow captives were marched hundreds of miles to a Hidatsa-Mandan village on the Missouri River. Eventually Sacagawea was sold to a French trader, Toussaint Charbonneau, along with another young Shoshone woman, and both became his wives.

In November 1804, an expedition led by Meriwether Lewis and William Clark set up winter camp near this Hidatsa village. The U.S. government had sent Lewis and Clark to document flora and fauna in the Louisiana Territory, enhance trade, and explore routes to the Northwest. Charbonneau, who spoke French and Hidatsa, and Sacagawea, who spoke several Indian languages, joined the expedition as interpreters in April 1805.

The only woman in the party, Sacagawea gave birth during the journey and then traveled with her infant son strapped to her back. Although no portraits of her exist, her presence was crucial, as Clark noted in his journal: "The Wife of Chabono our interpreter we find reconsiles all the Indians, as to our friendly intentions." Sacagawea helped persuade native leaders to assist the expedition, but her extensive knowledge of the terrain and fluency in Indian languages were equally important.

COMPARING THE AMERICAN HISTORIES of Parker Cleaveland and Sacagawea highlights the distinct ways that individuals contributed to the development of the United States and of national identities. Cleaveland was part of a generation of intellectuals who symbolized Americans' ingenuity. Although Sacagawea was not considered learned, her understanding of Indian languages and western geography was crucial to Lewis and Clark's success. Like many other Americans, Sacagawea and Cleaveland forged new identities as the young nation developed. Still, racial, class, and gender differences made it impossible to create a single American identity. At the same time, Democratic-Republican leaders sought to shape a new national identity by promising to limit federal power and enhance state authority and individual rights. Instead, western expansion, international crises, and Supreme Court decisions all contributed to the growth of federal power.

The Dilemmas of National Identity

In his inaugural address in March 1801, President Thomas Jefferson argued that the vast distance between Europe and the United States was a blessing, allowing Americans to develop their own unique culture and institutions. For many Americans, education offered one means of ensuring a distinctive national identity. Public schools could train American children in republican values, while the wealthiest among them could attend private academies and colleges. Newspapers, sermons, books, magazines, and other printed works could also help forge a common identity among the nation's far-flung citizens. Even the presence of Indians and Africans contributed to art and literature that were uniquely American. In addition, the construction of a new capital city to house the federal government offered a potent symbol of nationhood.

Yet these developments also illuminated political and racial dilemmas in the young nation. The decision to move the U.S. capital south from Philadelphia was prompted by concerns among southern politicians about the power of northern economic and political elites. The very construction of the capital, in which enslaved and free workers labored side by side, highlighted racial and class differences. Educational opportunities differed by race and class as well as by sex. How could a singular notion of American identity be forged in a country where differences of race, class, and sex loomed so large?

Education for a New Nation

The desire to create a specifically American culture emerged as soon as the Revolution ended. In 1783 Noah Webster, a schoolmaster, declared that "America must be as independent in *literature as in Politics*, as famous for *arts* as for *arms*." To promote his vision, Webster published the *American Spelling Book* (1810) and the *American Dictionary of the English Language* (1828). His books were widely used in the nation's expanding network of schools and academies and led to more standardized spelling and pronunciation of commonly used words.

Before the Revolution, public education for children was widely available in New England and the Middle Atlantic region. In the South, only those who could afford private schooling — perhaps 25 percent of the boys and 10 percent of the girls — received any formal instruction. Few young people enrolled in high school in any part of the colonies. Following the Revolution, state and national leaders proposed ambitious plans for public education, and in 1789 Massachusetts became the first state to insist that each town provide free schools for local children, though towns set attendance policies.

The American colonies boasted nine colleges that provided higher education for young men, including Harvard, Yale, King's College (Columbia), Queen's College (Rutgers), and the College of William and Mary. After independence, many Americans worried that these institutions were tainted by British and aristocratic influences. New colleges based on republican ideals were essential.

Frontier towns offered opportunities for colleges to enrich the community and benefit the nation. The relative isolation of these villages ensured that students would focus on education. And frontier colleges provided opportunities for ethnic and religious groups outside the Anglo-American mainstream — like Scots-Irish Presbyterians — to cement their place in American society. The young nation benefited but, once again, at the expense of Indians and their lands. For example, the founding of Franklin College in Athens, Georgia encouraged white settlement in the state's interior, an area largely populated by the Creek and Cherokee.

Frontier colleges were organized as community institutions composed of extended families, where administrators, faculty, and their wives guided students, hosted social events, and hired local workers, including servants and slaves. Women were viewed as exemplars of virtue in the new nation, and professors' wives served as maternal figures for young adults away from home. Families of modest means could send their sons

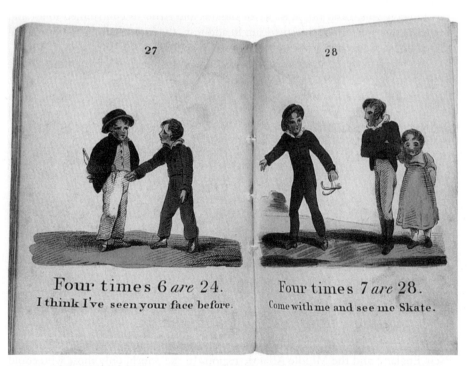

Marmaduke Multiply's Merry Method of Making Minor Mathematics, c. 1815   After Noah Webster introduced his American Spelling Book in 1810, math instructors introduced books for young people like the one shown here. The book uses rhymes and colorful illustrations to teach students multiplication tables. More and more educational books for children were published as public schools multiplied in the decades following the Revolution. Granger

to these less expensive colleges, depending on faculty couples to expand their intellect and provide moral guidance. In some towns, students at local female academies joined college men at chaperoned events to cultivate proper relations between the sexes. Female academies multiplied as well, with institutions such as the Young Ladies Academy of Philadelphia and the Albany (New York) Female Academy opening in the decades after the Revolution. Others, like the Moravian Female Seminary in Bethlehem, Pennsylvania, expanded their curriculum in the 1780s to provide young women with a wider range of intellectual and practical knowledge.

Literary and Cultural Developments

Older universities also contributed to the development of a national identity. A group known as the Hartford Wits, most of them Yale graduates, gave birth to a new literary tradition. Its members identified mainly as Federalists and published paeans to democracy, satires about Shays's Rebellion, and plays about the proper role of the central government in a republican nation. Developments in Europe, particularly liberal social ideas and Romantic beliefs in human perfectibility, also shaped American art, literature, philosophy, and architecture in the early nineteenth century. European Romantics, like the English poet William Wordsworth, the German philosopher Immanuel Kant, and the French painter Eugêne Delacroix, challenged Enlightenment ideas of rationality by insisting on the importance of human passion, the mysteries of nature, and the virtues of common folk.

American novelists in the early republic drew on these ideas as they sought to educate readers about virtue. Advances in printing and the manufacture of paper increased the circulation of novels, a literary genre developed in Britain and continental Europe at the turn of the eighteenth century. Improvements in girls' and young women's education then produced a growing audience for novels among women. American authors like Susanna Rowson and Charles Brockden Brown placed ordinary women and men in moments of high drama that tested their moral character. Novelists also emphasized new marital ideals, by which husbands and wives became affectionate partners and companions in creating a home and family.

Washington Irving was one of the most well-known literary figures in the early republic. He wrote a series of popular folktales, including "The Legend of Sleepy Hollow" and "Rip Van Winkle," that were published in his *Sketchbook* in 1820. They drew on Dutch culture in the Hudson valley region and often poked fun at more celebratory tales of early American history. In one serious essay, Irving challenged popular accounts of colonial wars that ignored courageous actions by Indians while applauding white atrocities.

Still, books glorifying the nation's past were also enormously popular. Just as European Romantics emphasized individual, especially heroic, action, so too did America's earliest historical writers. Among the most influential were Mason Weems, author of the *Life of Washington* (1806), a celebratory if fanciful biography, and Mercy Otis Warren, who wrote a three-volume *History of the Revolution* (1805). The influence of American authors increased as residents in both urban and rural areas purchased growing numbers of books.

Artists, too, devoted considerable attention to historical themes, though in the late eighteenth century, they tended more to Enlightenment perspectives. Charles

Willson Peale painted Revolutionary generals while serving in the Continental Army and became best known for his portraits of George Washington. Samuel Jennings offered a more radical perspective on the nation's character by incorporating women and African Americans into works like *Liberty Displaying the Arts and Sciences* (1792), but highlighted the importance of learning and rationality. So, too, did William Bartram, the son of a botanist. He journeyed through the southeastern United States and Florida, and published beautiful, and scientifically accurate, engravings of plants and animals in his *Travels* (1791). Engravings were less expensive than paintings so circulated more widely, and many highlighted national symbols like flags, eagles, and Lady Liberty.

In 1780, the Massachusetts legislature established the American Academy of Arts and Sciences to promote American literature and science. Six years later, Philadelphia's American Philosophical Society created the first national prize for scientific endeavor. Philadelphia was home as well to the nation's first medical college, founded at the University of Pennsylvania. Frontier colleges like Bowdoin also promoted new scientific discoveries. As in the arts, American scientists built on developments in continental Europe and Britain but prided themselves on contributing their own expertise.

Religious Renewal

Amid the wave of scientific discoveries, religious leaders sought to reinvigorate American spirituality. However, this spiritual renewal was rooted less in established churches and educated ministers than in new religious organizations and popular preachers. Methodist and Baptist churches were especially vital to this development. In 1780, only fifty Methodist churches existed in the United States. By 1820, it was the largest denomination in the nation, followed closely by Baptists. Believing that everyone could gain salvation, the two denominations appealed to small farmers, workers, and the poor as well to women and African Americans. Women already formed a majority of worshippers in many congregations, and some women — black and white — joined the popular ministries at the turn of the nineteenth century, A few women attracted followings independent of any church. In the late 1770s, Jemima Wilkinson, a white Quaker, began calling herself "the Publick Universal Friend." She developed a gender-neutral persona and proclaimed herself the "Spirit of Light." Wilkinson adopted men's clothing and gained devoted followers across New England who referred to the preacher as "he" or "him." Around the same time, Mother Ann Lee migrated from England to the United States and founded the first community of American Shakers, named after the ecstatic dances woven into their worship. Lee insisted on celibacy for herself and her followers, and women and men lived in separate dorm-like buildings. Shakers established rural communities, supporting themselves through farming and furniture making. They adopted children and welcomed converts to ensure their growth. In the early nineteenth century, a few women in the African Methodist Episcopal (AME) Church also requested the right to preach. Initially Richard Allen turned down such requests. However, in 1817, after hearing Jarena Lee offer an impromptu sermon from her seat at Mother Bethel, Allen changed his mind. In 1819, Lee was officially ordained a minister, preaching to interracial audiences of Baptists and Methodists as well as the AME Church.

In the rural South and in frontier areas, Baptists, Methodists, and Presbyterians organized camp meetings, where a dozen or more preachers, mostly men and many without formal training, tapped into deep wells of spirituality. The first camp meeting, held in Cane Ridge, Kentucky in 1801, attracted some 10,000 men and women. Whites and blacks, enslaved and free, attended these meetings and were encouraged to dance, shout, sing, and pray. For the next two decades, camp meetings continued to attract large crowds across the South and West.

The Racial Limits of "American" Culture

As white Americans sought to create a distinct national identity, they often wielded native names and symbols. Some Americans, including whiskey rebels, followed in the tradition of the Boston Tea Party, dressing as Indians to protest economic and political tyranny. More affluent whites also embraced this practice. The Tammany society, first founded in Philadelphia in 1772, expanded to other cities in the late eighteenth century. The society, named after a seventeenth-century Delaware chief called Tammend, promoted patriotism and republicanism. Its thirteen branches, named after Indian tribes, attracted large numbers of lawyers, merchants, and skilled artisans, who called their meetings "wigwams" and their leaders "sachems."

Poets, too, focused on American Indians. In his 1787 poem "Indian Burying Ground," Philip Freneau offered a sentimental portrait that highlighted the supposedly lost heritage of a nearly extinct native culture in New England. The theme of lost cultures and heroic (if still savage) Indians became even more pronounced in American poetry in the following decades. Such sentimental portraits were decidedly less popular along the nation's frontier, where indigenous communities continued to fight for their lands and rights.

White authors and artists offered far less sympathetic depictions of Africans and African Americans. Some positive images were produced in the North, intended for the rare patrons who opposed slavery. Typical images of blacks were far more demeaning, exaggerating their perceived physical and intellectual differences from whites to suggest their innate inferiority. Similarly, whites in frontier regions generally focused on natives' supposed savagery and duplicity.

Whether the depictions were realistic, sentimental, or derogatory, Africans, African Americans, and American Indians were almost always presented to the American public through the eyes of whites. Educated blacks like the Reverend Richard Allen of Philadelphia or the Reverend Thomas Paul of Boston wrote mainly for African American audiences or corresponded privately with sympathetic whites. Similarly, cultural leaders among American Indians worked mainly within their own nations either to maintain traditional languages and customs or to introduce what they considered more positive Anglo-American ideas and beliefs.

The improved educational opportunities available to white Americans generally excluded blacks and Indians. Most southern planters had little desire to teach their slaves to read and write. Even in the North, states did not generally incorporate black children into their plans for public education. African Americans in cities with large free black populations established the most long-lived schools for their race. The Reverend Allen opened a Sunday school for children in 1795 at Mother Bethel

AME Church, and other free blacks formed literary and debating societies. Still, only a small percentage of African Americans received an education equivalent to that available to whites in the early republic.

U.S. political leaders were more interested in the education of American Indians, but government officials left their schooling to religious groups. Several denominations sent missionaries to the Seneca, Cherokee, and other tribes, and a few successful students were then sent to American colleges to be trained as ministers or teachers for their own people. Eleazar Wheelock established an Indian Charity School in Connecticut in the 1760s. In 1765, he sent the Reverend Samson Occam, a Mohegan Presbyterian minister, to England, where he raised 12,000 pounds for a new school. That school, Dartmouth College, opened in 1769 in Hanover, New Hampshire. However, it educated mainly white men. Angered by Wheelock's betrayal, Occam founded the Christian Indian community of Brothertown in eastern New York in the late eighteenth century. The Oneida then established New Stockbridge in central New York, welcoming Mohicans from western Massachusetts and Lenape from Delaware. Occom arranged for these villages to receive official charters in 1787. In April 1792, shortly before his death, he evicted white settlers from Brothertown.

While largely unsuccessful, the divergent approaches whites took to educating Indians and African Americans demonstrated their broader assumptions about these groups. Most white Americans believed that Indians were untamed and uncivilized, but not innately different from Europeans. Africans and African Americans, on the other hand, were assumed to be inferior, and most whites believed that no amount of education could change that. As U.S. frontiers expanded, white Americans considered ways to "civilize" Indians and incorporate them into the nation. The requirements of slavery made it much more difficult for whites to imagine African Americans as anything more than lowly laborers, despite free blacks who clearly demonstrated otherwise.

Aware of the limited opportunities available in the United States, some African Americans considered moving elsewhere. In the late 1780s, the Newport African Union Society in Rhode Island developed a plan to establish a community for American blacks in Africa. Many whites, too, viewed the settlement of blacks in Africa as a way to solve what they considered the nation's racial dilemma.

Over the next three decades, the idea of emigration (as blacks viewed it) or colonization (as whites saw it) received widespread attention. Those who opposed slavery hoped to persuade slave owners to free or sell their human property on the condition that the former slaves be shipped to Africa. Some assumed that free blacks could find opportunities in Africa not available to them in the United States. Other whites simply wanted to rid the nation of its race problem by ridding it of blacks. In 1817 a group of southern enslavers and northern merchants formed the **American Colonization Society (ACS)** to establish colonies of freed slaves and free-born American blacks in Africa. Although some African Americans supported this scheme, northern free blacks generally opposed it, viewing colonization as an effort originating "more immediately from prejudice than philanthropy." Ultimately the plans of the ACS proved impractical. Particularly as cotton production expanded from the 1790s on, few plantation owners were willing to emancipate their workers.

A New Capital for a New Nation

While the construction of Washington City, the new national capital, provided an opportunity to highlight America's distinctive culture and identity, it also revealed enslavement as a crucial part of that identity. The capital was situated along the Potomac River between Virginia and Maryland, an area where more than 300,000 enslaved workers lived. Between 1792 and 1809, hundreds of enslaved men and a few women were hired out by their owners to build the capital. Owners were paid $5 per month for each laborer. Enslaved men cleared trees and stumps, built roads, dug trenches, baked bricks, and cut and laid sandstone while enslaved women cooked, did laundry, and nursed the sick and injured. A small number performed skilled labor as carpenters or assistants to stonemasons and surveyors. Four hundred slaves, more than half the labor force, worked on the Capitol building.

Free blacks also participated in the development of Washington. Many worked alongside enslaved laborers, but a few gained professional positions. Benjamin Banneker, for example, a self-taught clock maker, astronomer, and surveyor, was hired as an assistant to the surveyor Major Andrew Ellicott. In 1791 Banneker helped to plot the 100-square-mile site on which the capital was to be built.

African Americans often worked alongside Irish immigrants, whose wages were kept in check by the availability of enslaved labor. Most workers, regardless of race, faced poor housing, sparse meals, malarial fevers, and limited medical care. Despite these obstacles, in less than a decade, a system of roads was laid out and cleared, the Executive Mansion was built, and the north wing of the Capitol was completed.

More prosperous immigrants and foreign professionals were also involved in creating the U.S. capital. Irish-born James Hoban designed the Executive Mansion. A French engineer, Pierre Charles L'Enfant, planned the city's streets. William Thornton, a Scottish-trained physician born in the West Indies, drew the blueprints for the Capitol building and in 1802 became head of the U.S. Patent Office. Englishman Benjamin Latrobe, who migrated to the United States in 1795, directed the building's construction and was later appointed Surveyor of Public Buildings by Thomas Jefferson. Perhaps what was most "American" about the new capital was the diverse nationalities and races of those who designed and built it.

Washington's founders envisioned the city as a beacon to the world, proclaiming the advantages of the nation's republican principles. But its location on a slow-moving river and its clay soil left the area hot, humid, and dusty in the summer and muddy and damp in the winter and spring. When John Adams and his administration moved to Washington in June 1800, they considered themselves on the frontiers of civilization. The tree stumps that remained on the mile-long road from the Capitol to the Executive Mansion made it nearly impossible to navigate in a carriage. On rainy days, when roads proved impassable, officials walked or rode horses to work. Many early residents painted Washington in harsh tones. New Hampshire congressional representative Ebenezer Matroon wrote a friend, "If I wished to punish a culprit, I would send him to do penance in this place . . . this swamp — this lonesome dreary swamp, secluded from every delightful or pleasing thing."

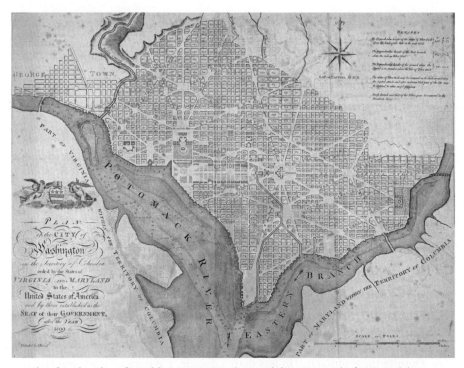

Plan for the City of Washington, 1795   The French-born Pierre L 'Enfant joined the Continental Army at age 23 in 1777 and served as a military engineer. Invited to design plans for Washington, he laid out a grand plan for broad boulevards, parks, and fountains, similar to those in major European cities. He also included a long mall stretching from the Potomac River east to the U.S. Capitol building.   From The New York Public Library, https://digitalcollections.nypl.org /items/510d47da-ef95-a3d9-e040-e00a18064a99

Despite its critics, Washington was the seat of federal power and thus played an important role in the social and political worlds of American elites. From January through March, the height of the social season, the wives of congressmen, judges, and other officials created a lively schedule of teas, parties, and balls in the capital city. When Thomas Jefferson became president, he opened the White House to visitors on a regular basis. Yet for all his republican principles, Jefferson moved into the Executive Mansion with a retinue of slaves.

In decades to come, Washington City would become Washington, D.C., a city with broad boulevards decorated with beautiful monuments to the American political experiment. And the Executive Mansion would become the White House, a proud symbol of republican government. Yet Washington was always characterized by wide disparities in wealth, status, and power, which were especially visible when enslaved laborers worked in the Executive Mansion's kitchen, laundry, and yard. President Jefferson's efforts to incorporate new territories into the United States only exacerbated these divisions by providing more economic opportunities for white planters, investors, and farmers while ensuring the expansion of slavery and the decimation of American Indians.

**REVIEW &
RELATE**
- How did developments in education, literature, and the arts contribute to the emergence of a distinctly American identity?
- How did African Americans and American Indians contribute to and challenge predominantly white views of American identity?

Extending Federal Power

Thomas Jefferson, like other Democratic-Republicans, envisioned the United States as a republic composed of small, independent farmers who had little need and less desire for expansive federal power. Despite Jefferson's early efforts to impose this vision on the government, developments in international affairs soon converged with Supreme Court rulings to expand federal power. But Jefferson, too, contributed to this expansion by purchasing the Louisiana Territory from France in 1803. The development of this vast territory increased federal authority and raised new questions about the place of Indians and African Americans in a republican society.

A New Administration Faces Challenges

In 1801 Democratic-Republicans worked quickly to implement their vision of limited federal power. Holding the majority in Congress, they repealed the whiskey tax and let the Alien and Sedition Acts expire. Jefferson significantly reduced government expenditures and immediately set about slashing the national debt, cutting it nearly in half by the end of his second term. Democratic-Republicans also worked to curb the powers granted to the Bank of the United States and the federal court system.

Soon, however, international upheavals forced Jefferson to make fuller use of his presidential powers. The U.S. government had paid tribute to the Barbary States of North Africa during the 1790s to gain protection for American merchant ships. The new president opposed this practice and in 1801 refused to continue the payments. The Barbary pirates quickly resumed their attacks, and Jefferson was forced to send the U.S. Navy and Marine Corps to retaliate. Although a combined American and Arab force did not achieve their objective of capturing Tripoli, the Ottoman viceroy agreed to negotiate a new agreement with the United States. Seeking to avoid all-out war, Congress accepted a treaty with the Barbary States that reduced the tribute payment.

Jefferson also followed the developing crisis in the West Indies during the 1790s. In 1791 slaves on the sugar-rich island of Saint Domingue launched a revolt against French rule. Inspired in part by the American Declaration of Independence, the **Haitian Revolution** escalated into a long and complicated conflict in which free people of color, white enslavers, and enslaved laborers formed competing alliances with British and Spanish forces as well as with leaders of the French Revolution. Finally, in December 1799, Toussaint L'Ouverture, a military leader and former slave, claimed the presidency of the new Republic of Haiti. But Napoleon Bonaparte seized power in France that same year and sent thousands of troops to reclaim the island. Toussaint was shipped off to France, where he died in prison. Many Haitians fled to the United States, but other Haitian rebels continued the fight.

The Haitian Revolution emboldened black people throughout the Americas as it frightened whites. In the United States, whites feared it might incite uprisings among the enslaved. In 1800 Gabriel, an enslaved blacksmith in Richmond, Virginia, plotted a rebellion. Inspired by the American and Haitian revolutions, supporters rallied around the demand for "Death or Liberty." Gabriel's plan failed when informants betrayed him to authorities. Nonetheless, news of the plot traveled across the South and terrified white residents. Their anxieties were heightened when in November 1803, prolonged fighting, yellow fever, and the loss of sixty thousand soldiers forced Napoleon to admit defeat in Haiti, and it became the first independent black-led nation in the Americas.

The Louisiana Purchase and Indian Societies

In France's defeat Jefferson saw an opportunity to gain navigation rights on the Mississippi River, which the French controlled. This was a matter of crucial concern to Americans living west of the Appalachian Mountains. Jefferson sent James Monroe to France to offer Napoleon $2 million to ensure Americans the right of navigation and deposit (i.e., offloading cargo from ships) on the Mississippi. To Jefferson's surprise, Napoleon offered instead to sell the entire Louisiana Territory for $15 million.

The president agonized over the constitutionality of this **Louisiana Purchase**. Since the Constitution contained no provisions for buying land from foreign nations, a strict interpretation would prohibit the purchase. In the end, though, the opportunity proved too tempting, and the president finally agreed to the purchase. Jefferson justified his decision by arguing that the territory would allow for the removal of more Indians from east of the Mississippi River, end European influence in the region, and expand U.S. trade networks. Opponents viewed the purchase as benefiting mainly agrarian interests and suspected Jefferson of trying to offset Federalist power in the Northeast. Still, the acquisition proved popular among ordinary Americans, most of whom focused on the opportunities it offered rather than the expansion of federal power it ensured.

Neither political party was concerned about the French, Spanish, or native peoples living in the region. When the Senate approved the purchase in October 1803, life had already changed dramatically for Indians in particular. In the late 1770s, Lakota Indians (called Sioux by Americans) expanded into the Black Hills of present-day South Dakota, forcing out the Cheyenne who had lived there. This mountainous region became a sacred site as well as the center of their bison- and horse-based society. Between 1779 and 1784, a smallpox epidemic ravaged Plains Indians, spreading along western trade routes and hitting children and pregnant women particularly hard. Some native bands lost 80 percent of their population, which led to further migration and a reconfiguration of communities. In the late eighteenth century, Russian traders—all male—discovered the value of sea otter pelts along North America's Northwest coast. Their rush to capture the trade before Spanish and American adventurers could do so introduced new diseases as well as cloth and metal goods to native societies, led to sexual assaults on women in the region, and produced drastic changes in native economies. In these difficult circumstances, some native Alutiiq women developed long-term relationships with Siberian peasants drawn into the dangerous work of capturing sea otters. These relationships, like those in French Canada, provided Russian men with assistance in gathering pelts and Alutiiq women with greater physical security and access to food, clothing, and other Russian trade goods.

At Jefferson's request, Congress had already appropriated funds for an expedition known as the **Corps of Discovery** to explore territory along the Missouri River. That expedition would now explore much of the Louisiana Territory. The president's personal secretary, Meriwether Lewis, headed the venture and invited fellow Virginian William Clark to serve as co-captain. The two set off with about forty-five men on May 14, 1804. For two years, they traveled thousands of miles up the Missouri River, through the northern plains, over the Rocky Mountains, and beyond the Louisiana Territory to the Pacific coast. Sacagawea and her husband joined them in April 1805, serving as guides and translators as they headed into the Rocky Mountains. Throughout the expedition, members meticulously recorded observations about local plants and animals as well as Indian residents, providing valuable evidence for young scientists like Parker Cleaveland and fascinating information for ordinary Americans.

Sacagawea was the only Indian to travel as a permanent member of the expedition, but many other native women and men assisted the Corps when it journeyed near their villages. They provided food and lodging for the Corps, hauled baggage up steep mountain trails, and traded food, horses, and other items. The one African American on the expedition, named York, also helped negotiate trade with local Indians. Although enslaved, York realized his value as a trader, hunter, and scout, and asked Clark for his freedom when the expedition ended in 1806. York did eventually become a free man, but it is not clear whether it was by Clark's choice or York's escape.

Other expeditions followed Lewis and Clark's venture. In 1806 Lieutenant Zebulon Pike led a group to explore the southern portion of the Louisiana Territory (Map 8.1). After traveling from St. Louis to the Rocky Mountains, the expedition entered Mexican territory. In early 1807, Pike and his men were captured by Mexican forces. They were returned to the United States at the Louisiana border that July. Pike had learned a great deal about lands that would eventually become part of the United States and about Mexican desires to overthrow Spanish rule, information that proved valuable over the next two decades.

Early in this series of expeditions, in November 1804, Jefferson easily won reelection as president. His popularity among farmers, already high, increased when Congress reduced the minimum allotment for federal land sales from 320 to 160 acres. This act allowed more farmers to purchase land on their own rather than via speculators. Yet by the time of Jefferson's second inauguration in March 1805, the president's vision of limiting federal power had been shattered by his own actions and those of the Supreme Court.

The Supreme Court Extends Its Reach

In 1801, just before the Federalist-dominated Congress turned over power to the Democratic-Republicans, it passed a new **Judiciary Act**. The act created six additional circuit courts and sixteen new judgeships, which President Adams filled with Federalist "midnight appointments" before he left office. Jefferson accused the Federalists of having "retired into the judiciary" and worried that "from that battery all

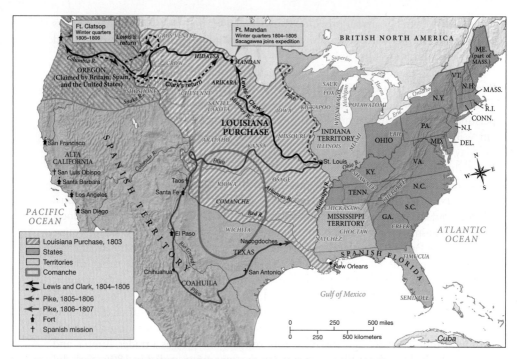

MAP 8.1   Lewis and Clark and Zebulon Pike Expeditions, 1804–1807
The expeditions led by Meriwether Lewis, William Clark, and Zebulon Pike illustrate the vast regions explored in just four years after the U.S. purchase of the Louisiana Territory. Journeying through and beyond the borders of that territory, the explorers gathered information about Indian nations, plants, animals, and the natural terrain even as Comanche and Shoshone nations, with access to horses, transformed the region.

the works of Republicanism are to be beaten down and destroyed." Meanwhile John Marshall, chief justice of the United States (1801–1835), insisted that the powers of the Supreme Court must be equal to and balance those of the executive and legislative branches.

One of the first cases to test the Court's authority involved a dispute over President Adams's midnight appointments. Jefferson's secretary of state, James Madison, refused to deliver the appointment papers to several of the appointees, including William Marbury. Marbury and three others sued Madison to receive their commissions. In *Marbury v. Madison* (1803), the Supreme Court ruled that it was not empowered to force the executive branch to give Marbury his commission. But in his decision, Chief Justice Marshall declared that the Supreme Court did have the duty "to say what the law is." He thus asserted a fundamental constitutional power: that the Supreme Court had the authority to decide which federal laws were constitutional. The following year, the Court also claimed the right to rule on the constitutionality of state laws. In doing so, the justices rejected Democratic-Republicans' claim that state legislatures had the power to repudiate federal law. Instead, the Supreme Court declared that federal laws took precedence over state laws.

Over the next dozen years, the Supreme Court continued to assert Federalist principles. In 1810 it insisted that it was the proper and sole arena for determining matters of constitutional interpretation. Then in 1819, the highest court reinforced its loose interpretation of the Constitution's implied powers clause in ***McCulloch v. Maryland***. This clause gave the federal government the right to "make all laws which shall be necessary and proper" for carrying out the explicit powers granted to it by the Constitution. Despite Democratic-Republicans' earlier opposition to a national bank, Congress chartered the Second Bank of the United States in 1816, and its branch banks issued notes that circulated widely in local communities. Legislators in Maryland, believing that branch banks had gained excessive power, approved a tax on their operations. Marshall's Court ruled that the establishment of the bank was "necessary and proper" for the functioning of the national government and rejected Maryland's right to tax the branch bank, claiming that "the power to tax involves the power to destroy."

By 1820 the Supreme Court, under the forceful direction of John Marshall, had established the power of judicial review—the authority of the nation's highest court to rule on cases involving states as well as the nation. From the Court's perspective, the judiciary was as important an institution in framing and preserving a national agenda as Congress or the president.

Democratic-Republicans Expand Federal Powers

Although Democratic-Republicans generally opposed Marshall's rulings, they, too, continued to expand federal power. Once again, international developments drove the administration's political agenda. By 1805 the security of the United States was threatened by continued conflicts between France and Great Britain. Both sought alliances with the young nation, and both ignored U.S. claims of neutrality. Indeed, each nation sought to punish Americans for trading with the other. Britain's Royal Navy began stopping American ships carrying sugar and molasses from the French West Indies and, between 1802 and 1811, impressed more than eight thousand sailors from such ships, including many American citizens. France claimed a similar right to stop U.S. ships that continued to trade with Great Britain.

Unable to convince foreign powers to recognize U.S. neutrality, Jefferson and Madison pushed for congressional passage of an embargo that they hoped would, like colonial boycotts, force Great Britain's hand. In 1807 Congress passed the **Embargo Act**, which prohibited U.S. ships from leaving their home ports until Britain and France repealed their restrictions on American trade. Although the act kept the United States out of war, it had a devastating impact on national commerce.

New England merchants immediately voiced their outrage, and some began sending goods to Europe via Canada. In response, Congress passed the Force Act, granting extraordinary powers to customs officials to end such smuggling. The economic pain caused by the rapid decline in trade spread well beyond the merchant class. Parker Cleaveland was forced to sell his home to the Bowdoin trustees and become their tenant. Farmers and urban workers as well as southern planters suffered the embargo's effects more directly. Exports nearly stopped, and sailors and dockworkers faced escalating unemployment. With the recession deepening, American concerns about the expansion of federal power reemerged. Congress and the president had not simply regulated international trade; they had brought it to a halt.

Still, despite the failure of the Embargo Act, many Americans viewed Jefferson favorably. He had devoted his adult life to the creation of the United States. He had purchased the Louisiana Territory, opening up vast lands to exploration, settlement, and development. This geographical boon encouraged inventors and artisans to pursue ideas that would help the early republic take full advantage of its resources and recover from its current economic plight. Some must have wondered, however, how a Democratic-Republican president had so significantly expanded the power of the federal government.

REVIEW & RELATE	• How did the Federalist-dominated courts and the Democratic-Republican president and Congress each contribute to the expansion of the federal government? • How did the purchase of the Louisiana Territory from France and international conflicts with France and Britain shape domestic issues in the late eighteenth and early nineteenth centuries?

Remaking America's Economic Character

As the United States expanded geographically, technological ingenuity became a highly valued commodity. The spread of U.S. settlements into new territories necessitated improved forms of transportation and communication and increased demands for muskets and other weapons to protect the nation's frontier. The growing population also fueled improvements in agriculture and manufacturing to meet demands for clothing, food, and farm equipment. And continued conflicts with Great Britain and France highlighted the nation's need to develop its natural resources and technological capabilities. Yet even though American ingenuity was widely praised, the daily lives of most Americans changed slowly. And for some, especially enslaved women and men, technological advances only added to their burdens.

Native Lands and American Migrations

Although Democratic-Republicans initially hoped to limit the powers of the national government, the rapid growth of the United States pulled in the opposite direction. An increased population, combined with the exhaustion of farmland along the eastern seaboard, fueled migration to the West as well as the growth of cities. These developments heightened conflicts with native tribes and over slavery, but they also encouraged innovations in transportation and communication and improvements in agriculture and manufacturing.

As white Americans encroached more deeply on lands settled by native peoples, Indian tribes were forced ever westward. As early as 1800, groups like the Shoshone, who originally inhabited the Great Plains, had been forced into the Rocky Mountains by Indians moving into the plains from the Mississippi and Ohio valleys (Map 8.2). Sacagawea must have realized that the expedition she accompanied would only increase pressure on the Shoshone and other tribes as white migration escalated.

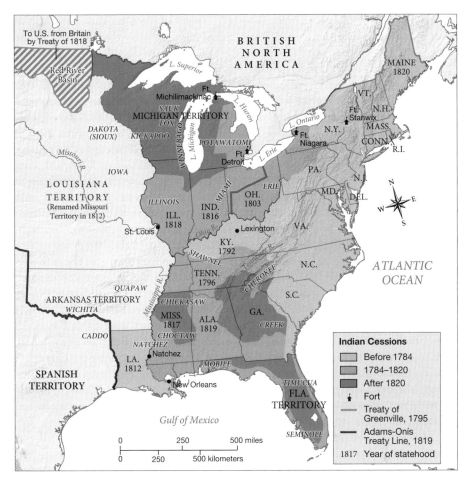

MAP 8.2   Indian Land Cessions, 1790–1820

With the ratification of the Constitution, the federal government gained greater control over Indian relations, including land cessions. At the same time, large numbers of white settlers poured into regions west of the Appalachian Mountains. The U.S. government gained most of this Indian land by purchase or treaty, but these agreements were often the consequence of military victories by the U.S. Army.

Indeed, President Jefferson ordered William Hull, Governor of Michigan Territory, to obtain Indian lands around military posts, such as Fort Detroit, to ensure American control should war erupt with Britain. Hull wrote Jefferson in December 1807, describing his meeting with native leaders, whom he addressed as "My Children." To Jefferson, Hull highlighted the economic benefits accruing to Indians; in discussions with Ottawa, Potawatomi, and other chiefs, he emphasized the military dangers created by ongoing tensions between the U.S. and Britain. Tribes would be "unmolested" if they agreed to cede lands and remain neutral in any future conflict. If they sided with the British, however, the United States would "lift the hatchet" and exterminate them. The 1807 Treaty of Detroit granted millions of acres of native land to the United States, encouraging more Americans to migrate west.

Thousands more moved to cities. Although the vast majority of Americans lived in rural areas, many young people sought job opportunities in manufacturing, skilled trades, and service work. Cities were defined at the time as places with 8,000 or more inhabitants, but New York City and Philadelphia both counted more than 100,000 residents by 1810. In New York a decade later, immigrants, most of them Irish, made up about 10 percent of the population and twice that percentage by 1825. At the same time, the number of African Americans in New York City increased to more than 10,000. Cities began to emerge along the nation's frontier as well. After the Louisiana Purchase, New Orleans became a key commercial center while western migration fueled cities like Cincinnati. Meanwhile Detroit, poised on the Canadian-U.S. border, maintained its multicultural population of French, British, American, Indian, and African American residents, the latter two groups including free and enslaved members. As the area gradually came under the authority of the nascent U.S. government, Detroit residents found themselves entangled in a complex web of laws and customs. Thus despite the supposed abolition of slavery via the Northwest Ordinance, many local enslavers managed to hold on to their human chattel even as the enslaved ran away, sued in court, and resisted in other ways. Smaller outposts further west, like Farnhamsburg (later Rock Island, Illinois), were founded by U.S. pioneers seeking trade with native communities. This post's location on the Mississippi River made it an important stop for migrants as trading posts multiplied throughout the Mississippi valley in the 1820s and 1830s. Continuing to serve as sites of exchange between Indians, French and American traders, and migrants, many created the foundation for later cities (Table 8.1).

Most Americans who headed west hoped to benefit from the increasingly liberal terms for land offered by the federal government. Yeomen farmers sought sufficient acreage to feed their families and grow some crops for sale. They were eager to settle in western sections of the original thirteen states, in the Ohio River valley, or in newly opened territories along the Missouri and Kansas Rivers. In the South, small farmers had to compete with slave-owning planters who headed west in the early nineteenth century. Migrants to the Mississippi valley also had to contend with a sizable population of Spanish and French residents, as well as Chickasaw and Creek Indians in the South and Shawnee, Chippewa, Sauk, and Fox communities farther north.

The development of roads and turnpikes hastened the movement of people and the transportation of goods. Frontier farmers wanted to get their produce to eastern markets quickly and cheaply. Before completion of the Lancaster Turnpike in Pennsylvania, it cost as much to carry wheat overland the sixty-two miles to Philadelphia as it did to ship it by sea from Philadelphia to London. Those who lived farther west faced even greater challenges. With the admission of Kentucky (1792), Tennessee (1796), and Ohio (1803) to the Union, demands for congressional support for building transportation routes grew louder. By 1819 five more states had been admitted along the Mississippi River, from Louisiana to Illinois.

During Jefferson's administration, secretary of the treasury Albert Gallatin urged Congress to fund roads and canals to enhance the economic development of the nation. He advocated a "great turnpike road" along the Atlantic seaboard from Maine

TABLE 8.1	PRICES AT GEORGE DAVENPORT'S TRADING POST, ROCK ISLAND, ILLINOIS, C. 1820		
Item	Price	Item	Price
Ax	$6.00	Large copper kettle	$30.00
Beaver trap	$8.00	Lead	$0.20 per pound
Black silk handkerchief	$2.00	Lead shot for guns	$1.00 per 5 pounds
Breechcloth	$3.00	Medium copper kettle	$10.00
Bridles	$2.00–$10.00	Muskrat spear	$2.00
Chain for staking down traps	$0.75 per 6 feet	Muskrat trap	$5.00
Combs	$1.00 per pair	Muslin or calico shirt	$3.00
File (for sharpening axes)	$2.00	Ordinary butcher knife	$0.50
Flannel	$1.00 per yard	Sheet iron kettle	$10.00
Flannel mantle	$3.00	Small copper kettle	$3.00
Gunflints	$1.00 per 15	Spurs	$6.00 per pair
Hand-size mirrors	$0.25	Tin kettle	$14.00
Heavy wool cloth	$10.00 per yard	Tomahawk	$1.50
Hoe	$2.00	Trade gun	$20.00–$25.00
Horn of gunpowder	$1.50	Wool blanket	$4.00
Horses	$35.00–$50.00	Wool mantle (short cloak or shawl)	$4.00

Source: Will Leinicke, Marion Lardner, and Ferrel Anderson, Two Nations, One Land (Rock Island, IL: Citizens to Preserve Black Hawk Park, 1981).

to Georgia as well as roads to connect the four main rivers that flowed from the Appalachians to the Atlantic Ocean. Although traditionally such projects were funded by the states, in 1815 Congress approved funds for a **National Road** from western Maryland through southwestern Pennsylvania to Wheeling, West Virginia. This so-called Cumberland Road was completed in 1818 and later extended into Ohio and Illinois.

Carrying people and goods by water remained faster and cheaper than transporting them over land, but rivers ran mainly north and south. In addition, although loads could be delivered quickly downstream, the return voyage was long and slow. While politicians advocated the construction of canals along east-west routes to link river systems, inventors and mechanics focused on building boats powered by steam to overcome the problem of sending goods upriver.

In 1804 Oliver Evans, a machinist in Philadelphia, invented a high-pressure steam engine attached to a dredge that cleaned the silt around the docks in Philadelphia harbor. He had insufficient funds, however, to pursue work on a steam-powered boat. Robert Fulton, a New Yorker, improved on Evans's efforts, using the low-pressure steam engine developed in England. In 1807 Fulton launched the first successful steamboat, the *Clermont*, which traveled some 150 miles up the Hudson River from

New York City to Albany in only thirty-two hours. The powerful Mississippi River proved a greater challenge, but by combining Evans's high-pressure steam engine with a flat-bottom hull that avoided the river's sandbars, mechanics who worked along the frontier improved Fulton's design and launched the steamboat era in the West.

Technology Reshapes Agriculture and Industry

Advances in agricultural and industrial technology paralleled the development of roads and steamboats. And new inventions spurred others, inducing a **multiplier effect** that inspired additional dramatic changes. Two inventions in particular—the spinning machine and the cotton gin—transformed the deeply intertwined realms of southern agriculture and northern industry.

American developments were closely tied to the earlier rise of industry in Great Britain. Before the eighteenth century, India was the chief supplier to Europe of raw cotton and cotton cloth. As Britain gained control of crucial areas of the Indian subcontinent, notably Bengal, in the 1750s, they transformed international trade and manufacturing. The wealth gained from Bengal was used to develop British manufacturing, and by the 1770s, the English had built spinning mills in which steam-powered machines spun raw cotton into yarn. Raw cotton was imported from British-occupied India without tariffs. Cotton cloth was then exported to India, where cheaper British goods undercut homemade cloth. Eager to maintain their monopoly on industrial technology and the market in cloth, the British made it illegal for engineers to emigrate. However, officials could not stop everyone who worked in a cotton mill from leaving. At age fourteen, Samuel Slater was hired as an apprentice in an English mill that used a yarn-spinning machine designed by Richard Arkwright. Slater was promoted to supervisor of the factory but in 1789, at age twenty-one, he emigrated to America, seeking greater opportunities. While working in New York City, he learned that Moses Brown, a wealthy Rhode Island merchant, was eager to develop a machine like Arkwright's. Funded by Rhode Island investors and assisted by local craftsmen, Slater designed and built a spinning mill in Pawtucket.

The mill opened in December 1790 and began producing yarn, which was then woven into cloth in private shops and homes. By 1815 a series of cotton mills dotted the Pawtucket River. These factories offered workers, most of whom were the wives and children of farmers, a steady income, and they ensured employment for weavers in the countryside. They also increased the demand for cotton in New England just as British manufacturers sought additional sources of the crop as well.

Ensuring a steady supply of cotton required another technological innovation, this one created by Eli Whitney. After graduating from Yale, Whitney agreed to serve as a private tutor for a planter family in South Carolina. On the ship carrying him south, Whitney met the widow Catherine Greene, who invited him to stay at her Mulberry Plantation near Savannah, Georgia. There local planters complained to him about the difficulty of making a profit on cotton. Long-staple cotton, grown in the Sea Islands, yielded enormous profits, but the soil in most of the South could sustain only the short-staple variety, which required hours of intensive labor to separate its sticky green seeds from the cotton fiber.

In 1793, in as little as ten days, Eli Whitney built a machine that could speed the process of deseeding short-staple cotton. Using mesh screens, rollers, and wire brushes, Whitney's **cotton gin** could clean as much cotton fiber in one hour as several workers could clean in a day. Recognizing the gin's value, Whitney received a U.S. patent, but because the machine was easy to duplicate, he never profited from his invention. He did, however, transform southern agriculture and northern industry.

Whitney had other ideas that proved more profitable. In June 1798, amid U.S. fears of a war with France, the U.S. government granted him an extraordinary contract to produce 4,000 rifles in eighteen months. Adapting the plan of Honoré Blanc, a French mechanic who devised a musket with interchangeable parts, Whitney demonstrated the potential for using machines to produce various parts of a musket, which could then be assembled in mass quantities. With Jefferson's enthusiastic support, the federal government extended Whitney's contract, and by 1809 his New Haven factory was turning out 7,500 guns annually. Whitney's factory became a model for the **American system of manufacturing**, in which water-powered machinery and the division of production into several small tasks allowed less skilled workers to produce mass quantities of a particular item. Moreover, the factories developed by Whitney and Slater became training grounds for younger mechanics and inventors who devised improvements in machinery or set out to solve new technological puzzles. Their efforts also transformed the lives of generations of workers—enslaved and free—who planted and picked the cotton, spun the yarn, wove the cloth, and sewed the clothes that cotton gins and spinning mills made possible.

Transforming Domestic Production

Slater and Whitney were among the most influential American inventors, but both required the assistance and collaboration of other inventors, machinists, and artisans to implement their ideas. The achievement of these enterprising individuals was seen by many Americans as part of a larger spirit of inventiveness and technological ingenuity that characterized U.S. identity. Although many Americans built on foreign ideas and models, a cascade of inventions appeared in the United States between 1790 and 1820.

Cotton gins and steam engines, steamboats and interchangeable parts, gristmills and spinning mills, clocks and woodworking lathes—each of these items and processes was improved over time and led to myriad other inventions. For instance, in 1811 Francis Cabot invented a power loom for weaving, a necessary step once spinning mills began producing more yarn than hand weavers could handle. Eventually clocks would be used to routinize the labor of workers in those mills so that they all arrived, ate lunch, and left at the same time.

Despite these rapid technological advances, the changes that occurred in the early nineteenth century were more evolutionary than revolutionary. Most political leaders and social commentators viewed gradual improvement as a blessing. For many Americans, the ideal situation consisted of either small mills scattered through the countryside or household enterprises that could supply neighbors with finer cloth, sturdier chairs, or other items that improved household comfort and productivity.

The importance of domestic manufacturing increased after passage of the Embargo Act as imports of cloth and other items fell dramatically. Small factories, like those along the Pawtucket River, increased their output, and so did ordinary housewives. Blacksmiths, carpenters, and wheelwrights busily repaired and improved the spindles, looms, and other equipment that allowed family members to produce more and better cloth from wool, flax, and cotton. These developments allowed some Americans, especially in towns and cities, to achieve a middling status between poorer laborers and wealthier elites. In this middling sector of society, new ideas about companionate marriage, which emphasized mutual obligations, may have encouraged husbands and wives to work more closely in domestic enterprises. While husbands generally carried out the heavier or more skilled parts of home manufacturing, like weaving, wives spun yarn and sewed together sections of cloth into finished goods.

At the same time, daughters, neighbors, and servants remained critical to the production of household items. In early nineteenth-century Hallowell, Maine, Martha Ballard labored alongside her daughters and a niece, producing cloth and food for domestic consumption, while she supplemented her husband's income as a surveyor by working as a midwife. Yet older forms of mutuality also continued, with neighbors sharing tools and equipment and those with specialized skills assisting neighbors in exchange for items they needed. Perhaps young couples imagined themselves embarking on more egalitarian marriages than those of their parents, but most still needed wider networks of support.

In wealthy households north and south, white servants and enslaved blacks took on a greater share of domestic labor in the late eighteenth and early nineteenth centuries. Most female servants in the North were white, young, and unmarried. Some arrived with children in tow or became pregnant on the job. Whether impregnated by consent or by force, these young women contributed to the rising rate of out-of-wedlock births following the Revolution. Meanwhile in the South, if enslaved household workers became pregnant their children added to the owner's labor supply. On larger plantations, owners increasingly assigned a few enslaved women to spin, cook, wash clothes, make candles, and wait on table. Plantation mistresses might also hire the wives of small farmers and landless laborers to spin cotton into yarn, weave yarn into cloth, and sew clothing for slaves and white children. While mistresses in both regions still engaged in household production, they expanded their roles as domestic managers.

However, most Americans at the turn of the nineteenth century continued to live on family farms, to produce or trade locally to meet their needs, and to use techniques handed down for generations. Yet by 1820 their lives, like those of wealthier Americans, were transformed by the expanding market economy, which over the next twenty years would inspire a market revolution. Gradually, more and more families would sew clothes with machine-spun thread made from cotton ginned in the American South, work their fields with newly invented cast-iron plows, and vary their diet by adding items shipped from other regions by steamboat.

Technology, Cotton, and Slaves

Some of the most dramatic technological changes occurred in agriculture, and none was more significant than the cotton gin, which led to the vast expansion of agricultural production and slavery in the South. This in turn fueled regional specialization, ensuring that residents in one area of the nation — the North, South, or West — depended on those in other areas. For instance, southern planters relied on the growing demand for cotton from northern manufacturers. At the same time, planters, merchants, manufacturers, and factory workers became more dependent on

The Cotton Gin, 1793
This colored lithograph by an anonymous American artist shows Eli Whitney's cotton gin at the center of complex transactions. Enslaved women and men haul and gin cotton. Meanwhile the planter appears to be bargaining with a cotton factor, or agent, who likely wants to purchase his crop for a northern manufacturer. Peter Newark American Pictures /Bridgeman Images

western farmers to produce grain and livestock to feed the nation. Despite their different relationships to agriculture and industry and to enslaved and free labor, Americans were increasingly bound to a **capitalist system** in which investment in and ownership of the means of production, distribution, and exchange was made and sustained primarily by private individuals and corporations rather than the government.

As cotton gins spread across the South, the system of slavery expanded into the interior of many states as well as into the lower Mississippi valley. While rice and sugar were also produced in the South, cotton quickly became the most important crop. In 1790 southern farms and plantations produced about 3,000 bales of cotton, each weighing about 300 pounds. By 1820, with the aid of the cotton gin, the South produced more than 330,000 bales annually (Table 8.2). For cotton growers, expansion meant increasing investments in cotton gins, wooden barrels, and most importantly, enslaved workers. For southern blacks, increased production meant increased burdens. Because seeds could be separated from raw cotton with much greater efficiency, farmers could plant vastly larger quantities of the crop. Although family members, neighbors, and hired hands performed this work on small farms with no or only a few slaves, wealthy planters, with perhaps a dozen enslaved workers, took advantage of rising cotton prices in the early eighteenth century to purchase and enslave more laborers.

The dramatic increase in the amount of cotton planted and harvested each year was paralleled by a jump in the size of the enslaved population. Thus, even as northern states began to abolish the institution, albeit slowly, southern enslavers dramatically increased the number of bondsmen and women they held. In 1790 there were fewer than 700,000 enslaved persons in the United States. By 1820 there were nearly 1.5 million. Still the demand increased even faster. Despite this population increase, growing competition for field hands drove up the price of the enslaved, which roughly doubled between 1795 and 1805.

TABLE 8.2	GROWTH OF COTTON PRODUCTION IN THE UNITED STATES, 1790–1830
Year	Production in Bales
1790	3,135
1795	16,719
1800	73,145
1805	146,290
1810	177,638
1815	208,986
1820	334,378
1825	532,915
1830	731,452

Source: Lewis Cecil Gray, *History of Agriculture in the Southern United States to 1860*, vol. 2 (Gloucester, MA: Peter Smith, 1958).

Although the international slave trade was banned in the United States in 1808, some planters smuggled in women and men from Africa and the Caribbean. Most planters, however, depended on enslaved women to bear more children, increasing the size of their labor force through natural reproduction. In addition, enslavers in the Deep South—from Georgia and the Carolinas west to Louisiana—began buying bound labor from farmers in Maryland and Virginia, where cotton and slavery were less profitable. Expanding slave markets in New Orleans and Charleston marked the continued importance of this domestic or internal slave trade as cotton moved west.

In the early nineteenth century, most white southerners believed that there was enough land to go around. And the rising price of cotton allowed small farmers to imagine they would someday be planters. Some southern Indians also placed their hopes in cotton. Cherokee and Creek Indians cultivated the crop, even purchasing enslaved blacks to increase production. Some Indian villages now welcomed ministers to their communities, hoping that embracing white culture might allow them to retain their current lands. Yet other native residents foresaw the increased pressure for land that cotton cultivation produced and organized to defend themselves from whites' invasion. Regardless of the policies adopted by Indians, cotton and slavery expanded rapidly into Cherokee- and Creek-controlled lands in the interior of Georgia and South Carolina. And the admission of the states of Louisiana, Mississippi, and Alabama between 1812 and 1819 marked the rapid spread of southern agriculture farther west.

Enslaved men and women played critical roles in the South's geographical expansion. Without their labor, neither cotton nor sugar could have become mainstays of the South's economy. The heavy work of carving out new plantations led most planters to select young enslaved men and women to move west, breaking apart families in the process. Some enslaved people resisted their removal and, if forced to go, used their role in the labor process to limit owners' control. They resisted by working slowly, breaking tools, and feigning illness or injury. Other enslaved women and men hid out temporarily as a respite from brutal work regimes or harsh punishments. Still others ran to areas controlled by Indians, hoping for better treatment, or to regions where slavery was no longer legal.

Yet given the power and resources wielded by whites, most enslaved people had to find ways to improve their lives within the system of bondage. The end of the international slave trade helped blacks in this regard since enslavers had to depend more on natural reproduction to increase their labor supply. To ensure that the enslaved lived longer and healthier lives, planters were forced to provide better food, shelter, and clothing. Some enslaved workers gained leverage to fish, hunt, or maintain small gardens to improve their diet. With the birth of more children, southern blacks also developed more extensive kinship networks, which often allowed other family members to care for children if their parents were compelled to move west. Enslavement was still brutal, but the enslaved made small gains that improved their chances of survival.

To find release from the oppressive burdens of daily life, enslaved southerners not only joined the camp meetings and religious revivals that burned across the southern frontier in the late eighteenth and early nineteenth century but also established their own religious ceremonies. These were often held in the woods or swamps at night, away from the prying eyes of planters and overseers.

Evangelical religion, combined with revolutionary ideals promoted in the United States and Haiti, proved a potent mix, and enslavers rarely lost sight of the potential dangers this posed to the system of bondage. Outright rebellions occurred only rarely, yet victory in Haiti and Gabriel's conspiracy in Virginia reminded the enslaved and owners alike that uprisings were possible. Clearly, the power of new American identities could not be separated from the dangers embedded in the nation's oppressive racial history.

REVIEW & RELATE	• How did new inventions and infrastructure improvements contribute to the development of the American economy? • Why did slavery expand and become more deeply entrenched in southern society in the early nineteenth century? What fears did this reinforce?

Conclusion: New Identities and New Challenges

The geographical and economic expansion that marked the period from 1790 to 1820 inspired scientific and technological advances as well as literary and artistic tributes to a distinctly American identity. For young ambitious men like Parker Cleaveland, Eli Whitney, Washington Irving, and Meriwether Lewis, the opportunities that opened in education, science, literature, and exploration offered possibilities for fame and financial success. While Whitney, Irving, and Lewis traveled widely, Cleaveland remained a professor of mathematics, mineralogy, and chemistry at Bowdoin, dying in Brunswick, Maine in 1858.

Lewis and Clark's efforts to open up the Louisiana Territory transformed the lives of many Americans. Along with the construction of roads, the invention of steamboats, and the introduction of iron plows, their Corps of Discovery opened up new lands for farming and also fueled the rise of western cities. Many white families sought fertile land, abundant wildlife, or opportunities for trade on the frontier. Yet these families often had to purchase land from speculators or compete with wealthy planters. And those who carved out farms might face Indians angered by the constant encroachment of white Americans on their lands.

New opportunities also appeared in eastern towns and cities as investors, inventors, and skilled artisans established factories and improved transportation. White women of middling or elite status could attend female academies, enter marriages based on ideals of companionship and mutual responsibilities, purchase rather than make cotton thread and cloth, and retain servants to perform the heaviest work. Yet these changes occurred gradually and unevenly. And while poorer white women might more easily find jobs in cotton mills or as servants, the pay was low and the hours long.

Transformations in white society introduced even more difficult challenges for African Americans. Despite the beginning of gradual emancipation in the North and the end of the international slave trade, slavery continued to grow. The invention of the cotton gin ensured the expansion of cotton cultivation into new areas, and many of the enslaved were forced to move west and leave family and friends behind. Enslaved women and men honed means of survival and resistance, but few could imagine a revolution like the one that took place in Haiti.

At the same time, all along the expanding U.S. frontier, American Indians faced continued pressure to leave their lands, embrace white culture, or both. In 1810 Sacagawea, Charbonneau, and their son Baptiste apparently traveled to St. Louis at the invitation of William Clark, who offered to pay for Baptiste's schooling. Sacagawea left Baptiste in Clark's care, and it is not clear whether she ever saw her son again. William Clark wrote "Se car ja we au Dead" on the cover of his cash book for 1825–1828, suggesting that she died during those years. By then, the Shoshone and Hidatsa were facing the onslaught of white settlement. They, along with Indians living in areas like Georgia, the Carolinas, and Tennessee, continued to resist U.S. expansion as they struggled to control the embattled frontier.

Indeed, the United States remained embattled throughout the early years of the republic. From 1790 to 1820, Great Britain, France, and the Barbary States of North Africa constantly challenged U.S. sovereignty from abroad while debates over slavery and conflicts over Indian lands multiplied at home. Moreover, as federal power expanded under Democratic-Republican rule, some Americans continued to worry about protecting the rights of states and of individuals. The American identities forged in the early republic would be continually tested as new challenges emerged and older conflicts intensified in the following decades.

Chapter 8 Review

KEY TERMS

American Colonization
   Society (ACS), 196
Haitian Revolution, 199
Louisiana Purchase, 200
Corps of Discovery, 201
Judiciary Act, 201
Marbury v. Madison, 202

McCulloch v. Maryland, 203
Embargo Act, 203
National Road, 207
multiplier effect, 208
cotton gin, 209
American system of manufacturing, 209
capitalist system, 211

REVIEW & RELATE

1. How did developments in education, literature, and the arts contribute to the emergence of a distinctly American identity?
2. How did African Americans and American Indians contribute to and challenge the predominantly white views of American identity?
3. How did the Federalist-dominated courts and the Democratic-Republican president and Congress each contribute to the expansion of the federal government?
4. How did the purchase of the Louisiana Territory from France and international conflicts with France and Britain shape domestic issues in the late eighteenth and early nineteenth centuries?
5. How did new inventions and infrastructure improvements contribute to the development of the American economy?
6. Why did slavery expand and become more deeply entrenched in southern society in the early nineteenth century? What fears did this reinforce?

TIMELINE OF EVENTS

1789	• Massachusetts institutes free public elementary education
1790	• Samuel Slater's spinning mill opens
1790–1820	• Cotton production in the South increases from 3,000 to 330,000 bales annually
	• U.S. slave population rises from 700,000 to 1.5 million
1791–1803	• Haitian Revolution
1792–1809	• New capital of Washington City constructed
1793	• Eli Whitney invents cotton gin
1801	• Judiciary Act
	• U.S. forces challenge Barbary pirates
	• Thousands attend camp meeting in Cane Ridge, Kentucky
1803	• Louisiana Purchase
	• *Marbury v. Madison*
1804–1806	• Corps of Discovery explores Louisiana Territory and Pacific Northwest
1807	• Robert Fulton launches first successful steamboat
	• Embargo Act
1810	• Population of New York and Philadelphia each exceeds 100,000
1817	• American Colonization Society founded
1819	• *McCulloch v. Maryland*
1820	• Washington Irving publishes *Sketchbook*
1828	• Noah Webster publishes *American Dictionary of the English Language*

9

Defending and Redefining the Nation

1809–1832

LEARNING OBJECTIVES

After reading this chapter you will be able to:

- Analyze the intertwined effects of conflicts on the frontier and with Britain on U.S. federal policies and the lives of white, black, and native Americans.

- Describe the role of state and federal governments in the nation's expansion and how expansion affected relations among increasingly distinct regions.

- Evaluate how the panic of 1819 and the Missouri Compromise affected and were affected by the nation's economic expansion and political divisions.

- Discuss how expanded voting rights for white working men, new racial restrictions, and continued debates over federal power led to political realignment.

- Explain the challenges that President Jackson faced in implementing federal policies on the tariff, the national bank, and the removal of the Cherokee.

COMPARING AMERICAN HISTORIES

Dolley Payne was raised on a Virginia plantation. But her Quaker parents, moved by the Society of Friends' growing antislavery sentiment, decided to free their slaves. In 1783, when Dolley was fifteen, the Paynes moved to Philadelphia. There, Dolley's father suffered heavy economic losses, and Dolley lost her first husband and her younger son to yellow fever. In 1794 the young widow met and married Virginia congressman James Madison. When the newly elected president Thomas Jefferson appointed Madison secretary of state in 1801, the couple moved to the new capital city of Washington.

216

Since Jefferson and his vice president, Aaron Burr, were widowers, **Dolley Madison** served as hostess for White House affairs. When James Madison succeeded Jefferson as president in 1809, he, too, depended on his wife's social skills and networks. Dolley held lively informal receptions to which she invited politicians, diplomats, cabinet officers, and their wives. These social events helped bridge the ideological differences that continued to divide Congress and proved crucial in creating a unified front when Congress declared war on Great Britain in 1812.

During the War of 1812, British forces attacked Washington City and burned the Executive Mansion, now called the White House. With the president away, his wife was left to secure important state papers, emerging as a symbol of national courage at a critical moment in the conflict. When peace came the following year, Dolley Madison quickly reestablished a busy social calendar to help mend divisions caused by the war.

In 1817, at the end of the president's second term, the Madisons left Washington just as a young trader named **John Ross** entered the political arena. Born in 1790 in the Cherokee nation, John (also known as Guwisguwi) was the son of a Scottish trader and his wife, who was both Cherokee and Scottish. John Ross was raised in an Anglo-Indian world in eastern Tennessee, where he played with Cherokee children and attended tribal events but was educated by private tutors and in Protestant missionary schools. At age twenty, Ross was appointed as a U.S. Indian agent among the Cherokee and during the War of 1812 served as an adjutant (or administrative assistant) in a Cherokee regiment.

After the war, Ross focused on business ventures in Tennessee, including the establishment of a plantation. He also became increasingly involved in Cherokee political affairs, using his bilingual skills and Protestant training to represent Indian interests to government officials. In 1819 Ross was elected president of the Cherokee legislature; and later, having moved to Georgia, he served as president of the Cherokee constitutional convention in 1827. The next year, after overseeing the first written constitution produced by an Indian nation, Ross was elected principal chief. Over the next decade, he battled to retain the Cherokee homeland against the pressures of white planters and politicians.

COMPARING THE AMERICAN HISTORIES of Dolley Madison and John Ross demonstrates that, while American politics was a white man's game, it was possible for those on the political margins to influence national developments. Both Madison and Ross sought to defend and expand the democratic ideals that defined the young nation. The First Lady helped to nurture a bipartisan political culture in

Washington, which was particularly important following the War of 1812. Despite the antislavery sentiments of her parents, however, she did not seem to struggle with the issue of slavery. However, that issue fueled tensions among Democratic-Republicans when the Missouri Territory sought statehood in 1819. Missouri's quest resulted from the nation's rapid geographical expansion. Its economic development proved more volatile, however, with the nation suffering its first major recession in 1819. Working men then demanded the right to vote to protect their economic interests. The Cherokee also asserted their rights. Ross encouraged Cherokees to embrace Anglo-American culture as a path to inclusion. But he could not overcome the power of planters and politicians to wrest valuable territory from his nation. President Andrew Jackson, elected in 1828, ensured Cherokee removal and supported slavery. Yet he was lauded as a democratic hero for his frontier background and promotion of workingmen's rights. While the United States successfully defended itself against British intervention, Americans still could not agree on who truly belonged in the nation.

Conflicts at Home and Abroad

When Thomas Jefferson completed his second term as president in March 1809, he was succeeded by his friend and ally James Madison. Like Jefferson, Madison sought to end foreign interference in American affairs and to resolve conflicts between native and white residents on the frontier. By 1815 the United States had weathered a series of domestic and foreign crises, including another war with Britain, but American sovereignty remained fragile. At the same time, even though Madison believed in a national government with limited powers, he, like Jefferson, ultimately expanded federal authority.

Tensions at Sea and on the Frontier

When President Madison took office, Great Britain and France remained embroiled in the Napoleonic Wars in Europe and refused to modify their policies toward American shipping or to recognize U.S. neutrality. American ships were subject to seizure by both nations, and British authorities continued to impress "deserters" into the Royal Navy. Just before Madison's inauguration in March 1809, Congress replaced the Embargo Act with the **Non-Intercourse Act**, which restricted trade with France and Britain and their colonies. Although the continued embargo against Britain encouraged U.S. manufacturing and the act allowed trade with other European nations, many Americans still opposed Congress using its power to constrain the right to trade.

In the midst of these crises, Madison also faced difficulties in the Northwest Territory. In 1794 General Anthony Wayne had won a decisive victory against a multi-tribe coalition at the **Battle of Fallen Timbers**. But this victory inspired two forceful native leaders to create a pan-Indian alliance in the Ohio River valley. The Shawnee prophet Tenskwatawa and his half-brother Tecumseh, a warrior, encouraged native peoples to resist white encroachments on their territory and to give up all aspects of white society and culture, including copper kettles, calico cloth, liquor, and other trade goods. These efforts, they believed, could create an Indian nation that stretched from the Canadian border to the Gulf of Mexico.

Indians in the upper Midwest rallied around the brothers. In 1808 Tenskwatawa and Tecumseh established the native community of Prophetstown along the

Tippecanoe River in Indiana Territory. The very next year, however, territorial governor William Henry Harrison lied to several Indian leaders about U.S. intentions in the region to persuade them to sign a treaty ceding three million acres of land to the United States for only $7,600. An enraged Tecumseh dismissed the treaty, claiming the land belonged to all the Indians together. Leaving Tenskwatawa in charge, he traveled south to urge the Cherokee and Choctaw to join his alliance.

In November 1811, in Tecumseh's absence and fearing the growing power of the Shawnee leaders, Governor Harrison attacked Prophetstown with 1,000 soldiers. With more troops and superior weapons, the U.S. army defeated the allied Indian forces, killed forty warriors, and burned Prophetstown to the ground. The rout damaged Tenskwatawa's stature as a prophet, and he and his supporters fled to Canada, where skirmishes continued along the U.S.-Canadian border. These conflicts with native tribes soon merged into a wider war with Britain.

War with Britain and Its Indian Allies

Convinced that British officials in Canada fueled Indian resistance, many Democratic-Republicans demanded an end to British intervention on the western frontier as well as British interference in transatlantic trade. Some called for the United States to declare war. Yet merchants in the Northeast feared the commercial disruptions that war entailed. Thus New England Federalists adamantly opposed a declaration of war.

For months, Madison avoided taking a clear stand. Then in March 1811, several dozen newly elected Democratic-Republicans, including Henry Clay of Kentucky and John C. Calhoun of South Carolina, joined Congress. Known as the War Hawks, they demanded that the United States end interference from Britain in the Old Northwest Territory and stop British ships from impressing American citizens. Finally, on June 1, 1812, with diplomatic efforts exhausted, Madison sent a secret message to Congress outlining U.S. grievances against Great Britain. Within weeks, Congress declared war by sharply divided votes in the House of Representatives and the Senate.

While supporters hoped a victory would raise America's stature in Europe, the nation was ill prepared to launch a major offensive against such an imposing foe. The cost of cuts in federal spending and military resources under President Jefferson now became apparent. Jefferson, for example, reduced the U.S. navy, established under President Adams, to only six small gunboats. Democratic-Republicans had also failed to recharter the Bank of the United States when it expired in 1811, so the nation lacked a vital source of credit. Nonetheless, many in Congress believed that Britain would be too engaged by its ongoing conflict with France to attack the United States.

Meanwhile U.S. commanders devised plans to attack Canada, but the U.S. army and navy proved no match for Great Britain and its Indian allies. Instead, Tecumseh, who was appointed a brigadier general in the British army, and British troops captured Detroit in August 1812. The victory encouraged other native tribes to ally with Britain. Joint British and Indian forces then launched successful attacks on Fort Dearborn, Fort Mackinac, and other points along the U.S.-Canadian border.

Even as U.S. forces faced numerous defeats, American voters reelected James Madison as president in November 1812. Madison won most western and southern states, where the war was most popular, but lost in New England and New York, where Federalist opponents held sway.

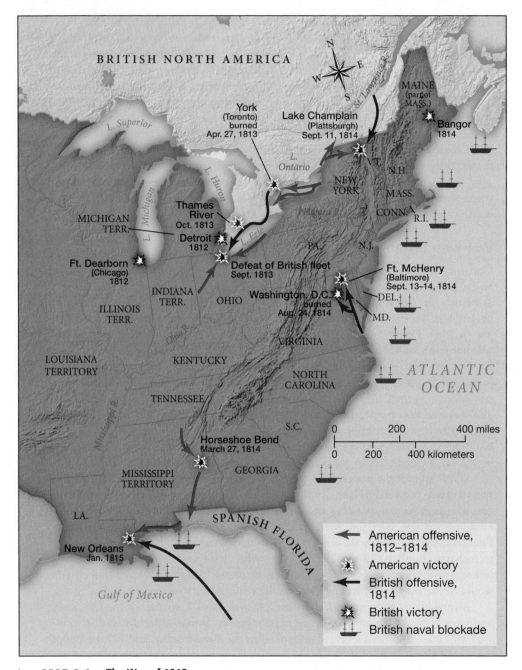

MAP 9.1   The War of 1812

Most conflicts in this war occurred in the Great Lakes region or around Washington, D.C. Yet two crucial victories occurred in the South. At Horseshoe Bend, troops under General Andrew Jackson and aided by Cherokee warriors defeated Creek allies of the British. At New Orleans, Jackson beat British forces shortly after a peace agreement was signed in Europe.

After a year of fighting, U.S. forces drove the British back into Canada in 1813 (Map 9.1). A naval victory on Lake Erie led by Commodore Oliver Perry proved crucial to U.S. success. Soon after, Tecumseh was killed in battle and U.S. forces burned York (present-day Toronto). Yet just as U.S. prospects in the war improved, New England Federalists demanded retreat. The war devastated the New England maritime trade, causing economic distress throughout the region. In 1813, state legislatures in New England withdrew their support for any invasion of "foreign British soil," and Federalists in Congress sought to block war appropriations and the deployment of local militia units into the U.S. army.

Meanwhile news arrived in March 1814 that Andrew Jackson and his Tennessee militiamen had defeated a force of Creek Indians, important allies of Tecumseh and Britain. The Creek had been fighting U.S. troops and their Cherokee allies, including John Ross, in the Mississippi Valley for ten months. At the **Battle of Horseshoe Bend**, in present-day Alabama, the combined U.S.-Cherokee forces killed eight hundred Creek warriors during the battle and the resulting retreat. Although some Americans were appalled at the slaughter, many white southerners were pleased when the Creek nation lost two-thirds of its tribal domain in the resulting treaty.

Battle of New Orleans On January 8, 1815, General Andrew Jackson's troops launched grapeshot and canister bombs against British forces in New Orleans in this final battle of the War of 1812. Jackson's troops included Indian allies, backcountry immigrants, and French-speaking black soldiers. This engraving by Francisco Scacki shows the slain British commander, Major General Sir Edward Pakenham, in the center foreground. Sarin Images/Granger

Despite such victories, the United States was no closer to winning the war. In August 1814, British ships carrying 5,000 soldiers sailed into Chesapeake Bay. They blockaded U.S. ports, launched attacks in Maryland, and marched toward Washington. As American troops retreated, Dolley Madison and an enslaved worker, Peter Jennings, gathered up government papers and valuable belongings before fleeing the White House. The redcoats then burned and sacked the capital city. U.S. troops quickly rallied, defeating the British in Maryland and expelling them from Washington and New York.

In December, as the British fleet landed thousands of troops at New Orleans, New England Federalists met secretly in Hartford, Connecticut to "deliberate upon the alarming state of public affairs." Some participants at the **Hartford Convention** called for New England states to secede from the nation. Most supported amendments to the U.S. Constitution that would eliminate the three-fifths clause, limit presidents to a single term and ensure they were elected from diverse states (ending Virginia's domination of the office), and require a two-thirds (rather than a simple) majority vote in Congress to declare war, impose embargoes, or admit new states.

The power of Federalists to put these policies in place was never tested. Despite the increase in troops, the British were losing steam as well. Representatives of the two countries met in Ghent, Belgium in December to negotiate a peace settlement. On Christmas Eve 1814, the **Treaty of Ghent** was signed, returning to each nation the lands it controlled before the war. When news of the Hartford Convention leaked out, Federalists appeared unpatriotic to many Americans. The party never recovered, despite retaining power in a few northern states and cities.

Another post-treaty event gained a far more positive response. In January 1815, U.S. troops under General Andrew Jackson attacked and routed the British army at New Orleans. The victory cheered most Americans, who, unaware that peace had already been achieved, proclaimed Jackson a national hero.

Although the War of 1812 achieved no formal territorial gains, it did represent an important defense of U.S. sovereignty and garnered international prestige for the young nation. At the same time, Indians on the western frontier lost a powerful ally when British representatives at Ghent failed to act as advocates for their allies. Thus, in practical terms, the U.S. government gained greater control over vast expanses of land in the Ohio and Mississippi River valleys.

REVIEW & RELATE	• How were conflicts with Indians in the West connected to ongoing tensions between the United States and Great Britain? • What were the long-term consequences of the War of 1812?

National Expansion and Regional Economies

By further expanding federal powers, the War of 1812 reinforced political changes that had been under way for more than a decade. At the Hartford Convention, Federalists who had once advocated broad national powers called for restrictions on federal authority. By contrast, Democratic-Republicans, who initially demanded restraints on federal power, now applauded its expansion. Indeed, Democratic-Republicans in Congress sought to use federal authority to settle boundary disputes in the West, make investments in transportation, and reestablish a national bank.

Some state governments also invested in roads and canals. Federal power was again asserted to settle disputes with Britain and Spain over U.S. borders in the North and the South. At the same time, more secure borders and state and federal investments in transportation fueled overseas trade and the development of increasingly distinct regional economies.

Governments Fuel Economic Growth

In 1800 Thomas Jefferson captured the presidency by advocating a reduction in federal powers and a renewed emphasis on the needs of small farmers and workingmen. Once in power, however, Jefferson and his Democratic-Republican supporters faced a series of economic and political developments that led many to embrace a loose interpretation of the U.S. Constitution and support federal efforts to aid economic growth.

Population growth and commercial expansion encouraged these federal efforts. In 1811 the first steamboat traveled down the Mississippi from the Ohio River to New Orleans; over the next decade, steamboat traffic expanded. This development helped western and southern residents but hurt trade on overland routes between northeastern seaports and the Ohio River valley. The federal government began construction of the Cumberland Road in 1811 to reestablish this regional connection by linking Maryland and Ohio. Congress passed additional bills to fund ambitious federal transportation projects, but President Madison vetoed much of this legislation, believing that it overstepped even a loose interpretation of the Constitution.

After the War of 1812, however, Democratic-Republican representative Henry Clay of Kentucky sketched out a plan to promote U.S. economic growth and advance commercial ties throughout the nation. Called the **American System**, it combined federally funded internal improvements, such as roads and canals, to aid farmers and merchants with federal tariffs to protect U.S. manufacturing. Western expansion fueled demand for these internal improvements. The non-Indian population west of the Appalachian Mountains more than doubled between 1810 and 1820, from 1,080,000 to 2,234,000. Many veterans of the War of 1812 settled there after receiving 160-acre parcels of land in the region as payment for service. These lands were largely territory taken from Britain's Indian allies. Congress admitted four new states to the Union in just four years: Indiana (1816), Mississippi (1817), Illinois (1818), and Alabama (1819). In the South, too, westward expansion depended on the dispossession of Creek and neighboring tribes.

Congress then negotiated with Indian nations to secure trade routes farther west. In the 1810s, Americans began trading along an ancient trail from Missouri to Santa Fe, a town in northern Mexico. But the trail cut across territory claimed by the Osage Indians. In 1825 Congress approved a treaty with the Osage to guarantee right of way for U.S. merchants. The Santa Fe Trail became a critical route for commerce between the United States and Mexico.

East of the Appalachian Mountains, state governments funded most internal improvement projects. The most significant of these was New York's **Erie Canal**, a 363-mile waterway stretching from the Mohawk River to Buffalo that was completed in 1825. Self-taught men directed this extraordinary engineering feat by which thousands of workers carved a swath forty feet wide and four feet deep through limestone cliffs, mountains, forests, and swamps. The canal, which rises 566 feet along its route, required the construction of 83 locks to lift and lower boats. The arduous and dangerous work was carried out mainly by Irish, Welsh, and German immigrants, many of whom settled along its route. Tolls on the Erie Canal quickly repaid the tremendous financial cost of its construction. Freight charges and shipping times plunged. And by linking western farmers to the Hudson River, the Erie Canal ensured that New York City became the nation's premier seaport (Map 9.2).

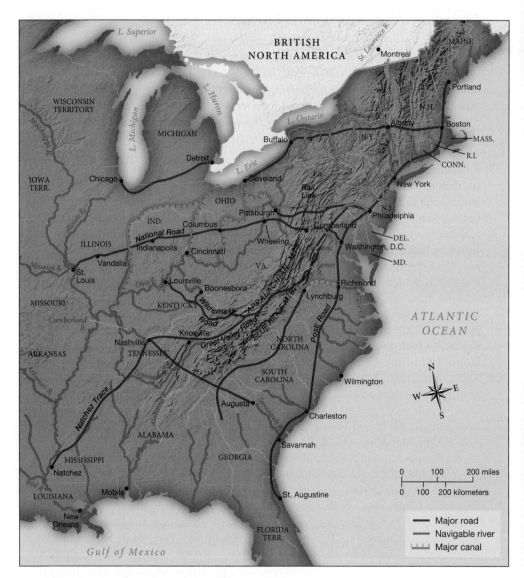

MAP 9.2   Roads and Canals to 1837

During the 1820s and 1830s, state and local governments as well as private companies built roads and canals to foster migration and commercial development. The Erie Canal, completed in 1825, was the most significant of these projects. Many other states, particularly in the Northeast and the old Northwest, sought to duplicate that canal's success over the following decade.

The Erie Canal's success inspired hundreds of similar projects in other states. While some of these projects failed, costing states huge sums of money, many succeeded. Canal boats carried manufactured goods from New England and the Middle Atlantic states to rural households in the Ohio River valley. They also created links across the Great Lakes. Western farmers could, thus ship agricultural products east more quickly and cheaply. Canals also linked smaller cities within Pennsylvania and Ohio, facilitating the rise of commercial and manufacturing centers like Harrisburg, Pittsburgh, and Cincinnati. Moreover, canals allowed vast quantities of coal to be transported out of the Allegheny Mountains, fueling industrial development throughout the Northeast.

Americans Expand the Nation's Borders

In 1816, in the midst of the nation's economic resurgence, Democratic-Republican James Monroe won an easy victory in the presidential election over Rufus King, a New York Federalist. John Quincy Adams was then serving as U.S ambassador in London, sent by President Madison to improve relations with Britain and resolve ongoing problems on the frontier. He negotiated treaties that limited U.S. and British naval forces on the Great Lakes, set the U.S.-Canadian border at the forty-ninth parallel, and established joint British-U.S. occupation of the Oregon Territory. In 1817 and 1818, the Senate approved these treaties, which resolved issues with Britain but further restricted Indian rights and power. By then President Monroe had recalled Adams to the United States to serve as his secretary of state.

While the U.S.-Canadian border was largely settled, Monroe harbored grave concerns about the nation's southern boundary. He sought to limit the power of Spain, which controlled Florida and vast territories in the West, and to stop Seminole Indians in Florida and Alabama from claiming lands the defeated Creeks ceded to the United States. Shifting from diplomacy to military force, the president sent General Andrew Jackson to force the Seminoles back into central Florida in 1817. He ordered Jackson to avoid direct conflict with Spanish forces for fear of igniting another war. However, in spring 1818 Jackson attacked two Spanish forts, hanged two Seminole chiefs, and executed two British citizens.

Jackson's attacks spurred outrage among Spanish and British officials and many members of Congress. The threat of conflict with Britain, Spain, and the Seminole tribe prompted President Monroe to establish the nation's first peacetime army. In the end, the British chose to ignore the execution of citizens engaged in "unauthorized" activities, while Spain decided to sell the Florida Territory to the United States. Indeed, in the **Adams-Onís Treaty** (1819), negotiated by John Quincy Adams, Spain ceded all its lands east of the Mississippi to the United States.

Success in acquiring Florida encouraged the administration to look for other opportunities to limit European influence in the Western Hemisphere. By 1822 Argentina, Chile, Peru, Colombia, and Mexico had all overthrown Spanish rule. That March, President Monroe recognized the independence of these southern neighbors, and Congress quickly established diplomatic relations with them. In his 1823 State of the Union address, President Monroe claimed that the Western Hemisphere was within the U.S. sphere of influence Although the United States did not have sufficient power to enforce what became known (in 1850) as the **Monroe Doctrine**, it declared its intention to challenge European interference in the hemisphere.

By the late 1820s, U.S. expanded its reach west and south as residents moved onto lands once belonging to Creeks and Spaniards and traded with newly independent Mexican territories. Southern whites began settling newly acquired areas of Georgia, Alabama, and Mississippi as well as Mexican-controlled lands in east Texas. At the same time, traders regularly traveled the Santa Fe Trail, and New England merchants began sending goods via clipper ships to Alta California, another Mexican territory.

Some Americans looked even farther afield. In the early nineteenth century, U.S. ships carried sea otter pelts and other Northwest coast merchandise across the Pacific, returning with Chinese porcelains and silks. In the early 1800s, the Alta California and China trades converged, expanding the reach of U.S. merchants and the demand for U.S. manufactured goods. Some Americans imagined controlling Pacific islands, especially Hawaii and Samoa.

Expanded trade routes along with wartime disruptions of European imports fueled the expansion of U.S. manufacturing, which improved opportunities for entrepreneurs and workers. By 1813 the area around Providence, Rhode Island boasted seventy-six spinning mills. Two years later, Philadelphia claimed pride of place as the nation's top industrial city, turning out glass, chemicals, metalwork, and leather goods.

Regional Economic Development

The roads, rivers, canals, and steamboats that connected a growing nation meant that people in one region could more easily exchange the goods they produced for those they needed. This development fostered the emergence of distinct but intertwined regional economies. In the South, for instance, vast Indian land cessions, the cotton gin, and a growing enslaved population ensured the expansion of cotton cultivation just as spinning mills in New England increased the demand for raw cotton in the North.

Important changes occurred within regions as well. Soil depletion caused by the over-production of tobacco and a fall in tobacco prices in Europe made enslaved labor less valuable in the upper South. When James and Dolley Madison returned to their Virginia plantation, Montpelier, in 1817, they experienced these problems firsthand. Plantation homes in such long-settled areas had become more fashionable as they incorporated luxury goods imported from China and Europe even as the soil in the region, depleted of nutrients, limited profits and made a shift to cotton impossible. While other Virginia enslavers sold their laborers to planters farther south and west, James Madison refused to break up enslaved families who had worked his plantation for decades. Thus the Madisons were forced to reduce their standard of living.

By the 1820s, more and more southern planters carefully calculated profits and risks, and many sought to extend slavery into areas once controlled by Creeks and Spaniards. They increased production of cash crops in the area, including sugar, rice, indigo, and especially cotton. Profits from this effort then provided funds to acquire more land and more enslaved workers. Initially, these enslavers needed young men to clear land and build houses, barns, and outbuildings so they purchased bondsmen from Virginia and Maryland. They also separated families on their eastern plantations to provide young workers for newer estates further west. Before the 1820s, men who traded in various goods also sold enslaved workers. After the 1820s, slave trading became a specialized occupation, one increasingly attractive to merchants north and south.

Ohio Farm and Indian Burial Ground, c. 1835–1860 American artist Charles Sullivan painted this scene in Montgomery County after moving to Ohio in the mid-1830s. It shows the diversified agriculture in this area of rolling hills and the Miamisburg Burial Mound, one of the largest conical Indian burial sites in the eastern United States. Sullivan painted native burial grounds throughout the region, some of which were later destroyed. Courtesy of the Ohio History Connection, no. Om2892_1831762_001

The southern cotton boom fueled economic transformations in the West and North that benefitted (mostly white) Americans across the nation. As cotton farmers and planters increased profits in the 1810s and 1820s, they purchased more grain and other agricultural goods from the Old Northwest. Towns like Cincinnati, located across the Ohio River from Kentucky, sprang up as regional centers for this growing commerce. Americans living in the Northeast increased their commercial connections with the South as well. Northern banks and merchants became deeply engaged in the southern cotton trade. They offered credit to planters, opened warehouses in cities like Savannah and Charleston, and sent agents into the countryside to bargain for cotton to be shipped north or to Europe. European countries also purchased large quantities of wheat. These regional ties both inspired and benefitted from state and federal investments in improved roads, canals, and ports.

The southern cotton boom thus helped fuel and fund northern industrial growth, a transportation revolution, and the building of larger and faster steamships and oceangoing vessels. Factory owners and merchants in New England could ship growing quantities of yarn, thread, and cloth along with shoes, tools, and leather goods to the South. Meanwhile, merchants in Philadelphia and Pittsburgh built ties to western farmers, exchanging manufactured goods for agricultural products. As importantly, in 1803 cotton became the nation's most valuable export. After 1815, with the end of the Napoleonic wars and the surge in European demand, cotton became an even more profitable export, adding to the riches of enslavers, planters, and northern merchants. Thus over time, even as America's regional economies became more distinctive, they also became increasingly interdependent.

Economic and Political Crises

Even as regional economies ensured economic interdependence, they inspired political differences. For instance, the growth in trade between regions led to an increase in commercial institutions, such as banks, the largest of which were established in the North. When the nation's first severe recession hit in 1819, many southern planters and midwestern farmers blamed it on the banks. In reality, falling prices for cotton and wheat abroad contributed to the recession along with banks' overextension of credit, much of it offered to southern planters and midwestern farmers who extended their reach into lands taken from the Shawnee, the Creek, and other Indian nations in the War of 1812. Whatever the cause, the interdependence of regional economies ensured that everyone suffered. Yet these economies were built on distinct forms of labor, with the South becoming increasingly dependent on enslaved labor and the North less so. When Missouri, situated between the Old Northwest Territory and expanding southern cotton lands, applied for statehood in 1819, these regional differences set off a furious national debate over slavery.

The Panic of 1819

The **panic of 1819** resulted from the convergence of numerous economic changes and lasted far longer than its name suggests. One important factor was irresponsible banking practices in the United States and a temporary, but substantial, decline in overseas demand for American cotton and wheat. Beginning in 1816, American banks, including the newly chartered Second Bank of the United States, loaned huge sums to settlers seeking newly opened land on the southern and northern frontiers as well as merchants and manufacturers expanding their businesses. In Alabama and other states, Indian land cessions provided the financial basis for state banks to develop credit schemes that worked so long as geographical and economic expansion continued. Moreover, many loans were not backed by sufficient collateral because banks assumed that continued economic growth would ensure repayment. In the South, planters often used enslaved workers as collateral. When agricultural production in Europe revived with the end of the Napoleonic Wars, the demand for American foodstuffs dropped sharply. Farm income plummeted by roughly one-third in the late 1810s, and in the South both individual lenders and bankers discovered that the same enslaved workers had been promised to more than one borrower. The results panicked lenders and led to dire consequences for the enslaved, who found themselves traded among angry owners or ordered to move by judges, who broke up families to untangle white men's corrupt bargains.

Thus in 1818, when the directors of the Second Bank tightened the credit they provided to branch banks, this curtailment led to economic panic. Some branch banks failed immediately. Others survived by calling in loans to companies and individuals, who in turn demanded repayment from those to whom they had extended credit. But disentangling the value of Indian land cessions and the ownership of enslaved workers proved challenging as both had become enmeshed in complex financial transactions. The chain of indebtedness pushed many people to the brink of economic ruin just as factory owners cut their orders for raw materials and their workforce. Merchants, too, decreased orders for new goods. Individuals and businesses faced bankruptcy and foreclosure, and property values fell sharply.

Bankruptcies, foreclosures, unemployment, and poverty spread across the country. Cotton farmers were especially hard hit by declining exports and falling prices. Planters who had gone into debt to purchase land in Alabama and Mississippi and more enslaved workers were unable to repay these loans. Many western residents, who had invested all they had in new farms, lost their land or simply stopped paying their mortgages. This further strained state banks, some of which collapsed, leaving the national bank holding mortgages on vast amounts of western territory.

Many Americans viewed banks as the cause of the panic. Some states defied the Constitution and the Supreme Court by trying to tax Second Bank branches or printing state banknotes with no specie (gold or silver) to back them. Some Americans called for government relief, but there was no system to provide the kinds of assistance needed. When Congress debated how to reignite the nation's economy, regional differences quickly appeared. Northern manufacturers called for higher tariffs to protect them from foreign competition, but southern planters argued that high tariffs raised the price of manufactured goods as agricultural profits declined. Meanwhile, workingmen and small farmers feared that their economic needs were being ignored by politicians tied to bankers, planters, manufacturers, and merchants.

Although the panic dissipated for many by 1823, the prolonged economic crisis shook national confidence. Citizens became more skeptical of federal authority and more suspicious of banks, especially citizens who continued to suffer economic hardship through the 1820s. Periodic cycles of economic expansion and contraction continued to shape the U.S. economy through the 1870s.

Slavery in Missouri

A second national crisis highlighted regional systems of labor. In February 1819 the Missouri Territory applied for statehood. New York congressman James Tallmadge Jr. proposed that Missouri be admitted only if it banned further importation of slaves and passed a gradual emancipation law. Southern congressmen blocked Tallmadge's proposals, but the northern majority in the House of Representatives then rejected Missouri's admission.

Southern politicians were outraged, claiming that since the Missouri Territory allowed slavery, so should the state of Missouri. With cotton production moving ever westward, southern congressmen wanted to ensure the availability of new lands. They also wanted to ensure the South's power in Congress. Because the northern population had grown more rapidly than that in the South, by 1819 northern politicians controlled the House of Representatives. Significant increases in the South's enslaved population did not offset this northern growth since slaves were counted as only three-fifths of a person for purposes of representation. The Senate, however, was evenly divided. If northerners could block the admission of slave states like Missouri while allowing the admission of free states, the balance of power in the Senate would also tip in the North's favor.

For southern planters, the decision on Missouri defined the future of slavery. With foreign trade in slaves outlawed since 1808, planters relied on natural increase and trading enslaved workers from older to newer areas of production to meet the demand for labor. Free blacks packed the congressional galleries in Washington to hear congressmen debate Missouri statehood, leading supporters of slavery to worry that any signs of weakness would fuel further resistance. Recent attacks on Georgia plantations by a coalition of fugitive slaves and Seminole Indians lent power to such fears.

In 1820 Representative Henry Clay of Kentucky forged a compromise that resolved the immediate issues and promised a long-term solution. Maine was to be admitted as a free state and Missouri as a slave state, thereby maintaining the balance between North and South in the U.S. Senate (Map 9.3). At the same time, Congress agreed that the southern border of Missouri—latitude 36°30'—was to serve as the boundary between slave and free states throughout the Louisiana Territory.

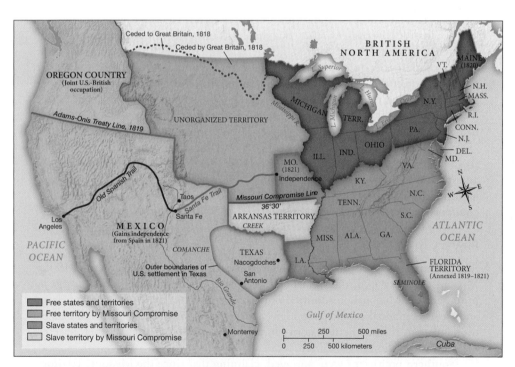

MAP 9.3   The Missouri Compromise and Westward Expansion, 1820s
The debate over the Missouri Compromise occurred as the United States began expanding farther westward. Within a few years of its adoption, the growth of U.S. settlements in eastern Texas and increased trade with a newly independent Mexico suggested the importance of drawing a clear boundary between slave and free states.

The **Missouri Compromise** ended the political crisis for the moment. Still, the debates made clear how quickly a disagreement over slavery could escalate into clashes that threatened the survival of the nation.

REVIEW & RELATE	• How did regional interdependency contribute to the panic of 1819? • What regional divisions did the conflict over slavery in Missouri reveal?

The Expansion and Limits of American Democracy

With the panic of 1819 and the debates over Missouri shaking many Americans' faith in their economic and political leaders and the frontier moving ever westward, the nation was ripe for change. Workingmen, small farmers, and frontier settlers, who had long been locked out of the electoral system by property qualifications and eastern elites, demanded the right to vote. The resulting political movement ensured voting rights for nearly all white men during the 1820s. Yet African Americans lost political and civil rights in the same period; and Indians fared poorly under the federal administrations brought to power by this expanded electorate. While some white women gained greater political influence as a result of the voting rights gained by fathers and husbands, they did not achieve independent political rights. Finally, as a wave of new voters entered the political fray, ongoing conflicts over slavery, tariffs, and the rights of Indian nations transformed party alignments.

Expanding Voting Rights

Between 1788 and 1820, the U.S. presidency was dominated by Virginia elites and after 1800 by Democratic-Republicans. With little serious political opposition at the national level, few people bothered to vote in presidential elections. Far more people engaged in political activities at the state and local levels. Many towns attracted large audiences to public celebrations on the Fourth of July and election days. Female participants sewed symbols of their partisan loyalties on their clothes and joined in parades and feasts organized by men.

The panic of 1819 increased political activity by laboring men, who were especially vulnerable to economic downturns. They now demanded the right to vote so they could hold politicians accountable. In New York State, Martin Van Buren, a rising star in the Democratic-Republican Party, led the fight to eliminate property qualifications for voting. At the state constitutional convention of 1821, the committee on suffrage argued that the only qualification for voting should be "the virtue and morality of the people." When Van Buren and the committee used the word *people*, however, they really meant white men.

Despite opposition from powerful and wealthy men, most states along the Atlantic seaboard had lowered or eliminated property qualifications on white male voters by 1825. Meanwhile states along the frontier that had joined the Union in the

First State Election Day in Detroit, c. 1837   This painting by Thomas Mickell Burnham depicts a lively election-day crowd. However, clouds loom overhead. Stevens Thomas Mason, the successful Democratic gubernatorial candidate, appears to buy votes while drunken men fill the streets and a small African American boy begs for coins. It is possible that the Whig Party commissioned the painting after its candidate lost.   Gift of Mrs. Samuel T. Carson/Bridgeman Images

1810s established universal white male suffrage from the beginning. And by 1824 three-quarters of the states (18 of 24) allowed voters, rather than state legislatures, to elect members of the Electoral College.

Yet as white workingmen gained political rights in the 1820s, democracy did not spread to other groups. Indian nations were considered sovereign entities, so native people voted in their own nations, not in U.S. elections. Moreover, tribes such as the Cherokee and the Iroquois, which had long granted women a political voice, began shifting to a male-dominated system that looked more like that of the United States. Native-born women had long been excluded from voting because of their perceived dependence on men. Among African Americans, men, too, faced growing restrictions on their political rights. No southern legislature had ever granted blacks the right to vote, and northern states began disfranchising them as well in the 1820s. In many cases, expanded voting rights for white men went hand in hand with new restrictions on black men. In New York State, for example, the constitution of 1821, which eliminated property qualifications for white men, raised property qualifications for African American voters.

When African American men protested their disfranchisement, some northern whites spoke out on their behalf. They claimed that denying rights to men who had in no way abused the privilege of voting set "an ominous and dangerous precedent." In response, opponents of black suffrage offered explicitly racist justifications. Some argued that black voting would lead to interracial socializing, even marriage. Others feared that black voters might hold the balance of power in close elections, forcing white civic leaders to accede to their demands. Gradually, racist arguments won the day, and by 1840, 93 percent of free blacks in the North were excluded from voting.

Racist Restrictions and Racial Violence

Restrictions on voting followed other constraints on African American men and women. As early as 1790, Congress limited naturalization (the process of becoming a citizen) to white aliens, that is, immigrants. It also excluded blacks from enrolling in federal militias. In 1820 Congress authorized city officials in Washington, D.C., to adopt a separate legal code governing free and enslaved blacks. This federal legislation encouraged states, in both the North and the South, to add their own restrictions, including the segregation of public schools, transportation, and accommodations. Some northern legislatures even denied African Americans the right to settle in their state.

In addition, blacks faced mob and state-sanctioned violence across the country. In the South such violence both brutalized African Americans and inspired some to rebel, particularly in port cities that were heavily involved in the slave trade. On January 8, 1811, free and enslaved blacks of French, West Indian, and U.S. backgrounds organized a rebellion on the outskirts of New Orleans, led by Charles Deslondes, who likely came from Haiti. White Louisianans seemed preoccupied in conflicts with Spaniards on their West Florida border. As dozens of black rebels took over sugar plantations, gathered hundreds of supporters, and marched toward New Orleans, word of the revolt finally spread to whites. White enslavers, seamen, and well-armed militias from New Orleans set upon black rebels at dawn on January 10. They killed dozens and captured many more. The captives were summarily tried and executed. Their heads were displayed on tall spikes in New Orleans and along the Mississippi River as a warning to other slaves.

In 1822 officials in another port city, Charleston, South Carolina, accused Denmark Vesey, a free black, of following Haitian revolutionary Toussaint L'Ouverture and plotting a conspiracy to emancipate the city's slaves. Vesey began life enslaved in the French Caribbean. Sold to slave trader Captain Vesey, he was resold to an enslaver in Charleston but was later returned to Captain Vesey. The young black man, known as Denmark, worked onboard ship for twenty years, taking Vesey's name and traveling to many ports and learning several languages. Denmark Vesey eventually purchased his freedom and returned to Charleston, where he worked as a carpenter, joined the mixed-race but white-dominated Second Presbyterian Church in 1817, and participated in black mutual aid societies. In challenging white assumptions about black inferiority, free blacks were often considered threatening by whites. And in 1822, Vesey helped organize a secret plot to liberate slaves in the city. However, shortly before the insurrection was to begin, white authorities seized ten black men, and Vesey realized that the plot had been discovered. Vesey and thirty-four of his co-conspirators were found guilty of insurrection and hanged. Although only two insurrectionists were tied to Charleston's African Methodist Episcopal Church, that center of black life was demolished.

Northern blacks also suffered from violent attacks by whites. Whites in cities across the region periodically rampaged through African American communities. Violence was often inspired by white fear over increases in the black population or immigrant anger over job competition. Both fueled white residents' outrage in Cincinnati in 1829, when attacks on black neighborhoods caused more than half of the city's black residents to flee. Many resettled in Ontario, Canada. They were joined by Philadelphia blacks after three days of rioting in August 1834. A dispute over seats on a merry-go-round led native-born and Irish mobs to tear down one church and sack another, destroy thirty black homes and several businesses, and beat dozens of black residents. Such attacks continued in northern cities throughout the 1830s.

Political Realignments

Restrictions on black political and civil rights converged with the continued decline of the Federalists. Federalist majorities in New York State had approved the gradual abolition law of 1799. In 1821 New York Federalists advocated equal rights for black and white voters as long as property qualifications limited suffrage to respectable citizens. But Federalists were losing power, and the concerns of African Americans were low on the Democratic-Republican agenda.

Struggles within the Democratic-Republican Party now turned to a large extent on the limits of federal power. Many Democratic-Republicans had come to embrace a more expansive view of federal authority and a looser interpretation of the U.S. Constitution. Others argued forcefully for a return to limited federal power and a strict construction of the Constitution. At the same time, rising young politicians — like Martin Van Buren and Andrew Jackson — joined newly enfranchised voters to seize control of the party from its longtime leaders.

The election of 1824 brought these conflicts to a head, splitting Democratic-Republicans into rival factions. By 1828 those factions coalesced into two distinct entities: the Democrats and the National Republicans. Unable to agree on a single presidential candidate in 1824, the Democratic-Republican congressional caucus fractured, backing four separate candidates: John Quincy Adams, Andrew Jackson, Henry Clay, and Secretary of the Treasury William Crawford.

As the race developed, Adams and Jackson emerged as the two strongest candidates. John Quincy Adams's stature rested on his diplomatic achievements and the reputation of his father, former president John Adams. He favored internal improvements and protective tariffs that would bolster northern industry and commerce. Jackson, who advocated limited federal power, relied largely on his fame as a war hero and Indian fighter to inspire popular support.

As a candidate who appealed to ordinary voters, Jackson held a decided edge. His supporters emphasized Jackson's humble origins, which appealed to small farmers and northern workers. Just as important, Jackson gained the support of Martin Van Buren, who also wanted to expand the political clout of the "common [white] man" and limit the reach of a central government that he insisted was becoming too powerful.

The four presidential candidates created a truly competitive race, and turnout at the polls increased significantly. Jackson won the popular vote by carrying Pennsylvania, New Jersey, the Carolinas, and much of the West and led in the Electoral College with 99 electors. But with no candidate gaining an absolute majority in the Electoral College, the Constitution called for the House of Representatives to choose the president from the three leading contenders — Jackson, Adams, and Crawford. Clay, who came in fourth, asked his supporters to back Adams, ensuring his election. Once in office, President Adams appointed Clay secretary of state. Jackson claimed that the two had engineered a "corrupt bargain," but Adams and Clay, who shared many ideas, formed a logical alliance.

Once in office, President Adams ran into vigorous opposition in Congress led by Van Buren. John C. Calhoun, a South Carolina Senator who had been elected vice president, also opposed most of Adams's policies. Van Buren argued against federal funding for internal improvements since New York State had financed the Erie Canal with its own monies. Calhoun, meanwhile, joined other southern politicians in opposing any expansion of federal power for fear it would be used to restrict the spread of slavery.

The most serious battle in Congress, however, involved tariffs. The tariff of 1816 had excluded most cheap English cotton cloth from the United States to aid New England manufacturing. In 1824 the tariff was extended to more expensive cotton and woolen cloth and to iron goods. During the presidential campaign, Adams and Clay appealed to northern voters by advocating even higher duties on these items. When Adams introduced tariff legislation that extended duties to raw materials like wool, hemp, and molasses, he gained support from both Jackson and Van Buren, who considered these tariffs beneficial to frontier farmers. Despite the opposition of Vice President Calhoun and congressmen from southeastern states, the tariff of 1828 was approved, raising duties on imports to an average of 62 percent.

The tariff of 1828, however, was Adams's only notable legislative victory. His foreign policy was also stymied by a hostile Congress. Adams thus entered the 1828 election campaign with little to show in the way of domestic or foreign achievements, and Jackson and his supporters took full advantage of the president's political vulnerability.

The Presidential Election of 1828

The election of 1828 tested the power of the two major factions in the Democratic-Republican Party and introduced a number of innovative techniques to create enthusiasm for the opposing candidates. President Adams followed the traditional approach of "standing" for office, telling supporters, "If my country wants my services, she must ask for them." To ensure that they would ask for his services, Henry Clay campaigned widely for Adams, earning the name the "Barbecue Orator." Jackson, too, refused to run for office, but encouraged his supporters, led by Van Buren, to take his case directly to the voters. Both benefited from the expansion of cheap newspapers and other printed materials that could reach voters in small towns and villages. Rising literacy rates ensured that more voters could read these partisan views.

Van Buren managed the first truly national political campaign in U.S. history, seeking to re-create the original Democratic-Republican coalition among farmers, northern artisans, and southern planters while adding a sizable constituency of frontier voters. Calhoun aided this effort, by again running for vice president but now supporting the Tennessee war hero despite their disagreement over tariffs. Jackson's supporters organized state nominating conventions rather than relying on the congressional caucus and established local Jackson committees in critical states like Virginia and New York. Jacksonians developed a logo, the hickory leaf, based on the candidate's nickname, "Old Hickory," which symbolized strength and resilience. Enthusiastic supporters formed local Hickory Clubs across the country.

Jackson's Tennessee background, rise to wealth, and reputation as an Indian fighter ensured his popularity among southern and western voters. He also reassured southerners that he advocated "judicious" duties on imports, suggesting that he might try to lower the 1828 rates. At the same time, his support of the tariff of 1828 and his military credentials created enthusiasm among northern workingmen and frontier farmers.

Meanwhile President Adams's advocates demeaned the "dissolute" and "rowdy" men who attended Jackson rallies. They also launched personal attacks on the candidate and his wife, Rachel. They questioned the timing of her divorce from her first husband and her remarriage to Jackson. A Cincinnati newspaper headline asked: "Ought a convicted adulteress and her paramour husband be placed in the highest offices of this free and Christian land?" Adams distanced himself from such partisan rhetoric, seeking to demonstrate his statesmanlike gentility. This strategy worked well when only men of wealth and property could vote. But with an enlarged electorate and an astonishing turnout of more than 50 percent of eligible voters, Adams's approach failed and Jackson became president (Figure 9.1).

The election of 1828 formalized a new party alignment. During the campaign Jackson and his supporters referred to themselves as "the Democracy" and forged a new national Democratic Party. In response Adams's supporters and the remaining diehard Federalists renamed themselves National Republicans. The competition

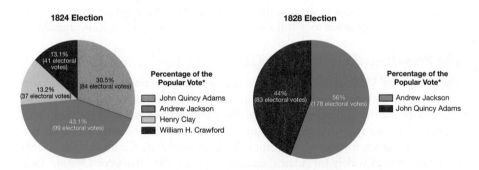

1824 Election

13.1% (41 electoral votes)
13.2% (37 electoral votes)
30.5% (84 electoral votes)
43.1% (99 electoral votes)

Percentage of the Popular Vote*
☐ John Quincy Adams
☐ Andrew Jackson
☐ Henry Clay
■ William H. Crawford

1828 Election

44% (83 electoral votes)
56% (178 electoral votes)

Percentage of the Popular Vote*
☐ Andrew Jackson
■ John Quincy Adams

*Popular vote percentages are approximate.

FIGURE 9.1   The Elections of 1824 and 1828 Andrew Jackson lost the 1824 election to John Quincy Adams when the decision was thrown into the House of Representatives. In 1828 Jackson launched the first popular campaign for president, mobilizing working-class white men who were newly enfranchised. Three times as many men — more than one million voters — cast ballots in 1828 than in 1824, ensuring Jackson's election as president. How did the greater number of candidates running in 1824 complicate the Electoral College system of selecting a president?

between **Democrats and National Republicans** heightened interest in national politics among ordinary voters and ensured that the innovative techniques introduced in 1828 would be widely adopted in future campaigns.

REVIEW & RELATE	• How and why did the composition of the electorate change in the 1820s? • In what ways did the 1828 presidential campaign represent a departure from earlier patterns in American politics?

Jacksonian Politics in Action

Jackson hoped to make government more responsive to the needs of white workers and frontier farmers. But the president's notion of democracy did not extend to Indians or African Americans. During his presidency, indigenous nations actively challenged his efforts to take more of their land, southern blacks continued to resist their enslavement, and growing numbers of free blacks demanded slavery's abolition. In addition, once President Jackson had to take clear positions on tariffs and other controversial issues, he could not please all of his constituents. He also confronted experienced adversaries like Henry Clay, Daniel Webster, and John Quincy Adams, who was elected to the House of Representatives from Massachusetts in 1830. The president thus faced considerable difficulty in translating popular support into public policy.

A Democratic Spirit?

On March 4, 1829, crowds of ordinary citizens came to see Jackson's inauguration. Jackson's wife, Rachel, had died of heart failure shortly after his election, leaving her husband devastated. Now Jackson, dressed in a plain black suit, walked alone to the Capitol as vast throngs of supporters waved and cheered. A somber Jackson read a brief inaugural address, took the oath of office, and then rode his horse through the crowds to the White House.

The size and enthusiasm of the crowds soon shattered the decorum of the inauguration. Author Margaret Bayard Smith reported mobs "scrambling, fighting, [and] romping" through the White House reception. Jackson was nearly crushed to death by "rabble" eager to shake his hand. Tubs of punch laced with rum, brandy, and champagne were finally placed on the lawn to draw the crowds outdoors.

While Jackson and his supporters viewed the event as a symbol of a new democratic spirit, others were less optimistic. Bayard Smith and other conservative political leaders saw echoes of the French Revolution in the unruly behavior of the masses. Supreme Court justice Joseph Story, too, feared "the reign of King 'Mob.'"

Tensions between the president and the capital's traditional leaders intensified when Jackson appointed Tennessee senator John Eaton as secretary of war. Eaton had had an affair with a woman thought to be of questionable character and later married her. When Jackson announced his plans to appoint Eaton to his cabinet, congressional leaders urged him to reconsider. The president appointed Eaton anyway, but the wives of Washington's leading politicians snubbed Mrs. Eaton. In a sign of women's growing influence in Washington, Jackson was eventually forced to ask Eaton to resign in what became known as the **Petticoat Affair**.

In the aftermath of Eaton's resignation, Jackson asked his entire cabinet to resign so he could begin anew. Afterward, however, his legislative agenda stalled in Congress, and National Republicans regained the momentum they had lost with Adams's defeat. The Petticoat Affair reinforced concerns that the president wielded his authority to reward friends, as did his reliance on an informal group of advisers, known as the Kitchen Cabinet. While his administration opened up government posts to a wider range of individuals, ensuring more democratic access, Jackson often selected appointees based on personal ties. He believed that "to the victor goes the spoils," and the resulting **spoils system**—continued by future administrations—assigned some federal posts as gifts for partisan loyalty rather than as jobs that required experience or expertise.

Confrontations over Tariffs and the Bank

The Democratic Party that emerged in the late 1820s was built on an unstable foundation. The coalition that formed around Jackson included northern workers who benefited from high tariffs as well as southern farmers and planters who did not. It brought together western voters who sought federal support for internal improvements and strict constructionists who believed such expenditures were unconstitutional. In nearly every legislative battle, then, decisiveness aroused conflict. In 1830 Congress passed four internal improvement bills with strong support from National Republicans. Jackson vetoed each one, which pleased his southern constituency but not his frontier supporters.

Southern congressmen, however, were more interested in his stand on tariffs. The tariff of 1828 enraged many southern planters and politicians, but most believed that once Jackson reached the White House, he would reverse course and reduce this **Tariff of Abominations**. Instead, he avoided the issue, and southern agriculture continued to suffer. Agricultural productivity in Virginia and other states of the Old South was already declining from soil exhaustion while prices for cotton and rice had not fully recovered after the panic of 1819. At the same time, southerners paid higher prices on many goods because of high tariffs.

Even as Calhoun campaigned with Jackson in 1828, the South Carolinian developed a philosophical argument to negate the effects of high tariffs on his state. In *The South Carolina Exposition and Protest*, published anonymously in 1828, Calhoun argued that states should have the ultimate power to determine the constitutionality of laws passed by Congress. When Jackson, after taking office, realized that his vice president advocated **nullification**—the right of individual states to declare individual laws void within their borders—it further damaged their relationship, which was already frayed by the Eaton affair.

When Congress debated the tariff issue in 1830, South Carolina senator Robert Hayne defended nullification. Claiming that the North intended to crush the South economically, he argued that only the right of states to nullify federal legislation could protect southern society. In response, Massachusetts senator Daniel Webster denounced nullification and the states' rights doctrine on which it was built. Jackson further antagonized southern political leaders by supporting Webster's position.

Matters worsened in 1832 when Congress confirmed the high duties set four years earlier. In response South Carolina held a special convention that approved an Ordinance of Nullification. It stated that duties on imports would not be collected in the state after February 1, 1833, and threatened secession if federal authorities tried to collect them.

The tariff crisis escalated in the fall of 1832 just as Jackson faced reelection. The tariff debates had angered many southerners, and Calhoun refused to run again as his vice president. Fortunately for Jackson, opponents in Congress had provided him with another issue that could unite his supporters and highlight his commitment to ordinary citizens: the renewal of the charter of the Bank of the United States.

Clay and Webster persuaded Nicholas Biddle, head of the bank, to request an early re-chartering of the bank. Jackson's opponents in Congress knew they had the votes to pass a new charter in the summer of 1832, and they hoped Jackson would veto the bill and thereby split the Democratic Party just before the fall elections. The Second Bank was a political quagmire. The bank had stabilized the economy during the 1820s by regularly demanding specie (gold or silver) payments from state-chartered banks. This kept those banks from issuing too much paper money and thereby prevented inflation and higher prices. This tight-money policy also kept banks from expanding too rapidly in the western states. Most financial elites applauded the bank's efforts, but its policies aroused hostility in the wider public. When state-chartered banks closed because of lack of specie, ordinary Americans were often stuck with worthless paper money. Tight-money policies also made it more difficult for individuals to get credit to purchase land, homes, or farm equipment.

As the president's opponents had hoped, Congress approved the new charter, and Jackson vetoed it. Yet rather than dividing the Democrats, Jackson's veto gained enormous support from voters across the country. In justifying his action, the president cast the Second Bank as a "monster" that was "dangerous to the liberties of the people" — particularly farmers, mechanics, and laborers — while promoting "the advancement of the few." Jackson also noted that since wealthy Britons owned substantial shares of the bank's stock, national pride demanded ending the Second Bank's reign over the U.S. economy. Jackson rode the enthusiasm for his bank veto to reelection over National Republican candidate Henry Clay. Within a year, the Second Bank was dead, deprived of government deposits by Jackson.

Soon after his reelection, however, the president faced a grave political crisis related to the tariff issue. Jackson now supported lower tariffs, but he was adamant in his opposition to nullification. In early 1833, he persuaded Congress to pass a Force Bill, which gave him authority to use the military to enforce national laws in South Carolina. At the same time, Jackson made clear that he would work with Congress to reduce tariffs, allowing South Carolina to rescind its nullification ordinance without losing face. Open conflict was averted, but the question of nullification was not resolved.

Contesting Indian Removal

On another long-standing issue — the acquisition of Indian land — Jackson gained the support of white southerners and most frontier settlers. Yet not all Americans agreed with his effort to force southern Indians off their lands. In the 1820s nations like the Cherokee gained the support of Protestant missionaries who hoped to "civilize" Indians by converting them to Christianity and "American" ways. In 1819

Congress had granted Protestant groups federal funds to advance these goals. Jackson, however, criticized such efforts and sided with political leaders who sought to force Cherokee and other native tribes to accept homelands west of the Mississippi River.

In 1825, three years before Jackson was elected president, Creek Indians in Georgia and Alabama were forcibly removed to the Unorganized Territory (previously part of Arkansas Territory and later called Indian Territory) based on a fraudulent treaty. Jackson supported this policy. When he became president, politicians and settlers in Georgia, Florida, the Carolinas, and Illinois demanded federal assistance to force remaining native communities out of their states.

Powerful nations, such as the Cherokee, vehemently protested their removal. The Cherokee had fought alongside Jackson at Horseshoe Bend in 1814. Thirteen years later, they adopted a republican form of government based on the U.S. Constitution. John Ross served as the president of the Cherokee constitutional convention in 1827 and a year later was elected principal chief. He and the other chiefs then declared themselves a sovereign nation within the borders of the United States. The Georgia legislature rejected Cherokee claims of independence and argued that Indians were simply guests of the state, a position that gained added significance when gold was discovered in Cherokee territory in 1829. Ross appealed to Jackson to recognize Cherokee sovereignty, but the president was affronted by what he saw as a challenge to his authority. He urged Congress to pass the **Indian Removal Act** in 1830, by which the Cherokee and other Indian nations would be forced to exchange their lands in the Southeast for a "clear title forever" on territory west of the Mississippi River. While some Cherokee leaders accepted removal and gave up their lands, the majority of Cherokees refused to accept these terms.

As the dispute between the Cherokee nation and Georgia unfolded, Jackson made clear his intention to implement the Indian Removal Act. In 1832 he sent federal troops into western Illinois to force Sauk and Fox peoples to move farther west. Instead, whole villages, led by Chief Black Hawk, fled to the Wisconsin Territory. Black Hawk and a thousand warriors confronted U.S. troops at Bad Axe, but the Sauk and Fox warriors were decimated in a brutal daylong battle. The survivors were forced to move west. Meanwhile the Seminole Indians prepared to go to war to protect their territory, while John Ross pursued legal means to resist removal through state and federal courts. The contest for Indian lands continued well past Jackson's presidency, but the president's desire to force indigenous nations westward would ultimately prevail.

REVIEW & RELATE
- What did President Jackson's response to the Eaton affair and Indian removal reveal about his vision of democracy?
- Which of Jackson's policies benefited or antagonized which groups of southerners?

Conclusion: The Nation Faces New Challenges

From the 1810s through the early 1830s, the United States was buffeted by a series of crises. Although early in the period geographical expansion and economic growth convinced the federal government to invest in internal improvements, the War of

1812 soon threatened the nation's stability and revealed significant regional divisions. The panic of 1819 then threw the nation into economic turmoil and led to demands for expanded voting rights for white men, while African American men experienced increased restrictions on their political participation. Regional differences rooted in different natural resources and economic priorities—manufacturing in the North, cotton and rice cultivation in the South, and family agriculture in the Midwest—were increasing in the 1810s. They led to greater interdependence across regions, but distinct economic needs and uncertainties intensified political debates over issues like tariffs. The admission of Missouri similarly heightened debates over slavery as white southerners saw themselves losing out to the North in population growth and political representation. At the same time, continued western expansion escalated conflicts with a diverse array of Indian nations.

In navigating these difficult issues, some Americans sought to find a middle ground. Dolley Madison worked to overcome partisan divisions through social networking. After the death of her husband, James, in 1836, she returned to Washington and transformed her home into a center of elite social life. Although her son's mismanagement of Montpelier forced her to sell the beloved estate, Dolley secured her old age when Congress purchased President James Madison's papers from her. Similarly, John Ross wielded his biracial heritage to seek rights for the Cherokee within a white-dominated world. Yet even as he served as a lobbyist for Cherokee interests in Washington, he also advocated acculturation to Anglo-American ways among the Cherokee. However, congressional passage of the Indian Removal Act challenged Ross's efforts to maintain his tribe's sovereignty and homeland. Henry Clay, too, was widely known for helping to forge compromises on issues like slavery and tariffs. In the 1820s, he brought a deeply divided Congress together, hoping that political leaders could eventually develop permanent solutions.

Despite the efforts of Madison, Ross, Clay, and others, differences often led to division in the 1820s and 1830s. Indeed, Clay's success in ensuring John Quincy Adams's selection as president in 1824 only furthered partisan divisions, leading to the emergence of two distinct political parties: the Democrats and the National Republicans. Andrew Jackson, who led the new Democratic Party, helped transform the process of political campaigning. He gave voice to white workers and frontier farmers, for example, by shutting the Second Bank of the United States. But he also introduced the spoils system to government and forced thousands of Indians off their lands. Indian removal, in turn, fostered the expansion of slavery southward and westward, which ensured future federal and sectional crises.

Dolley Madison, who lived into the late 1840s, and John Ross, who survived the Civil War, observed the continuing conflicts created by geographical expansion and partisan agendas. Ross, however, faced much more difficult circumstances as the Cherokee nation divided over whether to accept removal, facing internal dissent and pressure from the federal government for years.

Despite the dramatically different backgrounds and careers of Madison and Ross, both worked to bridge differences in the young nation, and both defended it against attack. Ultimately, however, neither had the power to overcome the partisan rivalries and economic crises that shaped the young nation or to halt the rising social, economic, and political tensions that would plague Americans in the decades to come.

Chapter 9 Review

KEY TERMS

Non-Intercourse Act, 218
Battle of Fallen Timbers, 218
Battle of Horseshoe Bend, 221
Hartford Convention, 222
Treaty of Ghent, 222
American System, 223
Erie Canal, 223
Adams-Onís Treaty, 225
Monroe Doctrine, 225

panic of 1819, 228
Missouri Compromise, 231
Democrats and National
   Republicans, 237
Petticoat Affair, 238
spoils system, 238
Tariff of Abominations, 238
nullification, 238
Indian Removal Act, 240

REVIEW & RELATE

1. How were conflicts with Indians in the West connected to ongoing tensions between the United States and Great Britain?

2. What were the long-term consequences of the War of 1812?

3. What role did government play in early-nineteenth-century economic development?

4. How and why did economic development—especially related to cotton—contribute to regional differences and shape regional ties?

5. How did regional interdependency contribute to the panic of 1819?

6. What regional divisions did the conflict over slavery in Missouri reveal?

7. How and why did the composition of the electorate change in the 1820s?

8. In what ways did the 1828 Presidential campaign represent a departure from earlier patterns in American politics?

9. What did President Jackson's response to the Eaton affair and Indian removal reveal about his vision of democracy?

10. Which of Jackson's policies benefited or antagonized which groups of southerners?

TIMELINE OF EVENTS

1809	• Non-Intercourse Act
1811	• First steamboat travels down the Mississippi
	• William Henry Harrison defeats Shawnees at Prophetstown
June 1812	• War of 1812 begins
1814	• Hartford Convention
March 1814	• Battle of Horseshoe Bend
August 1814	• British burn Washington City
December 1814	• Treaty of Ghent
1815	• Battle of New Orleans
1817–1818	• Andrew Jackson fights Spanish and Seminole forces in Florida
1818	• Great Britain and United States agree to joint occupation of Oregon Territory
1819	• Adams-Onís Treaty
1819–1823	• Panic of 1819
1820	• Missouri Compromise
1821	• White traders begin using Santa Fe Trail
1822	• Denmark Vesey organizes a slave rebellion
1823	• Monroe Doctrine proclaimed
1825	• Erie Canal completed
1828	• Tariff of 1828 (Tariff of Abominations)
	• John Ross elected principal chief of the Cherokee nation
1829	• Petticoat Affair
1830	• Indian Removal Act
1832	• South Carolina passes Ordinance of Nullification
1833	• Force Bill

10

Social and Cultural Ferment in the North

1820–1850

LEARNING OBJECTIVES

After reading this chapter you will be able to:

- Explain the growth of and changes in northern cities, including issues of immigration, class stratification, and gender roles.

- Analyze how industrialization transformed workers' lives, was affected by the boom and bust economic cycle, and contributed to class, ethnic, and racial tensions.

- Describe the range and appeal of religious movements that emerged in the 1830s and 1840s.

- Evaluate the emergence of reform movements and the strategies they embraced.

- Explain the importance of the transportation and communication revolution to the rise of antislavery movements and their impact on other social and political changes.

COMPARING AMERICAN HISTORIES

The great revival preacher **Charles Grandison Finney** was born in 1792 and raised in rural New York State. As a young man, Finney studied the law. But in 1821, like many others of his generation, he experienced a powerful religious conversion. No longer interested in a legal career, he turned to the ministry instead.

After being ordained in the Presbyterian Church, Finney joined "New School" ministers who rejected the more conservative traditions of the Presbyterian Church and embraced a vigorous evangelicalism. In the early 1830s the

Reverend Finney traveled throughout New York State preaching about Christ's place in a changing America. He held massive revivals in cities along the Erie Canal, most notably in Rochester, New York. He achieved his greatest success in places experiencing rapid economic development and an influx of migrants and immigrants, where the clash of cultures and classes fueled fears of moral decay.

Finney urged Christians to actively seek salvation. Once individuals reformed themselves, he said, they should work to abolish poverty, intemperance, prostitution, and slavery. He expected women to participate in revivals and good works but advised them to balance these efforts with their domestic responsibilities.

In many ways, **Amy Kirby Post** fit Finney's ideal. Born into a farm family in Jericho, New York, she found solace in spirituality and social reform. Like many other people in this period, Amy experienced the loss of loved ones. In 1825, at age twenty-three, Amy's fiancé died, and two years later she lost the sister to whom she was closest. The next year, Amy married a widower, Isaac Post. She mothered his two young children and bore five children of her own, two of whom died young. Yet Amy Post did not embrace evangelical revivals, but focused instead on the quiet piety preferred by her Quaker community.

Still, the personal upheavals Amy experienced in her twenties occurred amid heated controversies within the Society of Friends (Quakers). Elias Hicks claimed that the Society had abandoned its spiritual roots and become too much like a traditional church. His followers, called Hicksites, insisted that Quakers should reduce their dependence on disciplinary rules, elders, and preachers and rely instead on the "Inner Light"—the spirit of God dwelling within each individual. When the Society of Friends divided into Hicksite and Orthodox branches in 1827, Amy Kirby and Isaac Post joined the Hicksites.

In 1836 Amy Post moved with her husband and children to Rochester, New York. In a city marked by the spirit of Finney's revivals, Quakers emphasized quiet contemplation rather than emotional conversions, but the Society of Friends allowed members, including women, to preach when moved by the spirit. Quaker women also held separate meetings to discipline female congregants, evaluate marriage proposals, and write testimonies on important religious and social issues.

Amy Post's spiritual journey was increasingly shaped by the rising tide of abolition. Committed to ending slavery, she joined hundreds of local evangelical women in signing an 1837 antislavery petition. Four years later, she helped found the Western New York Anti-Slavery Society, which included Quakers and evangelicals, women and men, and blacks and whites. Post's growing commitment to abolition caused tensions in the Hicksite meeting since many members opposed working in "worldly" organizations alongside non-Quakers. In 1848 Post and other radical Friends formed a new, more activist-oriented Quaker meeting and joined the movement for women's rights as well as abolition.

COMPARING THE AMERICAN HISTORIES of Charles Finney and Amy Post shows how individuals responded to and helped shape the dynamic religious, social, and economic developments of the early nineteenth century. Finney changed the face of American religion, aided by masses of evangelical Protestants. The transportation and communication revolutions, the expansion of the market economy, and the rise of cities, especially in the northern United States, benefitted many Americans. However, they also made problems like poverty, unemployment, alcohol abuse, crime, and prostitution more visible, drawing people to Finney's message. Like many Americans, Amy Post migrated with her family along improved roads and canals to seek better economic opportunities. But as the moral stain of slavery continued to grow, she joined other Quakers and northern blacks in refusing to purchase slave-produced goods. Bursting traditional religious bonds, she also reconsidered what it meant to do God's work. For both Finney and Post, Rochester — the fastest-growing city in the nation between 1825 and 1835 — exemplified the possibilities and problems created by the market revolution, urban expansion, and rapid social change.

The Market Revolution

Commercial and industrial development, immigration from Europe, and migration from rural areas led to the rapid growth of cities in the northern United States from 1820 on. Such growth both built on and furthered the expansion of roads and canals, which were funded by federal and state governments in the 1810s and 1820s. By linking northern industries with western farms and southern plantations, these innovations in transportation fueled a **market revolution** as the manufacture of goods became better organized and innovations in industry, agriculture, and communication increased efficiency and productivity. These changes fostered urbanization, which, in turn, reinforced economic growth and innovation. However, it also created social upheaval. Cultural divisions intensified in urban areas where Catholics and Protestants, workers and the well-to-do, immigrants, African Americans, and native-born whites lived side by side. Class dynamics also changed with the development of a clear middle class of shopkeepers, professionals, and clerks.

Creating an Urban Landscape

Across the North, urban populations boomed. As commercial centers, seaports like New York and Philadelphia were the most populous cities in the early nineteenth century. Between 1820 and 1850, the number of cities with 100,000 inhabitants increased from two to six; five were seaports. The sixth was the river port of Cincinnati, Ohio. Smaller boomtowns, like Rochester, New York, emerged along inland waterways like the Erie Canal. Completed in 1825, it spurred agriculture, industry, and small business along its 363-mile route.

Development along the Erie Canal illustrates the ways that advancements in transportation transformed the surrounding landscape and ecology. As soon as the first stretch was completed in 1819, its economic benefits became clear. As the 40-foot-wide canal was extended across central and western New York State, settlers rushed to establish farms, mills, and ports. They chopped down millions of trees to construct homes and businesses and to open land for farms and orchards. Farmers shipped grain, cattle, and hogs to eastern markets or to emerging cities like Rochester. There, millers and butchers turned them into flour, beef, and pork, products that were now easier and cheaper to ship further onward. Newspapers multiplied, offering the latest news on crop prices and manufactured goods and advertising local services along the canal. The growing population of boatmen, merchants, and travelers depended on taverns for meals, rest, and information. Americans who lived along the Erie Canal, the Great Lakes, and major rivers could learn a great deal by spending time at taverns gathering news and information from far-flung ports.

As the population in western New York, the Old Northwest, and along the Great Lakes increased, residents demanded more and more manufactured goods. This demand fueled the growth of factories. Cotton, lumber, and flour mills were constructed near waterfalls for power, transforming isolated villages into mill towns while endangering the natural habitats of fish and wildlife. As thousands of newcomers cleared land in Ohio and Michigan, they expanded trade between areas fueled by the Erie Canal and the Great Lakes and older towns from New England to New York City. Midwesterners also shipped agricultural goods south via the Ohio and Mississippi Rivers, exchanging grain and other items for southern cotton, rice, and sugar. Southern trade also grew along the Atlantic coast, with cotton bales barely keeping up with the demand from New England factories.

Business and political leaders in Philadelphia and Baltimore, seeing the economic benefits created by the Erie Canal, demanded state funding for canals linking them to the Midwest. Where state funding proved insufficient, they persuaded English bankers and merchants to invest in American canals as well as railroads, which were just beginning to compete with waterways as a method to transport people and goods.

The Lure of Urban Life

As transportation improved and the economy expanded, cities across the North increased not only in size but also in diversity. During the 1820s, some 150,000 European immigrants entered the United States; during the 1830s, nearly 600,000; and during the 1840s, more than 1,700,000. This surge of immigrants included more Irish and German settlers than ever before as well as large numbers of Scandinavians. Many settled along the eastern seaboard. Others migrated west, including thousands of Irish immigrants who labored in difficult and dangerous conditions to build the Erie Canal. Some Irish workers quit these jobs to settle in local communities along the canal's route. Others added to the growth of frontier cities such as Cincinnati, St. Louis, and Chicago.

Late-eighteenth-century Irish immigrants, many of whom were Protestants, were joined by hundreds of thousands more in the 1830s and 1840s, when Irish Catholics poured into the United States. The Irish countryside was then plagued by bad weather, a potato blight, and harsh economic policies imposed by the English government. In 1845 to 1846 a full-blown famine forced thousands more Irish Catholic

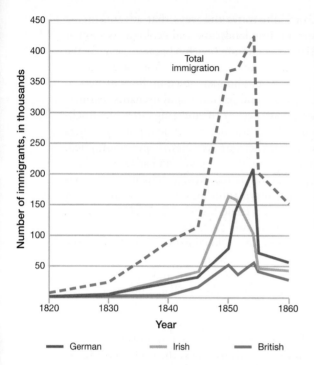

FIGURE 10.1 Immigration to the United States, 1820–1860
Famine, economic upheaval, and political persecution led masses of people from Ireland, Germany, and Britain to migrate to the United States from the 1820s through the 1850s. The vast majority settled in cities and factory towns in the North or on farms in the Midwest. An economic recession in the late 1850s finally slowed immigration, though only temporarily. What does this graph tell us about the growing diversity of the U.S. population?

families to emigrate. Young Irish women, who could easily find work as domestics or seamstresses, emigrated in especially large numbers. Poor harvests, droughts, failed revolutions, and repressive landlords convinced large numbers of Germans, including Catholics, Lutherans, and Jews, and Scandinavians to flee their homelands as well. By 1850 the Irish made up about 40 percent of immigrants to the United States, and Germans nearly a quarter (Figure 10.1).

These immigrants provided an expanding pool of cheap labor as well as skilled artisans, adding fuel to northern commerce and industry. Banks, mercantile houses, and dry-goods stores multiplied. Urban industrial enterprises included both traditional workshops and mechanized factories. Credit and insurance agencies emerged to aid entrepreneurs in their ventures. The increase in business also drove the demand for ships, warehouses, newspapers, and other commercial necessities, which created a surge in jobs for many urban residents.

Businesses focused on leisure also flourished. In the 1830s theater became affordable to working-class families, who attended comedies, musical revues, and morality plays. They also joined middle- and upper-class audiences at productions of Shakespeare and contemporary dramas. Minstrel shows mocked self-important capitalists but also portrayed African Americans in crude caricatures. One of the most popular characters was Jim Crow, who appeared originally in an African American song. In the 1820s Thomas Rice, a white performer who blacked his face with burnt cork, incorporated Jim Crow into a song-and-dance routine.

The lures of urban life were especially attractive to the young. Single men and women and newly married couples flocked to the largest cities, ensuring their continued growth. By 1850 half the residents of New York, Philadelphia, and other seaport cities were under sixteen years old. Young men sought work in factories, construction, and the maritime trades or in banks and commercial houses, while young women competed for jobs as seamstresses and domestic servants.

The Roots of Urban Disorder

While immigrant labor stimulated northern economic growth, immigrant families transformed the urban landscape. They crowded into houses and apartments and built ethnic institutions, including synagogues and convents — visible indicators of the growing diversity of northern cities. While most native-born Protestants applauded economic growth, cultural diversity aroused anxieties. Anti-Catholicism and anti-Semitism flourished in the 1830s and 1840s. Crude stereotypes portrayed Jews as manipulative moneylenders and Catholic nuns and priests as sexually depraved. Ethnic groups also battled stereotypes. Irishmen, for example, were often pictured as habitual drunkards.

Still, rising immigration did not deter rural Americans from seeking economic opportunities in the city. Native-born white men often set out on their own, but most white women settled in cities under the supervision of a husband, landlady, or employer. African Americans, too, sought greater opportunities in urban areas. In the 1830s, more blacks joined Philadelphia's vibrant African American community, attracted by its churches, schools, and mutual aid societies. New Bedford, Massachusetts, a thriving whaling center, recruited black workers and thus attracted fugitive slaves as well.

In urban areas, many individuals lived outside the bounds of traditional families. This led some single women and widows to create or to join "housefuls." Housefuls were groups of mostly unrelated women and men, often from different ethnic and racial backgrounds, bound together by economic ties. Many served as sites of commerce, labor, and daily life. Urban housefuls existed in boardinghouses and taverns run by women and in laundries or shops with living spaces above or behind. While they allowed women, immigrants, and free and enslaved blacks to survive outside traditional families, they were still marked by hierarchies of age, skill, literacy, and other measures of economic worth.

Wherever they lived, newcomers to cities faced many dangers. Some men sought to lure young women into the sex trade, and domestic servants were often subject to sexual abuse. Thieves and scam artists regularly victimized young men new to the city, while blacks and immigrants — men and women — confronted discrimination in housing and jobs as well as on the carriages and boats that carried them to their new homes. In addition, physical battles erupted on city streets between immigrant and native-born residents, Protestant and Catholic gangs, and white and black workers. Disease also spread quickly through densely populated neighborhoods. When innovations in transportation made it possible for more affluent residents to distance themselves from crowded inner cities, they moved to less congested neighborhoods on the urban periphery. Horse-drawn streetcar lines, first built in New York City in 1832, hastened this development.

By the 1840s, economic competition intensified, fueling violence among those driven to the margins. Native-born white employers and workers pushed Irish immigrants to the bottom of the economic ladder, where they competed with African Americans. Yet Irish workers insisted that their whiteness gave them a higher status than even the most skilled blacks. When black temperance reformers organized a parade in Philadelphia in August 1842, white onlookers—mostly Irish laborers—attacked the marchers, and the conflict escalated into a riot.

Americans who lived in small towns and rural areas regularly read news of urban violence and vice. Improvements in printing created vastly more and cheaper newspapers, while the construction of the first telegraph in 1844 ensured that news could travel more quickly from town to town. Newspaper offices served as centers of activity and exchange in towns and cities across the North. Readers were asked to "enquire of the printer" if they wished further details about announcements for events, tickets, and goods for sale or advertisements for fugitive slaves and runaway spouses. Subscribers, sellers, and advertisers also came and went amid the noise and clamor that accompanied the printing process. In cities, tabloids wooed readers with sensational stories of crime, sex, and scandal. Even more respectable newspapers reported on urban mayhem, while religious periodicals warned parishioners against urban immorality. In response to both a real and a perceived increase in crime, cities replaced voluntary night watchmen with paid police forces.

The New Middle Class

Members of the emerging middle class, which developed first in the North, included ambitious businessmen, successful shopkeepers, doctors, and lawyers as well as teachers, journalists, ministers, and other salaried employees. At the top rungs, successful entrepreneurs and professionals adopted affluent lifestyles. At the lower rungs, a growing cohort of salaried clerks and managers hoped that their hard work, honesty, and thrift would be rewarded with upward mobility.

Education, religious affiliation, and sobriety were important indicators of middle-class status. A well-read man who attended a well-established church and drank in strict moderation was marked as belonging to this new rank. He was also expected to own a comfortable home, marry a pious woman, and raise well-behaved children. The rise of the middle class inspired a flood of advice books, ladies' magazines, religious periodicals, and novels advocating new ideals of womanhood. These publications emphasized the centrality of child rearing and homemaking to women's identities. This **cult of domesticity** ideally restricted wives to home and hearth, where they provided their husbands with respite from the cares and corruptions of the world.

In reality, however, entrance to the middle class required the efforts of wives as well as husbands. While upper middle-class men were expected to provide financial security, women helped cement social and economic bonds by entertaining the wives of business associates, serving in charitable and temperance societies, and organizing Sabbath schools. Families struggling to enter the middle class might take in boarders or extended family members to help secure their financial status. The adoption of new marital ideals of affection and companionship also made the boundaries between public and domestic life more fluid. In many middle-class families, husbands and wives both participated in church, civic, and reform activities, even if they did so through single-sex organizations. At the same time, husbands joined in domestic activities in the evening, presiding over dinner or reading to children.

The ideal of separate spheres of work and home had even less relevance to the millions of women who toiled on farms and factories or as domestic servants,

John Aymar and Family, New York City, c. 1838 George Twibill Jr., a student of Samuel B. Morse, painted this family portrait. John Aymar imported rum and coffee, his occupation reflected in the ship masts peeking through the window. He stands over and behind his wife Elizabeth and their daughters, the quartet surrounded by the fine carpets, rich draperies, and expensive furnishings that proclaim their elite status. The Metropolitan Museum of Art, Gift of A. Grima Johnson, 2008

providing goods and services for middle-class and elite families. In turn, those middle-class families played a crucial role in the growing market economy and the jobs it created. Wives and daughters were responsible for much of the family's consumption. They purchased cloth, rugs, chairs, clocks, and housewares, and, if wealthy enough, European crystal and Chinese porcelain. Middling housewives bought goods once made at home, such as butter and candles, and arranged music lessons and other educational opportunities for their children.

Although increasingly recognized for their ability to consume wisely, middle-class women also performed significant domestic labor. While many could afford servants, they often joined domestics and daughters in household tasks. Except for those in the upper middle class, most women still cut and sewed garments, cultivated gardens, canned fruits and vegetables, cooked at least some meals, and entertained guests. As houses expanded in size and clothes became fancier, domestic servants shouldered the most laborious and time-consuming chores, while mothers and daughters performed lighter tasks. However, such work was increasingly invisible as husbands and fathers came to separate labor focused inwardly on the family from that focused outwardly in the market economy.

Middle-class men contributed significantly to the consumer economy. Of course, they created, invested in, and managed most industrial and commercial ventures.

Moreover, in carrying out business and professional obligations, many enjoyed restaurants, the theater, or sporting events. Men also attended plays and lectures with their wives and visited museums and circuses with their children. And they purchased hats, suits, mustache wax, and other accoutrements of middle-class masculinity.

REVIEW & RELATE

- How did the market revolution, including improvements like the Erie Canal, reshape the landscape and lives of Americans in the North?
- As northern cities became larger and more diverse in the first half of the nineteenth century, what changes and challenges did urban residents face and what values and beliefs did the new middle class embrace?

The Rise of Industry

In the mid-nineteenth century, industrial enterprises in the Northeast transformed the nation's economy even though they employed less than 10 percent of the U.S. labor force. In the 1830s and 1840s, factories grew considerably in size, and some investors, especially in textiles, constructed factory towns. New England textile mills relied increasingly on the labor of girls and young women, while urban workshops hired children, young women and men, and older adults. Although men still dominated the skilled trades, making chairs, clocks, shoes, hats, and fine clothing, employment in these trades slowly declined as industrial jobs expanded. An economic panic in 1837 exacerbated this trend and made it even more difficult for workers to organize across differences of skill, ethnicity, race, and sex.

Factory Towns and Women Workers

In the late 1820s investors and manufacturers joined forces to create factory towns in the New England countryside. The most famous mill town, Lowell, Massachusetts, was based on an earlier experiment in nearby Waltham. In the Waltham system, every step of the production process was mechanized; planned communities included factories, boardinghouses, government offices, and churches. Agents for the Waltham system recruited the daughters of New England farm families as workers, assuring parents that they would be watched over by managers and foremen as well as landladies. The young women were required to attend church and observe curfews while clocks and bells regulated their labor to ensure discipline and productivity.

Farm families needed more cash because of the growing market economy, and daughters in the mills could contribute to family finances and save money for the clothes and linens required for married life. Factory jobs also provided an alternative to marriage as young New England men moved west and left a surplus of women behind. Factory-owned boardinghouses provided a relatively safe, all-female environment for mill workers, and sisters and neighbors often lived together. Despite nearly constant supervision, many rural women viewed factory work as an adventure. They could set aside a bit of money for themselves, attend lectures and concerts, meet new people, and acquire a wider view of the world.

During the 1830s, however, working conditions began to deteriorate. Factory owners cut wages, lengthened hours, and sped up machines. Boardinghouses became overcrowded, and company officials regulated both rents and expenses so that higher prices for lodging did not necessarily mean better food or furnishings. Factory workers launched numerous strikes in the 1830s against longer hours, wage cuts, and speedups in factory production. The solidarity required to sustain these strikes was forged in boardinghouses and at church socials as well as on the factory floor. At age twelve, Harriet Robinson led a walkout at the Lowell Mills in 1836. In her memoir, written in 1898, she noted, "As I looked back at the long line that followed me, I was more proud than I have ever been since at any success I have achieved."

Despite mill workers' solidarity, it was difficult to overcome the economic power wielded by manufacturers. Working women's collective actions were generally short-lived, lasting only until a strike was settled. Then employees returned to their jobs until the next crisis hit. And as competition increasingly cut into profits, owners resisted mill workers' demands more vehemently. When the panic of 1837 intensified fears of job loss, women's organizing activities were doomed until the economy recovered.

The Decline of Craft Work and Workingmen's Responses

While the construction of factory towns expanded economic opportunities for young women, the gradual decline of time-honored crafts narrowed the prospects for workingmen. Craft workshops gradually increased in size and hired fewer skilled workers and more men who performed single tasks, like attaching soles to shoes. Many tasks also became mechanized during the nineteenth century. The final product was less distinctive than an entire item crafted by a skilled artisan, but it was less expensive and available in mass quantities.

The shift from craft work to factory work threatened to undermine workingmen's skills, pay, and labor conditions. Rather than skilled apprentices who worked alongside a master craftsman, masters began hiring foremen to regulate the workforce and installing bells and clocks to regulate the workday. This process of **deskilling** occurred over several decades in different trades. As it transformed shoemaking, printing, tailoring, and other trades, laboring men fought to maintain their status.

Some workers formed mutual aid societies to provide assistance in times of illness, injury, or unemployment. Others participated in religious revivals or joined fraternal orders to find the camaraderie they once enjoyed at work. The expansion of voting rights in the 1820s offered another avenue for action. The first workingmen's political party was founded in Philadelphia in 1827, and working-class men in the North joined forces to support politicians sympathetic to their needs. Most workingmen's parties focused on practical proposals: government distribution of free land in the West, abolishing compulsory militia service and imprisonment for debt, public funding for education, and regulations on banks and corporations. Although the electoral success of these parties was modest, in the 1830s Democrats and Whigs adopted many of their proposals.

Workingmen also formed unions to demand better wages and working conditions. In the 1820s and 1830s, skilled journeymen held mass meetings to protest employers' efforts to lengthen the workday, merge smaller workshops into larger factories, and cut wages. In New York City in 1834, labor activists formed a citywide federation, the General Trades Union, which provided support for striking workers. The National Trades Union was established later that year, with delegates representing more than twenty-five thousand workers across the North. These organizations aided skilled workers but refused admission to women and unskilled men.

It proved difficult to establish broader labor organizations. Most skilled men considered unskilled workers as competitors, not allies. Many workingmen also feared that women workers would undercut their wages and so refused to organize alongside them. And anti-immigrant and racist beliefs among many native-born Protestant workers interfered with organizing across racial and ethnic lines. With the onset of the panic of 1837, the common plight of workers became clearer. But the economic crisis made unified action nearly impossible as individuals sought to hold on to what little they had.

The Panic of 1837

The panic of 1837, which began in the South, hit northern cotton merchants hard (see "Van Buren and the Panic of 1837" in Chapter 11). With cotton shipments sharply curtailed, textile factories drastically cut production, unemployment rose, and merchants and investors went broke. Those still employed saw their wages cut in half. In Rochester, the Posts temporarily moved in with other family members and their oldest son left school to help save their pharmacy from foreclosure. Petty crime and prostitution also rose as men and women struggled to make ends meet.

In Lowell, hours increased and wages fell. Just as important, the process of deskilling intensified. Factory owners considered mechanization one way to improve their economic situation. A cascade of inventions, including power looms, steam boilers, and the steam press, transformed industrial occupations and led factory owners to invest more of their limited resources in machines. At the same time, the rising tide of immigrants provided a ready supply of relatively cheap labor. Artisans tried to maintain their traditional skills and status, but in many trades they were fighting a losing battle.

By the early 1840s, when the panic subsided, new technologies did spur new jobs. Factories demanded more workers to handle machines that ran at a faster pace. In printing, the steam press allowed publication of more newspapers and magazines, creating positions for editors, publishers, printers, engravers, reporters, and sales agents. Similarly, mechanical reapers sped the harvest of wheat and inspired changes in flour milling that required engineers to design machines and mechanics to build and repair them.

These changing circumstances fueled new labor organizations as well. Many of these unions comprised a particular trade or ethnic group, and almost all continued to address primarily the needs of skilled male workers. Textile operatives remained the one important group of organized female workers. In the 1840s, workingwomen even joined with workingmen in New England to fight for a ten-hour day. Slowly, however, farmers' daughters left the mills as desperate Irish immigrants flooded in and accepted lower wages, endangering the small improvements mill workers had gained.

For most women in need, charitable organizations offered more support than unions. Organizations like Philadelphia's Female Association for the Relief of Women and Children in Reduced Circumstances provided a critical safety net for many poor families since public monies for such purposes were limited. Although most northern towns and cities now provided some form of public assistance, they never had sufficient resources to meet local needs in good times, much less the extraordinary demands posed by the panic.

REVIEW & RELATE	• How and why did American manufacturing change during the first half of the nineteenth century? • How did new technologies, immigration, and the panic of 1837 change the economic opportunities and organizing strategies for northern workers?

Saving the Nation from Sin

In the first half of the nineteenth century, men and women of all classes and races embraced the Protestant religious revival known as the **Second Great Awakening**, through which they expressed deeply held beliefs and reclaimed a sense of the nation's godly mission. Still, evangelical Protestantism was not the only religious tradition to thrive in this period. Catholic churches and Jewish synagogues multiplied with immigration; and in the North, Quaker meetings and Unitarian congregations flourished as well. New religious groups also attracted thousands of followers while transcendentalists sought deeper engagements with nature as another path to spiritual renewal.

The Second Great Awakening

Although diverse religious traditions flourished in the United States, evangelical Protestantism proved the most powerful in the 1820s and 1830s. Evangelical churches hosted revivals, celebrated conversions, and organized prayer and missionary societies. This second wave of religious revivals had begun in Cane Ridge, Kentucky in 1801 and took root across the South. It then spread northward, transforming Protestant churches and the social fabric of northern life.

Ministers like Charles Grandison Finney adopted techniques first wielded by southern Methodists and Baptists: plain speaking, powerful images, and mass meetings. But Finney molded these techniques for a more affluent audience and held his "camp meetings" in established churches. By the late 1820s, boomtown growth along the Erie Canal aroused deep concerns among religious leaders about the rising tide of sin. In response, the Reverend Finney arrived in Rochester in September 1830. He began preaching in local Presbyterian churches, leading crowded prayer meetings that lasted late into the night. Individual supplicants walked to special benches designated for anxious sinners, who were prayed over in public. Female parishioners played crucial roles, encouraging their husbands, sons, friends, and neighbors to submit to God.

Thousands of Rochester residents joined in the evangelical experience as Finney's powerful message engulfed other denominations (Map 10.1). The significance of these revivals went far beyond an increase in church membership. Finney converted "the great mass of the most influential people" in the city: merchants, lawyers, doctors, master craftsmen, and shopkeepers. Equally important, he proclaimed that if Christians were "united all over the world the Millennium [Christ's Second Coming] might be brought about in three months." Preachers in Rochester and the surrounding towns took up his call, and converts committed themselves to preparing the world for Christ's arrival.

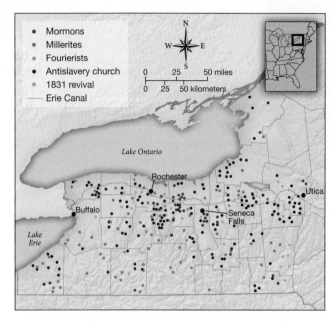

MAP 10.1   Religious Movements in the Burned-Over District, 1831–1848
Western and central New York State was burned over by the fires of religious revivalism in the 1830s and 1840s. But numerous other religious groups also formed or flourished in the region in these decades, including Quakers, Mormons, and Millerites. In the 1840s, Fourierist phalanxes, the Oneida community, and other utopian experiments were established here.

Source: Whitney R. Cross, *The Burned-Over District: The Social and Intellectual History of Enthusiastic Religion in Western New York, 1800–1850* (Ithaca, NY: Cornell University Press, 1950).

Developments in Rochester were replicated in cities across the North. Presbyterian, Congregational, and Episcopalian churches overflowed with middle-class and wealthy Americans, while Baptists and Methodists ministered to more laboring women and men. Black Baptists and Methodists evangelized in their communities, combining powerful preaching with rousing spirituals. In Philadelphia, African Americans built fifteen churches between 1799 and 1830. Black women joined men in evangelizing to their fellow African Americans as they continued to fight for the right to be ordained as ministers.

Tens of thousands of black and white converts embraced evangelicals' message of moral outreach. No reform movement gained greater impetus from the revivals than **temperance**, whose advocates sought to moderate and then ban the sale and consumption of alcohol. In the 1820s Americans fifteen years and older consumed six to seven gallons of distilled alcohol per person per year (about double the amount consumed today). Middle-class evangelicals, who once accepted moderate drinking as healthful, now insisted on eliminating alcohol consumption altogether.

New Visions of Faith and Reform

Although enthusiasm for temperance and other reforms waned during the panic of 1837 and many churches lost members, the Second Great Awakening continued in its aftermath. But evangelical ministers increasingly competed for souls with a variety of other religious groups, many of which also supported good works and social reform. The Society of Friends, the first religious group to refuse fellowship to slaveholders, expanded throughout the early nineteenth century, largely in the North and Midwest. Having divided in 1827 and again in 1848, the Society of Friends continued to grow. So, too, did its influence in reform movements as activists like Amy Post carried Quaker testimonies against alcohol, war, and slavery into the wider society. Unitarians also combined religious worship with social reform. They differed from other Christians by believing in a single unified higher spirit rather than the Trinity of the Father, the Son, and the Holy Spirit. Emerging mainly in New England in the early nineteenth century, Unitarian societies slowly spread west and south in the 1830s. Opposed to evangelical revivalism and dedicated to a rational approach to understanding the divine, Unitarians attracted prominent literary figures such as James Russell Lowell and Harvard luminaries like William Ellery Channing.

Other churches grew as a result of immigration. Dozens of Catholic churches were established to meet the needs of Irish and German immigrants. With the rapid increase in Catholic churches, Irish priests multiplied in the 1840s and 1850s, and women's religious orders became increasingly Irish as well. At the same time, synagogues, Hebrew schools, and Hebrew aid societies signaled the growing presence of Jewish immigrants, chiefly from Germany, in the United States. Between 1830 and 1860, new synagogues were built in Charleston, New Orleans, Baltimore, New York City, Cincinnati, and other cities. Most Catholics and Jews were less active in reform in the wider society and more focused on assisting their own congregants in securing a foothold in America.

Entirely new religious groups also flourished. One of the most important was the Church of Jesus Christ of Latter-Day Saints, or Mormons, founded by Joseph Smith. Smith began to receive visions from God at age fifteen and was directed to dig up gold plates inscribed with instructions for redeeming the Lost Tribes of Israel. *The Book of Mormon* (1830), based on these inscriptions, served, along with the Bible, as the scriptural foundation for Mormons. Smith served as their Prophet.

Smith founded not only a church but a theocracy (a community governed by religious leaders). In the mid-1830s Mormons established a settlement at Nauvoo, Illinois and recruited followers—black and white—from the eastern United States and England. When Smith voiced antislavery views, some local residents expressed outrage. But it was his claim to revelations sanctioning polygamy that led local authorities to arrest him and his brother. When a mob then lynched the Smith brothers, Brigham Young, a successful missionary, took over as Prophet. In 1846 he led 12,000 followers west, 5,000 of who settled near the Great Salt Lake, in what would soon become the Utah Territory. Isolated from anti-Mormon mobs, Young established a thriving theocracy. In this settlement, leaders practiced polygamy and though accepting black members, denied them the right to become priests.

New religious groups also formed by separating from established denominations. William Miller, a prosperous farmer and Baptist preacher, claimed that the Bible proved that the Second Coming of Jesus Christ would occur in 1843. Thousands of Americans joined the Millerites. When various dates for Christ's Second Coming passed without incident, however, Millerites developed competing interpretations for the failure and divided into distinct groups. The most influential group formed the Seventh-Day Adventist Church in the 1840s.

Transcendentalism

Another important movement for spiritual renewal was rooted in the transcendent power of nature. The founder of this transcendentalist school of thought was Ralph Waldo Emerson. Raised a Unitarian, Emerson began challenging the church's ideas. His 1836 essay entitled "Nature" expounded his newfound belief in a Universal Being. This Being existed as an ideal reality beyond the material world and was accessible through nature. Emerson's natural world was distinctly American and suggested that moral perfection could be achieved in the United States. Emerson expressed his ideas in widely read essays and books. He was also a popular speaker on the lyceum circuit, a new form of popular education and entertainment that drew tens of thousands of audience members in towns and cities across the country.

Emerson's hometown of Concord, Massachusetts served as a haven for writers, poets, intellectuals, and reformers drawn to **transcendentalism**. In 1840 Margaret Fuller, a close friend of Emerson, became the first editor of *The Dial*, a journal dedicated to transcendental thought. In 1844 she moved to New York City, where Horace Greeley hired her as a critic at the *New York Tribune*. In 1845, she published *Woman in the Nineteenth Century*, which combined transcendental ideas with arguments for women's rights.

Henry David Thoreau also followed the transcendentalist path. He grew up in Concord and read "Nature" while a student at Harvard in the mid-1830s. In July 1845 Thoreau moved to a cabin near Walden Pond and launched an experiment in simple living. A year later he was imprisoned overnight for refusing to pay his taxes as a protest against slavery and the Mexican-American War. In *Civil Disobedience* (1846), Thoreau argued that individuals of conscience had the right to resist government policies they believed to be immoral. Five years later, Thoreau published *Walden*, which highlighted the intertwined virtues of simple living, natural harmony, and social justice.

Thomas Cole, *View of the Round-Top in the Catskills Mountains*, 1827 Thomas Cole was born in England in 1801, migrated to America in 1818, and lived for many years in Catskill, New York with his wife and children until his death in 1848. Many of his paintings captured a romantic view of nature that combined a hint of wildness with the beauty of mountain mists and sunlit rivers shown here. Gift of Martha C. Karolik for the M. and M. Karolik/Bridgeman Images

Like Emerson, many American artists embraced the power of nature. Led by Thomas Cole, members of the Hudson River School painted romanticized landscapes from New York's Catskill and Adirondack Mountains. Some northern artists also traveled to the West, painting the region's grand vistas. Pennsylvanian George Catlin captured the dramatic scenery of western mountains, gorges, and waterfalls and painted moving portraits of Plains Indians.

REVIEW & RELATE	• What impact did the Second Great Awakening have in the North? • What new religious organizations and viewpoints emerged in the first half of the nineteenth century, *outside* of Protestant evangelical denominations?

Organizing for Change

Both religious commitments and secular problems spurred social activism in the 1830s and 1840s. In cities, small towns, and rural communities, Northerners founded organizations, launched campaigns, and established institutions to better the world around them. Still, reformers often disagreed over priorities and solutions. One major divide was between activists who employed moral arguments to persuade Americans to change and those who insisted that laws were the only effective means of changing behavior.

Varieties of Reform

Middle-class Protestants formed the core of many reform movements in the mid-nineteenth-century North. They had more time and money to devote to social reform than did their working-class counterparts and were less tied to traditional ways than their wealthy neighbors. Still, workers and farmers, African Americans and immigrants, Catholics and Jews also participated in efforts to improve society.

Reformers were sometimes forced to use different techniques. Since women were excluded from direct political participation, they established charitable associations, distributed food and medicine, constructed asylums, circulated petitions, organized boycotts, arranged meetings and lectures, and published newspapers and pamphlets. Other groups with limited political rights—African Americans and immigrants, for instance—embraced similar modes of action and also formed mutual aid societies. Native-born white men wielded these forms of activism alongside political campaigning and lobbying legislators. The reform techniques chosen were also affected by the goals of a particular movement. Moral suasion worked best with families, churches, and local communities, while legislation was more likely to succeed if the goal involved transforming people's behavior across a whole state or region.

In addition, many reformers used a variety of tactics and some changed their approach over time. For instance, reformers who sought to eradicate prostitution in the 1830s prayed in front of urban brothels and attempted to rescue "fallen" women. They soon launched *The Advocate of Moral Reform*, a monthly journal filled with morality tales, advice to mothers, and lists of men who visited brothels. In small towns, moral reformers sought to alert young women and men to the dangers of city life. By the 1840s, urban reformers opened Homes for Virtuous and Friendless Females to provide safe havens for vulnerable women. And across the country, moral reformers began petitioning state legislators to make punishments for men who hired prostitutes as harsh as those for prostitutes themselves.

The Problem of Poverty

Poverty had existed since the colonial era, but the panic of 1837 aroused greater public concern. Leaders of both government and private charitable endeavors increasingly linked relief to the moral character of those in need. Affluent Americans had long debated whether the poor would learn habits of industry and thrift if they were simply given aid without working for it. The debate was deeply gendered. Women and children were considered the worthiest recipients of aid, and middle and upper class women the appropriate dispensers of charity. Successful men, meanwhile, often linked poverty to weakness and considered giving pennies to a beggar an unmanly act that indulged the worst traits of the poor.

Towns and cities had long relegated the poorest residents to almshouses or workhouses. In the early nineteenth century, charitable societies sought to change the conditions that produced poverty. As the poor increased with urban growth, northern charitable ladies began visiting poor neighborhoods, offering blankets, clothing, food, and medicine to needy residents. But the problem seemed intractable, and many charitable organizations began building orphan asylums, hospitals, and homes for working women to provide deserving but vulnerable individuals with resources to improve their life chances.

Those considered the "undeserving" poor faced grimmer choices. They generally received assistance only through workhouses or jails. By the 1830s images of rowdy men who drank or gambled away what little they earned, prostitutes who tempted respectable men into vice, and immigrants who preferred idle poverty to virtuous labor became stock figures in debates over the causes of and responses to poverty.

At the same time, female reformers and novelists increasingly portrayed young poor women — if they were white and Protestant — as the victims of immoral men or unfortunate circumstance. In fictional tales, naive girls were seduced and abandoned by manipulative men. One of the first mass-produced books in the United States, Nathaniel Hawthorne's *The Scarlet Letter* (1850), was set in Puritan New England but addressed contemporary concerns about the seduction of innocents. It illustrated the social ostracism and poverty suffered by a woman who bore a child out of wedlock.

Other fictional tales placed the blame for fallen women on foreigners, especially Catholics. Such works drew vivid portraits of young nuns ravished by priests and then thrown out pregnant and penniless. These stories heightened anti-Catholic sentiment, which periodically boiled over into attacks on Catholic homes, schools, churches, and convents.

That sentiment intensified as economic competition increased between immigrants and native-born Americans. By the 1840s Americans who opposed immigration took the name **nativists** and launched public political campaigns that blamed foreigners for poverty and crime. Samuel F. B. Morse, an artist and inventor of the telegraph, was among the most popular anti-immigrant spokesmen. Nativists also physically assaulted immigrants, especially Irish Catholics. In May 1844 working-class nativists clashed with Irishmen in Philadelphia after shots were fired from a firehouse. A dozen nativists and one Irishman were killed the first day. The next night, nativists looted and burned Irish businesses and Catholic churches.

Many nativists blamed poverty among immigrants on their drinking habits. Others considered alcohol abuse, whether by native-born or immigrant Americans, the root cause of many social evils.

The Temperance Movement

Temperance advocates first organized officially in 1826 with the founding of the American Temperance Society. This all-male organization was led by clergy and businessmen and focused on alcohol abuse among working-class men. Religious revivals inspired the establishment of some 5,000 local chapters, and black and white men founded other temperance organizations as well. Over time, the temperance movement changed its goal from moderation to total abstinence, targeted middle-class and elite as well as working-class men, and welcomed women's support. Wives and mothers were expected to persuade male kin to stop drinking and sign a temperance pledge. In the 1830s, women founded dozens of temperance societies and funded the circulation of didactic tales, woodcuts, and etchings about the dangers of "demon rum."

Workingmen also embraced temperance as a way to gain dignity and respect. For Protestants, in particular, abstinence distinguished them from Irish Catholic workers. Some working-class temperance advocates criticized liquor dealers, whom they claimed directed "the vilest, meanest, most earth-cursing and hell-filling business ever followed." More turned to self-improvement. In the 1840s groups of laboring men formed Washingtonian societies—named in honor of the nation's founder—to help each other stop excessive drinking. Martha Washington societies appeared shortly thereafter, composed of the wives, mothers, and sisters of male alcoholics.

Despite the rapid growth of temperance organizations, moral suasion failed to reduce alcohol consumption significantly. Many temperance advocates thus turned to legal reform. In 1851 Maine was the first state to legally prohibit the sale of alcoholic beverages. By 1855 twelve more states had restricted the manufacture or sale of alcohol. Yet these stringent measures inspired a backlash. Hostile to the imposition of middle-class Protestant standards on the population at large, Irish workers in Maine organized the Portland Rum Riot in 1855. It led Maine to repeal its law the next year. Still, the diverse strategies used by temperance advocates did gradually reduce the consumption of beer, wine, and spirits across the United States.

Utopian Communities

While most reformers reached out to the wider society to implement change, some activists established self-contained communities to serve as models for others. The architects of these **utopian societies**, most formed in the North and Midwest, gained inspiration from European intellectuals and reformers as well as American religious and republican ideals.

In the 1820s Scottish and Welsh labor radicals such as Frances Wright, Robert Owen, and his son Robert Dale Owen established several utopian communities in the United States. They perceived the young republic as open to experiments in communal labor, gender equality, and (in Wright's case) racial justice. Their efforts ultimately failed, but they did arouse impassioned debate.

"Women Drawing Water, Bishop Hill Colony," c. 1860   This painting by Olaf Kraus captures the collective labor that characterized communal life at Bishop Hill Colony, Illinois. This utopian community was founded in 1846 by Eric Jansen, a critic of the Lutheran Church in Sweden. Forced to emigrate, he recruited 1400 other dissidents to join him on the American prairie. Kraus painted several scenes while living at Bishop Hill. Granger

Then in 1841, former Unitarian minister George Ripley established a transcendentalist community at Brook Farm in Massachusetts. Four years later, Brook Farm was reorganized according to the principles of the French socialist Charles Fourier. Fourier believed that cooperation across classes was necessary to temper conflicts inherent in capitalist society. He developed a plan for communities, called phalanxes, where residents chose jobs based on individual interest but were paid according to the contribution of each job to the community's well-being. Fourier also advocated equality for women. More than forty Fourierist phalanxes were founded in the northern United States during the 1840s.

The Oneida community was a more uniquely American experiment. John Humphrey Noyes established it in central New York in 1848. He believed that Christ's Second Coming had already occurred, and his followers embraced the communalism of the early Christian church. Noyes required members to relinquish their private property to the community and to embrace the notion of "complex marriage," in which women and men were free to have sexual intercourse with any consenting adult. He also introduced a form of birth control that sought to ensure women's freedom from constant childbearing and instituted communal child-rearing practices. Divorce and remarriage were also permitted. Despite the public outrage provoked by Oneida's economic and sexual practices, the community recruited several hundred residents and thrived for more than three decades.

REVIEW & RELATE

- How did efforts to alleviate poverty and temper alcohol consumption reflect the range of reform tactics and participants during the 1830s and 1840s?
- What connections can you identify between utopian communities and mainstream reform movements in the first half of the nineteenth century?

Abolitionism Expands and Divides

For a small percentage of Northerners, slavery was the ultimate injustice. While most Northerners considered it sufficient to rid their own region of human bondage, anti-slavery advocates argued that the North remained complicit in the institution. After all, enslaved workers labored under brutal conditions to provide cotton for New England factories, sugar and molasses for northern tables, and profits for urban traders. Free and enslaved blacks were the earliest advocates of abolition. As more whites joined the movement in the 1830s, the ongoing role of blacks, the unwillingness of many white churches to condemn slavery, and the propriety of women's activism stirred controversies. By the 1840s abolitionists also disagreed over whether to wield moral persuasion or organize politically and whether to focus on abolishing slavery in the South or preventing its extension into western territories. Although these debates could rupture individual organizations, they expanded the range of antislavery associations and campaigns.

The Beginnings of the Antislavery Movement

African Americans led the movement to abolish slavery from the American Revolution through at least the 1820s. They fled slavery and sued for their freedom during the Revolution, celebrated Haitian independence and honored Toussaint L'Overture, wrote antislavery poems and essays, and fought for gradual emancipation laws throughout the North. These black abolitionists gained allies, especially among white Quakers, who joined them in forming antislavery societies and petitioning state and federal governments to end slavery and the slave trade. In the 1820s these antislavery societies also published pamphlets, lectured to (usually small) audiences, and helped runaway slaves reach freedom.

In 1829 David Walker wrote the most militant antislavery statement, *Appeal . . . to the Colored Citizens of the World*. The free son of an enslaved father, Walker left his North Carolina home for Boston in the 1820s and became a writer for *Freedom's Journal*, the country's first African American newspaper. In his *Appeal*, Walker warned that slaves would claim their freedom by force if whites did not agree to emancipate them. Some northern blacks feared Walker's radical *Appeal* would unleash a white backlash. Quakers like Benjamin Lundy, editor of the *Genius of Universal Emancipation*, admired Walker's courage but rejected his call for violence. Nonetheless the *Appeal* circulated widely among free and enslaved blacks, with copies spreading from northern cities to Charleston, Savannah, New Orleans, and Norfolk.

William Lloyd Garrison, a white Bostonian who worked with Lundy, was inspired by Walker's radical stance. In 1831 he launched his own abolitionist newspaper, the ***Liberator***. He urged white antislavery activists to embrace the goal of immediate emancipation without compensation to slave owners, a position advocated by the English Quaker Elizabeth Heyrick in 1824.

The *Liberator* demanded that whites take an absolute stand against slavery but use moral persuasion rather than armed force to halt its spread. With like-minded black and white activists in Boston, Philadelphia, and New York City, Garrison organized the **American Anti-Slavery Society (AASS)** in 1833. Initially only men were invited to join, although Philadelphia Quaker Lucretia Mott attended the founding meeting with her husband James. By the end of the decade, the AASS boasted branches in dozens of towns and cities across the North. Members supported lecturers and petition drives, criticized churches that refused to denounce slavery, and proclaimed the U.S. Constitution a proslavery document. Some Garrisonians also participated in the work of the **underground railroad**, a secret network of black and white activists who assisted fugitives fleeing enslavement (Map 10.2).

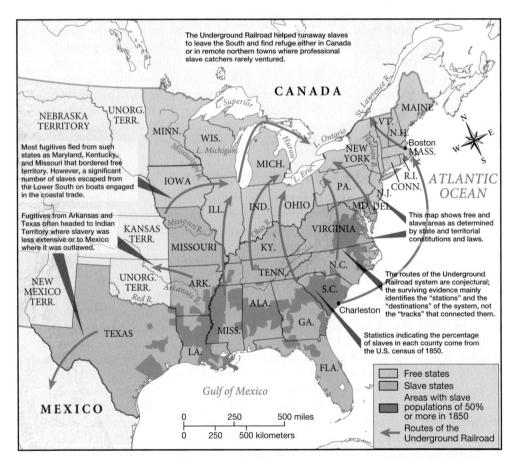

MAP 10.2   The Underground Railroad c. 1850
Free blacks and their white allies aided men and women who fled slavery from the 1790s on. By 1840, the system became more organized with individual conductors offering safe havens along well-worn routes. Former fugitives, most famously Harriet Tubman, joined the effort. In states like Arkansas and Texas, enslaved people often ran west rather than north, seeking aid from Indians or Mexicans.

Maria Stewart, a free black widow in Boston, spoke out against slavery in 1831–1832 in lectures to mixed-sex audiences. In addition to demanding abolition, she insisted that northern blacks take more responsibility for ending slavery and fighting discrimination. While Stewart gained large audiences, some black Bostonians criticized her for demeaning her own race or merely for being a woman. In 1833 free black and white Quaker women, led by Charlotte Forten and Lucretia Mott, formed the Philadelphia Female Anti-Slavery Society, which advocated abolition and the boycott of cotton, sugar, and other slave-produced goods. Two years later, Sarah and Angelina Grimké joined the Philadelphia society and the AAAS. Daughters of a prominent South Carolina planter, they moved to Philadelphia and converted to Quakerism. As white Southerners, their denunciations of slavery carried particular weight. Yet like Maria Stewart, their public stance as women aroused fierce opposition. In 1837 Congregationalist ministers in Massachusetts decried their presence in front of "promiscuous" audiences of men and women, but 1,500 female millworkers still turned out to hear them at Lowell's city hall.

The growing abolitionist movement quickly expanded to the frontier, where debates over slave and free territory were especially intense. In 1836 Ohio claimed more antislavery groups than any other state, and Ohio women initiated a petition drive to abolish slavery in the District of Columbia. The petition campaign, which spread across the North, inspired the first national meeting of women abolitionists in 1837. Other antislavery organizations, like the AASS, which had initially excluded women, now eagerly recruited them. Still, many local societies remained all-white or all-black and single-sex.

Abolition Gains Ground and Enemies

The growth of the abolitionist movement shocked many Northerners, and in the late 1830s violence often erupted in response to antislavery agitation. Northern manufacturers and merchants were generally hostile, fearing abolitionists' effect on the profitable trade in cotton, sugar, cloth, and rum. And white workingmen feared increased competition for jobs. In the 1830s mobs routinely attacked antislavery meetings, lecturers, and presses. At the 1838 Antislavery Convention of American Women at Philadelphia's Pennsylvania Hall, mobs forced black and white women to flee and then burned the hall to the ground.

Massive antislavery petition campaigns in 1836 and 1837 generated opposition in and between the North and South. Thousands of abolitionists, including Amy Post and her husband, Isaac, signed petitions to ban slavery in the District of Columbia, end the internal slave trade, and oppose the annexation of Texas. Some evangelical women considered such efforts part of their Christian duty, but most ministers (including Finney) condemned antislavery work as outside women's sphere. In response, most female evangelicals retreated from direct involvement in the movement. Others continued their efforts but faced excommunication by their churches. Meanwhile incensed Southern politicians persuaded Congress to pass the gag rule in 1836, which tabled all antislavery petitions without discussion.

But gag rules did not silence abolitionists. Indeed new groups of activists, most importantly self-emancipated slaves, offered potent personal tales of the horrors of bondage. The most famous fugitive abolitionist was Frederick Douglass. Born enslaved in Maryland around 1818, he fled to New Bedford, Massachusetts in 1838. He met Garrison in 1841, joined the AASS, and four years later published his life story, *Narrative of the Life of Frederick Douglass, as Told by Himself.* Having revealed his identity as a fugitive from slavery, Douglass sailed for England, where he launched a successful two-year lecture tour. While he was abroad, British abolitionists purchased Douglass's freedom from his owner, and Douglass returned to Massachusetts a free man.

In 1847 he decided to launch his own antislavery newspaper, the *North Star*, a decision that Garrison and other white AASS leaders opposed. Nonetheless, Douglass moved to Rochester, New York, with his wife Anna and their children. Douglass had found staunch allies in the city's black and white communities while lecturing in the region. These included Amy and Isaac Post, black barber James P. Morris, and members of the interracial and mixed-sex Western New York Anti-Slavery Society. That society and the all-black Union Anti-Slavery Sewing Society raised funds crucial for sustaining the *North Star*. Rochester men also organized single-sex abolitionist societies in the 1830s and 1840s as local anti-abolitionists became more outspoken. The latter included newspaper editor Horatio Warner, who forced a local school to reject Rosetta Douglass, Frederick and Anna's daughter, as a student. He and other anti-abolitionist editors regularly demeaned blacks and attacked abolitionists.

Many white abolitionists were eager to hear fugitive slaves tell their dramatic stories, but they did not necessarily embrace racial equality. Indeed, many white abolitionists opposed slavery but believed that blacks were racially inferior; others claimed to support racial equality but assumed that black abolitionists would defer to white leaders. The independent efforts of Douglass and other black activists significantly expanded the antislavery movement but also revealed the limits of many white abolitionists' views.

Conflicts also arose over the responsibility of churches to challenge slavery. The major Protestant denominations included southern as well as northern churches. If mainstream churches — Presbyterians, Baptists, Methodists — refused communion to enslavers, their southern branches would secede. Still, from the 1830s on, abolitionists pressured churches to take Christian obligations seriously and denounce human bondage. Individual congregations responded, but aside from the Society of Friends, larger denominations failed to follow suit.

In response, abolitionists urged parishioners to break with churches that admitted slaveholders as members. Antislavery preachers pushed the issue, and some worshippers "came out" from mainstream churches to form antislavery congregations. White Wesleyan Methodists and Free Will Baptists joined African American Methodists and Baptists in insisting that their members oppose slavery. Although these churches remained small, they served as a living challenge to mainstream denominations.

Abolitionism and Women's Rights

Women were increasingly active in the AASS and the "come outer" movement, but their growing participation aroused opposition even among abolitionists. In 1836–1837, female societies formed the backbone of antislavery petition campaigns demanding an end to slavery and the slave trade in Washington, D.C. In 1837, the Anti-Slavery Convention of American Women met in New York City, and participants discussed abolition as well as the rights of women, including African American women. More women also joined the lecture circuit, notably Abby Kelley, a fiery orator who demanded that women be granted an equal role in the movement. But when Garrison and his supporters appointed Kelley to the AASS business committee in May 1840, angry debates erupted over the propriety of women participating "in closed meetings with men." Of the 1,000 abolitionists in attendance, some 300 walked out in protest. The dissidents, including many evangelical men, soon formed a new organization, the American and Foreign Anti-Slavery Society, which excluded women from public lecturing and office holding but encouraged them to support men's efforts.

Those who remained in the AASS continued to expand women's roles. In 1840 local chapters appointed a handful of female delegates, including Lucretia Mott of Philadelphia, to the World Anti-Slavery Convention in London. The majority of men at the meeting, however, rejected the female delegates' credentials. Women were then forced to watch the proceedings from a separate section of the hall, confirming for some that women could be effective in campaigns against slavery only if they gained more rights for themselves.

As more women and blacks traveled to antislavery conventions, they confronted the difficulties of finding suitable accommodations. Most U.S. hotels and boarding houses were racially segregated and many were unwilling to house single women alongside men. Fortunately, many radical abolitionists were also active in the movement for health reform. One of its leaders, Sylvester Graham, advocated vegetarianism, sexual restraint, and temperance. Some of his followers established Graham boardinghouses in northern cities, offering food, beds, and spaces for socializing to black and white women and men. Graham Houses also provided safe haven for fugitive slaves. While rarely advertising these aspects of their work for fear of anti-abolitionist attacks, the Graham name reassured abolitionists and fugitives that they were welcome.

In spring 1844 and 1848, women in the Daughters of Zion, several of whom were abolitionists, petitioned the African Methodist Episcopal Church to grant women licenses to preach. Although some male leaders supported the claim, the conference majority twice rejected the request. In July 1848, a small circle of women, including Lucretia Mott and a young American she met in London, Elizabeth Cady Stanton, along with three progressive Quakers organized the first convention focused explicitly on women's rights. Held in Stanton's hometown of Seneca Falls, New York, the convention attracted three hundred white women and men. James Mott, husband of Lucretia, presided over the convention, and Frederick Douglass spoke, but women dominated the proceedings. One hundred participants, including Amy Post, signed the **Declaration of Sentiments**, which called for women's equality in everything from education and employment to legal rights and voting. Two weeks later, Post helped organize a second convention in Rochester. There participants elected a woman, Abigail Bush, to preside; invited working-class women to testify about their plight; and explicitly demanded equal rights for women of "every complexion," that is race. Douglass again offered his support.

Although abolitionism provided much of the impetus for women's rights advocates, other movements also contributed. Strikes by seamstresses and mill workers in the 1830s and 1840s highlighted women's economic needs. Utopian communities experimented with gender equality, and temperance reformers focused attention on domestic violence and sought changes in divorce laws. A diverse coalition also advocated for married women's property rights in the 1840s. Women's rights were debated among New York's Seneca Indians as well. Like the Cherokee, Seneca women had lost traditional rights over land and tribal policy as their nation adopted Anglo-American ways. In the summer of 1848, the creation of a written constitution threatened to enshrine these losses in writing. The Seneca constitution did strip women of their dominant role in selecting chiefs but protected their right to vote on the sale of tribal lands. Earlier in 1848, revolutions had erupted against repressive regimes in France and elsewhere in Europe. Antislavery newspapers covered developments in detail, including European women's demands for political and civil recognition. Women's rights meetings continued to draw on these ideas and influences over the next decade.

The Rise of Antislavery Parties

As women's rights advocates demanded female suffrage, debates over the role of partisan politics in the antislavery campaign intensified. Keeping slavery out of western territories depended on the actions of Congress, as did abolishing slavery in the nation's capital and ending the internal slave trade. Moral suasion had seemingly done little to change minds in Congress or in the South. To force abolition onto the national political agenda, the **Liberty Party** was formed in 1840. Many Garrisonians were appalled at the idea of participating in national elections when the federal government supported slavery in numerous ways, from the three-fifths compromise to allowing slavery in newly acquired territories. Still, the Liberty Party gained significant support among abolitionists in New York, the Middle Atlantic states, and the Midwest.

The 1840 election was also notable for the participation of women in campaign events. Whig candidate William Henry Harrison encouraged women to support the campaign. "Mother [Elizabeth] Clarkson" of Indiana gave numerous speeches on his behalf, and local Whig committees brought wagonloads of women to Harrison's rallies. The Liberty Party, too, welcomed public support from women. Harrison's victory opened the door to women's participation across the political spectrum.

Both Whigs and Democrats had avoided the antislavery issue to keep their southern and northern wings intact, but that strategy became more difficult once the Liberty Party entered campaigns. In 1840 that party won less than 1 percent of the popular vote but organized rallies that attracted large crowds. In 1844 the party more than doubled its votes, which was sufficient to deny Henry Clay a victory in New York State and thus ensure the election of James K. Polk (see "Expanding to Oregon and Texas" in chapter 11).

When President Polk led the United States into war with Mexico, interest in the Liberty Party surged. In 1848 it gained the support of antislavery Whigs, also called Conscience Whigs; northern Democrats who opposed the extension of slavery into the territories; and African American leaders like Frederick Douglass, who began questioning Garrisonians' view that only moral suasion could end slavery. Yet more practically minded political abolitionists soon founded the **Free-Soil Party**, which quickly subsumed the Liberty Party. Free-Soilers focused less on the moral wrongs of slavery than on the benefits of keeping western territories free for northern whites seeking economic opportunity. The Free-Soil Party nominated Martin Van Buren, a former Democrat, for president in 1848 and won 10 percent of the popular vote.

Once again, the result was to send a slaveholder to the White House — Zachary Taylor, a Mexican War hero. Nonetheless, the Free-Soil Party had gained far more support than the Liberty Party, raising fears in the South and in the two major parties that the battle over slavery could no longer be contained.

REVIEW & RELATE	• How did the American Anti-Slavery Society differ from earlier abolitionist organizations? • How did conflicts over gender, race, and tactics shape the development of the abolitionist movement in the 1830s and 1840s?

Conclusion: From the North to the Nation

Charles Grandison Finney followed these political developments from Oberlin College, where he served as president in the 1840s. Skeptical that electoral politics could transform society, he continued to view individual conversions as the wellspring of change. As the nation expanded westward, he trained ministers to travel the frontier converting American Indians to Christianity and reminding pioneering families of their religious obligations. Amy Post took a more militant stand, rejecting any participation in a government that accepted slavery and fomented war. She disagreed with Douglass's decision to support the Liberty Party, but recognized that moral persuasion alone might never convince planters to end slavery.

The efforts of the tens of thousands of Northerners inspired by religious and reform movements between 1820 and 1850 had a greater impact because of the growth of cities and improvements in transportation and communication. It was far easier by the 1830s for evangelicals, Quakers, Mormons, transcendentalists, utopian communalists, and other activists to spread their ideas through sermons, lectures, newspapers, pamphlets, and conventions.

Urban development was driven by the migration of native-born Americans from rural areas and small towns as well as the increase in immigration from Ireland, Germany, and other European nations. The panic of 1837 fueled an economic crisis that lasted several years and temporarily stalled the market revolution. But the panic also inspired many Americans to organize against poverty, intemperance, prostitution, and other urban problems. At the same time, the concentration of workers, immigrants, and free blacks in cities allowed them to unite and claim rights for themselves. For workers, the need to organize was heightened by the growth of factories even as the increasing diversity of the labor force aroused tensions among distinct racial and ethnic groups. Numerous attacks occurred against free blacks, who competed for jobs with immigrants and poor whites even as the antislavery movement expanded across the North.

Of the numerous reform movements that emerged in this period, abolition carried the most powerful national implications by 1850. The growth of abolitionist sentiment was related in part to the rapid expansion of slavery. Yet the increase in the size of southern plantations and their spread westward also ensured a steady supply of raw materials, such as cotton, that drove commercial and industrial development across the North. Such developments fueled significant transformations across the South as well.

Chapter 10 Review

KEY TERMS

market revolution, 246
cult of domesticity, 250
deskilling, 253
Second Great Awakening, 255
temperance, 256
transcendentalism, 258
nativists, 260
utopian societies, 261
*Appeal . . . to the Colored
   Citizens of the World,* 263

Liberator, 263
American Anti-Slavery
   Society (AASS), 264
underground railroad, 264
Declaration of Sentiments, 267
Liberty Party, 268
Free-Soil Party, 268

REVIEW & RELATE

1. How did the market revolution, including improvements like the Erie Canal, reshape the landscape and lives of Americans in the North?

2. As northern cities became larger and more diverse in the first half of the nineteenth century, what changes and challenges did urban residents face and what values and beliefs did the new middle class embrace?

3. How and why did American manufacturing change during the first half of the nineteenth century?

4. How did new technologies, immigration, and the panic of 1837 change the economic opportunities and organizing strategies for northern workers?

5. What impact did the Second Great Awakening have in the North?

6. What new religious organizations and viewpoints emerged in the first half of the nineteenth century, *outside* of Protestant evangelical denominations?

7. How did efforts to alleviate poverty and temper alcohol consumption reflect the range of reform tactics and participants during the 1830s and 1840s?

8. What connections can you identify between utopian communities and mainstream reform movements in the first half of the nineteenth century?

9. How did the American Anti-Slavery Society differ from earlier abolitionist organizations?

10. How did conflicts over gender, race, and tactics shape the development of the abolitionist movement in the 1830s and 1840s?

TIMELINE OF EVENTS

1820–1850	• Northern cities grow; immigration surges
1823	• Lowell mills built
1826	• American Temperance Society founded
1827	• First workingmen's political party founded
1829	• David Walker publishes *Appeal . . . to the Colored Citizens of the World*
1830	• Joseph Smith publishes *The Book of Mormon*
1830–1831	• Second Great Awakening in Rochester, New York
1833	• William Lloyd Garrison founds American Anti-Slavery Society (AASS)
1834	• National Trades Union founded
1837	• Anti-Slavery Convention of American Women
1837–1842	• Panic of 1837
1840	• American Anti-Slavery Society splits over the role of women
	• Liberty Party formed
	• World Anti-Slavery Convention, London
1844	• Congress funds construction of the first telegraph line
May 1844	• Anti-immigrant violence in Philadelphia
1845	• Frederick Douglass publishes *Narrative of the Life of Frederick Douglass*
	• Margaret Fuller publishes *Woman in the Nineteenth Century*
1845–1846	• Irish potato famine
1846	• Henry David Thoreau publishes *Civil Disobedience*
1848	• Women ask to be ordained in the African Methodist Episcopal Church
	• Free-Soil Party formed
July 1848	• Seneca Falls Woman's Rights Convention
1851	• Maine prohibits the sale of alcoholic beverages

11

Slavery Expands South and West

1830–1850

LEARNING OBJECTIVES

After reading this chapter you will be able to:

- Explain the development of a plantation society and the impact on planters and their families as well as enslaved workers and their families.

- Discuss the importance of enslaved labor and the development of a distinctive slave culture, including forms of resistance.

- Analyze the differences among southern whites as slavery expanded and compare the techniques used by planters to control free and enslaved blacks and non-slaveholding whites.

- Evaluate the challenges that Indians, the panic of 1837, Texas independence, and the Whig Party posed for the Democratic Party.

- Evaluate the ways that the idea of manifest destiny shaped national elections and intensified debates over slavery.

COMPARING AMERICAN HISTORIES

José Antonio Menchaca was born in Spanish Texas in January 1800. His parents and nine siblings were known as Tejanos, people of Mexican descent living in Texas. His Spanish great-great-grandfather on his mother's side had been one of the founders of San Antonio de Bexar in 1718. José Antonio was raised there and learned to read, write, and speak both Spanish and English. In 1826, he married Teresa Ramón, and they had four children.

After U.S. citizens living in Texas declared their independence from Mexico in 1835, Menchaca joined the Texian Army and served alongside other Tejanos under Captain Juan Seguin. He was stationed at the Alamo Mission in San Antonio in 1836 when word came that Mexican president Antonio Lopez de Santa Anna was leading an army to reclaim the territory. Captain Seguin and Alamo co-commander James Bowie convinced Menchaca to leave the fortress and move his family to Seguin's isolated ranch. Seguin, too, left the Alamo to recruit more Tejano volunteers. Thus Menchaca and Seguin were gone when Mexican soldiers defeated Texas forces at the Alamo.

Soon after, Menchaca rejoined Seguin's forces as an officer. Sam Houston, who had taken leadership of the Texas forces, met up with Seguin's company on March 11 and announced that delegates to the Convention of 1836 had declared Texas an independent nation. American scouts captured Mexican horsemen carrying mail for General Santa Anna, and Menchaca translated the letters for Houston that revealed detailed information about Mexican strategies. Concerned that the Anglos in his own army would not differentiate between Mexican enemies and their Tejano allies, Houston ordered the latter to stay behind. Seguin convinced him to allow his men to fight. Houston agreed but insisted that they place cardboard in their hatbands as a sign that they were Texas allies. The combined forces routed the Mexican Army at the battle of San Jacinto in April 1836, ensuring Texas independence. Menchaca was among the soldiers honored by the Congress of the Republic of Texas in 1838.

Solomon Northup, a free-born African American, also ended up on the nation's southern frontier. However, his residence in Louisiana was not of his own choosing. His father Mintus had been born into slavery in New York State but was freed by his master's will in 1797. He moved to Minerva, New York, married a free woman of color, and had two sons. Solomon, born in 1807 or 1808, married Anne Hampton when he was in his early twenties. He worked transporting goods on the region's waterways and made extra cash playing the fiddle while Anne worked as a cook. In 1834, the couple moved to Saratoga Springs, New York, where they raised their three children.

In March 1841 Northup met two white circus performers who hired him to play the fiddle for them on tour. They paid his wages up front and told him to obtain documents proving his free status. After reaching Washington, D.C., however, Northup was drugged, chained, and sold to James Birch, a notorious enslaver. Northup was resold in New Orleans to William Ford, who changed his name to Platt. Ford put him to work as a raftsman while Northup tried unsuccessfully to get word to his wife.

In 1842 Ford sold "Platt" to a neighbor, John Tibeats, who, unlike Ford, whipped and abused his enslaved workers. When Tibeats attacked Northup with an ax, he fought back and fled to Ford's house. His former owner shielded him from Tibeats' wrath and arranged his sale to the planter Edwin Epps. For the next ten years, Northup worked the cotton fields on Epps's plantation.

Finally, in 1852 Samuel Bass, a Canadian carpenter who openly acknowledged his antislavery views, came to work on Epps's house. Northup persuaded Bass to send a letter to his wife in Saratoga Springs. Anne Northup, astonished to hear that her husband was still alive, took the letter to lawyer Henry Northup, the son of Mintus's former owner. After months of legal efforts, a local judge freed Solomon Northup in January 1853.

COMPARING THE AMERICAN HISTORIES of José Antonio Menchaca and Solomon Northup illuminates clashes over western expansion and slavery. By siding with U.S. rebels, Menchaca and his family benefited when Texas gained its independence from Mexico. Establishing a home in San Antonio, Menchaca was elected alderman and then mayor of the city, achieving prosperity as well as political influence. His three daughters helped expand the multicultural population of the region by marrying into Anglo-American, French, and German families. In Texas and across the lower South, enslaved labor remained central to economic success and fueled market and industrial revolutions throughout the nation. Cities like New Orleans benefitted from both slavery's expansion and cotton's critical role in national and international trade. Still, from the 1830s to the 1850s, slave ownership became concentrated in the hands of a decreasing proportion of white southern families. Slave traders played a crucial role in slavery's expansion, inspiring some traders to capture free blacks like Solomon Northup and sell them into slavery. Northup labored in the harsh conditions of frontier Louisiana for masters who wielded distinct forms of brutality. He saw how the growing concentration of enslaved workers on individual plantations could both strengthen African American communities and fracture them. The enslaved laborers were also affected by the volatility of the cotton market, which created enormous economic uncertainty across the South. Planters insisted that expanding into new lands to cultivate more cotton was the only way to perpetuate economic growth, ensuring that more enslaved families would be separated from their loved ones. Democratic administrations in Washington, D.C. bolstered this expansionist effort by forcibly removing the last Indian nations from the Southeast, supporting independence and statehood for Texas, and proclaiming war on Mexico. These policies intensified clashes with Indian nations, heightened conflicts over slavery, and inspired the emergence of the Whig Party.

Planters Expand the Slave System

The cotton gin, developed in the 1790s, ensured the growth of southern agriculture into the 1850s. As the cotton kingdom spread west, those who owned the largest plantations forged a distinctive culture around the institution of slavery. While this slave-based agricultural economy limited the development of cities, technology, and educational institutions, the **planters** who wielded economic and political power calculated the benefits of the system. The South did become more dependent on the North for many of its needs, but the enormous profits from cotton, sugar, and rice allowed the planter class to live a luxurious lifestyle. Moreover, with northern businesses deeply entwined with the cotton economy, planters felt assured of northern support for policies supporting slavery. These included westward expansion, which dramatically increased the trade of enslaved people across the South. That trade shattered black families and fueled new forms of slave resistance and a growing abolition movement in the North. Still, southern planters and enslavers viewed themselves as national leaders, both the repository of traditional American values and the engine of economic progress.

A Plantation Society Develops in the South

Plantation slavery existed throughout the Americas in the early nineteenth century. Extensive plantations worked by large numbers of enslaved people existed in the West Indies and South America. In the U.S. South, however, the volatile cotton market and a scarcity of fertile land kept most plantations relatively small before 1830. But over the next two decades, territorial expansion and profits from cotton, rice, and sugar allowed successful enslavers to build grand houses and purchase a variety of luxury goods.

As plantations grew, a wealthy aristocracy sought to ensure productivity by employing harsh methods of discipline. Even planters considered progressive in their application of modern principles of agriculture, such as James Henry Hammond of South Carolina, used the whip liberally. By these means, they hoped to ensure that their estates generated sufficient profits to support a lavish lifestyle.

Increased attention to comfort and luxury helped make the heavy workload of plantation mistresses tolerable. Mistresses were expected to manage their own families and enslaved domestic workers as well as feeding, clothing, and medical care for the entire labor force. They also organized social events, hosted relatives and friends for extended stays, and sometimes directed the plantation in their husband's absence.

Still, plantation mistresses were relieved of the most arduous labor by enslaved women, who cooked, cleaned, and washed for the family, cared for the children, and even nursed the babies. Wealthy white women benefited from the best education, the greatest access to music and literature, and the finest clothes and furnishings. The pedestal on which plantation mistresses stood was shaky, built on a patriarchal system in which husbands and fathers held enormous power. Thus, most wives tried to ignore the sexual relations that husbands initiated with enslaved women. Catherine Hammond did not. After discovering James's sexual abuse of an enslaved mother and daughter, she moved to Charleston with their two youngest children. Others, however, took out their anger and frustration on enslaved women already victimized by their husbands. Moreover, many mistresses brought enslaved women or men to their marriage. These female enslavers traded them in slave markets, often through male agents, or hired them out as wet nurses so other plantation mistresses could avoid nursing their own children. They also bestowed them as gifts or bequests to family members and friends, tearing apart families as their husbands did.

Not all enslavers were wealthy planters like the Hammonds, with fifty or more slaves and extensive landholdings. Far more planters in the 1830s and 1840s owned between twenty and fifty enslaved people, and an even larger number of farmers owned just three to six enslaved workers. As Hammond wrote a friend in 1847, "The planters here are essentially what the nobility are in other countries. They stand at the head of society & politics."

Urban Life in the Slave South

The political and economic supremacy of enslavers had broad repercussions. The richest men in the South invested in enslaved labor, land, and household goods, with little left to develop industry, technology, or urban institutions. The largest factory in the South, the Tredegar Iron Works in Richmond, Virginia, employed several hundred free and enslaved African Americans by 1850. Most southern industrialists, however, like South Carolina textile manufacturer William Gregg, employed poor white women and children. But neither Tredegar nor scattered textile mills fundamentally reshaped the region's economy.

Even as the South fell behind in urban development, its port cities were central to economic growth throughout the nation. Northern agents, especially cotton brokers (called factors), directed much of the trade in Baltimore, Charleston, Savannah, and New Orleans. This trade formed another link in the economic bonds between North and South. Port cities were also home to the largest slave markets in the region. At the same time, nearly one-third of southern whites had no access to cash and instead bartered goods and services, which restricted the growth of smaller towns and cities across the South.

Cities were home to the largest numbers of free blacks in the South. The growing demand for cheap domestic labor in urban areas and planters' greater willingness to emancipate less valuable single enslaved women meant that free black women generally outnumbered men in southern cities. These women worked mainly as washerwomen, cooks, and general domestics, while free black men labored as skilled artisans, dockworkers, or sailors. Free blacks competed for the latter jobs with enslaved laborers and growing numbers of European immigrants who flocked to port cities in the 1840s and 1850s. The presence of immigrants and free blacks and the reputation of ports as escape hatches for enslaved runaways ensured that these cities remained volatile even as they drove the South's economy.

The scarcity of cities other than ports and of industry curtailed the development of internal transportation systems in the South. State governments invested little in roads, canals, and railroads. Most small farmers traded goods locally, and most planters used the South's extensive river system to ship goods to port cities, which were then carried on ships to the North, Europe, or the West Indies. Only Virginia and Maryland, with their proximity to the nation's capital, developed extensive road and rail networks.

The Consequences of Slavery's Expansion

Outside the South, industry and agriculture increasingly benefited from technological innovation. Planters, however, continued to rely on intensive manual labor and focused on fertilizer and crop rotation rather than machines to enhance productivity. The limited use of new technologies—such as iron plows or seed drills—resulted from a lack of investment capital (which was tied up in land and labor) and planters' refusal to purchase expensive equipment that enslaved workers might break or sabotage. These enslavers also relied on continually expanding the acreage under cultivation.

One result of these practices was that a declining percentage of white Southerners came to control vast estates with large numbers of enslaved laborers.

Between 1830 and 1850, the absolute number of both slaves and enslavers grew. But enslavers became a smaller proportion of all white Southerners because the white population grew faster than the number of enslavers. At the same time, distinctions among wealthy planters, small enslavers, and whites who owned no slaves also increased.

Planters' concern with productivity and profits and the concentration of more enslaved people on large plantations did have limited benefits for some black women and men. The end of the international slave trade in 1808 forced planters to rely more heavily on natural reproduction to increase their labor force. Thus many planters thought more carefully about how they treated their enslaved laborers, who were increasingly viewed as "valuable property." It was no longer good business to work enslaved people to death or cripple them by severe punishments.

Yet as slavery expanded westward, enslaved families were increasingly torn apart. By the late 1820s, enslaved workers were no longer most likely to be sold with other family members. Instead, those between fourteen and forty-five were sold in far larger numbers than younger and older workers and enslaved men far more often than women. Not until the 1850s did natural increase begin balancing out the sex ratios along with enslaved men developing new families. During the 1830s and 1840s, enslavers willingly broke up families to ensure the necessary supply of young healthy men on the plantation frontier.

Moreover, owners continued to whip enslaved workers and made paltry investments in their diet and health care. Most enslaved people lived in small houses or huts with dirt floors and little furniture or clothing. They ate a diet high in calories, especially fats and carbohydrates, but with little meat, fish, fresh vegetables, or fruits. The high mortality rate among enslaved infants and children—more than twice that of white children to age five—reflected this limited care.

The spread of slavery into Mississippi, Louisiana, Alabama, Missouri, and eventually Texas affected both white and black families, though certainly not equally. The younger sons of wealthy planters were often forced to move to the frontier, and their families generally lived in rough quarters on isolated plantations. A woman traveler noted that the men "think only of making money, and their houses are hardly fit to live in." A planter's wife complained, "Mississippi and Alabama are a dreary waste." Such moves were far more difficult for enslaved laborers, however. Between 1830 and 1850, more than 440,000 enslaved people were forced to move from the Upper South to the Lower South (Map 11.1), often tearing them away from their families. On the southern frontier, they endured incredibly harsh conditions as they cleared and cultivated new lands.

At the same time, slave markets blossomed in key cities across the South. Solomon Northup was held in one in Washington, D.C., where a woman named Eliza watched as her son Randall was "won" by a planter from Baton Rouge. She promised "to be the most faithful slave that ever lived" if he would also buy her and her daughter. The enslaver threatened the desperate mother with a hundred lashes and refused her entreaties. As slavery spread westward, such scenes were repeated thousands of times. Shattered family ties meant that enslaved workers on the frontier, like those initially shipped from Africa, had to forge new kinds of bonds, including fictive kin where blood relatives did not exist.

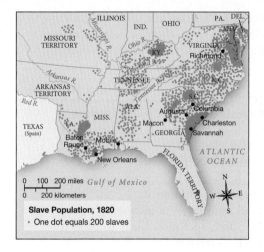

Slave Population, 1820
· One dot equals 200 slaves

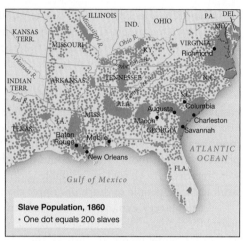

Slave Population, 1860
· One dot equals 200 slaves

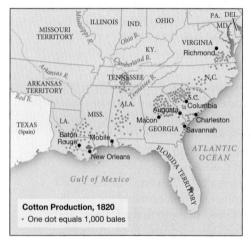

Cotton Production, 1820
· One dot equals 1,000 bales

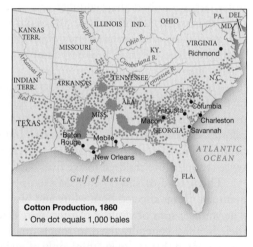

Cotton Production, 1860
· One dot equals 1,000 bales

MAP 11.1   The Spread of Slavery and Cotton, 1820–1860
While tobacco, rice, and sugar remained important crops in a few states, cotton became the South's and the nation's major export. The need to find more fertile fields led planters to migrate to Alabama, Mississippi, and Louisiana. As a result of cotton's success, the number of enslaved people increased dramatically, the internal slave trade expanded, and labor demands intensified.

REVIEW & RELATE	• What role did the planter elite play in southern society and politics? • What were the consequences of the dominance of enslave-based plantation agriculture for the southern economy?

Slave Society and Culture

Because enslaved labor formed the backbone of the southern economy, enslaved workers gained some leverage against owners and overseers. But blacks did not simply define themselves in relation to whites. They also developed relationships, identities, and cultural practices within the slave quarters. Many also found small ways to resist their enslavement on an everyday basis. Others resisted more openly, and a small number continued to organize rebellions against the system of slavery.

Enslaved Labor Fuels the Economy

The labor of enslaved blacks drove the nation's economy. In 1820 the South produced some 500,000 bales of cotton, much of it exported to England. By 1850 the region produced nearly 3 million bales, feeding textile mills in New England and abroad. A decade later, cotton accounted for nearly two-thirds of the U.S. export trade and added nearly $200 million a year to the American economy.

Enslaved laborers, of course, saw little of this wealth. Carpenters, blacksmiths, and other skilled enslaved workers were sometimes hired out and allowed to keep a small amount of the money they earned. They traveled to nearby households, compared their circumstances to those on other plantations, and sometimes made contact with free blacks. Some skilled enslaved laborers also learned to read and write and had access to tools and knowledge denied to field hands. Still, they were constantly hounded by whites who demanded travel passes and deference, and they were often suspected of involvement in rebellions.

Enslaved household workers sometimes received old clothes and bedding or leftover food from their owners. Yet they were under the constant surveillance of whites, and women especially were vulnerable to sexual abuse. Moreover, the work they performed was physically demanding. Fugitive slave James Curry recalled that his mother, a cook in North Carolina, rose early each morning to milk cows, bake bread, and churn butter. She was responsible for meals for her owners and the enslaved laborers. In summer, she cooked her last meal around eight o'clock, after which she milked the cows again. Then she returned to her quarters, put her children to bed, and often fell asleep while mending clothes.

Once enslaved children reached the age of ten to twelve, they were put to work full-time, usually in the fields. Although field labor was defined by its relentless pace and drudgery, it also brought together large numbers of enslaved people for the entire day and thus helped forge bonds among them. Songs provided a rhythm for their work and offered enslaved people the chance to communicate their frustrations or hopes.

Field labor was generally organized by task or by gang. Under the task system, typical on rice plantations, enslaved worker could return to their quarters once the day's task was completed. This left time for them to cultivate gardens, fish, or mend clothes. In the gang system, widely used on cotton plantations, men and women worked in groups under the supervision of a driver. Often working from sunup to sundown, they swept across fields hoeing, planting, or picking.

Many planters considered the work regimens they set as little different from northern factory owners who used bells and clocks to ensure that laborers spent maximum time at their machines. Indeed, some enslavers argued that their workers were better off because they provided them with housing, food, clothing, and health care, however minimal.

"A Slave Wedding," c. 1800   This rare water color painting of an African American wedding probably dates from the turn of the nineteenth century. The distance between the slave quarters and the plantation house suggests this may be a South Carolina scene. The enslaved women and men are dressed in their finest clothing and the musicians appear to be playing African-style instruments made from gourds.   MPI/Getty Images

Developing an African American Culture

Amid hard work and harsh treatment, enslaved people created social bonds and a rich culture of their own. For generations, African Americans continued to employ African names, like Cuffee and Binah. Even if masters gave the enslaved English names, workers might use African names in the slave quarters to sustain family memories and community networks. Elements of West African and Caribbean languages, agricultural techniques, medical practices, forms of dress, folktales, songs and musical instruments, dances, and courtship rituals demonstrated the continued importance of these cultures to African Americans. This hybrid culture was disseminated as enslaved workers hauled cotton to market, forged families across plantation boundaries, or were sold south and west. It was also passed across generations through storytelling, music, rituals, and health care. Most slave births were attended by black midwives, and African American healers sought southern equivalents to herbal cures used in West Africa.

Religious practices offer an important example of this blended culture. Africans from Muslim communities often continued to pray to Allah even if they were also required to attend Protestant churches, while black Protestant preachers developed rituals that combined African and American elements. In the early nineteenth century, many enslaved people eagerly embraced the evangelical teachings offered by Baptist and Methodist preachers, which echoed some of the expressive spiritual forms in West Africa. On Sundays, enslaved workers listened in the morning to white ministers proclaim slavery as God's will. Yet in the evening they might gather again to hear their own preachers declare God's love and the possibilities of liberation, at least in the hereafter. Enslaved people often incorporated drums, dancing, or other West African elements into these worship services.

Although most black preachers were men, a few enslaved women gained a spiritual following. Many female slaves embraced religion enthusiastically, hoping that Christian baptism might substitute for West African rituals that protected newborn babies. Enslaved women sometimes called on church authorities to intervene when white owners, overseers, or even enslaved men abused them. They also considered the church one means of sanctifying slave marriages that were not recognized legally.

Resistance and Rebellion

Many enslavers worried that black preachers and West African folktales inspired blacks to resist enslavement. Fearing defiance, planters went to incredible lengths to control their enslaved population. Although they were largely successful in quelling open revolts, they were unable to eliminate more subtle forms of opposition, like slowing the pace of work, feigning illness, and damaging equipment. More overt forms of resistance—such as truancy and running away, which disrupted work and lowered profits—also proved impossible to stamp out.

The forms of everyday resistance enslaved laborers employed varied in part on their location and resources. Skilled artisans, mostly men, could do more substantial damage because they used more expensive tools, but they were less able to protect themselves through pleas of ignorance. Field laborers could often damage only hoes, but they could do so regularly without exciting suspicion. Enslaved house workers could burn dinners, scorch shirts, break china, and even poison owners. Often considered the most loyal slaves, they were also among the most feared because of their intimate contact with white families. Single male slaves were the most likely to run away, planning their escape to get as far away as possible before their absence was noticed. Women who fled plantations were more likely to hide out for short periods in the local area. Eventually, isolation, hunger, or concern for children led most of these truants to return if slave patrols did not find them first.

Despite their rarity, efforts to organize slave uprisings, such as those planned in New Orleans in 1811 and in Charleston in 1822, continued to haunt southern whites. Rebellions in the West Indies, especially the one in Saint Domingue (Haiti), also echoed through the early nineteenth century. Then in 1831 a seemingly obedient slave named Nat Turner organized a revolt in rural Virginia that stunned whites across the South. A religious visionary who believed that God had given him a mission, Turner worked through family and friendship networks, including men and women, to execute that mission. On the night of August 21, he and his followers killed his owners, the Travis family, and then headed to nearby plantations in Southampton County. The insurrection led to the deaths of 57 white men, women, and children and liberated more than 50 enslaved people. But on August 22, outraged white militiamen burst on the scene and eventually captured the black rebels. Turner hid out for two months but was eventually caught, tried, and hung. Virginia executed 55 other African Americans suspected of assisting Turner.

Nat Turner's rebellion instilled panic among white Virginians, who beat and killed some 200 blacks with no connection to the uprising. White Southerners worried they might be killed in their sleep by seemingly submissive slaves. News of the rebellion traveled through enslaved communities as well, inspiring both pride and anxiety. The execution of Turner and his followers reminded African Americans how far whites would go to protect the institution of slavery.

A mutiny on the Spanish slave ship *Amistad* in 1839 reinforced white Southerners' fears of rebellion. When Africans being transported for sale in the West Indies seized control of the ship near Cuba, the U.S. navy captured the vessel and imprisoned the enslaved rebels. But international treaties outlawing the Atlantic slave trade and pressure applied by abolitionists led to a court case in which former president John Quincy Adams defended the right of the Africans to their freedom. The widely publicized case reached the U.S. Supreme Court in 1841, and the Court freed the rebels. While abolitionists cheered the ruling, white Southerners were shocked that the justices would liberate enslaved men.

REVIEW & RELATE	• How did enslaved African Americans create ties of family, community, and culture?
	• How did enslaved African Americans resist efforts to control and exploit their labor?

Planters Tighten Control

Fears of rebellion led to stricter regulations of black life, and actual uprisings temporarily reinforced white solidarity. Yet yeomen farmers, poor whites, and middle-class professionals all voiced some doubts about the ways in which slavery affected southern society. To ensure white unity, planters wielded their economic and political authority, highlighted bonds of kinship and religious fellowship, and promoted an ideology of white supremacy. Their efforts intensified as northern states and other nations began eradicating slavery.

Harsher Treatment for Southern Blacks

Slave revolts led many southern states to impose harsher controls, but Nat Turner's rebellion led some white Virginians to question slavery itself. In December 1831, the state assembly established a special committee to consider the crisis. Representatives from western counties, where slavery was never profitable, argued for gradual abolition laws and the colonization of the state's black population in Africa. Hundreds of women in the region sent petitions to the Virginia legislature supporting these positions.

While advocates of colonization gained significant support, eastern planters vehemently opposed abolition or colonization, and leading intellectuals argued for the benefits of slavery. Professor Thomas Dew, president of the College of William and Mary, insisted that enslavers performed godly work in raising Africans from the status of brute beast to civilized Christian. "Every one acquainted with southern slaves," he claimed, "knows that the slave rejoices in the elevation and prosperity of his master." In the fall of 1832 the Virginia legislature embraced Dew's proslavery argument, rejected gradual emancipation, and imposed new restrictions on enslaved and free blacks.

From the 1820s to the 1840s, more stringent codes were passed across the South. Most southern legislatures prohibited owners from manumitting their enslaved workers, made it illegal for whites to teach the enslaved to read or write, placed new limits on independent black churches, abolished slaves' limited access to courts, outlawed slave marriage, banned antislavery literature, defined rape as a crime only against white women, and outlawed assemblies of more than three blacks without a white person present.

States also regulated the lives of free blacks. Some prohibited free blacks from residing within their borders, others required large bonds to ensure good behavior, and most forbade free blacks who left the state from returning. The homes of free blacks could be raided at any time, and the children of free black women were subject to stringent apprenticeship laws that kept many in virtual slavery.

Such measures proved largely successful in controlling enslaved workers, but there was a price to pay. Restricting education and mobility for blacks hindered schooling and transportation for poor whites as well. Moreover, characterizing the region's primary labor force as savage and lazy discouraged investment in industry and other forms of economic development. And the regulations increased tensions between poorer whites, who were often responsible for enforcement, and wealthy whites, who benefited most clearly from their imposition.

White Southerners without Slaves

Yeomen farmers, independent owners of small plots who owned few or no enslaved workers, had a complex relationship with the South's plantation economy. Many were related to enslavers, and they often depended on planters to ship their crops to market. Some made extra money by hiring themselves out to planters. Yet yeomen farmers also recognized that their economic interests and daily experiences often diverged from those of planters. This was particularly clear on slavery's frontier, where many yeoman farmers had to carve fields out of forests without the benefit of enslaved workers. They joined with friends and neighbors for barn raisings, corn shuckings, quilting bees, and other collective endeavors that combined labor with sociability. Church services and church socials also brought small farm families together.

While most yeomen farmers believed in slavery, they sometimes challenged planters' authority and assumptions. In the Virginia slavery debates, for example, small farmers from western districts advocated gradual abolition. As growing numbers gained the right to vote in the 1830s and 1840s, they voiced their concerns in county and town meetings and in local courts. They advocated more liberal policies toward debtors and demanded greater representation in state legislatures. They also protested planters' obstruction of common lands and waterways, such as building dams upriver that deprived farmers downriver of fishing rights. Yeomen farmers questioned certain ideals embraced by elites. Although plantation mistresses considered manual labor beneath them, the wives and daughters of small farmers often worked in the fields, hauled water, and chopped wood. Still, yeomen farmers' ability to diminish planter control was limited by the continued importance of cotton to the southern economy.

White Southerners who owned no property at all had fewer means of challenging planters' power. These poor whites depended on hunting and fishing in frontier areas, performing day labor on farms and plantations, or working on docks or as servants in southern cities. Poor whites competed with free and enslaved blacks for employment and often harbored resentments as a result. Yet some, including poor immigrants from Ireland, Wales, and Scotland, built alliances with blacks based on their shared economic plight.

Some poor whites remained in the same community for decades, establishing themselves on the margins of society. They attended church regularly, performed day labor for affluent families, and taught their children to defer to those higher on the social ladder. Other poor whites moved frequently and survived by combining legal and illegal ventures. They might perform day labor while also stealing food from local farmers. These men and women often had few ties to local communities and little religious training or education. Although poor whites unnerved southern elites by flouting the law and sometimes befriending poor blacks, they could not mount a significant challenge to planter control.

The South's small but growing middle class distanced themselves from poorer whites in pursuit of stability and respectability. They worked as doctors, lawyers, teachers, and shopkeepers and often looked to the North for models to emulate. Many were educated in northern schools and developed ties with their commercial or professional counterparts in that region. They were avid readers of newspapers, religious tracts, and literary periodicals published in the North and South. And like middle-class Northerners, southern businessmen often depended on their wives' social and financial skills to succeed.

Nonetheless, middle-class southern men shared many of the social attitudes and political priorities of enslavers. They participated alongside planters in benevolent, literary, and temperance societies and agricultural reform organizations. Most middle-class Southerners also adamantly supported slavery. In fact, some suggested that bound labor might be useful to industry. Despite the emergence of a small middle class, however, the gap between rich and poor continued to expand in the South.

Planters Seek to Unify Southern Whites

Planters faced another challenge as nations in Europe and South America began to abolish slavery. In the United States, antislavery views were first widely expressed by free blacks and Quakers in northern and Middle Atlantic states. By the 1830s, they gained growing support among evangelical Protestants in the United States and Great Britain and among political radicals in Europe. Slave rebellions in Saint Domingue and the British West Indies in the early nineteenth century intensified these concerns. In 1807 the British Parliament had forbidden the sale of enslaved people within its empire, and in 1834 emancipated all those who remained enslaved. France followed suit in 1848. As Spanish colonies such as Mexico and Nicaragua gained their independence in the 1820s and 1830s, they, too, eradicated the institution. Meanwhile gradual abolition laws in the northern United States slowly eliminated slavery there. Although slavery continued in Brazil and in Spanish colonies such as Cuba, and serfdom remained in Russia, international attitudes toward human bondage had shifted significantly.

In response, planters wielded their political and economic power to forge tighter bonds among white Southerners. According to the three-fifths compromise in the U.S. Constitution, areas with large enslaved populations gained more representatives in Congress than those without. The policy also applied to state elections, giving such areas disproportionate power in state politics. In addition, planters used their resources to provide credit for those in need, offer seasonal employment for poorer whites, transport crops to market for yeomen farmers, and help out in times of crisis. Few whites could afford to antagonize these affluent benefactors.

Wealthy planters also emphasized ties of family and faith. James Henry Hammond, for example, regularly assisted his siblings and other family members financially. Many enslavers worshipped alongside their less well-to-do neighbors, and both pastor and congregation benefited from maintaining good relations with the wealthiest congregants. Most church members, like many relatives and neighbors, genuinely admired and respected planter elites who looked out for them.

While planters continued to insist that the U.S. Constitution protected slavery and the right of states to enforce their own labor systems, they did not take white solidarity for granted. From the 1830s on, they relied on the ideology of **white supremacy** to cement the belief that all whites, regardless of class or education, were superior to all blacks. Following on Thomas Dew, southern elites argued with growing vehemence that the moral and intellectual failings of blacks meant that slavery was not just a necessary evil but a positive good. At the same time, they insisted that blacks harbored deep animosity toward whites, which could be controlled only by regulating every aspect of their lives. Combining racial fear and racial pride, planters forged bonds with poor and middling whites to guarantee their continued dominance. They also continued to seek support from state and national legislators.

REVIEW & RELATE	• What groups made up white southern society? How did their interests overlap or diverge? • How and why did the planter elite seek to reinforce white solidarity?

Democrats Face Political and Economic Crises

Southern planters depended on federal power to expand and sustain the system of slavery. Despite differences on tariffs, both President Andrew Jackson and his successor, Martin Van Buren, stood with southern planters in support of Indian removal and independence for Texas from Mexico. But Van Buren faced a more well-organized opposition in the **Whig Party**, which formed in 1834. When later that decade U.S. rebels in Texas faced powerful resistance from Mexican and Comanche forces and a prolonged and severe economic panic gripped the nation, the Whigs found their opportunity to end Democratic control of the federal government. Over the next two decades, a **Second Party System** formed that pitted Whigs against Democrats on a wide range of economic, cultural, and political issues.

The Battle for Texas

As southern agriculture expanded westward, some whites looked toward Texas for fresh land. White Southerners had begun moving into eastern Texas in the early nineteenth century, but the Adams-Onís Treaty of 1819 guaranteed Spanish control of the territory. Then in 1821 Mexicans overthrew Spanish rule and claimed Texas as part of the new Republic of Mexico. But Mexicans faced serious competition from Comanche Indians, who controlled vast areas in northern Mexico and launched frequent raids into Texas.

Eager to increase settlement in the area and to create a buffer against the Comanches, the Mexican government granted U.S. migrants some of the best land in eastern Texas. It hoped these settlers would eventually spread into the interior, where Comanche raids had devastated Mexican communities. To entice more Southerners, the Mexican government negotiated a special exemption for U.S. planters when it outlawed slavery in 1829. But rather than spreading into the interior, American migrants stayed east of the Colorado River, out of reach of Comanche raids and close to U.S. markets in Louisiana.

Moreover, U.S. settlers resisted assimilation into Mexican society. Instead, they continued to worship as Protestants, speak English, send their children to separate schools, and trade mainly with the United States. By 1835 the 27,000 white Southerners and their 3,000 enslaved workers far outnumbered the 3,000 **Tejanos** (Mexican Texans) living in eastern Texas.

Forming a majority of the east Texas population and eager to expand their plantations and trade networks, growing numbers of U.S. settlers demanded independence. Then in 1836 Mexicans elected a strong nationalist leader, General Antonio López de Santa Anna, as president. He sought to calm Tejanos angered by their vulnerability to Comanche attacks and to curb U.S. settlers seeking further concessions. However, when Santa Anna appointed a military commander to rule Texas, U.S. migrants organized a rebellion and, on March 2, declared their independence. José Antonio Menchaca and many other Tejanos, long neglected by authorities in Mexico City, sided with the rebels. But the rebellion appeared to be short-lived. On March 6, 1836, General Santa Anna crushed settlers defending the **Alamo** in San Antonio. Soon thereafter, he captured the U.S. settlement at Goliad.

At this point, Santa Anna was convinced that the uprising was over. But the U.S. government, despite its claims of neutrality, aided the rebels with funds and army officers. American newspapers picked up the story of the Alamo and published accounts of the battle, describing the Mexican fighters as brutal butchers bent on saving Texas for the Catholic Pope. These stories, though more fable than fact, increased popular support for the war at a time when many Americans were increasingly hostile to Catholic immigrants in the United States.

At this point, the ability of Menchaca and other Tejanos to translate documents captured from Mexican couriers provided the entrée American forces needed. As hundreds of armed volunteers headed to Texas, General Sam Houston led rebel forces in a critical victory at San Jacinto in April 1836. While the Mexican government refused to recognize rebel claims, it did not try to regain the lost territory. Few of the U.S. volunteers arrived in time to participate in the fighting, but some settled in the newly liberated region. The Comanche nation quickly recognized the Republic of Texas and developed trade relations with residents to gain access to the vast U.S. market. Still, Santa Anna's failure to recognize Texas independence kept the U.S. government from granting the territory statehood for fear it would lead to war with Mexico. Texans shared that fear. Thus, Menchaca commanded a frontier company that patrolled the area between the San Antonio River and the Rio Grande. In 1842, Mexican soldiers did seek to reclaim San Antonio, but Menchaca's company helped defend the city and defeat the Mexicans.

Presidents Jackson and Van Buren also worried that admitting a new slave state might split the national Democratic Party. To limit debate on slavery, Congress had passed a **gag rule** in March 1836 that tabled all antislavery petitions without being read. Nevertheless, thousands of antislavery activists continued to flood the House of Representatives with petitions opposing the annexation of Texas.

Indians Resist Removal

The United States also faced continued challenges from Indian nations. After passage of the Indian Removal Act in 1830, Congress hoped to settle the most powerful eastern Indian tribes on land west of the Mississippi River. But some Indian peoples resisted. The Seminole, who had battled U.S. forces in the 1810s, continued to fight their removal. While federal authorities forcibly removed the majority of Seminoles to Indian Territory between 1832 and 1835, a minority fought back. Jackson and his military commanders expected that this **Second Seminole War** would be short-lived. However, they misjudged the Seminoles' strength; the power of their charismatic leader, Osceola; and the resistance of black fugitives living among the Seminoles.

The conflict continued long after Jackson left the presidency. During the seven-year guerrilla war, 1,600 U.S. troops died. U.S. military forces defeated the Seminole in 1842 only by luring Osceola into an army camp with false promises of a peace settlement. Instead, officers took him captive, finally breaking the back of the resistance. Still, to end the conflict, the U.S. government had to allow fugitive slaves living among the Seminoles to accompany the tribe to Indian Territory.

Unlike the Seminole, members of the Cherokee nation challenged removal by peaceful means, believing that their prolonged efforts to coexist with white society would ensure their success. Indian leaders like John Ross had urged Cherokees to embrace Christianity, white gender roles, and a republican form of government as the best means to ensure control of their communities. (See Chapter 9, "Cherokee Engage White America.") Large numbers had done so, but in 1829 and 1830, Georgia officials sought to impose new regulations on the Cherokee living within the state's borders. Tribal leaders took them to court, using evidence of their Americanization to claim their rights as an autonomous nation. In 1831 *Cherokee Nation v. Georgia* reached the U.S. Supreme Court, which denied a central part of the Cherokee claim. It ruled that all Indians were "domestic dependent nations" rather than fully sovereign governments. Yet the following year, in *Worcester v. Georgia*, the Court declared that the state of Georgia could not impose *state* laws on the Cherokee, for they had "territorial boundaries, within which their authority is exclusive," and that both their land and their rights were protected by the federal government.

President Jackson, who sought Cherokee removal, argued that only the tribe's removal west of the Mississippi River could ensure its "physical comfort," "political advancement," and "moral improvement." Most southern whites, seeking to expand cotton production or mine gold in Cherokee territory, agreed. But Protestant women and men in the North launched a massive petition campaign in 1830 supporting the Cherokees' right to their land. Cherokee women also renewed their protests against removal, and the tribe as a whole forestalled action through Jackson's second term.

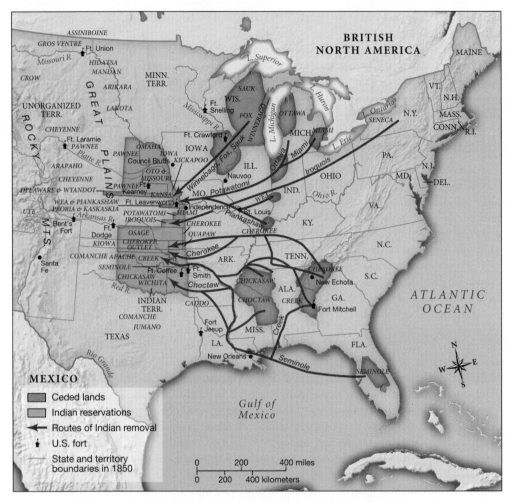

MAP 11.2   Indian Removals and Relocations, 1820s–1840s

In the 1820s and 1830s, the federal government used a variety of tactics, including military force, to expel Indian nations residing east of the Mississippi River. As these tribes resettled in the West, white migration along the Oregon and other trails began to increase. The result, by 1850, was the forced relocation of many western Indian nations as well.

In December 1835, however, U.S. officials convinced a small group of Cherokee men—without tribal sanction—to sign the **Treaty of New Echota**. It proposed the exchange of 100 million acres of Cherokee land in the Southeast for $68 million and 32 million acres in Indian Territory. Outraged Cherokee leaders like John Ross lobbied Congress to reject the treaty. But in May 1836, Congress approved the treaty by a single vote and set the date for final removal two years later (Map 11.2).

In 1838, the U.S. army forcibly removed Cherokees who had not yet resettled in Indian Territory. That June, General Winfield Scott, assisted by 7,000 U.S. soldiers, forced some 15,000 Cherokees into forts and military camps. Indian families spent

Seminole Warriors Attack the U.S. Block House, 1837   This hand-colored lithograph offers a rare glimpse of well-armed Seminole warriors attacking a U.S. fort. The image likely shows a December 1835 attack on a fort along the Withlacoochee River. T. J. Gray and James of Charleston, South Carolina, published a series of Florida scenes in the early nineteenth century depicting Seminole villages and U.S. forts and towns. Library of Congress, LC-DIG-ppmsca-19924

the next several months without sufficient food, water, sanitation, or medicine. In October, when the Cherokees finally began the march west, torrential rains were followed by snow. Although the U.S. army planned for a trip of less than three months, the journey actually took five months. As supplies ran short, many Indians died, including John Ross's wife. The remaining Cherokees completed this **Trail of Tears** in March 1839. But thousands remained near starvation a year later.

Following the Trail of Tears, Seneca Indians petitioned the federal government to stop their removal from western New York. Federal agents had negotiated the Treaty of Buffalo Creek with several Iroquois leaders in 1838. But some Seneca chiefs claimed the negotiation was marred by bribery and fraud. With the aid of Quaker allies, the Seneca petitioned Congress and the president for redress. Perhaps reluctant to repeat the Cherokee and Seminole debacles, Congress approved a new treaty in 1842 that allowed the Seneca to retain two of their four reservations in western New York.

By the 1840s, native peoples forced into Indian Territory had rebuilt their institutions and traditions. The Cherokee established Protestant churches and the first public schools west of the Mississippi. The Choctaw, too, opened public schools and became one of the first communities in the United States to offer girls and women equal access to education. The Choctaw also reached out to help people suffering hardship elsewhere. Hearing news of the Irish famine, the tribe sent relief money to starving communities in Ireland, creating a bond between the two peoples that continues into the twenty-first century.

Van Buren and the Panic of 1837

Although President Jackson proposed the Indian Removal Act, it was President Martin Van Buren who confronted ongoing challenges from Indian nations. When Van Buren ran for president in 1836, the Whigs hoped to defeat him by bringing together diverse supporters: evangelical Protestants who objected to Jackson's Indian policy, financiers and commercial farmers who advocated internal improvements and protective tariffs, merchants and manufacturers who favored a national bank, and Southerners who were antagonized by the president's heavy-handed use of federal authority. But the Whigs could not agree on a single candidate, and this lack of unity allowed Democrats to prevail. Although Van Buren won the popular vote by only a small margin (50.9 percent), he secured an easy majority in the electoral college.

Inaugurated on March 4, 1837, President Van Buren soon faced a major financial crisis. The **panic of 1837** started in the South and was rooted in the changing fortunes of American cotton in Great Britain. Capitalist calculations undergirded economic development in all regions of the United States. In the 1820s and 1830s, southern planters borrowed huge sums from British banks to expand landholdings and purchase more enslaved laborers, sure that King Cotton would provide the profits to repay their loans. Northern cotton factors and southern entrepreneurs also borrowed funds to improve southern port facilities. At the same time, British banks lent large sums to states such as New York to fund internal improvements, which drove the market revolution but also fueled inflation.

In late 1836, the Bank of England, faced with bad harvests at home and a declining demand for textiles, tightened credit to limit the flow of money out of the country. This forced British investors to call in their loans, which drove up interest rates in the United States just as cotton prices started to fall. Some American cotton merchants were forced to declare bankruptcy. The banks where they held accounts, mainly in the South, then failed. Ninety-eight of them did so in March and April 1837 alone. Cotton prices continued to fall, cut by nearly half in less than a year. Land values declined dramatically, and port cities came to a standstill. Cotton communities on the southern frontier collapsed as overextended planters lost or abandoned newly cleared fields. Their enslaved workers faced even worse conditions than usual as enslavers lost money and credit.

Because regional economies were increasingly intertwined, the panic radiated throughout the United States. Northern brokers, shippers, and merchants were devastated by losses in the cotton trade, and northern banks were hit by unpaid debts incurred for canals and other internal improvements. In turn, entrepreneurs who borrowed money to expand their businesses defaulted in large numbers, and shopkeepers, artisans, factory workers, and farmers in the North and Midwest suffered unemployment and foreclosures.

In the North and West, many Americans blamed Jackson's war against the Bank of the United States for precipitating the panic, and Americans everywhere were outraged at Van Buren's refusal to intervene in the crisis. While it is unlikely that any federal policy could have resolved the nation's economic problems, the president's apparent disinterest in the plight of the people inspired harsh criticisms from ordinary citizens as well as political opponents. Worse, despite brief signs of recovery in 1838, the depression deepened in 1839 and continued for four more years.

The Whigs Win the White House

Eager to exploit the weakness of Van Buren and the Democrats, the Whig Party organized its first national convention in fall 1840 and united behind military hero William Henry Harrison. Harrison was born to a wealthy planter family in Virginia, but he was portrayed as a self-made man who lived in a simple log cabin in Indiana. His running mate, John Tyler, another Virginia gentleman and a onetime Democrat, joined the Whigs because of his opposition to Jackson's stand on nullification. Whig leaders hoped he would attract southern votes. Taking their cue from Democrats, the Whigs organized rallies, barbecues, parades, and mass meetings. They turned the tables on their foe by portraying Van Buren as an aristocrat and Harrison as a war hero and friend of the common man. The Whigs supported American innovation and the entrepreneurial spirit, proclaimed prosperous farmers and skilled workers the backbone of the country, and insisted on their moral and religious superiority to Democrats. At the same time, eager to remind voters that Harrison had defeated Tenskwatawa at the Battle of Tippecanoe, the Whigs adopted the slogan "Tippecanoe and Tyler Too."

The Whigs also welcomed women into the campaign. By 1840 thousands of women had circulated petitions against Cherokee removal, organized temperance and antislavery societies, promoted religious revivals, and joined charitable associations. They embodied the kind of moral force that the Whig Party claimed to represent. In October 1840, Whig senator Daniel Webster spoke to a gathering of 1,200 women, calling on them to encourage their brothers and husbands to vote for Harrison.

The Whig strategy paid off handsomely on election day. Harrison won easily, and the Whigs gained a majority in Congress. Yet the election's promise was shattered when Harrison died of pneumonia a month after his inauguration. Whigs in Congress now had to deal with John Tyler, whose sentiments were largely southern and Democratic. Vetoing many Whig efforts at reform, Tyler allowed the Democratic Party to regroup and set the stage for close elections in 1844 and 1848.

REVIEW & RELATE

- How did westward expansion affect white Southerners, white Northerners, enslaved blacks, and American Indians in the 1830s and 1840s?
- What economic and political developments led to a Whig victory in the election of 1840?

The National Government Looks to the West

Despite the Whig victory in 1840, planters wielded considerable clout in Washington, D.C., because of the importance of cotton to the U.S. economy. In turn, Southerners needed federal support to expand into more fertile areas. With the economic panic of 1837–1843 finally over, the presidential election of 1844 turned on this issue. Democratic candidate James K. Polk demanded continued expansion into Mexico and Oregon. After Polk was elected, Britain and Mexico contested his claims, as did the Comanche. Still, the United States won vast Mexican territories in 1848, which intensified conflicts with Indians and debates over slavery.

Expanding to Oregon and Texas

Southerners eager to expand the plantation economy were at the forefront of the push for territorial expansion. Yet expansion was not merely a southern strategy. Northerners demanded that the United States reject British claims to the Oregon Territory, and some northern politicians and businessmen advocated acquiring Hawaii and Samoa to benefit U.S. trade. In 1844 the Democratic Party built on these expansionist dreams to recapture the White House.

The Democrats nominated a Tennessee congressman and governor, James K. Polk. The Whigs, unwilling to nominate Tyler for president, chose Kentucky senator Henry Clay. Polk declared himself in favor of the annexation of Texas. Clay, meanwhile, waffled on the issue. This proved his undoing when the Liberty Party, a small antislavery party founded in 1840, denounced annexation. Liberty Party candidate James G. Birney captured just enough votes in New York State to throw the state and the election to Polk.

In February 1845, a month before Polk took office, Congress passed a joint resolution annexing the Republic of Texas and granting it statehood. That summer, John L. O'Sullivan, editor of the *Democratic Review*, captured the American mood by declaring that nothing must interfere with "the fulfillment of our manifest destiny to overspread the continent allotted by Providence." This vision of **manifest destiny** — of the nation's God-given right to expand its borders — defined Polk's presidency.

With the Texas question seemingly resolved, President Polk turned his attention to Oregon, which stretched from the forty-second parallel to latitude 54°40′ and was jointly occupied by Great Britain and the United States. In 1842, three years before Polk took office, glowing reports of the mild climate and fertile soil around Puget Sound had inspired thousands of farmers and traders to flood into Oregon's Willamette Valley. Alarmed by this "Oregon fever," the British tried to confine Americans to areas south of the Columbia River. But U.S. settlers demanded access to the entire territory. President Polk encouraged migration into Oregon but was unwilling to risk war with Great Britain. Instead, diplomats negotiated a treaty in 1846 that extended the border with British Canada (the forty-ninth parallel) to the Pacific Ocean. Over the next two years, Congress admitted Iowa and Wisconsin to statehood, reassuring northern residents that expansion benefited all regions of the nation.

Some Americans hoped to gain even more territory by claiming northern Mexico and California for the United States. Spanish missions and forts, built in the late eighteenth century, dotted the Pacific Coast from San Diego to San Francisco. When Mexico achieved independence in 1821, it took control of this missionary and military network. Diseases carried by the Spanish and forced labor in their missions and forts had decimated some Indian tribes in the region. As Mexican soldiers took control, some married into Indian families, gaining land and social status and nurturing compound cultures. More often, however, diseases, guns, thefts of food and animals, sexual assault, and forced labor continued to debilitate native peoples.

Indians in areas newly claimed by the U.S. government faced these same dangers. In addition, as the U.S. government forced eastern tribes to move west of the Mississippi, tensions increased with Indian nations already there (see Map 11.2). Thus when the Cherokee were removed to Indian Territory, they confronted their traditional enemies, the Creek. Others, such as the Osage, whose society was forged around gender complementarity, managed to sustain much of their culture and economy despite accepting Christian missions and being forced to relocate in the Midwest. However, when white settlement pushed them onto ever less fertile land, women could no longer farm as productively and male hunters then became more critical to the community. Other native peoples were decimated by disease, including the Mandan, hosts to the Lewis and Clark expedition in 1803. When smallpox struck the Mandan in the 1830s, the Lakota and Dakota (Sioux) strengthened their domination of the region.

The flood of U.S. migrants into Texas and the southern plains also transformed relations among Indian nations and between Indians and Mexico. In the face of Spanish and then Mexican claims on their lands, for example, the Comanche forged alliances with former foes like the Wichita and the Osage. The Comanche also developed commercial ties with tribes in Indian Territory and with both Mexican and Anglo-American traders. They thereby hoped to benefit from the imperial ambitions of the United States and Mexico while strengthening bonds among Indians in the region.

For Mexicans and Tejanos, Comanche expansion was increasingly problematic. Mexico did not have sufficient resources to sustain the level of gift giving that Spanish authorities used to maintain peace. As a result, Comanche warriors launched continual raids against Mexican and Tejano settlements, failing to abide by the border between the two groups. But the Comanche also developed commercial relations with residents of New Mexico, who flaunted trade regulations promulgated in Mexico City. By 1846 Comanche trade and diplomatic relations with New Mexican settlements had seriously weakened the hold of Mexican authorities on their northern provinces. In Texas, José Antonio Menchaca was appointed an agent to native traders, including Comanche, and soon became a merchant himself.

Pursuing War with Mexico

With Texas now part of the United States, Mexico faced growing tensions with U.S. officials over the state's western border. Mexico insisted on the Nueces River as the boundary line, while Americans claimed all the land to the Rio Grande. In January 1846, Polk secretly sent emissary John Slidell to negotiate a border treaty with Mexico. But Polk also sent U.S. troops under General Zachary Taylor across the Nueces River. Mexican officials refused to see Slidell and instead sent their own troops across the Rio Grande. Meanwhile, U.S. naval commanders prepared to seize San Francisco Bay from the Mexicans if war was declared. The Mexican government responded by sending more troops into the disputed Texas territory.

When fighting erupted near the Rio Grande in May 1846 (Map 11.3), Polk claimed that "American blood had been shed on American soil" and declared a state of war. Many Whigs in Congress opposed the declaration, arguing that the president had provoked the conflict. However, antiwar Whigs failed to convince the Democratic majority, and Congress voted to finance the war. Although northern abolitionists protested vehemently, most Americans — North and South — considered westward expansion a boon.

Once the war began, battles erupted in a variety of locations. In May 1846, U.S. troops defeated Mexican forces in Palo Alto and Resaca de la Palma. A month later, the U.S. army captured Sonoma, California with the aid of local settlers. John Frémont then led U.S. forces to Monterey, where the navy launched a successful

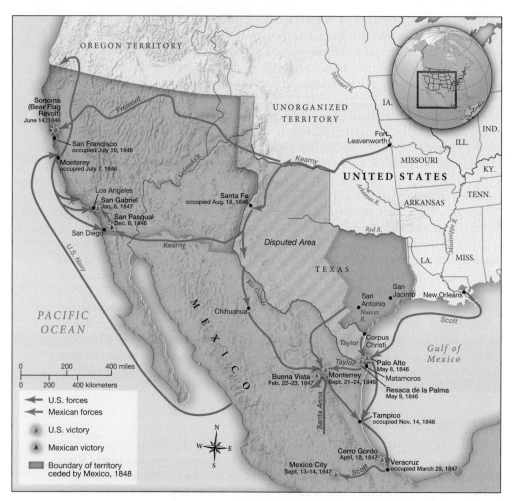

MAP 11.3   The Mexican-American War, 1846–1848
Although a dispute over territory between the Nueces River and the Rio Grande initiated the Mexican-American War, most of the fighting occurred between the Rio Grande and Mexico City. In addition, U.S. forces in California launched battles to claim independence for that region even before gold was discovered there.

attack and declared the California territory part of the United States. That fall, U.S. troops gained important victories at Monterrey, Mexico, just west of the Rio Grande, and Tampico, along the Gulf coast.

Despite major U.S. victories, General Santa Anna, who reclaimed the presidency of Mexico during the war, refused to give up. In February 1847, his troops attacked U.S. forces at Buena Vista and nearly secured a victory. Polk then agreed to send General Winfield Scott to Veracruz with 14,000 soldiers. Capturing the port in March, Scott's army headed to Mexico City. After a crushing defeat of Santa Anna at Cerro Gordo, the president-general was removed from power and the new Mexican government sought peace.

"Hanging of the San Patricios," 1847   In 1846–1847 more than two hundred immigrants, most of them Irish Catholics who defected from U.S. Army units, joined the Mexican Army. They formed the Batallón de San Patricios, which fought fiercely in many battles. When dozens were captured after the Battle of Chapultepec, the soldiers were convicted of desertion. Samuel Chamberlain painted one of two mass hangings that followed.   Herbert Orth/Contributor/The LIFE Images Collection/Getty Images

With victory ensured, U.S. officials faced a difficult decision: How much Mexican territory should they claim? The U.S. army in central Mexico faced continued guerrilla attacks. Meanwhile Whigs and some northern Democrats denounced the war as a southern conspiracy to expand slavery. In this context, Polk agreed to limit U.S. claims to the northern regions of Mexico. The president signed the **Treaty of Guadalupe Hidalgo** in February 1848, committing the United States to pay Mexico $15 million in return for control over Texas north and east of the Rio Grande plus California and the New Mexico territory.

Debates over Slavery Intensify

News of the U.S. victory traveled quickly across the United States. In the South, planters imagined slavery spreading into the lands acquired from Mexico. Northerners, too, applauded the expansion of U.S. territory but focused on California as a center for agriculture and commerce. Still, the acquisition of new territory heightened sectional conflicts. Debates over slavery had erupted during the war, fueled by abolitionist outrage. A few northern Democrats joined Whigs in denouncing "the power of SLAVERY" to "govern the country, its Constitutions and laws."

In August 1846, Democratic congressman David Wilmot of Pennsylvania proposed outlawing slavery in all territory acquired from Mexico so that the South could not profit from the war. While the **Wilmot Proviso** passed in the House, southern and proslavery northern Democrats defeated it in the Senate. Many Northerners shared these Democrats' views on African Americans. Legislators in Oregon Territory, too far north for slavery to be an issue, nonetheless excluded African Americans from settling within its borders. The first such law took effect in 1844, and the last of Oregon's exclusionary laws was not repealed until 1926. Ohio, Indiana, Illinois, and other Midwestern states also restricted or denied blacks the right to settle.

It was the question of slavery in the territories acquired from Mexico, however, that fueled the presidential election of 1848. With Polk declining to run for a second term, Democrats nominated Lewis Cass, a Michigan senator and ardent expansionist. Hoping to keep northern antislavery Democrats in the party, Cass argued that residents in each territory should decide whether to make the region free or slave. This strategy put the slavery question on hold but satisfied almost no one.

The Whigs, too, hoped to avoid the slavery issue for fear of losing southern votes. They nominated Mexican-American War hero General Zachary Taylor, a Louisiana enslaver who had no declared position on slavery in the western territories. But they sought to reassure their northern wing by nominating Millard Fillmore of Buffalo, New York, for vice president. As a member of Congress in the 1830s, Fillmore had opposed the annexation of Texas.

The Liberty Party, disappointed in the Whig ticket, decided to run its own candidate for president. Its leaders hoped to expand their support by reconstituting themselves as the Free-Soil Party. This party focused more on excluding enslaved labor from western territories than on the moral injustice of slavery. The party nominated former president Martin Van Buren and appealed to small farmers and urban workers hoping to benefit from western expansion.

Once again, the presence of a third party affected the outcome of the election. While Whigs and Democrats tried to avoid the slavery issue, Free-Soilers demanded attention to it. By focusing on the exclusion of slavery in western territories rather than its abolition, the party won more adherents in northern states. Indeed, Van Buren won enough northern Democrats so that Cass lost New York State and the 1848 election. Zachary Taylor and the Whigs won, but only by placing a southern enslaver in the White House.

REVIEW & RELATE	• How did the battle over Texas affect relations among Indian nations, among white Americans, and between Indians and whites? • How did the Mexican-American War reshape national politics and intensify debates over slavery?

Conclusion: Geographical Expansion and Political Division

By the mid-nineteenth century, the United States stood at a crossroads. Most Americans considered expansion advantageous and necessary for a strong economy. Planters certainly considered it critical to slavery's success. Yet as the number of enslaved workers and the size of plantations grew, planters also sought to impose stricter controls over blacks, enslaved and free, and to bind non-slaveowning whites more firmly to their interests. Enslaved blacks, meanwhile, developed an increasingly rich culture by combining traditions and rituals from Africa and the Caribbean with U.S. customs and beliefs. This African American culture served as one form of resistance against slavery's brutality. Many enslaved laborers resisted in other ways as well: sabotaging tools, feigning illness, running away, or committing arson or theft. Smaller numbers engaged in outright rebellions.

While most white Northerners were willing to leave slavery alone where it already existed, many hoped to keep it out of newly acquired territories. In this sense, the removal of the Cherokee did not disturb most Northerners since it was largely white yeoman farmers, they believed, who would benefit from access to their land. Still some northern whites, especially evangelical women, opposed removal on moral grounds. At the same time, many Northerners supported statehood for Texas despite abolitionist protests. When it came to the Mexican-American War, however, more Northerners — black and white — feared victory would largely benefit southern planters. Some yeomen farmers and middle-class professionals in the South also questioned whether extending slavery benefited the region economically and politically.

The vast lands gained from Mexico in 1848 intensified debates over slavery and led small but growing numbers of white Northerners to join African Americans, American Indians, and newly created Mexican Americans in protesting U.S. expansion. Tejano leaders, including José Antonio Menchaca, had supported statehood and the U.S. war against Mexico, eager to ensure the region's security. Still, after the war, Menchaca spoke out for Tejano veterans, who claimed they were denied proper compensation for their service.

These debates occurred amid a political realignment fueled by the panic of 1837. The extended depression allowed the newly formed Whig Party to gain support for its economic and reform agenda. In 1840 Whigs captured the White House and Congress just as a new antislavery force, the Liberty Party, emerged. But just four years later, James K. Polk's support of westward expansion and manifest destiny returned Democrats to power. The political volatility continued when the U.S. defeat of Mexico intensified debates over slavery, fractured the Democratic Party, and inspired the founding of the Free-Soil Party.

Political realignments continued over the next decade, as growing antislavery sentiment in the North confronted proslavery claims in the South. In 1853 Solomon Northup shocked thousands of antislavery readers with his book *Twelve Years a Slave*, which vividly described the horrors of the slave trade and life in bondage. His book and others alarmed planters, who continued to claim that slavery was a divine blessing. Yet in insisting on the benefits of enslaved labor, the planter elite reinforced conflicts with Northerners, whose lives were increasingly shaped by commercial and industrial development and the expansion of free labor.

Chapter 11 Review

KEY TERMS

planters, 274
Nat Turner's rebellion, 281
yeomen farmers, 283
white supremacy, 285
Whig Party, 285
Second Party System, 285
Tejanos, 286
Alamo, 286

gag rule, 287
Second Seminole War, 287
Treaty of New Echota, 288
Trail of Tears, 289
panic of 1837, 290
manifest destiny, 292
Treaty of Guadalupe Hidalgo, 295
Wilmot Proviso, 296

REVIEW & RELATE

1. What role did the planter elite play in southern society and politics?
2. What were the consequences of the dominant position of slave-based plantation agriculture for the southern economy?
3. How did enslaved African Americans create ties of family, community, and culture?
4. How did enslaved African Americans resist efforts to control and exploit their labor?
5. What groups made up white southern society? How did their interests overlap or diverge?
6. How and why did the planter elite seek to reinforce white solidarity?
7. How did westward expansion affect white Southerners, white Northerners, enslaved blacks, and American Indians in the 1830s and 1840s?
8. What economic and political developments led to a Whig victory in the election of 1840?
9. How did the battle over Texas affect relations among Indian nations, among white Americans, and between Indians and whites?
10. How did the Mexican-American War reshape national politics and intensify debates over slavery?

TIMELINE OF EVENTS

1830	• Indian Removal Act
1830–1850	• 440,000 enslaved people from Upper South sold to owners in Lower South
1831	• *Cherokee Nation v. Georgia*
	• Nat Turner leads slave uprising in Virginia
	• Virginia's Assembly establishes special committee on slavery
1832	• *Worcester v. Georgia*
1834	• Britain abolishes slavery in its territories
1835–1842	• Second Seminole War
1836	• Treaty of New Echota
March 2, 1836	• U.S. settlers declare eastern Texas an independent republic
March 6, 1836	• General Santa Anna crushes U.S. rebels at the Alamo
March 1836	• Congress passes gag rule
1837–1843	• Panic of 1837 triggers extended depression
1838–1839	• Cherokee driven west on Trail of Tears
1840	• Whigs win the presidency and gain control of Congress
1841	• Solomon Northup sold into slavery
1842	• Seneca Indians win treaty to remain in New York
1845	• U.S. annexes Texas
1846	• U.S. settles dispute with Great Britain over Oregon
May 1846– February 1848	• Mexican-American War
August 1846	• David Wilmot proposes Wilmot Proviso
March 1848	• Treaty of Guadalupe Hidalgo

12

Imperial Ambitions and Sectional Crises

1842–1861

LEARNING OBJECTIVES

After reading this chapter you will be able to:

- Compare the experiences of different groups living in and migrating to the West, including Mexicans, Mexican Americans, and American Indians.

- Explain how geographical expansion heightened sectional conflicts and how those conflicts shaped and were shaped by federal policies like the Compromise of 1850 and the Fugitive Slave Act.

- Analyze the ways that the spread of antislavery sentiments, partisan politics, and federal court decisions intensified sectional divisions.

- Evaluate the importance of John Brown's raid and the election of Abraham Lincoln as president in convincing southern states to secede from the Union.

COMPARING AMERICAN HISTORIES

John C. Frémont, a noted explorer and military leader, rose from humble beginnings. He was born out of wedlock to Anne Beverley Whiting Pryor of Savannah, Georgia, who abandoned her wealthy husband and ran off with a French immigrant. Frémont attended the College of Charleston, where he excelled at mathematics, but was eventually expelled for neglecting his studies. In 1833, at age twenty, he was hired to teach aboard a navy ship through the help of an influential South Carolina politician. He then obtained a surveying position to map new railroad lines and Cherokee lands in Georgia and was finally appointed a second lieutenant in the Corps of Topographical Engineers.

In 1840 Lieutenant Frémont moved to Washington, D.C., where he worked on maps and reports based on his surveys. The following year, he eloped with Jessie Benton, the daughter of Missouri senator Thomas Hart Benton. Despite the scandal, Senator Benton supported his son-in-law's selection for a federally funded expedition to the West. In 1842 Frémont and his guide, Kit Carson, led twenty-three men along the emerging Oregon Trail. Two years later, John returned to Washington, where Jessie helped him turn his notes into a vivid report on the Oregon Territory and California. Congress published the report, which inspired a wave of hopeful migrants to head west.

Frémont's success was tainted, however, by a quest for personal glory. On a federal mapping expedition in 1845, he left his post and headed to Sacramento, California. In early 1846, he stirred support among U.S. settlers there for war with Mexico. His brash behavior nearly provoked a bloody battle. Frémont then fled to the Oregon Territory, where he and Kit Carson initiated conflicts with local Indians. As the United States moved closer to war with Mexico, Frémont returned to California to support Anglo-American settlers' efforts to declare the region an independent republic. After the war, Frémont worked tirelessly for California's admission to the Union and served as one of the state's first senators. With his wife's encouragement, he embraced abolition and in 1856 was nominated for president by the new Republican Party.

Dred Scott also traveled the frontier in the 1830s and 1840s, but not of his own free will. Born a slave in Southampton, Virginia around 1800, his master, Peter Blow, moved west to Alabama in 1818 and then to St. Louis, Missouri, in 1830, taking Scott with him. Three years later, Blow sold Scott to Dr. John Emerson, an assistant surgeon in the U.S. army. In 1836 Emerson took Scott to Fort Snelling in the free territory of Wisconsin Territory. There Scott met Harriet Robinson, a young enslaved African American. Her master, an Indian agent, allowed the couple to marry in 1837 and transferred ownership of Harriet to Dr. Emerson. When Emerson moved back to St. Louis, the Scotts returned with him. After the doctor's death in 1843, the couple was hired out to local residents by Emerson's widow.

In April 1846, the Scotts initiated lawsuits to gain their freedom. The Missouri Supreme Court had ruled in earlier cases that enslaved people who resided for any time in free territory must be freed, and the Scotts had lived and married in Wisconsin. In 1850 the Missouri Circuit Court ruled in the Scotts' favor. However, the Emerson family appealed the decision to the state supreme court, with Harriet's case to follow the outcome of her husband's. Two years later, that court ruled against all precedent and overturned the lower court's decision. Dred Scott then appealed to the U.S. Supreme Court, but it, too, ultimately ruled against the Scotts, leaving them enslaved.

COMPARING THE AMERICAN HISTORIES of John Frémont and Dred Scott demonstrates how the explosive combination of westward expansion and growing regional divisions over the issue of slavery split the nation by 1861. Whereas Frémont joined expeditions to map and conquer the West, Scott followed the migrations of enslavers and soldiers. Both Frémont and Scott were supported by strong women, and both men advocated government action to end slavery. Only Frémont, however, had the right to vote, run for office, and join the Republican Party. From their different positions, these two men reflected the dramatic changes that occurred as westward expansion pushed the issues of empire and slavery to the center of national debate.

Claiming the West

During the 1830s and 1840s, national debates over slavery intensified. The most important battles now centered on western territories gained through victory in the war with Mexico. Before 1848, government-sponsored expeditions had opened up vast new lands for American pioneers seeking opportunity, and migrants moved west in growing numbers. Following the Mexican-American War and the discovery of gold in California, tens of thousands of men rushed to the Pacific coast seeking riches. But the West was already home to a diverse population that included Indians, Mexicans, Mormons, and missionaries. Pioneers converged, and often clashed, with these groups.

Traveling the Overland Trail

In the 1830s a growing number of migrants followed overland trails to the far West. In 1836 Narcissa Whitman and Eliza Spaulding joined a group traveling to the Oregon Territory, the first white women to make the trip. They accompanied their husbands, both Presbyterian ministers, who hoped to convert the region's Indians. Their letters to friends and co-worshippers back east described the rich lands and needy souls in the Walla Walla valley. Such missives were widely shared and encouraged further migration.

The panic of 1837 also prompted families to head west. Thousands of U.S. migrants and European immigrants sought better economic prospects in Oregon, the Rocky Mountain region, and the eastern plains, while Mormons continued to settle in Salt Lake City. Some pioneers opened trading posts where Indians exchanged goods with Anglo-American settlers or with merchants back east. Small settlements developed around these posts and near the expanding system of U.S. forts that dotted the region.

For many pioneers, the journey on the **Oregon Trail** began at St. Louis. From there, they traveled by wagon train across the Great Plains and the Rocky Mountains to the Pacific coast. By 1860 some 350,000 Americans had made the journey, claimed land from the Mississippi River to the Pacific that once belonged to native peoples, and transformed the United States into an expanding empire.

Because the journey west required funds for wagons and supplies, most pioneers were of middling status. The majority of pioneers made the three- to six-month journey with family members to help share the labor. Men, mainly farmers, comprised some 60 percent of these western migrants, but women and children traveled in significant numbers, often alongside relatives or neighbors from back east. Some courageous families headed west alone, but most traveled in wagon trains—from a few wagons to a few dozen—that provided support and security.

Traditional gender roles often broke down on the trail, and even conventional domestic tasks posed novel problems. Women had to cook unfamiliar food over open fires in all kinds of weather and with only a few pots and utensils. They washed laundry in rivers or streams and on the plains hauled water from great distances. Wood, too, was scarce on the plains, and women and children gathered buffalo dung (called "chips") for fuel. Men frequently had to gather food rather than hunt and fish, or they had to learn to catch strange (and sometimes dangerous) animals, such as jack rabbits and rattlesnakes. Few men were prepared for the dangerous work of floating wagons across rivers. Nor were many of them expert in shoeing horses or fixing wagon wheels, tasks that were performed by skilled artisans at home.

Expectations changed dramatically when men took ill or died. Then wives often drove the wagon, gathered or hunted for food, and learned to repair axles and other wagon parts. When large numbers of men were injured or ill, women might serve as scouts and guides or pick up guns to defend wagons under attack by Indians or wild animals. Yet despite their growing burdens, pioneer women gained little power over decision making. Moreover, the addition of men's jobs to women's responsibilities was rarely reciprocated. Few men cooked, did laundry, or cared for children on the trail.

In one area, however, relative equality reigned. Men and women were equally susceptible to disease, injury, and death during the journey. Accidents, gunshot wounds, drownings, broken bones, and infections affected people on every wagon train. Some groups were struck as well by deadly epidemics of measles or cholera. In addition, about 20 percent of women on the overland trail became pregnant, which posed even greater dangers than usual given the lack of medical services and sanitation. About the same percentage of women lost children or spouses on the trip west. Overall, about one in ten to fifteen migrants died on the western journey.

The Gold Rush

Despite the hazards, more and more Americans traveled overland to the Pacific coast, although only a few thousand Americans initially settled in California. Some were agents sent there by eastern merchants to purchase fine leather made from the hides of Spanish cattle. Several agents married into families of elite Mexican ranchers, known as Californios, and adopted their culture, even converting to Catholicism.

However, the Anglo-American presence in California changed dramatically after 1848 when gold was discovered at Sutter's Mill in northeastern California. Beginning in 1849 news of the discovery brought tens of thousands of settlers from the eastern United States, South America, Europe, and Asia. In the **gold rush**, "forty-niners" raced to claim riches in California, and men vastly outnumbered women.

The rapid influx of gold seekers heightened tensions between newly arrived whites, local Indians, and Californios. Forty-niners confiscated land owned by Californios, shattered the fragile ecosystem in the California mountains, and forced Mexican and Indian men to labor for low wages or a promised share in uncertain profits. New conflicts erupted when migrants from Asia and South America joined the search for wealth. Forty-niners from the United States regularly stole from and assaulted these foreign-born competitors.

Gold Rush Miners, 1849 These prospectors were two of some 80,000 who traveled to California after gold was discovered. While many Chinese miners were run off their claims, these two men, dressed in a mix of Chinese and American attire, panned for gold with the tools of their trade—pickax, hoe, and pan. A shed in the background may have served as their home. Granger

The gold rush also led to the increased exploitation of women as thousands of male migrants demanded food, shelter, laundry, and medical care. While some California women earned a good living by renting rooms, cooking meals, washing clothes, or working as prostitutes, many faced exploitation and abuse. Indian and Mexican women were especially vulnerable to sexual harassment and rape, while many Chinese women were imported specifically to provide sexual services for male miners.

Chinese men were also victims of abuse by whites, who ran them off their claims. Yet some Chinese men used the skills traditionally assigned them in their homeland—cooking and washing clothes—to earn a far steadier income than prospecting for gold could provide. Other men also took advantage of the demand for goods and services. Levi Strauss, a German Jewish immigrant, moved from New York to San Francisco to open a dry-goods store in 1853. He soon made his fortune producing canvas and then denim pants that could withstand harsh weather and long wear.

A Crowded Land

While U.S. promoters of migration continued to depict the West as open territory, it was in fact the site of competing national ambitions in the late 1840s. Despite granting statehood to Texas in 1845 and winning the war against Mexico in 1848, the United States had to battle for control of the Great Plains with powerful Indian nations, like the Lakota and Dakota and the Cheyenne (Map 12.1).

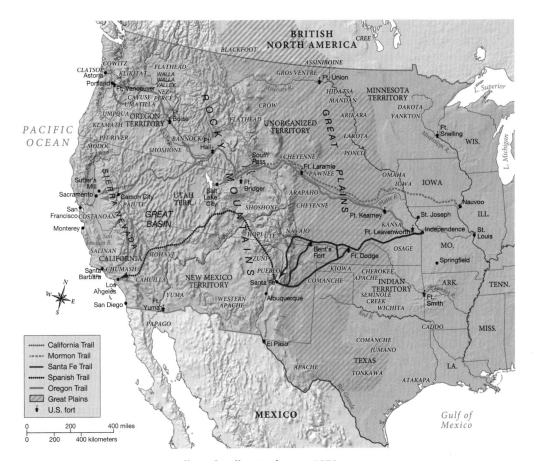

MAP 12.1   Western Trails and Indian Nations, c. 1850
As wagon trains and traders journeyed west in rapidly growing numbers during the 1830s and 1840s, the United States established forts along the most well-traveled routes. At the same time, Indians claimed or were forced into new areas through the pressure of Indian removals, white settlement, and the demands of hunting, trade, and agriculture.

Although attacks on wagon trains were rare, Indians did threaten frontier settlements throughout the 1840s and 1850s. Settlers often retaliated, and U.S. army troops joined them in efforts to push Indians back from areas newly claimed by whites. Yet in many parts of the West, Indians were as powerful as whites, and they did not cede territory without a fight. The Reverend Marcus Whitman and his wife, Narcissa, became victims of their success in promoting western settlement when pioneers brought a deadly measles epidemic to the region, killing thousands of Cayuse and Nez Percé Indians. In 1847, convinced that whites brought disease but no useful medicine, a group of Cayuse Indians killed the Whitmans and ten other white settlers.

Yet violence against whites could not stop the flood of migrants into the Oregon Territory. Indeed, attacks by one Indian tribe were often used to justify assaults on any Indian tribe. Thus John Frémont and Kit Carson, whose party was attacked by Modoc

Indians in Oregon in 1846, retaliated by destroying a Klamath Indian village and killing its inhabitants. The defeat of Mexico and the discovery of gold in California only intensified such conflicts. Over the next quarter century, vigilante violence, kidnapping, disease, the destruction of hunting and fishing grounds and farmlands, and mass murders reduced California's native population from about 150,000 to 30,000.

Although Indians and white Americans were the main players in many battles, Indian nations also competed with each other. In the southern plains, drought and disease exacerbated those conflicts in the late 1840s and dramatically changed the balance of power there. In 1845 the southern plains were struck by a dry spell, which lasted on and off until the mid-1860s. In 1848, smallpox ravaged Comanche villages, and a virulent strain of cholera was introduced into the region the next year by forty-niners traveling to California. In the late 1840s, the Comanche nation was the largest Indian group, with about twenty thousand members; by the mid-1850s, less than half that number remained.

Yet the collapse of the Comanche empire was not simply the result of outside forces. As the Comanche expanded their trade networks and incorporated smaller Indian nations into their orbit, they overextended their reach. Most important, they allowed too many bison to be killed to meet the needs of their Indian allies and the demand of Anglo-American and European traders. The Comanche also herded growing numbers of horses, which required expansive grazing lands and winter havens in the river valleys, which forced bison onto more marginal lands. Opening the Santa Fe Trail to commerce multiplied the problems by destroying vegetation and polluting springs, thereby diminishing resources in more of the region. The prolonged drought completed the depopulation of the bison on the southern plains. Without bison, the Comanche lost a trade item critical to sustaining their commercial and political control. As the Comanche empire collapsed, former Indian allies sought to advance their own interests. These developments reignited Indian wars on the southern plains as tens of thousands of pioneers poured through the region.

African Americans also participated in these western struggles. A few southeastern tribes forced into Indian Territory brought enslaved blacks with them, but some enslaved workers were also freed and married Seminole or Cherokee spouses. The Creek proved harsh masters, prompting some of those enslaved to escape north to free states or south to Mexican or Comanche territory. As southern officers in the U.S. army moved to frontier outposts, they carried more enslaved people into the region. Many, including Dr. John Emerson, changed posts frequently, taking enslaved workers like Dred Scott into both slave and free territories. Still, it was white planters who brought the greatest numbers of African Americans into Texas, Missouri, and Kansas, pushing the frontier of slavery ever westward. At the same time, free blacks joined the migration voluntarily in hopes of finding better economic opportunities and less overt racism in the West.

REVIEW & RELATE	• Why did Americans go west in the 1830s and 1840s, and what was the journey like? • What groups competed for land and resources in the West? How did disease, drought, and violence shape this competition?

Expansion and the Politics of Slavery

The place of slavery in the West aroused intense political debates as territories in the region began to seek statehood. Debates over the eradication of slavery and limits on its expansion had shaped the highly contested presidential election of 1848. After the Mexican-American War, the debate intensified and focused more specifically on slavery's westward expansion. Each time a territory achieved the requirements for statehood, a new crisis erupted. To resolve these crises required strong political leadership, judicial moderation, and a spirit of compromise among the American people. None of these conditions prevailed. Instead, passage of the Fugitive Slave Act in 1850 aroused deeper hostilities, and President Franklin Pierce (1853–1857) encouraged further expansion but failed to address the crises that ensued.

California and the Compromise of 1850

In the winter of 1849, just before President Zachary Taylor's March inauguration, California applied for admission to the Union as a free state. Some California political leaders opposed slavery on principle. Others wanted to "save" the state for whites by outlawing slavery, discouraging free black migration, and restricting the rights of Mexican, Indian, and Chinese residents. Yet the internal debates among Californians were not uppermost in the minds of politicians. Southerners were concerned about the impact of California's free-state status on the sectional balance in Congress, and southern Whigs in particular were shocked when President Taylor suggested that the Senate should simply admit California as requested.

Other debates percolated in Congress at the same time. Many Northerners were horrified by the spectacle of slavery and slave trading in the nation's capital and argued that it damaged America's international reputation. Southerners, meanwhile, complained that the Fugitive Slave Act of 1793 was being widely ignored in the North. A boundary dispute between Texas and New Mexico irritated western legislators, while Texas claimed that debts it accrued while an independent republic and during the Mexican-American War should be assumed by the federal government.

Senator Henry Clay of Kentucky, the Whig leader who had hammered out the Missouri Compromise in 1819 and 1820, again tried to resolve the many conflicts that stalled congressional action. He offered a compromise by which California would be admitted as a free state; the remaining land acquired from Mexico would be divided into two territories — New Mexico and Utah — and slavery there would be decided by popular sovereignty; the border dispute between New Mexico and Texas would be decided in favor of New Mexico, but the federal government would assume Texas's war debts; the slave trade (but not slavery) would be abolished in the District of Columbia; and a new and more effective fugitive slave law would be approved. Although Clay's compromise offered something to everyone, his colleagues did not immediately embrace it.

By March 1850, after months of passionate debate, the sides remained sharply divided, as did their most esteemed leaders. John C. Calhoun, a proslavery senator from South Carolina, refused to support any compromise that allowed Congress to decide the fate of slavery in the western territories. William H. Seward, an antislavery Whig senator from New York, proclaimed he could not support a compromise that forced Northerners to help hunt down fugitives from slavery. Although Daniel Webster, a Massachusetts Whig, urged fellow senators to support the compromise to preserve the Union, Congress adjourned with the fate of California undecided.

Before the Senate reconvened in September 1850, however, the political landscape changed in unexpected ways. Henry Clay retired the previous spring, leaving the Capitol with his last great legislative effort unfinished. On March 31, 1850, Calhoun died; his absence from the Senate made compromise more likely. Then in July, President Taylor died unexpectedly, and his vice president, Millard Fillmore, became president. Fillmore then appointed Webster as secretary of state, removing him from the Senate as well.

In fall 1850, with President Fillmore's support, a younger cohort of senators and representatives steered the **Compromise of 1850** through Congress, one clause at a time. This tactic allowed legislators to support only those parts of the compromise they found palatable. In the end, all the provisions passed, and Fillmore quickly signed the bills into law.

The Compromise of 1850, like the Missouri Compromise thirty years earlier, fended off a sectional crisis but signaled future problems. Would popular sovereignty prevail when later territories sought admission to the Union, and would Northerners abide by a fugitive slave law that called on them to aid directly in the capture of enslaved runaways?

The Fugitive Slave Act Inspires Northern Protest

The fugitive slave laws of 1793 and 1824 mandated that all states aid in apprehending and returning enslaved runaways to their enslavers. The **1850 Fugitive Slave Act** was different in two important respects. First, it eliminated jury trials for alleged fugitives. Second, the law required individual citizens, not just state officials, to help return runaways. The act angered many Northerners who believed that the federal government had gone too far in protecting the rights of enslavers and thereby aroused sympathy for the abolitionist cause.

Before 1850, free blacks led the effort to aid fugitives, including David Ruggles in New York City; William Still in Philadelphia; and, after his own successful escape, Frederick Douglass. Among their staunchest allies were white Quakers such as Amy and Isaac Post in Rochester, Lucretia Mott in Philadelphia, Thomas Garrett in Chester County, Pennsylvania, and Levi and Catherine Coffin in Newport, Indiana. Political abolitionists, like wealthy reformer Gerrit Smith, of Peterboro, New York, also aided the cause.

Following passage of the Fugitive Slave Act, the number of enslavers and hired slave catchers pursuing fugitives increased dramatically. But so, too, did the number of northern abolitionists helping blacks escape. Once escaped runaways crossed into free territory, most contacted free blacks or sought out Quaker, Baptist, or Methodist meetinghouses whose members might be sympathetic to their cause. They then began the journey along the underground railroad, from house to house or barn to barn, until they found safe haven. Harriet Tubman, herself a fugitive, returned south repeatedly and freed dozens of family members and other enslaved men and women. Abolitionists purchased the freedom of a few fugitives, including sisters Mary and Emily Edmondson who had been sold to slave traders after a failed escape attempt

Anti-Fugitive Slave Law Convention, Cazenovia, New York, 1850 This rare daguerreotype captures abolitionists, outraged over the Fugitive Slave Law, at a massive protest meeting. Some 2,000 participants met in an apple orchard. Frederick Douglass sits at the left side of the table. The Edmondson sisters, in plaid shawls, stand behind him on either side of Gerrit Smith. The sisters were among fifty former enslaved people who attended the meeting. Digital image courtesy of the Getty's Open Content Program

in 1848. Fugitives often followed disparate paths, depending on "conductors" to get them from one stop to the next. Despite its limits, the underground railroad was an important resource for fugitives seeking refuge in Canada or hoping to blend into free black communities stateside.

Free blacks were even more endangered after passage of the Fugitive Slave Act since slave catchers believed that they harbored fugitives in their midst. In Chester County, Pennsylvania, on the Maryland border, newspapers reported on at least a dozen free blacks who were kidnapped or arrested as runaways in the first three months of 1851. One provision of the Fugitive Slave Act encouraged such arrests: Commissioners were paid $10 for each slave sent back but only $5 if a runaway was not returned. Without the right to a trial, a free black could easily be sent south as a fugitive.

At the same time, a growing number of Northerners challenged the federal government's right to enforce the law. Blacks and whites organized protest meetings throughout the free states. At a meeting in Boston in 1851, William Lloyd Garrison denounced the law: "We execrate it, we spit upon it, we trample it under our feet." On July 5, 1852, Frederick Douglass asked a mixed-race audience, "What to the American slave, is your 4th of July? I answer, a day that reveals to him . . . the gross injustice and cruelty to which he is the constant victim." He then declared, "There is not a nation on the earth guilty of practices more shocking and bloody than are the people of these United States at this very hour."

Some abolitionists established vigilance committees to rescue fugitives who had been arrested. In Syracuse in October 1851, Jermaine Loguen, Samuel Ward, and the Reverend Samuel J. May led a well-organized crowd that broke into a Syracuse courthouse and rescued a fugitive known as Jerry. They successfully hid him from authorities before spiriting him to Canada.

Meanwhile Americans continued to debate the law's effects. John Frémont, one of the first two senators from California, helped defeat a federal bill that would have imposed harsher penalties on those who assisted runaways. And Congress felt growing pressure to calm the situation, including from foreign officials who were horrified by the violence required to sustain slavery in the United States. Black abolitionists denounced the Fugitive Slave Act across Canada, Ireland, and England, intensifying foreign concern over the law. Great Britain and France had abolished slavery in their West Indian colonies and could not support what they saw as extreme policies to keep the institution alive in the United States. Yet southern enslavers refused to compromise further, and increasingly northern abolitionists refused as well.

Pierce Encourages U.S. Expansion

In the presidential election of 1852, the Whigs and the Democrats tried once again to appeal to voters across the North-South divide by running candidates who either skirted the slavery issue or voiced ambiguous views. The Democrats nominated Franklin Pierce of New Hampshire. A northern opponent of abolition, Pierce had served in his state legislature and in Congress from 1833 to 1842. He also fought in the Mexican-American War and rose to brigadier general. The Whigs rejected President Millard Fillmore, who angered many by supporting popular sovereignty and vigorous enforcement of the Fugitive Slave Act. They turned instead to General Winfield Scott of Virginia. General Scott had never expressed any proslavery views and had served with distinction in the war against Mexico. The Whigs thus hoped to gain southern support while maintaining their northern base. The Free-Soil Party, too, hoped to expand its appeal by nominating John Hale, a New Hampshire Democrat.

Franklin Pierce's eventual victory left the Whigs and the Free-Soilers in disarray. Seeking a truly proslavery party, a third of southern Whigs threw their support to the Democrats in the election. Many Democrats who had supported Free-Soilers in 1848 were driven to vote for Pierce by their enthusiasm over the admission of California as a free state. But despite the Democratic triumph, that party also remained fragile. The nation now faced some of its gravest challenges under a president with no firm base of support and a cabinet that included men of widely differing views. When confronted with difficult decisions, Pierce received contradictory advice and often pursued his own expansionist vision.

Early in his administration, Pierce focused on expanding U.S. trade and extending the "civilizing" power of the nation to other parts of the world. Trade with China had declined in the 1840s, but the United States had begun commercial negotiations with Japan in 1846. In July 1853, President Fillmore sent U.S. emissary Commodore Matthew C. Perry, a renowned naval officer and founder of the Naval Engineer Corps, to obtain a mutual trade agreement with Japan. That treaty was signed shortly after Pierce was inaugurated. Over the next four years, Pierce implemented expanded commercial ties and enhanced diplomatic relations with Japan, and the United States supported the island nation against its traditional enemies, China, Russia, and Europe.

Many Americans were also eager to expand U.S. power in the Caribbean and Central America. For decades, U.S. politicians, particularly Southerners, had looked to gain control of Cuba, Mexico, and Nicaragua. A "Young America" movement within the Democratic Party imagined manifest destiny reaching southward as well as westward. Southern planters eager to expand became even more insistent about the ways that enslaved laborers benefited from the supposed care owners took in their spiritual and physical well-being.

In hopes of stirring up rebellious Cubans against Spanish rule, some Democrats joined with private adventurers to send three unauthorized expeditions, known as **filibusters**, to invade Cuba. In 1854 the capture of one of the filibustering ships led to an international incident. Spanish officials confiscated the ship, and southern Democrats urged Pierce to seek an apology and redress from Spain. But many northern Democrats rejected any effort to obtain another slave state, and Pierce was forced to renounce the filibusters.

Other politicians still pressured Spain to sell Cuba to the United States. These included Pierce's secretary of state, William Marcy, and the U.S. ambassador to Great Britain, James Buchanan, as well as ministers to France and Spain. In October 1854 these ministers met in Ostend, Belgium and sent a letter to Pierce urging the conquest of Cuba. When the **Ostend Manifesto** was leaked to the press, Northerners were outraged. They viewed the episode as "a dirty plot" to gain more slave territory and forced Pierce to give up plans to obtain Cuba. In 1855 a private adventurer named William Walker, who had organized four filibusters to Nicaragua, invaded that country and set himself up as ruler. He then invited southern enslavers to come to Nicaragua and establish plantations. Pierce and many Democrats endorsed his plan, but neighboring Hondurans forced Walker from power in 1857 and executed him three years later. Although Pierce's expansionist dreams often failed, his efforts heightened sectional tensions.

REVIEW & RELATE
- What steps did legislators take in the 1840s and early 1850s to resolve the issue of the expansion of slavery? Were they successful?
- How were slavery and American imperialist ambitions intertwined in the 1840s and 1850s?

Sectional Crises Intensify

The political crises of the early 1850s created a lively trade in antislavery literature. This cultural turmoil, combined with the weakness and fragmentation of the existing political parties, helped give rise to the Republican Party in 1854. The Republican Party soon absorbed enough Free-Soilers, Whigs, and northern Democrats to become a major political force. The events that drove these cultural and political developments included the publication of *Uncle Tom's Cabin*, continued challenges to the Fugitive Slave Act, a battle over the admission of Kansas to the Union, and a Supreme Court ruling in the *Dred Scott* case.

Popularizing Antislavery Sentiment

The Fugitive Slave Act forced Northerners to reconsider their role in sustaining the institution of slavery. In 1852, just months before Franklin Pierce was elected president, their concerns were heightened by the publication of the novel **Uncle Tom's Cabin** by Harriet Beecher Stowe. Stowe's father, Lyman Beecher, and brother Henry were among the nation's leading evangelical clergy, and her sister Catharine had opposed Cherokee removal and promoted women's education. Stowe was inspired to write *Uncle Tom's Cabin* by passage of the Fugitive Slave Act in 1850. Published in both serial and book forms, the novel created a national sensation.

Uncle Tom's Cabin built on accounts by former slaves as well as tales gathered by abolitionist lecturers and writers, which gained growing attention in the North. The autobiographies of Frederick Douglass (1845), William Wells Brown (1847), Josiah Henson (1849), and Henry Bibb (1849) set the stage for Stowe's novel. So, too, did the expansion of the antislavery press, which by the 1850s included dozens of newspapers. Antislavery poems and songs also circulated widely and were performed at abolitionist conventions and fund-raising fairs. The daguerreotype, an early form of photography, allowed abolitionists to create and circulate images of leading lecturers, fugitive slaves, and popular antislavery performers. Sojourner Truth created cartes-de-visite images to sell at her lectures, and Frederick Douglass became one of the most photographed individuals in the nineteenth century.

Still, nothing captured the public's attention as did *Uncle Tom's Cabin*. Read by millions in the United States and England and translated into French and German, the book reached a mass audience. Its sentimental portrait of saintly enslaved people and its vivid depiction of cruel masters and overseers offered white Northerners a way to identify with enslaved blacks. Although some African Americans expressed frustration that a white woman's fictional account gained far more readers than their factual narratives, most recognized the book's contribution to the antislavery cause.

Still, the real-life stories of fugitives from bondage could often surpass their fictional counterparts for drama. In May 1854 abolitionists sought to free fugitive Anthony Burns from a Boston courthouse, where his enslaver was attempting to reclaim him. They failed to secure his release, and Burns was soon marched to the docks to be shipped south. Twenty-two companies of state militia held back tens of thousands of angry Bostonians who lined the streets. A year later, supporters purchased Burns's freedom from his master, but the incident raised anguished questions among local residents. In a city that was home to so many intellectual, religious, and abolitionist leaders, Bostonians wondered how they had come so far in aiding and abetting slavery.

The Kansas-Nebraska Act Stirs Dissent

Kansas provided the first test of the effects of *Uncle Tom's Cabin* on northern sentiments toward slavery's expansion. As white Americans displaced Indian nations from their homelands, diverse groups of Indians settled in the northern half of the Louisiana Territory. This unorganized region had once been considered beyond the reach of white settlement, but Democratic senator Stephen Douglas of Illinois was eager to have a transcontinental railroad run through his home state. He needed the federal government to gain control of land along the route he proposed and thus argued for the establishment of a vast Nebraska Territory. But to support his plan, Douglas also needed to convince southern congressmen, who sought a route through their own region. According to the Missouri Compromise, states lying above the southern border of Missouri were automatically free. To gain southern support, Douglas sought to reopen the question of slavery in the territories.

When politicians began discussing further encroachment on unorganized western lands in 1851, Indian Commissioner George Manypenny reminded Congress that "the rights of person or property now pertaining to the Indians in said Territories" were inviolate, and that all lands held by Indians could "constitute no part of the [new] Territories . . . until ceded by treaty or otherwise." Numerous native peoples had been forced into this territory, including the Lakota, Dakota, Cheyenne, Navajo, and Crow. However, pressure for expansion proved unstoppable. By March 1853, Manypenny reported that "fifty-two treaties with various Indian tribes have been entered into. . . . [T]he quantity of land acquired by these treaties. . . is about one hundred and seventy-four millions of acres. . . ." Despite his previous concerns, he now proudly claimed that in "no former equal period of our history have so many treaties been made, or such vast accessions of land obtained."

In January 1854 Douglas introduced the **Kansas-Nebraska Act** to Congress. The act not only extinguished the treaty rights of any tribes remaining in the region but also repealed the Missouri Compromise. Two new territories — Kansas and Nebraska — would be carved out of the unorganized lands, and voters in each would determine whether to enter the nation as a slave or a free state (Map 12.2). The act spurred intense opposition from most Whigs and some northern Democrats who wanted to retain the Missouri Compromise line. Months of fierce debate followed, but the bill was ultimately voted into law.

Passage of the Kansas-Nebraska Act enraged many Northerners who considered the dismantling of the Missouri Compromise a sign of the rising power of the South. They were infuriated that the South — or what some now called the "Slave Power" — had again benefited from northern politicians' willingness to compromise. Although few of these opponents considered the impact of the law on Indians, the act shattered treaty rights protecting a dozen native tribes. These Plains Indians lost half the land they had held by treaty as thousands of settlers swarmed into the newly organized territories. Nor did settlers abide by treaty provisions. The resulting upheaval aided stronger nations. The Lakota, Dakota, Arapaho, and Cheyenne forged an alliance that allowed them to dominate smaller tribes in the region. In 1854–1855, conflicts between white settlers and Indians erupted across the Great Plains. In one instance, an anxious U.S. lieutenant fired on a Brulé (Sioux) man who he accused of stealing a cow. In the resulting exchange of shots, the lieutenant and his men were killed. The U.S. army then sent six hundred troops to retaliate. They killed eighty-five Brulé residents. Incidents such as this triggered cycles of violence in the region for decades.

As tensions escalated across the nation, Americans faced the 1854 congressional elections. The Democrats, increasingly viewed as supporting the priorities of enslavers, lost badly in the North. But the Whig Party also proved weak, having failed to stop the Slave Power from extending its leverage over federal policies. A third party, the American Party, was founded in the early 1850s and attracted native-born workers and Protestant farmers who were drawn to its anti-immigrant and anti-Catholic message. They continued to seek limits on immigrants' political power and

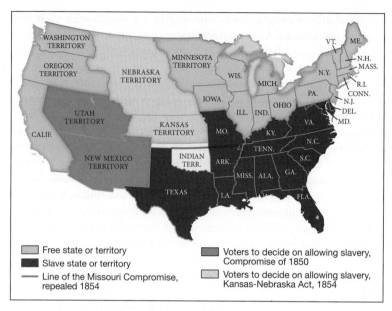

MAP 12.2   Kansas-Nebraska Territory

From 1820 on, Congress attempted to limit sectional conflict. But the Missouri Compromise (1820) and the Compromise of 1850 failed to resolve disagreements over slavery's expansion. The creation of the Kansas and Nebraska territories in 1854 heightened sectional conflict and ensured increased hostilities with Indians in the region.

cultural influence. Responding to these political realignments, another new party, led by antislavery Whigs and Free-Soilers — the **Republican Party** — was founded in the spring of 1854. Among its early members was a Whig politician from Illinois, Abraham Lincoln.

Although established only months before the fall 1854 elections, the Republican Party gained significant support in the Midwest, particularly in state and local campaigns. Meanwhile the American Party gained control of the Massachusetts legislature and nearly captured New York. These victories marked the demise of the Whigs and the Second Party System. Unlike the Whig Party, however, with its national constituency, the Republican Party was rooted solely in the North. Like Free-Soilers, the Republicans argued that slavery should not be extended into new territories. But the Republicans also advocated a program of commercial and industrial development and internal improvements to attract a broader base than earlier antislavery parties. The Republican Party attracted both ardent abolitionists and men whose main concern was keeping western territories open to free white men. This latter group was more than willing to accept slavery where it already existed.

Bleeding Kansas and the Election of 1856

The 1854 congressional elections exacerbated sectional tensions by bringing representatives from a strictly northern party — the Republicans — into Congress. But the conflicts over slavery reached far beyond the nation's capital. After passage of the Kansas-Nebraska Act, advocates and opponents of slavery poured into Kansas in anticipation of a vote on whether the state would enter the Union slave or free.

As Kansas prepared to hold its referendum, settlers continued to arrive daily, making it difficult to determine who was eligible to vote. In 1855 Southerners installed a proslavery government at Shawnee Mission, while abolitionists established a stronghold in Lawrence. Violence erupted when proslavery settlers invaded Lawrence, killing one resident, demolishing newspaper offices, and plundering shops and homes. Fearing that southern settlers in Kansas were better armed than antislavery Northerners in the territory, eastern abolitionists raised funds to ship rifles to Kansas.

In 1856 longtime abolitionist John Brown carried his own rifles to Kansas. Four of his sons already lived in the territory. A deeply religious man, Brown believed in the complete equality of blacks and whites. Brown held views similar to those of David Walker, whose 1829 appeal warned that enslaved people would eventually rise up and claim their freedom by force. To retaliate for proslavery attacks on Lawrence, the Browns and two friends kidnapped five proslavery advocates from their homes along Pottawatomie Creek and hacked them to death. The so-called Pottawatomie Massacre infuriated southern settlers, who then drew up the Lecompton Constitution, which declared Kansas a slave state. President Pierce made his support of the proslavery government clear, but Stephen Douglas publicly criticized his position to great acclaim from Republicans and Democrats. Pierce and Douglas then struggled over control of the Democratic Party. Congress remained divided over the issue or Kansas. While it deliberated, armed battles continued in Kansas. In the first six months of 1856, more than fifty settlers—on both sides of the conflict—were killed in what became known as **Bleeding Kansas**.

Fighting also broke out on the floor of Congress. Republican senator Charles Sumner of Massachusetts delivered an impassioned speech against the continued expansion of the Slave Power. In denouncing "The Crime against Kansas," he launched scathing attacks on planter politicians and specifically claimed that South Carolina senator Andrew Butler had "taken the harlot slavery" as his mistress. Butler's nephew, Preston Brooks, a Democratic member of the House of Representatives, rushed to defend his family's honor. He assaulted Sumner in the Senate chamber, beating him senseless with a cane. Sumner, who never fully recovered from his injuries, was considered a martyr in the North. Meanwhile Brooks was celebrated in the South, where supporters sent him canes decorated with the slogan "Hit him again!"

The presidential election of 1856 began amid an atmosphere poisoned by violence and recrimination. The Democratic Party nominated James Buchanan of Pennsylvania, a proslavery advocate. Western hero John C. Frémont headed the Republican Party ticket. The American Party, in its final presidential contest, selected former president Millard Fillmore as its candidate. The strength of nativism in politics was waning, however, and Fillmore won only the state of Maryland. Meanwhile Frémont attracted cheering throngs as he traveled across the West and North. Large numbers of women turned out to see Jessie Frémont, the first presidential candidate's wife to play a significant role in a campaign. Frémont carried most of the North and the West. Buchanan captured the South along with Pennsylvania, Indiana, and Illinois. Although Buchanan won only 45.2 percent of the popular vote, he received a comfortable majority in the electoral college, securing his victory. The nation was becoming increasingly divided along sectional lines, and President Buchanan would do little to resolve these differences.

The *Dred Scott* Decision

Just two days after Buchanan's inauguration, the Supreme Court finally announced its decision in the *Dred Scott* case (see "Comparing American Histories"). Led by Chief Justice Roger Taney, a proslavery Southerner, the majority ruled that an enslaved person was not a citizen and therefore could not sue in court. Indeed, Taney claimed that black men had no rights that a white man was bound to respect. The ruling annulled Dred Scott's suit and meant that he and his wife remained enslaved. But the ruling went further. The **Dred Scott decision** declared that Congress had no constitutional authority to exclude slavery from any territory, thereby nullifying the Missouri Compromise and any future effort to restrict slavery's expansion. Many Northerners were outraged, now convinced that a Slave Power conspiracy had taken hold of the federal government, including the judiciary.

In 1858, when Stephen Douglas faced reelection to the U.S. Senate, the Republican Party nominated Abraham Lincoln, a successful lawyer from Springfield, Illinois, to oppose him. The candidates participated in seven debates in which they explained their positions on slavery in the wake of the *Dred Scott* decision. Pointing to the landmark ruling, Lincoln asked Douglas how he could favor popular sovereignty, which allowed residents to keep slavery out of a territory, and yet support the *Dred Scott* decision, which protected slavery in all territories. Douglas claimed that if residents did not adopt local legislation to protect enslavers' property, they could thereby exclude slavery for all practical purposes. At the same time, he accused Lincoln of advocating "negro equality," a position that went well beyond his opponent's views. Lincoln did support economic opportunity for free blacks, but not political or social equality. Nor did he politically support the abolition of slavery. Still, the Republican candidate did declare that "this government cannot endure permanently half slave and half free. . . . It will become all one thing or all the other."

The Lincoln-Douglas debates attracted national attention, but the Illinois legislature selected the state's senator. Narrowly controlled by Democrats, it returned Douglas to Washington. Although the senator retained his seat, he was concerned by how far the Democratic Party had tilted toward the South. Indeed, the Democratic Party was splitting into southern and northern wings, and the nation was on the verge of civil war.

| REVIEW & RELATE | • What factors contributed to the spread of antislavery sentiment in the North beyond committed abolitionists? |
| | • How did the violence in Kansas and the *Dred Scott* decision reflect and intensify the growing sectional divide within the nation? |

From Sectional Crisis to Southern Secession

During the 1850s, a profusion of abolitionist lectures, conventions, and literature swelled antislavery sentiment in the North as did exhibits and images of instruments of torture used by enslavers. Mainstream newspapers regularly covered rescues of fugitives, the bloody crisis in Kansas, and political and judicial debates over slavery. Republican candidates in state and local elections also kept concerns about slavery's expansion and southern power alive. News of an uprising of Mexicans in Texas in summer 1859 disturbed some Americans, but nothing riveted the nation's attention as much as John Brown's raid on the federal arsenal at Harpers Ferry, Virginia that October. Less than a year later, Republican Abraham Lincoln captured the White House. In the wake of his election, seven southern states seceded from the Union. Lincoln tested their resolve by sending supplies to Fort Sumter in Charleston harbor, leading to the first battle of what would become the Civil War.

Cortina's War and John Brown's Raid

While Americans in the eastern United States debated issues of expansion and slavery, those living on lands acquired through the Mexican-American War confronted their own racial conflicts. In 1848, Mexicans living in the northern regions of their country suddenly became citizens of the United States. In the following years, many Mexicans were deprived of their land and legal rights, assaulted, incarcerated, and murdered. Juan Nepomuceno Cortina was born in 1824 to a wealthy Mexican family living south of the Rio Grande River. In his early twenties he fought with the Mexican Army against the United States. After the U.S. victory, he watched his family and his neighbors in Brownsville (now Texas) cheated out of land and cattle, reduced to second-class citizenship, and mistreated by newly appointed sheriffs and the Texas Rangers. In July 1859, after watching one of his Mexican farmhands being brutalized by a U.S. Marshall, Cortina ordered the Marshall to stop. When he did not, Cortina shot him in the shoulder. The conflict escalated, and Cortina organized a group of Mexicans to launch a successful raid on Brownsville. In September, they proclaimed the city the Republic of the Rio Grande and raised the Mexican flag.

U.S. residents formed an armed unit, the Brownsville Tigers, to retake the city. Cortina's men retreated into Mexico but continued to raid farms and homes in Texas. As battles continued, Cortina called on Texas Governor Sam Houston to protect the rights of Mexican residents. To Mexicans, Cortina proclaimed: "The voice of revelation whispers to me that to me is entrusted the work of breaking the chains of your slavery." Eventually, the Texas Rangers and U.S. Army joined the fight. By late December, they forced Cortina's troops deeper into Mexico though sporadic battles continued through winter 1860. Despite his defeat, Cortina remained a folk hero to Mexicans in Texas, served as governor of a northern Mexican state, and continued to lead cross-border raids on Anglo-American ranchers for the next fifteen years.

John Brown was also committed to changing society through force of arms. After joining the bloody battles in Kansas, Brown became more convinced that direct action was the only answer. Following the Pottawatomie killings, he went into hiding and reappeared back east, where he hoped to initiate an uprising to overthrow slavery. Brown focused his efforts on the federal arsenal in **Harpers Ferry, Virginia**. With eighteen followers—five African Americans and thirteen whites, including three of his sons—Brown planned to capture the arsenal and distribute arms to enslaved people in the surrounding area. He hoped this action would ignite a rebellion that would destroy the plantation system throughout the South. Brown tried to convince Frederick Douglass to join the venture, but Douglass considered it a foolhardy plan. Brown did manage to persuade a small circle of white abolitionists to bankroll the effort.

John Brown, c. 1847 Black portraitist Augustus Washington took this early daguerreotype of John Brown. A decade before he joined his sons in Kansas, Brown raises his hand, pledging to dedicate his life to the destruction of slavery. He holds the flag of the "Subterranean Pass Way," a militant version of the underground rail road Brown created in New York's far northern woodlands. Smithsonian Institution Libraries/Science Source

On the night of October 16, 1859, Brown and his men kidnapped some leading townsmen and seized the arsenal. Local residents were stunned but managed to alert authorities, and state militia swarmed into Harpers Ferry. The next day, federal troops arrived, led by Colonel Robert E. Lee. With troops flooding into the town, Brown and his men were soon under siege, trapped in the arsenal. Fourteen rebels were killed, including two of Brown's sons. On October 18, Brown and three others were captured.

As word of the daring raid spread, Brown was hailed as a hero by many devoted abolitionists and depicted as a madman by southern planters. Southern whites were sure the raid was part of a widespread conspiracy led by power-hungry abolitionists. Federal authorities moved quickly to quell enslavers' fears and end the episode. Brown rejected his lawyer's advice to plead insanity, and a local jury found him guilty of murder, criminal conspiracy, and treason. He was hanged on December 2, 1859.

John Brown's execution unleashed a massive outpouring of grief, anger, and uncertainty across the North. Abolitionists organized parades, demonstrations, bonfires, and tributes to the newest abolitionist martyr. Even many Quakers and other pacifists viewed John Brown as a hero for giving his life in the cause of emancipation. But most northern politicians and editors condemned the raid as a rash act that could only intensify sectional tensions.

Among southern whites, fear and panic greeted the raid on Harpers Ferry, and the execution of John Brown did little to quiet their outrage. By this time, southern intellectuals had developed a sophisticated proslavery argument that, to them, demonstrated the benefits of bondage for African Americans and its superiority to the northern system of wage labor. They argued that enslavers provided care and guidance for blacks from birth to death. Considering blacks too childlike to fend for themselves, proslavery advocates saw no problem with the enslaved providing labor and obedience in return for their care. Such arguments failed to convince abolitionists, who highlighted the brutality, sexual abuse, and shattered families that marked the system of bondage. In this context, Americans on both sides of the sectional divide considered the 1860 presidential election critical to the nation's future.

The Election of 1860

Brown's hanging set the tone for the 1860 presidential campaign. The Republicans met in Chicago five months after Brown's execution and distanced themselves from the more radical wing of the abolitionist movement. The party platform condemned both John Brown and southern "Border Ruffians," who initiated the violence in Kansas. The platform accepted slavery where it already existed, but continued to advocate its exclusion from western territories. Finally, the platform insisted on the need for federally funded internal improvements and protective tariffs. The Republicans nominated Abraham Lincoln as their candidate for president. Recognizing the impossibility of gaining significant votes in the South, the party focused instead on winning large majorities in the Northeast and Midwest.

The Democrats met in Charleston, South Carolina. Stephen Douglas was the leading candidate. However when Mississippi senator Jefferson Davis introduced a resolution to protect slavery in the territories, Douglas's northern supporters rejected it, heightening southern concerns about Douglas's commitment to the institution. President Buchanan also came out against Douglas, and the Democratic convention ended without choosing a candidate. Instead, various factions met separately. A group of largely northern Democrats met in Baltimore and nominated Douglas. Southern Democrats selected John Breckinridge, the vice president, an enslaver, and an advocate of annexing Cuba. The Constitutional Union Party, comprised mainly of former southern Whigs, advocated "no political principle other than the Constitution of the country, the union of the states, and the enforcement of the laws." Its members nominated Senator John Bell of Tennessee.

Although Lincoln won barely 40 percent of the popular vote, he carried a clear majority in the electoral college. With the admission of Minnesota and Oregon to the Union in 1858 and 1859, free states outnumbered slave states eighteen to fifteen, and Lincoln won all but one of them. Lincoln did not win a single Southern electoral vote. However, since free states were more populous than slave states, they controlled a larger number of electoral votes. Douglas ran second to Lincoln in the popular vote, but Bell and Breckinridge captured more electoral votes than Douglas because of their success in the South. Despite a deeply divided electorate, Lincoln became president (Map 12.3).

Although many abolitionists were wary of the Republicans, who were willing to leave slavery alone where it existed, most were nonetheless relieved at Lincoln's victory and hoped he would become more sympathetic to their views once in office. Meanwhile, southern whites, especially those in the deep South, were furious that a Republican had won the White House without carrying a single southern state.

From Secession to War

On December 20, 1860, six weeks after Lincoln's election, the legislature of South Carolina announced that because "a sectional party" had engineered "the election of a man to the high office of President of the United States whose opinions and

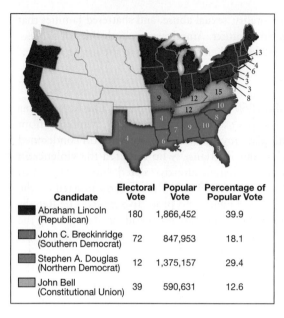

MAP 12.3   The Election of 1860
Four candidates vied for the presidency in 1860, and the voters split along clearly sectional lines. Although Stephen Douglas ran a vigorous campaign and gained votes in all regions of the country, he won a majority only in Missouri. Lincoln triumphed in the North and far West, and Breckinridge in most of the South.

Candidate	Electoral Vote	Popular Vote	Percentage of Popular Vote
Abraham Lincoln (Republican)	180	1,866,452	39.9
John C. Breckinridge (Southern Democrat)	72	847,953	18.1
Stephen A. Douglas (Northern Democrat)	12	1,375,157	29.4
John Bell (Constitutional Union)	39	590,631	12.6

purposes are hostile to slavery," the people of South Carolina dissolve their union with "the other states of North America." In early 1861, Mississippi, Florida, Alabama, Georgia, Louisiana, and Texas followed suit. Representatives from these states met on February 8 in Montgomery, Alabama, where they adopted a provisional constitution, elected Jefferson Davis as their president, and established the **Confederate States of America** (Map 12.4).

President Buchanan did nothing to stop the secession movement. When the crisis occurred, Buchanan listened to the slave owners in his cabinet and other southern sympathizers living in Washington, D.C. Following Lincoln's election, he claimed that the federal government had no right to intervene when southern states seceded. Some Northerners were shocked as Deep South states seceded, but others supported their right to leave. Many believed those states would return to the Union when they realized they could not survive on their own. In addition, with Virginia and other Upper South slave states still part of the nation, the secession movement seemed doomed to failure. Indeed, Northerners applauded the admission of Kansas as a free state in January 1861 just as the first southern states left the Union.

In the midst of the crisis, Kentucky senator John Crittenden proposed a compromise that gained significant support. Congress approved the first part of his plan, which called for a constitutional amendment to protect slavery from federal interference in any state where it already existed. But the second part of the **Crittenden plan** would extend the Missouri Compromise line (latitude 36°30′) to the California border and bar slavery north of that line. South of that line, however, slavery would be protected, including in any territories "acquired hereafter." Fearing that passage would encourage southern planters to again seek territory in Cuba, Mexico, or Central America, Republicans rejected the proposal. Compromise seemed increasingly unlikely.

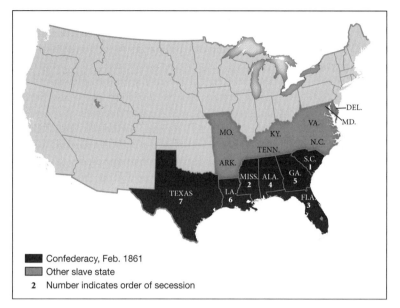

MAP 12.4　The Original Confederacy

Seven states in the Lower South seceded from the United States and formed the Confederate States of America in February 1861. While the original Confederacy was too limited in population and resources to defend itself against the U.S. government, its leaders hoped that other slave states would soon join them.

Confederate secessionists accused the federal government of failing to implement fully the Fugitive Slave Act and the *Dred Scott* decision. They were convinced that a Republican administration would do little to support southern interests. White Southerners also feared that Republican rule might inspire a mass uprising of slaves. Secession allowed them to maintain control over the South's black population.

Still, many legislators in the Upper South hoped a compromise could be reached, and Lincoln hoped to woo Confederates back into the Union. Most northern merchants, manufacturers, and bankers approved, wanting to maintain their economic ties to southern planters. Yet Lincoln also realized he must demonstrate Union strength to curtail further secessions. He focused on **Fort Sumter** in South Carolina's Charleston harbor, where a small Union garrison was running low on food and medicine. On April 8, 1861, Lincoln dispatched ships to the fort but promised to use force only if Confederates blocked his effort to send supplies.

The Confederate government now had to choose. It could attack the Union vessels and bear responsibility for starting a war or permit a "foreign power" to maintain a fort in its territory. President Davis and his advisers chose the aggressive course, demanding Fort Sumter's immediate and unconditional surrender. The commanding officer refused, and on April 12 Confederate guns opened fire. Two days later, Fort Sumter surrendered. On April 15, Lincoln called for 75,000 volunteers to put down the southern insurrection.

Whites in the Upper South then reconsidered secession. Some small farmers and landless whites were drawn to Republican promises of free labor and free soil and remained suspicious of the goals and power of secessionist planters. Yet the majority of southern whites, rich and poor, feared that Republicans would free the enslaved and introduce racial amalgamation, the mixing of whites and blacks, in the nation.

Lincoln used the powers of his office to keep border states that still allowed slavery—Maryland, Delaware, Missouri, and Kentucky—in the Union. He waived the right of habeas corpus (which protects citizens against arbitrary arrest and detention), jailed secessionists, arrested state legislators, and limited freedom of the press. Still, four other slave states—North Carolina, Virginia, Tennessee, and Arkansas—seceded. Virginia, with its strategic location near the nation's capital, was by far the most significant. In early April, Virginia legislators had opposed secession by a significant margin. After Fort Sumter, they reversed course, and seceded. The Confederate capital was soon moved to Richmond, which was also home to the South's largest iron manufacturer, critical for producing weapons and munitions.

At the same time, the firing on Fort Sumter prompted most Northerners to line up behind Lincoln's call to arms. Manufacturers and merchants rushed to support the president, while northern workers, including immigrants, responded to the call for volunteers. They assumed that the Union, with its greater resources and manpower, could quickly set the nation right. New York editor Horace Greeley proclaimed, "Jeff Davis and Co. will be swingin' from the battlements at Washington at least by the 4th of July."

| **REVIEW & RELATE** | • How and why did John Brown's raid on Harpers Ferry move the country closer to civil war? |
| | • How did Lincoln's election and the federal effort to resupply Fort Sumter affect southern politicians attitudes toward secession? |

Conclusion: A Nation Divided

Dred Scott did not live to see Abraham Lincoln take the oath of office in March 1861. Following the Supreme Court's 1857 ruling, Scott was returned to Irene Emerson, who had married abolitionist Calvin Chaffee. Unwilling to be the owner of the most well-known slave in America, Chaffee quickly returned Dred Scott and his family to his original owners, the Blow family. The Blows then freed the Scotts. For the next year and a half, before dying of tuberculosis, Dred Scott lived as a free man. Although Harriet and their daughters lived to see slavery abolished, in the spring of 1861 they could not imagine how that goal would be reached.

In 1860 John C. Frémont believed the nation was headed to war; and he was willing, once again, to serve a country he had helped expand. His work as a surveyor and soldier opened new territories to white settlement, and the gold rush then ensured California's admission to the Union. Yet what Frémont and others considered the nation's manifest destiny decimated Indian nations as well as the property, civil rights, and lives of many Mexicans. Despite the efforts of the Comanche and other tribes to fend off white encroachment, the U.S. government and white settlers claimed more and more territory. It was debates over the future of these western territories that heightened conflicts over slavery.

While some Confederate enslavers hoped to expand the nation into Cuba, Nicaragua, and other southern regions, Northerners fought all such schemes. Outraged by the Fugitive Slave Act and appalled by Bleeding Kansas, militant activists applauded John Brown's raid at Harpers Ferry. As important, more moderate Northerners increasingly opposed the expansion of slavery and voted for Lincoln in 1860. His election inspired seven southern states to secede, and his efforts to resupply Fort Sumter brought the nation face-to-face with civil war.

Chapter 12 Review

KEY TERMS

Oregon Trail, 302
gold rush, 303
Compromise of 1850, 308
Fugitive Slave Act of 1850, 308
filibusters, 311
Ostend Manifesto, 311
Uncle Tom's Cabin, 312
Kansas-Nebraska Act, 313

Republican Party, 314
Bleeding Kansas, 315
Dred Scott decision, 316
Harpers Ferry, Virginia, 317
Confederate States of America, 320
Crittenden plan, 320
Fort Sumter, 321

REVIEW & RELATE

1. Why did Americans go west in the 1830s and 1840s, and what was the journey like?
2. What groups competed for land and resources in the West? How did disease, drought, and violence shape this competition?
3. What steps did legislators take in the 1840s and early 1850s to resolve the issue of the expansion of slavery? Were they successful?
4. How were slavery and American imperialist ambitions intertwined in the 1840s and 1850s?
5. What factors contributed to the spread of antislavery sentiment in the North beyond committed abolitionists?
6. How did the violence in Kansas and the *Dred Scott* decision reflect and intensify the growing sectional divide within the nation?
7. How and why did John Brown's raid on Harpers Ferry move the country closer to civil war?
8. How did Lincoln's election and the federal effort to resupply Fort Sumter affect southern politicians' attitudes toward secession?

TIMELINE OF EVENTS

1842	• John C. Frémont leads expedition along the Oregon Trail
1848	• Gold discovered in California
1850	• Compromise of 1850
	• Fugitive Slave Act
1852	• Harriet Beecher Stowe publishes *Uncle Tom's Cabin*
1854	• U.S.-Japanese treaty allows for mutual trading
	• Republican Party founded
	• Kansas-Nebraska Act
1854–1858	• Period of violence in Bleeding Kansas
1857	• *Dred Scott* case
1858	• Lincoln-Douglas debates
1859	• Cortina War in Texas
	• John Brown's raid on Harpers Ferry
November 1860	• Abraham Lincoln elected president
December 1860	• South Carolina secedes from the Union
January 1861	• Mississippi, Florida, Alabama, Georgia, Louisiana, and Texas secede
February 1861	• Confederate States of America established
March 1861	• Lincoln inaugurated as president
April 1861	• Confederate attack on Fort Sumter
	• Virginia secedes

13

Civil War

1861–1865

LEARNING OBJECTIVES

After reading this chapter you will be able to:

- Explain why southern states seceded and describe the advantages and disadvantages that marked the Confederacy and the Union at the beginning of the Civil War.

- Describe the changing roles of African Americans, free and enslaved, in the war and the growing sentiment for emancipation in the North.

- Evaluate how the war changed northern and southern political priorities and the lives of soldiers and civilians.

- Identify turning points in the Civil War, including key battles in the eastern and western theaters of war, and explain the factors that led to Union victory and the abolition of slavery.

COMPARING AMERICAN HISTORIES

Born into slavery in 1818, **Frederick Douglass** became a celebrated orator, editor, and abolitionist in the 1840s. In 1845 Douglass published his autobiography, *Narrative of the Life of Frederick Douglass*, which described his enslavement in Maryland, his defiance against his masters, and his eventual escape to New York in 1838 with the help of Anna Murray, a free black servant.

After marrying in New York, Frederick and Anna moved to New Bedford, Massachusetts, and changed their last name to Douglass to avoid capture. In 1841 the American Anti-Slavery Society hired Frederick to present his vivid tale of enslaved life to public audiences. Four years later, Douglass launched a British lecture tour that attracted enthusiastic audiences. Supporters in Britain purchased his freedom, and Douglass returned to Massachusetts a free man in 1847.

Late that year, Frederick moved to Rochester, New York with Anna and their children to launch his abolitionist paper, the *North Star*. Over the next four years, Douglass gradually shifted his support from the Garrisonians to political abolitionism. When war erupted in April 1861, he lobbied President Lincoln relentlessly to make emancipation a war aim.

Initially Douglass feared that Lincoln was more committed to reconstituting the Union than abolishing slavery. But when the president issued the Emancipation Proclamation in January 1863, Douglass spoke enthusiastically on its behalf. He also argued that it was essential for black men to serve in the Union army. When African Americans were finally allowed to join in 1862–1863, Douglass helped recruit volunteers but he later protested discrimination against black troops and the denial of black civil rights.

Like Douglass, Rose O'Neal was born on a Maryland plantation, but she was white and free. Her father was John O'Neal, a planter who was killed in 1817 when Rose was about four. In her teens, she and her sister moved to Washington, D.C., where their aunt ran a fashionable boardinghouse. Her boarders included John C. Calhoun, whose states' rights views Rose eagerly embraced. Rose was welcomed into elite social circles and in 1835 married Virginian Robert Greenhow, who worked for the State Department.

Rose O'Neal Greenhow quickly became a favorite Washington hostess, entertaining congressmen, cabinet ministers, and foreign diplomats. Ardent proslavery expansionists, the Greenhows supported efforts to acquire Cuba and expand slavery into western territories. When Robert died in 1854, Rose and their four children remained in D.C. and continued to entertain powerful political leaders.

In May 1861, as the Civil War commenced, a U.S. army captain about to join the Confederate cause recruited Greenhow to head an espionage ring in Washington, D.C. With her close ties to southern sympathizers in the capital, Greenhow gathered intelligence on Union plans. Although she initially avoided suspicion, by August 1861 Greenhow was investigated and placed under house arrest. After continuing to smuggle out letters, she was sent to the Old Capitol Prison in January 1862. When Greenhow again managed to transmit information, she was exiled to Richmond, where Confederate president Jefferson Davis hailed her as a hero.

COMPARING THE AMERICAN HISTORIES of Frederick Douglass and Rose O'Neal Greenhow illustrates the ways that Americans, black and white, northern and southern, men and women, were shaped by and shaped the war that followed the firing on Fort Sumter. They were among hundreds of thousands of Americans who saw the war as a means to achieve their goals: a free nation, a haven for slavery, or a reunited country. Although the Confederacy launched the war, it lagged behind the Union in population, industrial and agricultural production, and railroad lines. These differences became more important as the war unfolded. Initially, however, skilled officers and knowledge of the southern terrain benefited the Confederate army as white, American Indian, and Mexican American men chose sides. On the home front, North and South, hundreds of thousands of Americans labored on farms and in factories, hospitals, and burgeoning government offices to support the war effort. After 1862, tens of thousands of African Americans joined the Union army and navy, and growing numbers of women of all races labored as cooks, laundresses, nurses, and even soldiers. The next year, the Emancipation Proclamation ensured that a Union victory would eradicate slavery. As the war dragged on, antiwar protests erupted North and South, fueled by inflation, conscription acts, and mounting casualties. Finally in 1865, the greater resources of the North, complemented by General Ulysses S. Grant's hard war strategy, led to Union victory and the final abolition of slavery.

The Nation at War, 1861–1862

When southern troops fired on northern ships seeking to resupply Fort Sumter, civil war finally erupted. The Union and the Confederacy faced very different tasks in the war. The South had to defend its territory and force the federal government to halt military action. The North had a more complicated challenge. Initially, northern political leaders believed that enslavers mainly drove secession. Lincoln and his supporters had hoped that early Union victories combined with battle deaths and property destruction would lead most southern whites to embrace reconciliation. However, this plan depended on early Union victories. Instead Confederates won early battles, and the North was forced to invade the South and isolate it from potential allies. As the conflict escalated in 1861 and 1862, both the Union and the Confederacy confronted the costs of war as well as conflicts over its meaning. Should the Union not only seek to defeat the South but also to abolish slavery? How could the Confederacy maintain the system of slavery in the midst of wartime mobilization? And how would Indians, African Americans, Mexican Americans, and immigrants envision their part in the Civil War?

Both Sides Prepare for War

At the onset of the war, the Union held a decided advantage in resources and population. The Union states held more than 60 percent of the U.S. population, and the Confederate population included several million enslaved blacks. Not only would enslaved men not be armed for combat, but some men and women would also use the disruptions of war to claim their freedom. The Union also far outstripped the Confederacy in manufacturing and even led the South in agricultural production. The North's many miles of railroad track ensured greater ease in moving troops and supplies. And the Union could launch far more ships to blockade southern ports (Figure 13.1).

Yet Union forces were less prepared for war than the Confederates, who had been organizing troops and gathering munitions for months. To match their efforts, Winfield Scott, general in chief of the U.S. army, told Lincoln he would need at least 300,000 men committed to serve for two or three years. Scott believed that massing

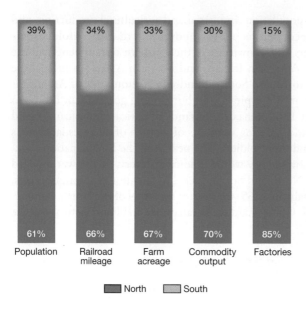

FIGURE 13.1
Economies of the North and South, 1860
This figure provides graphic testimony to the enormous advantages in resources the North held on the eve of the Civil War. The North led the South in population, farm acreage, and railroad mileage as well as factories and commodity output. Over four years of war, how might the differences in each area affect the ability of the Union and the Confederacy to pursue their objectives?
Source: Data from Stanley Engerman, "The Economic Impact of the Civil War," in *The Reinterpretation of American Economic History*, ed. Robert W. Fogel and Stanley Engerman (New York: Harper and Row, 1971).

such huge numbers of soldiers would force the Confederacy to negotiate a peace. But fearing to unnerve Northerners, the president asked for only 75,000 volunteers for three months. Moreover, rather than forming a powerful national army led by seasoned officers, Lincoln left recruitment, organization, and training largely to the states. The result was disorganization and the appointment of officers based more on political connections than military expertise.

Confederate leaders also initially relied on state militia units and volunteers, but they prepared for a prolonged war from the start. Before the firing on Fort Sumter, President Davis signed up 100,000 volunteers for a year's service. Moreover, the labor provided by enslaved workers allowed a large proportion of white working-age men to volunteer for military service without harming southern agricultural production, at least initially. And Southerners were likely to be fighting mainly on home territory, where they had expert knowledge of the terrain. When the final four states joined the Confederacy, the southern army also gained important military leadership. It ultimately recruited 280 West Point graduates, including Robert E. Lee, Thomas "Stonewall" Jackson, James Longstreet, and others who had proved their mettle in the Mexican-American War.

The South's advantages were apparent in the first major battle of the war though Confederate troops were also aided by information on Union plans sent by Rose Greenhow. When 30,000 Union troops marched on northern Virginia on July 21, 1861, Confederate forces were ready. At the **Battle of Bull Run** (or **Manassas**), later known as the First Battle of Bull Run, 22,000 Confederates repelled the Union attack. Civilians from Washington who traveled to the battle site to view the combat had to flee for their lives to escape Confederate artillery.

Despite Union defeats at Bull Run and at Wilson's Creek, Missouri that August, the Confederate army did not launch major strikes against Union forces. Meanwhile the Union navy began blockading the South's deep-water ports. By the time the armies settled into winter camps in 1861–1862, both sides had come to realize that the war was likely to be a long and costly struggle.

Wartime Roles of African Americans, Indians, and Mexican Americans

The outbreak of war intensified debates over abolition. Some 225,000 African Americans lived in the free states, and many offered their services in an effort to end slavery. African American leaders in Cleveland proclaimed, "Today, as in the times of '76, we are ready to go forth and do battle in the common cause of our country." But Secretary of War Simon Cameron had no intention of calling up black soldiers.

Northern optimism about a quick victory contributed to the rejection of African American volunteers. Union leaders feared that whites would not enlist if they had to serve alongside blacks. In addition, Lincoln and his advisers were initially wary of letting a war to preserve the Union become a war against slavery, and they feared that any further threat to slavery might drive the four slave states that remained in the Union into the Confederacy. This political strategy, however, depended on quick and overwhelming victories. With most U.S. soldiers posted on the western frontier and a third of officers joining the Confederacy, early victories were few. Nonetheless a rush of volunteers allowed Union troops to push into Virginia while the Union navy captured crucial islands along the Confederate coast.

Regardless of official policy, wherever Union forces appeared, enslaved southerners considered freedom a possibility. Enslaved workers living near battle sites circulated information on Union troop movements. Virginia enslavers, increasingly worried about losing their workers, began sending them to more distant plantations or Confederate army units. Still, some enslaved people fled and headed to Union camps. Many enslavers tracked fugitives behind Union lines and demanded their return. Some Union commanders denied fugitives entrance to their camps or returned them to their masters. But a few Union officers recognized the fugitives' practical value. Enslaved men and women knew the local geography and could provide critical labor that freed white soldiers to fight. In addition, their loss drained the Confederate labor supply. In May 1861 at Fort Monroe, Virginia, Union General Benjamin Butler offered fugitive slaves military protection and asked his superiors in Washington to develop a general policy on the matter.

Lincoln endorsed Butler's proposal that fugitive slaves be accepted into Union camps and allowed to work there. In August 1861, Congress passed a Confiscation Act that proclaimed that any owner whose enslaved workers were used by the Confederate army would lose all claim to them. The act thus recognized fugitives as **contraband** of war, that is property forfeited by Confederates' act of rebellion. Yet the act did not free these fugitives but rather placed them under Union protection.

This allowed the Union to strike at the institution of slavery without proclaiming a general emancipation that might prompt those border states where slavery remained legal to secede. Indeed, some Union officers in border states continued to return fugitives to their enslavers despite passage of the Confiscation Act. Although the act was far from a clear-cut declaration of freedom, it spurred the hopes of northern abolitionists and enslaved southerners.

WeeJukeKah/James Bird, 1900 This studio portrait of Civil War veteran and scout WeeJukeKah was taken in Black River Falls, Wisconsin, home of his Ho-Chunk (Winnebago) tribe. He wears a suit and a U.S. Army hat with two crossed arrows, which indicate that he was part of Company A of the Omaha Scouts, a group of 72 Ho-Chunk soldiers led by 6 white officers. Charles Van Schaick/Wisconsin Historical Society/Getty Images

While Northerners continued to debate African Americans' role in the war effort, the Union army recruited a wide array of other ethnic and racial groups, including American Indians. Unlike blacks, however, Indians did not all support the Union. The Comanche negotiated with both Union and Confederate agents while raiding the Texas frontier for horses and cattle. The Confederacy also gained significant support from slaveholding Indians who had earlier been removed from the Southeast. The Cherokee split over the war as they had over removal. General Stand Watie led a pan-Indian force into battle for the Confederates. Although John Ross initially joined the Confederates, he later led a group of Cherokee into Union army ranks alongside the Osage, Delaware, Seneca, and other Indian nations. Ely Parker, a Seneca sachem and engineer, became a lieutenant colonel in the Union army, serving with General Ulysses S. Grant.

Indians played crucial roles in a number of important early battles, particularly on the Confederate side. Cherokee and Seminole warriors fought valiantly with Confederates at the Battle of Pea Ridge in Arkansas in March 1862, but were defeated by a smaller but better supplied Union force. In August 1862 Indians contributed to the Confederate victory at the Second Battle of Bull Run and the following month participated in the bloodiest single day of battle in U.S. history at Antietam (Sharpsburg). That same August, starving Dakota warriors whose treaty rights were violated and annuity payments withheld attacked white traders, settlers, and soldiers. In the largest native uprising in U.S. history, the Dakota killed hundreds of settlers. An unknown number of Dakota were killed by U.S. troops. When the army regained control in October, the Minnesota Governor sought to execute 303 Dakota prisoners, some of whom had opposed the uprising. President Lincoln intervened, sparing the lives of 265 Dakota. Thirty-eight others were hung.

Mexican Americans and Tejanos faced difficult choices when recruited by Confederate and Union officers. In May 1861, Juan Nepomuceno Cortina, whose Tejano and Mexican troops had earlier fought Anglo Texans, aided the Union at the Battle of Zapata but were defeated by the 33rd Texas Confederate Cavalry. The 33rd was led by Mexican American Captain Santos Benavides, who had also fought against Apaches and other Indians. Cortina retreated into Mexico but continued to fight against Confederate soldiers and local militias along the Texas frontier while Captain

Benavides sought to recapture fugitive slaves in Mexico. Benavides also secured passage of a huge cotton shipment to a Mexican port after the U.S. Navy blockaded most southern ports. The sale of this cotton was crucial to the Confederate Treasury.

Hoping to gain control of the West's gold and silver mines, New Mexican Confederates launched an attack on Glorieta Pass, near Santa Fe, in March 1862. But a Union troop composed of Colorado miners ended that Confederate dream. New Mexico was home to many Union units, including the New Mexico Volunteer Infantry. Its 157 Mexican American officers comprised the most in any single unit fighting for the Union. It was led by Lieutenant Colonel Diego Archuleta, who was swiftly promoted to brigadier general.

While both Union and Confederate armies recruited American Indian and Mexican American regiments, African Americans were initially barred from enlisting as soldiers on either side. However, the constant call for black enlistment by Frederick Douglass and other leading abolitionists helped transform the attitudes of northern whites. So, too, did a series of Union military defeats. In spring 1862, Confederate general Stonewall Jackson won a series of stunning victories against three Union armies in Virginia's Shenandoah Valley. That June and July, General Robert E. Lee fought Union forces under General George B. McClellan to a standstill in the Seven Days Battle near Richmond. Then in August, Lee, Jackson, and General James Longstreet joined together to defeat Union troops at the Second Battle of Bull Run (Map 13.1).

MAP 13.1   Early Civil War Battles, 1861–1862
In 1861 and 1862, the Confederate army stunned Union forces with a series of dramatic victories in Virginia, Missouri, and Texas. However, the Union army won a crucial victory at Antietam (Sharpsburg); gained control of Confederate territory in Tennessee, Arkansas, and Mississippi; fended off Confederate troops in New Mexico Territory; and established a successful blockade of Confederate ports.

As the war turned against the North, the North turned against slavery. In April 1862 Congress had approved a measure to abolish slavery in the District of Columbia, symbolizing this significant shift in Union sentiment. During that bloody summer, Congress passed a second confiscation act, declaring that the enslaved people of anyone who supported the Confederacy should be "forever free of their servitude, and not again held as slaves." In July Congress also approved a militia act that allowed African Americans to serve in "any military or naval service for which they may be found competent."

Support for the 1862 militia act built on the lobbying of black leaders as well as the testimony of Union soldiers. In April 1862 a Union blockade led to the capture of New Orleans, while the **Battle of Shiloh** in Tennessee provided the army entrée to the Mississippi valley. There Union troops came face-to-face with slavery. Few of these soldiers were abolitionists, but many were shocked by what they saw, including instruments of torture. One Union soldier reported he had seen "enough of the horror of slavery to make one an Abolitionist forever." In addition, enslaved blacks provided important intelligence to northern officers, making clear their value to the Union effort.

Whether in victory or defeat, rising death tolls also increased support for African American enlistment. The Battle of Shiloh was the bloodiest battle in American history to that point. Earlier battles had resulted in a few hundred or even a few thousand casualties, but with more than 23,000 casualties, Shiloh raised the carnage to a new level. As the war continued, such brutal battles became routine. The Union army would need every available man—white, black, Indian, and Mexican American—to sustain its effort against the Confederates.

Indian and Mexican American regiments had already proven themselves in battle. African Americans followed suit. In October 1862 a group of black soldiers in the First Kansas Colored Volunteers repulsed Confederates at a battle in Missouri. In the South, white abolitionists serving as Union officers organized former slaves into units like the First South Carolina Volunteers in January 1863. A few months later, another black regiment—the Massachusetts Fifty-fourth—attracted recruits from across the North, including Frederick Douglass's three sons. For the next two years, tens of thousands of African American soldiers fought valiantly in dozens of battles.

Union Politicians Consider Emancipation

By the fall of 1862, African Americans and abolitionists had gained widespread support for emancipation as a necessary goal of the war. Lincoln and his cabinet realized that embracing abolition as a war aim would likely prevent international recognition of southern independence. As Massachusetts senator Charles Sumner proclaimed, "You will observe that I propose no crusade for abolition. [Emancipation] is to be presented strictly as a measure of military necessity." Still, some Union politicians feared that emancipation might arouse deep animosity in the slaveholding border states and drive them from the Union.

From the Confederate perspective, international support was critical. Official recognition from European nations might persuade the North to accept southern independence. More immediately, recognition would ensure markets for southern agriculture and access to manufactured goods and war materiel. Confederate officials were especially focused on Britain, the leading market for cotton and a leading producer of industrial products. President Davis considered sending Rose Greenhow to England to promote the Confederate cause.

Fearing that the British might capitulate to Confederate pressure, abolitionist lecturers toured Britain, reminding residents of their early leadership in the antislavery cause. The Union's formal commitment to emancipation would certainly increase British support for its position and prevent diplomatic recognition of the Confederacy. By the summer of 1862, Lincoln was convinced, but he wanted to wait for a military victory before making a formal announcement regarding emancipation.

Instead, the Union suffered a series of defeats that summer, and Lee marched his army into Union territory in Maryland. On September 17, Longstreet joined Lee in a fierce battle along Antietam Creek as Union troops brought the Confederate advance to a standstill near the town of Sharpsburg. Union forces suffered more than 12,000 casualties and the Confederates more than 10,000, the bloodiest single day of battle in U.S. history. Yet because Lee and his army were forced to retreat, Lincoln claimed the **Battle of Antietam** as a great victory. Five days later, the president announced his preliminary **Emancipation Proclamation** to the assembled cabinet, promising to free the enslaved in all seceding states.

On January 1, 1863, Lincoln signed the final edict, proclaiming that enslaved people in areas still in rebellion were "forever free" and inviting them to enlist in the Union army. Over the next two years, tens of thousands of enslaved men fled southern plantations and fought in the Union Army alongside equal numbers of free blacks who volunteered to ensure the Confederacy's defeat. Still, the proclamation was a moderate document in many ways. Its provisions exempted from emancipation the 450,000 slaves in the loyal border states, as well as more than 300,000 enslaved people in Union-occupied areas of Tennessee, Louisiana, and Virginia. The proclamation also justified the abolition of southern slavery on military, not moral, grounds. Despite its limits, the Emancipation Proclamation inspired joyous celebrations among free blacks and white abolitionists, who viewed it as the first step toward slavery's final eradication.

REVIEW & RELATE	• Why did American Indians, Mexicans and Tejanos, and African Americans choose to join Union or Confederate forces? • What events occurred to turn the Civil War into a war to end slavery?

War Transforms the North and the South

For soldiers and civilians seeking to survive the upheaval of war, political pronouncements rarely alleviated the dangers they faced. The war's extraordinary death tolls shocked Americans on both sides. On the home front, the prolonged conflict created labor shortages and severe inflation in both North and South. The war initially disrupted industrial and agricultural production as men were called to service, but the North recovered quickly by building on its prewar industrial base, technological know-how, and women's labor. In the South, manufacturing increased, with enslaved laborers pressed into service as industrial workers. But this further diminished the plantation labor force as more white women were forced into managerial roles. With most of the war fought on southern soil and the Union Navy blockading Confederate ports, shortages loomed everywhere. By 1863, these dramatic transformations inspired dissent and protest as rising death tolls and rising prices made the costs of war ever clearer.

Life and Death on the Battlefield

Few soldiers entered the conflict knowing what to expect. A young private wrote that his idea of combat had been that the soldiers "would all be in line, all standing in a nice level field fighting, a number of ladies taking care of the wounded, etc., etc., but it isn't so." Improved weaponry turned battles into scenes of bloody carnage. The shift from smoothbore muskets to rifles, which had grooves that spun the bullet, made weapons far more effective at longer distances. The use of minié balls—small bullets with a deep cavity that expanded upon firing—increased fatalities as well. By 1863 Union army sharpshooters acquired new repeating rifles with metal cartridges. With more accurate rifles and deadlier bullets, the rival armies increasingly relied on heavy fortifications, elaborate trenches, and distant mortar and artillery fire when they could. Still, casualties continued to rise, especially since the trenches served as breeding grounds for disease.

The hardships and discomforts of war extended beyond combat itself. As General Lee complained before Antietam, many soldiers fought in ragged uniforms and without shoes. Rations, too, ran short. Food was dispensed sporadically and was often spoiled. Many Union troops survived primarily on an unleavened biscuit called hardtack as well as small amounts of meat and beans and enormous quantities of coffee. Their diet improved over the course of the war, however, as the Union supply system grew more efficient while Confederate troops subsisted increasingly on cornmeal and fatty meat. As early as 1862, Confederate soldiers began gathering food from the haversacks of Union dead.

For every soldier who died as a result of combat, three died of disease. Measles, dysentery, typhoid, and malaria killed thousands who drank contaminated water, ate tainted food, and were exposed to the elements. And infected soldiers on both sides carried yellow fever and malaria into towns where they built fortifications. Prisoner-of-war camps were especially deadly locales. Debilitating fevers in a camp near Danville, Virginia spread to the town, killing civilians as well as soldiers.

The sufferings of African American troops were particularly severe. The death rate from disease for black Union soldiers was nearly three times greater than that for white Union soldiers, reflecting their poorer health upon enlistment, the hard labor they performed, and the minimal medical care they received in the field. Southern blacks who began their army careers in contraband camps fared even worse, with a camp near Nashville losing a quarter of its residents to death in just three months in 1864.

For all soldiers, medical assistance was primitive. Antibiotics did not exist, antiseptics were still unknown, and anesthetics were scarce. Union medical care improved with the **U.S. Sanitary Commission**, which was established by the federal government in June 1861 to promote and coordinate better medical treatment for soldiers. Nonetheless, a commentator accurately described most field hospitals as "dirty dens of butchery and horror," where amputations often occurred with whiskey as the only anesthetic.

As the horrors of war sank in, large numbers of soldiers deserted or refused to reenlist. As volunteers declined and deserters increased, both the Confederate and the Union governments were forced to institute conscription laws to draft men into service.

The Northern Economy Expands

As the war dragged on, the North's economic advantages became more apparent. Initially, the effects of the war on northern industry had been little short of disastrous. Raw cotton for textiles disappeared, southern planters stopped ordering shoes, and trade fell off precipitously. By 1863, however, the northern economy was in high gear and could provide more arms, food, shoes, and clothing to its troops as well as for those back home. As cotton production declined, woolen manufacturing doubled, and northern iron and coal production increased 25 to 30 percent during the war. Northern factories turned out weapons and ammunition while shipyards built the fleets that blockaded southern ports.

These economic improvements were linked to a vast expansion in the federal government's activities. War Department orders fueled the industrial surge. It also created the U.S. Military Railroads unit to construct tracks in newly occupied southern territories and granted large contracts to northern railroads to carry troops and supplies. With southern Democrats out of federal office, Congress also raised tariffs on imported goods to protect northern industries. In addition, the government hired thousands of "sewing women," who were contracted to make uniforms for Union soldiers. Other women joined the federal labor force as clerical workers to sustain the expanding bureaucracy and the voluminous amounts of government-generated paperwork.

That paperwork multiplied exponentially when the federal government created a national currency and a national banking system. Before the Civil War, private banks (chartered by the states) issued their own banknotes, which were used in most economic transactions. During the war, Congress revolutionized this system, giving the federal government the power to create currency, issue federal charters to banks, and take on national debt. The government then flooded the nation with treasury bills, commonly called greenbacks. The federal budget mushroomed as well—from $63 million in 1860 to nearly $1.3 billion in 1865. By the end of the war, the federal bureaucracy had become the nation's largest single employer.

Northern manufacturers faced one daunting problem: a shortage of labor. Over half a million workers left their jobs to serve in the Union army, and others were hired by the expanding federal bureaucracy. Manufacturers dealt with the problem primarily by mechanizing more tasks and by hiring more women and children, native-born and immigrant. Combining the lower wages paid to these workers with production speedups, manufacturers improved their profits while advancing the Union cause.

Urbanization and Industrialization in the South

Although Southerners had gone to war to protect a largely rural lifestyle, the war encouraged the growth of cities and industry. The creation of a large governmental and military bureaucracy brought thousands of Southerners to the Confederate capital of Richmond. As the war expanded, refugees from the countryside also flooded into Atlanta, Savannah, Columbia, and Mobile.

Industrialization contributed to urban growth as well. With the South unable to buy industrial goods from the North and limited in its trade with Europe, military necessity spurred southern industry. Clothing and shoe factories had "sprung up almost like magic" in Natchez and Jackson, Mississippi. The Tredegar Iron Works in Richmond expanded significantly as well, employing more than 2,500 men, black and white. More than 10,000 people labored in war industries in Selma, Alabama, where one factory produced cannons. With labor in short supply, widows and orphans, enslaved blacks, and white men too old or injured to fight were recruited for industrial work in many cities.

Women Aid the War Effort

Women of all classes and both races contributed to the war effort. Thousands filled jobs in agriculture, industry, and the government that were traditionally held by men while others assisted the military effort more directly. Most Union and Confederate officials initially opposed women's direct engagement in the war. Yet it was women's voluntary organization of relief efforts that inspired the federal government to establish the U.S. Sanitary Commission. By 1862 tens of thousands of women volunteered funds and assistance through hundreds of local chapters across the North. They hosted fund-raising fairs, coordinated sewing and knitting circles, rolled bandages, and sent supplies to the front lines.

With critical shortages of medical staff, some female nurses and doctors eventually gained acceptance in northern hospitals and field camps. In the North, Dorothea Dix, who had worked to improve treatment of the mentally ill, convinced Secretary of War Edwin Stanton to appoint her superintendent of nursing for the Union Army. She required nurses to be Protestant and plain looking, and Congress agreed to pay them $12 a month (one-third of what male nurses made). Some women gained positions independently of Dix's leadership. Mary Ann "Mother" Bickerdyke, a widow in her forties, showed incredible stamina and skill nursing men on the battlefield. Dr. Mary Walker, a rare female physician, also donated her services, working in field hospitals and prisoner of war camps. Since she usually dressed in men's clothing, wounded soldiers did not always recognize that a woman was caring for them.

Susie King Taylor was among the many black women who provided medical care during the war. Enslaved in South Carolina, she fled at age fifteen to a coastal island occupied by Union forces. There she laundered clothes, cleaned musketry, and served as a nurse in a segregated military hospital for black soldiers. She and other African American nurses received $10 per month, $2 less than their white counterparts. Catholic nuns also served on battlefields and in hospitals, aiding Union and Confederate soldiers. They worked in groups, their habits serving as their uniform. Despite widespread anti-Catholic prejudice, they were more widely praised by military officers due in part to their clear organization and deference to male leadership. By the end of the war, northern women almost entirely replaced men as military nurses.

In the South, too, women performed much of the medical care. But without government support, nursing was never recognized as a legitimate profession for women, and most nurses worked out of their own homes. As a result, a Confederate soldier's

Loreta Janeta Velazquez/Harry T. Buford, c. 1876 While attending school in New Orleans, Cuban-born Janeta Velazquez eloped with a Texas soldier. When the Civil War erupted, she joined her husband disguised as Lieutenant Buford. Soon widowed, she continued to serve as a Confederate soldier and spy until wounded in the Battle of Shiloh. In 1876, she published her memoir, *The Woman in Battle*, a mix of fact and fiction. The Granger Collection, New York

chance of dying from wounds or disease was greater than those of his Union counterpart. Southern women also worked tirelessly to supply soldiers with clothes, blankets, munitions, and food. But this work, too, was often performed locally and by individuals rather than as part of a coordinated Confederate effort.

Some Union and Confederate women played more unusual roles in the war. A few dozen women joined Rose Greenhow in gathering information for military and political leaders. One of the most effective spies on the Union side was the fugitive slave Harriet Tubman, who gathered intelligence in South Carolina, including from many enslaved blacks, between 1862 and 1864. Even more women served as couriers, carrying messages across battle lines to alert officers of critical changes in military orders or in the enemy's position.

In addition, at least four hundred women disguised themselves as men and fought as soldiers. There were likely hundreds more who fought for short periods of time or whose sex was never discovered. Sarah Edmonds took the name Franklin Thompson and enlisted as a private in the Second Michigan Infantry in Detroit in May 1861. She worked as a regimental nurse as well as a courier. Her regiment participated in several major battles, including First Manassas, Fredericksburg, and Antietam. After contracting malaria in April 1863, Edmonds deserted, fearing that doctors would discover her sex. On the Confederate side, Cuban-born Loretta Janeta Velazquez joined the army alongside her husband disguised as Harry Buford. After her husband was killed in battle, she continued to fight, serving as an officer in several regiments. Her identity was only discovered when she wrote her memoirs in 1876. Some female soldiers continued to live as men after the war; others once again donned women's clothes and embraced traditional gender roles.

Women on the home front also sought to influence wartime policies, especially in the North. Their most important effort followed the Emancipation Proclamation when Elizabeth Cady Stanton, Susan B. Anthony, and Lucy Stone founded the **Women's National Loyal League**. The League launched a massive petition drive to broaden Lincoln's policy, and female volunteers collected 260,000 signatures. Black and white signers, two-thirds of them women, demanded a congressional act "emancipating all persons of African descent" everywhere in the nation.

Dissent and Protest in the Midst of War

The war also inspired dissent and protest North and South. Dissent roiled border states from the start of the war. From 1861 on, battles raged among residents in the border state of Missouri, with Confederate sympathizers refusing to accept living in a Union state. Pro-southern residents formed militias and staged guerrilla attacks on Union supporters. The militias, with the tacit support of Confederate officials, claimed thousands of lives during the war and forced the Union army to station troops in the area.

By 1863, frustration spread north and south as casualties increased, numbers of volunteers declined, and inflation soared. Some white Northerners had always opposed emancipation, based on racial prejudice or fear that a flood of black migrants would increase competition for jobs. Then, just two months after the Emancipation Proclamation went into effect, a new law deepened concerns among many working-class Northerners. The **Enrollment Act**, passed by Congress in March 1863, established a draft system to ensure sufficient soldiers for the Union army. While draftees were to be selected by an impartial lottery, the law allowed a person with $300 to pay the government in place of serving or to hire another man as a substitute. Many workers deeply resented the draft's profound inequality.

Dissent turned to violence in July 1863 when the new law went into effect. Riots broke out in cities across the North. In New York City, where inflation caused tremendous suffering and a large immigrant population solidly supported the Democratic Party, implementation of the draft triggered four days of the worst rioting Americans had ever seen. Women and men — including many Irish and German immigrants — attacked Republican draft officials, wealthy businessmen, and the free black community. Between July 13 and 16, rioters lynched at least a dozen African Americans and looted and burned the city's Colored Orphan Asylum. The violence ended only when Union troops put down the riots by force. By then, more than one hundred New Yorkers, most of them black, lay dead.

By 1864 inflation, which eroded the earnings of rural and urban residents, fueled further protests in the North. Women, children, and old men took over much of the field labor in the Midwest, trying to feed their families and the army while struggling to pay their bills. Factory workers, servants, and day laborers felt the pinch as well. With federal greenbacks flooding the market and military production a priority, the price of consumer goods climbed about 20 percent faster than wages. Although industrialists garnered huge profits, workers suffered. A group of Cincinnati seamstresses complained to President Lincoln in 1864 about employers "who fatten on their contracts by grinding immense profits out of the labor of their operatives." At the same time, employers persuaded some state legislatures to prohibit strikes in wartime. The federal government, too, supported business over labor. When workers at the Parrott arms factory in Cold Spring, New York struck for higher wages in 1864, the government declared martial law and arrested the strike leaders.

Northern Democrats saw the widening unrest as a political opportunity. Although some Democratic leaders supported the war effort, many others — whom opponents called **Copperheads**, after the poisonous snake — rallied behind Ohio politician Clement L. Vallandigham in opposing the war. Presenting themselves as the "peace party," these Democrats enjoyed considerable success in eastern cities where inflation was rampant and immigrant workers were caught between low wages and military service. The party was also strong in parts of the Midwest, like Missouri, where sympathy for the southern cause and antipathy to African Americans ran deep.

In the South, too, some whites expressed growing dissatisfaction with the war. Jefferson Davis signed a conscription act in April 1862, a year before Lincoln, inciting widespread opposition. Here, too, men could hire a substitute if they had enough money, and an October 1862 law exempted men owning twenty or more enslaved workers from military service. Thus, large planters, many of whom served in the Confederate legislature, had effectively exempted themselves from fighting. As one Alabama farmer fumed, "All they want is to get you pumpt up and go to fight for their infernal negroes, and after you do their fighting you may kiss their hine parts for all they care."

Small farmers were also hard hit by policies that allowed the Confederate army to take whatever supplies it needed. The army's forced acquisition of farm produce intensified food shortages that had been building since early in the war. Moreover, the lack of an extensive railroad or canal system in the South limited the distribution of what food was available.

Food shortages drove up prices on basic items like bread and corn, while the Union blockade and the focus on military needs dramatically increased prices on other consumer goods. As the Confederate government issued ever more treasury notes to finance the war, inflation soared 2,600 percent in less than three years. In spring 1863 food riots led by working-class women erupted in cities across the South, including the Confederate capital of Richmond.

Some state legislatures then tried to control food prices, but Richmond workers continued to voice their resentment. In fall 1863 a group proclaimed, "From the fact that he consumes all and produces nothing, we know that without [our] labor and production the man with money could not exist."

The devastation of the war added to all these grievances. Since most battles were fought in the Upper South or along the Confederacy's western frontier, small farmers in these regions saw their crops, animals, and fields devastated. A phrase that had seemed cynical in 1862 — "A rich man's war and a poor man's fight" — became the rallying cry of the southern peace movement in 1864. Secret peace societies flourished mainly among small farmers and in regions, like the western mountains, where plantation slavery did not develop. A secret organization centered in North Carolina provided Union forces with information on southern troop movements and encouraged desertion by Confederates. In some mountainous areas, draft evaders and deserters formed guerrilla groups that attacked draft officials and actively impeded the war effort. Women joined these efforts, hiding deserters, raiding grain depots, and burning the property of Confederate officials.

When enslavers led the South out of the Union in 1861, they had assumed the loyalty of yeomen farmers, the deference of southern ladies, and the privileges of the southern way of life. Far from preserving social harmony and social order, however, the war undermined ties between elite and poor Southerners, between planters and small farmers, and between women and men. Although most white Southerners still supported the Confederacy in 1864 and internal dissent alone did not lead to defeat, it did weaken the ties that bound soldiers to their posts in the final two years of the war.

REVIEW & RELATE	• In what ways did the war reshape the economy and gender roles in the North and the South?
	• How did the death toll, inflation, and social conflicts heightened by the war fuel dissent and protest in the North and the South?

The Tide of War Turns, 1863–1865

In spring 1863, amid turmoil on the home front, General Robert E. Lee's army defeated a Union force twice its size at Chancellorsville, Virginia. The victory set the stage for a Confederate thrust into Pennsylvania, but Lee's decision to go on the offensive proved the Confederacy's undoing. In July 1863 the Union won two decisive military victories: at Gettysburg, Pennsylvania and Vicksburg, Mississippi. At the same time, the flood of African Americans, including those formerly enslaved, into Union army camps transformed the very meaning of the war. By 1864, with the momentum favoring the Union, General Ulysses S. Grant implemented policies of hard war that forced the Confederacy to consider surrender.

Key Victories for the Union

In mid-1863 Confederate commanders believed the tide was turning in their favor. Following victories at Fredericksburg and Chancellorsville, General Lee launched an invasion of northern territory. While the Union army maneuvered to protect Washington, D.C., General Joseph Hooker resigned as head of the Union Army of the Potomac. On June 28, Lincoln appointed George A. Meade as the new Union commander, and the general immediately faced a major engagement at the **Battle of Gettysburg** in Pennsylvania. If Confederates won a victory there, European countries might finally recognize the southern nation and force the North to accept peace.

Neither Lee nor Meade set out to launch a battle in this small Pennsylvania town. But Lee was afraid of outrunning his supply lines, and Meade wanted to keep Confederates from gaining control of the roads that crossed at Gettysburg. So between July 1 and July 3, the opposing armies fought a desperate battle with Union troops occupying the high ground and Confederate forces launching deadly assaults from below (Map 13.2). Ultimately, Gettysburg proved a disaster for the South: More than 4,700 Confederates were killed, including a large number of officers; another 18,000 were wounded, captured, or missing. Although the Union suffered similar casualties, it had more men to lose, and it could claim victory.

As Lee retreated to Virginia, the South suffered another devastating defeat. Troops under General Grant had been pounding Vicksburg, Mississippi since May 1863. The **siege of Vicksburg** ended with the surrender of Confederate forces on July 4. This victory was even more important strategically than Gettysburg (Map 13.2). Combined with a victory five days later at Port Hudson, Louisiana, the Union army controlled the entire Mississippi valley, the richest plantation region in the South. This series of victories also effectively cut Louisiana, Arkansas, and Texas off from the rest of the Confederacy, ensuring Union control of the West. In November 1863 Grant's troops achieved another major victory at Chattanooga, opening up much of the South's remaining territory to invasion. Thousands of enslaved workers deserted their plantations, and many joined the Union war effort.

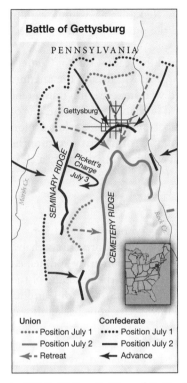
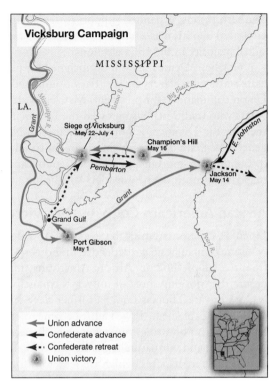

MAP 13.2   Battles of Gettysburg and Vicksburg, 1863
The three-day Battle of Gettysburg and the six-week siege of Vicksburg led to critical victories for the Union. Together, these victories forced General Lee's troops back into Confederate territory and gave the Union control of the Mississippi River. Still, the war was far from over. Confederate troops controlled the southern heartland, and Northerners wearied of the ever-increasing casualties.

That same month, November 1863, President Lincoln spoke at the official dedication ceremony for the National Cemetery at Gettysburg, Pennsylvania. In his **Gettysburg Address**, Lincoln tied the war against slavery to the fulfillment of the nation's founding ideal "that all men are created equal." He insisted that the United States "shall have a new birth of freedom—and that government of the people, by the people, and for the people, shall not perish from the earth." Only in this way, he declared, could Americans ensure that the "honored dead" had not "died in vain."

As 1864 dawned, the Union had twice as many forces in the field as the Confederacy, whose soldiers were suffering from low morale, high mortality, and dwindling supplies. Although some difficult battles lay ahead, the war of attrition—in which the larger, better-supplied Union forces slowly wore down their Confederate opponents—had begun to pay dividends.

The changing Union fortunes increased support for Lincoln and his congressional allies. Union victories and the Emancipation Proclamation also convinced Great Britain not to recognize the Confederacy as an independent nation. And the heroics of African American soldiers, who engaged in direct and often brutal combat against southern troops, expanded support for emancipation. Republicans, who now fully embraced abolition as a war aim, were nearly assured the presidency and a congressional majority in the 1864 elections.

Northern Democrats still campaigned for peace and the readmission of Confederate states with slavery intact. They nominated George B. McClellan, the onetime Union commander, for president. McClellan attracted working-class and immigrant voters who traditionally supported the Democrats and bore the heaviest burdens of the war. But Democratic hopes for victory in November were crushed when Union general William Tecumseh Sherman captured Atlanta, Georgia just two months before the election. Lincoln and the Republicans won easily, giving the party a clear mandate to continue the war to its conclusion.

African Americans Contribute to Victory

Lincoln's election secured the eventual downfall of slavery, but the movement to eradicate human bondage depended on numerous actors. Most importantly, perhaps, from the fall of 1862 on, African Americans enlisted in the Union army and helped ensure that nothing short of universal emancipation would be the outcome of the war. As Private Thomas Long, a former slave serving with the First South Carolina Volunteers, explained: "If we hadn't become sojers, all might have gone back as it was before. . . . But now tings can neber go back, because we have showed our energy and our courage and our naturally manhood."

In the border states, which were exempt from the Emancipation Proclamation, enslaved men were adamant about enlisting since those who served in the Union army were granted their freedom. Because of this provision, enslavers in these states did everything in their power to prevent their enslaved workers from joining the army. Despite these efforts, between 25 and 60 percent of military-age enslaved men in the four border states stole away and joined the Union army. By the end of the war, nearly 200,000 black men had served officially in the army and navy, and some 37,000 blacks had given their lives for the Union.

Yet despite their courage and commitment, black soldiers felt the sting of racism. They were segregated in camps, given the most menial jobs, and often treated as inferiors by white soldiers and officers. Particularly galling was the Union policy of paying black soldiers less than whites. African American soldiers openly protested this discrimination even after a black sergeant who voiced his views was charged with mutiny and executed by firing squad in February 1864. The War Department finally equalized wages four months later.

One primary concern of African American soldiers was to liberate enslaved people as Union armies moved deeper into the South. At the same time, thousands of enslaved southerners headed for Union lines. Even those forced to remain on plantations learned when Union troops were nearby and talked openly of emancipation. "Now they gradually threw off the mask," an enslaved laborer remembered, "and were not afraid to let it be known that the 'freedom' in their songs meant freedom of the body in this world."

From the first year of the war, the federal government recognized enslaved men and women who reached Union lines as contraband of war. Southern blacks seeking freedom quickly turned so-called "contraband" camps into **refugee communities**.

Union army camps stretched from eastern Virginia to Kansas and from northern Kentucky to southern Louisiana. Black men hoped to gain freedom and wages by fighting for the Union, but the women, children, and elderly they brought with them had to fend for themselves once their men left to fight. Women refugees sometimes worked as cooks, nurses, or laundresses for the army, but many had to survive on meager rations and aid from other refugees. Moreover, while some camps remained open for years, most moved with the battlefront. As that front shifted quickly in the final eighteen months of war, thousands of refugees were left behind, often in easy reach of their former enslavers. Nonetheless, hundreds of thousands of black refugees fled to Union lines, depriving enslavers of their labor while building free communities.

The Final Battles of a Hard War

In the spring of 1864, the war in the East entered its final stage. That March, Lincoln placed General Grant in charge of all Union forces. Grant embarked on a strategy of **hard war**, in which soldiers not only attacked military targets but also destroyed civilian crops, livestock, fields, and property to undermine morale and supply chains. Grant was also willing to accept huge casualties to achieve victory. Over the next year, he led his troops overland through western Virginia in an effort to take Richmond. Meanwhile, General Philip Sheridan devastated "The Breadbasket of the Confederacy" in Virginia's Shenandoah Valley, and General Sherman laid waste to the remnants of the plantation system in Georgia and the Carolinas.

Grant's troops headed toward Richmond, where Lee's army controlled strong defensive positions. The Confederates won a series of narrow, bloody victories, but Grant continued to push forward. Although Lee lost fewer men, they were losses he could not afford. Combining high casualties with deserters, Lee's army was melting away with each engagement. Although soldiers and civilians—North and South—called Grant "the butcher" for his seeming lack of regard for human life, the Union general was not deterred.

In the fall of 1864, implementing hard war tactics, Sheridan rendered the Shenandoah Valley a "barren waste." Called "the burning" by local residents, Sheridan's soldiers torched fields, barns, and homes and destroyed thousands of bushels of grain along with livestock, shops, and mills. His campaign demoralized civilians in the region and denied Confederate troops crucial supplies.

In the preceding months, Sherman had laid siege to Atlanta, but on September 2 his forces swept around the city and destroyed the roads and rails that connected it to the rest of the Confederacy. When General John B. Hood and his Confederate troops abandoned their posts, Sherman telegraphed Lincoln: "Atlanta is ours, and fairly won." That victory cut the South in two, but Sherman continued on. **Sherman's March to the Sea** introduced hard war tactics to Southerners along the three-hundred-mile route from the Atlantic coast north through the Carolinas. His troops cut a path of destruction fifty to sixty miles wide. They confiscated or destroyed millions of pounds of cotton, corn, wheat, and other agricultural items; tore up thousands of miles of railroad tracks; and burned Columbia, the South Carolina capital. As Eleanor Cohen Seixas, whose family had earlier fled to Columbia for safety, recorded in her journal, "The fires raged fearfully all night" and the "vile Yankees took from us clothing, food, jewels, all our cows, horses, carriages, etc."

Despite later claims that Sherman's men ravaged white women, instances of such behavior were rare, although Union soldiers did ransack homes and confiscate food and clothing.

Enslaved blacks hoped that Sherman's arrival marked their emancipation. During his victorious march, nearly 18,000 enslaved men, women, and children fled ruined plantations and sought to join the victorious troops. To their dismay, soldiers refused to take them along. Union officers realized that they could not care for this vast number of people and carry out their military operations. Still, some Union soldiers abused African American men, raped black women, or stole their few possessions, treating them as enemies rather than allies. At the same time, angry Confederates captured many blacks who were turned away, killing some and re-enslaving others.

These actions caused a scandal in Washington. In January 1865, Lincoln dispatched Secretary of War Edwin Stanton to Georgia to investigate the charges. At an extraordinary meeting in Savannah, Stanton and Sherman met with black ministers to hear their complaints and hopes. The ministers spoke movingly of the war lifting "the yoke of bondage." Freed blacks, they argued, "could reap the fruit of their own labor" and, if given land, "take care of ourselves, and assist the Government in maintaining our freedom." In response, Sherman issued **Field Order Number 15**, setting aside more than 400,000 acres of captured Confederate land to be divided into small plots for the formerly enslaved. The order proved highly controversial, but it offered blacks some hope of significant change.

If many African Americans were disappointed by the actions of Union soldiers in the East, American Indians were even more devastated by developments in the West. Despite Indian nations' substantial aid to Union armies, any hope of being rewarded for their efforts vanished by 1864. Tens of thousands of whites migrated west of the Mississippi River during the Civil War, and congressional passage of the Homestead Act in 1864 increased the numbers. At the same time, the U.S. army grew exponentially during the war, using its increased power to assault western Indian nations.

Attacks on Indians were not an extension of hard war policies, but rather a government-sanctioned effort to terrorize native communities. Beginning in 1862, the Dakota went to war with the United States over broken treaties. After being defeated, four hundred warriors were arrested by military officials and thirty-eight executed. In 1863 California Volunteers slaughtered more than two hundred men, women, and children in a Shoshone-Bannock village in Idaho. Meanwhile thousands of white settlers had been flooding into Colorado after gold was discovered in 1858, forcing Cheyenne and Arapaho Indians off their land. In 1864 officers at nearby Fort Lyon promised these Indians refuge at Sand Creek. Instead, Colonel John M. Chivington led his Third Colorado Calvary in a rampage that left 125 to 160 Indian men, women, and children dead. The Sand Creek Massacre ensured that white migrants traveling in the region would be subject to Indian attacks for years to come. At the same time, in the Southwest, the Navajo were defeated by U.S. troops and their Ute allies and forced into a four-hundred-mile trek to a reservation in New Mexico.

U.S. army officers considered "winning the West" one way to restore national unity once the Civil War ended. For Indian nations, the increased migration, expanded military presence, and sheer brutality they experienced in 1863 and 1864 boded ill for their future, whichever side won the Civil War.

The War Comes to an End

As the defeat of the Confederacy loomed, the U.S. Congress finally considered abolishing slavery throughout the nation. With intense pressure from Frederick Douglass and other abolitionists, petitioning by the Women's National Loyal League, the valiant efforts of Ohio Congressman James Ashley, and President Lincoln's lobbying of wavering senators, Congress passed the **Thirteenth Amendment** to the U.S. Constitution on January 31, 1865. It prohibited slavery and involuntary servitude anywhere in the United States. Some northern and western states had already enacted laws to ease racial inequities. Ohio, California, and Illinois repealed statutes barring blacks from testifying in court and serving on juries. Then, in May 1865, Massachusetts passed the first comprehensive public-accommodations law in U.S. history, ensuring equal treatment in stores, schools, theaters, and other social spaces. Cities from San Francisco to Cincinnati and New York also desegregated their streetcars.

Hoping to stave off defeat, southern leaders also began rethinking their racial policies. The Confederate House passed a law to recruit enslaved men into the army in February 1865, but the Senate defeated the measure. It was too late to make a difference anyway.

In early April 1865, with Sherman heading toward Raleigh, North Carolina, Grant captured Petersburg, Virginia and then drove Lee and his forces out of Richmond. Seasoned African American troops led the final assault on the city and were among the first Union soldiers to enter the Confederate capital. On April 9, after a brief engagement at Appomattox Court House, Virginia, Lee surrendered to Grant. Within hours, Lee's troops began heading home.

Yet the war was not quite over. Sporadic fighting continued until June 23, when Cherokee General Stand Watie finally surrendered to Union forces in Oklahoma. Union General Gordon Granger also confronted Confederate intransigence. In mid-June, he arrived in Galveston to assume command of the Texas District and discovered that African Americans were still being held as enslaved laborers. On June 19, he issued General Order #3, which informed the "people of Texas" that "all slaves are free." Blacks in Texas and elsewhere continue to celebrate **Juneteenth** as their Emancipation Day. For African Americans enslaved by the Creek, Cherokee, and other southeastern tribes battles over rights lasted far longer. Post–Civil War treaties promised them tribal citizenship as well as freedom. But as Indian nations with limited resources gained federal benefits, including hospitals, housing, and scholarship funds, tribal governments excluded black members. These issues continue to be litigated.

Northerners considered Lee's surrender the end of the war. Joyous celebrations erupted, and both blacks and whites hoped that the reunited nation would be stronger and more just. Their jubilation was short-lived. On April 14, Abraham Lincoln was shot at Ford's Theatre by a Confederate fanatic named John Wilkes Booth. The president died the next day, creating great uncertainty about how peace and national unity would be achieved.

REVIEW & RELATE	• How did African Americans claim their freedom and what roles did they play in the defeat of the Confederacy? How did the war affect white racial views in the North? • How did the Union win the war against the Confederacy while defeating Indians in the West?

Richmond in Ruins, April 1865 This photograph shows the Richmond and Petersburg Railroad Depot following the capture of the Confederate capital by General Grant and his troops in April 1865. The black man sitting amid the devastation no doubt realized that Richmond's fall marked the defeat of the South. Library of Congress, Prints and Photographs Division, Washington, D.C. [LC-DIG-cwpb-02709]

Conclusion: An Uncertain Future

The Civil War devastated and transformed the nation. The deadliest conflict in American history—some 600,000 to 750,000 Americans died in the war—the Civil War freed nearly 4 million Americans who had been enslaved. Soldiers who survived brought new experiences and ideas back to their families and communities. But many were also marked—like the formerly enslaved—by deep physical and emotional wounds. The war transformed the home front as well. Northern and southern women entered the labor force and the public arena in numbers never before imagined. The northern economy flourished and the South became more urbanized, but the Confederacy was left economically ruined. Meanwhile the federal government significantly expanded during the war. It also initiated programs, like the Homestead Act, that fueled migration, intensifying conflicts in the West that led to further devastation among Indian nations. Altogether, the Civil War dramatically accelerated the pace of economic, political, and social change, transforming American society both during the war and for decades afterward.

Still, the legacies of the war were far from certain in 1865. Wartime protests reflected a growing sense of class inequalities while the abolition of slavery highlighted ongoing racial disparities. Moreover, even in defeat, white Southerners honored Lee and other "heroes" of the "Lost Cause" with portraits, parades, and statues. Confederate women also worked tirelessly to preserve the memory of ordinary Confederate soldiers and of heroines like Rose O'Neal Greenhow, who had drowned in 1864 while returning from a mission to gain support in Europe.

Victorious Northerners celebrated wartime heroes as well but recognized that much still needed to be done. Frederick Douglass joined other former abolitionists in seeking to enfranchise African American men to secure their rights as free people, as black and white antislavery women headed south to open schools for freedpeople. Douglass and his allies had no illusions about the lengths to which many whites would go to protect their traditional privileges. And, indeed, many northern whites, exhausted by four years of war, hoped to leave the problems of slavery and secession behind. Others sought to benefit from rebuilding the South to ensure the nation's economic future. While most black and some white Southerners worked with Republicans to create a New South, far more whites embraced the Lost Cause legacy, which highlighted the valor of Confederate soldiers and denigrated the efforts of African Americans to build new lives in freedom. These competing visions—between Northerners and Southerners and within each group—would shape the uncertainties of peace in ways few could imagine at the end of the war.

Chapter 13 Review

KEY TERMS

Battle of Bull Run (Manassas), 328
contraband, 329
Battle of Shiloh, 332
Battle of Antietam, 333
Emancipation Proclamation, 333
U.S. Sanitary Commission, 334
Women's National Loyal League, 337
Enrollment Act, 338
Copperheads, 338

Battle of Gettysburg, 340
siege of Vicksburg, 340
Gettysburg Address, 341
refugee communities, 342
hard war, 343
Sherman's March to the Sea, 343
Field Order Number 15, 344
Thirteenth Amendment, 345
Juneteenth, 345

REVIEW & RELATE

1. What roles did American Indians, Mexicans and Tejanos, and African Americans play in supporting the Union or the Confederacy?
2. What events occurred to turn the Civil War into a war to end slavery?
3. In what ways did the war reshape economic priorities and gender roles in the North and the South?
4. How did the death toll, inflation, and social conflicts fuel dissent and protest in the North and the South?
5. How did African Americans claim their freedom and what roles did they play in the defeat of the Confederacy? How did the war affect white racial views in the North?
6. How did the Union win the war against the Confederacy while defeating Indians in the West?

TIMELINE OF EVENTS

1861	• Fort Sumter attacked
	• Enslaved workers declared "contraband"
	• U.S. Sanitary Commission established
	• Battle of Bull Run (Manassas)
	• Confiscation Act passed
1862	• Battle of Shiloh
	• Conscription act signed in South
	• Battle of Antietam
1863	• Emancipation Proclamation signed
	• Enrollment Act passed in North
	• Bread riots in Richmond
	• New York City draft riots
	• Battle of Gettysburg
	• Siege of Vicksburg
	• Gettysburg Address
1864	• Atlanta falls
	• Sand Creek Massacre
	• Sherman's "March to the Sea"
1865	• More than 200,000 African Americans serve in the Union army and navy
	• Field Order Number 15
	• Thirteenth Amendment passed
	• Lee surrenders to Grant
	• Lincoln assassinated

14

Emancipation and Reconstruction

1863–1877

LEARNING OBJECTIVES

After reading this chapter you will be able to:

- Describe the challenges newly freed African Americans faced and how they responded to them.
- Analyze the influence of the president and Congress on Reconstruction policy and evaluate the successes and shortcomings of the policies they enacted.
- Evaluate the changes that took place in the society and economy of the South during Reconstruction.
- Explain how and why Reconstruction came to an end by the mid-1870s.

COMPARING AMERICAN HISTORIES

Jefferson Franklin Long spent his life improving himself and the lives of others of his race. Born enslaved in Alabama in 1836, Long showed great resourcefulness in profiting from the limited opportunities available to him. His master, a tailor who moved his family to Georgia, taught him the trade, but Long taught himself to read and write. When the Civil War ended, he opened a tailor shop in Macon, Georgia. His business success allowed him to venture into Republican Party politics. Elected as Georgia's first black congressman in 1870, Long fought for the political rights of freed slaves. In his first appearance on the House floor, he opposed a bill that would allow former Confederate officials to return to Congress, noting that many belonged to secret societies, such as the Ku Klux Klan, that intimidated black citizens. Despite his pleas, the measure passed, and Long decided not to run for reelection.

By the mid-1880s, Long had become disillusioned with the ability of black Georgians to achieve their objectives via electoral politics. Instead, he counseled African Americans to turn to institution building as the best hope for social and economic advancement. Long helped found the Union Brotherhood Lodge, a black mutual aid society with branches throughout central Georgia, which provided social and economic services for its members. He died in 1901, as political disfranchisement and racial segregation swept through Georgia and the rest of the South.

Jefferson Long and **Andrew Johnson** shared many characteristics, but their views on race could not have been more different. Whereas Long fought for the right of self-determination for African Americans, Johnson believed that whites alone should govern. Born in 1808 in Raleigh, North Carolina, Johnson grew up in poverty. At the age of thirteen or fourteen, he became a tailor's apprentice and, after moving to Tennessee in 1826, like Long, opened a tailor shop. The following year, Johnson married and began to prosper, purchasing a farm and a small number of enslaved workers.

As he made his mark in Greenville, Tennessee, Johnson became active in Democratic Party politics. A social and political outsider, Johnson gained support by championing the rights of workers and small farmers against the power of the southern aristocracy. Political success followed, and by the time the Civil War broke out, he was a U.S. senator.

When the Civil War erupted, Johnson remained loyal to the Union even after Tennessee seceded in 1861. President Abraham Lincoln rewarded Johnson by appointing him as military governor of Tennessee. In 1864 the Republican Lincoln chose the Democrat Johnson to run with him as vice president. Less than six weeks after their inauguration in March 1865, Johnson became president upon Lincoln's assassination.

Fate placed Reconstruction in the hands of Andrew Johnson. The brutal Civil War had come to a close, but the hard work of reunion remained. Toward this end, President Johnson oversaw the reestablishment of state governments in the former Confederate states. Even as southern states passed measures that restricted black civil and political rights, President Johnson declared them fit for rejoining the Union. Most Northerners reached a different conclusion. Having won the bloody war, they feared losing the peace to Johnson and the defeated South.

COMPARING THE AMERICAN HISTORIES of Andrew Johnson and Jefferson Long highlights hard-fought battles to determine the fate of the postwar South and the meaning of freedom for newly emancipated African Americans. Former enslaved people sought to reunite their families, obtain land, and gain an education. President Johnson rejected their pleas for assistance to fulfill these aims.

However, Congress passed laws to ensure civil rights and extend the vote to African American men, although African American women, like white women, remained disfranchised. In the South, whites attempted to restore their economic and political power over African Americans by resorting to intimidation and violence. By 1877, they succeeded in bringing Reconstruction to an end with the consent of the federal government.

Emancipation

Even before the war came to a close, Reconstruction had begun on a small scale. During the Civil War, blacks remaining in Union-occupied areas, such as the South Carolina Sea Islands, gained some experience with freedom. When Union troops arrived, most southern whites fled, but enslaved workers chose to stay on the land. Some farmed for themselves, but most worked for northern whites who moved south to demonstrate the profitability of free black labor. After the war, however, former plantation owners returned. Rather than work for these whites, freedpeople preferred to establish their own farms. If forced to hire themselves out, they insisted on negotiating the terms of their employment. Wives and mothers often refused to labor for whites at all in favor of caring for their own families. These conflicts reflected the priorities that would shape the actions of freedpeople across the South in the immediate aftermath of the war. For freedom to be meaningful, it had to include economic independence, the power to make family decisions, and the right to control some community decisions.

African Americans Embrace Freedom

When U.S. troops arrived in Richmond, Virginia in April 1865, the city's enslaved population knew that freedom was, finally, theirs. Four days after Union troops arrived, 1,500 African Americans, including a large number of soldiers, packed First African Baptist, the largest of the city's black churches. During the singing of the hymn "Jesus My All to Heaven Is Gone," they raised their voices at the line "This is the way I long have sought." As news of the Confederacy's defeat spread, newly freed African Americans across the South experienced similar emotions. Many years later, Houston H. Holloway, an enslaved Georgian who had been sold three times before he was twenty years old, recalled the day of emancipation: "I felt like a bird out a cage. Amen. Amen, Amen. I could hardly ask to feel any better than I did that day."

For southern whites, however, the end of the war brought fear, humiliation, and uncertainty. From their perspective, the jubilation of former slaves poured salt in their wounds. In many areas, blacks celebrated their freedom under the protection of Union soldiers. When the army moved out, freedpeople suffered deeply for their enthusiasm. Whites beat, whipped, raped, and shot blacks who they felt had been too joyous in their celebration or too helpful to the Yankee invaders. As one North Carolina freedman testified, the Yankees "tol' us we were free," but once the army left, the planters "would get cruel to the slaves if they acted like they were free."

Newly freed blacks also faced less visible dangers. During the 1860s, disease swept through the South and through the contraband camps that housed many former slaves; widespread malnutrition and poor housing heightened the problem.

A smallpox epidemic that spread south from Washington, D.C. killed more than sixty thousand freedpeople.

Despite the dangers, southern blacks eagerly pursued emancipation. They moved; they married; they attended school; they demanded wages; they refused to work for whites; they gathered together their families; they created black churches and civic associations; they held political meetings. Sometimes, black women and men acted on their own, pooling their resources to advance their freedom. At other times, they received help from private organizations—particularly northern missionary and educational associations—staffed mostly by former abolitionists, free blacks, and evangelical Christians.

Emancipated slaves also called on federal agencies for assistance and support. The most important of these agencies was the newly formed Bureau of Refugees, Freedmen, and Abandoned Lands, popularly known as the **Freedmen's Bureau**. Created by Congress in 1865 and signed into law by President Lincoln, the bureau provided ex-slaves with economic and legal resources. The Freedmen's Bureau also aided many freedpeople in achieving one of their primary goals: obtaining land. A South Carolina freedman summed up the feeling of the newly emancipated. "Give us our own land and we take care of ourselves," he remarked. "But without land, the old masters can hire or starve us, as they please." During the last years of the war, the federal government had distributed to freedpeople around 400,000 acres of abandoned land from the South Carolina Sea Islands to Florida. Immediately after hostilities ceased, the Freedmen's Bureau made available hundreds of thousands of additional acres to recently emancipated slaves.

Reuniting Families Torn Apart by Slavery

The first priority for many newly freed blacks was to reunite families torn apart by slavery. Men and women traveled across the South to find family members. Well into the 1870s and 1880s, parents ran advertisements in newly established black newspapers, providing what information they knew about their children's whereabouts and asking for assistance in finding them. Milly Johnson wrote to the Freedmen's Bureau in March 1867, after failing to locate the five children she had lost under slavery. She finally located three of them, but any chance of discovering the whereabouts of the other two disappeared because the records of the slave trader who purchased them burned during the war. Despite such obstacles, thousands of formerly enslaved children were reunited with their parents in the 1870s.

Husbands and wives, or those who considered themselves as such despite the absence of legal marriage under slavery, also searched for each other. Those who lived on nearby plantations could live together for the first time. Those whose spouse had been sold to distant plantations had a more difficult time. They wrote (or had letters written on their behalf) to relatives and friends who had been sold with their mate; sought assistance from government officials, churches, and even their former masters; and traveled to areas where they thought their spouse might reside.

These searches were complicated by long years of separation and the lack of any legal standing for slave marriages. In 1866 Philip Grey, a Virginia freedman, located his wife, Willie Ann, and their daughter Maria, who had been sold away to Kentucky years before. Willie Ann was eager to reunite with her husband, but in the years since being sold, she had remarried and borne three children. Her second husband had

Winslow Homer, *A Visit from the Old Mistress*, 1876   Civil War correspondent and artist Winslow Homer visited Virginia in the mid-1870s and visually captured the tensions existing between freedpeople and former owners. Here, a former mistress visits the home of three black women. Although the house is humble, one woman refuses to stand for the "old mistress" and the other two, one holding a freeborn child, eye her warily.   Smithsonian American Art Museum, Washington, D.C./Art Resource, NY

joined the Union army and was killed in battle. When Willie Ann wrote to Philip in April 1866, she explained her new circumstances, concluding: "If you love me you will love my children and you will have to promise me that you will provide for them all as well as if they were your own. . . . I know that I have lived with you and loved you then and love you still."

Most black spouses who found each other sought to legalize their relationship. A superintendent for marriages for the Freedmen's Bureau in northern Virginia reported that he gave out seventy-nine marriage certificates on a single day in May 1866. In another case, four couples went right from the fields to a local schoolhouse, still dressed in their work clothes, where a parson married them.

Of course, some of the formerly enslaved hoped that freedom would allow them to leave unhappy relationships. Having never been married under the law, couples could simply separate and move on. Complications arose, however, if they had children. In Lake City, Florida in 1866, a Freedmen's Bureau agent asked his superiors for advice on how to deal with Madison Day and Maria Richards. They refused to legalize the relationship forced on them under slavery, but both sought custody of their three children. As with white couples in the mid-nineteenth century, the father was granted custody on the assumption that he had the best chance of providing for the children financially.

As was the custom and law of that time, wives were subordinate to their husbands. One North Carolina freedman said of his wife, "I consider her my property." This rankled Frances Gage, an antislavery and women's rights activist, who declared, "You give us a nominal freedom, but you leave us under the heel of our husbands." Yet there was an important trade-off that black women hoped to receive from this patriarchal arrangement: protection for themselves and their children.

Freedom to Learn

Seeking land and reuniting families were only two of the many ways that southern blacks proclaimed their freedom. Learning to read and write was another. The desire to learn was all but universal. Enslaved persons had been forbidden to read and write. With emancipation they pursued what had been denied them. A newly liberated father in Mississippi proclaimed, "If I nebber does nothing more while I live, I shall give my children a chance to go to school, for I considers education [the] next best ting to liberty."

A variety of organizations opened schools for formerly enslaved persons during the 1860s and 1870s. By 1870 nearly a quarter million blacks were attending one of the 4,300 schools established by the Freedmen's Bureau. Black and white churches and missionary societies sent hundreds of teachers, black and white, into the South to establish schools in former plantation areas. Their attitudes were often paternalistic and the schools were segregated, but the institutions they founded offered important educational resources for African Americans.

Parents worked hard to keep their children in school during the day. As children gained the rudiments of education, they passed on their knowledge to parents and older siblings whose jobs prevented them from attending school. Still, many adult freedpeople insisted on getting a bit of education for themselves. In New Bern, North Carolina, where many blacks labored until eight o'clock at night, a teacher reported that they then spent at least an hour "in earnest application to study."

Freedpeople sought education for a variety of reasons. Some viewed it as a sign of liberation. Others knew the importance of reading the labor contracts they signed if they were ever to challenge exploitation by whites. Some freedpeople were eager to correspond with relatives, others to read the Bible. Growing numbers hoped to participate in politics, particularly the public meetings organized by blacks in cities across the South. When such gatherings set priorities for the future, the establishment of public schools was high on the list.

Despite the enthusiasm of blacks and the efforts of the federal government and private agencies, schooling remained severely limited throughout the South. A shortage of teachers and of funding kept enrollments low among blacks and whites alike. The isolation of black farm families and the difficulties in eking out a living limited the resources available for education. By 1880, only about a quarter of African Americans were literate.

Freedom to Worship and the Leadership Role of Black Churches

One of the constant concerns freedpeople expressed was the desire to read the Bible and interpret it for themselves. A few black congregations had existed under slavery, but most slaves were forced to listen to white preachers who claimed that God created slavery.

From the moment of emancipation, freedpeople gathered at churches to cele-brate community events. Black Methodist and Baptist congregations spread rapidly across the South following the Civil War. In these churches, African Americans were no longer forced to sit in the back benches or punished for moral infractions defined by white masters. Now blacks invested community resources in their own religious institutions where they filled the pews, hired the preachers, and selected boards of deacons and elders. Churches were the largest structures available to freedpeople in many communities and thus were used by a variety of community organizations. They often served as schools and hosted picnics, dances, weddings, funerals, festivals, and other events that brought blacks together. Church leaders also often served as arbiters of community standards of morality.

In the early years of emancipation black churches also served as important sites for political organizing. Some black ministers worried that political concerns would overwhelm spiritual devotions. Others agreed with the Reverend Charles H. Pearce of Florida, who declared, "A man in this State cannot do his whole duty as a minister except he looks out for the political interests of his people." Whatever the views of ministers, black churches were among the few places where African Americans could express their political views free from white interference.

REVIEW & RELATE

- What were freedpeople's highest priorities in the years immediately following the Civil War? Why?
- How did freedpeople define freedom? What steps did they take to make freedom real for themselves and their children?

National Reconstruction

Presidents Abraham Lincoln and Andrew Johnson viewed Reconstruction as a process of national reconciliation. They sketched out terms by which the former Confederate states could reclaim their political representation in the nation without serious penal-ties. Congressional Republicans, however, had a more thoroughgoing reconstruction in mind. Like many African Americans, Republican congressional leaders expected the South to extend constitutional rights to the freedmen and to provide them with the political and economic resources to sustain their freedom. Over the next decade, these competing visions of Reconstruction played out in hard-fought and tumultu-ous battles over the meaning of the South's defeat and the emancipation of blacks.

Abraham Lincoln Plans for Reunification

In December 1863, even as battles continued, President Lincoln issued a **Proclamation of Amnesty and Reconstruction**, outlining his vision of the postwar world. Lincoln declared that defeated states would have to accept the abolition of slavery, but then new governments could be formed when 10 percent of those eligible to vote in 1860 (which in practice meant white southern men but not blacks) swore an oath of allegiance to the United States. Lincoln's plan granted amnesty to all but the highest-ranking Confederate officials, and the restored voters in each state would elect members to a constitutional convention and representatives to take their seats in Congress. In the next year and a half, Arkansas, Louisiana, and Tennessee—which were already under Union control—reestablished their governments under Lincoln's conciliatory "Ten Percent Plan."

Republicans in Congress had other ideas. Radical Republicans argued that the Confederate states should be treated as "conquered provinces" subject to congressional supervision. In 1864 Congress passed the Wade-Davis bill, which established much higher barriers for readmission to the Union than did Lincoln's plan. For instance, the Wade-Davis bill substituted 50 percent of voters for the president's 10 percent requirement. Lincoln put a stop to this harsher proposal by using a pocket veto—refusing to sign it within ten days of Congress's adjournment.

Although Lincoln and congressional Republicans disagreed about many aspects of postwar policy, Lincoln was flexible, and his actions mirrored his desire both to heal the Union and to help southern blacks. For example, the president supported the **Thirteenth Amendment**, abolishing slavery, which passed Congress in January 1865 and was sent to the states for ratification. In March 1865, Lincoln signed the law to create the Freedmen's Bureau. That same month, the president expressed his sincere wish for reconciliation between the North and the South. "With malice toward none, with charity for all," Lincoln declared in his second inaugural address, "let us strive on to finish the work . . . to bind up the nation's wounds." Lincoln would not, however, have the opportunity to implement his approach to Reconstruction. When he was assassinated in April 1865, it fell to Andrew Johnson, a very different sort of politician, to lead the country through the process of reintegration.

Andrew Johnson and Presidential Reconstruction

The nation needed a president who could transmit northern desires to the South with clarity and conviction and ensure that they were carried out. Instead, the nation got a president who substituted his own aims for those of the North, refused to engage in meaningful compromise, and misled the South into believing that he could achieve restoration quickly. In the 1864 election, Lincoln chose Johnson, a southern Democrat, as his running mate in a thinly veiled effort to attract border-state voters. The vice presidency was normally an inconsequential role, so it mattered little to Lincoln that Johnson was out of step with many Republican Party positions.

As president, however, Johnson's views took on profound importance. Born into rural poverty, Johnson had no sympathy for the southern aristocracy. Yet he had been a slave owner, so his political opposition to slavery was not rooted in moral convictions. Instead, it sprang from the belief that slavery gave plantation owners inordinate power and wealth, which came at the expense of the majority of white Southerners, who owned no slaves. Johnson saw emancipation as a means to "break down an odious and dangerous [planter] aristocracy," not to empower blacks. Consequently, he was unconcerned with the fate of African Americans in the postwar South. Six months after taking office, President Johnson rescinded the wartime order to distribute confiscated land to freedpeople in the Sea Islands. He saw no reason to punish the Confederacy's leaders, because he believed that the end of slavery would doom the southern aristocracy. He hoped to bring the South back into the Union as quickly as possible and then let Southerners take care of their own affairs.

Johnson's views, combined with a lack of political savvy and skill, ensured his inability to work constructively with congressional Republicans, even the moderates who constituted the majority. Moderate Republicans shared the prevalent belief of their time that blacks were inferior to whites, but they argued that the federal government needed to protect the enslaved people who were newly emancipated. Senator Lyman Trumbull of Illinois, for example, warned that without national legislation, ex-slaves would "be tyrannized over, abused, and virtually reenslaved." The moderates expected southern states, where 90 percent of African Americans lived, to extend basic civil rights to the freedpeople, including equal protection, due process of law, and the right to work and hold property.

Nearly all Republicans shared these positions, but the Radical wing of the party wanted to go further. Led by Senator Charles Sumner of Massachusetts and Congressman Thaddeus Stevens of Pennsylvania, this small but influential group advocated suffrage, that is voting rights, for African American men as well as the redistribution of southern plantation lands to the formerly enslaved. Stevens called on the federal government to provide freedpeople "a homestead of forty acres of land," which would give them some measure of autonomy. These efforts failed, and the Republican Party proved unable to pass a comprehensive land distribution program that enabled freed blacks to gain economic independence. Nonetheless, whatever disagreements between Radicals and moderates, all Republicans believed that Congress should have a strong voice in determining the fate of the former Confederate states. From May to December 1865, with Congress out of session, they waited to see what Johnson's restoration plan would produce, ready to assert themselves if his policies deviated too much from their own.

At first, it seemed as if Johnson would proceed as they hoped. He appointed provisional governors to convene new state constitutional conventions and urged these conventions to ratify the Thirteenth Amendment, abolishing slavery, and revoke the states' ordinances of secession. He also allowed the majority of white Southerners to obtain amnesty and a pardon by swearing their loyalty to the U.S. Constitution, but he required those who had held more than $20,000 of taxable property—the members of the southern aristocracy—to petition him for a special pardon to restore their rights. Republicans expected him to be harsh in dealing with his former political foes. Instead, Johnson relished the reversal of roles that put members of the southern elite at his mercy. As the once prominent petitioners paraded before him, the president granted almost all of their requests for pardons.

By the time Congress convened in December 1865, Johnson was satisfied that the southern states had fulfilled his requirements for restoration. Moderate and Radical Republicans disagreed, seeing few signs of change or contrition in the South. Mississippi, for example, rejected ratification of the Thirteenth Amendment. As a result of Johnson's liberal pardon policy, many former leaders of the Confederacy won election to state constitutional conventions and to Congress. Indeed, Georgians elected Confederate vice president Alexander H. Stephens to the U.S. Senate. As one white Mississippian candidly forecast, "Our negroes . . . will learn that freedom and independence are different things."

Indeed they did. Far from providing freedpeople with basic civil rights, the southern states passed a variety of **black codes** intended to reduce African Americans to a condition as close to slavery as possible. Some laws prohibited blacks from

Mourning at Stonewall Jackson's Gravesite, 1866 Many Northerners were concerned that the defeat of the Confederacy did not lessen white Southerners' devotion to the "Lost Cause" or the heroism of soldiers who fought to maintain a society based on the domination of African Americans. Women, who led the efforts to memorialize Confederate soldiers, are shown at the gravesite of General Stonewall Jackson in Lexington, Virginia. Virginia Military Institute Archives

bearing arms; others outlawed intermarriage and excluded blacks from serving on juries. The codes also made it difficult for blacks to leave plantations unless they proved they could support themselves. Other provisions sought to reduce the independence of black families. They empowered southern courts to assign black children to white employers without parental consent. Echoing the slave past, laws like these were designed to ensure that white landowners had a supply of cheap black labor despite the Thirteenth Amendment abolishing slavery.

Northerners viewed this situation with alarm. In their eyes, the postwar South looked very similar to the Old South, with a few cosmetic adjustments. If the black codes prevailed, one Republican proclaimed, "then I demand to know of what practical value is the amendment abolishing slavery?" Others wondered what their wartime sacrifices meant if the South admitted no mistakes, was led by the same people, and continued to oppress its black inhabitants.

Johnson and Congressional Resistance

Faced with growing opposition in the North, Johnson stubbornly held his ground. He insisted that the southern states had followed his plan and were entitled to resume their representation in Congress. Republicans objected, and in December 1865 they barred the admission of southern lawmakers. But Johnson refused to compromise. In January 1866, the president rejected a bill passed by Congress to extend the life of the Freedmen's Bureau for two years. A few months later, he vetoed the Civil Rights Act, which Congress had passed to protect freedpeople from the restrictions placed on them by the black codes. These bills represented a consensus among moderate and Radical Republicans on the federal government's responsibility toward the formerly enslaved.

Johnson justified his vetoes on both constitutional and personal grounds. He and other Democrats contended that so long as Congress refused to admit southern representatives, it could not legally pass laws affecting the South. The president also condemned the Freedmen's Bureau bill because it infringed on the right of states to handle internal affairs such as education and economic policies. Johnson's vetoes exposed his racism and his lifelong belief that the evil of slavery lay in the harm it did to poor whites, not to enslaved blacks. Johnson argued that the bills he vetoed discriminated against whites, who would receive no benefits under them, and thus put whites at a disadvantage with blacks receiving government assistance. Johnson's private secretary reported in his diary, "The president has at times exhibited a morbid distress and feeling against the Negroes."

Johnson's actions united moderates and Radicals against him. In April 1866, Congress repassed both the Freedmen's Bureau extension and Civil Rights Act over the president's vetoes. In June, lawmakers adopted the **Fourteenth Amendment**, which incorporated many of the provisions of the Civil Rights Act, and submitted it to the states for ratification (see Appendix). Reflecting its confrontational dealings with the president, Congress wanted to ensure more permanent protection for African Americans than simple legislation could provide. Lawmakers also wanted to act quickly, as the situation in the South seemed to be deteriorating rapidly. In May 1866, a race riot had broken out in Memphis, Tennessee. For a day and a half, white mobs, egged on by local police, went on a rampage, during which they terrorized blacks and burned their homes and churches. "The late riots in our city," the white editor of a Memphis newspaper asserted, "have satisfied all of one thing, that the *southern man* will not be ruled by the *negro*." A few months later, the New Orleans police, dominated by ex-Confederates, led a mob against black and white Republicans, killing thirty-four African Americans and three whites.

The Fourteenth Amendment defined citizenship to include African Americans, thereby nullifying the ruling in the *Dred Scott* case of 1857, which declared that blacks were not citizens. It extended equal protection and due process of law to all persons, not only citizens. The amendment repudiated Confederate debts, which some state governments had refused to do, and it barred Confederate officeholders from holding elective office unless Congress removed this provision by a two-thirds vote. Although most Republicans were upset with Johnson's behavior, at this point they were not willing to embrace the Radical position entirely. Rather than granting the right to vote to black males at least twenty- one years of age, the Fourteenth Amendment gave the states the option of excluding blacks and accepting a reduction in congressional representation if they did so.

Johnson remained inflexible. Instead of counseling the southern states to accept the Fourteenth Amendment, which would have sped up their readmission to the Union, he encouraged them to reject it. In the fall of 1866, Johnson decided to take his case directly to northern voters before the midterm congressional elections.

Campaigning for candidates who shared his views, he embarked on a swing through the Midwest. Out of touch with northern opinion, Johnson attacked Republican lawmakers and engaged in shouting matches with audiences. On election day, Republicans increased their majorities in Congress and now controlled two-thirds of the seats, providing them with greater power to override presidential vetoes.

Congressional Reconstruction

When the Fortieth Congress convened in 1867, Republican lawmakers charted a new course for Reconstruction. With moderates and Radicals united against the president, Congress intended to force the former Confederate states not only to protect the basic civil rights of African Americans but also to grant them the vote. Moderates now agreed with Radicals that unless blacks had access to the ballot, they would not be able to sustain their freedom. Extending the suffrage to African Americans also aided the fortunes of the Republican Party in the South by adding significant numbers of new voters. By the end of March, Congress enacted three Military Reconstruction Acts. Together they divided ten southern states into five military districts, each under the supervision of a Union general (Map 14.1). The male voters of each state, regardless of race, were to elect delegates to a constitutional convention; only former Confederate officials were disfranchised. The conventions were required to draft constitutions that guaranteed black suffrage and ratified the Fourteenth Amendment. Within a year, North Carolina, South Carolina, Florida, Alabama, Louisiana, and Arkansas had fulfilled these obligations and reentered the Union. In December 1866, only 0.5 percent of adult black males could vote in the United States; a year later the figure soared to 80.5 percent, with all of the gains made in the states subject to the military Reconstruction Acts.

Having ensured congressional Reconstruction in the South, Republican lawmakers turned their attention to disciplining the president. Johnson continued to resist their policies and used his power as commander in chief to order generals in the military districts to soften the intent of congressional Reconstruction. In response, Congress passed the Command of the Army Act in 1867, which required the president to issue all orders to army commanders in the field through the General of the Army in Washington, D.C., Ulysses S. Grant. The Radicals knew they could count on Grant to carry out their policies. Even more threatening to presidential power, Congress passed the **Tenure of Office Act**, which prevented Johnson from firing cabinet officers sympathetic to congressional Reconstruction. This measure barred the chief executive from removing from office any appointee that the Senate had ratified previously without returning to the Senate for approval.

Convinced that the new law was unconstitutional and outraged at this effort to limit his power, the quick-tempered Johnson chose to confront the Radical Republicans directly rather than seek a way around a congressional showdown. In February 1868, Johnson fired Secretary of War Edwin Stanton, a Lincoln appointee and a Radical sympathizer, without Senate approval. In response, congressional Radicals prepared articles of impeachment.

In late February, the House voted 126 to 47 to impeach Johnson, the first president ever to be impeached, or charged with unlawful activity. The case then went to trial in the Senate, where the chief justice of the United States presided

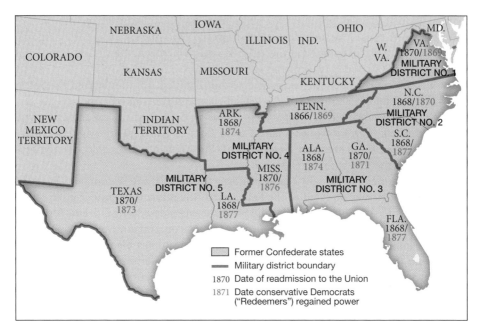

MAP 14.1　Reconstruction in the South
In 1867 Congress enacted legislation dividing the former Confederate states into five military districts. All the states were readmitted to the Union by 1870, and white conservative Democrats (Redeemers) had replaced Republicans in most states by 1875. Only in Florida, Louisiana, and South Carolina did federal troops remain until 1877.

and a two-thirds vote was necessary for conviction and removal from office. After a six-week hearing, the Senate fell one vote short of convicting Johnson. Most crucial for Johnson's fate were the votes of seven moderate Republicans who refused to find the president guilty of violating his oath to uphold the Constitution. They were convinced that Johnson's actions were insufficient to merit the enormous step of removing a president from office. Although Johnson remained in office, Congress effectively ended his power to shape Reconstruction policy.

The Republicans had restrained Johnson, and in 1868 they won back the presidency. Ulysses S. Grant, the popular Civil War general, ran against Horatio Seymour, the Democratic governor of New York. Although an ally of the Radical Republicans, Grant called for reconciliation with the South. He easily defeated Seymour, winning nearly 53 percent of the popular vote and 73 percent of the electoral vote.

The Struggle for Universal Suffrage

In February 1869, Congress passed the **Fifteenth Amendment** to protect black male suffrage, which had initially been guaranteed by the Military Reconstruction Acts. A compromise between moderate and Radical Republicans, the amendment prohibited voting discrimination based on race, but it did not deny states the power to impose qualifications based on literacy, payment of taxes, moral character, or any other standard that did not directly relate to race. Subsequently, the wording of the amendment provided loopholes for white leaders to disfranchise large numbers of African Americans. The amendment did, however, cover the entire nation, including the North, where states like Connecticut, Kansas, Michigan, New York, Ohio, and Wisconsin still excluded blacks from voting.

The Fifteenth Amendment sparked serious conflicts not only within the South but also among old abolitionist allies. The American Anti-Slavery Society had disbanded with emancipation. Immediately following the war, the many members who believed that important work remained to be done to guarantee the rights of freedpeople formed the **American Equal Rights Association**. However, its members divided over the Fifteenth Amendment.

Some women's rights advocates, including Elizabeth Cady Stanton and Susan B. Anthony, had earlier objected to the Fourteenth Amendment because it inserted the word *male* into the Constitution for the first time when describing citizens. Although they had supported abolition before the war, Stanton and Anthony worried that postwar policies intended to enhance the rights of southern black men would further limit the rights of women. While most African American activists embraced the Fifteenth Amendment, a few voiced concern. At a meeting of the Equal Rights

Frances Ellen Watkins Harper Born a free person of color in Baltimore, Frances Ellen Watkins Harper distinguished herself as a poet, a teacher, and an abolitionist. After the Civil War, she became a staunch advocate of women's suffrage and a supporter of the Fifteenth Amendment, which set her at odds with the suffragists Susan B. Anthony and Elizabeth Cady Stanton. Documenting the American South, University Library, The University of North Carolina at Chapel Hill, http://docsouth.unc.edu/neh/brownhal/ill22.html

Association in 1867, Sojourner Truth noted, "There is quite a stir about colored men getting their rights, but not a word about colored women."

At the 1869 meeting of the Equal Rights Association, differences over the measure erupted into open conflict. Stanton and Anthony denounced suffrage for black men only, and Stanton now supported her position on racial grounds. She claimed that the "dregs of China, Germany, England, Ireland, and Africa" were degrading the U.S. polity and argued that white, educated women should certainly have the same rights as immigrant and African American men. Black and white supporters of the Fifteenth Amendment, including Frances Ellen Watkins Harper, Wendell Phillips, Abby Kelley, and Frederick Douglass, denounced Stanton's bigotry. Believing that southern black men urgently needed suffrage to protect their newly won freedom, they argued that ratification of the Fifteenth Amendment would speed progress toward the enfranchisement of women, black and white.

This conflict led to the formation of competing organizations committed to women's suffrage. The National Woman Suffrage Association, established by Stanton and Anthony, allowed only women as members and opposed ratification of the Fifteenth Amendment. The American Woman Suffrage Association, which attracted the support of women and men, white and black, supported ratification. Less than a year later, in the spring of 1870, the Fifteenth Amendment was ratified and went into effect.

Since the amendment did not grant the vote to either white or black women, women suffragists attempted to use the Fourteenth Amendment to achieve their goal. In 1875 Virginia Minor, who had been denied the ballot in Missouri, argued that the right to vote was one of the "privileges and immunities" granted to all citizens under the Fourteenth Amendment. In *Minor v. Happersett*, the Supreme Court ruled against her, and most women were denied national suffrage for decades thereafter.

REVIEW & RELATE	• What was President Johnson's plan for reconstruction? How were his views out of step with those of most Republicans? • What characterized congressional Reconstruction? What priorities were reflected in congressional Reconstruction legislation?

Remaking the South

With President Johnson's power effectively curtailed, reconstruction of the South moved quickly. New state legislatures, ruled by a coalition of southern whites and blacks and white northern migrants, enacted political, economic, and social reforms that improved the overall quality of life in the South. Despite these changes, many black and white Southerners barely eked out a living under the planter-dominated sharecropping system. Moreover, the biracial Reconstruction governments lasted a relatively short time, as conservative whites used a variety of tactics, including terror and race baiting, to defeat their opponents at the polls.

Whites Reconstruct the South

During the first years of congressional Reconstruction, two groups of whites occupied the majority of elective offices in the South. A significant number of native-born Southerners joined Republicans in forging postwar constitutions and governments.

Before the war, some had belonged to the Whig Party and opposed secession from the Union. Western sections of Alabama, Georgia, North Carolina, and Tennessee had demonstrated a fiercely independent strain, and many residents had remained loyal to the Union. Small merchants and farmers who detested large plantation owners also threw in their lot with the Republicans. Even a few ex-Confederates, such as General James A. Longstreet, decided that the South must change and allied with the Republicans. The majority of whites who continued to support the Democratic Party viewed these whites as traitors. They showed their distaste by calling them **scalawags**, an unflattering term meaning "scoundrels."

At the same time, Northerners came south to support Republican Reconstruction. They had varied reasons for making the journey, but most considered the South a new frontier to be conquered culturally, politically, and economically. Some—white and black—had served in the Union army during the war, liked what they saw of the region, and decided to settle there. Some of both races came to provide education and assist the freedpeople in adjusting to their new lives. As a relatively underdeveloped area, the South also beckoned fortune seekers and adventurers who saw opportunities to get rich. Southern Democrats denounced such northern interlopers, particularly whites, as **carpetbaggers**, suggesting that they invaded the region with all their possessions in a satchel, seeking to plunder it and then leave. While Northerners did seek economic opportunity, they were acting as Americans always had in settling new frontiers and pursuing dreams of success. In fact, much of the animosity directed toward them resulted primarily not from their mere presence, but from their efforts to ally with African Americans in reshaping the South.

Black Political Participation and Economic Opportunities

Still, the primary targets of southern white hostility were African Americans who attempted to exercise their hard-won freedom. Blacks constituted a majority of voters in five states—Alabama, Florida, South Carolina, Mississippi, and Louisiana—while in Georgia, North Carolina, Texas, and Virginia they fell short of a majority. They did not use their ballots to impose black rule on the South, as many white Southerners feared. Only in South Carolina did African Americans control the state legislature, and in no state did they manage to elect a governor. Nevertheless, for the first time in American history, blacks won a wide variety of elected positions. More than six hundred blacks served in state legislatures; another sixteen, including Jefferson Long, held seats in the U.S. House of Representatives; and two from Mississippi were chosen to serve in the U.S. Senate.

Former slaves showed enthusiasm for politics in other ways, too. African Americans considered politics a community responsibility, and in addition to casting ballots, they held rallies and mass meetings to discuss issues and choose candidates. Although they could not vote, women attended these gatherings and helped influence their outcome. Covering a Republican convention in Richmond in October 1867, held in the First African Baptist Church, the *New York Times* reported that "the entire colored population of Richmond" attended. In addition, freedpeople formed mutual aid associations to promote education, economic advancement, and social welfare programs, all of which they saw as deeply intertwined with politics.

Southern blacks also bolstered their freedom by building alliances with sympathetic whites. These interracial political coalitions produced considerable reform in the South. They created the first public school systems; provided funds for social services, such as poor relief and state hospitals; upgraded prisons; and rebuilt the South's transportation system. Moreover, the state constitutions that the Republicans wrote brought a greater measure of political democracy and equality to the South by extending suffrage to poor white men as well as black men. Some states allowed married women greater control over their property and liberalized the criminal justice system. In effect, these Reconstruction governments brought the South into the nineteenth century.

Obtaining political representation was one way in which African Americans defined freedom. Economic independence constituted a second. Without government-sponsored land redistribution, however, the options for southern blacks remained limited. Lacking capital to purchase farms, most entered into various forms of tenant contracts with large landowners. **Sharecropping** proved the most common arrangement. Blacks and poor whites became sharecroppers for much the same reasons. They received tools and supplies from landowners and farmed their own plots of land on the plantation. In exchange, sharecroppers turned over a portion of their harvest to the owner and kept the rest for themselves.

The benefits of sharecropping proved less valuable to black farmers in practice than in theory. To tide them over during the growing season, croppers had to purchase household provisions on credit from a local merchant, who was often also their landlord. At the mercy of store owners who kept the books and charged high interest rates, tenants usually found themselves in considerable debt at the end of the year. To satisfy the debt, merchants devised a crop lien system in which tenants pledged a portion of their yearly crop to satisfy what they owed. Falling prices for agricultural crops in this period ensured that most indebted tenants did not receive sufficient return on their produce to get out of debt and thus remained bound to their landlords. For many African Americans, sharecropping turned into a form of virtual slavery.

The picture for black farmers was not all bleak, however. About 20 percent of black farmers managed to buy their own land. Through careful management and extremely hard work, black families planted gardens for household consumption and raised chickens for eggs and meat. Despite its pitfalls, even sharecropping provided a limited measure of independence and allowed some blacks to accumulate small amounts of cash.

Following the war's devastation, many of the South's white small farmers, known as yeomen, also fell into sharecropping. Meanwhile, many planters' sons abandoned farming and became lawyers, bankers, and merchants. Despite these changes, one thing remained the same: White elites ruled over blacks and poor whites, and they kept these two economically exploited groups from uniting by fanning the flames of racial prejudice.

Economic hardship and racial bigotry drove many blacks to leave the South. In 1879 former slaves, known as **Exodusters**, pooled their resources to create land companies and purchase property in Kansas on which to settle. They encouraged an exodus of some 25,000 African Americans from the South. Kansas was ruled by the Republican Party and had been home to the great antislavery martyr John Brown. As one hopeful freedman from Louisiana wrote to the Kansas governor in 1879, "I am anxious to reach your state . . . because of the sacredness of her soil washed in the blood of humanitarians for the cause of black freedom." Yet poor-quality land

and unpredictable weather often made farming on the Great Plains hard and unrewarding. Nevertheless, for many black migrants, the chance to own their own land
and escape the oppression of the South was worth the hardships. In 1880 the census
counted 40,000 blacks living in Kansas.

White Resistance to Congressional Reconstruction

Despite the Republican record of accomplishment during Reconstruction, white
Southerners did not accept its legitimacy. They accused interracial governments of
conducting a spending spree that raised taxes and encouraged corruption. Indeed,
taxes did rise significantly, but mainly because legislatures funded much-needed educational and social services. Corruption on building projects and railroad construction was common during this time. Still, it is unfair to single out Reconstruction
governments and especially black legislators as inherently depraved since their Democratic opponents acted the same way when given the opportunity. Economic scandals
were part of American life after the Civil War. As enormous business opportunities
arose in the postwar years, many economic and political leaders made unlawful deals
to enrich themselves. Furthermore, southern opponents of Reconstruction exaggerated its harshness. In contrast to revolutions and civil wars in other countries, only
one rebel was executed for war crimes (the commandant of Andersonville Prison in
Georgia); only one high-ranking official went to prison (Jefferson Davis); no official
was forced into exile, though some fled voluntarily; and most rebels regained voting
rights and the ability to hold office within seven years after the end of the rebellion.

    Most important, these Reconstruction governments had only limited
opportunities to transform the South. By the end of 1870, civilian rule had returned
to all of the former Confederate states, and they had reentered the Union. Republican
rule did not continue past 1870 in Virginia, North Carolina, and Tennessee and did
not extend beyond 1871 in Georgia and 1873 in Texas. In 1874 Democrats deposed
Republicans in Arkansas and Alabama; two years later, Democrats triumphed in
Mississippi. In only three states — Louisiana, Florida, and South Carolina — did
Reconstruction last until 1877.

    The Democrats who replaced Republicans trumpeted their victories as bringing
"redemption" to the South. Of course, these so-called **Redeemers** were referring
to the white South. For black Republicans and their white allies, redemption
meant defeat. Democratic victories came at the ballot boxes, but violence,
intimidation, and fraud paved the way. In 1865 in Pulaski, Tennessee General
Nathan Bedford Forrest organized Confederate veterans into a social club called
the **Knights of the Ku Klux Klan (KKK)**. Spreading throughout the South, its
followers donned robes and masks to hide their identities and terrify their victims.
Gun-wielding Ku Kluxers rode on horseback to the homes and churches of black
and white Republicans to keep them from voting. When threats did not work, they
beat and murdered their victims. In 1871, for example, 150 African Americans were
killed in Jackson County in the Florida Panhandle. A black clergyman lamented,
"That is where Satan has his seat." There and elsewhere, many of the individuals
targeted had managed to buy property, gain political leadership, or in other ways
defy white stereotypes of African American inferiority. Other white supremacist
organizations joined the Klan in waging a reign of terror. During the 1875 election

in Mississippi, which toppled the Republican government, armed terrorists killed hundreds of Republicans and scared many more away from the polls.

To combat the terror unleashed by the Klan and its allies, Congress passed three **Force Acts** in 1870 and 1871. These measures empowered the president to dispatch officials into the South to supervise elections and prevent voting interference. Directed specifically at the KKK, one law barred secret organizations from using force to violate equal protection of the laws. In 1872 Congress established a joint committee to probe Klan tactics, and its investigations produced thirteen volumes of gripping testimony about the horrors perpetrated by the Klan. Elias Hill, a freedman from South Carolina who had become a Baptist preacher and teacher, was one of those who appeared before Congress. He and his brother lived next door to each other. The Klansmen went first to his brother's house, where, as Hill testified, they "broke open the door and attacked his wife, and I heard her screaming and mourning [moaning]. . . . At last I heard them have [rape] her in the yard." When the Klansmen discovered Elias Hill, they dragged him out of his house and beat, whipped, and threatened to kill him. On the basis of such testimony, the federal government prosecuted some 3,000 Klansmen. Only 600 were convicted, however. As the Klan disbanded in the wake of federal prosecutions, other vigilante organizations arose to take its place.

REVIEW & RELATE	• What role did black people play in remaking southern society during Reconstruction? • How did southern whites fight back against Reconstruction? What role did terrorism and political violence play in this effort?

The Unraveling of Reconstruction

The violence, intimidation, and fraud perpetrated by white Redeemers does not fully explain the unraveling of Reconstruction. By the early 1870s most white Northerners had come to believe that they had done more than enough for black Southerners, and it was time to focus on other issues. Growing economic problems intensified this feeling. Still reeling from the amount of blood shed during the war, white Americans, north and south, turned their attention toward burying and memorializing the Civil War dead. White America was once again united, if only in the shared belief that it was time to move on, consigning the issues of slavery and civil rights to history.

The Republican Retreat

Most northern whites shared the racial prejudices of their counterparts in the South. Although they had supported protection of black civil rights and suffrage, they still believed that African Americans were inferior to whites and were horrified by the idea of social integration. They began to sympathize with southern whites' racist complaints that blacks were not capable of governing honestly and effectively.

In 1872 a group calling themselves Liberal Republicans challenged the reelection of President Grant. Financial scandals had racked the Grant administration. This high-level corruption reflected other get-rich-quick schemes connected to economic speculation and development following the Civil War. Outraged by the rising level of immoral behavior in government and business, Liberal Republicans nominated Horace Greeley, editor of the *New York Tribune*, to run against Grant. They linked government corruption to the expansion of federal power that accompanied Reconstruction and called for the removal of troops from the South and amnesty for all former Confederates. They also campaigned for civil service reform, which would base government employment on a merit system and abolish the "spoils system"—in which the party in power rewarded loyal supporters with political appointments—that had been introduced by Andrew Jackson in the 1820s.

The Democratic Party believed that Liberal Republicans offered the best chance to defeat Grant, and it endorsed Greeley. Despite the scandals that surrounded him, Grant remained popular. Moreover, the main body of Republicans "waved the bloody shirt," reminding northern voters that a ballot cast for the opposition tarnished the memory of brave Union soldiers killed during the war. The president won reelection with an even greater margin than he had four years earlier. Nevertheless, the attacks against Grant foreshadowed the Republican retreat on Reconstruction. Among the Democrats sniping at Grant was Andrew Johnson. Johnson had returned to Tennessee, and in 1874 the state legislature chose the former president to serve in the U.S. Senate. He continued to speak out against the presence of federal troops in the South until his death in 1875.

Congressional and Judicial Retreat

By the time Grant began his second term, Congress was already considering bills to restore officeholding rights to former Confederates who had not yet sworn allegiance to the Union. Black representatives, including Georgia congressman Jefferson Long, as well as some white lawmakers, remained opposed to such measures, but in 1872 Congress removed the penalties placed on former Confederates by the Fourteenth Amendment and permitted nearly all rebel leaders the right to vote and hold office. Two years later, for the first time since the start of the Civil War, the Democrats gained a majority in the House of Representatives and prepared to remove the remaining troops from the South.

Republican leaders also rethought their top priority with economic concerns increasingly replacing racial considerations. In 1873 a financial panic resulting from the collapse of the Northern Pacific Railroad triggered a severe economic depression lasting late into the decade. Tens of thousands of unemployed workers across the country worried more about finding jobs than they did about black civil rights. Businessmen, too, were plagued with widespread bankruptcies. When strikes erupted across the country in 1877, most notably the Great Railway Strike, in which more than half a million workers walked off the job, employers asked the U.S. government to remove troops from the South and dispatch them against strikers in the North and West.

While white Northerners sought ways to extricate themselves from Reconstruction, the Supreme Court weakened enforcement of the civil rights acts. In 1873 the *Slaughterhouse* cases defined the rights that African Americans were entitled to under the Fourteenth Amendment very narrowly. Reflecting the shift from moral to economic concerns, the justices interpreted the amendment as extending greater protection to corporations in conducting business than to blacks. As a result, blacks had to depend on southern state governments to protect their civil rights, the same state authorities that had deprived them of their rights in the first place. In *United States v. Cruikshank* (1876), the high court narrowed the Fourteenth Amendment further, ruling that it protected blacks against abuses only by state officials and agencies, not by private groups such as the Ku Klux Klan. Seven years later, the Court struck down the Civil Rights Act of 1875, which had extended "full and equal treatment" in public accommodations for persons of all races.

The Presidential Compromise of 1876

The presidential election of 1876 set in motion events that officially brought Reconstruction to an end. The Republicans nominated the governor of Ohio, Rutherford B. Hayes, who was chosen partly because he was untainted by the corruption that plagued the Grant administration. The Democrats selected their own anticorruption crusader, Governor Samuel J. Tilden of New York.

The outcome of the election depended on twenty disputed electoral votes, nineteen from the South and one from Oregon. Tilden won 51 percent of the popular vote, but Reconstruction political battles in Florida, Louisiana, and South Carolina put the election up for grabs. In each of these states, the outgoing Republican administration certified Hayes as the winner, while the incoming Democratic regime declared for Tilden.

The Constitution assigns Congress the task of counting and certifying the electoral votes submitted by the states. Normally, this is a mere formality, but 1876 was different. Democrats controlled the House, Republicans controlled the Senate, and neither branch would budge on which votes to count. Hayes needed all twenty for victory; Tilden needed only one. To break the logjam, Congress created a fifteen-member Joint Electoral Commission, composed of seven Democrats, seven Republicans, and one independent. Ultimately, a majority voted to count all twenty votes for the Republican Hayes, making him president (Map 14.2).

Still, Congress had to ratify this count, and disgruntled southern Democrats in the Senate threatened a filibuster — unlimited debate — to block certification of Hayes. With the March 4, 1877, date for the presidential inauguration creeping perilously close and no winner officially declared, behind-the-scenes negotiations finally settled the controversy. A series of meetings between Hayes supporters and southern Democrats led to a bargain. According to the agreement, Democrats would support Hayes in exchange for the president appointing a Southerner to his cabinet, withdrawing the last federal troops from the South, and endorsing construction of a transcontinental railroad through the South. This **compromise of 1877** averted a crisis over presidential succession, underscored increased southern Democratic influence within Congress, and marked the end of strong federal protections for African Americans in the South.

REVIEW & RELATE	• Why did northern interest in Reconstruction wane in the 1870s? • What common values and beliefs among white Americans were reflected in the compromise of 1877?

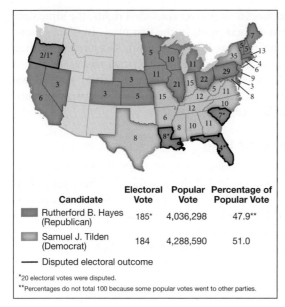

Candidate	Electoral Vote	Popular Vote	Percentage of Popular Vote
Rutherford B. Hayes (Republican)	185*	4,036,298	47.9**
Samuel J. Tilden (Democrat)	184	4,288,590	51.0
—— Disputed electoral outcome			

*20 electoral votes were disputed.

**Percentages do not total 100 because some popular votes went to other parties.

MAP 14.2   The Election of 1876

The presidential election of 1876 got swept up in Reconstruction politics. Democrats defeated Republicans in Florida, Louisiana, and South Carolina, but both parties claimed the electoral votes for their candidates. A federal electoral commission set up to investigate the twenty disputed votes, including one from Oregon, awarded the votes and the election to the Republican, Rutherford B. Hayes.

Conclusion: The Legacies of Reconstruction

Reconstruction was, in many ways, profoundly limited. Notwithstanding the efforts of the Freedmen's Bureau, African Americans did not receive the landownership that would have provided them with economic independence and bolstered their freedom from the racist assaults of white Southerners. The civil and political rights that the federal government conferred did not withstand the efforts of former Confederates to disfranchise and deprive the freedpeople of equal rights. The Republican Party shifted its priorities, and Democrats gained enough political power nationally to short-circuit federal intervention, even as numerous problems remained unresolved in the South. Northern support for racial equality did not run very deep, so white Northerners, who shared many of the prejudices of white Southerners, were happy to extricate themselves from further intervention in southern racial matters. Nor was there sufficient support to give women, white or black, the right to vote. Finally, federal courts, with growing concerns over economic rather than social issues, sanctioned Northerners' retreat by providing constitutional legitimacy for abandoning black Southerners and rejecting women's suffrage in court decisions that narrowed the interpretation of the Fourteenth and Fifteenth Amendments.

Despite all of this, Reconstruction did transform the country. As a result of Reconstruction, slavery was abolished and the legal basis for freedom was enshrined in the Constitution. Indeed, blacks exercised a measure of political and economic freedom during Reconstruction that never entirely disappeared over the decades to come. In many areas, freedpeople, exemplified by Congressman Jefferson Franklin Long and many others, asserted what they never could have during slavery—control over their lives, their churches, their labor, their education, and their families. What they could not practice during their own time, their descendants would one day revive through the promises codified in the Fourteenth and Fifteenth Amendments.

African Americans transformed not only themselves; they transformed the nation. The Constitution became much more democratic and egalitarian through inclusion of the Reconstruction amendments. Reconstruction lawmakers took an important step toward making the United States the "more perfect union" that the nation's Founders had pledged to create. Reconstruction established a model for expanding the power of the federal government to resolve domestic crises that lay beyond the abilities of states and ordinary citizens. It remained a powerful legacy for elected officials who dared to invoke it. And Reconstruction transformed the South to its everlasting benefit. It modernized state constitutions, expanded educational and social welfare systems, and unleashed the repressed potential for industrialization and new forms of economic development that the preservation of slavery had restrained. Ironically, Reconstruction did as much for white Southerners as it did for black Southerners in liberating them from the past.

Chapter 14 Review

KEY TERMS

Freedmen's Bureau, 352
Proclamation of Amnesty and
   Reconstruction, 355
Thirteenth Amendment, 356
black codes, 357
Fourteenth Amendment, 359
Tenure of Office Act, 360
Fifteenth Amendment, 361
American Equal Rights Association, 362

scalawags, 364
carpetbaggers, 364
sharecropping, 365
Exodusters, 365
Redeemers, 366
Knights of the Ku Klux Klan (KKK), 366
Force Acts, 367
compromise of 1877, 369

REVIEW & RELATE

1. What were freedpeople's highest priorities in the years immediately following the Civil War? Why?
2. How did freedpeople define freedom? What steps did they take to make freedom real for themselves and their children?
3. What was President Johnson's plan for reconstruction? How were his views out of step with those of most Republicans?
4. What characterized congressional Reconstruction? What priorities were reflected in congressional Reconstruction legislation?
5. What role did black people play in remaking southern society during Reconstruction?
6. How did southern whites fight back against Reconstruction? What role did terrorism and political violence play in this effort?
7. Why did northern interest in Reconstruction wane in the 1870s?
8. What common values and beliefs among white Americans were reflected in the compromise of 1877?

TIMELINE OF EVENTS

1863   • Lincoln issues Proclamation of Amnesty and Reconstruction

1865   • Ku Klux Klan formed

            • Freedmen's Bureau established

            • Thirteenth Amendment passed

            • Lincoln assassinated; Andrew Johnson becomes president

1866   • Freedmen's Bureau and Civil Rights Act extended over Johnson's presidential veto

            • Fourteenth Amendment passed

1867   • Military Reconstruction Acts

            • Command of the Army and Tenure of Office Acts passed

1868   • Andrew Johnson impeached

1869   • Fifteenth Amendment passed

            • Women's suffrage movement splits over support of Fifteenth Amendment

1870   • 250,000 blacks attend schools established by the Freedmen's Bureau

            • Civilian rule returns to the South

1870–1872 • Congress takes steps to curb Ku Klux Klan violence in the South

1873   • Financial panic sparks depression

1873–1883 • Supreme Court limits rights of African Americans

1875   • Civil Rights Act passed

1877   • Rutherford B. Hayes becomes president

            • Reconstruction ends

1879   • Black Exodusters migrate from South to Kansas

15

The West

1865–1896

LEARNING OBJECTIVES

After reading this chapter you will be able to:

- Analyze the motives and incentives that led to settling of the trans-Mississippi West and the technological developments that encouraged it.

- Evaluate the strategies used by the U.S. government to control the lives of Native Americans in the West and Indians' reactions to these efforts.

- Compare the roles of the mining and lumber industries in the economic and social development of the West.

- Summarize the factors that led to the rise of commercial ranching and contrast the image of life in the West for ranchers and farmers with the reality.

- Analyze the cultural diversity of the far West and the ethnic tensions that followed from this diversity.

COMPARING AMERICAN HISTORIES

Born in 1860, Phoebe Ann Moses grew up east of the Mississippi, seventy miles north of Cincinnati, Ohio. One of seven surviving children, she was sent to an orphanage at the age of nine, after her father died and her mother could not care for all her children. After working for a farm family, she ran away at the age of twelve and found a new home with a recently remarried widow. There, Phoebe Ann learned to ride and hunt and became an expert shot with a rifle. At fifteen, she entered a shooting contest and defeated a professional marksman, Frank Butler. The two married in 1876. Phoebe Ann changed her professional name to **"Annie Oakley,"** and she and Butler toured the Midwest in an act that featured precision shooting.

In 1884 Oakley and Butler met William F. "Buffalo Bill" Cody in New Orleans. In 1883, as the western frontier began to recede and the U.S. government relocated Native Americans who lived there, Cody attempted to recapture and reinvent the frontier experience by staging "Wild West" shows. A year later, he hired Oakley, with Butler serving as her manager. For the next fifteen years, Oakley was the star of the show. Wearing a fringed skirt, an embroidered blouse, and a broad felt hat, she stood atop her horse and performed amazing feats of marksmanship. Oakley toured Europe and fascinated heads of state and audiences alike with her version of "western authenticity." Fans at home and overseas displayed great nostalgia for a fast-diminishing era. When the census of 1890 reported that no open land was left to settle and thus no western frontier was left to conquer, Oakley's popularity soared. She continued performing in Wild West shows until her death in 1926.

While Annie Oakley portrayed the Wild West, **Geronimo** had lived it. Born to a Chiricahua Apache family in what was then northern Mexico (present-day Arizona and New Mexico), Geronimo led Apaches in a constant struggle against Spain, Mexico, and the United States. In 1851 a band of Mexicans raided an Apache camp, murdering Geronimo's mother, wife, and three children. After fighting Mexicans, Geronimo clashed with U.S. troops and evaded capture until 1877, when an Indian agent arrested him in New Mexico. Sent to a reservation, Geronimo escaped and for eight years engaged in daring raids against his foes. In 1886 two Chiricahua scouts led the U.S. military to Geronimo. Against an army of five thousand soldiers, the Apache warrior, with a band of eighteen fighters and some women and children, finally surrendered and was eventually relocated by the U.S. government to Fort Sill, Oklahoma.

The once-elusive warrior decided to take advantage of his legendary reputation and America's growing fascination with the mythic West. He sold photos of himself and pieces of his clothing; he appeared at the 1904 World's Fair in St. Louis, selling bows and arrows and autographs; and in 1905 he rode in President Theodore Roosevelt's inaugural parade as an example of a "tamed" Indian. Despite all of this, Geronimo never gave up the idea of returning to his birthplace. As long as the U.S. government prohibited him from going back to his ancestral lands in the Southwest, he considered himself a "prisoner of war." And so he remained until his death in 1909.

THE AMERICAN HISTORIES of Annie Oakley and Geronimo were profoundly different, yet they both contributed to the creation of a shared story, the myth of the American West. The West has great fascination in American culture. Stories about the frontier have romanticized both cowboys and Indians. These stories have also glorified individualism, self-help, and American ingenuity and minimized cooperation, organization, and the role of foreign influence in developing the West. As the American histories of Annie Oakley and Geronimo make clear, reality presents a more complicated picture of a diverse region initially inhabited by native peoples who were pushed aside by the arrival of white settlers and immigrants. In the areas known as the Great Plains and the far West, women took on new roles, and new cities emerged to accommodate the influx of miners, ranchers, and farmers.

Opening the West

The area west of the Mississippi was not hospitable to farmers and other adventurers lured by the appeal of cheap land and a fresh start. These pioneers demonstrated rugged determination; however, they could not have settled the West on their own. Federal policy and foreign investment played a large role in encouraging and financing the development of the West. Railroads were essential in transforming the region (Map 15.1).

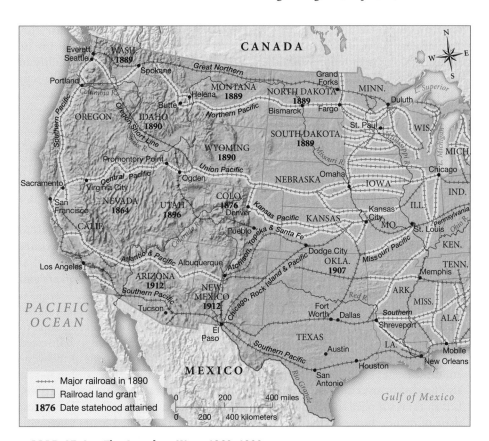

MAP 15.1 The American West, 1860–1900
Railroads played a key role in the expansion and settlement of the American West. The network of railroads running throughout the West opened the way for extensive migration from the East and for the development of a national market. None of this would have been possible without the land grants provided to the railroads by the U.S. government.

The Great Plains

In the mid-nineteenth century, the western frontier lay in the **Great Plains**. Lying on both sides of the Rocky Mountains, the Great Plains plateau was a semiarid territory with an average yearly rainfall sufficient to sustain short grasslands but not many trees. Prospects for sedentary farmers in this dry region did not appear promising. In 1878 geologist John Wesley Powell issued a report that questioned whether the land beyond the easternmost portion of the Great Plains could support small farming. Lack of rainfall, he argued, would make it difficult or even impossible for homesteaders to support themselves on family farms of 160 acres. Instead, he recommended that for the plains to prove economically sustainable, settlers would have to work much larger stretches of land, around 2,560 acres (4 square miles). This would provide ample room to raise livestock under dry conditions.

Powell's words of caution did little to dissuade Americans who intended to pursue Thomas Jefferson's vision of small farmers who would populate U.S. territories and demonstrate democratic values. Rejecting the idea that the Great Plains should remain a "perpetual desert," Charles Dana Wilber, a land speculator and journalist, asserted that "in reality there is no desert anywhere except by man's permission or neglect." Along with millions of others, he had great faith in Americans' ability to turn the Great Plains into a place where Jefferson's republican vision could take root and prosper.

Federal Policy and Foreign Investment

Despite the popular association of the West with individual initiative and self-sufficiency, the federal government played a huge role in facilitating the settlement of the West. National lawmakers enacted legislation offering free or cheap land to settlers and to mining, lumber, and railroad companies. The U.S. government also provided subsidies for transporting mail and military supplies, recruited soldiers to subdue Indian people who stood in the way of expansion, and appointed officials to govern the territories. Through these efforts, the government provided a necessary measure of safety and stability for new businesses to start up and grow as well as interconnected transportation and communication systems to supply workers and promote opportunities to develop new markets across North America.

Along with federal policy, foreign investment helped fuel development of the West. Lacking sufficient funds of its own, the United States turned to Europe to finance the sale of public bonds and private securities. European firms also invested in American mines, with the British leading the way. The development of the western cattle range—the symbol of the American frontier and the heroic cowboy—was also funded by overseas financiers. At the height of the cattle boom in the 1880s, British firms supplied some $45 million to underwrite ranch operations. The largest share of money, however, that flowed from Europe to the United States came with the expansion of the railroads, the most important ingredient in opening the West (Figure 15.1).

The **transcontinental railroad** became the gateway to the West. In 1862 the Republican-led Congress appropriated vast areas of land that railroad companies could use to lay their tracks or sell to raise funds for construction. The Central Pacific

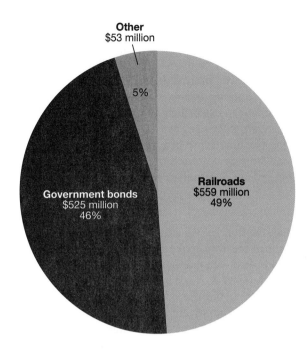

Other
$53 million

5%

Railroads
$559 million
49%

Government bonds
$525 million
46%

FIGURE 15.1 British Foreign Investment in the United States, 1876 British investment was an important source of funding for westward expansion following the Civil War. Nearly half of all British loans went toward financing railroad construction, which required large capital expenditures. The British also invested heavily in government bonds and to a lesser extent in cattle ranching and mining enterprises. Why did American railroads attract so much British investment?
Source: Data from Mina Wilkins, *The History of Foreign Investment in the United States to 1914* (Cambridge, MA: Harvard University Press, 1989), 164.

Company built from west to east, starting in Sacramento, California. The construction project attracted thousands of Chinese railroad workers. From the opposite direction, the Union Pacific Company began laying track in Council Bluffs, Iowa, and hired primarily Irish workers. In May 1869, the Central Pacific and Union Pacific crews met at Promontory Point, Utah. Workmen from the two companies drove a golden spike to complete the connection. For many Americans recovering from four years of civil war and still embroiled in southern reconstruction, the completion of the transcontinental railroad renewed their faith in the nation's ingenuity and destiny. A wagon train had once taken six to eight weeks to travel across the West. That trip could now be completed by rail in seven days. The railroad allowed both people and goods to move faster and in greater numbers than before. The West was now open not just to rugged pioneers but to anyone who could afford a railroad ticket.

The building of the railroads also provided new business opportunities, albeit more questionable. For example, Union Pacific promoters created a fake construction company called the Crédit Mobilier, which they used to funnel government bond and contract money into their own pockets. They also bribed congressmen to avoid investigation into their sordid dealings. Despite these efforts, in 1872 Congress exposed this corruption.

REVIEW & RELATE
- What role did the federal government play in opening the West to settlement and economic exploitation?
- Explain the determination of Americans to settle in land west of the Mississippi River despite the challenges the region presented.

Indians and Resistance to Expansion

American pioneers may have thought they were moving into a wilderness, but the West was home to large numbers of American Indians. Before pioneers and entrepreneurs could go west to pursue their economic dreams, the U.S. government would decide to remove this obstacle to American expansion. Through treaties — most of which Americans broke — and war, white Americans conquered the Indian tribes inhabiting the Great Plains during the nineteenth century. After the native population was largely subdued, those who wanted to reform Indian policy focused on carving up tribal lands and forcing Indians to assimilate into American society.

Indian Civilizations

Long before white settlers appeared, the frontier was already home to diverse peoples. The many native groups who inhabited the West spoke distinct languages, engaged in different economic activities, and competed with one another for power and resources. The descendants of Spanish conquistadors had also lived in the Southwest and California since the late sixteenth century, pushing the boundaries of the Spanish empire northward from Mexico. Indeed, Spaniards established the city of Santa Fe as the territorial capital of New Mexico years before the English landed at Jamestown, Virginia in 1607.

By the end of the Civil War, around 350,000 Indians were living west of the Mississippi. They constituted the surviving remnants of the 1 million people who had occupied the land for thousands of years before Europeans set foot in America. Nez Percé, Ute, and Shoshone Indians lived in the Northwest and the Rocky Mountain region; Lakota, Cheyenne, Blackfoot, Crow, and Arapaho tribes occupied the vast expanse of the central and northern plains; and Apaches, Comanches, Kiowas, Navajos, and Pueblos made up the bulk of the population in the Southwest. Some of the tribes, such as the Cherokee, Creek, and Shawnee, had been forcibly removed from the East during Andrew Jackson's presidency in the 1830s.

Indian tribes each adapted in unique ways to the geography and climate of their home territories, spoke their own language, and had their own history and traditions. Some were hunters, others farmers; some nomadic, others sedentary. In New Mexico, for example, Apaches were expert horsemen and fierce warriors, while the Pueblo Indians built homes out of adobe and developed a flourishing system of agriculture. Also, they cultivated the land through methods of irrigation that foreshadowed modern practices. The Pawnees in the Great Plains periodically set fire to the land to improve game hunting and the growth of vegetation. Indians on the southern plains gradually became enmeshed in the market economy for bison robes, which they sold to American traders (Map 15.2).

The lives of all Indian peoples were affected by the arrival of Europeans, but the consequences of cross-cultural contact varied considerably depending on the circumstances of each tribe. Whites trampled on Indian hunting grounds, polluted streams with acid run-off from mines, and introduced Indians to liquor. They inflicted the greatest damage through diseases for which Indians lacked the immunity that Europeans and white Americans had acquired. By 1870, smallpox had wiped out half the population of Plains Indians, and cholera, diphtheria, and measles caused serious but lesser harm. Nomadic tribes such as the Lakota Sioux were able to flee

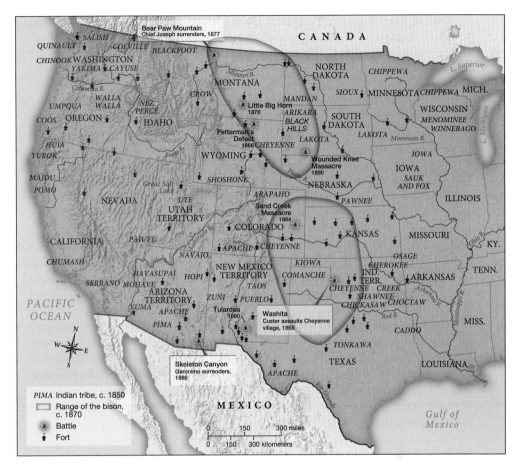

MAP 15.2   The Indian Frontier, 1870
Western migration posed a threat to the dozens of Indian tribes and the immense herds of bison in the region. The tribes had signed treaties with the U.S. government recognizing the right to live on their lands. The presence of U.S. forts did not protect the Indians from settlers who invaded their territories.

the contagion, while agrarian tribes such as the Mandan suffered extreme losses. As a result, the balance of power among Plains tribes shifted to the more mobile Sioux. Indians engaged in warfare with their enemies in disputes over hunting grounds, horses, and honor. However, the introduction of guns by European and American traders transformed Indian warfare into a much more deadly affair than had existed previously. And by the mid-nineteenth century, some tribes had become so deeply engaged in the commercial fur trade with whites that they had depleted their own hunting grounds.

Indian peoples taught their customs, which they considered divinely inspired, to their children in systematic fashion. Ancestral worship played a large part in this education. Mothers recounted to their children tales of heroic ancestors they wished them to emulate. The young learned their lessons through an array of songs, ceremonies, myths, and true stories.

Native Americans had their own approach toward nature and the land they inhabited. Most tribes did not accept private ownership of land, as whites did. Indians recognized the concept of private property in ownership of their horses, weapons, tools, and shelters, but they viewed the land as the common domain of their tribe, for use by all members. "The White man knows how to make everything," the Hunkpapa Lakota chieftain Sitting Bull remarked, "but he does not know how to distribute it." This communitarian outlook also reflected native attitudes toward the environment. Indians considered human beings not as superior to the rest of nature's creations, but rather as part of an interconnected world of animals, plants, and natural elements.

Bison (commonly known as buffalo) played a central role in the religion and society of many Indian tribes. By the mid-nineteenth century, approximately thirty million bison grazed on the Great Plains. Before acquiring guns, Indians used a variety of means to hunt their prey, including bows and arrows and spears. Some rode their horses to chase bison and stampede them over cliffs. The meat from the buffalo provided food; its hide provided material to construct tepees and make blankets and clothes; bones were crafted into tools, knives, and weapons; dried bison dung served as an excellent source of fuel. The Plains Indians dressed up in colorful outfits, painted their bodies, and danced to the almighty power of the buffalo and the spiritual presence within it.

Indian hunting societies, such as the Lakota Sioux and Apache, contained gender distinctions. The task of riding horses to hunt bison became men's work; women then prepared the buffalo hides when the hunters returned. Women saw themselves as an integral part of providing food, shelter, and clothing for the members of their tribe. Similarly, the religious belief that the spiritual world touched every aspect of the material world gave women an opportunity to experience this transcendent power without the mediation of male leaders.

Federal Policy toward Indians before 1870

Initially, the U.S. government treated western Indians as autonomous nations and recognized their stewardship over the land they occupied. In 1851 the **Treaty of Fort Laramie** confined tribes on the northern plains to designated areas in an attempt to keep white settlers from encroaching on their land. A treaty two years later applied these terms to tribes on the southern plains. Indians kept their part of the agreement, but white miners did not. They roamed through Indian hunting grounds in search of ore and faced little government enforcement of the existing treaties. In fact, the U.S. military made matters considerably worse. On November 29, 1864, a peaceful band of 700 Cheyennes and Arapahos under the leadership of Chief Black Kettle gathered at Sand Creek, Colorado, supposedly under guarantees of U.S. protection. Instead, Colonel John M. Chivington and his troops launched an attack, despite a white flag of surrender hoisted by the Indians, and brutally killed some 270 Indians, mainly women and children. A congressional investigation later determined that the victims "were mutilated in the most horrible manner." Although there was considerable public outcry over the incident, the government did nothing to increase enforcement of its treaty obligations. In almost all disputes between white settlers and Indians, the government sided with the whites, regardless of the Indians' legal rights. In 1867, the government signed the **Treaty of Medicine Lodge**, which provided reservation lands for the Comanche, Kiowa-Apache, and Southern Arapaho to settle. Despite this agreement, white hunters soon invaded this territory and decimated the buffalo herds.

The duplicity of the U.S. government had consequences for tribes' relationships among each other. The Sand Creek massacre unleashed Indian wars throughout the central plains, where the Lakota Sioux led the resistance from 1865 to 1868. After two years of fierce fighting, both sides signed a second Treaty of Fort Laramie, which gave northern tribes control over the "Great Reservation" set aside in parts of present-day Montana, Wyoming, North Dakota, and South Dakota. Another treaty placed the southern tribes in a reservation carved out of western Oklahoma. Meanwhile, the government recognized no differences among the tribes. In issuing his annual report in 1868, the Commissioner of Indian Affairs recommended that the Indians' "barbaric dialects should be blotted out and the English language substituted" in order to "fuse" different tribes "into one homogeneous mass."

Reconstruction and Indians

Much of federal policy toward Indians was shaped during the period of Reconstruction (see Chapter 14). When Ulysses S. Grant became president in 1869, he endorsed the passage of the Fifteenth Amendment and pledged to support the goals of the Military Reconstruction Act in the South. His next priority, he declared in his inaugural address, was "the proper treatment of the original occupants of this land—the Indians." He went on to affirm, "I will favor any course toward them which tends to their civilization and ultimate citizenship." However, Indians in the West did not receive any of the benefits granted by the post–Civil War Thirteenth, Fourteenth, and Fifteenth Amendments. In fact, the Fourteenth Amendment excluded from citizenship tribal Indians.

Despite President Grant's hopeful message, Indian Reconstruction sought to destroy and subjugate native tribes. The Nez Perce tribe was coerced to sign a treaty ceding most of its land to the United States. Intending to flee to Canada, Chief Joseph led the Nez Percé out of the Pacific Northwest in 1877 in a daring march of 1,400 miles as federal troops pursued them. The Nez Percé were finally intercepted in the mountains of northern Montana, just thirty miles from the border. Subsequently, the government relocated them to the southwestern territory of Oklahoma. In 1879 Chief Joseph pleaded with lawmakers in Congress to return his people to their home and urged the U.S. government to live up to the original intent of the treaties. His words carried some weight, and the Nez Percé returned under armed escort to a reservation in Washington.

The treaties did not produce a lasting peace. Though most of the tribes relocated onto reservations, some refused. The Apache chief Victorio explained why he would not resettle his people on a reservation. "We prefer to die in our own land under the tall cool pines," he declared. "We will leave our bones with those of our people. It is better to die fighting than to starve." General William Tecumseh Sherman, commander of the military forces against the Indians, ordered the army to wage a merciless war of annihilation "against all hostile Indians till they are obliterated or beg for mercy." In November 1868, Lieutenant Colonel George Armstrong Custer took Sherman at his word and assaulted a Cheyenne village, killing more than one hundred Indians. Nearly a decade later, in 1876, the Indians, this time Lakota Sioux,

Indian Drawing of Battle of Little Big Horn This ink-on-paper drawing by Amos Bad Heart Buffalo (1869–1913) depicts the June 1876 Battle of Little Big Horn, also known as Custer's Last Stand. It portrays the retreat of Major Marcus Reno's forces. The painted warrior on the white horse who is shooting a soldier from his saddle is Crazy Horse, the Sioux chieftain. The Stapleton Collection/Bridgeman Images

exacted revenge by killing Custer and his troops at the **Battle of the Little Big Horn** in Montana. Yet this proved to be the final victory for the Lakota nation, as the army mounted an extensive and fierce offensive against them that shattered their resistance.

Among the troops that battled the Indians were African Americans. Known as **buffalo soldiers**, they represented a cross section of the postwar black population looking for new opportunities that were now available after their emancipation. Some blacks enlisted to learn how to read and write; others sought to avoid unpleasant situations back home. In 1875, the army had around 25,500 men, and African Americans comprised about 10 percent of the regular army and about 20 percent of the cavalry. As was the practice during the Civil War, black soldiers served in segregated units under white commanders. A few gained more glory than money. In May 1880, Sergeant George Jordan of the Ninth Cavalry led troops under his command to fend off Apache raids in Tularosa, New Mexico, for which he was awarded the Congressional Medal of Honor.

Indian Defeat

By the late 1870s, Indians had largely succumbed to U.S. military supremacy. The tribes contained agile horsemen and skilled warriors, but the U.S. army was backed by the power of an increasingly industrial economy. Telegraph lines and railroads provided logistical advantages in the swift deployment of U.S. troops and the ability of the central command to communicate with field officers. Although Indians had acquired firearms, the army boasted an essentially unlimited supply of superior weapons. The diversity of Indians and historic rivalries among tribes also made it difficult for them to unite against their common enemy. The federal government exploited these divisions by hiring Indians to serve as army scouts against their traditional tribal foes.

The wholesale destruction of the bison was the final blow to Indian independence. As railroads pushed their tracks beyond the Mississippi, they cleared bison from their path by sending in professional hunters with high-powered rifles to shoot the animals. At the same time, buffalo products such as shoes, coats, and hats became fashionable in the East. By the mid-1880s, hunters had killed more than thirteen million bison. As a result of the relentless move of white Americans westward and conspicuous consumption back east, bison herds were almost annihilated.

Faced with decimation of the bison, broken treaties, and their opponents' superior military technology, Native Americans' capacity to wage war collapsed. Indians had little choice but to settle on shrinking reservations that the government established for them. The absence of war, however, did not bring them security. In the late 1870s, gold discoveries in the Black Hills of North Dakota ignited another furious rush by miners onto lands supposedly guaranteed to the Lakota people. Rather than honoring its treaties, the U.S. government forced the tribes to relinquish still more land. General Custer's Seventh Cavalry was part of the military force trying to push Indians out of this mining region, when it was annihilated at the Little Big Horn in 1876. Elsewhere, Congress opened up a portion of western Oklahoma to white homesteaders in 1889. Although this land had not been assigned to specific tribes relocated in Indian Territory, more than eighty thousand Indians from various tribes lived there. This government-sanctioned land rush opened the door for whites to acquire more land at the expense of the Indians. A decade later, Congress officially ended Indian control of Indian Territory.

To add to the humiliation of Native Americans, the U.S. Supreme Court ruled in *Elk v. Wilkins* (1884) that although Indians were born in the United States, they were not entitled to citizenship under the Fourteenth Amendment. A Winnebago Indian born on a reservation, John Elk moved to Omaha, Nebraska. He lived among whites and renounced his allegiance to his tribe. When he tried to register to vote, he was turned down. After Elk filed litigation to obtain the right to vote, the high court turned him down. In a 7-2 opinion, the justices decided that Elk was born a Winnebago and owed his allegiance to the tribe in perpetuity. Thus, no Indian had birthright citizenship.

Reforming Indian Policy

As reservations continued to shrink under expansionist assault and government acquiescence, a movement arose to reform Indian policy. Largely centered in the East, where few Indians lived, reformers came to believe that the future welfare of Indians lay not in sovereignty but in assimilation. In 1881 Helen Hunt Jackson published *A Century of Dishonor*, her exposé of the unjust treatment the Indians had received. Roused by this depiction of the Indians' plight, groups such as the Women's National Indian Association joined with ministers and philanthropists to advocate the transformation of native peoples into full-fledged Americans.

Judged by the standards of their own time, these well-intentioned reform-ers wanted to save the Indians from the brutality and corrupt behavior they had endured, and they believed they were acting in the Indians' best interests. The most advanced thinking among anthropologists at the time offered an approach that sup-ported assimilation as the only alternative to extinction. The influential Lewis Mor-gan, author of *Ancient Society* (1877), concluded that all cultures evolved through three stages: savagery, barbarism, and civilization. Indians occupied the lower rungs, but reformers argued that by adopting white values they could become civilized.

Reformers faced opposition from white Americans who doubted that Indian assimilation was possible. For many Americans, secure in their sense of their own superiority, the decline and eventual extinction of the Indian peoples was an inevita-ble consequence of what they saw as Indians' innate inferiority. For example, a Wyo-ming newspaper predicted: "The same inscrutable Arbiter that decreed the downfall of Rome has pronounced the doom of extinction upon the red men of America."

Reformers found their legislative spokesman in long-time Republican Senator Henry Dawes of Massachusetts. As legislative director of the Boston Indian Citi-zenship Association, Dawes shared Christian reformers' belief that becoming a true American would save both the Indians and the soul of the nation. Dawes had the same paternalistic attitude toward Indians as he had toward freed slaves. He believed that if both degraded groups worked hard and practiced thrift and individual initia-tive in the spirit of Dawes's New England Puritan forebears, they would succeed. The key for Dawes was private ownership of land.

Passed in 1887, the **Dawes Act** ended tribal rule and divided Indian lands into 160-acre parcels. The act allocated one parcel to each family head. The government held the lands in trust for the Indians for twenty-five years; at the end of this period, the Indians would receive American citizenship. In return, the Indians had to aban-don their religious and cultural rites and practices, including storytelling and the use of medicine men. Whatever lands remained after this reallocation—and the amount was considerable—would be sold on the open market, and the profits from the sales would be placed in an educational fund for Indians.

Unfortunately, like most of the policies it replaced, the Dawes Act proved detrimental to Native Americans. Indian families received inferior farmlands and inadequate tools to cultivate them, while speculators reaped profits from the sale of the "excess" Indian lands. A little more than a decade after the Dawes Act went into effect, Indians controlled 77 million acres of land, down sharply from the 155 million acres they held in 1881. Additional legislation in 1891 forced Indian parents to send their children to boarding schools or else face arrest. At these educational institutions, Indian children were given "American" names, had their long hair cut, and wore uniforms in place of their native dress. The program for boys provided manual and vocational training and that for girls taught domestic skills, so that they could emulate the gender roles in middle-class American families. However, this schooling offered few skills of use in an economic world undergoing industrial transformation.

Indian Assimilation and Resistance

Not all Indians conformed to the government's attempt at forced acculturation. Some refused to abandon their traditional social practices, and others rejected the white man's version of private property and civilization. Even on reservations, Indians found ways to preserve aspects of their native traditions. Through close family ties, they communicated to sons and daughters their languages, histories, and cultural practices. Parents refused to grant full control of their children to white educators and often made sure that schools were located on or near reservations where they fit into the pattern of their lives. Yet, many others displayed more complicated approaches to survival in a world that continued to view Indians with prejudice. Geronimo and Sitting Bull participated in pageants and Wild West shows but refused to disavow their heritage. Ohiyesa, a Lakota also known as Charles Eastman, went to boarding school, graduated from Dartmouth College, and earned a medical degree from Boston University. He supported passage of the Dawes Act, believed in the virtues of an American education, and worked for the Bureau of Indian Affairs. At the same time, he spoke out against government corruption and fraud perpetrated against Indians. Reviewing his life in his later years, Eastman/Ohiyesa reflected: "I am an Indian and while I have learned much from civilization . . . I have never lost my Indian sense of right and justice."

Disaster loomed for those who resisted assimilation and held on too tightly to the old ways. In 1888 the prophet Wovoka, a member of the Paiute tribe in western Nevada, had a vision that Indians would one day regain control of the world and that whites would disappear. He believed that the Creator had provided him with a **Ghost Dance** that would make this happen. The dance spread to thousands of Lakota Sioux in the northern plains. Seeing the Ghost Dance as a sign of renewed Indian resistance, the army attempted to put a stop to the revival. On December 29, 1890, the Seventh Cavalry chased three hundred ghost dancers to Wounded Knee Creek on the Pine Ridge Reservation in present-day South Dakota. In a confrontation with the Lakota leader Big Foot, a gunshot accidentally rang out during a struggle with one of his followers. The cavalry then turned the full force of their weaponry on the Indians, killing 250 Native Americans, many of them women and children.

The message of the massacre at Wounded Knee was clear for those who raised their voices against Americanization. As Black Elk, a spiritual leader of the Oglala Lakota tribe, asserted: "A people's dream died there. . . . There is no center any longer, and the sacred tree is dead." It may not have been the policy of the U.S. government to exterminate the Indians as a people, but it was certainly U.S. policy to destroy Indian culture and society once and for all.

REVIEW & RELATE	• How and why did federal Indian policy change during the nineteenth century? • Describe some of the ways that Indian peoples responded to federal policies. Which response do you think offered their greatest chance for survival?

The Mining and Lumber Industries

Among the settlers pouring into Indian Territory in the Rocky Mountains were miners in search of gold and silver. These prospectors envisioned instant riches that would come from a lucky strike. The vast majority found only backbreaking work, danger, and frustration. Miners continued to face hardship and danger as industrial mining operations took over from individual prospectors, despite the efforts of some miners to fight for better wages and working conditions. By 1900 the mining rush had peaked, and many of the boomtowns that had cropped up around the mining industry had emptied out. Still, mining companies and the workers they attracted forged big cities of diverse peoples and commerce. Closely related to mining, the lumber industry was less demographically diverse but also followed the pattern of domination by big business.

The Business of Mining

The discovery of gold in California in 1848 had set this mining frenzy in motion. Over the next thirty years, successive waves of gold and silver strikes in Colorado, Nevada, Washington, Idaho, Montana, and the Dakotas lured individual prospectors with shovels and wash pans. One of the biggest finds came with the **Comstock Lode** in the Sierra Nevada, where miners extracted around $350 million worth of silver (in nineteenth century dollars). One of those who came to try to share in the wealth was Samuel Clemens. Like most of his fellow miners, Clemens did not find his fortune in Nevada and soon turned his attention to writing, finally achieving success as the author called Mark Twain.

Like Twain, many of those who flocked to the Comstock Lode and other mining frontiers were men. Nearly half were foreign-born, many of them coming from Mexico or China. Using pans and shovels, prospectors could find only the ore that lay near the surface of the earth and water and could not afford to buy the equipment needed to dig out the vast deposits of gold and silver buried deep in the earth. As a result, western mining became a business run by men with the financial resources necessary to purchase industrial mining equipment.

When mining became an industry, prospectors became wageworkers. In Virginia City, Nevada miners labored for $4 a day, an amount that barely covered the expenses of life in a mining boomtown. Moreover, the work was extremely dangerous. Mine shafts extended down more than a thousand feet, and working temperatures regularly exceeded 100 degrees Fahrenheit. Noxious fumes, fires, and floods of scalding water flowed through the shafts, and other threats killed or disabled thousands each year.

Struggling with low pay and dangerous work, western miners sought to organize. In the mid-1860s, unions formed in the Comstock Lode areas of Virginia City and Gold Hill, Nevada. Although these unions had some success, they also provoked a violent backlash from mining companies determined to resist union demands. Companies hired private police forces to help break strikes. Such forces were often assisted by state militias deployed by elected officials with close ties to the companies. For example, in 1892 the governor of Idaho crushed an unruly strike by calling up the National Guard, a confrontation that resulted in the deaths of seven strikers. A year later, in 1893, mine workers formed one of the most militant labor organizations in the nation, the Western Federation of Miners. Within a decade, it had attracted fifty thousand members, though membership excluded Chinese, Mexican, and Indian workers.

Life in the Mining Towns

Men worked the mines, but women arrived as well in search of economic opportunity. In Storey County, Nevada, the heart of the Comstock Lode, the 1875 census showed that women made up about half the population. Most employed women worked long hours as domestics in boardinghouses, hotels, and private homes. Prostitution, which was legal, accounted for the single-largest segment of the female workforce. Most prostitutes were between the ages of nineteen and twenty-four, and they entered this occupation because few other well-paying jobs were available to them. Prostitutes faced constant danger, and many were victims of physical abuse, robbery, and murder.

As early as the 1880s, gold and silver discoveries had played out in the Comstock Lode. Boomtowns, which had sprung up almost overnight, became ghost towns as gold and silver deposits dwindled. Even more substantial places like Virginia City, Nevada experienced a severe decline as the veins of ore ran out. One revealing sign of the city's plummeting fortunes was the drop in the number of prostitutes, which declined by more than half by 1880. The mining business then shifted from gold and silver to copper, lead, and zinc, centered in Montana and Idaho. As with the early prospectors in California and Nevada, these miners eventually became wageworkers for giant consolidated mining companies. By the end of the nineteenth century, the Amalgamated Copper Company and the American Smelting and Refining Company dominated the industry.

Mining towns that survived settled into a more complex pattern of urban living. At its height in the 1870s, Virginia City contained 25,000 residents and was among the largest cities west of the Mississippi River. It provided schools and churches and featured such cultural amenities as theaters and opera houses. Though the population in mining towns remained predominantly young and male, the young men were increasingly likely to get married and raise families. Residents lived in neighborhoods divided by class and ethnicity. For example, in Butte, Montana the west side of town became home to the middle and upper classes. Mine workers lived on the east side in homes subdivided into apartments and in boardinghouses. The Irish lived in one section; Finns, Swedes, Serbs, Croatians, and Slovenes in other sections. Each group formed its own social, fraternal, and religious organizations to relieve the harsh conditions of overcrowding, poor sanitation, and discrimination. Residents of the east side relied on one another for support and frowned on those who deviated from their code of solidarity. "They didn't try to outdo the other one," one neighborhood woman remarked. "If you did, you got into trouble. . . . If they thought you were a little richer than they were, they wouldn't associate with you." Although western mining towns retained distinctive qualities, in their social and ethnic divisions they came to resemble older cities east of the Mississippi River.

The Lumber Boom

The mining industry created a huge demand for timber, as did the railroad lines that operated in the West. Initially small logging firms moved into the Northwest and California, cut down all the trees they could, sent them to nearby sawmills for processing, and moved on. By 1900, a few large firms came to dominate the industry and acquired vast tracts of forests. Frederick Weyerhaeuser purchased 900,000 acres of prime timberland in the Western Cascades of Oregon, largely bringing an end to the often chaotic competition of small firms that had characterized the industry in its early days. Increasingly, the western lumber industry became part of a global market that shipped products to Hawaii, South America, and Asia.

Loggers and sawmill workers did not benefit from these changes. Exclusively male, large numbers of workers came from Scandinavia, and only a few were Asian or African American. Men died or lost limbs in cutting down the trees, transporting them in the rivers, or processing the wood in sawmills. As lumber camps and mill villages became urbanized, those who gained the most were the merchants and bankers who supplied the goods and capital.

REVIEW & RELATE	• How and why did the nature of mining in the West change during the second half of the nineteenth century? • How did the mining and lumber industries reshape the frontier landscape?

The Cattle Industry and Commercial Farming

Like mining and lumber, cattle ranching and farming in the West increasingly became dominated by big business. Foreign investors from England, Scotland, Wales, and South America poured in money to fund the cattle industry and placed day-to-day control of their ranches in the hands of experienced corporate managers. Cowboys functioned as industrial laborers. They worked long hours in tough but boring conditions on the open range. Similarly, commercial farmers who headed west endured great hardships in trying to raise crops in an often inhospitable climate. Extreme weather and falling crop prices, however, forced many ranchers and farmers out of business, and their lands and businesses were snatched up by larger, more consolidated commercial ranching and agricultural enterprises. Despite difficult physical and economic conditions, many of the women and men who ranched and farmed in the West showed grit and determination not only in surviving but in improving their lives as well.

The Life of the Cowboy

There is no greater symbol of the frontier West than the cowboy. As portrayed in novels and film, the cowboy hero was the essence of manhood, an independent figure who fought for justice and defended the honor and virtue of women. Never the aggressor, he fought to protect law-abiding residents of frontier communities.

This romantic image excited generations of American readers and later movie and television audiences. In reality, cowboys' lives were much more mundane. Rather than working as independent adventurers, they increasingly operated in an industrial setting dominated by large cattle companies. Cowpunchers worked for paltry monthly wages, put in long days herding cattle, and spent part of the night guarding them on the open range. Their major task was to make the 1,500-mile **Long Drive** along the Chisholm Trail. Beginning in the late 1860s, cowboys moved cattle from ranches in Texas through Oklahoma to rail depots in Kansas towns such as Abilene and Dodge City; from there, cattle were shipped by train eastward to slaughterhouses in Chicago. Life along the trail was monotonous, and riders had to contend with bad weather, dangerous work, and disease.

Numbering around forty thousand and averaging twenty-four years of age, the cowboys who rode through the Great Plains from Texas to Kansas came from diverse backgrounds. The majority, about 66 percent, were white, predominantly Southerners who had fought for the South during the Civil War. Most of the rest were divided evenly between Mexicans and African Americans, some of whom were former slaves and others Union veterans of the Civil War.

Besides experiencing rugged life on the range, black and Mexican cowboys faced racial discrimination. Jim Perry, an African American who rode for the three-million-acre XIT Ranch in Texas for more than twenty years, complained: "If it weren't for my damned old black face I'd have been boss of one of these divisions long ago." Mexican *vaqueros*, or cowboys, earned one-third to one-half the wages of whites, whereas blacks were usually paid on a par with whites. Because the cattle kingdoms first flourished during Reconstruction, racial discrimination and segregation carried over into the Southwest. On one drive along the route to Kansas, a white boss insisted that a black cowboy eat and sleep separately from whites and shot at him when he refused to heed this order. Nevertheless, the proximity in which cowboys worked and the need for cooperation to overcome the pitfalls of the long drive made it difficult to enforce rigid racial divisions on the open range.

The Rise of Commercial Ranching

Commercial ranches absorbed cowboys into their expanding operations. Spaniards had originally imported cattle into the Southwest, and by the late nineteenth century some five million Texas longhorn steers grazed in the area. The extension of railroads across the West opened up a quickly growing market for beef in the East. The development of refrigerated railroad cars guaranteed that meat from slaughtered cattle could reach eastern consumers without spoiling. With money to be made, the cattle industry rose to meet the demand. Fewer than 40 ranchers owned more than 20 million acres of land. Easterners and Europeans joined the boom and invested money in giant ranches. By the mid-1880s, approximately 7.5 million head of cattle roamed the western ranges, and large cattle ranchers became rich. Cattle ranching had become fully integrated into the national commercial economy.

Then the bubble burst. Ranchers, who were already raising more cattle than the market could handle, increasingly faced competition from cattle producers in Canada and Argentina. Prices spiraled downward. Another source of competition came from homesteaders who moved into the plains and fenced in their farms with barbed wire, thereby reducing the size of the open range. Yet the greatest disaster occurred from 1885 to 1887. Two frigid winters, together with a torrid summer drought, destroyed 90 percent of the cattle on the northern plains of the Dakotas, Montana, Colorado, and Wyoming. Under these conditions, outside capital to support ranching diminished, and many of the great cattle barons went into bankruptcy. This economic collapse consolidated the remaining cattle industry into even fewer hands. The cowboy, never more than a hired hand, became a laborer for large corporations.

Commercial Farming

Like cowboys, farm families endured hardships to make their living in the West. They struggled to raise crops in an often inhospitable climate in hopes that their yields would be sold for a profit. Falling crop prices, however, led to soaring debt and

"Vaqueros in a Horse Corral," 1877   In this lithograph, James Walker captures vaqueros (cowboys) on a Texas ranch corralling horses. "Vaquero" is derived from the Spanish word for "cow," and "corral" comes from Spanish for "enclosure" or "pen." Originating in Spain and brought to Mexico, vaquero culture influenced the development of the southwestern United States and California. Peter Newark Pictures/Bridgeman Images

forced many farmers into bankruptcy and off their land, while others were fortunate enough to survive and make a living.

The federal government played a major role in opening up the Great Plains to farmers, who eventually clashed with cattlemen. The Republican Party of Abraham Lincoln had opposed the expansion of slavery in order to promote the virtues of free soil and free labor for white men and their families. In 1862, during the Civil War, preoccupation with battlefield losses did not stop the Republican-controlled Congress from passing the **Homestead Act**. As an incentive for western migration, the act established procedures for distributing 160-acre lots to western settlers, on condition that they develop and farm their land. What most would-be settlers did not know, however, was that lots of 160 acres were not viable in the harsh, dry climate of the Great Plains.

Reality did not deter pioneers and adventurers. In fact, weather conditions in the region temporarily fooled them. The decade after 1878 witnessed an exceptional amount of rainfall west of the Mississippi. Though not precisely predictable, this cycle of abundance and drought had been going on for millennia. In addition, innovation and technology bolstered dreams of success. Farmers planted hardy strains of wheat imported from Russia that survived the fluctuations of dry and wet and hot and cold weather. Machines produced by industrial laborers in northern factories to the east allowed farmers to plow tough land and harvest its yield. Steel-tipped plows, threshers, combines, and harvesters expanded production greatly, and windmills and pumping equipment provided sources of power and access to scarce water. These improvements in mechanization led to a significant expansion in agricultural pro-duction, which helped to lower food prices for consumers.

The people who accepted the challenge of carving out a new life were a diverse lot. The Great Plains attracted a large number of immigrants from Europe, some two million by 1900. Minnesota and the Dakotas welcomed communities of settlers from Sweden and Norway. Nebraska housed a considerable population of Germans, Swedes, Danes, and Czechs. About one-third of the people who migrated to the northern plains came directly from a foreign country.

Railroads and land companies lured settlers to the plains with tales of the fab-ulous possibilities that awaited their arrival. The federal government had given rail-roads generous grants of public land on which to build their tracks as well as parcels surrounding the tracks that they could sell off to raise revenue for construction. Western railroads advertised in both the United States and Europe, proclaiming that migrants to the plains would find "the garden spot of the world."

Having enticed prospective settlers with exaggerated claims, railroads offered bargain rates to transport them to their new homes. Families and friends often jour-neyed together and rented an entire car on the train, known as "the immigrant car," in which they loaded their possessions, supplies, and even livestock. Often migrants came to the end of the rail line before reaching their destination. They completed the trip by wagon or stagecoach.

Commercial advertising alone did not account for the desire to journey west-ward. Settlers who had made the trip successfully wrote to relatives and neighbors back east and in the old country about the chance to start fresh. Linda Slaughter, the wife of an army doctor in the Dakotas, gushed: "The farms which have been opened in the vicinity of Bismarck have proven highly productive, the soil being kept moist by frequent rains. Vegetables of all kinds are grown with but little trouble."

Those who took the chance shared a faith in the future and a willingness to work hard and endure misfortune. They found their optimism and spirits sorely tested. Despite the company of family members and friends, settlers faced a lonely existence on the vast expanse of the plains. Homesteads were spread out, and a feeling of isola-tion became a routine part of daily life.

With few trees around, early settlers constructed sod houses. These structures let in little light but a good deal of moisture, keeping them gloomy and damp. A Nebraskan who lived in this type of house jokingly remarked: "There was running water in our sod house. It ran through the roof." Bugs, insects, and rodents, like the rain, often found their way inside to make living in such shelters even more uncomfortable.

If these dwellings were bleak, the climate posed even greater challenges. After the unusually plentiful rainfall in the late 1870s and early 1880s, severe drought fol-lowed. Before that, a plague of grasshoppers ravaged the northern plains in the late 1870s, destroying fruit trees and plants. Intense heat in the summer alternated with frigid temperatures in the winter. The Norwegian American writer O. E. Rolvaag, in *Giants in the Earth* (1927), described the extreme hardships that accompanied the fierce weather: "Blizzards from out of the northwest raged, swooped down and stirred up a greyish-white fury, impenetrable to human eyes. As soon as these mon-sters tired, storms from the northeast were sure to come, bringing more snow."

Women Homesteaders

The women of the family were responsible for making homesteads more bearable. Mothers and daughters were in charge of household duties, cooking the meals, canning fruits and vegetables, and washing and ironing clothing. Women contributed significantly to the economic well-being of the family by occasionally taking in boarders and selling milk, butter, and eggs.

In addition, a surprisingly large number of single women staked out homestead claims by themselves. Some were young, unmarried women seeking, like their male counterparts, economic opportunity. Others were widows attempting to take care of their children after their husband's death. One such widow, Anne Furnberg, settled a homestead in the Dakota Territory in 1871. Born in Norway, she had lived with her husband and son in Minnesota. After her husband's death, the thirty-four-year-old Furnberg moved with her son near Fargo and eventually settled on eighty acres of land. She farmed, raised chickens and a cow, and sold butter and eggs in town. The majority of women who settled in the Dakotas were between the ages of twenty-one and twenty-five, had never been married, and were native-born children of immigrant parents. A sample of nine counties in the Dakotas shows that more than 4,400 women became landowners. Nora Pfundheler, a single woman, explained her motivation: "Well I was 21 and had no prospects of doing anything. The land was there, so I took it."

Once families settled in and towns began to develop, women, married and single, directed some of their energies to moral reform and extending democracy on the frontier. Because of loneliness and grueling work, some men turned to alcohol for relief. Law enforcement in newly established communities was often no match for the saloons that catered to a raucous and drunken crowd. In their roles as wives, mothers, and sisters, many women tried to remove the source of alcohol-induced violence that disrupted both family relationships and public decorum. In Kansas in the late 1870s, women flocked to the state's Woman's Christian Temperance Union, founded by Amanda M. Way. Although they did not yet have the vote, in 1880 these women vigorously campaigned for a constitutional amendment that banned the sale of liquor.

Temperance women also threw their weight behind the issue of women's suffrage. In 1884 Kansas women established the statewide Equal Suffrage Association, which delivered to the state legislature a petition with seven thousand signatures in support of women's suffrage. Their attempt failed, but in 1887 women won the right to vote and run for office in all Kansas municipal elections. Julia Robinson, who campaigned for women's suffrage in Kansas, recalled the positive role that some men played: "My father had always said his family of girls had just as much right to help the government as if we were boys, and mother and he had always taught us to expect Woman Suffrage in our day." Kansas did not grant equal voting rights in state and national elections until 1912, but women obtained full suffrage before then in many western states.

Farming on the Great Plains

Surviving loneliness, drudgery, and bad weather still did not guarantee financial success for homesteaders. In fact, the economic realities of farming on the plains proved formidable. Despite the image of yeomen farmers—individuals engaged in

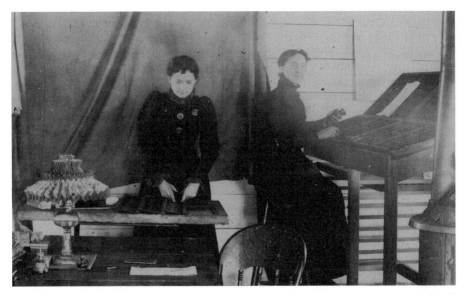

Women at Work in Kansas Women pioneers in the West worked in a variety of jobs besides homemakers and farmers. In the 1880s, these two women worked as typesetters for the *Kansas Workman*, a weekly newspaper that supported equal rights for workers. Women were often chosen for this job of arranging tiny pieces of lead, inky type because it required sure fingers and sober attention to detail. Kansas State Historical Association

subsistence farming with the aid of wives and children — most agriculture was geared to commercial transactions. Few farmers were independent or self-reliant. Farmers depended on barter and short-term credit. They borrowed from banks to purchase the additional land necessary to make agriculture economically feasible in the semi-arid climate. They also needed loans to buy machinery to help increase production and to sustain their families while they waited for the harvest.

Instead of raising crops solely for their own use, farmers concentrated on the cash crops of corn and wheat. The price of these commodities depended on the vagaries of an international market that connected American farmers to growers and consumers throughout the world. When supply expanded and demand remained relatively stable during the 1880s and 1890s, prices fell. This deflation made it more difficult for farmers to pay back their loans, and banks moved to foreclose.

Under these challenging circumstances, almost half of the homesteaders in the Great Plains picked up and moved either to another farm or to a nearby city. Large operators bought up the farms they left behind and ran them like big businesses. As had been the case in mining, logging, and ranching, western agriculture was increasingly commercialized and consolidated over the course of the second half of the nineteenth century.

The federal government unwittingly aided this process of commercialization and consolidation, to the benefit of large companies. The government sought to make bigger plots of land available in regions where small farming had proved impractical. The Desert Land Act (1877) offered 640 acres to settlers who would irrigate the land, but it brought small relief for farmers because the land was too dry. These properties soon fell out of the hands of homesteaders and into those of cattle ranchers. The Timber and Stone Act (1878) allowed homesteaders to buy 160 acres of forestland at $2.50 an acre. Lumber companies hired "dummy entrymen" to file claims and then quickly transferred the titles and added the parcels to their growing tracts of woodland.

REVIEW & RELATE	• How did market forces contribute to the boom and bust of the cattle ranching industry and commercial farming? • How did women homesteaders on the Great Plains in the late nineteenth century respond to frontier challenges?

Diversity in the Far West

Some pioneers settled on the Great Plains or moved west for reasons beyond purely economic motives. The Mormons, for example, settled in Utah to find a religious home. The West Coast states of Washington, Oregon, and especially California, with their abundant resources and favorable climates, beckoned adventurers to travel beyond the Rockies and settle along the Pacific Ocean. The far West attracted many white settlers and foreign immigrants—especially Chinese—who encountered Spaniards and Mexicans already inhabiting the region. This interweaving among diverse cultural groups sparked clashes that produced more oppression than opportunity for nonwhites.

Mormons

Unlike miners, cowboys, and farmers, **Mormons** sought refuge in the West for religious reasons. By 1870 the migration of Mormons (members of the Church of Jesus Christ of Latter-Day Saints) into the Utah Territory had attracted more than 85,000 settlers, most notably in Salt Lake City. Originally traveling to Utah under the leadership of Brigham Young in the late 1840s, Mormons had come under attack from opponents of their religion and the federal government for several reasons. Most important, Mormons believed in polygamy, the practice of having more than one wife at a time. Far from seeing the practice as immoral, Mormon doctrine held polygamy as a blessing that would guarantee both husbands and wives an exalted place in the afterlife. Non-Mormons denounced polygamy as a form of involuntary servitude. In reality, only a small minority of Mormon men had multiple wives, and most of these polygamists had only two wives.

Mormons also departed from the mainstream American belief in private property. The church considered farming a communal enterprise. To this end, church elders divided land among their followers, so that, as Brigham Young explained, "each person perform[ed] his several duties for the good of the whole more than for individual aggrandizement."

In the 1870s, the federal government took increased measures to control Mormon practices. In *Reynolds v. United States* (1879), the Supreme Court upheld the criminal conviction of a polygamist Mormon man. Previously in 1862 and 1874, Congress had banned plural marriages in the Utah Territory. Congress went further in 1882 by passing the Edmunds Act, which disfranchised men engaging in polygamy. In 1887

Congress aimed to slash the economic power of the church by limiting Mormon assets to $50,000 and seizing the rest for the federal Treasury. A few years later, under this considerable pressure, the Mormons officially abandoned polygamy.

Related to the attack on polygamy was the question of women's suffrage. In 1870 voters in Utah endorsed a referendum granting women the right to vote, which enfranchised more than seventeen thousand women. Emmeline B. Wells, a Mormon woman who defended both women's rights and polygamy, argued that women "should be recognized as . . . responsible being[s]," capable of choosing plural marriage of their own free will. Opponents of enfranchisement contended that as long as polygamy existed, extending the vote to "enslaved" Mormon women would only perpetuate the practice because they would vote the way their husbands did. This point of view prevailed, and the Edmunds-Tucker Act (1887) rescinded the right to vote for women in the territory. Only with the rejection of polygamy did Congress accept statehood for Utah in 1896. The following year, the state extended the ballot to women.

Californios and Mexican Americans

As with the nation's other frontiers, migrants to the West Coast did not find uninhabited territory. Besides Indians, the largest group that lived in California consisted of Spaniards and Mexicans. Since the eighteenth century, these **Californios** had established themselves as farmers and ranchers. The 1848 Treaty of Guadalupe Hidalgo, which ended the Mexican-American War, supposedly guaranteed the property rights of Californios and granted them U.S. citizenship, but reality proved different. Mexican American miners had to pay a "foreign miners tax," and Californio landowners lost their holdings to squatters, settlers, and local officials. By the end of the nineteenth century, about two-thirds of all land originally owned by Spanish-speaking residents had fallen into the hands of Euro-American settlers. By this time, many of these once wealthy Californios had been forced into poverty and the low-wage labor force. The loss of land was matched by a diminished role in the region's government, as economic decline, ethnic bias, and the continuing influx of white migrants combined to greatly reduce the political influence of the Californio population.

Spaniards and Mexicans living in the Southwest met the same fate as the Californios. When Anglo cattle ranchers began forcing Mexican Americans off their land near Las Vegas, New Mexico, a rancher named Juan Jose Herrera assembled a band of masked night riders known as Las Gorras Blancas (The White Caps). According to fliers that they distributed promoting their grievances, the group sought "to protect the rights and interests of the people in general and especially those of the helpless classes." Enemies of "tyrants," they desired a "free ballot and fair court." In 1889 and 1890, as many as seven hundred White Caps burned Anglo fences, haystacks, barns, and homes. In the end, however, Spanish-speaking inhabitants could not prevent the growing number of whites from pouring onto their lands and isolating them politically, economically, and culturally. The most notorious of these Anglo-American landgrabbers was the Santa Fe Ring. Consisting of lawyers, politicians, and speculators, they convinced the federal government to grant them millions of acres of public land on which thousands of Mexican American farmers had lived and worked. Despite these incursions, Mexican Americans remained a majority of the territorial population throughout the late nineteenth century. With this ethnic majority in mind, Congress twice refused New Mexico's application for statehood in the 1870s and 1880s. Not until 1912 did New Mexico become a state, no longer with Mexican Americans in the majority.

The impact on Mexican Americans in California, New Mexico, and Texas was devastating. By seizing their land and erecting legal barriers to keep them from retrieving it, Anglos damaged the economic prospects of a majority of Mexicans. Once property owners, many Mexican Americans became landless tenant farmers or low-paid wage laborers in mines and ranches. Also, they remained vulnerable to extra-legal, vigilante violence by Anglos if they stepped out of their subordinate place. Between 1861 and 1900, an estimated 287 Mexican Americans were lynched. As might be expected given the history of the region, disputes over property and economic resources triggered a large number of these brutal killings.

The Chinese

California and the far West also attracted a large number of Chinese immigrants. Migration to California and the West Coast was part of a larger movement in the nineteenth century out of Asia that brought impoverished Chinese to Australia, Hawaii, Latin America, and the United States. The Chinese migrated for several reasons in the decades after 1840. Economic dislocation related to the British Opium Wars (1839–1842 and 1856–1860), along with bloody family feuds and a decade of peasant rebellion from 1854 to 1864, propelled migration. Faced with unemployment and starvation, the Chinese sought economic opportunity overseas.

Chinese immigrants were attracted first by the 1848 gold rush and then by jobs building the transcontinental railroad. By 1880 the Chinese population had grown to 200,000, most of whom lived in the West. San Francisco became the center of the transplanted Chinese population, which congregated in the city's Chinatown. Under the leadership of a handful of businessmen, Chinese residents found jobs, lodging, and meals, along with social, cultural, and recreational outlets. Most of those who came were young, unmarried men who intended to earn enough money to return to China and start anew. The relatively few women who immigrated came as servants or prostitutes.

For many Chinese, the West proved unwelcoming. When California's economy slumped in the mid-1870s, many whites looked to the Chinese as scapegoats. White workingmen believed that Chinese laborers in the mines and railroads undercut their demands for higher wages. They contended that Chinese would work for less because they were racially inferior people who lived degraded lives. Anti-Chinese clubs mushroomed in California during the 1870s, and they soon became a substantial political force in the state. The Workingmen's Party advocated laws that restricted Chinese labor, and it initiated boycotts of goods made by Chinese people. Vigilantes attacked Chinese in the streets and set fire to factories that employed Asians. The Workingmen's Party and the Democratic Party joined forces in 1879 to craft a new state constitution that blatantly discriminated against Chinese residents. In many ways, these laws resembled the Jim Crow laws passed in the South that deprived African Americans of their freedom following Reconstruction (discussed in chapter 16).

Pressured by anti-Chinese sentiment on the West Coast, the U.S. government enacted drastic legislation to prevent any further influx of Chinese. The **Chinese Exclusion Act** of 1882 banned Chinese immigration into the United States and prohibited those Chinese already in the country from becoming naturalized American citizens. The exclusion act, however, did not stop anti-Chinese assaults.

In the mid-1880s, white mobs drove Chinese out of Eureka, California; Seattle and Tacoma, Washington; and Rock Springs, Wyoming. These attacks were often organized. In 1885, the Tacoma mayor and police led a mob that rounded up 700 Chinese residents and forced them to leave the city on a train bound for Portland.

REVIEW & RELATE	• What migrant groups were attracted to the far West? What drew them there? • Explain the rising hostility to the Chinese and other minority groups in the late-nineteenth-century far West.

Conclusion: The Ambiguous Legacy of the West

The legacy of the pioneering generation of Americans has proven mixed. Men and women pioneers encountered numerous obstacles posed by difficult terrain, forbidding climate, and unfamiliar inhabitants of the land they sought to harness. They built their homes, tilled the soil to raise crops, and mined the earth to remove the metals it contained. They developed cities that would one day rival those back east: San Francisco, Los Angeles, Seattle, and Denver. These pioneers served as the advance guard of America's expanding national and international industrial and commercial markets. As producers of staple crops and livestock and consumers of manufactured goods, they contributed to the expansion of America's factories, railroads, and telegraph communication system. The nation would memorialize their spirit as a model of individualism and self-reliance.

In fact, settlement of the West required more than individual initiative and self-determination. Without the direct involvement of the federal government, settlers would not have received free or inexpensive homesteads and military protection to clear native inhabitants out of their way. Without territorial governors and judges appointed by Washington to preside over new settlements, there would have been even less law, order, and justice than appeared in the rough-and-tumble environment of the West. Railroads, mining, and cattle ventures all relied heavily on foreign investors. Moreover, all the individualism and self-reliance that pioneers brought would not have saved them from the harsh conditions and disasters they faced without banding together as a community and pitching in to create institutions that helped them collectively. Despite their desire to achieve success, various pioneers—farmers, prospectors, cowboys—mostly found it difficult to make it on their own and began working for larger farming, mining, and ranching enterprises, with many of them becoming wageworkers. And for an experience that has been portrayed as a predominantly male phenomenon, settlement of the West depended largely on women.

Pioneers did not fully understand the land and people they encountered. More from ignorance than design, settlers engaged in agricultural, mining, and ranching practices that damaged fragile ecosystems. The settlement of the West nearly wiped out the bison and left Native Americans psychologically demoralized, culturally endangered, and economically impoverished. Some Indians willingly adopted white ways, but most of them fiercely resisted acculturation. Other minorities in the West, such as Mexicans and Chinese, also experienced harsh treatment at the hands of whites and suffered greatly.

Chapter 15 Review

KEY TERMS

Great Plains, 376
transcontinental railroad, 376
Treaty of Fort Laramie, 380
Treaty of Medicine Lodge, 380
Battle of the Little Big Horn, 382
buffalo soldiers, 382
Dawes Act, 384

Ghost Dance, 385
Comstock Lode, 386
Long Drive, 388
Homestead Act, 390
Mormons, 394
Californios, 395
Chinese Exclusion Act, 396

REVIEW & RELATE

1. What role did the federal government play in opening the West to settlement and economic exploitation?
2. Explain the determination of Americans to settle in land west of the Mississippi River despite the challenges the region presented.
3. How and why did federal Indian policy change during the nineteenth century?
4. Describe some of the ways that Indian peoples responded to federal policies. Which response do you think offered their greatest chance for survival?
5. How and why did the nature of mining in the West change during the second half of the nineteenth century?
6. How did the mining and lumber industries reshape the frontier landscape?
7. How did market forces contribute to the boom and bust of the cattle ranching industry and commercial farming?
8. How did women homesteaders on the Great Plains in the late nineteenth century respond to frontier challenges?
9. What migrant groups were attracted to the far West? What drew them there?
10. Explain the rising hostility to the Chinese and other minority groups in the late-nineteenth-century far West.

TIMELINE OF EVENTS

1848	• Gold discovered in California
1851	• First Treaty of Fort Laramie
1862	• Homestead Act
1864	• Sand Creek massacre
1865–1868	• Lakota Sioux lead Indian resistance
Late 1860s	• Large-scale cattle drives begin
1868	• Second Treaty of Fort Laramie
1869	• Transcontinental railroad completed
1870s	• Gold discovered in Black Hills of North Dakota
1876	• Battle of the Little Big Horn
1877	• Desert Land Act
	• Timber and Stone Act
1881	• Helen Hunt Jackson publishes *A Century of Dishonor*
1882	• Edmunds Act
	• Chinese Exclusion Act
1884	• Annie Oakley joins William Cody's Wild West show
1885–1887	• Cattle industry collapses
1886	• Geronimo captured
1887	• Dawes Act
	• Kansas women win right to vote in municipal elections
1889–1890	• Mexican American White Caps attack Anglo property
1890	• Massacre at Wounded Knee
1893	• Western Federation of Miners formed

16

Industrial America

1877–1900

LEARNING OBJECTIVES

After reading this chapter you will be able to:

- Summarize the causes of American industrialization and evaluate the impact of industrialization on business and the economy.

- Analyze popular doctrines guiding social and economic policy during the industrial age and evaluate prominent critiques of these ideas.

- Describe new lifestyles that emerged from industrialization and explain how Americans reacted to anxieties about changing gender and racial roles that resulted.

- Describe the forces that constrained and influenced national politics in the late 1800s.

COMPARING AMERICAN HISTORIES

In 1848 Will and Margaret Carnegie left Scotland and sailed to America, hoping to find a better life for themselves and their children. Once settled in Pittsburgh, Pennsylvania, the family went to work, including thirteen-year-old Andrew, who found a job in a textile mill. For $1.25 per week, he dipped spools into an oil bath and fired the factory furnace—tasks that left him nauseated by the smell of oil and frightened by the boiler. Nevertheless, like the hero of the rags-to-riches stories that were so popular in his era, **Andrew Carnegie** persevered, rising from poverty to great wealth through a series of jobs and clever investments. As a teenager, he worked in a telegraph office. A superintendent of the Pennsylvania Railroad Company noticed Andrew's aptitude and made him his personal assistant and telegrapher. While in this position, Carnegie learned about the railroad industry and purchased stock in a sleeping car company; the returns from that investment tripled his annual salary. Carnegie then became a railroad superintendent in western Pennsylvania, and by the time he was thirty-five, he had grown wealthy from his investments in a wide variety of industries.

Andrew Carnegie eventually founded the greatest steel company in the world and became one of the wealthiest men of his time. He also became one of the era's greatest philanthropists, fulfilling his sense of community obligation by giving away a great deal of his fortune.

John Sherman also believed in public service, but for him it would come through politics. Born in Lancaster, Ohio in 1823, Sherman became a lawyer like his father, an Ohio Supreme Court judge. Like Carnegie, Sherman made shrewd investments that brought him wealth, although not on the same scale as Carnegie.

Sherman decided to enter politics and in 1854 won election from Ohio to the House of Representatives as a member of the newly created Republican Party. He rose up the leadership ranks as Republicans came to national power with the election of Abraham Lincoln to the presidency in 1860. From 1861 to 1896, Sherman held a variety of major political positions, including U.S. senator from Ohio and secretary of the treasury under President Rutherford B. Hayes. After his term as treasury secretary ended, he returned to the Senate and wielded power as one of the top Republican Party leaders. With his background as chair of the Senate Finance Committee and as secretary of the treasury, Sherman was the most respected Republican of his time in dealing with monetary and financial affairs. Sherman believed that government should encourage business. His most famous accomplishment, the Sherman Antitrust Act, which authorized the government to break up organizations that restrained competition, embodied this belief. It enacted limited reforms without harming powerful business interests.

THE AMERICAN HISTORIES of Andrew Carnegie and John Sherman began very differently. Both men played a prominent role in developing the government-business partnership that was crucial to the rapid industrialization of the United States. Carnegie's organization and management skills helped shape the formation of large-scale business. At the same time, Sherman and his fellow lawmakers provided support for that enterprise, using the power of government to reduce risks for businessmen and to increase incentives for economic expansion. They often did so in ways that made politics more corrupt and made politicians less respected. Nevertheless, the public took politics seriously and turned out at the polls in great numbers. Corporate leaders joined with the clergy and writers to defend the established hierarchy of wealth and power. These businessmen used the doctrines of laissez-faire and Social Darwinism to justify their ruthless practices in the name of progress.

Industrialization and big business reshaped the nation. Railroads expanded national and international markets for American factory goods. Innovations and new inventions promoted business consolidation. Industrialization even brought changes to the agricultural South, all within the framework of racial segregation. Great fortunes were made, and the rich showcased their lavish lifestyles. Corporate consolidation also created a new middle class. The men of this group used their leisure to create new social and professional organizations while the women devoted more time to clubs and charitable associations.

America Industrializes

Between 1870 and 1900, the United States grew into a global industrial power. Transcontinental railroads spurred this breathtaking transformation, linking regional markets into a national market; at the same time, railroads themselves served as a massive new market for raw materials and new technologies. Building on advantages developed over the course of the nineteenth century, the Northeast, Midwest, and West led the way in the new economy, while efforts to industrialize the South met with uneven success. Men like Andrew Carnegie became both the heroes and the villains of their age. They engaged in ruthless practices that would lead some to label the new industrialists "robber barons," but they also created systems of industrial organization and corporate management that altered the economic landscape of the country and changed the place of the United States in the world.

The New Industrial Economy

The industrial revolution of the late nineteenth century originated in Europe. Great Britain was the world's first industrial power, but by the 1870s Germany had emerged as a major challenger for industrial dominance, increasing its steel production at a rapid rate and leading the way in the chemical and electrical industries. The dynamic economic growth and innovation stimulated by industrial competition quickly crossed the Atlantic.

Industrialization transformed the American economy. As industrialization took hold, the U.S. gross domestic product, the output of all goods and services produced annually, quadrupled—from $9 billion in 1860 to $37 billion in 1890. During this same period, the number of Americans employed by industry doubled. Moreover, the nature of industry itself changed, as small factories catering to local markets were displaced by large-scale firms producing for national and international markets. The midwestern cities of Chicago, Cincinnati, and St. Louis joined Boston, New York, and Philadelphia as centers of factory production, while the exploitation of the natural resources in the West took on an increasingly industrial character. Trains, telegraphs, and telephones connected the country in ways never before possible.

From 1870 to 1913, the United States experienced an extraordinary rate of growth in industrial output: In 1870 American industries turned out 23.3 percent of the world's manufacturing production; by 1913 this figure had jumped to 35.8 percent. In fact, U.S. output in 1913 almost equaled the combined total for

Europe's three leading industrial powers: Germany, the United Kingdom, and France. By the end of the nineteenth century, the United States was surging ahead of northern Europe as the manufacturing center of the world.

At the heart of the American industrial transformation was the railroad. Large-scale business enterprises would not have developed without a national market for raw materials and finished products. A consolidated system of railroads crisscrossing the nation facilitated the creation of such a market (Figure 16.1). In addition, railroads were direct consumers of industrial products, stimulating the growth of a number of industries through their consumption of steel, wood, coal, glass, rubber, brass, and iron. Finally, railroads contributed to economic growth by increasing the speed and efficiency with which products and materials were transported.

Before railroads could create a national market, they had to overcome several critical problems. In 1877 railroad lines dotted the country in haphazard fashion. They primarily served local markets and remained unconnected at key points. This lack of coordination stemmed mainly from the fact that each railroad had its own track gauge (the width between the tracks), making shared track use impossible and long-distance travel extremely difficult.

The consolidation of railroads solved many of these problems. In 1886 railroad companies finally agreed to adopt a standard gauge. Railroads also standardized time zones, thus eliminating confusion in train schedules. During the 1870s, towns and cities each set their own time zone, a practice that created discrepancies among them. In 1882 the time in New York City and in Boston varied by 11 minutes and 45 seconds. The following year, railroads agreed to coordinate times and divided the country into four standard time zones. Most cities soon cooperated with the new system, but not until 1918 did the federal government legislate the standard time zones that the railroads had first adopted.

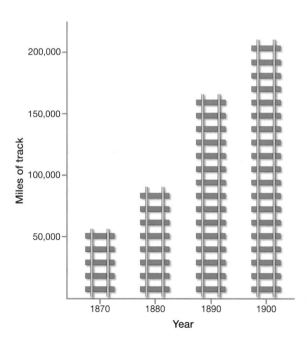

FIGURE 16.1　Expansion of the Railroad System, 1870–1900 The great expansion of the railroads in the late nineteenth century fueled the industrial revolution and the growth of big business. Connecting the nation from East Coast to West Coast, transcontinental railroads created a national market for natural resources and manufactured goods. The biggest surge in railroad construction occurred west of the Mississippi River and in the South. Describe the political and technological forces that promoted enormous railroad expansion from 1870–1900.

Innovation and Inventions

In addition to railroads, there were other engines of industrialization. American technological innovation created new industries, while expanding the efficiency and productivity of old ones. In 1866 a transatlantic telegraph cable connected the United States and Europe, allowing businessmen on both sides of the ocean to pursue profitable commercial ventures. New inventions also allowed business offices to run more smoothly: Typewriters were invented in 1868, carbon paper in 1872, adding machines in 1891, and mimeograph machines in 1892. As businesses grew, they needed more space for their operations. The construction of towering skyscrapers in the 1880s in cities such as Chicago and New York was made possible by two innovations: structural steel, which had the strength to support tall buildings, and elevators.

Alexander Graham Bell's telephone revolutionized communications. By 1880 fifty-five cities offered local service and catered to a total of 50,000 subscribers, most of them business customers. In 1885, Bell established the American Telephone and Telegraph Company (AT&T), and long-distance service connected New York, Boston, and Chicago. By 1900 around 1.5 million telephones were in operation.

Perhaps the greatest technological innovations that advanced industrial development came in steel manufacturing. In 1859 Henry Bessemer, a British inventor, designed a furnace that burned the impurities out of melted iron and converted it into steel. The open-hearth process, devised by another Englishman, William Siemens, further improved the quality of steel by removing additional impurities from the iron. Railroads replaced iron rails with steel because it was lighter, stronger, and more durable than iron. Steel became the major building block of industry, furnishing girders and cables to construct manufacturing plants and office structures. As production became cheaper and more efficient, steel output soared from 13,000 tons in 1860 to 28 million tons in the first decade of the twentieth century.

Factory machinery needed constant lubrication, and the growing petroleum industry made this possible. A new drilling technique devised in 1859 tapped into pools of petroleum located deep below the earth's surface. In the post–Civil War era, new distilling techniques transformed petroleum into lubricating oil for factory machinery. This process of "cracking" crude oil also generated lucrative by-products for the home, such as kerosene and paraffin for heating and lighting and salve to soothe cuts and burns. After 1900, the development of the gasoline-powered, internal combustion engine for automobiles opened up an even richer market for the oil industry.

Locomotives also benefited from innovations in technology. Improvements included air brakes and automatic coupling devices to attach train cars to each other. Elijah McCoy, a trained engineer and the son of former slaves, was forced because of racial discrimination to work at menial railroad jobs shoveling coal and lubricating train parts every few miles to keep the gears from overheating. This experience encouraged him to invent and patent an automatic lubricating device to improve efficiency.

By the late nineteenth century technological progress was increasingly an organized, collaborative effort. Thomas Alva Edison and his team served as the model. In 1876 Edison set up a research laboratory in Menlo Park, New Jersey. Housed in a two-story, white frame building, Edison's "invention factory" was staffed by a team

The Thomas Edison Team at Menlo Park　Thomas A. Edison relied on cooperation to produce the inventions pouring out of his Menlo Park, New Jersey laboratory. In this photograph, Edison is seated in the center surrounded by members of his team. Fred Ott sits on the left and George Gouraud on the right. Standing (left to right) are W. K. L. Dickson, Charles Batchelor, A. Theodore Wangemann, John Ott, and Charles Brown. Edison and his associates first invented the phonograph in 1877, and they are gathered around their "perfected" wax-recording phonograph, completed in 1888. Library of Congress, 3a15704

of inventors and craftsmen. In 1887 Edison opened another laboratory, ten times bigger than the one at Menlo Park, in nearby Orange, New Jersey. These facilities pioneered the research laboratories that would become a standard feature of American industrial development in the twentieth century.

Edison's laboratories produced inventions that revolutionized American business and culture. The phonograph and motion pictures changed the way people spent their leisure time. The electric light bulb illuminated people's homes and made them safer by eliminating the need for candles and gas lamps, which were fire hazards. It also brightened city streets, making them available for outdoor evening activities, and lit up factories so that they could operate all night long.

Like his contemporaries who were building America's huge industrial empires, Edison cashed in on his workers' inventions. He joined forces with the Wall Street banker J. P. Morgan to finance the Edison Electric Illuminating Company, which in 1882 provided lighting to customers in New York City. Goods produced by electric equipment jumped in value from $1.9 million in 1879 to $21.8 million in 1890. In 1892, Morgan helped Edison merge his companies with several competitors and reorganized them as the General Electric Corporation, which became the industry leader.

Building a New South

Although the largely rural South lagged behind the North and the Midwest in manufacturing, industrial expansion did not bypass the region. Well aware of global economic trends and eager for the South to achieve its economic potential, southern business leaders and newspaper editors saw industrial development as the key to the creation of a **New South**. Attributing the Confederate defeat in the Civil War to the North's superior manufacturing output and railroad supply lines, New South proponents hoped to modernize their economy in a similar fashion. One of those boosters was Richard H. Edmonds, editor of the *Manufacturers' Record*. He extolled the virtues of the "real South" of the 1880s, characterized by "the music of progress — the whirr of the spindle, the buzz of the saw, the roar of the furnace, the throb of the locomotive." Edmonds envisioned a South that would move beyond regional separatism and become fully integrated into the national economy.

Railroads were the key to achieving such economic integration, so after the Civil War new railroad tracks were laid throughout the South. This expanded railroad system created direct connections between the North and the South, and it facilitated the growth of the southern textile industry. Seeking to take advantage of plentiful cotton, cheap labor, and the improved transportation system, investors built textile mills throughout the South. Victims of falling prices and saddled with debt, sharecroppers and tenant farmers moved into mill towns in search of better employment. Mill owners preferred to hire girls and young women, who worked for low wages, to spin cotton and weave it on the looms. To do so, however, owners had to employ their entire family, for mothers and fathers would not let their daughters relocate without their supervision. Whatever attraction the mills offered applied only to whites. The pattern of white supremacy in the post-Reconstruction South kept blacks out of all but the most menial jobs.

Blacks contributed greatly to the construction of railroads in the New South, but they did not do so as free men. Convicts, most of whom were African American, performed the exhausting work of laying tracks through hills and swamps. Southern states used the **convict lease** system, in which blacks, usually imprisoned for minor offenses, were hired out to private companies to serve their time or pay off their fine. The convict lease system brought additional income to the state and supplied cheap labor to the railroads and planters, but it left convict laborers impoverished and virtually enslaved.

The South attracted a number of industries besides textile manufacturing. In the 1880s, James B. Duke established a cigarette manufacturing empire in Durham, North Carolina. Nearby tobacco fields provided the raw material that black workers prepared for white workers, who then rolled the cigarettes by machine. Acres of timber pines in the Carolinas, Florida, and Alabama sustained a lucrative lumber industry. Rich supplies of coal and iron in Alabama fostered the growth of the steel industry in Birmingham (Map 16.1).

Despite this frenzy of industrial activity, the New South in many ways resembled the Old South. Southern entrepreneurs still depended on northern investors to supply much of the capital for investment. Investors were attracted by the low wages that prevailed in the South, but low wages also meant that southern workers remained poor and, in many cases, unable to buy the manufactured goods produced by industry. Efforts to diversify agriculture beyond tobacco and cotton were constrained by a sharecropping system based on small, inefficient plots. In fact, even though industrialization did make considerable headway in the South, the economy remained overwhelmingly agricultural. This suited many white southerners who wanted to hold on to the individualistic, agrarian values they associated with the Old South. Tied to old ideologies and a system of forced labor, modernization in the South could go only so far.

Industrial Consolidation

In the North, South, and West, nineteenth-century industrialists strove to minimize or eliminate competition. To gain competitive advantages and increase profits, industrial entrepreneurs concentrated on reducing production costs, charging lower prices,

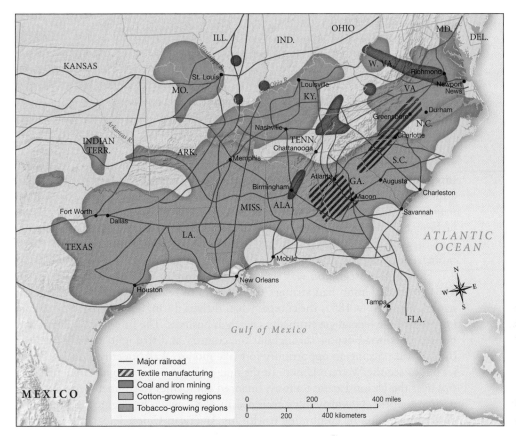

MAP 16.1　**The New South, 1900**
Although the South remained largely agricultural by 1900, it had made great strides toward building industries in the region. This so-called New South boasted an extensive railway network that provided a national market for its raw materials and manufactured goods, including coal, iron, steel, and textiles. Still, the southern economy in 1900 depended primarily on raising cotton and tobacco.

and outselling the competition. Successful firms could then acquire rival companies that could no longer afford to compete, creating an industrial empire in the process.

Building such industrial empires was not easy, however, and posed creative challenges for business ventures. Heavy investment in machinery resulted in very high fixed costs (or overhead) that did not change much over time. Because overhead costs remained stable, manufacturers could reduce the per-unit cost of production by increasing the output of a product—what economists call "economy of scale." Manufacturers aimed to raise the volume of production and find ways to cut variable costs—for labor and materials, for example. Through such savings, a factory owner could sell his product more cheaply than his competitors and gain a larger share of the market.

A major organizational technique for reducing costs and underselling the competition was **vertical integration**. "Captains of industry," as their admirers called them, did not just build a business; they created a system—a network of firms, each contributing to the final product. Men like Andrew Carnegie controlled the various phases of production from top to bottom (vertical), extracting the raw materials, transporting them to the factories, manufacturing the finished products, and shipping them to market. By using vertical integration, Carnegie eliminated middlemen and guaranteed regular and cheap access to supplies. He also lowered inventories and gained increased flexibility by shifting segments of the labor force to areas where they were most needed. His credo became "Watch the costs and the profits will take care of themselves."

Businessmen also employed another type of integration—**horizontal integration**. This approach focused on gaining greater control over the market by acquiring firms that sold the same products. John D. Rockefeller, the founder of the mammoth Standard Oil Company, specialized in this technique. In the mid-1870s, he brought a number of key oil refiners into an alliance with Standard Oil to control four-fifths of the industry. At the same time, the oil baron ruthlessly drove out of business or bought up marginal firms that could not afford to compete with him.

Horizontal integration was also a major feature in the telegraph industry. By 1861 Western Union had strung 76,000 miles of telegraph line throughout the nation. Founded in 1851, the company had thrived during the Civil War by obtaining most of the federal government's telegraph business. The firm had 12,600 offices housed in railroad depots throughout the country and strung its lines adjacent to the railroads. Seeing an opportunity to make money, Wall Street tycoon Jay Gould set out to acquire Western Union. In the mid-1870s, Gould, who had obtained control over the Union Pacific Railway, financed companies to compete with the giant telegraph outfit. Gould finally succeeded in 1881, when he engineered a takeover of Western Union by combining it with his American Union Telegraph Company. Gould made a profit of $30 million on the deal. On February 15, the day after the agreement, the *New York Herald Tribune* reported: "The country finds itself this morning at the feet of a telegraphic monopoly," a business that controlled the market and destroyed competition.

Bankers played a huge role in industrial consolidation. No one did it more skillfully than John Pierpont Morgan. In the 1850s, Morgan started his career working for a prominent American-owned banking firm in London, and in 1861 he created his own investment company in New York City. Morgan played the central role in channeling funds from Britain to support the construction of major American railroads. During the 1880s and 1890s, Morgan orchestrated the refinancing of several ailing railroads. To maintain control over these enterprises, the Wall Street financier placed his allies on their boards of directors and selected the companies' chief operating officers. Morgan then turned his talents for organization to the steel industry. In 1901 he was instrumental in merging Carnegie's company with several competitors in which he had a financial interest. United States Steel, Morgan's creation, became the world's largest industrial corporation, worth $1.4 billion. By the end of the first decade of the twentieth century, Morgan's investment house held more than 340 directorships in 112 corporations, amounting to more than $22 billion in assets, all at a time when there was no income tax.

The Growth of Corporations

With economic consolidation came the expansion of corporations. Before the age of large-scale enterprise, the predominant form of business ownership was the partnership. Unlike a partnership, a **corporation** provided investors with "limited liability." This meant that if the corporation went bankrupt, shareholders could not lose more than they had invested. Limited liability encouraged investment by keeping the shareholders' investment in the corporation separate from their other assets. In addition, corporations provided "perpetual life." Partnerships dissolved on the death of a partner, whereas corporations continued to function despite the death of any single owner. This form of ownership brought stability and order to financing, building, and perpetuating complex business endeavors.

Capitalists devised new corporate structures to gain greater control over their industries. Rockefeller's Standard Oil Company led the way by creating the **trust**, a monopoly formed by a small group of leading stockholders from several firms who manage the consolidated enterprise. To evade state laws against monopolies, Rockefeller created a petroleum trust. He combined other oil firms across the country with Standard Oil and placed their owners on a nine-member board of trustees that ran the company. Subsequently, Rockefeller created another method of bringing rival businesses together. Through a holding company, he obtained stock in a number of other oil companies and held them under his control.

Between 1880 and 1905, more than three hundred mergers occurred in 80 percent of the nation's manufacturing firms. Great wealth became heavily concentrated in the hands of a relatively small number of businessmen. Around two thousand businesses, a tiny fraction of the total number, dominated 40 percent of the nation's economy.

In their drive to consolidate economic power and shield themselves from risk, corporate titans generally had the courts on their side. In *Santa Clara County v. Southern Pacific Railroad Company* (1886), the Supreme Court decided that under the Fourteenth Amendment, which originally dealt with the issue of federal protection of African Americans' civil rights, a corporation was considered a "person." In effect, this ruling gave corporations the same right of due process that the framers of the amendment had meant to give to former slaves. In the 1890s, a majority of the Supreme Court embraced this interpretation. The right of due process shielded corporations from government regulation of the workplace, including the passage of legislation reducing the number of hours in the workday.

Yet trusts did not go unopposed. In 1890 Congress passed the **Sherman Antitrust Act**, which outlawed monopolies that prevented free competition in interstate commerce. The bill passed easily with bipartisan support because it merely codified legal principles that already existed. Senator Sherman and his colleagues intended to limit underhanded actions that destroyed competition. However, the judicial system shielded large corporations. In *United States v. E.C. Knight Company* (1895), a case against the "sugar trust," the Supreme Court rendered the Sherman Act virtually toothless by ruling that manufacturing was a local activity within a state and that, even if it was a monopoly, it was not subject to congressional regulation. This ruling left most trusts in the manufacturing sector beyond the jurisdiction of the Sherman Antitrust Act.

As the expanding labor force worked to produce a rapidly rising volume of goods, efficiency experts sought to cut labor costs and make the production process operate more smoothly. Frederick W. Taylor, a Philadelphia engineer and businessman, developed the principles of scientific management. Based on his concept of reducing manual labor to its simplest components and eliminating independent action on the part of workers, managers introduced time-and-motion studies. Using a stopwatch, they calculated how to break down a job into simple tasks that could be performed in the least amount of time. From this perspective, workers were no different from the machines they operated. With production soaring, marketing and advertising managers were called upon to devise new techniques to gauge consumer interests and stimulate their demands.

Another vital factor in creating large-scale industry was the establishment of retail outlets that could sell the enormous volume of goods pouring out of factories. As consumer goods became less expensive, retail outlets sprang up to serve the growing market for household items. Customers could shop at department stores—such as Macy's in New York City, Filene's in Boston, Marshall Field's in Chicago, May's in Denver, Nordstrom's in Seattle, and Jacome's in Tucson—where they were waited on by an army of salesclerks. Or they could buy the cheaper items in Frank W. Woolworth's five and ten cent stores, which opened in towns and cities nationwide. Chain supermarkets—such as the Great Atlantic and Pacific Tea Company (A&P), founded in 1869—sold fruits and vegetables packed in tin cans. They also sold foods from the meatpacking firms of Gustavus Swift and Philip Armour, which shipped them on refrigerated railroad cars. Mail-order catalogs allowed Americans in all parts of the country to buy consumer goods without leaving their home. The catalogs of Montgomery Ward (established in 1872) and Sears, Roebuck (founded in 1886) offered tens of thousands of items. Rural free delivery (RFD), instituted by the U.S. Post Office in 1891, made it easier for farmers and others living in the countryside to obtain these catalogs and buy their merchandise without having to travel miles to the nearest post office. By the end of the nineteenth century, the industrial economy had left its mark on almost all aspects of life in almost every corner of America.

REVIEW & RELATE	• What were the key factors behind the acceleration of industrial development in late-nineteenth-century America?
	• How did industrialization change the way American businessmen thought about their companies and the people who worked for them?

Laissez-Faire, Social Darwinism, and Their Critics

American industrialization developed as rapidly as it did in large part because it was reinforced by traditional ideas and values. The notion that hard work and diligence would result in success meant that individuals felt justified, even duty-bound, to strive to achieve upward mobility and accumulate wealth. Those who succeeded believed that they had done so because they were more talented, industrious, and resourceful than others. Prosperous businessmen regarded competition and the free market as essential to the health of an economic world they saw based on merit. Yet these same businessmen also created trusts that destroyed competition, and they depended on the government for resources and protection. This contradiction, along with the profoundly unequal distribution of wealth that characterized the late-nineteenth-century economy, generated a good deal of criticism of business tycoons and their beliefs.

The Doctrines of Success

Those at the top of the new industrial order justified their great wealth in a manner that most Americans could understand. The ideas of the Scottish economist Adam Smith, in *The Wealth of Nations* (1776), had gained popularity during the American Revolution. Advocating **laissez-faire** ("let things alone"), Smith contended that an "Invisible Hand," guided by natural law, guaranteed the greatest economic success if the government let individuals pursue their own self-interest unhindered by outside and artificial influences. In the late nineteenth century, businessmen and their conservative allies on the Supreme Court used Smith's doctrines to argue against restrictive government regulation. They equated their right to own and manage property with the personal liberty protected by the Fourteenth Amendment. Thus the Declaration of Independence, with its defense of "life, liberty, and the pursuit of happiness," and the Constitution, which enshrined citizens' political freedom, became instruments to guarantee unfettered economic opportunity and safeguard private property.

The view that success depended on individual initiative was reinforced in schools and churches. The McGuffey Readers, widely used to educate children, taught moral lessons of hard work, individual initiative, reliability, and thrift. The popular dime novels of Horatio Alger portrayed the story of young men who rose from "rags to riches." Americans could also hear success stories in houses of worship. Russell Conwell, pastor of the Grace Baptist Church in Philadelphia, delivered a widely printed sermon entitled "Acres of Diamonds," which equated godliness with riches and argued that ordinary people had an obligation to strive for material wealth. "I say that you ought to get rich, and it is your duty to get rich," Conwell declared, "because to make money honestly is to preach the gospel."

A concern for the welfare of children expressed in the McGuffey Readers and the pulp fiction of Horatio Alger reflected a larger societal problem. Thirteen percent of white children and thirty percent of black children lived with a single parent, most likely a woman. By 1900, 20 to 30 percent of all children under sixteen had lost one parent. Thus, the orphans that Horatio Alger wrote about were not a far-fetched idea.

If economic success was a matter of personal merit, it followed that economic failure was as well. The British philosopher Herbert Spencer proposed a theory of social evolution based on this premise in his book *Social Statics* (1851). Imagining a future utopia, Spencer wrote, "Man was not created with an instinct for his own degradation, but from the lower he has risen to the higher forms. Nor is there any conceivable end to his march to perfection." In his view, those at the top of the economic ladder were closer to perfection than were those at the bottom. Any effort to aid the unfortunate would only slow the march of progress for society as a whole.

Spencer's book proved extremely popular, selling nearly 400,000 copies in the United States by 1900. Publication of Charles Darwin's landmark *On the Origin of Species* (1859) appeared to provide some scientific legitimacy for Spencer's view. The British naturalist argued that plants, animals, and humans progressed or declined because of their ability or inability to adapt favorably to the environment and transmit these characteristics to future generations. The connection between the two men's ideas led some people decades later to label Spencer's theory **"Social Darwinism."**

Doctrines of success, such as Social Darwinism, gained favor because they helped Americans explain the rapid economic changes that were disrupting their lives. Although most ordinary people would not climb out of poverty to middle-class respectability, let alone affluence, they clung to ideas that promised hope. Theories such as Spencer's that linked success with progress provided a way for those who did not do well to understand their failure and blame themselves for their own inadequacies. At the same time, the notion that economic success derived from personal merit legitimized the fabulous wealth of those who did rise to the top.

Capitalists such as Carnegie found a way to soften both the message of extreme competition and its impact on the American public. Denying that the government should help the poor, they proclaimed that men of wealth had a duty to furnish some assistance. In his famous essay **"The Gospel of Wealth"** (1889), Carnegie argued that the rich should act as stewards of the wealth they earned. As trustees, they should administer their surplus income for the benefit of the community. Carnegie distinguished between charity (direct handouts to individuals), which he deplored, and philanthropy (building institutions that would raise educational and cultural standards), which he advocated. Carnegie was particularly generous in funding libraries (he provided the buildings but not the books) because they allowed people to gain knowledge through their own efforts.

Capitalists may have sung the praises of individualism and laissez-faire but this approach did not extend to industrial competition. Successful industrialists in the late nineteenth century sought to destroy competition. Their efforts over the course of several decades produced giant corporations that measured the worth of individuals by calculating their value to the organization. As John D. Rockefeller, the master of consolidation, proclaimed, "The day of individual competition in large affairs is past and gone."

Capitalists also sought government involvement that would favor business. Industrialists did not want the federal government to take any action that *retarded* their economic efforts, but they favored the use of the government's power to *promote* their enterprises and to stimulate entrepreneurial energies. Manufacturers pushed for congressional passage of high tariffs to protect goods from foreign competition and to foster development of the national marketplace. Industrialists demanded that federal and state governments dispatch troops when labor strikes threatened their businesses. They persuaded Washington to provide land grants for railroad construction and to send the army to clear Native Americans and bison from their tracks. They argued for state and federal courts to interpret constitutional and statutory law in a way that shielded property rights against attacks from workers. In large measure, capitalists succeeded not in spite of governmental support but because of it.

Challenges to Laissez-Faire

Proponents of government restraint and unbridled individualism did not go unchallenged. Critics of laissez-faire created an alternative ideology for those who sought to organize workers and expand the role of government as ways of restricting capitalists' power over labor and ordinary citizens.

Lester Frank Ward attacked laissez-faire in his book *Dynamic Sociology* (1883). Ward did not disparage individualism but viewed the main function of society as "the organization of happiness." Contradicting Herbert Spencer, Ward maintained that societies progressed when government directly intervened to help citizens — even the unfortunate. Rejecting laissez-faire, he argued that what people "really need is more government in its primary sense, greater protection from the rapacity of the favored few."

Some academics supported Ward's ideas. Most notably, economist Richard T. Ely applied Christian ethics to his scholarly assessment of capital and labor. He condemned the railroads for dragging "their slimy length over our country, and every turn in their progress is marked by a progeny of evils." In his book *The Labor Movement* (1886), Ely suggested that the ultimate solution for social ills resulting from industrialization lay in "the union of capital and labor in the same hands, in grand, wide-reaching, co-operative enterprises."

Two popular writers, Henry George and Edward Bellamy, added to the critique of materialism and greed. In *Progress and Poverty* (1879), George lamented: "Amid the greatest accumulations of wealth, men die of starvation." He blamed the problem on rent, which he viewed as an unjustifiable payment on the increase in the value of land. His remedy was to have government confiscate rent earned on land by levying a single tax on landownership. Though he advocated government intervention, he did not envision an enduring role for the state once it had imposed the single tax. By contrast, Bellamy imagined a powerful central government. In his novel *Looking Backward, 2000–1887* (1888), Bellamy attacked industrialists who "maim and slaughter workers by thousands." In his view, the federal government should take over large-scale firms, administer them as workers' collectives, and redistribute wealth equally among all citizens.

Neither Bellamy, George, Ward, nor Ely endorsed the militant socialism of Karl Marx. The German philosopher predicted that capitalism would be overthrown and replaced by a revolutionary movement of industrial workers that would control the means of economic production and establish an egalitarian society. Although his ideas gained popularity among European labor leaders, they were not widely accepted in the United States during this period. Most critics believed that the American political system could be reformed without resorting to the extreme solution of a socialist revolution. They favored a cooperative commonwealth of capital and labor, with the government acting as an umpire between the two.

REVIEW & RELATE	• In the late nineteenth century, how did many Americans explain individual economic success and failure? • How did the business community view the role of government in the economy at the end of the nineteenth century?

Society and Culture in the Gilded Age

Wealthy people in the late nineteenth century used their fortunes to support lavish lifestyles. For many of them, especially those with recent wealth, opulence rather than good taste was the standard of adornment. This tendency inspired writer Mark Twain and his collaborator Charles Dudley Warner to describe this era of wealth creation as the **Gilded Age**. Glittering on the outside, the enormous riches covered up the unbridled materialism and political rottenness that lay below the surface.

Twain and Warner had the very wealthy in mind when they coined the phrase, but others further down the social ladder found ways to participate in the culture of consumption. The rapidly expanding middle class enjoyed modest homes furnished with mass-produced consumer goods. Women played the central role in running the household, as most wives remained at home to raise children. Women and men often spent their free time attending meetings and other events sponsored by social, cultural, and political organizations. Such prosperity was, however, largely limited to whites. For the majority of African Americans still living in the South, life proved much harder. In response to black aspirations for social and economic advancement, white politicians imposed a rigid system of racial segregation on the South. Although whites championed the cause of individual upward mobility, they restricted opportunities to achieve success to whites only.

Wealthy and Middle-Class Leisure-Time Pursuits

Industrialization and the rise of corporate capitalism led to the expansion of the wealthy upper class as well as the expansion of the middle class, and new lifestyles emerged. Urban elites lived lives of incredible material opulence. J. P. Morgan, William Vanderbilt, and John D. Rockefeller built lavish homes in New York City. High-rise apartment buildings also catered to the wealthy. Overlooking Central Park, the nine-story Dakota Apartments boasted fifty-eight suites, a banquet hall, and a wine cellar. Millionaire residents furnished their stately homes with an eclectic mix of priceless art objects and furniture in a jumble of diverse styles. The rich and famous established private social clubs, sent their children to exclusive prep schools and colleges, and worshipped in the most fashionable churches.

Second homes, usually for use in the summer, were no less expensively constructed and decorated. Besides residences in Manhattan and Newport, Rhode Island, the Vanderbilts constructed a "home away from home" in the mountains of Asheville, North Carolina. The Biltmore, as they named it, contained 250 rooms, 40 master bedrooms, and an indoor swimming pool.

The wealthy also built and frequented opera houses, concert halls, museums, and historical societies as testimonies to their taste and sophistication. For example, the Vanderbilts, Rockefellers, Goulds, and Morgans financed the completion of the Metropolitan Opera House in New York City in 1883. When the facility opened, a local newspaper commented about the well-heeled audience: "The Goulds and the Vanderbilts and people of that ilk perfumed the air with the odor of crisp greenbacks." Upper-class women often traveled abroad to visit the great European cities and ancient Mediterranean sites.

Industrialization and the rise of corporate capitalism also brought an array of white-collar workers in managerial, clerical, and technical positions. These workers formed a new, expanded middle class and joined the businesspeople, doctors, lawyers, teachers, and clergy who constituted the old middle class. More than three million white-collar workers were employed in 1910, nearly three times as many as in 1870.

Middle-class families decorated their residences with mass-produced furniture, musical instruments, family photographs, books, periodicals, and a variety of memorabilia collected in their leisure time. They could relax in their parlors and browse through mass-circulation magazines and popular newspapers. Or they could read some of the era's outpouring of fiction, including romances, dime novels, westerns, humor, and social realism, an art form that depicted working-class life.

With more money and time on their hands, middle-class women and men were able to devote their efforts to charity. They joined a variety of social and professional organizations that were arising to deal with the problems accompanying industrialization (Table 16.1). During the 1880s, charitable organizations such as the American Red Cross were established to provide disaster relief. In 1892 the General Federation of Women's Clubs was founded to improve women's educational and cultural lives. Four years later, the National Association of Colored Women organized to help relieve suffering among the black poor, defend black women, and promote the interests of the black race.

During these swiftly changing times, adults became increasingly concerned about the nation's youth and sought to create organizations that catered to young

TABLE 16.1	AN AGE OF ORGANIZATIONS, 1876–1896	
Category	**Year of Founding**	**Organization**
Charitable	1881	American Red Cross
	1887	Charity Organization Society
	1889	Educational Alliance
	1893	National Council of Jewish Women
Sports/Fraternal	1876	National League of Baseball
	1882	Knights of Columbus
	1888	National Council of Women
	1892	General Federation of Women's Clubs
	1896	National Association of Colored Women
Professional	1883	Modern Language Association
	1884	American Historical Association
	1885	American Economic Association
	1888	American Mathematical Society

people. Formed before the Civil War in England and expanded to the United States, the Young Men's Christian Association (YMCA) grew briskly during the 1880s as it erected buildings where young men could socialize, build moral character, and engage in healthy physical exercise. The Young Women's Christian Association (YWCA) provided similar opportunities for women. African Americans also participated in "Y" activities through the creation of racially separate branches.

Changing Gender Roles

Economic changes led to adjustments in lifestyles and gender roles during the industrial era. Middle-class women generally remained at home, caring for the house and children, often with the aid of a servant. Whereas in the past farmers and artisans had worked from the home, now most men and women accepted as natural the separation of the workplace and the home caused by industrialization and urbanization. Although the birthrate and marriage rates among the middle class dropped during the late nineteenth century, wives were still expected to care for their husbands and family first to fulfill their feminine duties. Even though daughters increasingly attended colleges reserved for women, their families viewed education as a means of providing refinement rather than a career. One physician summed up the prevailing view that women could only use their brains "but little and in trivial matters" and should concentrate on serving as "the companion or ornamental appendage to man."

Middle-class women were part of a new consumer culture. Department stores, chain stores, ready-made clothes, and packaged goods, from Jell-O and Kellogg's Corn Flakes to cake mixes, competed for the money and loyalty of female consumers. Hairdressers, cosmetic companies, and department stores offered a growing and ever-changing assortment of styles. The expanding array of consumer goods did not, however, decrease women's domestic workload. They had more furniture to dust, fancier meals to prepare, changing fashions to keep up with, higher standards of cleanliness to maintain, and more time to devote to entertaining. The availability of mass-produced goods to assist the housewife in her chores made her role as consumer highly visible, while making her role as worker nearly invisible.

For the more socially and economically independent young women—those who attended college or beauty and secretarial schools—new worlds of leisure opened up. Bicycling, tennis, and croquet became popular sports for women in the late nineteenth century. So, too, did playing basketball, both in colleges and through industrial leagues. Indeed, women's colleges made sports a requirement, to offset the stress of intellectual life and produce a more well-rounded woman.

Middle-class men enjoyed new leisure pursuits, too. During the late nineteenth century 5.5 million men (of some 19 million adult men in the United States) joined fraternal orders, such as the Odd Fellows, Masons, Knights of Pythias, and Elks. These fraternities were divided along class lines with the Masons attracting the wealthiest, the Odd Fellows those in the middle, and the Knights of Pythias bringing in those lower down on the economic ladder. The fraternal orders offered middle-class men a network of business contacts and a communal, masculine social environment otherwise lacking in their lives. This notion of fraternity, however, did not apply to all. These organizations were racially exclusive, and African American men had to form their own lodges.

Women Bicyclists In the 1890s, with improvements in technology, middle-class women had both more leisure time and access to easy-to-ride bicycles. This photograph shows women at an early stage of the bicycle craze before changes in fashion allowed women to wear less-restrictive clothing that permitted exposed ankles and visible bloomers. In 1895, a Nebraska newspaper commented on the larger social implications of women bicyclists: The bicycle took "old-fashioned, slow-going notions of the gentler sex," and replaced them with "some new woman, mounted on her steed of steel." Robert Alexander/Getty Images

In fact, historians have referred to a "crisis of masculinity" afflicting a segment of middle- and upper-class men in the late nineteenth and early twentieth centuries. Middle-class occupations whittled away the sense of autonomy that men had experienced in an earlier era when they worked for themselves. The emergence of corporate capitalism had swelled the ranks of the middle class who held salaried jobs in managerial departments. At the same time, the expansion of corporations and big business stimulated a demand for clerical workers, female as well as male. This offered women many new opportunities to enter the job market. Along with this development, the push for women's rights, especially the right to vote, and women's increasing involvement in civic associations threatened to reduce absolute male control over the public sphere.

Responding to this gender crisis, middle-class men sought ways to exert their masculinity. Psychologists like G. Stanley Hall warned that unless men returned to a primitive state of manhood, they risked becoming spiritually paralyzed. To avoid this, went their advice, men should build up their bodies and engage in strenuous activities to improve their physical fitness.

Men turned to sports to cultivate their masculinity. Besides playing baseball and football, they could attend various sporting events. Baseball became the national pastime, and men could root for their home team and establish a community with the thousands of male spectators who filled up newly constructed ballparks. Baseball, a game played by elites in New York City in the 1840s, soon became a commercially popular sport. It spread across the country as baseball clubs in different cities competed with each other. The sport came into its own with the creation of the professional National League in 1876, and the introduction of the World Series in 1903 between the winners of the National League and the American League pennant races.

Boxing also became a popular spectator sport in the late nineteenth century. Bare-knuckle fighting—without the protection of gloves—epitomized the craze to display pure masculinity. A boxing match lasted until one of the fighters was knocked out, leaving both fighters bloody and battered.

During the late nineteenth century, middle-class women and men also had increased opportunities to engage in different forms of sociability and sexuality. Gay men and lesbians could find safe havens in New York City's Greenwich Village and Chicago's North Side for their own entertainment. Although treated by medical experts as sexual "inverts" who might be cured by an infusion of "normal" heterosocial contact, gay men and lesbians began to emerge from the shadows of Victorian-era sexual constraints around the turn of the twentieth century. "Boston marriages" constituted another form of relationship between women. The term apparently came from Henry James's book *The Bostonians* (1886), which described a female couple living together in a monogamous, long-term relationship. This type of relationship appealed to financially independent women who did not want to get married. Many of these relationships were sexual, but some were not. In either case, they offered women of a certain class an alternative to traditional, heterosexual marriage.

Black America and Jim Crow

While wealthy and middle-class whites experimented with new forms of social behavior, African Americans faced greater challenges to preserving their freedom and dignity. In the South, where the overwhelming majority of blacks lived, post-Reconstruction governments adopted various techniques to keep blacks from voting. To circumvent the Fifteenth Amendment, southern states devised suffrage qualifications that they claimed were racially neutral, and the Supreme Court ruled in their favor. They instituted the poll tax, a tax that each person had to pay in order to cast a ballot. Poll taxes fell hardest on the poor, a disproportionate number of whom were African American. Disfranchisement reached its peak in the 1890s, as white southern governments managed to deny the vote to most of the black electorate (Map 16.2). Literacy tests officially barred the uneducated of both races, but they were administered in a manner that discriminated against blacks while allowing illiterate whites to satisfy the requirement. Many literacy tests contained a loophole called a "grandfather clause." Under this exception, men whose father or grandfather had voted in 1860—a time when white men but not black men, most of whom were slaves, could vote in the South—were excused from taking the test.

In the 1890s, white southerners also imposed legally sanctioned racial segregation on the region's black citizens. Commonly known as **Jim Crow** laws (named for a character in a minstrel show, where whites performed in blackface), these new statutes denied African Americans equal access to public facilities and ensured that blacks lived apart from whites. In 1883, when the Supreme Court struck down the 1875 Civil Rights Act, it gave southern states the freedom to adopt measures confining blacks to separate schools, public accommodations, seats on transportation, beds

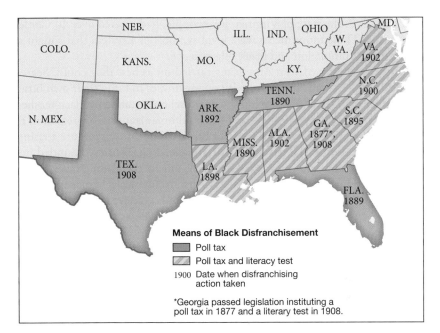

MAP 16.2   **Black Disfranchisement in the South, 1889–1908**
After Reconstruction, black voters posed a threat to the ruling Democrats by occasionally joining with third-party insurgents. To repel these challenges, Democratic Party leaders made racial appeals to divide poor whites and blacks. Chiefly in the 1890s and early twentieth century, white leaders succeeded in disfranchising black voters (and some poor whites), mainly by adopting poll taxes and literacy requirements.

in hospitals, and sections of graveyards. In 1896 the Supreme Court sanctioned Jim Crow, constructing the constitutional rationale for legally keeping the races apart. In **Plessy v. Ferguson**, the high court ruled that a Louisiana law providing for "equal but separate" accommodations for "whites" and "coloreds" on railroad cars did not violate the equal protection clause of the Fourteenth Amendment. In its decision, the Court concluded that civil rights laws could not change racial destiny. "If one race be inferior to the other socially," the justices explained, "the Constitution of the United States cannot put them on the same plane." In practice, however, white southerners obeyed the "separate" part of the ruling but never provided equal services. If blacks tried to overstep the bounds of Jim Crow in any way that whites found unacceptable, they risked their lives. Between 1884 and 1900, nearly 1,700 blacks were lynched in the South. Victims were often subjected to brutal forms of torture before they were hanged or shot.

Along with Jim Crow and disfranchisement laws, southerners buttressed white supremacy by erecting monuments to the political and military leaders of their Lost Cause Confederacy. Immediately following the Civil War, white southerners remembered their dead soldiers through memorials and grave markers. In the 1890s and for decades following, they erected public monuments in town squares to communicate their message that although the Confederacy had lost the Civil War, it had won the peace. By 1899, the state of Virginia, for example, had erected over 40 Confederate monuments. These monuments were vivid symbols of a system that sought to perpetuate white domination and black subservience.

In everyday life, African Americans carried on as best they could. Segregation provided many African Americans with opportunities to build their own businesses; control their own churches; develop their own schools, staffed by black teachers; and form their own civic associations and fraternal organizations. Segregation, though harsh and unequal, did foster a sense of black community, promote a rising middle class, and create social networks that enhanced racial pride. Founded in 1898, the North Carolina Life Insurance Company, one of the leading black-owned and black-operated businesses, employed many African Americans in managerial and sales positions. Burial societies ensured that their members received a proper funeral when they died. As with whites, black men joined lodges such as the Colored Masons and the Colored Odd Fellows, while women participated in the YWCA and the National Association of Colored Women. A small percentage of southern blacks resisted Jim Crow by migrating to the North, where blacks still exercised the right to vote, more jobs were open to them, and segregation was less strictly enforced.

REVIEW & RELATE	• What role did consumption play in the society and culture of the Gilded Age? • How did industrialization contribute to heightened anxieties about gender roles and race?

National Politics in the Era of Industrialization

Politicians played an important role in the expanding industrial economy that provided new opportunities for the wealthy and the expanding middle class. For growing companies and corporations to succeed, they needed a favorable political climate that would support their interests. Businessmen frequently looked to Washington for assistance. Marcus Alonzo Hanna, a wealthy industrialist, considered Ohio senator John Sherman "our main dependence in the Senate for the protection of our business interests." During this era, the office of the president was a weak and largely administrative post and legislators and judges were highly influenced and sometimes directly controlled by business leaders. For much of this period, the two national political parties battled to a standoff, which resulted in congressional gridlock with little accomplished. Yet spurred by fierce partisan competition, political participation grew among the electorate.

The Weak Presidency

James Bryce, a British observer of American politics, devoted a chapter of his book *The American Commonwealth* (1888) to "why great men are not chosen presidents." He believed that the White House attracted mediocre occupants because the president functioned mainly as an executor. The stature of the office had shrunk following the impeachment of Andrew Johnson and the reassertion of congressional power during Reconstruction. Presidents considered themselves mainly as the nation's top administrator. They did not see their roles as formulating policy or intervening on behalf of legislative objectives. With the office held in such low regard, great men became corporate leaders, not presidents.

Perhaps aware that they could expect little in the way of assistance or imagination from national leaders, voters refused to give either Democrats or Republicans solid support. No president between Ulysses S. Grant and William McKinley won back-to-back elections or received a majority of the popular vote. The only two-time winner, the Democrat Grover Cleveland, lost his bid for reelection in 1888 before triumphing again in 1892.

Nevertheless, the presidency attracted accomplished individuals. Rutherford B. Hayes (1877–1881), James A. Garfield (1881), and Benjamin Harrison (1889–1893) all had served ably in the Union army as commanding officers during the Civil War and had prior political experience. The nation greatly mourned Garfield following his assassination in 1881 by Charles Guiteau, a disgruntled applicant for federal patronage. Upon Garfield's death, Chester A. Arthur (1881–1885) became president. He had served as a quartermaster general during the Civil War, had a reputation as being sympathetic to African American civil rights, and had run the New York City Customs House effectively. Grover Cleveland (1885–1889, 1893–1897) first served as mayor of Buffalo and then as governor of New York. All of these men, as even Bryce admitted, worked hard, possessed common sense, and were honest. However, they were uninspiring individuals who lacked qualities of leadership that would arouse others to action.

Congressional Inefficiency

The most important factor in the weakened presidency was the structure of Congress, which prevented the president from providing vigorous leadership. Throughout most of this period, Congress remained narrowly divided. Majorities continually shifted from one party to the other. For all but two terms, Democrats controlled the House of Representatives, while Republicans held the majority in the Senate. Divided government meant that during his term in office no late-nineteenth-century president had a majority of his party in both houses of Congress. Turnover among congressmen in the House of Representatives, who were elected every two years, was quite high, and there was little power of incumbency. The Senate, however, provided more continuity and allowed senators, with six-year terms of office, to amass greater power than congressmen could.

For all the power that Congress wielded, it failed to govern effectively or efficiently. In the House, measures did not receive adequate attention on the floor because the Speaker did not have the power to control the flow of systematic debate. Committee chairmen held a tight rein over the introduction and consideration of legislation and competed with one another for influence in the chamber. Congressmen showed little decorum as they conducted business on the House floor and often chatted with each other or read the newspaper rather than listen to the speakers at the podium.

The Senate, though more manageable in size and more stable in membership (only one-third of its membership stood for reelection every two years), did not function much more smoothly. Senators valued their own judgments and business interests more than party unity. The position of majority leader, someone who could impose discipline on his colleagues and design a coherent legislative agenda, had not yet been created. Woodrow Wilson, the author of *Congressional Government* (1885) and a future president, concluded: "Our government is defective as it parcels out power and confuses responsibility." Under these circumstances, neither the president nor Congress governed efficiently.

The Business of Politics

Many lawmakers viewed politics as a business enterprise that would line their pockets with money. One cabinet officer grumbled, "A Congressman is a hog! You must take a stick and hit him on the snout!" Senators were elected by state legislatures, and these bodies were often controlled by well-funded corporations that generously spread their money around to gain influence. In both branches of Congress, party leaders handed out patronage to supporters regardless of their qualifications for the jobs (a practice known as the spoils system). Modern-day standards of ethical conduct did not exist; nor did politicians see a conflict of interest in working closely with corporations. Indeed, there were no rules to prevent lawmakers from accepting payments from big business. Most congressmen received free passes from railroads and in turn voted on the companies' behalf. To be fair, most politicians such as Senator Sherman did not see a difference between furthering the legislative agenda of big corporations and promoting the nation's economic interests. Nevertheless, the public held politicians in very low esteem because they resented the influence of corporate money in politics.

The 1890 Congress stands out as an example of fiscal irresponsibility. Known as the **Billion Dollar Congress**, the same Republican legislative majority that passed the Sherman Antitrust Act adopted the highest tariff in U.S. history. Sponsored by Ohio congressman William McKinley, a close associate of the industrialist Marcus Hanna, it lavishly protected manufacturing interests. Congress also spent enormous sums on special projects to enrich their constituents and themselves. Republicans spent so much money on extravagant enterprises that they wiped out the federal budget surplus.

Increasingly throughout the 1890s, corporate leaders and their political allies joined together in favor of extending American influence and control over foreign markets and natural resources abroad, especially in Central America and the Pacific regions. They agreed that cyclical fluctuations in the domestic economy required overseas markets to assure high profits. To accomplish this would necessitate building up American military and commercial power.

An Energized and Entertained Electorate

Despite all the difficulties of the legislative process, political candidates eagerly pursued office and conducted extremely heated campaigns. The electorate considered politics a form of entertainment. Political parties did not stand for clearly stated issues or offer innovative solutions; instead, campaigns took on the qualities of carefully staged performances. Candidates crafted their oratory to arouse the passions and prejudices of their audiences, and their managers handed out buttons, badges, and ceramic and glass plates stamped with the candidates' faces and slogans.

Partisanship helped fuel high political participation. During this period, voter turnout in presidential elections was much higher than at any time in the twentieth century. Region, as well as historical and cultural allegiances, replaced ideology as the key to party affiliation. The wrenching experience of the Civil War had cemented voting loyalties for many Americans. After Reconstruction, white southerners tended to vote Democratic; northerners and newly enfranchised southern blacks generally voted Republican. However, geography alone did not shape political loyalties; a sizable contingent of Democratic voters remained in the North, and southern whites and blacks periodically abandoned both the Democratic and Republican parties to vote for third parties.

Religion played an important role in shaping party loyalties during this period of intense partisanship. The Democratic Party tended to attract Protestants of certain sects, such as German Lutherans and Episcopalians, as well as Catholics. These faiths emphasized religious ritual and the acceptance of personal sin. They believed that the government should not interfere in matters of morality, which should remain the province of Christian supervision on earth and divine judgment in the hereafter. By contrast, other Protestant denominations, such as Baptists, Congregationalists, Methodists, and Presbyterians, highlighted the importance of individual will and believed that the law could be shaped to eradicate ignorance and vice. These Protestants were more likely to cast their ballots for Republicans, except in the South, where regional loyalty to the Democratic Party trumped religious affiliation.

Some people went to the polls because they fiercely disliked members of the opposition party. Northern white workers in New York City or Cincinnati, Ohio, for example, might vote against the Republican Party because they viewed it as the party of African Americans. Other voters cast their ballots against Democrats because they identified them as the party of Irish Catholics, intemperance, and secession.

Although political parties commanded fierce loyalties, the parties remained divided internally. For example, the Republicans pitted "Stalwarts" against "Half Breeds." The Stalwarts presented themselves as the "Old Guard" of the Republican Party, what they called the "Grand Old Party" (GOP). The Half Breeds, a snide name given to them by the Stalwarts, claimed to be more open to new ideas and less wedded to the old causes that the Republican Party promoted, such as racial equality. In the end, however, the differences between the two groups had less to do with ideas than with which faction would have greater power within the Republican Party.

Overall, the continuing strength of party loyalties produced equilibrium as voters cast their ballots primarily along strict party lines. The outcome of presidential elections depended on key "undecided" districts in several states in the Midwest and in New York and nearby states, which swung the balance of power in the electoral college. Indeed, from 1876 to 1896 all winning candidates for president and vice president came from Ohio, Indiana, Illinois, New York, and New Jersey.

REVIEW & RELATE

- What accounted for the inefficiency and ineffectiveness of the federal government in the late nineteenth century?
- How would you explain the high rates of voter turnout and political participation in an era of uninspiring politicians and governmental inaction?

1892 Presidential Campaign Plate Before radio, television, and the Internet, political parties advertised candidates in a variety of colorful ways, including banners, buttons, ribbons, and ceramic and glass plates. Voters, who turned out in record numbers during the late nineteenth century, coveted these items. This plate shows the 1892 Democratic presidential ticket of Grover Cleveland and Adlai Stevenson, who won the election. Collection of Steven F. Lawson

Conclusion: Industrial America

From 1877 to 1900, American businessmen demonstrated a zeal for organization. Prompted by new technology that opened up national markets of commerce and communication, business entrepreneurs created large-scale corporations that promoted industrial expansion. Borrowing from European investors and importing and improving on European technology, by 1900 U.S. industrialists had surpassed their overseas counterparts.

Capitalists made great fortunes and lived luxurious lifestyles, emulating the fashions of European elites. Most corporate leaders did not rise from poverty but instead came from the upper middle class and had access to education and connections. Those like Andrew Carnegie, who rose from rags to riches, were the exceptions. The wealthy explained their success as the result of individual effort and hard work. This idea was reinforced in schoolbooks such as the McGuffey Readers, the novels of Horatio Alger, and religious sermons like those of Russell Conwell.

Although most working Americans did not achieve much wealth during this era of industrialization, they had faith in the possibility of improving their economic positions. Members of the middle class lived less extravagantly than did the wealthy; nonetheless, they enjoyed the comforts of the growing consumer economy. Although Jim Crow restricted the black middle class and a heightened sense of masculinity inhibited opportunities available to white women, both groups managed to carve out ways to lift themselves economically and socially.

In gaining success, the wealthy exchanged individualism for organization, competition for consolidation, and laissez-faire for government support. Without pro-business policies from Washington lawmakers and favorable decisions from the Supreme Court, big business would not have developed as rapidly as it did in this era. To prosper, corporations needed sympathetic politicians—whether to furnish free land for railroad expansion, enact tariffs to protect manufacturers, or protect private property. Even when a public outcry led to the regulation of trusts, the pro-business senator John Sherman and his colleagues shaped the legislation so as to minimize damage to corporate interests. In general, national politicians avoided engaging in fierce ideological conflicts, but they, too, organized. The political parties they fashioned encouraged a high level of political participation among voters.

It remained for those who did not share in the glittering wealth of the Gilded Age to find ways to resist corporate domination. While corporate leaders and the expanding middle class enjoyed the fruits of industrial capitalism, workers, farmers, and reformers sought to remedy the economic, social, and political ills that accompanied industrialization.

Chapter 16 Review

KEY TERMS

New South, 405
convict lease, 406
vertical integration, 407
horizontal integration, 408
corporation, 409
trust, 409
Sherman Antitrust Act, 409

laissez-faire, 411
Social Darwinism, 412
"The Gospel of Wealth," 412
Gilded Age, 414
Jim Crow, 418
Plessy v. Ferguson, 419
Billion Dollar Congress, 422

REVIEW & RELATE

1. What were the key factors behind the acceleration of industrial development in late-nineteenth-century America?
2. How did industrialization change the way American businessmen thought about their companies and the people who worked for them?
3. In the late nineteenth century, how did many Americans explain individual economic success and failure?
4. How did the business community view the role of government in the economy at the end of the nineteenth century?
5. What role did consumption play in the society and culture of the Gilded Age?
6. How did industrialization contribute to heightened anxieties about gender roles and race?

7. What accounted for the inefficiency and ineffectiveness of the federal government in the late nineteenth century?

8. How would you explain the high rates of voter turnout and political participation in an era of uninspiring politicians and governmental inaction?

TIMELINE OF EVENTS

1859	• Charles Darwin publishes *On the Origin of Species*
	• Henry Bessemer improves steel production process
1860–1890	• U.S. gross domestic product quadruples
1866	• Transatlantic telegraph cable completed
1868	• Typewriter invented
1870–1900	• U.S. becomes a global industrial power
1870–1910	• Number of U.S. white-collar workers triples
1870s	• John D. Rockefeller takes control of oil refining business
1872	• Montgomery Ward established
1876	• Thomas Edison establishes research laboratory
1881	• James Garfield assassinated
1884–1900	• 1,700 blacks lynched in the South
1885	• Alexander Graham Bell founds American Telephone and Telegraph
1886	• U.S. railroads adopt standard gauge
	• *Santa Clara County v. Southern Pacific Railroad Company*
1889	• Andrew Carnegie publishes "The Gospel of Wealth"
1890	• Sherman Antitrust Act
1890s	• African Americans disfranchised in the South
1895	• *United States v. E.C. Knight Company*
1896	• *Plessy v. Ferguson*
1901	• United States Steel established

17

Workers and Farmers in the Age of Organization

1877–1900

LEARNING OBJECTIVES

After reading this chapter you will be able to:

- Explain how industrialization spurred the formation of labor organizations and how the government, in turn, responded to unionization.

- Analyze how industrialization affected rural life and how farmers responded to these changes.

- Compare the responses of industrial workers and farmers to the rise of big business.

- Explain the causes of the depression of 1893 and its consequences for workers, farmers, and politics.

COMPARING AMERICAN HISTORIES

John McLuckie worked at Andrew Carnegie's steel works in Homestead, Pennsylvania. In this town of some eleven thousand residents, where nearly everyone worked for Carnegie, the popular McLuckie was twice elected mayor and headed the Amalgamated Association of Iron and Steel Workers, one of the largest unions in the country. Although McLuckie earned a relatively decent income for that time, steelworkers and other industrial laborers had little power over the terms and conditions under which they worked. Visiting fraternal lodges and saloons, where steelworkers congregated, he spread the message of standing up to corporate leaders. "The constitution of this country," McLuckie declared, "guarantees all men the right to live, but in order to live we must keep up a continuous struggle."

In 1892 McLuckie faced the fight of his life when he battled with Carnegie and his plant manager, Henry Clay Frick, over wages and working conditions at the Homestead plant. Like Carnegie, the owners of a host of industries had created giant organizations that produced great wealth but also reshaped the working conditions of ordinary Americans. Toward the end of the nineteenth century, workers who labored for these industrial giants sought greater control over their employment by organizing unions to increase their power to negotiate with their employers. The events that unfolded in Homestead in 1892 revealed that workers were vastly outmatched in their struggle with management.

Mary Elizabeth Clyens was the daughter of Irish Catholic parents who came to the United States as part of the great wave of Irish immigration that began in the 1840s. Mary was raised in western Pennsylvania but moved to Kansas in 1870 to teach at a Catholic girls' school. There she met and married Charles L. Lease, a pharmacist turned farmer. The couple, however, could not support themselves and their children through farming, and in 1883 the Leases moved to Wichita. In Wichita, Mary found a much wider scope to express her interests and beliefs than she had on the farm. She joined a variety of organizations and worked in support of Irish independence, women's suffrage, and movements to advance the cause of industrial workers and farmers exploited by big business, railroads, and banks.

Mary Elizabeth Lease entered state and national politics through the Populist Party, which formed in 1890 to challenge the power of large corporations and their political allies, promote the interests of small farmers, and create an alliance between farmers and industrial workers. A mesmerizing speaker, she urged her audiences, according to reporters, to "raise less corn and more hell." Lease offered a variety of remedies for late-nineteenth-century America's economic and political ills, including nationalizing railroad and telegraph lines, increasing the currency supply, and expanding popular democracy. She also agitated for women's rights and voiced her determination "to place the mothers of this nation on an equality with the fathers." Following the collapse of the Populist Party in 1896, Lease and her family moved to New York City. She worked as a journalist, divorced her husband, and remained active as a speaker for educational reform and birth control until her death in 1931.

THE AMERICAN HISTORIES of John McLuckie and Mary Elizabeth Lease were linked by the economic and political forces that shaped the lives of both factory workers and farmers in industrialized America. Even though the culture of rural America was quite different from that of the nation's industrial towns and cities, farmers and workers faced many of the same problems. Over the course of the late nineteenth century, both groups had seen control over the nature and terms of their work pass from the individual worker or farmer to large corporations and financial institutions. McLuckie and Lease were part of a larger effort by laborers and farmers to fight for their own interests against the concentrated economic and political power of big business and to regain control of their lives and their work. In the 1890s, a severe economic depression made the situation even worse for farmers and industrial workers. Many of them joined the newly formed Populist Party to challenge the two major political parties for failing to represent their concerns.

Working People Organize

Industrialists were not the only ones who built organizations to promote their economic interests. Like their employers, working men and women also saw the benefits of organizing to increase their political and economic leverage. Determined to secure decent wages and working conditions, workers joined labor unions, formed political parties, and engaged in a variety of collective actions, including strikes. However, workers' organizations were beset by internal conflicts over occupational status, race, ethnicity, and gender. They proved no match for the powerful alliance between corporations and the federal government that stood against them, and they failed to become a lasting national political force. Workers fared better in their own communities, where family, neighbors, and local businesses were more likely to come to their aid.

The Industrialization of Labor

The industrialization of the United States transformed the workplace, bringing together large numbers of laborers under difficult conditions. In 1870 few factories employed 500 or more workers. Thirty years later, more than 1,500 companies had workforces of this size. Just after the Civil War, manufacturing employed 5.3 million workers; thirty years later, the figure soared to more than 15.1 million. Most of these new industrial workers came from two main sources. First, farmers like the Leases who could not make a decent living from the soil moved to nearby cities in search of factory jobs. Although mostly white, this group also included blacks who sought to escape the oppressive conditions of sharecropping. Between 1870 and 1890, some 80,000 African Americans journeyed from the rural South to cities in the South and the North to search for employment. Second, the economic opportunities in America drew millions of immigrants from Europe over the course of the nineteenth century. Immigrant workers initially came from northern Europe. However, by the end of the nineteenth century, the number of immigrants from southern and eastern European countries had surpassed those coming from northern Europe.

Inside factories, **unskilled workers**, those with no particular skill or expertise, encountered a system undergoing critical changes, as small-scale manufacturing gave way to larger and more mechanized operations. Immigrants, who made up the bulk of unskilled laborers, had to adjust both to a new country and to unfamiliar, unpleasant, and often dangerous industrial work. A traveler from Hungary who visited a steel mill in Pittsburgh that employed many Hungarian immigrants compared the factories to prisons where "the heat is most insupportable, the flames most choking." Nor were any government benefits—such as workers' compensation or unemployment insurance—available to industrial laborers who were hurt in accidents or laid off from their jobs.

Skilled workers, who had particular training or abilities and were more difficult to replace, were not immune to the changes brought about by industrialization and the rise of large-scale businesses. In the early days of manufacturing, skilled laborers operated as independent craftsmen. They provided their own tools, worked at their own pace, and controlled their production output. This approach to work enhanced their sense of personal dignity, reflected their notion of themselves as free citizens, and distinguished them from the mass of unskilled laborers. Mechanization, however, undercut their autonomy by dictating both the nature and the speed of production through practices of scientific management. Instead of producing goods, skilled workers increasingly applied their craft to servicing machinery and keeping it running smoothly. While owners reaped the benefits of the mechanization and regimentation of the industrial workplace, many skilled workers saw such "improvements" as a threat to their freedom.

Still, most workers did not oppose the technology that increased their productivity and resulted in higher wages. Compared to their mid-nineteenth-century counterparts, industrial laborers now made up a larger share of the general population, earned more money, and worked fewer hours. During the 1870s and 1880s, the average industrial worker's real wages (actual buying power) increased by 20 percent. At the same time, the average workday declined from ten and a half hours to ten hours. From 1870 to 1890, the general price index dropped 30 percent, allowing consumers to benefit from lower prices.

The lives of industrial workers remained extremely difficult. Although workers as a group saw improvements in wages and hours, they did not earn enough income to support their families adequately. Also, there were widespread disparities based on job status, race, ethnicity, sex, and region. Skilled workers earned more than unskilled workers. Whites were paid more than blacks, who were mainly shut out of better jobs. Immigrants from northern Europe, who had settled in the United States before southern Europeans, tended to hold higher-paying skilled positions. Southern factory workers, whether in textiles, steel, or armaments, earned less than their northern counterparts. Women, an increasingly important component of the industrial workforce, earned, on average, only 25 percent of what men did.

Between 1870 and 1900, the number of female wageworkers grew by 66 percent, accounting for about one-quarter of all nonfarm laborers. The majority of employed women, including those working in factories, were single and between the ages of sixteen and twenty-four. Overall, only 5 percent of married women worked outside the home, although 30 percent of African American wives were employed. Women workers were concentrated in several areas. White and black women continued to serve as maids and domestics. Others took over jobs that were once occupied by men. They became teachers, nurses, clerical workers, telephone operators, and department store salesclerks. Other women toiled in manufacturing jobs requiring fine eye-hand coordination, such as cigar rolling and work in the needle trades and textile industry.

Women also turned their homes into workplaces. In crowded apartments, they sewed furs onto garments, made straw hats, prepared artificial flowers, and fashioned jewelry. Earnings from piecework (work that pays at a set rate per unit) were even lower than factory wages, but they allowed married women with young children to contribute to the family income. When sufficient space was available, families rented rooms to boarders, and women provided meals and housekeeping for the lodgers. Some female workers found other ways to balance work with the needs and constraints of family life. To gain greater autonomy in their work, black laundresses began cleaning clothes in their own homes rather than their white employers' homes, so that they could control their own work hours. In 1881 black washerwomen in Atlanta conducted a two-week strike to secure higher fees from white customers.

Manufacturing also employed many child workers. By 1900 about 10 percent of girls and 20 percent of boys between the ages of ten and fifteen worked, and at least 1.7 million children under the age of sixteen held jobs. Employers often exposed children to dangerous and unsanitary conditions. Most child workers toiled long, hard hours breathing in dust and fumes as they labored in textile mills, tobacco plants, print shops, and coal mines. In Indiana, young boys worked the night shift in dark, windowless glass factories. Children under the age of ten, known as "breaker boys," climbed onto filthy coal heaps and picked out unprocessed material. Working up to twelve-hour days, these children received less than a dollar a day.

The burden of child labor fell more heavily on some groups than others. Among children between the ages of ten and nineteen, black males (66 percent) and black females (44 percent) were more likely to work than white males (43 percent) and white females (13.1 percent). Immigrant boys and girls were also more likely to be employed than their American-born counterparts. Thus, these disparities in child labor indicated the relatively higher earnings of white and native-born families.

Women and children worked because the average male head of household could not support his family on his own pay, despite the increase in real wages. As Carroll D. Wright, director of the Massachusetts Bureau of the Statistics of Labor, reported in 1882, "A family of workers can always live well, but the man with a family of small children to support, unless his wife works also, has a small chance of living properly." For example, in 1883 in Joliet, Illinois, a railroad brakeman tried to support his wife and eight children on $360 a year. A state investigator described the way they lived: "Clothes ragged, children half dressed and dirty. They all sleep in one room regardless of sex. The house is devoid of furniture, and the entire concern is as wretched as could be imagined." Not all laborers lived in such squalor, but many wageworkers barely lived at subsistence level.

Although the average number of working hours dropped during this era, many laborers put in more than 10 hours a day on the job. In the steel industry, blast-furnace operators toiled 12 hours a day, 7 days a week. They received a day off every 2 weeks, but only if they worked a 24-hour shift. Given the long hours and back-breaking work, it is not surprising that accidents were a regular feature of industrial life. Each year tens of thousands were injured on the job, and thousands died as a result of mine cave-ins, train wrecks, explosions in industrial plants, and fires at textile mills and garment factories. Railroad employment was especially unsafe — accidents ended the careers of one in six workers.

Agricultural refugees who flocked to cotton mills in the South also faced dangerous working conditions. Working twelve-hour days breathing the lint-filled air from the processed cotton posed health hazards. Textile workers also had to place their hands into heavy machinery to disentangle threads, making them extremely vulnerable to serious injury. Wages scarcely covered necessities, and on many occasions

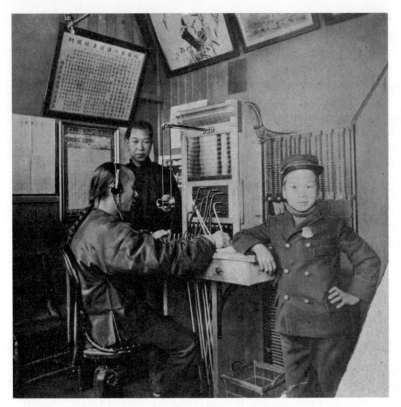

Chinese American Telephone Operator   The invention of the telephone brought jobs to many Americans, especially women. Yet not all operators were women, as this photograph shows. San Francisco's Chinatown employed workers from its own community, and in this photo a Chinese man works as a telephone operator while a child in a school uniform and another man stand by him. Library of Congress, Prints and Photographs Division [LC-USZ62-37204]

families did not know where their next meal was coming from. North Carolina textile worker J. W. Mehaffry complained that the mill owners "were slave drivers" who "work their employees, women, and children from 6 a.m. to 7 p.m. with a half hour for lunch." Mill workers' meals usually consisted of potatoes, cornbread, and dried beans cooked in fat. This diet, without dairy products and fresh meat, led to outbreaks of pellagra, a debilitating disease caused by niacin (vitamin B3) deficiency.

Although wages and working hours improved slightly for some workers, employers kept the largest share of the increased profits that resulted from industrialization. In 1877 John D. Rockefeller collected dividends at the rate of at least $720 an hour, roughly double what his average employee earned in a year. Despite some success stories, prospects for upward mobility for most American workers remained limited. A manual worker might rise into the ranks of the semiskilled but would not make it into the middle class. And to achieve even this small upward mobility required putting the entire family to work and engaging in rigorous economizing, what one historian called "ruthless underconsumption." Despite their best efforts, most Americans remained part of the working class.

Organizing Unions

Faced with improving but inadequate wages and with hazardous working conditions, industrial laborers sought to counter the concentrated power of corporate capitalists by joining forces. They attempted to organize **unions**—groups of workers seeking rights and benefits from their employers through their collective efforts. Union organizing was prompted by attitudes that were common among employers. Most employers were convinced that they and their employees shared identical interests, and they believed that they were morally and financially entitled to establish policies on their workers' behalf. They refused to engage in negotiations with labor unions (a process known as **collective bargaining**). Although owners appreciated the advantages of companies banding together to eliminate competition or to lobby for favorable regulations, similar collective efforts by workers struck them as unfair, even immoral. It was up to the men who supplied the money and the machines—rather than the workers—to determine what was a fair wage and what were satisfactory working conditions. In 1877 William H. Vanderbilt, the son of transportation tycoon Cornelius Vanderbilt, explained this way of thinking: "Our men feel that although I . . . may have my millions and they the rewards of their daily toil, still we are about equal in the end. If they suffer, I suffer, and if I suffer they cannot escape." Needless to say, many workers disagreed.

Industrialists expected their paternalistic values to reduce grievances among their workforce. They sponsored sports teams, set up social clubs, and offered cultural activities. The railroad magnate George Pullman built a model village to house his workers. In return, capitalists demanded unquestioned loyalty from their employees.

Yet a growing number of working people failed to see the relationship between employer and employee as mutually beneficial. Increasingly, they considered labor unions to be the best vehicle for communication and negotiation between workers and owners. Though not the first national workers' organization, the **Noble Order of the Knights of Labor**, founded by Uriah Stephens in 1869, initiated the most extensive and successful campaign after the Civil War to unite workers and challenge the power of corporate capitalists. "There is no mutuality of interests . . . [between] capital and labor," the Massachusetts chapter of the Knights proclaimed. "It is the iron heel of a soulless monopoly, crushing the manhood out of sovereign citizens." In fact, the essential premise of the Knights was that all workers shared common interests that were very different from those of owners.

The Knights did not really begin to flourish until Terence V. Powderly became Grand Master of the organization in 1879. Powderly advocated the eight-hour workday, the abolition of child labor, and equal pay for women. Under his leadership, the Knights accepted African Americans, immigrants, and women as members, though they excluded Chinese immigrant workers, as did other labor unions. As a result, the Knights experienced a surge in membership from 9,000 in 1879 to nearly a million in 1885, about 10 percent of the industrial workforce.

Rapid growth proved to be a mixed blessing. As membership grew, Powderly and the national organization exercised less and less control over local chapters. In fact, local chapters often defied the central organization by engaging in strikes, a tactic Powderly had officially disavowed. Nonetheless, members of the Knights struck successfully against the Union Pacific Railroad and the Missouri Pacific Railroad in 1885. The following year, on May 1, 1886, local assemblies of the Knights joined a nationwide strike to press for an eight-hour workday. However, this strike was soon overshadowed by events in Chicago that would prove to be the undoing of the Knights (Figure 17.1).

For months before the general strike, the McCormick Harvester plant in Chicago had been at the center of an often violent conflict over wages and work conditions. On May 3, 1886, police killed two strikers in a clash between union members and strikebreakers who tried to cross the picket lines. In response, a group of anarchists led by the German-born activist August Spies called for a rally in **Haymarket Square** to protest police violence. Consisting mainly of foreign-born radicals, such anarchists believed that government represented the interests of capitalists and stifled freedom for workers. Anarchists differed among themselves, but they generally advocated tearing down government authority, restoring personal freedom, and forming worker communes to replace capitalism. To achieve their goals, anarchists like Spies advocated the violent overthrow of government.

The Haymarket rally began at 8:30 in the evening of May 4 and attracted no more than 1,500 people, who listened to a series of speeches as rain fell. By 10:30 p.m., when the crowd had dwindled to some 300 people, 180 policemen decided to break it up. As police moved into the square, someone set off a bomb. The police fired back, and when the smoke cleared, seven policemen and four protesters lay dead. Most of the fatalities and injuries resulted from the police crossfire. A subsequent trial convicted eight anarchists of murder, though there was no evidence that any of them had planted the bomb or used weapons. Four of them, including Spies, were executed. Although Powderly and other union leaders denounced the anarchists and the bombing, the incident greatly tarnished the labor movement. Capitalists and

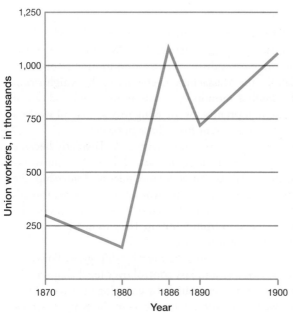

FIGURE 17.1   Union Membership, 1870–1900
Union membership fluctuated widely in the late nineteenth century. After reaching a low point in 1880, the number of union members rebounded. However, membership plummeted after 1886 only to soar again in the 1890s. Explain the rise and fall of union membership from 1880 through 1900.

Source: Data from Richard B. Freeman, "Spurts in Union Growth: Defining Moments and Social Processes," working paper 6012, National Bureau of Economic Research, Cambridge, MA, 1997.

their allies in the press attacked labor unionists as radicals prone to violence and denounced strikes as un-American. Following the Haymarket incident, the membership rolls of the Knights plunged to below 500,000. By the mid-1890s, the Knights had fewer than 20,000 members.

As the Knights of Labor faded, the **American Federation of Labor (AFL)** grew in prominence, offering an alternative vision of unionization. Instead of one giant industrial union that included all workers, skilled and unskilled, the AFL organized only skilled craftsmen—the labor elite—into trade unions. In 1886 Samuel Gompers became president of the AFL. Gompers considered trade unions "the business organizations of the wage earners to attend to the business of the wage earners" and favored the use of strikes. No social reformer, the AFL president concentrated on obtaining better wages and hours for workers so that they could share in the prosperity generated by industrial capitalism. By 1900 the AFL had around a million members. It achieved these numbers by recruiting the most independent, highest-paid, and least replaceable segment of the labor force—white male skilled workers. Unlike the Knights, the AFL had little or no place for women and African Americans in its ranks.

As impressive as the AFL's achievement was, the union movement as a whole experienced only limited success in the late nineteenth century. Only about one in fifteen industrial workers belonged to a union in 1900. Union membership was low for a variety of reasons. First, the political and economic power of corporations and the prospects of retaliation made the decision to sign up for union membership a risky venture. Second, the diversity of workers made organizing a difficult task. Foreign-born laborers came from many countries and were divided by language, religion, ethnicity, and history. Moreover, European immigrants quickly adopted native-born whites' racial prejudices against African Americans. Third, despite severe limitations in social mobility, American workers generally retained their faith in the benefits of the capitalist system. Finally, the government used its legal and military authority to side with employers and suppress militant workers.

Southern workers were the most resistant to union organizing. The agricultural background of mill workers left them with a heightened sense of individualism and isolation. In addition, their continued connection to family and friends in the countryside offered a potential escape route from industrial labor. Employers' willingness to use racial tensions to divide working-class blacks and whites prevented them from joining together to further their common economic interests.

Clashes between Workers and Owners

Despite the difficulties of organizing workers, labor challenged some of the nation's largest industries in the late nineteenth century. Faced with owners' refusal to recognize or negotiate with unions, workers marshaled their greatest source of power: withholding their labor and going on strike. Employers in turn had powerful weapons at their command to break strikes. They could recruit strikebreakers and mobilize private and public security forces to protect their businesses. That workers went on strike against such odds testified to their desperation and courage (Map 17.1).

Workers in the United States were not alone in their efforts to combat industrial exploitation. In England, laborers organized for better wages and working conditions. In 1888 in London, young women who worked at a match factory staged a

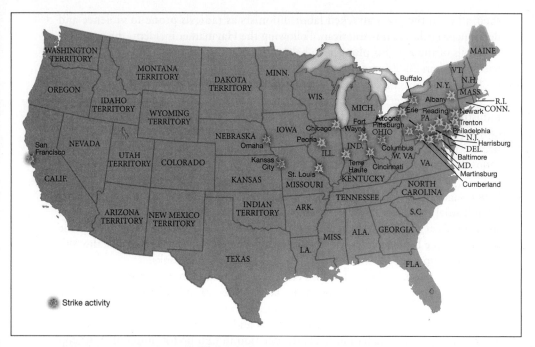

MAP 17.1   The Great Railroad Strike
This nationwide strike, precipitated by falling wages during the Depression of 1873, started in West Virginia and Pennsylvania and spread to Chicago, St. Louis, and San Francisco. The strike brought a halt to rail traffic as over 100,000 workers and another half a million sympathizers walked off their jobs. Violence broke out in Pittsburgh, resulting in more than twenty deaths. Federal troops were eventually dispatched to end the strike. Many workers quickly recognized the need to form unions to gain power to stand up against employers and the government.

walkout to protest the exorbitant fines that employers imposed on them for arriving even one minute late to work. With community support, they won their demands. From 1888 to 1890, the number of strikes throughout Europe grew from 188 to 289. In 1890 thousands of workers in Budapest, Hungary rose up to protest unsafe working conditions. European workers also campaigned for the right to vote, which unlike white male American workers, they were denied on economic grounds.

In the United States in the 1890s, labor mounted several highly publicized strikes. Perhaps the most famous was the 1892 **Homestead strike**. Steelworkers at Carnegie's Homestead, Pennsylvania factory near Pittsburgh played an active role in local politics and civic affairs. Residents generally believed that Andrew Carnegie's corporation paid decent wages that allowed them to support their families and buy their own homes. In 1892 craftsmen earned $180 a month, and they appeared to have Carnegie's respect. Others, like John McLuckie, earned less than half that amount, and unskilled workers made even less.

In 1892, with steel prices falling, Carnegie decided to replace some of his skilled craftsmen with machinery, cut wages, save on labor costs, and bust McLuckie's union, the Amalgamated Association of Iron and Steel Workers. Knowing that his actions would provoke a strike and seeking to avoid the negative publicity that would result, Carnegie left the country and went to Scotland, leaving his plant manager, Henry Clay Frick, in charge.

Fiercely anti-union, Frick prepared for the strike by building a three-mile, fifteen-foot-high fence, capped with barbed wire and equipped with searchlights, around three sides of the Homestead factory. A hated symbol of the manager's hostility, the fence became known as "Fort Frick." Along the fourth side of the factory flowed the Monongahela River. Frick had no intention of negotiating seriously with the union on a new contract, and on July 1 he ordered a lockout. Only employees who rejected the union and accepted lower wages could return to work. The small town rallied around the workers, and the union members won a temporary victory. On July 6, barge-loads of armed Pinkerton detectives (an independent police force), hired by Frick to protect the plant, set sail toward the factory entrance alongside the Monongahela. From the shore, union men shot at the barges and set fire to a boat they pushed toward the Pinkertons. When the smoke cleared, the Pinkertons surrendered and hastily retreated onshore as women and men chased after them.

This triumph proved costly for the union. The battle left nine strikers and three Pinkerton detectives dead. Frick convinced the governor of Pennsylvania to send in state troops to protect the factory and the strikebreakers. Frick's efforts to end the strike spurred some radicals to action. Emma Goldman, an anarchist who advocated the violent overthrow of capitalism, declared that a blow against Frick would "strike terror in the enemy's ranks and make them realize that the proletariat of America had its avengers." On July 23, Alexander Berkman, Goldman's partner, who had no connection with the union, entered Frick's office and shot the steel executive in the neck, leaving him wounded but alive. The resulting unfavorable publicity, together with the state's prosecution of the union, broke the strike. Subsequently, steel companies blacklisted the union leaders for life, and McLuckie fled Pennsylvania and wound up nearly penniless in Arizona.

Like Andrew Carnegie, George Pullman considered himself an enlightened employer, one who took good care of the men who worked in his luxury sleeping railcar factory outside Chicago. However, also like the steel titan, Pullman placed profits over personnel. In 1893 a severe economic depression prompted Pullman to cut wages without correspondingly reducing the rents that his employees paid for living in company houses. This dual blow to worker income and purchasing power led to a fierce strike the following year. The Pullman workers belonged to the American Railway Union, headed by Eugene V. Debs. After George Pullman refused to negotiate, the union voted to go on strike.

In the end, the **Pullman strike** was broken by the federal government. President Grover Cleveland ordered federal troops to get the railroads operating, but the workers still refused to capitulate. Richard Olney, Cleveland's attorney general, then obtained an order from the federal courts to restrain Debs and other union leaders from continuing the strike. The government used the Sherman Antitrust Act to punish unions for conspiring to restrain trade, something it had rarely done with respect to large corporations. Refusing to comply, Debs and other union officials were charged with contempt, convicted under the Sherman Antitrust Act, and sent to jail. The strike collapsed.

Debs remained unrepentant. After serving his jail sentence, he became even more radical. In 1901 he helped establish the Socialist Party of America. German exiles who came to the United States following revolutions in Europe in 1848 had brought with them the revolutionary ideas of the German philosopher Karl Marx. Marx argued that capital and labor were engaged in a class struggle that would end with the violent overthrow of capitalist government and its replacement by communism. Marxist ideas attracted a small following in the United States, mainly among the foreign-born population. By contrast, other types of European socialists, including the German Social Democratic Party, appealed for working-class support by advocating the creation of a more just and humane economic system through the ballot box, not by violent revolution. Debs favored this nonviolent, democratic brand of socialism and managed to attract a broader base of supporters by articulating socialist doctrines in the language of cooperation and citizenship that many Americans shared. Debsian socialism appealed not only to industrial workers but also to dispossessed farmers and miners in the Southwest and Midwest.

Western miners had a history of labor activism, and by the 1890s they were ready to listen to radical ideas. Shortly after the Homestead strike ended in 1892, silver miners in Coeur d'Alene, Idaho walked out after owners slashed their wages. Employers refused to recognize any union, obtained an injunction against the strike, imported strikebreakers to run the mines, and persuaded Idaho's governor to impose martial law, in which the military took over the normal operation of civilian affairs. The work stoppage lasted four months, resulting in the arrest of six hundred strikers. Although the workers lost, the following year they succeeded in forming the Western Federation of Miners, which continued their fight.

The **Industrial Workers of the World (IWW)**, which emerged largely through the efforts of the Western Federation of Miners, sought to raise wages, improve working conditions, and gain union recognition for the most exploited segments of American labor. The IWW, or "Wobblies" as they were popularly known, sought to unite all skilled and unskilled workers in an effort to overthrow capitalism. The Wobblies favored strikes and direct-action protests rather than collective bargaining or mediation. At their rallies and strikes, they often encountered government force and corporation-inspired mob violence. Nevertheless, the IWW had substantial appeal among lumberjacks in the Northwest, dockworkers in port cities, miners in the West, farmers in the Great Plains, and textile workers in the Northeast.

Even though industrialists usually had state and federal governments as well as the media on their side, workers continued to press for their rights. Workers used strikes as a last resort when business owners refused to negotiate or recognize their demands to organize themselves into unions. Although most late-nineteenth-century strikes failed, striking unionists nonetheless called for collective bargaining, higher wages, shorter hours, and improved working conditions—an agenda that unions and their political allies would build on in the future.

Working-Class Leisure in Industrial America

Despite the hardships industrial laborers faced in the late nineteenth century, workers carved out recreational spaces that they could control and that offered relief from their backbreaking toil. For many, Sunday became a day of rest that took on a secular flavor.

Working-class leisure patterns varied by gender, race, and region. Women did not generally attend spectator sporting events, such as baseball and boxing matches, which catered to men. Nor did they find themselves comfortable in union halls and saloons, where men found solace in drink. Working-class wives preferred to gather to prepare for births, weddings, and funerals or to assist neighbors who had suffered some misfortune.

Once employed, working-class daughters found a greater measure of independence and free time by living in rooming houses on their own. Women's wages were only a small fraction of men's earnings, so workingwomen rarely made enough money to support a regular social life. Still, they found ways to enjoy their free time. Some single women went out in groups, hoping to meet men who would pay for drinks, food, or a vaudeville show. Others dated so that they knew they would be taken care of for the evening. Some of the men who "treated" on a date assumed a right to sexual favors in return, and some of these women then expected men to provide them with housing and gifts in exchange for an ongoing sexual relationship. Thus emotional and economic relationships became intertwined.

Fun at Coney Island, c.1898   Circuses and amusement parks were two forms of entertainment that attracted working-class and middle-class audiences. This poster announces the performance of Barnum and Bailey's "Greatest Show on Earth" at the water carnival in Coney Island. Clowns, boxers, divers, and log rollers would be among the variety of performers at the beach. Library of Congress, LC-DIG-ppmsca-54817

Around the turn of the twentieth century, dance halls flourished as one of the mainstays of working-class communities. Huge dance palaces were built in the entertainment districts of most large cities. They made their money by offering music with lengthy intermissions for the sale of drinks and refreshments. Women and men also attended nightclubs, some of which were racially integrated. In so-called redlight districts of the city, prostitutes earned money entertaining their clients with a variety of sexual pleasures.

Not all forms of leisure were strictly segregated along class lines. A number of forms of cheap entertainment appealed not only to working-class women and men but also to their middle-class counterparts. By the turn of the twentieth century, most large American cities featured amusement parks. Brooklyn's Coney Island stood out as the most spectacular of these sprawling playgrounds. In 1884, the world's first roller coaster was built at Coney Island, providing thrills to those brave enough to ride it. In Chicago at the 1893 World's Columbian Exposition, residents enjoyed the new Ferris wheel, which soared 250 feet in the air. Vaudeville houses—with their minstrel shows (whites in blackface) and comedians, singers, and dancers—brought howls of laughter to working-class audiences. Nickelodeons charged five cents to watch short films. Live theater generally attracted more wealthy patrons; however, the Yiddish theater, which flourished on New York's Lower East Side, and other immigrant-oriented stage productions appealed mainly to working-class audiences.

Itinerant musicians entertained audiences throughout the South. Lumber camps, which employed mainly African American men, offered a popular destination for these musicians. Each camp contained a "barrelhouse," also called a honky tonk or a juke joint. Besides showcasing music, the barrelhouse also gave workers the opportunity to "shoot craps, dice, drink whiskey, dance, every modern devilment you can do," as one musician who played there recalled. From the Mississippi delta emerged a new form of music—the blues. W. C. Handy, "the father of the blues," discovered this music in his travels through the delta, where he observed southern blacks performing songs of woe, accompanying themselves with anything that would make a "musical sound or rhythmical effect, anything from a harmonica to a washboard." Meanwhile in New Orleans, an amalgam of black musical forms evolved into jazz. Musicians such as "Jelly Roll" Morton experimented with a variety of sounds, putting together African and Caribbean rhythms with European music, mixing pianos with clarinets, trumpets, and drums. Blues and jazz spread throughout the South.

In mountain valley mill towns, southern whites preferred "old-time" music, but with a twist: they modified the lyrics of traditional ballads and folk songs, originally enjoyed by British settlers, to extol the exploits of outlaws and adventurers. Country music, which combined romantic ballads and folk tunes to the accompaniment of guitars, banjos, autoharps, dulcimers, and organs, emerged as a distinct brand of music by the twentieth century. As with African Americans, in the late nineteenth century working-class and rural whites found new and exciting types of music to entertain them in their leisure. Religious music also appealed to both white and black audiences and drew crowds to evangelical revivals.

Mill workers also amused themselves by engaging in social, recreational, and religious activities. Women visited each other and exchanged confidences, gossip, advice on child rearing, and folk remedies. Men from various factories organized baseball teams that competed in leagues. Managers of a mill in Charlotte, North Carolina, admitted that they "frequently hired men better known for their batting averages than their work records."

Farmers Organize

Like industrial workers, farmers experienced severe economic hardships and a loss of political power in the face of rapid industrialization. The introduction of new machinery such as the combine harvester, introduced in 1878, led to substantial increases in the productivity of American farms. Soaring production, however, led to a decline in agricultural prices in the late nineteenth century, a trend that was accelerated by increased agricultural production around the world. In addition, the role of agriculture in the economy was steadily declining and taking second place to commerce and industry. Agriculture had slipped from a majority of economic production in 1860 to 40 percent in 1890, behind manufacturing and mining. Faced with an economic crisis caused by falling prices and escalating debt, farmers fought back, creating new organizations to champion their collective economic and political interests.

Farmers Unite

From the end of the Civil War to the mid-1890s, increased production of wheat and cotton, two of the most important American crops, led to a precipitous drop in the price for these crops. Falling prices created a debt crisis for many farmers. Most American farmers were independent businessmen who borrowed money to pay for land, seed, and equipment. When their crops were harvested and sold, they repaid their debts with the proceeds. As prices fell, farmers increased production in an effort to cover their debts. This tactic led to a greater supply of farm produce in the marketplace and even lower prices. Unable to pay back loans, many farmers lost their property in foreclosures to the banks that held their mortgages and furnished them credit.

To make matters worse, farmers lived isolated lives. Spread out across vast acres of rural territory, farmers had few social and cultural diversions. Even more than the families of industrial workers, farmers put their children to work; rural youngsters were 8 percent more likely to work than their urban counterparts. As the farm economy declined, more and more of their children left the monotony of rural America behind and headed for cities in search of new opportunities and a better life. Early efforts to organize farmers were motivated by a desire to counteract the isolation of rural life by creating new forms of social interaction and cultural engagement. In 1867, Oliver H. Kelly founded the Patrons of Husbandry to brighten the lonely existence of rural Americans through educational and social activities. Known as **Grangers** (from the French word for "granary"), the association grew rapidly in the early 1870s, especially in the Midwest and the South. Between 1872 and 1874, approximately fourteen thousand new Grange chapters were established.

Grangers also formed farm cooperatives to sell their crops at higher prices and pool their purchasing power to buy finished goods at wholesale prices. The Grangers' interest in promoting the collective economic interests of farmers led to their increasing involvement in politics. Grangers endorsed candidates who favored their cause, and perhaps their most important objective was the regulation of shipping and grain storage prices. In many areas, individual railroads had monopolies on both of these services, and were able to charge farmers higher-than-usual rates to store and ship their crops. By electing sympathetic state legislators, Grangers managed to obtain regulations that placed a ceiling on the prices railroads and grain elevators could charge. The Supreme Court temporarily upheld these victories in *Munn v. Illinois* (1877). In 1886, however, in *Wabash v. Illinois* the Supreme Court reversed itself and struck down these state regulatory laws as hindering the free flow of interstate commerce.

Another apparent victory for regulation came in 1887 when Congress passed the Interstate Commerce Act, establishing the **Interstate Commerce Commission (ICC)** to regulate railroads. Although big businessmen could not prevent occasional government regulation, they managed to render it largely ineffective. In time, railroad advocates came to dominate the ICC and enforced the law in favor of the railway lines rather than the shippers. Implementation of the Sherman Antitrust Act also favored big business. From the standpoint of most late-nineteenth-century capitalists, national regulations often turned out to be more of a help than a hindrance.

By the late 1880s, the Grangers had abandoned electoral politics and once again devoted themselves strictly to social and cultural activities. A number of factors explain the Grangers' return to their original mission. First, prices began to rise for some crops, particularly corn, relieving the economic pressure on midwestern farmers. Second, the passage of regulatory legislation in a number of states convinced some Grangers that their political goals had been achieved. Finally, a lack of marketing and business experience led to the collapse of many agricultural collectives.

The withdrawal of the Grangers from politics did not, however, signal the end of efforts by farmers to form organizations to advance their economic interests. While farmers in the midwestern corn belt experienced some political success and an economic upturn, farmers farther west in the Great Plains and in the Lower South fell more deeply into debt, as the price of wheat and cotton on the international market continued to drop. In both of these regions, farmers organized **Farmers' Alliances**. In the 1880s, Milton George formed the Northwestern Farmers' Alliance. At the same time, Dr. Charles W. Macune organized the much larger Southern Farmers' Alliance. Southern black farmers, excluded from the Southern Farmers' Alliance, created a parallel Colored Farmers' Alliance. The Alliances formed a network of recruiters to sign up new members. No recruiter was more effective than Mary Elizabeth Lease, who excited farm audiences with her forceful and colorful rhetoric, delivering 160 speeches in the summer of 1890 alone. The Southern Farmers' Alliance advocated a sophisticated plan to solve the farmers' problem of mounting debt. Macune devised a proposal for a **subtreasury system**. Under this plan, the federal government would locate offices near warehouses in which farmers could store nonperishable commodities. In return, farmers would receive federal loans for 80 percent of the current market value of their produce. In theory, temporarily taking crops off the market would decrease supply and, assuming demand remained stable, lead to increased prices. Once prices rose, farmers would return to the warehouses, redeem their crops, sell them at the higher price, repay the government loan, and leave with a profit.

The first step toward creating a nationwide farmers' organization came in 1889, when the Northwestern and Southern Farmers' Alliances agreed to merge. Alliance leaders, including Lease, saw workers as fellow victims of industrialization, and they invited the Knights of Labor to join them. They also attempted to lower prevailing racial barriers by bringing the Colored Farmers' Alliance into the coalition. The following year, the National Farmers' Alliance and Industrial Union held its convention in Ocala, Florida. The group adopted resolutions endorsing the subtreasury system, as well as recommendations that would promote the economic welfare of farmers and extend political democracy to "the plain people." These proposals included tariff reduction, government ownership of banks and railroads, and political reforms to extend democracy, such as direct election of U.S. senators.

Finally, the Alliance pressed the government to increase the money supply by expanding the amount of silver coinage in circulation. In the Alliance's view, such a move would have two positive, and related, consequences. First, the resulting inflation would lead to higher prices for agricultural commodities, putting more money in farmers' pockets. Second, the real value of farmers' debts would decrease, since the debts were contracted in pre-inflation dollars and would be paid back with inflated currency. Naturally, the eastern bankers who supplied farmers with credit opposed such a policy. In fact, in 1873 Congress, under the leadership of Senator John Sherman, had halted the purchase of silver by the Treasury Department, a measure that helped reduce the money supply. Later, however, under the Sherman Silver Purchase Act (1890), the government resumed buying silver, but the act placed limits on its purchase and did not guarantee the creation of silver coinage by the Treasury. In the past, some members of the Alliance had favored expanding the money supply with greenbacks (paper money). However, to attract support from western silver miners, Alliance delegates emphasized the free and unlimited coinage of silver. Alliance supporters met with bitter disappointment, though, as neither the Republican nor the Democratic Party embraced their demands. Rebuffed, farmers took an independent path and became more directly involved in national politics through the formation of the Populist Party.

Populists Rise Up

In 1892 the National Farmers' Alliance moved into the electoral arena as a third political party. The People's Party of America, known as the **Populists**, held its first nominating convention in Omaha, Nebraska, in 1892. In addition to incorporating the Alliance's Ocala planks into their platform, they adopted recommendations to broaden the party's appeal to industrial workers. Populists endorsed a graduated income tax, which would impose higher tax rates on higher income levels, the eight-hour workday, and immigration restriction, which stemmed from the unions' desire to keep unskilled workers from glutting the market and depressing wages. Reflecting the influence of women such as Mary Lease, the party endorsed women's suffrage.

The party did not, however, offer specific proposals to prohibit racial discrimination or segregation. Rather, the party focused on remedies to relieve the economic plight of impoverished white and black farmers in general.

In 1892 the Populists nominated for president former Union Civil War general James B. Weaver. Although Weaver came in third behind the Democratic victor, Grover Cleveland, and the Republican incumbent, Benjamin Harrison, he managed to win more than 1 million popular votes and 22 electoral votes.

At the state level, Populists performed even better. They elected 10 congressional representatives, 5 U.S. senators, 3 governors, and 1,500 state legislators. Two years later, the party made even greater strides by increasing its total vote by 42 percent and achieving its greatest strength in the South. This electoral momentum positioned the Populists to make an even stronger run in the next presidential election. The economic depression that began in 1893 and the political discontent it generated enhanced Populist chances for success.

REVIEW & RELATE	• Why was life so difficult for American farmers in the late nineteenth century?
	• What were the similarities and differences between farmers' and industrial workers' efforts to organize in the late nineteenth century?

The Depression of the 1890s

When the Philadelphia and Reading Railroad went bankrupt in early 1893, it set off a chain reaction that pushed one-quarter of American railroads into insolvency. As a result, on May 5, 1893, "Black Friday," the stock market collapsed in a panic, triggering the **depression of 1893**. Making this situation worse, England and the rest of industrial Europe had experienced an economic downturn several years earlier. In the early 1890s foreign investors began selling off their American stocks, leading to a flow of gold coin out of the country and further damage to the banking system. Hundreds of banks failed, which hurt the businesspeople and farmers who relied on a steady flow of bank credit. By the end of 1894, nearly 12 percent of the American workforce remained unemployed. The depression became the chief political issue of the mid-1890s and resulted in a realignment of power between the two major parties. Unable to capitalize on depression discontent, however, the Populist Party split apart and collapsed.

Depression Politics

President Grover Cleveland's handling of the depression, accompanied by protest marches and labor strife, only made a bad situation worse. In the spring of 1894, Jacob Coxey, a Populist reformer from Ohio, led a march on Washington, D.C., demanding that Cleveland and Congress initiate a federal public works program to provide jobs for the unemployed. Though highly critical of the favored few who dominated the federal government, Coxey had faith that if "the people . . . come in a body like this, peaceably to discuss their grievances and demanding immediate relief,

Congress . . . will heed them and do it quickly." After traveling for a month from Ohio, Coxey led a parade of some five hundred unemployed people into the nation's capital. Attracting thousands of spectators, **Coxey's army** attempted to mount their protest on the grounds of the Capitol building. In response, police broke up the demonstration and arrested Coxey for trespassing. Cleveland turned a deaf ear to Coxey's demands for federal relief and also disregarded protesters participating in nearly twenty other marches on Washington.

In the coming months, Cleveland's political stock plummeted further. He responded to the Pullman strike in the summer of 1894 by obtaining a federal injunction against the strikers and dispatching federal troops to Illinois to enforce it. The president's action won him high praise from the railroads and conservative business interests, but it showed millions of American workers that the Cleveland administration did not have a solution for ending the suffering caused by the depression. "While the people should patriotically and cheerfully support their Government," the president declared, "its functions do not include the support of the people."

Making matters worse, Cleveland convinced Congress to repeal the Sherman Silver Purchase Act. This angered western miners, who relied on strong silver prices, along with farmers in the South and Great Plains who were swamped by mounting debt. At the same time, the removal of silver as a backing for currency caused private investors to withdraw their gold deposits from the U.S. Treasury. To keep the government financially solvent, Cleveland worked out an agreement with a syndicate led by J. P. Morgan to help sell government bonds, a deal that netted the banker a huge profit. In the midst of economic suffering, this deal looked like a corrupt bargain between the government and the rich.

In 1894 Congress also passed the Wilson-Gorman Act, which raised tariffs on imported goods. Intended to protect American businesses by keeping the price of imported goods high, it also deprived foreigners of the necessary income with which to buy American exports. This drop in exports did not help economic recovery. The Wilson-Gorman Act did include a provision that the Populists and other reformers endorsed: a progressive income tax of 2 percent on all annual earnings over $4,000. No federal income tax existed at this time, so even this mild levy elicited cries of "socialism" from conservative critics, who challenged the tax in the courts. In *Pollack v. Farmers Loan and Trust* (1895), the Supreme Court declared the income tax unconstitutional and denounced it as the opening wedge in "a war of the poor against the rich; a war constantly growing in intensity and bitterness."

With Cleveland's legislative program in shambles and his inability to solve the depression abundantly clear, the Democrats suffered a crushing blow at the polls. In the congressional elections of 1894, the party lost an astonishing 120 seats in the House. This defeat offered a preview of the political shakeup that loomed ahead.

Political Realignment in the Election of 1896

The presidential election of 1896 marked a turning point in the political history of the nation. Democrats nominated William Jennings Bryan of Nebraska, a farmers' advocate. He embodied the belief that farmers still formed the backbone of the republic despite the fact they no longer dominated the nation economically. "Burn down your cities," Bryan declared, "and leave our farms, and your cities will spring up again as if by magic; but destroy our farms and the grass will grow in the streets of every city in the country." Bryan also favored silver coinage and when he vowed that he would not see Republicans "crucify mankind on a cross of gold," the Populists endorsed him as well.

Republicans nominated William McKinley, the governor of Ohio and a supporter of the gold standard and high tariffs on manufactured and other goods. McKinley's campaign manager, Marcus Alonzo Hanna, an ally of Ohio senator John Sherman, raised an unprecedented amount of money, about $16 million, mainly from wealthy industrialists who feared that the free and unlimited coinage of silver would debase the U.S. currency. Hanna saturated the country with pamphlets, leaflets, and posters, many of them written in the native languages of immigrant groups. He also hired a platoon of speakers to fan out across the country denouncing Bryan's free silver cause as financial madness. By contrast, Bryan raised about $1 million.

The outcome of the election transformed the Republicans into the majority party in the United States. McKinley won 51 percent of the popular vote and 61 percent of the electoral vote. More important than this specific contest, however, was that the election proved critical in realigning the two parties. Voting patterns shifted with the 1896 election, giving Republicans the edge in party affiliation among the electorate not only in this contest but also in presidential elections over the next three decades (Map 17.2).

What happened to produce this critical realignment in electoral power? The main ingredient was Republicans' success in forming a coalition that included both corporate capitalists and their workers. Many urban dwellers and industrial workers took out their anger on Cleveland's Democratic Party and Bryan as its standard-bearer for failing to end the depression. In addition, Bryan, who hailed from Nebraska and reflected small-town agricultural America and its values, could not win over the swelling numbers of urban immigrants who considered Bryan's world alien to their experience.

The election of 1896 broke the political stalemate in this age of organization. The core of Republican backing came from industrial cities of the Northeast and

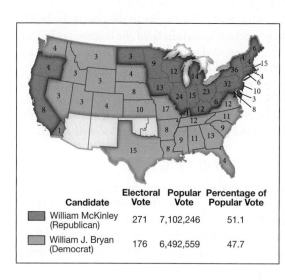

Candidate	Electoral Vote	Popular Vote	Percentage of Popular Vote
William McKinley (Republican)	271	7,102,246	51.1
William J. Bryan (Democrat)	176	6,492,559	47.7

MAP 17.2 The Election of 1896 William McKinley's election in 1896 resulted in a realignment of political power in the United States that lasted until 1932. Republicans became the nation's majority party by forging a coalition of big business and urban industrial workers from the Northeast and Midwest. Democratic strength was confined to the South and to small towns and rural areas of the Great Plains and Rocky Mountain states.

Midwest. Republicans won support from their traditional constituencies of Union veterans, business people, and African Americans and added to it the votes of a large number of urban wageworkers. The campaign persuaded voters that the Democratic Party represented the party of depression and that Republicans stood for prosperity and progress. They were soon able to take credit for ending the depression when, in 1897, gold discoveries in Alaska helped increase the money supply and foreign crop failures raised American farm prices. Democrats managed to hold on to the South as their solitary political base.

The Decline of the Populists

The year 1896 also marked the end of the Populists as a national force, as the party was torn apart by internal divisions over policy and strategy. Populist leaders such as Tom Watson of Georgia did not want the Populist Party to emphasize free silver above the rest of its reform program. Northern Populists, who either had fought on the Union side during the Civil War or had close relatives who did, such as Mary Lease whose father and brother died on the Union side, could not bring themselves to join the Democrats, the party of the old Confederacy. Nevertheless, the Populist Party officially backed Bryan, but to retain its identity, the party nominated Watson for vice president on its own ticket. After McKinley's victory, the Populist Party collapsed.

In addition to losing the presidential election, several other problems plagued the third party. The nation's recovery from the depression removed one of the Populists' prime sources of electoral attraction. Despite appealing to industrial workers, the Populists were unable to capture their support. The free silver plank attracted silver miners in Idaho and Colorado, but the majority of workers failed to identify with a party composed mainly of farmers. As consumers of agricultural products,

Wilmington, North Carolina Massacre, 1898 In 1898, Populists in alliance with the Republican Party in Wilmington, N.C. elected a white mayor and a biracial city council. Two days after the election, on November 10, armed members of the defeated Democratic Party, the party of white supremacy, overthrew the new city government. A mob of around 2,000 white men, some of whom are pictured above, set fire to the city's black newspaper building. White terrorists killed at least fifteen people and forced more than 2,000 blacks to flee the city permanently. The success of this coup d'état dealt Populism a mortal blow. Library of Congress, Prints and Photographs Division [LC-USZ62-51942]

industrial laborers did not see any benefit in raising farm prices. Populists also failed to create a stable, biracial coalition of farmers. Most southern white Populists did not truly accept African Americans as equal partners, even though these groups had mutual economic interests.

To eliminate Populism's insurgent political threat, southern opponents found ways to disfranchise black and poor white voters. During the 1890s, southern states inserted into their constitutions voting requirements that virtually eliminated the black electorate and greatly diminished the white electorate. Seeking to circumvent the Fifteenth Amendment's prohibition against racial discrimination in the right to vote, conservative white lawmakers adopted regulations based on wealth and education because blacks were disproportionately poor and had lower literacy rates. They instituted poll taxes, which imposed a fee for voting, and literacy tests, which asked questions designed to trip up black would-be voters. In 1898 the Supreme Court upheld the constitutionality of these voter qualifications in *Williams v. Mississippi*. Recognizing the power of white supremacy, the Populists surrendered to its appeals.

Tom Watson provides a case in point. He started out by encouraging racial unity but then switched to divisive politics. In 1896 the Populist vice presidential candidate called on citizens of both races to vote against the crushing power of corporations and railroads. By whipping up antagonism against blacks, his Democratic opponents appealed to the racial pride of poor whites to keep them from defecting to the Populists. Chastened by the outcome of the 1896 election and learning from the tactics of his political foes, Watson embarked on a vicious campaign to exclude blacks from voting. "What does civilization owe the Negro?" he bitterly asked. "Nothing! Nothing! NOTHING!!!" Only by disfranchising African Americans and maintaining white supremacy, Watson and other white reformers reasoned, would poor whites have the courage to vote against rich whites.

Nevertheless, even in defeat the Populists left an enduring legacy. Many of their political and economic reforms — direct election of senators, the graduated income tax, government regulation of business and banking, and a version of the subtreasury system (called the Commodity Credit Corporation, created in the 1930s) — became features of reform in the twentieth century. Perhaps their greatest contribution, however, came in showing farmers that their old individualist ways would not succeed in the modern industrial era. Rather than re-creating an independent political party, most farmers looked to organized interest groups, such as the Farm Bureau, to lobby on behalf of their interests.

REVIEW & RELATE	• How did the federal government respond to the depression of 1893? • What were the long-term political consequences of the depression of 1893?

Conclusion: A Passion for Organization

From 1877 to 1900, industrial workers and farmers joined the march toward organization led by the likes of Carnegie, Rockefeller, and Morgan. These wealthy titans of industry and finance had created the large corporations that transformed the rhythms and meanings of life in workplaces, farms, and leisure activities. Working people such as John McLuckie met the challenges of the new industrial order by organizing unions. Lacking the power of giant companies and confronted by the federal government's use of force to break up strikes, labor unions nevertheless carved out sufficient space for workers to join together in their own defense to resist absolute corporate rule. At the same time, farmers, perhaps the most individualistic workers, and their advocates, such as Mary Elizabeth Lease, created organizations that proposed some of the most forward-looking solutions to remedy the ills accompanying industrialization. Though the political fortunes of the Grangers and Populists declined, their message persisted: Resourceful and determined workers and farmers could, and should, join together to ensure survival not just of the fittest but of the neediest as well.

Under the pressure of increased turmoil surrounding industrialization and a brutal economic depression, the political system reached a crisis in the 1890s. Despite the historic shift in party loyalties brought about by the election of William McKinley, it remained to be seen whether political party realignment could furnish the necessary leadership to address the problems of workers and farmers. The events of the 1890s convinced many Americans, including many in the middle class, that the hands-off approach to social and economic problems that had prevailed in the past was no longer acceptable. In cities and states across the country, men and women took up the cause of reform. They had to wait for national leaders to catch up to them.

Chapter 17 Review

KEY TERMS

unskilled workers, 429
skilled workers, 430
unions, 433
collective bargaining, 433
Noble Order of the Knights
 of Labor, 433
Haymarket Square, 434
American Federation of
 Labor (AFL), 435
Homestead strike, 436
Pullman strike, 437

Industrial Workers of the World
 (IWW), 438
Grangers, 441
Interstate Commerce Commission
 (ICC), 442
Farmers' Alliances, 442
subtreasury system, 442
Populists, 443
depression of 1893, 444
Coxey's army, 445

REVIEW & RELATE

1. How did industrialization change the American workplace? What challenges did it create for American workers?

2. How did workers resist the concentrated power of industrial capitalists in the late nineteenth century, and why did such efforts have only limited success?

3. Why was life so difficult for American farmers in the late nineteenth century?

4. What were the similarities and differences between farmers' and industrial workers' efforts to organize in the late nineteenth century?

5. How did the federal government respond to the depression of 1893?

6. What were the long-term political consequences of the depression of 1893?

TIMELINE OF EVENTS

1865–1895	• U.S. manufacturing jobs jump from 5.3 million to 15.1 million
1867	• Grange founded
1869	• Knights of Labor founded
1870–1900	• Number of female wageworkers increases by 66 percent
1877	• Great Railroad Strike
1879	• Terence Powderly becomes leader of Knights of Labor
1880s	• Northwestern, Southern, and Colored Farmers' Alliances formed
1886	• Haymarket Square violence
	• American Federation of Labor founded
1887	• Interstate Commerce Act
1889	• Northwestern and Southern Farmers' Alliances merge
1890	• Sherman Silver Purchase Act
1890s	• Southern states restrict blacks' right to vote
1892	• Homestead steelworkers' strike
	• Populist Party established
1893	• Depression triggered by stock market collapse
1894	• Pullman strike
	• Coxey's army marches to Washington
	• Sherman Silver Purchase Act repealed
1896	• Populist William Jennings Bryan runs for president
1897	• Populist Party declines
1901	• Eugene Debs establishes Socialist Party of America

Cities, Immigrants, and the Nation

1880–1914

LEARNING OBJECTIVES

After reading this chapter you will be able to:

- Explain the reasons late nineteenth- and early twentieth-century immigrants came to the United States and evaluate how they were received by native-born Americans.

- Explain why farmers, small-town residents, and African Americans from the South migrated to cities, and summarize the challenges and technological changes they encountered.

- Assess the benefits and liabilities of urban political machines and compare those who supported and opposed them.

COMPARING AMERICAN HISTORIES

In the fall of 1905, **Beryl Lassin** faced a difficult choice. Living in a *shtetl* (a Jewish town) in western Russia, Lassin had few if any opportunities as a young blacksmith. Beryl and his wife, Lena, lived at a dangerous time in Russia. Jews were subject to periodic pogroms, state-sanctioned outbreaks of anti-Jewish violence carried out by local Christians. Beryl also faced a discriminatory military draft that required conscripted Jews to serve twenty-year terms in the army, far longer than Christians. Beryl decided he should quickly follow his wife's brother to the United States. With the understanding that his wife would follow as soon as possible, Beryl set sail for America on October 7, 1905. He was crammed into the steerage belowdecks with hundreds of other passengers. Ten days later he disembarked in New York harbor at Ellis Island, the processing center for immigrants, where he stood in long lines and underwent a strenuous medical examination to ensure that he was fit to enter the country. Once he proved he had someplace to go, Beryl boarded a ferry across the Hudson that took him to a new life in the United States.

Less than a year later, Lena joined her husband. Over the next decade, the couple had five children. Shortly after the youngest girl was born, Lena died and Beryl, now called Ben, was forced to place his children in a group home and foster care. The children were reunited with their father when Ben remarried, but life was still difficult. To make ends meet, his three eldest boys left school and went to work. Still, Ben's family managed to leave the crowded Lower East Side for Harlem and then the Bronx. Ben preferred to speak in Yiddish and never learned to read English. Nor did he become an American citizen. His children, however, were all citizens because they had been born in the United States.

On June 8, 1912, another immigrant followed a similar route but ended up taking a different path. Seventeen years old and unmarried, **Maria Vik Takacs** decided to leave her home in rural Hungary. As a Catholic, Maria did not experience the religious persecution that Beryl did. Like many other Hungarians, Maria left to help support her family back in the old country. She had an aunt living in the United States, and she came across with a Hungarian couple who escorted young women for domestic service in America.

Maria, too, landed at Ellis Island and passed the rigorous entry exams. Soon she boarded a train for Rochester in western New York. There she worked as a cook for a German physician, learned English, and led an active social life within the local Hungarian community. She married Karoly (Charles) Takacs, a cabinetmaker from Hungary, who had come to avoid the military draft. Charles became a U.S. citizen in May 1916. By marrying him, Mary, as she was now called, became a citizen as well.

The couple purchased a farm in Middleport, New York. Because so many Hungarians lived in the area, Mary only began to speak more English when the oldest of her four children entered kindergarten.

The American histories of Beryl and Maria took one to the urban bustle of New York City, the other to a quiet rural village in western New York State. However, as different as their lives in America were, neither regretted their choice to immigrate. Like millions of others, they had come to America to build better lives for themselves and their families, and both saw their children and grandchildren succeed in ways that they could have only dreamed of in their native countries. Indeed, two grandchildren of Beryl and Maria, Steven Lawson and Nancy Hewitt, respectively—became historians, got married, and wrote this textbook. The experiences of these families, like countless others, reflect the complicated ways that immigrants' lives were transformed at the same time the nation itself was being transformed.

LASSIN AND VIK were part of a flood of immigrants who entered the United States from 1880 to the outbreak of World War I in 1914. Unlike the majority of earlier immigrants, who had come from northern Europe, most of the more than 20 million people who arrived during this period came from southern and eastern Europe. A smaller number of immigrants came from Asia and Mexico. Most remained in cities, which grew as a result. Urban immigrants were welcomed by political bosses, who saw in them a chance to gain the allegiance of millions of new voters. At the same time, their coming upset many middle- and upper-class city dwellers who blamed these new arrivals for lowering the quality of urban life.

A New Wave of Immigrants

For more than three hundred years following the settlement of the North American colonies, the majority of immigrants to America were white northern European Protestants. During this same time, blacks had been brought forcibly from Africa and enslaved, mainly by way of the West Indies and the Caribbean. By the end of the nineteenth century, a new pattern of immigration emerged, one that included greater ethnic and religious diversity. These new immigrants often encountered hostility from those whose ancestors had arrived generations earlier, and faced the difficult challenge of retaining their cultural identities while becoming assimilated as Americans.

Immigrants Arrive from Many Lands

Immigration to the United States was part of a worldwide phenomenon. In addition to the United States, European immigrants also journeyed to other countries in the Western Hemisphere, especially Canada, Argentina, Brazil, and Cuba. Others left China, Japan, and India and migrated to Southeast Asia and Hawaii. From England and Ireland, migrants ventured to other parts of the British empire. As with those who came to the United States, these immigrants left their homelands to find new job opportunities or to obtain land to start their own farms. In countries like Australia, New Zealand, and South Africa, white settlers often pushed aside native peoples to make communities for themselves. Whereas most immigrants chose to relocate voluntarily, some made the move bound by labor contracts that limited their movement during the terms of the agreement. Chinese, Mexican, and Italian workers made up a large portion of this group.

The late nineteenth century saw a shift in the country of origin of immigrants to the United States: Instead of coming from northern and western Europe, many now came from southern and eastern European countries, most notably Italy, Greece, Austria-Hungary, Poland, and Russia. Most of those settling on American shores after 1880 were Catholic or Jewish and hardly knew a word of English. They tended to be even poorer than immigrants who had arrived before them, coming mainly from rural areas and lacking suitable skills for a rapidly expanding industrial society. Even after relocating to a new land and a new society, such immigrants struggled to break patterns of poverty that were, in many cases, centuries in the making.

Immigrants came from other parts of the world as well. From 1860 to 1924, some 450,000 Mexicans migrated to the U.S. Southwest. Many traveled to El Paso,

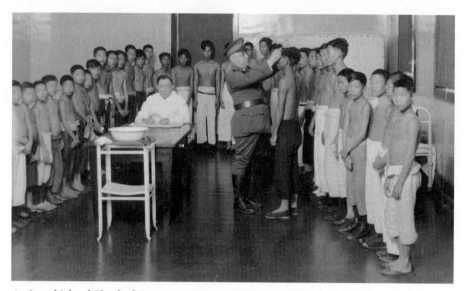

Angel Island Physical Exam   Beginning in 1910, tens of thousands of Chinese tried to immigrate to the United States through Angel Island in San Francisco Bay. Thousands were detained for long periods until they could prove their identities and demonstrate they had relatives in the country. One of the hurdles they had to overcome was the medical examination. In this photo taken in 1923, a group of Chinese boys waits to see the doctor while a military official inspects one of them.   National Archives

Texas, near the Mexican border, and from there hopped aboard one of three railroad lines to jobs on farms and in mines, mills, and construction. Cubans, Spaniards, and Bahamians traveled to the Florida cities of Key West and Tampa, where they established and worked in cigar factories. Although Congress excluded Chinese immigration after 1882, it did not close the door to migrants from Japan. Unlike the Chinese, the Japanese had not competed with white workers for jobs on railroad and other construction projects. Moreover, Japan was a major world power in the late nineteenth century and held American respect by defeating Russia in the Russo-Japanese War of 1904–1905. Some 260,000 Japanese arrived in the United States during the first two decades of the twentieth century. Many of them settled on the West Coast, where they worked as farm laborers and gardeners and established businesses catering to a Japanese clientele. Nevertheless, Japanese immigrants were considered part of an inferior "yellow race" and encountered discrimination in their West Coast settlements.

Despite the 1882 **Chinese Exclusion Act**, tens of thousands of Chinese attempted to immigrate, many claiming to be family members of those already in the country. Some first went to Canada or Mexico, but few managed to cross the border illegally. In 1910 the government established an immigration station at Angel Island in San Francisco Bay. In contrast to Ellis Island, Angel Island served mainly as a detention center where Chinese immigrants were imprisoned for months, even years, while they sought to prove their eligibility to enter the United States. Nevertheless, over the next thirty years, some 50,000 Chinese successfully passed through Angel Island.

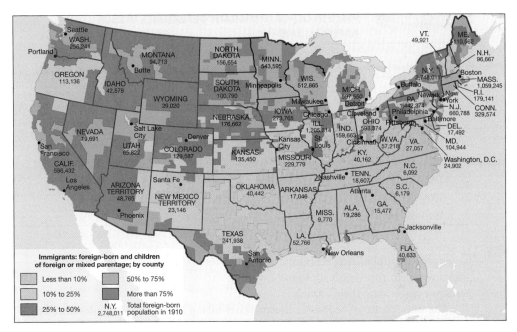

MAP 18.1   Immigrants in the U.S., 1910

By 1910, immigrants had come to the United States from primarily Europe, Asia, Mexico, and Latin America. They tended to settle near their ports of entry in cities, where they usually joined people from their own country who had settled previously. The pattern of settlement varied widely among regions of the country, as the map shows.

This wave of immigration changed the composition of the American population. By 1910 one-third of the population was foreign-born or had at least one parent who came from abroad. Foreigners and their children made up more than three-quarters of the population of New York City, Detroit, Chicago, Milwaukee, Cleveland, Minneapolis, and San Francisco. Immigration, though not as extensive in the South as in the North, also altered the character of southern cities. About one-third of the population of Tampa, Miami, and New Orleans consisted of foreigners and their descendants. The borderland states of Texas, New Mexico, Arizona, and southern California contained similar percentages of immigrants, most of whom came from Mexico (Map 18.1).

Mexican immigration began to increase significantly after the Chinese Exclusion Act shut off Chinese immigration, thereby creating a demand for cheap labor in mining and agriculture in the Southwest. American companies and commercial farmers were eager to hire Mexican immigrants because they considered them docile and physically strong enough to handle unhealthy working and living conditions. More important, they saw Mexicans as temporary residents who would return to their nearby homeland upon completing their jobs. The number of Mexican nationals living in the United States doubled from 100,000 in 1890 to 200,000 in 1910. It would increase even further with the outbreak of the Mexican Revolution in 1910.

These immigrants came to the United States largely for economic, political, and religious reasons. Nearly all were poor and expected to find ways to make money in America. U.S. railroads and steamship companies advertised in Europe and recruited

TABLE 18.1	PERCENTAGE OF IMMIGRANT DEPARTURES VERSUS ARRIVALS, 1875–1914		
Year	Arrivals	Departures	Percentage of Departures to Arrivals
1875–1879	956,000	431,000	45%
1880–1884	3,210,000	327,000	10%
1885–1889	2,341,000	638,000	27%
1890–1894	2,590,000	838,000	32%
1895–1899	1,493,000	766,000	51%
1900–1904	3,575,000	1,454,000	41%
1905–1909	5,533,000	2,653,000	48%
1910–1914	6,075,000	2,759,000	45%

passengers by emphasizing economic opportunities in the United States. Early immigrants wrote to relatives back home extolling the virtues of what they had found, perhaps exaggerating their success.

The importance of economic incentives in luring immigrants is underscored by the fact that millions returned to their home countries after they had earned sufficient money. Of the more than 27 million immigrants from 1875 to 1919, 11 million returned home (Table 18.1). Immigrants facing religious or political persecution in their homeland, like Beryl Lassin, were the least likely to return.

Creating Immigrant Communities

In cities such as New York, Boston, and Chicago, immigrants occupied neighborhoods that took on the distinct ethnic characteristics of the groups that inhabited them. A cacophony of different languages echoed in the streets as new residents continued to communicate in their mother tongues. The neighborhoods of immigrant groups often were clustered together, so residents were as likely to learn phrases in their neighbors' languages as they were to learn English.

The formation of **ghettos** — neighborhoods dominated by a single ethnic, racial, or class group — eased immigrants' transition into American society. Living within these ethnic enclaves made it easier for immigrants to find housing, hear about jobs, buy food, and seek help from those with whom they felt most comfortable. **Mutual aid societies** sprang up to provide social welfare benefits, including insurance payments and funeral rites. Group members established social centers where immigrants could play cards or dominoes, chat and gossip over tea or coffee, host dances and benefits, or just relax among people who shared a common heritage. In San Francisco's Chinatown, the largest Chinese community in California, such organizations usually consisted of people who had come from the same towns in China. These groups performed a variety of services, including finding jobs for their members, resolving disputes, campaigning against anti-Chinese discrimination, and sponsoring parades and other cultural activities. One society member explained: "We are strangers in a strange country. We must have an organization to control our country fellows and develop our friendship."

The same impulse to band together occurred in immigrant communities throughout the nation. On the West Coast, Japanese farmers joined *kenjinkai*, which not only provided social activities but also helped first-generation immigrants locate jobs and find housing. In Ybor City, Tampa's cigar-making section, mutual aid organizations rose to meet the needs of Spaniards, Cubans, Afro-Cubans, and Italians. El Centro Asturiano constructed a building that contained a 1,200-seat theater, "$4,000 worth of modern lighting fixtures, a cantina, and a well stocked *biblioteca* (library)." Cubans constructed their own palatial clubhouse, El Circulo Cubano, with stained-glass windows, a pharmacy, a theater, and a ballroom. The modest La Union Martí-Maceo catered to Tampa's Afro-Cubans and sponsored its own baseball team. The establishment of such clubs and cultural centers speaks to the commitment of immigrant groups there and elsewhere to enhance their communities.

Besides family and civic associations, churches and synagogues provided religious and social activities for urban immigrants. Between 1865 and 1900, the number of Catholic churches nationwide more than tripled. Like mutual aid societies, churches offered food and clothing to those who were ill or unable to work and fielded sports teams to compete in recreational leagues. Immigrants altered the religious practices and rituals in their churches to meet their own needs and expectations, many times over the objections of their clergy. Various ethnic groups challenged the orthodox practices of the Catholic Church and insisted that their parishes adopt religious icons that they had worshipped in the old country. These included patron saints or protectresses from Old World towns, such as the Madonna del Carmine, whom Italian Catholics in New York's East Harlem celebrated with an annual festival that their priests considered a pagan ritual. Women played the predominant role in running these street festivities. German Catholics challenged Vatican policy by insisting that each ethnic group have its own priests and parishes. Some Catholics, like Mary Vik, who lived in rural areas that did not have a Catholic Church in the vicinity, attended services with local Christians from other denominations.

Religious worship also varied among Jews. German Jews had arrived in the United States in an earlier wave of immigration than eastern European Jews. By the early twentieth century, they had achieved some measure of economic success and founded Reform Judaism, with Cincinnati, Ohio as its center. This brand of Judaism relaxed strict standards of worship, including absolute fidelity to kosher dietary laws, and allowed prayers to be said in English. By contrast, eastern European Jews, like Beryl Lassin, observed the traditional faith, maintained a kosher diet, and prayed in Hebrew.

With few immigrants literate in English, foreign-language newspapers proliferated to inform their readers of local, national, and international events. Between the mid-1880s and 1920, 3,500 new foreign-language newspapers came into existence. These newspapers helped sustain ethnic solidarity in the New World as well as maintain ties to the Old World. Newcomers could learn about social and cultural activities in their communities and keep abreast of news from their homeland.

Saloons were a central institution of immigrant culture, where men spent a good deal of leisure time. They read newspapers written in their native languages, swapped information about job opportunities, enjoyed time away from overcrowded tenements, discussed politics, and fostered bonds of masculinity exclusive of women.

However, the excessive drinking associated with saloons put a severe strain on family health and finances, especially when inebriated husbands and fathers lost their tempers at home or squandered their wages on alcohol.

Like other communities with poor, unskilled populations, immigrant neighborhoods bred crime. Young men joined gangs based on ethnic heritage and battled with those of other immigrant groups to protect their turf. Adults formed underworld organizations—some of them tied to international criminal syndicates, such as the Mafia—that trafficked in prostitution, gambling, robbery, and murder. Tongs (secret organizations) in New York City's and San Francisco's Chinatowns controlled the opium trade, gambling, and prostitution in their communities. A survey of New York City police and municipal court records from 1898 concluded that some Jews "are prominent in their commission of forgery, violation of corporation ordinance, as disorderly persons (failure to support wife or family), both grades of larceny, and of the lighter grade of assault."

Crime was not the only social problem that plagued immigrant communities. Newspapers and court records reported husbands abandoning wives and children, engaging in drunken and disorderly conduct, or abusing their family. Boarders whom immigrant families took into their homes for economic reasons also posed problems. Cramped spaces created a lack of privacy, and male boarders sometimes attempted to assault the woman of the house while her husband and children were out to work or in school. Finally, generational conflicts within families began to develop as American-born children of immigrants questioned their parents' values. Thus the social organizations and mutual aid societies that immigrant groups established were more than a simple expression of ethnic solidarity and pride. They were also a response to the very real problems that challenged the health and stability of immigrant communities.

Hostility toward Recent Immigrants

On October 28, 1886, the United States held a gala celebration for the opening of the Statue of Liberty in New York harbor, a short distance from Ellis Island. French sculptors Frédéric-Auguste Bartholdi and Alexandre-Gustave Eiffel had designed the monument to appear at the Centennial Exposition in Philadelphia in 1876. Ten years overdue, the statue arrived in June 1885, but funds were still needed to finish construction of a base on which the sculpture would stand. Ordinary people dipped into their pockets for spare change, contributing to a campaign that raised $100,000 so that Lady Liberty could finally hold her uplifted torch for all to see. In 1903 the inspiring words of Emma Lazarus, a Jewish poet, were inscribed on the pedestal welcoming new generations of immigrants.

> Give me your tired, your poor,
> Your huddled masses yearning to breathe free,
> The wretched refuse of your teeming shore,
> Send these, the homeless, tempest-tossed to me,
> I lift my lamp beside the golden door!

Despite the welcoming inscription on the Statue of Liberty, many Americans whose families had arrived before the 1880s considered the influx of immigrants from southern and eastern Europe, Mexico, the Caribbean, and Asia at best a necessary evil and at worst a menace. Industrialists counted on immigrants to provide cheap labor. Existing industrial workers saw the newcomers as a threat to their economic livelihoods and believed that their arrival would result in greater competition for jobs and lower wages. And, while most immigrants came to America to find work and improve the lives of their families, a small portion antagonized and frightened capitalists and middle-class Americans with radical calls for the reorganization of society and the overthrow of the government. Of course, the vast majority of immigrants were not radicals, but many radicals were recent immigrants. During times of labor-management strife, this fact made it easier for businessmen and their spokesmen in the press to associate all immigrants with anti-American radicalism.

Anti-immigrant fears linked to ideas about race and ethnicity had a long history in the United States. In 1790 Congress passed a statute restricting citizenship to those deemed white. Among those excluded from citizenship were Native Americans, who were regarded as "savages," and African Americans, most of whom were slaves at the time. In 1857 the Supreme Court ruled that even free blacks were not citizens, while at the same time declaring that Native Americans could become citizens. From the very beginning of the United States, largely Protestant lawmakers debated whether Catholics and Jews qualified as whites. Although lawmakers ultimately included Catholics and Jews within their definition of "white," over the next two centuries Americans viewed racial categories as not simply matters of skin color. Ethnicity (country or culture of origin) and religion became absorbed into and intertwined with racial categories. A sociological study of Homestead, Pennsylvania published in 1910 broke down the community along the following constructed racial lines: "Slav, English-speaking European, native white, and colored." Russian Jewish immigrants such as Beryl Lassin were recorded as Hebrews rather than as Russians, suggesting that Jewishness was seen by Christian America as a racial identity.

Natural scientists and social scientists gave credence to the idea that some races and ethnic groups were superior and others were inferior. Referring to Darwin's theory of evolution, biologists and anthropologists constructed measures of racial hierarchies, placing descendants of northern Europeans with lighter complexions—Anglo-Saxons, Teutonics, and Nordics—at the top of the evolutionary scale. Those with darker skin were deemed inferior "races," with Native Americans, African Americans, and Chinese at the bottom. Scholars attempting to make disciplines such as history more "scientific" accepted these racial classifications. The prevailing sentiment of this era reflected demeaning images of many immigrant groups: Irish as drunkards, Mexicans and Cubans as lazy, Italians as criminals, Hungarians as ignorant peasants, Jews as cheap and greedy, and Chinese as drug addicts. These characteristics supposedly resulted from inherited biological traits, rather than from extreme poverty or other environmental conditions.

Newer immigrants, marked as racially inferior, became a convenient target of hostility. Skilled craftsmen born in the United States viewed unskilled workers from abroad who would work for low wages as a threat to their attempts to form unions and keep wages high. Middle-class city dwellers blamed urban problems on the rising tide of foreigners. In addition, Protestant purists felt threatened by Catholics and Jews and believed these "races" incapable or unworthy of assimilation into what they considered to be the superior white, Anglo-Saxon, and Protestant culture.

Nativism—the belief that foreigners pose a serious danger to one's native society and culture—arose as a reactionary response to immigration. In 1887 Henry F. Bowers of Clinton, Iowa founded the American Protective Association. The group proposed restricting Catholic immigration, making English a prerequisite to American citizenship, and prohibiting Catholics from teaching in public schools or holding public offices. New England elites, such as Massachusetts senator Henry Cabot Lodge and writer John Fiske, argued that southern European, Semitic, and Slavic races did not fit into the "community of race" that had founded the United States. In 1893 Lodge and fellow Harvard graduates established the Immigration Restriction League and lobbied for federal legislation that would exclude adult immigrants unable to read in their own language.

To preserve their status and power and increase the size of the native-born population, nativists embraced the idea of **eugenics**—a pseudoscience that advocated "biological engineering"—and supported the selective breeding of "desirable" races to counter the rapid population growth of "useless" races. Accordingly, eugenicists promoted the institutionalization of people deemed "unfit," sterilization of those considered mentally impaired, and the licensing and regulation of marriages to promote better breeding. In pushing for such measures, eugenicists believed that they were following the dictates of modern science and acting in a humane fashion to prevent those deemed unfit from causing further harm to themselves and to society.

Others took a less harsh approach. As had been the case with Native Americans, reformers stressed the need for immigrants to assimilate into the dominant culture, embrace the values of individualism and self-help, adopt American styles of dress and grooming, and exhibit loyalty to the U.S. government. They encouraged immigrant children to attend public schools, where they would learn to speak English and adopt American cultural rituals by celebrating holidays such as Thanksgiving and Columbus Day and reciting the pledge of allegiance, introduced in 1892. Educators encouraged adult immigrants to attend night classes to learn English.

The Assimilation Dilemma

If immigrants were not completely assimilated, neither did they remain the same people who had lived on the farms and in the villages of Europe, Asia, Mexico, and the Caribbean. Some, like Mary Vik, sought to become full-fledged Americans or at least see that their children did so. Writer Israel Zangwill, an English American Jew, furnished the enduring image of assimilation in his 1908 play *The Melting-Pot*. Zangwill portrayed people from distinct backgrounds entering the cauldron of American life, mixing together, and emerging as citizens identical to their native-born counterparts.

However, the image of America as a **melting pot** worked better as an ideal than as a mirror of reality. Immigrants during this period never fully lost the social, cultural, religious, and political identities they had brought with them. And, anti-immigrant sentiment of many native-born Americans perceived them as strangers and aliens. The same year that Zangwill's play was published, Alfred P. Schultz, a New York physician, provided a dim view of the prospects of assimilation in his book *Race or Mongrel*. Schultz dismissed the melting pot theory that public schools could convert the children of all races into Americans.

While recent immigrants faced the dilemma of assimilating, sociologist W. E. B. Du Bois analyzed the predicament experienced by African Americans following Reconstruction. In *The Souls of Black Folk* (1903), Du Bois wrote that African Americans felt a "two-ness," an identity carved out of their African heritage together with their lives as slaves and free people in America. This "double-consciousness . . . two souls, two thoughts, two unreconciled strivings" describes the particular identity of African Americans at the turn of the century. While this echoes the experience of the diverse groups who arrived in the country after 1880, African Americans were faced with systemic racial segregation and oppression unlike any other group of people experienced.

REVIEW & RELATE	• What challenges did new immigrants to the United States face? • What steps did immigrants take to meet these challenges?

Becoming an Urban Nation

In the half century after the Civil War, the population of the United States quadrupled, but the urban population soared sevenfold. In 1870 one in five Americans lived in cities with a population of 8,000 or more. By 1900 one in three resided in cities of this size. In 1870 only Philadelphia and New York had populations over half a million. Twenty years later, in addition to these two cities, Chicago's population exceeded 1 million; St. Louis, Boston, and Baltimore had more than 500,000 residents; and Cleveland, Buffalo, San Francisco, and Cincinnati boasted populations over 250,000. Urbanization was not confined to the Northeast and Midwest. Denver's population jumped from 4,700 in 1870 to more than 107,000 in 1890. During that same period, Los Angeles grew nearly fivefold, from 11,000 to 50,000, and Birmingham leaped from 3,000 to 26,000. This phenomenal urban growth also brought remarkable physical changes to the cities, as tall buildings reached toward the skies, electric lights brightened the nighttime hours, and water and gas pipes, sewers, and subways snaked below the ground.

The New Industrial City

Although cities have long been a part of the landscape, Americans have felt ambivalent about their presence. Many Americans have shared Thomas Jefferson's idea that democratic values were rooted in the soil of small, independent farms. In contrast to the natural environment of rural life, cities have been perceived as artificial creations in which corruption and contagion flourish. In the 1890s, the very identity of Americans seemed threatened as the frontier came to an end. Some agreed with the historian Frederick Jackson Turner, who believed the closing of the western frontier endangered the existence of democracy because it removed the opportunity for the pioneer spirit that built America to regenerate. Rural Americans were especially uncomfortable with the country's increasingly urban life. When the small-town lawyer Clarence Darrow moved to Chicago in the 1880s he was horrified by the "solid, surging sea of human units, each intent upon hurrying by." Still, like Darrow, millions of people were drawn to the new opportunities cities offered.

TABLE 18.2	PERCENTAGE OF RURAL AND URBAN POPULATION IN U.S., 1880–1910	
Year	Rural	Urban
1880	71.8	28.2
1890	64.9	35.1
1900	60.4	39.5
1910	54.4	45.6

Source: U.S. Department of Commerce, Bureau of the Census, Table 4, https://www.census.gov/population/censusdata/table-4.pdf

Urban growth in America was part of a long-term worldwide phenomenon. Between 1820 and 1920, some 60 million people globally moved from rural to urban areas. Most of them migrated after the 1870s, and millions journeyed from towns and villages in Europe to American cities (Table 18.2). Yet the number of Europeans who migrated internally was greater than those who went overseas. As in the United States, Europeans moved from the countryside to urban areas in search of jobs. Many migrated to the city on a seasonal basis, seeking winter employment in cities and then returning to the countryside at harvest time.

Before the Civil War, commerce was the engine of growth for American cities. Ports like New York, Boston, New Orleans, and San Francisco became distribution centers for imported goods or items manufactured in small shops in the surrounding countryside. Cities in the interior of the country located on or near major bodies of water, such as Chicago, St. Louis, Cincinnati, and Detroit, served similar functions. As the extension of railroad transportation led to the development of large-scale industry, these cities and others became industrial centers as well.

Industrialization contributed to rapid urbanization in several ways. It drew those living on farms, who either could not earn a satisfactory living or were bored by the isolation of rural areas, into the city in search of better-paying jobs and excitement. One rural dweller in Massachusetts complained: "The lack of pleasant, public entertainments in this town has much to do with our young people feeling discontented with country life." In addition, while the mechanization of farming increased efficiency, it also reduced the demand for farm labor. In 1896 one person could plant, tend, and harvest as much wheat as it had taken eighteen farmworkers to do sixty years before.

Industrial technology and other advances also made cities more attractive and livable places. Electricity extended nighttime entertainment and powered streetcars to convey people around town. Improved water and sewage systems provided more sanitary conditions, especially given the demands of the rapidly expanding population. Structural steel and electric elevators made it possible to construct taller and taller buildings, which gave cities such as Chicago and New York their distinctive skylines. Scientists and physicians made significant progress in the fight against the spread of contagious diseases, which had become serious problems in crowded cities.

Many of the same causes of urbanization in the Northeast and Midwest applied to the far West. The development of the mining industry attracted business and labor to urban settlements. Cities grew up along railroad terminals, and railroads stimulated urban growth by bringing out settlers and creating markets. By 1900, the proportion of residents in western cities with a population of at least ten thousand was greater than in any other section of the country except the Northeast. More so than in the East, Asians and Hispanics inhabited western urban centers along with whites and African Americans. In 1899 Salt Lake City boasted the publication of two black newspapers as well as the president of the Western Negro Press Association. Western cities also took advantage of the latest technology, and in the 1880s and 1890s electric trolleys provided mass transit in Denver and San Francisco.

In addition to immigrants who populated the cities across the nation, before 1890 the rise in urban population came mainly from Americans on the move. Young men and young women left the farm to seek their fortune. The female protagonist of Theodore Dreiser's novel *Sister Carrie* (1900) abandons small-town Wisconsin for the lure of Chicago. In real life, mechanization on farms created many "Sister Carries" by making women less valuable in the fields. The possibility of purchasing mass-produced goods from mail-order houses such as Sears, Roebuck also left young women less essential as homemakers because they no longer had to sew their own clothes and could buy labor-saving appliances from catalogs.

Similar factors drove rural black women and men into cities. Plagued by the same poverty and debt that white sharecroppers and tenants in the South faced, blacks suffered from the added burden of racial oppression and violence in the post-Reconstruction period. From 1870 to 1890, the African American population of Nashville, Tennessee, soared from just over 16,000 to more than 29,000. In Atlanta, Georgia, the number of blacks jumped from slightly above 16,000 to around 28,000.

Economic opportunities were more limited for black migrants than for whites. African American migrants found work as cooks, janitors, and domestic servants. Many found employment as manual laborers in manufacturing companies — including tobacco factories, which employed women and men; tanneries; and cottonseed oil firms — and as dockworkers. Although the overwhelming majority of blacks worked as unskilled laborers for very low wages, others opened small businesses such as funeral parlors, barbershops, and construction companies or went into professions such as medicine, law, banking, and education that catered to residents of segregated black neighborhoods. Despite considerable individual accomplishments, by the turn of the twentieth century most blacks in the urban South had few prospects for upward economic mobility.

In 1890, although 90 percent of African Americans lived in the South, a growing number were moving to northern cities to seek employment and greater freedom. Boll weevil (beetle) infestations during the 1890s decimated cotton production and forced sharecroppers and tenants off farms. At the same time, blacks saw significant erosion of their political and civil rights in the last decade of the nineteenth century. Most black citizens in the South were denied the right to vote and experienced rigid, legally sanctioned racial segregation in all aspects of public life. Between 1890 and 1914 approximately 485,000 African Americans left the South. By 1914 New York, Chicago, and Philadelphia each counted more than 100,000 African Americans among their population. An African American woman expressed her enthusiasm about the employment she found in Chicago, where she earned $3 a day working in a railroad yard. "The colored women like this work," she explained, because "we make more money . . . and we do not have to work as hard as at housework," which required working sixteen-hour days, six days a week.

African American Family, 1900   Despite the rigid racial segregation and oppression that
African Americans faced in the late nineteenth century, some black families found ways to
achieve economic success and upward mobility. With its piano and fine furniture, the home of this
African American family reflects middle-class conventions of the period. The father is a graduate
of Hampton Institute, a historically black university founded after the Civil War to educate
freedpeople. Library of Congress, Prints and Photographs Division [LC-USZ62-38150]

Although many blacks found they preferred their new lives to the ones they had
led in the South, the North did not turn out to be the promised land of freedom.
Black newcomers encountered discrimination in housing and employment. Residential segregation confined African Americans to racial ghettos. Black workers found it
difficult to obtain skilled employment despite their qualifications, and women and
men most often toiled as domestics, janitors, and part-time laborers.

Nevertheless, African Americans in northern cities built communities that preserved and reshaped their southern culture and offered a degree of insulation against
the harshness of racial discrimination. A small black middle class appeared consisting
of teachers, attorneys, and small business owners. In 1888 African Americans organized the Capital Savings Bank of Washington, D.C. Ten years later, two black real
estate agents in New York City were worth more than $150,000 each, and one agent
in Cleveland owned $100,000 in property. The rising black middle class provided
leadership in the formation of mutual aid societies, lodges, and women's clubs. Newspapers such as the *Chicago Defender* and *Pittsburgh Courier* furnished local news to
their subscribers and reported national and international events affecting people of

color. As was the case in the South, the church was at the center of black life in north-ern cities. More than just religious institutions, churches furnished space for social activities and the dissemination of political information. By the first decade of the twentieth century, more than two dozen churches had sprung up in Chicago alone. Whether housed in newly constructed buildings or in storefronts, black churches pro-vided worshippers freedom from white control. They also allowed members of the northern black middle class to demonstrate what they considered to be respectability and refinement. This meant discouraging enthusiastic displays of "old-time religion," which celebrated more exuberant forms of worship. As the Reverend W. A. Black-well of Chicago's AME Zion Church declared, "Singing, shouting, and talking [were] the most useless ways of proving Christianity." This conflict over modes of religious expression reflected a larger process that was under way in black communities at the turn of the twentieth century. As black urban communities in the North grew and developed, tensions and divisions emerged within the increasingly diverse black com-munity, as a variety of groups competed to shape and define black culture and identity.

Expand Upward and Outward

As the urban population increased, cities expanded both up and out. Before 1860, the dominant form of brick and stone construction prevented buildings from rising more than four or five stories. However, as cities became much more populous, land values soared. Steep prices prompted architects to make the most of small, expensive plots of land by finding ways to build taller structures. Architects began using cast-iron columns instead of the thick, heavy walls of brick that limited floor space. The resulting "cloudscrapers" raised the urban skyline to ten stories. The development of structural steel, which was stronger and more durable than iron, turned cloudscrap-ers into **skyscrapers**, which stretched some thirty stories into the air. With the devel-opment of the electric elevator and the radiator, which replaced fireplaces with hot water circulated through pipes, even taller skyscrapers came to loom over downtown business districts in major cities.

Cities also expanded horizontally, as new transportation technology made it possible for residents to move around a much larger urban landscape. In the mid-nineteenth century in cities such as Boston and Philadelphia, pedestrians could still walk from one end of the city to the other within an hour. If residents preferred, they could pay a fare and hop on board a horse-drawn railcar. These vehicles moved slowly and left tons of horse manure in the streets. To avoid such problems, in 1873 San Francisco, followed by Seattle and Chicago, installed a system of cable-driven trolley cars. At first, these trolleys proved slow and unreliable. But by 1914, advances in transportation converted walking cities into riding cities.

Electricity provided the transportation breakthrough. In 1888 naval engineer Frank J. Sprague completed the first electric trolley line in Richmond, Virginia. Electric-powered streetcars traveled twice as fast as horse-drawn railcars and left little mess on the streets. Subways could run underground without asphyxiating passen-gers and workmen with a steam engine's smoke and soot. Boston opened the first subway in 1897, followed by New York City in 1904.

Bridges spanning large rivers and waterways also helped extend the boundar-ies of the inner city. In 1883 the Brooklyn Bridge opened, connecting Manhattan with the city of Brooklyn. Designed and engineered by John Augustus Roebling, and completed by his son Washington and Washington's wife Emily, the bridge had taken thirteen years to construct and cost twenty men their lives. It stretched more than a mile across the East River and was broad enough for a footpath, two double carriage lanes, and two railroad lines. During its first year in operation, more than 11 million people passed over the bridge; today, more than 51 million vehicles cross the bridge each year.

The electrification of public transportation and the construction of bridges made it feasible for some people to live considerable distances from their workplace. In the eighteenth and nineteenth centuries, middle- and upper-class merchants and professionals usually lived near their shops and offices in the heart of the city, surrounded by their employees. After 1880, the huge influx of immigration brought large numbers of impoverished workers to city centers. The resulting traffic congestion and overcrowded housing pushed wealthier residents to seek more open spaces in which to build houses. The new electric trolley lines allowed middle-class urbanites to move miles away from downtown areas. In 1850 the Boston metropolis spread in a radius of two to three miles around the city and had a population of 200,000. In 1900 suburban Boston ringed the city in a ten-mile radius, with a population of more than 1 million. Increasingly, cities divided into two parts: an inner commercial and industrial core housing the working class, and outer communities occupied by a wealthier class of white, older-stock Americans.

How the Other Half Lived

As the middle and upper classes fled the industrial urban center for the suburbs, the working poor moved in to replace them. They lived in old factories and homes and in shanties and cellars. Because land values were higher in the city, rents were high and the poorest people could least afford them. To make ends meet, families crowded into existing apartments, sometimes taking in boarders to help pay the rent. This led to increased population density and overcrowding in the urban areas where immigrants lived. On New York's Lower East Side, the population density was the highest in the world. Such overcrowding fostered communicable diseases and frustration, giving the area the nicknames "typhus ward" and "suicide ward."

Overcrowding combined with extreme poverty turned immigrant neighborhoods into slums, which were characterized by substandard housing. Impoverished immigrants typically lived in multiple-family apartment buildings called **tenements** (legally defined as containing more than three families). First constructed in 1850, these early dwellings often featured windowless rooms and little or no plumbing and heating. In 1879 a New York law reformed the building codes to require minimal plumbing facilities and to stipulate that all bedrooms (but not all rooms) have a window. Constructed on narrow 25-by-100-foot lots, these five- and six-story buildings included four small apartments on a floor and had only two toilets off the hallway. Tenements stood right next to each other, with only an air shaft separating them. Although these dwellings marked some improvement in living conditions, they proved miserable places to live in—dark, damp, and foul smelling. In 1895 a federal government housing inspector observed that the air shafts provided "imperfect light and ventilation" and that "refuse matter or filth of one kind or another [was] very apt to accumulate at the bottom, giving rise to noxious odors." The air shafts also operated as a conduit for fires that moved swiftly from one tenement to another.

In fact, the density of late-nineteenth-century cities could turn individual fires into citywide disasters. The North Side of Chicago burned to the ground in 1871, and Boston and Baltimore suffered catastrophic fires as well. On April 18, 1906, an earthquake in San Francisco set the city ablaze, causing about 1,500 deaths. Such fires could, however, have long-term positive consequences. The great urban conflagrations encouraged construction of fireproof buildings made of brick and steel instead of wood. In addition, citizens organized fire watches and established municipal fire departments to replace volunteer companies. An unintended side effect, fires provided cities with a chance to rebuild. Chicago's skyscrapers and its system of urban parks were built on land cleared by fire.

In 1890 Jacob Riis, a Danish immigrant, newspaperman, and photographer, illustrated the brutal conditions endured by tenement families such as Beryl Lassin's on New York's Lower East Side. "In the stifling July nights," he wrote in *How the Other Half Lives*, "when the big barracks are like fiery furnaces, their very walls giving out absorbed heat, men and women lie in restless, sweltering rows, panting for air and sleep." Under these circumstances, Riis lamented, an epidemic "is excessively fatal among the children of the poor, by reason of the practical impossibility of isolating the patient in a tenement." Despite their obvious problems, tenements soon spread to other cities such as Cleveland, Cincinnati, and Boston, and one block might have ten of these buildings, housing as many as four thousand people.

With all the misery they spawned as places to live, tenements also functioned as workplaces. Czech immigrants made cigars in their apartments from six in the morning until nine at night, seven days a week, for about 6 cents an hour. By putting an entire family to work, they could make $15 a week and pay their rent of $12 a month. Clothing contractors in particular saw these tenement **sweatshops** as a cheap way to produce their products. By jamming two or three sewing machines into an apartment and paying workers a fixed amount for each item they produced, contractors kept their costs down and avoided factory regulations.

Even when immigrants left sweatshop apartments and went to work in factories, they continued to face exploitation. The 600 Jewish and Italian clothing workers, most of whom were women, who toiled in the **Triangle Shirtwaist Company**, located in New York City's Greenwich Village, worked long hours for little pay. On March 25, 1911, a fire broke out on the eighth story of the factory and quickly spread to the ninth and tenth floors. The fire engines' ladders could not reach that high, and one of the exits on the ninth floor was locked to keep workers from stealing material. One hundred forty-six people died in the blaze—some by jumping out the windows, but most by getting trapped behind the closed exit door. In the aftermath of the fire, Rose Schneiderman, a Polish Jewish immigrant who had led a strike at the Triangle Shirtwaist Company in 1909, addressed a memorial gathering at the Metropolitan Opera House. Following public outrage over the fire and through the efforts of reformers, New York City established a Bureau of Fire Protection, required safety devices in buildings, and prohibited smoking in factories. Furthermore, this tragedy spearheaded legislative efforts to improve working conditions in general, protect women workers, and abolish child labor.

Slums compounded the potential for disease, poor sanitation, fire, congestion, and crime. Living on poor diets, slum dwellers proved particularly vulnerable to epidemics. Cholera, yellow fever, and typhoid killed tens of thousands. Tuberculosis was even deadlier. An epidemic that began in a slum neighborhood could easily spread into more affluent areas of the city. Children suffered the most. Almost one-quarter of the children born in American cities in 1890 did not live to celebrate their first birthdays.

Contributing to the outbreak of disease was faulty sewage disposal, a problem that vexed city leaders. Until the invention of the modern indoor flush toilet in the late nineteenth century, people relied on outdoor toilets, with as many as eight hundred people using a single facility. All too often, cities dumped human waste into rivers that also supplied drinking water. In 1881 the exasperated mayor of Cleveland called the Cuyahoga River "an open sewer through the center of the city." At the same time, the great demand for water caused by the population explosion resulted in lower water pressure. Consequently, residents in the upper floors of tenements had to carry buckets of water from the lower floors. Until cities overcame their water and sanitation challenges, epidemics plagued urban dwellers.

Urban crowding created other problems as well. Traffic moved slowly through densely populated cities. Pedestrians and commuters had to navigate around throngs of people walking on sidewalks and streets, peddlers selling out of pushcarts, and piles of garbage cluttering the walkways. Streets remained in poor shape. In 1889 the majority of Cleveland's 440 miles of streets consisted of sand and gravel. Chicago did not fare much better. In 1890 most road surfaces were covered with wooden blocks, and three-quarters of the city's more than 2,000 miles of streets remained unpaved. Rainstorms quickly made matters worse by turning foul-smelling, manure-filled streets into mud.

Poverty and overcrowding contributed to increased crime. The U.S. murder rate quadrupled between 1880 and 1900, at a time when the murder rates in most European cities were declining. In New York City, crime thrived in slums with the apt names of "Bandit's Roost" and "Hell's Kitchen," and groups of young hoodlums preyed on unsuspecting citizens. Poverty forced some of the poor to turn to theft or prostitution. One twenty-year-old prostitute, who supported her sickly mother and four brothers and sisters, lamented: "Let God Almighty judge who's to blame most, I that was driven, or them that drove me to the pass I'm in." Rising criminality led to the formation of urban police departments, though many law officers supplemented their incomes by collecting graft (illegal payments) for ignoring criminal activities.

REVIEW & RELATE	• What factors contributed to rapid urban growth in the late nineteenth century? • How did the American cities of 1850 differ from those of 1900? What factors account for these differences?

Urban Politics at the Turn of the Century

The problems that booming cities faced in trying to absorb millions of immigrants proved formidable and at times seemed insurmountable. From a governmental standpoint, cities had limited authority over their own affairs. They were controlled by state legislatures and needed state approval to raise revenues and pass regulations. For the most part, there were no zoning laws to regulate housing construction. Private companies owned public utilities, and competition among them produced unnecessary duplication and waste. The government services that did exist operated on a segmented basis, with the emphasis on serving wealthier neighborhoods at the expense of the city at large. Missing was a vision of the city as a whole, working as a single unit.

Political Machines and City Bosses

City government in the late nineteenth century was fragmented. Mayors usually did not have much power, and decisions involving public policies such as housing, transportation, and municipal services often rested in the hands of private developers. Bringing some order out of this chaos, the **political machine** functioned to give cities the centralized authority and services that they otherwise lacked. At the head of the machine was the political **boss**. Although the boss himself (and they were all men) held some public office, his real authority came from leadership of the machine. These organizations maintained a tight network of loyalists throughout city wards (districts), each of which contained designated representatives responsible for catering to the needs of their constituents. Whether Democratic or Republican, political machines did not care about philosophical issues; they were concerned primarily with staying in power.

The strength of political machines rested in large measure on immigrants. The organization provided a kind of public welfare when private charity could not cope satisfactorily with the growing needs of the poor. Machines doled out turkeys on holidays, furnished a load of coal for the winter, provided jobs in public construction, arranged for shelter and meals if tenement houses burned down, and intervened with the police and the courts when a constituent got into trouble. Bosses sponsored baseball clubs, held barbecues and picnics, and attended christenings, bar mitzvahs, weddings, and funerals. For enterprising members of immigrant groups—and this proved especially true for the Irish during this period—the machine offered upward mobility out of poverty as they rose through its ranks. Not all immigrants benefited from political bosses equally, however. In San Francisco, Abe Ruef, whose parents were French Jews, became a political boss around the turn of the twentieth century. His sympathies for immigrants did not extend to the Chinese, however. Following the 1906 earthquake, he led an effort to expel residents of the city's Chinatown.

The poor were not the only group that benefited from connections to political machines. The machine and its functionaries helped businessmen maneuver through the maze of contradictory and overlapping codes regulating building and licenses that impeded their routine course of activities. In addition to assisting legitimate businessmen, the machine facilitated the underworld commerce of vice, prostitution, and gambling by acting as an arbiter to keep this trade within established boundaries—all for a cut of the illegal profits.

In return for these services, the machine received the votes of immigrants and money from businessmen. When challenged by reformers or other political rivals, the machine readily engaged in corrupt election practices to maintain its power. Mobilizing the "graveyard vote," bosses took names from tombstones to pad lists of

Boss Abe Ruef   In 1908 Abe Ruef, the political boss of San Francisco, was tried and convicted on charges of bribery and influence peddling. Ruef served four and a half years of a fourteen-year sentence at San Quentin. This photo captures a worried-looking Ruef listening to his attorney, Henry Ach, outside the courthouse during his trial. Courtesy of the Bancroft Library, University of California, Berkeley, call no. BANC PIC 1905.02623-A

registered voters. They also hired "repeaters" to vote more than once under phony names and did not flinch from dumping whole ballot boxes into the river or using hired thugs to scare opponents from the polls.

Bosses enriched themselves through graft and corruption. They secured protection money from both legitimate and illegitimate business interests in return for their services. In the 1860s and 1870s, Boss William Marcy Tweed, the head of Tammany Hall, New York City's political machine, swindled the city out of a fortune while supervising the construction of a lavish three-story courthouse in lower Manhattan. The original budget for the building was $250,000, but the city spent more than $13 million on the structure. The building remained unfinished in 1873, when Tweed was convicted on fraud charges and went to jail. In later years, Tammany Hall's George Washington Plunkitt distinguished this kind of "dishonest graft" from the kind of "honest graft" that he practiced. If he received inside information about a future sale of city property, Plunkitt reasoned, why shouldn't he get a head start, buy it at a low price, and then sell it at a higher figure? As he delighted in saying, "I seen my opportunities and I took 'em." Still, courts did not see such behavior so favorably. In 1908, San Francisco's Boss Ruef was convicted of bribery and imprisoned at San Quentin.

The services of political machines came at a high cost. Corruption and graft led to higher taxes on middle-class residents. Much of the proceeds of machine activities went into the private coffers of machine bosses and other functionaries. The romanticized image of the political boss as a modern-day Robin Hood who stole from the rich and gave to the poor is greatly exaggerated. Trafficking in vice might have run more smoothly under the coordination of the machine, but the safety and health of city residents hardly improved. Most important, although immigrants and the poor did benefit from an informal system of social welfare, the machine had no interest in resolving the underlying causes of their problems. As the dominant urban political party organization, the machine cared little about issues such as good housing, job safety, and sufficient wages. It remained for others to provide alternative approaches to relieving the plight of the urban poor.

Urban Reformers

The men and women who criticized the political bosses and machines — and the corruption and vice they fostered — usually came from the ranks of the upper middle class and the wealthy. Their solutions to the urban crisis typically centered around toppling the political machine and replacing it with a civil service that would allow government to function on the basis of merit rather than influence peddling and cronyism. Both locally and nationally, they pushed for civil service reform. In 1883 Congress responded to this demand by passing the **Pendleton Civil Service Reform Act**, which required federal jobs to be awarded on the basis of merit, as determined by competitive examinations, rather than through political connections. As for the immigrants who supported machine politics, these reformers preferred to deal with them from afar and expected that through proper education they might change their lifestyles and adopt American ways.

Another group of Americans from upper- and middle-class backgrounds put aside whatever prejudices they might have held about working-class immigrants and dealt directly with newcomers to try to solve various social problems. These reformers — mostly young people, and many of them women and college graduates — took up residence in **settlement houses** located in urban slums. Settlement houses offered a variety of services to community residents, including day care for children; cooking, sewing, and secretarial classes; neighborhood playgrounds; counseling sessions; and meeting rooms for labor unions. Settlement house organizers understood that immigrants gravitated to the political machine or congregated in the local tavern not because they were inherently immoral but because these institutions helped mitigate their suffering and, in some cases, offered concrete paths to advancement. Although settlement house workers wanted to Americanize immigrants, they also understood immigrants' need to hold on to remnants of their original culture. By 1900 approximately one hundred settlement houses had been established in major American cities.

Religiously inspired reform provided similar support for slum dwellers. Some Protestant ministers began to argue that immigrants' problems resulted not from chronic racial or ethnic failings but from their difficult environment. Some of them preached Christianity as a "social gospel," which included support for civil service reform, antimonopoly regulation, income tax legislation, factory inspection laws, and workers' right to strike.

Despite the efforts of social gospel advocates and the charitable organizations that arose to help relieve human misery, private attempts to combat the various urban ills, however well-meaning, proved insufficient. The problems were structural, not personal, and one group or even several operating together did not have the resources or power to make urban institutions more efficient, equitable, and humane. If reformers were to succeed in tackling the most significant social problems and make lasting changes in American society and politics, they would have to enlist state and federal governments.

REVIEW & RELATE	• What role did political machines play in late-nineteenth-century cities? • Who led the opposition to machine control of city politics, and what solutions and alternatives did they offer?

Conclusion: A Nation of Cities

Immigrants from southern and eastern Europe, as well as from Asia and points south, who came to the United States between the 1880s and 1914 survived numerous hardships as they strove to create better lives for their families. They persevered despite discrimination, overcrowding in slums, and dangerous working conditions, long hours, and low wages. Immigrants joined neighborhood groups—houses of worship, fraternal organizations, burial societies, political machines, and settlement houses—to promote their own welfare. Some achieved success and returned to their homelands. Most of those who remained in the United States, like Mary Vik and Ben Lassin, struggled to earn a living but managed to pave the way for their children and grandchildren to obtain better education and jobs. Mary's granddaughter, Nancy A. Hewitt, earned a Ph.D. in history from the University of Pennsylvania, and Ben's grandson, Steven F. Lawson, earned a doctorate in history from Columbia University. They became university professors and, through their teaching and writing, have tried to preserve their grandparents' legacy.

Immigrants were not the only group on the move in the late nineteenth century. Rural dwellers left their farms seeking new job opportunities as well as the excitement cities provided. Among them, African Americans migrated in search of political freedom and economic opportunity. They relocated from the rural South to the urban South and North, where they continued to encounter discrimination. Yet cities gave them more leeway to develop their own communities and institutions than they had before. And African Americans in the North were allowed to vote, a tool they would use to gain equality in the future. Nevertheless, because of long-standing patterns of racism, supported by law, African Americans would struggle much longer than did white immigrants to obtain equality and justice.

Few public institutions attempted to aid immigrants or racial minorities as they made the difficult transition to urban and industrial life. Yet immigrants did participate in urban politics through the efforts of political bosses and their machines who sought immigrant votes. In return, political machines provided immigrants with rudimentary social and political services. Political machines, however, bred corruption, along with higher taxes to fund their extravagances. Dishonest government prompted middle- and upper-class urban dwellers to take up reform in order to sweep the political bosses out of office and diminish the power of their immigrant supporters, as we will see in the next chapter.

Chapter 18 Review

KEY TERMS

Chinese Exclusion Act, 454
ghettos, 456
mutual aid societies, 456
nativism, 460
eugenics, 460
melting pot, 460
skyscrapers, 465

tenements, 466
sweatshops, 467
Triangle Shirtwaist Company, 467
political machine, 469
boss, 469
Pendleton Civil Service Reform Act, 471
settlement houses, 471

REVIEW & RELATE

1. What challenges did new immigrants to the United States face?

2. What steps did immigrants take to meet these challenges?

3. What factors contributed to rapid urban growth in the late nineteenth century?

4. How did the American cities of 1850 differ from those of 1900? What factors account for these differences?

5. What role did political machines play in late-nineteenth-century cities?

6. Who led the opposition to machine control of city politics, and what solutions and alternatives did they offer?

TIMELINE OF EVENTS

1880–1914	• Period of significant immigration to United States
1882	• Chinese Exclusion Act
1883	• Pendleton Civil Service Reform Act
	• Brooklyn Bridge opens
1886	• Statue of Liberty opens
1887	• American Protective Association formed
1892	• U.S. schools adopt pledge of allegiance
1893	• Immigration Restriction League founded
1897	• Boston opens first subway system in the United States
1903	• W. E. B. Du Bois publishes *The Souls of Black Folk*
1906	• San Francisco earthquake
1908	• Israel Zangwill publishes *The Melting-Pot*
	• San Francisco's Boss Ruef convicted of bribery
1911	• Triangle Shirtwaist Company fire in New York City

19

Progressivism and the Search for Order

1900–1917

LEARNING OBJECTIVES

After reading this chapter you should be able to:

- Compare progressivism with Populism.
- Describe the problems progressives tried to address.
- Explain the reasons progressives engaged in moral reform and evaluate how their views of immigrants shaped their efforts.
- Analyze how the notions of efficiency, openness, and accountability influenced the progressives' approach to political and environmental reform.
- Compare the ways in which the federal government handled progressive reform during the administrations of Presidents Theodore Roosevelt, William Howard Taft, and Woodrow Wilson.

COMPARING AMERICAN HISTORIES

Gifford Pinchot grew up on a Connecticut estate where he learned to hunt, fish, and enjoy nature. Yet Pinchot rejected a life of leisure and instead sought to make his mark through public service by working to conserve and protect America's natural resources. After graduating from Yale in 1889, Pinchot had to study forestry abroad. No American university offered a forestry program, reflecting the predominant view that, for all practical purposes, the nation's natural resources were unlimited. As a consequence, Pinchot took courses at the French National School of Forestry, where the curriculum treated forests as crops that needed care and replenishing.

474

On his return in 1890, Pinchot began finding likeminded Americans who had begun to see the need to conserve the nation's natural resources and protect its wild spaces. Drawing on his scientific training and his experiences in Europe, Pinchot advocated the use of natural resources by sportsmen and businesses under carefully regulated governmental authority. Appointed to head the Federal Division of Forestry in 1898, Pinchot found a vigorous ally in the White House when Theodore Roosevelt took office in 1901. In 1907 Pinchot began to speak of the need for *conservation*, which he defined as the use of America's natural resources "for the benefit of the people who live here now." This use of resources included responsible business practices in industries such as logging and mining.

Not all environmentalists agreed. In contrast to Pinchot, author and nature photographer **Geneva (Gene) Stratton-Porter** focused her energies on *preservation*, the protection of public land from any private development. Born in 1863 in Wabash County, Indiana, Stratton-Porter grew up roaming through fields, watching birds, and observing "nature's rhythms." After marrying in 1886, Stratton-Porter took up photography and hiked into the wilderness of Indiana to take pictures of wild birds.

Stratton-Porter built a reputation as a nature photographer. She also published a series of widely read novels and children's books that revealed her vision of the harmony between human beings and nature. She urged readers to preserve the environment so that men and women could lead a truly fulfilling existence on earth and not destroy God's creation. One area on which she and Pinchot agreed was support for national parks.

THE AMERICAN HISTORIES of Gifford Pinchot and Gene Stratton-Porter reveal the efforts of two of the many individuals who searched for ways to limit the damaging impact of modernization on the United States. From roughly 1900 to 1917, many Americans sought to bring order out of the chaos accompanying rapid industrialization and urbanization. Despite the magnitude of the issues, those who believed in the need to combat the problems of industrial America possessed an optimistic faith—sometimes derived from religious principles, sometimes from a secular outlook—that they could relieve the stresses and strains of modern life. Such people were united by faith in the notion that if people joined together and applied human intelligence to the task of improving the nation, progress was inevitable. So widespread was this hopeful conviction that we call this period the Progressive Era.

In pursuit of progress and stability, some reformers tried to control the behavior of groups they considered a threat to the social order. Equating difference with disorder, many progressives tried to impose white middle-class standards of behavior on diverse immigrant populations. Some sought to eliminate the "problem" altogether by curtailing immigration from southern and eastern Europe. Others advocated birth control as a means to preserve the lives of childbearing women, but also to promote ethnic and racial engineering. In addition, progressives fought for women's suffrage, consumer protection, regulation of business, and good government reform. Many white progressives, particularly in the South, favored racial segregation and disfranchisement of African Americans. At the same time, however, black progressives and their white allies created organizations dedicated to securing racial equality. Despite their disparate and sometimes conflicting aims, progressives maintained a passion for change as a means of improving the nation.

The Roots of Progressivism

At the turn of the twentieth century, many Americans believed that the nation was in dire need of reform. Two decades of westward expansion, industrialization, urbanization, and skyrocketing immigration had transformed the country in unsettling ways. In the aftermath of the social and economic turmoil that accompanied the depression of the 1890s, many members of the middle and upper classes were convinced that unless they took remedial measures, the country would collapse under the weight of class conflict. Progressives advocated governmental intervention, yet they sought change without radically altering capitalism or the democratic political system. Not everyone endorsed progressives' goals, however. Conservatives continued to support individualism and the free market as the determinant of political and economic power, and radicals pressed for the socialist reorganization of the economy and the democratization of politics. Yet the public showed widespread support for progressivism by electing the reformers Theodore Roosevelt and Woodrow Wilson as presidents.

Progressive Origins

Progressives contended that old ways of governing and doing business did not address modern conditions. In one sense, they inherited the legacy of the Populist movement of the 1890s. Progressives attacked laissez-faire capitalism, and by regulating monopolies they aimed to limit the power of corporate trusts. Like the Populists, progressives advocated instituting an income tax as well as a variety of initiatives designed to give citizens a greater say in government. Progressives differed from Populists in fundamental ways. Perhaps most important, progressives were interested primarily in urban and industrial America, while the Populist movement had emerged in direct response to the problems that plagued rural America.

Progressives were heirs to the intellectual critics of the late nineteenth century who challenged laissez-faire and rejected Herbert Spencer's doctrine of the "survival of the fittest." **Pragmatism** greatly influenced progressives. Pragmatists contended that the meaning of truth could be discovered only through experience. Ideas had to be measured by their practical consequences. From pragmatists, progressive reformers derived a skepticism toward rigid dogma and instead relied on human experience to guide social action.

Progressive reformers also drew inspiration from the religious ideals of the **social gospel**. In *Christianity and the Social Crisis* (1907), Walter Rauschenbusch urged Christians to embrace the teachings of Jesus on the ethical obligations for social justice and to put these teachings into action by working among the urban poor. Washington Gladden argued that unregulated private enterprise was "inequitable" and compared financial speculators to vampires "sucking the life-blood of our commerce."

Progressive leaders such as Theodore Roosevelt and Gifford Pinchot combined the moral fervor of the social gospel with the rationalism of scientific efficiency.

Pragmatism and the social gospel appealed to members of the new middle class. Before the Civil War, the middle class had consisted largely of ministers, lawyers, physicians, and small proprietors. The growth of large-scale businesses during the second half of the nineteenth century expanded the middle class, which now included men and women whose professions grew out of industrialization, such as engineering, corporate management, and social work. Progressivism drew many of its most devoted adherents from this new middle class.

Muckrakers

The growing desire for reform at the turn of the century received a boost from investigative journalists known as **muckrakers**. Popular magazines such as *McClure's* and *Collier's* sought to increase their readership by publishing exposés of corruption in government and the shady operations of big business. Filled with details uncovered through intensive research, these articles had a sensationalist appeal that both informed and aroused their mainly middle-class readers. In 1902 journalist Ida Tarbell lambasted the ruthless and dishonest business practices of the Rockefeller family's Standard Oil Company, the model of corporate greed. Journalists Lincoln Steffens wrote about machine bosses' shameful rule in many American cities and Ida B. Wells wrote scathing articles and pamphlets condemning the lynching of African Americans. Other muckrakers exposed fraudulent practices in insurance companies, child labor, drug abuse, and prostitution.

REVIEW & RELATE	• What late-nineteenth-century trends and developments influenced the progressives? • Why did the progressives focus on urban and industrial America?

Humanitarian and Social Justice Reform

Progressivism took different paths based on the interests and concerns of its participants. Although many of the reform efforts overlapped, it is useful to examine them in specific categories. Humanitarian reformers focused on the plight of urban immigrants, African Americans, and the underprivileged. They tried to improve housing and working conditions for impoverished city dwellers. Their motives were not always purely altruistic. Unless living standards improved, many reformers reasoned, immigrants and racial minorities would "contaminate" the cities' middle-class inhabitants with communicable diseases, escalating crime, and threats to traditional cultural norms. These reformers also supported suffrage for women, whose votes, they believed, would help purify electoral politics and elect candidates committed to social and moral reform.

Female Progressives and the Poor

Women played the leading role in efforts to improve the lives of the impoverished. Jane Addams had toured Europe after graduating from a women's college in Illinois. The Toynbee Hall settlement house (see "Urban Reformers," in chapter 18) in London impressed her for its work in helping poor residents of the area. After returning home to Chicago in 1889, Addams and her friend Ellen Starr established **Hull House** as a center for social reform. Hull House inspired a generation of young women to work directly in immigrant communities. Many were college-educated, professionally trained women who were shut out of jobs in male-dominated professions. Staffed mainly by women, settlement houses became all-purpose urban support centers providing recreational facilities, social activities, and educational classes for neighborhood residents. Calling on women to take up **civic housekeeping**, Addams maintained that women could protect their households from the chaos of industrialization and urbanization only by attacking the sources of that chaos in the community at large.

Settlement houses and social workers occupied the front lines of humanitarian reform, but they found considerable support from women's clubs. Formed after the Civil War, these local groups provided middle-class women places to meet, share ideas, and work on common projects. By 1900 these clubs counted 160,000 members. Initially devoted to discussions of religion, culture, and science, club women began to help the needy and lobby for social justice legislation. "Since men are more or less closely absorbed in business," one club woman remarked about this civic awakening, "it has come to pass that the initiative in civic matters has devolved largely upon women." Starting out in towns and cities, club women carried their message to state and federal governments and campaigned for legislation that would establish social welfare programs for working women and their children.

In an age of strict racial segregation, African American women formed their own clubs. They sponsored day care centers, kindergartens, and work and home training projects. The activities of black club women, like those of white club women, reflected a class bias, and they tried to lift up poorer blacks to ideals of middle-class womanhood. Yet in doing so, they challenged racist notions that black women and men were incapable of raising healthy and strong families. By 1916 the National Association of Colored Women (NACW), whose motto was "lifting as we climb," boasted 1,000 clubs and 50,000 members.

One organization that attracted both white and black women in the South was the Young Women's Christian Association (YWCA). College women created student chapters of the "Y," which they devoted to working with the poor in settlement houses, prisons, orphanages, and other areas of public service. Two white sisters in North Carolina, Grace and Katharine Lumpkin, tried to carry out the social gospel mission of Walter Rauschenbusch and pledged "to lend to those less fortunate a helping hand" without concern for "culture, wealth, or pedigree." Black women such as Juliette Derricotte, Juanita Saddler, and Frances Williams built up college YWCA chapters on black campuses, though operating mainly in a segregated environment.

White working-class women also organized, but because of employment discrimination there were few, if any, black female industrial workers to join them. Building on the settlement house movement and together with middle-class and wealthy women, working-class women founded the National Women's Trade Union League (WTUL) in 1903. Recognizing that many women needed to earn an income to help support their families, the WTUL was dedicated to securing higher wages, an eight-hour day, and improved working conditions. Believing women to be physically weaker than men, most female reformers advocated special legislation to protect women in the workplace. They campaigned for state laws prescribing the maximum number of hours women could work, and they succeeded in 1908 when they won a landmark victory in the Supreme Court in *Muller v. Oregon*, which upheld an Oregon law establishing a ten-hour workday for women. These reformers also convinced lawmakers in forty states to establish pensions for mothers and widows. In 1912 their focus shifted to the federal government with the founding of the Children's Bureau in the Department of Commerce and Labor. Headed by Julia Lathrop, the bureau collected sociological data and devised a variety of publicly funded social welfare measures. In 1916 Congress enacted a law banning child labor under the age of fourteen (it was declared unconstitutional in 1918). In 1921 Congress passed the Shepherd-Towner Act, which allowed nurses to offer maternal and infant health care information to mothers.

Not all women believed in the idea of protective legislation for women. In 1898 Charlotte Perkins Gilman published *Women and Economics*, in which she argued against the notion that women were ideally suited for domesticity. She contended that women's reliance on men was unnatural: "We are the only animal species in which the female depends on the male for food." Emphasizing the need for economic independence, Gilman advocated the establishment of communal kitchens that would free women from household chores and allow them to compete on equal terms with men in the workplace. Emma Goldman, an anarchist critic of capitalism and middle-class sexual morality, also spoke out against the kind of marriage that made women "keep their mouths shut and their wombs open." These women considered themselves as feminists—women who aspire to reach their full potential and gain access to the same opportunities as men. Even those less radical than Gilman and Goldman, such as Louisa Dana Haring of Chicago, argued that the 1908 *Muller* opinion would hinder sexual equality. "If men want to curtail the hours of work for women," Haring wrote, "let them see to it that the rates per hour are raised, so as to afford compensation for loss of time." She went on to point out the obvious: "Who ever heard of limiting a working woman in a home (where she often does the rudest, heaviest sort of work) to eight hours of toil a day?"

Fighting for Women's Suffrage

Before 1900 women did not have the full right to vote, except in a handful of western states. Although the Fourteenth and Fifteenth Amendments extended citizenship to African Americans and protected the voting rights of black men, they left women, both white and black, ineligible to vote. Following Reconstruction, the two major organizations campaigning for women's suffrage at the state and national levels—Susan B. Anthony and Elizabeth Cady Stanton's National Woman Suffrage Association and Lucy Stone and Julia Ward Howe's American Woman Suffrage Association—failed to achieve major victories. In 1890 the two groups combined to form the National American Woman Suffrage Association, and by 1918 women could vote fully in fifteen states and the territory of Alaska (Map 19.1).

Suffragists included a broad coalition of supporters and based their campaign on a variety of arguments. Reformers such as Jane Addams attributed corruption in politics to the absence of women's maternal influence. In this way, mainstream suffragists couched their arguments within traditional conceptions of women as family

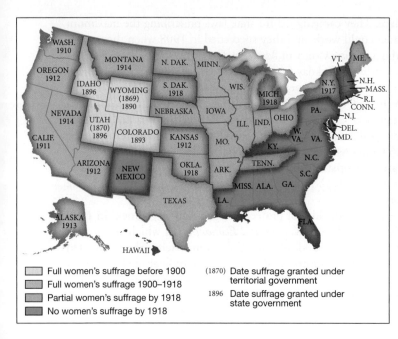

MAP 19.1
Women's Suffrage
Western states and territories were the first to approve women's suffrage. Yet even as western states enfranchised women, most placed restrictions on or excluded African American, American Indian, Mexican American, and Asian American women. States granting partial suffrage allowed women to vote only in certain contests, such as local, primary, or presidential elections.

Full women's suffrage before 1900

Full women's suffrage 1900–1918

Partial women's suffrage by 1918

No women's suffrage by 1918

(1870) Date suffrage granted under territorial government

1896 Date suffrage granted under state government

nurturers and claimed that men should see women's vote as an expansion of traditional household duties into the public sphere. By contrast, suffragists such as Alice Paul rejected such arguments, asserting that women deserved the vote on the basis of their equality with men as citizens. She founded the National Woman's Party and in 1923 proposed that Congress adopt an Equal Rights Amendment to provide full legal equality to women.

Both male and female opponents fought against women's suffrage. They believed that women were best suited by nature to devote themselves to their families and leave the world of politics to men. Suffrage critics insisted that extending the right to vote to women would destroy the home, lead to the moral degeneracy of children, and tear down the social fabric of the country.

Campaigns for women's suffrage did not apply to women of all races and classes. White suffragists in the South supported white female enfranchisement while maintaining racial prejudice against black men and women. Outspoken white suffragists such as Rebecca Latimer Felton from Georgia, Belle Kearney from Mississippi, and Kate Gordon from Louisiana contended that allowing southern white women to vote would preserve white supremacy by offsetting any black men's votes granted by the Fifteenth Amendment. Due to restrictive poll tax requirements, extending the vote to white women would benefit only those in the middle and upper classes who had enough family income to pay in order to vote.

Many middle-class women outside the South used similar reasoning, but they targeted newly arrived immigrants instead of African Americans. Many Protestant women and men viewed Catholics and Jews from southern and eastern Europe as racially inferior and spiritually dangerous. They blamed such immigrants for the ills of the cities in which they congregated, and some suffragists believed that the vote of middle-class Protestant women would help clean up the mess the immigrants created.

African American women challenged these racist arguments and mounted their own drive for female suffrage. They had an additional incentive to press for enfranchisement. As the target of white sexual predators during slavery and its aftermath, some black women saw the vote as a way to address this problem. "The ballot," Nannie Helen Burroughs, the founder of the NACW remarked, is the black woman's "weapon of moral defense." Although they did not gain much support from white suffragists, by 1916 African American women worked through the NACW and formed suffrage clubs throughout the nation.

The women's suffrage campaign adopted a variety of tactics. Reformers launched orderly parades on foot and in automobiles through the streets of American cities and towns. Growing numbers of working-class and immigrant women joined these parades, which gained widespread publicity. In attempting to promote suffrage, advocates embraced consumer culture. Macy's and other department stores sold blouses, skirts, and pins in suffrage colors—gold, white, and purple. Suffragists decorated store windows and created posters and slogans to appeal to diverse voters. Radical activists such as Alice Paul conducted confrontational demonstrations in Washington, D.C., in front of the gates of the White House. As a result, they were arrested, sent to prison, and force-fed after embarking on a hunger strike. Although

Nannie Burroughs and the National Women's Baptist Convention, c.1905 Nine African American women stand with Nannie Burroughs holding a banner reading, "Banner State Woman's National Baptist Convention." This organization, which Burroughs co-founded, provided support for southern black women in their efforts to promote education, suffrage, and anti-lynching measures. Library of Congress, LC-DIG-ds-13272

mainstream suffrage leaders denounced these new tactics, they gained much-needed publicity for the movement, which in turn aided the lobbying efforts of more moderate activists. In 1919 Congress passed the Nineteenth Amendment, granting women the vote. The following year, the amendment was ratified by the states.

The campaign for women's suffrage in the United States was part of an international movement. Victories in New Zealand (1893), Australia (1902), and Norway (1913) spurred on American suffragists. Indeed, Alice Paul and other radical American activists found inspiration in the militant tactics employed by some in the British suffrage movement.

Progressivism and African Americans

As with suffrage, social justice progressives faced huge barriers in the fight for racial equality. By 1900 white supremacists in the South had disfranchised most black voters and imposed a rigid system of segregation in education and all aspects of public life, which they enforced with violence. From 1884 to 1900, approximately 2,500 people were lynched, most of them southern blacks. Antiblack violence also took the form of race riots that erupted in southern cities. Farther north, in Springfield, Illinois, a riot broke out in 1908 when the local sheriff tried to protect two black prisoners from a would-be lynch mob. This confrontation triggered two days of white violence against blacks, some of whom fought back, leaving twenty-four businesses and forty homes destroyed and seven people (two blacks and five whites) dead.

As the situation for African Americans deteriorated, black leaders responded in several ways. Booker T. Washington espoused an approach that his critics called accommodation but that he defended as practical. Born a slave and emancipated at age nine, Washington attended Hampton Institute, run by sympathetic whites in his home state of Virginia. School officials believed that African Americans would first have to build up their character and accept the virtues of abstinence, thrift, and industriousness before seeking a more intellectual education. In 1881 Washington founded **Tuskegee Institute** in Alabama, which he modeled on Hampton. In 1895, he received an enthusiastic reception from white business and civic leaders in Atlanta for his message urging African Americans to remain in the South, accept racial segregation, concentrate on moral and economic development, and avoid politics. At the same time, he called on white leaders to protect blacks from the growing violence directed at them.

White leaders in both the South and the North embraced Washington, and he became the most powerful African American of his generation. Although he discouraged public protests against segregation, he emphasized racial pride and solidarity among African Americans. Yet Washington was a complex figure who secretly financed and supported court challenges to electoral disfranchisement and other forms of racial discrimination.

Washington's enormous power did not discourage opposing views among African Americans. Ida B. Wells, like Washington, had been born a slave. In 1878 she took a job in Memphis as a teacher. Six years later, Wells sued the Chesapeake & Ohio Railroad for moving her from the first-class "Ladies Coach" to the segregated smoking car because she was black. She won her case in the lower court, but her victory was reversed by the Tennessee Supreme Court. Undeterred, she began writing for the newspaper *Free Speech*, and when her articles exposing injustices in the Memphis school system got her fired from teaching, she took up journalism full-time.

Unlike Washington, Wells believed that black leaders had to speak out vigorously against racial inequality and lynching. On March 9, 1892, three black men in Memphis were murdered by a white mob. The victims had operated a grocery store that became the target of hostility from white competitors. The black businessmen fought back and shot three armed attackers in self-defense. In support of their actions, Wells wrote, "When the white man . . . knows he runs as great a risk of biting the dust every time his Afro-American victim does, he will have greater respect for Afro-American life." Subsequently arrested for their armed resistance, the three men were snatched from jail and lynched.

In response to Wells's articles about the Memphis lynching, a white mob burned down her newspaper's building. She fled to Chicago, where she published a report refuting the myth that the rape of white women by black men was the leading cause of lynching. She concluded that racists used this brand of violence to ensure that African Americans would not challenge white supremacy. Wells waged her campaign throughout the North and in Europe. She also joined the drive for women's suffrage, which she hoped would give black women a chance to use their votes to help combat racial injustice.

W. E. B. Du Bois also rejected Washington's accommodationist stance and urged blacks to demand first-class citizenship. In contrast to Washington's and Wells's families, Du Bois's ancestors were free blacks, and he grew up in Great Barrington, Massachusetts. He earned a Ph.D. in history from Harvard. Du Bois agreed with Washington about advocating self-help as a means for advancement, but he did not believe this effort would succeed without a proper education and equal voting rights. In *The Souls of Black Folk* (1903), Du Bois argued that African Americans needed a liberal arts education. Du Bois contended that a classical, humanistic education would produce a cadre of leaders, the "Talented Tenth," who would guide African Americans to the next stage of their development. African American leaders should demand the universal right to vote, and only then, Du Bois contended, would African Americans gain equality, self-respect, and dignity as a race.

Du Bois was an intellectual who put his ideas into action. In 1905 he spearheaded the creation of the Niagara Movement, a group that first met on the Canadian side of Niagara Falls. The all-black organization demanded the vote and equal access to public facilities for African Americans. By 1909 internal squabbling and a shortage of funds had crippled the group. That same year, however, Du Bois became involved in the creation of an organization that would shape the fight for racial equality throughout the twentieth century: the **National Association for the Advancement of Colored People (NAACP)**. In addition to Du Bois, Ida B. Wells, and veterans of the Niagara Movement, white activists such as Jane Addams joined in forming the organization. Beginning in 1910, the NAACP initiated court cases challenging racially discriminatory voting practices and other forms of bias in housing and criminal justice. Its first victory came in 1915, when its lawyers convinced the Supreme Court to strike down the grandfather clause that discriminated against black voters (*Guinn v. United States*).

African Americans also pursued social justice initiatives outside the realm of politics. Southern blacks remained committed to securing a quality education for their children after whites failed to live up to their responsibilities under *Plessy v. Ferguson*. Black schools remained inferior to white schools, and African Americans did not receive a fair return from their tax dollars; in fact, a large portion of their payments helped subsidize white schools.

Black women played a prominent role in promoting education. For example, in 1901 Charlotte Hawkins Brown set up the Palmer Memorial Institute outside of Greensboro, North Carolina. In these endeavors, black educators received financial assistance from northern philanthropists, white club women interested in moral uplift of the black race, and religious missionaries seeking converts in the South. By 1910 more than 1.5 million black children went to school in the South, most of them taught by the region's 28,560 black teachers. Thirty-four black colleges existed, and more than 2,000 African Americans held college degrees.

Progressivism and Indians

Like African Americans, Native Americans struggled against injustice. Indian muckrakers criticized government policies and anti-Indian attitudes, but the magazines that exposed the evils of industrialization often ignored their plight. Instead, Indian reformers turned to the *Quarterly Journal*, published by the Society of American Indians, to air their grievances. Carlos Montezuma was the most outspoken critic of Indian policy. A Yavapai tribe member from Arizona, he called for the abolition of the Indian Office as an impediment to the welfare of Native Americans. Montezuma argued that Native Americans had to free themselves to gain their independence and advocated for extending full citizenship and equal rights to all Indians. Arthur C. Parker, an anthropologist from the eastern tribe of the Seneca, challenged the notion that Indians suffered mainly because of their own backwardness. In scathing articles, he condemned the United States for robbing American Indians of their cultural and economic independence. One Indian who wrote for non-Indian magazines such as *Harper's Weekly* was Zitkala-Ša. This Sioux woman published essays exposing the practices of boarding schools designed to assimilate Indians. Non-Indian anthropologists such as Franz Boas and Ruth Benedict added their voices to those of Indian journalists in attacking traditional views of Native Americans as inferior and uncivilized.

Indian reformers did not succeed in convincing state and federal governments to pass legislation to address their concerns. Nevertheless, activists did succeed in filing thirty-one complaints with the U.S. Court of Claims for monetary compensation for federal payments to which they were entitled but had not received. Like other exploited groups during the Progressive Era, Indians created organizations, such as the Black Hills Treaty Council and others, to pressure the federal government and to publicize their demands.

REVIEW & RELATE	• What role did women play in the early-twentieth-century fight for social justice? • How did social reformers challenge discrimination against women, racial and ethnic minorities, and Indians?

Morality and Social Control

In many cases, progressive initiatives crossed the line from social reform to social control. Convinced that the "immorality" of the poor was the cause of social disorder, some reformers sought to impose middle-class standards of behavior and morality on the lower economic classes. As with other forms of progressivism, reformers interested in social control were driven by a variety of motives. Regardless, efforts to prohibit alcohol, fight prostitution, and combat juvenile delinquency often involved attempts to repress the poor. So, too, did protective health measures such as birth control. Some social control progressives went even further in their efforts to impose their own morality, calling for restrictions on immigration, which they saw as a cultural threat.

Prohibition

Prohibition campaigns began long before the Civil War but scored few important successes until 1881, when Kansas became the first state whose constitution banned the consumption of alcohol. Women spearheaded the prohibition movement by forming the **Woman's Christian Temperance Union (WCTU)** in 1874 under the leadership of Frances Willard. Willard built the temperance movement around the need to protect the home. Husbands and fathers who drank excessively were also likely to abuse their wives and children and to drain the family finances. Prohibiting the consumption of alcohol would therefore help combat these evils. At the same time, the quality of family and public life would be improved if women received the right to vote and young children completed their education without having to go to work.

After Willard's death in 1898, the Anti-Saloon League (ASL) became the dominant force in the prohibition movement. Established in 1893, the league grew out of evangelical Protestantism. The group had particular appeal in the rural South, where Protestant fundamentalism flourished. Between 1906 and 1917, twenty-one states, mostly in the South and West, banned liquor sales. However, concern over alcohol was not confined to these regions. Middle-class progressives in northern cities, who identified much of urban decay with the influx of immigrants, saw the tavern as a breeding ground for immoral activities. In 1913 the ASL convinced Congress to pass the Webb-Kenyon Act, which banned the transportation of alcoholic beverages into dry states. After the United States entered World War I in 1917, reformers argued that prohibition would help win the war by conserving grain used to make liquor and by saving soldiers from intoxication. The Eighteenth Amendment, ratified in 1919, made prohibition the law of the land until it was repealed in 1933.

Prostitution, Narcotics, and Juvenile Delinquency

Alarmed by the increased number of brothels and "streetwalkers" that accompanied the growth of cities, progressives sought to eliminate prostitution. Some framed the issue in terms of public health, linking prostitution to the spread of sexually transmitted diseases. Others presented it as an effort to protect female virtue. Such reformers were generally interested only in white women, who, unlike African American and Asian women in similar circumstances, were considered sexual innocents coerced into prostitution. Still others claimed that prostitutes themselves were to blame, seeing women who sold their sexual favors as inherently immoral.

Reformers offered two different approaches to the problem. Taking the moralistic solution, Representative James R. Mann of Chicago steered through Congress the White Slave Trade Act (known as the Mann Act) in 1910, banning the transportation of women across state lines for immoral purposes. By contrast, the American Social Hygiene Association, founded in 1914, subsidized scientific research into sexually transmitted diseases, funded investigations to gather more information, and drafted model ordinances for cities to curb prostitution. By 1915 every state had laws making sexual solicitation a crime.

Prosecutors used the Mann Act to enforce codes of racial as well as sexual behavior. In 1910 Jack Johnson, an African American boxer, defeated the white heavyweight champion, Jim Jeffries. His victory upset some white men who were obsessed with preserving their racial dominance and masculine integrity. Johnson's relationships with white women further angered some whites, who eventually succeeded in bringing down the outspoken black champion by prosecuting him on morals charges in 1913.

Moral crusaders also sought to eliminate the use and sale of narcotics. By 1900 approximately 250,000 people in the United States were addicted to opium, morphine, or cocaine—far fewer, however, than those who abused alcohol. On the West Coast, immigration opponents associated opium smoking with the Chinese and tried to eliminate its use as part of their wider anti-Asian campaign. In alliance with the American Medical Association, reformers convinced Congress to pass the Harrison Narcotics Control Act of 1914, prohibiting the sale of narcotics except by a doctor's prescription.

Progressives also tried to combat juvenile delinquency, and this effort often involved attempts to control disadvantaged youth, especially immigrant children. Inspired by new ideas about children as a distinct category—not simply small adults—reformers succeeded in establishing a juvenile court system that focused on rehabilitation rather than punishment for youthful offenders. Juvenile courts conducted civil rather than criminal proceedings, thereby allowing local officials greater flexibility as they extended their supervision of boys and girls over such noncriminal behavior as smoking, truancy, and sexual activity. Rehabilitation of delinquent boys, regardless of their suspect behavior, often turned into punitive treatment. Fewer girls got caught up in the juvenile courts, but those who did appeared mainly on charges of "sexual precocity." In replacing criminal penalties with juvenile rehabilitation progressive reformers sought to impose middle-class norms on disadvantaged youth.

Birth Control

The health of women and families occupied reformers such as Margaret Sanger, the leading advocate of birth control. Working as a nurse mainly among poor immigrant women in New York City, she witnessed the damage that unrestrained childbearing produced on women's health. According to Sanger, contraception—the use of artificial means to prevent pregnancy—would save the lives of mothers by preventing unwanted childbearing and avoiding unsafe and illegal abortions, and would keep families from having large numbers of children they could not afford. Moreover,

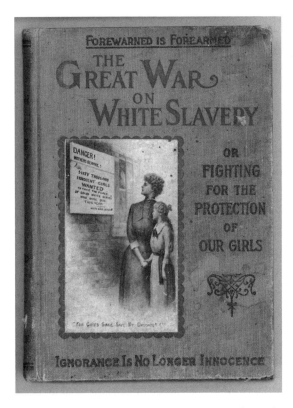

Sanger believed that if women were freed from the anxieties of becoming pregnant, they would experience more sexual enjoyment and make better companions for their spouses. Her arguments for birth control also had a connection to eugenics. Contraception, she believed, would "raise the quality" of the white race by reducing the chances of immigrants and women from ethnic and racial minorities reproducing so-called unfit children.

Sanger and her supporters encountered enormous opposition. It was illegal to sell contraceptive devices or furnish information about them. Nevertheless, in 1916 Sanger opened up the nation's first birth control clinic in an immigrant section of Brooklyn. The police quickly closed down the facility and arrested Sanger. Undeterred, she continued to agitate for her cause and push to change attitudes toward women's health and reproductive rights.

Immigration Restriction

Sanger wanted to lessen the problems faced by immigrant women. However, other moral reformers sought to restrict immigration itself. Anti-immigrant sentiment often reflected racial and religious bigotry, as reformers concentrated on preventing Catholics, Jews, and all non-Europeans from entering the United States. Social scientists validated these prejudices by categorizing darker-skinned immigrants as inferior races. The harshest treatment was reserved for Asians. In 1908 President Theodore Roosevelt entered into an executive agreement with Japan that reduced Japanese immigration to the United States. In 1913 the California legislature passed a statute barring Japanese immigrants from buying land, a law that twelve other states subsequently enacted.

In 1917 reformers succeeded in further restricting immigration. Congress passed legislation to ban people who could not read English or their native language from entering the country. The act also denied entry to other undesirables: "alcoholics," "feeble-minded persons," "epileptics," "people mentally or physically defective," "professional beggars," "anarchists," and "polygamists." In barring people considered unfit to enter the country, lawmakers intended to keep out those who could not support themselves and might become public wards of the state and, in the case of anarchists and polygamists, those who threatened the nation's political and religious values.

REVIEW & RELATE	• What practices and behaviors of the poor did social control progressives find most alarming? Why? • What role did anti-immigrant sentiment play in motivating and shaping progressives' social control initiatives?

Good Government Progressivism

In an effort to diminish the power of corrupt urban political machines and unregulated corporations, progressives pushed for good government reforms, promoting initiatives they claimed would produce greater efficiency, openness, and accountability in government. Many of the progressives' proposed reforms appeared, at least on the surface, to give citizens more direct say in their government; however, a closer look reveals a more complicated picture.

Municipal and State Reform

Cities were at the forefront of government reform during the Progressive Era. Municipal governments failed to keep up with the problems of accelerated urban growth. Political machines distributed city services within a system bloated by corruption and graft. Upper-middle-class businessmen and professionals fed up with wasteful and inefficient political machines sought to institute new forms of government that functioned more rationally and cost less.

The adoption of the commission form of government was a hallmark of urban reform. Commission governments replaced the old form of a mayor and city council with elected commissioners, each of whom ran a municipal department as if it were a business. By 1917 commissions had spread to more than four hundred cities throughout the country. Governments with a mayor and city council also began to appoint city managers, who functioned as chief operating officers, to foster business-like efficiency. The head of the National Cash Register Company, who helped bring the city manager system to Dayton, Ohio, praised it for resembling "a great business enterprise whose stockholders are the people."

Reformers also adopted direct primaries for voters to select candidates rather than allowing a handful of machine politicians to decide elections behind closed doors. To reverse the influence of immigrants who supported their own ethnic candidates and to topple the machines that catered to them, municipal reformers replaced district elections with citywide "at-large" elections. Ethnic enclaves lost not only their ward representatives but also a good deal of their influence because citywide election campaigns were expensive, shifting power to those who could afford to run. Working- and lower-class residents of cities still retained the right to vote, but their power was diluted.

In the South, where fewer immigrants lived, white supremacists employed these tactics to further disfranchise African Americans. Southern lawmakers diminished whatever black political power remained by adopting at-large elections and commission governments. Throughout the South, direct primary contests (or "white primaries") were closed to blacks.

Urban progressivism did produce a number of mayors who carried out genuine reforms. Elected in 1901, Cleveland mayor Tom L. Johnson implemented measures to assess taxes more equitably, regulate utility companies, and reduce public transportation fares. Samuel "Golden Rule" Jones, who served as Toledo's mayor from 1897 to 1903, supported social justice measures by establishing an eight-hour workday for municipal employees, granting them paid vacations, and prohibiting child labor. Under Mayor Hazen Pingree, who served from 1889 to 1896, Detroit constructed additional schools and recreational facilities and put the unemployed to work on municipal projects during economic hard times.

Progressives also took action at the state level. Robert M. La Follette, Republican governor of Wisconsin from 1901 to 1906, led the way by initiating a range of reforms to improve the performance of state government and increase its accountability to constituents. During his tenure as governor, La Follette dismantled the statewide political machine by instituting direct party primaries, an expanded civil service, a law forbidding direct corporate contributions to political parties, a strengthened railroad regulatory commission, and a graduated income tax. In 1906 La Follette entered the U.S. Senate, where he battled for further reform.

Other states picked up and expanded La Follette's progressive agenda. In 1913 three-quarters of the states ratified the Seventeenth Amendment, which mandated that U.S. senators would be elected by popular vote instead of being chosen by state legislatures. This constituted another effort to remove the influence of money from politics.

Conservation and Preservation of the Environment

The penchant for efficiency that characterized government progressivism also shaped progressive efforts to conserve natural resources. As chief forester in the Department of Agriculture, Gifford Pinchot emphasized the efficient use of resources and sought ways to reconcile the public interest with private profit motives. His approach often won support from large lumber companies, which had a long-term interest in sustainable forests. Large companies also saw conservation as a way to drive their smaller competitors out of business, as large companies could better afford the additional costs associated with managing healthy forests.

This gospel of efficiency faced a stiff test in California. After the devastating earthquake of 1906, San Francisco officials, coping with water and power shortages, asked the federal government to approve construction of a hydroelectric dam and reservoir in **Hetch Hetchy valley**, located in Yosemite National Park (Map 19.2). Pinchot supported the project because he saw it as the best use of the land for the greatest number of people. The famed naturalist John Muir strongly disagreed. He campaigned

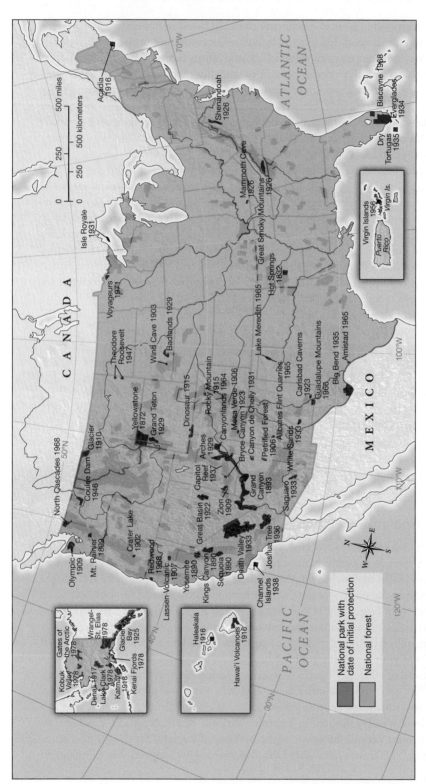

MAP 19.2   National Parks and Forests

In 1872, the federal government created the first national park at Yellowstone, which spread over portions of the future states of Wyoming, Montana, and Idaho. President Theodore Roosevelt added six sites — Crater Lake, Wind Cave, Petrified Forest, Lassen Volcanic, Mesa Verde, and Zion — to the park system. The construction of a dam and reservoir in Yosemite National Park's Hetch Hetchy Valley divided conservationists Gifford Pinchot and John Muir during the Roosevelt administration.

to save Hetch Hetchy from "ravaging commercialism" and warned against choosing economic gains over spiritual values. After a bruising seven-year battle, Pinchot (by this time a private citizen) triumphed. Still, this incursion into a national park helped spur the development of environmentalism as a political movement.

Besides the clash with preservationists, the Hetch Hetchy Dam project reveals progressive conservationists' racial bias. Conservationists such as Pinchot may have seen themselves as acting in the public interest, but their definition of "the public" did not include all Americans. In planning for the Hetch Hetchy Dam, progressives did not consult with the Mono Lake Paiutes who lived in Yosemite and who were most directly affected by the project. Conservation was meant to serve the interests of white San Franciscans and not those of the Indian inhabitants of Yosemite.

REVIEW & RELATE	• Who gained and who lost political influence as a result of progressive reforms? • How did a commitment to greater efficiency shape progressives' political and environmental initiatives?

Presidential Progressivism

The problems created by industrialization and the growth of big business were national in scope. Recognizing this fact, prominent progressives sought national leadership positions, and two of them, Presidents Theodore Roosevelt and Woodrow Wilson, instituted progressive reforms during their terms. In the process, they reinvigorated the presidency, an office that had declined in power and importance during the late nineteenth century.

Theodore Roosevelt and the Square Deal

Born into a moderately wealthy New York family, Theodore Roosevelt graduated from Harvard in 1880 and entered government service. Elected as governor of New York in 1898, two years later he became William McKinley's vice president. After McKinley's assassination in 1901, Roosevelt took over the presidency.

Roosevelt brought an activist style to the presidency. He considered his office a **bully pulpit**—a platform from which to promote his programs and from which he could rally public opinion. To this end, he used his energetic and extroverted personality to establish an unprecedented rapport with the American people.

For all his exuberance and energy, President Roosevelt pursued a moderate domestic course. Like his progressive colleagues, he opposed ideological extremism in any form. Roosevelt believed that as head of state he could serve as an impartial arbiter among competing factions and determine what was best for the public. To him, reform was the best defense against revolution.

As president, Roosevelt sought to provide economic and political stability, what he referred to as a "Square Deal." The coal strike that began in Pennsylvania in 1902 gave Roosevelt an opportunity to play the role of defender of the public good. Miners had gone on strike for an eight-hour workday, a pay increase of 20 percent, and recognition of their union. Union representatives agreed to have the president create a panel to settle the dispute, but George F. Baer, president of the Reading Railroad, which also owned the mines, pledged that he would never agree to the workers' demands. Disturbed by what he considered the owners' "arrogant stupidity," Roosevelt threatened to dispatch federal troops to take over and run the mines. When the owners backed down, the president established a commission that hammered out a compromise, which raised wages and reduced working hours but did not recognize the union.

At the same time, Roosevelt tackled the problems caused by giant business trusts. In February 1902, the president instructed the Justice Department to sue the Northern Securities Company under the Sherman Antitrust Act. Financed by J. P. Morgan, Northern Securities held monopoly control of the northernmost transcontinental railway lines. In 1904 the Supreme Court ordered that the Northern Securities Company be dissolved, ruling that the firm had restricted competition. With this victory, Roosevelt affirmed the federal government's power to regulate business trusts that violated the public interest. Overall, Roosevelt initiated twenty-five suits under the Sherman Antitrust Act, including litigation against the tobacco and beef trusts and the Standard Oil Company, which earned him the title of "trustbuster."

Roosevelt distinguished between "good" trusts, which acted responsibly, and "bad" trusts, which abused their power. Railroads had earned an especially bad reputation with the public for charging higher rates to small shippers and those in remote regions while granting rebates to favored customers, such as Standard Oil. In 1903 Roosevelt helped persuade Congress to pass the Elkins Act, which outlawed railroad rebates. Three years later, the president increased the power of the Interstate Commerce Commission to set maximum railroad freight rates. Also in 1903 Roosevelt secured passage of legislation that established the Department of Commerce and Labor. Within this cabinet agency, the Bureau of Corporations gathered information about large companies in an effort to promote fair business practices.

Soaring in popularity, Roosevelt easily won reelection in 1904. During the next four years, the president applied antitrust laws even more vigorously than before. He steered through Congress various reforms concerning the railroads, such as the Hepburn Act (1906), which standardized shipping rates. Roosevelt charted a middle course between preservationists and conservationists. He reserved 150 million acres of timberland as part of the national forests, but he authorized the expenditure of more than $80 million in federal funds to construct dams, reservoirs, and canals largely in the West.

Not all reform came from Roosevelt's initiative. Congress passed two notable consumer laws in 1906 that reflected the multiple and sometimes contradictory forces that shaped progressivism. That year, Upton Sinclair published *The Jungle*, a muckraking novel that portrayed the impoverished lives of immigrant workers in Packingtown (Chicago) and the deplorable working conditions they endured. Outraged readers responded to the vivid description of the shoddy and filthy ways the meatpacking industry slaughtered animals and prepared beef for sale. The largest and most efficient meatpacking firms had financial reasons to support reform as well. They were losing money because European importers refused to purchase tainted meat. Congress responded by passing the Meat Inspection Act, which benefited consumers and provided a way for large corporations to eliminate competition from smaller, marginal firms that could not afford to raise standards to meet the new federal meat-processing requirements.

In 1906 Congress also passed the Pure Food and Drug Act, which prohibited the sale of adulterated and fraudulently labeled food and drugs. The impetus for

TABLE 19.1	NATIONAL PROGRESSIVE LEGISLATION
1903	Department of Labor and Commerce established to promote fair business practices
	Elkins Act
1906	Pure Food and Drug Act
	Meat Inspection Act; Hepburn Act
1910	White Slave Trade Act
1913	Underwood Act reduces tariffs to benefit farmers
	Sixteenth Amendment (graduated income tax)
	Seventeenth Amendment (election of senators by popular vote)
	Federal Reserve System
1914	Harrison Narcotics Control Act
	Federal Trade Commission
	Clayton Antitrust Act
1916	Adamson Act provides eight-hour workday for railroad workers
	Keating-Owen Act outlaws child labor in firms engaged in interstate commerce
	Workmen's Compensation Act
1919	Eighteenth Amendment (prohibition)
1920	Nineteenth Amendment (women's suffrage)

this law came from consumer groups, medical professionals, and government scientists. Dr. Harvey Wiley, a chemist in the Department of Agriculture, drove efforts for reform from within the government. He considered it part of his professional duty to eliminate harmful products (Table 19.1).

Roosevelt initially gave African Americans reason to believe that they, too, would get a square deal. In October 1901, at the outset of his first term, Roosevelt invited Booker T. Washington to a dinner at the White House, outraging white supremacists in the South. Though Roosevelt dismissed this criticism, he never invited another black guest. Also in his first term, Roosevelt supported the appointment of a few black Republicans to federal posts in the South.

Nevertheless, Roosevelt lacked a commitment to black equality and espoused the racist ideas of eugenics then in fashion. He deplored the declining birthrate of native-born white Americans compared with that of eastern and southern European newcomers and African Americans, whom he considered inferior. He argued that unless Anglo-Saxon women produced more children, whites would end up committing "race suicide." "If the women flinch from breeding," Roosevelt worried, "the . . . death of the race takes place even quicker."

Once he won reelection in 1904, Roosevelt had less political incentive to defy the white South. He stopped cooperating with southern black officeholders and maneuvered to build the Republican Party in the region with all-white support. However, his most reprehensible action involved an incident that occurred in Brownsville, Texas, in 1906. White residents of the town charged that black soldiers stationed at Fort Brown shot and killed one man and wounded another. Roosevelt ordered that unless the alleged perpetrators stepped forward, the entire regiment would receive dishonorable discharges without a court-martial. Roosevelt never doubted the guilt of the black soldiers, and when no one admitted responsibility, he summarily dismissed 167 men from the military.

Roosevelt's racial attitudes also shaped his policies with respect to American Indians. Like nearly all Americans, Roosevelt believed that Native Americans were inferior to Anglo-Saxons. The president contended that enlightened white people had the duty to assimilate "primitive" Indians and make them more "civilized." Roosevelt was an enthusiastic supporter of the 1887 Dawes Act, which sold off Native lands and attempted to convert Indians into small farmers as a "vast pulverizing engine to break up the tribal mass." Within this paternalistic and racist framework, Roosevelt did act against corruption in the Bureau of Indian Affairs and initiated investigations into the treatment of Indians on reservations. The president thought that education for Indians should be "elementary and largely industrial," and their need of higher education was "very, very limited." In 1902, his administration issued an order requiring Indian men on reservations to cut their hair short, arguing that this "will be a great step in advance and will certainly hasten their progress towards civilization." Native Americans found it deeply offensive.

Taft Retreats from Progressivism

When Roosevelt decided not to seek another term as president in 1908, choosing instead to back William Howard Taft as his successor, he thought he was leaving his reform legacy in capable hands. A Roosevelt loyalist, Taft easily defeated the Democratic candidate, William Jennings Bryan, who was running for the presidency for the third and final time.

Taft's presidency did not proceed as Roosevelt and his progressive followers had hoped. Taft proved a weak leader and frequently took stands opposite to Roosevelt and the progressives, such as in the field of conservation. When Pinchot criticized Taft's secretary of the interior, Richard Ballinger, for returning restricted Alaskan coal mines to private mining companies in 1910, Taft fired Pinchot. Taft did not oppose conservation — he transferred more land from private to public control than did Roosevelt — but his dismissal of Pinchot angered conservationists.

Subsequently, Roosevelt turned against his handpicked successor. After returning from overseas in 1910, Roosevelt became increasingly troubled by Taft's missteps. The loss of the House of Representatives to the Democrats in the 1910 elections raised alarms among Roosevelt Republicans. A year later, relations between the ex-president and the incumbent further deteriorated when Roosevelt attacked Taft for filing antitrust litigation against U.S. Steel for a deal that the Roosevelt administration had approved in 1907. Ironically, Roosevelt, known as a trustbuster, believed that filing more lawsuits under the Sherman Antitrust Act yielded diminishing returns, whereas Taft, the conservative, initiated more antitrust litigation than did Roosevelt.

The Election of 1912

Convinced that only he could lead the party to victory, Roosevelt announced his candidacy for the 1912 Republican presidential nomination. Despite Roosevelt's popularity among rank-and-file Republicans, Taft still controlled the party machinery and the majority of convention delegates. Losing to Taft on the first ballot, an embittered Roosevelt formed a third party to sponsor his run for the presidency. Roosevelt excitedly told thousands of supporters gathered in Chicago that he felt "as strong as a BULL MOOSE," which became the nickname for Roosevelt's new **Progressive Party**.

In accepting the nomination, Roosevelt articulated the philosophy of **New Nationalism**. He argued that the federal government should use its power to fight against the forces of special privilege and for social justice for the majority of Americans. To this end, the Progressive Party platform advocated income and inheritance taxes, an eight-hour workday, the abolition of child labor, workers' compensation, fewer restrictions on labor unions, and women's suffrage.

The Democrats also nominated a progressive candidate, Woodrow Wilson, the reform governor of New Jersey. As an alternative to Roosevelt's New Nationalism, Wilson offered his **New Freedom**. As a Democrat and a southerner (he was born in Virginia), Wilson had a more limited view of government than did the Republican Roosevelt. Wilson envisioned a society of small businesses, with the government's role confined to ensuring open competition among businesses and freedom for individuals to make the best use of their opportunities. Wilson's New Freedom did not embrace social reform and rejected federal action in support of women's suffrage and the elimination of child labor.

Eugene V. Debs, the Socialist Party candidate who had been imprisoned for his leadership in the Pullman strike, was a fourth candidate in the race. He favored overthrowing capitalism through peaceful, democratic methods and replacing it with government ownership of business and industry for the benefit of the working class.

The Republican Party split decided the outcome of the election. The final results gave Roosevelt 27 percent of the popular vote and Taft 23 percent. Together they had a majority, but because they were divided, Wilson became president, with 42 percent of the popular vote and 435 electoral votes. Finishing fourth, Debs did not win any electoral votes, but he garnered around a million popular votes (6 percent).

Woodrow Wilson and the New Freedom Agenda

Once in office, Wilson hurried to fulfill his New Freedom agenda. An admirer of the British parliamentary system, Wilson viewed the president as an active and strong leader whose job was to provide his party with a legislative program. The 1912 elections had given the Democrats control over Congress, and Wilson expected his party to support his New Freedom measures.

Tariff reduction came first. The Underwood Act of 1913 reduced import duties, a measure that appealed to southern and midwestern farmers who sought lower prices on the manufactured goods they bought that were subject to the tariff. The law also incorporated a reform that progressives had adopted from the Populists: the graduated income tax (tax rates that increase at higher levels of income). The ratification of the Sixteenth Amendment in 1913 provided the legal basis for the income tax after the Supreme Court had previously declared such a levy unconstitutional. The graduated income tax was meant to advance the cause of social justice by moderating income inequality. The need to recover revenues lost from lower tariffs provided an additional practical impetus for imposing the tax. Because the law exempted people earning less than $4,000 a year from paying the income tax, more than 90 percent of Americans owed no tax. Those with incomes exceeding this amount paid rates ranging from 1 percent to 6 percent on $500,000 or more.

Woodrow Wilson's New Freedom Before Woodrow Wilson was elected president in 1912 he had been a college professor of political science and president of Princeton University. Having stepped out of the university's ivory tower into the White House, Wilson was prepared to "educate" his opponents about their economic and civic duties to the nation. How does this political cartoon depict this? Sarin Images/Granger

Also in 1913, Wilson pressed Congress to consider banking reform. Farmers favored a system supervised by the government that afforded them an ample supply of credit at low interest rates. Eastern bankers wanted reforms that would stabilize a system plagued by cyclical financial panics, the most recent in 1907, while keeping the banking system under the private control of bankers. The resulting compromise created the Federal Reserve System. The act established twelve regional banks. These banks lent cash reserves to member banks in their districts at a "rediscount rate," a rate that could be adjusted according to the fluctuating demand for credit. Federal Reserve notes became the foundation for a uniform currency. The Federal Reserve Board, appointed by the president and headquartered in Washington, D.C., supervised the system. Nevertheless, as with other progressive agencies, the experts selected to oversee the new banking system came from within the banking industry itself. Although farmers won a more rational and flexible credit supply, Wall Street bankers retained considerable power over the operation of the Federal Reserve System.

Next, President Wilson took two steps designed to help resolve the problem of economic concentration. First, in 1914 he persuaded Congress to create the Federal Trade Commission. The commission had the power to investigate corporate activities and prohibit "unfair" practices (which the law left undefined). Wilson's second measure directly attacked monopolies. Enacted in 1914, the Clayton Antitrust Act strengthened the Sherman Antitrust Act by banning certain corporate operations, such as price discrimination and overlapping membership on company boards, which undermined economic competition. The statute also exempted labor unions from prosecution under antitrust legislation, reversing the policy initiated by the federal government in the wake of the Pullman strike.

By the end of his second year in office, Wilson had achieved most of his New Freedom objectives. In response to political pressure and looking ahead to reelection, he was forced to widen his progressive agenda and support measures he had previously rejected. With the Republican Party once again united after the electoral fiasco of 1912, Wilson looked to gain support from Roosevelt's constituency by supporting New Nationalism social justice measures. In 1916 he signed into law the Adamson Act, which provided an eight-hour workday and overtime pay for railroad workers; the Keating-Owen Act, outlawing child labor in firms that engaged in interstate commerce; and the Workmen's Compensation Act, which provided insurance for federal employees in case of injury. In supporting programs that required greater intervention by the federal government, Wilson had placed political expediency ahead of his professed principles. He would later show a similar flexibility when he lent his support to a women's suffrage amendment, a cause he had long opposed.

Despite facing a challenge from a united Republican Party, Wilson won the 1916 election against former New York governor Charles Evans Hughes with slightly less than 50 percent of the vote. Wilson's reelection owed little to support from African Americans. W. E. B. Du Bois, who backed Wilson in 1912 for pledging to "assist in advancing the interest of [the black] race," had become disillusioned with the president. The southern-born Wilson had surrounded himself with white appointees from the South. Despite black protests, Wilson held a screening in the White House of the film *Birth of a Nation*, which glorified the Ku Klux Klan and denigrated African Americans. Making the situation worse, Wilson introduced racial segregation into government offices and dining facilities in the nation's capital, and blacks lost jobs in post offices and other federal agencies throughout the South. In Wilson's view, segregation was in the "best interests" of African Americans.

Still, President Wilson achieved much of the progressive agenda—more, in fact, than he had intended to when he first came to office. By the beginning of his second term, the federal government had further extended regulation over the activities of corporations and banks. Big business and finance still wielded substantial power, but Wilson had steered the government on a course that also benefited ordinary citizens, including passage of social justice measures he had initially opposed.

REVIEW & RELATE	• How did the progressive agenda shape presidential politics in the first two decades of the twentieth century? • How did the progressive policies of Presidents Roosevelt and Wilson apply to African Americans and Indians?

Conclusion: The Progressive Legacy

By the end of the Progressive Era, Americans had come to expect more from their government. They were more confident that their food and medicine were safe, that children would not have to sacrifice their health and education by going to work, that women laborers would not be exploited, and that political officials would be more responsive to their wishes. As a result of the efforts of environmentalists as different as Gifford Pinchot and Gene Stratton-Porter, the nation expanded its efforts both to conserve and to preserve its natural resources. These and other reforms accomplished what Theodore Roosevelt, Woodrow Wilson, and their fellow progressives wanted: to bring order out of chaos.

In challenging laissez-faire and championing governmental intervention, progressives sought to balance individualism with social justice and social control.

Despite well-intentioned political reforms, middle- and upper-class progressives generally were more interested in augmenting their ability to advance their own agenda than in expanding opportunities for political participation for all Americans. Confident that they spoke for the "interests of the people," progressives believed that increasing their own political power would be good for the nation as a whole.

Progressivism was not for whites only, but racism constrained the progressive movement. Native Americans campaigned and organized to get the federal government to repair its broken promises of justice. Blacks were active participants in progressivism, whether through extending educational opportunities, working in settlement houses, campaigning for women's suffrage, or establishing the NAACP. Nevertheless, racism was also a characteristic of progressivism. White southern reformers generally favored disfranchisement and segregation. Northern whites did not prove much more sympathetic. Immigrants also found themselves unwelcome targets of moral outrage as progressives forced these newcomers to conform to middle-class standards of social behavior. Campaigns for temperance, moral reform, and birth control all shared a desire to mold people deemed inferior into proper citizens, uncontaminated by chronic vice and corruption.

Progressivism included a range of disparate and overlapping efforts to reorder political, social, moral, and physical environments. Except for the brief existence of the Progressive Party in 1912, reformers did not have a tightly knit organization or a fixed agenda. Leaders were more likely to come from the middle class, but support came from the rich as well as the poor, depending on the issue. Of course, many Americans did not embrace progressive principles, as conservative opponents continued to hold power and to fight against reform. Nevertheless, by 1917 a combination of voluntary changes and government intervention had cleared the way to regulate corporations, increase governmental efficiency, and promote social justice. Progressives succeeded in ameliorating conditions that might have produced violent revolution and more disorder. In time, they would bring their ideas to reordering international affairs.

Chapter 19 Review

KEY TERMS

pragmatism, 476
social gospel, 476
muckrakers, 477
Hull House, 478
civic housekeeping, 478
suffragists, 479
Tuskegee Institute, 482
National Association for the
    Advancement of Colored People
    (NAACP), 483

Woman's Christian Temperance
    Union (WCTU), 485
Hetch Hetchy valley, 489
bully pulpit, 491
Progressive Party, 495
New Nationalism, 495
New Freedom, 495

REVIEW & RELATE

1. What late-nineteenth-century trends and developments influenced the progressives?
2. Why did the progressives focus on urban and industrial America?
3. What role did women play in the early-twentieth-century fight for social justice?
4. How did social reformers challenge discrimination against women, racial and ethnic minorities, and Indians?
5. What practices and behaviors of the poor did social control progressives find most alarming? Why?
6. What role did anti-immigrant sentiment play in motivating and shaping progressives' social control initiatives?
7. Who gained and who lost political influence as a result of progressive reforms?
8. How did a commitment to greater efficiency shape progressives' political and environmental initiatives?
9. How did the progressive agenda shape presidential politics in the first two decades of the twentieth century?
10. How did the policies of Presidents Roosevelt and Wilson apply to African Americans and Indians?

TIMELINE OF EVENTS

1874	• Woman's Christian Temperance Union founded
1889	• Jane Addams and Ellen Starr establish Hull House
1890	• National American Woman Suffrage Association formed
1895	• Booker T. Washington delivers Atlanta address
1900	• First commission form of government established in Galveston, Texas
1902	• President Roosevelt settles coal strike

1903	• National Women's Trade Union League founded
	• Roosevelt orders male Indians on reservations to cut hair
1906	• Meat Inspection Act and Pure Food and Drug Act
1908	• Race riot in Springfield, Illinois
1909	• National Association for the Advancement of Colored People founded
1910	• President Taft fires Gifford Pinchot
1912	• Roosevelt forms Progressive Party
	• Children's Bureau of the Department of Commerce and Labor established
1913	• Sixteenth Amendment (graduated income tax) ratified
	• Federal Reserve System created
1914	• Harrison Narcotics Control Act
	• Federal Trade Commission created Clayton Antitrust Act
1916	• Keating-Owen Act
	• Workmen's Compensation Act
1919	• Eighteenth Amendment (prohibition) ratified
1920	• Nineteenth Amendment (women's vote) ratified

20

Empire, Wars, and Pandemic

1898–1919

LEARNING OBJECTIVES

After reading this chapter you will be able to:

- Analyze the reasons behind U.S. imperialism in the 1890s and early twentieth century.

- Compare the interventions in Cuba and the Philippines and their effects on U.S. attitudes toward nation building.

- Compare Roosevelt's "big stick" diplomacy, Taft's dollar diplomacy, and Wilson's moral diplomacy and identify their benefits and drawbacks.

- Summarize the reasons for U.S. intervention in World War I and evaluate their relative importance.

- Evaluate the domestic effects of World War I on U.S. economics, culture, politics, and public health.

COMPARING AMERICAN HISTORIES

Alfred Thayer Mahan came from a military family. Born in 1840, he grew up in West Point, New York, where his father served as dean of the faculty at the U.S. Military Academy. Seeking to emerge from his father's shadow, Alfred attended the U.S. Naval Academy, receiving his commission in 1861, just as the Civil War was getting under way. His wartime experience convinced him that the navy needed a dramatic overhaul.

After the war, Captain Mahan built his reputation as a military historian and strategist at the U.S. Naval War College. In 1890 he published *The Influence of Sea Power upon History,* in which he argued that great imperial powers in modern history had succeeded because they possessed strong navies and merchant marines. In his view, sea power had allowed these nations to defeat their enemies, conquer territories, and establish colonies. Appearing at a time when European nations were embarking on a new round of empire building, this book had an enormous influence on U.S. imperialists, including Theodore Roosevelt. Mahan's work reinforced the belief of men like Roosevelt that the long-term prospects of the United States depended on the acquisition of strategic outposts in Asia and the Caribbean that could guarantee U.S. access to overseas markets.

As the economic and strategic importance of the Caribbean grew in the minds of imperial strategists such as Mahan and Roosevelt, the Cuban freedom fighter **José Martí** developed a very different vision of the region's future. Born in 1853, Martí got involved in the fight for Cuban independence from Spain as a teenager. In 1869, at age seventeen, he was arrested for protest activities during a revolutionary uprising against Spain. Sentenced to six years of hard labor, Martí was released after six months and was forced into exile. He returned to Cuba in 1878, only to be arrested and deported again the following year.

Martí settled in the United States, and with other Cuban exiles, he continued to promote Cuban independence and the establishment of a democratic republic under the banner of the Cuban Revolutionary Party. He conceived of the idea of Cuba Libre (Free Cuba) not just as a struggle for political independence but also as a social revolution that would erase unfair distinctions based on race and class.

When Cubans once again rebelled against Spain in 1895, Martí returned to Cuba to fight alongside his comrades. On May 19, only three months after he had returned to Cuba, Martí died in battle. Cuba ultimately won its independence from Spain, but Martí's vision of Cuba Libre was only partially realized. In 1898 the United States intervened on the side of the Cuban rebels, guaranteeing their victory but not their freedom.

BY COMPARING THE AMERICAN HISTORIES of Alfred Thayer Mahan and José Martí, we see disparate understandings of the United States' relationship with the rest of the world. Up until the late nineteenth century, most Americans associated colonialism with the European powers and saw overseas expansion as incompatible with U.S. values. In this context, they shared Martí's point of view. The imperialism espoused by Mahan and others therefore represented a reversal of traditional U.S. attitudes. Supporters of U.S. imperialism saw the acquisition and control of overseas territories, by force if necessary, as essential to the protection of U.S. interests. This perspective would come to dominate U.S. foreign policy in the early twentieth century. Theodore Roosevelt and Woodrow Wilson, progressive presidents who sanctioned intervention in economic and moral issues at home, supported vigorous intervention in world affairs. Just as they used government power to institute economic, political, and social reforms at home, so too did many progressives advocate U.S. intervention to reshape world affairs. Although Roosevelt and Wilson differed in style and approach, in foreign affairs they asserted America's right to use its power to secure order and thwart revolution wherever U.S. interests were seen to be threatened. Having become a major power on the world stage in the early twentieth century, the United States chose to enter World War I, in which rival European alliances battled for imperial domination. The end of the war did not bring peace; indeed, the war helped spread a worldwide influenza pandemic.

The Awakening of Imperialism

In the decades following the Civil War, the U.S. government concentrated on set-tling the western territories, decimating Native Americans, and extracting the region's resources. In many ways, westward expansion and the conquest of Indians in the nineteenth century foreshadowed international expansion. Arguments based on racial superiority and the nation's duty to expand became justifications for expansion in North America and overseas. By the end of the nineteenth century sweeping eco-nomic, cultural, and social changes led many in the United States to conclude that the time had come for the country to assert its power beyond its borders. In 1893, the influential U.S. historian Frederick Jackson Turner argued that the ending of the frontier necessitated a "wider field" for the "exercise [of] American energy" and rein-vigorating the nation's political, economic, and cultural strengths. Convinced of the argument for empire advanced by Mahan and other imperialists, U.S. officials led the nation in a burst of overseas expansion from 1898 to 1904, in which the United States acquired Guam, Hawaii, the Philippines, and Puerto Rico; established a pro-tectorate in Cuba; and exercised force to build a canal through Panama. These gains paved the way for subsequent U.S. intervention in Haiti, the Dominican Republic, and Nicaragua.

The Economics of Expansion

The industrialization of the United States and the growth of corporate capitalism stimulated imperialist desires in the late nineteenth century. Throughout its early his-tory, the United States had sought overseas markets for exports. However, the impor-tance of exports to the U.S. economy increased dramatically in the second half of the nineteenth century, as industrialization gained momentum. In 1870 U.S. exports totaled $500 million. By 1910 the value of U.S. exports had increased threefold to $1.7 billion (Figure 20.1).

The bulk of U.S. exports went to the developed markets of Europe and Can-ada. Although the less economically advanced nations of Latin America and Asia did not have the same ability to buy U.S. products, businessmen still considered these regions—especially China, with its large population—as future markets for U.S. industries.

The desire to expand foreign markets remained a steady feature of U.S. busi-ness interests. The fear that the domestic market for manufactured goods was shrink-ing gave this expansionist hunger greater urgency. The fluctuating business cycle of boom and bust that characterized the economy in the 1870s and 1880s reached its

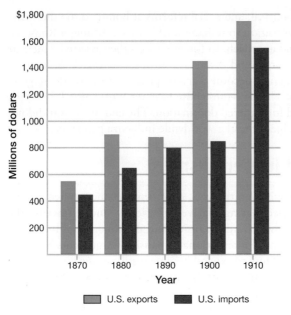

FIGURE 20.1   U.S. Exports and Imports, 1870–1910 As U.S. industrial power expanded at the end of the nineteenth century, exports increased dramatically. Between 1870 and 1910, U.S. exports more than tripled. Imports rose as well but were restrained by protective tariffs. How did the desire for overseas trade influence U.S. expansion overseas?

peak in the depression of the 1890s. The social unrest that accompanied this depression worried business and political leaders about the stability of the country. The way to sustain prosperity and contain radicalism, many businessmen agreed, was to find foreign markets for U.S. goods. Senator William Frye of Maine argued, "We must have the market [of China] or we shall have revolution."

Similar commercial ambitions led many in the United States to covet Hawaii. U.S. missionaries first visited the Hawaiian Islands in 1820. As missionaries tried to convert native peoples to Christianity, U.S. businessmen sought to establish plantations on the islands, especially to grow sugarcane. In exchange for duty-free access to the U.S. sugar market, white Hawaiians signed an agreement in 1887 that granted the United States exclusive rights to a naval base at Pearl Harbor in Honolulu.

The growing influence of white sugar planters on the islands alarmed native Hawaiians. In 1891 Queen Liliuokalani, a strong nationalist leader who voiced the slogan "Hawaii for the Hawaiians," sought to increase the power of the indigenous peoples she governed, at the expense of the sugar growers. In 1893 white plantation owners, with the cooperation of the U.S. ambassador to Hawaii and 150 U.S. marines, overthrew the queen's government. Once in command of the government, they entered into a treaty of annexation with the United States. However, President Grover Cleveland opposed annexation and withdrew the treaty. Nevertheless, planters remained in power and waited for a suitable opportunity to seek annexation.

Cultural Justifications for Imperialism

Imperialists linked overseas expansion to economic considerations but race was also a key component in their arguments for empire. Many in the United States and western Europe deemed themselves superior to nonwhite peoples of Latin America, Asia, and Africa. Buttressing their arguments with racist studies claiming to demonstrate scientifically the "racial superiority" of white Protestants, imperialists asserted a "natural right" of conquest and world domination.

Imperialists added an ethical dimension to this ideology by contending that "higher civilizations" had a duty to uplift inferior nations. In *Our Country* (1885), the Congregationalist minister Josiah Strong proclaimed the superiority of the Anglo-Saxon, or white northern European, race and the responsibility of the United States to spread its Christian way of life throughout the world. Secular intellectuals, such as historian John Fiske, praised the English race for settling the United States and predicted that English society and culture would become "predominant" in the less civilized parts of the globe.

As in Hawaii, Christian missionaries served as foot soldiers for the advancing U.S. commercial empire. In fact, there was often a clear connection between religious and commercial interests. For example, in 1895 industrialists John D. Rockefeller Jr. and Cyrus McCormick created the World Student Christian Federation, which dispatched more than five thousand young missionaries throughout the world, many of them women. China became a magnet for U.S. missionary activity. Many Americans hoped that, under missionary supervision, the Chinese would become consumers of both U.S. ideas and U.S. products.

Gender and Empire

Gender anxieties provided additional motivation for U.S. imperialism. In the late nineteenth century, with the Civil War long over, many in the United States worried that the rising generation of U.S. men lacked opportunities to test and strengthen their manhood. In 1897 Mississippi congressman John Sharp Williams lamented the waning of "the dominant spirit which controlled in this Republic [from 1776 to 1865] . . . one of honor, glory, chivalry, and patriotism." The depression of the 1890s hit working-class men hard, causing them to question their self-worth as they lost the ability to support their families. By embracing the imperialist project, they would regain their manly honor.

The growing presence of women as political activists in campaigns for suffrage and moral, humanitarian, and governmental reforms threatened male identity. Concerned over the feminization of politics, Alfred Thayer Mahan warned that women's suffrage would undermine the nation's military security because women lacked the will to use physical force. He asserted that giving women the vote would destroy the "constant practice of the past ages by which to men are assigned the outdoor rough action of life and to women that indoor sphere which we call the family."

Males in the United States could reassert their manhood by adopting a militant spirit. Known as **jingoists**, war enthusiasts such as Theodore Roosevelt and Alfred Thayer Mahan saw war as necessary to the development of a generation of men who could meet the challenges of the modern age. "No greater danger could befall civilization than the disappearance of the warlike spirit (I dare say war) among civilized men," Mahan asserted. "There are too many barbarians still in the world." Mahan and Roosevelt promoted naval power, and by 1900 the U.S. fleet contained seventeen battleships and six armored cruisers, making it the third most powerful navy in the world, up from twelfth place in 1880. Having built a powerful navy, the United States would soon find opportunities to use it.

REVIEW & RELATE

- What role did economic developments play in prompting calls for a U.S. empire? What role did social and cultural developments play?
- Why did the United States embark on building an empire in the 1890s and not decades earlier?

The War with Spain

The United States went to war with Spain over Cuba in 1898 because U.S. policymakers decided that Cuban independence from Spain was in the United States' economic and strategic interests. Victory over Spain, however, brought the United States much more than control over Cuba. In the peace negotiations following the war, the United States acquired a significant portion of Spain's overseas empire, turning the United States into a major imperial power. To Americans, the war has traditionally been called the Spanish-American War, but this term fails to take into account the significant role played by the Cuban people and subsequently by the Filipino people who were also under Spanish rule.

Revolution in Cuba

The Cuban War for Independence began in 1895 around the concept of *Cubanidad*—pride of nation. José Martí envisioned that this war of national liberation from Spain would provide land to impoverished peasants and offer genuine racial equality for the large Afro-Cuban population that had been liberated from slavery less than a decade earlier, in 1886. "Our goal," the revolutionary leader declared in 1892, "is not so much a mere political change as a good, sound, and just and equitable system." Black Cubans, such as Antonio Maceo, flocked to the revolutionary cause and constituted a significant portion of the senior ranks in the rebel army.

The insurgents fought a brilliant guerrilla war. Facing some 200,000 Spanish troops, 50,000 rebels ground them down in a war of attrition. Within eighteen months, the rebellion had spread across the island and garnered the support of all segments of the Cuban population. By the end of 1897, the Spanish government offered the rebels a series of reforms that would give the island home rule within the empire but not independence. Sensing victory, the insurgents held out for total separation to realize their vision of **Cuba Libre**, an independent Cuba with social and racial equality.

The revolutionaries had every reason to feel confident as they wore down Spanish troops. First, they had help from the climate. One-quarter of Spanish soldiers had contracted yellow fever, malaria, and other tropical illnesses and remained confined to hospitals. Second, mounting a successful counterinsurgency would have required far more troops than Spain could spare. Its forces were spread too thin around the globe to keep the empire intact. Finally, antiwar sentiment was mounting in Spain, and on January 12, 1898 Spanish troops mutinied in Havana. Speaking for many, a former president of Spain asserted: "Spain is exhausted. She must withdraw her troops and recognize Cuban independence before it is too late."

The War of 1898

With the Cuban insurgents on the verge of victory, President William McKinley favored military intervention as a way to increase U.S. control of postwar Cuba. By intervening before the Cubans won on their own, the United States could determine the postwar relationship and protect its vital interests in the Caribbean, including the private property rights of U.S. landowners in Cuba.

The U.S. press helped build support for U.S. intervention by framing the war as a matter of U.S. honor. William Randolph Hearst's *New York Journal* competed with Joseph Pulitzer's *New York World* to see which could provide the most lurid coverage of Spanish atrocities. Known disparagingly as **yellow journalism**, these sensationalist newspaper accounts aroused jingoistic outrage against Spain.

On February 15, 1898, the battleship *Maine*, anchored in Havana harbor, exploded, killing 266 U.S. sailors. Newspapers in the United States blamed Spain. The *World* shouted the rallying cry "Remember the *Maine*! To hell with Spain!" Assistant Secretary of the Navy Theodore Roosevelt seconded this sentiment by denouncing the explosion as a Spanish "act of treachery." Why the Spaniards would choose to blow up the *Maine* and provoke war with the United States while already losing to Cuba remained unanswered, but the incident was enough to turn U.S. opinion toward war.

On April 11, 1898, McKinley asked Congress to declare war against Spain. The declaration included an amendment proposed by Senator Henry M. Teller of Colorado declaring that Cuba "ought to be free and independent." Yet in endorsing independence, the war proclamation asserted the right of the United States to remain involved in Cuban affairs until it had achieved "pacification." On April 21, the United States officially went to war with Spain. In going to war, McKinley embarked on an imperialistic course that had been building since the early 1890s. The president signaled the broader expansionist concerns behind the war when, shortly after it began, he successfully steered a Hawaiian annexation treaty through Congress.

It was fortunate for the United States that the Cuban insurgents had seriously weakened Spanish forces before the U.S. fighters arrived. The U.S. army lacked sufficient strength to conquer Cuba on its own, and McKinley had to mobilize some 200,000 National Guard troops and assorted volunteers. Theodore Roosevelt resigned from his post as assistant secretary of the navy and organized his own regiment, called "Rough Riders." U.S. forces lacked battle experience; supplies were inadequate; their uniforms were not suited for the hot, humid climate of a Cuban summer; and the soldiers did not have immunity from tropical diseases.

African American soldiers, who made up about one-quarter of the troops, encountered racial discrimination and violence. As more and more black troops arrived in southern U.S. ports for deployment to Cuba, they faced increasingly hostile crowds. In Tampa, Florida, where troops gathered from all over the country to be transported to Cuba, racial tensions exploded on June 8. Intoxicated white soldiers from Ohio grabbed a two-year-old black boy from his mother and used him for target practice, shooting a bullet through his shirtsleeve. In retaliation, African American soldiers stormed into the streets and exchanged gunfire with whites, leaving three whites and twenty-seven black soldiers wounded.

African American Soldiers and the War of 1898   This photograph shows a group portrait of African American soldiers in Company E, 9th United States Volunteer Infantry who were sent to Cuba in the war against Spain. Black soldiers were recruited because it was mistakenly believed that they were "immune" to tropical diseases such as yellow fever, which killed white soldiers in Cuba. Black soldiers were organized in segregated units under the command of white officers, such as the one on the left side of the photograph.   Library of Congress, LC-DIG-ppmsca-54528

Despite military inexperience, logistical problems, and racial tensions, the United States quickly defeated the weakened Spanish military, and the war was over four months after it began. During this war, 460 U.S. soldiers died in combat, while more than 5,000 lost their lives to disease. The subsequent peace treaty ended Spanish rule in Cuba, ceded Puerto Rico and the Pacific island of Guam to the United States, and recognized U.S. occupation of the Philippines until the two countries could arrange a final settlement. U.S. foreign-policy strategists could now construct the empire that Mahan had envisioned.

The Pacification of Cuba

Although Congress had adopted the **Teller Amendment** in 1898 pledging Cuba's independence from Spain, President McKinley and his supporters insisted that Cuban self-rule would come only after pacification. Racial prejudice and cultural chauvinism blinded Americans to the contributions Cubans had made to defeat Spain. One U.S. officer reported to the *New York Times*: "The typical Cuban I encountered was a treacherous, lying, cowardly, thieving, worthless half-breed mongrel, born of a mongrel spawn of [Spain], crossed upon the fetches of darkest Africa and aboriginal America." José Martí may have been fighting for racial equality, but the U.S. government certainly was not.

U.S. officials presumed that Cuba was unfit to be independent and kept the island under U.S. military occupation until 1902. Cuba's transition to self-rule came with the adoption of a governing document based on the U.S. Constitution. However, the Cuban constitution came with strings attached. In March 1901, Congress passed the **Platt Amendment**, introduced by Senator Orville Platt of Connecticut, which limited Cuban sovereignty. The amendment prohibited the Cuban government from signing treaties with other nations without U.S. consent, permitted the United States to intervene in Cuba to preserve independence and remove threats to economic stability, and leased Guantánamo Bay to the United States as a naval base. U.S. officials pressured Cuban leaders to incorporate the Platt Amendment into their constitution. When U.S. occupation ended in 1902, Cuba was not fully independent.

The Philippine War

Before invading Cuba, the United States had won a significant battle against Spain on the other side of the world. At the outset of the war, the U.S. Pacific Fleet, under the command of Commodore George Dewey, attacked Spanish forces in their colony of the Philippines. Dewey defeated the Spanish flotilla in Manila Bay on May 1, 1898. Two and a half months later, U.S. troops followed up with an invasion of Manila, and Spanish forces promptly surrendered (Map 20.1).

While pacifying Cuba, the U.S. government had to decide what action to take in the Philippines. Imperialists viewed U.S. control of the islands as an important step forward in the quest for entry into the China market. The Philippines could serve as a naval station for the merchant marine and the navy to safeguard potential trade with the Asian mainland. Also, President McKinley believed that if the United States did not act, another European power would take Spain's place, something he thought would be "bad business and deplorable."

With this in mind, McKinley decided to annex the Philippines. As with Cuba, McKinley and most U.S. citizens believed that nonwhite Filipinos were not yet capable of self-government. Thus, McKinley set out "to educate the Filipinos, and uplift and Christianize them." As was often the case with imperialism, assumptions about racial superiority were used as justification for the pursuit of economic and strategic advantage.

The president's plan ran into vigorous opposition. Anti-imperialists in Congress took a strong stand against annexing the Philippines. Their cause drew support from such prominent Americans as industrialist Andrew Carnegie, social reformer Jane Addams, writer Mark Twain, and labor organizer Samuel Gompers, all of whom joined the **Anti-Imperialist League**, founded in November 1898. Progressives like Addams who were committed to humanitarian reforms at home questioned whether the United States should exploit colonial people overseas. Union leaders feared that annexation would prompt the migration of cheap laborers into the country and undercut wages. Others worried about the financial costs of supporting military forces across the Pacific. Most anti-imperialists had racial reasons for rejecting the

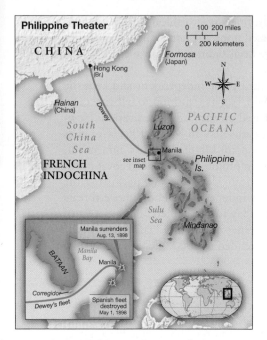

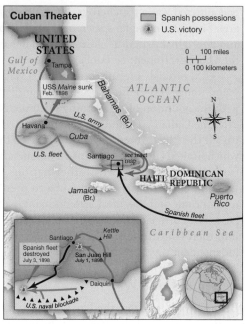

MAP 20.1   The War of 1898

The United States and Spain fought the War of 1898 (sometimes referred to as the Spanish-American War) on two fronts—the Philippines and Cuba. Naval forces led by Commodore George Dewey made the difference in the U.S. victory by defeating the Spaniards first in Manila Bay and then off the coast of Cuba. In Cuba, rebels had seriously weakened the Spanish military before U.S. ground troops secured victory.

treaty. Like imperialists, they considered Asians to be inferior to Europeans. In fact, many anti-imperialists held an even dimmer view of the capabilities of people of color than did their opponents, rejecting the notion that Filipinos could be "civilized" under U.S. tutelage.

Despite this opposition, McKinley and the imperialists won out. Approval of the treaty annexing the Philippines in 1898 marked the beginning of problems for the United States. As in Cuba, a popular revolt had preceded U.S. occupation. At first, Filipino people welcomed the Americans as liberators, but once it became clear that U.S. rule would simply replace Spanish rule, the Filipinos rebelled again. Led by Emilio Aguinaldo, rebel forces fought back against the 70,000 U.S. troops sent by this latest colonial power. The Filipino insurgents used guerilla tactics of raids, ambushes, and sabotage against the U.S. army.

U.S. forces responded in kind, adopting harsh methods to suppress the uprising. General Jacob H. Smith ordered his troops to "kill and burn, and the more you kill and burn, the better you will please me" (sentiments that caused a public outcry when made known back in the United States, and which led to his court-martial). U.S. counterinsurgency efforts, which indiscriminately targeted combatants and civilians alike, alienated the native population. An estimated 200,000 Filipino civilians died between 1899 and 1902. The Americans' taste for war and sacrifice quickly waned, as nearly 5,000 Americans died in the Philippine War, far more combat deaths than in Cuba. Anti-imperialists claimed that the United States acted as a bully, taking the position of "a strong man" fighting against "a weak and puny child."

Amid growing casualties on the battlefield and antiwar sentiment at home, the conflict ended with a U.S. military victory. In March 1901, U.S. forces captured Aguinaldo and broke the back of the rebellion. Exhausted, the Filipino leader asked his comrades to lay down their arms. In July 1901, McKinley appointed Judge William Howard Taft of Ohio as the first civilian governor to oversee the government of the Philippines. For the next forty-five years, except for a brief period of Japanese rule during World War II, the United States remained in control of the islands.

REVIEW & RELATE	• Why did the United States go to war with Spain in 1898? • In what ways did the War of 1898 mark a turning point in the relationship between the United States and the rest of the world?

Extending U.S. Imperialism, 1899–1913

The War of 1898 turned the United States into an imperial nation. Once the war was over, and with its newly acquired empire in place, the United States sought to achieve even greater global power. President Theodore Roosevelt and his successors achieved Captain Mahan's dream of building a Central American canal and wielded U.S. military and financial might in the Caribbean with little restraint. At the same time, the United States took a more active role in Asian affairs.

Theodore Roosevelt and "Big Stick" Diplomacy

After President McKinley was assassinated in 1901, Vice President Theodore Roosevelt succeeded him as president. A progressive reformer at home, Roosevelt advocated using military power to protect U.S. commercial and strategic interests as well as to preserve international order. "It is contemptible for a nation, as for an individual," Roosevelt instructed Congress, "[to] proclaim its purposes, or to take positions which are ridiculous if unsupported by potential force, and then to refuse to provide this force." This Progressive Era interventionist, inspired by Captain Mahan's writings, welcomed his nation's new role as an international policeman.

To fulfill his international agenda, Roosevelt sought to demonstrate U.S. might and preserve order in the Caribbean and Central and South America. The building of the Panama Canal provides a case in point. Mahan considered a canal across Central America as vital because it would provide faster access to Asian markets and improve the U.S. navy's ability to patrol two oceans effectively. The United States took a step toward realizing Mahan's goal in 1901, when it signed the Hay-Pauncefote Treaty with Britain, granting the United States the right to construct such a canal. A French company had already begun construction at a site in Panama and had completed two-fifths of the operation; when it ran out of money, it sold its holdings to the United States.

Before the United States could resume building the canal, it had to negotiate with the South American country of Colombia, which controlled Panama. Secretary of State John Hay and Colombian representatives reached an agreement highly favorable to the United States, which the Colombian government refused to ratify. When Colombia held out for a higher price, Roosevelt accused the Colombians of being "utterly incapable of keeping order" in Panama and declared that transit across Panama was vital to world commerce. In 1903 the president supported a pro-U.S. uprising by sending warships into the harbor of Panama City, an action that prevented the Colombians from quashing the insurrection. Roosevelt signed a treaty with the new government of Panama granting the United States the right to build the canal and exercise "power and authority" over it. In 1914, under U.S. control, the Panama Canal opened to sea traffic.

With the United States controlling Cuba, the Panama Canal, and Puerto Rico, President Roosevelt intended to deter any threats to U.S. power in the region. The economic instability of Central American and Caribbean nations gave Roosevelt the opportunity to brandish what he called a "big stick" to keep these countries in check and prevent intervention by European powers also interested in the area. In 1904, when the government of the Dominican Republic was teetering on the edge of bankruptcy and threatened to default on $22 million in European loans, Roosevelt sprang into action. He announced U.S. opposition to any foreign intervention to reclaim debts, a position that echoed the principles of the Monroe Doctrine, which in 1823 proclaimed that the United States would not tolerate outside intervention in the Western Hemisphere. Roosevelt added his own corollary to the Monroe Doctrine by affirming the right of the United States to intervene in the internal affairs of any country in Latin America or the Caribbean that displayed "chronic wrong-doing" and could not preserve order and manage its own affairs. The **Roosevelt Corollary** proclaimed that the countries of Central America and the Caribbean had to behave according to U.S. wishes or face American military invasion.

Opening the Door in China

Roosevelt displayed U.S. power in other parts of the world. His major concern was protecting the **Open Door** policy in China that his predecessor McKinley had engineered to secure naval access to the Chinese market. By 1900 European powers had already dominated foreign access to Chinese markets, leaving scant room for newcomers. When the United States sent 2,500 troops to China in August 1900 to help quell a nationalist rebellion against foreign involvement known as the Boxer uprising, European competitors in return were compelled to allow the United States free trade access to China.

In 1904 the Russian invasion of the northern Chinese province of Manchuria prompted the Japanese to attack the Russian fleet. Roosevelt admired Japanese military prowess, but he worried that if Japan succeeded in driving the Russians out of the area, it would cause "a real shifting of equilibrium as far as the white races are concerned." To prevent that from happening, Roosevelt convened a peace conference in Portsmouth, New Hampshire, in 1905. Under the agreement reached at the conference, Japan received control over Korea and parts of Manchuria but pledged to support the United States' Open Door policy. In 1906 the president sent sixteen U.S. battleships on a trip around the globe in a show of force meant to demonstrate that the United States was serious about taking its place as a premier world power.

When Roosevelt's secretary of war, William Howard Taft, became president (1909–1913), he continued his predecessor's foreign policy with slight modification. Proclaiming that he would rather substitute "dollars for bullets," Taft encouraged private bankers to invest money in the Caribbean and Central America, a policy known as **dollar diplomacy**.

Yet Taft did not rely on financial influence alone. He dispatched more than 2,000 U.S. troops to the region to guarantee economic stability. In 1909 when rebels in Nicaragua threatened. U.S. fruit and mining companies in the nation, Taft sent in U.S. marines to police the country, deter further uprisings, and oversee the economy. They remained there for another twenty-five years, thereby placing Nicaragua under U.S. "protection."

| REVIEW & RELATE | • How did the United States assert its influence and control over Latin America in the early twentieth century? |
| | • How did U.S. policies in Latin America mirror U.S. policies in Asia? |

Wilson and American Foreign Policy, 1912–1917

When Woodrow Wilson became president in 1913, he pledged to open a new chapter in the United States' relations with Latin America and the rest of the world. Disdaining power politics and the use of force, Wilson vowed to place diplomacy and moral persuasion at the center of U.S. foreign policy. Despite Wilson's stated commitment to the peaceful resolution of international issues, during his presidency the U.S. military intervened repeatedly in Latin America, and U.S. troops fought on European soil in the global conflict that contemporaries called the Great War.

Diplomacy and War

Though he voiced a preference for moral diplomacy, Wilson preserved the U.S. sphere of influence in the Caribbean using much the same methods as had Roosevelt and Taft. To protect U.S. investments, the president sent marines to Haiti in 1915, to the Dominican Republic in 1916, and to Cuba in 1917.

The most serious challenge to Wilson's diplomacy came in Mexico. The **Mexican revolution** in 1911 spawned a civil war among various insurgent factions. The resulting instability threatened U.S. interests in Mexico, particularly oil. When Mexicans refused to accept Wilson's demands to install leaders he considered "good men," Wilson withdrew diplomatic recognition from Mexico. In a disastrous attempt to influence Mexican politics, Wilson sent the U.S. navy to the port of Veracruz on April 22, 1914, leading to a bloody clash that killed 19 Americans and 126 Mexicans. The situation worsened after Wilson first supported and then turned against one of the rebel competitors for power in Mexico, General Francisco "Pancho" Villa. In response to this betrayal, Villa and 1,500 troops rode across the border and attacked the town of Columbus, New Mexico. In July 1916, Wilson ordered General John Pershing to send 10,000 army troops into Mexico in an attempt to capture Villa. The operation was a complete failure that further angered Mexican leaders and confirmed their sense that Wilson had no respect for Mexican sovereignty.

At the same time as the situation in Mexico was deteriorating, a more serious problem was developing in Europe. On June 28, 1914, a Serbian nationalist, intending to strike a blow against Austria-Hungary, assassinated the Austrian archduke Franz Ferdinand in Sarajevo, the capital of the province of Bosnia. This terrorist attack plunged Europe into a world war. On August 4, 1914, the Central Powers — Germany, the Ottoman empire, and Austria-Hungary — officially declared war against the Allies — Great Britain, France, and Russia. (Italy joined the Allies in 1915.)

For the first three years of the Great War, Wilson kept the United States neutral. Though privately he supported the British, the president urged Americans to remain "impartial in thought as well as action." Peace activists sought to keep Wilson to his word. In 1915 women reformers and suffragists such as Jane Addams and Carrie Chapman Catt organized the Women's Peace Party to keep the United States out of the war.

Wilson faced two key problems in maintaining neutrality. First, the United States had closer and more important economic ties with the Allies than with the Central Powers, a disparity that would only grow as the war went on. The Allies purchased more than $750 million in U.S. goods in 1914, a figure that quadrupled over the next three years. By contrast, the Germans bought approximately $350 million worth of U.S. products in 1914; by 1917 the figure had shrunk to $30 million. When the Allies did not have the funds to pay for U.S. goods, they sought loans from private bankers. Initially, the Wilson administration resisted such requests. In 1915, however, Wilson reversed course. Concerned that failure to keep up the prewar level of commerce with the Allies would hurt the country economically, the president authorized private loans. The gap in financial transactions with the rival war powers grew even wider; by 1917 U.S. bankers had loaned the Allies $2.2 billion, compared with just $27 million to Germany.

The second problem facing Wilson arose from Great Britain's and Germany's differing war strategies. As the superior naval power, Britain established a blockade of the North Sea to quarantine Germany and starve it into submission. The British navy violated international law by mining the waters to bottle up the German fleet and keep foreign ships from supplying Germany with food and medicines. Although Wilson protested this treatment, he did so weakly. He believed that the British could pay compensation for such violations of international law after the war.

Confronting a strangling blockade, Germany depended on the newly developed U-boat (*Unterseeboot*, or submarine) to counter the British navy. In February 1915, Germany declared a blockade of the British Isles and warned citizens of neutral nations to stay off British ships in the area. U-boats, which were lighter and sleeker than British battleships, relied on surprise. This strategy violated the rules of engagement under international maritime law, which required belligerent ships to allow civilians to leave passenger liners and cargo ships before firing. The British complicated the situation for the Germans by flying flags of neutral countries on merchant vessels and arming them with small "defensive" weapons. If U-boats played by the rules and surfaced before inspecting merchant ships, they risked being blown out of the water by disguised enemy guns.

Under these circumstances, U.S. neutrality could not last long. On May 15, 1915, catastrophe struck. Without surfacing and identifying itself, a German submarine off the Irish coast attacked the British luxury liner *Lusitania*, which had departed from New York City en route to England. Although the ship's stated objective was to provide passengers with transport, its cargo contained a large supply of ammunition for British weapons. The U-boat's torpedoes rapidly sank the ship, killing 1,198 people, including 128 Americans.

Outraged Americans called on the president to respond; some, including Theodore Roosevelt, advocated the immediate use of military force. Despite his pro-British sentiments, Wilson resisted going to war. Instead, he held the Germans in "strict accountability" for their action. Wilson demanded that Germany refrain from further attacks against passenger liners and offer a financial settlement to the *Lusitania*'s survivors. Unwilling to risk war with the United States, Germany consented.

Wilson had only delayed the United States' entry into the war. By pursuing a policy of neutrality that treated the combatants unequally and by insisting that Americans had a right to travel on the ships of belligerent nations, the president diminished the chance that the United States would stay out of the war.

Throughout 1916, Wilson pursued two separate but interrelated policies that embodied the ambivalence that he and the U.S. people shared about the war. On the one hand, with Germany alternating between continued U-boat attacks and apologies, the president sought to build the country's military preparedness in the event of war. He signed into law the National Defense Act, which increased the size of the army, navy, and National Guard. On the other hand, with U.S. public opinion divided on the Great War, Wilson chose to run for reelection as a peace candidate. The Democrats adopted the slogan "He kept us out of war" and also emphasized the president's substantial record of progressive reform. Wilson won a narrow victory against Charles Evans Hughes, the former governor of New York, who wavered between advocating peace and criticizing Wilson for not sufficiently supporting the Allies.

Making the World Safe for Democracy

As 1917 dawned, the bloody war dragged on. Neither side wanted a negotiated peace because each counted on victory to gain sufficient territory and financial compensation to justify the great sacrifices in human lives and materiel caused by the conflict. Nevertheless, Wilson tried to persuade the belligerents to abandon the battlefield for the bargaining table. On January 22, 1917, he declared that the world needed a "peace without victory," one based on self-determination, freedom of the seas, respect for international law, and the end of hostile alliances.

Germany quickly rejected Wilson's proposal. The United States had never been truly neutral, and Germany's leaders saw no reason to believe that the situation would change. In 1915 and again in 1916, to prevent the United States from entering the war, Germany had pledged to refrain from using its U-boats against passenger and merchant ships. However, on February 1, 1917 the Germans changed course and resumed unrestricted submarine warfare, calculating that they could defeat the Allies before the United States declared war. In response, Wilson used his executive power to arm merchant ships, bringing the United States one step closer to war.

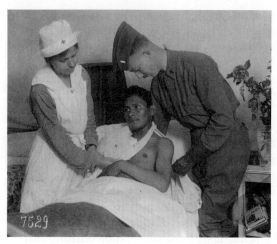

An American Nurse Comforts a Wounded Soldier, 1918 Women played important roles as nurses and ambulance drivers in combat areas during World War I. The nurse in this photograph, Ethel Goede, attends a wounded American soldier from the Choctaw Nation in Oklahoma. The nurse and Army surgeon, standing at the right, worked in the American Military Hospital No. 5 at Auteuil, France, a tent hospital put up and supported by the American Red Cross, which recruited women volunteer nurses. Library of Congress, LC-A6199-7529

The country moved even closer to war after the **Zimmermann telegram** became public. On February 24, the British turned over to Wilson an intercepted message from Arthur Zimmermann, the German foreign minister, to the Mexican government. The note revealed that Germany had offered Mexico an alliance in the event that the United States joined the Allies. If the Central Powers won, Mexico would receive the territory it had lost to the United States in the mid-nineteenth century—Texas, New Mexico, and Arizona. When U.S. newspapers broke the story several days later, it inflamed public opinion and provided the Wilson administration another reason to fear a German victory.

In late February and March, German U-boats sank several armed U.S. merchant ships, and on April 2, 1917 President Wilson asked Congress to declare war against Germany and the other Central Powers. After four days of vigorous debate led by opponents of the war—including Senator Robert M. La Follette of Wisconsin and the first female elected representative, Jeanette P. Rankin from Montana—Congress voted to approve the war resolution.

For three years, President Wilson had resisted calls for war. However, Wilson finally decided that only by going to war would he be able to ensure that the United States played a role in shaping the peace. "The world must be made safe for democracy," he informed Congress in his war message, and he had concluded that the only way to guarantee this outcome was by helping to defeat Germany. This need became even more urgent when in November 1917 the Russian Revolution installed a Bolshevik (Communist) regime that negotiated a separate peace with the Central Powers (Map 20.2).

It would take a while for Americans to make their presence felt in Europe. The United States needed a large army, which it created through the draft. The Selective Service Act of 1917 conscripted 3 million men by war's end. Mobilizing such a large force required substantial time, and the **American Expeditionary Forces (AEF)**, established in 1917 under General Pershing, did not make much of an impact until 1918. Before then, U.S. warships joined the British in escorting merchant vessels, combating German submarines, and laying mines in the North Sea. The United States also provided crucial funding and supplies to the Allies as their reserves became depleted.

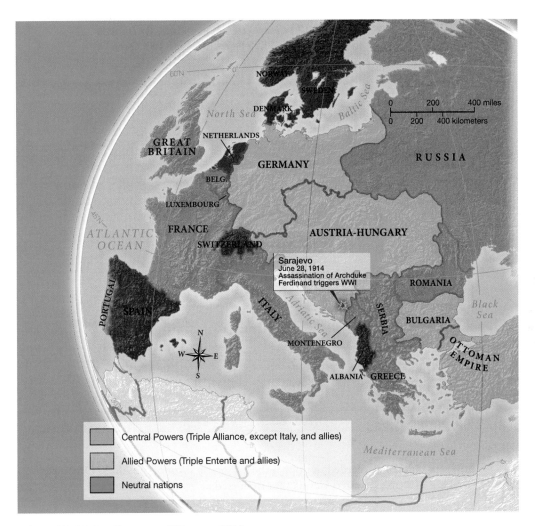

MAP 20.2   **European Alliances, 1914**
Pre-war alliances helped precipitate World War I. The assassination of Archduke Ferdinand of Austria-Hungry by a Serbian revolutionary in Sarajevo set the countries in the Austro-Hungarian and German-led Central Alliance against the British-French-Russian Entente, as the map shows.

The AEF finally began to make an impact in Europe in May 1918. From May through September, more than 1 million U.S. troops helped the Allies repel German offensives in northern France near the Belgian border. One momentous battle in the Argonne Forest lasted two months until the Allies broke through enemy lines and pushed toward Germany. Nearly 50,000 U.S. troops died in the fierce fighting, and another 230,000 were injured (Table 20.1). Like their European counterparts, who suffered a staggering 8 to 10 million casualties, Americans experienced the horrors of war magnified by new technology. Dug into filthy trenches, soldiers dodged rapid machine-gun fire, heavy artillery explosions, and poison gas shells. In the end,

TABLE 20.1	WORLD WAR I CASUALTIES PERCENTAGE OF DEATHS IN MOBILIZED FORCES IN WORLD WAR I BY COUNTRY		
Country	**Total Mobilized Forces**	**Deaths**	**Percentage**
Allied Powers			
Romania	750,000	335,706	45%
Russia	12,000,000	1,700,000	14%
Canada	424,000	56,694	14%
Italy	5,615,000	650,000	12%
British Empire	8,904,467	908,307	10%
Portugal	100,000	7,222	7%
Serbia	707,343	45,000	6%
Belgium	267,000	13,716	5%
United States	4,734,991	116,516	2%
Greece	230,000	5,000	2%
Japan	800,000	300	.03%
Central Powers			
Germany	11,000,000	1,773,700	16%
Austria-Hungary	7,800,000	1,200,000	15%
Turkey	2,850,000	325,000	11%
Bulgaria	1,200,000	87,500	7%

however, the AEF succeeded in tipping the balance in favor of the Allies. On November 11, 1918, an exhausted Germany surrendered.

REVIEW & RELATE
- In what ways, if any, did President Wilson's approach to Latin American affairs differ from that of his predecessors?
- Why did President Wilson find it so difficult to keep the United States out of World War I?

Fighting the War at Home

Modern global warfare required full mobilization at home. In preparing to support the war effort, the country drew on recent experience. The progressives' passion for organization, expertise, efficiency, and moralistic control was harnessed to the effort of placing the economy on a wartime footing and rallying the American people behind the war. In the process, the government gained unprecedented control over American life. The war effort also produced unforeseen economic and political opportunities.

Government by Commission

Progressives had relied on government commissions to regulate business practices as well as health and safety standards. In July 1917 the Wilson administration followed suit by establishing the **War Industries Board (WIB)** to supervise the purchase of military supplies and to gear up private enterprise to meet demand. The WIB was largely ineffective until the president found the right man to lead it. In March 1918, he chose Wall Street financier Bernard Baruch, who recruited staff from business enterprises that the board regulated. Baruch prodded businesses into compliance mainly by offering lucrative contracts rather than by coercion. Ultimately, the WIB created a government partnership with the corporate sector that would last beyond the war.

Labor also experienced significant gains through government regulation. Shortages of workers and an outbreak of strikes hampered the war effort. In April 1918, Wilson created the **National War Labor Board (NWLB)** to settle labor disputes. The agency consisted of representatives from unions, corporations, and the public. In exchange for obtaining a "no strike pledge" from organized labor, the NWLB supported an eight-hour workday with time-and-a-half pay for overtime, labor's right to collective bargaining, and equal pay for equal work by women.

While the NWLB fell short of reaching this last goal, the war employed more than a million women who had not held jobs before. As military and government services expanded, women found greater opportunities as telephone operators, nurses, and clerical workers. At the same time, the number of women employed as domestic servants declined. Women took over formerly male jobs driving street-cars, delivering ice, assembling airplane motors, operating drill presses, oiling rail-road engines, and welding parts. Yet women's incomes continued to lag significantly behind those of men performing the same tasks.

Americans experienced the expanding scope of government intervention most directly through the efforts of three new agencies that regulated consumption and travel. Wilson appointed Herbert Hoover to head the Food Administration. Hoover sought to increase the military and civilian food supply mainly through voluntary conservation measures. He generated a massive publicity campaign urging Americans to adopt "wheatless Mondays," "meatless Tuesdays," and "porkless Thursdays and Saturdays." The government also mobilized schoolchildren to plant vegetable gardens to increase food production for the home front.

Consumers saved gas and oil under the prodding of the Fuel Administration. The agency encouraged fuel "holidays" along the line of Hoover's voluntary restrictions and created daylight savings time to conserve fuel by adding an extra hour of sunlight to the end of the workday. The Fuel Administration also offered higher prices to coal companies to increase productivity. The Railroad Administration acted more forcefully than most other agencies. Troop and supply shipments depended on the efficient operation of the railways. The administration controlled the railroads during the war, coordinating train schedules, overseeing terminals and regulating ticket prices, upgrading tracks, and raising workers' wages.

Winning Hearts and Minds

Faced with significant antiwar sentiment, Wilson waged a campaign to rally support for his aims and to stimulate patriotic fervor. To generate enthusiasm and ensure loyalty, the president appointed journalist George Creel to head the **Committee on Public Information (CPI)**, which focused on generating propaganda. Creel recruited a vast network of lecturers to speak throughout the country and spread patriotic messages. The committee coordinated rallies to sell bonds and raise money to fund the war. The CPI persuaded reporters to censor their war coverage, and most agreed in order to avoid government intervention. The agency helped produce films depicting the Allies as heroic saviors of humanity and the Central Powers as savage beasts. The CPI also distributed colorful and sometimes lurid posters emphasizing the depravity of the enemy and the nation's moral responsibility to defeat the Central Powers.

Propaganda did not prove sufficient, however, and Americans remained deeply divided about the war. To suppress dissent, Congress passed the Espionage Act in 1917 and the Sedition Act a year later. Both limited freedom of speech by criminalizing certain forms of expression. The **Espionage Act** prohibited antiwar activities, including interfering with the draft. It also banned the mailing of publications

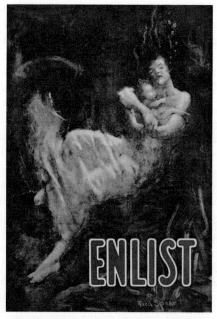

World War I Posters Many of the wartime posters were aimed at rallying women to provide help on the home front and mobilizing men to defend women by joining the military. The poster on the left was put out by the Young Women's Christian Association (YWCA) and the one at the right, illustrated by Fred Spear for the Boston Committee of Public Safety, shows a mother and her infant drowning with the sinking of the Lusitania in 1915. Left: Marka/Universal Images Group via Getty Images; right: Gift of John T. Spaulding/Bridgeman Images

advocating forcible interference with any laws. The **Sedition Act** punished individuals who expressed beliefs disloyal or abusive to the U.S. government, flag, or military uniform. Of the slightly more than two thousand prosecutions under these laws, only a handful concerned charges of actual sabotage or espionage. Most defendants brought to trial were critics who merely spoke out against the war. In 1918, for telling a crowd that the military draft was a form of slavery, the Socialist Party's Eugene V. Debs was tried, convicted, and sentenced to ten years under the Espionage Act. (President Warren G. Harding pardoned Debs in 1921.) The Justice Department also went after the Industrial Workers of the World (IWW), which continued to initiate labor strikes during the war. The government broke into the offices of the IWW, ransacked the group's files for evidence of disloyalty, and arrested more than 130 members.

Government efforts to promote national unity and punish those who did not conform prompted local communities to enforce "one hundred percent Americanism." Civic groups banned the playing of German music and operas from concert halls, and schools prohibited teaching the German language. Foods with German origins were renamed—sauerkraut became "liberty cabbage," and hamburgers became "liberty sandwiches." Such sentiments were expressed in a more sinister fashion when mobs assaulted German Americans.

Prejudice toward German Americans was further inflamed by the formation of the **American Protective League (APL)**, a quasi-official association endorsed by the Justice Department. Consisting of 200,000 chapters throughout the country, the APL employed individuals to spy on German residents suspected of disloyal behavior. Most often, APL agents found little more than German immigrants who merely retained attachments to family and friends in their homeland.

Anti-immigrant bias, shared by many progressive reformers, flourished in other ways as well. The effort to conserve manpower and grain supplies bolstered the impulse to control standards of moral behavior, particularly those associated with immigrants, such as drinking. This anti-immigrant prejudice in part explains the ratification of the Eighteenth Amendment in 1919, prohibiting the sale of all alcoholic beverages. Yet not all the moral indignation unleashed by the war resulted in restriction of freedom. After considerable wartime protest and lobbying, women suffragists succeeded in securing the right to vote.

President Wilson's goal "to make the world safe for democracy" appealed to oppressed racial minorities. They hoped the war would push the United States to live up to its rhetoric and extend freedom at home. Nearly 400,000 African Americans served in the war and more than 40,000 saw combat, but most were assigned to service units and worked in menial jobs. The army remained segregated, and few black officers commanded troops. Despite this discrimination, W. E. B. Du Bois echoed African Americans' hope that their patriotism would be rewarded at the war's end: "We of the colored race have no ordinary interest in the outcome."

The same held true for American Indians. More than ten thousand Indians participated in the war. Recruited from Arizona, Montana, and New York, they fought in the major battles in France and Belgium. Unlike African Americans, they did not fight in segregated units and saw action as scouts and combat soldiers. They gained recognition by communicating messages in their native languages to confuse the

Germans listening in. Aware of the contradiction between their poor treatment historically by the U.S. government and the nation's democratic war aims, they expected that their wartime patriotism would bring them a greater measure of justice. However, like African Americans, they would be disappointed.

1918–1919 Influenza Pandemic

While fighting the war, the United States had to battle a global outbreak of deadly influenza. A highly contagious virus transmitted through the air, the disease infected around 500 million people, or about one-third of the world's population. The flu killed an estimated 50 million people globally and approximately 675,000 in the U.S. In many American cities and towns, bodies piled up due to a shortage of morticians, gravediggers, and coffins. Funerals were confined to fifteen minutes.

The origin of the influenza **pandemic** (a disease prevalent in a country, continent, or the world) remains a mystery, but at the time it was considered to have begun in Spain. Classified as an H1N1 virus, influenza came in three waves, starting in March 1918. This outbreak was relatively mild, but during the fall season a much more severe contagion struck. The third, less serious, wave broke out in the winter of 1918–1919, and by spring it had largely run its course. The virus briefly returned a year later but with comparatively little effect. The pandemic hit those in the twenty-to-forty age range especially hard, more so than in the very young and elderly. The majority of deaths occurred from pneumonia.

More American soldiers died from the flu than were killed on battlefields during World War I. Approximately 40 percent of men in the Navy and 36 percent in the Army became ill. In fact, soldiers helped spread the virus throughout Europe and the U.S. Housed in crowded military bases and transported in congested ships heading overseas and back, troops easily transmitted the disease to each other and to civilians. One of the first recorded outbreaks of the virus took place in Kansas at Camp Funston. On March 4, 1918, the first soldier reported ill at this Army training camp for soldiers preparing for assignment in Europe. Within two weeks, over 1,000 soldiers went to the hospital and 38 died. Those who survived carried the disease within the United States and to Europe as part of the American Expeditionary Force. Civilians became readily infected, including President Woodrow Wilson, who survived, and Friedrich Trump, the future president's grandfather, who did not.

African Americans were more susceptible to illnesses such as tuberculosis and pneumonia and their life expectancy was lower than whites. During the era of Jim Crow, health care for blacks was separate and unequal, leaving them at greater risk to disease. Surprisingly then, reports from black communities and public health officials indicate that African Americans contracted influenza at a lower rate than did whites for reasons that remain unclear. In contrast, the effects of the pandemic varied among Native American tribes. Less than 1 percent of Indians died from influenza in Oklahoma, Wyoming, Kansas, and Michigan, whereas 4 to 6 percent perished from the disease in Arizona, Colorado, Mississippi, New Mexico, and Utah. Navajo communities in particular were seriously affected. Despite the variations, Indians suffered heavily because the federal government failed to provide adequate health care on the reservations. Higher death rates also occurred among newly arrived immigrants from eastern and southern Europe and Mexico.

The pandemic placed a severe strain on the health care system. Many physicians and nurses were serving in the military, and medical students had to take their place. The Red Cross created a National Committee on Influenza to gather medical supplies and mobilize nurses and volunteers. President Wilson never spoke publicly about the virus nor did the U.S. Public Health Service provide much leadership; the surgeon general merely warned people to stay out of crowds and advised them to breathe fresh air. This left cities and towns with the prime responsibility of dealing with the pandemic. Local public health departments distributed masks to be worn in public, and San Francisco levied a $5 fine on individuals caught not wearing a mask. St. Louis initiated quarantines and shut down schools, churches, and theaters. In New York City, Boy Scout troops patrolled the streets warning residents not to spit on the sidewalk. In contrast, Philadelphia allowed a massive war bond parade in September 1918, causing an eruption in the number of infections and resulting in over 12,000 deaths.

Although research scientists and physicians worked hard to develop a vaccine and treatments for the flu, they did not succeed. Doctors tried almost anything they could think of to treat the ill; most prescribed aspirin and some chose quinine (used to treat malaria) or injected patients with typhoid vaccine. Other approaches degenerated into quackery, such as advising patients to sniff boric acid and baking soda to flush out the nasal cavities or ingesting hydrogen peroxide, iodine, and even low doses of toxic strychnine on the theory that some form of "internal disinfection" was necessary to cleanse the body. Whereas President Wilson had adapted progressive techniques of efficiency and order to mobilize Americans on the home front during the war, his administration failed to lead the way in applying similar methods against the pandemic.

Waging Peace

In January 1918, just before the onset of the pandemic and ten months before the war ended, President Wilson presented Congress with his plan for peace. Wilson bundled his ideas in the **Fourteen Points**, principles that he hoped would prevent future wars. Based on his assessment of the causes of the Great War, Wilson envisioned a generous peace treaty that included freedom of the seas, open diplomacy and the abolition of secret treaties, free trade, self-determination for colonial subjects, and a reduction in military spending. More important than any specific measure, Wilson's proposal hinged on the creation of the **League of Nations**, a body of large and small nations that would guarantee peaceful resolution of disputes and back up decisions through collective action, including the use of military force as a last resort.

Following the armistice that ended the war on November 11, 1918, Wilson personally took his message to the Paris Peace Conference, the postwar meeting of the victorious Allied nations that would set the terms of the peace. The first sitting president to travel overseas, Wilson was greeted in Paris by joyous crowds. While in Paris, Wilson contracted influenza from which he never fully recovered.

For nearly six months, Wilson tried to convince reluctant Allied leaders to accept the central components of his plan. Having exhausted themselves financially and having suffered the loss of a generation of young men, the Allies intended to scoop up the spoils of victory and make the Central Powers pay dearly. The European Allies intended to hold on to their respective colonies regardless of Wilson's call for self-determination, and as a nation that depended on a strong navy, Britain refused to limit its options concerning freedom of the seas. Perhaps Georges Clemenceau, France's president, best expressed his colleagues' skepticism about Wilson's idealistic vision: "President Wilson and his Fourteen Points bore me. Even God Almighty has only ten!"

During the conference, Wilson was forced to compromise on a number of his principles in order to retain the cornerstone of his diplomacy — the establishment of the League of Nations. He abandoned his hope for peace without bitterness by agreeing to a "war guilt" clause that levied huge economic reparations on Germany for starting the war. He was willing to sacrifice some of his ideals because the league took on even greater importance in the wake of the 1917 Communist revolution in Russia. Wilson needed the league to keep the peace, giving war-ravaged and recovering nations the opportunity to choose U.S.-style economic freedom and political democracy over communism. In the end, the president won agreement for the establishment of his cherished League of Nations. The **Treaty of Versailles**, signed at the royal palace just outside Paris, authorized the league to combat aggression against any member nation through collective military action.

The Failure of Ratification

In July 1919, after enduring bruising battles in Paris, Wilson returned to Washington, D.C., only to face another wrenching struggle in the Senate over ratification of the Versailles treaty. The odds were stacked against Wilson from the start. The Republicans held a majority in the Senate, and Wilson needed the support of two-thirds of the Senate to secure ratification. Henry Cabot Lodge, the Republican chairman of the Senate Foreign Relations Committee, opposed Article X of the League of Nations covenant, which sanctioned collective security arrangements against military aggression. Lodge argued that such an alliance compromised the United States' independence in conducting its own foreign relations. Lodge had at least thirty-nine senators behind him, more than enough to block ratification. Conceding the need to protect the country's national self-interest, the president agreed to modifications to the treaty so that the Monroe Doctrine and America's obligations in the Caribbean and Central America were kept intact. Lodge, however, was not satisfied and insisted on adding fourteen "reservations" limiting compliance with the treaty, including strong language affirming Congress's right to declare war before agreeing to a League of Nations military action.

Wilson's stubbornness more than equaled Lodge's, and the president refused to compromise. Making matters worse, Wilson faced resistance from sixteen lawmakers dubbed "irreconcilables," who opposed the league under any circumstances. Mainly Republicans from the Midwest and West, they voiced the traditional U.S. rejection of entangling alliances.

To break the logjam, Wilson attempted to rally public opinion behind him. In September 1919, he embarked on a nationwide speaking tour to carry his message directly to the American people. Over a three-week period, he traveled eight thousand miles by train, keeping a grueling schedule that exhausted him. After a stop in Pueblo, Colorado, on September 25, Wilson collapsed and canceled the rest of his trip. On October 2, Wilson suffered a massive stroke that nearly killed him. The effects of the stroke, which left him partially paralyzed, emotionally unstable, and mentally impaired, dimmed any remaining hopes of compromise. The full extent of his illness was kept from the public, and his wife, Edith, ran the White House for the next eighteen months.

Still fresh from their grisly experiences with the global influenza pandemic, many Americans seemed wary of binding themselves to an international agency such as the league. On November 19, 1919, the Senate rejected the amended treaty. The following year, Wilson had one final chance to obtain ratification, but still he refused to accept reservations despite members of his own party urging compromise. In March 1920, treaty ratification failed one last time, falling just seven votes short of the required two-thirds majority. The United States never signed the Treaty of Versailles or joined the League of Nations, weakening the league and diminishing the prospects for long-term peace.

REVIEW & RELATE	• Compare the U.S. government's efforts to manage the economy and public opinion with its response to the influenza pandemic during World War I. • How did President Wilson's wartime policies and his efforts to shape the peace that followed reflect his progressive roots?

Conclusion: A U.S. Empire

In the final decade of the nineteenth century, the United States transformed itself into an imperial power. Presidents McKinley and Roosevelt carried out the strategy outlined by Captain Mahan to enlarge the navy, construct a canal linking the Atlantic and Pacific Oceans, and acquire coaling stations and bases in the Pacific to service the fleet. U.S. officials disregarded the nationalistic aspirations of freedom fighters such as José Martí in Cuba and Emilio Aguinaldo in the Philippines in favor of the imperial spoils gained from winning the War of 1898. The United States justified intervention on moral grounds predicated on racist beliefs, much as it had in conquering the Indians during westward expansion. As a fit and manly nation, the United States felt responsible for uplifting "inferior" peoples to "civilized" standards and make them capable of self-government. This justification quickly wore thin. To crush the rebellion in the Philippines, the military engaged in atrocities that called into question the honor and virtue of the United States. Once it achieved victory in the Philippines, the nation concentrated its efforts on maintaining territories primarily for commercial purposes. Within the few short years from 1898 to 1904, this commercial empire had fallen into place.

The Progressive Era presidents, Roosevelt and Wilson, created and sustained a U.S. empire. They disagreed significantly in approach — Roosevelt favoring force, Wilson preferring negotiations — but in practice they shared a willingness to use military power to protect national interests. These two presidents helped construct the modern American state, an expanded federal government in cooperation with responsible corporate leaders. This relationship reached its peak during World War I. In mobilizing the home front, the Wilson administration blurred the line between public and private business by expanding the reach of government over the economy and curtailing personal liberty. However, this move toward nationalization was hardly complete, as the failure of Wilson to offer a central strategy to combat the 1918 influenza pandemic shows.

In 1917, because of its heavy reliance on trade with foreign countries, especially in Europe, the United States confronted its first major international crisis of the twentieth century. Wilson reluctantly led the country into war to guarantee a world order in which reasonable nations attempted to resolve controversies through negotiation, not violence. The failure of the United States to join the League of Nations, for which the president bore much of the responsibility, shattered his own idealistic dream.

Nevertheless, the United States did not isolate itself from participation in the world. The country emerged from the war in excellent financial shape; it had become the leading foreign creditor; its industrial capacity had greatly expanded; and its commercial empire in the Caribbean and Central America remained intact. It would take another two decades for policymakers to realize that the country's refusal to support a strong collective response to expansionist aggression posed serious dangers for U.S. commerce and values.

Chapter 20 Review

KEY TERMS

jingoists, 505
Cuba Libre, 506
yellow journalism, 507
Teller Amendment, 508
Platt Amendment, 509
Anti-Imperialist League, 509
Roosevelt Corollary, 512
Open Door, 512
dollar diplomacy, 513
Mexican revolution, 513
Zimmermann telegram, 516
American Expeditionary
    Forces (AEF), 516

War Industries Board (WIB), 519
National War Labor Board
    (NWLB), 519
Committee on Public Information
    (CPI), 520
Espionage Act, 520
Sedition Act, 521
American Protective
    League (APL), 521
pandemic, 522
Fourteen Points, 523
League of Nations, 523
Treaty of Versailles, 524

REVIEW & RELATE

1. What role did economic developments play in prompting calls for a U.S. empire? What role did social and cultural developments play?

2. Why did the United States embark on building an empire in the 1890s and not decades earlier?

3. Why did the United States go to war with Spain in 1898?

4. In what ways did the War of 1898 mark a turning point in the relationship between the United States and the rest of the world?

5. How did the United States assert its influence and control over Latin America in the early twentieth century?

6. How did U.S. policies in Latin America mirror U.S. policies in Asia?

7. In what ways, if any, did President Wilson's approach to Latin American affairs differ from that of his predecessors?

8. Why did President Wilson find it so difficult to keep the United States out of World War I?

9. Compare the U.S. government's efforts to manage the economy and public opinion with its response to the influenza pandemic during World War I.

10. How did President Wilson's wartime policies and his efforts to shape the peace that followed reflect his progressive roots?

TIMELINE OF EVENTS

1880–1900	• U.S. creates third most powerful navy
1893	• U.S. plantation owners overthrow Queen Liliuokalani of Hawaii
1895–1898	• Cuban War for Independence
1898	• U.S. battleship *Maine* explodes
	• The War of 1898
	• Anti-Imperialist League founded
1899–1902	• Philippine-American War
1901	• Platt Amendment passed
1904	• Roosevelt Corollary announced
1909	• U.S. intervenes in Nicaragua on behalf of U.S. fruit and mining companies
1914	• Panama Canal opens
	• World War I begins
1915	• German submarine sinks the *Lusitania*
1916	• Wilson sends U.S. troops into Mexico to capture Pancho Villa
1917	• Zimmermann telegram
	• United States enters World War I
	• Espionage Act
	• War Industries Board established
	• Committee on Public Information established
1918	• Sedition Act
	• National War Labor Board established
	• Germany surrenders, ending World War I
	• Influenza pandemic spreads throughout the world
1919	• Influenza pandemic reaches its peak and subsides
	• Wilson loses battle for ratification of Treaty of Versailles

21

The Twenties

1919–1929

LEARNING OBJECTIVES

After reading this chapter you will be able to:

- Explain the causes of the anti-communist panic, labor unrest, and escalating racial tensions following World War I.

- Evaluate the importance of the second industrial revolution, the creation of the consumer culture, urbanization, and the federal government in promoting economic expansion.

- Describe how white and black popular culture challenged traditional morality and gender roles.

- Examine the tensions between nativists and immigrants and fundamentalism and modernism, and explain how these culture wars affected federal policies.

- Explain the dominance of the Republican Party over the Progressive and Democratic Parties and analyze the political flaws that led to the Great Depression.

COMPARING AMERICAN HISTORIES

Pursuit of the American dream kept **David Curtis (D. C.) Stephenson** on the move. Born in 1891 to Texas sharecroppers, Stephenson moved with his family to the Oklahoma Territory in 1901. After quitting school at age sixteen, he drifted around for more than a decade, working for a string of newspapers and gaining a reputation as a heavy drinker. In 1915 he married and settled down; however, he soon lost his newspaper job, abandoned his pregnant wife, and hit the road working for one newspaper

528

after another in between binges of drunkenness. His wife divorced him, and in 1917 Stephenson joined the army to fight in World War I. Despite a series of drunken brawls and sexual misadventures, he received an honorable discharge in 1919.

Stephenson remarried and settled in Indiana, where he found financial and political success. In 1920 he joined the Ku Klux Klan (KKK), the Reconstruction-era organization that had reemerged in 1915 in Georgia. The newly revived Klan spread beyond the South, targeting African Americans, recent immigrants, Jews, and Catholics as enemies of traditional Protestant family values. Stephenson directed Klan operations in twenty-three states, building a profitable empire on fear, prejudice, and get-rich-quick schemes. A few years later, however, his Klan career ended with his arrest and conviction on rape and second-degree murder charges.

Ossian Sweet also pursued the American dream. Like Stephenson, he rose from humble beginnings. The descendant of enslaved people, Sweet was born in 1895 and grew up in central Florida. Hoping to shield him from the dangers of Jim Crow, Sweet's parents sent him north when he was thirteen years old.

After attending Wilberforce University in Ohio and Howard Medical School in Washington, D.C., Sweet moved to Detroit in 1921 to open a medical practice. He married, and in 1924 the Sweets decided to buy a house in a working-class neighborhood occupied exclusively by whites. Before the Sweets moved in, their white neighbors, with Klan backing, began organizing to keep them out.

When the Sweet family moved into their house on September 8, 1925, they encountered a hostile crowd in the street. Dr. Sweet had brought some backup with him. Armed to resist the mob, the Sweets and their defenders fired their weapons at the crowd after rocks smashed through the upstairs windows of the house. When the shooting stopped and the police restored calm, one white man lay dead and another wounded. Dr. Sweet; his wife, Gladys; and the other nine occupants of his house went on trial on first-degree murder charges. Hired by the NAACP, Clarence Darrow represented the eleven defendants and after two trials — the first ended in a hung jury — won an acquittal in 1926.

THE AMERICAN HISTORIES of Ossian Sweet and D. C. Stephenson illustrate the competing forces that shaped the 1920s. Both men achieved a measure of financial success, but they did so in the post–World War I atmosphere of growing social friction and intense racial resentments. When Sweet's parents decided to send him north, they were responding to the racial violence that plagued the South, but they were also demonstrating their belief that a better life was possible for their son. By contrast, Stephenson grew wealthy by tapping into the same racial tensions that shaped the Sweets' lives. Many whites who considered themselves "100 percent Americans" believed that racial and ethnic minorities threatened their power. The fear of Communist infiltration heightened their concerns over immigration, and changes in morality and gender roles further aroused their fears. Although the general prosperity of the period masked the tensions lying beneath the surface, it did not eliminate them. Rampant consumerism concealed the unequal prosperity fostered by Republican Party policies that later led to the Great Depression. As the experiences of D. C. Stephenson and Ossian Sweet show, the decade following the end of World War I opened up fresh avenues for economic prosperity as well as new sites for cultural clashes exacerbated by the tensions of modern America.

Social Turmoil

The return of peace in 1918 brought with it problems that would persist into the 1920s. Government efforts to suppress opposition to U.S. involvement in World War I fostered an atmosphere of fear and repression that continued after the war. The influenza epidemic that killed hundreds of thousands of Americans and millions of people around the world further heightened anxiety. Finally, the abrupt transition away from a wartime economy produced inflation, labor unrest, and escalating racial tensions.

The Red Scare, 1919–1920

The success of the Bolshevik Revolution in Russia in 1917 and the subsequent creation of the Union of Soviet Socialist Republics terrified officials of capitalist countries in western Europe and the United States. This fear was exacerbated in 1919 with the creation of the Comintern, an association of Communists who pledged to incite revolution in capitalist countries around the world. This sparked panic over Communist-inspired radicalism known as the **Red scare**, which set the stage for the suppression of dissent.

On March 3, 1919, in *Schenck v. United States* the Supreme Court invoked the Espionage Act to uphold the conviction of Charles Schenck, the general secretary of the Socialist Party, for mailing thousands of leaflets opposing the military draft. Delivering the Court's unanimous opinion, Justice Oliver Wendell Holmes ruled that during wartime Congress has the authority to prohibit individuals from using words that create "a clear and present danger" to the safety of the country. Although the trial record failed to show that Schenck's leaflets had convinced any young men to resist conscription, the Court upheld his conviction. Later that year in *Abrams v. United States*, the Court further limited free speech by sustaining the guilty verdict of five anarchists who distributed leaflets denouncing U.S. military efforts to overthrow the Bolshevik regime.

Postwar economic problems increased the anxiety of American citizens, reinforcing officials who sought to restore order by suppressing radicals. Industries were slow to convert their plants from military to civilian production, and consumer goods therefore remained in short supply. The war had brought jobs and higher wages on the home front, and consumers who had been restrained by wartime rationing were eager to spend their savings. With demand greatly exceeding supply, however, prices soared by 77 percent. At the same time, farmers, who had benefited from wartime conditions, faced falling crop prices as European nations resumed agricultural production and the federal government ended price supports.

A series of strikes launched by labor unions in 1919 contributed to the fear that the United States was under assault by sinister, radical forces. As skyrocketing inflation undercut wages and employers launched a new round of union-busting efforts, labor went on the offensive. In 1919 more than four million workers went on strike nationwide. In September, striking Boston policemen left the city unguarded, resulting in widespread looting and violence. Massachusetts governor Calvin Coolidge sent in the National Guard to break the strike and restore order.

Public officials and newspapers decried the violence, but they also greatly exaggerated the peril. Communists and socialists did support some union activities, but few of the millions of workers who struck for higher wages and better working conditions had ties to extremists. The major prewar radical organization, the Industrial Workers of the World, never recovered from the government harassment that had crippled it during World War I. However, scattered acts of violence allowed government and business leaders to stir up anxieties about the Communist threat. On May 1, 1919, radicals sent more than thirty incendiary devices through the mail to prominent Americans, though authorities defused the bombs before they reached their targets. The following month, bombs exploded in eight cities, including one at the doorstep of the home of A. Mitchell Palmer, the attorney general of the United States.

After the attack, Palmer launched a government crusade to root out Communists. Palmer traced the source of radicalism to recent immigrants, mainly those from Russia and eastern and southern Europe. To track down suspected radicals, Palmer selected J. Edgar Hoover to head the General Intelligence Division in the Department of Justice. In November 1919, government agents in twelve cities rounded up and arrested hundreds of foreigners, including the anarchist and feminist Emma Goldman. Goldman and some 250 other people caught in the government dragnet were soon deported to Russia. Over the next few months, the **Palmer raids** continued in more than thirty cities. Authorities arrested at least four thousand suspected radicals, interrogated them without legal counsel, and held them incommunicado without stipulating the charges against them. Of the thousands arrested, the government found reason to deport 556. The raids did not uncover any extensive plots to overthrow the U.S. government, nor did they lead to the arrest of the bombers.

More deportations would have taken place had it not been for Louis F. Post. As acting secretary of labor, Post had authority over the Immigration Bureau, which handled deportations. A reformer and supporter of workers' rights, Post concluded that many of the Palmer raids had been conducted without proper search warrants and prisoners interrogated without access to a lawyer. Consequently, Post freed some 3,000 prisoners and halted further deportations despite the opposition of Palmer and Hoover.

Post's actions helped reduce public enthusiasm for the Palmer raids. In 1920 a group of pacifists, progressives, and constitutional lawyers formed the American Civil Liberties Union (ACLU) to monitor government abridgments of the Bill of Rights. Although the Palmer raids ended, the Red scare persisted. After Hoover became director of the Bureau of Investigation (later renamed the Federal Bureau of

Investigation) in 1921, he continued spying and collecting information on suspected radicals and increasing his power over the next several decades.

Racial Violence in the Postwar Era

Racial strife also heightened postwar anxieties. Drawn by the promise of wartime industrial jobs, more than 400,000 African Americans left the South beginning in 1917 and 1918 and headed north hoping to escape poverty and racial discrimination. (By 1930 another 800,000 blacks had left the South.) This exodus became known as the **great migration**. During World War I, many blacks found work in steel production, meatpacking, shipbuilding, and other heavy industries, but most were relegated to low-paying jobs. Still, as a carpenter earning $95 a month wrote from Chicago to a friend back in Hattiesburg, Mississippi: "I should have been here 20 years ago. I just begin to feel like a man." Most African American women remained employed as domestic workers, but more than 100,000 obtained manufacturing jobs.

For many blacks, however, the North was not the "promised land" they expected. Instead, they encountered bitter opposition from white migrants from the South competing for employment and scarce housing. As black and white veterans returned from the war, racial hostilities exploded. In 1919 race riots erupted in twenty-five cities throughout the country, including one in Washington, D.C., which Ossian Sweet witnessed firsthand. The previous year, W. E. B. Du Bois of the NAACP had urged the black community to "close ranks" to fight Germany, but the racial violence against blacks in 1919 embittered him. "By the God of Heaven," Du Bois wrote, "we are cowards and jackasses if now that that war is over, we do not marshal every ounce of our brain and brawn to fight a sterner, longer, more unbending battle against the forces of hell in our own land."

The worst of these disturbances occurred in Chicago. On a hot July day, a black youth swimming at a Lake Michigan beach inadvertently crossed over into an area of water customarily reserved for whites. In response, white bathers shouted at the swimmer and hurled stones at him. The black swimmer drowned, and word of the incident quickly spread through white and black neighborhoods. For thirteen days, mobs of blacks and whites attacked each other, ransacked businesses, and torched homes. Over the course of the riots, at least 15 whites and 23 blacks died, 178 whites and 342 blacks were injured, and more than 1,000 black families were left homeless.

Two years later, on May 31 and June 1, 1921, whites launched a killing spree against the black community of Tulsa, Oklahoma. Known at the time as "the Negro Wall Street," the Greenwood district of Tulsa contained numerous black businesses and churches and was the home of African American professionals. However, status and wealth did not protect the residents of the area from the power of white supremacy. After a black man was arrested for allegedly assaulting a white woman in an elevator, white mobs gathered around the jail, threatening to lynch him. Thwarted in their attempts, a crowd of over 2,000 gun-toting whites headed into Greenwood, where a contingent of armed blacks, many of whom were World War I veterans, fought back. Outnumbered by the white vigilantes, they were forced to retreat. During the fracas, city police deployed aircraft to drop firebombs on black businesses and residences, setting Greenwood ablaze. After the smoke cleared, at least thirty-six

The Tulsa Race Massacre, 1921 This photograph captures what once was a section of the thriving black business district of Greenwood in Tulsa, Oklahoma, after racist white mobs burned it down and left an estimated 300 dead. A black man surveys the charred ruins in the aftermath of the massacre. Oklahoma Historical Society/Getty Images

people lay dead, twenty-six blacks and ten whites, though recent investigations place the death toll in the **Tulsa Massacre** at around 300. Some 800 victims lay in hospital beds and another 6,000 black residents were locked up in internment centers for several days. Thousands of African Americans fled the city, as thirty-five blocks remained devastated from the fires. Nevertheless, black Tulsans took the initiative to rebuild Greenwood despite white opposition.

REVIEW & RELATE	• What factors combined to produce the turmoil of the immediate postwar period? • What factors contributed to the rise in racial tensions that accompanied the transition from wartime to peacetime?

Prosperity, Consumption, and Growth

Despite the turbulence of the postwar period, the 1920s were a time of vigorous economic growth and urbanization. Between 1922 and 1927, the economy grew by 7 percent a year. Unemployment rates remained low, as producers added new workers in an effort to keep up with increasing consumer demand. Aligning themselves with big business, government officials took an active role in stimulating industrial and economic growth. The average purchasing power of wage earners soared, but many Americans were left out of this economic boom.

Government Promotion of the Economy

The general prosperity of the 1920s owed a great deal to backing by the federal government. Republicans controlled the presidency and Congress, and though they claimed to stand for principles of laissez-faire and opposed various economic and social reforms, they were willing to use governmental power to support large corporations and the wealthy.

Senator Warren G. Harding of Ohio, who was elected president in 1920, declared that he and his party wanted "less government in business and more business in government." Harding's cabinet appointments reflected this goal. Treasury Secretary Andrew Mellon, a banker and an aluminum company titan, believed that the government should stimulate economic growth by reducing taxes on the rich, raising tariffs to protect manufacturers from foreign competition, and trimming the budget. The Republican Congress enacted much of this agenda. During the Harding administration, tax rates for the wealthy, which had skyrocketed during World War I, plummeted from 66 percent to 20 percent. Mellon believed that those on the lower rungs of the economic ladder would prosper once businesspeople invested the extra money they received from tax breaks into expanding production. Supposedly, the wealth would trickle down through increased jobs and purchasing power. At the same time, Republicans turned Progressive Era regulatory agencies such as the Federal Trade Commission and the Federal Reserve Board into boosters for major corporations and financial institutions by weakening enforcement.

Secretary of Commerce Herbert Hoover had an even greater impact than Mellon in cementing the government–business partnership during the 1920s. Hoover believed that the federal government had a role to play in promoting business activities and in lessening economic suffering. He insisted on voluntary cooperation between the public and private sectors. Hoover favored the creation of trade associations in which businesses would collaborate to stabilize production levels, prices, and wages. In turn, the Commerce Department would provide helpful data and information to improve productivity and trade.

Hoover's vision fit into a larger Republican effort to weaken unions by promoting voluntary business-sponsored worker welfare initiatives. For example, under the **American Plan**, some firms established health insurance and pension plans for their workers. As early as 1914, Henry Ford provided his autoworkers over twenty-two years old "a share in the profits of the house" equal to a minimum wage of $5 a day, and he cut the workday from nine hours to eight. Unions were further damaged by a series of Supreme Court rulings that restricted strikes and overturned hard-won victories such as child labor legislation and minimum wage laws. By 1929 union membership had dropped from approximately five million to three million, or about 10 percent of the industrial labor market.

Scandals during the Harding presidency diminished its luster but did not stall Republican economic policy. The **Teapot Dome scandal** grabbed the most headlines. In 1921 Interior Secretary Albert Fall collaborated with Navy Secretary Edwin

Denby to transfer potential oil fields to the Interior Department. Fall then parceled out these properties to private companies. As a result, Harry F. Sinclair's Mammoth Oil Company received a lease to develop the Teapot Dome section in Wyoming. In return for this handout, Sinclair delivered more than $300,000 to Fall. In the wake of congressional hearings, Fall and Sinclair were convicted on a number of criminal charges and sent to jail.

Harding's sudden death from a heart attack in August 1923 brought Vice President Calvin Coolidge to the presidency. Coolidge distanced himself from the scandals of his predecessor's administration but reaffirmed Harding's economic policies. "The chief business of the American people is business," President Coolidge remarked.

Americans Become Consumers

The 1920s marked a period of economic expansion and general prosperity. National income rose from approximately $63 billion to $88 billion, and per capita income jumped from $641 to $847, an increase of 32 percent. The purchasing power of wage earners climbed approximately 20 percent.

This great spurt of economic growth in the 1920s resulted from technological innovation and scientific management techniques (Figure 21.1). Perhaps the greatest innovation came with the introduction of the assembly line. First used in the automobile

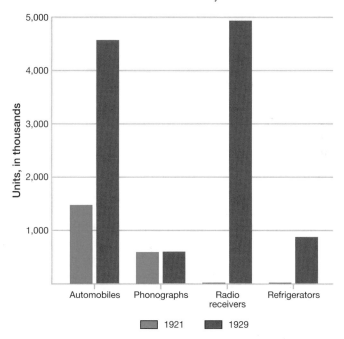

FIGURE 21.1 Production of Consumer Goods, 1921 and 1929
Rising per capita income, lower manufacturing costs, urban electrification, and advertising spurred the production of consumer goods in the 1920s. According to this figure, what were the most popular consumer goods in this period and how did they serve to bring Americans from all regions together?

industry before World War I, the assembly line moved the product to a worker who performed a specific task before sending it along to the next worker. Perfected by Henry Ford, this system saved enormous time, costs, and energy by emphasizing repetition, accuracy, and standardization, which allowed Ford to lower prices.

Besides the automobile, the **second industrial revolution** focused on the production of consumer-oriented goods. The electrification of urban homes created demand for a wealth of new labor-saving appliances. Refrigerators, washing machines, toasters, and vacuum cleaners appealed to middle-class housewives whose husbands could afford to purchase them. Wristwatches replaced bulkier pocket watches. Radios became the chief source of home entertainment.

Although such household items changed the lives of many Americans, the automobile had the most profound impact. Auto sales soared in the 1920s from a total of 1.5 million to 5 million, fueling the growth of related industries such as steel, rubber, petroleum, and glass. In 1929 Ford and his competitors at General Motors, Chevrolet, and Oldsmobile employed nearly 4 million workers, and around one in eight American workers toiled in factories connected to automobile production.

The automobile also changed day-to-day living patterns. Although most roads and highways consisted of dirt and contained rocks and ruts, enough were paved to extend the boundaries of suburbs farther from the city. By the end of the 1920s, around 17 percent of Americans lived in suburbia. Cars allowed families to travel to vacation destinations at greater distances from their homes, like to the resorts of Florida and the national parks in the Rocky Mountains and on the West Coast. Even the roadside landscape changed, as gas stations, diners, and motels sprang up to serve motorists.

The automobile also provided new dating opportunities for young men and women. At the turn of the twentieth century, a young man courted a woman by going to her home and sitting with her on the sofa or out on the porch under the watchful eyes of her parents and family members. With the arrival of the automobile, couples could get away from adult supervision and drive to a "lover's lane," where they could express their feelings with greater physicality than before.

Although Ford and other manufacturers succeeded in lowering prices, they still had to convince Americans to spend their hard-earned money to purchase their products. Turning for help to the fledgling advertising industry, manufacturers nearly tripled their spending on advertising over the course of the 1920s. Firms pitched their products around price and quality, but advertisers also played on consumers' unexpressed fears, unfulfilled desires, hopes for success, and sexual fantasies. The producers of Listerine mouthwash transformed a product previously used to disinfect hospitals into one that fought the dreaded but made-up disease of halitosis (bad breath). Advertisers invited consumers to measure success by their ability to buy new products. Purchasing a General Electric all-steel refrigerator not only would preserve food longer but also would enhance the owners' reputation among their neighbors.

Although average wages and incomes rose during the 1920s, the majority of Americans did not have the disposable income to afford new consumer goods. To resolve this problem, companies extended credit in dizzying amounts. By 1929 consumers purchased 60 percent of their cars and 80 percent of their radios and furniture on credit — mainly through the installment plan. "Buy now and pay later" became the motto of corporate America.

Chevrolet Advertisement, 1920s The 1920s boom in the production of automobiles posed a challenge for business marketers and advertisers. They had to convince consumers that items once considered as luxuries were now necessities that would improve their lives. Many of these advertisements were directed at middle-class women who, as housewives, managed the family budget. The Chevrolet Motor Company aimed this advertisement at women by appealing to its car's easy handling and low price. Image Courtesy of The Advertising Archives

Urbanization

The growth of cities helped promote the spread of the consumer-oriented economy. Increasingly clustered in urban areas, people had more convenient access to department stores and chain stores. Advertisers targeted city residents because they were easier to reach and a large middle class of shoppers provided a growing market.

The census of 1920 reported that for the first time in U.S. history a majority of Americans lived in cities. In 1910 just over 54 percent of the nation lived in small towns and villages with fewer than 2,500 people. A decade later, only 49 percent inhabited these areas. The end of World War I brought a decline in demand for American agricultural goods, and about six million residents left their farms and villages and moved to cities. By 1930 the percentage of those living in rural America dropped to 44 percent. The war had pushed large numbers of African Americans out of the rural South for jobs in the cities. Also, with war's end, immigration from southern and eastern Europe resumed.

The West grew faster than any other region of the country, and its cities boomed. From 1910 to 1930, the population of the United States increased by 33.5 percent; at the same time, the population of the West soared by nearly 59 percent. In northern California, the bay area cities of San Francisco, Oakland, and Berkeley nearly doubled in population. Seattle, Portland, Denver, and Salt Lake City also rose in prominence. After the war, western city leaders boasted of the business and employment opportunities and beautiful landscapes that awaited migrants to their urban communities (Map 21.1).

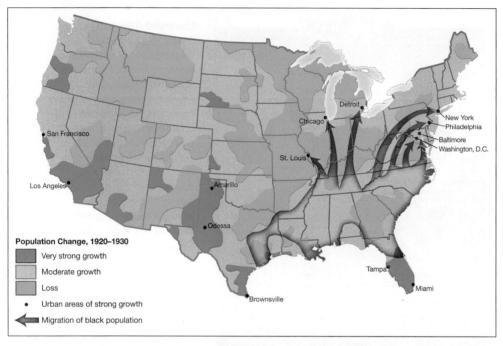

MAP 21.1   The Shift from Rural to Urban Population, 1920–1930
Throughout late nineteenth and early twentieth centuries the population of the nation had shifted from
rural to urban areas. In the 1920s this migration continued, especially among African Americans in the
South and Latinos in the Southwest and West. Many of these migrants from rural to urban landscapes
actually stayed in the same region, particularly Latinos.

Los Angeles stood out for its growth, which skyrocketed from 319,000 residents
in 1910 to over 1.2 million in 1930. The mild, sunny climate of southern California
attracted midwesterners and northeasterners who were tired of rugged winters. Promoters enticed new residents to buy up real estate, which could be purchased cheaply
and sold for a big profit. The city offered a dependable public transit system that
connected Los Angeles and neighboring counties. During the 1920s, the motion picture industry settled here, and its movies delighted audiences throughout the nation.
This urban boom boosted economic growth and, along with it, consumer spending.

Perilous Prosperity

Prosperity in the 1920s was real enough, but behind the impressive financial indicators flashed warnings that profound danger loomed ahead. Perhaps most important,
the boom was accompanied by growing income inequality. A majority of workers
lived below the poverty line, and farmers plunged deeper into debt. Corporate profits
increased much faster than wages, resulting in a disproportionate share of the wealth
going to the rich. The combined income of the top 1 percent of families was greater
than that of the 42 percent at the bottom (Figure 21.2); 66 percent lived below the
income level necessary to maintain an adequate standard of living.

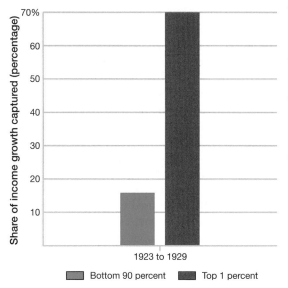

FIGURE 21.2 Income Inequality, 1923–1929 Although the U.S. economy expanded rapidly in the early 1920s, the accumulation of vast wealth among a small percentage of Americans created growing inequality. Explain the dangers this created for the overall economy in the 1920s.

Income inequality was a critical problem because America's new mass-production economy depended on ever-increasing consumption, and higher income groups could consume only so much. While the expansion of consumer credit helped hide this fundamental weakness, the low wages earned by most Americans drove down demand over time. Cutbacks in demand forced manufacturers to reduce production, thereby reducing jobs and increasing unemployment, which in turn dragged down the demand for consumer goods even further. As a result, by 1926 automobile sales had begun to slow, as did new housing construction — signs of an economy heading for trouble.

At the same time, the wealthy few used their disproportionate wealth to speculate in the stock market and risky real estate ventures. To encourage investments, brokers promoted buying stocks on margin (credit) and required down payments of only a fraction of the market price. Without vigilant governmental oversight, banks and lending agencies extended credit without taking into account what would happen if a financial panic occurred and they were suddenly required to call in their loans. To make matters worse, the banking system operated on shaky financial grounds, combining savings facilities with speculative lending operations. With minimal interference from the Federal Trade Commission, businesspeople frequently managed firms in a reckless way that created a high level of interdependence among them. This interlocking system of corporate ownership and control meant that the collapse of one company could bring down many others, while also imperiling the banking houses that had generously financed them.

Rampant real estate speculation in Florida foreshadowed these dangers. In many cases, investors bought properties sight unseen, and assumed that land values would continue to increase. However, after severe storms in 1926 and 1928, land prices spiraled downward, speculators defaulted on bank loans, and financial institutions collapsed.

Throughout the 1920s, income plummeted for farmers as well. Declining world demand following the end of World War I, together with increased productivity because of the mechanization of agriculture, drove down farm prices. Between 1925 and 1929, falling wheat and cotton prices cut farm income in half. The collapse of farm prices had the most devastating effects on tenants and sharecroppers, who were forced off their lands through mortgage foreclosures. Around three million displaced farmers migrated to cities.

Internationally, the United States encountered serious economic obstacles. World War I had destroyed European economies, leaving them ill equipped to repay the $11 billion they had borrowed from the United States. Much of the Allied recovery depended on obtaining the reparations imposed on Germany at the conclusion of World War I. Germany, however, was in even worse shape than France and Britain and could not meet its obligations. Consequently, the U.S. government negotiated a deal by which American banks loaned money to Germany, which used the money to pay reparations to Britain and France, which in turn used Germany's reparations payments to repay debts owed to U.S. banks. What appeared a satisfactory resolution at the time ultimately proved a calamity. With this revolving-door solution, U.S. bankers were at the mercy of spiraling credit and unstable European economies. Compounding the problem, Republican administrations in the 1920s supported high tariffs on imports, thereby reducing foreign manufacturers' revenues, making it more difficult for these countries to pay off their debts.

REVIEW & RELATE	• Describe the relationship between business and government in the 1920s. • Why was a high level of consumer spending so critical to 1920s prosperity, and why was the economic expansion of the 1920s ultimately unsustainable?

Challenges to Social Conventions

While most of the nation ignored growing evidence of the fragility of American prosperity, the social and cultural consequences of the second industrial revolution ushered in new, distinctly modern cultural patterns. Advertising and credit, two of the mainstays of modern capitalism, sought to bypass the time-honored virtues of saving and living within one's means. Conventional sexual standards came under assault from the growth of the film and automobile industries, which influenced clothing styles and dating practices. In addition to moral and social behavior, traditional racial assumptions came under attack. African American writers and artists condemned racism, drew on their rich racial legacies, and produced a cultural renaissance. Other blacks, led by the Jamaican immigrant Marcus Garvey, rejected the integrationist strategy of the NAACP in favor of black nationalism.

Breaking with the Old Morality

Challenges to the virtues of thrift and sacrifice were accompanied by a transformation of the moral codes of late-nineteenth-century America, especially those relating to sex. The entertainment industry played a large role in promoting relaxed attitudes toward sexual relations to a mass audience throughout the nation.

By the 1920s, Hollywood film studios had blossomed into major corporations, and movies were shown in ornate theaters in cities and towns across the country. The star system was born, and matinee idols influenced fashions and hairstyles. Female stars dressed as "flappers" and wooed audiences. Representing the liberated **new woman**, flappers sported short hair and short skirts, used ample makeup (formerly associated with prostitutes), smoked cigarettes in public, drank illegal alcoholic beverages, and gyrated to jazz tunes on the dance floor.

While Americans enjoyed new entertainment opportunities most remained faithful to traditional values. By 1929 approximately 40 percent of households owned a radio. Shows such as *The General Motors Family* and *The Maxwell House Hour* blended product advertising with family entertainment. *Amos 'n' Andy* garnered large audiences by satirizing black working-class life, which, intentionally or not, reinforced racist stereotypes. In cities like New York and Chicago, immigrants could tune in to foreign-language radio programs aimed at non-English-speaking groups, which offered listeners an outlet for preserving their ethnic identity in the face of the increasing homogeneity fostered by the national consumer culture.

The most spirited challenge to both traditional values and the modern consumer culture came from a diverse group of intellectuals known as the **Lost Generation**. Author Gertrude Stein coined the term to describe the disillusionment that many of her fellow writers and artists felt after the ravages of World War I. Already concerned about the impact of mass culture and corporate capitalism on individualism and free thought, they focused their talents on criticizing what they saw as the hypocrisy of old values and the conformity ushered in by the new. In the novel *This Side of Paradise* (1920), F. Scott Fitzgerald complained that his generation had "grown up to find all Gods dead, all wars fought, all faith in man shaken." In a series of novels, including *Main Street* (1920), *Babbitt* (1922), and *Elmer Gantry* (1927), Sinclair Lewis ridiculed the narrow-mindedness of small-town life, the empty materialism of businessmen, and the insincerity of evangelical preachers. Journalist Henry Louis (H. L.) Mencken picked up these subjects in the pages of his magazine, *The American Mercury*. From his vantage point in Baltimore, Maryland, he lampooned the beliefs and behavior of Middle America.

Scholars joined literary and social critics in challenging conventional ideas. Sigmund Freud, an Austrian psychoanalyst, shifted emphasis away from culture to individual consciousness. His disciples stressed the role of the unconscious mind and the power of the sex drive in shaping human behavior, beliefs that gained traction not only in university education but also in advertising appeals.

Scholars also discredited conventional wisdom about race. Challenging studies that purported to demonstrate the intellectual superiority of whites over blacks, Columbia University anthropologist Franz Boas argued that any apparent intelligence gap between the races resulted from environmental factors and not heredity. His student Ruth Benedict further argued that the culture of so-called primitive tribes, such as the Pueblo Indians, produced a less stressful and more emotionally connected lifestyle than that of more advanced societies.

The Harlem Renaissance

The greatest challenge to conventional notions about race came from African Americans. The influx of southern black migrants to the North during and after World War I created a black cultural renaissance, with New York City's Harlem and the South Side of Chicago leading the way. Gathered in Harlem — with a population of more than 120,000 African Americans in 1920 and growing every day — a group of black writers paid homage to the **New Negro**, the second generation born after emancipation. These New Negro intellectuals refused to accept white supremacy. They expressed pride in their race and demanded full citizenship and participation in American society. Black writers and poets drew on themes from African American life and history for inspiration in their literary works.

The poets, novelists, and artists of the **Harlem Renaissance** captured the imagination of blacks and whites alike. Many of these artists increasingly rejected white standards of taste as well as staid middle-class black values. Writers Langston Hughes and Zora Neale Hurston in particular drew inspiration from the vernacular of African American folk life. In 1926 Hughes defiantly asserted: "We younger Negro artists who create now intend to express our dark-skinned selves without fear or shame. If white people are pleased, we are glad. If they are not, it doesn't matter."

Black music became a vibrant part of mainstream American popular culture in the 1920s. Musicians such as Ferdinand "Jelly Roll" Morton, Louis Armstrong, Edward "Duke" Ellington, and singer Bessie Smith developed and popularized two of America's most original forms of music — jazz and the blues. These unique compositions grew out of the everyday experiences of black life and expressed the thumping rhythms of work, pleasure, and pain. Such music did not remain confined to dance halls and clubs in black communities; it soon spread to white musicians and audiences for whom jazz rhythms meant emotional freedom and the expression of sexuality.

Marcus Garvey and Black Nationalism

In addition to providing a fertile ground for African American intellectuals, Harlem became the headquarters of the most significant alternative black political vision of the 1920s. In 1916 the Jamaican-born Marcus Mosiah Garvey settled in Harlem and became the leading exponent of black nationalism. In 1914 Garvey had set up the **Universal Negro Improvement Association (UNIA)** in Jamaica, an organization through which he promoted racial separation and pride as well as economic self-help through black business ownership. Unlike the leaders of the NAACP, who sought equal access to American institutions and cooperation with whites, Garvey favored a "Back to Africa" movement that would ultimately repatriate many black Americans to their ancestral homelands on the African continent. His recently acquired Black Star Line steamship company planned to transport passengers between the United States, the West Indies, and Africa. Together with the indigenous black African majority, transplanted African Americans would help overthrow colonial rule and use their power to assist black people throughout the world.

Garvey also tapped into the racial discontent of African Americans for whom living in the United States had proved so difficult. He denounced what he saw as the accommodationist efforts of the NAACP and declared, "To be a Negro is no disgrace, but an honor, and we of the UNIA do not want to become white." Ironically, the UNIA and D. C. Stephenson's Klan agreed on the necessity of racial separation. Garvey's appeals to black manhood were accompanied by a celebration of black womanhood. He set up the Black Cross Nurses, and his wife, Amy Jacques

Marcus Garvey   Dressed in military regalia topped off with a plumed hat, the Jamaican immigrant Marcus Garvey embodied the spirit of black nationalism after World War I. His Universal Negro Improvement Association, headquartered in Harlem, attracted a sizable following in the United States, the Caribbean, Central America, Canada, and Africa. Garvey advocated black political and economic independence.   New York Daily News Archive/Getty Images

Garvey, went beyond her husband's traditional notions of femininity to extol the accomplishments of black women in politics and culture. Garveyism became the first mass African American movement in U.S. history and was especially effective in recruiting working-class blacks. UNIA branches were established in thirty-eight states throughout the North and South and attracted some 500,000 members.

Given his ideas and outspokenness, Garvey soon made powerful enemies. Du Bois and fellow members of the NAACP despised him. The black socialist labor leader A. Philip Randolph, who saw the UNIA program as just another form of exploitative capitalism, labeled Garvey an "unquestioned fool and ignoramus." Yet Garvey's downfall came from his own business practices. Convicted in 1925 of mail fraud related to his Black Star Line, Garvey served two years in federal prison until President Coolidge commuted his term and had the Jamaican citizen deported.

REVIEW & RELATE	• How did new forms of entertainment challenge traditional morality and traditional gender roles? • Describe the black cultural and intellectual renaissance that flourished in the 1920s.

Culture Wars

Many segments of the population resisted attacks on traditional cultural and racial values. Rallying around the concepts of ethnic and racial purity, Protestant fundamentalism, and "family values," defenders of an older America attempted to roll back the tide of modernity. The enactment of prohibition was their greatest victory.

Prohibition

After decades of efforts to combat the use of alcohol, in 1919 the Eighteenth Amendment, banning its manufacture and sale, was ratified. That same year Congress passed the Volstead Act, which set up the legal machinery to enforce the amendment. Supporters claimed that prohibition would promote family stability, improve morals, and prevent crime. They took aim at the ethnically diverse culture of saloons associated with urban immigrants.

This attempt to promote traditional values proved difficult to enforce. In rural areas "moonshiners" took grain and processed it into liquor. In big cities, clubs known as speakeasies offered illegal alcohol and the entertainment to keep their customers satisfied. Treasury Department agents roamed the country destroying stills and raiding speakeasies, but liquor continued to flow. Nevertheless, prohibition did reduce alcohol consumption, but crime flourished. Gangsters paid off police, bribed judges, and turned cities into battlegrounds between rival criminal gangs, reinforcing the notion among small-town and rural dwellers that urban life eroded American values. By the end of the decade, most Americans welcomed an end to prohibition.

Nativists versus Immigrants

Prohibition reflected the surge in nativist (anti-immigrant) and racist thinking that revealed long-standing prejudices — earlier attempts at temperance reform had been largely aimed at immigrants. The end of World War I brought a new wave of Catholic and Jewish emigration from eastern and southern Europe, triggering religious prejudice among Protestants. Just as immigrants had been linked to socialism and anarchism in the 1880s and 1890s, old-stock Americans associated these immigrants with immoral behavior and political radicalism and saw them as a threat to traditional U.S. culture and values. As in the late nineteenth century, native-born workers saw immigrants as a source of cheap labor that threatened their jobs and wages.

The **Sacco and Vanzetti case** provides the most dramatic evidence of this nativism. In 1920 a botched robbery in South Braintree, Massachusetts, resulted in the murder of two employees. Police charged Nicola Sacco and Bartolomeo Vanzetti with the crime. These two Italian immigrants shared radical political views as anarchists and World War I draft evaders. The subsequent trial revolved around their foreign birth and ideology more than the facts pertaining to their guilt or innocence. The presiding judge at the trial referred to the accused as "anarchistic bastards" and "damned dagos" (a derogatory term for "Italians"). Convicted and sentenced to death, Sacco and Vanzetti lost their appeals for a new trial. Criticism of the verdict came from all over the world. Workers in Mexico, Argentina, Uruguay, France, and Morocco organized vigils and held rallies in solidarity with the condemned men. Despite such support, the two men were executed in the electric chair in 1927.

The Sacco and Vanzetti case provides an extreme example of 1920s nativism, but the anti-immigrant views that contributed to the two men's conviction and execution were commonplace during the period. For example, Henry Ford contended that immigrants did not understand "the principles which have made our [native] civilization," and he blamed the influx of foreigners for society's "marked deterioration" during the 1920s. He stirred up anti-immigrant prejudices mainly by targeting Jews. Believing that an international Jewish conspiracy was attempting to subvert Christian societies, Ford serialized in his company newspaper the so-called *Protocols of the Elders of Zion*, an anti-Semitic tract concocted in czarist Russia to justify pogroms against Jews. Ford continued to publish it even after the document was proved a fake.

Ford joined other nativists in supporting legislation to restrict immigration. In 1924 Congress passed the **National Origins Act**, a quota system on future immigration. The measure limited entry by any foreign group to 2 percent of the number of people of that nationality who resided in the United States in 1890. The statute's authors were interested primarily in curbing immigration from eastern and southern Europe, which had increased after 1890. Quotas established for northern Europe went unfilled, while those for southern and eastern Europe could not accommodate the vast number of people who sought admission. The law continued to bar East Asian immigration altogether. However, immigration from Mexico and elsewhere in the Western Hemisphere was exempted from the quotas of the Nation Origins Act because farmers in the Southwest needed Mexican laborers to tend their crops and pressured the government to excuse them from coverage. In a related measure, in 1924 Congress established the Border Patrol to control the flow of undocumented immigration from Mexico. Nevertheless, *legal* immigration to the United States from Mexico increased during the 1920s.

With immigration of those considered "undesirable" severely if not completely curtailed, some nativist reformers shifted their attention to Americanization. Speaking about immigrants, educator E. P. Cubberly said, "Our task is to break up their groups and settlements, to assimilate and amalgamate these people as a part of our American race, to implant in their children the northern-European conception of righteousness, law and order, and popular government." Business corporations conducted Americanization and naturalization classes on factory floors. Schools, patriotic societies, fraternal organizations, women's groups, and labor unions launched citizenship classes.

In the Southwest and on the West Coast, whites aimed their Americanization efforts at the growing population of Mexican Americans. Subject to segregated education,

Mexican Americans were expected to speak English in their classes. Anglo school administrators and teachers generally believed that Mexican Americans were suited only for farmwork and manual trades. For Mexican Americans, therefore, Americanization meant vocational training and preparation for low-status, low-wage jobs.

To challenge discrimination against Mexican Americans, the League of United Latin American Citizens (LULAC) was formed in Corpus Christi, Texas in 1929. Mexican American veterans of World War I mainly took the lead and were soon joined by women from middle-class civic clubs. The league adopted the same non-partisan, nonviolent, legalistic approach as did the NAACP in furthering racial equality, and campaigned to end discrimination against Mexican Americans at the ballot box, the workplace, and in schools. To this end, the league filed court cases and conducted voter registration drives. LULAC favored assimilation into American culture without Mexican Americans abandoning their heritage. Declaring its loyalty to the United States and supporting English as the official language, the league nevertheless affirmed: "We solemnly declare . . . to maintain a sincere and respectful reverence for our racial origins of which we are proud."

American Indians continued to face great challenges. During World War I, to save money the federal government had ceased appropriating funds for public health programs aimed at benefiting reservation Indians. With the war over, the government failed to restore the funds. Throughout the 1920s, rates of tuberculosis, eye infections, and infant mortality spiked among the Indian population. Boarding schools continued to promote menial service jobs for Indian students. Worse still, in Oklahoma with its large Native American population, a series of murders took place in Osage County. A 1921 federal law required members of the Osage tribe who received land allotments, many of which were atop rich oil reserves, to have a white guardian until they demonstrated "competency" to manage their parcels. Local white businessmen and lawyers made a good deal of money acting as guardians for the Osage. A federal investigation by J. Edgar Hoover's Bureau of Investigation discovered that some whites, besides engaging in fraud, committed murder to obtain the oil rights of the Osage. Only a few of the perpetrators were brought to trial and convicted. To protect this tribe, in 1925 Congress enacted a law prohibiting non-Osage from inheriting land allotments.

While these tragic events unfolded in Osage County, Congress passed landmark legislation on behalf of Native Americans. In 1924, the **Indian Citizenship Act** granted citizenship and the right to vote to all American Indians. Nevertheless, most Indians remained outside the economic and political mainstream of American society with meager government help.

Chinese residents also continued to face discrimination and segregation. The Chinese Exclusion Act remained in operation, making it difficult for nurturing family life. By 1920, Chinese men outnumbered Chinese women by seven to one. Furthermore, immigration restrictions prohibited Chinese workingmen from bringing their wives into the country. The 1924 National Origins Act made matters worse by banning all Asian women from entering the country. That same year the Supreme Court upheld the segregation of Chinese children in public schools.

Chinese communities faced problems similar to those experienced by other ethnic groups. Tensions developed between those born in China and their American-born children over assimilation. One Chinese American who grew up in San Francisco noted, "There was endless discussion about what to do about the dilemma of being *caught in between*." Many Chinese parents prohibited their children from speaking English at home and sent them to Chinese-language schools after public school. Chinese American children found cultural preservation efforts an onerous burden as they increasingly partook in America's growing consumer culture.

Despite attempts at Americanization, ethnic groups did not dissolve into a melting pot and lose their cultural identities. First-generation Americans — the children of immigrants — learned English, enjoyed American popular culture, and dressed in fashions of the day. Yet in cities around the country where immigrants had settled, ethnic enclaves remained intact and preserved the religious practices and social customs of their residents. Americanization may have watered down the "vegetable soup" of American diversity, but it did not eliminate the variety and distinctiveness of its flavors. Even the conservative U.S. Supreme Court weighed in favorably on the side of ethnic pluralism. During World War I Nebraska had enacted an anti-German measure prohibiting the teaching of any language other than English in its public schools. In *Meyer v. Nebraska* (1923), the Supreme Court struck down this law and affirmed that constitutional protections against unreasonable state restrictions applied to language minorities.

Resurrection of the Ku Klux Klan

Nativism received its most spectacular boost from the reemergence of the Ku Klux Klan in 1915. Originally dedicated to terrorizing emancipated African Americans and their white Republican allies in the South during Reconstruction, the KKK branched out during the 1920s to the North and West. In addition to blacks, the new Klan targeted Catholics and Jews, as well as anyone who was alleged to have violated community moral values. The organization consisted of a cross section of native-born Protestants primarily from the middle and working classes who sought to reverse a perceived decline in their social and economic power. Revived by W. J. Simmons, a former Methodist minister, the new Klan celebrated its founding at Stone Mountain, Georgia, near Atlanta. There, Klansmen bowed to the twin symbols of their cause, the American flag and a burning cross that represented their fiery determination to stand up for Christian morality and against all those considered "un-American." By the mid-1920s, Klan membership totaled more than three million men and women. Not confined to rural areas, the revived Klan counted a significant following in D. C. Stephenson's Indianapolis and Ossian Sweet's Detroit, as well as in Chicago, Denver, Portland, and Seattle. Rural dwellers who had moved into cities with large numbers of black migrants and recent immigrants found solace in Klan vows to preserve "Native, white, Protestant supremacy."

The KKK also appealed to white women who desired to reestablish traditional values. In the face of challenges to conventional values, a changing sexual morality, and the flaunting of prohibition, wives joined their husbands as devoted followers. Protestant women appreciated the Klan's message condemning abusive husbands and fathers and the group's affirmation of the status of white Protestant women as the embodiment of virtue.

Like the original Klan, its successor resorted to terror tactics. Acting under cover of darkness and concealed in robes and hoods, Klansmen burned crosses to scare their victims, many of whom they beat, kidnapped, tortured, and murdered. To gain greater legitimacy and to appeal to a wider audience, the Klan participated in electoral politics. The KKK succeeded in electing governors in Georgia and Oregon, a

U.S. senator from Texas, numerous state legislators, and other officials in California, Indiana, Michigan, Ohio, and Oklahoma. Politicians routinely joined the Klan to advance their careers, whether they shared its views or not.

The Klan did not go unchallenged. Organizations such as the Anti-Defamation League, founded by the Jewish service organization B'Nai B'rith in 1913, investigated and exposed the activities of anti-Semitic groups like the KKK. They were joined by the Catholic Holy Names Society, another target of the Klan, which in 1924 mobilized 10,000 marchers to Washington, D.C., to counter the Klan and promote religious tolerance. More than a dozen states, both in the North and South, passed laws aimed at the KKK, which banned the wearing of masks or hoods in public as a means of intimidation. More than these efforts, the conviction and imprisonment in 1925 of the Klan leader D. C. Stephenson for rape and murder dealt a severe blow to the KKK.

Fundamentalism versus Modernism

Protestant fundamentalists also fought to uphold long-established values against modern-day incursions. Around 1910, two wealthy Los Angeles churchgoers had subsidized and distributed a series of booklets called *The Fundamentals*, informing readers that the Bible offered a true account of the genesis and development of humankind and the world and that its words had to be taken literally. After 1920, believers of this approach to interpreting the Bible became known as "fundamentalists." Their preachers spread the message of old-time religion through carnival-like revivals, and ministers used the new medium of radio to broadcast their sermons. Fundamentalism's appeal was strongest in the Midwest and the South — the so-called Bible belt — where residents felt deeply threatened by the secular aspects of modern life that left their conventional religious teachings open to skepticism and scorn.

Nothing bothered fundamentalist Protestants as much as Charles Darwin's theory of evolution. In *On the Origin of Species* (1859), Darwin replaced the biblical story of creation with a scientific theory of the emergence and development of life that centered on evolution and natural selection. Fundamentalists rejected this explanation and repudiated the views of fellow Protestants who attempted to reconcile Darwinian evolution with God's Word by reading the Bible as a symbolic representation of what might have happened. To combat any other interpretation but the biblical one, in 1925 lawmakers in Arkansas, Florida, Mississippi, Oklahoma, and Tennessee made it illegal to teach in public schools and colleges "any theory that denies the story of the Divine Creation of man as taught in the Bible."

Shortly after the anti-evolution law passed, the town of Dayton, Tennessee decided to take advantage of it to attract new investment to the area. The townspeople recruited John Scopes, a general science high school teacher, to defy the law by lecturing from a biology textbook that presented Darwin's theory. With help from the ACLU, which wanted to challenge the restrictive state statute on the grounds of free speech and academic freedom, Dayton turned an ordinary judicial hearing into the "trial of the century."

When court convened in July 1925, millions of people listened over the radio to the first trial ever broadcast. Reporters from all over the country descended on Dayton to keep their readers informed of the proceedings.

Clarence Darrow headed the defense team. A controversial criminal lawyer from Chicago, who in a few months would defend Ossian Sweet, Darrow doubted the existence of God. On the other side, William Jennings Bryan, three-time Democratic candidate for president and secretary of state under Woodrow Wilson, assisted the prosecution. As a Protestant fundamentalist, Bryan believed that accepting scientific evolution would undermine the moral basis of politics and that communities should have the right to determine their children's school curriculum. A minister summed up what the fundamentalists considered to be at stake: "[Darwin's theory] breeds corruption, lust, immorality, greed, and such acts of criminal depravity as drug addiction, war, and atrocious acts of genocide."

The presiding judge ruled that scientists could not take the stand to defend evolution because he considered their testimony "hearsay," given that they had not been present at the creation. The jury took only eight minutes to declare Scopes guilty, but his conviction was overturned by an appeals court on a technicality. Yet fundamentalists remained as certain as ever in their beliefs, and anti-evolution laws stayed in force until the 1970s. The trial served to highlight a cultural division over the place of religion in American society that persists to the present day.

REVIEW & RELATE	• What was the connection between anti-immigrant sentiment and the defense of tradition during the 1920s? • Who challenged the new morality associated with modernization? Why?

Politics and the Fading of Prosperity

These cultural clashes tore the Democratic Party apart, leaving Republicans in command of national politics. As it attracted urban immigrants to its ranks alongside its customary base of white southerners, the Democratic Party tried to reconcile the tensions between traditional and modern America. Its failure to do so kept Republicans in power despite growing evidence of their inability to resolve serious economic problems. Although many progressives continued to press for reform, they were all but powerless to prevent the coming economic crisis.

The Battle for the Soul of the Democratic Party

The 1924 presidential election exposed serious fault lines within the Democratic Party. Since Reconstruction, Democrats had dominated the South. Southern Democrats shared fundamentalist religious beliefs and support for prohibition that usually placed them at odds with big-city Democrats. The northern urban wing of the party represented immigrants who rejected prohibition as contrary to their cultural practices. These distinctions, however, were not absolute — some rural dwellers opposed prohibition, and some urbanites supported temperance.

Delegates to the 1924 Democratic convention in New York City disagreed over a party platform and a presidential candidate. When northeastern urban delegates attempted to insert a plank condemning the Ku Klux Klan for its intolerance, they lost by a thin margin. The sizable number of convention delegates who either belonged to or had been backed by the Klan ensured the proposal's defeat.

The selection of the presidential ticket proved even more divisive. Urban Democrats favored New York governor Alfred E. Smith, who came from an Irish

Catholic immigrant family and had grown up on New York City's Lower East Side. The epitome of everything that rural Democrats despised, Smith also denounced prohibition. After a fierce contest, the pride of New York City lost the nomination to John W. Davis, a West Virginia Protestant and a defender of prohibition. Left deeply divided going into the general election, Davis lost to Calvin Coolidge in a landslide (Map 21.2).

In 1928, the delicate cultural equilibrium within the Democratic Party had shifted in favor of the urban forces. With Stephenson and the Klan discredited and no longer a force in Democratic politics, the delegates nominated Al Smith as their presidential candidate.

The Republicans selected Herbert Hoover, one of the most popular men in the United States. Affectionately called "the Great Humanitarian" for his European relief efforts after World War I, Hoover served as secretary of commerce during the Harding and Coolidge administrations. His name became synonymous with the Republican prosperity of the 1920s. In accepting his party's nomination for president in 1928, Hoover optimistically declared: "We in America today are nearer to the final triumph over poverty than ever before in the history of the land." A Protestant supporter of prohibition from a small town, Hoover was everything Smith was not.

Hoover chose Charles Curtis as his vice-presidential running mate. Curtis's mother belonged to the Kaw Nation in Kansas. Curtis was a firm believer in Indian assimilation, and as a congressman he had successfully sponsored a bill that extended the Dawes Act to Indian territory in Oklahoma. Before campaigning for vice-president, he had served as Senate majority leader.

The outcome of the 1928 election proved predictable. Hoover trounced Smith with 58 percent of the popular vote and more than 80 percent of the electoral vote. Charles Curtis became the first vice-president of Native American ancestry. Despite the weakening economy, Smith lost usually reliable Democratic votes to religious and ethnic prejudices. The New Yorker prevailed only in Massachusetts, Rhode Island, and six southern states but failed to win his home state. A closer look at the election returns showed a significant party realignment under way. Smith succeeded in identifying the Democratic Party with

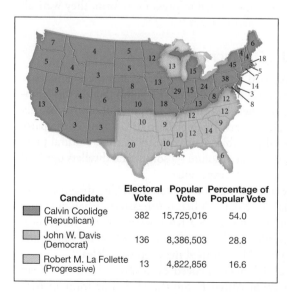

Candidate	Electoral Vote	Popular Vote	Percentage of Popular Vote
Calvin Coolidge (Republican)	382	15,725,016	54.0
John W. Davis (Democrat)	136	8,386,503	28.8
Robert M. La Follette (Progressive)	13	4,822,856	16.6

MAP 21.2 The Election of 1924

Republican Calvin Coolidge, who became president in August 1923 on the death of Warren Harding, continued Harding's policies of limited government regulation and corporate tax cuts. Coolidge easily defeated Democrat John Davis, whose strength was confined to the South. Running as the Progressive Party candidate, Senator Robert La Follette won 16 percent of the popular vote but carried only his home state of Wisconsin, with 13 electoral votes.

urban, ethnic-minority voters and attracting them to the polls. Despite the landslide loss, he captured the twelve largest cities in the nation, all of which had gone Republican four years earlier. To break the Republicans' national dominance, the Democrats would need a candidate who appealed to both traditional and modern Americans. Smith's candidacy, though ending in defeat, laid the foundation for future Democratic political success.

Lingering Progressivism

The Democrats and Republicans were not the only parties that attracted voters in the 1920s. Some voters continued to cast their ballot for the Socialist Party. Others took the opportunity to voice their disapproval of Republican policies by voting for the remaining progressive candidates. Progressives did manage to hold on to seats in Congress, and in 1921 they helped pass the Shepherd-Towner Act, which appropriated federal funds to establish maternal and child centers. Senator Thomas J. Walsh of Montana, a progressive Democrat, led the investigation into the Teapot Dome scandal. But their efforts to restrict the power of the Supreme Court, reduce tax cuts for the wealthy, nationalize railroads, and extend agricultural relief to farmers were rebuffed by conservative legislative majorities. They did succeed in winning congressional passage of an amendment banning child labor, but it failed to win ratification by two-thirds of the states. In 1924, reformers nominated Senator Robert M. La Follette of Wisconsin to run for president on a revived Progressive Party ticket, but he came in a distant third. The Progressive Party collapsed soon after La Follette died in 1925.

Still, progressivism managed to stay alive on the local and state levels. Gifford Pinchot, a Roosevelt ally and a champion of conservation, twice won election as governor of Pennsylvania starting in 1922. Social workers continued their efforts to alleviate urban poverty and lobby for government assistance to the poor. Even at the national level, women in the Children's Bureau maintained the progressive legacy by supporting assistance to families and devising social welfare proposals. Progressivism did not disappear during the 1920s, but it did fight an uphill and often losing battle during an age of conservative political ascendancy. Its weakness contributed to the government's failure to check the worst corporate and financial practices, a failure that would play a role in the nation's economic collapse.

Financial Crash

On October 29, 1929, a day that became known as **Black Tuesday**, stock market prices tumbled. Over the previous five years, the rising market, bolstered by optimistic buyers, earned huge profits for investors, and the value of stocks nearly doubled. In late October, panicked sellers sent stock prices into free fall. Although only 2.5 percent of Americans owned stock, the stock market collapse had an enormous impact on the economy and the rest of the world. Because so much of the stock boom depended on generous margin requirements (a down payment of only 5 to 10 percent), when investor-borrowers got caught short by falling prices, they could not repay the financial institutions that had extended them credit. Banks and lending agencies, with their interlocking management and overextension of credit, had difficulty withstanding the turmoil unleashed by the tumbling stock market.

The 1929 crash signaled the start of the decade-long Great Depression. The seeds for this economic catastrophe had been planted far earlier. The causes stemmed from flaws in an economic system that produced a great disparity of wealth, inadequate consumption, overextension of credit both at home and abroad, and the government's unwillingness to relieve the plight of farmers. Republican administrations made matters worse by lowering taxes on the rich and raising tariffs to benefit manufacturers. The Federal Reserve Board exacerbated the situation by keeping interest rates high, thereby making it difficult for people to get loans and repay debts. The failure was not that of the United States alone; the depression affected capitalist nations throughout the world. The stock market collapse crushed whatever confidence the American public had that the unfettered law of supply and demand and laissez-faire economics could ensure prosperity.

REVIEW & RELATE	• How did divisions within the Democratic Party contribute to Republican political dominance in the 1920s? • What underlying economic weaknesses led to the Great Depression?

Conclusion: The Transitional Twenties

The 1920s signaled the tense transition of the United States from a rural, small-town society to an urban, industrial one. Factories roared with the noise of new products aimed at the mass of American consumers. Automobiles, fueled by gasoline, traveled up and down streets and highways. Electricity powered household appliances and ran movie projectors in theaters throughout the nation. People living throughout the country had similar opportunities to buy consumer products and partake in a mass culture made possible by movies and radio. Producing for a mass market, industrial giants like Henry Ford transformed the nature of work and pleasure. The assembly line revolutionized the pace of labor and turned it into a standardized routine. The automobile transformed dating patterns and opened up new opportunities for the exploration of romance and sex.

Yet the roar of consumption and the excitement of breaking the ties of social and cultural conventions proved fleeting. Most Americans lived at or below the poverty line and earned just enough for bare necessities. They could live beyond their means through an ample supply of credit, but their poverty contrasted with the increasing concentration of wealth in the hands of the richest Americans. The stock market crash of 1929 and the ensuing Great Depression exposed the shortcomings of the corporate business world, inadequate oversight by the federal government, and an overreliance on the private sector to look after the nation's economic health.

The weaknesses of the economy were often overshadowed by the clash over cultural differences. Guardians of traditional morality and values worried about the effects of more than fifty years of industrialization, immigration, and urbanization. Issues such as the enforcement of prohibition, the teaching of evolution in the schools, and the debate about whether a Catholic should be elected president dominated political discussion, while efforts to assist farmers and workers were unsuccessful. These battles marked a turning point in U.S. history — the transition from a traditional, rural, Protestant society to an urban, ethnically and religiously diverse one. The widespread popularity of D. C. Stephenson's Ku Klux Klan throughout the South and the North demonstrated that the older America of white, northern European Protestants did not intend to relinquish political or cultural power without a struggle. At the same time, ethnic minorities represented by Al Smith had no intention of backing down. Neither did millions of African Americans, whether they joined the NAACP, as did Ossian Sweet, or supported Marcus Garvey's UNIA. During the next decade, Americans from all backgrounds would battle more than cultural threats; they would fight for their economic survival.

Chapter 21 Review

KEY TERMS

Red scare, 530
Palmer raids, 531
great migration, 532
Tulsa Massacre, 533
American Plan, 534
Teapot Dome scandal, 534
second industrial revolution, 536
new woman, 541
Lost Generation, 541

New Negro, 542
Harlem Renaissance, 542
Universal Negro Improvement
    Association (UNIA), 542
Sacco and Vanzetti case, 545
National Origins Act, 545
Indian Citizenship Act, 546
Black Tuesday, 551

REVIEW & RELATE

1. What factors combined to produce the turmoil of the immediate postwar period?
2. What factors contributed to the rise in racial tensions that accompanied the transition from wartime to peacetime?
3. Describe the relationship between business and government in the 1920s.
4. Why was a high level of consumer spending so critical to 1920s prosperity, and why was the economic expansion of the 1920s ultimately unsustainable?
5. How did new forms of entertainment challenge traditional morality and traditional gender roles?
6. Describe the black cultural and intellectual renaissance that flourished in the 1920s.
7. What was the connection between anti-immigrant sentiment and the defense of tradition during the 1920s?
8. Who challenged the new morality associated with modernization? Why?
9. How did divisions within the Democratic Party contribute to Republican political dominance in the 1920s?
10. What underlying economic weaknesses led to the Great Depression?

TIMELINE OF EVENTS

1915	• Ku Klux Klan revived
1917–1918	• Great migration begins
1917	• Russian Revolution begins
1918–1920	• Worldwide influenza epidemic
1919	• Ratification of Eighteenth Amendment (Prohibition); Volstead Act passed
	• 4 million workers go on strike nationwide
	• Race riots
	• Radicals mail bombs
	• Palmer raids begin
1919–1929	• Harlem Renaissance
1920	• American Civil Liberties Union (ACLU) formed
1921	• J. Edgar Hoover becomes director of the Bureau of Investigation
	• Teapot Dome scandal
	• Tulsa Massacre
1924	• Indian Citizens Act Passed
	• National Origins Act passed
	• Charles Dawes negotiates reduction in Germany's reparations payments
1925–1929	• U.S. farm income drops by 50 percent
1925	• Scopes trial
1927	• Sacco and Vanzetti executed
1928	• Democrat Al Smith loses presidential election to Republican Herbert Hoover
1929	• Stock market crash sparks Great Depression
	• Formation of League of United Latin American Citizens (LULAC)

22

Depression, Dissent, and the New Deal

1929–1940

LEARNING OBJECTIVES

After reading this chapter you will be able to:

- Evaluate the Hoover administration's response to the Great Depression and its impact on the rural poor, working people, and racial and ethnic minorities.
- Describe the major New Deal programs and assess their positive and negative effects on the groups they were designed to help.
- Explain how the New Deal expanded its scope after 1935 and why it came to an end in 1938.

COMPARING AMERICAN HISTORIES

In 1901, at the age of fifteen, Anna Eleanor Roosevelt saw her uncle Theodore succeed William McKinley as president. Like other girls of her generation, Eleanor was expected to marry and become a "charming wife." Eleanor appeared well on her way toward doing so when she married her distant cousin Franklin Delano Roosevelt in 1905. Over a ten-year period, Eleanor gave birth to six children, further reinforcing her status as a traditional woman of her class.

Two events, however, altered the expected course of her life. First, thirteen years into her marriage **Eleanor Roosevelt** discovered that her husband was having an affair with her social secretary, Lucy Mercer. She did not divorce him but made it clear that she would stay with him primarily as a mother to their children and a political partner. Second, in 1921 Franklin contracted polio. Although he recovered, he would never walk again or stand without the aid of braces. This physical hardship allowed Eleanor to gain increased political influence with Franklin. After her husband won the presidency in 1932, Eleanor did not function as a typical First Lady. She played a very public role promoting her husband's agenda, and she also took advantage of her own extensive contacts in labor unions, civil rights organizations, and women's groups to advance a variety of causes. In many ways more liberal than her husband, Eleanor was a fierce advocate for the rights of women, racial minorities, workers, and the poor. Behind the scenes, she pushed her husband to move further to the political left.

Eleanor Roosevelt's proximity to power provided her with a unique position from which to confront the problems of her day. In contrast, **Luisa Moreno** provides a striking example of an activist whose American story bears little resemblance to that of Roosevelt. A native of Guatemala, Moreno moved to Mexico and then New York City. In the midst of the Great Depression, she worked as a seamstress in a sweatshop to support her young child and unemployed husband. Like tens of thousands of people disillusioned with capitalism, in 1930 she joined the Communist Party but quit several years later.

In 1935 Moreno went to Florida to organize cigar workers for the American Federation of Labor (AFL). Despite numerous successes, she grew tired of the AFL's refusal to recruit unskilled workers and jumped to the United Cannery, Agricultural, Packing, and Allied Workers of America (UCAPAWA), an affiliate of the Congress of Industrial Organizations (CIO).

Moreno promoted the advancement of Latinos throughout the United States. In 1939 she helped create El Congreso de Pueblos de Habla Española (The Congress of Spanish-Speaking People). Besides championing equal access to jobs, education, housing, and health care, the organization pressed to end the segregation of Latinos in schools and public accommodations. Moreno was not nearly as well-known as Eleanor Roosevelt, but she worked just as hard to fight poverty, exploitation, and racial bigotry on behalf of people whom President Franklin Roosevelt called "the forgotten Americans."

THE AMERICAN HISTORIES of Eleanor Roosevelt and Luisa Moreno are very different, but both of their lives were shaped in fundamental ways by the same global catastrophe, the Great Depression. Even before the Great Depression, most Americans lived at or near the poverty level, surviving month to month. By 1933, millions of Americans had lost even this tenuous hold on economic security, as unemployment reached a record 25 percent. The Republican administration of President Herbert Hoover depended on private charity and voluntary efforts to meet the needs of downtrodden Americans afflicted by the Depression, but these efforts fell short of the vast need that grew during the Depression and left many frustrated. Proclaiming the establishment of a New Deal for America, Franklin Roosevelt expanded the power of the federal government by initiating relief, recovery, and reform measures, all the while drawing critics on the political left and right. In seeking to break from the past, Roosevelt occasionally overextended his reach, as he did in challenging the Supreme Court. Despite its successes, the New Deal did not end the depression and left racial and ethnic minorities and the rural and urban poor still suffering.

The Great Depression

Herbert Hoover had the unenviable task of assuming the presidency in 1929 just as the economy was about to crumble. Given his long history of public service, he seemed the right man for the job. Hoover, however, was unwilling to make a fundamental break with conventional economic approaches and proved unable to effectively communicate his genuine concern for the plight of the poor. Despite his sincere efforts, the depression deepened. As this happened, many Americans, made desperate by their economic plight and angered by the inadequate response of their government, took to the streets in protest.

Hoover Faces the Depression

National prosperity was at its peak when the Republican Hoover entered the White House in March 1929. Hoover brought to the presidency a blend of traditional and progressive ideas. He believed that government and business should form voluntary partnerships to work toward common goals. He argued that the government should extend its influence lightly over the economy—to encourage and persuade sensible behavior, but not to impose itself on the private sector.

The Great Depression sorely tested Hoover's beliefs. Having placed his faith in cooperation rather than coercion, the president relied on voluntarism to get the nation through hard economic times. Hoover hoped that management and labor, through gentle persuasion, would hold steady on prices and wages. In the meantime, for those in dire need, the president turned to local communities and private charities. Hoover expected municipal and state governments to shoulder the burden of providing relief to the needy, just as they had during previous economic downturns.

Hoover's remedies failed to rally the country back to good economic health. Initially, businesspeople responded positively to the president's request to maintain the status quo, but when the economy did not bounce back, they lost confidence and defected. Nor did local governments and private agencies have the funds to provide relief to all those who needed it. With tax revenues in decline, some 1,300 municipalities across the country had gone bankrupt by 1933. Benevolent societies and religious groups could handle short-term misfortunes, but they could not cope with the ongoing disaster of mass unemployment (Figure 22.1).

As confidence in recovery fell and the economy sank deeper into depression, President Hoover shifted direction. He persuaded Congress to lower income tax rates and to allocate an unprecedented $423 million for federal public works projects. In 1929 the president signed into law the Agricultural Marketing Act, a measure aimed at raising prices for long-suffering farmers.

Hoover's recovery efforts fell short, however. He retreated from initiating greater spending because he feared government deficits more than unemployment. With federal

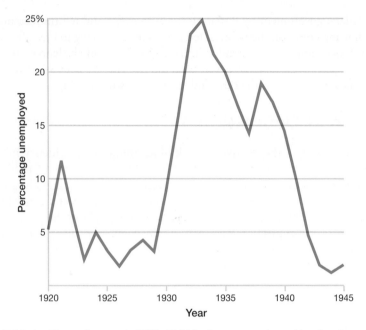

FIGURE 22.1 Unemployment, 1920–1945 Business prosperity and immigration restriction ensured low unemployment during most of the 1920s. When unemployment rose dramatically in the late 1920s, President Hoover failed to handle the crisis. During the 1930s, President Roosevelt's New Deal took initiatives to lower unemployment. What does this figure indicate about the effectiveness of New Deal programs on unemployment?

accounting sheets showing a rising deficit, Hoover reversed course in 1932 and joined with Congress in sharply raising income, estate, and corporate taxes on the wealthy. This effectively slowed down investment and new production, throwing millions more American workers out of jobs. The Hawley-Smoot Act, passed by Congress in 1930, made matters worse. In an effort to replenish revenues and protect American farmers and companies from foreign competition, the act increased tariffs on agricultural and industrial imports. However, other countries retaliated by raising their import duties, which hurt American companies because it diminished demand for American exports.

In an exception to his aversion to spending, Hoover lobbied Congress to create the Reconstruction Finance Corporation (RFC) to supply loans to troubled banks, railroads, and insurance companies. By injecting federal dollars into these critical enterprises, the president and lawmakers expected to produce dividends that would trickle down from the top of the economic structure to the bottom. In 1932 Congress gave the RFC a budget of $1.5 billion to employ people in public works projects, a significant allocation for those individuals hardest hit by the depression.

This departure from Republican economic philosophy failed to reach its goal. The RFC spent its budget too cautiously, and its funds reached primarily those institutions that could best afford to repay the loans, ignoring the companies in the greatest difficulty. Wealth never trickled down. Hoover was not indifferent to the plight of others, but he was incapable of breaking away from his ideological preconceptions. He refused to support expenditures for direct relief for basic needs (what today we call welfare) and hesitated to extend assistance for work relief because he believed that it would ruin individual initiative and character.

Hoover and the United States did not face the Great Depression alone; it was a worldwide calamity. By 1933 Germany, France, and Great Britain were all facing mass unemployment. In this climate of extreme social and economic unrest, authoritarian dictators came to power in a number of European countries, including Germany, Italy, Spain, and Portugal. Each claimed that his country's social and economic problems could be solved only by placing power in the hands of a single, all-powerful leader.

Hoovervilles and Dust Storms

The depression hit all areas of the United States hard. In large cities, families crowded into apartments with no gas or electricity and little food to put on the table. In Los Angeles, people cooked their meals over wood fires in backyards. In many cities, the homeless constructed makeshift housing consisting of cartons, old newspapers, and cloth—what journalists derisively dubbed Hoovervilles. Thousands of hungry citizens wound up living under bridges in Portland, Oregon; in wrecked autos in city dumps in Brooklyn, New York, and Stockton, California; and in abandoned coal furnaces in Pittsburgh.

Rural workers fared no better. Landlords in West Virginia and Kentucky evicted coal miners and their families from their homes in the dead of winter, forcing them to live in tents. Farmers in the Great Plains, who were already experiencing foreclosures,

Soup Kitchen, 1931 At the height of the Great Depression, these unemployed men stand in a long line outside a Chicago soup kitchen waiting for a meal. Without major government relief efforts for the unemployed during the Hoover administration, such men depended mainly on the efforts of charity. In this instance, the notorious gangster Al Capone set up this establishment before going to federal prison for tax evasion in 1932. National Archives, photo no. 306-NT-165319c

were little prepared for the even greater natural disaster that laid waste to their farms. In the early 1930s, dust storms swept through western Kansas, eastern Colorado, western Oklahoma, the Texas Panhandle, and eastern New Mexico, in an area that came to be known as the Dust Bowl, destroying crops and plant and animal life (Map 22.1). The storms resulted from both climatological and human causes. A series of droughts had destroyed crops and turned the earth into sand, which gusts of wind deposited on everything that lay in their path. Though they did not realize it at the time, plains farmers, by focusing on growing wheat for income, had neglected planting trees and grasses that would have kept the earth from eroding and turning into dust.

As the storms continued through the 1930s, most residents—approximately 75 percent—remained on the plains. Millions, however, headed for California looking for relief from the plague of swirling dirt and hoping to find jobs in the state's fruit and vegetable fields. Although they came from several states besides Oklahoma, these migrants came to be known as "Okies," a derogatory term used by those who resented and looked down on the poverty-stricken newcomers to their communities. John Steinbeck's novel *The Grapes of Wrath* (1939) portrayed the plight of the fictional Joad family as storms and a bank foreclosure destroyed their Oklahoma farm and sent them on the road to California.

Challenges for Racial Minorities

Given the demographics of the workforce, the overwhelming majority of Americans who lost their jobs were white men; yet racial and ethnic minorities, including African Americans, Latinos, and Asian Americans, suffered disproportionate hardship. Racial discrimination had kept these groups from achieving economic and political equality, and the Great Depression added to their woes.

Traditionally the last hired and the first fired, blacks occupied the lowest rungs on the industrial and agricultural ladders. "The depression brought everybody down a peg or two," the African American poet Langston Hughes wryly commented. "And the Negroes had but few pegs to fall." Despite the great migration to the North during and after World War I, three-quarters of the black population still lived in the South. Mainly sharecroppers and tenant farmers, black southerners were mired in debt that they could not repay as crop prices plunged to record lows during the 1920s. As white landowners struggled to save their farms

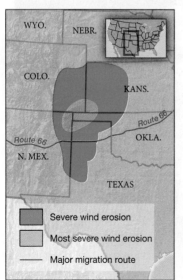

MAP 22.1   **The Dust Bowl**
Although "Okies" was the term used for the migrants escaping the Dust Bowl and heading to California, as depicted in John Steinbeck's classic novel *Grapes of Wrath*, Oklahoma was not the only state from where they came. Many of those who fled the terrible windstorms also journeyed from their homes in Kansas, Texas, and Colorado. Seen at the time as a natural phenomenon, the dust storms in fact originated from man-made agricultural practices that eroded the soil.

by introducing machinery to cut labor costs, they forced black sharecroppers off the land and into even greater poverty. Nor was the situation better for black workers employed at the lowest-paying jobs as janitors, menial laborers, maids, and laundresses. On average, African Americans earned $200 a year, less than one-quarter of the average wage of white factory workers.

The economic misfortune that African Americans experienced was compounded by the fact that they lived in a society rigidly constructed to preserve white supremacy. The 25 percent of blacks living in the North faced racial discrimination in employment, housing, and the criminal justice system, but at least they could express their opinions and desires by voting. By contrast, black southerners remained segregated and disfranchised by law. The depression also exacerbated racial tensions, as whites and blacks competed for the shrinking number of jobs. Lynching, which had declined during the 1920s, surged upward—in 1933 twenty-four blacks lost their lives to this form of terrorism.

Events in Scottsboro, Alabama, reflected the special misery African Americans faced during the Great Depression. Trouble erupted in 1931 when two young, unemployed white women, Ruby Bates and Victoria Price, snuck onto a freight train heading to Huntsville, Alabama. Before the train reached the Scottsboro depot, a fight broke out between black and white men on top of the freight car occupied by the two women. After the train pulled in to Scottsboro, the local sheriff arrested nine black youths between the ages of twelve and nineteen. Charges of assault quickly escalated into rape, when the women told authorities that the black men in custody had molested them on board the train.

The defendants' court-appointed attorney was less than competent and had little time to prepare his clients' cases. It probably made no difference, as the all-white male jury swiftly convicted the accused and awarded the harshest of sentences; only the youngest defendant was not given the death penalty. The Supreme Court spared the lives of the **Scottsboro Nine** by overturning their guilty verdicts in 1932 on the grounds that the defendants did not have adequate legal representation and again in 1935 because blacks had been systematically excluded from the jury pool. Although Ruby Bates had recanted her testimony and there was no physical evidence of rape, retrials in 1936 and 1937 produced the same guilty verdicts, but this time the defendants did not receive the death penalty—a minor victory considering the charges. State prosecutors dismissed charges against four of the accused, all of whom had already spent six years in jail. Despite international protests against this racist injustice, the last of the remaining five did not leave jail until 1950.

Racism also worsened the impact of the Great Depression on Spanish-speaking Americans. Mexicans and Mexican Americans made up the largest segment of the Latino population living in the United States. Concentrated in the Southwest and California, they worked in a variety of low-wage factory jobs and as migrant laborers in fruit and vegetable fields. The depression reduced the Mexican-born population living in the United States in two ways. The federal government, in cooperation with state and local governments and private businesses, deported (or what officials called "repatriation") around one million Mexicans, a majority of whom were American citizens. Los Angeles officials organized more than a dozen deportation trains transporting thousands of Mexicans to the border. Many others returned to Mexico voluntarily when demand for labor in the United States dried up.

The exodus eased off by 1933, as the number of migrants no longer posed an economic threat and the Roosevelt administration adopted more humane policies. Those who remained endured growing hardships. Relief agencies refused to provide them with the same benefits as whites. Like African Americans, they encountered discrimination in public schools, in public accommodations, and at the ballot box. Conditions remained harshest for migrant workers toiling long hours for little pay and living in overcrowded and poorly constructed housing. In both fields and factories, employers had little incentive to improve the situation because there were plenty of white migrant workers to fill their positions.

The transient nature of agricultural work and the vulnerability of Mexican laborers made it difficult for workers to organize, but Mexican Americans played a pivotal role in forming some forty agricultural unions in California during the 1930s. Mexican American laborers engaged in dozens of strikes in California and Texas. Most ended in defeat, but a few, such as a strike of pecan shellers in San Antonio, Texas, led by Luisa Moreno, won better working conditions and higher wages. Toward the end of the decade, strikers in California's San Joaquin Valley won pay raises after the state labor commission concluded: "Without question civil rights of strikers have been violated." Despite these hard-fought victories, the condition of Latinos remained precarious.

On the West Coast, Asian Americans also remained economically and politically marginalized. Japanese immigrants eked out livings as small farmers, grocers, and gardeners, despite California laws preventing them from owning land. Many of their college-educated U.S.-born children found few professional opportunities available to them, and they often returned to work in family businesses. The depression magnified the problem. Like other racial and ethnic minorities, Japanese people found it harder to find even the lowest-wage jobs now that unemployed whites were willing to take them. As a result, about one-fifth of Japanese immigrants returned to Japan during the 1930s.

Chinese people suffered a similar fate. Although some 45 percent of Chinese Americans had been born in the United States and were citizens, people of Chinese ancestry remained isolated in ethnic communities along the West Coast. Discriminated against in schools and most occupations, many operated restaurants and laundries. During the depression, those Chinese who did not obtain assistance through governmental relief turned instead to their own community organizations and to extended families to help them through the hard times.

Filipino immigrants had arrived on the West Coast after the Philippines became a territory of the United States in 1901. Working as low-wage agricultural laborers, they were subject to the same kind of racial animosity as other minorities. Filipino farmworkers organized agricultural labor unions and conducted numerous strikes in California, but like their Mexican counterparts they were brutally repressed. In 1934 anti-Filipino hostility reached its height when Congress passed the Tydings-McDuffie Act. The measure accomplished two aims at once: The act granted independence to the Philippines, and it restricted Filipino immigration into the United States.

Families under Strain

With millions of men unemployed, women faced increased family responsibilities. Stay-at-home wives had to care for their children and provide emotional support for out-of-work husbands who had lost their role as the family breadwinner. Despite the loss of income, homemakers continued their daily routines of shopping, cooking, cleaning, and child rearing.

Disproportionate male unemployment led to an increase in the importance of women's income. The depression hit male-dominated industries like steel mills and automakers the hardest. As a result, men were more likely to lose their jobs than women. Although more women held on to their jobs, their often meager wages had to go further because many now had to support unemployed fathers and husbands. During the 1930s, federal and local governments sought to increase male employment by passing laws to keep married women from holding civil service and teaching positions. Nonetheless, more and more married women entered the workplace, and by 1940 the proportion of women in the job force had grown by about 25 percent.

As had been the case in previous decades, a higher proportion of African American women than white women worked outside the home in the 1930s. By 1940 about 40 percent of African American women held jobs, compared to about 25 percent of white women. Racial discrimination played a key role in establishing this pattern. Black men faced higher unemployment rates than did their white counterparts, and what work was available was often limited to the lowest-paying jobs. As a result, black women faced greater pressure to supplement family incomes. Still, unemployment rates for black women reached as high as 50 percent during the 1930s.

Despite increased burdens, most American families remained intact and discovered ways to survive the economic crisis. They pared down household budgets, made do without telephones and new clothes, and held on to their automobiles for longer periods of time. What money they managed to save they often spent on movies. Comedies, gangster movies, fantasy tales, and uplifting films helped viewers forget their troubles, if only for a few hours. Radio remained the chief source of entertainment, and radio sales doubled in the 1930s as listeners tuned in to soap operas, comedy and adventure shows, news reports, and musical programs.

Organized Protest

As the depression deepened, angry citizens found ways to express their discontent. Farmers had suffered economic hardship longer than any other group. Even before 1929, they had seen prices spiral downward, but in the early 1930s agricultural income plummeted 60 percent, and one-third of farmers lost their land (Figure 22.2). Some farmers decided that the time had come for drastic action. In the summer of 1932, Milo Reno, an Iowa farmer, created the Farm Holiday Association to organize farmers to keep their produce from going to market and thereby raise prices. Strikers from the association blocked roads and bullied other reluctant farmers by smashing their truck windshields and headlights and slashing their tires. When law enforcement officials arrested fifty-five demonstrators in Council Bluffs, thousands of farmers marched on the jail and forced their release. Despite armed attempts to prevent foreclosures and the intentional destruction of vast quantities of farm produce, the Farm Holiday Association failed to achieve its goal of raising prices.

Disgruntled urban residents also resorted to protest. Although the Communist Party remained a tiny group of just over 10,000 members in 1932, it played a large role in organizing the dispossessed. In major cities such as New York, Communists set up unemployment councils and led marches and rallies demanding jobs and

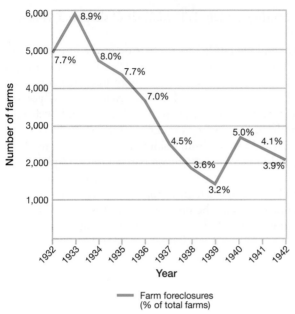

FIGURE 22.2 Farm Foreclosures, 1932–1942 A drop of 60 percent in prices led to a wave of farm foreclosures and rural protests in the early 1930s. From 1934 on, federal programs that promoted rural electrification, crop allotments, commodity loans, and mortgage credits allowed many farmers to retain their land. What does this figure reveal about the pattern of farm foreclosures?

food. In Harlem, the party endorsed rent strikes by African American apartment residents against their landlords. Party members did not confine their activities to the urban Northeast. They also went south to defend the Scottsboro Nine and to organize industrial workers in the steel mills of Birmingham and sharecroppers in the surrounding rural areas of Alabama. On the West Coast, Communists unionized seamen and waterfront workers and led strikes. They also recruited writers, directors, and actors in Hollywood.

One of the most visible protests of the early 1930s centered on the Ford factory in Dearborn, Michigan. As the depression worsened after 1930, Henry Ford, who had initially pledged to keep employee wages steady, changed his mind and reduced wages. On March 7, 1932, spearheaded by Communists, three thousand autoworkers marched from Detroit to Ford's River Rouge plant in nearby Dearborn. When they reached the factory town, they faced policemen indiscriminately firing bullets and tear gas, which killed four demonstrators. The attack provoked great outrage. Around forty thousand mourners attended the funeral of the four protesters; sang the Communist anthem, the "Internationale"; and surrounded the caskets, which were draped in a red banner emblazoned with a picture of Bolshevik hero Vladimir Lenin.

Protests spread beyond Communist agitators. The federal government faced an uprising by some of the nation's most patriotic and loyal citizens—World War I veterans. Scheduled to receive a $1,000 bonus for their service, unemployed veterans could not wait until the payment date arrived in 1945. Instead, in the spring of 1932 a group of ex-soldiers from Portland, Oregon set off on a march on Washington, D.C., to demand immediate payment of the bonus by the federal government. By the time they reached the nation's capital, the ranks of this **Bonus Army** had swelled to around twenty thousand veterans. They camped in the Anacostia Flats section of the city, constructed ramshackle shelters, and in many cases moved their families in with them.

Although many veterans eventually returned home, much of the Bonus Army remained in place until late July. When President Hoover decided to clear the capital of the protesters, violence ensued. Rather than engaging in a measured and orderly removal, General Douglas MacArthur overstepped presidential orders and used excessive force to disperse the veterans and their families. The Third Cavalry, commanded by George S. Patton, torched tents and sent their residents fleeing from the city.

In this one-sided battle, the biggest loser was President Hoover. Through four years of the country's worst depression, Hoover had lost touch with the American people. His cheerful words of encouragement fell increasingly on deaf ears. As workers, farmers, and veterans stirred in protest, Hoover appeared aloof, standoffish, and insensitive.

REVIEW & RELATE	• How did President Hoover respond to the problems and challenges created by the Great Depression? • How did different segments of the American population experience the depression?

The New Deal

The nation was ready for a change, and on election day 1932, with hard times showing no sign of abating, Democratic presidential candidate Franklin Delano Roosevelt, the governor of New York, defeated Hoover easily. Roosevelt won 57 percent of the popular votes and garnered an overwhelming 472 electoral votes. He attracted a coalition of the poor: farmers and city dwellers, laborers and immigrants, northerners and southerners (the majority of African Americans did not join the coalition until 1936). Roosevelt's sizable victory provided him with a mandate to take the country in a bold new direction. However, few Americans, including Roosevelt himself, knew exactly what the new president meant to do or what his pledge of a New Deal would mean for the country.

Roosevelt Restores Confidence

As a presidential candidate, Roosevelt presented no clear, coherent policy. He did not spell out how his plans for the country would differ from Hoover's, but he did refer broadly to providing a "new deal" and bringing to the White House "persistent experimentation." Roosevelt's appeal derived more from the genuine compassion he was able to convey than from his promises. In this context, Eleanor Roosevelt's evident concern for people's suffering and her history of activism made Franklin Roosevelt even more attractive.

Instead of any fixed ideology, FDR, as he was popularly known, followed what one historian has called "pragmatic humanism." A seasoned politician who understood the need for flexibility, Roosevelt blended principle and practicality. "It is common sense," Roosevelt explained, "to take a method and try it. If it fails, admit it frankly and try another. But above all, try something." More than any president before him, FDR created an expectation among Americans that the federal government would take concrete action to improve their lives. A Colorado woman expressed her appreciation to Eleanor Roosevelt: "Your husband is great. He seems

Franklin Delano Roosevelt Campaigning in Kansas, 1932   New York governor Franklin D. Roosevelt promises a "new deal" to farmers in Topeka, Kansas, as he campaigns for president in 1932 as the Democratic candidate. Photographers were careful not to show that Roosevelt was unable to use his legs, which were paralyzed after he contracted polio in 1921. His son James, seated at the left, often propped up his father so that it appeared he could stand on his own, as he is doing in this photograph. Roosevelt forged a coalition of farmers and urban workers and easily defeated the incumbent Hoover. Franklin D. Roosevelt Library

lovable even tho' he is a 'politician.' " The New Deal would take its twists and turns, but Roosevelt never lost the support of the majority of Americans.

Starting with his inaugural address, in which he declared that "the only thing we have to fear is fear itself," Roosevelt took on the task of rallying the American people and restoring their confidence in the future. Using the power of radio to communicate directly, Roosevelt delivered regular fireside chats in which he boosted morale and informed his audience of the steps the government was taking to help solve their problems. Roosevelt's **New Deal** would provide relief, put millions of people to work, raise prices for farmers, extend conservation projects, revitalize America's financial system, and rescue capitalism.

Steps toward Recovery

President Roosevelt took swift action on entering office. In March 1933 he issued an executive order shutting down banks for several days to calm the panic that gripped many Americans in the wake of bank failures and the loss of their life's savings. Shortly after, Congress passed the administration's Emergency Banking Act, which subjected banks to Treasury Department inspection before they reopened, reorganized the banking system, and provided federal funds to bail out banks on the brink of closing. This assertion of federal power allowed solvent banks to reopen. Boosting confidence further, Congress passed the Glass-Steagall Act in June 1933. The measure created the **Federal Deposit Insurance Corporation (FDIC)**, insuring personal savings accounts up to $5,000, and detached commercial banks from investment banks to avoid risky speculation. The president also sought tighter supervision of the stock market. By June 1934 Roosevelt had signed into law measures setting up the Securities and Exchange Commission (SEC) to regulate the stock market and ensure that corporations gave investors accurate information about their portfolios.

The regulation of banks and the stock exchange did not mean that Roosevelt was antibusiness. He affirmed his belief in a balanced budget and sought to avoid a $1 billion deficit by cutting government workers' salaries and lowering veterans' pensions. Roosevelt also tried to keep the budget under control by ending prohibition, which would allow the government to tax alcohol sales and eliminate the cost of enforcement. The Twenty-first Amendment, ratified in 1933, ended the more than decade-long experiment with temperance.

As important as these measures were, the Roosevelt administration had much more to accomplish before those hardest hit by the depression felt some relief. Roosevelt viewed the Great Depression as a crisis analogous to war and adapted many of the bureaus and commissions used during World War I to ensure productivity and mobilize popular support to fit the current economic emergency. Many former progressives lined up behind Roosevelt, including women reformers and social workers who had worked in government and private agencies during the 1920s. At his wife Eleanor's urging, Roosevelt appointed one of them, Frances Perkins, as the first woman to head a cabinet agency—the Department of Labor.

Rehabilitating agriculture and industry stood at the top of the New Deal's priority list. Farmers came first. In May 1933 Congress passed the **Agricultural Adjustment Act**, aimed at raising prices by reducing production. The Agricultural Adjustment Administration (AAA) paid farmers subsidies to produce less in the future, and for farmers who had already planted their crops and raised livestock, the agency paid them to plow under a portion of their harvest, slaughter hogs, and destroy dairy products. By 1935 the program succeeded in raising farm income by 50 percent. Large farmers remained the chief beneficiaries of the AAA because they could afford to cut back production. In doing so, especially in the South, they forced off the land sharecroppers who no longer had plots to farm. Even when sharecroppers managed to retain a parcel of their acreage, AAA subsidies went to the landowners, who did not always distribute the designated funds owed to the sharecroppers. Though poor white farmers felt the sting of this injustice, the system of white supremacy existing in the South guaranteed that blacks suffered most.

The Roosevelt administration exhibited its boldest initiative in creating the **Tennessee Valley Authority (TVA)** in 1933, to bring low-cost electric power to rural areas and help redevelop the entire Tennessee River valley region through flood-control projects. In contrast to the AAA and other farm programs in which control stayed in private hands, the TVA owned and supervised the building and operation of public power plants. For farmers outside the Tennessee River valley, the Rural Electrification Administration helped them obtain cheap electric power starting in 1935, and for the first time tens of thousands of farmers experienced the modern conveniences that electricity brought (though most farmers would not get electric power until after World War II).

Roosevelt and Congress also acted to deal with the soil erosion problem behind the dust storms. In 1933 the Department of the Interior established a Soil Erosion Service, and two years later Congress created a permanent Soil Conservation Service in the Department of Agriculture. Although these measures would prove beneficial in the long run, they did nothing to prevent even more severe storms from rolling through the Dust Bowl in 1935 and 1936.

At the same time, Roosevelt concentrated on industrial recovery. In 1933 Congress passed the National Industrial Recovery Act, which established the **National Recovery Administration (NRA)**. This agency allowed business, labor, and the public (represented by government officials) to create codes to regulate production, prices, wages, hours, and collective bargaining. Designers of the NRA expected that if wages rose and prices remained stable, consumer purchasing power would climb, demand would grow, and businesses would put people back to work. For this plan to work, businesspeople needed to keep prices steady by absorbing some of the costs of higher wages. Businesses that joined the NRA displayed the symbol of the blue eagle to signal their patriotic participation.

However, the NRA did not function as planned, nor did it bring the desired recovery. Businesses did not exercise the necessary restraint to keep prices steady. Large manufacturers dominated the code-making committees, and because Roosevelt had suspended enforcement of the antitrust law, they could not resist taking collective action to force smaller firms out of business. The NRA legislation guaranteed labor the right to unionize, but the agency did not vigorously enforce collective bargaining. The government failed to intervene to redress the imbalance of power between labor and management because Roosevelt depended primarily on big business to generate economic improvement. Moreover, the NRA had created codes for too many businesses, and government officials could not properly oversee them all. In 1935 the Supreme Court delivered the final blow to the NRA by declaring it an unconstitutional delegation of legislative power to the president.

Direct Assistance and Relief

Economic recovery programs were important, but they took time to take effect, and many Americans needed immediate help. Thus, relief efforts and direct job creation were critical parts of the New Deal. Created in the early months of Roosevelt's term, the Federal Emergency Relief Administration (FERA) provided cash grants to states to revive their bankrupt relief efforts. Roosevelt chose Harry Hopkins, the chief of New York's relief agency, to head the FERA and distribute its initial $500 million appropriation. On the job for two hours, Hopkins had already spent $5 million. He did not calculate whether a particular plan "would work out in the long run," because, as he remarked, "people don't eat in the long run — they eat every day."

Harold Ickes, secretary of the interior and director of the Public Works Administration (PWA), oversaw efforts to rebuild the nation's infrastructure. Funding architects, engineers, and skilled workers, the PWA built the Grand Coulee, Boulder, and Bonneville dams in the West; the Triborough Bridge in New York City; 70 percent of all new schools constructed between 1933 and 1939; and a variety of municipal buildings, sewage plants, port facilities, and hospitals.

Yet neither the FERA nor the PWA provided enough relief to the millions who faced the winter of 1933–1934 without jobs or the money to heat their homes. In response, Hopkins persuaded Roosevelt to launch a temporary program to help needy Americans get through this difficult period. Both men favored "work relief" — giving people jobs rather than direct welfare payments whenever practical. The Civil Works Administration (CWA) lasted four months, but in that brief time it employed more than 4 million people on about 400,000 projects that built 500,000 miles of roads, 40,000 schools, 3,500 playgrounds, and 1,000 airports.

One of Roosevelt's most successful relief programs was the **Civilian Conservation Corps (CCC)**, created shortly after he entered the White House. The CCC recruited unmarried men between the ages of eighteen and twenty-five for a two-year stint, putting them to work planting forests; cleaning up beaches, rivers, and parks; and building bridges and dams. Participants received $1 per day, and the government sent $25 of the $30 in monthly wages directly to their families, helping make this the most popular of all New Deal programs. The CCC employed around 2.5 million men and lasted until 1942.

New Deal Critics

Despite the unprecedented efforts of the Roosevelt administration to spark recovery, provide relief, and encourage reform between 1933 and 1935, the country remained in depression, and unemployment still hovered around 20 percent. Roosevelt found himself under attack from both the left and the right. On the right, conservatives questioned New Deal spending and the growth of big government. On the left, the president's critics argued that he had not done enough to topple wealthy corporate leaders from power and relieve the plight of the downtrodden.

In 1934 officials of the Du Pont Corporation and General Motors formed the American Liberty League. From the point of view of the league's founders, the New Deal was little more than a vehicle for the spread of socialism and communism. The organization spent $1 million attacking what it considered to be Roosevelt's "dictatorial" policies and his assaults on free enterprise. The league, however, failed to attract support beyond a small group of northern industrialists, Wall Street bankers, and disaffected Democrats.

Corporate leaders also harnessed Christian ministers to promote their pro-capitalism, anti–New Deal message. The United States Chamber of Commerce and the National Association of Manufacturers allied with clergymen to challenge "creeping socialism." In 1935 the Reverend James W. Fifield founded Spiritual Mobilization and, from the pulpit of his wealthy First Congregational Church in Los Angeles, praised capitalism as a pillar of Christianity and attacked the "pagan statism" of the New Deal.

Roosevelt also faced criticism from the left. Communist Party membership reached its peak of around 75,000 in 1938, and though the party remained relatively small in numbers, it attracted intellectuals and artists whose voices could reach the larger public. Party members led unionizing drives in both the North and the South and displayed great talent and energy in organizing workers where resistance to unions was greatest. In the mid-1930s, the party followed the Soviet Union's anti-fascist foreign policy and joined with left-leaning, non-Communist groups, such as unions and civil rights organizations, to oppose the growing menace of fascism in

Europe, particularly in Germany and Italy. As a result, the Communist Party joined New Deal liberals, unions, socialists, and civil rights advocates in the **Popular Front**, an alliance for social change rather than revolution. By the end of the decade, however, the Popular Front dissolved as the Communist Party lost credibility after the Soviet Union reversed its anti-Nazi foreign policy.

The greatest challenge to Roosevelt came from a trio of talented men who reflected diverse beliefs. Francis Townsend, a retired California physician, proposed a "Cure for Depressions." In 1934 he formed the Old-Age Revolving Pensions Corporation, whose title summed up the doctor's idea. Townsend would have the government give all Americans over the age of sixty a monthly pension of $200 if they retired and spent the entire stipend each month. Retirements would open up jobs for younger workers, and the income these workers received, along with the pension for the elderly, would pump ample funds into the economy to promote recovery. The government would fund the Townsend plan with a 2 percent "transaction" or sales tax. By 1936 Townsend Clubs had attracted about 3.5 million members throughout the country, and one-fifth of all adults in the United States signed a petition endorsing the Townsend plan.

While Townsend appealed mainly to the elderly, Charles E. Coughlin, a priest from the Detroit area, attracted Catholics and a lower-middle-class following. Father Coughlin used his popular national radio broadcasts to talk about economic and political issues. Originally a Roosevelt supporter, in 1934 Coughlin created the National Union for Social Justice and began criticizing the New Deal for catering to greedy bankers. He spoke to millions of radio listeners about the evils of the Roosevelt administration, the godless Communists who had allegedly infested it, and international bankers — coded language referring to Jews — who supposedly manipulated it. As the decade wore on, his strident anti-Semitism and his growing fondness for fascist dictatorships abroad overshadowed his economic justice message, and Catholic officials ordered him to stop broadcasting.

Huey Pierce Long of Louisiana posed the greatest political threat to Roosevelt. Unlike Townsend and Coughlin, Long had built and operated a successful political machine, first as governor and then as U.S. senator, taking on the special interests of oil and railroad corporations in his home state. Early on he had backed Roosevelt, but Long found the New Deal wanting. In 1934 Long established the Share Our Wealth society, promising to make "every man a king" by presenting families with a $5,000 homestead and a guaranteed annual income of $2,000. To accomplish this, Long proposed levying heavy income and inheritance taxes on the wealthy. Although the financial calculations behind his bold plan did not add up, Share Our Wealth clubs counted some seven million members. The swaggering senator departed from most of his segregationist southern colleagues by appealing to a coalition of disgruntled farmers, industrial workers, and African Americans. Before Long could help lead a third-party campaign for president, he was shot and killed in 1935.

REVIEW & RELATE

- What steps did Roosevelt take to stimulate economic recovery and provide relief to impoverished Americans during his first term in office?
- What criticisms did Roosevelt's opponents level against the New Deal?

The New Deal Moves to the Left

Facing criticism from within his own party about the pace and effectiveness of the New Deal, and with the 1936 election looming, Roosevelt moved to the left. He adopted harsher rhetoric against recalcitrant corporate leaders; beefed up economic and social programs for the unemployed, the elderly, and the infirm; and revived measures to redress the power imbalance between management and labor. In doing so, he fashioned a New Deal political coalition that would deliver a landslide victory in 1936 and allow the Democratic Party to dominate electoral politics for the next three decades.

Expanding Relief Measures

Even though the New Deal had helped millions of people, millions of others still felt left out, as the popularity of Townsend, Coughlin, and Long indicated. "We the people voted for you," a Columbus, Ohio worker wrote the president in disgust, "but it is a different story now. You have faded out on the masses of hungry, idle people. . . . The very rich is the only one who has benefited from your new deal."

In 1935 the president seized the opportunity to win his way back into the hearts of impoverished "forgotten Americans." Although Roosevelt favored a balanced budget, political necessity forced him to embark on deficit spending to expand the New Deal. Federal government expenditures would now exceed tax revenues, but New Dealers argued that these outlays would stimulate job creation and economic growth, which ultimately would replenish government coffers. Based on the highly successful but short-lived Civil Works Administration, the **Works Progress Administration (WPA)** provided jobs for the unemployed with a far larger budget, starting out with $5 billion. To ensure that the money would be spent, Roosevelt appointed Harry Hopkins to head the agency. Although critics condemned the WPA for employing people on unproductive "make-work" jobs, overall the WPA did a great deal of good. The agency constructed or repaired more than 100,000 public buildings, 600 airports, 500,000 miles of roads, and 100,000 bridges. The WPA employed about 8.5 million workers during its eight years of operation.

The WPA also helped artists, writers, and musicians. Under its auspices, the Federal Writers Project, the Federal Art Project, the Federal Music Project, and the Federal Theater Project encouraged the production of cultural works and helped bring them to communities and audiences throughout the country. Writers Richard Wright, Ralph Ellison, Clifford Odets, Saul Bellow, John Cheever, Margaret Walker, and many others nourished both their works and their stomachs while employed by the WPA. Some painters, such as Jacob Lawrence, worked in the "easel division"; others created elaborate murals on the walls of post offices and other government buildings. Historians and folklorists researched and prepared city and state guides and interviewed black ex-slaves whose narratives of the system of bondage would otherwise have been lost.

In addition to the WPA, the National Youth Administration (NYA) employed millions of young people. Their work ranged from clerical assignments and repairing automobiles to building tuberculosis isolation units and renovating schools. Heading the NYA in Texas, the young Lyndon B. Johnson worked hard to expand educational and construction projects to unemployed whites and blacks. The Division of Negro Affairs, headed by the Florida educator Mary McLeod Bethune and the only racial minority group subsection in the NYA, ensured that African American youths would benefit from the programs sponsored by the agency.

Despite their many successes, these relief programs had a number of flaws. The WPA paid participants relatively low wages. The $660 in annual income earned by the average worker fell short of the $1,200 that a family needed to survive. In addition, the WPA limited participation to one family member. In most cases, this meant the male head of the household. As a result, women made up only about 14 percent of WPA workers, and even in the peak year of 1938, the WPA hired only 60 percent of eligible women. With the exception of the program for artists, most women hired by the WPA worked in lower-paying jobs than men.

Establishing Social Security

The elderly required immediate relief and insurance in a country that lagged behind the rest of the industrialized world in helping its aged workforce. In August 1935, the president rectified this shortcoming and signed into law the **Social Security Act**. The measure provided that at age sixty-five, eligible workers would receive retirement

TABLE 22.1	**MAJOR NEW DEAL MEASURES, 1933–1938**	
Year	**Legislation**	**Purpose**
1933	National Industrial Recovery Act	Government, business, labor cooperation to set prices, wages, and production codes
	Agricultural Adjustment Act	Paid farmers to reduce production to raise prices
	Civilian Conservation Corps	Jobs for young men in conservation
	Public Works Administration	Construction jobs for the unemployed
	Federal Emergency Relief Act	Relief funds for the poor
	Tennessee Valley Authority	Electric power and flood control to rural areas
	Glass-Steagall Act	Insured bank deposits and separated commercial from investment banking
1934	Securities and Exchange Commission	Regulated the stock market
1935	Social Security Act	Provided retirement pensions, unemployment insurance, aid to the disabled, and payments to women with dependent children
	Wagner Act	Guaranteed collective bargaining for unions
	Works Progress Administration	Provided jobs to 8 million unemployed
1938	Fair Labor Standards Act	Established minimum hourly wage and maximum weekly working hours

payments funded by payroll taxes on employees and employers. The law also extended beyond the elderly by providing unemployment insurance for those temporarily laid off from work and welfare payments for the disabled who were permanently out of a job as well as for destitute, dependent children of single parents.

The Social Security program had significant limitations. The act excluded farm, domestic, and laundry workers, who were among the neediest Americans and were disproportionately African American. The reasons for these exclusions were largely political. The president needed southern Democrats to support this measure, and as a Mississippi newspaper observed: "The average Mississippian can't imagine himself chipping in to pay pensions for able bodied Negroes to sit around in idleness." The system of financing pensions also proved unfair. The payroll tax, which imposed the same fixed percentage on all incomes, was a regressive tax, one that fell hardest on those with lower incomes. Nor did Social Security take into account the unpaid labor of women who remained in the home to take care of their children.

Even with its flaws, Social Security revolutionized the expectations of American workers. It created a compact between the federal government and its citizens, and workers insisted that their political leaders fulfill their moral responsibilities to keep the system going. President Roosevelt recognized that the tax formula might not be economically sound, but he had a higher political objective in mind. He believed that payroll taxes would give contributors the right to collect their benefits and that "with those taxes in there, no damn politician can ever scrap my social security program."

Organized Labor Strikes Back

In 1935 Congress passed the **National Labor Relations Act**, also known as the Wagner Act for its leading sponsor, Senator Robert F. Wagner Sr. of New York. The law created the National Labor Relations Board (NLRB), which protected workers' right to organize labor unions without owner interference. During the 1930s, union membership rolls soared from fewer than 4 million workers to more than 10 million, including more than 800,000 women. At the outset of the depression, barely 6 percent of the labor force belonged to unions, compared with 33 percent in 1940.

Government efforts boosted this growth, but these spectacular gains were due primarily to workers' grassroots efforts set in motion by economic hard times. The number of striking workers during the first year of the Roosevelt administration soared from nearly 325,000 to more than 1.5 million. Organizers such as Luisa Moreno traveled the country to bring as many people as possible into the union movement. The most important development within the labor movement occurred in 1935, with the creation of the CIO. After the AFL, which consisted mainly of craft unions, rejected a proposal by John L. Lewis of the United Mine Workers to incorporate industrial workers under its umbrella, Lewis and representatives of seven other AFL unions defected and formed the CIO. Unlike the AFL, the new union sought to recruit a wide variety of workers without respect to race, gender, or region. Long excluded from the AFL, African American workers flocked to the CIO. Although they still encountered racial discrimination, especially in the South, they did participate in interracial organizing throughout the country. In 1937 the CIO mounted a full-scale organizing campaign. More than 4.5 million workers participated in some 4,700 strikes. Unions found new ways to protest poor working conditions

and arbitrary layoffs. Members of the United Auto Workers (UAW), a CIO affiliate, launched a **sit-down strike** against General Motors (GM) in Flint, Michigan,
to win union recognition, higher wages, and better working conditions. Strikers
refused to work but remained in the plants, shutting them down from the inside.
When the company sent in local police forces to evict the strikers on January 11,
1937, the barricaded workers bombarded the police with spare machine parts and
anything that was not bolted down. The community rallied around the strikers, and
wives and daughters called "union maids" formed the Women's Emergency Brigade,
which supplied sit-downers with food and water and kept up their morale. Neither
the state nor the federal government interfered with the work stoppage, and after six
weeks GM acknowledged defeat and recognized the UAW.

The following year, the New Deal added a final piece of legislation sought by
organized labor. The **Fair Labor Standards Act** (1938) established minimum wages
at 40 cents an hour and maximum working hours at forty per week. By the end
of the decade "big labor," as the AFL and CIO unions were known, had become a
significant force in American politics and a leading backer of the New Deal.

A Half Deal for Racial Minorities

President Roosevelt made significant gestures on behalf of African Americans. He
appointed Mary McLeod Bethune and Robert Weaver to staff New Deal agencies
and gathered an informal "Black Cabinet" in the nation's capital to advise him on
matters pertaining to race. The Roosevelt administration also established the Civil
Liberties Unit (later renamed Civil Rights Section) in the Department of Justice,
which investigated racial discrimination. Eleanor Roosevelt acted as a visible symbol
of the White House's concern with the plight of blacks. In 1939 Eleanor Roosevelt
quit the Daughters of the American Revolution, a women's organization, when it
refused to allow black singer Marian Anderson to hold a concert in Constitution
Hall in Washington, D.C. Instead, the First Lady brought Anderson to sing on the
steps of the Lincoln Memorial.

The New Deal inspired African Americans to form new groups, further to the
left than the NAACP, in the struggle for racial and economic justice. Created in
1935, the National Negro Congress (NNC) consisted of civil rights activists, black
intellectuals, black religious leaders, black and white labor organizers, Communists,
and those opposed to the rise of fascism in Europe. A. Philip Randolph, a socialist
and head of the Brotherhood of Pullman Car Porters, served as its president, but
resigned in 1940 due to concern over increasing Communist influence. In 1937,
the Southern Negro Youth Congress (SNYC), an offshoot of the NNC, formed in
Richmond, Virginia. This interracial organization of young southerners, many of
whom were college educated, conducted boycotts of businesses practicing racial
discrimination in employment, conducted voter registration drives in African
American communities, and promoted unions. Like the National Negro Congress,
the SNYC did not exclude Communists, which drew opposition from the NAACP
and other anti-Communist, civil rights organizations, following the collapse of
the Popular Front. Perhaps the greatest measure of Franklin Roosevelt's impact on
African Americans came when large numbers of black voters switched from the
Republican to the Democratic Party in 1936, a pattern that has lasted to the present

Mary McLeod Bethune and Eleanor Roosevelt President Roosevelt appointed prominent African Americans to positions in his administration. One member of his so-called "Black Cabinet" was Mary McLeod Bethune. A founder of the National Council of Negro Women, she served as director of Negro activities in the National Youth Administration. This 1937 photograph shows her seated next to her close friend, First Lady Eleanor Roosevelt, and Aubrey Williams, executive director of the National Youth Administration and a white southern liberal. Bettmann/Getty Images

day. "Go turn Lincoln's picture to the wall," a black observer commented after the election. "That debt has been paid in full."

Yet overall the New Deal did little to break down racial inequality. President Roosevelt believed that the plight of African Americans would improve, along with that of all downtrodden Americans, as New Deal measures restored economic health. Black leaders disagreed. They argued that the NRA's initials stood for "Negroes Ruined Again" because the agency displaced black workers and approved lower wages for blacks than for whites. The AAA dislodged black sharecroppers. New Deal programs such as the CCC and those for building public housing maintained existing patterns of segregation. The Federal Housing Administration created "redlining" maps, which outlined neighborhoods where African Americans lived in red ink. This alerted banks to forgo real estate loans for those seeking to move into these communities. Owning a home is the major form of building wealth for most Americans, and redlining disadvantaged black homeownership. From 1934 to 1952, 98 percent of Federal Housing Administration loans went to whites. In addition, both the Social Security Act and the Fair Labor Standards Act omitted from coverage jobs that black and brown Americans were most likely to hold. In fact, the New Deal's big labor/big government alliance left out non-unionized industrial and agricultural workers, many of whom were African American and lacked bargaining power. Overall, "the federal government," as the historian Ira Katznelson writes, "functioned as a commanding instrument of white privilege."

This pattern of halfway reform persisted for other racial minorities. Since the end of the Indian wars in 1890, many Native Americans had lived in poverty, forced onto reservations where they were offered few economic opportunities and where whites carried out a relentless assault on their culture. By the early 1930s, American Indians earned an average income of less than $50 a year—compared with $800 for whites—and their unemployment rate was three times higher than that of white Americans. For the most part, they lived on lands that whites had given up on as unsuitable for farming or mining. The policy of assimilation established by the Dawes Act of 1887 had exacerbated the problem by depriving Indians of their cultural identities as well as their economic livelihoods. In 1934 the federal government reversed its course. Spurred on by John Collier, the commissioner of

The Indian New Deal   John Collier, commissioner of Indian affairs under President Roosevelt, favored a New Deal for Native Americans. An advocate for Indian culture, Collier implemented reform legislation that replaced the policy of Indian assimilation with that of self-determination. In this photo he appears with two Native Americans in the Southwest. MPI/Getty Images

Indian affairs, Congress passed the **Indian Reorganization Act (IRA)**, which terminated the Dawes Act, authorized self-government for those living on reservations, extended tribal landholdings, and pledged to uphold native customs and language.

Although the IRA brought economic and social improvements for Native Americans, many problems remained. Despite his considerable efforts, Collier approached Indian affairs from the top down. One historian remarked that Collier had "the zeal of a crusader who knew better than the Indians what was good for them." The Indian commissioner failed to appreciate the diversity of native tribes and administered laws that contradicted Native American political and economic practices. For example, the IRA required the tribes to operate by majority rule, whereas many of them reached decisions through consensus, which respected the views of the minority. Although 174 tribes accepted the IRA, 78 tribes, including the Seneca, Crow, and Navajo, rejected it.

Decline of the New Deal

Roosevelt's shift to the left paid political dividends, and in 1936 the president won reelection by a landslide. His sweeping victory proved to be one of the rare critical elections that signified a fundamental political realignment. Democrats replaced Republicans as the majority party in the United States, overturning thirty-six years of Republican rule. While Roosevelt had won convincingly in 1932, not until 1936 did the president put together a stable coalition that could sustain Democratic dominance for many years to come.

In 1936 Roosevelt trounced Alfred M. Landon, the Republican governor of Kansas, and Democrats increased their congressional majorities by staggering margins. The vote broke down along class lines. Roosevelt won the votes of 80 percent of union members, 81 percent of unskilled workers, and 84 percent of people on relief, compared with only 42 percent of high-income voters. Millions of new voters came out to the polls, and most of them supported Roosevelt's New Deal coalition of the poor, farmers, urban ethnic minorities, unionists, white southerners, and African Americans.

The euphoria of his triumph, however, proved short-lived. An overconfident Roosevelt soon reached beyond his electoral mandate and within two years found himself unable to extend the New Deal. In 1937 Roosevelt devised a **court-packing plan** to ensure support of New Deal legislation and asked Congress to increase the size of the Supreme Court. He justified this as a matter of reform, claiming that the present nine-member Court could not handle its workload. Roosevelt attributed a good deal of the problem to the advanced age of six of the nine justices, who were over seventy years old. Under his proposal, the president would make one new appointment for each judge over the age of seventy who did not retire so long as the bench did not exceed fifteen members. In reality, Roosevelt schemed to "pack" the Court with supporters to prevent it from declaring New Deal legislation such as Social Security and the Wagner Act unconstitutional.

The plan backfired. Conservatives charged Roosevelt with seeking to destroy the separation of powers enshrined in the Constitution among the executive, legislative, and judicial branches. In the end, the president failed to expand the Supreme Court, but he preserved his legislative accomplishments. In a series of rulings, the chastened Supreme Court approved Social Security, the Wagner Act, and other New Deal legislation. Nevertheless, the political fallout from the court-packing fight damaged the president and his plans for further legislative reform.

Roosevelt's court-packing plan alienated many southern Democratic members of Congress who previously had sided with the president. Traditionally suspicious of the power of the federal government, southern lawmakers worried that Roosevelt was going too far toward centralizing power in Washington at the expense of states' rights. Southern Democrats formed a coalition with conservative northern Republicans who shared their concerns about the expansion of federal power and excessive spending on social welfare programs. Their antipathy toward labor unions further bound them. Although they held a minority of seats in Congress, this **conservative coalition** could block unwanted legislation by using the filibuster in the Senate (unlimited debate that could be shut down only with a two-thirds vote). After 1938 these conservatives made sure that no further New Deal legislation passed.

Roosevelt also lost support for New Deal initiatives because of the recession of 1937, which FDR's policies had triggered. When federal spending soared after passage of the WPA and other relief measures adopted in 1935, the president lost his economic nerve for deficit spending. He called for reduced spending, which increased unemployment and slowed economic recovery. In addition, as the Social Security payroll tax took effect, it reduced the purchasing power of workers, thereby exacerbating the impact of reduced government spending. Making the situation worse, pension payments were not scheduled to begin for several years. This "recession within the depression" further eroded congressional support for the New Deal.

The country was still deep in depression in 1939. Unemployment was at 17 percent, with more than 11 million people out of work. Most of those who were poor at the start of the Great Depression remained poor. Recovery came mainly to those who were temporarily impoverished as a result of the economic crisis. The distribution of wealth remained skewed toward the top. In 1933 the richest 5 percent of the population controlled 31 percent of disposable income; in 1939 the latter figure stood at 26 percent.

Against this backdrop of persistent difficult economic times, the president's popularity began to fade. In the midterm elections of 1938, Roosevelt campaigned against Democratic conservatives in an attempt to reinvigorate his New Deal coalition. His efforts failed and upset many ordinary citizens who associated the tactic with that used by European dictators who had recently risen to power. As the decade came to a close, Roosevelt turned his attention away from the New Deal and increasingly toward a new war in Europe that threatened to engulf the entire world.

> **REVIEW & RELATE**
> - Why and how did the New Deal shift to the left in 1934 and 1935?
> - Despite the president's landslide victory in 1936, why did the New Deal stall during Roosevelt's second term in office?

Conclusion: New Deal Liberalism

The Great Depression produced enormous economic hardships that the Hoover administration fell far short of relieving. Although Hoover's successor, Franklin Roosevelt, failed to end the depression, in contrast he provided unprecedented economic assistance to the poor as well as the rich. The New Deal expanded the size of the federal government from 605,000 employees to more than 1 million during the 1930s. Moreover, the New Deal rescued the capitalist system, doing little to alter the fundamental structure of the American economy. Despite subjecting businesses to greater regulation, it left corporations, the stock market, farms, and banks in the hands of private enterprise. By the end of the 1930s, large corporations had more power over markets than ever before. Income and wealth remained unequally distributed, nearly to the same extent as they had been before Roosevelt took office in 1933.

Roosevelt forged a middle path between reactionaries and revolutionaries at a time when the fascist tyrants Adolf Hitler and Benito Mussolini gained power in Germany and Italy, respectively, and Joseph Stalin ruthlessly consolidated his rule in the Communist Soviet Union. By contrast, the American president expanded democratic capitalism, bringing a broader cross section of society to the decision-making table. Roosevelt's "broker state" of multiple competing interests provided for greater democracy than a government dominated exclusively by business elites. This system did not benefit those who remained unorganized and wielded little power, African Americans, Latinos, and Native Americans. The redlining policies of the Federal Housing Authority reinforced the structural racism rooted in centuries of white supremacy. Still, these marginalized groups did receive greater recognition and self-determination from the federal government. Indeed, these and other groups helped shape the New Deal. As Eleanor Roosevelt's history shows, women played key roles in campaigning for social welfare legislation. Others, like Luisa Moreno, helped organize workers and promoted ethnic pride among Latinos in the face of deportations. African Americans challenged racism and pressured the federal government to distribute services more equitably. American Indians won important democratic and cultural reforms, and though Asian Americans continued to encounter considerable discrimination on the West Coast, they joined to help each other. President Roosevelt also solidified the institution of the presidency as the focal point for public leadership. His cheerfulness, hopefulness, and pragmatism rallied millions of individuals behind him. Even after Roosevelt died in 1945, the public retained its expectation that leadership would come from the White House.

Through his programs and his force of personality, Franklin Roosevelt convinced Americans that he cared about their welfare and that the federal government would not ignore their suffering. However, he was not universally beloved: Millions of Americans despised him because they thought he was leading the country toward socialism, and he did not solve all the problems the country faced — it would take government spending for World War II to end the depression. Still, together with his wife, Eleanor, Franklin Roosevelt conveyed a sense that the American people belonged to a single community, capable of banding together to solve the country's problems, no matter how serious they were or how intractable they might seem.

Chapter 22 Review

KEY TERMS

Scottsboro Nine, 561
Bonus Army, 564
New Deal, 566
Federal Deposit Insurance
   Corporation (FDIC), 567
Agricultural Adjustment Act, 567
Tennessee Valley Authority
   (TVA), 567
National Recovery Administration
   (NRA), 568
Civilian Conservation Corps (CCC), 569

Popular Front, 570
Works Progress Administration
   (WPA), 571
Social Security Act, 572
National Labor Relations Act, 573
sit-down strike, 574
Fair Labor Standards Act, 574
Indian Reorganization Act (IRA), 576
court-packing plan, 577
conservative coalition, 577

REVIEW & RELATE

1. How did President Hoover respond to the problems and challenges created by the Great Depression?
2. How did different segments of the American population experience the depression?
3. What steps did Roosevelt take to stimulate economic recovery and provide relief to impoverished Americans during his first term in office?
4. What criticisms did Roosevelt's opponents level against the New Deal?
5. Why and how did the New Deal shift to the left in 1934 and 1935?
6. Despite the president's landslide victory in 1936, why did the New Deal stall during Roosevelt's second term in office?

TIMELINE OF EVENTS

1931	• Scottsboro Nine tried for rape
1932–1939	• Dust Bowl storms
1932	• Reconstruction Finance Corporation created
	• River Rouge autoworkers' strike
	• Farm Holiday Association formed
	• Bonus Army marches
1933	• Roosevelt moves to stabilize banking and financial systems
	• Agricultural Adjustment Act passed
	• Federal Emergency Relief Administration created
	• Tennessee Valley Authority created
	• National Recovery Administration created
	• Civilian Conservation Corps created
1934	• Indian Reorganization Act passed
	• Francis Townsend forms Old-Age Revolving Pensions Corporation
	• Huey Long establishes Share Our Wealth movement
	• Securities and Exchange Commission created
1935	• Charles E. Coughlin organizes National Union for Social Justice
	• Works Progress Administration created
	• Social Security Act passed
	• National Labor Relations Act passed
	• Congress of Industrial Organizations founded
1937	• Sit-down strike against General Motors
	• Roosevelt proposes to increase the size of the Supreme Court
1938	• Fair Labor Standards Act passed

23

World War II

1933–1945

LEARNING OBJECTIVES

After reading this chapter you will be able to:

- Evaluate the key reasons behind U.S. intervention in World War II as well as the arguments of those who opposed it.
- Analyze the effects the war had on the U.S. economy and on the lives of women and families.
- Compare and contrast the treatment of racial minority groups and their responses on the home front.
- Explain the Allied military strategy in fighting World War II on the European and Pacific fronts, including how it affected the decision to drop the atomic bomb on Japan, U.S.-Soviet relations, and the Holocaust.

COMPARING AMERICAN HISTORIES

One month after Japan attacked the U.S. naval base at Pearl Harbor on December 7, 1941, President Franklin Roosevelt approved a full-scale effort to develop an atomic bomb. As scientific director of this top-secret program, physicist **J. Robert Oppenheimer** orchestrated the work of more than 3,000 scientists, technicians, and military personnel at the Los Alamos Laboratories near Santa Fe, New Mexico. The son of German American Jews, Oppenheimer helped Jews gain asylum in the United States when the Nazis started persecuting them in the early 1930s.

On July 16, 1945, Oppenheimer and his team successfully tested their new weapon. The explosion lit up the predawn sky with a blast so powerful that it broke a window 125 miles away. A mushroom cloud shot up 41,000 feet into the sky over ground zero, where a 1,200-foot-wide crater had formed. Oppenheimer understood that the world had been permanently transformed. Quoting from Hindu scriptures, he remembered thinking at the moment of the explosion, "I am become death, destroyer of worlds." Weeks later, in early August 1945, the United States dropped two atomic bombs on Japan, which resulted in over 200,000 deaths.

While Oppenheimer and his team remained cloistered at Los Alamos, **Fred Korematsu** and some 112,000 Japanese Americans lived in internment camps, imprisoned for no other reason than their Japanese ancestry. Born in Oakland, California, in 1919 to Japanese immigrants, Fred grew up like many first-generation Americans. His parents spoke Japanese at home and maintained the cultural traditions of their native land, while their sons learned English in public school, ate hamburgers, and played football and basketball like other children their age. Following graduation from high school, Korematsu worked on the Oakland docks as a welder.

After the 1941 bombing of Pearl Harbor, residents on the West Coast turned their anger on the Japanese and Japanese Americans living among them. As assimilated as Fred Korematsu and many other Nisei (the U.S.-born children of Japanese immigrants) had become, white Americans doubted their loyalty. As a result, Korematsu soon lost his job.

On March 21, 1942, President Roosevelt issued Executive Order 9066 authorizing military commanders on the West Coast to take any measures necessary to promote national security. On May 9, the military ordered Korematsu's family to report to Tanforan Racetrack in San Mateo, from which they would be transported to internment camps throughout the West. Although the rest of his family complied with the order, Fred refused. Three weeks later, he was arrested and then transferred to the Topaz internment camp in south-central Utah. Found guilty of violating the original evacuation order, Korematsu received a sentence of five years of probation. When he appealed his conviction to the U.S. Supreme Court in 1944, the high court upheld the verdict.

THE AMERICAN HISTORIES of Fred Korematsu and J. Robert Oppenheimer were shaped by the profound changes brought about by war. Korematsu was subjected to the full force of anti-Japanese sentiment that followed the attack on Pearl Harbor, while Oppenheimer played a key role in developing a weapon that he believed would shorten the war.

The war that these two men experienced in such different ways marked a critical point for the United States in the twentieth century. World War II finally ended the Great Depression, cementing the trend toward government intervention in the economy that had begun with the New Deal. With the war fought almost entirely on foreign soil, the United States converted its factories to wartime production and became the "arsenal of democracy," putting millions of Americans to work in the process, including African Americans, other racial and ethnic minorities, and women.

The war also provided opportunities for African Americans to press for civil rights, while at the same time the government trampled on the civil liberties of Japanese Americans. All Americans contributed to the war effort through rationing and higher taxes. Overseas, soldiers fought fierce battles in Europe, Africa, and Asia. The combined military power of the Allies, led by the United States, Great Britain, and the Soviet Union, finally defeated the Axis nations of Germany, Italy, and Japan, but not until the fighting had killed 60 to 70 million people, more than half of whom were civilians, and ushered in the Atomic Age.

The Road toward War

The end of World War I did not bring peace and prosperity to Europe. The harsh peace terms imposed on the Central Powers in 1919 left the losers, especially Germany, deeply resentful. The war saddled both sides with a huge financial debt and produced economic instability, which contributed to the Great Depression. In the Far East, Japanese invasions of China and Southeast Asia threatened America's Open Door policy (see "Opening the Door in China" in chapter 20). The failure of the United States to join the League of Nations dramatically reduced the organization's ability to maintain peace and stability. German expansionism in Europe in the late 1930s moved President Roosevelt and the nation toward war, but it took the Japanese attack on Pearl Harbor to bring the United States into the global conflict.

The Growing Crisis in Europe

Despite its failure to join the League of Nations, the United States did not withdraw from international affairs in the 1920s. It participated in arms control negotiations; signed the Kellogg-Briand Pact, which outlawed war as an instrument of national policy but proved unenforceable; and expanded its foreign investments in Central and Latin America, Asia, the Middle East, and western Europe. In 1933 a new possibility for trade emerged when the Roosevelt administration extended diplomatic recognition to the Soviet Union (USSR).

Overall, the country did not retreat from foreign affairs so much as it refused to enter into collective security agreements that would restrain its freedom of action. To the extent that American leaders practiced isolationism, they did so mainly in the political sense of rejecting internationalist organizations such as the League of Nations, institutions that might require military cooperation to implement their decisions.

The experience of World War I had reinforced this brand of political isolationism, which was reflected in an outpouring of antiwar sentiments in the late 1920s and early 1930s. Best-selling novels like Ernest Hemingway's *Farewell to Arms* (1929), Erich Maria Remarque's *All Quiet on the Western Front* (1929), and Dalton Trumbo's *Johnny Got His Gun* (1939) presented graphic depictions of the horror and futility of war. Beginning in 1934, Senate investigations chaired by Gerald Nye of North Dakota concluded that bankers and munitions makers—"merchants of death," as one contemporary writer labeled them—had conspired to push the United States into war in 1917. Nye's hearings appealed to popular antibusiness sentiment in Depression-era America.

Following the Nye Committee hearings, Congress passed a series of **Neutrality Acts**, each designed to make it more difficult for the United States to become entangled in European armed hostilities. In 1935 Congress prohibited the sale of munitions to either warring side and authorized the president to warn Americans against traveling on passenger liners of belligerent nations. The following year, lawmakers added private loans to the ban, and in 1937 they required belligerents to pay cash for nonmilitary purchases and ship them on their own vessels—so-called cash-and-carry provisions.

Events in Europe, however, made U.S. neutrality ever more difficult to maintain. After rising to power as chancellor of Germany in 1933, Adolf Hitler revived Germany's economic and military strength despite the Great Depression. Hitler installed National Socialism (Nazism) at home and established the empire of the Third Reich abroad. The *Führer* (leader) whipped up patriotic fervor by scapegoating and persecuting Communists and Jews. To garner support for his actions, Hitler manipulated German feelings of humiliation for losing World War I and having been forced to sign the "war guilt" clause and pointed to the disastrous effects of the country's inflation-ridden economy. In 1936 Hitler sent troops to occupy the Rhineland between Germany and France in blatant violation of the Treaty of Versailles.

Hitler did not stop there. Citing the need for more space for the Germanic people to live, he pushed for German expansion into eastern Europe. In March 1938 he forced Austria to unite with Germany. In September of that year Hitler signed the Munich Accord with Great Britain and France, allowing Germany to annex the Sudetenland, the mainly German-speaking, western region of Czechoslovakia. Hitler still wanted more land and was convinced that his western European rivals would not stop him, so in March 1939 he sent German troops to invade and occupy the rest of Czechoslovakia. Hitler proved correct; Britain and France did nothing in response, a policy critics called **appeasement**.

Hitler's Italian ally, Benito Mussolini, joined him in war and conquest. In 1935 Italian troops invaded Ethiopia. The following year, both Germany and Italy intervened in the Spanish civil war, providing military support for General Francisco Franco in his effort to overthrow the democratically elected, socialist republic of Spain. While the United States and Great Britain remained on the sidelines, only the Soviet Union officially assisted the Loyalist defenders of the Spanish republic. In violation of American law, private citizens, many of whom were Communists, volunteered to serve on the side of the Spanish Loyalists and fought on the battlefield as the Abraham Lincoln Brigade. Other sympathetic Americans, such as J. Robert Oppenheimer, provided financial assistance for the anti-Franco government. Despite these efforts, Franco's forces seized control of Spain in early 1939, another victory for Hitler and Mussolini.

The Challenge to Isolationism

As Europe drifted toward war, public opinion polls revealed that most Americans wanted to stay out of any European conflict. The president, however, thought it likely that, to protect its own economic and political interests, the United States would eventually need to assist the Western democracies. Still, Roosevelt had to tread lightly in the face of the Neutrality Acts that Congress had passed between 1935 and 1937 and overwhelming public opposition to American involvement in Europe.

Germany's aggression in Europe eventually led to full-scale war. When Germany invaded Poland in September 1939, Britain and France declared war on Germany and Italy. Just before the invasion, the Soviet Union had signed a nonaggression agreement with Germany, which carved up Poland between the two nations and permitted the USSR to occupy the neighboring Baltic states of Latvia, Lithuania, and Estonia. Soviet leader Joseph Stalin had few illusions about Hitler's ultimate design on his own nation, but he concluded that by signing this pact he could secure his country's western borders and buy additional time. (In June 1941 the Germans broke the pact and invaded the Soviet Union.)

Roosevelt responded to the outbreak of war by reaffirming U.S. neutrality. Despite his sympathy for the Allies, which most Americans had come to share, the president stated his hope that the United States could stay out of the war: "Let no man or woman thoughtlessly or falsely talk of America sending its armies to European fields."

With the United States on the sidelines, German forces marched toward victory. By the spring of 1940, German armies had launched a *Blitzkrieg* (lightning war) across Europe, defeating and occupying Denmark, Norway, the Netherlands, Belgium, and Luxembourg. With German victories mounting, committed opponents of American involvement in foreign wars organized the **America First Committee**. America First tapped into the feeling of isolationism and concern among a diverse group of Americans who did not want to get dragged into another foreign war.

The greatest challenge to isolationism occurred in June 1940 when France fell to the German onslaught and Nazi troops marched into Paris. Britain now stood virtually alone, and its position seemed tenuous. The British had barely succeeded in evacuating their forces from France by sea when the German *Luftwaffe* (air force) began a bombing campaign on London and other targets in the Battle of Britain.

The surrender of France and the Battle of Britain drastically changed Americans' attitude toward entering the war. Before Germany invaded France, 82 percent of Americans thought that the United States should not aid the Allies. After France's defeat, in a complete turnaround, some 80 percent of Americans favored assisting Great Britain in some way. However, four out of five Americans polled opposed immediate entry into the war. As a result, the politically astute Roosevelt presented U.S. assistance to Britain as a way to prevent American military intervention by allowing Great Britain to defeat the Germans on its own.

Despite public opinion, the Roosevelt administration found ways of helping Britain. On September 2, 1940, the president sent fifty obsolete destroyers to the British in return for leases on British naval bases in Newfoundland, Bermuda, and the British West Indies. Two weeks later, on September 16, Roosevelt persuaded Congress to pass the Selective Service Act, the first peacetime military draft in U.S. history, which quickly registered more than 16 million men.

This political maneuvering came as Roosevelt campaigned for an unprecedented third term in 1940. He defeated the Republican Wendell Willkie, a Wall Street lawyer who shared Roosevelt's anti-isolationist views. Both candidates accommodated voters' desire to stay out of the European war, and Roosevelt went so far as to promise American parents: "Your boys are not going to be sent into any foreign war."

Roosevelt's campaign promises did not halt the march toward war. Roosevelt succeeded in pushing Congress to pass the **Lend-Lease Act** in March 1941. With

Britain running out of money and its shipping devastated by German submarines, this measure circumvented the cash-and-carry provisions of the Neutrality Acts. The United States would lend or lease equipment, but no one expected the recipients to return the used weapons and other commodities. To protect British ships carrying American supplies, the president extended naval and air patrols in the North Atlantic. In response, German submarines began sinking U.S. ships. By May 1941, Germany and the United States were engaged in an undeclared naval war.

The United States Enters the War

Financially, militarily, and ideologically, the United States had aligned itself with Britain, and Roosevelt expected that the nation would soon be formally at war. As Germany and Italy successfully expanded their empires, they endangered U.S. economic interests and democratic values. President Roosevelt believed that American security abroad was threatened by the German Nazis and Italian Fascists. After passage of the Lend-Lease Act, American and British military planners agreed that defeating Germany would become the top priority if the United States entered the war. In August 1941, Roosevelt and British prime minister Winston Churchill met in Newfoundland, where they signed the **Atlantic Charter**, a lofty statement of war aims that included principles of freedom of the seas, self-determination, free trade, and "freedom from fear and want" — ideals that laid the groundwork for the establishment of a postwar United Nations. At the same meeting, Roosevelt promised Churchill that the United States would protect British convoys in the North Atlantic as far as Iceland while the nation waited for a confrontation with Germany that would rally the American public in support of war. The president got what he wanted. After several attacks on American ships by German submarines in September and October, the president persuaded Congress to repeal the neutrality legislation of the 1930s and allow American ships to sail across the Atlantic to supply Great Britain. By December, the nation was close to open war with Germany.

The event that finally prompted the United States to enter the war, however, occurred not in the Atlantic but in the Pacific Ocean. For nearly a decade, U.S. relations with Japan had deteriorated over the issue of China's independence and maintaining the Open Door to Chinese markets. The United States did little to challenge the Japanese invasion and occupation of Manchuria in 1931, but after Japanese armed forces moved farther into China in 1937, the United States supplied arms to China.

Relations worsened in 1940 when the Japanese government signed the Tripartite Pact with Germany and Italy, which created a mutual defense agreement among the Axis powers. That same year, Japanese troops invaded northern Indochina, and Roosevelt responded by embargoing sales of products that Japan needed for war. This embargo did not deter the Japanese; in July they occupied the remainder of Indochina to gain access to the region's natural resources. The Roosevelt administration retaliated by freezing Japanese assets and cutting off all trade with Japan.

On the quiet Sunday morning of December 7, 1941, Japan attacked the U.S. Pacific Fleet stationed at Pearl Harbor in Honolulu, Hawaii. This surprise air and naval assault killed more than 2,400 Americans and seriously damaged ships and aircraft. The bombing raid abruptly ended isolationism and rallied the American public behind President Roosevelt, who pronounced December 7 "a date which will live in infamy." The next day, Congress overwhelmingly voted to go to war with Japan, and on December 11 Germany and Italy declared war on the United States in response. In little more than a year after his reelection pledge to keep the country out of war, Roosevelt sent American men to fight overseas. Still, an overwhelming majority of Americans now considered entry into the war as necessary to preserve freedom and democracy against assaults from fascist and militaristic nations.

REVIEW & RELATE	• How did American public opinion shape Roosevelt's foreign policy in the years preceding U.S. entry into World War II? • What events in Europe and the Pacific ultimately brought the United States into World War II?

The Home-Front Economy

The global conflict had profound effects on the American home front. World War II ended the Great Depression, restored economic prosperity, and increased labor union membership. At the same time, it smoothed the way for a closer relationship between government and private defense contractors, later referred to as the **military-industrial complex**. The war extended U.S. influence in the world and offered new economic opportunities at home. Despite fierce and bloody military battles throughout the world, Americans kept up morale by rallying around family and community.

Managing the Wartime Economy

To mobilize for war, President Roosevelt increased federal spending to unprecedented levels. Federal government employment during the war expanded to an all-time high of 3.8 million workers, setting the foundation for a large, permanent Washington bureaucracy. War orders fueled economic growth, productivity, and employment. The gross domestic product increased from the equivalent of nearly $900 billion in 1939 (in 1990 prices) to nearly $1.5 trillion (in 1990 prices) at the end of the war (Figure 23.1), union membership rose from around 9 million to nearly 15 million, and unemployment dropped from 8 million to less than 1 million. The armed forces helped reduce unemployment significantly by enlisting 12 million men and women, 7 million of whom had been unemployed.

All regions of the country experienced wartime prosperity. The industrial areas of the Northeast and Midwest once again boomed, as automobile factories converted to building tanks and other military vehicles, oil refineries processed gasoline to fuel them, steel and rubber companies manufactured parts to construct these vehicles and the weapons they carried, and textile and shoe plants furnished uniforms and boots for soldiers to wear. As farmers provided food for the nation and its allies, farm production soared. The economy diversified geographically. Fifteen million Americans—11 percent of the entire population—migrated between 1941 and 1945. The war transformed the agricultural South into a budding industrial region. The federal government poured more than $4 billion in contracts into the South to operate military camps, contract with textile factories to clothe the military, and use its ports to build and launch warships. The availability of jobs in southern cities attracted

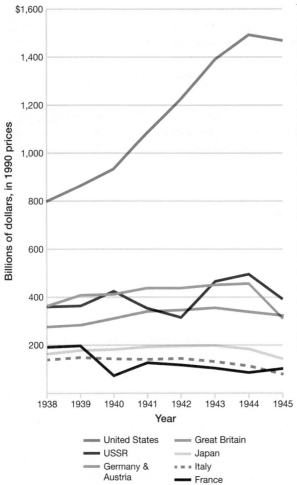

FIGURE 23.1 Real Gross Domestic Product of the Great Powers, 1938–1945 Although World War II stalled or damaged the economic productivity of most of the warring nations, the U.S. economy grew dramatically between 1938 and 1944. With all the battles taking place outside the continental United States, the demand for food, weapons, ships, airplanes, gasoline, and other items by Great Britain and other Allied powers fueled this growth. Explain why the war and not the New Deal succeeded in ending the Great Depression. Data from Mark Harrison, ed., *The Economics of World War II: Six Great Powers in International Comparison* (Cambridge: Cambridge University Press, 1998), 11.

sharecroppers and tenant farmers, black and white, away from the countryside and promoted urbanization while reducing the region's dependency on the plantation economy.

No region was changed more by the war than the West. The West Coast prospered because it was the gateway to the Pacific war. The federal government established aircraft plants and shipbuilding yards in California, Oregon, and Washington, resulting in extraordinary population growth in Los Angeles, San Diego, San Francisco, Portland, and Seattle. The West's population grew three times as fast as the rest of the nation's. Los Angeles led the way in attracting defense contracts, as its balmy climate proved ideal for test-flying the aircraft that rolled off its assembly lines.

Following the attack on Pearl Harbor, Congress passed the War Powers Act, which authorized the president to reorganize federal agencies any way he thought necessary to win the war. In 1942 the president established the **War Production Board** to oversee the economy. The agency enticed business corporations to meet ever-increasing government orders by negotiating lucrative contracts that helped underwrite their costs, lower their taxes, and guarantee large profits. The government also suspended antitrust enforcement, giving private companies great leeway in running their enterprises. Much of the antibusiness hostility generated by the Great Depression evaporated as the Roosevelt administration recruited business executives to supervise government agencies. Indeed, the close relationship between the federal government and business that emerged during the war produced the military-industrial complex, which would have a vast influence on the future development of the economy.

In the first three years of the war, the United States increased military production by some 800 percent. American factories accounted for more than half of worldwide manufacturing output. By 1945 the United States had produced 86,000 tanks, nearly 300,000 airplanes, 15 million rifles and machine guns, and 6,500 ships.

Financing this enormous enterprise took considerable effort. The federal government spent more than $320 billion, ten times the cost of World War I. To pay for the war, the federal government sold $100 billion in bonds, only about half of what was needed. The rest came from increased income tax rates, which for the first time affected low- and middle-income workers, who had paid little or no tax before. At the same time, the tax rate for the wealthy was boosted to 94 percent. In addition to paying higher taxes, American consumers shouldered the burden of shortages and high prices.

Building up the armed forces was the final ingredient in the mobilization for war. In 1940 about 250,000 soldiers were serving in the U.S. military. By 1945 American forces had grown to more than 12 million men and women through voluntary enlistments and a draft of men between the ages of eighteen and forty-five. The military reflected the diversity of the U.S. population. The sons of immigrants fought alongside the sons of older-stock Americans. Although the military tried to exclude homosexuals, many managed to join the fighting forces. Some 700,000 African Americans served in the armed forces, but civilian and military officials confined them to segregated units in the army, assigned them to menial work in the navy, and excluded them from the marines. The Army Air Corps created a segregated fighting unit of black soldiers who trained at Tuskegee Institute in Alabama, and these Tuskegee airmen, like their counterparts among the ground forces, distinguished themselves in battle. Women could not fight in combat, but 140,000 joined the Women's Army Corps, and 100,000 joined the navy's WAVES (Women Accepted for Voluntary Emergency Service). In these and other service branches, women contributed mainly as nurses and performed transportation and clerical duties.

Women also played an important but secretive role in bolstering Allied military efforts. The navy and army recruited thousands of women college students and small-town school teachers to Washington, D.C., where they worked on deciphering German and Japanese diplomatic and military codes. These young, unmarried women worked very long, tedious hours during the week as well as on weekends, and succeeded in providing the U.S. military with secret information of enemy planning. In this way, they joined the efforts already begun by British female codebreakers operating at Bletchley Park, England.

The government relied on corporate executives to manage wartime economic conversion, but without the sacrifice and dedication of American workers, their efforts would have failed. The demands for wartime production combined with the departure of millions of American workers to the military created a labor shortage that gave unions increased leverage. By 1945 the membership rolls of organized labor had grown from 9 million to nearly 14 million. In 1942 the Roosevelt administration established the **National War Labor Board**, which regulated wages, hours, and working conditions and authorized the government to take over plants that refused to abide by its decisions. Unions at first refrained from striking but later in the war organized strikes to protest the disparity between workers' wages and corporate profits. In 1943 Congress responded by passing the Smith-Connally Act, which prohibited walkouts in defense industries and set a thirty-day "cooling-off" period before unions could go out on strike.

New Opportunities for Women

World War II opened up new opportunities for women in the paid workforce. Between 1940 and the peak of wartime employment in 1944, the number of employed women rose by more than 50 percent, to 6 million. Given severe labor shortages caused by increased production and the exodus of male workers into the armed forces, for the first time in U.S. history married working women outnumbered single working women. At the start of the war, about half of women employees held poorly paid clerical, sales, and service jobs. Women in manufacturing labored mainly in low-wage textile and clothing factories. During the war, however, the overall number of women in manufacturing grew by 141 percent; in industries producing directly for war purposes, the figure jumped by 463 percent. By contrast, the number of women in domestic service dropped by 20 percent. As women moved into defense-related jobs, their incomes also improved.

As impressive as these figures are, they do not tell the whole story. First, although married women entered the job market in record numbers, most of these workers were older and without young children. Women over the age of thirty-five accounted for 60 percent of those entering the workforce. The government did little to encourage young mothers to work, and few efforts were made to provide assistance for child care for those who did. In contrast to this situation, in Great Britain child care programs were widely available. Second, openings for women in manufacturing jobs did not guarantee equality. Women received lower wages for labor comparable to the work that men performed, and women did not have the same chances for advancement. Typical union benefits, such as seniority, hurt women, who were generally the most recent hires. In fact, some contracts stipulated that women's tenure in jobs previously held by men would last only for the duration of the war.

Gender stereotypes continued to dominate the workforce and society in general. Magazine covers with the image of "Rosie the Riveter," a woman with her sleeves rolled up and her biceps bulging, became a symbol for the recruitment of women, but reality proved different. Women who took war jobs were viewed not so much as war workers but as women temporarily occupying "men's jobs" during the emergency. As the war drew to a close, public relations campaigns shifted gears and encouraged the same women they had recently recruited to prepare to return home. And nearly all of the brilliant women codebreakers in Washington, D.C., were ordered to go back home.

Everyday Life on the Home Front

Morale on the home front remained generally high during the war, as prosperity returned and American casualties proved relatively light compared with those of other allied nations. As in World War I, the government set up an agency, the Office of War Information, to promote patriotism and urge Americans to contribute to the

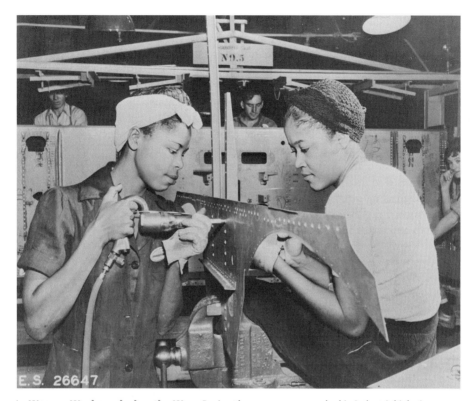

Women Workers during the War   During the war, women worked in industrial jobs in unprecedented numbers. Corporations and the federal government actively recruited women through posters and advertisements and promised women that factory work was something that would benefit them, their families, and their nation. This image spotlights two African American women, Luedell Mitchell and Lavada Cherry, real life "Rosie the Riveters," working at the El Segundo, California plant of Douglas Aircraft. As the Allies neared victory, however, the message changed, and women were urged to prepare to return to the home to open up jobs for returning soldiers. Library of Congress, 8e01286

war effort any way they could. Schoolchildren collected scrap metal and rubber to donate to the production of military vehicles and weapons. With rationing in effect and food in short supply, the government encouraged families in towns and cities to grow "victory gardens" for their own fruits and vegetables. Mothers and daughters helped staff USO (United Service Organizations) dances and recreational activities for soldiers headquartered in the United States. Americans also contributed to the war effort by adhering to restrictions on the consumption of consumer goods. Rationing cards restricted purchases of gasoline for cars and for food such as meat, butter, and sugar.

Hollywood kept the American public entertained, and movie attendance reached a record high of more than 100 million viewers. Films portrayed the heroism of soldiers on battlefields in Guadalcanal and Bataan. They celebrated the courage of Russian allies in propaganda epics such as *Mission to Moscow* (1943) and explored the depth of personal and political loyalties in classics such as *Casablanca* (1943). Hollywood stars such as Betty Grable kept up servicemen's spirits by posing for photos that GIs pinned up in their lockers, tents, and equipment.

For many Americans, life went on, but not quite in the same way. Around 15 million Americans moved during the war, with more than half of them relocating out of state. With husbands at war and wives at work, many children became "latchkey kids" who stayed home alone after school until their mothers or fathers returned from their jobs. With less parental supervision, juvenile delinquency rose, resulting in increased teenage arrests for robbery, vandalism, and loitering. With the end of the Great Depression and with more young people working, marriage rates increased, and couples wed at a younger age. By 1945 the winding down of the war and the rapidly increasing number of marriages produced the first signs of a "baby boom." At the same time, the stresses of life during wartime, including long separations of husbands and wives, also resulted in higher divorce rates.

REVIEW & RELATE	• How did the war accelerate the trend that began during the New Deal toward increased government participation in the economy? • How did the war affect life on the home front for the average American?

Fighting for Equality at Home

The war also had a significant impact on race relations. The fight to defeat Nazism, a doctrine based on racial prejudice and white supremacy, offered African Americans a chance to press for equal opportunity at home. By contrast, Japanese Americans experienced intensified discrimination and oppression as wartime anti-Japanese hysteria led to the internment of Japanese Americans, an erosion of their civil rights. They were freed toward the end of the war, but their incarceration left scars. Finally, Mexican Americans and American Indians benefited from wartime jobs and military service but continued to experience prejudice.

The Origins of the Civil Rights Movement

In 1941 A. Philip Randolph, the head of the Brotherhood of Sleeping Car Porters, applied his labor union experience to the struggle for civil rights. He announced that he planned to lead a 100,000-person march on Washington, D.C., in June 1941 to protest racial discrimination in government and war-related employment as well as segregation in the military. Although Randolph believed in an interracial alliance of working people, he insisted that the march should be all-black to show that African Americans could lead their own movement. Inching the country toward war, but not yet engaged militarily, President Roosevelt wanted to avoid any embarrassment the proposed march would bring to the forces supporting democracy and freedom. With his wife, Eleanor, serving as go-between, Roosevelt agreed to meet with Randolph and worked out a compromise. Randolph called off the march, and in return, on June 25, 1941, the president issued Executive Order 8802, creating the **Fair Employment Practice Committee (FEPC)**. Roosevelt refused to order the desegregation of the military, but he set up a committee to investigate inequality in the armed forces. Although the FEPC helped African Americans gain a greater share of jobs in key industries than they had before, the effect was limited because the agency did not have enforcement power.

The march on Washington movement was emblematic of rising civil rights activity. Black leaders proclaimed their own "two-front war" with the symbol of the **Double V** to represent victory against racist enemies both abroad and at home. The National Association for the Advancement of Colored People (NAACP) continued its policy of fighting racial discrimination in the courts. In 1944 the organization won a significant victory in a case from Texas, *Smith v. Allwright*, which outlawed all-white Democratic primary elections in the traditionally one-party South. As a result of the decision, the percentage of African Americans registered to vote in the South doubled between 1944 and 1948. In 1942 early civil rights activists also founded the interracial Congress of Racial Equality (CORE) in Chicago. CORE protested directly against racial inequality in public accommodations. Its members organized "sit-ins" at restaurants and bowling alleys that refused to serve African Americans. Students at Howard University in Washington, D.C., used the same tactics, with some success, to protest racial exclusion from restaurants and cafeterias in the nation's capital. Although these demonstrations did not get the national attention that postwar protests would, they constituted the prelude to the civil rights movement.

Population shifts on the home front during World War II exacerbated racial tensions, resulting in violence. As jobs opened up throughout the country at military installations and defense plants, hundreds of thousands of African Americans moved from the rural South to the urban South, the North, and the West. Cities could not handle this rapid influx of people and failed to provide sufficient housing to accommodate those who migrated in search of employment. Competition between white and black workers for scarce housing spilled over into tensions in crowded transportation and recreational facilities. In 1943 the stress caused by close wartime contact between the races exploded in more than 240 riots. The most serious one occurred in Detroit, where federal troops had to restore order after whites and blacks fought with each other following an altercation at a popular amusement park that killed thirty-four people.

Struggles for Mexican Americans

Immigration from Mexico increased significantly during the war. To address labor shortages in the Southwest and on the Pacific coast and departing from the deportation policies of the 1930s, in 1942 the United States negotiated an agreement with Mexico for contract laborers (*braceros*) to enter the country for a limited time to work as farm laborers and in factories. *Braceros* had little or no control over their living spaces or working conditions. They conducted numerous strikes for higher wages in the agricultural fields of the Southwest and Northwest. Most U.S. residents of Mexican ancestry were American citizens. Like other Americans, they settled into jobs to help fight the war, while more than 300,000 Mexican Americans served in the armed forces.

The war heightened Mexican Americans' consciousness of their civil rights. As one Mexican American World War II veteran recalled: "We were Americans, not 'spics' or 'greasers.' Because when you fight for your country in a World War, against an alien philosophy, fascism, you are an American and proud to be in America." In southern California, newspaper publisher Ignacio Lutero Lopez campaigned against segregation in movie theaters, swimming pools, and other public accommodations. He organized boycotts against businesses that discriminated against or excluded Mexican Americans. Wartime organizing led to the creation of the Unity Leagues, a coalition of Mexican American business owners, college students, civic leaders, and GIs that pressed for racial equality. In Texas, Mexican Americans joined the League of United Latin American Citizens (LULAC), a largely middle-class group that challenged racial discrimination and segregation in public accommodations. Members of the organization emphasized the use of negotiations to redress their grievances, but when they ran into opposition, they resorted to economic boycotts and litigation. The war encouraged LULAC to expand its operations throughout the Southwest.

Mexican American citizens encountered hostility from recently transplanted whites and longtime residents. Tensions were greatest in Los Angeles. A small group of Mexican American teenagers joined gangs and identified themselves by wearing zoot suits — colorful, long, loose-fitting jackets with padded shoulders and baggy pants tapered at the bottom. Not all zoot-suiters were gang members, but many outside their communities failed to make this distinction and found the zoot-suiters' dress and swagger provocative. On the night of June 4, 1943, squads of sailors stationed in Long Beach invaded Mexican American neighborhoods in East Los Angeles and indiscriminately attacked both zoot-suiters and those not dressed in this garb, setting off four days of violence. Mexican American youths tried to fight back. The **zoot suit riots** ended as civilian and military authorities restored order. In response, the Los Angeles city council banned the wearing of zoot suits in public.

American Indians

Some twenty-five thousand Native Americans served in the military during the war, a disproportionately higher representation than their numbers in the population. Although the Iroquois nation challenged the right of the United States to draft Indians, in 1942 it separately declared war against the Axis powers. Like most other Americans, Native Americans joined up for a variety of reasons: patriotism, concern over the threat of fascism, and a desire to escape the impoverishment and drudgery of home life. The armed forces used Navajo soldiers in the Pacific theater to confuse the Japanese by sending coded messages in their tribal language. In addition to those serving in the military, another forty thousand Indians worked in defense-related industries. The migration of Indians off reservations opened up new opportunities and fostered increased pride in the part they played in winning the war. Nevertheless, for most Indians the war did not improve their living conditions or remove hostility to their tribal identities.

The Ordeal of Japanese Americans

World War II marked a significant crossroads for the protection of civil liberties. In general, the federal government did not repress civil liberties as harshly as it had during World War I, primarily because opposition to World War II was not nearly as great. The chief potential for radical dissent came from the Communist Party, but after the Germans attacked the Soviet Union in June 1941, Communists and their sympathizers rallied behind the war effort and did whatever they could to stifle any protest that threatened the goal of defeating Germany. On the other side of the political spectrum, after the attack on Pearl Harbor conservative isolationists in the America First Movement quickly threw their support behind the war.

Of the three ethnic groups associated with the Axis enemy — Japanese, Germans, and Italians — Japanese Americans received by far the worst treatment from the civilian population and state and federal officials. German immigrants had experienced animosity and repression on the home front during World War I but, like Italian immigrants, had generally assimilated into the wider population. In addition, German Americans and Italian Americans had spread out across the country, while Japanese Americans remained concentrated in distinct geographical pockets along the West Coast. Although German Americans and Italian Americans experienced prejudice, they had come to be considered racially white. Nevertheless, the government arrested about 1,500 Italians considered "enemy aliens" and placed around 250 of them in internment camps. It also arrested more than 11,000 Germans, some of them American citizens, who were considered a danger.

The **internment**, or forced relocation and detainment, of Italians and Germans in the United States paled in comparison with that of the Japanese. Nearly all people of Japanese descent lived along the West Coast. Government officials relocated all of those living there — citizens and noncitizens alike — to camps in Arizona, Arkansas, California, Colorado, Idaho, Texas, Utah, and Wyoming. In Hawaii, the site of the Japanese attack on Pearl Harbor, the Japanese population, nearly one-third of the territory's population, was too large to transfer and instead lived under martial law. The few thousand Japanese Americans living elsewhere in the continental United States remained in their homes.

It did not matter that Fred Korematsu had been born in the United States, had a white girlfriend of Italian heritage, and counted whites among his best friends. His parents had come from Japan, and for much of the American public, his racial heritage meant that he was not a true American. As one American general put it early in the war, "A Jap's a Jap. It makes no difference whether he is an American citizen or not." Along with more than 100,000 people of Japanese descent, two-thirds of whom were American citizens, Korematsu spent most of the war held in an internment camp. Japanese Americans lost their freedom and protection under the Bill of Rights and the Fourteenth Amendment. Despite scant evidence that Japanese Americans were disloyal or harbored spies or saboteurs, U.S. officials chose to believe that as a group they threatened national security. The government established a system that questioned German Americans and Italian Americans on an individual basis if their loyalty came under suspicion. By contrast, U.S. officials identified all Japanese Americans and Japanese resident aliens with the nation that had attacked Pearl Harbor, and incarcerated them. In this respect, the United States was not unique. Following the United States' lead, Canada interned its Japanese population, more than 75 percent of whom held Canadian citizenship.

For their part, Japanese Americans did their best to manage during this upheaval. They had been forced to sell their possessions and dispose of their homes and businesses quickly, either selling or renting them at very low prices or simply abandoning them. They left their neighborhoods with only what they could carry. They lived in wooden barracks divided into one-room apartments and shared communal toilets, showers, laundries, and dining facilities. The camps provided schools, recreational activities, and opportunities for religious worship, except for Shintoism, the official religion of Japan. Some internees attempted to farm, but the arid land on which the camps were located made this nearly impossible. Inmates who worked at jobs within a camp earned monthly wages of $12 to $19, far less than they would have received outside the camps.

Japanese Americans responded to their internment in a variety of ways. Many formed community groups, and some expressed their reactions to the emotional upheaval by writing of their experiences or displaying their feelings through artwork. Contradicting beliefs that their ancestry made them disloyal or not real Americans, some 18,000 men joined the army, and many fought gallantly in some of the war's fiercest battles on the European front with the 442nd Regiment, one of the most heavily decorated units in the military. Nisei soldiers were among the first, along with African American troops, to liberate Jews from German concentration camps. Others, like Fred Korematsu, remained in the camps and challenged the legality of President Roosevelt's executive order, which had allowed military officials to exclude Japanese Americans from certain areas and evacuate them from their homes. However, the Supreme Court ruled against him and others. Finally, in December 1944, shortly after he won election to his fourth term as president, Roosevelt rescinded Executive Order 9066.

In contrast to the treatment of Japanese Americans, the status of Chinese Americans improved markedly during the war. Of the more than 100,000 Chinese living in the United States, approximately 13,000 served in the Army. Forty percent of these soldiers were not native-born citizens. With China under Japanese occupation, Congress repealed the Chinese Exclusion Act in 1943, making the Chinese, including those in the military, the first Asians who could become naturalized citizens. Chinese American men also fought in integrated military units like their Filipino peers. For the first time, the war opened up jobs to Chinese American men and women outside their ethnic economy.

Despite the violation of the civil liberties of Japanese American citizens, the majority did not become embittered against the United States. Rather, most of the internees returned to their communities after the war and resumed their lives, still intent on pursuing the American dream from which they had been so harshly excluded; however, some 8,000 Japanese Americans renounced their U.S. citizenship and repatriated to Japan in 1945. After briefly moving to Detroit, Korematsu returned to San Leandro, California, with his wife and two children. Still, Korematsu had trouble finding regular employment because he had a criminal record for violating the exclusion order. In the name of national security the government had established the precedent of incarcerating groups deemed "suspect." It took four decades for the U.S. government to admit its mistake and apologize, and in 1988 Congress awarded reparations of $20,000 to each of the 60,000 living internees. In 1998 President Bill Clinton awarded Korematsu the Presidential Medal of Freedom — the highest decoration a civilian can receive.

| REVIEW & RELATE | • What new challenges and opportunities did the war present to racial minority groups?
• Why were Japanese Americans singled out as a particular threat to national security? |

Global War

World War II pitted the "Grand Alliance" of Great Britain, the Soviet Union, the French government in exile, and the United States against the Axis powers of Germany, Japan, and Italy. From the outset, the United States deployed military forces to contain Japanese aggression, but its most immediate concern was to defeat Germany. Before battles in Europe, Asia, and four other continents concluded, more than 60 million people perished, including 405,000 Americans. Six million Jewish civilians died in the Holocaust, the Nazi regime's genocidal effort to eradicate Europe's Jewish population. Another 9 million civilians—Slavic peoples, Romani, Jehovah's Witnesses, homosexuals, the disabled, and Communists—also were systematically murdered by the Nazis. The Soviet Union experienced the greatest losses—nearly 27 million soldiers and civilians, more than two-fifths of all those killed.

War in Europe

United against Hitler, the Grand Alliance divided over how quickly to mount a counterattack directly on Germany. The Soviet Union, which bore the brunt of the fighting in trying to repel the German army's invasion, demanded the opening of a **second front** through France and into Germany to take the pressure off its forces. The British wanted to fight first in northern Africa and southern Europe, in part to remove Axis forces from territory that endangered their economic interests in the Mediterranean and the Middle East and in part to buy time to rebuild their depleted fighting strength. President Roosevelt understood the Soviet position, but worried about losing public support early in the war if the United States experienced heavy casualties. He approved his military advisers' plans for an invasion of France from England in 1943, but in the meantime he agreed with Churchill to fight the Germans and Italians on the periphery of Europe.

From a military standpoint, this circuitous approach proved successful. In October 1942 British forces in North Africa overpowered the Germans at El Alamein, pushing them out of Egypt and removing their threat to the Suez Canal. The following month, British and American troops landed in Algeria and Morocco. After some early defeats, the combined strength of British and American ground, air, and naval forces drove the Germans out of Africa in May 1943.

These military victories failed to relieve political tensions among the Allies. Although the Soviets had managed to stop the German offensive against Stalingrad, the deepest penetration of enemy troops into their country, Stalin expected the second front to begin as promised in the spring of 1943. He was bitterly disappointed when Roosevelt postponed the cross–English Channel invasion of France until 1944. To Stalin, it appeared as if his allies were looking to gain a double triumph by letting the Communists and Nazis beat each other into submission.

Instead of opening a second front in France, British, American, and Canadian troops invaded Italy from its southern tip in July 1943. Their initial victories quickly led to the removal of Mussolini and his retreat to northern Italy, where he lived under German protection (Map 23.1). Not until June 4, 1944, did the Allies occupy Rome in central Italy and force the Germans to retreat.

To overcome Stalin's dissatisfaction with the postponement of opening the second front, President Roosevelt issued orders to give the Soviets unlimited access to Lend-Lease supplies to sustain their war efforts and to care for their citizens. In November 1943, Roosevelt, Churchill, and Stalin met in Tehran, Iran. Roosevelt and Stalin seemed to get along well. Stalin agreed to deploy troops against Japan after the war in Europe ended, and Roosevelt agreed to open the second front within six months. Churchill joined Roosevelt and Stalin in supporting the creation of an international organization to ensure postwar peace.

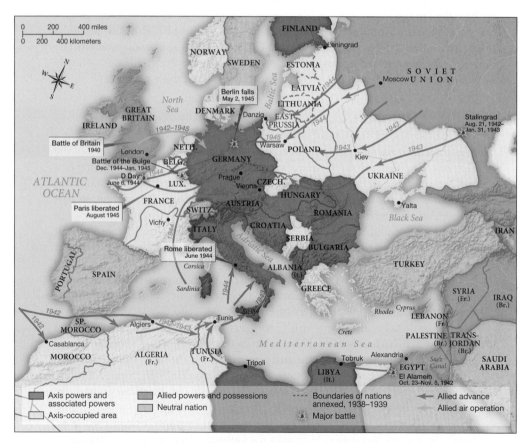

MAP 23.1   **World War II in Europe, 1941–1945**
By late 1941, the Axis powers had brought most of Europe and the Mediterranean region under their control. But between 1942 and 1945, the Allied powers drove them back. Critical victories at Leningrad and Stalingrad, in North Africa, and on the beaches of Normandy forced the retreat, and then the defeat, of the Axis powers.

This time the Americans and British kept their word, and the Allies finally embarked on the second-front invasion. On June 6, 1944—called **D Day**—more than 1.5 million American, British, and Canadian troops crossed the English Channel in 4,000 boats and landed on the beaches of Normandy, France. Despite deadly machine-gun fire from German troops placed on higher ground, the Allied forces managed to establish a beachhead. The bravery and discipline of the troops, along with their superior numbers, overcame the Germans and opened the way for the Allies to liberate Paris in August 1944. By the end of the year, the Allies had regained control of the rest of France and most of Belgium.

Amid these Allied victories, Roosevelt ran for a fourth term against Republican challenger Thomas E. Dewey, governor of New York. He dumped from the campaign ticket his vice president, Henry A. Wallace, a liberal on economic and racial issues, and replaced him with Senator Harry S. Truman of Missouri, who was more acceptable to southern voters. Despite his declining health, Roosevelt won easily.

War in the Pacific

With the Soviet Union bearing the brunt of the fighting in eastern Europe, the United States shouldered the burden of fighting Japan. U.S. military commanders began a two-pronged counterattack in the Pacific in 1942. General Douglas MacArthur, whose troops had escaped from the Philippines as Japanese forces overran the islands in May 1942, planned to regroup in Australia, head north through New Guinea, and return to the Philippines. At the same time, Admiral Chester Nimitz directed the U.S. Pacific Fleet from Hawaii toward Japanese-occupied islands in the western Pacific. If all went well, MacArthur's ground troops and Nimitz's naval forces would combine with General Curtis LeMay's air forces to overwhelm Japan. This strategy was known as "**island-hopping**." Accordingly, American and allied forces would leapfrog over heavily fortified Japanese positions and concentrate their resources on lightly defended Japanese islands that would provide bases capable of sustaining the campaign to attack the nation of Japan.

All went according to plan in 1942. Shortly after the Philippines fell to the Japanese, the Allies won a major victory in May in the Battle of the Coral Sea, off the northwest coast of Australia. The following month, the U.S. navy achieved an even greater victory when it defeated the Japanese in the Battle of Midway Island, northwest of Hawaii. In August, the fighting moved to the Solomon Islands, east of New Guinea, where U.S. forces waged fierce battles at Guadalcanal Island. After six months of heavy casualties on both sides, the Americans finally dislodged the Japanese. By late 1944, American, Australian, and New Zealand troops had put the Japanese on the defensive.

In 1945 the United States mounted its final offensive against Japan. In preparation for an invasion of the Japanese home islands, American marines won important battles on Iwo Jima and Okinawa, two strategic islands off the coast of Japan. The fighting proved costly—on Iwo Jima alone, the Japanese fought and died nearly to the last man while killing 6,000 Americans and wounding 20,000 others. At the same time, the U.S. Army Air Corps conducted firebomb raids over Tokyo and other major cities, killing some 330,000 Japanese civilians. These attacks were conducted by newly developed B-29 bombers, which could fly more than 3,000 miles and could

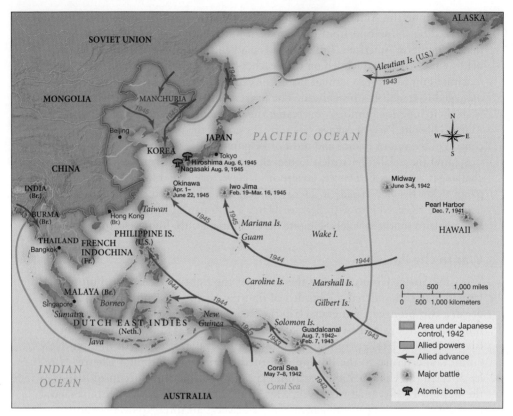

MAP 23.2   World War II in the Pacific, 1941–1945
After bombing Pearl Harbor on December 7, 1941, Japan captured the Philippines and wrenched control of Asian colonies from the British, French, and Dutch and then occupied eastern China. The Allied powers, led by U.S. forces, eventually defeated Japan by winning a series of hard-fought victories on Central Pacific islands and by bombing Hiroshima and Nagasaki.

be dispatched from Pacific island bases captured by the U.S. military. The purpose of this strategic bombing was to destroy Japan's economic capability to sustain the war rather to destroy their military forces. At the same time, the navy blockaded Japan, further crippling its economy and reducing its supplies of food, medicine, and raw materials (Map 23.2). Still, the Japanese government refused to surrender and indicated its determination to resist by launching *kamikaze* attacks (suicidal airplane crashes) on American warships and airplanes.

Ending the War

With victory in sight in both Europe and the Pacific, the Allies addressed problems of postwar relations. In February 1945 Roosevelt and Churchill met with Stalin in the resort city of Yalta in the Ukraine. There they clashed over the question of the postwar government of Poland and whether to recognize the claim of the Polish government in exile in London, which the United States and Great Britain supported, or that of the pro-Soviet government, which had spent the war in the USSR. The loosely worded **Yalta Agreement**, which resulted from the conference, called for the establishment of permanent governments in Poland and the rest of eastern Europe through free elections.

Despite this controversy, the Allies left Yalta united over other issues. They renewed their commitment to establishing the United Nations, and the Soviets reaffirmed their intention to join the war against Japan three months after Germany's surrender. The Allies also reached a tentative agreement on postwar Germany. The United States, Great Britain, the Soviet Union, and France would divide the country into four zones, each occupied by one of the powers. They would further subdivide Berlin into four sectors because the capital city fell within the Soviet occupation area. As with the accord over Poland, the agreement concerning Germany created tension after the war.

The Yalta Conference concluded just as the final assault against Germany got under way. The Germans had launched one last offensive in mid-December 1944. Mobilizing troops from remaining outposts in Belgium, they attacked Allied forces in the Battle of the Bulge. After an initial German drive into enemy lines, American and British fighting men recovered and sent the Germans retreating across the Rhine

Roosevelt, Churchill, and Stalin at Yalta, 1945   This photograph taken in February 1945 shows, from left to right, a smiling Prime Minister Winston Churchill, President Franklin Roosevelt, and Soviet Premier Joseph Stalin at the Yalta conference in Crimea. The so-called "Big Three" allies met to discuss postwar plans for Germany and Eastern Europe. In poor health at the time of the meeting, two months later Roosevelt died of a stroke. National Archives, no. 531340

River and back into Germany. Pushing from the west, American general Dwight D. Eisenhower stopped at the Elbe River, where he had agreed to meet up with Red Army troops who were charging from the east to Berlin. After an intense assault by the Soviets, the German capital of Berlin fell, and on April 25 Russian and American forces linked up in Torgau on the Elbe River. They achieved this triumph two weeks after Franklin Roosevelt died at the age of sixty-three from a cerebral hemorrhage. On April 30, 1945, with Berlin shattered, Hitler committed suicide in his bunker. A few days earlier, Italian antifascist partisans had captured and executed Mussolini in northern Italy. On May 2, German troops surrendered in Italy, and on May 7 the remnants of the German government formally surrendered. The war in Europe ended the next day.

With the war over in Europe, the United States made its final push against Japan. Since 1942, J. Robert Oppenheimer and his team of scientists and engineers had labored feverishly to construct an atomic bomb. Few people knew about the top-secret **Manhattan Project**, and Congress appropriated $2 billion without knowing its true purpose.

Vice President Harry S. Truman did not learn about the details of the Manhattan Project until Roosevelt's death on April 12, and in July he found out about the first atomic test while en route to a conference in Potsdam, Germany, with Stalin and Churchill. He ordered the State Department to issue an ultimatum to the Japanese demanding their immediate surrender or else face annihilation. When Japan indicated that it would surrender if the United States allowed the country to retain its emperor, Hirohito, the Truman administration refused and demanded unconditional surrender. As a further blow to Japan, Stalin was ready to send the Soviet military to attack Japanese troops in Manchuria on August 8, which would seriously weaken Japan's ability to hold out.

On August 6 the *Enola Gay*, an American B-29 bomber, dropped an atomic bomb on Hiroshima. The weapon immediately killed 80,000 civilians, and tens of thousands later died slowly from radiation poisoning. Three days later, on August 9, Japan still had not surrendered, and the Army Air Corps dropped another atomic bomb on Nagasaki, killing more than 100,000 civilians. Five days later, on August 14, Japan announced that it would surrender; the formal surrender was completed on September 2.

At the time, very few Americans questioned the decision to drop atomic bombs on Japan. Truman believed that had Roosevelt been alive, he would have authorized use of the bombs. Newly on the job, Truman hesitated to reverse a decision already reached by his predecessor. He reasoned that his action would save American lives because the U.S. military would not have to launch a costly invasion of Japan's home islands. He also felt justified in giving the order because he sought retaliation for the surprise attack on Pearl Harbor and for Japanese atrocities against American soldiers, especially in the Philippines.

Evidence of the Holocaust

The end of the war revealed the full extent and horror of the **Holocaust** — Germany's calculated and methodical slaughter of certain religious, ethnic, and political groups. As Allied troops liberated Germany and Poland, they saw for themselves the brutality of the Nazi concentration camps that Hitler had set up to execute or work to death 6 million Jews and another 5 million "undesirables" — Slavs, Poles, Gypsies, homosexuals, the physically and mentally disabled, and Communists. At Buchenwald and Dachau in Germany and at Auschwitz in Poland, the Allies encountered the skeletal remains of inmates tossed into mass graves, dead from starvation, illness, and executions. Crematoria on the premises contained the ashes of inmates first poisoned and then incinerated. Troops also freed the "living dead," those still alive but seriously ill and undernourished.

These horrific discoveries shocked the public, but evidence of what was happening had appeared early in the war. Journalists like Varian Fry had outlined the Nazi atrocities against the Jews several years before. "Letters, reports, tables all fit together. They add up to the most appalling picture of mass murder in all human history," Fry wrote in the *New Republic* magazine in 1942.

The Roosevelt administration did little in response, despite growing evidence. It chose not to send planes to bomb the concentration camps or the railroad lines

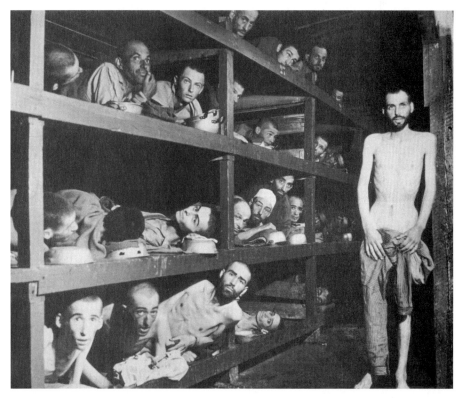

Holocaust Survivors When American troops of the 80th Army Division liberated the Buchenwald concentration camp in Germany, they found these emaciated victims of the Holocaust. Elie Wiesel (seventh from the left on the middle bunk next to the vertical post) went on to become an internationally famous writer who wrote about his wartime experiences and won the Nobel Peace Prize. H. Miller/Getty Images

leading to them, deeming it too risky militarily and too dangerous for the inmates. "The War Department," its assistant Secretary John J. McCloy wrote the director of the War Refugee Board in defending this decision, "is of the opinion that the suggested air operation is impracticable. It could be executed only by the diversion of considerable air support essential to the success of our forces now engaged in decisive operations and would in any case be of such very doubtful efficacy that it would not amount to a practical project." In a less defensible decision, the Roosevelt administration refused to relax immigration laws to allow Jews and other persecuted ethnic minorities to take refuge in the United States, and only 21,000 managed to find asylum. The State Department, which could have modified these policies, was staffed with anti-Semitic officials, and though President Roosevelt expressed sympathy for the plight of Hitler's victims, he believed that winning the war as quickly as possible was the best way to help them.

Nevertheless, even when it had been possible to rescue Jews, the United States balked. In 1939 a German liner, the SS *St. Louis*, embarked from Hamburg with 937 Jewish refugees aboard and set sail for Cuba. Blocked from entry by the Cuban government, the ship sailed for the coast of Florida, hoping to gain permission to enter the United States. However, the United States refused, maintaining that the passengers did not have the proper documents required under the Immigration Act of 1924. The ship then headed back to Europe, where the United Kingdom, Belgium, the Netherlands, and France took in the passengers. Unfortunately, in 1940, when the Nazis invaded Belgium, the Netherlands, and France and sent their Jewish residents to concentration camps, an estimated 254 of the *St. Louis* passengers died along with countless others.

Although not nearly to the same extent as in the Holocaust, the Japanese also committed numerous war atrocities. Around 50,000 U.S. soldiers and civilians became prisoners of war and about half of them were forced to work as slave laborers. From June 1942 to October 1943, the Japanese constructed a 300-mile railroad between Burma (Myanmar) and Thailand using 60,000 Allied prisoners of war and 200,000 Asian conscripts. Working under inhumane conditions, approximately 13,000 Allied prisoners of war and 80,000 Asian laborers died before the railway was completed. About 40 percent of American POWs died in Japanese captivity (in contrast only 1 percent died in Nazi camps). One reason why POWs were treated so poorly was because the Japanese believed that surrender was a cowardly act and those who did so were beneath contempt. Far more than the Americans and their allies, Chinese civilians and native residents of such countries as Burma and the Dutch East Indies (Indonesia) were brutalized and killed by the Japanese occupying forces.

REVIEW & RELATE	• How did the Allies win the war in Europe and in the Pacific, and how did tensions among them shape their military strategy and postwar plans? • Why did the United States fail to do more to help victims of the Holocaust?

Conclusion: The Impact of World War II

Franklin Roosevelt initially charted a course of neutrality before the United States entered World War II. Roosevelt believed that the rise of European dictatorships and their expansionist pursuits throughout the world threatened American national security. He saw signs of trouble early, but responding to antiwar sentiment from lawmakers and the American public, Roosevelt waited for a blatant enemy attack before declaring war. The Japanese attack on Pearl Harbor in 1941 provided that justification.

On the domestic front, World War II accomplished what Franklin Roosevelt's New Deal could not. Prosperity and nearly full employment returned only after the nation's factories began supplying the Allies and the United States joined in the fight against the Axis powers. Mobilization for war also furthered the tremendous growth and centralization of power in the federal government that had begun under the New Deal. Washington, D.C. became the chief source of authority to which Americans looked for solutions to problems concerning economic security and financial development. The federal government showed that it would use its authority to expand equal rights for African Americans. The war swung national power against racial discrimination, and various civil rights victories during the war served as precursors to the civil rights movement of subsequent decades. The war also heightened Mexican Americans' consciousness of oppression and led them to organize for civil rights. However, in neither case, nor that of American Indians, did the war erase white prejudice.

At the same time, the federal government trampled on the civil liberties of Japanese Americans. The president succumbed to wartime antagonism against Japanese immigrants and their children. With China a wartime ally, Chinese Americans escaped a similar fate. Yet like white and black Americans, the Nisei displayed their patriotism by distinguishing themselves as soldiers on the battlefields of Europe.

The war brought women into the workforce as never before, providing a measure of independence and distancing them from their traditional roles as wives and mothers. Nevertheless, the government and private employers made it clear that they expected most female workers to give up their jobs to returning servicemen and to become homemakers once the war ended.

Finally, the war thrust the United States onto the world stage as one of the world's two major superpowers alongside the Soviet Union. This position posed new challenges. In sole possession of the atomic bomb, the most powerful weapon on the planet, and fortified by a robust economy, the United States filled the international power vacuum created by the weakening and eventual collapse of the European colonial empires. The fragile alliance that had held together the United States and the Soviet Union shattered soon after the end of World War II. The Atomic Age, which J. Robert Oppenheimer helped usher in with a powerful weapon of mass destruction, and the government oppression that Fred Korematsu endured in the name of national security did not disappear. Rather, they expanded in new directions and shaped the lives of all Americans for decades to come.

Chapter 23 Review

KEY TERMS

Neutrality Acts, 584
appeasement, 584
America First Committee, 585
Lend-Lease Act, 585
Atlantic Charter, 586
military-industrial complex, 587
War Production Board, 588
National War Labor Board, 589
Fair Employment Practice
    Committee (FEPC), 592

Double V, 593
zoot suit riots, 594
internment, 595
second front, 597
D Day, 599
"island-hopping", 599
Yalta Agreement, 601
Manhattan Project, 602
Holocaust, 602

REVIEW & RELATE

1. How did American public opinion shape Roosevelt's foreign policy in the years preceding U.S. entry into World War II?
2. What events in Europe and the Pacific ultimately brought the United States into World War II?
3. How did the war accelerate the trend that began during the New Deal toward increased government participation in the economy?
4. How did the war affect life on the home front for the average American?
5. What new challenges and opportunities did the war present to racial minority groups?
6. Why were Japanese Americans singled out as a particular threat to national security?
7. How did the Allies win the war in Europe and in the Pacific, and how did tensions among them shape their military strategy and postwar plans?
8. Why did the United States fail to do more to help victims of the Holocaust?

TIMELINE OF EVENTS

1933	• United States extends diplomatic recognition to the Soviet Union
	• Adolf Hitler becomes chancellor of Germany
1935–1937	• Neutrality Acts
1939	• Germany occupies Czechoslovakia
	• Germany and Soviet Union invade Poland; World War II begins

1940	• Battle of Britain begins
	• Tripartite Pact signed
1941	• Lend-Lease Act
	• Fair Employment Practice Committee created
	• Atlantic Charter signed
	• Germany invades Soviet Union
December 7, 1941	• Pearl Harbor bombed
December 11, 1941	• Germany and Italy declare war on the United States
1942	• Congress of Racial Equality established
	• Manhattan Project approved
	• Roosevelt orders internment of Japanese Americans
1943	• Zoot suit riots
June 6, 1944	• D Day invasion begins
1945	• Final U.S. offensive against Japan, with victories at Iwo Jima and Okinawa
February 1945	• Yalta Conference
May 1945	• Germany surrenders
August 1945	• U.S. drops atomic bombs on Hiroshima and Nagasaki
September 1945	• Japan surrenders

24

The Opening of the Cold War

1945–1961

COMPARING AMERICAN HISTORIES

George Frost Kennan played a critical role in shaping the postwar confrontation between the United States and the Soviet Union. Kennan's views were based on extensive experience with the Soviets gained during two tours of duty serving as a diplomat at the U.S. Embassy in Moscow. During the first, from 1933 to 1937, he witnessed countless "enemies of the state" arrested, exiled, or executed in Stalin's purges. His experiences convinced him that there was little basis for a positive relationship between the United States and the Soviet Union.

Kennan's second tour as a lead U.S. diplomat in Moscow, from 1944 to 1946, came at a critical juncture in U.S.-Soviet relations. As the war drew to a close, tensions over the nature of the postwar world escalated, and by 1946 the wartime alliance had collapsed. Against this backdrop, Kennan warned that Stalin was committed to expanding communism throughout the world and advised President Harry S. Truman to adopt a policy of *containment*. In Kennan's view, all Soviet efforts at expansion should be met with firm resistance. At the same time, the United States should take an active role in rebuilding the economies of war-torn Western European countries, thereby reducing the appeal of communism to their populations. Kennan's concept of containment would become the basis for President Truman's Cold War foreign policy.

Kennan, however, was not a rigid cold warrior. As the Cold War intensified and expanded, Kennan argued that containment would work best through political and economic rather than military means. He soon insisted that his containment strategy had been misunderstood. Increasingly, his views fell out of favor at the State Department, and Kennan left in 1950 in a disagreement with the Truman administration's growing militarization of the conflict with the Soviet Union.

Julius and Ethel Rosenberg were casualties of the Cold War that Kennan helped shape. Accused of passing military secrets to the Soviet Union, they were tried for espionage in an atmosphere of growing anti-Communist fervor. Like other young idealists during the 1930s, Ethel became disillusioned with capitalism, joined the Young Communist League, and took part in labor union organizing in her hometown of New York City. Julius attended the City College of New York, where he, too, joined the Young Communist League. Three years after they met in 1936, Julius and Ethel married and started a family.

During World War II, Julius worked for the Army Signal Corps as an engineer. In 1945 he lost his job after a security investigation revealed his Communist Party membership. Five years later, the federal government charged that during World War II the Rosenbergs had provided classified information about the construction of the atomic bomb to the Soviet Union, charges they denied.

A jury found them guilty on April 5, 1951, and the presiding judge sentenced them to death. Despite an international campaign for clemency and after unsuccessful appeals to the Supreme Court, on June 19, 1953, the Rosenbergs were executed. Though recent evidence has confirmed Julius Rosenberg's role as a spy, the case against Ethel remains inconclusive. Without the heightened Cold War climate that then existed in the country, it is likely that neither would have gone to the electric chair

THE AMERICAN HISTORIES of both George Kennan and Julius and Ethel Rosenberg revolved around their views of communism and the Soviet Union. Kennan designed an approach to containing Soviet aggression based on his dealings with Stalin. The Rosenbergs believed in communism's promise of social and economic equality and saw the Soviet Union as a defense against Nazi aggression. The lives of

Kennan, the Rosenbergs, and all Americans would be profoundly shaped by the epic military and ideological battle between the superpowers as the Cold War expanded from the late 1940s through the 1950s, bringing with it increased interventions abroad, fear of communism within the United States, and changes in the executive power of the presidency.

The Origins of the Cold War 1945–1947

The wartime partnership between the United States and the Soviet Union (USSR) was an alliance of necessity. The two nations joined forces to combat Nazi aggression, putting aside ideological differences and a history of mutual distrust. As long as the Nazi threat existed, the alliance held, but as the war ended and attention turned to the postwar world, the allies became adversaries. The two nations did not engage directly in war, but they entered into a prolonged struggle for political, economic, and military dominance known as the **Cold War**.

Mutual Misunderstandings

The roots of the Cold War stretched back several decades. After the Bolshevik Revolution of 1917, the United States refused to grant diplomatic recognition to the Soviet Union and sent troops to Russia to support anti-Bolshevik forces seeking to overturn the revolution, an effort that failed. At the same time, the American government, fearing Communist efforts to overthrow capitalist governments, sought to wipe out communism in the United States by deporting immigrant radicals during the Red scare (see "The Red Scare, 1919–1920" in chapter 21). The United States continued to deny diplomatic recognition to the USSR until 1933, when President Roosevelt reversed this policy. Nevertheless, relations between the two countries remained uneasy.

World War II brought a thaw in tensions. President Roosevelt went a long way toward defusing Stalin's concerns at the Yalta Conference in 1945. The Soviet leader viewed the Eastern European countries that the USSR had liberated from the Germans, especially Poland, as a buffer to protect his nation from future attacks by Germany. Roosevelt understood Stalin's reasoning and recognized political realities: The Soviet military already occupied Eastern Europe, a state of affairs that increased Stalin's bargaining position. Still, the president attempted to balance Soviet influence by insisting that the Yalta Agreement include a guarantee of free elections in Eastern Europe.

By contrast, Roosevelt's successor, Harry S. Truman, took a much less nuanced approach to U.S.-Soviet relations than his predecessor. Stalin's ruthless purges within the Soviet Union in the 1930s and 1940s convinced Truman that the Soviet dictator was paranoid and extremely dangerous. He believed that the Soviets threatened "a barbarian invasion of Europe," and he intended to deter it. In his first meeting with Soviet foreign minister Vyacheslav Molotov in April 1945, Truman rebuked the Russians for failing to support free elections in Poland. Molotov, recoiling from the sharp tone of Truman's remarks, replied: "I have never been talked to like that in my life."

Despite this rough start, Truman did not immediately abandon the idea of cooperation with the Soviet Union. At the Potsdam Conference in Germany in July 1945, Truman and Stalin agreed on several issues. The two leaders reaffirmed the concept of free elections in Eastern Europe; Soviet troop withdrawal from the oil fields of northern Iran, which bordered the USSR; and the partition of Germany (and Berlin itself) into four Allied occupation zones.

Within six months of the war's end, however, relations between the two countries soured. The United States was the only nation in the world with the atomic bomb and boasted the only economy reinvigorated by the war. As a result, the Truman administration believed that it held the upper hand against the Soviets. With this in mind, the State Department offered the Soviets a $6 billion loan, which the country needed to help rebuild its war-ravaged economy. But when the Soviets undermined free elections in Poland in 1946 and established a compliant government, the United States withdrew the offer. Soviet troops also remained in northern Iran, closing off the oil fields to potential capitalist enterprises. The failure to reach agreement over international control of atomic energy proved the last straw. The United States wanted to make sure it would keep its atomic weapons, while the Soviets wanted the United States to destroy its nuclear arsenal. Clearly, the former World War II allies did not trust each other.

Truman had significantly underestimated the strength of the Soviet position. The Soviets were well on their way toward building their own atomic bomb, negating the Americans' nuclear advantage. The Soviets could also ignore the enticement of U.S. economic aid by taking resources from East Germany and mobilizing the Russian people to rebuild their country's industry and military. On February 9, 1946, Stalin delivered a tough speech to rally Russians to make sacrifices to enhance national security. By asserting that communism was "a better form of organization than any non-Soviet social system," he implied, according to George Kennan, that capitalist nations could not coexist with communism and that future wars were unavoidable unless communism triumphed over capitalism.

Whether Stalin meant this speech as an unofficial declaration of a third world war was not clear, but U.S. leaders interpreted it this way. A few days after Stalin spoke, Kennan sent an 8,000-word telegram from the U.S. Embassy in Moscow to Washington, blaming the Soviets for stirring up international tensions and confirming that Stalin could not be trusted. The following month, on March 15, former British prime minister Winston Churchill gave a speech in Truman's home state of Missouri. Declaring that "an iron curtain has descended across the Continent" of Europe, Churchill observed that "there is nothing [the Russians] admire so much as strength, and there is nothing for which they have less respect than for . . . military weakness." This comment reaffirmed Truman's sentiments expressed the previous year: "Unless Russia is faced with an iron fist and strong language another war is in the making." The message was clear: Unyielding resistance to the Soviet Union was the only way to avoid another world war.

Not all Americans agreed with this view. Led by Roosevelt's former vice president Henry Wallace, who served as Truman's secretary of commerce, critics voiced concern about taking a "hard line" against the Soviet Union. Stalin was pursuing a policy of expansion, they agreed, but for limited reasons. Wallace claimed that the Soviets merely wanted to protect their borders by surrounding themselves with friendly countries, just as the United States had done by establishing spheres of influence in the Caribbean. Except for Poland and Romania, Stalin initially accepted an array of governments in Eastern Europe, allowing free elections in Czechoslovakia, Hungary, and, to a lesser extent, Bulgaria. Only as Cold War tensions escalated did the Soviets tighten control over all of Eastern Europe. Critics such as Wallace considered this outcome the result of a self-fulfilling prophecy; by misinterpreting Soviet motives, the Truman administration pushed Stalin to counter the American hard line with a hard line of his own.

Thus, after World War II, the United States came to believe that the Soviet Union desired world revolution to spread communism, a doctrine hostile to free market individualism. At the same time, the Soviet Union viewed the United States as seeking to make the world safe for capitalism, thereby reducing Soviet chances to obtain economic resources and rebuild its war-shattered economy. Each nation tended to see the other's actions in the most negative light and to see global developments as a zero-sum game, one in which every victory for one side was necessarily a defeat for the other.

The Truman Doctrine

By 1947 U.S.-Soviet relations had reached a new low. International arms control had proved futile, the United States had gone to the United Nations to pressure the Soviets to withdraw from Iran, and the rhetoric from both sides had become warlike. From the American vantage point, Soviet actions to expand communism in Eastern Europe appeared to threaten democracies in Western Europe. By contrast, the Soviets viewed the United States as seeking to extend economic control over nations close to their borders and to weaken communism in the Soviet Union.

Events in Greece allowed Truman to take the offensive and apply Kennan's policy of containment. To maintain access to the Middle East and its Asian colonies, the United Kingdom considered it vitally important to keep Greece within its sphere of influence. In 1946 a civil war broke out in Greece between the right-wing monarchy and a coalition of insurgents consisting of members of the wartime anti-Nazi resistance, Communists, and non-Communist opponents of the repressive government. Exhausted by the war and in desperate financial shape, the British turned to the United States for help.

The Truman administration believed that the presence of Communists among the Greek rebels meant that Moscow was behind the insurgency. In fact, Stalin was not aiding the Greek revolutionaries; the assistance came from the Communist leader of Yugoslavia, Josip Broz (known then as Marshall Tito), who acted independently of the Soviets and would soon break with them. Following Kennan's lead in advocating containment, Truman incorrectly believed that all Communists around the world were ultimately controlled by the Kremlin.

While Truman was convinced that the United States had to intervene in Greece to contain the spread of communism, he still had to convince the Republican-controlled Congress and the American people to go along. To overcome potential opposition to its plans, the Truman administration exaggerated the danger of Communist influence in Greece. Truman sent Undersecretary of State Dean Acheson to testify before a congressional committee that, "like apples in a barrel infected by one rotten one, the corruption of Greece would infect Iran and all to the east." The administration's presentation of the issues to the American public was even more dramatic. On March 12, 1947, Truman gave a speech to a joint session of Congress that was broadcast over national radio to millions of listeners. He interpreted the civil war in Greece as a titanic struggle between freedom and totalitarianism that threatened the free world. "I believe," the president declared, "that it must be the policy of the United States to support free peoples who are resisting attempted subjugation by armed minorities or by outside pressures." Truman's rhetoric stretched the truth on many counts—the armed minorities to which the president referred had fought Nazi totalitarianism; the Soviets did not supply the insurgents; and the right-wing monarchy, propped up by the military, was hardly democratic. Nevertheless, Truman achieved his goal of frightening both lawmakers and the public, and Congress appropriated $400 million in military aid to fortify the existing governments of Greece and neighboring Turkey.

The **Truman Doctrine**, which pledged to protect democratic countries and contain the expansion of communism, was the cornerstone of American foreign policy throughout the Cold War. The United States committed itself to shoring up governments, whether democratic or dictatorial, as long as they were avowedly anti-Communist. Americans believed that the rest of the world's nations wanted to be like the United States and therefore would not willingly accept communism, which they thought could be imposed only from the outside by the Soviet Union and never reasonably chosen from within.

Although Truman misread Soviet intentions with respect to Greece, Stalin's regime had given him cause for worry. Soviet actions that imposed communism in Poland, along with the USSR's refusal to withdraw troops from the Baltic states of Latvia, Lithuania, and Estonia, reinforced the president's concerns about Soviet expansionism and convinced many in the U.S. government that Stalin had no intention of abiding by his wartime agreements. Difficulties in negotiating with the Soviets about international control of atomic energy further worried American foreign-policy makers about Russian designs for obtaining the atomic bomb.

The Marshall Plan and Economic Containment

U.S. diplomat George Kennan's version of containment called for economic and political aid to check Communist expansion. In this context, to forestall Communist inroads and offer humanitarian assistance to Europeans facing homelessness and starvation, the Truman administration offered economic assistance to the war-torn continent. In doing so, the United States also hoped to guarantee increased trade with Europe. In a June 1947 speech that drew heavily on Kennan's ideas, Secretary of State George Marshall sketched out a plan to provide financial assistance to Europe. Although he invited any country, including the Soviet Union, that experienced "hunger, poverty, desperation, and chaos" to apply for aid, Marshall did not expect Stalin to ask for assistance. To do so would require the Soviets to supply information to the United States concerning the internal operations of their economy and to admit to the failure of communism.

Following up Marshall's speech, Truman asked Congress in December 1947 to authorize $17 billion for European recovery. With conservative-minded Republicans still in control of Congress, the president's spending request faced steep opposition. The Soviet Union inadvertently came to Truman's political rescue. Stalin interpreted the proposed **Marshall Plan** of economic assistance as a hostile attempt by the United States to gain influence in Eastern Europe. To forestall this possibility, in late February 1948 the Soviets extinguished the remaining democracy in Eastern Europe by engineering a Communist coup in Czechoslovakia. Congressional lawmakers viewed this action as further proof of Soviet aggression. In April 1948, they approved the Marshall Plan, providing $13 billion in economic assistance to sixteen European countries over the next five years.

<table>
<tr><td>REVIEW & RELATE</td><td>• Why did American policymakers believe that containing Communist expansion should be the foundation of American foreign policy?
• What role did mutual misunderstandings and mistrust play in the emergence of the Cold War?</td></tr>
</table>

The Cold War Hardens, 1948–1953

After 1947 the Cold War intensified. Both sides increased military spending and took measures to enhance their military presence around the world. Fueled by growing distrust, the Soviet Union and the United States engaged in inflammatory rhetoric that added to the danger the conflict posed to world peace. In 1950 the United States, in cooperation with the United Nations, sent troops to South Korea to turn back an invasion from the Communist North. Truman took advantage of Cold War hostilities to expand presidential power through increased military spending and the creation of a vast national intelligence network.

Military Containment

The New Deal and World War II had increased the power of the president and his ability to manage economic and military crises. The Cold War further strengthened the presidency and shifted the balance of governmental power to the executive branch, creating what has been called the **imperial presidency**.

As the Cold War heated up, Congress granted the president enormous authority over foreign affairs and internal security. The National Security Act, passed in 1947, created the Department of Defense as a cabinet agency (replacing the Department of War), consolidated control of the various military services under its authority, and established the Joint Chiefs of Staff, composed of the heads of the army, navy, air force, and marines. To advise the president on military and foreign affairs, the act set up the **National Security Council (NSC)**, a group presided over by the national security adviser and consisting of the secretaries of state, defense, the army, the navy, and the air force and any others the president might appoint.

In addition to this panel, the National Security Act established the Central Intelligence Agency (CIA) as part of the executive branch. The CIA was given the responsibility of coordinating intelligence gathering and conducting espionage abroad to counter Soviet spying operations. Another new intelligence agency, the National Security Agency, created in 1949, monitored overseas communications through the latest technological devices. Together, these agencies enhanced the president's ability to conduct foreign affairs with little congressional oversight and out of public view.

By 1948 the Truman administration had decided that an economically healthy Germany, with its great industrial potential, provided the key to a prosperous Europe and consequently a depression-proof United States. Rebuilding postwar Germany would also fortify the eastern boundary of Europe against Soviet expansion. In mid-1948 the United States, the United Kingdom, and France consolidated their occupation zones, created the Federal Republic of Germany (West Germany), and initiated economic reforms to stimulate a speedy recovery. The Soviet Union saw a strong Germany as a threat to its national security and responded by closing the access roads from the border of West Germany to Berlin, located in the Soviet zone of East Germany, which effectively cut off the city from the West.

The Soviet blockade of West Berlin turned the Cold War even colder. Without provisions from the United States and its allies in West Germany, West Berliners could not survive. In an effort to break the blockade, Truman ordered a massive airlift, during which American and British planes transported more than 2.5 million tons of supplies to West Berlin. After nearly a year of these flights, the **Berlin airlift** ended in the spring of 1949 when the Russians lifted the blockade.

Meanwhile, in November 1948 Truman won election for a second term. He drew opposition from critics on his left and right for his handling of the Cold War, challenging both his aggressiveness toward the Soviets and his increased spending for containment. Nevertheless, most Americans stood behind his anti-Communist foreign policy as the Cold War continued.

The two superpowers kept the conflict alive when each fashioned military alliances to keep the other at bay. In April 1949, the United States joined eleven European countries in the **North Atlantic Treaty Organization (NATO)**. A peacetime military alliance, NATO established a collective security pact in which an attack on one member was viewed as an attack on all (Map 24.1). In 1949 the Russians followed suit by organizing the Council for Mutual Economic Assistance to help their satellite nations rebuild and six years later by creating the Warsaw Pact military alliance, the respective counterparts in Eastern Europe to the Marshall Plan and NATO.

Amid the growing militarization of the Cold War, 1949 brought two new shocks to the United States and its allies. First, in September the Russians successfully tested an atomic bomb. Second, Communist forces within China led by Mao Zedong and Zhou Enlai succeeded in overthrowing the U.S.-backed government of Jiang Jieshi and creating the People's Republic of China. These two events convinced many in the United States that the threat posed by communism was escalating rapidly.

In response, the National Security Council met to reevaluate U.S. strategy in fighting the Cold War. In April 1950 the NSC recommended to Truman that the United States intensify its containment policy both abroad and at home. The document it handed over to the president, entitled **NSC-68**, spelled out the need for action in ominous language. "The Soviet Union, unlike previous aspirants to hegemony," NSC-68 warned, "is animated by a new fanatic faith, antithetical to our own, and seeks to impose its absolute authority over the rest of the world. It is in this context that this Republic and its citizens . . . stand in their deepest peril." NSC-68 proposed that the United States develop an even more powerful nuclear weapon, the hydrogen bomb; increase military spending; and continue to negotiate NATO-style alliances around the globe. Departing from the original guidelines for the CIA, the president's advisers proposed that the United States engage in "covert means" to foment and support "unrest and revolt in selected strategic [Soviet] satellite countries." At home, they added, the government should prepare Americans for the Communist danger by enhancing internal security and civil defense programs.

Truman agreed with many of the principles behind NSC-68 but worried about the cost of funding it. Though the Democrats controlled both houses of Congress,

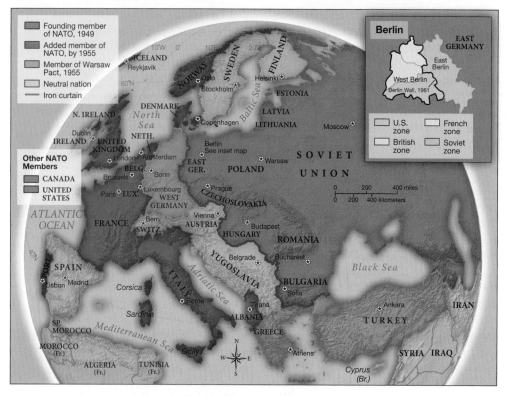

MAP 24.1   The Cold War in Europe, 1945–1955
In 1946, the four major victorious wartime allies divided Germany and Berlin into distinct sectors, leading to increasing conflict. Between 1949 and 1955, the descent of what Winston Churchill called the "iron curtain" of communism and the creation of rival security pacts headed by the United States and the Soviet Union hardened these postwar divisions into the Cold War.

there was little sentiment to raise taxes and slash the economic programs established during the New Deal. However, circumstances abruptly changed when, in June 1950, shortly after the president received the NSC report, Communist North Korea invaded U.S.-backed South Korea. In response to this attack, Truman took the opportunity to put into practice key recommendations of NSC-68.

The Korean War

Korea emerged from World War II divided between U.S. and Soviet spheres of influence. Above the 38th parallel, the Communist leader Kim Il Sung ruled North Korea with support from the Soviet Union. Below that latitude, the anti-Communist leader Syngman Rhee governed South Korea. The United States supported Rhee, but in January 1950 Secretary of State Dean Acheson commented that he did not regard South Korea as part of the vital Asian "defense perimeter" protected by the United States against Communist aggression. Truman had already removed remaining American troops from the country the previous year. On June 25, 1950, an emboldened Kim Il Sung sent military forces to invade South Korea, seeking to unite the country under his leadership.

Following the invasion Korea took on new importance to American policymakers. If South Korea fell, the president believed, Communist leaders would be "emboldened to override nations closer to our own shores." Thus the Truman Doctrine was now applied to Asia as it had previously been applied to Europe. This time, however, American financial aid would not be enough. It would take the U.S. military to contain the Communist threat.

Truman did not seek a declaration of war from Congress. Instead, he chose a multinational course of action. With the Soviet Union boycotting the United Nations over its refusal to admit the Communist People's Republic of China, on June 27, 1950, the United States obtained authorization from the UN Security Council to send a peacekeeping force to Korea. Fifteen other countries joined UN forces, but the United States supplied the bulk of the troops, as well as their commanding officer, General Douglas MacArthur. In reality, MacArthur reported to the president, not the United Nations.

U.S. Racial Integration of the Military in Korea, 1950 In 1948, President Truman issued an executive order to desegregate the armed forces. During the Korean War African American soldiers served in integrated combat units. On the top left of this November 20, 1950 photo, Sergeant First Class Major Cleveland, the African American squad leader of this racially integrated unit fighting with the 2nd Infantry Division, points out a Communist-led North Korean position to his machine gun crew. Corbis/Getty Images

Before MacArthur could mobilize his forces, the North Koreans had penetrated most of South Korea, except for the port of Pusan on the southwest coast of the peninsula. In a daring counterattack, on September 15, 1950, MacArthur dispatched land and sea forces to capture Inchon, northwest of Pusan on the opposite coast, to cut off North Korean supply lines. Joined by UN forces pushing out of Pusan, MacArthur's Eighth Army troops chased the enemy northward back over the 38th parallel.

Now Truman had to make a key decision. MacArthur wanted to invade North Korea, defeat the Communists, and unify the country. Instead of sticking to his original goal of containing Communist aggression against South Korea, Truman succumbed to the lure of liberating all of Korea from the Communists. MacArthur received permission to proceed, and on October 9 his forces crossed into North Korea. Within three weeks, UN troops marched through the country until they reached the Yalu River, which bordered China. With the U.S. military massed along their southern perimeter, the Chinese warned that they would send troops to repel the invaders if the Americans crossed the Yalu. Both General MacArthur and Secretary of State Acheson, guided by CIA intelligence, discounted this threat. The intelligence, however, was faulty. Truman approved MacArthur's plan to cross the Yalu, and on November 27, 1950, China sent more than 300,000 troops south into North Korea. Within two months, Communist troops regained control of North Korea, allowing them once again to invade South Korea. On January 4, 1951, the South Korean capital of Seoul fell to Chinese and North Korean troops (Map 24.2).

By the spring of 1951, the war had degenerated into a stalemate. UN forces succeeded in recapturing Seoul and repelling the Communists north of the 38th parallel. This time, with the American public anxious to end the war and with the presence of the Chinese promising an endless, bloody predicament, the president sought to replace combat with diplomacy. The American objective would be containment, not Korean unification.

Truman's change of heart infuriated General MacArthur, who was willing to risk an all-out war with China and to use nuclear weapons to win. After MacArthur spoke out publicly against Truman's policy by remarking, "There is no substitute for victory," the president removed him from command on April 11, 1951. Even with the change in strategy and leadership, the war dragged on for two more years, until July 1953, when a final armistice agreement was reached. By that time, the Korean War had cost the United States close to 37,000 lives and $54 billion.

The Korean War and the Imperial Presidency

The Korean War boosted the imperial presidency by allowing the president to bypass Congress and the Constitution to initiate wars in the name of "police actions." The war permitted Truman to expand his powers as commander in chief and augmented the strength of the national security state over which he presided. As a result of the Korean conflict, the military draft became a regular feature of American life for young men over the next two decades. The expanded peacetime military was active around the globe, operating bases in Europe, Asia, and the Middle East. During the war, the

MAP 24.2   The Korean War, 1950–1953

Considered a "police action" by the United Nations, the Korean War cost the lives of nearly 37,000 U.S. troops. Approximately 1 million Koreans were killed, wounded, or missing. Each side pushed deep into enemy territory, but neither could achieve victory. When hostilities ceased in 1953, a demilitarized zone near the original boundary line separated North and South Korea.

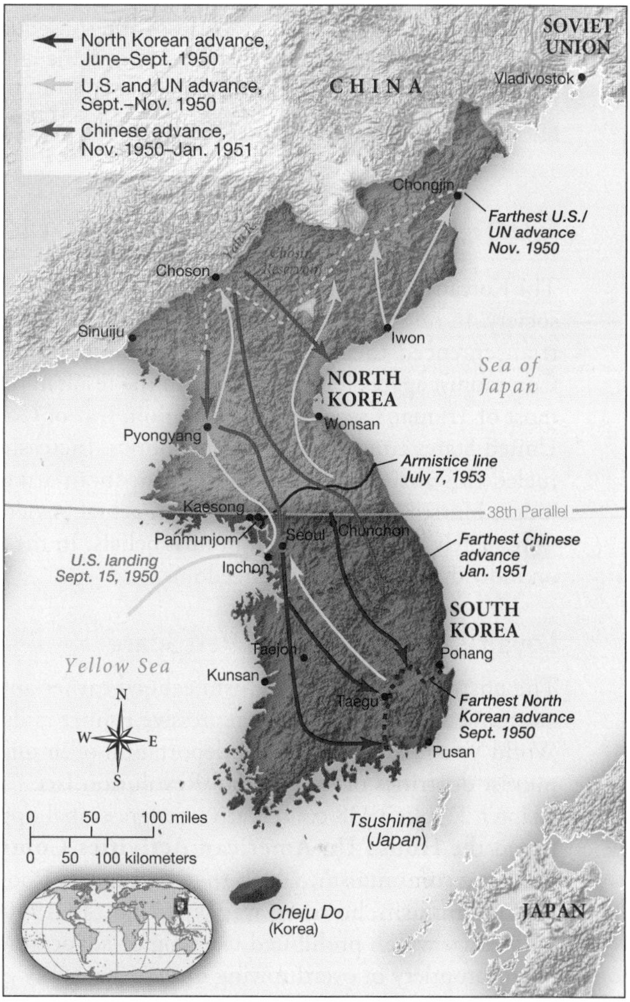

military budget rose from $13.5 billion to $50 billion, strengthening the connection between economic growth and permanent mobilization to fight the Cold War. The war also permitted President Truman to reshape foreign policy along the lines sketched in NSC-68, including the extension of U.S. influence in Southeast Asia. Consequently, he authorized economic aid to support the French against Communist revolutionaries in Vietnam.

Yet the power of the imperial presidency did not go unchecked. Congress deferred to Truman on key issues of military policy, but on one important occasion the Supreme Court stepped in to restrain him. The central issue grew out of a labor dispute in the steel industry. In 1952 the United Steel Workers of America threatened to go on strike for higher wages, which would have had a serious impact on war production as well as the economy in general. On May 2, after the steel companies refused the union's demands, Truman announced the government seizure and operation of the steel mills to keep them running. He argued that as president he had the "inherent right" to take over the steel plants.

The steel companies objected and brought the matter before the Supreme Court. On June 2, 1952, the Court ruled against Truman. It held that the president did not have the intrinsic authority to seize private property, even during wartime. For the time being, the Supreme Court affirmed some limitations on the unbridled use of presidential power even during periods of war.

REVIEW &
RELATE
• What were the causes and consequences of the militarization of
  the containment strategy in the late 1940s and early 1950s?
• How did the Korean War contribute to the centralization of
  power in the executive branch?

Combating Communism at Home, 1945–1954

The Korean War heightened fear of the threat of Communist infiltration in American society. In one striking example, the presiding judge in the Rosenbergs' espionage trial sentenced them to death because he believed their actions "caused . . . the Communist aggression in Korea, with the resultant casualties exceeding 50,000." For most of Truman's second administration, fear of Communist subversion within the United States consumed domestic politics. Increasing evidence of Soviet espionage fueled this anti-Communist obsession. In an atmosphere of fear, lawmakers and judges blurred the distinction between actual Soviet spies and political radicals who were merely attracted to Communist beliefs. In the process, these officials trampled on individual constitutional freedoms.

Loyalty and the Second Red Scare

The postwar fear of communism echoed earlier anti-Communist sentiments. The government had initiated the repressive Palmer raids during the Red scare following World War I, which led to the deportation of immigrants sympathetic to the Communist doctrines of the Russian Revolution (see "The Red Scare, 1919–1920" in chapter 21). In 1938 conservative congressional opponents of the New Deal established the **House Un-American Activities Committee (HUAC)** to investigate domestic communism, which they tied to the Roosevelt administration. Much of anticommunism, however, was bipartisan. In 1940 Roosevelt signed into law the Smith Act, which prohibited teaching or advocating the "duty, necessity, desirability, or propriety of overthrowing or destroying any government in the United States by force or violence" or belonging to any group with that aim. At the same time, President Roosevelt secretly authorized the FBI to monitor and wiretap individuals suspected of violating the act.

The Cold War produced the second Red scare. Just two weeks after his speech announcing the Truman Doctrine in March 1947, the president signed an executive order creating the **Federal Employee Loyalty Program**. Under this program, a board investigated federal employees to see if "reasonable grounds [existed] to suspect disloyalty." Soviet espionage was, in fact, a cause for legitimate concern. Spies operated in both Canada and the United States during and after World War II, and they had infiltrated the Manhattan Project.

The loyalty board concentrated its attention on individuals who espoused dissenting views on a variety of issues. It failed to uncover a single verifiable case of espionage or find even one actual Communist in public service. This lack of evidence did not stop the board from dismissing 378 government employees for their political beliefs and personal behavior. Some employees were fired because they were homosexuals and considered susceptible to blackmail by foreign agents. (Heterosexual men and women who were having extramarital affairs were not treated in the same manner.) The accused rarely faced their accusers and at times did not learn the nature of the charges against them. This disregard for due process of law spread as loyalty boards at state and municipal levels questioned and fired government employees, including public school teachers and state university professors.

Congress also investigated communism in the private sector, especially in industries that shaped public opinion. In 1947 HUAC broadened the anti-Red probe from Washington to Hollywood. Convinced that the film industry had come under Communist influence and threatened to poison the minds of millions of moviegoers, HUAC conducted hearings that attracted much publicity. HUAC cited for contempt ten witnesses, among them directors and screenwriters, for refusing to answer questions about their political beliefs and associations. These and subsequent hearings assumed the form of a ritual. The committee already had information from the FBI about the witnesses; HUAC really wanted the accused to confess their Communist heresy publicly and to show contrition by naming their associates. Those who did not comply were considered "unfriendly" witnesses and were put on an industry blacklist that deprived them of employment.

HUAC grabbed even bigger headlines in 1948. With Republicans in charge of the committee, they launched a probe of Alger Hiss, a former State Department official in the Roosevelt administration who had accompanied the president to the Yalta Conference. The hearings resulted from charges brought by former Soviet spy Whittaker Chambers that Hiss had passed him classified documents. Hiss denied the allegations, and President Truman dismissed them as a distraction. In fact, Democrats viewed the charges as a politically motivated attempt by Republicans to characterize the Roosevelt and Truman administrations as having been riddled with Communists.

Following Truman's victory in the 1948 presidential election, first-term Republican congressman Richard M. Nixon kept the Hiss affair alive. A member of HUAC, Nixon went to Chambers's farm and discovered a cache of State Department documents that Chambers had stored for safekeeping. Armed with this evidence, Nixon reopened the case. While the statute of limitations for espionage from the 1930s had expired, the federal government had enough evidence to prosecute Hiss for perjury—lying under oath about passing documents to Chambers. One trial produced a hung jury, but a second convicted Hiss; he was sentenced to five years in prison.

Hiss's downfall tarnished the Democrats, as Republicans charged them with being "soft on communism." It did not matter that Truman was a cold warrior who had advanced the doctrine of containment to stop Soviet expansionism or that he had instituted the federal loyalty program to purge Communists from government. In fact, in 1949 Truman tried to demonstrate his cold warrior credentials by authorizing the Justice Department to prosecute twelve high-ranking officials of the Communist Party for violating the Smith Act. In the 1951 decision in *Dennis v. United States*, the Supreme Court upheld the conviction of the Communist leaders on the grounds that they posed a "clear and present danger" to the United States by advocating the violent overthrow of the government. With no evidence of an immediate danger of a Communist uprising, the justices decided that "the gravity of the [Communist] evil" was enough to warrant conviction.

In 1950 the Truman administration also prosecuted Julius and Ethel Rosenberg. Unlike the *Dennis* case, which involved political beliefs, the Rosenbergs were charged with espionage. When the Russians successfully tested an atomic bomb in 1949, anyone accused of helping them obtain this weapon became "Public Enemy Number One." The outbreak of the Korean War the following year, in which tens of thousands of soldiers died, made the Rosenbergs appear as conspirators to murder. After a lengthy trial in 1951, the couple received the death penalty, rather than a possible thirty-year sentence, undoubtedly because they refused to confess and because the trial took place during the war.

By 1950 the anti-Communist crusade included Democrats and Republicans, liberals and conservatives. Liberals had the most to lose because conservatives could easily brand them as ideologically tainted. In his successful campaign to become a U.S. senator from California in 1950, Richard Nixon had accused his opponent, the liberal Democrat Helen Gahagan Douglas, of being "pink down to her underwear," not quite a Red but close enough. Liberal civil rights and civil liberties groups as well as labor unions were particularly vulnerable to such charges and rushed to rid their organizations of suspected Communists. Such efforts did nothing, however, to slow down conservative attacks. In 1950 Republicans supported legislation proposed by Senator Pat McCarran, a conservative Democrat from Nevada, which required Communist organizations to register with the federal government, established detention camps to incarcerate radicals during national emergencies, and denied passports to American citizens suspected of Communist affiliations. The severity of the entire measure proved too much for President Truman, and he vetoed it. Reflecting the bipartisan consensus on the issue, the Democratic-controlled Congress overrode the veto.

McCarthyism

Joseph Raymond McCarthy, a Republican senator from Wisconsin, took advantage of the phenomenon of postwar anticommunism, which was already in full swing from 1947 to 1950, and served as its most public and feared voice from 1950 until 1954. Senator McCarthy used his position as the head of the Permanent Investigation Subcommittee of the Committee on Government Operations to harass current and former government officials and employees who, he claimed, collaborated with the Communist conspiracy. He had plenty of assistance from members of his own party who considered McCarthy a potent weapon in their battle to reclaim the White House. Robert A. Taft, the respected conservative Republican senator from Ohio, told McCarthy "to keep talking and if one case doesn't work [you] should proceed with another." The press also courted the young senator by giving his charges substantial coverage on the front pages of daily newspapers and then shifting the story to the back pages when McCarthy's claims turned out to be false. McCarthy bullied people, exaggerated his military service, drank too much, and did not pull his punches in making speeches—but his anti-Communist tirades fit into mainstream Cold War politics.

Aware of the power of the Communists-in-government issue, McCarthy gave a speech in February 1950 in Wheeling, West Virginia. Waving sheets of paper in his hand, the senator announced that he had "the names of 205 men known to the Secretary of State as being members of the Communist Party and who nevertheless are still working and shaping the policy of the State Department." McCarthy cared more about the message than about the truth. As he continued campaigning for Republican congressional candidates across the country, he kept changing the number of alleged Communists in the government. When Senator Millard Tydings of Maryland, a Democrat who headed the Senate Foreign Relations Committee, launched an investigation of McCarthy's charges, he concluded that they were irresponsible and unfounded.

This finding did not stop McCarthy; if anything, it emboldened him to go further. He accused Tydings of being "soft on communism" and campaigned against his reelection in 1952. Tydings's defeat in the election scared off many critics from openly confronting McCarthy. McCarthy won reelection to the Senate, and when Republicans once again captured a majority in Congress, he became chair of the Permanent Investigations Subcommittee. Not only did he make false accusations and smear witnesses with anti-Communist allegations, he also dispatched two aides to travel to Europe and purge what they considered disreputable books from the shelves of overseas libraries sponsored by the State Department.

McCarthy stood out among anti-Communists for his brazen tactics. McCarthy publicly hurled charges so astounding, especially coming from a U.S. senator, that people thought there must be something to them. He specialized in the "multiple untruth," a concoction of allegations so complex and convoluted that it was impossible to refute them simply or quickly. By the time the accusations could be discredited, the damage was already done. The senator bullied and badgered witnesses, called them names, and if necessary furnished phony documents and doctored photographs linking them to known Communists.

In 1954 McCarthy finally went too far. After one of his aides got drafted and the army refused to give him a special commission, McCarthy accused the army of harboring Communists at Camp Kilmer and Fort Monmouth in New Jersey. To sort out these charges and to see whether the army had acted appropriately, McCarthy's own Senate subcommittee conducted an investigation, with the Wisconsin senator stepping down as chair. For two months, the relatively new medium of television broadcast live the army-McCarthy hearings, during which the cameras showed viewers for the first time how reckless McCarthy had become. As his public approval declined, the Senate decided that it could no longer tolerate McCarthy's outrageous behavior. The famous television journalist Edward R. Murrow ran an unflattering documentary on McCarthy on his evening program on CBS, which further cast doubt on the senator's character and veracity. In December 1954 the Senate voted to censure McCarthy for conduct unbecoming a senator, having violated senatorial decorum by insulting colleagues who criticized him. McCarthy retained his seat on the subcommittee and all his Senate prerogatives, but he never again wielded substantial power. In 1957 he died from acute hepatitis, a disease related to alcoholism.

The anti-Communist consensus did not end with the execution of the Rosenbergs in 1953 or the censure of Joseph McCarthy in 1954. Even J. Robert Oppenheimer, "the father of the atomic bomb," came under scrutiny. In 1954 the Atomic Energy Commission revoked Oppenheimer's security clearance for suspected, though unproven, Communist affiliations. That same year, Congress passed the Communist Control Act, which required "Communist infiltrated" groups to register with the federal government. Federal, state, and municipal governments required employees to take a loyalty oath affirming their allegiance to the United States and disavowing support for any organization that advocated the overthrow of the government. In addition, the blacklist continued in Hollywood throughout the rest of the decade. After the Supreme Court declared racial segregation in public schools unconstitutional in 1954, a number of southern states, including Florida and Louisiana, set up committees to investigate Communist influence in the civil rights movement. In a case concerning civil liberties, the Supreme Court still upheld HUAC's authority to investigate communism and to require witnesses who came before it to answer questions about their affiliations. Yet the Court did put a stop to the anti-Communist momentum. In 1957 the high court dealt a severe blow to enforcement of the Smith Act by ruling in *Yates v. United States* that the Justice Department could not prosecute someone for merely advocating an abstract doctrine favoring the violent overthrow of the government. In response, Congress tried, but failed, to limit the Supreme Court's jurisdiction in cases of this sort.

Although attacks against radicals in this period came to be known as **McCarthyism**, J. Edgar Hoover and the FBI did more to fuel the anti-Communist hysteria of the second Red scare than did the Wisconsin senator. Hoover and his bureau did even greater damage than McCarthy because they used their broad reach to disperse the information from Communist-hunters throughout the government in order to suppress any perceived anti-Communist activity. The FBI was involved in criminal prosecutions in the *Dennis* and *Rosenberg* cases, supplied evidence to congressional committees and loyalty boards, and wiretapped suspected targets and used undercover agents to monitor and harass them. The FBI under the long tenure of J. Edgar Hoover perpetuated a zealous policy of anticommunism in this era.

REVIEW & RELATE
- Why did fear of Communists in positions of influence escalate in the late 1940s and early 1950s?
- Why was McCarthyism much more powerful than Joseph McCarthy?

The Cold War Expands, 1953–1961

With the end of the Korean War in 1953, the United States and the Soviet Union each spent huge sums of money and manpower building up their arsenal of nuclear weapons and military forces. They did not engage directly on the battlefield, but they attempted to spread their influence around the world while protecting their spheres of influence closer to their borders. The growing presence of nuclear weapons hung over diplomatic crises wherever they emerged, occasionally prompting the leaders of the two most powerful nations to seek an accommodation.

Nuclear Weapons and Containment

In foreign affairs, President Dwight D. Eisenhower perpetuated Truman's containment doctrine while at the same time espousing the contradictory principle of "rolling back" communism in Eastern Europe. However, when Hungarians rose up against their Soviet-backed regime in 1956, the U.S. government did little in response. Rather than pushing back communism, the Eisenhower administration expanded the doctrine of containment around the world by entering into treaties to establish regional defense pacts.

Eisenhower's commitment to fiscal discipline had a profound effect on his foreign policy. The president worried that the alliance among government, defense contractors, and research universities — which he dubbed "the military-industrial complex" — would bankrupt the economy and undermine individual freedom. With this in mind, he implemented the **New Look** strategy, which placed a higher priority on building a nuclear arsenal and delivery system than on the more expensive task of maintaining and deploying armed forces on the ground throughout the world. Nuclear missiles launched from the air by air force bombers or fired from submarines would give the United States, as Secretary of Defense Charles Wilson asserted, "a bigger bang for the buck." With the nation now armed with nuclear weapons, the Eisenhower administration threatened "massive retaliation" in the event of Communist aggression.

The New Look may have saved money and slowed the rate of defense spending, but it had serious flaws. First, it placed a premium on "brinksmanship," taking Communist enemies to the precipice of nuclear destruction, risking the death of millions, and hoping the other side would back down. Second, massive retaliation did

Bomb Shelter, 1954 The successful test of an atomic bomb by the Soviets in 1949 followed by the Korean War prompted many Americans to begin preparing for a possible nuclear attack. This Houston, Texas family, including their dog, pose in their bomb shelter stocked with food, first aid supplies, weapons, and ammunition. John Dominis/The LIFE Picture Collection/Getty Images

TABLE 24.1	NUCLEAR WARHEADS, UNITED STATES, SOVIET UNION, UNITED KINGDOM, 1945–1960			
Country	1945	1950	1955	1960
United States	2	299	2,422	18,638
Soviet Union	0	5	200	1,605
United Kingdom	0	0	14	42

Source: Robert S. Norris & Hans M. Kristensen (2010). Global Nuclear Weapons Inventories, 1945–2010, Bulletin of the Atomic Scientists, 66:4, 77–83, DOI: 10.2968/066004008

The Cold War launched a nuclear arms race between the United States and its British ally and the Soviet Union. By 1960, the United States had lost its nuclear monopoly, but together with the United Kingdom its nuclear stockpile of warheads vastly outnumbered that of the Soviet Union.

not work for small-scale conflicts. For instance, in the event of a confrontation in Berlin, would the United States launch nuclear missiles toward Germany and expose its European allies in West Germany and France to nuclear contamination? Third, the buildup of nuclear warheads provoked an arms race by encouraging the Soviet Union to do the same. Peace depended on the superpowers terrifying each other with the threat of nuclear annihilation — that is, if one country attacked the other, retaliation was guaranteed to result in shared obliteration. This strategy was known as **mutually assured destruction**, and its acronym — **MAD** — summed up its nightmarish qualities. As each nuclear power increased its capacity to destroy the other many times over, the potential for mistakes and errors in judgment increased, threatening a nuclear holocaust that would leave little to rebuild. (See Table 24.1.)

National security concerns occupied a good deal of the president's time. Fearing that a Soviet nuclear attack could wipe out nearly a third of the population before the United States could retaliate, the Eisenhower administration stepped up civil defense efforts. Schoolchildren took part in "duck and cover" drills, in which teachers shouted "Take cover" and students hid under their desks. In the meantime, both the United States and the Soviet Union began producing intercontinental ballistic missiles armed with nuclear warheads. They also stepped up aboveground tests of nuclear weapons, which contaminated the atmosphere with dangerous radioactive particles.

Despite doomsday rhetoric of massive retaliation, Eisenhower generally relied more on diplomacy than on military action. Stalin's death in 1953 and his eventual replacement by Nikita Khrushchev in 1955 permitted détente, or a relaxation of tensions, between the two superpowers. In July 1955 Eisenhower and Khrushchev, together with British and French leaders, gathered in Geneva to discuss arms control. Nothing concrete came out of this summit, but Eisenhower and Khrushchev did ease tensions between the two nations. In a speech to Communist officials two years later, Khrushchev denounced the excesses of Stalin's totalitarian rule and reinforced hopes for a new era of peaceful coexistence between the Cold War antagonists. In 1958, Vice President Richard Nixon visited the Soviet Union, the first top elected official to do so since the onset of the Cold War, as a sign of warming relations between the two nations. Nixon and Khrushchev attended a U.S. exhibition in Moscow on July 24, 1959, where the two leaders debated the relative merits of capitalism and communism, while looking at an American kitchen that displayed the latest household appliances. This so-called "Kitchen Debate" did not dissuade Khrushchev from making a twelve-day visit to the United States later that year. Yet peaceful coexistence remained precarious. Just as President Eisenhower was about to begin his own tour of the Soviet Union in 1960, the Soviets shot down an American U-2 spy plane flying over their country. Eisenhower canceled his trip, and tensions resumed.

Decolonization

Between 1945 and 1960, three dozen new states in Asia, Africa, and the Middle East gained independence from their European colonial rulers. In addition, the United States granted full independence to the Philippines in 1946. This **decolonization** movement coincided with the freezing of Cold War relations between the United States and the Soviet Union. Both Presidents Truman and Eisenhower feared that as these former European colonies won their independence, the Soviets would seek to gain influence over them and swing the global balance of power to its side. In this battle over the allegiance of the newly freed and developing nations (what was called at the time the Third World), both the United States and the USSR jockeyed for position to win them over by offering economic and technical aid. While the United States promoted its democratic ideology, the Soviets countered with the argument that communism represented the masses and stood against imperialism.

The decolonization movement reconfigured the composition of the United Nations. In 1946, there were 35 member states in the world organization. As a result of decolonization, by 1961, membership in the UN had jumped to 104. Most of these new developing nations sought to rebuild their fragile economic and political systems and reclaim their cultural identities. These liberated countries remained wary of their former colonizers, most of whom were allied with the United States during the Cold War. Consequently, the United States had to walk a fine line between accommodating its European partners and gaining the trust of developing nations.

The difficulties proved challenging. Confronting the problem of Cold War alignments, these developing nations chose neutrality. At the **Bandung Conference** in Indonesia in 1955, twenty-nine Asian and African nations, many of them recently liberated, condemned continued colonization, particularly control in North Africa by France, a close U.S. ally, and asserted their intention to remain non-aligned with either side in the Cold War. The U.S. government took a dim view of this meeting and refused to send representatives. Especially worrisome to the United States, the Communist Chinese government made serious overtures to form closer relations with these nations.

Interventions in the Middle East, Latin America, and Africa

While relations between the Soviet Union and the United States thawed and then cooled during the Eisenhower era, the Cold War expanded into new regions. The efforts of Iranian, Guatemalan, and Cuban leaders to seize control of their countries' resources mirrored the surge of nationalism that swept through former European colonies in the 1950s. The United States frequently took a heavy handed approach when it suspected newly decolonized nations were edging to the side of the Soviets. In a manner first suggested in NSC-68, the Eisenhower administration deployed the CIA to help topple governments considered pro-Communist as well as to promote U.S. economic interests. For example, after Prime Minister Mohammed Mossadegh of Iran nationalized foreign oil corporations in 1953, the CIA engineered a successful coup that ousted his government and installed the pro-American shah Mohammad Reza Pahlavi in his place. Mossadegh was not a Communist, but by overthrowing him American oil companies obtained 40 percent of Iran's oil revenue.

In 1954 the economics of fruit and shipping replaced oil as the catalyst for U.S. intervention into a third-world nation within its own sphere of influence. The elected socialist regime of Jacobo Arbenz Guzmán in Guatemala had seized 225,000 acres of land held by the United Fruit Company, a powerful American company in which Secretary of State John Foster Dulles and his brother, CIA director Allen Dulles, held stock. According to the Dulles brothers, the land's seizure by the Guatemalan government posed a threat to the nearby Panama Canal. Eisenhower allowed the CIA to hatch a plot that resulted in a coup d'état, or government overthrow, that installed a right-wing military regime in Guatemala, which safeguarded both the Panama Canal and the United Fruit Company.

The success of the CIA's covert efforts in Guatemala prompted the Eisenhower administration to plan a similar action in Cuba, ninety miles off the coast of Florida. In 1959 Fidel Castro led an uprising and came to power in Cuba after overthrowing the American-backed dictator Fulgencio Batista. A Cuban nationalist in the tradition of José Martí, Castro sought to regain full control over his country's economic resources, including those owned by U.S. corporations. He appropriated $1 billion worth of American property and signed a trade agreement with the Soviet Union. To consolidate his political rule, Castro jailed opponents and installed a Communist regime. In 1960 President Eisenhower authorized the CIA to design a clandestine operation to overthrow the Castro government, but he left office before the invasion could occur.

Developing nations seeking to practice neutrality during the Cold War did so at their own peril. Such was the case in Egypt, which achieved independence from Great Britain in 1952. Two years later, under General Gamal Abdel Nasser, the country sought to modernize its economy by building the hydroelectric Aswan Dam on the Nile River. Nasser welcomed financial backing from the United States and the Soviet Union, but the Eisenhower administration refused to contribute so long as the Egyptians accepted Soviet assistance. In 1956 Nasser, falling short of funds, sent troops to take over the Suez Canal, the waterway run by Great Britain and through which the bulk of Western Europe's oil was shipped. He intended to pay for the dam by collecting tolls from canal users. In retaliation, Britain and France, the two European powers most affected by the seizure, invaded Egypt on October 29, 1956. Locked in a struggle with Egypt and other Arab nations since its creation in 1948, Israel joined the attack. The invading forces — all U.S. allies — had not warned the Eisenhower administration of their plans. Coming at the same time as the Soviet crackdown against the Hungarian revolution, the British-French-Israeli assault placed the United States in the difficult position of condemning the Soviets for intervening in Hungary while its anti-Communist partners waged war in Suez. Instead, Eisenhower cooperated with the United Nations to negotiate a cease-fire and engineer a pullout of the invading forces in Egypt. Ultimately, the Soviets proved the winners in this Cold War skirmish. The Suez invasion revived memories of European imperialism and fueled anti-Western sentiments and pan-Arab nationalism (a sense of unity among Arabs across national boundaries), which worked to the Soviets' advantage.

The Eisenhower administration soon moved to counter growing Soviet power in the region. In 1957, to throttle increasing Communist influence in the Middle East, Congress approved the **Eisenhower Doctrine**, which gave the president a free hand to use U.S. military forces in the Middle East "against overt armed aggression from any nation controlled by International Communism." In actuality, the Eisenhower administration proved more concerned with protecting access to oil fields from hostile Arab nationalist leaders than with any Communist incursion. In 1958, when an anti-American, non-Communist regime came to power in Iraq, the president sent 14,000 marines to neighboring Lebanon to prevent a similar outcome there.

Just before Eisenhower left office in January 1961, his administration intervened in a civil war in the newly independent Congo. This former colony of Belgium held valuable mineral resources, which Belgium and the United States coveted. After the Congo's first prime minister, Patrice Lumumba, stated his intentions to remain neutral in the Cold War, President Eisenhower and CIA director Allen Dulles declared him unreliable in the conflict with the Soviet Union. With the support of Belgian military troops and encouragement from the United States, the resource-rich province of Katanga seceded from the Congo in 1960. After the Congolese military, under the leadership of Joseph Mobuto, overthrew Lumumba's government, the CIA launched an operation that culminated in the execution of Lumumba on January 17, 1961. Several years later, Mobuto became president of the country, changed its name to Zaire, and allied with the West.

Early Intervention in Vietnam, 1954–1960

One offshoot of the Korean War was increased U.S. intervention in Vietnam, resulting in profound, long-term consequences. By the 1950s, Vietnamese revolutionaries (the Vietminh) had been fighting for independence from the French for decades. They were led by Ho Chi Minh, a revolutionary who had studied Communist doctrine in the Soviet Union but was not controlled by the Soviets. In fact, he modeled his 1945 Vietnamese Declaration of Independence on that of the United States. In 1954 the Vietminh defeated the French at the Battle of Dien Bien Phu. With the backing of the United States, the Soviet Union, and China, both sides agreed to divide Vietnam at the seventeenth parallel and hold free elections to unite the country in 1956.

President Dwight Eisenhower, who had brought the Korean War to a close in 1953, believed that if Vietnam fell to the Communists, the rest of Southeast Asia and Japan would "go over very quickly" like "a row of dominoes," threatening American strategic power in the Far East as well as free access to Asian markets. Convinced that Ho Chi Minh and his followers would win free elections, in 1955 the Eisenhower administration supported the anti-French, anti-Communist Ngo Dinh Diem to lead South Vietnam and then backed his regime's refusal to hold national elections in 1956. The anti-Communist interests of the United States had trumped its democratic promises. With the country now permanently divided, Eisenhower funneled economic aid to Diem to undertake needed land reforms that would strengthen his government and weaken the appeal of Ho Chi Minh. The president

The Battle of Dien Bien Phu, 1954 This photograph shows Vietnamese soldiers resting in a trench at Dien Bien Phu, site of the pivotal battle at which French colonial forces were defeated. Fighting began on March 13, 1954, and ended on May 7, when French troops surrendered. This photo, like most of those taken of the battle, was restaged shortly after the action, mainly for propaganda purposes. AFP/Getty Images

also dispatched CIA agents and military advisers to support the South Vietnamese government. However, Diem used most of the money to consolidate his power rather than implement reforms, which only widened opposition to his regime from Communists and non-Communists alike. This prompted Ho Chi Minh in 1959 to support the creation in the South of the National Liberation Front, or **Vietcong**, to wage a military insurgency against Diem. By the end of the decade, the Eisenhower administration had created a major diplomatic problem with no clear plan for its resolution.

REVIEW & RELATE

- In what ways did the Eisenhower administration continue the Cold War policies of President Truman? In what ways did it depart from his predecessor?
- How did U.S. intervention in Vietnam reflect the policy of containment?

Conclusion: The Cold War and Anticommunism

Anticommunism remained a potent weapon in political affairs as long as the Cold War operated in full force. When George Kennan designed the doctrine of containment in 1946 and 1947, he had no idea that it would lead to permanent military alliances such as NATO or to a war in Korea. He viewed the Soviet Union as an unflinching ideological enemy, but he believed that it should be contained through economic rather than military means. Despite his launching of the Marshall Plan and providing aid to the Greeks through the Truman Doctrine, President Truman soon departed from Kennan's vision by militarizing containment. Beginning with NATO and continuing with the Korean War, the Truman administration put into operation around the world the heightened military plans called for by NSC-68. Hard-line Cold War rhetoric portrayed the struggle as a battle between good and evil. Born out of different perceptions of national interests and mutual misunderstandings of the other side's actions, the Cold War became frozen in the language of competing moralistic assumptions and self-righteousness. Within this context, though some Americans rallied to obtain clemency for the Rosenbergs, most considered that they got just what they deserved.

The Eisenhower administration continued the policy of containment inherited from Truman. Eisenhower brought the Korean War to an end and attempted to slow down the rate of military spending. Nevertheless, in the name of checking Communist aggression, his administration did not hesitate to intervene in Latin America, the Middle East, Africa, and Southeast Asia. Both the United States and the Soviet Union built up their nuclear arsenals and developed speedier ways by air and sea to deliver these deadly weapons against each other. Occasionally, foreign crises riveted the attention of Americans on the perils of atomic brinksmanship with the Soviets, but the sheer horror of the possibility of nuclear war helped the two major Cold War powers avoid escalating existing conflicts into nuclear destruction. Such brinksmanship did little to quell mounting fears of Communist infiltration and espionage at home in the United States. Those fears led to the second Red scare, as well as a strengthened presidency, one given more powers with which to combat communism and maintain national security. Cold War spending helped boost the American economy, but the renewed prosperity it brought masked some serious trouble brewing at home over civil rights and teenage culture.

Chapter 24 Review

KEY TERMS

Cold War, 610
Truman Doctrine, 613
Marshall Plan, 613
imperial presidency, 614
National Security Council (NSC), 614
Berlin airlift, 615
North Atlantic Treaty Organization
    (NATO), 615
NSC-68, 615
House Un-American Activities
    Committee (HUAC), 620

Federal Employee Loyalty Program,
    620
McCarthyism, 624
New Look, 625
mutually assured destruction
    (MAD), 626
decolonization, 627
Bandung Conference, 627
Eisenhower Doctrine, 629
Vietcong, 630

REVIEW & RELATE

1. Why did American policymakers believe that containing Communist expansion should be the foundation of American foreign policy?
2. What role did mutual misunderstandings and mistrust play in the emergence of the Cold War?
3. What were the causes and consequences of the militarization of the containment strategy in the late 1940s and early 1950s?
4. How did the Korean War contribute to the centralization of power in the executive branch?
5. Why did fear of Communists in positions of influence escalate in the late 1940s and early 1950s?

6. Why was McCarthyism much more powerful than Joseph McCarthy?
7. In what ways did the Eisenhower administration continue the Cold War policies of President Truman? In what ways did it depart from his predecessor?
8. How did U.S. intervention in Vietnam reflect the policy of containment?

TIMELINE OF EVENTS

1938	• House Un-American Activities Committee (HUAC) established
1945	• Potsdam Conference
1946	• Kennan telegram outlines containment strategy
	• Churchill's "iron curtain" speech
1947	• Truman Doctrine articulated National Security Act passed
	• Central Intelligence Agency (CIA) established
	• Truman creates Federal Employee Loyalty Program
1948–1949	• Berlin blockade and airlift
	• Alger Hiss affair
1948	• Marshall Plan approved
1949	• National Security Agency established
	• Communists win Chinese civil war North Atlantic Treaty Organization (NATO) formed
	• Soviet Union successfully tests atomic weapon
1950–1953	• Korean War
1950–1954	• McCarthy's anti-Communist crusade
1950	• NSC-68 issued
1953	• Julius and Ethel Rosenberg executed for espionage
	• U.S. supports overthrow of Iranian government
1954	• French defeated in Vietnam
	• U.S. supports overthrow of Guatemalan government
1955	• U.S. supports Ngo Diem in South Vietnam
1855	• Bandung Conference of Non-Aligned Nations
1956	• Suez crisis
1958	• U.S. troops sent to Lebanon
1959	• Fidel Castro takes power in Cuba
	• The Vietcong formed
1961	• U.S. intervenes in the Congo

25

Troubled Innocence

1945–1961

LEARNING OBJECTIVES

After reading this chapter you will be able to:

- Explain the problems of converting from World War II to peacetime and describe the causes and effects of the postwar economic boom.

- Analyze how the 1950s popular culture reflected the expanding consumer-oriented economy and explain the challenges to mainstream culture posed by teenagers, women, and the Beat generation.

- Examine the growth of the civil rights movement and identify the strategies used to challenge segregation and discrimination in the 1950s.

- Evaluate the impact of President Eisenhower's domestic policies and accomplishments on the Republican Party and the nation.

COMPARING AMERICAN HISTORIES

Alan Freed shook up American youth culture in the 1950s by rebranding black music and making it popular with white teenagers. In 1951, at the age of twenty-nine, Aldon (Alan) James Freed was a white disc jockey, or "deejay," spinning records at a Cleveland, Ohio, radio station. He played rhythm and blues, an African American music style considered by many whites as "race music" that was only suitable for blacks. Calling himself Moondog, Freed howled like a dog and used sound effects to rattle his radio listeners. Although he initially appealed mainly to a black audience, Freed's radio show and live concerts of music he dubbed rock 'n' roll soon attracted white teenagers.

In 1954 Freed moved to New York City, where his evening rock 'n' roll radio broadcast became a number one hit with a broad audience. Three

633

years later, he hosted a nationally televised rock 'n' roll program, but only briefly. The American Broadcasting Company canceled Freed's show after four telecasts because of outrage from affiliate stations in the South after the black singer Frankie Lymon was shown dancing with a white girl.

The television incident was only the start of Freed's professional problems. In 1960 Freed was brought before a congressional committee investigating "payola," a common practice among deejays of receiving gifts from record companies in exchange for playing their records. His career sank further when, in 1962, Freed was convicted of commercial bribery by New York State. Impoverished and struggling with alcoholism, Freed died in 1965 at the age of forty-three.

Like Alan Freed, **Grace Metalious** sent shock waves through American popular culture in the 1950s. Metalious grew up in poverty in Manchester, New Hampshire. In 1943, while still a teenager, she married and became a mother and housewife. In 1956 Metalious published her first novel, *Peyton Place*, and the book sold more than three million copies the first year. Considered provocative and racy because of its discussion of sex, rape, and incest, the novel punctured myths about the straitlaced life of small-town America. It criticized small-minded conformity that enforced a double standard of sexual behavior on women.

Despite the book's popularity, Metalious was never seen as a serious writer. Detractors described her as an untalented author who disseminated filth. Metalious could not reconcile her success with the criticism she received and, like Alan Freed, increasingly turned to alcohol for comfort. In 1964, just eight years after publication of *Peyton Place*, she died at age thirty-nine of cirrhosis of the liver. Both Metalious and Freed challenged notions of conventional taste, and both found their lives upended by the backlash their work inspired.

THE AMERICAN HISTORIES of Alan Freed and Grace Metalious, both of whom attacked conformity, were made possible by the emergence of a mass-consumption economy fueled by technological innovation. The end of World War II had produced economic, social, and political challenges for Americans; however, the economic boom of the 1950s allowed many Americans to overcome them. A large number of families moved into the middle class and out to suburbia. Yet not everyone felt satisfied, and critics expressed their disapproval in diverse ways. Young people challenged their parents' culture. Writers and musicians experimented with freer forms of artistic expression and attacked the conformity they associated with mainstream America. And African Americans and other marginalized groups challenged racial segregation directly in the Supreme Court and through powerful community protests.

Peacetime Transition and the Boom Years

The notoriety of Grace Metalious and Alan Freed came at a time of renewed economic growth and prosperity in the United States. Although confronted with family upheaval, labor disruptions, and economic constraints immediately following the war, by 1950 Americans had more disposable income than they had enjoyed in decades. While President Truman struggled to hold together the New Deal coalition, consumers responded enthusiastically to the wide range of products that advertisers promised would improve their lives. The search for the good life propelled middle-class families from cities to the suburbs. At the same time, a postwar baby boom added millions of children to the population and created a market to supply them with goods from infancy and childhood to adolescence.

Peacetime Challenges, 1945–1948

Before Americans could work their way toward prosperity, they faced considerable challenges. Immediately after the war, consumers experienced shortages and high prices, businesses complained about tight regulations, and labor unions sought higher wages and a greater voice in companies' decision making. The return to peace also occasioned debates about whether married women should continue to work outside the home.

By mid-1946, 9 million American soldiers had returned to a changed world. The war had exerted pressures on traditional family life as millions of women had left home to work jobs that men had vacated. Most of the 150,000 women who served in the military received their discharge, and like their male counterparts they hoped to obtain employment. Many other women who had tasted the benefits of wartime employment also wanted to keep working and were reluctant to give up their positions to men.

The war disrupted other aspects of family life as well. During the war, husbands and wives had spent long periods apart, resulting in marital tensions and an increased divorce rate. The relaxation of parental authority during the war led to a rise in juvenile delinquency, which added to the anxieties of adults. In 1948 the noted psychiatrist William C. Menninger observed, "While we alarm ourselves with talk of . . . atom bombs, we are complacently watching the disintegration of our family life." Some observers worried that the very existence of the traditional American family was in jeopardy.

Economic Conversion and Labor Discontent

Even before the war ended, the U.S. government took some steps to meet postwar economic challenges. In 1944, for example, Congress passed the **Servicemen's Readjustment Act**, commonly known as the **GI Bill**, which offered veterans educational opportunities and financial aid as they adjusted to civilian life. Nevertheless, veterans, like other Americans, faced shortages in the supply of housing and consumer goods and high prices for available commodities.

The GI Bill Attending Pennsylvania State College under the GI Bill of Rights, William Oskay, Jr. pays $28 a month for the trailer home in which he is studying at a desk made from orange crates. Mrs. Oskay plays with their young daughter in the background. To gain extra money for clothing and entertainment, the enterprising Oskay sells sandwiches in fraternity houses, earning $3 or $4 a night. Bettmann/Getty Images

President Harry Truman ran into serious difficulty handling these and other problems. In the years immediately following the war, incomes fell, undermined by inflation and reduced overtime hours. As corporate profits rose, workers in the steel, automobile, and fuel industries struck for higher wages and a greater voice in company policies. Truman responded harshly. Labor had been one of Franklin Roosevelt's strongest allies, but his successor put that relationship in jeopardy. In 1946 the federal government took over railroads and threatened to draft workers into the military until they stopped striking. Truman took a tough stance, but in the end union workers received a pay raise, though it did little to relieve inflation.

Political developments forced Truman to change course with the labor unions. In the 1946 midterm elections, Republicans won control of Congress. Stung by this defeat, Truman sought to repair the damage his anti-union policies had done to the Democratic Party coalition. In 1947 Congress passed the **Taft-Hartley Act**, which hampered the ability of unions to organize and limited their power to strike if larger national interests were seen to be at stake. Seeking to regain labor's support, Truman vetoed the measure. Congress, however, overrode the president's veto, and the Taft-Hartley Act became law.

Truman, the New Deal Coalition, and the Election of 1948

Truman's handling of domestic and foreign affairs brought out several challengers for the 1948 election. Much of the opposition came from his own party. From the left, former Democratic vice president Henry Wallace ran on the Progressive Party ticket, backed by disgruntled liberals who opposed Truman's hard-line Cold War policies. From the right, Democratic governor Strom Thurmond of South Carolina campaigned mainly on preserving racial segregation in the South and headed up the States' Rights Party, known as the Dixiecrats. Both Wallace and Thurmond threatened to take Democratic votes from the president. However, Truman's strongest challenge came from the popular Republican governor of New York, Thomas E. Dewey.

Up against overwhelming odds, Truman managed to win the presidency. He out-campaigned Dewey, while Wallace and Thurmond failed to draw significant votes away from Truman. He succeeded in holding together the New Deal coalition of labor, racial and ethnic minority groups, farmers, and liberals and winning enough votes in the South to come out ahead.

By this time, most liberals had moved closer to the political center. Rejecting what they considered the ideological dogmatism of the extreme left and right, they favored a strong anti-Communist policy abroad and supported a brand of reform capitalism at home that encouraged economic growth rather than a redistribution of wealth to lift Americans into the middle class. In doing so, they also sought to avoid the political fallout from charges of Communist sympathizers-in-government hurled by Republicans.

Economic Boom

While the United States faced political challenges, the economy flourished in the decade and a half after the Second World War. Between 1945 and 1960, the gross national product (GNP) soared 250 percent and per capita income (total income divided by the population) grew 35 percent. During this fifteen-year period, the average real income (actual purchasing power) for American workers increased by as much as it had during the fifty years preceding World War II. Equally striking, 60 percent of Americans achieved middle-class status, and the number of salaried office workers rose 61 percent. Factory workers also experienced gains. Union membership leaped to the highest level in U.S. history, reaching nearly 17 million.

The affluence of the 1950s was much more equally distributed than the prosperity of the 1920s had been. As the middle class grew, the top 5 percent of wealthy families dropped in the percentage of total income they earned from 21.3 percent to 19 percent. Though poverty remained a persistent problem, the rate of poverty decreased, falling from 34 percent in 1947 to 22.1 percent in 1960 (Figure 25.1). A college education served as a critical marker of middle-class status. Traditionally, colleges and universities had been accessible only to the upper class. That began to change between 1940 and 1960 as the number of high school students who entered college more than doubled.

The market for consumer goods skyrocketed. TV sets became a household staple in the 1950s, and by 1960, 87 percent of Americans owned a television. Americans also continued to purchase automobiles—75 percent owned a car. With gas supplies plentiful and the price per gallon less than 30 cents, automakers concentrated on size, power, and style to compete for buyers. With more cars on the road, motel chains such as Holiday Inn sprang up along the highways. Fast-food establishments proliferated to feed motorists and their families.

Baby Boom

During the postwar years, with traditional gender roles largely reinstated and the economy booming, nuclear families began to grow. In the 1940s and 1950s the average age at marriage was younger than it had been in the 1930s. On average, men married for the first time at the age of just under twenty-three, and 49 percent

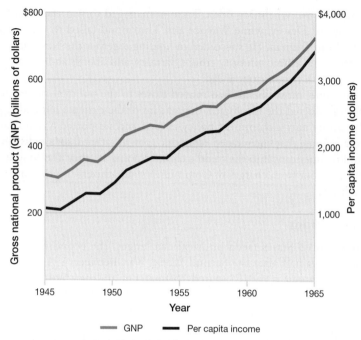

FIGURE 25.1   Economic Growth, 1945–1965 As industries shifted from war equipment to consumer goods, productivity remained high. More Americans entered the middle class in the two decades following World War II, while rising union membership ensured higher incomes for the working class. As a result, the purchasing power of most Americans increased in the immediate postwar period. What factors promoted the growth of the middle class in the 1950s?

of women married by nineteen. Couples also produced children at an astonishing rate. In the 1950s, the growth rate in the U.S. population approached that of India (Figure 25.2).

Marriage and parenthood reflected a culture spurred by the Cold War. Public officials and the media urged young men and women to build nuclear families in which the father held a paying job and the mother stayed at home and raised her growing family. Doing so would strengthen the moral fiber of the United States in its battle against Soviet communism.

Parents could also look forward to their children surviving diseases that had resulted in many childhood deaths in the past. In the 1950s, children received vaccinations against diphtheria, whooping cough, and tuberculosis before they entered school. The most serious illness affecting young children remained the crippling disease of polio, or infantile paralysis. In 1955 Dr. Jonas Salk developed a successful injectable vaccine against the disease. On April 12, 1955, news bulletins interrupted scheduled television programs to announce Salk's breakthrough, and, as one writer recalled, "citizens rushed to ring church bells and fire sirens, shouted, clapped, sang, and made every kind of joyous noise they could." By the mid-1960s polio was no longer a public health menace in the United States.

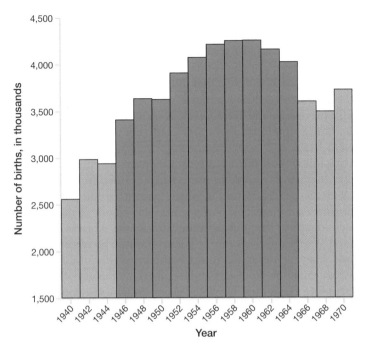

FIGURE 25.2   **The Baby Boom, 1946–1964** The U.S. population increased dramatically in the postwar decades. Economic prosperity made it easier to support large families, women's early age at marriage contributed to high fertility, and improved health care led to the survival of more children. As this figure shows, the baby boom experienced its peak in the 1950s. How much did the baby boom influence the flourishing of teenage culture that arose in the same period?

Changes in Living Patterns

With larger families and larger family incomes came an increased demand for better housing. The economic and demographic booms encouraged migration out of the cities so that growing families could have their own homes, greater space, and a healthier environment. To meet this demand, the federal government offered Americans opportunities to purchase their own homes. The Federal Housing Administration, created in the 1930s, provided long-term mortgages to qualified buyers at low interest rates. After the war, the Veterans Administration offered even lower mortgage rates and did not require substantial down payments for ex-GIs. The federal government also cooperated by building highways that allowed drivers to commute to and from the suburbs. By 1960 nearly 60 million people, one-third of the nation's population, lived in suburbs.

William Levitt, a thirty-eight-year-old veteran from Long Island, New York, devised the formula for attracting home buyers to the suburbs. In 1948, Levitt remarked: "No man who owns his own house and lot can be a Communist. He has too much to do." After World War II, Levitt, his father, and his brother saw opportunity in the housing crunch and pioneered the idea of adapting Henry Ford's mass-production principles to the housing industry. To build his subdivision of

Levittown in Hempstead, Long Island, twenty miles from Manhattan, he bulldozed 4,000 acres of potato fields and brought in trucks that dumped piles of building materials at exact intervals of sixty feet. Specialized crews then moved from pile to pile, each performing their assigned job. In July 1948, Levitt's workers constructed 180 houses a week, or 36 a day, in two shifts. Mass-production methods kept prices low, and Levitt quickly sold his initial 17,000 houses and soon built other subdivisions in Pennsylvania and New Jersey. With Levitt leading the way, the annual production of new single-family homes nearly doubled from 937,000 in 1946 to 1.7 million in 1950.

Although millions of Americans took advantage of opportunities to move to the suburbs, Levitt closed his subdivisions to African Americans. He was supported by the Federal Housing Administration which guaranteed financing for sales of housing in "all-white" communities. Many whites moved out of the cities because they were prejudiced against the growing number of southern blacks who migrated north during World War II and the influx of Puerto Ricans who came to the United States after the war. Many communities in the North adopted restrictive covenants, which prohibited resale of homes to blacks and members of other racial and ethnic minority groups, including Hispanics, Jews, and Asian Americans. Although the Supreme Court outlawed restrictive covenants in *Shelley v. Kraemer* (1948), housing discrimination remained prevalent in urban and suburban neighborhoods. Real estate brokers steered buyers from these marginalized groups away from white communities, and banks refused to lend money to black purchasers who sought to move into white locales, an illegal policy called redlining.

Nevertheless, a few African Americans succeeded in cracking suburban racial barriers, but at great risk. In August 1957, a black couple, William Myers, an electrical engineer, and his wife Daisy, managed to buy a house in Levittown, Pennsylvania. Once the Myers moved in, they faced two weeks of intimidation and assaults from mobs of hostile white community residents. When local police refused to protect them, the governor dispatched state troopers to keep them safe. Although the Myers succeeded in remaining in Levittown, their experience underscored the racially discriminatory housing practices that existed in the North.

No sections of the nation expanded faster than the West and the South. Attracted by the warmer climate and jobs in the defense, petroleum, and chemical industries, transplanted Americans swelled the populations of California, Texas, and Florida. The advent of air conditioning also made such moves much more feasible. California's population increased the most, adding nearly six million new residents between 1940 and 1960, including a large influx of Asians and Latinos. In 1957, in a sign of the times, New York City lost two of its baseball teams, the New York Giants and the Brooklyn Dodgers, to San Francisco and Los Angeles. This migration to the **Sun Belt**, as the southern and western states would be called, transformed the political and social landscapes of the nation.

REVIEW & RELATE	• How did the conversion from war to peacetime affect the economy, society, and politics in the United States? • What factors contributed to the economic and population growth of the 1950s, and how did they contribute to suburbanization and the growth in the Sun Belt?

William and Daisy Myers Integrate Levittown, 1957 Daisy Myers serves coffee to her husband William in their new $12,150 ranch-style house in Levittown, Pennsylvania. The first black family to move into this all-white community, on August 19, 1957, the Myers braved two weeks of threatening protests by their new neighbors and proclaimed: "We're here to stay," and they did. AP Images/Sam Myers

The Culture of the 1950s

In the 1950s, new forms of popular culture developed as the United States confronted difficult political, diplomatic, and social issues. Amid this turmoil, television played a large role in shaping people's lives, reflecting their desire for success and depicting the era as a time of innocence. The rise of teenage culture as a powerful economic force also influenced this portrayal of the 1950s. Teenage tastes and consumption patterns reinforced the impression of a simpler and more carefree time. Religion painted a similar picture, as attendance at houses of worship rose. Still, the decade held a more complex social reality. Cultural rebels—writers, actors, and musicians—emerged to challenge mainstream values. Women did not always act the suburban parts that television and society assigned them, and religion seemed to serve more of a communal, social function than an individual, spiritual one.

The Rise of Television

Few postwar developments had a greater impact on American society and politics than the advent of television. The three major television networks—the Columbia Broadcasting System (CBS), the National Broadcasting Company (NBC), and the American Broadcasting Company (ABC)—offered programs nationwide that appealed to mainstream tastes while occasionally challenging the public with serious drama, music, and documentaries. During the 1950s, television networks began to feature presidential campaign coverage, from the national nominating conventions to election-day vote tallies, and political advertisements began to fill the airwaves.

If some Americans recall the 1950s as a time of innocence, they have in mind television shows that depicted white families entertaining themselves, mediating quarrels peacefully, and relying on the wisdom of parents. In *The Adventures of Ozzie and Harriet*, the Nelsons raised two clean-cut sons. In *Father Knows Best*, the Andersons—a father and mother and their three children—lived a tranquil life in the suburbs, and the father solved whatever dilemmas arose. The same held true for the Cleaver family on *Leave It to Beaver*. Television portrayed working-class families in grittier fashion on shows such as *The Life of Riley*, whose lead character worked at a factory, and *The Honeymooners*, whose male protagonists were a bus driver and a sewer worker. Nevertheless, like their middle-class counterparts, these families stayed together and worked out their problems despite their more challenging financial circumstances.

By contrast, African American families received little attention on television. Black female actors usually appeared as maids, and the one show that featured an all-black cast, *The Amos 'n' Andy Show*, highlighted the racial stereotypes of the period. American Indians faced similar difficulties. Few appeared on television, and those who did served mainly as targets for "heroic" cowboys defending the West from "savage" Indians. One exception was Tonto, the Lone Ranger's sidekick. Played by Jay Silverheels, a Canadian Mohawk, he challenged the false image of the "hostile Indian" by showing his loyalty to his white partner and his commitment to the code of "civilized" justice.

Wild Ones on the Big Screen

If parents expected young people to behave like Ozzie and Harriet Nelson's sons, the popular culture industry provided teenagers with alternative role models. In *Rebel Without a Cause* (1955), actor James Dean portrayed a seventeen-year-old filled with anguish about his life. A sensitive but misunderstood young man, he muses that he wants "just one day when I wasn't all confused . . . [when] I wasn't ashamed of everything . . . [when] I felt I belonged some place." *The Wild One* (1954), which starred Marlon Brando, also popularized youthful angst. The leather-outfitted leader of a motorcycle gang, Brando rides into a small town, hoping to shake it up. When asked by a local resident, "What are you rebelling against?" he coolly replies, "Whaddya got?" Real gangs did exist on the streets of New York and other major cities. Composed of working-class youth from various ethnic and racial backgrounds, these gangs were highly organized, controlled their neighborhood turfs, and engaged in "rumbles" (fights) with intruders.

Rebel Without a Cause, 1955
James Dean starred in the movie *Rebel Without a Cause*, playing Jim Stark, a troubled teenager seeking an escape from his middle-class, suburban life. The movie explored the conflict between parents and teenagers, what we call today "the generation gap." Dean's outfit of leather jacket and blue jeans and his anguished demeanor both reflected and shaped teenage culture.
Everett Collection

Hollywood rarely portrayed women as rebels, but instead as mothers, understanding girlfriends, and dutiful wives. If they sought a career, like many of the women played by actor Doris Day, they pursued it only as long as necessary to meet the right man. The film industry also perpetuated an image of a tantalizing woman who utilized her attributes to seduce and outwit men. Marilyn Monroe in *The Seven Year Itch* (1955) and Elizabeth Taylor in *Cat on a Hot Tin Roof* (1958) both portrayed female characters as sexual beings.

The Influence of Teenage Culture

In 1941 *Popular Science* magazine coined the term *teenager*, and by the middle of the next decade members of this age group viewed themselves not as prospective adults but as a distinct group with its own identity, patterns of behavior, and tastes. Postwar prosperity provided teenagers with money to support their own choices and styles. In 1959 *Life* magazine found that teenagers had $10 billion at their disposal, "a billion more than the total sales of GM [General Motors]."

Teenagers owned 10 million record players, more than 1 million TV sets, and 13 million cameras. They spent 16 percent of their disposable income on entertainment, particularly the purchase of rock 'n' roll records. The comic book industry also attracted a huge audience among teenagers by selling inexpensive, illustrated, and easy-to-read pulp fiction geared toward romance and action adventure.

Public high schools reinforced teenage identity. Following World War II, high school attendance exploded. In 1930, 50 percent of white children attended high school; thirty years later, the figure had jumped to 90 percent. The percentage of black youths attending high school also grew, doubling from 1940 to 1960. For the first time, many white middle-class teenagers saw the fashions and heard the language of working-class youths close up and both emulated and feared what they encountered.

More than anything else, rock 'n' roll music set teenagers apart from their elders. The pop singers of the 1940s and early 1950s—such as Frank Sinatra, Perry Como, Rosemary Clooney, and Patti Page, who had appealed to both adolescents and parents—lost much of their teenage audience after 1954 to rock 'n' roll, with its heavy downbeat and lyrics evoking teenage passion and sexuality. Black artists such as Chuck Berry, Little Richard, and Antoine "Fats" Domino popularized the sound of classic, up-tempo rock.

Although blacks pioneered the sound of rhythm and blues, the music entered the mainstream largely through white artists. Born in Tupelo, Mississippi, and living in Memphis, Tennessee, Elvis Presley adapted the fashion and sensuality of black performers to his own style. Elvis's snarling singing and pelvic gyrations excited young people, both black and white, while upsetting their parents. In an era when matters of sex remained private or were not discussed at all and when African Americans were still treated as second-class citizens, a white man singing "black" music and shaking his body to its frenetic tempo caused alarm. When Elvis sang on the popular *Ed Sullivan Show* in 1956, cameras were allowed to show him only from the waist up to uphold standards of decency.

The Lives of Women

Throughout the 1950s, movies, women's magazines, mainstream newspapers, and medical and psychological experts informed women that only by embracing domesticity could they achieve personal fulfillment. Dr. Benjamin Spock's best-selling *Common Sense Book of Baby and Child Care* (1946) advised mothers that their children would reach their full potential only if wives stayed at home and watched over their offspring. In another best seller, *Modern Women: The Lost Sex* (1947), Ferdinand Lundberg and Marynia Farnham called the independent woman "a contradiction in terms." A 1951 study of corporate executives found that most businessmen viewed the ideal wife as one who devoted herself to her husband's career. College newspapers described female undergraduates who were not engaged by their senior year as "distraught." Certainly many women professed to find domestic lives fulfilling, but many others experienced anxiety and depression. Far from satisfied, these women suffered from what the social critic Betty Friedan would later call "a problem that has no name," a malady that derived from the unrewarding roles women were expected to play.

Although most married women with families did not work during the 1950s, the proportion of working wives doubled from 15 percent in 1940 to 30 percent in 1960, with the greatest increase coming among women over the age of thirty-five. Married women were more likely to work if they were African American or came from working-class immigrant families. Moreover, women's magazines offered readers a more complex message than domesticity. Alongside articles about and advertisements directed at stay-at-home mothers, these periodicals profiled career women, such as white Maine senator Margaret Chase Smith, black educator Mary McLeod Bethune, and sports figures such as white golf and tennis great Babe (Mildred) Didrikson Zaharias. At the same time, working women played significant roles in labor unions, where they fought to reduce disparities between men's and women's income and provide a wage for housewives, recognizing the importance of their unpaid work to maintaining families. Many other women joined clubs and organizations like the Young Women's Christian Association (YWCA), where they engaged in charitable and public service activities. Some participated in political organizations, such as Henry Wallace's Progressive Party, and peace groups, such as the Women's International League for Peace and Freedom, to campaign against the violence caused by racial discrimination at home and Cold War rivalries abroad.

Religious Revival

Along with marriage and the family, religion experienced a revival in the postwar United States. The arms race between the United States and the Soviet Union heightened the dangers of international conflict for ordinary citizens, and the social and economic changes that accompanied the Cold War intensified personal anxiety. Churchgoing underscored the contrast between the United States, a religious nation, and the "godless" communism of the Soviet Union. The link between religion and Americanism prompted Congress in 1954 to add "under God" to the pledge of allegiance and to make "In God We Trust" the national motto. A good American, one magazine proclaimed, could not be "un-religious."

Americans worshipped in growing numbers. Between 1940 and 1950, church and synagogue membership rose by 78 percent, and more than 95 percent of the population professed a belief in God. Yet religious affiliation appeared to reflect a greater emphasis on togetherness than on specific doctrinal beliefs. It offered a way to overcome isolation and embrace community in an increasingly alienating world.

Television spread religiosity into millions of homes. The Catholic bishop Fulton J. Sheen spoke to a weekly television audience of ten million and alternated his message of "a life worth living" with attacks on atheistic Communists. The Methodist minister Norman Vincent Peale, also a popular TV figure, combined traditional religious faith with self-help remedies prescribed in his best-selling book *The Power of Positive Thinking* (1952). The Reverend Billy Graham, from Charlotte, North Carolina, preached about the unhappiness caused by personal sin at huge outdoor crusades, which were broadcast on television.

Beats and Other Nonconformists

As many Americans migrated to the suburbs, spent money on leisure and entertainment, and cultivated religion, a small group of young poets, writers, intellectuals, musicians, and artists attacked mainstream politics and culture. Known as **Beats** (derived from "beaten down"), they offered stinging critiques of what they considered the sterility and conformity of white middle-class society. In 1956 Allen Ginsberg began his epic poem *Howl* with the line "I saw the best minds of my generation destroyed by madness, starving hysterical naked." In his novel *On the Road* (1957), Jack Kerouac praised the individual who pursued authentic experiences and mind-expanding consciousness through drugs, sexual experimentation, and living in the moment. At a time when whiteness was a standard of beauty and virtue, the Beats and authors such as Norman Mailer looked to African Americans as cultural icons, embracing a sense of spontaneity and coolness they attributed to blacks. The Beats formed their own artistic enclaves in New York City's Greenwich Village and San Francisco's North Beach and Haight-Ashbury districts.

The Beat writers frequently read their poems and prose to the rhythms of jazz, reflecting both their affinity with African American culture and the innovative explorations taking place in music. From the big bands of the 1930s and 1940s, postwar jazz musicians formed smaller trios, quartets, and quintets and experimented with sounds more suitable for serious listening than for dancing. The bebop rhythms of trumpeter Dizzy Gillespie and alto saxophonist Charlie Parker revolutionized jazz, as did trumpeter Miles Davis and tenor saxophonist John Coltrane, who experimented with more complex and textured forms of this music and took it to new heights. Like rock 'n' roll musicians, these black artists broke down racial barriers as their music attracted white audiences.

Homosexuals also attempted to live nonconformist lifestyles, albeit clandestinely. According to studies by researcher Dr. Alfred Kinsey of Indiana University, homosexuals made up approximately 10 percent of the adult population. During World War II, gay men and lesbians had the opportunity to meet other homosexuals in the military and in venues that attracted gay soldiers. Though homosexuality remained taboo and public displays of same-sex sexuality were criminalized, politically radical gay men organized against homophobia after the war. In 1951 they formed the Mattachine Society in Los Angeles, which then spread to the East Coast. In 1954 a group of lesbians founded the Daughters of Bilitis in San Francisco. Because of police harassment, most homosexuals refused to reveal their sexual orientation, which made sense practically but reduced their ability to counter anti-homosexual discrimination.

Kinsey also shattered myths about conformity among heterosexuals. In *Sexual Behavior in the Human Female* (1953), he revealed that 50 percent of the women he interviewed had had sexual intercourse before marriage, and 25 percent had had extramarital affairs. Kinsey's findings were supported by other data. Between 1940 and 1960, the frequency of out-of-wedlock births among all women rose from 7.1 newborns to 21.6 newborns per thousand women of childbearing age. The sexual relations that Grace Metalious depicted in *Peyton Place* reflected what many Americans practiced but did not talk about. The brewing sexual revolution went public in 1953 with the publication of *Playboy* magazine, founded by Hugh Hefner. Through a combination of serious articles and photographs of nude women, the magazine provided its chiefly male readers with a guide to pursuing sexual pleasure and a sophisticated lifestyle.

Like Metalious, many writers denounced the conformity and shallowness they found in suburban America. Novelist Sloan Wilson wrote about the alienating experience of suburban life in *The Man in the Gray Flannel Suit* (1955). In J. D. Salinger's novel *Catcher in the Rye* (1951), the young protagonist, Holden Caulfield, mocks the phoniness of the adult world while ending up in a mental institution. Journalists and scholars joined in the criticism, and they tapped into a growing feeling, especially among a new generation of young people, of the dangers of a mass culture based on standardization, compliance, and bureaucratization.

REVIEW & RELATE	• What trends in American popular culture did the television shows and popular music of the 1950s reflect? • How did artists, writers, and social critics challenge the mainstream politics and culture of the 1950s?

The Growth of the Civil Rights Movement

African Americans wanted what most other Americans desired after World War II —the opportunity to make a decent living, buy a nice home, raise a healthy family, and get the best education for their children. Yet blacks faced much greater obstacles than did whites in obtaining these dreams, particularly in the Jim Crow South. Determined to eliminate racial injustices, black Americans mounted a campaign against white supremacy in the decades after World War II. African Americans increasingly viewed their struggle as part of an international movement of black people in Africa and other nonwhites in the Middle East and Asia to obtain their freedom from Western colonial rulers. Embracing similar hopes, Asian Americans and Latinos pursued their own struggles for equality.

The Rise of the Southern Civil Rights Movement

With the war against Nazi racism over, African Americans expected to win first-class citizenship in the United States. During World War II, blacks waged successful campaigns to pressure the federal government to tackle discrimination and organizations such as the Congress of Racial Equality (CORE) and the NAACP attacked racial injustice. African American veterans, such as Medgar Evers in Mississippi, returned home to the South determined to build on these victories, especially by extending the right to vote. Yet African Americans found that most whites resisted demands for racial equality.

In 1946 violence surfaced as the most visible evidence of many white people's determination to preserve the traditional racial order. A race riot erupted in Columbia, Tennessee, in which blacks were killed and black businesses were torched. In South Carolina, Isaac Woodard, a black veteran still in uniform and on his way home on a bus, got into an argument with the white bus driver. When the local sheriff arrived, he pounded Woodard's face with a club, permanently blinding the ex-GI. In Mississippi, Senator Theodore Bilbo, running for reelection in the Democratic primary, told white audiences that they could keep blacks from voting "by seeing them the night before" the election. Groups such as the NAACP and the National Association of Colored Women demanded that the president take action to combat this reign of terror.

In December 1946, President Truman responded by issuing an executive order creating the President's Committee on Civil Rights. While the committee conducted its investigation, in April 1947, Jackie Robinson became the first black baseball player to enter the major leagues. This accomplishment proved to be a sign of changes to come.

After extensive deliberations, the committee, which consisted of blacks and whites, northerners and southerners, issued its report, **To Secure These Rights**, on October 29, 1947. Placing the problem of "civil rights shortcomings" within the context of the Cold War, the report argued that racial inequality and unrest could only aid the Soviets in their global anti-American propaganda efforts. "The United States is not so strong," the committee asserted, "the final triumph of the democratic ideal not so inevitable that we can ignore what the world thinks of us or our record." A far-reaching document, the report called for racial desegregation in the military, interstate transportation, and education, as well as extension of the right to vote. The following year, under pressure from African American activists, President Truman signed an executive order to desegregate the armed forces.

Even without federal action, African Americans moved to obtain civil rights. The anti-Communist attacks in the late 1940s and early 1950s against liberal and left-wing groups had damaged a number of interracial organizations, including the National Negro Congress and the Southern Negro Youth Congress. However, NAACP branches and local civic groups remained in the South to challenge white supremacy. These organizations dispatched black women and men to conduct voter registration drives throughout major cities and small towns in the South. By 1954, the percentage of black registered voters in the South had leaped from 3 percent in 1940 to 20 percent. These black freedom efforts, though fruitful, were very dangerous. In 1951, Harry T. Moore, the leader of the NAACP in Florida who had spearheaded voter registration campaigns, was killed along with his wife when the Ku Klux Klan detonated a bomb under their house.

School Segregation and the Supreme Court

Led by the NAACP, African Americans also launched a prolonged assault on school segregation. First the association filed lawsuits against states that excluded blacks from publicly funded law schools and universities. After victories in Missouri and

Maryland, the group's chief lawyer, Thurgood Marshall, convinced the Supreme Court in 1950 to disband the separate law school that Texas had established for blacks and admit them to the University of Texas Law School. At the same time, the Court eliminated separate facilities for black students at the University of Oklahoma graduate school and ruled against segregation in interstate rail transportation.

Before African Americans could attend college, they had to obtain a good education in public schools. Black schools typically lacked the resources provided to white schools, and the NAACP understood that southern officials would never live up to the "separate but equal doctrine" asserted in *Plessy v. Ferguson* (1896). African Americans sought to integrate schools not because they wanted their children to sit next to white students, but because they believed that integration offered the best and quickest way to secure quality education.

On May 17, 1954, in ***Brown v. Board of Education of Topeka, Kansas***, the Supreme Court overturned *Plessy*. In a unanimous decision read by Chief Justice Earl Warren, the Court concluded that "in the field of public education the doctrine of 'separate but equal' has no place. Separate educational facilities are inherently unequal." This ruling undercut the legal foundation for segregation and officially placed the law on the side of those who sought racial equality. Nevertheless, the ruling did not end the controversy; in fact, it led to more battles over segregation. In 1955 the Court issued a follow-up opinion calling for implementation with "all deliberate speed." But it left enforcement of *Brown* to federal district courts in the South, which consisted mainly of white southerners who espoused segregationist views. As a result, southern officials emphasized "deliberate" rather than "speed" and slowed the implementation of the *Brown* decision.

The Montgomery Bus Boycott

The *Brown* decision encouraged African Americans to protest against other forms of racial discrimination. In 1955 in Montgomery, Alabama, the Women's Political Council, a group of middle-class and professional black women, petitioned the city commission to improve bus service for black passengers. Among other things, they wanted blacks not to have to give up their seats to white passengers who boarded the bus after black passengers did. Their requests went unheeded until December 1, 1955, when Rosa Parks, a black seamstress and an NAACP activist, refused to give up her seat to a white man. Parks's arrest rallied civic, labor, and religious groups and sparked a bus boycott that involved nearly the entire black community. Instead of riding buses, black commuters walked to work or joined car pools. White officials refused to capitulate and fought back by arresting leaders of the **Montgomery Improvement Association**, the organization that coordinated the protest. Other whites hurled insults at blacks and engaged in violence. After more than a year of conflict, the Supreme Court ruled in favor of the complete desegregation of Montgomery's buses.

Out of this landmark struggle, Martin Luther King Jr. emerged as the civil rights movement's most charismatic leader. His personal courage and power of oratory inspired nearly all segments of the African American community. Twenty-six years old at the time of Parks's arrest, King was the pastor of the prestigious Dexter Avenue Baptist Church. Though King was familiar with the nonviolent methods

Montgomery Bus Boycott, 1956 Two months after African American residents of Montgomery, Alabama, began their boycott of the city buses to protest segregation and mistreatment, the black community kept up its boycott despite violence and intimidation. Black women had made up the majority of bus riders, and this photograph, taken on February 1, 1956, shows many of them walking to work or to stores for shopping. Don Cravens/Getty Images

of the Indian revolutionary Mohandas Gandhi and the civil disobedience of the nineteenth-century writer Henry David Thoreau, he drew his inspiration and commitment to these principles mainly from black church and secular leaders such as A. Philip Randolph and Bayard Rustin. King understood how to convey the goals of the civil rights movement to sympathetic white Americans, but his vision and passion grew out of black communities. At the outset of the Montgomery bus boycott, King noted proudly of the boycott: "When the history books are written in future generations, the historians will have to pause and say 'There lived a great people — a Black people — who injected new meaning and dignity into the veins of civilization.' "

The Montgomery bus boycott made King a national civil rights leader, but it did not guarantee him further success. In 1957 King and a like-minded group of southern black ministers formed the **Southern Christian Leadership Conference (SCLC)** to spread nonviolent protest throughout the region, but except in a few cities, such as Tallahassee, Florida, additional bus boycotts did not take hold.

White Resistance to Desegregation

Segregationists responded forcefully to halt black efforts to eliminate Jim Crow. In 1956, 101 southern congressmen issued a manifesto denouncing the 1954 *Brown* opinion and pledging to resist it through "lawful means." Other white southerners went beyond the law. In 1957 a federal court approved a plan submitted by the Little Rock, Arkansas School Board to integrate Central High School. However, the state's governor, Orval Faubus, obstructed the court ruling by sending the state National Guard to keep out nine black students chosen to attend Central High. Faced with blatant state resistance to federal authority, President Eisenhower placed the National Guard under federal control and sent in the 101st Airborne Division to restore order after a mob blocked the students from entering the school. These black pioneers, who became known as the **Little Rock Nine**, attended classes for the year under the protection of the National Guard but still encountered considerable harassment from white students. In defiance of the high court, other school districts, such as Prince

Edward County, Virginia, chose to close their public schools rather than desegregate. By the end of the decade, public schools in the South remained mostly segregated.

The white South used other forms of violence and intimidation to preserve segregation. The third incarnation of the Ku Klux Klan (KKK) appeared after World War II to strike back at growing African American challenges to white supremacy. This terrorist group threatened, injured, and killed blacks they considered "uppity." Following the *Brown* decision, segregationists also formed the White Citizens' Council (WCC). The WCC drew members largely from businessmen and professionals. The WCC generally intimidated blacks by threatening to fire them from jobs or denying them credit from banks. In Alabama, WCC members launched a campaign against radio stations playing the kind of rock 'n' roll music that Alan Freed popularized in New York City because they believed that it fostered close interracial contact.

The WCC and the KKK created a racial climate in the deep South that encouraged whites to believe they could get away with murder to defend white supremacy. In the summer of 1955, Emmett Till, a fourteen-year-old from Chicago who was visiting his great-uncle in Mississippi, was killed because he allegedly flirted with a white woman in a country store. Although the two accused killers were brought to trial, an all-white jury quickly acquitted them. The white woman, Carolyn Bryant, later admitted that her accusations were false.

The Sit-Ins

With boycotts petering out and white violence rising, African Americans, especially high school and college students, developed new techniques to confront discrimination, including sit-ins, in which protesters seat themselves in a strategic spot and refuse to move until their demands are met or they are forcibly evicted. These mass protests really got off the ground in February 1960, when four students at historically black North Carolina A&T University in Greensboro initiated sit-ins at the whites-only lunch counters in Woolworth and Kress department stores. Their demonstrations sparked similar efforts throughout the Southeast (Map 25.1).

A few months after the sit-ins began, a number of participants formed the **Student Nonviolent Coordinating Committee (SNCC)**. The organization's young members sought to challenge racial segregation in the South and to create interracial communities based on economic equality and political democracy. This generation of black and white sit-in veterans came of age in the 1950s at a time when Cold War democratic rhetoric and the Supreme Court's *Brown* decision raised their expectations for racial equality. Yet these young activists, including the Alabamian teenager and future congressman John Lewis, often saw their hopes dashed by southern segregationist resistance, including the murder of Emmett Till, which both horrified and helped mobilize them to fight for black equality.

Civil Rights Struggles in the North

Northern racism was systemic and powerful, but often invisible. Residential segregation reinforced racial segregation in public neighborhood schools. Banks used redlining to map out neighborhoods where African Americans could not obtain home mortgages. Public service jobs in many police and fire departments favored the descendants of white immigrants who had first held these posts in the late nineteenth

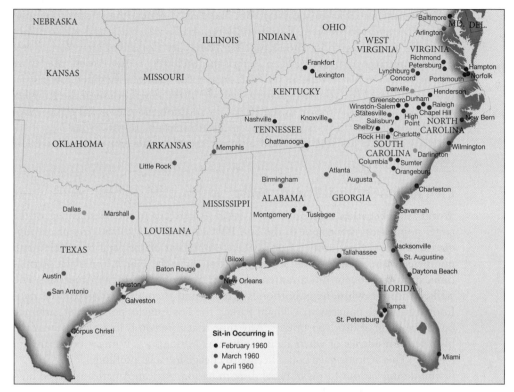

MAP 25.1   **Lunch Counter Sit-Ins, February–April 1960**
After starting slowly in the late 1950s, lunch counter sit-ins exploded in 1960 following a sit-in
by college students in Greensboro, North Carolina. Within three months, sit-ins erupted in fifty-
eight cities across the South. The participation of high school and college students revitalized
the civil rights movement and led to the formation of the Student Nonviolent Coordinating
Committee in April 1960.

century. Because blacks were commonly the last hired by most employers, seniority
rules worked against them when it came to cutting jobs. When private businesses
hired African Americans, they usually placed them in the lowest wage positions.
Some labor unions also practiced discrimination by excluding blacks from joining,
while others confined them to the lowest job categories.

Northern blacks also encountered discrimination in public accommodations.
Public swimming pools in Pittsburgh, Denver, Cleveland, and Buffalo, among other
cities, barred African Americans. Many restaurants refused to serve blacks. Palisades
Amusement Park, overlooking the Hudson River from New Jersey, was off-limits
to African Americans, as was the main amusement park in Cincinnati. Even with a
paycheck, one observer remarked, black workers "couldn't enjoy themselves, in terms
of theaters and other things. . . . They couldn't use their money for purposes of themselves or their families."

Despite widespread racial discrimination in the entire country, there were significant differences between the North and South. Most northern blacks could vote,

and cities such as Chicago and New York had elected African Americans to municipal offices and to Congress. Children living in adjacent black and white neighborhoods attended public schools together. The City College of New York, a free public university, admitted African Americans, including Colin Powell, the future secretary of state. Blacks rode on public transportation without the Jim Crow restrictions imposed in the South. Lynching was rare in the North, though the Ku Klux Klan flourished in the region in the 1920s. In addition, northern civil rights advocates made gradual inroads against racial discrimination. In the 1950s New York City passed a fair housing law and California created a fair employment practices commission.

Civil Rights Struggles in the West

World War II sparked a migration of African Americans to the West as part of the larger population movement to the Sun Belt. From 1940 to 1960, the black population in the region jumped from 4.9 to 5.4 percent of the total population and numbered more than 1.2 million. In the West, as in the North, the black population explosion brought unwarranted attention from police. African Americans who walked through white neighborhoods often found themselves targeted and confronted by white policemen. William Parker, the Los Angeles police chief, summed up the attitude of his department: "Any time that a person is in a place other than his place of residence or where he is conducting business . . . it might be a cause for inquiry." This attitude gave police license to engage in racial profiling.

Encountering various forms of racial discrimination, African Americans waged boycotts and sit-ins of businesses that refused blacks equal service in Lawrence, Kansas and Albuquerque, New Mexico. Perhaps the most significant protest occurred in Oklahoma City. In August 1958, the teenagers of the NAACP Youth Council and their adult adviser, Clara M. Luper, led sit-ins to desegregate lunch counters in downtown stores. Having succeeded in integrating a dozen facilities, the movement waged a six-year struggle to end discrimination in public accommodations throughout the city.

Other marginalized groups in the postwar West also struggled for equality. For Mexican Americans World War II inspired such challenges. In southern California, they formed Unity Leagues to protest segregation, and they often joined with African American groups in addressing discrimination. In 1947, the League of United Latin American Citizens (LULAC) won a case in federal court in *Mendez v. Westminster* prohibiting separate public schools for Mexican-American students. Spurred on by such efforts, Mexican Americans in 1949 succeeded in electing Edward Roybal to the Los Angeles City Council, the first American of Mexican descent to serve on that body since 1888. In Texas LULAC succeeded through litigation and boycotts in desegregating movie theaters, swimming pools, restaurants, and other public accommodations. LULAC also brought an end to discrimination in jury selection. Once Jackie Robinson integrated baseball in 1947, he opened the way for Afro-Hispanic ballplayers. Two years later, Orestes "Minnie" Miñoso, an Afro-Cuban, made it to the major leagues, playing for the Cleveland Indians.

World War II helped advance civil rights for Chinese Americans. In 1943 Congress repealed the exclusion law and followed up by passing the War Brides Act in 1945, which resulted in the admission of 6,000 Chinese women to the United States. However, the fall of China to the Communists in 1949 and the beginning of the Korean War the next year posed new challenges to Chinese communities on the West Coast. Although organizations such as the Six Companies of San Francisco denounced Communist China and pledged their loyalty to the United States, Cold War witch-hunts targeted the Chinese. With the Chinese Communists fighting against the United States in Korea, some regarded Chinese people in America with suspicion. "People would look at you in the street and think," one Chinese woman recalled, " 'Well you're one of the enemy.' " The federal government established a "Confession Program" by which Chinese people illegally in the country would be allowed to stay if they came forward, acknowledged their loyalty to the United States, and provided information about friends and relatives. Some 10,000 Chinese in San Francisco participated in this program.

Despite these hardships, Chinese Americans made great economic strides. Chinatowns shrank in population as their upwardly mobile residents moved to the suburbs. By 1959 Chinese Americans had a median family income of $6,207, compared with $5,660 for all Americans.

During the late 1940s and 1950s, Japanese Americans attempted to rebuild their lives following their wartime evacuation and internment. Overall, they succeeded. Many returned to the West Coast and although they found their neighborhoods occupied by other ethnic groups and their businesses in other hands, they took whatever jobs they could find and stressed education for their children. The McCarran-Walter Immigration Act of 1952 made it possible for Japanese aliens to become U.S. citizens. In addition, California repealed its Alien Land Law of 1913, which prohibited noncitizen Japanese from purchasing land. In 1955 about 40,000 Japanese Americans lived in Los Angeles, a figure slightly higher than the city's prewar population. Like other Americans, they began moving their families to suburbs such as Gardena, a half-hour ride from downtown Los Angeles. The federal government neither apologized for its wartime treatment of the Japanese nor awarded them financial compensation for their losses; this would happen three decades later.

REVIEW & RELATE	• What strategies did African Americans adopt in the 1940s and 1950s to fight segregation and discrimination? How did other racial and ethnic minorities pursue equality? • How and why did white southerners resist efforts to end segregation?

Domestic Politics in the Eisenhower Era

Despite the existence of civil rights protesters, rock 'n' roll upstarts, intellectual dissenters, and sexual revolutionaries, the 1950s seemed to many a tranquil, even dull period. This impression owes a great deal to the leadership of President Dwight D. Eisenhower. Serving two terms from 1953 to 1961, Eisenhower, or "Ike" as he was affectionately called, convinced the majority of Americans that their country was in good hands regardless of political turbulence at home and heated international conflicts abroad. By 1960, however, the nation was ready for a new generation of leadership.

Modern Republicanism

President Eisenhower, a World War II hero, radiated strength and trust, qualities the American people found very attractive as they rebuilt their lives and established families in the 1950s. In November 1952, Eisenhower coasted to victory over the Democratic candidate Adlai Stevenson, winning 55 percent of the popular vote and 83 percent of the electoral vote. The Republicans managed to win slim majorities in the Senate and the House, but within two years the Democrats regained control of Congress.

Eisenhower adopted **Modern Republicanism**, which tried to fit the traditional Republican Party ideals of individualism and fiscal restraint within the broad framework of Franklin Roosevelt's New Deal. As Eisenhower wrote to his brother, "Should any political party attempt to abolish social security, unemployment insurance, and eliminate labor laws and farm programs, you would not hear of that party again in our political history." With Democrats in control of Congress after 1954, Republicans agreed to raise Social Security benefits and to include coverage for some ten million additional workers. Congress and the president retained another New Deal mainstay, the minimum wage, and increased it from 75 cents to $1 an hour. Departing from traditional Republican criticism of big government, the Eisenhower administration added the Department of Health, Education, and Welfare to the cabinet in 1953.

In 1956 the Eisenhower administration sponsored the **National Interstate and Defense Highway Act**, which provided funds for the construction of 42,500 miles of roads throughout the country, boosting both suburbanization and national defense. In order to build this highway network, planners designed a road system that tore through black urban neighborhoods. Residents in the path of these highways lost their homes, businesses, churches, and entertainment centers. During the first twenty years of interstate highway construction over one million people, including 475,000 families, most of them African Americans, were displaced. An example of structural racism, the highway legislation produced longterm socioeconomic effects.

In 1958 Eisenhower signed into law the National Defense Education Act, which provided federal aid for instruction in science, math, and foreign languages and graduate fellowships and loans for college students. He portrayed the new law as a way to catch up with the Soviets, who the previous year had successfully launched the first artificial satellite, called *Sputnik*, into outer space.

For six of Eisenhower's eight years in office, the president had to work with Democratic majorities in Congress. Overall, he managed to forge bipartisan support for his proposals, most significantly civil rights. Under his administration's leadership, Republicans joined with Democrats, led by Senate Majority Leader Lyndon B. Johnson, to pass the first pieces of civil rights legislation since Reconstruction. In 1957 and 1960, Eisenhower signed into law two bills that extended the authority of the federal government to file court challenges against southern election officials who blocked African Americans from registering to vote. However, southern Democratic senators thwarted Congress from passing even stronger voting measures or acts that would have enforced school desegregation.

Eisenhower administration policy, however, did not work to the benefit of Native Americans. The federal government reversed many of the reforms instituted during the New Deal. In the 1950s the Bureau of Indian Affairs (BIA) adopted the policy of termination and relocation of Indian tribes. Those tribes deemed to have achieved the most "progress," such as the Flatheads of Montana, the Klamaths of Oregon, and the Hoopas of northern California, were treated as ordinary American citizens, which resulted in termination of their federal benefits and transfer of their tribal lands to state and local governments. The National Congress of American Indians fought unsuccessfully against this program.

The government also relocated Indians to urban areas. Between 1952 and 1960, the BIA encouraged more than 30,000 Indians to move from reservations to cities. The Indian population of Los Angeles grew to 25,000, including members of the Navajo, Sioux, and Cherokee nations. Although thousands of Indians took advantage of the relocation program, many had difficulty adjusting to urban life and fell into poverty.

The Eisenhower administration also repatriated undocumented Mexican laborers. The *bracero* program instituted in 1942, had permitted immigration from Mexico into the United States, but large agricultural growers sought an even greater supply of cheap labor. When Mexicans crossed the border illegally, simply seeking work, Mexico complained because it also needed a larger supply of agricultural workers. American labor groups protested that illegal immigrants took jobs away from Americans. In 1954, Eisenhower's Immigration and Naturalization Service rounded up undocumented Mexicans, mainly in Texas and California, and returned them to Mexico. Those deported often suffered harsh conditions, and seven deportees drowned after they jumped ship. "Operation Wetback," as the program was dubbed using a derogatory term for Mexicans, forced an estimated 250,000 to 1.3 million Mexicans to leave the United States.

The same year as the deportations began, the U.S. Supreme Court ruled in favor of Mexican Americans in *Hernandez v. Texas* (1954). The justices decided unanimously that the equal protection clause of the Fourteenth Amendment protects Mexican Americans as a distinct nationality group. The court found that a Texas county had deprived a defendant of his constitutional rights in a criminal trial, because the state systematically excluded Mexican Americans from serving on juries. Moreover, the case marked the first time in history that Mexican American attorneys—Carlos C. Cadena, Gustavo C. Garcia, and Johnny Herrara—argued before the Supreme Court.

The Election of 1960

Even after serving two terms, Eisenhower remained popular. However, he could not run for a third term, barred by the Twenty-second Amendment (1951), and Vice President Richard M. Nixon ran as the Republican candidate for president in 1960. Unlike Eisenhower, Nixon was not universally liked or respected. His reputation for unsavory political combat drew the scorn of Democrats, especially liberals. And Nixon had to fend off charges that Republicans, as embodied in the seventy-year-old Eisenhower, were out-of-date and out of new ideas.

The Democratic candidate for president in 1960, Senator John F. Kennedy of Massachusetts, promised to instill renewed "vigor" in the White House and get the country moving again. Yet Kennedy did not differ much from his Republican rival on domestic and foreign policy issues. While Kennedy employed a rhetoric of high-minded change, he had not compiled a distinguished record in the Senate. Moreover, his family's fortune had paved the way for his political career, and he had earned a well-justified reputation in Washington as a playboy and womanizer.

The outcome of the 1960 election turned on several factors. The country was experiencing a slight economic recession, reviving memories in older voters of the Great Depression, which had begun with the Republican Herbert Hoover in power. In addition, presidential candidates faced off on television for the first time, partici-pating in four televised debates. TV emphasized visual style and presentation. In the first debate, with Nixon having just recovered from a stay in the hospital and looking haggard, Kennedy convinced a majority of viewers that he possessed the presidential bearing for the job. Nixon performed better in the next three debates, but the dam-age had been done. Still, Kennedy had to overcome considerable religious prejudice to win the election. No Catholic had ever won the presidency, and the prejudices of Protestants, especially in the South, threatened to divert critical votes from Kennedy's Democratic base. While many southern Democrats supported Nixon, Kennedy bal-anced out these defections by gaining votes from the nation's Catholics, especially in northern states rich in electoral votes (Map 25.2).

Race also exerted a critical influence. Nixon and Kennedy had similar records on civil rights, and if anything, Nixon's was slightly stronger. However, on October 19, 1960, when Atlanta police arrested Martin Luther King Jr. for participating in a restaurant sit-in, Kennedy sprang to his defense, whereas Nixon kept his distance. Kennedy telephoned the civil rights leader's wife to offer his sympathy and used his influence to get King released from jail. As a result, Kennedy won back for Demo-crats 7 percent of black voters who had supported Eisenhower in 1956. Kennedy

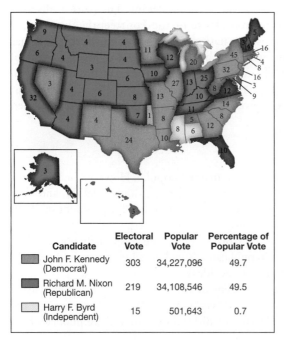

MAP 25.2   The Election of 1960
The 1960 presidential candidates differed little on major policy issues. John F. Kennedy gained the White House by winning back black voters who had supported Eisenhower, gaining crucial support from Catholic voters across the country, and appearing more presidential on the first televised debate in history. Still, his margin of victory was razor thin.

Candidate	Electoral Vote	Popular Vote	Percentage of Popular Vote
John F. Kennedy (Democrat)	303	34,227,096	49.7
Richard M. Nixon (Republican)	219	34,108,546	49.5
Harry F. Byrd (Independent)	15	501,643	0.7

triumphed by a margin of less than 1 percent of the popular vote, underscoring the importance of the African American electorate.

REVIEW & RELATE	• Why did Eisenhower adopt a moderate domestic agenda? What were his most notable domestic accomplishments and failures? • Why did Kennedy win the 1960 presidential election?

Conclusion: Postwar Politics and Culture

Following the end of World War II and a bumpy period of reconversion, the return of peace and prosperity fostered a baby boom that sent families scrambling for new housing and increasingly away from the cities. Suburbs grew as housing developers such as William Levitt built affordable, mass-produced homes and as the federal government provided loans and new highways that allowed suburban residents to commute to their urban jobs. With increased income, consumers purchased the latest models in automobiles as well as newly introduced televisions, reshaping how they spent their leisure time. As the wartime and baby boom generations entered their teenage years, their sheer numbers and general affluence helped make them a significant economic and cultural force. They poured their dollars into clothes, music, and other forms of entertainment, which reinforced their identity as teenagers and set them apart from adults.

The increasingly distinct teenage culture owed a great deal to African Americans, who contributed to the development of rock 'n' roll and revolutionized jazz and thereby influenced cultural challenges from teenage rebels and the beats. African Americans focused on tearing down the legal and institutional foundations of white supremacy. First in the courts and then in the streets, they confronted segregation and disfranchisement in the South. By the end of the 1950s, African Americans had persuaded the Supreme Court to reverse the doctrine of "separate but equal" that buttressed Jim Crow; they also won significant victories in desegregating buses in Montgomery, schools in Little Rock, and lunch counters in Greensboro. Black teenagers reinvigorated the civil rights movement through their boldness and energy, opening the path for even greater racial changes in the coming decade. In the North and West, African Americans faced a more subtle and enduring form of Jim Crow — **systemic racism** contained in housing practices, education, and criminal justice institutions. Other marginalized groups, inspired by the civil rights movement, pursued equal rights for themselves. In addition to struggles over racial equality, the 1950s witnessed serious tensions at home. Teenage cultural rebellion, sexual revolution, and McCarthyite witch-hunts, in addition to a bloody war in Korea, confronted the citizens of Alan Freed's and Grace Metalious's America. Nevertheless, the popular image of the 1950s as a tranquil and innocent period persists, with President Eisenhower remaining a symbol for the age. He provided moderate leadership that helped the country adjust to dramatic changes. His critics complained that the nation had lost its spirit of adventure, misplaced its ability to distinguish between community and conformity, failed to live up to ideals of racial and economic justice, and relinquished its primary place in the world. Nevertheless, most Americans emerging from decades of depression and war felt satisfied with the new lives they were building: They still liked Ike.

When the Republican Eisenhower left office in 1961, a new decade began with a Democratic president in charge. Yet the challenges that Eisenhower had faced and the diplomatic, social, and cultural forces that propelled them had not diminished. During the following years, many of the young people who had benefited from the peace and prosperity of the 1950s would lead the way in questioning the role of the United States in world affairs and its commitment to democracy, freedom, and equality at home.

Chapter 25 Review

KEY TERMS

Servicemen's Readjustment
  Act (GI Bill), 635
Taft-Hartley Act, 636
Levittown, 640
Sun Belt, 640
Beats, 645
To Secure These Rights, 647
Brown v. Board of Education of
  Topeka, Kansas, 648
Montgomery Improvement
  Association, 648

Southern Christian Leadership
  Conference (SCLC), 649
Little Rock Nine, 649
Student Nonviolent Coordinating
  Committee (SNCC), 650
Modern Republicanism, 654
National Interstate and Defense
  Highway Act, 654
systemic racism, 657

REVIEW & RELATE

1. How did the conversion from war to peacetime affect the economy, society, and politics in the United States?

2. What factors contributed to the economic and population growth of the 1950s, and how did they contribute to suburbanization and the growth in the Sun Belt?

3. What trends in American popular culture did the television shows and popular music of the 1950s reflect?

4. How did artists, writers, and social critics challenge the mainstream politics and culture of the 1950s?

5. What strategies did African Americans adopt in the 1940s and 1950s to fight segregation and discrimination? How did other racial and ethnic minorities pursue equality?

6. How and why did white southerners resist efforts to end segregation?

7. Why did Eisenhower adopt a moderate domestic agenda? What were his most notable domestic accomplishments and failures?

8. Why did Kennedy win the 1960 presidential election?

TIMELINE OF EVENTS

1940–1960	• Migration to Sun Belt swells region's population
1944	• Servicemen's Readjustment Act (GI Bill)
1945–1960	• U.S. gross national product soars 250 percent; 60 percent of Americans achieve middle-class status; union membership reaches new high
1947	• Taft-Hartley Act
	• President's Committee on Civil Rights issues *To Secure These Rights*
	• Jackie Robinson becomes the first black baseball player to enter the major leagues
1954–1958	• Eisenhower adopts Modern Republicanism and expands domestic programs
1954	• *Brown v. Board of Education of Topeka, Kansas* Supreme Court ruling
	• Operation Wetback
1955–1956	• Montgomery bus boycott
1955	• Jonas Salk develops polio vaccine
	• Emmett Till murdered
1956	• Grace Metalious publishes *Peyton Place*
	• National Interstate and Defense Highway Act
1957	• Martin Luther King Jr. and other black ministers form Southern Christian Leadership Conference (SCLC)
	• School desegregation in Little Rock, Arkansas, enforced
	• Soviet Union launches *Sputnik*
1960	• Student Nonviolent Coordinating Committee (SNCC) formed

26

Liberalism and Its Challengers

1960–1973

LEARNING OBJECTIVES

After reading this chapter you will be able to:

- Evaluate President Kennedy's approaches to liberalism at home and in foreign affairs.

- Explain how the civil rights movement succeeded in convincing the federal government to enact the Civil Rights Act of 1964 and the Voting Rights Act of 1965.

- Describe the major legislative accomplishments of the Great Society.

- Explain why U.S. intervention in Vietnam escalated in the 1960s.

- Examine the challenges to liberalism from the political left and right and analyze their similarities and differences.

COMPARING AMERICAN HISTORIES

As attorney general of California at the outset of World War II, **Earl Warren** helped convince President Franklin D. Roosevelt to order the relocation of 110,000 Japanese Americans. After the war, as governor, he continued to fight against perceived threats to national security by joining the anti-Communist crusade. In 1953 President Dwight D. Eisenhower appointed Warren to be chief justice of the United States, a choice that many observers saw as a safe conservative pick.

As chief justice, however, Warren defied expectations and instead led the Supreme Court in a liberal direction. In 1954 Warren wrote the landmark opinion ordering school desegregation in *Brown v. Board of Education of Topeka, Kansas*. The Warren Court did not shrink from controversy, and its rulings expanding the rights of accused criminals, banning prayer in public school classrooms, and upholding birth control as a right of privacy evoked harsh criticism from the police, religious fundamentalists, and conservative politicians.

Unlike Earl Warren, **Bayard Rustin** worked outside of regular political and social channels to achieve change. Rustin joined the Young Communist League in the 1930s because of its commitment to economic justice, racial equality, and international peace. As a committed pacifist, however, Rustin quit the organization in 1941 when the party supported U.S. intervention in World War II and retreated on its fight against racial discrimination during the war.

In 1942 Rustin helped found the Congress of Racial Equality (CORE), an interracial organization that pioneered nonviolent, direct-action protests against racial bias. Rustin was imprisoned from 1943 to 1946 for declining to perform alternative service after he refused to register for the military draft. Following his release, in 1947 Rustin helped plan and lead the Journey of Reconciliation, which challenged segregation on interstate buses in the South. In the 1950s and 1960s, he became an adviser to Martin Luther King Jr. and a major strategist in the civil rights movement.

Rustin remained active in various causes throughout his life. One of his last efforts was perhaps his most personal: the struggle against antigay prejudice. Rustin had to conceal his sexual identity at a time when the public and his political allies rejected homosexuals. In the 1980s, as the gay liberation movement grew more vocal, Rustin spoke out for tolerance and equality until his death in 1987.

THE AMERICAN HISTORIES of Earl Warren and Bayard Rustin demonstrate the complexity of social change. The federal government had the power to encourage social movements by interpreting the Constitution, enacting legislation, and enforcing the law in a manner that eliminated barriers to racial, sexual, and political equality. Yet federal action would not have happened without the pressure applied by activists like Rustin. As president, Lyndon Johnson took action with his Great Society programs, but his escalation of the war in Vietnam divided his party and generated opposition from young activists on the left. At the same time, efforts to promote equality and social justice, along with the military stalemate in Vietnam, produced a strong reaction from conservatives who sought to roll back liberal gains; pursue their own policies of small government, low taxes, and self-reliance; and bring about an end to the war.

The Politics of Liberalism

Hoping to build on the legacy of the New Deal, liberals sought to increase the role of the federal government in the economy, education, and health care. Most liberals supported a staunchly anti-Communist foreign policy, differing with Republicans more over means than over ends. Indeed, when Democrats recaptured the White House in 1960, they seized opportunities in Cuba and Southeast Asia to vigorously challenge the expansion of Soviet influence.

Kennedy's New Frontier

With victory in World War II and the revival of economic prosperity, liberal thinkers regained confidence in capitalism. Many saw the postwar American free-enterprise system as different from the old-style capitalism that had existed before Franklin Roosevelt's New Deal. In their view, this new "reform capitalism," or democratic capitalism, created abundance for all and not just for the elites. Rather than pushing for the redistribution of wealth, liberals now called on the government to help create conditions conducive to economic growth and increased productivity. The liberal economist John Kenneth Galbraith argued in *The Affluent Society* (1958) that increased public investments in education, research, and development were the key to American prosperity and progress.

These ideas guided the thinking of Democratic politicians such as Senator John F. Kennedy of Massachusetts. Elected president in 1960, the forty-three-year-old Kennedy brought good looks, charm, a beautiful wife, and young children to the White House. Kennedy pledged a **New Frontier** to battle "tyranny, poverty, disease, and war," but lacking strong majorities in Congress, he contented himself with making small gains on the New Deal's foundation. Congress expanded unemployment benefits, increased the minimum wage, extended Social Security benefits, and raised appropriations for public housing, but Kennedy's caution disappointed many liberals.

Kennedy, the Cold War, and Cuba

The Kennedy administration showed greater zeal in fighting the Cold War abroad. The president believed that America's reform capitalism should become a global model. Communism, like fascism before it, posed a fundamental threat to American interests and to other countries' ability to emulate the economic miracle of the United States. The faith of liberals in U.S. ingenuity, willpower, technological superiority, and moral righteousness encouraged them to reshape the "free world" in America's image.

President Kennedy's first Cold War battle took place in Cuba. Before his election, Kennedy learned of a secret CIA plan, devised by the Eisenhower administration, to topple Fidel Castro from power. After becoming president, Kennedy approved the scheme that Eisenhower had set in motion.

The operation ended disastrously. On April 17, 1961, the invasion force of between 1,400 and 1,500 Cuban exiles, trained by the CIA, landed by boat at the Bay of Pigs on Cuba's southwest coast. Kennedy refused to provide backup military forces for fear of revealing the U.S. role in the attack. Castro's troops defeated the insurgents in three days. CIA planners had underestimated Cuban popular support for Castro, falsely believing that the invasion would inspire a national uprising against the Communist regime. The Kennedy administration had blundered into a bitter foreign policy defeat (Map 26.1).

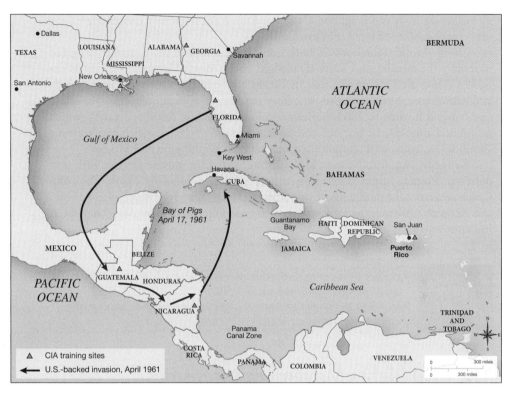

MAP 26.1   The Bay of Pigs Invasion, 1961
President Kennedy launched the Bay of Pigs invasion on April 17, 1961 to topple the Communist regime of Fidel Castro. The CIA secretly trained Cuban exiles in locations in the southern United States, Central America, and the Caribbean. After three days of fighting, the invasion failed and turned Castro into a national hero, thereby strengthening his leadership. Fearing further U.S. aggression, Castro turned to the Soviet Union to install missiles in Cuba for protection.

Two months later, Kennedy met Soviet leader Nikita Khrushchev at a summit meeting in Vienna. Khrushchev took advantage of the president's embarrassing defeat in Cuba to press his own demands. After the confrontational summit meeting raised tensions between the superpowers, Kennedy persuaded Congress to increase the defense budget, dispatch additional troops to Europe, and bolster civil defense. In August, the Soviets responded by constructing a wall through Berlin, making it more difficult for refugees to flee from East Berlin to West Berlin.

Despite the Bay of Pigs disaster, the United States continued its efforts to topple the Castro regime. Such attempts were uniformly unsuccessful, but a wary Castro invited the Soviet Union to install short- and intermediate-range missiles in Cuba to protect the country against any U.S. incursion. On October 22, 1962, Kennedy went on national television to inform the American people that the Soviets had placed missiles in Cuba. The Kennedy administration decided to blockade Cuba to prevent Soviet ships from supplying the deadly warheads that would make the missiles fully operational. If Soviet ships defied the blockade, the president would order air strikes on its island neighbor. Ordinary Americans nervously contemplated the very real possibility of nuclear destruction.

On the brink of nuclear war, both sides chose compromise. Khrushchev agreed to remove the missiles, and Kennedy pledged not to invade Cuba and secretly promised to dismantle U.S. missile sites in Turkey aimed at the Soviet Union. Kennedy and Khrushchev, having stepped back from the edge of nuclear holocaust, worked to ease tensions further. In 1963 they signed a Partial Nuclear Test Ban Treaty—which prohibited atmospheric but not underground testing—and installed an electronic "hot line" to ensure swift communications between Washington and Moscow.

Kennedy sought to balance his hard-line, anti-Communist policies with new outreach efforts to inspire developing nations to follow a democratic path. The Peace Corps program sent thousands of volunteers to teach and advise developing nations, and Kennedy's Alliance for Progress supplied economic aid to emerging democracies in Latin America.

REVIEW & RELATE	• How did President Kennedy's domestic agenda reflect the liberal political ideology of the early 1960s? • Evaluate Kennedy's and Khrushchev's actions in the Cuban missile crisis. How was war averted?

The Civil Rights Movement Intensifies, 1961–1968

At home, the most critical issue facing the nation in the early 1960s was the intensification of the civil rights movement. As a candidate, Kennedy had promised vigorous action on civil rights, but as president he did little to follow through on his promises. With southern Democrats occupying key positions in Congress and threatening to block any civil rights proposals, Kennedy sought to mollify this critical component of his political base. Following Kennedy's death in 1963, President Johnson succeeded in breaking the legislative logjam and signed into law three major pieces of civil rights legislation. He did so under considerable pressure from the civil rights movement. At the height of their triumphs, however, many civil rights activists became increasingly skeptical of nonviolence and integration and turned to the self-determination of black power.

Freedom Rides

Similar to Bayard Rustin's efforts in the 1940s to challenge discrimination, the Congress of Racial Equality took action. CORE mounted racially integrated **Freedom Rides** to test whether facilities in the South were complying with the 1960 Supreme Court ruling that outlawed segregated bus and train stations serving passengers who were traveling interstate. CORE alerted the Justice Department and the FBI of its plans for May 4, 1961, but the riders received no protection when Ku Klux Klan–dominated mobs in Anniston and Birmingham, Alabama attacked two of its buses, seriously wounding several activists.

After safety concerns forced CORE to forgo the rest of the trip, members of the Student Nonviolent Coordinating Committee (SNCC) rushed to Birmingham to continue the bus rides. The Kennedy administration urged them to reconsider, but Diane Nash, a SNCC founder, explained that although the group realized the peril of resuming the journey, "we can't let them stop us with violence. If we do, the movement is dead." When the replenished busload of riders reached Montgomery on May 20, they were brutally assaulted by a mob. Dr. Martin Luther King Jr. subsequently held a rally in a Montgomery church, where white mobs threatened the lives of King and the Freedom Riders inside the building. Faced with the prospect of more bloodshed, the Kennedy administration dispatched federal marshals to the scene and persuaded the governor to call out the Alabama National Guard to ensure the safety of everyone in the church.

The president and his brother, Attorney General Robert Kennedy, worked out a compromise to let the rides continue with minimal violence, and with minimal publicity. The Cold War worked in favor of the protesters. With the Soviet Union publicizing the violence against Freedom Riders in the South, the Kennedy administration attempted to preserve America's image abroad by persuading the Interstate Commerce Commission to issue an order prohibiting segregated transportation facilities. Still, southern whites resisted. When Freedom Riders encountered opposition in Albany, Georgia, in the fall of 1961, SNCC workers remained in Albany and helped local leaders organize residents against segregation and other forms of racial discrimination. Even with the assistance of Dr. King and the Southern Christian Leadership Conference (SCLC), the Albany movement stalled.

Kennedy Supports Civil Rights

Despite the setback in Albany, the civil rights movement kept up pressure on other fronts. In September 1962 Mississippi governor Ross Barnett tried to thwart the registration of James Meredith as an undergraduate at the University of Mississippi. Barnett's obstruction precipitated a riot on campus, and President Kennedy dispatched army troops and federalized the Mississippi National Guard to restore order, but not before two bystanders were killed.

The following year, King and the SCLC joined the Reverend Fred Shuttlesworth's movement in Birmingham, Alabama, in its battle against discrimination, segregation, and police brutality. With the white supremacist Eugene "Bull" Connor in charge of law enforcement, civil rights protesters, including children from age six to sixteen, encountered violent resistance, vicious police dogs, and high-powered water hoses. Connor ordered mass arrests, including Dr. King's, prompting the minister to write his famous "Letter from Birmingham Jail," in which he justified the use of nonviolent direct action. Seeking to defuse the crisis, President Kennedy sent an emissary in early May 1963 to negotiate a peaceful solution that granted concessions to Birmingham blacks and ended the demonstrations. On Sunday, September 15, 1963, however, the Ku Klux Klan dynamited Birmingham's Sixteenth Street Baptist Church, a freedom movement staging ground. The blast killed four young girls attending services.

Even before this brutal bombing, the president had finally embraced the nation's duty to guarantee equal rights regardless of race. On June 11, 1963, shortly after negotiating the Birmingham agreement, Kennedy delivered a nationally televised address. He acknowledged that the country faced a "moral crisis" heightened by the events in Birmingham, and he noted the difficulty of preaching "freedom around the world" while "this is a land of the free except for Negroes." He proposed congressional legislation to end segregation in public accommodations, increase federal power to promote school desegregation, and broaden the right to vote.

Events on the day Kennedy delivered his powerful speech reinforced the need for swift action. Earlier that morning, Alabama governor George C. Wallace stood in front of the administration building at the University of Alabama to block the entrance of two black undergraduates. To uphold the federal court decree ordering their admission, Kennedy deployed federal marshals and the Alabama National Guard, and Wallace, having dramatized his point, stepped aside. However, victory soon turned into tragedy. That evening Medgar Evers, the head of the NAACP in Mississippi, was shot and killed in the driveway of his Jackson home by the white supremacist Byron de la Beckwith. (Following two trials, de la Beckwith remained free until 1994, when he was retried and convicted for Evers's murder.)

Congress was still unwilling to act. To increase pressure on lawmakers, civil rights organizations held the **March on Washington for Jobs and Freedom** on August 28, 1963, carrying out an idea first proposed by A. Philip Randolph in 1941 (see "The Origins of the Civil Rights Movement" in chapter 23). With Randolph as honorary chair, his associate Bayard Rustin directed the proceedings as 250,000 black and white peaceful protesters rallied in front of the Lincoln Memorial. Two speakers in particular caught the attention of the crowd. John Lewis, the chairman of SNCC, expressed the frustration of blacks with both the Kennedy administration and Congress. "The revolution is at hand. . . . We will not wait for the President, nor the Justice Department, nor Congress," Lewis asserted. "But we will take matters into our own hands." In a more conciliatory tone, King delivered a speech expressing his dream for racial and religious brotherhood. Still, King issued a stern warning to "those who hope that the Negro needed to blow off steam and will now be content. . . . There will be neither rest nor tranquility in America until the Negro is granted his citizenship rights."

If civil rights leaders hoped to elicit additional support from the Kennedy administration, their hopes were dashed. On November 22, 1963, Lee Harvey Oswald shot President Kennedy as he rode in an open motorcade in Dallas, Texas. The assassination prompted an outpouring of public grief. In death, Kennedy achieved immense popularity, yet he left many problems unresolved. His legislative agenda, including civil rights, remained unfulfilled. It was up to Vice President Lyndon Johnson to step into the breach.

Freedom Summer and Voting Rights

Following Kennedy's death, President Johnson took charge of the pending civil rights legislation. Under his leadership, a bipartisan coalition passed the **Civil Rights Act of 1964**. The law prohibited discrimination in public accommodations, increased federal enforcement of school desegregation and the right to vote, and created the Community Relations Service, a federal agency authorized to help resolve racial conflicts. The act also contained a final measure to combat employment discrimination on the basis of race and sex.

Yet even as President Johnson signed the Civil Rights Act into law on July 2, black freedom forces launched a new initiative to secure the right to vote in the South. The 1964 act contained a voting rights provision but did little to address the main problems of the discriminatory use of literacy tests and poll taxes and the biased administration of registration procedures that kept the majority of southern blacks from registering. Beatings, killings, acts of arson, and arrests became a routine response to voting rights efforts. Although the Justice Department filed lawsuits against recalcitrant voter registrars and police officers, the government refused to send in federal personnel or instruct the FBI to safeguard vulnerable civil rights workers.

To focus national attention on this problem, SNCC, CORE, the NAACP, and the SCLC launched the **Freedom Summer** project in Mississippi. They assigned eight hundred volunteers from around the nation, mainly white college students, to work with local black community organizers on voter registration drives and in "freedom schools" to improve education for rural black youngsters. White supremacists fought back against what they perceived as an enemy invasion. In late June 1964, the Ku Klux Klan, in collusion with local law enforcement officials, killed three civil rights workers. This tragedy provoked national outrage, and President Johnson pressed the usually uncooperative FBI to find the culprits, which it did. However, civil rights workers continued to encounter white violence and harassment throughout Freedom Summer.

One outcome of the Freedom Summer project was the creation of the **Mississippi Freedom Democratic Party (MFDP)**. Because the regular state Democratic Party excluded blacks, the civil rights coalition formed an alternative Democratic Party open to everyone. In August 1964 the mostly black MFDP sent a delegation to the Democratic National Convention, meeting in Atlantic City, New Jersey, to challenge the seating of the all-white delegation from Mississippi. One MFDP delegate, Fannie Lou Hamer, who had lost her job for her voter registration activities, offered passionate testimony that was broadcast on television. President Johnson then hammered out a compromise that gave the MFDP two at-large seats, seated members of the regular delegation who took a loyalty oath, and prohibited racial discrimination in the future by any state Democratic Party. While both sides rejected the deal, four years later an integrated delegation, which included Hamer, represented Mississippi at the Democratic National Convention in Chicago.

Freedom Summer highlighted the problem of disfranchisement, but it took further demonstrations in Selma, Alabama, to resolve it. After state troopers shot and killed a black voting rights demonstrator in February 1965, Dr. King called for a march from Selma to the capital, Montgomery, to petition Governor Wallace to end the violence and allow blacks to vote. On Sunday, March 7, as black and white marchers, including John Lewis, left Selma, the sheriff's forces sprayed them with tear gas, beat them, and sent them running for their lives. A few days later, a white clergyman who had joined the protesters was killed by a group of white thugs. On March 21, following another failed attempt to march to Montgomery, King finally led protesters on the fifty-mile hike to the state capital, where they arrived safely four days later. Still, after the march, the Ku Klux Klan murdered a white female marcher from Michigan.

Events in Selma prompted President Johnson to take action. On March 15 he addressed a joint session of Congress and told lawmakers and a nationally televised audience that the black "cause must be our cause too." On August 6, 1965, the president signed the **Voting Rights Act**, which banned the use of literacy tests for voter registration, authorized a federal lawsuit against the poll tax (which succeeded in 1966), empowered federal officials to register disfranchised voters, and required seven southern states to submit any voting changes to Washington before they went into effect. With strong federal enforcement of the law, by 1968 a majority of black southerners and nearly two-thirds of black Mississippians could vote (Figure 26.1).

These civil rights victories had exacted a huge toll on the movement. SNCC and CORE came to distrust Presidents Kennedy and Johnson for failing to provide protection for voter registration workers. Furthermore, Johnson's attempt to broker a compromise at the 1964 Atlantic City Convention convinced MFDP supporters that the liberal president had sold them out. The once united movement showed signs of splintering.

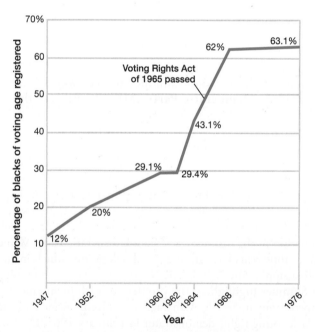

FIGURE 26.1   Black Voter Registration in the South, 1947–1976
After World War II, the percentage of black adults registered to vote in the South slowly but steadily increased, largely as a result of grassroots voting drives. Despite the Kennedy administration's support for voter registration drives, a majority of southern blacks remained prohibited from voting in 1964. The passage of the 1965 Voting Rights Act removed barriers such as literacy tests and poll taxes, strengthened the federal government's enforcement powers, and enabled more than 60 percent of southern blacks to vote by the late 1960s. Compare the growth of black voter registration during the Eisenhower (1953–1961), Kennedy (1961–1963), and Johnson (1963–1969) administrations.   Source: Data from David Garrow, *Protest at Selma* (New Haven, CT: Yale University Press, 1978), and U.S. Department of Commerce, Bureau of the Census, *Statistical Abstract of the United States*, 1976.

Civil Rights and Black Power

Increasingly after 1964, SNCC and CORE began exploring new ways of seeking freedom through strategies of black self-determination and self-defense. They were greatly influenced by Malcolm X. Born Malcolm Little, he had engaged in a life of crime, which landed him in prison. Inside jail, he converted to the Nation of Islam, a religious sect based partly on Muslim teachings and partly on the belief that white people were devils (not a doctrine associated with orthodox Islam). After his release from jail, Malcolm rejected his "slave name" and substituted the letter X to symbolize his unknown African forebears. Minister Malcolm helped convert thousands of disciples in black neighborhoods by denouncing whites and encouraging blacks to embrace their African heritage and beauty as a people. Favoring self-defense over nonviolence, he criticized civil rights leaders for failing to protect their communities. After 1963, Malcolm X broke away from the Nation of Islam, visited the Middle East and Africa, and accepted the teachings of traditional Islam. He moderated his anti-white rhetoric but remained committed to black self-determination. He had already influenced the growing number of disillusioned young black activists when, in 1965, members of the Nation of Islam murdered him, apparently in revenge for challenging the organization.

Black militants, echoing Malcolm X's ideas, challenged racial liberalism. They renounced the principles of integration and nonviolence in favor of black power and self-defense. Instead of welcoming whites within their organizations, black radicals believed that African Americans had to assert their independence from white America. In 1966 SNCC expelled white members and created an all-black organization. Stokely Carmichael, SNCC's chairman, proclaimed "black power" as the central goal of the freedom struggle and linked the cause of African American freedom to revolutionary conflicts in Cuba, Africa, and Vietnam.

Despite differences in tactics and philosophy, both the civil rights and black power movements grew out of the broader African American freedom struggle and sought full citizenship for African Americans without diminishing their black cultural heritage. Many civil rights leaders emerged from black universities, churches, and civic groups. Black power activists such as Stokely Carmichael had gained experience working in southern black communities during the civil rights movement. In addition, both movements maintained contact with African liberation struggles and supported their anti-colonial efforts.

Black power gained notoriety against a backdrop of riots in black neighborhoods, which erupted across the nation starting in the mid-1960s: in Harlem and Rochester, New York, in 1964; in Los Angeles in 1965; and in Cleveland, Chicago, Detroit, Newark, and Tampa in the following two years. Urban blacks, many in the North and West, faced problems of high unemployment, dilapidated housing, and police mistreatment that civil rights legislation had done nothing to correct. While many whites perceived the uprisings solely as an exercise in criminal behavior, many blacks viewed the violence as an expression of political discontent—as rebellions, not riots. Even nonviolence proponents such as Dr. King recognized the source of frustration behind the uprisings. "In the final analysis," King explained in 1967, "a riot is the language of the unheard. . . . Social justice and progress are the absolute guarantors of riot prevention." The Kerner Commission, appointed by President Johnson to

Malcolm X   A charismatic minister in the Nation of Islam, Malcom X preached a fiery message of black nationalism and self-defense, ideas that later merged into the ideology of black power. Though his message drew criticism from liberal whites and black civil rights leaders, Malcolm X appealed to many African Americans. In this July 27, 1963 rally in Harlem, he holds up a copy of Muhammed Speaks, the Nation of Islam newspaper.   Underwood Archives/Getty Images

assess urban disorders and chaired by Governor Otto Kerner of Illinois, concluded in 1968 that white racism remained at the heart of the problem: "Our nation is moving toward two societies, one black, one white—separate and unequal."

New groups emerged to take up the cause of black power. In 1966 Huey P. Newton and Bobby Seale, college students in Oakland, California, formed the **Black Panther Party**. Dressed in black leather, sporting black berets, and carrying guns, the Panthers appealed mainly to black men. The Panthers also sought to make improvements in their neighborhoods. They established day care centers and health facilities, often run by women, which gained the admiration of many in their communities. Much of this good work was overshadowed by violent confrontations with the police, which led to the deaths of Panthers in shootouts and the imprisonment of key party officials. By the early 1970s, government crackdowns on the Black Panthers had destabilized the organization and reduced its influence.

The assassination of Martin Luther King Jr. in 1968 furthered black disillusionment. King was shot and killed by James Earl Ray in Memphis, where he was supporting demonstrations by striking sanitation workers. In the wake of his murder, riots erupted in hundreds of cities throughout the country. Little noticed amid the fiery turbulence, President Johnson signed into law the 1968 Fair Housing Act, the final piece of civil rights legislation of his term.

**REVIEW &
RELATE**

- How did civil rights activists pressure state and federal
  government officials to enact their agenda?
- How were the civil rights and black power movements similar and
  in what ways were they different?

Federal Efforts toward Social Reform, 1964–1968

President Johnson's liberal accomplishments reached beyond civil rights, and he drew on Kennedy's legacy and his own considerable political skills to win passage of the most important items on the liberal agenda. While Johnson pressed ahead in the legislative arena, Chief Justice Earl Warren's Supreme Court issued rulings that extended social justice to marginalized people and favored those who believed in a firm separation of church and state, free speech, and a right to privacy.

The Great Society

In an address at the University of Michigan on May 22, 1964, President Johnson sketched out his dream for the **Great Society**, one that "rests on abundance and liberty for all. It demands an end to poverty and racial injustice, to which we are totally committed in our time."

Besides poverty and race, he outlined three broad areas in need of reform: education, the environment, and cities. Toward this end, the Elementary and Secondary School Act (1965) was the most far-reaching federal law ever passed. It provided federal funds directly to public schools to improve their quality. The Model Cities program (1966) set up the Department of Housing and Urban Affairs, which coordinated efforts at urban planning and rebuilding neighborhoods in decaying cities. The Department of Transportation sought to ensure a fast, safe, and convenient transportation system. In addition, the president pushed Congress to pass hundreds of environmental protection laws, including those dealing with air and water pollution, waste disposal, the use of natural resources, and the preservation of wildlife and wilderness areas.

The War on Poverty came with passage of the Economic Opportunity Act of 1964. Through this measure, Johnson wanted to offer the poor "a hand up, not a handout." Among its major components, the law provided job training, food stamps, rent supplements, redevelopment of depressed rural areas, remedial education (later to include the preschool program Head Start), a domestic Peace Corps called Volunteers in Service to America (VISTA), and a Community Action Program that empowered the poor to shape policies affecting their own communities. Between 1965 and 1968, expenditures targeted for the poor doubled, from $6 billion to $12 billion. The antipoverty program helped reduce the proportion of poor people from 20 percent in 1963 to 13 percent five years later, and it helped reduce the rate of black poverty from 40 percent to 20 percent during this same period.

Johnson intended to fight the War on Poverty through the engine of economic growth, which would create new jobs for the unemployed without redistributing wealth. With this in mind, he persuaded Congress to enact significant tax cuts. Johnson's tax cut, which applied across the board, stimulated the economy and sent the gross national product soaring from $591 billion in 1963 to $977 billion by the end of the decade. Despite the gains made, many liberals believed that Johnson's spending on the War on Poverty did not go far enough. Whatever the shortcomings, Johnson campaigned on his antipoverty and civil rights record in his bid to recapture the White House in 1964. His Republican opponent, Senator Barry M. Goldwater of Arizona, personified the conservative right wing of the Republican Party. The Arizona senator condemned big government, supported states' rights, and accused liberals of not waging the Cold War forcefully enough. His aggressive conservatism appealed to his grassroots base in small-town America, especially in southern California, the Southwest, and the South. His tough rhetoric, however, scared off moderate Republicans, resulting on election day in a landslide for Johnson as well as considerable Democratic majorities in Congress.

Flush with victory, Johnson pushed Congress to move quickly. Among its accomplishments, the Eighty-ninth Congress (1965–1967) subsidized health care for the elderly and the poor by creating Medicare and Medicaid, expanded voting rights for African Americans in the South, raised the minimum wage, and created national endowments for the fine arts and the humanities. The 1965 Immigration Act repealed discriminatory national origins quotas established in 1924, resulting in a shift of immigration from Europe to Asia and Central and South America (Table 26.1). With immigration on the rise, President Johnson signed into law the 1968 Bilingual Education Act, which provided federal funds to improve education for students who spoke little or no English.

The Warren Court

The Warren Court reflected this high tide of liberalism. In 1967, the justices overturned state laws prohibiting interracial marriages. A year later, fourteen years after the *Brown* decision, they ruled that school districts in the South could no longer maintain racially exclusive schools and must desegregate immediately. In a series of cases, the Warren Court ensured fairer legislative representation for blacks and whites by removing the disproportionate power that rural districts had held over urban districts.

The Supreme Court's most controversial rulings dealt with the criminal justice system, religion, and private sexual practices. Strengthening the rights of criminal defendants, the justices ruled in *Gideon v. Wainwright* (1963) that states had to provide indigents accused of felonies with an attorney, and in *Miranda v. Arizona* (1966) they ordered the police to advise suspects of their constitutional rights. The Court also moved into controversial territory concerning school prayer, contraception, and pornography. In 1962 the Court outlawed a nondenominational Christian prayer recited in New York State schools as a violation of the separation of church and state guaranteed by the First Amendment. Three years later, in *Griswold v. Connecticut*, the justices struck down a state law that banned the sale of contraceptives because such laws, they contended, infringed on an individual's right to privacy. In a 1966 case the justices ruled that states could not prohibit what they deemed pornographic material unless it was "utterly without redeeming social value," a standard that opened the door for the dissemination of sexually explicit books, magazines, and films. These verdicts unleashed a firestorm of criticism, especially from religious groups that accused the Warren Court of undermining traditional values of faith and decency.

REVIEW & RELATE
- What problems and challenges did Johnson's Great Society legislation target?
- In what ways did the Warren Court's rulings advance the liberal agenda?

TABLE 26.1   **MAJOR GREAT SOCIETY MEASURES, 1964–1968**

Year	Legislation or Order	Purpose
1964	Civil Rights Act	Prohibited discrimination in public accommodations, education, and employment
	Economic Opportunity Act	Established War on Poverty agencies: Head Start, VISTA, Job Corps, and Community Action Program
1965	Elementary and Secondary Education Act	Federal funding for elementary and secondary schools
	Medical Care Act	Provided Medicare health insurance for citizens sixty-five years and older and Medicaid health benefits for the poor
	Voting Rights Act	Banned literacy tests for voting, authorized federal registrars to be sent into seven southern states, and monitored voting changes in these states
	Executive Order 11246	Required employers to take affirmative action to promote equal opportunity and remedy the effects of past discrimination
	Immigration and Nationality Act	Abolished quotas on immigration that reduced immigration from non-Western and southern and eastern European nations
	Water Quality Act	Established and enforced federal water quality standards
	Air Quality Act	Established air pollution standards for motor vehicles
	National Arts and Humanities Act	Established National Endowment of the Humanities and National Endowment of the Arts to support the work of scholars, writers, artists, and musicians
1966	Model Cities Act	Approved funding for the rehabilitation of inner cities
1967	Executive Order 11375	Expanded affirmative action regulations to include women
1968	Civil Rights Act	Outlawed discrimination in housing
1968	Bilingual Education Act	Provided bilingual education for students of limited English-speaking ability

The Vietnam War, 1961–1969

While substantial progress was made on civil rights and liberal reforms at home, the Kennedy and Johnson administrations enjoyed far less success in fighting communism abroad. Following the overthrow of French colonial rule in Vietnam in 1954, the Cold War spread to Southeast Asia, where the United States applied the doctrine of containment (see "Early Intervention in Vietnam, 1954–1960" in chapter 24). Mistaking the situation in Vietnam as a war of outside Communist aggression, the United States deployed hundreds of thousands of troops to fight in what was, instead, a civil war.

Kennedy's Intervention in South Vietnam

President Kennedy believed that if Communists toppled one regime in Asia it would produce a "domino effect," with one country after another falling to the Communists. Kennedy also believed that aggressive nations that attacked weaker ones threatened world peace unless they were challenged.

Kennedy's containment efforts in Vietnam ran into difficulty because the United States did not control the situation on the ground. The U.S.-backed president of South Vietnam, Ngo Dinh Diem, had spent more than $1 billion of American aid on building up military and personal security forces to suppress political opposition rather than implement the economic and political reforms that he had promised. In 1961 Kennedy sent military advisers to help the South Vietnamese fight the Communists, but the situation deteriorated in 1963 when the Catholic Diem prohibited the country's Buddhist majority from holding religious celebrations. In protest, Buddhist monks committed suicide by setting themselves on fire, a grisly display captured on television news programs in the United States. With political opposition mounting against Diem and with the war going poorly, the Kennedy administration endorsed a military coup to replace the Diem government. On November 1, 1963, the coup leaders removed Diem from office, assassinated the deposed president and key members of his regime, and installed a military government.

Diem's death, however, did little to improve the war against the Communists. The National Liberation Front (Vietcong), Communist political and military forces living in South Vietnam and sponsored by Ho Chi Minh, had more support in the rural countryside than did the South Vietnamese government. The rebels promised economic and political reforms and recruited local peasants opposed to the corruption and ruthlessness of the Diem regime. The Kennedy administration committed itself to supporting Diem's successor, but by late November 1963 Kennedy seemed torn between sending more American troops and finding a way to negotiate a peace.

Johnson Escalates the War in Vietnam

When Lyndon Johnson took office after Kennedy's assassination, there were 16,000 American military personnel in Vietnam. Privately, Johnson harbored reservations about fighting in Vietnam, but he feared appearing soft on communism and was concerned that a demonstration of weakness would jeopardize congressional support for his domestic plans. Although Johnson eventually concluded that more U.S. forces had to be sent to Vietnam, he waited for the right moment to rally Congress and the American public behind an escalation of the war.

That moment came in August 1964. On August 2, North Vietnamese gunboats attacked an American spy ship sixty miles off the North Vietnamese coast in the Gulf of Tonkin. Two days later, another U.S. destroyer reported coming under torpedo attack, but because of stormy weather the second ship was not certain that it had been fired on. Neither ship suffered any damage. Despite the considerable uncertainty about what actually happened with the second ship, Johnson seized the opportunity to urge Congress to authorize military action. On August 7 Congress passed the **Gulf of Tonkin Resolution**, which provided the president with unlimited power to make military decisions regarding Vietnam.

After winning election in 1964, President Johnson stepped up U.S. military action. In March 1965, with North Vietnamese forces flooding into the South, the president initiated a massive bombing campaign called Operation Rolling Thunder. For more than three years, American planes dropped a million tons of bombs on North Vietnam, more than the total amount the United States used in World War II. Despite this massive firepower, the operation proved ineffective. A largely agricultural country, North Vietnam did not have the type of industrial targets best suited for air attacks. It stored its vital military resources underground and was able to reconstruct rudimentary bridges and roads to maintain the flow of troops into the South within hours after U.S. bombers had pounded them.

Responding to the need to protect American air bases and the persistent ineffectiveness of the South Vietnamese military, Johnson deployed ever-increasing numbers of ground troops to Vietnam. Troop levels rose from 16,000 in 1963 to 536,000 in 1968. The U.S. military also deployed napalm bombs, which spewed burning jellied gasoline, and Agent Orange, a chemical that denuded the Vietnamese countryside and produced long-term adverse health effects for those who came in contact with it, including American soldiers. These attacks added to the resentment of South Vietnamese peasants and helped the Vietcong gain new recruits.

The United States confronted a challenging guerrilla war in Vietnam. The Vietcong fought at night and blended in during the day as ordinary residents of cities and villages. They did not provide a visible target, and they recruited women and men of all ages, making it difficult for U.S. ground forces to distinguish friend from foe. In the end, the U.S. military effort alienated the population they were designed to safeguard.

On the ground, frustration also bred racism, as many American soldiers could not relate to the Vietnamese way of life and dismissed the enemy as "gooks." This attitude helped push some troops over the line between legitimate warfare and murder. Frustrated by rising casualties from an enemy they could not see, some American soldiers indiscriminately burned down villages and killed noncombatant civilians. Such contemptible behavior peaked in March 1968 when an American platoon murdered between 347 and 504 unarmed Vietnamese civilians in the village of My Lai, an event that came to be known as the My Lai massacre.

The My Lai carnage came in the wake of the **Tet Offensive**. On January 31, 1968, the Buddhist New Year of Tet, some 67,000 Communist forces mounted a

My Lai Massacre, 1968   On March 16, 1968, U.S. army soldiers killed hundreds of unarmed civilians—most of them women, children, and the elderly—in the village of My Lai. The soldiers left bodies piled in ditches that ran around the village. The massacre became public in 1969, but only one soldier was convicted by a military tribunal. Ronald S. Haeberle/The LIFE Images Collection/Getty Images

surprise offensive throughout South Vietnam that targeted major population centers (Map 26.2). For six hours, a suicide squadron of Vietcong surrounded the U.S. Embassy in Saigon. U.S. forces finally repelled the Tet Offensive, but the battle proved psychologically costly to the United States. Following it, the most revered television news anchor of the era, Walter Cronkite of CBS, turned against the war and expressed the doubts of a growing number of viewers when he announced: "To say that we are mired in stalemate seems the only reasonable, yet unsatisfactory conclusion."

Tet marked the beginning of the end of the war's escalation. On March 31, 1968, President Johnson ordered a halt to the bombing campaign and called for peace negotiations. He also stunned the nation by announcing that he would not seek reelection. By the time Johnson left the White House in 1969, peace negotiations had stalled and some 36,000 Americans had died in combat, along with 52,000 South Vietnamese troops. The escalation of the war had exacted another high price as well: It created a crisis of public confidence in government and turned many ordinary Americans into dissenters against the political establishment.

REVIEW & RELATE	• Why did Kennedy and Johnson escalate the Vietnam War? • How did the reality of the war on the ground compare with the political and military assumptions for fighting it?

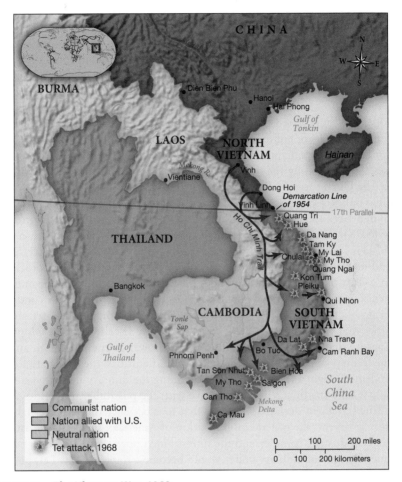

MAP 26.2   The Vietnam War, 1968
The United States wielded vastly more military personnel and weaponry than the Vietcong and North Vietnamese but faced a formidable challenge in fighting a guerrilla war in a foreign country. Massive American bombing failed to defeat the North Vietnamese or stop their troop movements and supply lines along the Ho Chi Minh Trail. The 1968 Tet Offensive demonstrated the shortcomings in the U.S. strategy.

Challenges to the Liberal Establishment

Even at its peak in the 1960s, liberalism faced major challenges from both the left and the right. Young activists became impatient with what they saw as the slow pace of social progress and were increasingly distressed by the escalation of the Vietnam War. At the same time, the right was disturbed by the failure of the United States to win the war as well as by the liberal reforms they believed diminished individual initiative and benefited racial minorities at the expense of the white middle class. Conservatives depicted the left as unpatriotic and out of step with mainstream American values. By 1969 Richard M. Nixon, a political conservative, had captured the White House.

The New Left

The civil rights movement had inspired many young people to activism. Combining ideals of freedom, equality, and community with direct-action protest, civil rights activists offered a model for those seeking to address a variety of problems, including the threat of nuclear devastation, the loss of individual autonomy in a corporate society, racism, poverty, sexism, and environmental degradation. The formation of SNCC in 1960 illuminated the possibilities for personal and social transformation and offered a movement culture founded on democracy.

Tom Hayden helped apply the ideals of SNCC to predominantly white college campuses. After spending the summer of 1961 registering voters in Mississippi and Georgia, the University of Michigan graduate student returned to campus eager to recruit like-minded students who questioned America's commitment to democracy.

Hayden became an influential leader of the **Students for a Democratic Society (SDS)**, which advocated the formation of a "New Left." They considered the "Old Left," which revolved around attraction to the Communist Party, as autocratic and no longer relevant. "We are people of this generation," SDS proclaimed, "bred in at least modest comfort, housed now in universities, looking uncomfortably to the world we inherit." In its **Port Huron Statement** (1962), SDS condemned mainstream liberal politics, Cold War foreign policy, racism, and research-oriented universities that cared little for their undergraduates. It called for the adoption of "participatory democracy," which would return power to the people. In an ironic twist, the framers of the manifesto picked up the rhetoric of the moderate Republican president, Dwight Eisenhower, in condemning the military-industrial complex. "Not only is ours the first generation to live with the possibility of world-wide cataclysm," the statement declared, "it is the first to experience the actual social preparation for cataclysm, the general militarization of American society." The attack on the military-industrial complex and the unrestrained power of the executive branch to conduct foreign and military policy would become a staple of New Left protest.

The New Left never consisted of one central organization; after all, many protesters challenged the very idea of centralized authority. In fact, SDS did not initiate the New Left's most dramatic early protest. In 1964 the University of California at Berkeley banned political activities just outside the main campus entrance in response to CORE protests against racial bias in local hiring. When CORE defied the prohibition, campus police arrested its leader, prompting a massive student uprising. Student activists then formed the **Free Speech Movement (FSM)**, which held rallies in front of the administration building, culminating in a nonviolent, civil rights–style sit-in. When California governor Edmund "Pat" Brown dispatched state and county police to evict the demonstrators, students and faculty joined in protest and forced the university administration to yield to FSM's demands for amnesty and reform. By the end of the decade, hundreds of demonstrations had erupted on campuses throughout the nation.

The Vietnam War accelerated student radicalism, and college campuses provided a strategic setting for antiwar activities. Like most Americans in the mid-1960s, undergraduates had only a dim awareness of U.S. activity in Vietnam. Yet all college men were eligible for the draft once they graduated and lost their student deferment. As more troops were sent to Vietnam, student protesters launched a variety of campaigns and demonstrations. Others resisted the draft by fleeing to Canada. Most college students, however, were not activists—between 1965 and 1968, only 20 percent of college students attended demonstrations. The activist minority, however, received extensive media attention and helped raise awareness about the difficulty of waging the Vietnam War abroad and maintaining domestic tranquility at home.

By the end of 1967, as the number of troops in Vietnam approached half a million, protests increased. Antiwar sentiment had spread to faculty, artists, writers, businesspeople, and elected officials. In April Martin Luther King Jr. delivered a powerful antiwar address at Riverside Church in New York City. "The world now demands," King declared, "that we admit that we have been wrong from the beginning of our adventure in Vietnam, that we have been detrimental to the life of the Vietnamese people." As protests spread and the government clamped down on dissenters, some activists substituted armed struggle for nonviolence. SDS split into factions, with the most prominent of them, the Weathermen, going underground and adopting violent tactics.

The Counterculture

The New Left's challenge to liberal politics attracted many students, and the **counterculture's** rejection of conventional middle-class values of work, sexual restraint, and rationality captivated even more. Cultural rebels emphasized living in the present, seeking immediate gratification, expressing authentic feelings, and reaching a higher consciousness through mind-altering drugs. Despite differences in approach, both the New Left and the counterculture expressed concerns about modern technology, bureaucratization, and the possibility of nuclear annihilation and sought new means of creating political, social, and personal liberation.

Rock 'n' roll became the soundtrack of the counterculture. In 1964 Bob Dylan's song "The Times They Are A-Changin'" became an anthem for youth rebellion. That same year, the Beatles, a British quartet influenced by 1950s black and white rock 'n' rollers, toured the United States and revolutionized popular music. Originally singing melodic compositions of teenage love and angst, the Beatles embraced the counterculture and began writing songs about alienation and politics, flavoring them with the drug-inspired sounds of psychedelic music. Although most of the songs that reached the top ten on the record charts did not undermine traditional values, the music of groups like the Beatles, the Rolling Stones, the Who, the Grateful Dead, Jefferson Airplane, and the Doors spread counterculture messages.

The counterculture viewed the elimination of sexual restrictions as essential for transforming personal and social behavior. The 1960s generation did not invent sexual freedom, but it did a great deal to shatter time-honored moral codes of monogamy, fidelity, and moderation. Promiscuity—casual sex, group sex, extramarital affairs, public nudity—and open-throated vulgarity tested public tolerance. Within limits, the broader culture reflected these changes. The Broadway production of the musical *Hair* showed frontal nudity, the movie industry adopted ratings of "X" and "R" that made films with nudity and profane language available to a wider audience, and new television comedy shows featured sketches with risqué content.

With sexual conduct in flux, society had difficulty maintaining the double standard of behavior that privileged men over women. The counterculture gave many women a chance to enjoy sexual pleasure that had long been denied them. The availability of birth control pills for women, introduced in 1960, made much of this sexual freedom possible. Although sexual liberation still carried more risks for women than for men, increased openness in discussing sexuality allowed many women to gain greater control over their bodies and their relationships.

Liberation Movements

The varieties of political protest and cultural dissent emboldened other oppressed groups to emancipate themselves. Women, Latinos, Native Americans, and gay Americans all launched liberation movements.

Despite passage of the Nineteenth Amendment in 1920, which gave women the right to vote, women did not have equal access to employment, wages, or education or control over reproduction. Nor did they have sufficient political power to remove these obstacles to full equality. Yet by 1960 nearly 40 percent of all women held jobs, and women made up 35 percent of college enrollments. The social movements of the 1960s—attracted large numbers of women. Groups like SNCC empowered female staff in community-organizing projects, and women also played central roles in antiwar efforts, leading many to demand their own movement for liberation.

The women's liberation movement also built on efforts of the federal government to address gender discrimination. In 1961 President Kennedy appointed the **Commission on the Status of Women**. The commission's report, *American Women*, issued in 1963, reaffirmed the primary role of women in raising the family but cataloged the inequities women faced in the workplace. In 1963 Congress passed the Equal Pay Act, which required employers to give men and women equal pay for equal work. The following year, the 1964 Civil Rights Act opened up further opportunities when it prohibited sexual bias in employment and created the Equal Employment Opportunity Commission (EEOC).

In 1963 Betty Friedan published a landmark book, *The Feminine Mystique*, which questioned society's prescribed gender roles and raised the consciousness of mostly college-educated women. In *The Feminine Mystique*, she described the post-college isolation and alienation experienced by her female friends who got married and stayed home to care for their children. However, not all women saw themselves reflected in Friedan's book. Many working-class women and those from African American and other racial and ethnic minority families had not had the opportunity to attend college or stay home with their children, and younger college women had not yet experienced the burdens of domestic isolation.

In October 1966, Betty Friedan and like-minded women formed the **National Organization for Women (NOW)**. With Friedan as president, NOW dedicated itself to moving society toward "true equality for all women in America, and toward a fully equal partnership of the sexes." NOW called on the EEOC to enforce women's employment rights more vigorously and favored passage of an Equal Rights Amendment (ERA), paid maternity leave for working women, the establishment of child care centers, and reproductive rights. Although NOW advocated job training programs and assistance for impoverished women, it attracted a mainly middle-class white membership. Some blacks were among its charter members, but most African American women chose to concentrate first on eliminating racial barriers that affected black women and men alike.

Young women, black and white, had also faced discrimination, sometimes in unexpected places. Even within the civil rights movement women were not always treated equally, often being assigned clerical duties. Men held a higher status within the antiwar movement because women were not eligible for the draft. Ironically, men's claims of moral advantage justified many of them in seeking sexual favors. "Girls say yes to guys who say no," quipped draft-resisting men who sought to put women in their traditional place.

As a result of these experiences, some women formed their own "consciousness-raising" groups to share their experiences of oppression in the family, the workplace, the university, and movement organizations. These women's liberationists went beyond NOW's emphasis on legal equality and attacked male domination, or patriarchy, as a crucial source of women's subordination. They criticized the nuclear family and cultural values that glorified women as the object of male sexual desires, and they protested creatively against discrimination. In 1968 radical feminists picketed the popular Miss America contest in Atlantic City, New Jersey, and set up a "Freedom Trash Can" into which they threw undergarments and cosmetics. Radical groups such as the Redstockings condemned all men as oppressors and formed separate female collectives to affirm their identities as women. In contrast, other feminists attempted to build the broadest possible coalition. In 1972 Gloria Steinem, a founder of NOW, established *Ms.* magazine in hope of attracting readers from across the feminist political spectrum. The magazine featured women's art and poetry alongside articles on sisterhood, child rearing, and abortion.

In 1973 feminists won a major battle in the Supreme Court over a woman's right to control reproduction. In ***Roe v. Wade***, the high court ruled that states could not prevent a woman from obtaining an abortion in the first three months of pregnancy but could impose some limits in the next two trimesters. In furthering the constitutional right of privacy for women, the justices classified abortion as a private medical issue between a patient and her doctor. This decision marked a victory for a woman's right to choose to terminate her pregnancy, but it also stirred up a fierce reaction from women and men who considered abortion to be the murder of an unborn child.

The Miss America Pageant Protest, 1968 In fighting for gender equality, the women's movement that emerged in the 1960s challenged all aspects of the male-dominated culture that considered women as sex objects. On September 7, 1968, feminists targeted the Miss America contest in Atlantic City, New Jersey. Protesters believed the pageant degraded women by producing a sex-driven ideal of femininity. An unidentified member of the Women's Liberation Party drops a brassiere, a garment protesters considered an instrument "of female torture," in the trash barrel. AP Images

Latinas joined the feminist movement, often forming their own organizations, but they, like black women, also joined men in struggles for racial equality and advancement. During the 1960s, the size of the Spanish-speaking population in the United States tripled from three million to nine million. They were a diverse group who hailed from many countries and backgrounds. In the 1950s, Cesar Chavez had emerged as the leader of oppressed Mexican farmworkers in California. In seeking the right to organize a union and gain higher wages and better working conditions, Chavez shared King's nonviolent principles. In 1962, along with Dolores Huerta, a fellow labor leader, Chavez formed the National Farm Workers Association, and in 1965 the union called a strike against California grape growers, one that attracted national support and finally succeeded after five years.

Another leader who fought for social and economic justice for Mexican Americans was Reies Tijerina. Beginning in the late 1950s in New Mexico, Tijerina, a Pentecostal minister, organized Mexican Americans to seek the return of lands confiscated by Anglos in violation of the 1848 Treaty of Guadalupe Hidalgo between the United States and Mexico. In 1963, Tijerina formed *La Alianza Federal de Mercedes* (Federal Alliance of Land Grants) and broadened his agenda to include first-class citizenship, economic opportunity, and the right to speak Spanish. In 1966 Tijerina led *Alianza* members in a takeover of government land in New Mexico's Carson National Forest. The next year they waged an armed raid on the Tierra Amarilla courthouse in northern New Mexico, attempting to make a citizen's arrest of the local district attorney for violating their civil rights and denying their claims to land grants. In 1970, the federal

Reies Tijerina and the Poor People's Campaign, 1968   Reies Tijerina (left), the Mexican American leader, stands alongside Native American leader Al Bridges (center) and the Reverend Ralph Abernathy (right), Martin Luther King Jr.'s successor. They are in Washington, D.C., preparing for the Poor People's March and encampment at the National Mall in front of the Capitol.
Bettmann/Getty Images

government convicted Tijerina on charges stemming from the courthouse raid, and he was sentenced to prison. As a result, the *Alianza* declined.

Young Mexican Americans, especially those in cities such as Los Angeles, supported Chavez, Huerta, and Tijerina and challenged moderate political leaders who favored cultural assimilation. Borrowing from the Black Panthers, Mexican Americans formed the Brown Berets, a self-defense organization. In 1969 some 1,500 activists gathered in Denver and declared themselves *Chicanos* (from *mejicano*, the Spanish word for "Mexican"), a term that expressed their cultural pride and identity. Chicanos created a new political party, **La Raza Unida (The United Race)**, to promote their interests, and the party and its allies sponsored demonstrations to fight for jobs, bilingual education, and the creation of Chicano studies programs in colleges. Chicano and other Spanish-language communities also took advantage of the protections of the Voting Rights Act, which in 1975 was amended to include sections of the country — from New York to California to Florida and Texas — where Hispanic literacy in English and voter registration were low.

Puerto Ricans organized the Young Lords Party (YLP). Originating as a youth gang in Chicago in 1969, the group soon spread to New York City. Like the Black Panthers, the organization established inner-city breakfast programs and medical clinics. The YLP supported bilingual education in public schools, condemned U.S. imperialism, favored independence for Puerto Rico, and supported women's reproductive rights. Under the leadership of José Cha Cha Jiménez, the Young Lords became a national organization.

Native Americans also joined the upsurge of activism. By 1970 some 800,000 people identified themselves as American Indians, many of whom lived in poverty on reservations. They suffered from inadequate housing, high alcoholism rates, low life expectancy, staggering unemployment, and lack of education. Conscious of their heritage as the first Americans, they determined to halt their deterioration by asserting pride in "red power" and established the **American Indian Movement (AIM)** in 1968. The following year, Indians occupied the abandoned prison island of Alcatraz in San Francisco Bay, where they remained until 1971. Among their demands, they offered to buy the island for $24 in beads and cloth—a reference to the purchase of Manhattan Island in 1626—and turn it into an Indian educational and cultural center. In 1972 AIM occupied the headquarters of the Federal Bureau of Indian Affairs in Washington, D.C. Demonstrators also seized the village of Wounded Knee, South Dakota, the scene of the 1890 massacre of Sioux residents by the U.S. army, to dramatize the impoverished living conditions on reservations. They held on for more than seventy days with eleven hostages until a shootout with the FBI ended the confrontation, killing one protester and wounding another.

The results of the red power movement proved mixed. Demonstrations focused media attention on the plight of Native Americans but did little to address their needs in meaningful ways. Nevertheless, courts became more sensitive to Indian claims and protected mineral and fishing rights on reservations.

One of the biggest obstacles faced by radical liberation movements came from federal and local governments. The FBI used its Counter Intelligence Program (COINTELPRO) to infiltrate these groups and stir up distrust and factionalism within them. In 1969, tipped off by an informer, the FBI joined with the Chicago Police Department in an armed, pre-dawn raid against Black Panthers, resulting in the shooting and killing of the popular leaders Fred Hampton and Mark Clark.

Asian American college students on the West Coast fought their own liberation struggle. At the University of California, Berkeley, and San Francisco State University, they participated in demonstrations against the Vietnam War and racism. In 1968 Asian American students at San Francisco State joined the Third World Liberation Front and, along with the Black Student Union, went on strike for five months, succeeding in the establishment of programs in Asian American and Black studies.

The children of newly arrived Chinese immigrants faced different problems, struggling in public schools that taught exclusively in English. Established in 1969, the Chinese for Affirmative Action filed a lawsuit against San Francisco school officials for discriminating against students with limited English-language skills. In *Lau v. Nichols* (1974), the Supreme Court upheld the group's claim, accelerating opportunities for bilingual education.

During this period many Japanese American high school and college students learned for the first time about their parents' and grandparents' internment during World War II. Like other activists, they expressed pride in their ethnic heritage and joined in efforts to publicize the injustices that earlier generations had endured. The activism of this third generation of Japanese helped convince the moderate Japanese American Citizens League in 1970 to endorse reparations for the internees, the first step in an ultimately successful two-decade effort.

Homosexuals were also marginalized and discriminated against in American society. Estimated at 4.5–5.5 percent of the population, gay men and lesbians remained largely invisible to the rest of society. In the 1950s, gay men and women created their own political and cultural organizations and frequented bars and taverns outside mainstream commercial culture, but most lesbians and gay men, like Bayard Rustin, hid their identities. There were, however, notable exceptions. During the early 1960s Frank Kameny, a member of the Mattachine Society, a group founded in the 1950s to protect the rights of gay men, led protesters in picketing the White House, the Pentagon, the United Nations, and the United States Civil Service Commission. Kameny had been fired by the federal government in the 1950s because he was gay.

In 1969, gay men and lesbians turned more militant in asserting their collective grievances. Police regularly cracked down on gay bars like the Stonewall Tavern in New York City's Greenwich Village. But on June 27, 1969, gay patrons battled back. The *Village Voice* called the **Stonewall riots** "a kind of liberation, as the gay brigade emerged from the bars, back rooms, and bedrooms of the Village and became street people." In the manner of black power, the New Left, and radical feminists, homosexuals organized the Gay Liberation Front, voiced pride in being gay, and demanded equality of opportunity regardless of sexual orientation.

As with other oppressed groups, LGBT people achieved victories slowly and unevenly. In the decades following the 1960s, they faced discrimination in employment, could not marry or receive domestic benefits, and were subject to violence for public displays of affection.

The Revival of Conservatism

These diverse social movements did a great deal to change the political and cultural landscapes of the United States, but they did not go unchallenged. Many white Americans worried about black militancy, opposed liberalism, and were even more dismayed by the radical offshoots they spawned. Conservatives soon attracted support from many Americans who did not see change as progress. Many believed that the political leadership of the nation did not speak for them about what constituted a great society.

The brand of conservatism that emerged in the 1960s united libertarian support for a laissez-faire political economy with opposition to social welfare policies and moralistic concerns for defeating communism and defending religious devotion, moral decency, and family values. Conservatives believed that the United States had to escalate the struggle against the evil of godless communism anywhere it posed a threat in the world, but they opposed internationalism as represented in the United Nations.

Conservative activists built on the foundation erected by writers such as William F. Buckley, the creator of the *National Review*, an influential journal of conservative ideas, and the novelist Ayn Rand. They also incorporated the ideas of the Reverend Billy Joe Hargis's Christian Crusade and Dr. Frederick Charles Schwartz's Christian Anti-Communist Crusade, both formed in the early 1950s. These groups promoted conspiracy theories about how the eastern liberal establishment intended to sell the country out to the Communists by supporting the United Nations, foreign aid, Social Security, and civil rights. The John Birch Society packaged these ideas in periodicals and radio broadcasts throughout the country and urged readers and listeners to remain vigilant to attacks against their freedom.

In the late 1950s and early 1960s, the conservative revival grew, mostly unnoticed, at the grassroots level in the suburbs of southern California and the Southwest. Bolstered by the postwar economic boom that centered around military research and development, these towns in the Sun Belt attracted college-educated engineers, technicians, managers, and other professionals from the Midwest Rust Belt seeking new economic opportunities. These migrants brought with them Republican loyalties as well as conservative political and moral values. Women played a large part in conservative causes, especially in protesting against public school curricula that they perceived as un-Christian and un-American. Young housewives built an extensive network of conservative study groups.

The conservative revival also found fertile recruiting ground on college campuses. In October 1960 some ninety young conservatives met at William Buckley's estate in Sharon, Connecticut to draw up a manifesto of their beliefs. "In this time of moral and political crisis," the framers of the Sharon Statement declared, "the foremost among the transcendent values is the individual's use of his God-given free will, whence derives his right to be free from the restrictions of arbitrary force." Based on this principle, the manifesto affirmed the conservative doctrines of states' rights, the free market, and anticommunism. Participants at the conference formed the **Young Americans for Freedom (YAF)**, which six months later boasted 27,000 members. In 1962 the YAF filled Madison Square Garden to listen to a speech by the one politician who excited them: Republican senator Barry M. Goldwater of Arizona.

Goldwater's book *The Conscience of a Conservative* (1960) attacked New Deal liberalism and advocated abolishing Social Security; dismantling the Tennessee Valley Authority, the government-owned public power utility; and eliminating the progressive income tax. His firm belief in states' rights put him on record against the ruling in *Brown v. Board of Education* and prompted him to vote against the Civil Rights

Act of 1964, positions that won him increasing support from conservative white southerners. However, Goldwater's advocacy of small government did not prevent him from supporting increased military spending to halt the spread of communism. The senator may have anticipated growing concerns about government excess, but his defeat in a landslide to Lyndon Johnson in the 1964 presidential election indicated that most voters perceived Goldwater's brand of conservatism as too extreme.

The election of 1964 also brought George C. Wallace onto the national stage as a leading architect of the conservative revival. As Democratic governor of Alabama, the segregationist Wallace had supported states' rights and opposed federal intervention to reshape social and political affairs. Wallace began to attract white northerners fed up with rising black militancy, forced busing to promote school integration, and open housing laws to desegregate their neighborhoods. Running in the Democratic presidential primaries in 1964, the Alabama governor garnered 34 percent of the votes in Wisconsin, 30 percent in Indiana, and 43 percent in Maryland.

More so than Goldwater, Wallace united a populist message against the political establishment with concern for white working-class Americans. Wallace voters identified with the governor as an "outsider." Many of them also backed Wallace for attacking privileged college students who, he claimed, mocked patriotism, violated sexual taboos, and looked down on hardworking, churchgoing, law-abiding Americans. How could "all those rich kids — from the fancy suburbs," one father wondered, "[avoid the draft] when my son has to go over there and maybe get his head shot off?" Both George Wallace and Barry Goldwater waged political campaigns against liberals for undermining the economic freedom of middle- and working-class whites and coddling what they considered "racial extremists" and "countercultural barbarians."

| **REVIEW & RELATE** | • How did organizations on the left challenge social, cultural, and economic norms in the 1960s?
• What groups were attracted to the 1960s conservative movement? Why? |

Conclusion: Liberalism and Its Discontents

The presidencies of John Kennedy and Lyndon Johnson marked the high point of liberal reform as well as Cold War military interventionism. Kennedy's New Frontier and Johnson's Great Society expanded the power of the national state to provide both compassionate government and bureaucratic regulation. Liberalism permitted greater freedom for racial, ethnic, and sexual minorities; expanded educational opportunities for the disadvantaged; reduced poverty; extended health care for the elderly; and began to clean up the environment. However, these expensive programs drew opposition from conservatives who saw big government as a threat to fiscal responsibility and individual liberty. Kennedy and Johnson's escalation of the Vietnam War fractured the liberal coalition of the 1960s and overshadowed their domestic accomplishments.

Kennedy and Johnson did not achieve their liberal agenda by themselves. The civil rights movement, with activists like Bayard Rustin, pushed the federal government into action. In addition, Earl Warren's Supreme Court affirmed the constitutionality of major pieces of reform legislation and charted a new course for expanding the guarantees of the Bill of Rights.

Although the Vietnam War tarnished liberalism, the struggles of African Americans, Asian Americans, women, Chicanos, Native Americans, and LGBT people continued. Indeed, the civil rights movement spurred other exploited groups to seek greater freedom, and they flourished in the late 1960s and early 1970s despite the waning of liberalism.

Liberalism began to unravel during the 1960s as its policies and programs prompted powerful attacks from radicals and conservatives alike. Indeed, over the next twenty-five years conservatives mobilized the American electorate and gained power by attacking liberal political, economic, and cultural values.

Chapter 26 Review

KEY TERMS

New Frontier, 662
Freedom Rides, 664
March on Washington for Jobs and Freedom, 666
Civil Rights Act of 1964, 666
Freedom Summer, 667
Mississippi Freedom Democratic Party (MFDP), 667
Voting Rights Act, 668
Black Panther Party, 670
Great Society, 671
Gulf of Tonkin Resolution, 675
Tet Offensive, 675
Students for a Democratic Society (SDS), 678

Port Huron Statement, 678
Free Speech Movement (FSM), 678
counterculture, 679
Commission on the Status of Women, 680
National Organization for Women (NOW), 680
Roe v. Wade, 681
La Raza Unida (The United Race), 683
American Indian Movement (AIM), 683
Stonewall riots, 684
Young Americans for Freedom (YAF), 685

REVIEW & RELATE

1. How did President Kennedy's domestic agenda reflect the liberal political ideology of the early 1960s?
2. Evaluate Kennedy's and Khrushchev's actions in the Cuban missile crisis. How was war averted?
3. How did civil rights activists pressure state and federal government officials to enact their agenda?
4. How were the civil rights and black power movements similar and in what ways were they different?
5. What problems and challenges did Johnson's Great Society legislation target?

6. In what ways did the Warren Court's rulings advance the liberal agenda?

7. Why did Kennedy and Johnson escalate the Vietnam War?

8. How did the reality of the war on the ground compare with the political and military assumptions for fighting it?

9. How did organizations on the left challenge social, cultural, and economic norms in the 1960s?

10. What groups were attracted to the 1960s conservative movement? Why?

TIMELINE OF EVENTS

1960	• Young Americans for Freedom founded
1961	• Kennedy sends military advisers to South Vietnam
	• Bay of Pigs invasion
	• Freedom Rides
	• Soviets build Berlin Wall
1962	• Port Huron Statement
	• Cuban missile crisis
1963–1968	• U.S. troops in Vietnam rise from 16,000 to 536,000
1963	• Betty Friedan publishes *The Feminine Mystique*
	• Partial Nuclear Test Ban Treaty
	• March on Washington for Jobs and Freedom
	• John F. Kennedy assassinated; Lyndon B. Johnson becomes president
1964–1966	• Great Society domestic programs enacted
1964	• Civil Rights Act of 1964
	• Freedom Summer
	• Gulf of Tonkin Resolution
1965	• Operation Rolling Thunder begins
	• Voting Rights Act
1966	• Black Panther Party formed
	• National Organization for Women (NOW) formed
1967	• Raid on Tierra Amarilla by Reies Tijerina and *La Alianza Federal de Mercedes*
1968	• American Indian Movement (AIM) founded
	• Martin Luther King Jr. assassinated
	• Tet Offensive begins
1969	• Stonewall Riots
1973	• *Roe v. Wade* Supreme Court decision

27

The Swing toward Conservatism

1968–1980

LEARNING OBJECTIVES

After reading this chapter you will be able to:

- Compare how President Nixon handled the Vietnam War and the Cold War.

- Evaluate the extent to which President Nixon shaped conservatism and the forces that led to his downfall.

- Evaluate President Carter's successes and failures in domestic and foreign politics.

- Explain how liberal activists addressed the issues of clean energy, equal rights for women, racial equality, and nuclear proliferation in the 1970s.

- Explain the rise of the New Right and compare it to Richard Nixon's approach to conservatism.

COMPARING AMERICAN HISTORIES

Louise Day Hicks fought against liberal notions of racial justice, thereby rallying support for conservatism. Born in 1916, Louise Day grew up in a relatively comfortable Irish Catholic home in South Boston. The daughter of a prominent judge, Hicks never moved far away from her working-class Irish community. Yet she crossed boundaries that most women of her age and neighborhood did not reach. A wife and a mother, she graduated from Boston University Law School in 1955, one of only nine women enrolled in her class of 232.

In 1961, Hicks entered the political arena, winning election to the Boston School Committee as "the only mother on the ballot." She became identified with the cause that would define her public career: opposition to racial integration in schools. Segregation existed in northern schools because of public policies that reinforced housing segregation and kept blacks from moving into white ethnic neighborhoods. Hicks refused to acknowledge the existence of this kind of segregation and lashed out at "racial agitators" and "pseudo-liberals."

In the late 1960s and 1970s, she rode to higher office on the white backlash to racial integration, first as a congresswoman and then as president of the Boston City Council. When a federal judge ordered busing to desegregate city schools in 1974, Hicks founded Restore Our Alienated Rights (ROAR). The group's protests created a good deal of havoc but failed to stop the court ruling. Through all this, Hicks remained a Democrat, but many of her white, working-class supporters in Boston and elsewhere joined the growing conservative coalition shaping the Republican Party.

Pauli Murray took a different path to advocate for her political beliefs. The descendant of Africans, Europeans, and Native Americans, Murray spent her life challenging racial and gender discrimination. Born Anna Pauline Murray in 1910 and orphaned at the age of thirteen, she moved to Durham to live with her mother's family. After graduating college in New York City, she applied for admission to the University of North Carolina Law School. Rejected by the all-white university, Murray moved to Washington, D.C., to attend historically black Howard University Law School, where she led demonstrations against segregated public accommodations in the city. In the decade following her graduation in 1944, she wrote a book about state segregation laws, which the NAACP cited in support of its successful arguments in *Brown v. Board of Education* (1954).

In the 1960s and 1970s, Murray devoted much of her energy toward issues of race and gender. President John F. Kennedy appointed her to a federal commission to investigate the status of women. Murray helped launch the National Organization for Women, supported the Equal Rights Amendment, and coined the term "Jane Crow" to define the dual racial and gender discrimination black women faced. In the 1970s, the pioneering Murray carved out a new career path by becoming the first African American woman ordained as an Episcopal priest.

Throughout her life, Murray wrestled with her sexual identity. Although she had married (and divorced) a man, she shared intimate relationships with women. Having lived before the emergence of the transgender movement, Murray, who thought of her inner self as male, would most likely have identified as queer.

THE AMERICAN HISTORIES of Louise Day Hicks and Pauli Murray reveal that while conservatism grew in the late 1960s and 1970s, liberalism persisted. Elected in 1968 in the conservative backlash to radical dissent, Richard Nixon ended the war in Vietnam and withdrew from the war on poverty. Although the Watergate scandal briefly interrupted conservative momentum, New Right conservatism continued to grow throughout the 1970s. It meshed traditional conservative support for lower taxes, deregulation, and anti-unionism with cultural and racial resentments. Still, liberalism survived the rise of conservatism. The women's movement and black freedom struggle turned in new directions. The environmental movement accelerated amidst several man-made disasters. The reduction of overseas oil supplies propelled interest in finding alternative sources of energy. Nevertheless, the political balance between conservatism and liberalism began tipping toward the right.

Nixon: War and Diplomacy, 1969–1974

In winning the presidency in 1968, Richard Nixon paid close attention to international affairs. Having pledged to end the war in Vietnam, it took him another four years to do so. A fierce anti-Communist, Nixon considered himself a realist in foreign affairs. He was concerned more with a stable world order than with promoting American ideals. Nixon and Secretary of State Henry Kissinger worked to establish closer relations with both the Communist People's Republic of China and the Soviet Union. While the Soviet Union and China competed for influence in Asia, Nixon exploited this conflict to keep these nuclear powers divided. His administration brought a thaw in Cold War relations, but he was less successful in navigating Arab-Israeli hostilities in the Middle East, a misstep that caused pain for consumers of gasoline and oil at home.

The Election of 1968

Nineteen sixty-eight was a turbulent year. In February, police shot indiscriminately into a crowd gathered for civil rights protests at South Carolina State University in Orangeburg, killing three students. In March, student protests at Columbia University led to a violent confrontation with the New York City police. On April 4, the murder of Martin Luther King Jr. sparked an outburst of rioting by blacks in more than one hundred cities throughout the country. The assassination of Democratic presidential aspirant Robert Kennedy in June further heightened the mood of despair. Adding to the unrest, demonstrators gathered in Chicago in August at the Democratic National Convention to press for an antiwar plank in the party platform. Thousands of protesters were beaten and arrested by Chicago police officers. Many Americans watched in horror as television networks broadcast the bloody clashes, but a majority of viewers sided with the police rather than the protesters.

Similar protests occurred around the world. In early 1968, university students outside Paris protested educational policies and what they perceived as their second-class status. When students at the Sorbonne in Paris joined them in the streets, police attacked them viciously. In June, French president Charles de Gaulle sent in tanks to break up the strikes but also instituted political and economic reforms. Protests erupted during the spring in Prague, Czechoslovakia, where President Alexander Dubček vowed to reform the Communist regime by initiating "socialism with a human face." In August the Soviet Union sent its military into Prague to crush the reforms, bringing this brief experiment in freedom remembered as the "Prague Spring" to a violent end. During the same year, student-led demonstrations erupted in Yugoslavia, Poland, West Germany, Italy, Spain, Japan, and Mexico.

It was against this backdrop of global unrest that Richard Nixon ran for president against the Democratic nominee Hubert H. Humphrey and the independent candidate, George C. Wallace, the segregationist governor of Alabama and a popular archconservative. To outflank Wallace on the right, Nixon declared himself the "law and order" candidate, a phrase that became a code for reining in black militancy. To win southern supporters, he pledged to ease up on enforcing federal civil rights legislation and oppose forced busing to achieve racial integration in schools. He criticized antiwar protesters and promised to end the Vietnam War with honor. Seeking to identify the Democratic party with social and cultural radicalism, Nixon geared his campaign message to the "silent majority" of voters — what one political analyst characterized as "the unyoung, the unpoor, and unblack." This conservative message appealed to many Americans who were fed up with domestic uprisings and war abroad.

Although Nixon won 301 electoral votes, 110 more than Humphrey, none of the three candidates received a majority of the popular vote (Map 27.1). Yet Nixon and Wallace together garnered about 57 percent of the popular vote, a dramatic shift to the right compared with Lyndon Johnson's landslide victory just four years earlier. The New Left had given way to an assortment of old and new conservatives, overwhelmingly white, who were determined to contain, if not roll back, the Great Society.

The Failure of Vietnamization

Vietnam plagued Nixon as it had his Democratic predecessor. Despite intimations during the campaign that he had a secret plan to end the war, Nixon's approach to Vietnam turned out to look much the same as Johnson's. Henry Kissinger, who served first as national security adviser and then as secretary of state, continued peace talks with the North Vietnamese, which Johnson had initiated. Over the next four years, Nixon and Kissinger devised a strategy that removed U.S. ground forces and turned over greater responsibility for the fighting to the South Vietnamese army, a process called **Vietnamization**.

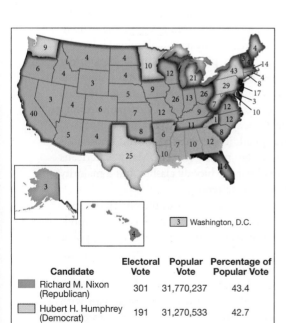

Candidate	Electoral Vote	Popular Vote	Percentage of Popular Vote
Richard M. Nixon (Republican)	301	31,770,237	43.4
Hubert H. Humphrey (Democrat)	191	31,270,533	42.7
George C. Wallace (American Independent)	46	9,906,141	13.5

3 ☐ Washington, D.C.

MAP 27.1   The Election of 1968
Democratic presidential candidate Hubert Humphrey lost across the South as white voters turned to Republican Richard Nixon or segregationist George Wallace. Many working-class whites in the North and West also shifted their allegiance to these "law and order" candidates, rejecting the civil rights and antipoverty agendas promoted by President Johnson and blaming Democrats for the turmoil over the Vietnam War.

Vietnamization did not mean an end to U.S. belligerence in the region. In 1969, at the same time that American troop levels were being drawn down, the president ordered secret bombing raids in Cambodia, a neutral country adjacent to South Vietnam that contained enemy forces and parts of the Ho Chi Minh Trail. Meant to pressure the North Vietnamese into accepting U.S. peace terms, the bombing accomplished little. In April 1970 Nixon ordered the invasion of Cambodia, which destabilized the country and eventually brought to power the Communist organization Khmer Rouge, which later slaughtered two million Cambodians. In 1971 the United States sponsored the South Vietnamese invasion of Laos, a neighboring country that harbored North Vietnamese troops and supply lines, which again yielded no battlefield gains. Finally, in December 1972, shortly before Christmas, the United States carried out a massive eleven-day bombing campaign of targets in North Vietnam meant to force the North Vietnamese government to reach a peace accord.

The intense bombing of North Vietnam did end formal U.S. involvement in the war. An agreement signed on January 27, 1973 stipulated that the United States would remove all American troops, the North Vietnamese would return captured U.S. soldiers, and North and South Vietnam would strive for peaceful national unification. This agreement did not bring peace and the war in Vietnam continued. In 1975 North Vietnamese and Vietcong forces captured Saigon, resulting in a Communist victory. This outcome came at a terrible cost. Some 58,000 American soldiers, 215,000 South Vietnamese soldiers, 1 million North Vietnamese and Vietcong soldiers, and an estimated 4 million South and North Vietnamese civilians were killed in the conflict.

The Nixon administration's war efforts generated great controversy at home. The invasion of Cambodia touched off widespread campus demonstrations in May 1970. At Kent State University in Ohio, four student protesters were shot and killed by the National Guard. Large crowds of antiwar demonstrators descended on Washington in 1969 and 1971, though the president refused to heed their message. Nevertheless, the American public, and not just radicals, had turned against the war. By 1972 more than 70 percent of those polled believed that the Vietnam War was a mistake. Growing numbers of Vietnam veterans also spoke out against the war. Contributing to this disillusionment, in 1971 the *New York Times* and the *Washington Post* published a classified report known as the **Pentagon Papers**. This document confirmed that the Kennedy and Johnson administrations had misled the public about the origins and nature of the Vietnam War. Congress reflected growing disapproval for the war by repealing the Gulf of Tonkin Resolution in 1970 after the Cambodian invasion. In 1973 Congress passed the **War Powers Act**, which required the president to consult with Congress within forty-eight hours of deploying military forces and to obtain a declaration of war from Congress if troops remained on foreign soil beyond sixty days.

The Cold War Thaws

Although the Vietnam War remained controversial for Nixon, his efforts toward easing tensions with the country's Cold War adversaries proved more successful, through a policy known as **détente**. Through secret negotiations, Kissinger prepared the way for Nixon to visit mainland China in 1972. After blocking the People's Republic of China's admission to the United Nations for twenty-two years, the United States announced that it would no longer oppose China's entry to the world organization.

The closer relations between China and the United States worried the USSR. Although both were Communist nations, the Soviet Union and China had pursued their own ideological and national interests. To check growing Chinese influence with the United States, Soviet premier Leonid Brezhnev invited President Nixon to Moscow in May 1972, the first time an American president had visited the Soviet Union since 1945. The main topic of discussion concerned arms control, and with the Soviet Union eager to make a deal in the aftermath of Nixon's trip to China, the two sides worked out the historic **Strategic Arms Limitation Treaty (SALT I)**, the first to curtail nuclear arms production during the Cold War. The pact restricted the number of antiballistic missiles that each nation could deploy and froze the number of intercontinental ballistic missiles and submarine-based missiles for five years.

Throughout the world, the United States chose to support dictatorship over democracy when its strategic or economic interests were at stake. In Chile, the United States overthrew the democratically elected socialist president Salvador Allende after he nationalized U.S. properties. In 1973 the Central Intelligence Agency (CIA) backed an operation that led to the murder of Allende, and the coup brought nearly two decades of dictatorial rule to that country. Under Nixon's leadership, the United States also supported repressive regimes in Nicaragua, South Africa, the Philippines, and Iran.

Crisis in the Middle East and at Home

Nixon's diplomatic initiatives, however, failed to resolve festering problems in the Middle East. Since its victory in the Six-Day War of 1967, Israel had occupied territory once controlled by Egypt and Syria as well as the former Palestinian capital of Jerusalem. On October 6, 1973, during the start of the Jewish High Holidays of Yom Kippur, Egyptian and Syrian troops, fortified with Soviet arms, launched a surprise attack on Israel. An Israeli counterattack, reinforced by a shipment of $2 billion of American weapons, repelled Arab forces, and the Israeli military stood ready to destroy the Egyptian army. To avoid a complete breakdown in the balance of power, the United States and the Soviet Union agreed to broker a cease-fire that left the situation the same as before the war.

U.S. involvement in the struggle between Israel and its Arab enemies exacerbated economic troubles at home. On October 17, 1973, in the midst of the Yom Kippur War, the **Organization of Petroleum Exporting Countries (OPEC)** imposed an oil embargo on the United States as punishment for its support of Israel. In 1960 the Persian Gulf countries of Saudi Arabia, Iran, Iraq, and Kuwait together with Venezuela had formed OPEC and used its control of petroleum supplies to set world prices. As a result of the embargo, the price of oil skyrocketed. The effect of high oil prices rippled through the economy, leading to increased inflation and unemployment. The crisis lasted until May 1974, when OPEC lifted its embargo following six months of diplomacy by Kissinger.

REVIEW & RELATE

- Compare Nixon's policies toward Vietnam with those toward the Soviet Union and China.
- How did Nixon's Middle East policy affect Americans at home?

Nixon and Politics, 1969–1974

Nixon had won the presidency in 1968 by forging a conservative coalition behind him and blaming liberals for the radical excesses of the 1960s. Nixon won reelection in 1972, but his victory was short-lived. In an effort to ensure an overwhelming victory, the Nixon administration engaged in illegal activities that subsequently came to light and forced the president to resign.

Pragmatic Conservatism

On the domestic front, Nixon had pledged during his 1968 campaign to "reverse the flow of power and resources from the states and communities to Washington." He kept his promise by dismantling Great Society programs, cutting funds for the War on Poverty, and eliminating the Office of Economic Opportunity. In 1972 the president adopted a program of revenue sharing, which transferred federal tax revenues to the states to use as they wished. Hoping to rein in the liberal Warren Court, Nixon nominated conservative justices to the Supreme Court.

However, in several areas Nixon departed from conservatives who favored limited government. In 1970 he persuaded Congress to pass the Environmental Protection Act, which strengthened federal oversight of industrial activities affecting the natural environment throughout the country. In 1972 the federal government increased its responsibility for protecting the health and safety of American workers through the creation of the Occupational Safety and Health Administration (OSHA). The Consumer Products Safety Commission was established to provide added security for the buying public. The president also signed a law banning cigarette advertising on radio and television because of the link between smoking and cancer.

Nixon also applied a pragmatic approach to racial issues. In general, he supported "benign neglect" and rejected new legislative attempts to use busing to promote school desegregation. In this way, Nixon courted southern conservatives in an attempt to deter George Wallace from mounting another third-party challenge in 1972. Still, Nixon made efforts to further civil rights. Expanding **affirmative action** programs begun under the Johnson administration, he adopted plans that required construction companies and unions to recruit racial minority workers according to their percentage in the local labor force. His support of affirmative action was part of a broader approach to encourage "black capitalism," a concept designed to convince African Americans to seek opportunity within the free-enterprise system rather than through government handouts. Moreover, in 1970 Nixon signed the extension of the 1965 Voting Rights Act, which lowered the voting age from twenty-one to eighteen for national elections. Support for the measure reflected the impact of the Vietnam War: If young men could fight at eighteen, then they should be able to vote at eighteen. In 1971 the Twenty-sixth Amendment was ratified to lower the voting age for state and local elections as well.

The Nixon Landslide and Watergate Scandal, 1972–1974

By appealing to voters across the political spectrum, Nixon won a monumental victory in 1972. The president invigorated the "silent majority" by demonizing his opponents and encouraging Vice President Spiro Agnew to aggressively pursue his strategy of polarization. Agnew called protesters "kooks" and "social misfits" and attacked the media and Nixon critics with heated rhetoric. As Nixon had hoped, George Wallace ran in the Democratic primaries. Wallace won impressive victories in the North as well as the South, but his campaign ended after an assassination attempt left him paralyzed. With Wallace out of the race, the Democrats helped Nixon look more centrist by nominating George McGovern, a liberal antiwar senator from South Dakota.

Winning in a landslide, Nixon captured more than 60 percent of the popular vote and nearly all of the electoral votes. Nonetheless Democrats retained control of Congress. Nixon would have little time to savor his victory, for within the next two years his conduct in the campaign would come back to destroy his presidency.

In the early hours of June 17, 1972, five men broke into Democratic Party headquarters in the Watergate apartment complex in Washington, D.C. What appeared initially as a routine robbery turned into the most infamous political scandal of the twentieth century. It was eventually revealed that the break-in had been authorized by the Committee for the Re-Election of the President in an attempt to steal documents from the Democrats.

President Nixon may not have known in advance the details of the break-in, but he did authorize a cover-up of his administration's involvement. Nixon ordered his chief of staff, H. R. Haldeman, to get the CIA and FBI to back off from a thorough investigation of the incident. To silence the burglars at their trials, the president promised them $400,000 and hinted at a presidential pardon after their conviction.

Nixon embarked on the cover-up to protect himself from revelations of his administration's other illegal activities. Several of the Watergate burglars belonged to a secret band of operatives known as "the plumbers," which had been formed in 1971 and authorized by the president to find and plug up unwelcome information leaks from government officials. On their first secret operation, the plumbers broke into the office of military analyst Daniel Ellsberg's psychiatrist to look for embarrassing personal information with which to discredit Ellsberg, who had leaked the *Pentagon Papers*. The president had other unsavory matters to hide. In an effort to contain leaks about the administration's secret bombing of Cambodia in 1969, the White House had illegally wiretapped its own officials and members of the press.

Watergate did not become a major scandal until months after the 1972 election. The trial judge forced one of the burglars to reveal the men's backers. This revelation led two *Washington Post* reporters, Bob Woodward and Carl Bernstein, to investigate the link between the administration and the plumbers. With the help of Mark Felt, a top FBI official whose identity long remained secret and whom the reporters called "Deep Throat," Woodward and Bernstein exposed the true nature of the crime. The Senate created a special committee in February 1973 to investigate the scandal. White House counsel John Dean, whom Nixon had fired, testified about discussing the cover-up with the president and his closest advisers. His testimony proved accurate after the committee learned that Nixon had secretly taped all Oval Office conversations. When the president refused to release the tapes to a special prosecutor, the Supreme Court ruled against him.

With Nixon's cover-up revealed, and impeachment and conviction likely, Nixon resigned on August 9, 1974. The scandal took a great toll on the administration:

Attorney General John Mitchell and Nixon's closest advisers, H. R. Haldeman and John Ehrlichman, resigned, and twenty-five government officials went to jail. Watergate also damaged the office of the president, leaving Americans wary and distrustful.

Vice President Gerald Ford served out Nixon's remaining term. The Republican representative from Michigan had replaced Vice President Spiro Agnew after Agnew resigned in 1973 following charges that he had taken illegal kickbacks while governor of Maryland. Ford chose Nelson A. Rockefeller, the moderate Republican governor of New York, as his vice president; thus, neither man had been elected to the office he now held. President Ford's most controversial and defining act took place shortly after he entered the White House. Explaining to the country that he wanted to quickly end the "national nightmare" stemming from Watergate, Ford pardoned Nixon for any criminal offenses he might have committed as president. Rather than healing the nation's wounds, this preemptive pardon polarized Americans and cost Ford considerable political capital.

REVIEW & RELATE	• Describe the conservative coalition that brought Nixon to power. • How did Nixon appeal to conservatism and how much did he depart from it?

Nixon Supporters Rally during Watergate, 1974 On July 29, 1974, while the House Judiciary Committee was voting to recommend the impeachment of President Nixon, his supporters held a prayer vigil in front of the Capitol. Although 57 percent of Americans thought Nixon should be removed from office, Nixon did retain support from the Republican rank and file, as this protest shows. Nevertheless, on August 9, he resigned. Keystone/Getty Images

The Presidency of Jimmy Carter, 1976–1980

Though deeply disillusioned by Vietnam and the Watergate scandal, most Americans hoped that, with these disasters behind them, better times lay ahead. This was not to be. Under the leadership of the Democratic president Jimmy Carter, the economy worsened as oil-producing nations in the Persian Gulf and Latin America raised the price of petroleum. Carter's efforts to revive the economy and rally the country behind energy conservation were ineffective. In foreign policy President Carter sought to negotiate with the Soviets over arms reduction while at the same time challenging them to do more to protect human rights. In practice, Carter found this balancing act difficult to sustain, and despite his desire to find ways to cooperate with the Soviets, relations between the superpowers deteriorated over the course of his term in office. Despite successful diplomatic efforts in the Middle East, trouble in the Persian Gulf added to the Carter administration's woes.

Jimmy Carter and the Limits of Affluence

Gerald Ford received the Republican presidential nomination in 1976 and ran against James Earl (Jimmy) Carter, a little-known former governor of Georgia, who used his "outsider" status to his advantage. Shaping his campaign with Watergate in mind, Carter stressed personal character over economic issues. As a moderate, post-segregationist governor of Georgia, Carter won the support of the family of Martin Luther King Jr. and other black leaders. Carter needed all the help he could get and eked out a narrow victory.

The greatest challenge Carter faced once in office was a faltering economy. America's consumer-oriented economy depended on cheap energy, a substantial portion of which came from sources outside the United States (Figure 27.1). Due to the 1973 OPEC oil embargo on the United States, the price of oil had skyrocketed. By the time Carter became president, American automobile drivers who had paid 30 cents a gallon for gas in 1970 were paying several times that amount.

Energy concerns helped reshape American industry. With energy prices rising, American manufacturers sought ways to reduce costs by moving their factories to nations that offered cheaper labor and lower energy costs. This outmigration of American manufacturing had two significant consequences. First, it weakened the American labor movement, particularly in heavy industry. In the 1970s, union membership dropped from 28 to 23 percent of the workforce and continued to decline over the next decade. Second, this process of deindustrialization accelerated a significant population shift that had begun during World War II from the old industrial areas of the Northeast and the Midwest (the Rust Belt) to the South and the Southwest (the Sun Belt), where cheaper costs and lower wages were enormously attractive to businesses (Map 27.2). Only 14 percent of southern workers were unionized in a region with a long history of opposition to labor organizing. Sun Belt cities such as Houston, Atlanta, Phoenix, and San Diego flourished, while steel and auto towns in Ohio, Michigan, and Pennsylvania decayed.

These monumental shifts in the American economy produced widespread pain. Higher gasoline prices affected all businesses that relied on energy, leading to serious inflation. To maintain their standard of living in the face of rising inflation and

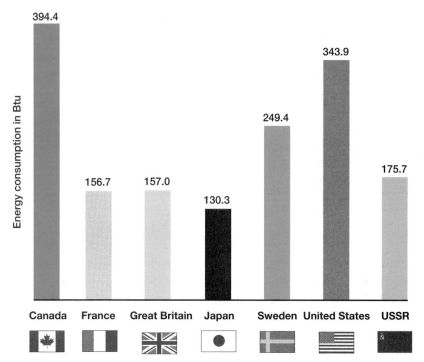

FIGURE 27.1 **Global Per Capita Energy Consumption** Next to Canada, in 1980 the United States consumed the largest amount of energy per capita, measured in British thermal units (Btu), among the major industrialized nations in the world. The source of most of this energy came (and still comes) from such fossil fuels as coal and oil. Greenhouse gas emissions from this fuel production and consumption have created an environmental hazard in the above nations, and those like China and India that experienced rapid industrialization in the decades following 1980. Besides industrialization, what other factors influence per capita energy consumption?

stagnant wages, many Americans went into debt, using a new innovation, the credit card, to borrow collectively more than $300 billion. The American economy had gone through inflationary spirals before, but they were usually accompanied by high employment, with wages helping to drive up prices. In the 1970s, however, rising prices were accompanied by growing unemployment, a situation that economists called "stagflation." With both inflation and unemployment occurring at the same time, economists were confounded, and many Americans felt they had lost control over their economy (Figure 27.2).

President Carter tried his best to find a solution. To reduce dependency on foreign oil, in 1977 Carter devised a plan for energy self-sufficiency, which he called the "moral equivalent of war." Critics called the proposal weak. A more substantial accomplishment came on August 4, 1977, when Carter signed into law the creation of the Department of Energy, with responsibilities covering research, development, and conservation of energy. In 1978, he backed the **National Energy Act**, which set gas emission standards for automobiles and provided incentives for installing alternate energy systems, such as solar and wind power, in homes and public buildings.

MAP 27.2   The Sun and Rust Belts
Dramatic economic and demographic shifts during the 1970s led to industrial development and population growth in the "Sun Belt" in the South and Southwest at the expense of the "Rust Belt" in the Northeast and Midwest. As manufacturers sought cheap, non-unionized labor, they moved factories to the South or overseas while defense industries and agribusiness fueled growth from Texas to California.

FIGURE 27.2   United States Unemployment Rate and Inflation Rate (the "Misery Index"), 1970–1980 The misery index is calculated by adding the unemployment rate to the annual rate of inflation. It measures how the average person is doing economically. High rates of unemployment and inflation drive up the misery index, indicating overall economic suffering. How do you explain the spike in the misery index in 1975 and 1980?

He also supported congressional legislation to spend $14 billion for public sector jobs as well as to cut taxes by $34 billion, which reduced unemployment but only temporarily.

In many other respects Carter embraced conservative principles. Believing in fiscal restraint, he rejected liberal proposals for national health insurance and more expansive employment programs. Instead, he signed into law bills deregulating the airline, banking, trucking, and railroad industries, measures that appealed to conservative proponents of free market economics.

The Perils of Détente

In the area of foreign policy Carter departed from Nixon. Whereas Nixon was a realist who considered the U.S. role in world affairs as an exercise in power politics, Carter was an idealist who made human rights a cornerstone of his foreign policy. Unlike previous presidents who had supported dictatorial governments as long as they were anti-Communist, Carter intended to hold such regimes to a higher moral standard. The Carter administration cut off military and economic aid to repressive regimes in Argentina, Uruguay, and Ethiopia. Still, Carter was not entirely consistent in his application of moral standards to diplomacy. Important U.S. allies around the world such as the Philippines, South Korea, and South Africa were hardly models of democracy, but national security concerns kept the president from severing ties with them.

One way that Carter tried to set an example of responsible moral leadership was by signing an agreement to return control of the Panama Canal Zone to Panama at the end of 1999. The treaty that President Theodore Roosevelt negotiated in 1903 gave the United States control over this ten-mile piece of Panamanian land forever. Panamanians resented this affront to their sovereignty, and Carter considered the occupation a vestige of colonialism.

The president's pursuit of détente with the Soviet Union was less successful. In 1978 the Carter administration extended full diplomatic recognition to China. After the fall of China to the Communists in 1949, the United States had supported Taiwan, an island off the coast of China, as an outpost of democracy against mainland China. In abandoning Taiwan by recognizing China, Carter sought to drive a greater wedge between China and the Soviet Union. Nevertheless, Carter did not give up on cooperation with the Soviets. In June 1979 Carter and Soviet leader Leonid Brezhnev signed **SALT II**, a new strategic arms limitation treaty. Six months later, however, the Soviet Union invaded Afghanistan to bolster its pro-Communist Afghan regime. President Carter viewed this action as a violation of international law and a threat to Middle East oil supplies, and he therefore persuaded the Senate to drop consideration of SALT II. In addition, Carter obtained from Congress a 5 percent increase in military spending, reduced grain sales to the USSR, and led a boycott of the 1980 Olympic Games in Moscow.

Of perhaps the greatest long-term importance was President Carter's decision to authorize the CIA to provide covert military and economic assistance to Afghan rebels resisting the Soviet invasion. Chief among these groups were the *mujahideen*, or warriors who wage jihad. Although portrayed as freedom fighters, these Islamic fundamentalists (including a group known as the Taliban) did not support democracy in

Afghan Mujahideen, January 1980   On December 25, 1979, Soviet troops invaded Afghanistan to suppress mujahideen guerrillas who were trying to overthrow the nation's secular, pro-Soviet regime. These rebel forces were among the guerrillas who defeated the Soviets after a decade of warfare and eventually established an Islamic theocracy. Pascal Manoukian/Sygma/GettyImages

the Western sense. Among the mujahideen who received assistance from the United States was Osama bin Laden, a Saudi Arabian Islamic fundamentalist.

Challenges in the Middle East

Before President Carter attempted to restrain the Soviet Union in Afghanistan, he did have some notable diplomatic successes. Five years after the 1973 Yom Kippur War, with relations between Israel and its Arab neighbors in a deadlock, Carter invited the leaders of Israel and Egypt to the United States. Following two weeks of discussions in September 1978 at the presidential retreat at Camp David, Maryland, Israeli prime minister Menachem Begin and Egyptian president Anwar Sadat reached an agreement on a "framework for peace." For the first time in its history, Egypt would extend diplomatic recognition to Israel in exchange for Israel's agreement to return the Sinai peninsula to Egypt, which Israel had captured and occupied since 1967. Carter facilitated Sadat's acceptance of the **Camp David accords** by promising to extend foreign aid to Egypt. The treaty, however, left unresolved controversial issues between Israelis and Arabs concerning the establishment of a Palestinian state and control of Jerusalem.

Whatever success Carter had in promoting peace in the Middle East suffered a serious setback in the Persian Gulf nation of Iran. In 1953 the CIA had helped overthrow Iran's democratically elected president, replacing him with a monarch and staunch ally, Mohammad Reza Pahlavi, the shah of Iran. For more than two decades, the shah ruled Iran with U.S. support, seeking to construct a modern, secular state allied with the United States. In doing so, he used repressive measures against Islamic fundamentalists, deploying his secret police to imprison, torture, and exile dissenters. In 1979 revolutionary forces headed by Ayatollah Ruholla Khomeini, an Islamic fundamentalist exiled by the shah, overthrew his government. Khomeini intended to end the growing secularism in Iran and reshape the nation according to strict Islamic law.

When the deposed shah needed treatment for terminal cancer, President Carter invited him to the United States for medical assistance as a humanitarian gesture, despite warnings from the Khomeini government that it would consider this invitation a hostile action. On November 4, 1979, the ayatollah ordered fundamentalist Muslim students to seize the U.S. Embassy in Tehran and hold its fifty-two occupants hostage until the United States returned the shah to Iran to stand trial. President Carter retaliated by freezing all Iranian assets in American banks, breaking off diplomatic relations, and imposing a trade embargo. As the impasse dragged on and with the presidential election of 1980 fast approaching, Carter launched a failed rescue attempt to free the hostages. Seeking to humiliate the president further, Khomeini released the hostages on January 20, 1981, the inauguration day of Carter's successor, Ronald Reagan.

REVIEW & RELATE
- How effective was President Carter in domestic politics?
- How did events in the Middle East, the Persian Gulf, and Afghanistan challenge the objectives of the Carter administration?

The Persistence of Liberalism in the 1970s

Many of the changes sought by liberals and radicals during the 1960s had entered the political and cultural mainstreams in the 1970s. The counterculture, with its long hairstyles and colorful clothes, also entered the mainstream, and rock continued to dominate popular music. Some Americans experimented with recreational drugs, and the remaining sexual taboos of the 1960s fell away. Many parents became resigned to seeing their daughters and sons living with boyfriends or girlfriends before getting married. And many of those same parents divorced their spouses.

Popular Culture

The antiwar movement and counterculture influenced popular culture in many ways. Rock musicians such as Bruce Springsteen, Jackson Browne, and Billy Joel sang of loss, loneliness, urban decay, and adventure. The film *M*A*S*H* (1970), though dealing with the Korean War, was a thinly veiled satire of the horrors of the Vietnam War, and in the late 1970s filmmakers began producing movies specifically about Vietnam and the toll the war took on ordinary Americans who served there. The television sitcom *All in the Family* gave American viewers the character of Archie Bunker, an opinionated, white, blue-collar worker, in a comedy that dramatized the contemporary political and cultural wars as conservative Archie taunted his liberal son-in-law with politically incorrect remarks about racial minorities, feminists, and liberals.

Women's Movement

In the 1970s the women's movement gained strength, but it also attracted powerful opponents. The 1973 Supreme Court victory for abortion rights in *Roe v. Wade* did not end the controversy. In 1976 Congress responded to abortion opponents by passing legislation prohibiting the use of federal funds for impoverished women seeking to terminate unintended pregnancies.

Feminists engaged in other debates in this decade, often clashing with more conservative women. The National Organization for Women (NOW) and its allies succeeded in getting thirty-five states out of a necessary thirty-eight to ratify the **Equal Rights Amendment (ERA)**, which prevented the abridgment of "equality of rights under law . . . by the United States or any State on the basis of sex." Pauli Murray, one of the founders of NOW, summed up the argument for why black women needed the ERA. "The Negro woman has suffered more than the addition of sex discrimination to race discrimination," Murray declared. "She . . . remains on the lowest rank of social and economic status in the United States."

In response, conservative women activists formed their own movement to block ratification. Phyllis Schlafly founded the Stop ERA organization to prevent the creation of a "unisex society." Despite the inroads made by feminists, traditional notions of femininity appealed to many women and to male-dominated legislatures. The remaining states refused to ratify the ERA, thus killing the amendment in 1982, when the ratification period expired.

Despite the failure to obtain ratification of the ERA, feminists achieved significant victories. In 1972 Congress passed the Educational Amendments Act. Title IX of this law prohibited colleges and universities that received federal funds from discriminating on the basis of sex, leading to substantial advances in women's athletics. Many more women sought relief against job discrimination through the Equal Employment Opportunity Commission, resulting in major victories. In the case of *Reed v. Reed* (1971) Ruth Bader Ginsburg, an attorney for the American Civil Liberties Union, convinced the Supreme Court that the Equal Protection Clause of the Fourteenth Amendment prohibited differential treatment based on sex. From 1973 to 1976, Ginsburg won another five cases before the Supreme Court, thereby reshaping the Fourteenth Amendment as an instrument for gender equality.

NOW membership continued to grow, and the number of battered women's shelters and rape crisis centers multiplied in towns and cities across the country. Women saw their ranks increase on college campuses, in both undergraduate and professional schools. Women also began entering politics in greater numbers, especially at the local and state levels. At the national level, women such as Shirley Chisholm and Geraldine Ferraro of New York, Louise Day Hicks of Massachusetts, Barbara Jordan of Texas, and Patricia Schroeder of Colorado won seats in Congress.

At the same time, women of color sought to broaden the definition of feminism to include struggles against race and class oppression as well as sex discrimination. In 1974 a group of black feminists, led by author Barbara Smith, organized the Combahee River Collective and proclaimed: "We . . . often find it difficult to separate race from class from sex oppression because in our lives they are most often experienced simultaneously." Chicana and other Latina feminists also sought to extend women's liberation beyond the confines of the white middle class. In 1987 feminist poet and writer Gloria Anzaldúa wrote: "Though I'll defend my race and culture when they are attacked by non-mexicanos . . . I abhor some of my culture's ways, how it cripples its women . . . our strengths used against us, lowly [women] bearing humility with dignity."

Environmentalism

Another outgrowth of 1960s liberal activism that flourished in the 1970s was the effort to clean up and preserve the environment. The publication of Rachel Carson's *Silent Spring* in 1962 had renewed awareness of what Progressive Era reformers called conservation. Carson expanded the concept of conservation to include ecology, which addressed the relationships of human beings and other organisms to their environments. By exploring these connections, she offered a revealing look at the devastating effects of pesticides on birds and fish, as well as on the human food chain and water supply.

This new environmental movement not only focused on open spaces and national parks but also sought to publicize urban environmental problems. By 1970, 53 percent of Americans considered air and water pollution to be one of the top issues facing the country, up from only 17 percent five years earlier.

Not everyone embraced environmentalism. As the **Environmental Protection Agency (EPA)** toughened emission standards, automobile manufacturers complained that the regulations forced them to raise prices and hurt an industry that was already feeling the threat of foreign competition, especially from Japan. Workers were also affected, as declining sales forced companies to lay off employees. Similarly, passage of the Endangered Species Act of 1973 pitted timber companies in the Northwest against environmentalists. The new law prevented the federal government from funding any projects that threatened the habitat of animals at risk of extinction.

Several disasters heightened public demands for stronger government oversight of the environment. In 1978 women living near Love Canal outside Niagara Falls, New York complained about unusually high rates of illnesses and birth defects in their community. Investigations revealed that their housing development had been constructed on top of a toxic waste dump. This discovery spawned grassroots efforts to clean up this area as well as other contaminated communities. In 1980 President Carter and Congress responded by passing the Comprehensive Environmental Response, Compensation, and Liability Act (known as Superfund) to clean up sites contaminated with hazardous substances. Further inquiries showed that the presence of such poisonous waste dumps disproportionately affected racial minorities and the poor. Critics called the placement of these waste locations near African American and other racial and ethnic minority communities "environmental racism" and launched a movement for environmental justice.

The burgeoning environmental movement worried that potential accidents in nuclear energy plants would pour radioactive contaminants into the environment and endanger surrounding communities. In 1976, over 1,400 activists were arrested protesting the construction of a nuclear power plant in Seabrook, New Hampshire. Some of the worst fears of the anti-nuclear movement nearly came to pass in March 1979 at the Three Mile Island nuclear power plant near Harrisburg, Pennsylvania. A broken valve at the plant leaked coolant and threatened the meltdown of the reactor's nuclear core. As officials quickly evacuated residents from the surrounding area, employees at the plant narrowly averted catastrophe by fixing the problem before an explosion occurred.

Racial Struggles Continue

The struggle for racial equality did not end with the 1960s. The coalition of civil rights organizations had disintegrated, but the National Association for the Advancement of Colored People remained active, as did local organizations in communities nationwide. Following passage of the 1965 Voting Rights Act, electoral politics became the new form of activism. In 1970 Congress placed a permanent ban on literacy tests for voting. By 1992 there were more than 7,500 black elected officials in the United States. Many of them had participated in the civil rights movement and subsequently worked to gain for their constituents the economic benefits that integration and affirmative action had not yet achieved. In 1975, Congress renewed the Voting Rights Act and added provisions safeguarding the ballot for language minorities, including holding bilingual elections.

The issue of school busing highlighted the persistence of racial discrimination. In the fifteen years following *Brown v. Board of Education*, few schools had been integrated. Starting in 1969, the U.S. Supreme Court ruled that genuine racial integration of the public schools must no longer be delayed. In 1971 the Court went even further in *Swann v. Charlotte-Mecklenburg Board of Education* by requiring school districts to bus pupils to achieve integration. Cities such as Charlotte, North Carolina; Lexington, Kentucky; and Tampa, Florida, embraced the ruling and carefully planned for it to succeed.

The decision was more controversial in other municipalities around the nation and it exposed racism as a national problem. In many northern communities racially discriminatory housing policies created segregated neighborhoods and, thus, segregated schools. When white parents in the Detroit suburbs objected to busing their children to inner-city, predominantly black schools, the Supreme Court in 1974 departed from the *Swann* case and prohibited busing across distinct school district boundaries. This ruling created a serious problem for integration efforts because many whites were fleeing the cities and moving to the suburbs where few blacks lived.

As the conflict over school integration intensified, violence broke out in communities throughout the country. In Boston, Massachusetts, busing opponents led by Louise Day Hicks tapped into the racial and class resentments of the largely white working-class population of South Boston, which was paired with the black community of Roxbury for busing, leaving mainly middle- and upper-class white communities unaffected. In the fall of 1974, battles broke out inside and outside the schools. Despite the violence, schools stayed open, and for the next three decades Boston remained under court order to continue busing.

Along with busing, affirmative action generated fierce controversy. From 1970 to 1977, with the acceleration of affirmative action programs, the number of African Americans attending college doubled, constituting nearly 10 percent of the student body, a few percentage points lower than the proportion of blacks in the national population. Though the average black family still earned a lower income than the average white family, black family income as a percentage of white family income had grown from 55.1 percent in 1965 to 61.5 percent ten years later. African Americans, however, still had a long struggle ahead to attain income and wages equal to whites. The situation was even worse for those who did not reach middle-class status: About 30 percent of African Americans slid deeper into poverty during the decade.

The case of Allan Bakke shaped the policy of affirmative action. In 1973, Bakke was rejected for admission into the medical school at the University of California at Davis. Of the one hundred available spaces in the incoming class, the university awarded sixteen spots to racial minorities, as part of its affirmative action policy to recruit a more racially and ethnically diverse student body. Contending that the policy amounted to reverse discrimination, Bakke sued the University of California at Davis. "I realize that the rationale for these quotas is that they attempt to atone for past racial discrimination," Bakke complained. "But insisting on a new racial bias in favor of minorities is not a just situation." In 1978, in *Regents of the University of California v. Bakke*, the U.S. Supreme Court struck down racial quotas as a component of affirmative action, but the justices permitted the use of race as one criterion in higher education admissions.

Despite the persistence of economic and educational inequality, many whites believed that affirmative action placed them at a disadvantage with blacks in the educational and economic marketplaces. In particular, many white men condemned policies that they thought recruited blacks at their expense. Polls showed that although most whites favored equal treatment of blacks, they disapproved of affirmative action as a form of "reverse discrimination." The furor over affirmative action did not end with the *Bakke* case, and over the next three decades affirmative action opponents succeeded in narrowing the use of racial considerations in employment and education.

Beyond voting rights, education, and affirmative action, one of the biggest concerns for African Americans remained treatment by the criminal justice system. Police officers patrolled black neighborhoods and arrested their residents disproportionately; trial juries convicted blacks disproportionately, and judges gave higher sentences disproportionately to African Americans. The lopsided imprisonment rates of blacks (and Latinos) played a substantial role in giving the United States the highest incarceration figures in the world.

A prisoner rights movement emerged. In September 1971 mainly black and Latino inmates at the Attica Correctional Facility, near Batavia, New York, rose up in protest of their treatment. Subject to overcrowding, censorship, and religious discrimination (against Muslims), more than 1,200 inmates overpowered their guards and seized forty-two prison staff. Influenced by the liberationist philosophies of Malcolm X and Martin Luther King Jr., and inspired by the revolutionary prisoner rights activists George Jackson and Angela Davis, the Attica rebels sought a variety of prison reforms. After peaceful negotiations collapsed over the issue of granting amnesty to the insurgents, Governor Nelson Rockefeller sent state troopers to regain control of the prison. The armed assault ended the rebellion and resulted in the deaths of thirty-three inmates and ten correctional officers. The Attica insurrection sparked awareness not just of prisoner rights but of systemic racism in criminal justice programs.

Mexican Americans Challenge Discrimination

During the late 1960s and 1970s, Mexican Americans campaigned for educational equality. School districts disproportionately assigned Mexican Americans into classes for the learning disabled and assigned them to vocational rather than college preparatory tracks. Mexican American students in East Los Angeles, San Antonio, Denver, and Houston conducted walkouts in protest of the lack of resources provided their schools.

Mexican American parents in San Antonio sued their school district, contending that financing education through property taxes placed their children at a disadvantage. They argued that the teacher-student ratio in their schools was substantially higher and the availability of books for pupils substantially lower compared to conditions in wealthier school districts. In *San Antonio Independent School District v. Rodriguez* (1973), however, the Supreme Court ruled that financing school systems through property taxes was not unconstitutional. Despite the unfavorable outcome, the case raised greater awareness about disparities in educational funding, and many states attempted to equalize school spending.

Mexican American college students also pressed their demands for equal rights. Formed in 1969, the Movimiento Estudiantil Chicano de Aztlán (Chicano Student Movement of Aztlán), known as MEChA, sought to promote Mexican American empowerment through political action. In the 1970s chapters arose on college campuses in Los Angeles, San Diego, and Riverside, California, and spread to Washington, Oregon, Colorado, Arizona, and Indiana. MEChA placed a premium on higher education in order to "contribute to the information of a complete person who truly

values life and freedom." The organization embraced the idea of *Chicanismo*, a political and cultural identity signaling a "rebirth of pride and confidence." These student radicals condemned Anglos for exploiting cheap Mexican labor and turning their *barrios* (neighborhoods) into colonies.

Chicano Power, 1970 The Brown Berets was a militant Chicano group supporting farm workers, educational and criminal justice reform, and antiwar activities. In this February 28, 1970 photo, two Chicana women stand together in Los Angeles, wearing matching uniforms during a National Chicano Moratorium Committee march in opposition to the war in Vietnam. David Fenton/Getty Images

The New Right Rises

The backlash against affirmative action and the ERA confirmed that liberal reformers were losing ground to conservatives. By the end of the 1970s, liberalism had become identified with special interests and elitism. At the same time, the pragmatic conservatism of Richard Nixon was being displaced by a harder edged brand of conservatism called the **New Right**. The New Right was founded on the budding conservatism of the 1960s as represented in the Sharon Statement and the presidential candidacy of Barry Goldwater. In the 1970s it expanded for a variety of reasons: the revolt against higher taxes, the backlash against the growth of the federal government, the disillusionment of former liberal intellectuals, and the growth of the Christian Right.

Tax Revolt

In the 1970s, working- and middle-class white resentment centered on big government spending and higher taxes. During that decade, taxation claimed 30 percent of the gross national product, up 6 percent from 1960. Although Americans still paid far less in taxes than their counterparts in Western Europe, Americans objected to raising state and federal taxes. Leading the tax revolt was the Sun Belt state of California. In a 1978 referendum, California voters passed Proposition 13, a measure that reduced property taxes and placed strict limits on the ability of local governments to raise them in the future. In the wake of Proposition 13, a dozen states enacted similar measures.

Economic conservatives also set their sights on reducing the federal income tax. They supported cutting personal and corporate taxes by a third in the belief that reducing taxes would encourage new investment and job creation. "Supply-side" economists argued that lowering tax rates would actually boost tax receipts: With lower taxes, companies and investors would have more capital to invest, leading to expanded job growth; with increased employment, more people would be paying taxes. At the same time, supply-side conservatives called for reduced government spending, especially in the social service sector, to ensure balanced budgets and to eliminate what they saw as unnecessary spending on domestic programs.

Neoconservatism

The New Right also benefited by the defection of disillusioned liberals. Labeled **neoconservatives**, intellectuals such as Irving Kristol, Norman Podhoretz, and Nathan Glazer reversed course and condemned the Great Society programs that they had originally supported. They believed that federal policies, such as affirmative action, had aggravated rather than improved the problems government planners intended to solve. They considered the New Left's opposition to the Vietnam War and its disapproval of foreign intervention a threat to national security.

Christian Conservatism

Perhaps the greatest spark igniting the New Right came from religious and social conservatives, mainly evangelical Christians and Catholics. Evangelicals considered themselves to have been "born again" — literally experiencing Jesus Christ's saving presence inside of them. By the end of the 1970s, evangelical Christians numbered around 50 million, about a quarter of the population. The Christian Right opposed abortion, gay rights, and sex education; attacked Supreme Court rulings banning prayer in the public schools; denounced Charles Darwin's theory of evolution in favor of divine creationism; supported the traditional role of women as mothers and homemakers; and backed a hard-line, anti-Communist stand against the Soviet Union. Certainly not all evangelical Christians held all of these beliefs; for example, President Carter, a born-again Christian, did not. Still, conservative Christians believed that the liberals and radicals of the 1960s had spread the secular creed of individual rights and personal fulfillment at the expense of established Christian values.

Social conservatives worried that the traditional nuclear family was in danger, as households consisting of married couples with children declined from 30 percent in the 1970s to 23 percent thirty years later, and the divorce rate soared. The number of unmarried couples living together doubled over the last quarter of the twentieth century. In 1970, 26.4 percent of infants were born to single mothers; by 1990 the rate had risen to 43.8. This increase was part of a trend in developed countries worldwide. Moreover, social conservatives united in fierce opposition to abortion, which the Supreme Court legalized in *Roe v. Wade*. They argued that an unborn fetus is a person and therefore has a right to life protected by the Constitution.

The direct impetus pushing conservative evangelicals into politics came when the Internal Revenue Service (IRS) removed tax-exempt status from a fundamentalist Christian college. Bob Jones University in South Carolina defended racial segregation on biblical grounds, but under pressure from the federal government began admitting some African American students in the mid-1970s. However, the school continued practicing discrimination by prohibiting interracial dating. In 1976, when the IRS revoked the university's tax-exempt status, conservative Christians charged that the federal government was interfering with religious freedom. This sparked a grassroots political campaign to rally Christian evangelicals around a host of grievances.

Television became an even greater instrument in the hands of New Right Christian preachers in the 1970s and 1980s. The Reverend Pat Robertson of Virginia founded the Christian Broadcasting Network, and ministers such as Jerry Falwell used the airwaves to great effect. What distinguished Falwell and Robertson from earlier evangelists like Billy Graham was their fusion of religion and electoral politics. In 1979 Falwell founded the Moral Majority, an organization that backed political candidates who supported a "family values" social agenda. Within two years of its creation, the Moral Majority counted four million members who were eager to organize in support of New Right politicians. The New Right also lined up advocacy groups such as the American Enterprise Institute and the Heritage Foundation to generate and promote conservative ideals. The alliance of economic, intellectual, and religious conservatives offered a formidable challenge to liberalism.

REVIEW & RELATE	• Explain the rise of the New Right in the 1970s.
	• How did Christian evangelicals influence the New Right?

Conclusion: The Swing toward Conservatism

The election of President Richard M. Nixon signaled discontent with the liberal policies and radical excesses of the 1960s. However, this conservative victory proved short-lived, as Nixon was forced to resign in disgrace as a result of the Watergate scandal. Before his resignation in 1973, Nixon had displayed a pragmatic conservatism that dismantled parts of the Great Society while at the same time signing into law measures that extended environmental protection and voting rights, including those for eighteen-year-olds. He issued executive orders expanding affirmative action.

The return of Democrats to the White House in 1977 did not restore 1960s-style liberalism. The presidential administration of Jimmy Carter acknowledged the conservative notions of limited government and a deregulated market economy while embracing key conservative social values, such as faith in God and prayer. Although Carter departed from conservatives on some key issues concerning the economy, race, and gender, he did not portray himself as the heir of the liberal ideals promoted by Franklin Roosevelt, Harry Truman, and Lyndon Johnson.

The movement toward conservatism grew slowly and sporadically. Nixon's pragmatic conservatism may have stalled in Washington, D.C., but in cities and states around the nation conservatives with a more rigid ideological bent than Nixon rallied their forces. The 1970s marked the rise of the New Right, which joined defectors from liberalism and exponents of conservative free market, anti-government principles with white members of the working class resentful of racial change, anti-abortion advocates, and proponents of right-wing Christian beliefs. The New Right sought to transform the politics of resentment toward the culture of the 1960s into the politics of revivalism, convincing many that traditional values once again might guide the nation.

The move to the right, however, did not stifle liberalism or dissent. For much of the 1970s, Democrats controlled Congress and although the Supreme Court shifted in a more conservative direction, the Court did not reject the precedents established by the Warren Court. The justices upheld abortion rights and, in the *Bakke* case, they limited affirmative action but did not overturn its constitutional foundation. Civil rights reformers, feminists such as Pauli Murray, environmentalists, and anti-nuclear activists continued to press their concerns and achieve victories. Nevertheless, racial problems persisted as conservatives attacked affirmative action and school busing to promote integration. Many of these battles shifted northward, as white, working-class, grassroots activists such as Louise Day Hicks fought against busing in particular and more generally against liberal elites, who, they believed, ignored them.

In foreign affairs, President Nixon ushered in a period of détente with the Soviet Union and the opening of diplomatic relations with Communist China. He brought an end to American military participation in Vietnam, but did so with less than honor. Throughout the rest of the world, Nixon pursued a muscular foreign policy, which often left the United States siding with dictators. His Middle East strategy in the 1973 Yom Kippur War produced a damaging gasoline crisis at home, which would be felt for years. Jimmy Carter built on Nixon's spirit of cooperation with the Soviet Union and China, only to see it end with renewed conflict with the Soviets. Where Nixon and previous presidents had failed, Carter succeeded in brokering a peace treaty between Egypt and Israel. However, his popularity plummeted after Iranian revolutionaries seized the American Embassy in Teheran and held its fifty-two occupants hostage for 444 days despite a failed rescue attempt.

Conservatism experienced its political ups and downs in the 1970s, but by the end of the decade it stood on the edge of transforming the political landscape of the nation. It remained for Ronald Reagan to lead the New Right forward.

Chapter 27 Review

KEY TERMS

Vietnamization, 692
Pentagon Papers, 693
War Powers Act, 693
détente, 693
Strategic Arms Limitation Treaty
   (SALT I), 694
Organization of Petroleum
   Exporting Countries (OPEC), 694
affirmative action, 695
Watergate, 696

National Energy Act, 699
SALT II, 701
mujahideen, 701
Camp David accords, 702
Equal Rights Amendment (ERA), 704
Environmental Protection Agency
   (EPA), 705
New Right, 709
neoconservatives, 709

REVIEW & RELATE

1. Compare Nixon's policies toward Vietnam with those toward the Soviet Union and China.
2. How did Nixon's Middle East policy affect Americans at home?
3. Describe the conservative coalition that brought Nixon to power.
4. How did Nixon appeal to conservatism and how much did he depart from it?
5. How effective was President Carter in domestic politics?
6. How did events in the Middle East, the Persian Gulf, and Afghanistan challenge the objectives of the Carter administration?
7. How and why did the social and cultural developments of the 1960s continue to create conflict and controversy in the 1970s?
8. Evaluate the strengths and weaknesses of liberalism in the 1970s.
9. Explain the rise of the New Right in the 1970s.
10. How did Christian evangelicals influence the New Right?

TIMELINE OF EVENTS

1970	• Invasion of Cambodia
	• Four students shot and killed at Kent State University
	• Gulf of Tonkin Resolution repealed
1971	• Environmental Protection Agency created
	• *Pentagon Papers* published
	• Attica prison uprising
1972	• Nixon visits China
	• SALT I signed
	• Watergate break-in
	• Passage of Title IX
	• Equal Rights Amendment submitted to states for ratification
	• *San Antonio Independent School District v. Rodriguez*
1973	• U.S. supports Israel in Yom Kippur War
	• Endangered Species Act passed
	• War Powers Act passed
	• U.S. agrees to withdraw from Vietnam
1973–1974	• OPEC oil embargo
1974	• Nixon resigns
1975	• North Vietnam defeats South Vietnam
1977	• Department of Energy created
1978	• Camp David accords
	• Proposition 13 passed in California
	• Bakke decision
1979	• Iran hostage crisis
	• SALT II signed; Congress does not ratify
	• Soviet Union invades Afghanistan
	• Three Mile Island accident
	• Moral Majority founded by Jerry Falwell

28

The Triumph of Conservatism, the End of the Cold War, and the Rise of the New World Order

1980–1992

LEARNING OBJECTIVES

After reading this chapter you will be able to:

- Assess the impact of Reaganomics and the ability of Presidents Reagan and Bush to deliver on the New Right's agenda.

- Analyze Ronald Reagan's role in ending the Cold War and fighting international terrorism.

- Describe how George H. W. Bush managed the end of the Cold War, and evaluate how he established a New World Order between the United States and the rest of the world.

COMPARING AMERICAN HISTORIES

As secretary of state, **George Pratt Shultz** presided over the end of the Cold War. A skilled mediator, Shultz believed in hard-nosed diplomacy, asserting that "negotiations are a euphemism for capitulation if the shadow of power is not cast across the bargaining table." Upon graduating from Princeton with an economics degree in 1942, Shultz joined the Marine Corps and served in the Pacific during World War II. After the war, he earned a Ph.D. in industrial economics and taught at the Massachusetts Institute of Technology and the University of Chicago. In 1955 he joined President Eisenhower's Council of Economic Advisors, the first of many government posts he would fill in the Kennedy, Johnson, and Nixon administrations before he left government for the corporate world.

In 1982 Shultz returned to Washington to serve as President Ronald Reagan's secretary of state. Like Reagan, Shultz believed that the United States needed to reassert itself as a global power and rebound from the insecurity and self-doubt that followed the Vietnam War. The president believed that a tough approach would bring peace, and he revived the fiery rhetoric and military preparedness of the darkest days of the Cold War. Reagan and Shultz also sided with anti-Communist dictators in Nicaragua and El Salvador who brutally repressed their political opponents. As an economist, Shultz doubted that the Soviet Union was financially able to sustain its military strength, and his predictions proved correct. Faced with an escalating arms race, a fresh group of Soviet leaders decided to pursue peaceful relations.

While President Reagan and Secretary of State Shultz advocated confrontation with the Soviet Union, **Demetria Martinez** took a very different approach to foreign affairs. Born in Albuquerque, New Mexico in 1960, Martinez came from a family with roots in Mexico. Her maternal grandmother, Lucy Jamarillo, migrated to New Mexico after the Mexican Revolution of 1910, and in the 1940s was elected county clerk in Albuquerque. Demetria's parents were educators, and her father, Ted, was the first Mexican American elected to the Albuquerque school board.

Demetria Martinez chose creative writing and journalism rather than electoral politics as a career. Following graduation from Princeton University in 1982, she returned to New Mexico and became a religion reporter for the *Albuquerque Journal.* As a journalist she came into contact with the **Sanctuary Movement**, a network of religious groups that provided asylum for undocumented immigrants from Central America. As part of a newspaper assignment in 1986, she travelled to Juarez, Mexico to interview two pregnant El Salvadoran women who sought sanctuary in the United States. Martinez and the two women crossed over the border to El Paso and then drove separately to Albuquerque. Martinez declined to write the story because she feared that U.S. immigration officials would find out the identity of the women and deport them. Instead she wrote a poem, "Nativity: For Two Salvadoran Women, 1986–1987."

Martinez became a catalyst for the Sanctuary Movement after she was indicted and tried by the federal government for criminal violation of immigration laws. Denying that she had illegally smuggled the two women into the United States and defending her right as a journalist under the First Amendment to interview the Salvadorans, she was acquitted by the jury.

Martinez went on to become an educator and prize-winning poet and author. She continues to promote Chicana causes and social justice through her writing and teaching.

THE AMERICAN HISTORIES of George Shultz and Demetria Martinez were shaped by decades of Cold War strife overseas and in Central America. Shultz and Martinez, however, stood on opposite sides. Advised by Secretary of State Shultz, President Ronald Reagan employed harsher anti-Soviet rhetoric than at any time since the early 1960s and accelerated the buildup of the military. With the end of the Cold War and the collapse of the Soviet Union and its empire, the United States became the world's sole superpower. At the same time, the United States had to operate in an increasingly globalized world and face tests of its strength in Central America, the Middle East, and the Persian Gulf. In contrast, Martinez directed her efforts toward publicizing the plight of refugees who tried to escape from Cold War era conflicts in El Salvador.

Not only did Reagan transform diplomatic relationships with the Soviet Union, he reshaped the nation's political priorities. The president implemented anti-union measures and signed legislation granting large tax cuts as well as reductions in spending for programs that helped the poor and needy. His administration also relaxed government regulations over business and succeeded in tipping the Supreme Court to the right through its conservative appointments. Social conservatives, too, made headway during the 1980s by defeating the Equal Rights Amendment.

The Reagan Revolution

The election of former California governor Ronald Reagan as president in 1980 reflected the spectacular growth in political power of the New Right. Reagan pushed the conservative economic agenda of lower taxes and business deregulation alongside the New Right's concern for traditional religious and family values. His presidency installed conservatism as the dominant political ideology for the remainder of the twentieth century.

Reagan and Reaganomics

A former movie actor, Reagan had transformed himself from a New Deal Democrat into a conservative Republican politician when he ran for governor of California in 1966. As governor, he implemented conservative ideas of free enterprise and small government and denounced Johnson's Great Society for threatening private property and individual liberty. His support for conservative economic and social issues carried him to the presidency.

In 1980 Reagan handily beat Jimmy Carter and John Anderson, a moderate Republican who ran as an independent candidate (Map 28.1). The high unemployment and inflation of the late 1970s worked in Reagan's favor. Reagan appealed to a coalition of conservative Republicans and disaffected Democrats, promising to cut taxes and reduce spending, and to end affirmative action. The 1980 and subsequent presidential elections demonstrated the rising political, economic, and social influence of the American South and West, especially as these regions continued their rapid population growth by drawing migrants from other areas of the nation. Finally, he energized members of the religious right, who flocked to the polls to support Reagan's demands for voluntary prayer in the public schools, defeat of the Equal Rights Amendment, and a constitutional amendment to outlaw abortion. In fact, the religious right attracted its most ardent supporters from the South and West.

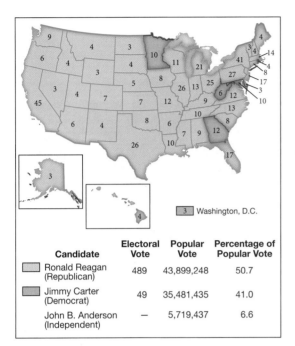

MAP 28.1 The Election of 1980

Ronald Reagan won 50.7 percent of the popular vote in the 1980 election, but his margin of victory over Jimmy Carter was much greater in the electoral vote. Reagan won the votes of the South and many disaffected Democrats in the urban North. A third-party candidate, John Anderson of Illinois, won 6.6 percent of the popular vote, demonstrating significant disapproval with both major parties.

Candidate	Electoral Vote	Popular Vote	Percentage of Popular Vote
Ronald Reagan (Republican)	489	43,899,248	50.7
Jimmy Carter (Democrat)	49	35,481,435	41.0
John B. Anderson (Independent)	—	5,719,437	6.6

Reagan's first priority was stimulating the stagnant economy. The president's strategy, known as **Reaganomics**, reflected the ideas of supply-side economists and conservative Republicans. Reagan subscribed to the idea of trickle-down economics in which the gains reaped at the top of a strong economy would trickle down to the benefit of those below, thus reducing the need for large government social programs. Stating that "government is not the solution to our problem; government is the problem," Reagan asked Congress for a huge income tax cut of 30 percent over three years, a reduction in spending for domestic programs of more than $40 billion, and new monetary policies to lower rising rates for loans.

The president did not operate in isolation from the rest of the world. He learned a great deal from Margaret Thatcher, the British prime minister who took office two years before Reagan. Thatcher combated inflation by slashing welfare programs, selling off publicly owned companies, and cutting back health and education programs. An advocate of supply-side economics, Thatcher reduced income taxes on the wealthy by more than 50 percent to encourage new investment. West Germany also moved toward the right under Chancellor Helmut Kohl, who reined in welfare spending. In the 1980s Reaganomics and Thatcherism dominated the United States and the two most powerful nations of Western Europe.

In March 1981 Reagan survived a nearly fatal assassin's bullet. More popular than ever after his recovery, the president persuaded the Democratic House and the Republican Senate to pass his economic measures in slightly modified form in the **Economic Recovery Tax Act**. These cuts in taxes and spending did not produce the immediate results Reagan sought—unemployment rose to 9.6 percent in 1983 from 7.1 percent in 1980. However, the government's tight money policies, as engineered by the Federal Reserve Board, reduced inflation from 14 percent in 1980 to 4 percent

Ronald Reagan Campaigns for President, 1980   Pledging to make America great again, Republican presidential candidate Ronald Reagan greets supporters at a senior citizens' retirement community in Seal Beach, California. During his 1980 campaign, Reagan expressed the cardinal tenet of antigovernment conservatism: "Government is like a baby, an alimentary canal with a big appetite at one end and no sense of responsibility at the other." AP Images/Walter Zeboski

in 1984. By 1984 the unemployment rate had fallen to 7.5 percent, while the gross national product grew by a healthy 4.3 percent, an indication that the recession, and the stagflation that came with it, had subsided.

The success of Reaganomics came at the expense of the poor and the lower middle class. The president reduced spending for food stamps, school lunches, Aid to Families with Dependent Children (welfare), and Medicaid, while maintaining programs that middle-class voters relied on, such as Medicare and Social Security. Rather than diminishing the government, the savings that came from reduced social spending went into increased military appropriations. Together with lower taxes, these expenditures benefited large corporations that received government military contracts and favorable tax write-offs.

As a result of Reagan's economic policies, financial institutions and the stock market earned huge profits. The Reagan administration relaxed antitrust regulations, encouraging corporate mergers to a degree unseen since the Great Depression. Fueled by falling interest rates, the stock market created wealth for many investors. The number of millionaires doubled during the 1980s, as the top 1 percent of families gained control of 42 percent of the nation's wealth and 60 percent of corporate stock. Reflecting this phenomenal accumulation of riches, television produced melodramas depicting the lives of oil barons (such as *Dallas* and *Dynasty*), whose characters lived glamorous lives filled with intrigue and extravagance. In *Wall Street* (1987), a film that captured the money ethic of the period, the main character utters the memorable line summing up the moment: "Greed, for lack of a better word, is good. Greed is right. Greed works."

Contrary to the promises of Reaganomics, the wealth did not trickle down and the gap between the rich and the poor widened. During the 1980s, the nation's share of poor people rose from 11.7 percent to 13.5 percent, representing 33 million Americans. Severe cutbacks in government social programs such as food stamps worsened the plight of the poor. Poverty disproportionately affected women and racial minorities. The number of homeless people grew to as many as 400,000 during the 1980s. The middle class also diminished from a high of 53 percent of families in the early 1970s to 49 percent in 1985.

The Reagan administration's relaxed regulation of the corporate sector also contributed to the unbalanced economy. The president aided big business by challenging labor unions. In 1981 air traffic controllers went on strike to gain higher wages and improved safety conditions. In response, the president fired the strikers who refused to return to work, and in their place he hired new controllers. Reagan's anti-union actions encouraged a decline in union membership throughout the 1980s, with union membership falling to 16 percent, its lowest level since the New Deal. Without union protection, wages failed to keep up with inflation, further increasing the gap between rich and poor.

Reagan continued the business deregulation initiated under Carter. Federal agencies concerned with environmental protection, consumer product reliability, and occupational safety saw their key functions shifted to the states, which made them less effective. Reagan also extended banking deregulation, which encouraged savings and loan institutions (S&Ls) to make risky loans to real estate ventures. When real estate prices began to tumble, savings and loan associations faced collapse and Congress appropriated over $100 billion to rescue them. Notwithstanding deregulation and small-government rhetoric, the number of federal government employees actually increased under Reagan by 200,000.

Reagan's landslide victory over Democratic candidate Walter Mondale in 1984 sealed the national political transition from liberalism to conservatism. Voters responded overwhelmingly to the improving economy, Reagan's defense of traditional social values, and his boundless optimism about America's future. Despite the landslide, the election was notable for the nomination of Representative Geraldine Ferraro of New York as Mondale's Democratic running mate, the first woman to run on a major party ticket for national office.

Reagan's second term did not produce changes as significant as did his first term. Democrats still controlled the House and in 1986 recaptured the Senate. The Reagan administration focused on foreign affairs and the continued Cold War with the Soviet Union, thus escalating defense spending. Most of the Reagan economic revolution continued as before, but with serious consequences. The federal deficit mushroomed, and by 1989 the nation was saddled with a $2.8 trillion debt, a situation that jeopardized the country's financial independence and the economic well-being of succeeding generations.

The president further reshaped the future through his nominations to the U.S. Supreme Court. Starting with the choice of Sandra Day O'Connor, the Court's first female justice, in 1981, Reagan's appointments moved the Court in a more conservative direction. The elevation of Associate Justice William Rehnquist to chief justice in 1986 reinforced this trend, which would have significant consequences for decades to come.

The Implementation of Social Conservatism

Throughout his two terms, President Reagan pushed the New Right's social agenda. Conservatives blamed political liberalism for what they saw as a decline in family values. Their solution was a renewed focus on conservative Christian principles. In addition to trying to remove evolution and sex education from the classroom and bring in prayer, the New Right stepped up its opposition to abortion and imposed limits on reproductive rights. The Reagan administration required family planning agencies seeking federal funding to notify parents of children under age eighteen before dispensing birth control, cut off financial aid to international organizations supporting abortion, and provided funds to promote sexual abstinence. Despite these efforts, conservatives could not convince the Supreme Court to overturn *Roe v. Wade*. However, they did see the Equal Rights Amendment go down to defeat in 1982 when it failed to get the required two-thirds approval from the states.

Social conservatives also felt threatened by more tolerant views of homosexuality. The gay rights movement, which began in the 1960s, strengthened during the 1970s as thousands of gay men and lesbians made known their sexual orientation, fought discrimination, and expressed pride in their sexual identity. Then, in the early 1980s, physicians traced an outbreak of a deadly illness among gay men to a virus that attacked the immune system (human immunodeficiency virus, or HIV), making it vulnerable to infections that were usually fatal. This disease, called **acquired immune deficiency syndrome (AIDS)**, was transmitted through bodily fluids during sexual intercourse, through blood transfusions, and by intravenous drug use. Scientists could not explain why the disease initially showed up among gay men in the United States; however, New Right critics insisted that AIDS was a plague visited on sexual deviants by an angry God. As the epidemic spread beyond the gay community, gay rights organizers and their heterosexual allies raised research money and public awareness. By the early 1990s, medical advances had begun to extend the lives of AIDS patients and manage the disease.

Increased immigration also troubled social conservatives as another reflection of the general societal breakdown. The number of immigrants to the United States rose dramatically in the 1970s and 1980s following the relaxation of foreign quota restrictions after 1965 (Figure 28.1). During these decades, immigrants came mainly from Mexico, Central America, the Caribbean, and eastern and southern Asia and tended to settle in California, Florida, Texas, New York, and New Jersey. By 1990 one-third of Los Angeles's and New York City's populations were foreign-born, figures similar to the high numbers of European immigrants at the turn of the twentieth century.

Confronted by anti-immigrant attacks from the New Right, Reagan walked a fine line on immigration. In 1982, the U.S. Supreme Court in *Plyler v. Doe* ruled that a county in Texas could not withhold funds from the education of children of undocumented Mexican immigrants. In 1986 Reagan supported the **Immigration Reform and Control Act**, which extended amnesty to undocumented aliens residing in the United States for a specified period. It permitted them

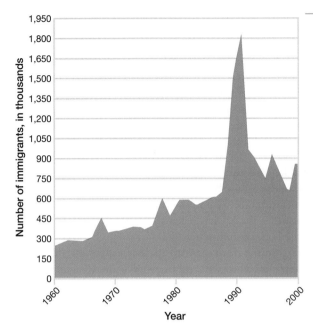

FIGURE 28.1 Immigrant Arrivals to the United States, 1960–2000 Immigration to the United States rose dramatically in the 1970s and 1980s, peaking in the early 1990s. Between 1970 and 2000, nearly 21 million immigrants arrived in the United States, mainly from Mexico, Central America, the Caribbean, and eastern and southern Asia. How do you explain the rise in immigration after 1965? Source: Data from 2000 Statistical Yearbook of the Immigration and Naturalization Service

to acquire legal status, while penalizing employers who hired new illegal workers. The measure allowed Reagan and the Republicans to appeal to Latino voters in the Sun Belt states while convincing the New Right that the administration intended to halt further undocumented immigration.

The president disagreed with New Right critics who questioned whether culturally diverse people could assimilate into American society. To the contrary, Reagan appointed Lauro F. Cavazos, a sixth generation Texan, as secretary of education, the first Latino to hold a cabinet position.

REVIEW & RELATE	• What was Reaganomics, and what were its most important long-term consequences? • How did conservative ideas shape the social, cultural, and political landscape of the 1980s and 1990s?

Reagan and the End of the Cold War, 1981–1988

President Reagan and Secretary of State George Shultz believed that the Cold War would be won only after the United States achieved military supremacy over the Soviet Union. Reagan also took strong measures to fight communism around the globe, from Central America to the Middle East. Yet military superiority alone would not defeat the Soviet Union. A shift of leadership within the USSR, as well as a worldwide protest movement for nuclear disarmament, helped bring an end to the Cold War and prepare the way for the dissolution of the Soviet empire.

"The Evil Empire"

In running for president in 1980, Reagan wrapped his hard-line anti-Communist message in the rhetoric of peace. "I've called for whatever it takes to be so strong that no other nation will dare violate the peace," he told the Veterans of Foreign Wars Convention on August 18, 1980. Once in the White House, Reagan left no doubt about his anti-Communist stance. He called the Soviet Union "the evil empire," regarding it as "the focus of evil in the modern world." The president planned to confront that evil with both words and deeds, backing up his rhetoric with a massive military buildup.

In a show of economic might, Reagan proposed the largest military budget in American history. The defense budget grew by about 7 percent per year, increasing from $157 billion in 1981 to around $282 billion in 1988. Reagan clearly intended to win the Cold War by outspending the Soviets, even if it meant running up huge deficits that greatly burdened the U.S. economy.

Reagan was unyielding in his initial dealings with the Soviet Union, and negotiations between the superpowers moved slowly and unevenly. The Reagan administration's "zero option" proposal called for the Soviets to dismantle all of their intermediate-range missiles in exchange for the United States agreeing to refrain from deploying any new medium-range missiles. The administration presented this option merely for show, expecting the Soviets to reject it. However, in 1982, after the Soviets accepted the principle of "zero option," Reagan sent negotiators to begin Strategic Arms Reduction Talks (START). Influenced by antinuclear protests in Europe, which had a great impact on European governments, the Americans proposed shelving the deployment of 572 Pershing II and cruise missiles in Europe in return for the Soviets' dismantling of Eastern European–based intermediate-range ballistic missiles that were targeted at Western Europe. The Soviets viewed this offer as perpetuating American nuclear superiority and rejected it.

Relations between the two superpowers deteriorated in September 1983 when a Soviet fighter jet shot down a South Korean passenger airliner, killing 269 people. The Soviets charged that the plane had veered off course and violated their airspace. Although the disaster resulted mainly from Soviet mistakes, Reagan chose to condemn this attack as further proof of the malign intentions of the USSR. The United States sent additional missiles to bases in West Germany, Great Britain, and Italy; in response, the Soviets abandoned the disarmament talks and replenished their nuclear arsenal in Czechoslovakia and East Germany. More symbolically, the Soviets boycotted the 1984 Olympic Games in Los Angeles, in retaliation for the U.S. boycott of the Olympics in Moscow four years earlier. As the two adversaries swung from peace talks to threats of nuclear confrontation, one European journalist observed: "The second Cold War has begun."

Human Rights and the Fight against Communism

The Reagan administration extended its Cold War position throughout the world, emphasizing anticommunism often at the expense of human rights. Reagan embraced the distinction made by his ambassador to the United Nations, Jeane Kirkpatrick, between non-Communist "authoritarian" nations, which were acceptable, and Communist "totalitarian" regimes, which were not.

Reagan considered the South African government an example of an acceptable authoritarianism, even though it practiced apartheid (white supremacy and racial separation) and torture. The fact that the South African Communist Party had joined the fight against apartheid reinforced Reagan's desire to support the white-minority, anti-Communist government. Interested in the country's vast mineral wealth, Reagan opted for what he called "constructive engagement" with South Africa, rather than condemn its racist practices. The Reagan administration did so even as protesters across the United States and the world spoke out against South Africa's repressive white-majority government and campaigned for divestment of public and corporate funds from South African companies. After years of pressure from the divestment movement on college campuses and elsewhere, in 1986 Congress passed the Comprehensive Anti-Apartheid Act, which prohibited new trade and investment in South Africa. President Reagan vetoed it, but Congress overrode the president's veto.

The president also exploited the fear of communism in Central America and the Caribbean, where for nearly a century the United States had guarded its sphere of influence. During the 1980s, the United States continued its economic isolation of Cuba via the trade embargo, and it sought to prevent other Communist or leftist governments from emerging in Central America and the Caribbean.

In the late 1970s Nicaraguan revolutionaries, known as the National Liberation Front or Sandinistas, had overthrown the tyrannical government of General Anastasio Somoza, a brutal dictator. President Jimmy Carter, who had originally supported Somoza's overthrow, halted all aid to Nicaragua in 1980 after the Sandinistas began nationalizing foreign companies and drawing closer to Cuba. Under Reagan, Secretary of State Shultz suggested a U.S. invasion of Nicaragua, reflecting the administration's belief that the revolution in Nicaragua had been sponsored by Moscow. Instead Reagan adopted a more indirect approach. In 1982 he authorized the CIA to train approximately two thousand guerrilla forces outside the country, known as Contras (Counterrevolutionaries), to overthrow the Sandinista government. Although Reagan praised the Contras as "the moral equivalent of our Founding Fathers," the group consisted of pro-Somoza reactionaries as well as anti-Marxist democrats who blew up bridges and oil dumps, burned crops, and killed civilians. In 1982 Congress, unwilling to support such actions, passed the **Boland Amendment**, which prohibited direct aid to the Contras. In the face of congressional opposition, Reagan and his advisers came up with a plan that would secretly fund the efforts of their military surrogates in Nicaragua. Reagan ordered the CIA and the National Security Council (NSC) to raise money from anti-Communist leaders abroad and wealthy conservatives at home. This effort, called "Project Democracy," raised millions of dollars, and by 1985 the number of Contra troops had swelled from 10,000 to 20,000. In violation of federal law, CIA director William Casey also authorized his agency to continue training the Contras in assassination techniques and other methods of subversion.

Elsewhere in Central America, the Reagan administration supported a corrupt right-wing government in El Salvador that, in an effort to put down an insurgency, sanctioned military death squads and killed forty thousand people during the 1980s. Despite the failings and abuses of the El Salvadoran government, Reagan insisted that Communist regimes in Nicaragua and Cuba were behind the Salvadoran insurgents. The United States sent more than $5 billion in aid to El Salvador and trained its military leaders to combat guerrilla forces (Map 28.2).

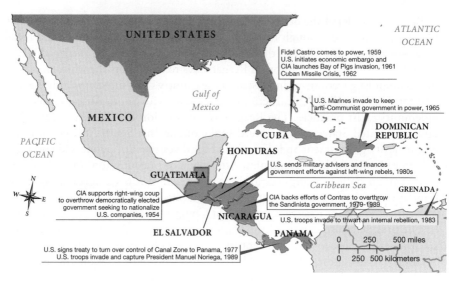

MAP 28.2   The United States in Central America and the Caribbean, 1954–1989
The United States had intervened in Central America and the Caribbean since the late 1890s to protect its sphere of interest. With the onset of the Cold War in the late 1940s, the United States intervened in the internal affairs of these nations to thwart what it viewed as the threat of Communist aggression, even if this meant supporting dictatorial regimes. As a result of such conflicts in the 1980s, many immigrants from Central America sought political asylum in the United States, mainly in Texas, New Mexico, Arizona, and California.

In addition to financing guerrilla wars in Central America, on October 25, 1983 Reagan sent 7,000 marines to invade the tiny Caribbean island of Grenada. After a coup toppled the leftist government of Maurice Bishop, who had received Cuban and Soviet aid, the United States stepped in, ostensibly to protect American medical school students in Grenada from political instability following the coup. A pro-American government was installed. The swift action in Grenada boosted Reagan's popularity.

While many Americans supported Reagan's strong anti-Communist stance, others opposed to the president's policy mobilized protests. Marches, rallies, and teach-ins were organized in cities and college campuses nationwide. U.S.-sponsored wars also drove many people to flee their dangerous, poverty-stricken countries and seek asylum in the United States. Between 1984 and 1990, 45,000 Salvadorans and 9,500 Guatemalans applied for asylum in the United States, but because the United States supported the established governments in those two nations, nearly all requests for refugee status were denied. Approximately five hundred American churches and synagogues established a sanctuary movement to provide safe haven for those fleeing Central American civil wars. Demetria Martinez's trial and acquittal in 1988 for allegedly smuggling undocumented immigrants into the United States gave a big boost to the sanctuary cause. Like other Christians, she was influenced by "liberation theology," a movement developed by Catholic clergymen in Latin America to promote social justice and political freedom.

In contrast, many other Americans, especially in California and Texas, began to view the influx of refugees from Central America with alarm. This immigration, both legal and illegal, meant an increase in medical and educational costs for state and local communities, which taxpayers considered a burden.

Fighting International Terrorism

Two days before the Grenada invasion in 1983, the U.S. military suffered a grievous blow halfway around the world. In the tiny country of Lebanon, wedged between Syrian occupation on its northern border and the Palestine Liberation Organization's (PLO) fight against Israel to the south, a civil war raged between Christians and Muslims. Reagan believed that stability in the region was in America's national interest. In 1982 the Reagan administration sent 800 marines, as part of a multilateral force that included French and Italian troops, to keep the peace. On October 23, 1983, a suicide bomber drove a truck into a marine barracks, killing 241 soldiers. Reagan withdrew the remaining troops.

The removal of troops did not end threats to Americans in the Middle East. Terrorism had become an ever-present danger, especially since the Iranian hostage crisis in 1979–1980. In 1985, 17 American citizens were killed in terrorist assaults, and 154 were injured. In one of those attacks, commandos of the Palestine Liberation Organization hijacked the Italian liner *Achille Lauro*, which was cruising from Egypt to Israel. One of the 450 passengers, the wheelchair-bound, elderly Jewish American Leon Klinghoffer, was murdered and thrown overboard. After three days, Egyptian authorities negotiated an end to the terrorist hijacking.

In response to the 1985 PLO cruise ship attack, the Reagan administration targeted the North African country of Libya for retaliation. Its military leader, Muammar al-Qaddafi, supported the Palestinian cause and provided sanctuary for terrorists. The Reagan administration had placed a trade embargo on Libya, and Secretary of State Shultz remarked: "We have to put Qaddafi in a box and close the lid." In 1986, after the bombing of a nightclub in West Berlin killed 2 American servicemen and injured 230, Reagan charged that Qaddafi was responsible. In late April the United States retaliated by sending planes to bomb the Libyan capital of Tripoli. Following the bombing, Qaddafi took a much lower profile against the United States. Reagan had demonstrated his nation's military might despite the retreat from Lebanon (Map 28.3).

In the meantime, the situation in Lebanon remained critical as the strife caused by civil war led to the seizing of American hostages. By mid-1984, seven Americans in Lebanon had been kidnapped by Shi'ite Muslims financed by Iran. Since 1980, Iran, a Shi'ite nation, had been engaged in a protracted war with Iraq, which was ruled by military leader Saddam Hussein and his Sunni Muslim party, the chief rival to the Shi'ites. With relations between the United States and Iran having deteriorated in the aftermath of the 1979 coup, the Reagan administration backed Iraq in this war. The fate of the hostages in Lebanon, however, motivated Reagan to make a deal with Iran. In late 1985 Reagan's national security adviser, Robert McFarlane, negotiated secretly with an Iranian intermediary for the United States to sell antitank missiles to Iran in exchange for the Shi'ite government using its influence to induce the Muslim kidnappers to release the hostages.

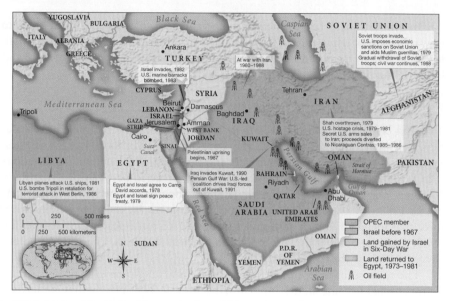

MAP 28.3   The United States in the Middle East, 1978–1991
The United States has historically needed access to the rich oil reserves of the Middle East. From the 1970s to the 1990s, both Democratic and Republican administrations were committed to the security of Israel, supportive of Afghan rebels fighting Soviet invaders, and opposed to the rising power of Islamic regimes. These principles often led to contradictory policies that further embroiled the United States in Middle East affairs.

Had the matter ended there, the secret deal might never have come to light. However, NSC aide Lieutenant Colonel Oliver North developed a plan to transfer the proceeds from the arms-for-hostages deal to fund the Contras in Nicaragua and circumvent the Boland Amendment, which prohibited direct aid to the rebels. Despite opposition from Secretary of State Shultz, Reagan liked North's plan, although the president seemed vague about the details, and some $10 million to $20 million of Iranian money flowed into the hands of the Contras.

In 1986 information about the **Iran-Contra affair** came to light. In the summer of 1987, televised Senate hearings exposed much of the tangled, covert dealings with Iran. In 1988 a special federal prosecutor indicted NSC adviser Vice Admiral John Poindexter (who had replaced McFarlane), North, and several others on charges ranging from perjury to conspiracy to obstruction of justice. Reagan took responsibility for the transfer of funds to the Contras, but he managed to weather the political crisis.

The Nuclear Freeze Movement

Reagan's tough talk and military buildup against the Soviet Union ignited protests against nuclear weapons in the United States and Europe. At the end of the Carter administration, the United States had promised NATO that it would station new missiles in England, Italy, West Germany, and Belgium. Reagan's decision to implement this policy sparked enormous protest. One such protest came in 1981 when women peace activists set up camp at Greenham Common in England outside of one of the military bases prepared to house the arriving missiles, one of twenty such camps in England. At the Greenham Common peace camp, protesters sang, danced, and performed skits to affirm women's solidarity for peace. Women came together not only to promote disarmament but also to empower themselves and create supportive communities dedicated to peace.

These activities were part of a larger **nuclear freeze movement** that began in 1980. Its proponents called for a "mutual freeze on the testing, production, and deployment of nuclear weapons and of missiles and aircraft designed primarily to deliver nuclear weapons." Grassroots activists also held town meetings throughout the United States to mobilize ordinary citizens to speak out against nuclear proliferation. In 1982 some 750,000 people rallied in New York City's Central Park to support a nuclear freeze resolution presented at the United Nations. Despite opposition from the United States and its NATO allies, measures favoring the freeze easily passed in the UN General Assembly. In the 1982 elections, peace groups placed nonbinding, nuclear freeze referenda on local ballots, which passed with wide majorities.

The following year, the Seneca Falls Women's Encampment for a Future of Peace and Justice set up operations in western New York next to an army depot that stored nuclear missiles. On July 30, 1983, peace activist Barbara Deming led a march of seventy-five female activists into the small town of Waterloo. Several miles into the walk the marchers found their way blocked by a few hundred counter-demonstrators

Ronald Reagan and Mikhail Gorbachev, 1987   After once calling the Soviet Union "the evil empire," President Ronald Reagan sits alongside Soviet leader Mikhail Gorbachev to sign the Intermediate-range Nuclear Forces (INF) agreement in the East Room of the White House on December 8, 1987. The agreement marked a turning point in the Cold War. Ronald Reagan Presidential Library

brandishing American flags and chanting, "Commies, go home!" The peace activists then sat down in nonviolent protest, and the police arrested Deming and fifty-three other protesters. Congress rejected the demonstrators' call for an "immediate freeze."

Yet the antinuclear movement in the United States and in Europe influenced Reagan. According to a 1982 public opinion poll, 57 percent of Americans favored an immediate nuclear freeze. Reagan acknowledged that he was more inclined to reconsider deploying missiles abroad because European leaders felt pressure from protesters in their home countries. The freeze movement inside and outside the United States created a favorable climate in which the president and Soviet leaders could negotiate a genuine plan for nuclear disarmament by the end of the decade.

The Road to Nuclear De-escalation

Ronald Reagan won reelection in 1984 by a landslide. Following his enormous victory, Reagan softened his militant stance and became more amenable to negotiating with the USSR. Reagan espoused conservative principles during his presidency, but he refused to let rigid dogma interfere with more pragmatic considerations to foster peace. Having earned political capital from his long fight against communism, he was prepared, as president, to spend it. By the time President Reagan left office, little remained of the Cold War.

In the mid-1980s, powerful changes were sweeping through the Soviet Union. In September 1985, Mikhail Gorbachev became general secretary of the Communist Party and head of the Soviet Union. Gorbachev introduced a program of economic and political reform. Through *glasnost* (openness) and *perestroika* (restructuring), the Soviet leader hoped to reduce massive state control over the declining economy and to extend democratic elections, as well as freedom of speech and freedom of the press. Gorbachev understood that the success of his reforms depended on reducing Cold War tensions with the United States and slowing the arms escalation that was bankrupting the Soviet economy. Gorbachev's *glasnost* brought the popular American musical performer Billy Joel to the Soviet Union in August 1987, staging the first rock concert in the country.

The changes that Gorbachev brought to the internal affairs of the Soviet Union carried over to the international arena. From 1986 to 1988, the Soviet leader negotiated in person with the American president, something that had not happened during Reagan's first term. In 1986 at a summit in Reykjavik, Iceland, the two leaders agreed to cut the number of strategic nuclear missiles in half. In 1987 the two sides negotiated an Intermediate Nuclear Forces Treaty, which provided for the destruction of existing intermediate-range missiles and on-site inspections to ensure compliance. The height of détente came in December 1987, when Gorbachev traveled to the United States to take part in the treaty-signing ceremony. Reagan no longer referred to the USSR as "the evil empire," and Gorbachev impressed Americans with his personal charm. The following year, Reagan flew to the Soviet Union, hugged Gorbachev at Lenin's Tomb, and told reporters, "They've changed," referring to the once and not-so-distant "evil empire." Citizens of the two adversarial nations breathed a collective sigh of relief; at long last, the icy terrain of the Cold War appeared to be melting.

The Presidency of George H. W. Bush, 1989–1993

After Reagan left office, his two-term vice president, George H. W. Bush, generally carried on his conservative legacy at home and abroad. While sharing most of Reagan's views, Bush called for a "kinder, gentler nation" in dealing with social justice and the environment. When Bush became president in 1989, he also encountered a very different Soviet Union from the one Reagan had faced a decade earlier and one that produced new challenges. The USSR was undergoing an internal revolution, which allowed Bush and the United States to take on a new role in a world that was no longer divided between capitalist and Communist nations and their allies. Globalization became the hallmark of the post–Cold War era, replacing previously dualistic economic and political systems, with mixed consequences. Following the collapse of the old world order, local and regional conflicts long held in check by the Cold War broke out along religious, racial, and ethnic lines.

"Kinder and Gentler" Conservatism

In his 1988 presidential campaign against Michael Dukakis, the Democratic governor of Massachusetts, Bush defended conservative principles when he promised, "Read my lips: No new taxes." The Republican candidate attacked Dukakis for his liberal positions and accused him of being soft on crime. Bush also affirmed his own opposition to abortion and support for gun rights and the death penalty.

Once in office Bush had to deal with problems that he inherited from his predecessor. Reagan's economic programs and military spending had left the nation with a mounting federal budget deficit and fears over inflation. Attempts to ward off inflation by raising interest rates had slowed economic growth. Then the real estate market faltered, resulting in the failure of a third of the nation's saving and loans associations. To make matters worse, oil prices spiked in 1990 after President Bush ordered the invasion of Iraq. As a result, the nation fell back into recession. Unemployment rose from 5.3 percent when Bush took office in 1989 to 7.5 percent by 1992, and state and local governments had difficulty paying for the educational, health, and social services that the Reagan and Bush administrations had transferred to them. To reverse the downward spiral, Bush abandoned his "no new taxes" pledge. In 1990 he supported a deficit reduction package that included more than $130 billion in new taxes, but which failed to solve the economic problems and angered Reagan conservatives. He also departed from anti-government conservatives when he signed the Americans with Disabilities Act (1990), extending a range of protections to some 40 million Americans with physical and mental handicaps.

Bush had a mixed record on the environment. In 1989 the oil tanker *Exxon Valdez* struck a reef off the coast of Alaska, dumping nearly 11 million gallons of oil into Prince William Sound. This disaster created pressure for stricter environmental legislation. In 1990 the president signed the Clean Air Act, which reduced emissions from automobiles and power plants. Bush refused to go further, and in 1992 he opposed international efforts to limit carbon dioxide emissions, greenhouse gases that contribute to climate change.

Bush courted conservatives in his nomination of Clarence Thomas in 1991 to fill the Supreme Court vacancy left by Justice Thurgood Marshall, the first African American justice. Thomas belonged to a rising group of conservative blacks who shared Republican views supporting private enterprise and the free market system and opposing affirmative action. As chief of the Equal Employment Opportunity Commission (EEOC) under Reagan, Thomas had generally weakened the agency's enforcement of racial and gender equality in the workplace. He also opposed abortion and denounced welfare. During the course of Thomas's Senate confirmation hearing, Anita Hill, Thomas's assistant at the EEOC, testified before the Senate Judiciary Committee and a nationally televised audience that Thomas had made unwanted sexual advances to her on and off the job, which she quit in 1983. Hill's charges of sexual harassment did not stop his confirmation. Thomas became one of the most conservative members of the Court. Membership in women's political associations—such as Emily's List, founded in 1984, and the Fund for a Feminist Majority, founded in 1987—soared following Hill's testimony.

Bush made less controversial but noteworthy appointments aimed at appealing to racial minority voters. He retained Lauro Cavazos as secretary of education and selected Manuel Lujan Jr. of New Mexico as secretary of the interior. Republicans maintained their political efforts to appeal to Latinos, particularly Mexican Americans, and broaden the base of their party.

The Breakup of the Soviet Union

Bush's first year in office coincided with upheavals in the Soviet-controlled Communist bloc, with Poland leading the way. In 1980 Polish dockworker Lech Walesa had organized **Solidarity**, a trade union movement conducting a series of popular strikes that forced the Communist government to recognize the group. Solidarity had ten million members and attracted various opponents of the Communist regime, including working-class democrats, Catholics, and nationalists who favored breaking ties with the Soviet Union. In 1981 Soviet leaders, disturbed by Solidarity's growing strength, forced the Polish government to crack down on the organization, arrest Walesa, and ban Solidarity. In 1989 Walesa and Solidarity seized on the changes ushered in by Mikhail Gorbachev's *glasnost* in the USSR to press their demands for democracy in Poland. The Soviets refused to intervene, and Poland conducted its first free elections since the beginning of the Cold War, electing Lech Walesa as president of the country. In July 1989, Gorbachev further broke from the past and announced that the Soviet Union would respect the national sovereignty of all the nations in the Warsaw Pact, which the Soviet Union had controlled since the late 1940s.

Gorbachev's proclamation spurred the end of communism throughout Eastern Europe. Within the next year, Soviet-sponsored regimes fell peacefully in Hungary and Czechoslovakia, replaced by elected governments. Bulgaria held free elections, which brought reformers to power. Only in Romania did Communist rulers put up a fight. There, it took a violent popular uprising to topple the brutal dictator Nicolae Ceausescu. The Baltic states of Latvia, Lithuania, and Estonia, which the Soviets had incorporated into the USSR at the outset of World War II, also regained their independence, sparking the political breakup of the Soviet Union itself.

Perhaps the most striking symbolism in the dismantling of the Soviet empire came in Germany, a country that had been divided between East and West states since 1945. With Communist governments collapsing around them, East Germans demonstrated against the regime of Erich Honecker. With no Soviet help forthcoming, Honecker decided to open the border between East and West Germany. On November 9, 1989, East and West Germans flocked to the Berlin Wall and jubilantly joined workers in knocking down the concrete barricade that divided the city. A year later, East and West Germany merged under the democratic, capitalist Federal Republic of Germany.

Gorbachev also brought an end to the costly nine-year Soviet-Afghan War. When the Soviets withdrew their last troops on February 15, 1989, they left Afghanistan in shambles. One million Afghans had perished, and another 5 million fled the country for Pakistan and Iran, resulting in the political destabilization of Afghanistan. Following a civil war, the Taliban, a group of Sunni Muslim fundamentalists, came to power in the mid-1990s and established a theocratic regime that, among other things, strictly regulated what women could wear in public and denied them educational and professional opportunities. The Taliban also provided sanctuary for many of the mujahideen rebels who had fought against the Soviets, including Osama bin Laden, who would use the country as a base for his al-Qaeda organization to promote terrorism against the United States.

Meanwhile, the Soviet Union disintegrated. Free elections were held in 1990, which ironically threatened Gorbachev's own power by bringing non-Communists to local and national political offices. Although an advocate of economic reform and political openness, Gorbachev remained a Communist and was committed to preserving the USSR. Challenges to Gorbachev came from both ends of the political spectrum. Boris Yeltsin, his former protégé, led the non-Communist forces that wanted Gorbachev to move more quickly in adopting capitalism; on the other side, hard-line generals in the Soviet army disapproved of Gorbachev's reforms and his cooperation with the United States. On August 18, 1991, a group of hard-core conspirators staged a coup against Gorbachev, placed him under house arrest, and surrounded the parliament building with troops. Yeltsin, the president of the Russian Republic, rallied fellow legislators and Muscovites against the plotters and brought the uprising to a peaceful end. Several months later, in early December, Yeltsin and the leaders of the independent republics of Belarus and Ukraine formed the Commonwealth of Independent States (CIS), consisting of the Russian Federation and eleven of fifteen former Soviet states. Shortly after, the CIS removed the hammer and sickle, the symbol of communism, from its flag.

Under these circumstances, on December 25, 1991, Gorbachev resigned. The next day, the Soviet legislative body passed a resolution dissolving the USSR. With the Soviet Union dismantled, Yeltsin, as head of the Russian Federation and the CIS, expanded the democratic and free market reforms initiated by Gorbachev (Map 28.4).

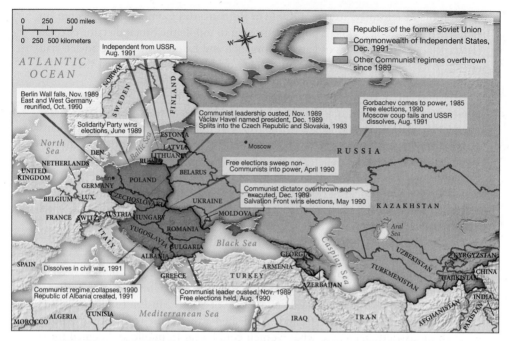

MAP 28.4   The Fall of Communism in Eastern Europe and the Soviet Union, 1989–1991
The collapse of Communist regimes in Eastern Europe was due in part to political and economic reforms initiated by Soviet premier Mikhail Gorbachev, including agreements with the United States to reduce nuclear arms. These changes inspired demands for free elections that were supported by popular uprisings, first in Poland and then in other former Soviet satellites.

Before Gorbachev left office, he completed one last agreement with the United States to curb nuclear arms. In mid-1991, just before conspirators staged their abortive coup, Gorbachev met with President Bush, who had traveled to Moscow to sign a strategic arms reduction treaty. Under this pact, each side agreed to reduce its bombers and missiles by one-third and to trim its conventional military forces. This accord led to a second strategic arms reduction treaty. Gorbachev's successor, Boris Yeltsin, met with Bush in January 1993, and the two agreed to destroy their countries' stockpile of multiple-warhead intercontinental missiles within a decade.

Globalization and the New World Order

With the end of the Cold War, cooperation replaced economic and political rivalry between capitalist and Communist nations in a new era of **globalization**—the extension of economic, political, and cultural interconnections among nations through commerce, migration, and communication. In 1976 the major industrialized democracies had formed the Group of Seven (G7). Consisting of the United States, the United Kingdom, France, West Germany, Italy, Japan, and Canada, the G7 nations met annually to discuss common problems related to issues of global concern, such as trade, health, energy, the environment, and economic and social

Globalization, 1980s Following the efforts of Presidents Nixon, Ford, and Carter to normalize relations with Communist China, companies established commercial enterprises there, including American fast-food chain restaurants. Here a Chinese soldier, standing beside a replica of Colonel Sanders, picks up his order at the bike ride-up window of a Kentucky Fried Chicken restaurant. Dave Bartruff/Getty Images

development. After the fall of communism, Russia joined the organization, which became known as G8. This group of countries represented only 14 percent of the globe's population but produced 60 percent of the world's economic output.

Globalization was accompanied by the extraordinary growth of multinational (or transnational) corporations—companies that operate production facilities or deliver services in more than one country. Between 1970 and 2000, the number of such firms soared from 7,000 to well over 60,000. By 2000 the 500 largest corporations in the world generated more than $11 trillion in revenues, owned more than $33 trillion in assets, and employed 35.5 million people. American companies left their cultural and social imprint on the rest of the world. Walmart greeted shoppers in more than 1,200 stores outside the United States, and McDonald's changed global eating habits with its more than 1,000 fast-food restaurants worldwide. As American firms penetrated other countries with their products, foreign companies changed the economic landscape of the United States. For instance, by the twenty-first century Japanese automobiles, led by Toyota and Honda, captured a major share of the American market, surpassing Ford and General Motors, once the hallmark of the country's superior manufacturing and salesmanship.

Globalization also affected popular culture and media. In the 1990s reality shows, many of which originated in Europe, became a staple of American television. The Swedish series *Expedition Robinson* was converted into *Survivor*, pitting contestants against each other in remote areas of the globe. At the same time, American programs such as *Cheers* and *Friends* were shown as reruns all over the world. As cable channels proliferated, American viewers of Hispanic or Asian origin could watch programs in their native languages. The Cable News Network (CNN), the British Broadcasting Corporation (BBC), and Al Jazeera, an Arabic-language television channel, competed for viewers with specially designed international broadcasts.

Globalization also had negative consequences. Organized labor in particular suffered a severe blow. By 2004 union membership in the United States had dropped to 12.5 percent of the industrial workforce. Fewer and fewer consumer goods bore the label "Made in America," as multinational companies shifted manufacturing jobs to low-wage workers in developing countries. Many of these foreign workers earned more than the prevailing wages in their countries, but by Western standards their pay was extremely low. There were few or no regulations governing working conditions or the use of child labor, and many foreign factories resembled the sweatshops of early-twentieth-century America. Not surprisingly, workers in the United States could not compete in this market. Furthermore, China, which by 2007 had become a prime source for American consumers, failed to regulate the quality of its products closely. Chinese-made toys, including the popular Thomas the Train, showed up in U.S. stores with excessive lead paint and had to be returned before endangering millions of children.

Globalization also posed a danger to the world's environment. As poorer nations sought to take advantage of the West's appetite for low-cost consumer goods, they industrialized rapidly, with little concern for the excessive pollution that accompanied their efforts. The desire for wood products and the expansion of large-scale farming eliminated one-third of Brazil's rain forests. The health of indigenous people suffered wherever globalization-related manufacturing appeared. In Taiwan and China, chemical byproducts of factories and farms turned rivers into polluted sources of drinking water and killed the rivers' fish and plants.

The older industrialized nations added their share to the environmental damage. Americans consumed electricity and gas produced overwhelmingly from coal and petroleum. The burning of fossil fuels by cars and factories released greenhouse gases, which has raised the temperature of the atmosphere and the oceans and contributed to the phenomenon known as global warming or climate change. Nearly all scientists believe that global warming threatens the stability of animal species and of human societies across the planet. However, after the industrialized nations of the world signed the Kyoto Protocol in 1998 to curtail greenhouse-gas emissions, the U.S. Senate refused to ratify it. Critics of the agreement maintained that it did not address the newly emerging industrial countries that polluted heavily and thus was unfair to the United States.

Globalization also highlighted health problems such as the AIDS epidemic. By the outset of the twenty-first century, approximately 33.2 million people worldwide suffered from the disease, though the number of new cases diagnosed annually had dropped to 2.5 million from more than 5 million a few years earlier. Africa remained the continent with the largest number of AIDS patients and the center of the epidemic. Increased education and the development of more effective pharmaceuticals to treat the illness reduced cases and prolonged the lives of those affected by the disease. Though treatments were more widely available in prosperous countries like the United States, agencies such as the United Nations and the World Health Organization, together with nongovernmental groups such as Partners in Health, were instrumental in offering relief in developing countries.

Managing Conflict after the Cold War

The end of the Cold War left the United States as the only remaining superpower. Though Reagan's Cold War defense spending had created huge deficits, the United States emerged from the Cold War with its economic and military strength intact. With the power vacuum created by the breakup of the Soviet Union, the question remained how the United States would use its strength to preserve world order and maintain peace.

Events in China showed the limitations of American military might. In May 1989, university students in Beijing and other major cities in China held large-scale protests to demand political and economic reforms in the country. Some 200,000 demonstrators consisting of students, intellectuals, and workers gathered in the capital city's huge Tiananmen Square, where they constructed a papier-mâché figure resembling the Statue of Liberty and sang songs borrowed from the African American civil rights movement. Deng Xiaoping, Mao Zedong's successor, cracked down on the demonstrations by declaring martial law and dispatching the army to disperse the protesters. Peaceful activists were mowed down by machine guns and stampeded by tanks. In response, President Bush merely issued a temporary ban on sales of weapons and nonmilitary items to China. When outrage over the Tiananmen Square massacre subsided, the president restored normal trade relations.

Flexing military muscle in Panama, however, was more feasible for the Bush administration than doing so in China. During the 1980s, the United States had developed a precarious relationship with Panamanian general Manuel Noriega. Although Noriega channeled aid to the Contras with the approval and support of the CIA, he angered the Reagan administration by maintaining close ties with Cuba. Noriega cooperated with the U.S. Drug Enforcement Agency in halting shipments of cocaine from Latin America headed for the United States at the same time that he helped Latin American drug kingpins launder their profits. In 1988 two Florida grand juries indicted the Panamanian leader on charges of drug smuggling and bribery, pressuring President Reagan to cut off aid to Panama and to ask Noriega to resign. Not only did Noriega refuse to step down, but he also nullified the results of the 1989 presidential election in Panama and declared himself the nation's "maximum leader."

After the United States tried unsuccessfully to foment an internal coup against Noriega, in 1989 the Panamanian leader proclaimed a "state of war" between the United States and his country. On December 28, 1989, President Bush launched Operation Just Cause, sending some 27,000 marines to invade Panama. Bush justified the invasion as necessary to protect the Panama Canal and the lives of American citizens, as well as to halt the drug traffic promoted by Noriega. In reality, the main purpose of the mission was to overthrow and capture the Panamanian dictator. The United States easily defeated its much weaker enemy. The U.S. government installed a new regime, and the marines captured Noriega and sent him to Florida to stand trial on the drug charges. In 1992 he was found guilty and sent to prison.

The Bush administration deployed much more military force in Iraq. Maintaining a steady flow of oil from the Persian Gulf was vital to U.S. strategic interests.

During the prolonged Iraq-Iran War in the 1980s, the Reagan administration had switched allegiance from one belligerent to the other to ensure that neither side emerged too powerful. Though the administration had orchestrated the arms-for-hostages deal with Iran, it had also courted the Iraqi dictator Saddam Hussein. U.S. support for Hussein ended in 1990, after Iraq sent 100,000 troops to invade the small oil-producing nation of Kuwait, on the southern border of Iraq.

President Bush responded aggressively. He warned the Iraqis that their invasion "will not stand." Oil was at the heart of the matter. Hussein needed to revitalize the Iraqi economy, which was devastated after a decade of war with Iran. Bush feared that the Iraqi dictator would also attempt to overrun Kuwait's neighbor Saudi Arabia, an American ally, thereby giving Iraq control of half of the world's oil supply. Bush was also concerned that an emboldened Saddam Hussein would then upset the delicate balance of power in the Middle East and pose a threat to Israel by supporting the Palestinians. The Iraqis were rumored to be quickly developing nuclear weapons, which Hussein could use against Israel.

Rather than act unilaterally, President Bush organized a multilateral coalition against Iraq. Secretary of State James Baker persuaded the United Nations to adopt a resolution calling for Iraqi withdrawal from Kuwait and imposing economic sanctions. Thirty-eight nations, including the Arab countries of Egypt, Saudi Arabia, Syria, and Kuwait, contributed 160,000 troops, roughly 24 percent of the 700,000 allied forces that were deployed in Saudi Arabia in preparation for an invasion if Iraq did not comply.

With military forces stationed in Saudi Arabia, Bush gave Hussein a deadline of January 15, 1991 to withdraw from Kuwait or else risk attack. However, the president faced serious opposition at home against waging a war for oil. Demonstrations occurred throughout the nation, and most Americans supported the continued implementation of economic sanctions, which were already causing serious hardships for the Iraqi people. In the face of widespread opposition, the president requested congressional authorization for military operations against Iraq. After long debate, Congress narrowly approved Bush's request.

Saddam Hussein let the deadline pass. On January 16, **Operation Desert Storm** began when the United States launched air attacks on Baghdad and other key targets in Iraq. After a month of bombing, Hussein still refused to capitulate, so a ground offensive was launched on February 24, 1991. More than 500,000 allied troops moved into Kuwait and easily drove Iraqi forces out of that nation; they then moved into southern Iraq. The vastly outmatched Iraqi army, worn out from its ten-year war with Iran, was quickly defeated. Desperate for help, Hussein ordered the firing of Scud missiles on Israel to provoke it into war, which he hoped would drive a wedge between the United States and its Arab allies. Despite sustaining some casualties, Israel refrained from retaliation. The ground war ended within one hundred hours, and Iraq surrendered. An estimated 100,000 Iraqis died; by contrast, 136 Americans perished (see Map 28.3).

With the war over quickly, President Bush resisted pressure to march to Baghdad and overthrow Saddam Hussein. Bush's stated goal had been to liberate Kuwait; he did not wish to fight a war in the heart of Iraq. The administration believed that such an expedition would involve house-to-house, urban guerrilla warfare. Marching on Baghdad would also entail battling against Hussein's elite Republican Guard, not the weaker conscripts who had put up little resistance in Kuwait. Bush's Arab allies opposed expanding the war, and the president did not want to risk losing their support. Finally, getting rid of Hussein might make matters worse by leaving Iran and its Muslim fundamentalist rulers the dominant power in the region.

Operation Desert Storm preserved the U.S. lifeline to oil in the Persian Gulf and succeeded because of its limited military objectives. President Bush and his advisers understood that the United States had triumphed because it had pieced together a genuine coalition of nations, including Arab ones, to coordinate diplomatic and military action. Military leaders had a clear and defined mission—the liberation of Kuwait—as well as adequate troops and supplies. When they carried out their purpose, the war was over. The Bush administration had applied the Cold War policy of limited containment in dealing with Hussein. This successful U.S. military intervention in the Middle East provided President Bush an opportunity to address other explosive issues in the region. Following the end of the Iraq war, Bush set in motion the peace process that brought the Israelis and Palestinians together to sign a 1993 agreement providing for eventual Palestinian self-government in the Gaza Strip and the West Bank. For the first time the United States officially recognized Yasser Arafat, the head of the PLO, whom both the Israelis and the Americans had considered a terrorist.

In several areas of the globe, the move toward democracy that had begun in the late 1980s proceeded peacefully into the 1990s. The oppressive, racist system of apartheid fell in South Africa, and antiapartheid activist Nelson Mandela was released after twenty-seven years in prison to become president of the country in 1994. In 1990 the dictator Augusto Pinochet stepped down as president of Chile and ceded control to a democratically elected candidate. That same year, the pro-Communist Sandinista government lost at the polls in Nicaragua, and in 1992 the ruling regime in El Salvador signed a peace accord with the rebels.

The 1992 Election

Despite his successes abroad, Bush's popularity plunged at home. After the president dispatched American troops and defeated Iraqi military forces in Kuwait in 1991, his approval rating stood at a whopping 89 percent. In sharp contrast, Bush's poll number plummeted to 34 percent in 1992. This precipitous decline resulted mainly from his inability to revive the sagging economy.

Bush ran for reelection against Governor William Jefferson (Bill) Clinton of Arkansas. Learning from the mistakes of Michael Dukakis as well as the successes of Reagan, Clinton ran as a centrist Democrat who promised to reduce the federal deficit by raising taxes on the wealthy and who supported conservative social policies such as the death penalty, tough measures against crime, and welfare reform. Though he did pledge to extend health care and opposed discrimination against homosexuals, Clinton relied on his mainstream southern Democratic credentials to deflect any claims that he was a liberal. Bush also faced a challenge from the independent candidate Ross Perot, a wealthy self-made businessman from Texas, whose campaign against rising government deficits won 19 percent of the popular vote, mostly at Bush's expense. In turn, Clinton defeated the incumbent by a two-to-one electoral margin.

REVIEW & RELATE

- What role did George H. W. Bush play in shaping the post–Cold War world?
- How did the end of the Cold War contribute to the growth of globalization?

Conclusion: Conservative Ascendancy and the End of the Cold War

The election of President Ronald Reagan represented the culmination of conservative ideas first set in motion by Republican Barry Goldwater's campaign for the White House in 1964. He emerged out of southern California where the movement to lower property taxes, increase community control over school curricula, rein in student protesters, disband affirmative action, and dismantle liberal programs had gained momentum in the 1960s and 1970s. First as governor of California and then as president, Reagan spearheaded the New Right movement. Although Reagan did not have a Republican-controlled Congress to work with throughout his presidency (Republicans held the Senate but not the House), he did succeed in reshaping government policies along more conservative lines.

Reagan's New Right regime bestowed a mixed legacy. The Reagan-Bush administrations reduced inflation and revived economic growth. But they also burdened the country with worrisome budget deficits and with fiscal and monetary policies that encouraged widespread, imprudent speculation on Wall Street and increased the power of giant corporations over political and economic life. Tax and spending cuts further enriched the wealthy but hurt the poor and the middle class. Americans learned about dangers to the environment and took some measures to correct them, but generally refused to alter their lifestyles. African Americans and women broke through barriers that denied them equal access to education and politics, but they confronted white male opposition to further progress. Although the sanctuary movement, highlighted by the trial of Demetria Martinez, provided refuge for undocumented immigrants from Central America fleeing political persecution and poverty, it encountered serious opposition from conservatives distressed by the economic and cultural consequences of immigration from south of the border.

Conservatives came to power amid major changes occurring in foreign affairs, most notably the proliferation and then the cessation of the Cold War. Some unlikely people were responsible for ending the Cold War. President Reagan, a militant anti-Communist crusader, together with his pragmatic and steady secretary of state, George Shultz, guided the United States through a policy of heightened military preparedness to push the Soviet Union toward peace. It was a dangerous gambit, but it worked; diplomacy rather than armed conflict prevailed. Reagan's Cold War strategy succeeded in part because during the 1980s a leader amenable to peace, Mikhail Gorbachev, governed the Soviet Union. He envisioned the end of the Cold War as a means of bringing political and economic reform to his beleaguered and bankrupt nation. What Reagan and Gorbachev began, their successors, George H. W. Bush and Boris Yeltsin, completed: the Cold War came to a conclusion, and the Soviet Union dismantled its empire and incorporated a measure of democracy and capitalism into Russia.

The activism of ordinary people around the world also helped transform the relationship between the superpowers. Antinuclear protesters in Western Europe and the United States kept up pressure on Western leaders to make continued nuclear expansion unacceptable. In Eastern Europe, Polish dockworker Lech Walesa and other fighters for democracy broke from the Soviet orbit and tore down the bricks and barbed-wire fences of the iron curtain.

The United States emerged as the winner of the Cold War, thereby gaining dominance as the world's sole superpower. Yet this did not necessarily guarantee peace. In assuming this preeminent role, the United States faced new threats to international security from governments and insurgents seeking to rebuild nations along ethnic and religious lines in the Middle East and the Persian Gulf. The collapse of the Soviet empire created a power vacuum that would be filled by a variety of unchecked and combustible local and regional forces intent on challenging the political and economic dominance of the United States. President Bush responded to such crises in Iraq and Panama decisively, but his response to China's crackdown at Tiananmen Square was far more tepid.

At the same time, globalization presented new opportunities and posed additional challenges. It promoted more international cooperation and freer trade among nations. Globalization also fostered greater communication and cultural exchanges around the world. However, globalization brought many problems as well. Rapid industrialization and exploration of new sources of wealth accelerated the environmental dangers of air and water pollution, climate change, and the destruction of primeval forests. As globalization shrank the world economically and culturally, the United States became the chief target of those who wanted to contain the influence of Western values. Terrorism, which transcended national borders, replaced communism as the leading enemy of the United States and its allies.

Chapter 28 Review

KEY TERMS

Sanctuary Movement, 715

Reaganomics, 717

Economic Recovery Tax Act, 717

acquired immune deficiency syndrome (AIDS), 720

Immigration Reform and Control Act, 720

Boland Amendment, 723

Iran-Contra affair, 726

nuclear freeze movement, 727

glasnost, 728

perestroika, 728

Solidarity, 730

globalization, 732

Operation Desert Storm, 736

REVIEW & RELATE

1. What was Reaganomics, and what were its most important long-term consequences?
2. How did conservative ideas shape the social, cultural, and political landscape of the 1980s and 1990s?
3. How did anticommunism shape Ronald Reagan's foreign policy?
4. What role did ordinary citizens play in prompting the superpowers to move toward nuclear de-escalation?
5. What role did George H. W. Bush play in shaping the post–Cold War world?
6. How did the end of the Cold War contribute to the growth of globalization?

TIMELINE OF EVENTS

1981	• Passage of the Economic Recovery Tax Act
1982	• Boland Amendment passed
	• 750,000 attend nuclear freeze rally in New York City
	• Ratification period expires for Equal Rights Amendment
1983	• Suicide bomb attack in Lebanon kills 241 U.S. soldiers
	• U.S. invasion of Grenada
1987	• Senate hearings on Iran-Contra affair
	• Intermediate Nuclear Forces Treaty signed
1989	• Tiananmen Square protests
	• Fall of the Berlin Wall
1990	• Bush signs Americans with Disabilities Act and Clean Air Act
1990–1991	• Soviet Union dismantled
1991	• U.S. pushes Iraq out of Kuwait
1993	• Second Strategic Arms Reduction Treaty signed

29

The Challenges of a Globalized World

1993 to the present

LEARNING OBJECTIVES

After reading this chapter you will be able to:

- Assess the impact of computer technology, globalization, and immigration on the United States.
- Evaluate President Clinton's responses to domestic and global issues.
- Explain the impact of the 9/11 attacks on President Bush's foreign policy and describe his compassionate conservatism at home.
- Analyze the reasons for Barack Obama's election as president and explain the challenges that faced his administration.
- Explain how Donald Trump reshaped the presidency.

COMPARING AMERICAN HISTORIES

William Henry Gates III started tinkering with computers at age thirteen. As a teenager in 1969, the enterprising Gates and some friends set up a business to make computerized traffic counters to gauge the speed of vehicles, for which they earned $20,000.

His brilliant mind and entrepreneurial inclinations led Gates to enroll at Harvard and then to drop out after spending more time at the university's computer center than he did in class. In 1974 he became interested in microcomputers as an alternative to large conventional computers. A year later, Gates formed a computer software company called Microsoft, envisioning the microcomputer on office desktops and in homes throughout America.

Bill Gates succeeded beyond all expectations. In 1980 Microsoft collaborated with International Business Machines (IBM) to create a software package for IBM's new line of personal computers. In 1986 Microsoft became a publicly traded company on the New York Stock Exchange. Within a decade, Gates became the richest man in America, and like industrial titans a century earlier, he donates generously to fund philanthropic activities worldwide. In 2000, along with his wife, he set up the Bill and Melinda Gates Foundation, the largest private foundation in the world, which seeks to extend health care, fight diseases such as malaria, tuberculosis, and HIV/AIDS, and promote economic development in poor and developing countries around the globe.

Digital technology played an important part in the life of **Alicia Garza** and the movement she helped found, **Black Lives Matter (BLM)**. Born in 1981, Alicia Schwartz Garza was raised by her African American mother and her Jewish stepfather in the San Francisco Bay area. She graduated from the University of California, San Diego with a degree in anthropology and sociology, and she became a community organizer. She came out as queer, and in 2008, she married Malachi Garza, a trans-male activist.

BLM grew out of Garza's 2013 Facebook post following the acquittal of a white Florida man who shot and killed Trayvon Martin, an unarmed black teenager who was about the same age as Garza's younger brother. Her post concluded: "Black people. I love you. I love us. Our lives matter." From the last three words emerged the hashtag, Black Lives Matter, and along with Patrisse Cullors and Opal Tometi, Garza built a social media platform that sparked the creation of the BLM movement.

The 2014 killing of another unarmed black youth, Michael Brown, by a policeman in Ferguson, Missouri, fueled BLM protests. In 2015, Garza led a Freedom Ride to Ferguson, which helped propel Black Lives Matter chapters throughout the country and internationally. As writer and activist, Alicia Garza continues to promote racial, gender, and economic equality on behalf of communities of color, LGBTQ (lesbian, gay, bisexual, transgender, queer), and the poor.

THE AMERICAN HISTORIES of Bill Gates and Alicia Garza were deeply affected by the twin forces of digital technology and systemic racism. Computers, the Internet, and cell phone technology reformulated commerce and social relations, furthering the globalization that emerged after the Cold War. Google, the Web, Facebook, and Twitter became household words and broke down domestic and global barriers that earlier technologies had not penetrated. Computer technology revolutionized political communication and organization, mobilized ordinary citizens into action, and expanded opportunities for disgruntled and oppressed citizens of foreign countries to overthrow despotic rulers. At the same time, the al-Qaeda terror attacks of September 11, 2001 placed the United States and its allies on a permanent war footing, resulting in wars against terrorism in Iraq and Afghanistan and increased surveillance of suspected terrorists and citizens alike. Amid these upheavals, Americans broke new ground by electing their first black president. Still, the nation faced historic burdens of institutionalized racism, as spotlighted in the wave of police killings of unarmed black citizens from Trayvon Martin to George Floyd. The 2016 election of Donald Trump as president underscored the political, economic, and cultural divisions that continued to divide the country and highlighted the challenges digital technology posed for national unity and security. Trump proved unable to handle a series of public health, economic, and racial crises and was defeated by Joseph Biden in the 2020 election.

Transforming American Society

The 1990s marked a period of great economic growth and technological advancement in the United States. Computers stood at the center of the technological revolution of the late twentieth and early twenty-first centuries, allowing both small and large businesses to reach new markets and transform the workplace. Digital technology also altered the way individuals worked, purchased goods and services, communicated, and spent their leisure time. As the Internet connected Americans to the rest of the world, corporate leaders embraced globalization as the key to economic prosperity. They put together business mergers so that their companies could operate more powerfully in the international market. Government officials generally supported their efforts by reducing regulations on business and financial practices. Globalization not only thrust American business enterprises outward but also brought a new population of immigrants to the United States.

The Computer Revolution

The first working computers were developed for military purposes during World War II and the Cold War and were enormous in size and cost. Engineers began to resolve the size issue with the creation of transistors. Invented in the late 1940s, these small electronic devices came into widespread use in running computers during the 1960s. The design of integrated circuits in the 1970s led to the production of microcomputers in which a silicon chip the size of a nail head did the work once performed by huge computers. Bill Gates was not the only one to recognize the potential market of microcomputers for home and business use. Steve Jobs, like Gates a college dropout, founded Apple Computer Company in 1976, Microsoft's biggest competitor.

Microchips and digital technology found a market beyond home and office computers. Over the last two decades of the twentieth century, computers came to operate everything from standard appliances such as televisions and telephones, to new electronic devices such as CD players, fax machines, and cell phones. Computers controlled traffic lights on the streets and air traffic in the skies. They changed the leisure patterns of youth: Many young people preferred to play video games indoors than to engage in outdoor activities. Consumers purchased goods online, and companies such as Amazon sold merchandise through the Internet without any retail stores. Soon computers became the stars of movies such as *The Matrix* (1999), *A.I. Artificial Intelligence* (2001), and *Iron Man* (2008).

The Internet—an open, global series of interconnected computer networks that transmit data, information, electronic mail, and other services—grew out of military research in the 1970s, when the Department of Defense constructed a system of computer servers connected to one another throughout the United States. The main objective of this network was to preserve military communications in the event of a Soviet nuclear attack. At the end of the Cold War, the Internet was repurposed for nonmilitary use, linking government, academic, business, and organizational systems. In 1991 the World Wide Web came into existence as a way to access the Internet and connect documents and other resources to one another through hyperlinks. In 2020 over 85 percent of people in the United States used the Internet, up from 50 percent in 2000. Internet use worldwide leapt ten fold, from nearly 361 million people in 2000 to over 4.6 billion in 2020.

The Changing American Population

As the technological revolution transformed the United States, an influx of immigrants began to alter the composition of the American population. The population of the United States grew from 202 million to 331 million between 1970 and 2020, and immigrants accounted for some 28 million of the increase.

Most newcomers in the 1980s and 1990s arrived from Latin America and South and East Asia. Relatively few Europeans (approximately 2 million) moved to the United States, though their numbers increased after the collapse of the Soviet empire in the early 1990s. Poverty and political unrest pushed migrants out of Mexico, Central America, and the Caribbean. At the beginning of the twenty-first century, Latinos (35 million) had surpassed African Americans (34 million) as the nation's largest racial minority group. With the arrival of Caribbean and African immigrants, black America was also becoming more diverse.

In addition to the 16 million immigrants who came from south of the U.S. border, another 9 million headed eastward from Asia, including Chinese, South Koreans, and Filipinos, together with refugees from Vietnam and Cambodia. By 2010 an estimated 3.18 million Indians from South Asia lived in the United States, most arriving after the 1960s. Indian Americans became the third-largest Asian American group behind Chinese and Filipinos. Another 1 to 2 million people came from predominantly Islamic nations such as Pakistan, Lebanon, Iraq, and Iran (Figure 29.1).

REVIEW & RELATE
- How did computers change life in the United States at the turn of the millennium?
- How has globalization affected immigration in recent decades?

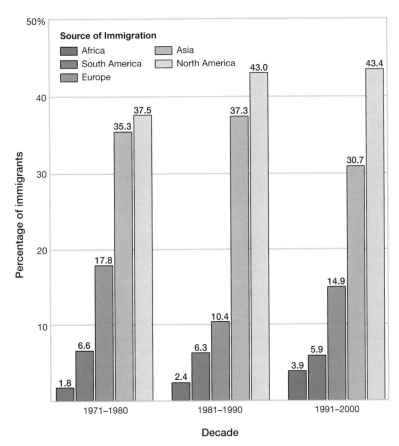

FIGURE 29.1 Immigrant Growth by Home Region, 1981–2010
In the late twentieth and early twenty-first centuries, immigration to the United States increased significantly, especially from North America (which in this figure includes Mexico, Central America, and the Caribbean). Asians formed the second largest group of immigrants, while Africans arrived in small but growing numbers. Compare each region's percentage of immigration in 1991 with 2010 and present the conclusions you can draw.
Source: Data from *2015 Yearbook of Immigration Statistics, Office of Immigration Statistics, U.S. Department of Homeland Security, December 2016.*

Political Polarization and Globalization in the Clinton Years

The first president born after 1945, President Bill Clinton had to deal with the challenges facing the post–Cold War world. He embraced globalization as the key to economic prosperity and showed his readiness to promote and defend U.S. national security. Despite achieving general prosperity and peace, Clinton could not escape the political polarization that divided the American electorate, and his tenure in office only intensified this schism.

Politics during the Clinton Administration

Born in Arkansas in 1946, William Jefferson (Bill) Clinton served five terms as Democratic governor of his home state. As governor, Clinton spoke out for equal opportunity, improved education, and economic development. After defeating President George H. W. Bush in 1992, Clinton entered the White House.

In 1993 Clinton sought to reverse a number of Reagan-Bush policies. He persuaded Congress to raise taxes on wealthy individuals and corporations, while his administration reduced defense spending following the end of the Cold War. Taken together, these measures stimulated a robust economic growth of 4 percent annually, established over 22 million jobs, lowered the national debt, and created a budget surplus. Clinton further departed from his Republican predecessors by signing executive orders expanding federal assistance for legal abortion. He also approved the 1993 Family and Medical Leave Act, which allowed parents to take up to twelve weeks of unpaid leave to care for newborn children without risk of losing their jobs. The president had less success opening the military to gay men and lesbians, though many already served secretly. His policy of "don't ask, don't tell" permitted lesbian, gay, and bisexual individuals to serve in the armed forces so long as they kept their sexual orientation a secret, a compromise that failed to end discrimination. The Clinton administration's most stinging defeat came when Congress failed to pass universal medical coverage.

Clinton tried to appeal to voters across the political spectrum on other issues. He signed a tough anticrime law that funded the recruitment of an additional 100,000 police officers to patrol city streets, while supporting gun control legislation. Although the prison population had been on the rise before the 1990s, Clinton's anticrime bill accelerated the rate of incarceration and had a disproportionate effect on African Americans and Latinos. Managing to overcome the powerful lobby of the National Rifle Association, in 1993 Clinton signed the Brady Bill, which imposed a five-day waiting period to check the background of gun buyers.

Conservatives were fiercely opposed to Clinton on several fronts. Right-wing talk radio hosts criticized the president and his wife, Hillary Rodham Clinton, a lawyer and leader in the effort to reform health care. Conservatives blamed the Clintons for all they considered wrong in society — feminism, abortion, affirmative action, and secularism. Criticism of pre-presidential dealings in a controversial real estate project known as Whitewater prompted the appointment in 1994 of a special prosecutor to investigate allegations of impropriety.

Facing conservative antagonism, the president and the Democratic Party fared poorly in the 1994 congressional elections, losing control of both houses of Congress. Republicans, led by House Minority Leader Newt Gingrich of Georgia, championed the **Contract with America**. This document embraced conservative principles, including a constitutional amendment for a balanced budget, reduced welfare spending, lower taxes, and term limits for lawmakers. It also marked a shift toward rigid partisan divisions in Congress. The election underscored the increasing influence of white evangelical Christians, who voted in large numbers for Republican candidates.

Stung by this defeat, Clinton tried to outmaneuver congressional Republicans by shifting rightward and championing welfare reform. In 1996 he signed the **Personal Responsibility and Work Opportunity Reconciliation Act**. It replaced the Aid to Families with Dependent Children provision of the Social Security law, the basis for welfare in the United States since the New Deal, with a new measure that required adult welfare recipients to find work within two years or lose the benefits provided to families earning less than $7,700 annually. The law also placed a lifetime limit of five years on these federal benefits. Also in 1996, the president approved the Defense of Marriage Act, which denied married same-sex couples the federal benefits granted to heterosexual married couples, including Social Security survivor's benefits.

In adopting such positions as welfare reform and antigay legislation, Clinton angered many of his liberal supporters but ensured his reelection in 1996. Running against Republican senator Robert Dole of Kansas and the independent candidate Ross Perot, Clinton captured 49 percent of the popular vote and 379 electoral votes. Dole received 41 percent of the vote, and Perot came in a distant third.

Declining support from his liberal base did not seriously undermine President Clinton, but sexual indiscretions nearly brought him down. Starting in 1995, Clinton had engaged in consensual sexual relations with Monica Lewinsky, a twenty-two-year-old White House intern. Clinton denied these charges under oath, but when Lewinsky testified about their sexual encounters, the president recanted his earlier statements. After an independent prosecutor concluded that Clinton had committed perjury and obstructed justice, the Republican-controlled House voted to impeach the president on December 19, 1998. However, on February 12, 1999, Republicans in the Senate failed to muster the necessary two-thirds vote to convict Clinton on the impeachment charges.

These impeachment efforts did not deter Clinton from improving the country's economy. In the midst of the sex scandal in 1998, the unemployment rate fell to 4.3 percent, the lowest level since the early 1970s. The rate of home ownership reached a record-setting 66 percent. As the "misery index"—a compilation of unemployment and inflation—fell, the gross domestic product grew by more than $250 billion. In 1999 the stock market's Dow Jones average reached a historic high of 10,000 points. That same year the president signed into law a measure that freed banks to merge commercial, investment, and insurance services, prohibited since 1933, giving them enormous leeway in undertaking profitable but risky ventures. The Clinton administration boasted that its economic policies had succeeded in canceling the Reagan-Bush budget deficit, yielding a surplus for the fiscal year 2000. This boom, however, did not affect everyone equally. African Americans and Latinos lagged behind whites economically; and the gap between rich and poor widened as the wealthiest 13,000 American families earned as much income as the poorest 20 million.

Global Challenges

Clinton embraced economic cooperation in Europe. In 1993 western European nations formed the European Union (EU), which encouraged free trade and investment among member nations. In 1999 the EU introduced a common currency, the euro, which nineteen nations have now adopted.

Clinton encouraged the formation of a similar economic partnership in North America. In 1993, together with the governments of Mexico and Canada, the U.S. Congress ratified the **North American Free Trade Agreement (NAFTA)**. The agreement removed tariffs and other obstacles to commerce and investment among the three countries to encourage trade. Between 1994 and 2004, trade among NAFTA nations increased by nearly 130 percent. Although Mexico saw a significant drop in poverty rates and a rise in real income, NAFTA harmed some workers in the United States. From 1994 to 2007, net manufacturing jobs dropped by 3,654,000 as U.S.

companies outsourced their production to Mexico, with its low wage and benefits structure. However, many more manufacturing jobs were lost to automation.

Clinton also actively promoted globalization through the World Trade Organization (WTO). Created in 1995, the WTO consists of more than 150 nations and seeks "to ensure that trade flows as smoothly, predictably, and freely as possible." The policies of the WTO generally benefit wealthier nations, such as the United States. From 1978 to 2000, the value of U.S. exports and imports jumped from 17 percent to 25 percent of the gross domestic product.

As the first president elected in the post–Cold War era, Clinton faced numerous foreign policy challenges during his two terms in office. No longer did the problems facing the United States result from customary military aggression by one nation against another; rather, the greatest threats came from the implosion of national governments into factionalism and genocide and the rise of Islamic extremists.

President Clinton responded boldly to violence in the Balkans, an area considered vital to U.S. national security. In 1989 Yugoslavia splintered after the ruling Communist regime crumbled. The predominantly Roman Catholic states of Slovenia and Croatia declared their independence from the largely Russian Orthodox Serbian population in Yugoslavia. In 1992 the mainly Muslim territory of Bosnia-Herzegovina also broke away, despite protests by its substantial Serbian population (Map 29.1). A civil war erupted between Serb and Croatian minorities and the Muslim-dominated Bosnian government. Supported by Slobodan Milošević, the leader of the neighboring province of Serbia, Bosnian Serbs wrested control of large parts of the region and slaughtered tens of thousands of Muslims through what they euphemistically called **ethnic cleansing**. In 1995 Clinton sponsored NATO bombing raids against the Serbs, dispatched 20,000 American troops as part of a multilateral peacekeeping force, and brokered a peace agreement. In 1999 renewed conflict erupted when Milošević's Serbian government attacked the province of Kosovo to eliminate its Albanian Muslim residents. Clinton and NATO initiated air strikes and placed troops on the ground that preserved Kosovo's independence.

The United States faced an even graver danger from Islamic extremists intent on waging a religious struggle (jihad) and establishing a transnational religious caliphate. The United States' close relationship with Israel placed it high on the list of terrorist targets, along with pro-American Muslim governments in Egypt, Pakistan, and Indonesia. In 1993 Islamic militants orchestrated the bombing of the World Trade Center's underground garage, killing six people and injuring more than one thousand. Five years later, terrorists blew up American embassies in Kenya and Tanzania, killing hundreds and injuring thousands of local workers and residents. In retaliation, Clinton ordered air strikes against terrorist bases in Sudan and Afghanistan. In 2000, al-Qaeda terrorists blew a gaping hole in the side of the USS *Cole*, a U.S. destroyer anchored in Yemen, killing seventeen American sailors. Terrorism would continue to plague the United States.

| REVIEW & RELATE | • How did conflicts between Democrats and Republicans affect President Clinton's accomplishments?
• Explain the new post–Cold War foreign policy threats that President Clinton faced. |

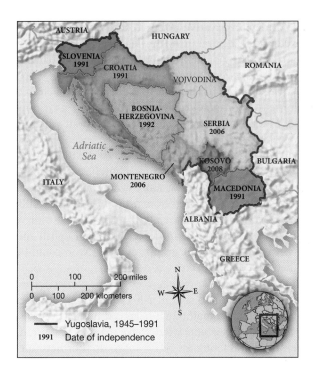

MAP 29.1   The Breakup of Yugoslavia, 1991–2008
With the collapse of Communist control of Yugoslavia in 1989, the country splintered along ethnic and religious lines, eventually forming seven separate nations. A civil war between Serbia and Croatia ended in 1995, but Serbs then attacked Muslims in Bosnia and Kosovo.

The Presidency of George W. Bush

In 2000 Americans celebrated the new millennium, looking forward with hope for the future. Yet within three years, the country endured a bruising presidential election, experienced unprecedented terrorism at home, and engaged in two wars abroad. President George W. Bush left the country as politically divided as his predecessor had.

Bush and Compassionate Conservatism

In 2000 the Democratic candidate, Vice President Al Gore, ran against George W. Bush, the Republican governor of Texas and son of the forty-first president. Gore ran on the coattails of the Clinton prosperity while Bush campaigned as a "compassionate conservative." Ralph Nader, an anti-corporate activist, ran under the banner of the Green Party, formed in 1991 to support environmentalism and social justice.

Although Gore won a narrow plurality of the popular vote (48.4 percent, compared with 47.8 percent for Bush and 2.7 percent for Nader), Bush won a slim majority of the electoral votes: 271 to 267. The key state in this Republican victory was Florida, where Bush led Gore by fewer than 500 popular votes. Counties with high proportions of African Americans and lower-income residents, who were more likely to support Gore, encountered significant difficulties and outright discrimination in voting. When litigation over the recount reached the U.S. Supreme Court in December 2000, the Court, which included conservative justices appointed by Ronald Reagan and George H. W. Bush, proclaimed Bush the winner.

George W. Bush appealed to his conservative political base by governing as boldly as if he had received a resounding electoral mandate. The president promoted the agenda of the evangelical Christian wing of the Republican Party. He spoke out against same-sex marriage, abortion, and federal support for stem cell research, a scientific procedure that used discarded embryos to find cures for diseases. Bush created a special office in the White House to coordinate faith-based initiatives, providing religious institutions with federal funds for social service activities without violating the First Amendment's separation of church and state.

Attending to the faithful made for good politics. At the turn of the twenty-first century, a growing number of churchgoers were joining megachurches. These congregations, mainly Protestant, each contained 2,000 or more worshippers. Between 1970 and 2005, the number of megachurches jumped from 50 to more than 1,300. Joel Osteen—the evangelical pastor of Lakewood Church in Houston, Texas—drew average weekly audiences of 43,000 people, with sermons available in English and Spanish. Such religious leaders held sway with large groups of voters who could be mobilized to significant political effect.

While courting people of faith, Bush also acknowledged economic conservatives. Congress gave the president tax-cut proposals to sign in 2001 and 2003, measures that favored the wealthiest Americans. Yet to maintain a balanced budget, the cardinal principle of fiscal conservatism, these tax cuts would have required a substantial reduction in spending, which Bush and Congress chose not to do. Furthermore, continued deregulation of business encouraged unsavory activities that resulted in corporate scandals and risky financial practices.

At the same time, Bush showed the compassionate side of his conservatism. His cabinet appointments reflected racial, ethnic, and sexual diversity. They included African Americans as secretary of state (Colin Powell) and national security adviser (Condoleezza Rice, who later succeeded Powell as secretary of state). His Latino appointments included Alberto Gonzalez as attorney general, Carlos Gutierrez as secretary of commerce, and Mel Martinez as secretary of housing and urban affairs. Compassionate conservatism also included educational reform for those attending school in underprivileged areas. In addition, in 2003 Bush signed into law the Medicare Prescription Drug, Improvement, and Modernization Act, which aimed to lower the cost of prescription drugs to some 40 million senior citizens enrolled in Medicare.

The Iraq War

President Bush spent less time on domestic issues when events vaulted him into the role of wartime president. On September 11, 2001, four commercial jets were hijacked by al-Qaeda operatives recruited by Osama bin Laden, and used as weapons to attack the World Trade Center and the Pentagon, killing 2,996 people. Bush then launched a war on terror, one that led to protracted and costly conflicts in Afghanistan and Iraq and the erosion of civil liberties at home. As part of that effort, in 2002 Congress created a cabinet-level superagency, the Department of Homeland Security, responsible for developing a national strategy against further terrorist threats. Two years later, Congress created the Office of the Director of National Intelligence to coordinate the work of security agencies more effectively.

President Bush at Ground Zero   On September 14, 2001, President George W. Bush toured the wreckage of the destroyed World Trade Center. Standing on a pile of rubble, he heard firefighters, police officers, and other rescuers shout, "USA, USA." He responded: "I can hear you. The rest of the world hears you. And the people who knocked these buildings down will hear all of us soon." Courtesy George W. Bush Presidential Library and Museum. (P7365-23a) © Tribune Content Agency, LLC. All Rights Reserved. Reprinted with permission.

In the immediate aftermath of the September 11 terrorist attacks, Bush acted decisively. The president dispatched U.S. troops to Afghanistan, whose Taliban leaders refused to turn over Osama bin Laden and other terrorists operating training centers in the country. A combination of anti-Taliban warlords and U.S. military forces toppled the Taliban regime and installed a pro-American government; however, the elusive bin Laden escaped into a remote area of Pakistan.

On the home front, the war on terror prompted passage of the **Patriot Act** in October 2001. The measure expanded the authority of law enforcement and immigration officials in detaining and deporting immigrants suspected of terrorism-related acts. The act also gave law enforcement agencies nearly unlimited authority to wiretap telephones, retrieve e-mail messages, and search the medical, financial, and library borrowing records of individuals, including U.S. citizens, suspected of involvement in terrorism overseas or at home. The computer age provided terrorist networks like al-Qaeda with the means to communicate quickly across national borders and to raise money and launder it into safe bank accounts online. Computer technology also gave U.S. intelligence agencies ways to monitor these communications and transactions.

Amid rising anti-Muslim sentiments, the overwhelming majority of Americans supported the Patriot Act. In the weeks and months following September 11, some people committed acts of violence against mosques, Arab American community centers and businesses, and individual Muslims and people they thought were Muslims. Despite some criticism of its harsh provisions, the Patriot Act was renewed in 2006 with only minor changes.

The Bush administration sought to expand the war on terror to reshape the politics of the Middle East and Persian Gulf along pro-American lines. In doing so, the United States and its European allies would ensure the flow of cheap oil to satisfy the energy demands of consumers in these countries. Furthermore, by replacing authoritarian regimes with democratic governments, the president envisioned a domino effect that would lead to the toppling of reactionary leaders. In crafting this strategy, Bush departed from the well-established, post–World War II policy of containing enemies short of going to war. Instead, the **Bush Doctrine** proposed undertaking preemptive war against despotic governments deemed a threat to U.S. national security, even if that danger was not imminent.

President Bush declared in January 2002 that Iraq was part of an "axis of evil," along with Iran and North Korea. Bush considered Saddam Hussein, the Iraqi dictator, undependable to protect U.S. oil interests in the region. Removing him, Bush believed, would also open a path to overthrowing the radical Islamic government of neighboring Iran, which had embarrassed the United States in 1979 and remained its sworn enemy.

Over the next two years, Bush convinced Congress and a majority of the American people that Iraq presented an immediate danger to the United States by falsely connecting Saddam Hussein to the 9/11 al-Qaeda terrorists. The president also accused Iraq of being well advanced in building and stockpiling "weapons of mass destruction," despite evidence to the contrary.

In March 2003, after a congressional vote of approval, U.S. military aircraft unleashed massive bombing attacks on Baghdad. Contrary to the approach taken by the first President Bush in the 1991 Gulf War, the United States did not wait for any overt act of aggression and created merely a nominal alliance of nations with only Great Britain supplying significant combat troops. Within weeks Hussein went into hiding, prompting Bush to declare that "major combat operations" had ended in Iraq.

This triumphant declaration proved premature. Hussein was captured several months later, but despite the presence of 130,000 U.S. and 30,000 British troops, the war dragged on. More American soldiers (over 4,000) died after the president proclaimed victory than had died during the invasion. The perception of the United States as an occupying power destabilized Iraq, leading to a civil war between the country's Shi'ite Muslim majority, which had been persecuted under Saddam Hussein, and its Sunni religious minority, which Hussein represented. In the northern part of the nation, the Kurdish majority, another group brutalized by Hussein, also battled Sunnis. Al-Qaeda forces, which previously had been absent from the country, joined the fray.

At the same time, Bush instituted the policy of incarcerating suspected al-Qaeda rebels in the U.S. military base in Guantánamo, Cuba, without due process of the law. The facility housed more than six hundred men classified as "enemy combatants," who were subject to extreme interrogation and were deprived of legal counsel.

Amid a protracted war in Iraq, President Bush won reelection in 2004 by promising to stay the course and deter further terrorism. Although the Democratic presidential candidate, Senator John Kerry of Massachusetts, criticized Bush's handling of Iraq, Bush eked out a victory, winning a slight majority of the popular vote (50.7 percent).

Bush's Second Term

Over the next four years President Bush's credibility suffered. Several issues — sectarian violence in Iraq, mounting death tolls, and the failures of the U.S.-supported Iraqi government — turned the majority of Americans against the war. Little changed, however, as American troops remained in Iraq and Afghanistan. The war on terror had become a permanent part of life in the United States.

With turmoil also continuing in the Persian Gulf, the threat of nuclear proliferation grew. Iraq did not have nuclear weapons in actuality, but Iran was developing nuclear capabilities. Iranian leaders claimed that they wanted nuclear technology for peaceful purposes, but the Bush administration believed that Iran's real purpose was to build nuclear devices to attack Israel and establish its supremacy in the region.

Bush's handling of a major natural disaster further diminished his popularity. On August 29, 2005, **Hurricane Katrina** slammed into Louisiana and Mississippi. This powerful storm devastated New Orleans, a city with a population of nearly 500,000, a majority of whom were African American. The flood surge caused levees to break, deluging large areas of the city and trapping 50,000 residents. Not only did local and state officials respond slowly and ineptly to the crisis, but so, too, did the federal government.

The flooding killed at least 1,800 residents of the Gulf coast, New Orleans's population dropped by around 130,000 residents, and critics blamed the president for his lack of leadership and slow response to the disaster.

REVIEW & RELATE	• How did President Bush put compassionate conservatism into action? • How did the war on terror affect American foreign policy in the Bush administration?

The Challenges Faced by President Barack Obama

The world was economically interconnected and fully concerned with combating terror when a severe recession began in 2008. Looking for new hope, many Americans rallied behind the presidential candidacy of Barack Obama. Obama's election ushered in reforms, but his victory did not eliminate the nation's deep political and cultural divisions or eradicate pervasive economic and social inequality.

The Great Recession

In 2008 the boom times of the previous decade came to a sudden halt. The stock market's Dow Jones average, which had hit a high of 14,000, fell 6,000 points, the steepest percentage drop since 1931. Americans who had invested their money in the stock market lost trillions of dollars. The gross domestic product fell by about 6 percent, a loss too great for the economy to absorb quickly. Millions of Americans lost their jobs, and many forfeited their homes when they could no longer afford to pay their mortgages. Unemployment jumped from 4.9 percent in January 2008 to 7.6 percent a year later. Confronted by this spiraling disaster, President Bush approved a $700 billion bailout plan to rescue the nation's largest banks and brokerage houses.

The causes of the **Great Recession** were many and had developed over a long period. Since the Reagan presidency, the federal government had relaxed regulation of the financial industry, while the Federal Reserve Bank encouraged excessive borrowing by keeping interest rates low and relaxed its oversight of Wall Street practices that placed ordinary investors' money at risk. Investment houses developed elaborate computer models that produced new and risky kinds of financial instruments, which went unregulated. Insurance companies such as American International Group marketed so-called credit default swaps as protection for risky securities, exacerbating the financial crisis.

The economy might have experienced a less severe downturn if there had been greater economic equality to bolster consumer spending. Instead, wealth remained concentrated in relatively few hands. In 2007 the top 1 percent of households owned 34.6 percent of all privately held wealth, and the next 19 percent held 50.5 percent. The other 80 percent of Americans owned only 15 percent of the wealth. This maldistribution of wealth made it extremely difficult to support an economy that required ever-expanding purchasing power and produced steadily rising personal debt (Figure 29.2).

With the interdependence of economies through globalization, the Great Recession spread rapidly throughout the world. Great Britain's banking system teetered on the edge of collapse. Other nations in the European Union (EU), most notably Greece and Spain, verged on bankruptcy and had to be rescued by stronger EU nations. Even in China, where the economy had boomed as a result of globalization, businesses shut down and unemployment rose as global consumer demand declined.

Obama and the Great Recession

In the midst of the Great Recession, the United States held the 2008 presidential election. The Republican candidate, John McCain, was a Vietnam War hero and a three-term senator from Arizona. His Democratic opponent, Barack Obama, had served four years in the Senate from Illinois. For their vice presidential running mates, McCain chose Sarah Palin, the first-term governor of Alaska, and Obama selected Joseph Biden, the senior senator from Delaware.

Obama overcame racial prejudices in the country by speaking eloquently about his background—the son of a black immigrant from Kenya and the grandson of a white World War II veteran from Kansas. The former community organizer also succeeded in building a nationwide, grassroots political movement through digital technology. He raised an enormous amount of campaign money from ordinary donors

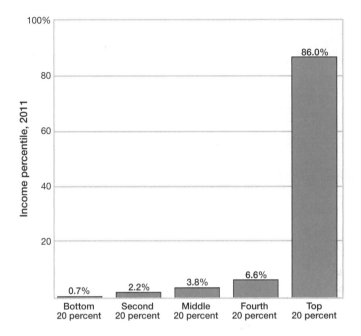

Note: Capital income includes taxable and nontaxable interest income, as well as income from dividends, capital gains, and corporate tax liability. Capital income does not include earned income in the form of salaries and wages.

FIGURE 29.2   Wealth Inequality (Capital Income), 2011
The decline of American manufacturing and the expansion of the low-wage service sector, combined with the rise of high-tech industries and unregulated investment banking, led to growing disparities of wealth in the early twenty-first century. Disparities exist even within the top 20th percentile, as the top 1 percent controlled more than half of all capital income in 2011. Compare the top 20 percent and the bottom 20 percent of Americans with respect to capital income.

through the Internet and used Web sites and text messaging to mobilize his supporters. Moreover, the public blamed the Bush administration for the recession, and Obama offered hope for economic recovery. Obama captured 53 percent of the popular vote, obtaining a majority of votes from African Americans, Latinos, women, and the young, who turned out in record numbers, and a comfortable 365 electoral votes. The Democrats also scored big victories in the House and Senate.

President Obama stemmed the tide of the Great Recession and turned its course toward economic recovery. He continued the Bush administration's bailout of collapsing banks and investment firms and expanded it to include American automobile companies. In 2009 the president supported passage of an economic stimulus plan that provided federal funds to state and local governments to create jobs and keep their employees on the public payroll.

In addition to restoring the economy, President Obama dealt with the health care problems that disproportionately affected the poor. He pushed Congress to pass the **Patient Protection and Affordable Care Act ("Obamacare")** in 2010, a

President Obama, Healer-in-Chief, 2015   In this June 26, 2015 photo, President Barack Obama sings "Amazing Grace" during his eulogy for the Reverend Clementa Pinckney in Charleston, South Carolina. Pinckney was one of the nine people murdered by a white supremacist shooter at Mother Emanuel African Methodist Episcopal Church in Charleston on June 17. AP Photo/David Goldman

measure mandating that all Americans had to obtain health insurance or face a tax penalty and that no one could be denied coverage for a preexisting condition. He also signed into law repeal of President Clinton's "don't ask, don't tell" policy, which discriminated against lesbian, gay, and bisexual service members in the military.

The 2010 Revolt against Obama

Despite such accomplishments, President Obama continued to encounter vigorous political opposition. Most Republican lawmakers refused to support his economic stimulus and health care reform bills. A group of Republican conservatives formed the **Tea Party movement** and attacked the president as a "socialist" for what they perceived as an effort to expand federal control over the economy and diminish individual liberty. The rise of the Tea Party intensified the partisanship within the country and added to the growing gridlock in Washington, D.C. The Tea Party flexed its electoral muscle in the 2010 midterm elections, successfully campaigning for Republican congressional and gubernatorial candidates who supported its positions. As a result, Republicans regained control of the House while the Democratic majority in the Senate narrowed.

Obama also encountered political difficulties from the left. Although the president saved the financial system from collapse, at the end of 2011 unemployment dropped from 10.2 percent to a still high 8.5 percent. With millions of people still out of work, a resurgent Wall Street rewarded its managers and employees with big financial bonuses. Large corporations earned millions of dollars in profits but did not create new jobs. In 2011 protesters in cities around the nation launched the Occupy Wall Street movement, which attacked corporate greed, economic inequality, and government ineffectiveness. High unemployment and crushing student loan debt and massive cuts in spending on education, social services, and infrastructure inspired many of these activists.

Obama's Second Term

With unemployment remaining high, economic growth moving at a slow pace, and a number of European nations unable to pay mounting debts, the economy loomed as the top issue in the 2012 presidential election. The Republican nominee, Mitt Romney, the former governor of Massachusetts, appealed to conservative voters by opposing Obamacare and embracing the social agenda of the Christian Right. Despite the slower-than-expected economic recovery, Obama won reelection by holding together his coalition of African American, Latino, female, young, and lower-income voters.

During President Obama's second term, the economy showed greater improvement. The unemployment rate dropped to 4.9 percent in February 2016, the lowest figure in eight years. From 2010 to 2014, the gross domestic product grew steadily by an average of more than 2 percent, and the strengthening economy cut the budget deficit significantly. However, as the economy recovered from recession, real wages declined and income and wealth inequality widened. The top 1 percent gained about 95 percent of the income growth since 2009, and the top 10 percent held its highest share of income since World War I. One reason for this widening gap was that since 2000 the United States lost 5 million good-paying manufacturing jobs, and many of the jobs created by the recovery were low-wage service positions, whereas the wealthiest Americans benefited from the soaring stock market and rising capital gains. Making the problem worse, union membership continued its long-term decline, eliminating the major vehicle for workers to increase their wages.

In two other areas, gay rights and the environment, the Obama administration made great strides. Initially Obama had supported civil unions rather than same-sex marriage, but in 2012 he declared his support for it. The following year, the Supreme Court struck down the 1996 Defense of Marriage Act, thereby extending recognition of same-sex marriage. Finally, in 2015, in *Obergefell v. Hodges* the Court legalized same-sex marriage nationwide. (In *Bostock v. Clayton County* [2020], the Court ruled that the Civil Rights Act of 1964 protects employees from discrimination because of sexual orientation or gender identity.) With respect to the environment, the Obama administration took climate change seriously, encouraged fuel efficiency and clean energy production, bolstered the Environmental Protection Agency, and extended protection of significant cultural and natural landmarks.

Latinos and Immigration

In the twenty-first century, Latinos constituted the chief source of immigration into the United States. This group consisted of Mexicans, Central and South Americans, and those from the Caribbean islands of Cuba, the Dominican Republic, and Puerto Rico (whose residents are U.S. citizens). In 2010, some 50 million Latinos lived in the United States, and many of these residents made the economy run by taking low wage jobs in service industries and agriculture. The influx in Latino immigration resulted in a rise in poverty in many Latino communities. In 2010, the poverty rate of Latinos was twice the national average and hovered at 30 percent. Still, Latinos held political office and proved successful in many areas of economic and cultural life. President Obama appointed four Latinos to serve in his cabinet, Hilda Solis, Ken Salazar, Thomas Perez, and Julian Castro.

Most Latinos favored immigration reform, especially the protection of undocumented children brought by their parents into the country. Congress had failed to pass the Development, Relief, and Education for Alien Minors (DREAM) Act, first introduced in 2001, which would have provided an opportunity for the children of undocumented immigrants in the United States to gain legal residency status. To protect these so-called "dreamers," in 2012 President Obama instituted the **Deferred Action for Childhood Arrivals (DACA)** policy, which allows children who have entered the country illegally to receive a renewable two-year extension of their residence in the United States along with eligibility for work permits.

Asian Americans

Immigrants continued to arrive from the South Asian countries of India, Pakistan, and Bangladesh and the East Asian nations of Japan, South Korea, Philippines, China, Vietnam, and Cambodia. Most came for economic opportunity, others for political reasons. By 2012, about 75 percent of Asian American adults had been born overseas.

In 2016, the Asian American population of 21 million constituted 6.5 percent of the total U.S. population, up from 1 percent in 1965. They tended to be better educated than any other immigrant group. Their higher educational levels paid off economically. In 2007, their median income of $66,000 was higher than that of whites. They were more likely than any ethnic group to live in mixed neighborhoods and marry across racial lines. President Obama appointed three Asian Americans to his cabinet, Eric Shinseki, Steven Chu, and Gary Locke.

Asian Americans were a diverse group. Those from South Korea, Japan, China, and India came from different backgrounds than those from Laos, Cambodia, and Bangladesh. Not all became successful, and many, particularly those from Cambodia and Laos, suffered from the same economic problems as did other marginalized groups. The income gap within the Asian American population was greater than for any other ethnic group. From 1970 to 2016, the difference in the standard of living between Asian Americans at the top and the bottom of the income ladder nearly doubled.

California modeled diversity as a result of immigration. By 2016, 27 percent of the state's population was foreign-born. The majority of Californians consisted of Latinos, Asian Americans, and African Americans, with whites in the minority. Immigrants also flocked to the Southwest and to northeastern and midwestern cities like New York City, Jersey City, Chicago, and Detroit. They fanned out across the Southeast, adding to the growing populations of Atlanta, Raleigh-Durham, Charlotte, Columbia, and Memphis and providing these cities with an unprecedented ethnic mixture.

By the middle of the twenty-first century the population of the United States may look much different than it did at the beginning. In 2012 the U.S. Census Bureau reported that nonwhite babies made up the majority of births for the first time. If the current trends in immigration and birthrates continue, the percentage of Latinos and Asian Americans in the nation will increase, while that of whites and blacks will decline. In addition, the racial and ethnic composition of the population has been transformed through intermarriage. In 2010 the Census Bureau disclosed that one of seven new marriages, or 14.6 percent, was interracial or interethnic. In 1961, when Barack Obama was born, the figure for interracial marriages was less than 0.1 percent. In an increasingly globalized nation, debates over immigration, race, and citizenship will continue.

African Americans and Systemic Racism

During his two terms, President Obama selected seven African Americans to positions in his cabinet, reflecting the racial and ethnic diversity reshaping contemporary America. Particularly noteworthy, he chose Eric Holder (2009–2015) and Loretta Lynch (2015–2017) to serve as attorney general. He also appointed a black woman, Susan Rice, to the key post of national security adviser.

Despite the political recognition gained by African Americans, racial conflicts continued to erupt. Blacks had long-standing grievances with the criminal justice system as a result of systemic racism. Whereas most whites saw police officers as protectors, blacks viewed them with suspicion or as threats to their safety. The 2013 acquittal of a white man in the killing of Trayvon Martin in Sanford, Florida triggered outrage. A series of subsequent police killings of unarmed blacks in Ferguson, Missouri; Cleveland, Ohio; Staten Island, New York; and Baltimore, Maryland launched Black Lives Matter, co-founded by Alicia Garza. As a result of federal investigations, in 2015 the Justice Department found a pattern of systemic racism in the Ferguson and Cleveland police departments and negotiated settlements that instituted reforms. Nevertheless, persistent problems remained not only in policing but in prison sentencing. The enforcement of drug laws put blacks at a serious disadvantage. Judges handed down longer sentences for possession of crack cocaine, more commonly used among inner city residents, than powder cocaine, more likely used by suburban whites. Over 28 percent of African American men can expect to be incarcerated over their lifetime, while whites have a 4 percent chance of imprisonment. The "prison-industrial complex" grew as states spent more money on building new prisons than on higher education. Disproportionate black imprisonment perpetuated the cycle of poverty and disfranchisement, as released African American felons had difficulty finding jobs and getting their right to vote restored.

African Americans also faced renewed barriers to voting. The Supreme Court in *Shelby v. Holder* (2013) ruled that a critical enforcement provision of the 1965 Voting Rights Act was no longer valid. In the wake of this decision, Republican state legislatures adopted voter identification requirements and voter suppression measures that made it more difficult for African Americans, Latinos, and Native Americans to cast ballots.

The Native American Struggle Continued

In 2020 nearly 7 million Native Americans lived in the United States. They continued to push for maintaining their tribal sovereignty at the same time as exercising their rights as U.S. citizens. Recent court victories had given them greater control over their internal affairs, including education and law enforcement. For example, in *McGirt v. Oklahoma* (2020) the Supreme Court ruled that most of the eastern portion of Oklahoma, including Tulsa, remains by treaty within the Indian nations of the Muscogee (Creek), Cherokee, Choctaw, Chickasaw, and Seminole. Native Americans living there are subject to tribal or federal courts rather than state jurisdiction. In addition, Indians have also established a network of thirty-eight tribal colleges, integrating indigenous traditions into their curriculum. In 2010, nearly 200,000 indigenous students were enrolled in colleges.

Most Native Americans, however, lived in poverty. Although the courts have given tribes control over gambling casinos, a lucrative enterprise, the jobs that gaming creates are low paying, and some reservations face unemployment rates of 80 percent. Indians on remote reservations did not have access to health facilities. Indigenous tribes continued to battle corporations over development of oil pipelines near their land and access to natural resources.

President Obama sought closer cooperation between the federal government and Native Americans. He convened annual White House Tribal Nations conferences. The president established the White House Council on Indian Affairs and appointed a record number of Native Americans to positions in his administration, among them Karen Driver of the Fond du lac Band (Chippewa); Tracy Goodluck, an Oneida/Muscogee; and Gina Jackson, a Te-Moak Western Shoshone. Despite this recognition, Native Americans remained a vulnerable population.

Obama and the World

Throughout Obama's two terms, his administration faced serious tests of its international leadership. In 2008 the president appointed Hillary Clinton, the former first lady and a senator from New York, as his secretary of state. The U.S. military increased combat troop withdrawals from Iraq and turned over security for the country to the newly elected Iraqi government. At the same time, the Obama administration stepped up the war in Afghanistan by increasing U.S. troop levels, which led to a rise in casualties. In 2011 he achieved dramatic success when U.S. special forces killed Osama bin Laden in his hideout in Pakistan. By 2016, with John Kerry now his secretary of state, the president had withdrawn most combat soldiers from Afghanistan. Yet Iraq remained unstable, and the outcome of the war against the Taliban in Afghanistan proved uncertain. Despite bin Laden's death, radical jihadists continued to pose a serious danger.

Other international challenges continued as well. From 2006 to 2013, instability in Asia, the Middle East, and the Persian Gulf also heightened U.S. security concerns and underscored the difficulties of achieving lasting peace in these regions (Map 29.2).

The Middle East posed the greatest threat with the rise of a new militant organization known as the **Islamic State of Iraq and Syria (ISIS)**. An offshoot of

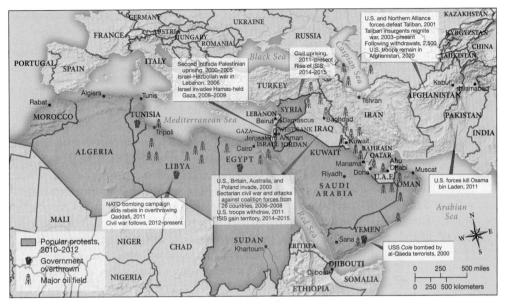

MAP 29.2   The Middle East, 2000–2020

Since 2000 the Middle East has been marked by both terrorism and democratic uprisings. After 9/11 the United States tried to transform Iraq and Afghanistan by military might, which led to prolonged wars. Yet popular rebellions in 2011, led by young people and fueled by new technology, created hope that change was possible. However, as of 2016 the military had regained power in Egypt, and Libya had descended into civil war. Syria remained involved in a brutal civil war. The terrorist, military organization ISIS captured sections of Syria as well as territory in Iraq, but in 2017 they were driven out of most of this territory by Syrian government, Russian, and American-backed military forces.

al-Qaeda, it grew out of the sectarian violence following the overthrow of Saddam Hussein in Iraq. ISIS took over parts of Syria and Iraq, prompting the United States and some Arab nations to launch air strikes against its forces.

The civil war in Syria had profound effects on the rest of the world. Starting in 2010, millions of Syrians fled their homes, and tens of thousands sought refuge in western Europe and the United States. This movement of refugees, greater than at any time since World War II, overwhelmed those European countries to which they first came—Greece, Hungary, and the Czech Republic. The EU split over how to manage the crisis. In 2015 President Obama pledged to accept 10,000 Syrian refugees into the United States during 2016, but that number paled in comparison to the numbers who needed safe havens. Meanwhile, the humanitarian crisis of providing food, shelter, and medical attention to the refugees grew.

Antiterrorist surveillance within the United States provoked growing controversy. Under the Patriot Act, the National Security Agency (NSA) began collecting and storing phone records of U.S. citizens. The NSA did not listen to the calls, but it drew on this bulk data to track suspected terrorists. In 2015, Congress passed legislation curtailing this massive, clandestine operation, which restored some balance between national security and individual privacy. On other foreign fronts, President

Obama launched bold departures. In 2014 he set in motion the normalization of diplomatic relations with Cuba and, the following year, along with several other world powers, negotiated an agreement with Iran on restricting its nuclear program. In contrast, relations with Russia deteriorated. In 2014 Russia, led by Vladimir Putin, annexed its former territory of the Crimea and in 2015 provided military support for pro-Russian separatists in Ukraine. In response the United States and the EU imposed economic sanctions on Russia but declined to take military action. Later in 2015 Russia sent military forces to Syria to support the government of the dictator Bashar al-Assad, a long-time ally, and fight his opponents, both ISIS and rebels backed by the United States.

The United States also faced global economic and environmental challenges. As China flourished economically, American workers lost jobs, and the Chinese amassed a nearly $200 billion trade surplus with the United States. In addition, the growth of manufacturing and the market economy in China resulted in the rising consumption of oil and gasoline. The increase in carbon emissions in China and other parts of Asia contributed to the problem of climate change, which ultimately threatens the delicate balance between the natural environment and human societies across the planet. Global warming in the past half century has resulted mainly from emissions of greenhouse gases into the atmosphere and the erosion of the ozone layer. Climbing temperatures cause the melting of glaciers, a rise in the sea level, extreme fluctuations of weather with severely damaging storms, and famines. Disruptions in industrial and agricultural production caused by storms and the subsequent expense of rebuilding have already had a negative impact on the U.S. and world economies. In December 2015 the United States joined 194 nations, including China and India, in signing the Paris Climate Agreement to reduce greenhouse gas emissions produced from fossil fuels.

REVIEW & RELATE	• What were the causes and consequences of the Great Recession? • What effects did the election and presidency of Barack Obama have on American politics, society, and the United States' relationship to the world?

The Presidency of Donald Trump

As Barack Obama's second term drew to a close in 2016, Americans elected Donald Trump to succeed him. The Republican Trump defeated the Democratic candidate Hillary Rodham Clinton, preventing her from becoming the first woman elected president. Despite this triumph, Trump and the Republican-controlled Congress found governing difficult.

The 2016 Election

A New York City real estate tycoon and a reality television host, Trump had never held political office or engaged in public service. In contrast, Hillary Clinton had an extensive record of public and political service: first lady, U.S. senator from New York, and secretary of state.

Running as an antiestablishment outsider, Trump adopted the slogan "Make America Great Again." He embraced right-wing, nativist populism against Mexican, Central American, and Muslim immigrants and opposed free trade agreements that he concluded shipped jobs overseas. As part of his "America First" stance, he criticized international military alliances such as NATO, a major component of U.S. foreign policy since World War II. His well-publicized moral lapses notwithstanding, Trump appealed to white Christian evangelicals by stating his opposition to abortion and pledging to appoint conservative judges to the Supreme Court who would overturn *Roe v. Wade.*

His nativist rhetoric echoed the beliefs of white nationalism, including neo-Nazis, the Ku Klux Klan, and whites who believed they were losing ground to other racial or ethnic groups. Obama's presidency had brought to a boil white racial resentments and provided fuel for Trump's candidacy. Even before running for president, Trump had called into question Obama's U.S. citizenship, despite substantial proof to the contrary, claiming that he had been born in Kenya and therefore was ineligible to become president. During the campaign, Trump appealed to white racial bitterness by attacking an American-born judge of Latino heritage and the Muslim parents of a dead war hero who criticized Trump for his racial and religious intolerance. He also stoked the flames of ethnic prejudice by calling unauthorized Mexican immigrants "rapists" and promising to build a wall between the U.S. and Mexican border and make the Mexican government pay for it.

Trump's appeal to certain segments of the U.S. electorate did not operate in a vacuum. Throughout western Europe anti-immigrant, right-wing nationalist parties were gaining ground. In a 2016 referendum, voters in the United Kingdom chose to withdraw from the European Union, a move known as Brexit (British exit). Nativist, anti-Muslim parties grew stronger in France, Germany, Austria, the Netherlands, and Scandinavia, though none gained control of their governments as they did in Hungary, Poland, and the Czech Republic.

Late in the campaign, when the online Web site WikiLeaks published e-mails stolen from the accounts of the Democratic National Committee and Hillary Clinton's campaign director, Trump tried to use them to his advantage. Seventeen U.S. intelligence agencies later concluded that Russian state-sponsored agents had hacked the accounts and given the e-mails to WikiLeaks. Russian hackers had pilfered the records in an attempt to promote negative publicity about the Clinton campaign and sow discord within the American electorate. Trump refused to acknowledge Russian meddling and instead praised Russia's authoritarian leader, Vladimir Putin.

Despite losing the popular vote by nearly 3 million ballots, Trump won in the Electoral College, 304–227. Trump captured six states that Obama had won in 2012, and the outcome turned on a total of 78,000 votes in Pennsylvania, Michigan, and Wisconsin. Trump's nativist agenda, along with sexist and white-identity appeals, resonated especially with older white men, residents of small towns and rural areas, workers who had lost their jobs to automation and globalization, and those who had less than a college education. Even a majority of white women (53 percent) gave Trump a slight edge, though Clinton did remain overwhelming popular among African American women.

Racial and cultural resentments proved most significant in the outcome. White attitudes toward African Americans, recent immigrants, and Muslims were the main indicators in determining support for Trump. The president-elect did not create these racial, ethnic, and religious resentments, but he exploited and legitimized them.

The Trump Presidency

From the outset of his administration, women like BLM's co-founder Alicia Garza played a leading role in challenging President Trump. The president's misogynist behavior and rhetoric mobilized millions of women and male allies to march in Washington, D.C., and major cities around the nation and the world to reject Trump's views and affirm that "women's rights are human rights." His election also inspired many women to run for political office.

The rage against Trump and his defeat of the first female, major-party candidate for president inspired a collective uprising against sexual degradation of women. "When Trump won the election, I felt a crushing sense of powerlessness," one woman declared. "And then I realized that I had to do something." Social media provided a means for women's activism. Originated by Tarana Burke, an African American social activist, and promoted by the actress Alyssa Milano, the **#MeToo movement** linked tens of millions of women who shared on Twitter and Facebook their stories of rape, sexual harassment, and sexual assault. As a result, by the end of 2017, numerous women had come forward with complaints of sexual misconduct by media, entertainment, and sports celebrities, corporate executives, and politicians of both political parties, often leading to the swift firing or resignation of these men.

Once in the White House, Trump did not reverse course and become more "presidential." Rather, he continued to subvert the norms of American politics. He used his Twitter account to insult those who disagreed with him, including fellow Republicans. He viewed all criticism as personal, and attacked the mainstream media as "the enemy of the American people," claiming it promoted "fake news."

President Trump had some success in achieving his agenda. Although Congress narrowly rejected his signature campaign promise to repeal and replace the Affordable Care Act, the president won passage of a Republican tax cut law that disproportionately favored corporations and the wealthy. The economic recovery that had begun under the Obama administration continued during the first three years of Trump's administration. The stock market soared, and unemployment figures tumbled to 3.6 percent. The president also secured ratification of his appointments of Neil Gorsuch, Brett Kavanaugh, and Amy Coney Barrett to the Supreme Court, thereby reinforcing the conservative majority on the bench. In 2018 he signed into law the First Step Act, a bipartisan reform measure aimed at reducing mass incarceration and the length of mandatory criminal sentencing. As commander-in-chief, the president furnished American military support to defeat ISIS in Iraq and Syria, forcing it to withdraw from major cities under its control.

Trump achieved even more by issuing executive orders. He managed to put into effect a ban on immigrants from primarily Muslim nations. He revoked Obama's DACA order allowing so-called "dreamers," to remain indefinitely. His administration cancelled the provisional residency permits of more than 200,000 immigrants from El Salvador, Haiti, and Honduras who had fled to the U.S. following natural disasters in their countries. The children subsequently born into these families were American citizens, and the deportation of one or both of their parents would create a humanitarian crisis. Cracking down on asylum-seeking Central American immigrants at the southern border with Mexico, in 2018 the Trump administration initiated a "zero tolerance" policy. **U.S. Immigration and Customs Enforcement (ICE)** agents separated over 5,000 children from their parents who faced deportation and locked them up in crowded and unsafe holding facilities. In 2018, a federal judge ordered the reunification of the separated families.

Trump used his executive power to weaken health care coverage as well as loosen protections for consumers and the environment. He appointed individuals to head cabinet offices and regulatory agencies who favored limited governance and privatization of public services, while denying scientific evidence of man-made global warning. He withdrew the United States from the Paris Climate Agreement; rolled back Obama-initiated trade and travel relations with Cuba; and decertified the Iran Nuclear Agreement. He issued some seventy executive orders either reversing or curtailing environmental and climate regulations he considered burdensome to the fossil fuel industry and other businesses. Trump took these actions in the face of ecological disasters resulting from climate change. Warmer temperatures in California, Oregon, and Washington State dried out forests, causing in 2020 a series of extensive fires that threatened life, property, and natural resources.

While many of these policies provoked outrage, the Trump presidency fueled greater controversy over issues of race. White nationalists became emboldened by Trump's election, and he in turn provided encouragement by choosing not to condemn them forcefully or consistently. At a rally in Charlottesville, Virginia, Nazis and Ku Klux Klan members paraded across the University of Virginia campus mocking Jews and other racial or ethnic groups. They were there to oppose removal of Confederate monuments, which offended African Americans and others for honoring the war to maintain slavery. When an anti-fascist protester was run down and killed by an automobile driven by a white nationalist, President Trump squandered the moral authority of his office by equating the white nationalist demonstrators with those who opposed them. During Trump's term, right-wing, white supremacist, anti-Semitic extremists posed the greatest threat of domestic terrorism.

Of greater concern to his presidency was the investigation into Russian interference in the 2016 election. Two congressional committees and a special prosecutor appointed by the Justice Department, Robert Mueller, looked into Russian hacking and possible collusion between members of the Trump campaign and Kremlin-sponsored operatives seeking to damage Hillary Clinton's campaign. One of the targets of the investigation was General Michael Flynn, who was forced to resign as National Security Advisor shortly after taking office. He subsequently pled guilty to lying to the FBI about his contacts with Russia (Trump later pardoned him). In 2019, Mueller reported that although the Trump campaign "welcomed" Russian interference in the election, there was no conclusive evidence that the campaign had "conspired" with Russian agents in their illegal activities. Nevertheless, Mueller found that Trump may have obstructed justice in attempting to thwart investigations into Russian interference, but he accepted the Justice Department's legal opinion that a sitting president could not be indicted on criminal charges. Despite evidence to the contrary, Trump called the charge of Russian interference a "hoax" perpetrated by his opponents to delegitimize his election.

Trump escaped criminal charges following the **Mueller Report**, but his subsequent actions led to impeachment. In July 2019, he telephoned the president of

Ukraine and asked him to dig up political dirt on former vice president Joe Biden, a possible Democratic opponent in the 2020 election, and his son for alleged corrupt activities in that country. In return, Trump indicated that he would release military assistance to the Ukrainian government to aid in its war against Russian-sponsored insurgents. The 2018 congressional elections had brought Democrats control of the House of Representatives. After investigating whether Trump had solicited foreign interference from Ukraine for his own political gain, a majority of the House voted along partisan lines to impeach the president for obstructing justice and obstructing Congress. With Republicans still a majority of the Senate, in February 2020 Democrats fell far short of winning the two-thirds vote necessary to convict Trump and remove him from office.

Pandemic, Protests, and Politics

In 2020, Trump faced a deadly threat to his presidency. Early in the year, the outbreak in China of a new virus, **COVID-19**, erupted into a worldwide pandemic, potentially as deadly as the 1918 influenza contagion. After the United States reported its first cases in late January, Trump banned air travel to China and European countries struck by the disease, but it was too late. At the end of February 2021, a year after the pandemic started, the United States experienced over 28 million cases and over 500,000 deaths, leading the world in the largest number of infections and deaths. With 4 percent of the global population, the United States counted 26 percent of the over 111 million worldwide coronavirus cases and 21 percent of the deaths.

The president made a bad situation worse. His administration was unprepared with a detailed plan to deal with the pandemic despite warnings from scientists. From the beginning, he played down the severity of the deadly virus claiming that he "didn't want to create panic." He misled the public by claiming the disease would quickly disappear. He refused to mobilize the full resources of the federal government and left it up to the states to deal with the crisis. He advocated a variety of treatments and drugs that either were of dubious value or potentially caused harmful side effects. Ignoring many of the recommendations of his health advisers, particularly the wearing of masks in close quarters and avoiding large gatherings, in October the president caught the virus and had to be hospitalized. Still, he continued to downplay the danger of the pandemic even as infections and deaths skyrocketed, and he placed his efforts behind "Operation Warp Speed," which he launched to encourage pharmaceutical companies to develop a vaccine. In December 2020 the Federal Drug Administration approved the first vaccines, but it would take many months for the general public to be inoculated.

The pandemic caused the most severe economic downturn since the Great Depression. The Gross Domestic Product fell sharply, and by December the unemployment rate, after briefly rising to over 14 percent, hovered around 7 percent, with higher figures for African Americans, Latinos, Native Americans, and women. The president and Congress twice reached a bipartisan agreement on legislation that provided funds to keep businesses afloat and extend unemployment payments, but never agreed on any wider plan to combat the disease.

COVID-19 underscored the systemic racism that plagued the United States. Marginalized groups and people of color tended to work in service and agricultural jobs that did not permit them to do telework at home, thus placing them at greater risk. Blacks, Latinos, and indigenous people suffered from disproportionately higher infection and death rates. They were more vulnerable because socioeconomic conditions, often a legacy of discrimination, forced them to live in dense, segregated housing through which the disease spread rapidly. They had more limited access to adequate health care, a higher level of distrust of the medical community, and relatedly a higher incidence of pre-existing conditions that made the effects of the virus more devastating.

The pandemic was not the only crisis that African Americans and other racial and ethnic minorities faced. While the country locked down from the virus, black people rose up to protest police brutality. Joined by a younger generation of whites, Latinos, and indigenous people, they challenged the pernicious effects of structural racism in the criminal justice system. The killings of Breonna Taylor by Louisville police and George Floyd by Minneapolis police sparked this uprising. Taylor died from gunfire after three police officers broke into her apartment mistakenly believing a suspected drug dealer was inside. When George Floyd was arrested, one policeman placed his knee on his neck as Floyd lay on the ground shouting that he could not breathe. Meanwhile three other police officers stood by and watched Floyd die over

Helen H. Richardson/MediaNews Group/The Denver Post via Getty Images

George Floyd and Breonna Taylor, Black Lives Matter, 2020 The police killings of George Floyd and Breonna Taylor sparked interracial demonstrations throughout the nation with the rallying cry of "Black Lives Matter." In the photo on the top, on June 7, 2020, public school students walk peacefully by a mural of George Floyd painted on a wall in Denver, Colorado. In the photo on the bottom taken on September 21, 2020, Tamika Palmer, mother of Breonna Taylor, stands in front of a mural of her daughter at Jefferson Square Park in Louisville, Kentucky, where protesters had demonstrated peacefully since Taylor's killing by police on March 13. Brandon Bell/Getty Images

the course of nine minutes. Bystanders videoed this, and millions watched in horror on television news programs and the Internet.

There had been police killings before but these incidents fueled outrage long bottled up. Led by Black Lives Matter, interracial demonstrations erupted around the country. Most protests were peaceful, but frustration turned rage into sporadic violence. Support grew for BLM. Minneapolis made substantial reforms in its policing, and Louisville reached a $12 million civil settlement with Breonna Taylor's family and promised to initiate police reforms. Government officials in the South removed Confederate monuments that glorified the institutional segregation and disfranchisement of the Jim Crow era. In contrast, President Trump condemned the protesters, called for law and order against "agitators" and "anarchists," defended retaining Confederate memorials, and sent in federal troops to tear-gas demonstrators.

The 2020 election took place amidst the swirl of pandemic, protests, and economic distress. These challenges proved too much for Donald Trump to overcome. His opponent, the former vice president Joseph Biden of Delaware, and his running mate, Senator Kamala Harris of California, triumphed. An African American and South Asian, Harris became the first woman vice president. The Biden-Harris ticket won by more than seven million popular votes and swept to victory in the Electoral College by a vote of 306–232.

Trump responded by falsely charging widespread election fraud. He sought to overturn the results of the election through frivolous court challenges and by pressuring Republicans in swing states and in Congress to reject Biden's victory and re-install him as president. On January 6, 2021, at a rally in Washington, D.C., President Trump incited a crowd to storm the Capitol and block the certification of the electoral votes for Biden and Harris. The violent mob invaded the Capitol, resulting in five deaths, before city police ended the insurrection. A week later, in a bipartisan vote, the House of Representative impeached Trump for inciting an insurrection, making him the only president in history to be impeached twice. Following Biden's inauguration, the Senate conducted the impeachment trial but fell short of the two-thirds vote to convict Trump. Although seven Republicans joined fifty Democrats — the largest bipartisan majority for conviction in history — the overwhelming majority of Republican senators voted in Trump's favor.

REVIEW & RELATE	• Explain how Donald Trump was elected president and describe the differences between campaigning for office and governing. • Explain how the pandemic and protests influenced American politics and society during the Trump administration.

Conclusion: Technology, Terror, and Pandemic in a Global Society

Since 1993 Americans have faced new forms of globalization, new technologies, and new modes of warfare. The computer revolution begun by Bill Gates and others helped change the way Americans gather information, communicate ideas, purchase goods, and conduct business. It has also shaped national and international conflicts. The September 11, 2001 attacks on the World Trade Center and the Pentagon demonstrated that terrorists could use computers and digital equipment to wreak havoc on the most powerful nation in the world. And Barack Obama's 2008 presidential campaign, protesters demonstrating against various Middle East dictatorships, and leaders such as Alicia Garza and Tarana Burke of the Black Lives Matter and #MeToo movements also wielded technology to promote their causes. On the other hand, in the interest of combating terrorism, the U.S. government has used this technology to monitor the activities of citizens it considers a threat to national security, thereby raising concerns about civil liberties.

The Bush administration responded to the 9/11 terrorist attacks by fighting wars in Iraq and Afghanistan. President Obama ended the Iraq War and steadily withdrew troops from Afghanistan, but neither administration was able to build stable governments in these countries. The rise of ISIS, which grew out of the fighting in Iraq, posed an even greater danger than did al-Qaeda to stability in the Middle East and the spread of terrorism throughout the world. At the same time, the United States and its allies faced a militarily revitalized Russia seeking to extend its influence in Ukraine and Syria, once again heightening the prospect of confrontation between the world's major nuclear powers.

Along with the computer revolution, globalization has encouraged vast economic transformations throughout the world. Presidents as politically different as Bill Clinton and George W. Bush supported deregulation, free trade, and other policies that fostered corporate mergers and allowed businesses to reach beyond U.S. borders for cheap labor, raw materials, and new markets. While the 1990s witnessed the fruits of the new global economy, in 2008 the dangers of financial speculation and intertwined national economies became strikingly clear with the onset of the Great Recession. This economic collapse has underscored the inequalities of wealth that continue to widen, aggravated by racial, ethnic, and gender disparities.

The Obama administration succeeded in ending the worst features of the recession and at the same time managed to extend health care coverage to the country's most vulnerable citizens. Yet Obama faced increased partisan congressional gridlock that made further reforms concerning immigration, job creation, racial justice, energy consumption, and the environment impossible. Indeed, it took the federal courts to extend marriage equality nationwide.

The election of Donald Trump in 2016 demonstrated that despite the accomplishments of the Obama administration, many Americans felt left out or fearful of that progress. Trump waged a political campaign based on racial, economic, and cultural grievances that carried over from the campaign into his presidency. Although Trump lost to Joe Biden in 2020, these divisions in the nation remain sharper than at any time since the turbulent 1960s. The cult of Donald Trump—Trumpism—continued its hold on the Republican Party.

It should be kept in mind that throughout its history, the United States has shown great strength in finding solutions to its problems. The nation has incorporated diverse populations into its midst, redefined old cultural identities and created new ones, expanded civil rights and civil liberties, extended economic opportunities, and joined other nations to fight military aggression and address other international concerns. The nation will have to draw on these strengths and continue to innovate and adapt to change if it expects to exert leadership in the world and maintain its greatness in the twenty-first century.

Chapter 29 Review

KEY TERMS

Black Lives Matter, 742
Contract with America, 746
Personal Responsibility and Work
　Opportunity Reconciliation Act,
　746
North American Free Trade Agree-
　ment (NAFTA), 747
ethnic cleansing, 748
Patriot Act, 751
Bush Doctrine, 752
Hurricane Katrina, 753
Great Recession, 754
Patient Protection and Affordable
　Care Act ("Obamacare"), 755

Tea Party movement, 756
Obergefell v. Hodges, 757
Deferred Action for Childhood
　Arrivals (DACA), 758
Islamic State of Iraq and Syria (ISIS),
　760
#MeToo movement, 764
U.S. Immigration and Customs
　Enforcement (ICE), 765
Mueller Report, 765
COVID-19, 766

REVIEW & RELATE

1. How did computers change life in the United States at the turn of the millennium?
2. How has globalization affected business consolidation and immigration in recent decades?
3. How did conflicts between Democrats and Republicans affect President Clinton's accomplishments?
4. Explain the new post–Cold War foreign policy threats that President Clinton faced.
5. How did President Bush put compassionate conservatism into action?
6. How did the war on terror affect American foreign policy in the Bush administration?
7. What were the causes and consequences of the Great Recession?
8. What effects did the election and presidency of Barack Obama have on American politics, society, and the United States' relationship to the world?
9. Explain how Donald Trump was elected president and describe the differences between campaigning for office and governing.
10. Explain how the pandemic and protests influenced American politics and society during the Trump administration.

TIMELINE OF EVENTS

1975	• Microsoft formed
1976	• Apple Computer Company formed
1980–1990s	• Immigration surges from Mexico, Central America, the Caribbean, and South and East Asia
1991	• World Wide Web created
1994	• Contract with America announced; Republicans win control of Congress
1996	• Personal Responsibility and Work Reconciliation Act passed
	• Defense of Marriage Act passed
1998	• President Clinton impeached
2000	• Supreme Court rules in favor of George W. Bush in contested presidential election
2001	• September 11 attacks on World Trade Center and Pentagon
	• U.S. troops invade Afghanistan; Patriot Act passed
2003–2011	• War in Iraq
2005	• Hurricane Katrina
2008	• Great Recession begins
	• Barack Obama elected president
	• Tea Party movement formed
2010	• Patient Protection and Affordable Care Act ("Obamacare")
2011	• Osama bin Laden killed
	• Occupy Wall Street movement formed
	• Black Lives Matter movement formed
2012	• Deferred Action for Childhood Arrivals (DACA) policy
2015	• Supreme Court legalizes same-sex marriage nationwide
	• Agreement signed by 195 nations to lower greenhouse gas emissions
	• Agreement with Iran restricting its nuclear weapons program
2016	• Donald Trump elected president
2017	• Women's March on Washington and formation of #MeToo movement
2019	• First impeachment of President Trump
2020	• Coronavirus pandemic
2021	• George Floyd and Breonna Taylor killings and Black Lives Matter protests for racial justice
	• Joseph Biden and Kamala Harris elected president and vice president
	• Trump incites insurrection at the Capitol and is impeached again

Appendix

The Declaration of Independence

In Congress, July 4, 1776.

The unanimous Declaration of the thirteen United States of America

When in the course of human events, it becomes necessary for one people to dissolve the political bands which have connected them with another, and to assume, among the powers of the earth, the separate and equal station to which the laws of nature and of nature's God entitle them, a decent respect to the opinions of mankind requires that they should declare the causes which impel them to the separation.

We hold these truths to be self-evident, that all men are created equal; that they are endowed by their Creator with certain unalienable rights; that among these, are life, liberty, and the pursuit of happiness. That, to secure these rights, governments are instituted among men, deriving their just powers from the consent of the governed; that, whenever any form of government becomes destructive of these ends, it is the right of the people to alter or to abolish it, and to institute a new government, laying its foundation on such principles, and organizing its powers in such form, as to them shall seem most likely to effect their safety and happiness. Prudence, indeed, will dictate that governments long established, should not be changed for light and transient causes; and, accordingly, all experience hath shown, that mankind are more disposed to suffer, while evils are sufferable, than to right themselves by abolishing the forms to which they are accustomed. But, when a long train of abuses and usurpations, pursuing invariably the same object, evinces a design to reduce them under absolute despotism, it is their right, it is their duty, to throw off such government and to provide new guards for their future security. Such has been the patient sufferance of these colonies, and such is now the necessity which constrains them to alter their former systems of government. The history of the present King of Great Britain is a history of repeated injuries and usurpations, all having, in direct object, the establishment of an absolute tyranny over these States. To prove this, let facts be submitted to a candid world: He has refused his assent to laws the most wholesome and necessary for the public good.

He has forbidden his governors to pass laws of immediate and pressing importance, unless suspended in their operation till his assent should be obtained; and, when so suspended, he has utterly neglected to attend to them.

He has refused to pass other laws for the accommodation of large districts of people, unless those people would relinquish the right of representation in the legislature; a right inestimable to them, and formidable to tyrants only.

He has called together legislative bodies at places unusual, uncomfortable, and distant from the depository of their public records, for the sole purpose of fatiguing them into compliance with his measures.

He has dissolved representative houses repeatedly for opposing, with manly firmness, his invasions on the rights of the people.

He has refused, for a long time after such dissolutions, to cause others to be elected; whereby the legislative powers, incapable of annihilation, have returned to the people at large for their exercise; the state remaining in the mean-time exposed to all the danger of invasion from without, and convulsions within.

He has endeavoured to prevent the population of these States; for that purpose, obstructing the laws for naturalization of foreigners, refusing to pass others to encourage their migration hither, and raising the conditions of new appropriations of lands.

He has obstructed the administration of justice, by refusing his assent to laws for establishing judiciary powers.

He has made judges dependent on his will alone, for the tenure of their offices, and the amount and payment of their salaries.

He has erected a multitude of new offices, and sent hither swarms of officers to harass our people, and eat out their substance.

He has kept among us, in times of peace, standing armies, without the consent of our legislature.

He has affected to render the military independent of, and superior to, the civil power.

He has combined, with others, to subject us to a jurisdiction foreign to our Constitution, and unacknowledged by our laws; giving his assent to their acts of pretended legislation:

For quartering large bodies of armed troops among us:

For protecting them by a mock trial, from punishment, for any murders which they should commit on the inhabitants of these States:

For cutting off our trade with all parts of the world:

For imposing taxes on us without our consent:

For depriving us, in many cases, of the benefit of trial by jury:

For transporting us beyond seas to be tried for pretended offences:

For abolishing the free system of English laws in a neighboring province, establishing therein an arbitrary government, and enlarging its boundaries, so as to render it at once an example and fit instrument for introducing the same absolute rule into these colonies:

For taking away our charters, abolishing our most valuable laws, and altering, fundamentally, the powers of our governments:

For suspending our own legislatures, and declaring themselves invested with power to legislate for us in all cases whatsoever.

He has abdicated government here, by declaring us out of his protection, and waging war against us.

He has plundered our seas, ravaged our coasts, burnt our towns, and destroyed the lives of our people.

He is, at this time, transporting large armies of foreign mercenaries to complete the works of death, desolation, and tyranny, already begun, with circumstances of cruelty and perfidy scarcely paralleled in the most barbarous ages, and totally unworthy the head of a civilized nation.

He has constrained our fellow citizens, taken captive on the high seas, to bear arms against their country, to become the executioners of their friends, and brethren, or to fall themselves by their hands.

He has excited domestic insurrections amongst us, and has endeavored to bring on the inhabitants of our frontiers, the merciless Indian savages, whose known rule of warfare is an undistinguished destruction of all ages, sexes, and conditions.

In every stage of these oppressions, we have petitioned for redress; in the most humble terms; our repeated petitions have been answered only by repeated injury. A prince, whose character is thus marked by every act which may define a tyrant, is unfit to be the ruler of a free people.

Nor have we been wanting in attention to our British brethren. We have warned them, from time to time, of attempts made by their legislature to extend an unwarrantable jurisdiction over us. We have reminded them of the circumstances of our emigration and settlement here. We have appealed to their native justice and magnanimity, and we have conjured them, by the ties of our common kindred, to disavow these usurpations, which would inevitably interrupt our connections and correspondence. They, too, have been deaf to the voice of justice and consanguinity. We must, therefore, acquiesce in the necessity which denounces our separation, and hold them as we hold the rest of mankind, enemies in war, in peace, friends.

We, therefore, the representatives of the United States of America, in general Congress assembled, appealing to the Supreme Judge of the world for the rectitude of our intentions, do, in the name, and by authority of the good people of these colonies, solemnly publish and declare, that these united colonies are, and of right ought to be, free and independent states: that they are absolved from all allegiance to the British Crown, and that all political connection between them and the state of Great Britain is, and ought to be, totally dissolved; and that, as free and independent states, they have full power to levy war, conclude peace, contract alliances, establish commerce, and to do all other acts and things which independent states may of right do. And, for the support of this declaration, with a firm reliance on the protection of Divine Providence, we mutually pledge to each other our lives, our fortunes, and our sacred honor.

The foregoing Declaration was, by order of Congress, engrossed, and signed by the following members:

JOHN HANCOCK

New Hampshire
Josiah Bartlett
William Whipple
Matthew Thornton

Massachusetts Bay
Samuel Adams
John Adams
Robert Treat Paine
Elbridge Gerry

Rhode Island
Stephen Hopkins
William Ellery

Connecticut
Roger Sherman
Samuel Huntington
William Williams
Oliver Wolcott

New York
William Floyd
Phillip Livingston
Francis Lewis
Lewis Morris

New Jersey
Richard Stockton
John Witherspoon
Francis Hopkinson
John Hart
Abraham Clark

Pennsylvania
Robert Morris
Benjamin Rush
Benjamin Franklin
John Morton
George Clymer
James Smith
George Taylor
James Wilson
George Ross
Caesar Rodney
George Read
Thomas M'Kean

Maryland
Samuel Chase
William Paca
Thomas Stone
Charles Carroll, of Carrollton

North Carolina
William Hooper
Joseph Hewes
John Penn

South Carolina
Edward Rutledge
Thomas Heyward, Jr.
Thomas Lynch, Jr.
Arthur Middleton

Virginia
George Wythe
Richard Henry Lee
Thomas Jefferson
Benjamin Harrison
Thomas Nelson, Jr.
Francis Lightfoot Lee
Carter Braxton

Georgia
Button Gwinnett
Lyman Hall
George Walton

Resolved, That copies of the Declaration be sent to the several assemblies, conventions, and committees, or councils of safety, and to the several commanding officers of the continental troops; that it be proclaimed in each of the United States, at the head of the army.

The Articles of Confederation and Perpetual Union

Agreed to in Congress, November 15, 1777.
Ratified March 1781.

Between the states of New Hampshire, Massachusetts Bay, Rhode Island and Providence Plantations, Connecticut, New York, New Jersey, Pennsylvania, Delaware, Maryland, Virginia, North Carolina, South Carolina, and Georgia.*

Article 1

The stile of this confederacy shall be "The United States of America."

Article 2

Each State retains its sovereignty, freedom and independence, and every power, jurisdiction, and right, which is not by this confederation expressly delegated to the United States, in Congress assembled.

Article 3

The said states hereby severally enter into a firm league of friendship with each other for their common defence, the security of their liberties and their mutual and general welfare; binding themselves to assist each other against all force offered to, or attacks made upon them, or any of them, on account of religion, sovereignty, trade, or any other pretence whatever.

Article 4

The better to secure and perpetuate mutual friendship and intercourse among the people of the different states in this union, the free inhabitants of each of these states, paupers, vagabonds, and fugitives from justice excepted, shall be entitled to all privileges and immunities of free citizens in the several states; and the people of each State shall have free ingress and regress to and from any other State, and shall enjoy therein all the privileges of trade and commerce, subject to the same duties, impositions, and restrictions, as the inhabitants thereof respectively; provided, that such restrictions shall not extend so far as to prevent the removal of property, imported into any State, to any other State of which the owner is an inhabitant; provided also, that no imposition, duties, or restriction, shall be laid by any State on the property of the United States, or either of them. If any person guilty of, or charged with treason, felony, or other high misdemeanor in any State, shall flee from justice and be found in any of the United States, he shall, upon demand of the governor or executive power of the State from which he fled, be delivered up and removed to the State having jurisdiction of his offence. Full faith and credit shall be given in each of these states to the records, acts, and judicial proceedings of the courts and magistrates of every other State.

Article 5

For the more convenient management of the general interests of the United States, delegates shall be annually appointed, in such manner as the legislature of each State shall direct, to meet

*This copy of the final draft of the Articles of Confederation is from the *Journals of the Continental Congress*, 9:907–925, November 15, 1777.

in Congress, on the 1st Monday in November in every year, with a power reserved to each State to recall its delegates, or any of them, at any time within the year, and to send others in their stead for the remainder of the year.

No State shall be represented in Congress by less than two, nor by more than seven members; and no person shall be capable of being a delegate for more than three years in any term of six years; nor shall any person, being a delegate, be capable of holding any office under the United States, for which he, or any other for his benefit, receives any salary, fees, or emolument of any kind.

Each State shall maintain its own delegates in a meeting of the states, and while they act as members of the committee of the states.

In determining questions in the United States, in Congress assembled, each State shall have one vote.

Freedom of speech and debate in Congress shall not be impeached or questioned in any court or place out of Congress: and the members of Congress shall be protected in their persons from arrests and imprisonments, during the time of their going to and from, and attendance on Congress, except for treason, felony, or breach of the peace.

Article 6

No State, without the consent of the United States, in Congress assembled, shall send any embassy to, or receive any embassy from, or enter into any conference, agreement, alliance, or treaty with any king, prince, or state; nor shall any person, holding any office of profit or trust under the United States, or any of them, accept of any present, emolument, office or title, of any kind whatever, from any king, prince, or foreign state; nor shall the United States, in Congress assembled, or any of them, grant any title of nobility.

No two or more states shall enter into any treaty, confederation, or alliance, whatever, between them, without the consent of the United States, in Congress assembled, specifying accurately the purposes for which the same is to be entered into, and how long it shall continue.

No state shall lay any imposts or duties which may interfere with any stipulations in treaties entered into by the United States, in Congress assembled, with any king, prince, or state, in pursuance of any treaties already proposed by Congress to the courts of France and Spain.

No vessels of war shall be kept up in time of peace by any State, except such number only as shall be deemed necessary by the United States, in Congress assembled, for the defence of such State or its trade; nor shall any body of forces be kept up by any State, in time of peace, except such number only as, in the judgment of the United States, in Congress assembled, shall be deemed requisite to garrison the forts necessary for the defence of such State; but every State shall always keep up a well regulated and disciplined militia, sufficiently armed and accoutred, and shall provide, and constantly have ready for use, in public stores, a due number of field pieces and tents, and a proper quantity of arms, ammunition and camp equipage.

No State shall engage in any war without the consent of the United States, in Congress assembled, unless such State be actually invaded by enemies, or shall have received certain advice of a resolution being formed by some nation of Indians to invade such State, and the danger is so imminent as not to admit of a delay till the United States, in Congress assembled, can be consulted; nor shall any State grant commissions to any ships or vessels of war, nor letters of marque or reprisal, except it be after a declaration of war by the United States, in Congress assembled, and then only against the kingdom or state, and the subjects thereof, against which war has been so declared, and under such regulations as shall be established by the United States, in Congress assembled, unless such State be infested by pirates, in which case vessels of war may be fitted out for that occasion, and kept so long as the danger shall continue, or until the United States, in Congress assembled, shall determine otherwise.

Article 7

When land forces are raised by any State for the common defence, all officers of or under the rank of colonel, shall be appointed by the legislature of each State respectively, by whom such forces shall be raised, or in such manner as such State shall direct; and all vacancies shall be filled up by the State which first made the appointment.

Article 8

All charges of war and all other expences, that shall be incurred for the common defence or general welfare, and allowed by the United States, in Congress assembled, shall be defrayed out of a common treasury, which shall be supplied by the several states, in proportion to the value of all land within each State, granted to or surveyed for any person, as such land and the buildings and improvements thereon shall be estimated according to such mode as the United States, in Congress assembled, shall, from time to time, direct and appoint.

The taxes for paying that proportion shall be laid and levied by the authority and direction of the legislatures of the several states, within the time agreed upon by the United States, in Congress assembled.

Article 9

The United States, in Congress assembled, shall have the sole and exclusive right and power of determining on peace and war, except in the cases mentioned in the 6th article; of sending and receiving ambassadors; entering into treaties and alliances, provided that no treaty of commerce shall be made, whereby the legislative power of the respective states shall be restrained from imposing such imposts and duties on foreigners as their own people are subjected to, or from prohibiting the exportation or importation of any species of goods or commodities whatsoever; of establishing rules for deciding, in all cases, what captures on land or water shall be legal, and in what manner prizes, taken by land or naval forces in the service of the United States, shall be divided or appropriated; of granting letters of marque and reprisal in times of peace; appointing courts for the trial of piracies and felonies committed on the high seas, and establishing courts for receiving and determining, finally, appeals in all cases of captures; provided, that no member of Congress shall be appointed a judge of any of the said courts.

The United States, in Congress assembled, shall also be the last resort on appeal in all disputes and differences now subsisting, or that hereafter may arise between two or more states concerning boundary, jurisdiction or any other cause whatever; which authority shall always be exercised in the manner following: whenever the legislative or executive authority, or lawful agent of any State, in controversy with another, shall present a petition to Congress, stating the matter in question, and praying for a hearing, notice thereof shall be given, by order of Congress, to the legislative or executive authority of the other State in controversy, and a day assigned for the appearance of the parties by their lawful agents, who shall then be directed to appoint, by joint consent, commissioners or judges to constitute a court for hearing and determining the matter in question; but, if they cannot agree, Congress shall name three persons out of each of the United States, and from the list of such persons each party shall alternately strike out one, the petitioners beginning, until the number shall be reduced to thirteen; and from that number not less than seven, nor more than nine names, as Congress shall direct, shall, in the presence of Congress, be drawn out by lot; and the persons whose names shall be so drawn, or any five of them, shall be commissioners or judges to hear and finally determine the controversy, so always as a major part of the judges who shall hear the cause shall agree in the determination; and if either party shall neglect to attend at the day appointed, without shewing reasons which Congress shall judge sufficient, or, being present, shall refuse to strike, the Congress shall proceed to nominate three persons out of each State, and the secretary of Congress shall strike in behalf of such party absent or refusing; and the judgment and sentence of the court to be appointed, in the manner before prescribed, shall be final and conclusive; and if any of the parties shall refuse to submit to the authority of such court, or to appear or defend their claim or cause, the court shall nevertheless proceed to pronounce sentence or judgment, which shall, in like manner, be final and decisive, the judgment or sentence and other proceedings begin, in either case, transmitted to Congress, and lodged among the acts of Congress for the security of the parties concerned: provided, that every commissioner, before he sits in judgment, shall take an oath, to be administered by one of the judges of the supreme or superior court of the State where the cause shall be tried, "well and truly to hear and determine the matter in question, according to the best of his judgment, without favour, affection, or hope of reward:" provided, also, that no State shall be deprived of territory for the benefit of the United States.

All controversies concerning the private right of soil, claimed under different grants of two or more states, whose jurisdictions, as they may respect such lands and the states which passed such grants, are adjusted, the said grants, or either of them, being at the same time claimed to have originated antecedent to such settlement of jurisdiction, shall, on the petition of either party to the Congress of the United States, be finally determined, as near as may be, in the same manner as is before prescribed for deciding disputes respecting territorial jurisdiction between different states.

The United States, in Congress assembled, shall also have the sole and exclusive right and power of regulating the alloy and value of coin struck by their own authority, or by that of the respective states; fixing the standard of weights and measures throughout the United States; regulating the trade and managing all affairs with the Indians not members of any of the states; provided that the legislative right of any State within its own limits be not infringed or violated; establishing and regulating post offices from one State to another throughout all the United States, and exacting such postage on the papers passing through the same as may be requisite to defray the expences of the said office; appointing all officers of the land forces in the service of the United States, excepting regimental officers; appointing all the officers of the naval forces, and commissioning all officers whatever in the service of the United States; making rules for the government and regulation of the said land and naval forces, and directing their operations.

The United States, in Congress assembled, shall have authority to appoint a committee to sit in the recess of Congress, to be denominated "a Committee of the States," and to consist of one delegate from each State, and to appoint such other committees and civil officers as may be necessary for managing the general affairs of the United States, under their direction; to appoint one of their number to preside; provided that no person be allowed to serve in the office of president more than one year in any term of three years; to ascertain the necessary sums of money to be raised for the service of the United States, and to appropriate and apply the same for defraying the public expences; to borrow money or emit bills on the credit of the United States, transmitting, every half year, to the respective states, an account of the sums of money so borrowed or emitted; to build and equip a navy; to agree upon the number of land forces, and to make requisitions from each State for its quota, in proportion to the number of white inhabitants in such State; which requisitions shall be binding; and thereupon, the legislature of each State shall appoint the regimental officers, raise the men, and cloathe, arm, and equip them in a soldier-like manner, at the expence of the United States; and the officers and men so cloathed, armed, and equipped, shall march to the place appointed and within the time agreed on by the United States, in Congress assembled; but if the United States, in Congress assembled, shall, on consideration of circumstances, judge proper that any State should not raise men, or should raise a smaller number than its quota, and that any other State should raise a greater number of men than the quota thereof, such extra number shall be raised, officered, cloathed, armed, and equipped in the same manner as the quota of such State, unless the legislature of such State shall judge that such extra number cannot be safely spared out of the same, in which case they shall raise, officer, cloathe, arm, and equip as many of such extra number as they judge can be safely spared. And the officers and men so cloathed, armed, and equipped, shall march to the place appointed and within the time agreed on by the United States, in Congress assembled.

The United States, in Congress assembled, shall never engage in a war, nor grant letters of marque and reprisal in time of peace, nor enter into any treaties or alliances, nor coin money, nor regulate the value thereof, nor ascertain the sums and expences necessary for the defence and welfare of the United States, or any of them: nor emit bills, nor borrow money on the credit of the United States, nor appropriate money, nor agree upon the number of vessels of war to be built or purchased, or the number of land or sea forces to be raised, nor appoint a commander in chief of the army or navy, unless nine states assent to the same; nor shall a question on any other point, except for adjourning from day to day, be determined, unless by the votes of a majority of the United States, in Congress assembled.

The Congress of the United States shall have power to adjourn to any time within the year, and to any place within the United States, so that no period of adjournment be for a longer duration than the space of six months, and shall publish the journal of their proceedings monthly, except such parts thereof, relating to treaties, alliances or military operations, as, in their judgment, require secrecy; and the yeas and nays of the delegates of each State on any question shall be entered on the journal, when it is desired by any delegate; and the delegates of a State, or any of them, at his, or their request, shall be furnished with a transcript of the said journal, except such parts as are above excepted, to lay before the legislatures of the several states.

Article 10

The committee of the states, or any nine of them, shall be authorized to execute, in the recess of Congress, such of the powers of Congress as the United States, in Congress assembled, by the consent of nine states, shall, from time to time, think expedient to vest them with; provided, that no power be delegated to the said committee, for the exercise of which, by the articles of confederation, the voice of nine states, in the Congress of the United States assembled, is requisite.

Article 11

Canada acceding to this confederation, and joining in the measures of the United States, shall be admitted into and entitled to all the advantages of this union; but no other colony shall be admitted into the same, unless such admission be agreed to by nine states.

Article 12

All bills of credit emitted, monies borrowed and debts contracted by, or under the authority of Congress before the assembling of the United States, in pursuance of the present confederation, shall be deemed and considered as a charge against the United States, for payment and satisfaction whereof the said United States and the public faith are hereby solemnly pledged.

Article 13

Every State shall abide by the determinations of the United States, in Congress assembled, on all questions which, by this confederation, are submitted to them. And the articles of this confederation shall be inviolably observed by every State, and the union shall be perpetual; nor shall any alteration at any time hereafter be made in any of them, unless such alteration be agreed to in a Congress of the United States, and be afterwards confirmed by the legislatures of every State.

These articles shall be proposed to the legislatures of all the United States, to be considered, and if approved of by them, they are advised to authorize their delegates to ratify the same in the Congress of the United States; which being done, the same shall become conclusive.

The Constitution of the United States*

Agreed to by Philadelphia Convention, September 17, 1787.
Implemented March 4, 1789.

Preamble

We the people of the United States, in order to form a more perfect union, establish justice, insure domestic tranquility, provide for the common defense, promote the general welfare, and secure the blessings of liberty to ourselves and our posterity, do ordain and establish this Constitution for the United States of America.

Article I

Section 1. All legislative powers herein granted shall be vested in a Congress of the United States, which shall consist of a Senate and a House of Representatives.

Section 2. The House of Representatives shall be composed of members chosen every second year by the people of the several States, and the electors in each State shall have the qualifications requisite for electors of the most numerous branch of the State Legislature.

No person shall be a Representative who shall not have attained to the age of twenty-five years, and been seven years a citizen of the United States, and who shall not, when elected, be an inhabitant of that State in which he shall be chosen.

Representatives and direct taxes shall be apportioned among the several States which may be included within this Union, according to their respective numbers, *which shall be determined by adding to the whole number of free persons, including those bound to service for a term of years and excluding Indians not taxed, three-fifths of all other persons.* The actual enumeration shall be made within three years after the first meeting of the Congress of the United States, and within every subsequent term of ten years, in such manner as they shall by law direct. The number of Representatives shall not exceed one for every thirty thousand, but each State shall have at least one Representative; and until such enumeration shall be made, *the State of New Hampshire shall be entitled to choose three, Massachusetts eight, Rhode Island and Providence Plantations one, Connecticut five, New York six, New Jersey four, Pennsylvania eight, Delaware one, Maryland six, Virginia ten, North Carolina five, South Carolina five, and Georgia three.*

When vacancies happen in the representation from any State, the Executive authority thereof shall issue writs of election to fill such vacancies.

The House of Representatives shall choose their Speaker and other officers; and shall have the sole power of impeachment.

Section 3. The Senate of the United States shall be composed of two Senators from each State, *chosen by the legislature thereof,* for six years; and each Senator shall have one vote.

Immediately after they shall be assembled in consequence of the first election, they shall be divided as equally as may be into three classes. The seats of the Senators of the first class shall be vacated at the expiration of the second year, of the second class at the expiration of the fourth year, and of the third class at the expiration of the sixth year, so that one-third may be chosen every second year; and if vacancies happen by resignation or otherwise, during the recess of the legislature of any State, the Executive thereof may make temporary appointments until the next meeting of the legislature, which shall then fill such vacancies.

No person shall be a Senator who shall not have attained to the age of thirty years, and been nine years a citizen of the United States, and who shall not, when elected, be an inhabitant of that State for which he shall be chosen.

*Passages no longer in effect are in italic type.

The Vice-President of the United States shall be President of the Senate, but shall have no vote, unless they be equally divided.

The Senate shall choose their other officers, and also a President pro tempore, in the absence of the Vice-President, or when he shall exercise the office of President of the United States.

The Senate shall have the sole power to try all impeachments. When sitting for that purpose, they shall be on oath or affirmation. When the President of the United States is tried, the Chief Justice shall preside: and no person shall be convicted without the concurrence of two-thirds of the members present.

Judgment in cases of impeachment shall not extend further than to removal from the office, and disqualification to hold and enjoy any office of honor, trust or profit under the United States: but the party convicted shall nevertheless be liable and subject to indictment, trial, judgment and punishment, according to law.

Section 4. The times, places and manner of holding elections for Senators and Representatives shall be prescribed in each State by the legislature thereof; but the Congress may at any time by law make or alter such regulations, except as to the places of choosing Senators.

The Congress shall assemble at least once in every year, and such meeting *shall be on the first Monday in December, unless they shall by law appoint a different day.*

Section 5. Each house shall be the judge of the elections, returns and qualifications of its own members, and a majority of each shall constitute a quorum to do business; but a smaller number may adjourn from day to day, and may be authorized to compel the attendance of absent members, in such manner, and under such penalties, as each house may provide.

Each house may determine the rules of its proceedings, punish its members for disorderly behavior, and with the concurrence of two-thirds, expel a member.

Each house shall keep a journal of its proceedings, and from time to time publish the same, excepting such parts as may in their judgment require secrecy; and the yeas and nays of the members of either house on any question shall, at the desire of one fifth of those present, be entered on the journal.

Neither house, during the session of Congress, shall, without the consent of the other, adjourn for more than three days, nor to any other place than that in which the two houses shall be sitting.

Section 6. The Senators and Representatives shall receive a compensation for their services, to be ascertained by law and paid out of the treasury of the United States. They shall in all cases except treason, felony and breach of the peace, be privileged from arrest during their attendance at the session of their respective houses, and in going to and returning from the same; and for any speech or debate in either house, they shall not be questioned in any other place.

No Senator or Representative shall, during the time for which he was elected, be appointed to any civil office under the authority of the United States, which shall have been created, or the emoluments whereof shall have been increased, during such time; and no person holding any office under the United States shall be a member of either house during his continuance in office.

Section 7. All bills for raising revenue shall originate in the House of Representatives; but the Senate may propose or concur with amendments as on other bills.

Every bill which shall have passed the House of Representatives and the Senate, shall, before it become a law, be presented to the President of the United States; if he approve he shall sign it, but if not he shall return it with objections to that house in which it shall have originated, who shall enter the objections at large on their journal, and proceed to reconsider it. If after such reconsideration two-thirds of that house shall agree to pass the bill, it shall be sent, together with the objections, to the other house, by which it shall likewise be reconsidered, and, if approved by two-thirds of that house, it shall become a law. But in all such cases the votes of both houses shall be determined by yeas and nays, and the names of the persons voting for and against the bill shall be entered on the journal of each house respectively. If any bill shall not be returned by the President within ten days (Sundays excepted) after it shall have been presented to him, the same shall be a law, in like manner as if he had signed it, unless the Congress by their adjournment prevent its return, in which case it shall not be a law.

Every order, resolution, or vote to which the concurrence of the Senate and House of Representatives may be necessary (except on a question of adjournment) shall be presented to the President of the United States; and before the same shall take effect, shall be approved by him, or being disapproved by him, shall be repassed by two-thirds of the Senate and House of Representatives, according to the rules and limitations prescribed in the case of a bill.

Section 8. The Congress shall have power

To lay and collect taxes, duties, imposts, and excises, to pay the debts and provide for the common defense and general welfare of the United States; but all duties, imposts and excises shall be uniform throughout the United States;

To borrow money on the credit of the United States;

To regulate commerce with foreign nations, and among the several States, and with the Indian tribes;

To establish an uniform rule of naturalization, and uniform laws on the subject of bankruptcies throughout the United States;

To coin money, regulate the value thereof, and of foreign coin, and fix the standard of weights and measures;

To provide for the punishment of counterfeiting the securities and current coin of the United States;

establish post offices and post roads;

To promote the progress of science and useful arts by securing for limited times to authors and inventors the exclusive right to their respective writings and discoveries;

To constitute tribunals inferior to the Supreme Court;

To define and punish piracies and felonies committed on the high seas and offences against the law of nations;

To declare war, grant letters of marque and reprisal, and make rules concerning captures on land and water;

To raise and support armies, but no appropriation of money to that use shall be for a longer term than two years;

To provide and maintain a navy;

To make rules for the government and regulation of the land and naval forces;

To provide for calling forth the militia to execute the laws of the Union, suppress insurrections and repel invasions;

To provide for organizing, arming, and disciplining the militia, and for governing such part of them as may be employed in the service of the United States, reserving to the States respectively the appointment of the officers, and the authority of training the militia according to the discipline prescribed by Congress;

To exercise exclusive legislation in all cases whatsoever, over such district (not exceeding ten miles square) as may, by cession of particular States, and the acceptance of Congress, become the seat of the government of the United States, and to exercise like authority over all places purchased by the consent of the legislature of the State, in which the same shall be, for erection of forts, magazines, arsenals, dock-yards, and other needful buildings;—and

To make all laws which shall be necessary and proper for carrying into execution the foregoing powers, and all other powers vested by this Constitution in the government of the United States, or in any department or officer thereof.

Section 9. *The migration or importation of such persons as any of the States now existing shall think proper to admit shall not be prohibited by the Congress prior to the year one thousand eight*

hundred and eight; but a tax or duty may be imposed on such importation, not exceeding ten dollars for each person.

The privilege of the writ of habeas corpus shall not be suspended, unless when in cases of rebellion or invasion the public safety may require it.

No bill of attainder or ex post facto law shall be passed.

No capitation, or other direct, tax shall be laid, unless in proportion to the census or enumeration herein before directed to be taken.

No tax or duty shall be laid on articles exported from any State.

No preference shall be given by any regulation of commerce or revenue to the ports of one State over those of another; nor shall vessels bound to, or from, one State be obliged to enter, clear, or pay duties in another.

No money shall be drawn from the treasury, but in consequence of appropriations made by law; and a regular statement and account of the receipts and expenditures of all public money shall be published from time to time.

No title of nobility shall be granted by the United States: and no person holding any office of profit or trust under them, shall, without the consent of the Congress, accept of any present, emolument, office, or title, of any kind whatever, from any king, prince, or foreign state.

Section 10. No State shall enter into any treaty, alliance, or confederation; grant letters of marque and reprisal; coin money; emit bills of credit; make anything but gold and silver coin a tender in payment of debts; pass any bill of attainder, ex post facto law, or law impairing the obligation of contracts, or grant any title of nobility.

No State shall, without the consent of Congress, lay any imposts or duties on imports or exports, except what may be absolutely necessary for executing its inspection laws: and the net produce of all duties and imposts, laid by any State on imports or exports, shall be for the use of the treasury of the United States; and all such laws shall be subject to the revision and control of the Congress.

No State shall, without the consent of Congress, lay any duty of tonnage, keep troops, or ships of war in time of peace, enter into any agreement or compact with another State, or with a foreign power, or engage in war, unless actually invaded, or in such imminent danger as will not admit of delay.

Article II

Section 1. The executive power shall be vested in a President of the United States of America. He shall hold his office during the term of four years, and, together with the Vice-President, chosen for the same term, be elected as follows:

Each State shall appoint, in such manner as the legislature thereof may direct, a number of electors, equal to the whole number of Senators and Representatives to which the State may be entitled in the Congress; but no Senator or Representative, or person holding an office of trust or profit under the United States, shall be appointed an elector.

The electors shall meet in their respective States, and vote by ballot for two persons, of whom one at least shall not be an inhabitant of the same State with themselves. And they shall make a list of all the persons voted for, and of the number of votes for each; which list they shall sign and certify, and transmit sealed to the seat of government of the United States, directed to the President of the Senate. The President of the Senate shall, in the presence of the Senate and House of Representatives, open all the certificates, and the votes shall then be counted. The person having the greatest number of votes shall be the President, if such number be a majority of the whole number of electors appointed; and if there be more than one who have such majority, and have an equal number of votes, then the House of Representatives shall immediately choose by ballot one of them for President; and if no person have a majority, then from the five highest on the list said house shall in like manner choose the President. But in choosing the President the votes shall be taken by States, the representation from each State having one vote; a quorum for this purpose shall consist of a member or members from two-thirds of the States, and a majority of all the States shall be necessary to a choice. In every case, after the choice of the President, the person having the greatest number of votes of the electors shall be the Vice-President. But if there should remain two or more who have equal votes, the Senate shall choose from them by ballot the Vice-President.

The Congress may determine the time of choosing the electors, and the day on which they shall give their votes; which day shall be the same throughout the United States.

No person except a natural-born citizen, *or a citizen of the United States at the time of the adoption of this Constitution,* shall be eligible to the office of President; neither shall any person be eligible to that office who shall not have attained to the age of thirty-five years, and been fourteen years a resident within the United States.

In cases of the removal of the President from office or of his death, resignation, or inability to discharge the powers and duties of the said office, the same shall devolve on the Vice-President, and the Congress may by law provide for the case of removal, death, resignation, or inability, both of the President and Vice-President, declaring what officer shall then act as President, and such officer shall act accordingly, until the disability be removed, or a President shall be elected.

The President shall, at stated times, receive for his services a compensation, which shall neither be increased nor diminished during the period for which he shall have been elected, and he shall not receive within that period any other emolument from the United States, or any of them.

Before he enter on the execution of his office, he shall take the following oath or affirmation:—"I do solemnly swear (or affirm) that I will faithfully execute the office of the President of the United States, and will to the best of my ability preserve, protect and defend the Constitution of the United States."

Section 2. The President shall be commander in chief of the army and navy of the United States, and of the militia of the several States, when called into the actual service of the United States; he may require the opinion, in writing, of the principal officer in each of the executive departments, upon any subject relating to the duties of their respective offices, and he shall have power to grant reprieves and pardons for offenses against the United States, except in cases of impeachment.

He shall have power, by and with the advice and consent of the Senate, to make treaties, provided two-thirds of the Senators present concur; and he shall nominate, and by and with the advice and consent of the Senate, shall appoint ambassadors, other public ministers and consuls, judges of the Supreme Court, and all other officers of the United States, whose appointments are not herein otherwise provided for, and which shall be established by law: but Congress may by law vest the appointment of such inferior officers, as they think proper, in the President alone, in the courts of law, or in the heads of departments.

The President shall have power to fill up all vacancies that may happen during the recess of the Senate, by granting commissions which shall expire at the end of their next session.

Section 3. He shall from time to time give to the Congress information of the state of the Union, and recommend to their consideration such measures as he shall judge necessary and expedient; he may, on extraordinary occasions, convene both houses, or either of them, and in case of disagreement between them, with respect to the time of adjournment, he may adjourn them to such time as he shall think proper; he shall receive ambassadors and other public ministers; he shall take care that the laws be faithfully executed, and shall commission all the officers of the United States.

Section 4. The President, Vice-President and all civil officers of the United States shall be removed from office on impeachment for, and on conviction of, treason, bribery, or other high crimes and misdemeanors.

Article III

Section 1. The judicial power of the United States shall be vested in one Supreme Court, and in such inferior courts as the Congress may from time to time ordain and establish. The judges, both of the Supreme and inferior courts, shall hold their offices during good behavior, and shall, at stated times, receive for their services a compensation which shall not be diminished during their continuance in office.

Section 2. The judicial power shall extend to all cases, in law and equity, arising under this Constitution, the laws of the United States, and treaties made, or which shall be made, under their authority;—to all cases affecting ambassadors, other public ministers and consuls;—to all cases of admiralty and maritime jurisdiction;—to controversies to which the United States shall be a party;—to controversies between two or more States;—between a State and citizens of another State;—between citizens of different States;—between citizens of the same State claiming lands under grants of different States, and between a State, or the citizens thereof, and foreign states, citizens or subjects.

In all cases affecting ambassadors, other public ministers and consuls, and those in which a State shall be party, the Supreme Court shall have original jurisdiction. In all the other cases before mentioned, the Supreme Court shall have appellate jurisdiction, both as to law and fact, with such exceptions, and under such regulations, as the Congress shall make.

The trial of all crimes, except in cases of impeachment, shall be by jury; and such trial shall be held in the State where said crimes shall have been committed; but when not committed within any State, the trial shall be at such place or places as the Congress may by Law have directed.

Section 3. Treason against the United States shall consist only in levying war against them, or in adhering to their enemies, giving them aid and comfort. No person shall be convicted of treason unless on the testimony of two witnesses to the same overt act, or on confession in open court.

The Congress shall have power to declare the punishment of treason, but no attainder of treason shall work corruption of blood, or forfeiture except during the life of the person attainted.

Article IV

Section 1. Full faith and credit shall be given in each State to the public acts, records, and judicial proceedings of every other State. And the Congress may by general laws prescribe the manner in which such acts, records, and proceedings shall be proved, and the effect thereof.

Section 2. The citizens of each State shall be entitled to all privileges and immunities of citizens in the several States.

A person charged in any State with treason, felony, or other crime, who shall flee from justice, and be found in another State, shall on demand of the executive authority of the State from which he fled, be delivered up, to be removed to the State having jurisdiction of the crime.

No Person held to service or labor in one State, under the laws thereof, escaping into another, shall, in consequence of any law or regulation therein, be discharged from such service or labor, but shall be delivered up on claim of the party to whom such service or labor may be due.

Section 3. New States may be admitted by the Congress into this Union; but no new State shall be formed or erected within the jurisdiction of any other State; nor any State be formed by the junction of two or more States, or parts of States, without the consent of the legislatures of the States concerned as well as of the Congress.

The Congress shall have power to dispose of and make all needful rules and regulations respecting the territory or other property belonging to the United States; and nothing in this Constitution shall be so construed as to prejudice any claims of the United States, or of any particular State.

Section 4. The United States shall guarantee to every State in this Union a republican form of government, and shall protect each of them against invasion; and on application of the legislature, or of the executive (when the legislature cannot be convened), against domestic violence.

Article V

The Congress, whenever two-thirds of both houses shall deem it necessary, shall propose amendments to this Constitution, or, on the application of the legislatures of two-thirds of the several States, shall call a convention for proposing amendments, which, in either case, shall be valid to all intents and purposes, as part of this Constitution, when ratified by the legislatures of three-fourths of the several States, or by conventions in three-fourths thereof, as the one or the other mode of ratification may be proposed by the Congress; *provided that no amendments which may be made prior to the year one thousand eight hundred and eight shall in any manner affect the first and fourth clauses in the ninth section of the first article;* and that no State, without its consent, shall be deprived of its equal suffrage in the Senate.

Article VI

All debts contracted and engagements entered into, before the adoption of this Constitution, shall be as valid against the United States under this Constitution, as under the Confederation.

This Constitution, and the laws of the United States which shall be made in pursuance thereof; and all treaties made, or which shall be made, under the authority of the United States, shall be the supreme law of the land; and the judges in every State shall be bound thereby, anything in the Constitution or laws of any State to the contrary notwithstanding.

The Senators and Representatives before mentioned, and the members of the several State legislatures, and all executive and judicial officers, both of the United States and of the several States, shall be bound by oath or affirmation to support this Constitution; but no religious test shall ever be required as a qualification to any office or public trust under the United States.

Article VII

The ratification of the conventions of nine States shall be sufficient for the establishment of this Constitution between the States so ratifying the same.

Done in convention by the unanimous consent of the States present, the seventeenth day of September in the year of our Lord one thousand seven hundred and eighty-seven and of the Independence of the United States of America the twelfth. In witness whereof we have hereunto subscribed our names.

GEORGE WASHINGTON, President and Deputy from Virginia

New Hampshire
John Langdon
Nicholas Gilman

Massachusetts
Nathaniel Gorham
Rufus King

Connecticut
William Samuel
 Johnson
Roger Sherman

New York
Alexander Hamilton

New Jersey
William Livingston
David Brearley
William Paterson
Jonathan Dayton

Pennsylvania
Benjamin Franklin
Thomas Mifflin
Robert Morris

George Clymer
Thomas FitzSimons
Jared Ingersoll
James Wilson
Gouverneur Morris

Delaware
George Read
Gunning Bedford, Jr.
John Dickinson
Richard Bassett
Jacob Broom

Maryland	**North Carolina**	Charles Pinckney
James McHenry	William Blount	Pierce Butler
Daniel of St. Thomas Jenifer	Richard Dobbs Spaight	
Daniel Carroll	Hugh Williamson	**Georgia**
		William Few
Virginia	**South Carolina**	Abraham Baldwin
John Blair	John Rutledge	
James Madison, Jr.	Charles Cotesworth Pinckney	

Amendments to the Constitution
(including six unratified amendments)

Amendment I

[RATIFIED **1791**]

Congress shall make no law respecting an establishment of religion, or prohibiting the free exercise thereof; or abridging the freedom of speech, or of the press; or the right of the people peaceably to assemble, and to petition the government for a redress of grievances.

Amendment II

[RATIFIED **1791**]

A well-regulated militia being necessary to the security of a free State, the right of the people to keep and bear arms shall not be infringed.

Amendment III

[RATIFIED **1791**]

No soldier shall, in time of peace, be quartered in any house without the consent of the owner, nor in time of war, but in a manner to be prescribed by law.

Amendment IV

[RATIFIED **1791**]

The right of the people to be secure in their persons, houses, papers, and effects, against unreasonable searches and seizures, shall not be violated, and no warrants shall issue but upon probable cause, supported by oath or affirmation, and particularly describing the place to be searched, and the persons or things to be seized.

Amendment V

[RATIFIED **1791**]

No person shall be held to answer for a capital, or otherwise infamous crime, unless on a presentment or indictment of a grand jury, except in cases arising in the land or naval forces, or in the militia, when in actual service in time of war or public danger; nor shall any person be subject for the same offence to be twice put in jeopardy of life or limb; nor shall be compelled in any criminal case to be a witness against himself, nor be deprived of life, liberty, or property, without due process of law; nor shall private property be taken for public use without just compensation.

Amendment VI

[RATIFIED **1791**]

In all criminal prosecutions, the accused shall enjoy the right to a speedy and public trial, by an impartial jury of the State and district wherein the crime shall have been committed, which district shall have been previously ascertained by law, and to be informed of the nature and cause of the accusation; to be confronted with the witnesses against him; to have compulsory process for obtaining witnesses in his favor, and to have the assistance of counsel for his defence.

Amendment VII

[RATIFIED **1791**]

In suits at common law, where the value in controversy shall exceed twenty dollars, the right of trial by jury shall be preserved, and no fact tried by a jury shall be otherwise reexamined in any court of the United States, than according to the rules of the common law.

Amendment VIII

[RATIFIED **1791**]

Excessive bail shall not be required, nor excessive fines imposed, nor cruel and unusual punishments inflicted.

Amendment IX

[RATIFIED **1791**]

The enumeration in the Constitution, of certain rights, shall not be construed to deny or disparage others retained by the people.

Amendment X

[RATIFIED **1791**]

The powers not delegated to the United States by the Constitution, nor prohibited by it to the States, are reserved to the States respectively, or to the people.

Unratified Amendment

[REAPPORTIONMENT AMENDMENT (PROPOSED BY CONGRESS SEPTEMBER **25, 1789,** ALONG WITH THE BILL OF RIGHTS)]

After the first enumeration required by the first article of the Constitution, there shall be one Representative for every thirty thousand, until the number shall amount to one hundred, after which the proportion shall be so regulated by Congress, that there shall be not less than one hundred Representatives, nor less than one Representative for every forty thousand persons, until the number of Representatives shall amount to two hundred; after which the proportion shall be so regulated by Congress, that there shall not be less than two hundred Representatives, nor more than one Representative for every fifty thousand persons.

Amendment XI

[RATIFIED **1798**]

The judicial power of the United States shall not be construed to extend to any suit in law or equity, commenced or prosecuted against one of the United States by citizens of another State, or by citizens or subjects of any foreign state.

Amendment XII

[RATIFIED **1804**]

The electors shall meet in their respective States, and vote by ballot for President and Vice-President, one of whom, at least, shall not be an inhabitant of the same State with themselves; they shall name in their ballots the person voted for as President, and in distinct ballots the person voted for as Vice-President, and they shall make distinct lists of all persons voted for as President, and of all persons voted for as Vice-President, and of the number of votes for each, which lists they shall sign and certify, and transmit sealed to the seat of government of the United States, directed to the President of the Senate;—the President of the Senate shall, in the presence of the Senate and House of Representatives, open all the certificates and the votes shall then be counted;—the person having the greatest number of votes for President shall be the President, if such number be a majority of the whole number of electors appointed; and if no person have such majority, then from the persons having the highest numbers not exceeding three on the list of those voted for as President, the House of Representatives shall choose immediately, by ballot, the President. But in choosing the President, the votes shall be taken by States, the representation from each State having one vote; a quorum for this purpose shall consist of a member or members from two-thirds of the States, and a majority of all the States shall be necessary to a choice. And if the House of Representatives shall not choose a President whenever the right of choice shall devolve upon them, before *the fourth day of March* next following, then the Vice-President shall act as President, as in the case of the death or other constitutional disability of the President.

The person having the greatest number of votes as Vice-President shall be the Vice-President, if such number be a majority of the whole number of electors appointed; and if no person have a majority, then from the two highest numbers on the list the Senate shall choose the Vice-President; a quorum for the purpose shall consist of two-thirds of the whole number of Senators, and a majority of the whole number shall be necessary to a choice. But no person constitutionally ineligible to the office of President shall be eligible to that of Vice-President of the United States.

Unratified Amendment

[TITLES OF NOBILITY AMENDMENT (PROPOSED BY CONGRESS MAY **1, 1810**)]

If any citizen of the United States shall accept, claim, receive or retain any title of nobility or honor or shall, without the consent of Congress, accept and retain any present, pension, office or emolument of any kind whatever, from any emperor, king, prince or foreign power, such person shall cease to be a citizen of the United States, and shall be incapable of holding any office of trust or profit under them or either of them.

Unratified Amendment

[CORWIN AMENDMENT (PROPOSED BY CONGRESS MARCH **2, 1861**)]

No amendment shall be made to the Constitution which will authorize or give to Congress the power to abolish or interfere, within any State, with the domestic institutions thereof, including that of persons held to labor or service by the laws of said State.

Amendment XIII

[RATIFIED **1865**]

Section 1. Neither slavery nor involuntary servitude, except as a punishment for crime whereof the party shall have been duly convicted, shall exist within the United States, or any place subject to their jurisdiction.

Section 2. Congress shall have power to enforce this article by appropriate legislation.

Amendment XIV

[RATIFIED **1868**]

Section 1. All persons born or naturalized in the United States, and subject to the jurisdiction thereof, are citizens of the United States and of the State wherein they reside. No State shall make or enforce any law which shall abridge the privileges or immunities of citizens of the United States; nor shall any State deprive any person of life, liberty, or property, without due process of law; nor deny to any person within its jurisdiction the equal protection of the laws.

Section 2. Representatives shall be appointed among the several States according to their respective numbers, counting the whole number of persons in each State, excluding Indians not taxed. But when the right to vote at any election for the choice of Electors for President and Vice-President of the United States, Representatives in Congress, the executive and judicial officers of a State, or the members of the legislature thereof, is denied to any of the *male* inhabitants of such State, being *twenty-one* years of age and citizens of the United States, or in any way abridged, except for participation in rebellion, or other crime, the basis of representation therein shall be reduced in the proportion which the number of such male citizens shall bear to the whole number of *male* citizens *twenty-one* years of age in such State.

Section 3. No person shall be a Senator or Representative in Congress, or Elector of President and Vice-President, or hold any office, civil or military, under the United States, or under any State, who, having previously taken an oath, as a member of Congress, or as an officer of the United States, or as a member of any State legislature, or as an executive or judicial officer of any State, to support the Constitution of the United States, shall have engaged in insurrection or rebellion against the same, or given aid or comfort to the enemies thereof. Congress may, by a vote of two-thirds of each house, remove such disability.

Section 4. The validity of the public debt of the United States, authorized by law, including debts incurred for payment of pensions and bounties for services in suppressing insurrection or rebellion, shall not be questioned. But neither the United States nor any State shall assume or pay any debt or obligation incurred in aid of insurrection or rebellion against the United States, or any claim for the loss or emancipation of any slave; but all such debts, obligations, and claims shall be held illegal and void.

Section 5. The Congress shall have power to enforce, by appropriate legislation, the provisions of this article.

Amendment XV

[RATIFIED **1870**]

Section 1. The right of citizens of the United States to vote shall not be denied or abridged by the United States or by any State on account of race, color, or previous condition of servitude.

Section 2. The Congress shall have power to enforce this article by appropriate legislation.

Amendment XVI

[RATIFIED **1913**]

The Congress shall have power to lay and collect taxes on incomes, from whatever source derived, without apportionment among the several States, and without regard to any census or enumeration.

Amendment XVII

[RATIFIED 1913]

Section 1. The Senate of the United States shall be composed of two Senators from each State, elected by the people thereof, for six years; and each Senator shall have one vote. The electors in each State shall have the qualifications requisite for electors of [voters for] the most numerous branch of the State legislatures.

Section 2. When vacancies happen in the representation of any State in the Senate, the executive authority of such State shall issue writs of election to fill such vacancies: Provided, that the Legislature of any State may empower the executive thereof to make temporary appointments until the people fill the vacancies by election as the Legislature may direct.

Section 3. *This amendment shall not be so construed as to affect the election or term of any Senator chosen before it becomes valid as part of the Constitution.*

Amendment XVIII

[RATIFIED 1919; REPEALED 1933 BY AMENDMENT XXI]

Section 1. *After one year from the ratification of this article the manufacture, sale, or transportation of intoxicating liquors within, the importation thereof into, or the exportation thereof from the United States and all territory subject to the jurisdiction thereof, for beverage purposes, is hereby prohibited.*

Section 2. *The Congress and the several States shall have concurrent power to enforce this article by appropriate legislation.*

Section 3. *This article shall be inoperative unless it shall have been ratified as an amendment to the Constitution by the legislatures of the several States, as provided by the Constitution, within seven years from the date of the submission thereof to the States by the Congress.*

Amendment XIX

[RATIFIED 1920]

Section 1. The right of citizens of the United States to vote shall not be denied or abridged by the United States or by any State on account of sex.

Section 2. Congress shall have the power to enforce this article by appropriate legislation.

Unratified Amendment

[CHILD LABOR AMENDMENT (PROPOSED BY CONGRESS JUNE 2, 1924)]

Section 1. *The Congress shall have power to limit, regulate, and prohibit the labor of persons under eighteen years of age.*

Section 2. *The power of the several States is unimpaired by this article except that the operation of State laws shall be suspended to the extent necessary to give effect to legislation enacted by Congress.*

Amendment XX

[RATIFIED 1933]

Section 1. The terms of the President and Vice-President shall end at noon on the 20th day of January, and the terms of Senators and Representatives at noon on the 3rd day of January, of the years in which such terms would have ended if this article had not been ratified; and the terms of their successors shall then begin.

Section 2. The Congress shall assemble at least once in every year, and such meeting shall begin at noon on the 3rd day of January, unless they shall by law appoint a different day.

Section 3. If, at the time fixed for the beginning of the term of the President, the President-elect shall have died, the Vice-President-elect shall become President. If a President shall not have been chosen before the time fixed for the beginning of his term, or if the President-elect shall have failed to qualify, then the Vice-President-elect shall act as President until a President shall have qualified; and the Congress may by law provide for the case wherein neither a President-elect nor a Vice-President-elect shall have qualified, declaring who shall then act as President, or the manner in which one who is to act shall be selected, and such person shall act accordingly until a President or Vice-President shall have qualified.

Section 4. The Congress may by law provide for the case of the death of any of the persons from whom the House of Representatives may choose a President whenever the right of choice shall have devolved upon them, and for the case of the death of any of the persons from whom the Senate may choose a Vice-President whenever the right of choice shall have devolved upon them.

Section 5. Sections 1 and 2 shall take effect on the 15th day of October following the ratification of this article.

Section 6. This article shall be inoperative unless it shall have been ratified as an amendment to the Constitution by the Legislatures of three-fourths of the several States within seven years from the date of its submission.

Amendment XXI

[RATIFIED **1933**]

Section 1. The eighteenth article of amendment to the Constitution of the United States is hereby repealed.

Section 2. The transportation or importation into any State, Territory, or Possession of the United States for delivery or use therein of intoxicating liquors, in violation of the laws thereof, is hereby prohibited.

Section 3. This article shall be inoperative unless it shall have been ratified as an amendment to the Constitution by conventions in the several States, as provided in the Constitution, within seven years from the date of the submission thereof to the States by the Congress.

Amendment XXII

[RATIFIED **1951**]

Section 1. No person shall be elected to the office of the President more than twice, and no person who has held the office of President, or acted as President, for more than two years of a term to which some other person was elected President shall be elected to the office of President more than once. But this article shall not apply to any person holding the office of President when this Article was proposed by the Congress, and shall not prevent any person who may be holding the office of President, or acting as President, during the term within which this Article becomes operative from holding the office of President or acting as President during the remainder of such term.

Section 2. This article shall be inoperative unless it shall have been ratified as an amendment to the Constitution by the legislatures of three-fourths of the several States within seven years from the date of its submission to the States by the Congress.

Amendment XXIII

[RATIFIED **1961**]

Section 1. The District constituting the seat of Government of the United States shall appoint in such manner as the Congress may direct: A number of electors of President and Vice-President equal to the whole number of Senators and Representatives in Congress to which the District would be entitled if it were a State, but in no event more than the least populous State; they shall be in addition to those appointed by the States, but they shall be considered for the purposes of the election of President and Vice-President, to be electors appointed by a State; and they shall meet in the District and perform such duties as provided by the twelfth article of amendment.

Section 2. The Congress shall have the power to enforce this article by appropriate legislation.

Amendment XXIV

[RATIFIED **1964**]

Section 1. The right of citizens of the United States to vote in any primary or other election for President or Vice-President, for electors for President or Vice-President, or for Senator or Representative in Congress, shall not be denied or abridged by the United States or any State by reason of failure to pay any poll tax or other tax.

Section 2. The Congress shall have the power to enforce this article by appropriate legislation.

Amendment XXV

[RATIFIED **1967**]

Section 1. In case of the removal of the President from office or of his death or resignation, the Vice-President shall become President.

Section 2. Whenever there is a vacancy in the office of the Vice-President, the President shall nominate a Vice-President who shall take office upon confirmation by a majority vote of both Houses of Congress.

Section 3. Whenever the President transmits to the President pro tempore of the Senate and the Speaker of the House of Representatives his written declaration that he is unable to discharge the powers and duties of his office, and until he transmits to them a written declaration to the contrary, such powers and duties shall be discharged by the Vice-President as Acting President.

Section 4. Whenever the Vice-President and a majority of either the principal officers of the executive departments or of such other body as Congress may by law provide, transmit to the President pro tempore of the Senate and the Speaker of the House of Representatives their written declaration that the President is unable to discharge the powers and duties of his office, the Vice-President shall immediately assume the powers and duties of the office as Acting President.

Thereafter, when the President transmits to the President pro tempore of the Senate and the Speaker of the House of Representatives his written declaration that no inability exists, he shall resume the powers and duties of his office unless the Vice-President and a majority of either the principal officers of the executive department[s] or of such other body as Congress may by law provide, transmit within four days to the President pro tempore of the Senate and the Speaker of the House of Representatives their written declaration that the President is unable to discharge the powers and duties of his office. Thereupon Congress shall decide the issue, assembling within forty-eight hours for that purpose if not in session. If the Congress, within twenty-one days after receipt of the latter written declaration, or, if Congress is not in session, within twenty-one days after Congress is required to assemble, determines by two-thirds vote of both Houses that the President is unable to discharge the powers and duties of his office, the Vice-President shall continue to discharge the same as Acting President; otherwise, the President shall resume the powers and duties of his office.

Amendment XXVI

[RATIFIED **1971**]

Section 1. The right of citizens of the United States, who are eighteen years of age or older, to vote shall not be denied or abridged by the United States or by any State on account of age.

Section 2. The Congress shall have power to enforce this article by appropriate legislation.

Unratified Amendment

[EQUAL RIGHTS AMENDMENT (PROPOSED BY CONGRESS MARCH **22, 1972**; SEVEN-YEAR DEADLINE FOR RATIFICATION EXTENDED TO JUNE **30, 1982**)]

Section 1. *Equality of rights under the law shall not be denied or abridged by the United States or by any State on account of sex.*

Section 2. *The Congress shall have the power to enforce, by appropriate legislation, the provisions of this article.*

Section 3. *This amendment shall take effect two years after the date of ratification.*

Unratified Amendment

[D.C. STATEHOOD AMENDMENT (PROPOSED BY CONGRESS AUGUST **22, 1978**)]

Section 1. *For purposes of representation in the Congress, election of the President and Vice-President, and article V of this Constitution, the District constituting the seat of government of the United States shall be treated as though it were a State.*

Section 2. *The exercise of the rights and powers conferred under this article shall be by the people of the District constituting the seat of government, and as shall be provided by Congress.*

Section 3. *The twenty-third article of amendment to the Constitution of the United States is hereby repealed.*

Section 4. *This article shall be inoperative, unless it shall have been ratified as an amendment to the Constitution by the legislatures of three-fourths of the several states within seven years from the date of its submission.*

Amendment XXVII

[RATIFIED **1992**]

No law, varying the compensation for the services of the Senators and Representatives, shall take effect, until an election of Representatives shall have intervened.

Admission of States to the Union

State	Year of Admission	State	Year of Admission
Delaware	1787	Michigan	1837
Pennsylvania	1787	Florida	1845
New Jersey	1787	Texas	1845
Georgia	1788	Iowa	1846
Connecticut	1788	Wisconsin	1848
Massachusetts	1788	California	1850
Maryland	1788	Minnesota	1858
South Carolina	1788	Oregon	1859
New Hampshire	1788	Kansas	1861
Virginia	1788	West Virginia	1863
New York	1788	Nevada	1864
North Carolina	1789	Nebraska	1867
Rhode Island	1790	Colorado	1876
Vermont	1791	North Dakota	1889
Kentucky	1792	South Dakota	1889
Tennessee	1796	Montana	1889
Ohio	1803	Washington	1889
Louisiana	1812	Idaho	1890
Indiana	1816	Wyoming	1890
Mississippi	1817	Utah	1896
Illinois	1818	Oklahoma	1907
Alabama	1819	New Mexico	1912
Maine	1820	Arizona	1912
Missouri	1821	Alaska	1959
Arkansas	1836	Hawaii	1959

Presidents of the United States

President	Term	President	Term
George Washington	1789–1797	Grover Cleveland	1893–1897
John Adams	1797–1801	William McKinley	1897–1901
Thomas Jefferson	1801–1809	Theodore Roosevelt	1901–1909
James Madison	1809–1817	William H. Taft	1909–1913
James Monroe	1817–1825	Woodrow Wilson	1913–1921
John Quincy Adams	1825–1829	Warren G. Harding	1921–1923
Andrew Jackson	1829–1837	Calvin Coolidge	1923–1929
Martin Van Buren	1837–1841	Herbert Hoover	1929–1933
William H. Harrison	1841	Franklin D. Roosevelt	1933–1945
John Tyler	1841–1845	Harry S. Truman	1945–1953
James K. Polk	1845–1849	Dwight D. Eisenhower	1953–1961
Zachary Taylor	1849–1850	John F. Kennedy	1961–1963
Millard Fillmore	1850–1853	Lyndon B. Johnson	1963–1969
Franklin Pierce	1853–1857	Richard M. Nixon	1969–1974
James Buchanan	1857–1861	Gerald R. Ford	1974–1977
Abraham Lincoln	1861–1865	Jimmy Carter	1977–1981
Andrew Johnson	1865–1869	Ronald Reagan	1981–1989
Ulysses S. Grant	1869–1877	George H. W. Bush	1989–1993
Rutherford B. Hayes	1877–1881	Bill Clinton	1993–2001
James A. Garfield	1881	George W. Bush	2001–2009
Chester A. Arthur	1881–1885	Barack Obama	2009–2017
Grover Cleveland	1885–1889	Donald J. Trump	2017–2021
Benjamin Harrison	1889–1893	Joseph R. Biden	2021–Present

Glossary

acquired immune deficiency syndrome (AIDS): Immune disorder that reached epidemic proportions in the United States in the 1980s. (p. 720)

Adams-Onís Treaty: Treaty negotiated by John Quincy Adams and signed in 1819 by which Spain ceded all of its lands east of the Mississippi River to the United States. (p. 225)

affirmative action: Programs meant to overcome historical patterns of discrimination against minorities and women in education and employment. By establishing guidelines for hiring and college admissions, the government sought to advance equal opportunities for minorities and women. (p. 695)

Agricultural Adjustment Act: New Deal legislation that raised prices for farm produce by paying farmers subsidies to reduce production. Large farmers reaped most of the benefits from the act. The Supreme Court declared it unconstitutional in 1936. (p. 567)

Alamo: Texas fort captured by General Santa Anna on March 6, 1836, from rebel defenders. Sensationalist accounts of the siege of the Alamo increased popular support in the United States for Texas independence. (p. 286)

Albany Congress: June 1754 meeting in Albany, New York, of Iroquois and colonial representatives meant to facilitate better relations between Britain and the Iroquois Confederacy. Benjamin Franklin also put forward a plan for colonial union that was never implemented. (p. 112)

Alien and Sedition Acts: 1798 security acts passed by the Federalist-controlled Congress. The Alien Act allowed the president to imprison or deport noncitizens; the Sedition Act placed significant restrictions on political speech. (p. 185)

America First Committee: Isolationist organization founded by Senator Gerald Nye in 1940 to keep the United States out of World War II. (p. 585)

American Anti-Slavery Society (AASS): Abolitionist society founded by William Lloyd Garrison in 1833 that became the most important northern abolitionist organization of the period. (p. 264)

American Colonization Society (ACS): Organization formed in 1817 to establish colonies of freed slaves and freeborn blacks in Africa. The ACS was led by a group of white elites whose primary goal was to rid the nation of African Americans. (p. 196)

American Equal Rights Association: Group of black and white women and men formed in 1866 to promote gender and racial equality. The organization split in 1869 over support for the Fifteenth Amendment. (p. 362)

American Expeditionary Forces (AEF): Established in 1917 after the United States entered World War I. These Army troops served in Europe under the command of General John J. Pershing. (p. 516)

American Federation of Labor (AFL): Trade union federation founded in 1886. Led by its first president, Samuel Gompers, the AFL sought to organize skilled workers into trade-specific unions. (p. 435)

American Indian Movement (AIM): An American Indian group, formed in 1968, that promoted "red power" and condemned the United States for its continued mistreatment of Native Americans. (p. 683)

American Plan: Voluntary program initiated by businesses in the early twentieth century to protect worker welfare. The American Plan was meant to undermine the appeal of labor unions. (p. 534)

American Protective League (APL): An organization of private citizens that cooperated with the Justice Department and the Bureau of Investigation during World War I to spy on German residents suspected of disloyal behavior. (p. 521)

American System: Plan proposed by Henry Clay to promote the U.S. economy by combining federally funded internal improvements to aid farmers with federal tariffs to protect U.S. manufacturing and a national bank to oversee economic development. (p. 223)

American system of manufacturing: Production system focused on water-powered machinery, division of labor, and the use of interchangeable parts. The introduction of the American system in the early nineteenth century greatly increased the productivity of American manufacturing. (p. 209)

Anti-Imperialist League: An organization founded in 1898 to oppose annexation of the Philippines. Some feared that annexation would bring competition from cheap labor; others considered Filipinos racially inferior and the Philippines unsuitable as an American territory. (p. 509)

Antifederalists: Opponents of ratification of the Constitution. Antifederalists were generally more rural and less wealthy than the Federalists. (p. 174)

Appeal . . . to the Colored Citizens of the World: Radical abolitionist pamphlet published by David Walker in 1829. Walker's work inspired some white abolitionists to take a more radical stance on slavery. (p. 263)

appeasement: The policy of England and France in 1938 that allowed the Nazis to annex Czechoslovak territory in exchange for Hitler promising not to take further land, a pledge he soon violated. (p. 584)

Articles of Confederation: Plan for national government proposed by the Continental Congress in 1777 and ratified in March 1781. The Articles of Confederation gave the national government limited powers, reflecting widespread fear of centralized authority. (p. 150)

Atlantic Charter: August 1941 agreement between Franklin Roosevelt and Winston Churchill that outlined potential war aims and cemented the relationship between the United States and Britain. (p. 586)

Atlantic economy: The systematic exchange of goods and people between Europe and the Americas that emerged in the seventeenth century. (p. 33)

Aztecs: Spanish term for the Mexica, an indigenous people who built an empire in present-day Mexico in the centuries before the arrival of the Spaniards. The Aztecs built their empire through conquest. (p. 5)

Bacon's Rebellion: 1676 uprising in Virginia led by Nathaniel Bacon. Bacon and his followers, many of whom were former servants, were upset by the Virginia governor's unwillingness to send troops to intervene in conflicts between settlers and Indians and by the lack of representation of western settlers in the House of Burgesses. (p. 42)

Bandung Conference: A conference of twenty-nine Asian and African nations held in Indonesia in 1955; the countries declared their neutrality in the Cold War struggle between the United States and the Soviet Union and condemned colonialism. (p. 627)

Battle of Antietam: Fought in September 1862, this Civil War battle was the bloodiest single day in U.S. military history, but it gave Abraham Lincoln the victory he sought before announcing the Emancipation Proclamation. (p. 333)

Battle of Bull Run (Manassas): First major battle of the Civil War at which Confederate troops routed Union forces in July 1861. (p. 328)

Battle of Bunker Hill: Early Revolutionary War battle in which British troops narrowly defeated patriot militias, emboldening patriot forces. (p. 139)

Battle of Fallen Timbers: Battle at which U.S. General Anthony Wayne won a major victory over a multi-tribe coalition of American Indians in the Northwest Territory in 1794. (p. 218)

Battle of Gettysburg: Key July 1863 battle that helped turn the tide for the Union. The Union victory at Gettysburg, combined with a victory at Vicksburg that same month, positioned the Union to push farther into the South. (p. 340)

Battle of Horseshoe Bend: In 1814, Tennessee militia led by Andrew Jackson fought alongside Cherokee warriors to defeat Creek forces allied with Britain during the War of 1812. (p. 221)

Battle of Oriskany: In one of the bloodiest Revolutionary War battles, a force of German-American farmers and Oneida Indians deterred British troops and their Indian allies in central New York State, leaving British forces further east vulnerable to attack by the Continental Army. (p. 146)

Battle of Saratoga: Key Revolutionary War battle fought at Saratoga, New York. The patriot victory there in October 1777 provided hope that the colonists could prevail and increased the chances that the French would formally join the patriot side. (p. 148)

Battle of Shiloh: April 1862 battle in Tennessee that provided the Union entrance to the Mississippi valley. Shiloh was the bloodiest battle in American history to that point. (p. 332)

Battle of the Little Big Horn: 1876 battle in the Montana Territory in which Lieutenant Colonel George Armstrong Custer and his troops were massacred by Lakota Sioux. (p. 382)

Battle of Yorktown: Decisive battle in which the surrender of British forces on October 19, 1781, at Yorktown, Virginia, effectively sealed the patriot victory in the Revolutionary War. (p. 157)

Beats: A small group of young poets, writers, intellectuals, musicians, and artists who attacked mainstream American politics and culture in the 1950s. (p. 645)

benign neglect: British colonial policy from about 1700 to 1760 that relaxed supervision of internal colonial affairs as long as the North American colonies produced sufficient raw materials and revenue; also known as *salutary neglect.* (p. 122)

Beringia: Land bridge that linked Siberia and Alaska during the Wisconsin period. Migrants from northeast Asia used this bridge to travel to North America. (p. 3)

Berlin airlift: During the Berlin blockade by the Soviets from 1948 to 1949, the U.S. and British governments dispatched their air forces to transport food and supplies to West Berlin. (p. 615)

Bill of Rights: The first ten amendments to the Constitution. These ten amendments helped reassure Americans who feared that the federal government established under the Constitution would infringe on the rights of individuals and states. (p. 176)

Billion Dollar Congress: The Republican-controlled Congress of 1890 that spent huge sums of money to promote business and other interests. (p. 422)

black codes: Racial laws passed in the immediate aftermath of the Civil War by southern legislatures. The black codes were intended to reduce free African Americans to a condition as close to slavery as possible. (p. 357)

Black Death: The epidemic of bubonic plague that swept through Europe beginning in the mid-fourteenth century and wiped out roughly half of Europe's population. (p. 9)

Black Lives Matter: Social protest movement begun in the wake of the shooting death of Trayvon Martin by an armed civilian in 2013. Organized by protestors around the social media hashtag Black Lives Matter, the movement expanded throughout the nation after police killings of unarmed African Americans in Ferguson, Missouri; Staten Island, New York; Cleveland, Ohio; and Baltimore, Maryland in 2014 and 2015. (p. 742)

Black Panther Party: Organization founded in 1966 by Huey P. Newton and Bobby Seale to advance the black power movement in black communities. (p. 670)

Black Tuesday: October 29, 1929, crash of the U.S. stock market. The 1929 stock market crash marked the beginning of the Great Depression. (p. 551)

Bleeding Kansas: The Kansas Territory during a period of violent conflicts over the fate of slavery in the mid-1850s. The violence in Kansas intensified the sectional division over slavery. (p. 315)

Boland Amendment: 1982 act of Congress prohibiting direct aid to the Nicaraguan Contra forces. (p. 723)

Bonus Army: World War I veterans who marched on Washington, D.C., in 1932 to demand immediate payment of their service bonuses. President Hoover refused to negotiate and instructed the U.S. army to clear the capital of protesters, leading to a violent clash. (p. 564)

boss: Leader of a political machine. Men like "Boss" George Washington Plunkitt of New York's Tammany Hall wielded enormous power over city life. (p. 469)

Boston Massacre: 1770 clash between colonial protesters and British soldiers in Boston that led to the death of five colonists. The bloody conflict was used to promote the patriot cause. (p. 128)

***Brown v. Board of Education of Topeka, Kansas*:** Landmark 1954 Supreme Court case that overturned the "separate but equal" principle established by *Plessy v. Ferguson* and applied to public schools. Few schools in the South were racially desegregated for more than a decade. (p. 648)

buffalo soldiers: African American cavalrymen who fought in the West against the Indians in the 1870s and 1880s and served with distinction. (p. 382)

bully pulpit: Term used by Theodore Roosevelt to describe the office of the presidency. Roosevelt believed that the president should use his office as a platform to promote his programs and rally public opinion. (p. 491)

Bush Doctrine: President George W. Bush's proposal to engage in preemptive war against despotic governments, such as Iraq, deemed to threaten U.S. national security, even if the danger was not imminent. (p. 752)

Californios: Spanish and Mexican residents of California. Before the nineteenth century, Californios made up California's economic and political elite. Their position, however, deteriorated after the conclusion of the Mexican-American War in 1848. (p. 395)

Camp David accords: 1978 peace accord between Israel and Egypt facilitated by the mediation of President Jimmy Carter. (p. 702)

capitalist system: Economy in which private individuals and corporations rather than the government primarily own and sustain the means of production, distribution, and exchange. (p. 211)

carpetbaggers: Derogatory term for white Northerners who moved to the South in the years following the Civil War. Many white Southerners believed that such migrants were intent on exploiting their suffering. (p. 364)

Chinese Exclusion Act: 1882 act that banned Chinese immigration into the United States and prohibited those Chinese already in the country from becoming naturalized American citizens. (p. 396, 454)

Church of England: National church established by Henry VIII after he split with the Catholic Church. (p. 31)

civic housekeeping: Idea promoted by Jane Addams for urban reform by using women's traditional skills as domestic managers; caregivers for children, the elderly, and the needy; and community builders. (p. 478)

Civil Rights Act of 1964: Wide-ranging civil rights act that, among other things, prohibited discrimination in public accommodations and employment and increased federal enforcement of school desegregation. (p. 666)

Civilian Conservation Corps (CCC): New Deal work program that hired young, unmarried men to work on conservation projects. The CCC employed about 2.5 million men and lasted until 1942. (p. 569)

Coercive Acts (Intolerable Acts): 1774 act of Parliament passed in response to the Boston Tea Party. The Coercive Acts were meant to force the colonists into submission, but they only resulted in increased resistance. Colonial patriots called them the Intolerable Acts. (p. 129)

Cold War: The political, economic, and military conflict, short of direct war on the battlefield, between the United States and the Soviet Union that lasted from 1945 to 1991. (p. 610)

collective bargaining: The process of negotiation between labor unions and employers. (p. 433)

Columbian exchange: The biological exchange between the Americas and the rest of the world. Although the initial impact of the Columbian exchange was strongest in the Americas and Europe, it was soon felt all over the world. (p. 17)

Commission on the Status of Women: Commission appointed by President Kennedy in 1961. The commission's 1963 report, *American Women*, highlighted employment discrimination against women and recommended legislation requiring equal pay for equal work regardless of sex. (p. 680)

committee of correspondence: Type of committee first established in Massachusetts to circulate concerns and reports of protests and other events to leaders in other colonies in the aftermath of the Sugar Act. (p. 123)

Committee on Public Information (CPI): Committee established in 1917 to create propaganda and promote censorship to generate enthusiasm for World War I and stifle antiwar dissent. (p. 520)

***Common Sense*:** Pamphlet arguing in favor of independence written by Thomas Paine and published in 1776. *Common Sense* was widely read and had an important impact on the debate over declaring independence from Britain. (p. 140)

Compromise of 1850: Series of acts following California's application for admission as a free state. Meant to quell sectional tensions over slavery, the act was intended to provide something for all sides but ended up fueling more conflicts. (p. 308)

compromise of 1877: Compromise between Republicans and southern Democrats that resulted in the election of Rutherford B. Hayes. Southern Democrats agreed to support Hayes in the disputed presidential election in exchange for his promise to end Reconstruction. (p. 369)

Comstock Lode: Massive silver deposit discovered in the Sierra Nevada in the late 1850s. (p. 386)

Confederate States of America: Nation established in 1861 by the eleven slave states that seceded between December 1860 and April 1861. (p. 320)

conquistadors: Spanish soldiers who were central to the conquest of the civilizations of the Americas. Once conquest was complete, conquistadors often extracted wealth from the people and lands they now ruled. (p. 19)

conservative coalition: Alliance of southern Democrats and conservative northern Republicans in Congress that thwarted passage of New Deal legislation after 1938. (p. 577)

Continental Congress: Congress convened in Philadelphia in 1774 in response to the Coercive Acts. The delegates hoped to reestablish the freedoms colonists had enjoyed in earlier times. (p. 130)

contraband: Designation assigned to escaped slaves by Union general Benjamin Butler in May 1861. By designating slaves as property forfeited by the act of rebellion, the Union was able to strike at slavery without proclaiming a general emancipation. (p. 329)

Contract with America: A document that called for reduced welfare spending, lower taxes, term limits for lawmakers, and a constitutional amendment for a balanced budget. In preparation for the 1994 midterm congressional elections, Republicans, led by Representative Newt Gingrich, drew up this proposal. (p. 746)

convict lease: The system used by southern governments to furnish mainly African American prison labor to plantation owners and industrialists and to raise revenue for the states. In practice, convict labor replaced slavery as the means of providing a forced labor supply. (p. 406)

Copperheads: Northern Democrats who did not support the Union war effort. Such Democrats enjoyed considerable support in eastern cities and parts of the Midwest. (p. 338)

corporation: A form of business ownership in which the liability of shareholders in a company is limited to their individual investments. The formation of corporations in the late nineteenth century greatly stimulated investment in industry. (p. 409)

Corps of Discovery: Expedition organized by the U.S. government to explore the Louisiana Territory. Led by Meriwether Lewis and William Clark, the expedition set out in May 1804 and journeyed to the Pacific coast and back by 1806 with the aid of interpreters like Sacagawea. (p. 201)

cotton gin: Machine invented by Eli Whitney in 1793 to deseed short-staple cotton. The cotton gin dramatically reduced the time and labor involved in deseeding, facilitating the expansion of cotton production in the South and West. (p. 209)

counterculture: Young cultural rebels of the 1960s who rejected conventional moral and sexual values and used drugs to reach a higher consciousness. These so-called hippies bonded together in their style of clothes and taste in rock 'n' roll music. (p. 679)

court-packing plan: Proposal by President Franklin Roosevelt in 1937 to increase the size of the Supreme Court and reduce its opposition to New Deal legislation. Congress failed to pass the measure, and the scheme increased resentment toward Roosevelt. (p. 577)

COVID-19: An infectious disease caused by a novel coronavirus that first appeared in China in 2019 and is responsible for the worldwide pandemic that followed. (p. 766)

Coxey's army: 1894 protest movement led by Jacob Coxey. Coxey and five hundred supporters marched from Ohio to Washington, D.C., to protest the lack of government response to the depression of 1893. (p. 445)

Crittenden plan: A political compromise over slavery which failed after seven southern states seceded from the Union in early 1861. It would have protected slavery from federal interference where it already existed and extended the Missouri Compromise line to California. (p. 320)

Crusades: Eleventh- and twelfth-century campaigns to reclaim the Holy Land for the Roman Catholic Church. The Crusades were, on the whole, a military failure, but they did stimulate trade and inspire Europeans to seek better connections with the larger world. (p. 9)

Cuba Libre: Vision of Cuban independence developed by José Martí, who hoped that Cuban independence would bring with it greater social and racial equality. (p. 506)

cult of domesticity: New ideals of womanhood that emerged alongside the middle class in the 1830s and 1840s that advocated women's relegation to the domestic sphere where they could devote themselves to the care of children, the home, and hard-working husbands. (p. 250)

D Day: June 6, 1944, invasion of German-occupied France by Allied forces. The D Day landings opened up a second front in Europe and marked a major turning point in World War II. (p. 599)

Dawes Act: 1887 act that ended federal recognition of tribal sovereignty and divided Indian land into 160-acre parcels to be distributed to Indian heads of household. The act dramatically reduced the amount of Indian-controlled land and undermined Indian social and cultural institutions. (p. 384)

Declaration of Independence: Document declaring the independence of the colonies from Great Britain. Drafted by Thomas Jefferson and then debated and revised by the Continental Congress, the Declaration was made public on July 4, 1776. (p. 141)

Declaration of Sentiments: Call for women's rights in marriage, family, religion, politics, and law issued at the 1848 Seneca Falls convention. It was signed by 100 of the 300 participants. (p. 267)

decolonization: The period after World War II through the 1960s when countries in Asia, Africa, and the Middle East gained independence from their European colonial rulers. In 1946 the United States gave the Philippines independence. (p. 627)

Deferred Action for Childhood Arrivals (DACA): This policy, initiated under the administration of Barack Obama in 2012, allows children who entered the country illegally to receive a two-year extension of their residency in the U.S. along with eligibility for work permits. (p. 758)

Democratic-Republicans: Political party that emerged out of opposition to Federalist policies in the 1790s. The Democratic-Republicans chose Thomas Jefferson as their presidential candidate in 1796, 1800, and 1804. (p. 183)

Democrats and National Republicans: Two parties that resulted from the split of the Democratic-Republicans in the early 1820s. Andrew Jackson emerged as the leader of the Democrats. (p. 237)

depression of 1893: Severe economic downturn triggered by railroad and bank failures. The severity of the depression, combined with the failure of the federal government to offer an adequate response, led to the realignment of American politics. (p. 444)

deskilling: The replacement of skilled labor with unskilled labor and machines. (p. 253)

détente: An easing of tense relations with the Soviet Union during the Cold War. This process moved unevenly through the 1970s and early 1980s but accelerated when Soviet leader Mikhail Gorbachev came to power in the mid-1980s. (p. 693)

dollar diplomacy: Term used by President Howard Taft to describe the economic focus of his foreign policy. Taft hoped to use economic policies and the control of foreign assets by American companies to influence Latin American nations. (p. 513)

Double V: The slogan African Americans used during World War II to state their twin aims to fight for victory over Fascism abroad and victory over racism at home. (p. 593)

***Dred Scott* decision:** 1857 Supreme Court case centered on the status of Dred Scott and his family. In its ruling, the Court denied the claim that black men had any rights and blocked Congress from excluding slavery from any territory. (p. 316)

Dunmore's Proclamation: 1775 proclamation issued by the British commander Lord Dunmore that offered freedom to all enslaved African Americans who joined the British army. The proclamation heightened concerns among some patriots about the consequences of independence. (p. 140)

Economic Recovery Tax Act: Act signed into law by President Ronald Reagan in 1981, that slashed income and estate taxes especially on those in the highest income brackets. (p. 717)

Eisenhower Doctrine: A doctrine guiding intervention in the Middle East. In 1957 Congress granted President Dwight Eisenhower the power to send military forces into the Middle East to combat alleged Communist aggression. Eisenhower sent U.S. marines into Lebanon in 1958 under this doctrine. (p. 629)

Emancipation Proclamation: January 1, 1863, proclamation that declared all slaves in areas still in rebellion "forever free." While stopping short of abolishing slavery, the Emancipation Proclamation was, nonetheless, seen by blacks and abolitionists as a great victory. (p. 333)

Embargo Act: 1807 act that prohibited American ships from leaving their home ports until Britain and France repealed restrictions on U.S. trade. The act had a devastating impact on American commerce. (p. 203)

encomienda: System first established by Christopher Columbus by which Spanish leaders in the Americas received land and the labor of all Indians residing on it. From the Indian point of view, the encomienda system amounted to little more than enslavement. (p. 14)

Enlightenment: European cultural movement that emphasized rational and scientific thinking over traditional religion and superstition. Enlightenment thought appealed to many colonial elites. (p. 99)

Enrollment Act: March 1863 Union draft law that provided for draftees to be selected by an impartial lottery. A loophole in the law that allowed wealthy Americans to escape service by paying $300 or hiring a substitute created widespread resentment. (p. 338)

enslavers: Those who traded or owned enslaved people; see also planters. (p. 74)

Enterprise of the Indies: Christopher Columbus's proposal to sail west across the Atlantic to Japan and China. In 1492 Columbus gained support for the venture from Ferdinand and Isabella of Spain. (p. 14)

Environmental Protection Agency (EPA): Federal agency established by Richard Nixon in 1971 to regulate activities that resulted in pollution or other environmental degradation. (p. 705)

Equal Rights Amendment (ERA): A proposed amendment that prevented the abridgment of "equality of rights under law . . . by the United States or any State on the basis of sex." Not enough states had ratified the amendment by 1982, when the ratification period expired, so it was not adopted. (p. 704)

Erie Canal: Canal built in the early 1820s that made water transport from the Great Lakes to New York City possible. The success of the Erie Canal inspired many similar projects and ensured New York City's place as the premier international port in the United States. (p. 223)

Espionage Act: 1917 act that prohibited antiwar activities, including opposing the military draft. It punished speech critical of the war as well as deliberate actions of sabotage and spying. (p. 520)

ethnic cleansing: Ridding an area of a particular ethnic minority to achieve ethnic homogeneity. In the civil war between Serbs and Croatians in Bosnia from 1992 to 1995, the Serbian military attempted to eliminate the Croatian population through murder, rape, and expulsion. (p. 748)

eugenics: The pseudoscience of producing genetic improvement in the human population through selective breeding. Proponents of eugenics often saw ethnic and racial minorities as genetically "undesirable" and inferior. (p. 460)

Exodusters: Blacks who migrated from the South to Kansas in 1879 seeking land and a better way of life. (p. 365)

Fair Employment Practice Committee (FEPC): Committee established in 1941 to help African Americans gain a greater share of wartime industrial jobs. (p. 592)

Fair Labor Standards Act: 1938 law that provided a minimum wage of 40 cents an hour and a forty-hour workweek for employees in businesses engaged in interstate commerce. (p. 574)

Farmers' Alliances: Regional organizations formed in the late nineteenth century to advance the interests of farmers. The most prominent of these organizations were the Northwestern Farmers' Alliance, the Southern Farmers' Alliance, and the Colored Farmers' Alliance. (p. 442)

Federal Deposit Insurance Corporation (FDIC): Federal agency created in 1933 through New Deal legislation, that insured bank deposits up to $5,000, a figure that would substantially rise over the years. (p. 567)

Federal Employee Loyalty Program: Program established by President Truman in 1947 to investigate federal employees suspected of disloyalty and Communist ties. (p. 620)

Federalists: Supporters of ratification of the Constitution, many of whom came from urban and commercial backgrounds. (p. 174)

Field Order Number 15: Order issued by General William Sherman in January 1865, setting aside more than 400,000 acres of Confederate land to be divided into plots for former slaves. Sherman's order came in response to pressure from African American leaders. (p. 344)

Fifteenth Amendment: Amendment to the Constitution prohibiting the abridgment of a citizen's right to vote on the basis of "race, color, or previous condition of servitude." From the 1870s on, southern states devised numerous strategies for circumventing the Fifteenth Amendment. (p. 361)

filibusters: Unauthorized military expeditions launched by U.S. adventurers to gain control of Cuba, Nicaragua, and other Spanish territories in the 1850s. (p. 311)

Force Acts: Three acts passed by the U.S. Congress in 1870 and 1871 in response to vigilante attacks on southern blacks. The acts were designed to protect black political rights and end violence by the Ku Klux Klan and similar organizations. (p. 367)

Fort Sumter: Union fort that guarded the harbor in Charleston, South Carolina. The Confederacy's decision to fire on the fort and block resupply in April 1861 marked the beginning of the Civil War. (p. 321)

Fourteen Points: The core principles President Woodrow Wilson saw as the basis for lasting peace, including freedom of the seas, open diplomacy, and self-determination for colonial peoples. (p. 523)

Fourteenth Amendment: Amendment to the Constitution defining citizenship and protecting individual civil and political rights from abridgment by the states. Adopted during Reconstruction, the Fourteenth Amendment overturned the *Dred Scott* decision. (p. 359)

Free Speech Movement (FSM): Movement protesting policies instituted by the University of California at Berkeley that restricted free speech. In 1964 students at Berkeley conducted sit-ins and held rallies against these policies. (p. 678)

Freedmen's Bureau: Federal agency created in 1865 to provide ex-slaves with economic and legal resources. The Freedmen's Bureau played an active role in shaping black life in the postwar South. (p. 352)

Freedom Rides: Integrated bus rides through the South organized by CORE and SNCC in 1961 to test compliance with Supreme Court rulings on segregation. (p. 664)

Freedom Summer: 1964 civil rights project in Mississippi launched by SNCC, CORE, the SCLC, and the NAACP. Some eight hundred volunteers, mainly white college students, worked on voter registration drives and in freedom schools to improve education for rural black youngsters. (p. 667)

Free-Soil Party: Party founded by political abolitionists in 1848 to expand the appeal of the Liberty Party by focusing less on the moral wrongs of slavery and more on the benefits of providing economic opportunities for northern whites in western territories. (p. 268)

Fugitive Slave Act of 1850: Act strengthening earlier fugitive slave laws, passed as part of the Compromise of 1850. The Fugitive Slave Act provoked widespread anger in the North and intensified sectional tensions. (p. 308)

gag rule: Rule passed by the House of Representatives in 1836 to table, or postpone action on, all antislavery petitions without hearing them read to stifle debate over slavery. It was renewed annually until it was rescinded in 1844. (p. 287)

Gettysburg Address: Speech given by Abraham Lincoln in November 1863, at a dedication of the National Cemetery created at Gettysburg, Pennsylvania. (p. 341)

ghettos: Neighborhoods dominated by a single ethnic, racial, or class group. (p. 456)

Ghost Dance: Religious ritual performed by the Paiute Indians in the late nineteenth century. Following a vision he received in 1888, the prophet Wovoka believed that performing the Ghost Dance would cause whites to disappear and allow Indians to regain control of their lands. (p. 385)

Gilded Age: Term coined by Mark Twain and Charles Dudley Warner to describe the late nineteenth century. The term referred to the opulent and often ostentatious lifestyles of the era's superrich. (p. 414)

***glasnost*:** Policy of political "openness" initiated by Soviet leader Mikhail Gorbachev in the 1980s. Under *glasnost*, the Soviet Union extended democratic elections, freedom of speech, and freedom of the press. (p. 728)

globalization: The extension of economic, political, and cultural relationships among nations, through commerce, migration, and communication. Globalization expanded in the late twentieth century because of free trade agreements and the relaxation of immigration restrictions. (p. 732)

Glorious Revolution: 1688 rebellion that forced James II from the English throne and replaced him with William and Mary. The Glorious Revolution led to greater political and commercial autonomy for the British colonies. (p. 58)

gold rush: The rapid influx of migrants into California after the discovery of gold in 1848. Migrants came from all over the world seeking riches. (p. 303)

"The Gospel of Wealth": 1889 essay by Andrew Carnegie in which he argued that the rich should act as stewards of the wealth they earned, using their surplus income for the benefit of the community. (p. 412)

Grangers: Members of an organization founded in 1867 to meet the social and cultural needs of farmers. Grangers took an active role in the promotion of the economic and political interests of farmers. (p. 441)

Great Awakening: Series of religious revivals in colonial America that began in 1720 and lasted to about 1750. (p. 101)

great migration: Population shift of more than 400,000 African Americans who left the South beginning in 1917–1918 and headed north and west hoping to escape poverty and racial discrimination. During the 1920s another 800,000 blacks left the South. (p. 532)

Great Plains: Semiarid territory in central North America. (p. 376)

Great Recession: The severe economic decline in the United States and throughout the world that began in 2008, leading to bank failures, high unemployment, home foreclosures, and large federal deficits. (p. 754)

Great Society: President Lyndon Johnson's vision of social, economic, and cultural progress in the United States. (p. 671)

Gulf of Tonkin Resolution: 1964 congressional resolution giving President Lyndon Johnson wide discretion in the use of U.S. forces in Vietnam. The resolution followed reported attacks by North Vietnamese gunboats on two American destroyers. (p. 675)

Haitian Revolution: Revolt against French rule by free and enslaved blacks in the 1790s on the island of Saint Domingue. The revolution led in 1803 to the establishment of Haiti, the first independent black-led nation in the Americas. (p. 199)

hard war: The strategy promoted by General Ulysses S. Grant in which Union forces destroyed civilian crops, livestock, fields, and property to undermine Confederate morale and supply chains. (p. 343)

Harpers Ferry, Virginia: Site of an 1859 raid on a federal arsenal led by John Brown, who hoped to inspire an uprising by enslaved Americans. (p. 317)

Harlem Renaissance: The work of African American writers, artists, and musicians that flourished following World War I through the 1920s. (p. 542)

Hartford Convention: 1814 convention of Federalists opposed to the War of 1812. Delegates to the convention considered a number of constitutional amendments, as well as the possibility of secession. (p. 222)

Haymarket Square: Site of 1886 rally and violence in Chicago. In the aftermath of the events in Haymarket Square, the union movement in the United States went into temporary decline. (p. 434)

Hetch Hetchy valley: Site of a controversial dam built to supply San Francisco with water and power in the aftermath of the 1906 earthquake. The dam was built over the objections of preservationists such as John Muir. (p. 489)

Holocaust: The Nazi regime's genocidal effort to eradicate Europe's Jewish population during World War II, which resulted in the deaths of six million Jews. (p. 602)

Homestead Act: 1862 act that established procedures for distributing 160-acre lots to western settlers, on condition that they develop and farm their land, as an incentive for western migration. (p. 390)

Homestead strike: 1892 strike by steelworkers at Andrew Carnegie's Homestead steel factory. The strike collapsed after a failed assassination attempt on Carnegie's plant manager, Henry Clay Frick. (p. 436)

Hopewell people: Indian people who established a thriving culture near the Mississippi River in the early centuries C.E. (p. 7)

horizontal integration: The ownership of as many firms as possible in a given industry by a single owner. John D. Rockefeller pursued a strategy of horizontal integration when he bought up rival oil refineries. (p. 408)

horticulture: A form of agriculture in which people work small plots of land with simple tools. (p. 4)

House Un-American Activities Committee (HUAC): U.S. House of Representatives committee established in 1938 to investigate domestic communism. After World War II, HUAC conducted highly publicized investigations of Communist influence in government and the entertainment industry. (p. 620)

House of Burgesses: Local governing body in Virginia established by the English crown in 1619. (p. 39)

Hull House: This settlement house, based on Toynbee Hall in England, was established by Jane Addams and Ellen Starr in Chicago in 1889. It served as a center of social reform and provided educational and social opportunities for working-class poor and immigrant women and their children. (p. 478)

Hurricane Katrina: Storm that hit the Gulf coast states of Louisiana, Mississippi, and Alabama in 2005. The hurricane caused massive flooding in New Orleans after levees broke. Federal, state, and local government responses to the storm were inadequate and highlighted racial and class inequities. (p. 753)

Immigration Reform and Control Act: Law signed by President Ronald Reagan in 1986, which extended amnesty to undocumented immigrants in the United States for a specified period and allowed them to obtain legal status. At the same time the law penalized employers who hired new illegal workers. (p. 720)

imperial presidency: Term used to describe the growth of presidential powers during the Cold War, particularly with respect to war-making powers and the conduct of national security. (p. 614)

import duty: Tax imposed on goods imported into the colonies, paid by the importer rather than directly by the consumer; also known as a *tariff*. (p. 123)

impressment: The forced enlistment of civilians into the army or navy. The impressment of residents of colonial seaports into the British navy was a major source of complaint in the eighteenth century. (p. 105)

Incas: Andean people who built an empire in the centuries before the arrival of the Spaniards. At the height of their power in the fifteenth century, the Incas controlled some sixteen million people. (p. 5)

indentured servants: Servants contracted to work for a set period of time without pay. Many early migrants to the English colonies indentured themselves in exchange for the price of passage to North America. (p. 39)

Indian Citizenship Act: 1924 legislation that extended the right to vote and citizenship to all American Indians. (p. 546)

Indian Removal Act: 1830 act by which Indian peoples in the East were forced to exchange their lands for territory west of the Mississippi River. Andrew Jackson was an ardent supporter of Indian removal. (p. 240)

Indian Reorganization Act (IRA): 1934 act that ended the Dawes Act, authorized self-government for those living on reservations, extended tribal landholdings, and pledged to uphold native customs and language. (p. 576)

Industrial Workers of the World (IWW): Organization that grew out of the activities of the Western Federation of Miners in the 1890s and formed by Eugene V. Debs. Known as Wobblies, the IWW attempted to unite all skilled and unskilled workers in an effort to overthrow capitalism. (p. 438)

internment: The relocation of persons seen as a threat to national security to isolated camps during World War II. Nearly all people of Japanese descent living on the West Coast were forced to sell or abandon their possessions and relocate to internment camps during the war. (p. 595)

Interstate Commerce Commission (ICC): Regulatory commission established by Congress in 1887. The commission investigated interstate shipping, required railroads to make their rates public, and could bring lawsuits to force shippers to reduce "unreasonable" fares. (p. 442)

Intolerable Acts: *See* Coercive Acts.

Iran-Contra affair: Ronald Reagan administration scandal involving the funneling of funds from an illegal arms-for-hostages deal with Iran to the Nicaraguan Contras in the mid-1980s. (p. 726)

Islamic State of Iraq and Syria (ISIS): Jihadist terrorist group originally founded in 1999, which gained strength from the sectarian violence that grew out of the 2003 U.S. invasion of Iraq. The group captured territory in Iraq and Syria and claimed responsibility for terrorist attacks in Paris, San Bernardino, California, and Lebanon. (p. 760)

"island-hopping": This strategy, employed by the U.S. in World War II in the Pacific, directed American and Allied forces to avoid heavily fortified Japanese islands and concentrate on less heavily defended islands in preparation for a combined air, land, and sea invasion of Japan. (p. 599)

Jamestown: The first successful English colony in North America. Settled in 1607, Jamestown was founded by soldiers and adventurers under the leadership of Captain John Smith. (p. 37)

Jay Treaty: 1796 treaty that required British forces to withdraw from U.S. soil, required American repayment of debts to British firms, and limited U.S. trade with the British West Indies. (p. 179)

Jim Crow: Late-nineteenth-century statutes that established legally defined racial segregation in the South. Jim Crow legislation helped ensure the social and economic subordination of southern blacks. (p. 418)

jingoists: Superpatriotic supporters of the expansion and use of military power. Jingoists such as Theodore Roosevelt longed for a war in which they could demonstrate America's strength and prove their own masculinity. (p. 505)

Judiciary Act: Act passed in 1801 by the Federalist-controlled Congress to expand the federal court system by creating sixteen circuit (regional) courts, with new judges appointed for each, just before Democratic-Republicans took control of the presidency and Congress. (p. 201)

Juneteenth: June 19, 1865, the day when General Gordon Granger informed all enslaved people in Texas that they were free. The day is still celebrated by many African Americans as Emancipation Day. (p. 345)

Kansas-Nebraska Act: 1854 act creating the territories of Kansas and Nebraska out of what was then Indian land. The act stipulated that the issue of slavery would be settled by a popular referendum in each territory. (p. 313)

King William's War: 1689–1697 war that began as a conflict over competing French and English interests on the European continent but soon spread to the American frontier. Both sides pulled Indian allies into the war. (p. 62)

Knights of the Ku Klux Klan (KKK): Organization formed in 1865 by General Nathan Bedford Forrest to enforce prewar racial norms. Members of the KKK used threats and violence to intimidate blacks and white Republicans. (p. 366)

La Raza Unida (The United Race): A Chicano political party, formed in 1969, that advocated job opportunities for Chicanos, bilingual education, and Chicano cultural studies programs in universities. (p. 683)

laissez-faire: French for "let things alone." Advocates of laissez-faire believed that the marketplace should be left to regulate itself, allowing individuals to pursue their own self-interest without any government restraint or interference. (p. 411)

League of Nations: The international organization proposed by Woodrow Wilson after the end of World War I to ensure world peace and security in the future through mutual agreement. The United States failed to join the league because Wilson and his opponents in Congress could not work out a compromise. (p. 523)

Lend-Lease Act: March 1941 law permitting the United States to lend or lease military equipment and other commodities to Great Britain and its allies. Its passage marked the end of American neutrality before the U.S. entered World War II. (p. 585)

Levittown: Suburban subdivision built in Long Island, New York, in the 1950s in response to the postwar housing shortage. Subsequent Levittowns were built in Pennsylvania and New Jersey. (p. 640)

***Liberator*:** Radical abolitionist newspaper launched by William Lloyd Garrison in 1831. Through the *Liberator*, Garrison called for immediate, uncompensated emancipation of slaves. (p. 263)

Liberty Party: Antislavery political party formed in 1840. The Liberty Party, along with the Free-Soil Party, helped place slavery at the center of national political debates. (p. 268)

Little Rock Nine: Nine African American students who, in 1957, became the first black students to attend Central High School in Little Rock, Arkansas. Federal troops were required to overcome the resistance of white officials and to protect the students. (p. 649)

Long Drive: Cattle drive from the grazing lands of Texas to rail depots in Kansas. Once in Kansas, the cattle were shipped eastward to slaughterhouses in Chicago. (p. 388)

Lost Generation: A term used by the writer Gertrude Stein to describe the writers and artists disillusioned with the consumer culture of the 1920s. (p. 541)

Louisiana Purchase: U.S. government's 1803 purchase from France of the vast territory stretching from the Mississippi River to the Rocky Mountains and from New Orleans to present-day Montana, doubling the size of the nation. (p. 200)

loyalist: A colonial supporter of the British during the Revolutionary War. Loyalists came from all economic backgrounds and had a variety of motives for siding with the British. (p. 142)

Manhattan Project: Code name for the secret program to develop an atomic bomb. The project was launched in 1942 and directed by the United States with the assistance of Great Britain and Canada. (p. 602)

manifest destiny: Term coined by John L. O'Sullivan in 1845 to describe what he saw as the nation's God-given right to expand its borders. Throughout the nineteenth century, the concept of manifest destiny was used to justify U.S. expansion. (p. 292)

***Marbury v. Madison*:** 1803 Supreme Court decision that established the authority of the Supreme Court to rule on the constitutionality of federal laws. (p. 202)

March on Washington for Jobs and Freedom: August 28, 1963, rally by civil rights organizations in Washington, D.C., that brought increased national attention to the movement. (p. 666)

market revolution: Innovations in agriculture, industry, communication, and transportation in the early 1800s fueled increased efficiency and productivity and linked northern industry with western farms and southern plantations. (p. 246)

Marshall Plan: Post–World War II European economic aid package developed by Secretary of State George Marshall. The plan helped rebuild Western Europe and served American political and economic interests in the process. (p. 613)

Maya: People who established large cities in the Yucatán peninsula. Mayan civilization was strongest between 300 and 800 C.E. (p. 5)

Mayflower Compact: Written constitution created by the Pilgrims upon their arrival in Plymouth. The Mayflower Compact was the first written constitution adopted in North America. (p. 45)

McCarthyism: Term used to describe the harassment and persecution of suspected political radicals. Senator Joseph McCarthy was one of many prominent government figures who helped incite anti-Communist hysteria in the early 1950s. (p. 624)

McCulloch v. Maryland: 1819 Supreme Court decision that reinforced the federal government's ability to employ an expansive understanding of the implied powers clause of the Constitution. (p. 203)

#MeToo Movement: The social movement of black and white women—spurred on by the election of Donald Trump as president—linked tens of millions of women through social media networks in opposition to sexual harassment and abuse in workplaces and educational institutions. In 2017, it conducted massive marches throughout the U.S. and the world. (p. 764)

melting pot: Popular metaphor for immigrant assimilation into American society. According to this ideal, all immigrants underwent a process of Americanization that produced a homogeneous society. (p. 460)

mercantilism: Economic system centered on the maintenance of a favorable balance of trade for the home country, with more gold and silver flowing into that country than flowed out. Seventeenth- and eighteenth-century British colonial policy was heavily shaped by mercantilism. (p. 68)

metis: Term for mixed-race children of French men and Indian women in colonial North America. (p. 35)

Mexican revolution: 1911 revolution in Mexico, which led to nearly a decade of bloodshed and civil war. (p. 513)

Middle Passage: The brutal voyage of slave ships laden with human cargo from Africa to the Americas. The voyage was the middle segment in a triangular journey that began in Europe, went first to Africa, then to the Americas, and finally back to Europe. (p. 70)

military-industrial complex: The government-business alliance related to the military and national defense that developed out of World War II and greatly influenced future development of the U.S. economy. (p. 587)

Mississippi Freedom Democratic Party (MFDP): Political party formed in 1964 to challenge the all-white state Democratic Party for seats at the 1964 Democratic presidential convention and run candidates for public office. Although unsuccessful in 1964, MFDP efforts led to subsequent reform of the Democratic Party and the seating of an interracial convention delegation from Mississippi in 1968. (p. 667)

Missouri Compromise: 1820 act that allowed Missouri to enter the Union as a slave state and Maine to enter as a free state and established the southern border of Missouri as the boundary between slave and free states throughout the Louisiana Territory. (p. 231)

Modern Republicanism: The political approach of President Dwight Eisenhower that tried to fit traditional Republican Party ideals of individualism and fiscal restraint within the broad framework of the New Deal. (p. 654)

Monroe Doctrine: Assertion by President James Monroe in 1823 that the Western Hemisphere was part of the U.S. sphere of influence. Although the United States lacked the power to back up this claim, it signaled an intention to challenge Europeans for authority in the Atlantic world. (p. 225)

Montgomery Improvement Association: Organization founded in Montgomery, Alabama, in 1955 to coordinate the boycott of city buses by African Americans. (p. 648)

Mormons: Religious sect that migrated to Utah to escape religious persecution; also known as the Church of Jesus Christ of Latter-Day Saints. (p. 394)

muckrakers: Investigative journalists who specialized in exposing corruption, scandal, and vice. Muckrakers helped build public support for progressive causes. (p. 477)

Mueller Report: The report of Robert Mueller, special counsel for the Justice Department, into Russian interference in the 2016 presidential election. The report concluded that agents of the Russian government used social media and Internet hacking against the Democratic presidential candidate Hillary Clinton. The report concluded that Donald Trump cooperated with but did not conspire with the Russians. (p. 765)

mujahideen: Religiously inspired Afghan rebels who resisted the Soviet invasion of Afghanistan in 1979. (p. 701)

multiplier effect: The diverse changes spurred by a single invention, including other inventions it spawns and the broader economic, social, and political transformations it fuels. (p. 208)

mutual aid societies: Voluntary associations that provide a variety of economic and social benefits to their members. (p. 456)

mutually assured destruction (MAD): Defense strategy built around the threat of a massive nuclear retaliatory strike. Adoption of the doctrine of mutually assured destruction contributed to the escalation of the nuclear arms race during the Cold War. (p. 626)

Nat Turner's rebellion: 1831 slave uprising in Virginia led by Nat Turner. Turner's rebellion instilled panic among white Southerners, leading to tighter control of African Americans and reconsideration of the institution of slavery. (p. 281)

National Association for the Advancement of Colored People (NAACP): Organization founded by W. E. B. Du Bois, Ida B. Wells, Jane Addams, and others in 1909 to fight for racial equality. The NAACP strategy focused on fighting discrimination through the courts. (p. 483)

National Energy Act: Legislation signed into law by President Jimmy Carter in 1978, which set gas emissions standards for automobiles and provided incentives for installing alternative energy systems, such as wind and solar power. (p. 699)

National Interstate and Defense Highway Act: 1956 act that provided funds for construction of 42,500 miles of roads throughout the United States. (p. 654)

National Labor Relations Act: 1935 act (also known as the Wagner Act) that created the National Labor Relations Board (NLRB). The NLRB protected workers' right to organize labor unions without owner interference. (p. 573)

National Organization for Women (NOW): Feminist organization formed in 1966 by Betty Friedan and like-minded activists. (p. 680)

National Origins Act: 1924 act establishing immigration quotas by national origin. The act was intended to severely limit immigration from southern and eastern Europe as well as prohibit all immigration from East Asia. (p. 545)

National Recovery Administration (NRA): New Deal agency established in 1933 to create codes to regulate production, prices, wages, hours, and collective bargaining. The NRA failed to produce the intended results and was eventually ruled unconstitutional. (p. 568)

National Republicans: *See* Democrats and National Republicans.

National Road: Road constructed using federal funds that ran from western Maryland through southwestern Pennsylvania to Wheeling, West Virginia; also called the Cumberland Road. Completed in 1818, the road was part of a larger push to improve the nation's infrastructure. (p. 207)

National Security Council (NSC): Council created by the 1947 National Security Act to advise the president on military and foreign affairs. The NSC consists of the national security adviser and the secretaries of state, defense, the army, the navy, and the air force. (p. 614)

National War Labor Board (NWLB): Government agency created in 1918 to settle labor disputes. The NWLB consisted of representatives from unions, corporations, and the public. (p. 519)

National War Labor Board: Taking the same name of its World War I predecessor, this World War II board was established in 1942 to oversee labor-management relations. The board regulated wages, hours, and working conditions and authorized the government to take over plants that refused to abide by its decisions. (p. 589)

nativism: The belief that foreigners pose a serious danger to a nation's society and culture. Nativist sentiment rose in the United States as the size and diversity of the immigrant population grew. (pp. 260, 460)

nativists: Anti-immigrant Americans who launched public campaigns against foreigners in the 1840s. Nativism emerged as a response to increased immigration to the United States in the 1830s and 1840s, particularly the large influx of Catholic immigrants. (p. 260)

Navigation Acts: Acts passed by Parliament in the 1650s and 1660s that prohibited smuggling, established guidelines for legal commerce, and set duties on trade items. In the 1760s, British authorities sought to enforce these laws fully, leading to resistance by colonists. (pp. 69, 122)

neoconservatives: Disillusioned liberals who condemned the Great Society programs they had originally supported. Neoconservatives were particularly concerned about affirmative action programs, the domination of campus discourse by New Left radicals, and left-wing criticism of the use of American military and economic might to advance U.S. interests overseas. (p. 709)

Neutrality Acts: Legislation passed between 1935 and 1937 to make it more difficult for the United States to become entangled in overseas conflicts. The Neutrality Acts reflected the strength of isolationist sentiment in 1930s America. (p. 584)

New Deal: The policies and programs that Franklin Roosevelt initiated to combat the Great Depression. The New Deal represented a dramatic expansion of the role of government in American society. (p. 566)

New Freedom: Term used by Woodrow Wilson to describe his limited-government, progressive agenda. Wilson's New Freedom was offered as an alternative to Theodore Roosevelt's New Nationalism. (p. 495)

New Frontier: President John F. Kennedy's domestic agenda. Kennedy promised to battle "tyranny, poverty, disease, and war," but, lacking strong majorities in Congress, he achieved relatively modest results. (p. 662)

New Jersey Plan: A proposal to the 1787 Constitutional Convention that highlighted the needs of small states by creating one legislative house in the federal government and granting each state equal representation in it. (p. 172)

New Light clergy: Colonial clergy who called for religious revivals and emphasized the emotional aspects of spiritual commitment. The New Lights were leaders in the Great Awakening. (p. 99)

New Look: The foreign policy strategy implemented by President Dwight Eisenhower that emphasized the development and deployment of nuclear weapons in an effort to cut military spending. (p. 625)

New Nationalism: Agenda articulated by Theodore Roosevelt in his 1912 presidential campaign. Roosevelt called for increased regulation of large corporations, a more active role for the president, and the extension of social justice using the power of the federal government. (p. 495)

New Negro: 1920s term for the second generation of African Americans born after emancipation and who stood up for their rights. (p. 542)

New Right: The conservative coalition of old and new conservatives, as well as disaffected Democrats. The New Right came to power with the election of Ronald Reagan in 1980. (p. 709)

New South: Term popularized by newspaper editor Henry Grady in the 1880s, a proponent of the modernization of the southern economy. Grady believed that industrial development would lead to the emergence of a "New South." (p. 405)

new woman: 1920s term for the modern, sexually liberated woman. The new woman, popularized in movies and magazines, flouted traditional morality. (p. 541)

Noble Order of the Knights of Labor: Labor organization founded in 1869 by Uriah Stephens. The Knights sought to include all workers in one giant union. (p. 433)

Non-Intercourse Act: Act passed by Congress in 1809 allowing Americans to trade with every nation except France and Britain. The act failed to stop the seizure of American ships or improve the economy. (p. 218)

North American Free Trade Agreement (NAFTA): Free trade agreement approved in 1993 by the United States, Canada, and Mexico. (p. 747)

North Atlantic Treaty Organization (NATO): Cold War military alliance intended to enhance the collective security of the United States and Western Europe. (p. 615)

Northwest Ordinance: Act of the confederation congress that provided for the survey, sale, and eventual division into states of the Northwest Territory. The 1787 act clarified the process by which territories could become states. (p. 165)

NSC-68: April 1950 National Security Council document that advocated the intensification of the policy of containment both at home and abroad. (p. 615)

nuclear freeze movement: 1980s protests calling for a mutual freeze on the testing, production, and deployment of nuclear weapons and of missiles and aircraft designed primarily to deliver nuclear weapons. (p. 727)

nullification: The doctrine that individual states have the right to declare federal laws unconstitutional and, therefore, void within their borders. South Carolina attempted to invoke the doctrine of nullification in response to the tariff of 1832. (p. 238)

Obergefell v. Hodges: The 2015 U.S. Supreme Court decision legalizing same-sex marriage throughout the nation. (p. 757)

Old Light clergy: Colonial clergy from established churches who supported the religious status quo in the early eighteenth century. (p. 99)

Open Door: 1899 policy in which Secretary of State John Hay informed the nations occupying China that the United States had the right of equal trade in China. (p. 512)

Operation Desert Storm: Code name of the 1991 allied air and ground military offensive that pushed Iraqi forces out of Kuwait. (p. 736)

Oregon Trail: The route west from the Missouri River to the Oregon Territory. By 1860, some 350,000 Americans had made the three- to six-month journey along the trail. (p. 302)

Organization of Petroleum Exporting Countries (OPEC): Organization formed by oil-producing countries to control the price and supply of oil on the global market. (p. 694)

Ostend Manifesto: This 1854 letter from U.S. ambassadors and the Secretary of State to President Franklin Pierce urged him to conquer Cuba. When it was leaked to the press, Northerners voiced outrage at what they saw as a plot to expand slave territories. (p. 311)

Palmer raids: Government roundup of some 6,000 suspected alien radicals in 1919–1920, ordered by Attorney General A. Mitchell Palmer and his assistant J. Edgar Hoover. The raids resulted in the deportation of 556 immigrants. (p. 531)

pandemic: A disease prevalent in a country, continent, or the world. Examples include the Black Death, the 1918 influenza pandemic, and the 2020 coronavirus pandemic. (pp. 9, 522, 766)

panic of 1819: The nation's first severe recession. This panic, which lasted for a decade in some areas, resulted from irresponsible banking practices, the declining European demand for American goods, and the expansion of settlement and slavery into Indian lands. (p. 228)

panic of 1837: Severe economic recession that began shortly after Martin Van Buren's presidential inauguration. The panic of 1837 started in the South and was rooted in the changing fortunes of American cotton in Great Britain. (p. 290)

Patient Protection and Affordable Care Act (Obamacare): Passed in 2010, this law expanded health insurance to millions of Americans previously uncovered through a variety of measures including extension of Medicaid, setting up of health-insurance exchanges, allowing children to remain under their parents' coverage until the age of twenty-six, and preventing insurance companies from excluding coverage based on pre-existing conditions. (p. 755)

patriarchal family: Model of the family in which fathers have absolute authority over wives, children, and servants. Most colonial Americans accepted the patriarchal model of the family, at least as an ideal. (p. 88)

Patriot Act: 2001 law passed in response to the September 11 terror attacks. It eased restrictions on domestic and foreign intelligence gathering and expanded governmental power to deport immigrants. (p. 751)

Peace of Paris: 1763 peace treaty that brought the Seven Years' War to a close. Under the terms of the treaty, Britain gained control of North America east of the Mississippi River and of present-day Canada. (p. 115)

Pendleton Civil Service Reform Act: 1883 act that required federal jobs to be awarded on the basis of merit through competitive exams rather than through political connections. (p. 471)

Pentagon Papers: Classified report on U.S. involvement in Vietnam leaked to the press in 1971. The report confirmed that the Kennedy and Johnson administrations had misled the public about the origins and nature of the Vietnam War. (p. 693)

Pequot War: 1636–1637 conflict between New England settlers, their Narragansett allies, and the Pequots. The English saw the Pequots as both a threat and an obstacle to further English expansion. (p. 49)

perestroika: Policy of economic "restructuring" initiated by Soviet leader Mikhail Gorbachev. Gorbachev hoped that by reducing state control he could revive the Soviet economy. (p. 728)

Personal Responsibility and Work Opportunity Reconciliation Act: 1996 act reforming the welfare system in the United States. The law required adults on the welfare rolls to find work within two years or lose their welfare benefits. (p. 746)

Petticoat Affair: 1829 political conflict over Andrew Jackson's appointment of John Eaton as secretary of war. Eaton was married to a woman of allegedly questionable character, and the wives of many prominent Washington politicians organized a campaign to snub her. (p. 238)

Pietists: German protestants who decried the power of established churches and urged individuals to follow their hearts rather than their heads in spiritual matters. Pietism had a profound influence on the leaders of the Great Awakening. (p. 99)

Pilgrims: Group of English religious dissenters who established a settlement at Plymouth, Massachusetts, in 1620. Unlike more mainstream Protestants, the Pilgrims were separatists who aimed to sever all connections with the Church of England. (p. 45)

Pinckney Treaty: 1796 treaty that defined the boundary between U.S. and Spanish territory in the South and opened the Mississippi River and New Orleans to U.S. shipping. (p. 182)

planters: Southern whites who owned the largest plantations and forged a distinct culture and economy around the institution of slavery. (p. 274)

Platt Amendment: 1901 act of Congress limiting Cuban sovereignty. American officials pressured Cuban leaders to incorporate the amendment into the Cuban constitution. (p. 509)

Plessy v. Ferguson: 1896 Supreme Court ruling that upheld the legality of Jim Crow legislation. The Court ruled that as long as states provided "equal but separate" facilities for whites and blacks, Jim Crow laws did not violate the equal protection clause of the Fourteenth Amendment. (p. 419)

political machine: Urban political organizations that dominated many late-nineteenth-century cities. Machines provided needed services to the urban poor, but they also fostered corruption, crime, and inefficiency. (p. 469)

Popular Front: A coalition formed in the mid-1930s of Communist Party members, New Deal liberals, unions, socialists, and civil rights advocates for social change rather than revolution. (p. 570)

Populists: The People's Party of America, formed in 1892. The Populists sought to appeal to both farmers and industrial workers. (p. 443)

Port Huron Statement: Students for a Democratic Society manifesto written in 1962 that condemned liberal politics, Cold War foreign policy, racism, and research-oriented universities. It called for the adoption of "participatory democracy." (p. 678)

Powhatan Confederacy: Large and powerful Indian confederation in Virginia. The Jamestown settlers had a complicated and contentious relationship with the leaders of the Powhatan Confederacy. (p. 37)

pragmatism: Philosophy that holds that truth can be discovered only through experience and that the value of ideas should be measured by their practical consequences. Pragmatism had a significant influence on the progressives. (p. 476)

Proclamation Line of 1763: Act of Parliament that restricted colonial settlement west of the Appalachian Mountains. The Proclamation Line sparked protests from rich and poor colonists alike. (p. 118)

Proclamation of Amnesty and Reconstruction: 1863 proclamation that established the basic parameters of President Abraham Lincoln's approach to

Reconstruction. Lincoln's plan would have readmitted the South to the Union on relatively lenient terms. (p. 355)

Progressive Party: Third party formed by Theodore Roosevelt in 1912 to facilitate his candidacy for president. Nicknamed the "Bull Moose Party," the Progressive Party split the Republican vote, allowing Democrat Woodrow Wilson to win the election. (p. 495)

proprietary colonies: Colonies granted to individuals, rather than held directly by the crown or given to chartered companies. Proprietors of such colonies, such as William Penn of Pennsylvania, had considerable leeway to distribute land and govern as they pleased. (p. 58)

Protestantism: Religious movement initiated in the early sixteenth century that resulted in a permanent division within European Christianity. Protestants differed with Catholics over the nature of salvation, the role of priests, and the organization of the church. (p. 30)

Pueblo revolt: 1680 uprising of Pueblo Indians against Spanish forces in New Mexico that led to the Spaniards' temporary retreat from the area. The uprising was sparked by mistreatment and the suppression of Indian culture and religion. (p. 60)

Pullman strike: 1894 strike by workers against the Pullman railcar company. When the strike disrupted rail service nationwide, threatening the delivery of the mail, President Grover Cleveland ordered federal troops to get the railroads moving again. (p. 437)

Puritans: Radical English Protestants who hoped to reform the Church of England. The first Puritan settlers in the Americas arrived in Massachusetts in 1630. (p. 46)

Reaganomics: Ronald Reagan's economic policies based on the theories of supply-side economists and centered on tax cuts and cuts to domestic programs. (p. 717)

Red scare: The fear of Communist-inspired radicalism in the wake of the Russian Revolution. The Red scare following World War I culminated in the Palmer raids on suspected radicals. (p. 530)

Redeemers: White, conservative Democrats who challenged and overthrew Republican rule in the South during Reconstruction. (p. 366)

redemptioners: Immigrants who borrowed money from shipping agents to cover the costs of transport to America, loans that were repaid, or "redeemed," by colonial employers. Redemptioners worked for their "redeemers" for a set number of years. (p. 74)

refugee communities: Settlements of formerly enslaved peoples during the Civil War. The Union recognized enslaved people who reached Union Army camps as contraband of war, but southern blacks turned these settlements into refugee communities to sustain themselves under desperate circumstances. (p. 342)

Regulators: Local organizations formed in North and South Carolina to protest and resist unpopular policies from 1766–1771. After first seeking redress through official institutions, Regulators went on to establish militias and other institutions of self-governance. (p. 128)

Renaissance: The cultural and intellectual flowering that began in Italy in the fifteenth century and then spread north. The Renaissance occurred at the same time that European rulers were pushing for greater political unification of their states. (p. 10)

republican motherhood: In the 1790s, some leaders supported women's education so that they could instruct their sons in principles of republican government. (p. 170)

Republican Party: Party formed in 1854 that was committed to stopping the expansion of slavery and advocated economic development and internal improvements. Although their appeal was limited to the North, the Republicans quickly became a major political force. (p. 314)

Roe v. Wade: The 1973 Supreme Court opinion that affirmed a woman's constitutional right to abortion. (p. 681)

Roosevelt Corollary: 1904 addition to the Monroe Doctrine that affirmed the right of the United States to intervene in the internal affairs of Caribbean and Latin American countries to preserve order and protect American interests. (p. 512)

Sacco and Vanzetti case: 1920 case in which Nicola Sacco and Bartolomeo Vanzetti were convicted of robbery and murder. The trial centered on the defendants' foreign birth and political views, rather than the facts pertaining to their guilt or innocence. (p. 545)

Sanctuary Movement: A network of religious groups that provided asylum for undocumented immigrants from Central America in the 1980s. (p. 715)

SALT II: 1979 strategic arms limitation treaty agreed on by President Jimmy Carter and Soviet leader Leonid Brezhnev. After the Soviet Union invaded Afghanistan, Carter persuaded the Senate not to ratify the treaty. (p. 701)

scalawags: Derisive term for white Southerners who supported Reconstruction. (p. 364)

Scottsboro Nine: Nine African American youths convicted of raping two white women in Scottsboro, Alabama, in 1931. The Communist Party played a key role in defending the Scottsboro Nine and in bringing national and international attention to their case. (p. 561)

Second Continental Congress: Assembly of colonial representatives that served as a national government during the Revolutionary War. Despite limited formal powers, the Continental Congress coordinated the war effort and conducted negotiations with outside powers. (p. 138)

second front: The invasion by U.S., British, and Canadian forces into German-occupied France to take pressure off the Soviet forces fighting the Germans on the eastern front. Josef Stalin had called for the invasion in 1942. The attack in western Europe did not begin until 1944, fostering resentment in Stalin. (p. 597)

Second Great Awakening: Evangelical revival movement that began in the South in the early nineteenth century and then spread to the North. The social and economic changes of the first half of the nineteenth century were a major spur to religious revivals, which in turn spurred social reform movements. (p. 255)

second industrial revolution: Revolution in technology and productivity that reshaped the American economy in the early twentieth century. (p. 536)

Second Party System: When the Whig Party formed in 1834, they posed the first significant challenge to Democratic Party control in two decades. (p. 285)

Second Seminole War: 1835–1842 war between the Seminoles, including fugitive slaves who had joined the tribe, and the U.S. government over whether the Seminoles would be forced to leave Florida and settle west of the Mississippi River. Despite substantial investments of men, money, and resources, it took seven years for the United States to achieve victory. (p. 287)

Sedition Act: 1918 act appended to the Espionage Act. It punished individuals for expressing opinions deemed hostile to the U.S. government, flag, or military. (p. 521)

Servicemen's Readjustment Act (GI Bill): 1944 act that offered educational opportunities and financial aid to veterans as they readjusted to civilian life. Known as the GI Bill, the law helped millions of veterans build new lives after the war. (p. 635)

settlement houses: Community centers established by urban reformers in the late nineteenth century. Settlement house organizers resided in the institutions they created and were often female, middle-class, and college educated. (p. 471)

sharecropping: A system that emerged as the dominant mode of agricultural production in the South in the years after the Civil War. Under the sharecropping system, sharecroppers received tools and supplies from landowners in exchange for a share of the eventual harvest. (p. 365)

Shays's Rebellion: 1786 rebellion by western Massachusetts farmers caused primarily by economic turmoil in the aftermath of the Revolutionary War. (p. 171)

Sherman Antitrust Act: 1890 act that outlawed monopolies that prevented free competition in interstate commerce. (p. 409)

Sherman's March to the Sea: Hard war tactics employed by General William Tecumseh Sherman to capture Atlanta and huge swaths of Georgia and the Carolinas, devastating this crucial region of the Confederacy in 1864. (p. 343)

siege of Vicksburg: After a prolonged siege, Union troops forced Confederate forces to surrender at Vicksburg, Mississippi, leading to Union control of the rich Mississippi River valley. (p. 340)

sit-down strike: A strike in which workers occupy their place of employment. In 1937 the United Auto Workers conducted sit-down strikes in Flint, Michigan, against General Motors to gain union recognition, higher wages, and better working conditions. The union won its demands. (p. 574)

skilled workers: Workers with particular training and skills. Skilled workers were paid more and were more difficult for owners to replace than unskilled workers. (p. 430)

skyscrapers: Buildings more than ten stories high that first appeared in U.S. cities in the late nineteenth century. Urban crowding and high prices for land stimulated the drive to construct taller buildings. (p. 465)

slave laws: A series of laws that defined slavery as a distinct status based on racial identity and which passed that status on through future generations. (p. 78)

Social Darwinism: The belief associated with the late nineteenth and early twentieth centuries and popularized by Herbert Spencer, that drew upon some of the ideas of Charles Darwin. Stressing individual competition and the survival of the fittest, Social Darwinism was used to justify economic inequality, racism, imperialism, and hostility to federal government regulation. (p. 412)

social gospel: Religious movement that advocated the application of Christian teachings to social and economic problems. The ideals of the social gospel inspired many progressive reformers. (p. 476)

Social Security Act: Landmark 1935 act that created retirement pensions for most Americans, as well as unemployment insurance. (p. 572)

Solidarity: Polish trade union movement led by Lech Walesa. During the 1980s, Solidarity played a central role in ending Communist rule in Poland. (p. 730)

Sons of Liberty: Boston organization first formed to protest the Stamp Act. The Sons of Liberty spread to other colonies and played an important role in the unrest leading to the American Revolution. (p. 124)

Southern Christian Leadership Conference (SCLC): Organization founded in 1957 by Martin Luther King Jr. and other black ministers to encourage nonviolent protests against racial segregation and disfranchisement in the South. (p. 649)

spoils system: Patronage system introduced by Andrew Jackson in which federal offices were awarded on the basis of political loyalty. The system remained in place until the late nineteenth century. (p. 238)

Stamp Act: 1765 act of Parliament that imposed a duty on all transactions involving paper items. The Stamp Act prompted widespread, coordinated protests and was eventually repealed. (p. 124)

Stonewall riots: The 1969 violence between gays and New York City police after the police raided the Stonewall Inn, a gay bar in Greenwich Village whose patrons fought the police in response to harassment. This encounter helped launch the gay liberation movement. (p. 684)

Stono rebellion: 1739 uprising by enslaved Africans and African Americans in South Carolina. In the aftermath of the uprising, white fear of slave revolts intensified. (p. 79)

Strategic Arms Limitation Treaty (SALT I): 1972 agreement between the United States and Soviet Union to curtail nuclear arms production during the Cold War. The pact froze for five years the number of antiballistic missiles (ABMs), intercontinental ballistic missiles (ICBMs), and submarine-based missiles that each nation could deploy. (p. 694)

Student Nonviolent Coordinating Committee (SNCC): Civil rights organization that grew out of the sit-ins of 1960. The organization focused on taking direct action and political organizing to achieve its goals. (p. 650)

Students for a Democratic Society (SDS): Student activist organization formed in the early 1960s that advocated the formation of a "New Left" that would overturn the social and political status quo. (p. 678)

subtreasury system: A proposal by the Farmers' Alliances in the 1880s for the federal government to extend loans to farmers and store their crops in warehouses until prices rose and they could buy back and sell their crops to repay their debts. (p. 442)

suffragists: Supporters of voting rights for women. Campaigns for women's suffrage gained strength in the late nineteenth and early twentieth centuries and culminated in ratification of the Nineteenth Amendment in 1920. (p. 479)

Sugar Act: 1764 act of Parliament that imposed an import tax on sugar, coffee, wines, and other luxury items. The Sugar Act sparked colonial protests that would escalate over time as new revenue measures were enacted. (p. 123)

Sun Belt: The southern and western part of the United States. After World War II, millions of Americans moved to the Sun Belt, drawn by the region's climate and jobs in the defense, petroleum, and chemical industries. (p. 640)

sweatshops: Small factories or shops in which workers toiled under adverse conditions. Business owners, particularly in the garment industry, turned tenement apartments into sweatshops. (p. 467)

systemic racism: A form of racism that is embedded in U.S. legal, cultural, political, and economic institutions as a result of the history of enslavement and Jim Crow. It results in discrimination in criminal justice, employment, housing, health care, voting, and education. Also known as institutional racism. (p. 657)

Taft-Hartley Act: 1947 law that curtailed unions' ability to organize. It prevented unions from barring employment to non-union members and authorized the federal government to halt a strike for eighty days if it interfered with the national interest. (p. 636)

Tariff of Abominations: White Southerners' name for the 1828 Congressional tariff act that benefited northern manufacturers and merchants at the expense of agriculture, especially southern plantations. (p. 238)

Tea Party movement: A loose coalition of conservative and libertarian forces that arose around 2008. Generally working within the Republican Party, the Tea Party advocates small government, low taxes, and reduced federal deficits. (p. 756)

Teapot Dome scandal: Oil and land scandal during the Warren Harding administration that highlighted the close ties between big business and the federal government in the early 1920s. (p. 534)

Tejanos: Mexican residents of Texas. Although some Tejano elites allied themselves with American settlers, most American settlers resisted the adoption of Tejano culture. (p. 286)

Teller Amendment: Amendment to the 1898 declaration of war against Spain stipulating that Cuba should be free and independent. The amendment was largely ignored in the aftermath of America's victory. (p. 508)

temperance: The movement to moderate and then ban the sale and consumption of alcohol. The American temperance movement emerged in the early nineteenth century as part of the larger push for improving society from the 1820s to the 1850s. (p. 256)

tenements: Multifamily apartment buildings that housed many poor urban dwellers at the turn of the twentieth century. Tenements were crowded, uncomfortable, and dangerous. (p. 466)

Tennessee Valley Authority (TVA): New Deal agency that brought low-cost electricity to rural Americans and redeveloped the Tennessee River valley through flood-control projects. The agency built, owned, and supervised a number of power plants and dams. (p. 567)

Tenure of Office Act: Law passed by Congress in 1867 to prevent President Andrew Johnson from removing cabinet members sympathetic to the Republican Party's approach to congressional Reconstruction without Senate approval. Johnson was impeached, but not convicted, for violating the act. (p. 360)

Tet Offensive: January 31, 1968, offensive mounted by Vietcong and North Vietnamese forces against population centers in South Vietnam. The offensive was turned back, but it shocked many Americans and increased public opposition to the war. (p. 675)

Thirteenth Amendment: Amendment to the Constitution abolishing slavery. The Thirteenth Amendment was passed in January 1865 and sent to the states for ratification. (pp. 345, 356)

three-fifths compromise: Compromise between northern and southern delegates to the 1787 Constitutional Convention to count enslaved persons as three-fifths of a free person in apportioning representation in the House of Representatives and taxation by the federal government. (p. 173)

***To Secure These Rights*:** Report issued by President Harry Truman's Committee on Civil Rights in 1947 that advocated extending racial equality. Among its recommendations was the desegregation of the military, which Truman instituted by executive order in 1948. (p. 647)

Townshend Act: 1767 act of Parliament that instituted an import tax on a range of items including glass, lead, paint, paper, and tea. The Townshend Act prompted a boycott of British goods and contributed to violence between British soldiers and colonists. (p. 126)

Trail of Tears: The forced march of some 15,000 Cherokees from Georgia to Indian Territory. Inadequate planning, food, water, sanitation, and medicine led to the deaths of thousands of Cherokees. (p. 289)

transcendentalism: A movement founded by Ralph Waldo Emerson in the 1830s that proposed that individuals look inside themselves and to nature for spiritual and moral guidance rather than to the dogmas of formal religion. Transcendentalism attracted a number of important American writers and artists to its vision. (p. 258)

transcontinental railroad: A railroad linking the East and West Coasts of North America. Completed in 1869, the transcontinental railroad facilitated the flow of migrants and the development of economic connections between the West and the East. (p. 376)

Treaty of Fort Laramie: 1851 treaty that sought to confine tribes on the northern plains to designated areas in an attempt to keep white settlers from encroaching on their land. In 1868, the second Treaty of Fort Laramie gave northern tribes control over the "Great Reservation" in parts of present-day Montana, Wyoming, North Dakota, and South Dakota. (p. 380)

Treaty of Fort Stanwix: 1784 treaty in which U.S. commissioners coerced Iroquois delegates into ceding vast tracts of land in western New York and the Ohio River Valley to the United States. (p. 165)

Treaty of Ghent: Accord signed in December 1814 ending the War of 1812 and returning to U.S. and Britain the lands each controlled before the war. (p. 222)

Treaty of Greenville: 1795 treaty signed following the Battle of Fallen Timbers through which Indians in the Northwest Territory were forced to cede vast tracts of land to the United States. (p. 181)

Treaty of Guadalupe Hidalgo: 1848 treaty ending the Mexican-American War. By the terms of the treaty, the United States acquired control over Texas north and east of the Rio Grande plus the New Mexico territory, which included present-day Arizona and New Mexico and parts of Utah, Nevada, and Colorado. The treaty also ceded Alta California, which had declared itself an independent republic during the war, to the United States. (p. 295)

Treaty of Medicine Lodge: 1867 treaty that provided reservation lands for the Comanche, Kiowa-Apache, and Southern Arapaho to settle. Despite this agreement, white hunters soon invaded this territory and decimated the buffalo herd. (p. 380)

Treaty of New Echota: 1836 treaty in which a group of Cherokee men agreed to exchange their land in the Southeast for money and land in Indian Territory. Despite the fact that the treaty was obtained without tribal sanction, it was approved by the U.S. Congress. (p. 288)

Treaty (Peace) of Paris: 1783 treaty that formally ended the conflict between Britain and its North American colonies. The newly established United States gained benefits from the treaty. (p. 157)

Treaty of Versailles: Signed in 1919, this treaty officially ended World War I. President Woodrow Wilson went to France and played a major role in drafting the treaty, which established a League of Nations to prevent future wars. However, the U.S. Senate refused to ratify the treaty. (p. 524)

Triangle Shirtwaist Company: Site of an infamous industrial fire in New York City in 1911. Inadequate fire safety provisions in the factory led to the deaths of 146 workers. (p. 467)

Truman Doctrine: U.S. pledge to contain the expansion of communism around the world. Based on the idea of containment, the Truman Doctrine was the cornerstone of American foreign policy throughout the Cold War. (p. 613)

trust: Business monopolies formed in the late nineteenth and early twentieth centuries through mergers and consolidation that inhibited competition and controlled the market. (p. 409)

Tulsa Massacre: The invasion in 1921 by a mob of over 2,000 armed white supremacists into the African American Greenwood neighborhood of Tulsa,

Oklahoma. The mob killed twenty-six blacks and burned down businesses and homes. (p. 533)

Tuscarora War: War launched by Tuscarora Indians from 1711 to 1715 against European settlers in North Carolina and their allies from the Yamasee, Catawba, and Cherokee nations. The Tuscaroras forfeited their lands when they signed the peace treaty and many then joined the Iroquois Confederacy to the north. (p. 65)

Tuskegee Institute: African American educational institute founded in 1881 by Booker T. Washington. Following Washington's philosophy, the Tuskegee Institute focused on teaching industrious habits and practical job skills. (p. 482)

U.S. Immigration and Customs Enforcement (ICE): Federal agency created in 2003 under the Department of Homeland Security. It is used to keep undocumented immigrants from entering the United States and deporting those who do enter illegally. (p. 765)

U.S. Sanitary Commission: Federal organization established in June 1861 to improve and coordinate the medical care of Union soldiers. Northern women played a key role in the work of the commission. (p. 334)

Uncle Tom's Cabin: Novel published in 1852 by Harriet Beecher Stowe. Meant to publicize the evils of slavery, the novel struck an emotional chord in the North and was an international best seller. (p. 312)

underground railroad: A series of routes from southern plantation areas to northern free states and Canada along which abolitionist supporters, known as conductors, provided hiding places and transportation for runaway slaves seeking freedom. (p. 264)

unions: Groups of workers seeking rights and benefits from their employers through their collective efforts. (p. 433)

Universal Negro Improvement Association (UNIA): Organization founded by Marcus Garvey in 1914 to promote black self-help, pan-Africanism, and racial separatism. (p. 542)

unskilled workers: Workers with little or no specific expertise. Unskilled workers, many of whom were immigrants, made up the vast majority of the late-nineteenth-century industrial workforce. (p. 429)

utopian societies: Communities formed in the first half of the nineteenth century to embody alternative social and economic visions and to create models for society at large to follow. (p. 261)

Valley Forge: Site of Continental Army winter encampment in 1777–1778. Despite the harsh conditions, the Continental Army emerged from its encampment at Valley Forge as a more effective fighting force. (p. 148)

vertical integration: The control of all elements in a supply chain by a single firm. For example, Andrew Carnegie, a vertically integrated steel producer, sought to own suppliers of all the raw materials used in steel production. (p. 407)

Vietcong: The popular name for the National Liberation Front (NLF) in South Vietnam, which was formed in 1959. The Vietcong waged a military insurgency against the U.S.-backed president, Ngo Dinh Diem, and received support from Ho Chi Minh, the leader of North Vietnam. (p. 630)

Vietnamization: President Richard Nixon's strategy of turning over greater responsibility for the fighting of the Vietnam War to the South Vietnamese army. (p. 692)

Virginia and Kentucky Resolutions: Resolutions passed by legislatures in Virginia and Kentucky that declared the Alien and Sedition Acts (1798) "void and of no force" in their states. (p. 185)

Virginia Plan: Plan put forth at the beginning of the 1787 Constitutional Convention that introduced the ideas of a strong central government, a bicameral legislature, and a system of representation based on population. (p. 172)

Voting Rights Act: 1965 act that eliminated many of the obstacles to African American voting in the South and resulted in dramatic increases in black participation in the electoral process. (p. 668)

Walking Purchase: 1737 treaty that allowed Pennsylvania to expand its boundaries at the expense of the Delaware Indians. The treaty, quite possibly a forgery, allowed the British to add territory that could be walked off in a day and a half. (p. 97)

War Industries Board (WIB): Government commission created in 1917 to supervise the purchase of military supplies and oversee the conversion of the economy to meet wartime demands. The WIB embodied a government-business partnership that lasted beyond World War I. (p. 519)

War of the Spanish Succession: 1702–1713 war over control of Spain and its colonies; also called Queen Anne's War. Although the Treaty of Utrecht that ended the war in 1713 was intended to bring peace through the establishment of a balance of power, imperial conflict continued to escalate. (p. 63)

War Powers Act: 1973 act that required the president to consult with Congress within forty-eight hours of deploying military forces and to obtain a declaration of war from Congress if troops remained on foreign soil beyond sixty days. (p. 693)

War Production Board: Board established in 1942 to oversee the economy during World War II. The War Production Board was part of a larger effort to convert American industry to the production of war materials. (p. 588)

Watergate: Scandal and cover-up that forced the resignation of Richard Nixon in 1974. The scandal revolved around a break-in at Democratic Party headquarters in 1972 and subsequent efforts to conceal the administration's involvement in the break-in. (p. 696)

Whig Party: Political party formed in the 1830s to challenge the power of the Democratic Party. The Whigs attempted to forge a diverse coalition from around the country by promoting commercial interests and moral reforms. (p. 285)

Whiskey Rebellion: Uprising by western Pennsylvania farmers who led protests against the excise tax on whiskey in the early 1790s. (p. 180)

white supremacy: An ideology promoted by southern planters and intellectuals that maintained that all whites, regardless of class or education, were superior to all blacks. (p. 285)

Wilmot Proviso: 1846 proposal by Democratic congressman David Wilmot of Pennsylvania to outlaw slavery in all territory acquired from Mexico. The proposal was defeated, but the fight over its adoption foreshadowed the sectional conflicts of the 1850s. (p. 296)

Woman's Christian Temperance Union (WCTU): Organization founded in 1874 to campaign for a ban on the sale and consumption of alcohol. In the late nineteenth century, under Frances Willard's leadership, the WCTU supported a broad social reform agenda. (p. 485)

Women's National Loyal League: Organization founded by abolitionist women during the Civil War to press Lincoln and Congress to enact universal emancipation. (p. 337)

Works Progress Administration (WPA): New Deal agency established in 1935 to put unemployed Americans to work on public projects ranging from construction to the arts. (p. 571)

XYZ affair: 1798 incident in which French agents demanded bribes before meeting with American diplomatic representatives. (p. 184)

Yalta Agreement: Agreement negotiated at the 1945 Yalta Conference by Roosevelt, Churchill, and Stalin about the fate of postwar eastern Europe. The Yalta Agreement did little to ease growing tensions between the Soviet Union and its Western allies. (p. 601)

Yamasee War: A pan-Indian war from 1715 to 1717 led by the Yamasee who intended, but failed, to oust the British from South Carolina. (p. 65)

yellow journalism: Sensationalist news accounts meant to provoke an emotional response in readers. Yellow journalism contributed to the growth of public support for American intervention in Cuba in 1898. (p. 507)

yeomen farmers: Southern independent landowners who did not own slaves. Although yeomen farmers had connections to the South's plantation economy, many realized that their interests were not always identical to those of the planter elite. (p. 283)

Young Americans for Freedom (YAF): A group of young conservatives from college campuses formed in 1960 in Sharon, Connecticut. The group favored free market principles, states' rights, and anticommunism. (p. 685)

Zimmermann telegram: 1917 telegram in which Germany offered Mexico an alliance in the event that the United States entered World War I. The telegram's publication in American newspapers helped build public support for war. (p. 516)

zoot suit riots: Series of riots in 1943 in Los Angeles, California, sparked by white hostility toward Mexican Americans. White sailors attacked Mexican American teenagers who dressed in zoot suits — suits with long jackets with padded shoulders and baggy pants tapered at the bottom. (p. 594)

Index

Letters in parentheses following page numbers refer to figures *(f)*, illustrations *(i)*, maps *(m)*, and tables *(t)*.

Abenaki people, 113
Abernathy, Ralph, 682*(i)*
Abolitionism, 263–269
    antislavery parties and, 268
    beginnings of, 263–265
    Civil War, 329
    Douglass in, 326
    Finney in, 245
    Fugitive Slave Act and, 309
    gag rule on, 265, 286
    gradual, 234
    growth of, 265–266
    Harpers Ferry raid and, 316–319
    literature in, 312
    Missouri statehood and, 218
    Mormons in, 257
    planters' efforts to unify southern whites
        against, 284–285
    Post in, 245
    Quakers in, 168
    Republican Party and, 314, 319
    universal suffrage and, 361–363
    women's rights and, 266–268
Abortion
    birth control and, 486
    Bush, George H. W., on, 729
    Christian Right on, 710
    in colonial era, 84
    New Right and, 720
    Roe v. Wade and, 681, 704, 720, 763
Abraham Lincoln Brigade, 584
Abrams v. United States, 530
Accommodation, 483
Acheson, Dean, 616, 618
Achille Lauro (ship), 725
Acoma people, 32*(i)*
Acquired immune deficiency syndrome
    (AIDS), 720, 734
"Acres of Diamonds" (Conwell), 411
Act of Religious Toleration (1649), 41
Adams, Abigail, 170

Adams, John
    as ambassador, 160
    Declaration of Independence and, 140–141
    judges appointed by, 201
    in peace term negotiations, 157
    as president, 183–185
    as vice president, 175
    on Washington, D.C., 197
Adams, John Quincy, 225, 234–235
    Amistad mutiny and, 282
    election of 1828, 235–236
    Jackson and, 237
Adams, Samuel, 124, 126
    Boston Massacre and, 127
    in Continental Congress, 131
    "Rights of the Colonies," 129
Adamson Act (1916), 493*(t)*
Adams-Onis Treaty (1819), 225
Adams-Onis Treaty line, 205*(m)*
Addams, Jane, 477–479, 483, 509
Adding machines, 404
Adventures of Ozzie and Harriet, The (TV
    show), 641
Advertising
    effect of, on social conventions, 540
    in twenties, 536, 537*(i)*
Advocate of Moral Reform, The, 259
Affirmative action, 673*(t)*, 684
    controversy over, 706
    Nixon and, 695
Affluent Society, The (Galbraith), 662
Afghanistan
    air strikes against, 748
    mujahideen assisted in, 701–702, 702*(i)*,
        726*(m)*
    Obama on, 760
    Soviet withdrawal from, 731
Africa
    AIDS in, 734
    Back to Africa movement, 542
    in Columbian exchange, 17–18, 18*(m)*

Africa (*Continued*)
  immigrants from, 745(*f*)
  Portuguese trade with, 10–11
  resettlement of blacks in, 195
  slave trade, 9, 11–13
  trade with, 67
  World War II in, 597
African Americans
  in American Revolution, 136–137,
      140–141, 143–144, 144(*i*), 157
  Beat culture and, 645–646
  black nationalism and, 542–544, 543(*i*)
  buffalo soldiers, 382
  citizenship of, 370, 459
  after the Civil War, 344
  in Civil War, 326–327, 329–332, 342–344
  Civil War death rates of, 334
  in Civil War draft riots, 338
  colonial era, 95
  colonial fertility rates among, 90
  cowboys, 398
  cultural divisions and, 246
  cultural influence of, 657
  culture of, 280–281, 297
  depictions of, in early republic, 195
  economic opportunities for, 364–366
  education of, 195, 354, 483
  election of 1960, 656, 656(*m*)
  employment of women, 430
  excluded from Social Security, 573
  Exodusters, 365
  Freedmen's Bureau and, 370
  freedom of religion and, 354–355
  in Gilded Age, 414
  in Great Depression, 560–561, 563
  great migration of, 532
  Harlem Renaissance and, 541–542
  housing segregation and, 640
  identity of, 461
  Irish immigrants in conflict with,
      249–250
  as itinerant musicians, 440
  Jim Crow and, 396, 418–420
  in Korean War, 617(*i*)
  lynchings of, 419, 477, 482, 561
  migration north by, 429, 472
  minstrel shows and, 248
  New Deal and, 573–576
  police shootings of, 759
  political participation of, 364–366
  Populists and, 448

  post-Revolution struggle of for rights,
      168–169
  progressivism and, 476, 478, 482–483, 498
  religion and, 98, 101, 168, 465
  in religious renewal of the 18th century,
      194
  Republican Party and, 423
  resettlement of, in Africa, 195
  in rock 'n' roll, 643
  in Second Great Awakening, 256
  sharecropping and, 365
  in social reform movements, 259
  in Spanish-American War, 507
  Square Deal and, 493
  systemic racism and, 759
  in teenage culture, 643
  on television, 642
  in unions, 433
  in urbanization, 249, 463–465
  violence against, 232–233, 350, 366–367,
      419, 529, 532
  voting rights for, 232, 361–363
  in western cities, 463
  in western migration, 306
  westward migration of after World War II,
      652
  in Wilmington, North Carolina massacre,
      447(*i*)
  Wilson supported by, 497
  women, in workforce, 644
  women, rights and roles of, 170
  women's clubs, 478
  women's suffrage and, 479, 480(*m*)
  in World War I, 521
  in World War II, 589, 592–593
  YMCA/YWCA and, 416
African Methodist Episcopal Church, 168,
      196, 234, 465
Agent Orange, 675
Agnew, Spiro, 695–697
Agricultural Adjustment Act (1933), 567,
      572(*t*), 575
Agricultural Marketing Act (1929), 557
Agriculture
  African, 11
  braceros in, 593
  in Civil War, 339
  colonial era, 75–77
  Columbian exchange in, 17–18, 18(*m*)
  commercial, in West, 388–394
  cotton production and, 210–213

debt in, 441
development of, 9–10
Dust Bowl and, 560
family labor in, 89, 89(i)
farmer organization and, 441–443
French Revolution and, 179
Granger movement in, 441–443
in Great Depression, 557, 561–563
Great Plains, 376, 392–394, 397
horticulture as, 3–4
industrialization and, 406
Japanese immigrants in, 454
market revolution and, 246
Mayan, 5
Mediterranean, 9
Mexican Americans in, 655, 682
migrant laborers in, 562
New Deal and, 567
in New South, 406
in North vs. South, 328
organized protests in, 563–565
plantation, 226–227
political crises from indebted farmers in,
    170–171
population growth and, 206
Populists and, 447
production levels in, 441
after the Revolution, 162
sharecropping, 365
Shays's Rebellion and, 163
soil exhaustion and, 238
southern, 226–227
technology in, 208–209, 389
transportation improvements and, 247
unions in, 438
Whiskey Rebellion and, 180
after World War I, 537, 540
yeomen farmers and westward
    migration, 206
Aguinaldo, Emilio, 510
AIDS (acquired immune deficiency
    syndrome), 720, 734
Aid to Families with Dependent Children,
    718, 746
Air controllers strike, 719
Air Quality Act (1965), 673(t)
Alabama
    black majority in, 364
    desegregation blocked in, 665
    Freedom Rides in, 664
    Freedom Summer in, 667

lumber industry in, 406
readmitted to the Union, 360
resistance to desegregation in, 650
Scottsboro Nine, 561
secession of, 320
slavery in, 278(m)
statehood of, 212
steel industry in, 406
Alamance Creek, Battle of, 128
Alamo, 286
Alarcón, Hernando de, 22(m)
Alaska
    coal mining in, 494
    Exxon Valdez oil spill, 729–730
    gold discoveries in, 447
    women's suffrage in, 479
Alaska, settlement of, 3, 4(m)
Al-Assad, Bashar, 762
Albany, Georgia, 665
Albany Congress, 112
Albuquerque Journal, 715
Alcatraz occupation, 683
Alcoholism, immigrants and, 458
Aleut people, 3
Alger, Horatio, 411, 424
Algeria, in World War II, 597
Algonquian Indians, 35, 42
Alien Act (1798), 184
Alien and Sedition Acts (1798), 185
Alien Land Law (1913), 653
Al Jazeera, 734
Allen, Ethan, 119, 138
Allen, Richard, 169, 195
Allende, Salvador, 694
Alliance for Progress, 664
Allies (World War I), 513–518, 517(m)
Allies (World War II), 583
All in the Family (TV show), 703
All Quiet on the Western Front (Remarque), 583
Almshouses, 260
Al-Qadaffi, Muammar, 725
Al-Qaeda, 731, 748, 769
    9/11 attacks by, 743
    Hussein linked to, 752
    in Iraq War, 752
Amalgamated Association of Iron and Steel
    Workers, 427, 436
Amalgamated Copper Company, 387
Amazon, 744
America, naming of, 2, 16
America First, 763

America First Committee, 585
America First Movement, 595
American Academy of Arts and Sciences, 194
American and Foreign Anti-Slavery Society, 267
American Anti-Slavery Society (AASS), 264, 267, 325, 362
American Broadcasting Company (ABC), 634
American Broadcasting System (ABS), 641
American Civil Liberties Union (ACLU), 531, 548
American Colonization Society (ACS), 196
American Commonwealth, The (Bryce), 420
American Dictionary of the English Language (Webster), 191
American Duties Act (England, 1764), 123
American Economic Association, 415*(t)*
American Enterprise Institute, 710
American Equal Rights Association, 362
American Expeditionary Forces (AEF), 516–517
American Federation of Labor (AFL), 435, 556, 573
American Historical Association, 415*(t)*
American Indian Movement (AIM), 683
American Indians, 3–8, 494, 546
    in American Revolution, 141, 146, 152
    assimilation of, 384–385, 575–576
    bison and, 306, 379*(m)*, 380
    British conflicts with, 116–119, 117*(m)*
    casinos, 760
    citizenship of, 459, 547
    civilizations of, 378–380, 379*(m)*
    in Civil War, 329–332, 344
    colonial expansion and conflict with, 96*(m)*, 96–98
    Columbian exchange with, 17–18, 18*(m)*, 25
    conflicts in New England, 49, 52
    Continental Congress and, 152
    cotton cultivation by, 212
    cultural diversity among, 3–5, 8*(m)*
    defeat of, 382–383
    depictions of in early republic, 193, 195
    Dutch colonization and, 35–36
    education of, 195, 383
    encomienda and, 14
    English colonies and, 38
    enslavement and torture of, 24, 65
    epidemics among, 378–379
    expansion and conflict with, 165–167

federal policy on, 380–381, 383–384
French trade and conflict with, 33–35
frontier colleges and, 192
frontier conflicts with, 116–119, 117*(m)*, 178
gold rush and, 303
Great Awakening and, 101
imperialism toward, 503
inclusion of, 218
Indian Wars, 112–114, 115*(m)*, 116–119
Jackson and, 225, 237, 239–240
Kansas-Nebraska Act and, 313
land cessions by, 205*(m)*
land treaties with, 165
Lewis and Clark expedition aided by, 190
liberation movement of, 683
mapmaking by, 16–17
measles and, 305
migration of, to Americas, 3–4, 4*(m)*
New Deal and, 575–576, 576*(i)*, 655
northern, 6–8
Northwest Ordinance on, 165, 167
pan-Indian alliances among, 181, 182*(m)*
praying towns and, 47
progressivism and, 484, 498
Prophetstown and, 219
relocated from reservations, 655
removal of, 239–240, 287–289, 288*(m)*
resistance to European encroachment, 63–66, 64*(m)*
resistance to Western settlement, 378–385
Santa Fe Trail and, 223
slavery among, 306
Supreme Court rulings, 760
on television, 642
terrorization of, 344
under Eisenhower, 654–655
voting rights of, 232
in War of 1812, 220*(m)*, 221
western settlement and, 304–306, 305*(m)*
westward migration and, 204, 205*(m)*, 206
women, rights and roles of, 170
women's suffrage and, 480*(m)*
in World War I, 521
in World War II, 592, 594
Americanization, 546–547
American League of Baseball, 418
American Liberty League, 569
American Mathematical Society, 415*(t)*
American Medical Association, 486
American Mercury, The (magazine), 541

American Party, 313–315
American Philosophical Society, 194
American Plan, 534
American Protective Association, 460
American Protective League (APL), 520(i)
American Railway Union, 437
American Red Cross, 415, 415(t)
American Revolution (1775–1783), 135–161
    choosing sides in, 141–144
    commitment to independence in, 143–144
    debt after, 164, 167, 177, 179
    Declaration of Independence in, 140–141
    eruption of armed conflict, 137–139
    fighting in, 144–149, 147(m), 152
    financing, 152
    France in, 146, 148, 151
    governing during, 149–153
    legacies of, 159–160
    neutral parties in, 143
    in North, 146, 147(m)
    peace after, 157
    slavery question in, 150–151
    Southern fighting in, 155–157
    victory in, 158–159
    Western fighting in, 154(m)
    women in, 136–137
American Smelting and Refining Company,
    387
American Spelling Book (Webster), 191
Americans with Disabilities Act (1990), 729
American System, 223
American system of manufacturing, 209
American Telephone and Telegraph Company
    (AT&T), 404
American Temperance Society, 261
American Union Telegraph Company, 408
American Woman Suffrage Association, 479
American Women, 680
AME Zion Church, 465
Amherst, Jeffrey, 114
Amish, neutrality of in American Revolution,
    143
Amistad, 282
Amos'n' Andy Show, The (TV show), 541, 642
Amusement parks, 440
Anarchists, 434, 437, 531
Anasazi people, 8(m)
Ancient Society (Morgan), 383
Anderson, John, 716, 717(m)
Anderson, Marion, 574
Andersonville Prison, 366

Angel Island, 454
Anglicanism, 31
Anglo-Saxons, 505
Anthony, Susan B., 337, 362, 362(i), 479
Anthropology, on Indians, 484, 541
Anti-authoritarianism, 140
Antietam, battle of (1862), 330,
    331(m), 333
Antifederalists, 174
"Anti-Fugitive Slave Law Convention,
    Cazenovia, New York," 309(i)
Anti-immigrant fears, 458–460, 521
Anti-imperialism, 509
Anti-Imperialist League, 509
Anti-Muslim sentiments, 752, 763
Anti-Saloon League, 485
Anti-Semitism, 249
    Coughlin and, 570
    in the State Department during World War
        II, 604
    in the twenties, 545
Antislavery Convention of American Women,
    265
Anti-Slavery Societies, 245
Anzaldua, Gloria, 705
Apache Indians, 60
    civilization of, 378
    reservation land for, 381
Apartheid, 723, 737
Appeal...to the Colored Citizens of the World
    (Walker), 263
Appeasement, 584
Apple Computer Company, 743
Appomattox Court House, 345
Apprentices, 13, 73–74, 283
Arafat, Yasser, 737
Arapaho Indians
    Kansas-Nebraska Act and, 313
    Sand Creek Massacre, 344, 380–381
Arawak people, 16–17
Argentina, 453, 701
Argonne, battle of the (1918), 517
Arizona, 6, 455, 595
    Arkansas, 360, 595
Arkwright, Richard, 208
Armour, Philip, 410
Armstrong, Louis, 542
Army, first peacetime, 225
Army Air Corps, 589
Army-McCarthy hearings, 623
Arnold, Benedict, 139, 146, 156

Arthur, Chester A., 421
Articles of Confederation, 150, 155, 171, 186
Arts, 193–194
  Harlem Renaissance and, 542
  nineteenth century, 258*(i)*
  in the twenties, 541–542
  Works Progress Administration and, 571
Asheville, North Carolina, 414
Ashley, James, 345
Asian Americans
  civil rights movement and, 652–653
  in the Great Depression, 560, 562
  immigration of, 758–759
  liberation movement of, 684
  quota system on, 545
  women's suffrage and, 480*(m)*
Assembly line, 535, 552
Assimilation
  Americanization in the twenties and,
    546–547
  of immigrants, 460, 744
  of Indians, 384–385, 484, 575–576
  melting pot metaphor for, 460
Aswan Dam, 628
Atlanta, Georgia, 336
  African Americans in, 463
  Civil War capture of, 342–343
Atlantic Charter, 586
Atlantic slave trade, 70–71
Atlatl, 7
Atomic Age, 605
Attucks, Crispus, 127
A&T University, 650
Auschwitz, 603
Australia, 453
  women's suffrage in, 482
  in World War II, 599
Austria, unification with Germany, 584
Austria-Hungary, in World War I, 514, 517*(m)*
Authoritarianism, 559
  totalitarianism vs., 722
Automobiles
  bailouts of manufacturers, 755
  emission standards for, 699
  factories in World War II, 587
  influence of, on American life, 536
  internal combustion engine and, 404
  production and consumption of, 535*(f)*,
    535–536, 537*(i)*
  sales decline in the twenties, 539
  sexual norms and, 540

  after World War II, 637
Avilés, Pedro Menéndez de, 21
Axis, World War I, 583
Axis of evil, 752
Aylión, Lucas Vazquez de, 15*(m)*
Aztecs, 4*(m)*, 5, 8*(m)*, 15*(m)*, 25
  demographic disaster among, 17
  mapmaking, 17
  Spanish and, 2, 19

B-29 bombers, 599
Babbitt (Lewis), 541
Baby boom, 592, 637–638, 639*(f)*, 657
Back to Africa movement, 542
Bacon, Nathaniel, 42–43
Bacon's Rebellion, 42
Bad Axe, Battle of, 240
Bad Heart Buffalo, Amos, 382*(i)*
Baer, George F., 491–492
Bahamas, immigrants from, 454
Baker, James, 736
Bakke, Allan, 707
Balboa, Vasco Nuñez de, 15*(m)*, 16
Balkans, 748
Ballard, Martha, 210
Ballinger, Richard, 494
Baltimore
  Black Lives Matter in, 759
  fire in, 467
  police killings in, 759
  population of, 461
  transportation revolution in, 247
Bandung Conference, 627
Bangladesh, 758
Bank of the United States, 177, 199, 219
  Jackson and, 239
  Second, 203
Banks and banking
  African Americans in, 463
  bailouts of, 755
  Black Tuesday and, 551
  deregulation of under Reagan, 719
  Farmers' Alliance on, 443
  in the Great Depression, 566
  in industrial consolidation, 408
  panic of 1819 and, 228–229
  redlining by, 575, 640
  regulation of, 567
  in the twenties, 539–540
  under Jackson, 239
  Wilson's reforms of, 496

Banneker, Benjamin, 197
Baptist churches
    abolitionism and, 266
    black, 355
    renewal in, 194
    Second Great Awakening and, 255
Baptiste, 214
Barbados, 41–43, 44(m), 58
    slave laws in, 78
    slave markets, 61
Barbary pirates, 163, 199
Barnett, Ross, 665
Barrelhouses, 440
Barrett, Amy Coney, 764
Barrios, 708
Bartholdi, Frédéric-Auguste, 458
Bartram, William, 194
Baruch, Bernard, 519
Baseball, 417–418, 440, 647, 652
Bass, Samuel, 274
Bates, Ruby, 561
Batista, Fulgencio, 628
Battle of Britain, 585
Battle of the Little Big Horn (1876), 382, 382(i)
Bay of Pigs, Cuba, 662(m), 662–663
Beans, 4
Beatles, 679
Beats, 645–646
Beecher, Catharine, 312
Beecher, Henry, 312
Beecher, Lyman, 312
Beef trust, 492
Begin, Menachim, 702
Belarus, 731
Belgium, in World War II, 585
Bell, Alexander Graham, 404
Bell, John, 319, 320(m)
Bellamy, Edward, 413
Bellow, Saul, 571
Benedict, Ruth, 484, 541
Benezet, Anthony, 169
Benign neglect, 122
Benton, Jessie, 301
Benton, Thomas Hart, 301
Beringia, 3, 4(m)
Bering Strait, land bridge in, 3, 4(m)
Berkeley, California, 537
    Asian American and Black studies at, 684
    New Left in, 678
Berkeley, William, 42–43

Berkman, Alexander, 437
Berlin airlift, 615
Berlin Wall, 663, 731
Bernstein, Carl, 696
Berry, Chuck, 643
Bessemer, Henry, 404
Bethune, Mary McLeod, 572, 574, 575(i), 644
Bett, Mum, 150
Bibb, Henry, 312
Bickerdyke, Mary Ann "Mother," 336
Bicycles, 417(i)
Biddle, Nicholas, 239
Biden, Joseph, 754
    election of 2020, 754, 768
    Trump and, 766
Big Foot, 385
Big labor, 574
"Big stick" diplomacy, 511–512
Bilbo, Theodore, 647
Bilingual education, 683–684
Billion Dollar Congress, 422
Bill of Rights, 150, 174, 176
    Alien and Sedition Acts and, 185
    Japanese American internment and, 595
    Red scare abridgment of, 531
Biltmore, 414
Bin Laden, Osama, 702, 731, 750–751, 760
Birmingham, Alabama, 406, 564
    Freedom Rides in, 664
    Kennedy's intervention in, 666
    population of, 461
Birney, James G., 292
Birth control, 486–487
Birth of a Nation (film), 497
Birthrate
    baby boom, 637–638, 639(f)
    nineteenth century, 416
Bishop, Maurice, 724
Bishop Hill Colony, Illinois, 262(i)
Bison, 306
    role of, for Indians, 379(m), 380
    slaughter of, 383
    white hunters in decimating, 380
"Black Cabinet," 574
Black capitalism, 695
Black codes, 357, 359
Black Cross Nurses, 542
Black Death, 9
Black Elk, 385
Black Friday (1893), 444

Black Hawk, 240

Black Hills Treaty Council, 484

Black Kettle, 380

Blacklisting, 621

Black Lives Matter (BLM), 742, 759, 768

Black nationalism, 540, 542–544

Black Panther Party, 669

Black power, 669–670

Black Star Line, 544

Black Student Union, 684

Black Tuesday, 551

Blackwell, W. A., 465

Blanc, Honoré, 209

Bleeding Kansas, 314–316, 323

Bletchley Park, England, 589

Blitzkrieg, 585

Bloomers, 417(i)

Blow, Peter, 301

Blues, 440, 542

Boas, Franz, 484, 541

Bob Jones University, 710

Boland Amendment, 723

Boll weevils, 463

Bolsheviks, 516, 530, 610

Bomb shelters, 625(i)

Bonaparte, Napoleon, 199

Bonneville Dam, 568

Bonus Army, 564

Book of Mormon, The, 257

Book printing, 16

Boom and bust cycles, 503

Boomtowns, 246, 255, 386

Boone, Daniel, 153

Booth, John Wilkes, 345

Border Patrol, 545

Bosnia-Herzegovina, 748, 749(m)

Bosses, political, 469–471, 477

Boston

    Davenport's sermons in, 102

    desegregation in, 706

    fire in, 467

    fugitive slaves in, 312

    immigrant communities in, 456

    industry in, 402

    police strike in, 531

    population of, 461

    public market in, 105

    school busing in, 706

    suburbs around, 466

    time zone in, 403

Boston Almshouse, 75

Boston Committee of Public Safety, 520(i)

Bostonians, The (James), 418

Boston Indian Citizenship Association, 384

Boston marriages, 418

Boston Massacre, 127–128

Boston Tea Party, 129, 184

Boulder Dam, 568

Bouquet, Henry, 114, 118(i)

Bowdoin College, 189, 194, 203

Bowers, Henry F., 460

Boxer uprising (1900), 512

Boxing, 418, 486

Braceros, 593, 655

Braddock, Edward, 113

Bradford, William, 45, 47

Brady Bill (1993), 746

Brant, Joseph, 142, 146

Brant, Molly, 146

Brazil, immigration to, 453

Bread riots, 104

Breaker boys, 431

Breckinridge, John, 319, 320(m)

Brexit, 763

Brezhnev, Leonid, 694, 701

Bridges, Al, 682(i)

Bright, Joseph, 91

Brinkmanship, 625

Britain, Battle of, 585

British Broadcasting Corporation (BBC), 734

British South Seas Company, 68

Brook Farm, 262

Brooklyn, New York, Hooverville in, 559

Brooklyn Bridge, 465

Brooklyn Dodgers, 640

Brooks, Preston, 315

Brotherhood of Sleeping Car Porters, 592

Brown, Charles Brockden, 193

Brown, Charlotte Hawkins, 484

Brown, Edmund "Pat," 678

Brown, John, 315, 317–318, 323

    Exodusters and, 365

Brown, Michael, 742

Brown, Moses, 208

Brown Berets, 683, 708(i)

Browne, Jackson, 703

Brownsville, Texas, 493–494

Brown v. Board of Education of Topeka, Kansas, 648–650

    Goldwater on, 685

    school busing and, 706

    Warren in, 660

Broz, Josip, 612
Bryan, William Jennings, 445–446, 446*(m)*, 494
    Populists and, 446
    in the Scopes trial, 548
Bryce, James, 404
Bubonic plaque, 9
Buchanan, James, 311, 315–316, 319–320
Buchenwald concentration camp, 603, 603*(i)*
Buckley, William F., 685
Budapest, Hungary, strikes in, 436
Buddhism, in Vietnam, 674
Buffalo, New York, 461
Buffalo soldiers, 382
Bulgaria, fall of the Soviet regime in, 730
Bull Moose Party, 495
Bull Run
    first battle of (1861), 328, 331*(m)*
    second battle of (1862), 330
Bully pulpit, 491
Bunker Hill, battle of (1775), 138*(i)*, 139, 162
Bureau of Corporations, 492
Bureau of Indian Affairs (BIA), 655, 683
Bureau of Investigation, 531
Burgoyne, John, 146, 147*(m)*
Burke, Tarana, 764, 769
Burned-over district, 256*(m)*
Burns, Anthony, 312
Burr, Aaron, 183, 185, 217
Burroughs, Nannie Helen, 481
Bus boycott, Montgomery, 648–649, 649*(i)*
Bush, Abigail, 267
Bush, George H. W., 729–737
    in the election of 1992, 737
    Noriega and, 735
    Operation Desert Storm and, 736–737
Bush, George W., 749–753
    9/11 attacks and, 750*(i)*, 769
    Iraq War and, 750–753
    second term of, 753
Bush Doctrine, 752
Business
    management in, 402, 410
    technology and transformation of, 743–744
Business, women in, after the Revolution, 170
Butler, Andrew, 315
Butler, Benjamin, 329
Butler, Frank, 374
Butte, Montana, 387

Cabeza de Vaca, Alvar Nuñez, 15*(m)*, 21, 22*(m)*
Cable News Network (CNN), 734
Cabot, Francis, 209
Cabot, John, 15, 15*(m)*, 23
Cabot, Sebastian, 15
Cabrillo, Juan Rodriguez, 22*(m)*
Caddo Indians, 60, 65–66
Cadena, Carlos C., 655
Cahokia people, 7
Calhoun, John C., 235, 307–308, 326
California, 226
    agricultural worker strikes in, 562, 682
    Alien Land Law in, 653
    anti-Chinese assaults in, 396
    Asian Americans in the Great Depression, 562
    Chinese immigrants in, 396
    civil rights movement in, 652
    Compromise of 1850 and, 308
    expansion into, 292
    gold rush in, 302–304, 304*(i)*, 386
    growth of, in the twenties, 538, 538*(m)*
    Hetch Hetchy valley in, 489, 491
    immigrants in, 454–455, 758
    internment camps in, 595
    Japanese internment camps in, 582
    Ku Klux Klan in, 547
    lumber industry in, 387
    native cultures in, 7
    Okies in, 560
    refugees in, 725
    statehood of, 322
    tax revolt in, 709
    after World War II, 640
    in World War II, 588
California Trail, 305*(m)*
Californios, 395
Calvert, Cecilius, 40
Calvert, Leonard, 41
Calvin, John, 31, 47
Calvinism, 35, 47
Cambodia, 758
    immigrants from, 744, 745*(f)*
    invasion of, 693
Cameron, Simon, 329
Camp David accords, 702
Camp followers, 145, 148
Camp Kilmer, 623

Camp meetings, 195
Canada
    border established with, 225
    British control over, 114, 115(m)
    Embargo Act and, 203
    energy consumption per capita in, 699(f)
    exports to, 503
    fugitive slaves in, 309–310
    in the Group of Seven (G7), 732
    immigration to, 453
    Japanese American internment in, 595
    NAFTA and, 747
Canals, 223–225, 246–247
    to 1837, 224(m)
Cane Ridge, Kentucky, camp meeting at,
        195, 255
Cape Verde Islands, 14
Capitalism, 11
    black, 695
    communism on, 611
    Haymarket incident and, 434–435
    laissez-faire, 410–413
    New Deal and, 569, 577
    progressivism and, 476
    reform, after World War II, 637, 662
    social gospel and, 476
    socialism and, 438
Capitol, U.S., 197, 768
Capone, Al, 559(i)
Captains of industry, 407
Caravels, 10
Carbon paper, 404
Caribbean, 757
    immigrants from, 720, 721(f), 744, 745(f)
    imperialism in, 502
    Roosevelt Corollary on, 512
    Wilson and, 513
Carlos V (King of Spain), 24
Carmichael, Stokely, 669
Carnegie, Andrew, 400–402, 408
    Homestead strike and, 428, 436
    Morgan and, 408
    on philanthropy, 412
    on the Philippines, 509
Carnegie, Margaret, 400
Carnegie, Will, 400
Carolina(s). *See also* North Carolina; South
        Carolina
    labor in, 58
    land conflicts in, 119
    rise of slavery in, 76

    slavery in, 78–79
Carolina Grant, 44(m)
Carpetbaggers, 364
Carson, Kit, 301, 305
Carson, Rachel, 705
Carta Marina, 2
Carter, Jimmy, 698–703, 711
    the Christian Right and, 710
    economic policies and, 698–701
    in the election of 1980, 716, 717(m)
    foreign policy under, 701–703
Cartier, Jacques, 22–23
Casablanca (film), 592
Casey, William, 723
Cash-and-carry provisions, 584
Cash crops, 393
Casinos, 760
Cass, Lewis, 296
Castro, Fidel, 628, 662, 662(m)
Castro, Julian, 758
Catawba people, 65
Catherine of Aragon, 31
Catholics
    blamed for fallen women, 260
    Crusades, 9
    cultural divisions and, 246
    immigrants, 257, 453, 457, 544
    immigrants as white or not, 459
    immigration restrictions against, 459
    Inquisition by, 10
    Irish immigrants, 98, 247–248
    Ku Klux Klan on, 548
    in Maryland, 40–41
    nativists on, 260
    the New Right and, 710
    prejudice against, 249
    as president, 656
    Protestant Reformation and, 30–31
    reconquest of Spain, 10
    Spanish conquest and, 31–33, 32(i)
    in the twenties, 544
Catlin, George, 259
Cat on a Hot Tin Roof (film), 643
Cattle ranches, 388–394
    commercial, 389
    foreign investment in, 376, 376(f), 388
Cavalier, René-Robert, 60
Cavazos, Lauro F., 721
Cayuga Indians, 142
Cayuse Indians, 305
Cazenovia, New York, 309(i)

Ceausescu, Nicolae, 731
Cell phones, 743
Census, U.S.
  of 1920, 537
Centennial Exposition (1876), 458
Central America, anticommunist interventions in, 723
Central Intelligence Agency (CIA), 614
  Bay of Pigs and, 662, 662(m)
  intervention in Afghanistan, 701–702
  intervention in Chile, 694
  intervention in Nicaragua, 723
  interventions in the Middle East, Latin America, and Africa, 627–629
  Vietnam intervention by, 630
  Watergate scandal and, 696
Central Pacific Company, 376–377
Central Powers, 513–518, 517(m)
Century of Dishonor, A (Jackson), 383
Chaffee, Calvin, 322
Chamberlain, Samuel, 295(i)
Chambers, Whittaker, 621
Champlain, Samuel de, 33
Chancellorsville, battle of (1863), 340
Channing, William Ellery, 257
Chapultepec, Battle of, 295(i)
Charbonneau, Toussaint, 190, 214
Charitable organizations, 254, 259
  Gilded Age, 415(t), 415–416
  in the Great Depression, 557
Charity, philanthropy vs., 412
Charity Organization Society, 415(t)
Charles I (King of England), 49
Charles II (King of England), 43, 49, 57–58
Charles II (King of Spain), 63
Charleston, South Carolina, 71–72, 227
  American Revolution in, 154(m), 156
  slave market in, 212
  slave trade in, 77(i)
  Vesey conspiracy in, 233–234
Charlotte, North Carolina, 440
Chattanooga, battle of (1863), 340
Chavez, Cesar, 682
Cheever, John, 571
Cherokee Nation v. Georgia, 287
Cherokee people, 63, 64(m), 65
  alliances of, 113
  in American Revolution, 142
  civilization of, 378
  in Civil War, 330, 345
  frontier colleges and, 192

frontier conflicts with, 114
land conflicts with, 167
removal of, 240, 287–289, 288(m)
Ross, 217
Sand Creek massacre of, 380–381
Trail of Tears, 289
in War of 1812, 220(m), 221
women's rights among, 268
Chesapeake & Ohio Railroad, 482
Chesapeake region
  life expectancy in, 90
  rice cultivation in, 78
  slavery in, 78
  women's status in, 87–88
Chevrolet, 536, 537(i)
Cheyenne Indians, 304
  Custer and, 381
  Kansas-Nebraska Act and, 313
  Sand Creek Massacre, 344
Chicago
  African American population of, 463
  fire in, 467
  gays and lesbians in, 418
  ghetto riots in, 669
  the great migration to, 532
  Haymarket Square, 434
  immigrant communities in, 455
  immigrants in, 455
  industry in, 402
  Irish immigrants in, 247
  Ku Klux Klan in, 547
  race riots of 1919 in, 532
  railroad strike in, 436(m)
  settlement houses in, 478
  skyscrapers in, 404
  soup kitchens in, 559(i)
  streets in, 468
  trolleys in, 465
  World's Columbian Exposition, 440
Chicago Defender (newspaper), 464
Chicanismo, 708
Chicanos, 683
Chickasaw Indians, 167
Child care, in World War II, 590
Child labor, 431, 467
  globalization and, 734
  muckrakers on, 477
  outlawed, 493(t), 497
  progressivism on, 479
  in the twenties, 534
  unions on, 433

Children
  baby boom, 637–638, 639(f)
  colonial era, 90
  of former slaves, 352
  labor of, 431
  latchkey kids, 592
Children's Bureau, 479
Chile, Pinochet in, 737
China
  Boxer uprising in, 512
  climate change and, 762
  colonial-era trade, 67
  communist revolution in, 615
  energy consumption in, 699(f)
  immigrants from, 744, 745(f)
  Japanese invasion of Manchuria, 586
  missionaries in, 505
  Open Door policy in, 512–513, 583, 586
  Opium Wars in, 396
  Philippine war and, 509
  Tiananmen Square massacre, 735
  trade with, 179, 226, 310, 504
China, People's Republic of, 615
  Korean War and, 616–618
  Nixon and, 691, 693
  overtures of in the Middle East, Latin
    America, and Africa, 627
  Vietnam and, 629
Chinatowns, 432(i), 456, 458, 653
Chinese Americans
  affirmative action and, 684
  civil rights movement and, 652–653
  in the Great Depression, 562
  in the twenties, 546–547
  in World War II, 596
Chinese Exclusion Act (1882), 396, 454–455,
    546
  repealed, 596
Chinese for Affirmative Action, 684
Chinese immigrants
  in California gold rush, 304, 304(i)
  labor contracts with, 453
  legislation against, 396, 454
  opium and, 486
  Rock Springs massacre of, 397
  as telephone operators, 432(i)
  in the twenties, 546–547
  in unions, 433
  in the West, 396–397
Chisholm, Shirley, 704
Chisholm Trail, 388

Chivington, John M., 344
Choctaw Indians, 66, 113, 167
Cholera, 305, 378, 468
Christian Anti-Communist Crusade, 685
Christian Broadcasting Network, 710
Christian Crusade, 685
Christianity
  conversion of native peoples to, 24
  Crusades in, 9
  the New Right and, 710
  "New School" ministers, 244
  reconquest of Spain, 10
  revivals in, 83–84
  Second Great Awakening, 255–256
  slavery justified in, 12
  social gospel in, 471, 476
Christianity and the Social Crisis
    (Rauschenbusch), 476
Christian Right, 710
  Bush, George W., and, 750
  Contract with America and, 746
Chu, Steven, 758
Chumash Indians, 7
Churchill, Winston, 586, 598
  on the iron curtain, 611, 616(m)
  Yalta Agreement and, 600
Church of England, 31, 40
  in colonial America, 58
  Pilgrims and, 45
  Puritans and, 45, 47–48
Cigarette manufacturing, 406
Cincinnati, Ohio, 206, 227
  growth of, 246
  industry in, 402
  Irish immigrants in, 247
  population of, 461
  Reform Judaism in, 457
  seamstresses in, 338
Citizenship
  of African Americans, 359
  of Californios, 395
  immigrants and, 459
  of Indians, 459
  of Japanese Americans, 595–596, 653
  racial restrictions on, 233
  voting rights and, 479
City bosses, 469–471
City managers, 489
Civic housekeeping, 478
Civil disobedience, 648–649
Civil Disobedience (Thoreau), 258

Civilian Conservation Corps (CCC), 569, 572(t)
Civil Liberties Unit, 574
Civil rights
  of freedpeople, 357
  Mexican Americans, 593
  racial restrictions on, 233
  in Reconstruction, 350
  Red scare abridgment of, 530–531
  in the 1960s, 664–670
  in state constitutions, 150
  in World War II, 592–593, 596, 604
Civil Rights Act (1866), 359
Civil Rights Act (1875), 369, 418
Civil Rights Act (1964), 666–667, 673(t), 680
Civil Rights Act (1968), 673(t)
Civil rights movement, 605, 646–653
  black power and, 669–670
  Freedom Rides in, 664–665
  Freedom Summer in, 666–668
  Kennedy's support of, 665–666
  Kennedy vs. Nixon in, 656
  Mexican American, 593–594
  Montgomery bus boycott in, 648–649, 649(i)
  origins of, 592–593
  rise of the Southern, 646–647
  school busing and, 706
  school segregation and, 647–650
  sit-ins in, 650
  suspected Communist influence in, 624
  voting rights and, 666–668
  in the West, 652–653
  white resistance to desegregation and, 649–650
  women in, 681
Civil Rights Section, 574
Civil service, 470, 563
Civil War, 324–347
  African Americans in, 329–332
  American Indians in, 329–332
  brutality of, 334–335, 345, 372
  dissent and protests in, 338–339
  early battles in, 328, 331(m)
  emancipation after, 351–355
  end of, 345
  final battles of, 343–344
  Johnson, Andrew, in, 350
  key Union victories in, 340–342
  life and death on the battlefield in, 334–335
  Mahan in, 501
  northern economic expansion in, 335
  partisanship after, 423
  preparations for, 327–329
  Reconstruction after, 355–363
  secession of the South and, 321(m)
  telegraphs in, 408
  transformations from, 333–340
  turn in tide of, 340–345
  women in, 336–337, 337(i)
  women spies in, 326
Civil Works Administration (CWA), 569, 571
Clark, George Rogers, 153–154
Clark, William, 201
  journals of, 190
  route traveled by, 202(m)
  on Sacagawea, 214
  Sacagawea and, 190
Clarke, Charity, 127
Clay, Henry, 223, 230, 235, 236(f), 307–308
  election of 1832, 239
  election of 1844, 268, 292
Clayton Antitrust Act (1914), 493(t), 496
Clean Air Act (1990), 709
"Clear and present danger" doctrine, 530, 621
Cleaveland, Martha, 189–190
Cleaveland, Parker, 189–190, 203, 213
Clemenceau, Georges, 524
Clemens, Samuel, 386, 414
Clerical workers, 415, 430
Clermont (steamboat), 207
Cleveland, Grover, 421, 424(i)
  depression of 1893 and, 445
  in election of 1892, 444
  Hawaii annexation and, 504
Cleveland, Major, 617(i)
Cleveland, Ohio
  Black Lives Matter in, 759
  ghetto riots in, 669
  immigrants in, 455
  police killings in, 759
  population of, 461
  progressivism in, 489
  sewage disposal in, 468
  streets in, 468
Cleveland Indians, 652
Climate change, 757, 762
Clinton, Bill, 596, 737
  domestic and economic policy of, 745–747
  global challenges facing, 747–748
  impeachment of, 747

Clinton, Henry, 151, 155
Clinton, Hillary Rodham, 746
  in the 2016 election, 762
  as secretary of state, 760
Clooney, Rosemary, 643
Cloth industry
  in American Revolution, 143
  English, 46
  family labor in, 89
  global trade in, 67
  Navigation Acts and, 69
  in Rhode Island, 226
  in South Carolina, 57
  technology in, 208
Clothing factories
  in tenements, 467
  Triangle Shirtwaist fire and, 467
  in World War II, 587
Clovis people, 4*(m)*
Clyens, Mary Elizabeth, 428
Coal mining, 431
Coatzacoalcos, 1
Codebreakers, 589
Codfish, 47
Cody, William F. "Buffalo Bill," 374
Coercive Acts (England, 177), 129–131
Coeur d'Alene, Idaho, 438
Coffin, Catherine, 308
Coffin, Levi, 308
Colbert, Jean-Baptiste, 69
Cold Spring, New York, 338
Cold War, 616*(m)*
  anticommunism and, 630
  civil rights movement and, 647, 650
  conflict management after, 735–737
  containment policy in, 609
  end of the, 715–716, 721–728
  espionage in, 621
  expansion of, 624–630
  fall of the Soviet Union and, 730–732, 732*(m)*
  fighting communism at home in, 620–624
  hardening of positions in, 614–620
  human rights and, 722–725
  the Internet and, 744
  Kennedy and, 662*(m)*, 662–664
  Korean War in, 616–618
  McCarthyism in, 622–624
  Middle East, Latin America, and Africa interventions in, 627–629
  military containment in, 614–616

  mutual misunderstandings in, 610–612
  Nixon and, 691, 693–694
  nuclear de-escalation and, 728
  nuclear freeze movement and, 726–728
  opening of the, 608–632
  origins of, 610–614
  Red scare in, 620–622
  space race in, 654
  timeline of, 632
  the Truman Doctrine in, 612–613
  Vietnam and, 629–630, 674
  Wallace on, 611
Cole, Thomas, 258*(i)*, 259
Collective bargaining, 433
Colleges and universities
  colonial era, 47, 99
  desegregation of, 647
  frontier, 192–194
  after World War II, 637
Collier, John, 575, 576*(i)*
Collier's (magazine), 477
Colombia, Panama Canal and, 511–512
Colonial America, 55–82
  comparing histories of, 55–57
  consumer cultures in, 71–72
  costs and benefits of empire in, 67–72
  diversity in, 95
  economic competition in, 93–95
  English colonies in, 57–59, 59*(t)*
  ethnicity and racial diversity in, 76*(m)*
  European claims in, 57–62
  European wars and, 62–63
  expansion and conflict in, 96*(m)*, 96–98
  finding work in, 73–74
  French colonies, 60–61
  grievances against the British, 120–121
  imperial conflicts and, 112–119
  Indian alliances and conflict in, 62–63, 64*(m)*
  labor in, 55–56, 73–80
  Native American resistance in, 61–72, 64*(m)*
  political awakenings in, 103–107
  religion in, 83–87, 99–103
  resistance to Britain in, 123–131
  rural conditions, 75–77
  sex ratios in, 88, 88*(t)*
  southern frontier conflicts, 66–67
  Spanish colonies, 59–60
  trade and, 67–68, 68*(m)*
  unity in, 120–122

Colonies, 28–51
  Dutch, 35–36
  English, 22–23, 44*(m)*, 57–59*(t)*
  expansion and conflict in, 96–98
  French, 23, 33–34, 44*(m)*, 98
  New England, 45–51
  proprietary, 58
  Protestant Reformation and, 30–31
  Spanish, 44*(m)*, 59–60
  West Indies, 43, 44*(m)*
Colorado
  cattle ranching in, 389
  Indians displaced in, 344
  internment camps in, 595
  Populists and, 447
  Pueblo people in, 6–7
Colored Farmers' Alliance, 442
Colored Masons, 420
Colored Odd Fellows, 420
Colored Orphan Asylum, 338
Coltrane, John, 645
Columbia, Tennessee, race riot in, 647
Columbia Broadcasting System (CBS), 641
Columbian exchange, 17–18, 18*(m)*, 25
Columbus, Christopher, 14–15, 15*(m)*
Comanche people, 60, 202*(m)*, 306
  battle for Texas and, 286
  civilization of, 378
  in Civil War, 330
  epidemics among, 305
  in Texas, 291, 293
Combahee River Collective, 704
Come outer movement, 266
Comintern, 530
Command of the Army Act (1867), 360
Commission governments, 488
Commission on the Status of Women, 680
Committee for the Re-Election of the
    President, 696
Committee on Public Information (CPI), 520
Committees of correspondence, 123,
    128–129
Commodity Credit Corporation, 448
Common law, 88
Common Sense (Paine), 136, 140
Common Sense Book of Baby and Child Care
    (Spock), 644
Commonwealth of Independent States, 731
Communication
  newspapers in, 250
  telephone, 404

Communism, 438
  capitalism vs., 611
  in China, 615
  Chinese Americans and, 653
  Eisenhower Doctrine on, 628–629
  fall of the Soviet Union and, 730–732,
      732*(m)*
  fear of in the twenties, 530–531
  human rights and the fight against,
      722–725
  Kennedy and, 662*(m)*, 662–664
  Levitt on housing and, 639
  McCarthyism and, 622–624
  Reagan on, 721
  Red scare and, 530–531, 620–622
  religious revival in the 1950s and, 645
  Russian Revolution and, 516, 524
  in Vietnam, 629–630, 674–676
Communist Control Act (1954), 623
Communist Party
  in the Great Depression, 563–564
  Moreno in, 556
  on New Deal, 569
  Smith Act violations by, 621
  in World War II, 595
Community Relations Service, 666
Como, Perry, 643
Companionate marriage, 190, 210
Compassionate conservatism, 749–750
Comprehensive Anti-Apartheid Act (1986),
    723
Comprehensive Environmental Response,
    Compensation, and Liability Act
    (1980), 705
Compromise of 1850, 307, 314*(m)*
Compromise of 1877, 369
Computers, 741–744
Comstock Lode, 386
Concentration camps, 596, 603*(i)*
Concord, battle of, 137–138
Coney Island, 440
Confederate States of America, 320–321*(m)*
  amnesty for officials from, 355
  compared with the Union states, 327
  conflict and dissent in, 338–339
  devotion to the "Lost Cause" in, 358*(i)*
  end of the war and, 345
Confederate monuments, 419–420, 765, 768
Confession Program, 653
Congo, civil war in, 629
Congregational Church, 256

Congress
  gag rule of 1836, 265
  industrialization and, 421–422
  inefficiency of, 421–422
  New Deal and, 577
  police actions and, 618
  war powers and, 693
Congressional Government (Wilson), 422
Congress of Industrial Organizations (CIO),
    556, 573–574
Congress of Racial Equality (CORE), 593, 661
  Freedom Rides, 664
  Freedom Summer and, 667
  Free Speech Movement and, 678
Connecticut, 49
  Constitution ratified by, 175, 175(t)
  land claims of, 166(m)
  royal charter of, 57
Connor, Eugene "Bull," 665
Conquistadors, 19, 25, 378
Conscience Whigs, 268
Consciousness-raising groups, 681
Conservation
  energy, 698
  Pinchot on, 474–475
Conservatism
  Bush, George H. W., and, 729–737
  Bush, George W., and, 749–750
  Carter and, 698–703
  Christian, 710
  on the Clintons, 746
  compassionate, 749–750
  "kinder and gentler," 729–730
  liberalism challenged by, 677
  neoconservatives in, 709
  the New Right in, 709–710
  persistence of liberalism and, 703–708
  pragmatic, 695
  Reaganomics and, 716–719
  revival of in the 1960s, 684–686
  social, 720–721
  the swing toward, 689–713
  tax revolt and, 709
  Tea Party movement, 756
Conservative coalition, 577
Constitution
  amendments to, 176
  Bill of Rights in, 173–174, 176
  Constitutional Convention and, 172–174
  Hartford Convention on, 222
  imperial presidency and, 618
  implied powers clause in, 203
  interpretation of by political parties, 234
  laissez-faire and, 411
  ratification of, 164, 174–175, 175(t)
  Reconstruction amendments, 371
  slavery abolished in, 345
  Supreme Court's authority in interpreting,
    203
Constitutional Convention (1787), 172–174
Constitutional Union Party, 319, 320(m)
Consumer culture
  colonial, 71–72
  in the Gilded Age, 414–416
  middle class in, 250–252
  in the 1950s, 657
  teenage culture and, 643
  in the twenties, 535–536
  women in, 416
Consumer Products Safety Commission, 695
Consumer safety, 492, 695
Containment policy, 609, 630
  Bush Doctrine on, 752
  economic, 613–614
  military containment, 614–616
  nuclear weapons in, 624–627
  Operation Desert Storm and, 736–737
Continental Army, 137
  back pay of, 157, 164
  building, 139
  camp followers, 145, 148
  flags sewn for, 143
  formation of, 137
  Hamilton in, 163
  military takeover threatened by, 164
  mutiny in, 156
  raising funds for, 152
  Shays in, 163
  smallpox in, 146
  victories of, 145–146, 156–157
Continental Congress, 131, 137
  alliance with France and, 152
  Articles of Confederation and, 150
  Continental Army and, 139, 152, 164
  Declaration of Independence and, 140
  Indian affairs and, 153
  land claims and, 155
  peace offer rejected by, 145
  recruiting supporters by, 142
  return of, to Philadelphia, 146
  Second, 138
  on slavery, 151

Contraband, 329
Contraception, 486–487, 672, 720
Contract with America, 746
Contras, 723, 726
Convict lease system, 406
Convicts, transportation of, 74
Conwell, Russell, 411, 424
Coolidge, Calvin, 531, 535
    in the election of 1924, 550, 550(m)
    Garvey deported by, 544
Copperheads, 338
Copper mining, 387
Corbin, Margaret, 149
Corn, 4
Cornplanter, 165
Cornstalk, 143
Cornwallis, Charles, 154(m), 155–156
Coronado, Francisco Vásquez de, 21, 22(m)
Corporations, 402
    growth of, 409–410
    management of, 402
    multinational, 733
    profits of, in the twenties, 539
    support of, in the twenties, 534
Corps of Discovery, 201
Cortés, Hernán, 2, 15(m), 19–20, 25
Cosby, William, 106
Cotton, 196
    boll weevil infestations, 463
    Civil War and, 335
    in economic development, 226–227
    falling prices in the twenties, 540
    manufacturing, 208
    Navigation Acts on, 69
    in the New South, 407(m)
    panic of 1837 and, 254, 290
    plantation society and, 274–275
    slavery and, 210–213, 274–275, 278(m)
    southern economy and, 279
    technology and expanded production of,
        210–213, 212(t)
Cotton, John, 29
Cotton gin, 209, 211, 211(i), 274
Coughlin, Charles E., 570–571
Council Bluffs, Iowa, 563
Council of Economic Advisors, 714
Council of Trent, 31
Councils for Trade and Plantations, 57
Counterculture, 679–680, 703
Counter-Reformation, 31
Country music, 440

Court-packing plan, 577
COVID-19, 766–767
Cowboys, 376, 388–389
Coxey, Jacob, 444
Coxey's army, 444
Craft work, decline of, 253–254
Crater Lake, 490(m)
Crawford, William, 234–235, 236(f)
Crazy Horse, 382(i)
Creationism, 548, 710
Credit
    effect of, on social conventions, 540
    in the twenties, 536, 539
Crédit Mobilier, 377
Creek people, 65
    alliances of, 113
    in American Revolution, 142
    civilization of, 378
    frontier colleges and, 192
    land conflicts with, 167
Creel, George, 520
Crime
    in cities, 468
    in immigrant neighborhoods, 458
    nativists on, 260
Crimea, annexation of, 762
Criminal justice system
    Black Lives Matter and, 759
    juvenile, 486
    Warren court on, 672
Crisis of masculinity, 417
Crittenden, John, 320
Crittenden plan, 320
Croatia, 748, 749(m)
Cronkite, Walter, 676
Crop systems, 9
Cross Keys, battle of (1862), 331(m)
"Cross of gold" speech (Bryan), 446
Crow Indians, Indian Reorganization Act and,
    576
Crusades, 9
Cuba, 19, 502
    Bay of Pigs, 662(m), 662–663
    CIA intervention in, 628
    filibusters to, 311
    immigrants from, 454, 457
    immigration to, 453
    independence from Spain, 502, 506
    normalization of diplomatic relations with,
        762
    pacification of, 508–509

Cuba (*Continued*)
  protectorate in, 503
  Spanish exploration from, 21, 22(*m*)
  U.S. intervention in, 507, 510(*m*), 513
  War for Independence in, 506
Cuba Libre, 502, 506
Cuban missile crisis, 662(*m*), 662–664
Cubberly, E. P., 545
Cullors, Patrisse, 742
Cult of domesticity, 250
Culture
  African American, 280–281, 297, 464–465
  assimilation and, 460
  Gilded Age, 414–420
  globalization and, 733
  immigrants and, 453
  as justification for imperialism, 504–505
  popular, in the 1970s, 703
  of the 1950s, 641–646
  teen, 639(*f*)
Cumberland Road, 207, 223
"Cure for Depressions" (Townsend), 570
Currency
  in Civil War, 335
  Continentals in American Revolution, 152
  after the Revolution, 167
  silver backing of, 443, 445
Currency Act (England, 1764), 123–124
Curtis, Charles, 550
Custer, George Armstrong, 381–383, 382(*i*)
Custis, Martha, 111
Cuzco, 6
Czechoslovakia
  Communist coup in, 613
  fall of the Soviet regime in, 730
  German annexation of, 584
  Prague Spring in, 691
Czech Republic, 761

Dachau, 603
da Gama, Vasco, 11
Dakota Apartments, New York City, 414
Dakota Territory, 391
Dance halls, 440
Darragh, Lydia, 148
Darrow, Clarence, 461, 529, 548
Darwin, Charles, 412, 459, 548, 710
Daughters of Bilitis, 645
Daughters of Liberty, 124
Davenport, George, 207(*t*)
Davenport, James, 102

Davis, Jefferson, 320
  Britain and, 333
  conscription act by, 339
  on Greenhow, 326
  imprisonment of, 366
Davis, John W., 550, 550(*m*)
Davis, Miles, 645
Dawes, Henry, 384
Dawes Act (1887), 384–385, 575
Day, Doris, 643
Day, Madison, 353
Dayton, Ohio, 488
Dayton, Tennessee, 548
D Day (1944), 599
Dean, James, 642
Dean, John, 696
Dearborn, Michigan, Ford factory strike, 564
Death penalty, 729
Debs, Eugene V., 437–438
  conviction of under the Espionage Act, 521
  in election of 1912, 495
Debt
  of farmers after the Revolution, 170–171
  of farmers in the nineteenth century,
    441–442
  in the Great Depression, 560
  Hamilton's agenda on, 177
  panic of 1819 and, 228–229
  after the Revolution, 159, 164, 167
  under Reagan, 719
Declaration of Independence, 140, 411
  French Revolution influenced by, 179
  signers of, in Constitutional Convention, 172
Declaration of Sentiments, 267
Declaratory Act (England, 1766), 126
Decolonization, 627
Deep Throat, 696
Defense of Marriage Act (1996), 746, 757
Deferred Action for Childhood Arrivals
    (DACA), 758, 764
Deforestation, 8
De Galle, Charles, 691
De Kalb, Johann Baron, 148
Delacroix, Eugêne, 193
Delaware, 58, 175, 175(*t*)
Delaware Indians, 96(*m*), 96–97
  alliance with France, 113
  in American Revolution, 143, 153
  in Civil War, 330
  land treaties with, 165
Deming, Barbara, 727

Democratic National Convention
  of 1964, 667
  of 1968, 691
Democratic Party, 234, 311
  abolitionism and, 268
  African Americans in, 574
  anti-Chinese movement in, 396
  after the Civil War, 370
  Civil War and, 342
  congressional majority by, 421
  constituents of, 423
  Copperheads, 338
  election of 1828, 236–237
  election of 1852 and, 310
  in election of 1860, 319, 320(m)
  in election of 1896, 445–447, 446(m)
  in election of 1912, 495
  Greeley endorsed by, 368
  Hiss affair and, 621
  Johnson, Andrew, in, 350
  on Kansas-Nebraska Act, 313
  Mississippi Freedom, 667
  New Deal and, 570, 576–577
  Redeemers, 366
  Second Party System, 285
  Truman and, 636
  in the twenties, 549–550
  Van Buren and, 290
  in Wilmington, North Carolina massacre,
    447(i)
  workingmen's interests and, 253
Democratic-Republicans, 183–187
  Bank of the United States and, 219
  on expansion, 222
  expansion of federal powers by, 203–204
  federal power limited by, 199
  national identity and, 191
  political realignments and, 234–235
  Second Bank of the United States and, 203
  on voting rights, 231
Democratic Review, 292
Demographics
  baby boom, 592, 637–638, 639(f)
  late twentieth to twenty-first century,
    745(f)
  nineteenth century, 247–248
  Sun and Rust Belt, 700(m)
  of western migration, 302
Denby, Edward, 534–535
Deng Xiaoping, 735
Denmark, in World War II, 585

Dennis v. United States, 621, 624
Denver
  growth of in the twenties, 537
  Ku Klux Klan in, 547
  population of, 461
Department of Agriculture, 568
Department of Commerce and Labor, 492
Department of Defense, 614, 744
Department of Energy, 699
Department of Health, Education, and
    Welfare, 654
Department of Homeland Security, 750
Department of Housing and Urban Affairs,
    671
Department of the Interior, 568
Department of Transportation, 671
Department stores, 410, 416, 430
Deportation
  in the Great Depression, 561
  of radicals in the Red scare, 531, 620
  of undocumented Mexicans, 655
Depression of 1893, 444–445
Deregulation
  under Carter, 701
  under Reagan, 716, 719
Desegregation, 657
  busing in, 707
  Kennedy and, 665–666
  for Mexican Americans, 652
  Supreme Court on, 648–649
  white resistance to, 649–650
Desegregation, of public transportation, 345
Desert Land Act (1877), 393
Deskilling of labor, 253–254
De Soto, Hernando, 21
Détente, 626, 693, 701–702
Detroit
  ghetto riots in, 669
  immigrants in, 455
  Ku Klux Klan in, 547
  progressivism in, 489
  race riots in, 593
  school busing in, 706
De Ulloa, Francisco, 22(m)
Development, Relief, and Education for Alien
    Minors (DREAM) Act, 758
Dew, Thomas, 282, 285
Dewey, George, 509, 510(m)
Dewey, Thomas E., 599, 636
Dial, The, 258
D'Iberville, Pierre LeMoyne, 61

Dickinson, John, 126, 131, 138
Dien Bien Phu, 629
Diet
    of factory workers, 432
    in the Great Depression, 559*(i)*
    during World War I, 519
Digital technology, 741–744
Diphtheria, 18*(m)*, 378, 638
Diseases, 13
    child mortality and, 90
    in Civil War, 334
    Columbian exchange in, 17–18, 18*(m)*, 20, 20*(f)*, 25
    impact of, on Indians, 378
    in Jamestown, 37
    missionaries and, 35
    native depopulation from, 23
    Pilgrims and, 45
    tenements and, 466, 468
    trade and, 68
    urban crowding and, 467
    vaccinations against, 638
    western settlement and, 305
Disk jockeys, 633–634
Dissent, suppression of, 530–531
District of Columbia
    Compromise of 1850 on, 307
    slavery in, 265, 307
Diversity
    Americanization efforts and, 546–547
    colonial era, 76*(m)*
    nineteenth century, 247–248, 248*(f)*
    religious, 102*(m)*
    in the West, 394–397
    in western cities, 463
Division of labor, 178
Division of Negro Affairs, 572
Divorce
    colonial era, 91
    legalization of, 170
    in Oneida community, 262
    in the 1970s, 703
    in World War II, 592
Dixiecrats, 636
Dole, Robert, 747
Dollar diplomacy, 513
Domestication of animals, 9
Domestic labor
    in the 1950s, 644
    women in, 430, 590–592
    as women's purpose, 637

Domestic labor, cult of domesticity and, 250
Domestic production, 209–210
Dominican Republic, 503, 512–513
Domino, Antoine "Fats," 643
"Don't ask, don't tell" policy, 746, 756
Double V, 593
Douglas, Helen Gahagan, 622
Douglas, Stephen, 312, 316
    election of 1860, 319, 320*(m)*
    Harpers Ferry raid and, 317
Douglass, Frederick, 254, 265, 268, 309*(i)*
    autobiography of, 312, 325
    Fifteenth Amendment and, 363
    Fugitive Slave Act and, 309
    voting rights and, 346, 363
Draft, military
    American Revolution, 152
    Civil War, 338
    of Indians, 594
    Korean War, 618
    Rustin's refusal to register for, 661
    Vietnam War, 678
    World War I, 516
    World War II, 585, 594
Drake, Francis, 33
Dreamers, 758
Dred Scott decision, 301, 316, 321, 359
Dreiser, Theodore, 463
Drinker, Elizabeth, 148
Driver, Karen, 760
Drug abuse
    Beats on, 645
    counterculture and, 679
    muckrakers on, 477
    progressivism on, 486
Du Bois, W. E. B., 461, 483, 497, 521, 532
    on Garvey, 543
"Duck and cover" drills, 626
Due process, Guantánamo prisoners and, 752
Dukakis, Michael, 729, 737
Duke, James B., 406
Dulles, Allen, 628–629
Dulles, John Foster, 628
Dunkards, 121
Dunmore, Lord, 140–141, 151
Dunmore's Proclamation, 140–141
Du Pont Corporation, 569
Dust Bowl, 559–560, 560*(m)*
Dutch West India Company, 36
Dylan, Bob, 679
Dynamic Sociology (Ward), 413

Eastern Europe
as buffer between Germany and the USSR, 610–611
fall of Communism in, 730–731, 732(m)
the Marshall Plan in, 613
East India Company, 129
Eastman, Charles, 385
Eaton, John, 237
Economic depressions
of 1893, 444–445
Black Tuesday and, 551
the Great Depression, 551–552, 555–579
imperialism and, 504
panic of 1819 and, 228–229
panic of 1837, 254–255, 269, 290
panic of 1873, 368
after the Revolution, 167
after World War I, 530
Economic growth, 223–225
regional, 226–228
slavery in, 279
Economic Opportunity Act (1964), 671, 673(t)
Economic policy
of Carter, 698–701
of Clinton, Bill, 745–747
Economic policy, under Hamilton, 176–178
Economic Recovery Tax Act (1982), 717
Economy
industrial, 402–403
19th century, 222–228
Economy of scale, 407
Edict of Nantes, 33
Edison, Thomas Alva, 404–405
Edison Electric Illuminating Company, 405–406
Edmonds, Richard H., 405–406
Edmondson, Emily, 308, 309(i)
Edmondson, Mary, 308, 309(i)
Edmunds Act (1882), 395
Edmunds-Tucker Act (1887), 395
Education
for African Americans, 354, 483
in arts and sciences, 194
bilingual, 683–684
Cold War and, 654
colonial era, 98
desegregation of, 647–650
in early republic, 191–193, 192(i), 195
for free blacks, 169
GI Bill and, 635, 636(i)

Great Society programs in, 671–672, 673(t)
of Indians, 385, 484
of Latinos, 556
of Mexican Americans, 652
middle class and, 250–252
segregation in, 418
of slaves, 283
teenage culture and, 643
for women, 170
women teachers in, 430
Educational Alliance, 415(t)
Educational Amendments Act (1972), 704
Edwards, Jonathan, 100
Egypt
Camp David accords, 702
Cold War conflict over, 628
Six-Day War, 694
uprisings in, 761(m)
in World War II, 597
Ehrlichman, John, 697
Eiffel, Alexandre-Gustave, 458
Eighteenth Amendment, 485, 493(t), 521, 544
Eisenhower, Dwight D., 658
black voter registration and, 668(f)
containment under, 624–627, 631
Council of Economic Advisors, 714
domestic politics under, 653–657
interventions in the Middle East, Latin America, and Africa, 628–629
on the military-industrial complex, 624, 678
Modern Republicanism and, 654–655
reelection of, 654
Vietnam and, 629
Warren appointed by, 660
in World War II, 602
Eisenhower Doctrine, 629
El Alamein, battle of (1942), 597
El Centro Asturiano, 457
El Circulo Cubano, 457
El Congreso de Pueblos de Habla Española, 556
Election(s)
of 1796, 183
of 1800, 185–186
of 1824, 234–235, 236(f)
of 1828, 235–237, 236(f)
of 1836, 290
of 1844, 268, 292

Election(s) (*Continued*)
   of 1848, 268, 296
   of 1852, 310
   of 1854, 313
   of 1860, 319, 320*(m)*
   of 1876, 369, 370*(m)*
   of 1892, 444
   of 1894, 444–445
   of 1896, 445–447, 446*(m)*
   of 1912, 494–495
   of 1916, 497, 515
   of 1924, 549, 550*(m)*
   of 1928, 550
   of 1944, 599
   of 1948, 621, 636–637
   of 1960, 655–657, 656*(m)*
   of 1964, 672, 686
   of 1968, 691–692, 692*(m)*
   of 1972, 695–697
   of 1976, 698
   of 1980, 716, 717*(m)*
   of 1984, 719
   of 1988, 728
   of 1992, 737, 746
   of 1996, 746
   of 2000, 749
   of 2008, 754–756
   of 2012, 757
   of 2016, 743, 762–764
   of 2020, 743
   Farmers' Alliance on, 442
   progressive reforms of, 488
   television coverage of, 641
Electoral college, 173
   determination of electors to, 185
   political parties and, 183
Electricity
   consumer goods in the twenties and,
     535*(f)*, 536
   lighting and, 405, 465
   New Deal programs for, 567–568
   rural electrification, 567–568
   social change from, 552
   urbanization and, 465
Electric trolleys, 463
Elementary and Secondary School Act (1965),
   671, 673*(t)*
Elementary Treatise on Mineraology and Geology
   (Cleaveland), 189–190
Elevators, 465
Eliot, John, 47

Elizabeth I (Queen of England), 23, 33
Elkins Act (1903), 492, 493*(t)*
Elk v. Wilkins, 383
Ellicott, Andrew, 197
Ellington, Edward "Duke," 542
Ellis Island, 451, 454, 458
Ellison, Ralph, 571
Ellsberg, Daniel, 696
Elmer Gantry (Lewis), 541
Elmina Castle, 11
El Paso, Texas, 453–454
El Salvador, 723
Ely, Richard T., 413
Emancipation, 351–355
   African American embrace of, 351–352
   education and, 354
   family reunification and, 352–354
   freedom of religion and, 354–355
   universal suffrage and, 361–363
Emancipation Proclamation (1863), 326–327,
   333
   exemptions from, 342
   women's support of, 337
Embargo Act (1807), 203, 209, 218
Emergency Banking Act (1933), 566
Emerson, Irene, 322
Emerson, John, 301, 306
Emerson, Ralph Waldo, 257–258
Emily's List, 730
Encomienda, 14, 19, 32
Endangered Species Act (1973), 705
Enemy combatants, 753
Energy crisis, 698
Energy use, 698, 699*(f)*
England
   civil war in, 49
   colonial government by, 66
   colonial policies of, 120–123
   colonial resistance against, 123–131
   colonial trade, 67–72
   colonies of, 28–30, 37–51, 57–59, 59*(t)*,
     64*(m)*
   convicts transported by, 74
   emergence of slavery and, 41
   exploration by, 15, 15*(m)*, 19, 22–23
   France and, wars between, 62–63, 151
   Glorious Revolution in, 85, 98
   immigration from, 453
   impressment by, 105–106, 120
   Indian Wars and, 112–114
   mercantilism in, 68–69

New England colonies, 45–51
Oregon Territory and, 292
panic of 1837 and, 290
Protestant Reformation in, 31
Queen Anne's War and, 63
slavery outlawed in, 284
slave trade, 13, 70–71, 284
trade and, 11
war debts of, 122
War of 1812, 219–222, 220(m)
West Indies colonies, 43, 44(m)
English language
bilingual education and, 684
immigration restrictions based on, 488
Enlightenment, 99, 103, 105, 120
American Revolution and, 140
Romanticism and, 193
Enola Gay, 602
Enrollment Act (1863), 338
Enterprise of the Indies, 13
Entrepreneurs, nineteenth century, 250
Enumerated articles, 69
Environment
climate change and, 757, 762
the Dust Bowl and, 560
energy consumption and, 699(f)
Exxon Valdez oil spill and, 729–730
Obama on, 757, 762
Progressivism on, 475, 489–491
under Johnson, 671
Environmentalism, 497
in the 1970s, 705–706
Taft and, 494
Environmental Protection Act (1970), 695
Environmental Protection Agency (EPA), 705
Environmental racism, 705
Epidemics, 468
AIDS, 720, 734
influenza, 530
smallpox, 17, 18(m), 20(i), 45, 47, 49,
139, 146, 293, 306, 352
yellow fever, 178, 180
Episcopal Church, 256, 423
Epps, Edwin, 273
Equal Employment Opportunity Commission
(EEOC), 680, 704, 730
Equal Pay Act (1963), 680
Equal Rights Amendment, 480, 680, 704
defeated, 716, 720
Erie Canal, 223–225, 224(m), 246–247, 255
Erikson, Leif, 13

Erik the Red, 13
Espionage Act (1917), 520, 530
Essay on Female Education (Rush), 170
Esteban, 21, 22(m)
Estonia, 585, 613, 731
Ethiopia, repressive regime in, 701
Ethnic cleansing, 748
Eugenics, 460, 493
Eureka, California, 397
Europe
antinuclear protests in, 722
Columbian exchange with, 17–18, 18(m)
crisis leading to World War II in, 583–584
crossing of the Atlantic, 14–15
expanding reach of, 9–13
exploration of the Americas, 14–16, 15(m)
exports to, 503
long-distance trade networks, 10–11
mapmaking and printing, 16–17
the Marshall Plan in, 613
Mediterranean world, 9–10
refugees in, 761
slave trade with Africa, 9, 11–13
European Union (EU), 747
Brexit, 763
the Great Recession and, 754
refugees in, 761
Evangelicalism, 213
abolitionism and, 245, 265
the New Right and, 710
prohibition and, 486
Second Great Awakening and, 255–256
Evans, Oliver, 207
Evers, Medgar, 666
Evolution, 710
fundamentalism on, 548
racism and, 459
social, 411
Excise taxes, on whiskey, 178
Executive Mansion, 197–198, 217
Executive Order 9066, 582, 596
Executive Order 11375, 673(t)
Exodusters, 365
Exxon Valdez oil spill, 729–730

Factionalism, 174
Factory towns, 252–253
Fair Employment Practice Committee (FEPC),
592
Fairfax, William, 110
Fair Housing Act (1968), 670

Fair Labor Standards Act (1938), 572(t), 574
Faith-based initiatives, 750
Fake news, 764
Fall, Albert, 534–535
Fallen Timbers, battle of, 181, 218
Falwell, Jerry, 710
Families
    African American, 464(i)
    in American Revolution, 149
    colonial era, 75–77, 87–93
    in domestic production, 210
    in frontier colleges, 192–193
    in the Great Depression, 562–563
    immigrant, generational conflict in, 458
    middle-class, 250–252
    patriarchal, 88, 90–93
    reunified after slavery, 352–354
    slave, 211
    on television, 641–642
    women's status and, 87–88
    working, 88–89
    after World War II, 635, 637–638
Family and Medical Leave Act (1993), 746
Family values
    the Christian Right and, 710
    Reagan and, 720
    women's rights and, 746
Farewell to Arms (Hemingway), 583
Farm Bureau, 448
Farmers' Alliances, 443
Farm foreclosures, 563, 564(f)
Farm Holiday Association, 563
Farnham, Marynia, 644
Fascism, 570
Fast food, 637, 733
Father Knows Best (TV show), 641
Faubus, Orval, 649
Faulkner, Abigail, 87
Federal Bureau of Indian Affairs, 683
Federal Bureau of Investigation (FBI)
    Freedom Summer and, 667
    House Un-American Activities Committee
      and, 620
    in the Red scare, 531
    Red scare and, 624
    Watergate scandal and, 696
Federal Deposit Insurance Corporation
    (FDIC), 567
Federal Division of Forestry, 475
Federal Emergency Relief Administration
    (FERA), 568, 572(t)

Federal Employee Loyalty Program, 620
Federal Housing Administration, 639
Federal Housing Authority, 640
Federalist Papers, The (Madison, Jay, and
    Hamilton), 174
Federalists, 174–175, 179, 186–187
    election of 1800, 185–186
    in first party system, 183–186
    Louisiana Purchase and, 200
    political realignments and, 234
    Supreme Court and, 203
    in War of 1812, 219
    Whiskey Rebellion and, 180
Federal Reserve Board, 496
    Great Depression and, 552
    the Great Recession and, 754
    in the 1980s, 719
    in the twenties, 534
Federal Reserve System, 493(t), 496
Federal Trade Commission, 493(t), 496, 534,
    539
Felt, Mark, 696
Felton, Rebecca Latimer, 480
Female Association for the Relief of
    Women and Children in Reduced
    Circumstances, 254
Feme covert, 88
Feminine Mystique, The (Friedan), 680
Feminism
    progressivism and, 479
    in the 1970s, 704–705
    women's liberation and, 680–682
Ferdinand, Archduke, 517(m)
Ferdinand II of Aragon, 10
Ferguson, Missouri, 742, 759
Ferraro, Geraldine, 704, 719
Ferris wheel, 440
Fertility rates, colonial era, 90
Field Order Number 15, 344
Fifield, James W., 569
Fifteenth Amendment, 363, 370
    Jim Crow laws and, 418
    poll taxes and, 448
    women's suffrage and, 479
Filibusters, 311
Filipino immigrants, 562, 596
Fillmore, Millard, 296, 308, 310
Film industry
    Communists in, 564
    computers and, 744
    counterculture and, 679

in the Great Depression, 564
House Un-American Activities Committee
    and, 620–621
in the 1950s, 642–643
in the 1970s, 703
sexual values and, 541
in the twenties, 541
in World War II, 591–592
Finney, Charles Grandison, 244–246, 255,
    269
Fire departments, 467
Fires, 467
Fireside chats, 566
First African Baptist Church, Richmond,
    Virginia, 351
First South Carolina Volunteers, 332
First Step Act, 764
Fiske, John, 460, 505
Fitzgerald, F. Scott, 541
Flappers, 541
Flathead Indians, 655
Flint, Michigan, GM strike in, 574
Flood-control projects, 567
Florida, 59
    black majority in, 364
    ceded to England, 115
    civil rights movement investigation
        in, 624
    conflict with Indians in, 225
    in the 2000 election, 749
    immigrants in, 454
    Indian resistance to cattle ranching in, 59
    Ku Klux Klan in, 366
    lumber industry in, 406
    Ponce de León in, 16
    readmitted to the Union, 360
    real estate speculation in, 539
    secession of, 320
    slave raids in, 64
    Spanish exploration of, 21
    after World War II, 640
Floyd, George, 743, 767, 767(i)
Flynn, Michael, 765
Food Administration, 519, 520(i)
Force Act (1807), 203
Force Acts (1870, 1871), 367
Force Bill (1833), 239
Ford, 733
Ford, Gerald, 697
Ford, Henry, 534, 536, 545, 564
Ford River Rouge plant, 564

Foreign policy
    Shultz on, 715
    the Truman Doctrine in, 612–613
    under Bush, George W., 750–753
    under Carter, 701–703
    under Clinton, 747–748
    under Eisenhower, 624–625, 628–629
    under Roosevelt, Theodore, 502, 511–512
    under Taft, 513
    under Truman, 619
    under Wilson, 502, 513–518
Forgotten Americans, 556, 571
Forrest, Nathan Bedford, 366
Fort(s), 64(m), 302
Fort Brown, 493–494
Fort Crown Point, 114
Fort Dearborn, 219
Fort Detroit, 116, 154
Fort Donelson, battle of (1862), 331(m)
Fort Duquesne, 111, 113
Fort Frontenac, 114
Fort Henry, battle of (1862), 331(m)
Fort Lee, 145
Fort Lyon, 344
Fort Mackinac, 219
Fort Michilimackinac, 154
Fort Monmouth, 623
Fort Monroe, 329
Fort Mose, 80
Fort Niagara, 153
Fort Pitt, 114
Fort Sill, 374
Fort Stanwix, 146, 165
Fort Sumter, 328, 331(m)
Fort Ticonderoga, 114, 138–139, 146
Fort Washington, 145, 149
Forty-niners, 303
Fossil fuels, 699(f)
Fourier, Charles, 262
Fourierist phalanxes, 256(m), 262
Fourteen Points (Wilson), 523
Fourteenth Amendment, 359, 370
    corporate personhood and, 409
    Japanese American internment
        and, 595
    property rights as personal liberty in, 411
    ratification of, 359
    United States v. Cruikshank and, 369
    women excluded from voting in, 363
    women's suffrage and, 479
Frame of Government, 58

France
  American Revolution and, 148, 151
  appeasement by, 584
  Bandung Conference and, 627
  colonial expansion and conflict, 98
  colonies of, 60–61, 64(m)
  Counter-Reformation in, 31
  Embargo Act and, 203
  energy consumption per capita in, 699(f)
  European wars with, 62–63
  exploration by, 15(m), 19, 23
  fall of to Germany, 585
  the Great Depression in, 559
  in the Group of Seven (G7), 732
  Haitian Revolution and, 199
  Indian conflicts with, 61, 61(i)
  industrialization in, 403
  Louisiana Purchase from, 190, 200–201
  mercantilism in, 68–69
  in Paris Peace Conference, 524
  protests in 1968, 691
  seizures of U.S. ships by, 183
  on slavery, 284
  slavery abolished in, 310
  trade and, 11
  Vietnam and, 629, 674
  after World War I, 540
  in World War I, 514
  in World War II, 585, 599, 601
  World War II declared by, 585
  XYZ affair, 184
Franciscans, 31–32, 32(i), 60
Franco, Francisco, 584
Franklin, Benjamin, 72, 99
  Declaration of Independence and, 141
  as envoy to Paris, 148, 151
  first political cartoon by, 113(i)
  Paine and, 135
  Paxton Boys and, 117
  in peace term negotiations, 157
  Plan of Union by, 112
Franklin College, 192
Franz Ferdinand, assassination of, 514
Fraternal organizations, 415(t), 416, 420
Free blacks
  abuse of, in Sherman's March to the Sea,
    344
  church governance and, 168
  in development of Washington,
    D.C., 197
  education for, 354

  emigration of, to Africa, 196
  on Fugitive Slave Act, 309
  job competition from, 269
  migration of, from the South, 168
  political participation by, 364–366
  in southern cities, 276
Freed, Alan, 633–635, 650
Freedmen's Bureau, 352, 370
  creation of, 356
  Johnson on, 359
  marriage certificates from, 353
  schools, 354
Freedom of assembly, 179
Freedom of religion
  for African Americans, 354–355
  French Revolution and, 179
  the New Right and, 710
Freedom of speech
  French Revolution and, 179
  limits on, in the Red scare, 530
Freedom Rides, 664
Freedom Schools, 667
Freedom's Journal, 263
Freedom Summer, 666–668
Freedom Trash Can, 681
Free silver, 445, 447
Free-Soil Party, 268, 296, 311
  election of 1852 and, 310
Free Speech Movement (FSM), 678
Free Speech (newspaper), 483
Free trade agreements, 746
Free Will Baptists, 266
Frelinghuysen, Theodorus, 100
Fremont, Jessie, 315
Frémont, John C., 300–302, 305, 310, 322
  election of 1856, 315
French and Indian War, 120, 122
French Revolution (1789–1799), 160, 179,
    186
Freneau, Philip, 195
Freud, Sigmund, 541
Frick, Henry Clay, 437
Friedan, Betty, 644, 680
Frontier
  as American symbol, 461–462
  antislavery parties and, 268
  conflicts with Indians along, 66–67, 116–
    119, 165–167, 178, 181–182, 182(m),
    239–240
  consequences of slavery in, 276–277
  education in, 191–193

Indian resistance to settlement along, 378–385

migration to, 178

mining towns, 386–387

official closing of, 503

after the Revolution, 164, 171, 181–182, 186–187

Whiskey Rebellion and, 180

women homesteaders in, 392, 393(i)

Front Royal, battle of (1862), 331(m)

Fry, Varian, 603

Frye, William, 504

Fuel Administration, 519

Fugitive Slave Act (1850), 307

opposition to, 308–310

Fugitive slaves

in abolitionism, 266

in Civil War, 329

Constitutional Convention on, 173

as contraband of war, 329

in New Bedford, 249

stories of, 312

underground railroad and, 264, 264(i), 264(m)

Fuller, Margaret, 258

Fulton, Robert, 207

Fundamentalism, 548–549

Fundamentals, The, 548

Fund for a Feminist Majority, 730

Furnberg, Anne, 392

Fur trade, 23, 33

Dutch, 36

French, 61–62

Gabriel (slave), 200, 213

Gadsden, Christopher, 125, 129, 131

Gage, Thomas, 138(i)

Gag rule (1836), 265, 287

Galbraith, John Kenneth, 662

Gallatin, Albert, 206

Gambling, 458

Gandhi, Mohandas, 648

Gang labor, 279

Gangs

immigrants in, 458

in the 1950s, 642

nineteenth century, 249

Garcia, Gustavo C., 655

Garfield, James A., 421

Garrison, William Lloyd, 263, 266–268, 309

Garvey, Amy Jacques, 542–543

Garvey, Marcus, 540, 542–544, 543(i)

Garza, Alicia, 742, 759, 769

Gas emission standards, 699

Gates, Bill, 741–743, 768

Gates, Horatio, 156

Gay Liberation Front, 684

Gay liberation movement, 661, 684

Gaza Strip, 737

Gender discrimination, women's liberation and, 680–682

Gender roles

among Indians, 380

colonial, 89–90

imperialism and, 505

industrialization and, 416–418

progressivism on, 480

in the 1970s, 703

in western migration, 303

women's liberation and, 680–682

after World War II, 635

in World War II, 590

General Electric Corporation, 405

General Federation of Women's Clubs, 415, 415(t)

General Intelligence Division, 531

General Motors, 536, 569, 574, 733

General Motors Family, The (radio show), 541

General Trades Union, 254

Genêt, Edmond, 179

Genius of Universal Emancipation, 263

Genocide

in the Balkans, 748

the Holocaust, 597, 602–604, 603(i)

George, Henry, 413

George, Milton, 442

George II (King of England), 66, 103

George III (King of England), 115, 122, 125, 141

Georgia, 59

American Revolution in, 154

black voters in, 364

Cherokee in, 217, 240

Constitution ratified by, 175, 175(t)

cotton and slavery in, 212

first black congressman from, 349

immigrants to, 66

Ku Klux Klan in, 547

land claims of, 166(m)

secession of, 320

German immigrants, 76, 95, 96*(m)*
    in Civil War draft riots, 338
    Democratic Party and, 423
    as farmers, 391
    religion and, 457
    in 1820s, 247, 248*(f)*
    socialism and, 438
    suspicion of in World War I, 521
    in World War II, 595
German Social Democratic Party, 438
Germany
    deal with Mexico, 515
    expansionism of, 584
    the Great Depression in, 559
    in the Group of Seven (G7), 732
    Hitler's rise in, 584
    Holocaust in, 602–604, 603*(i)*
    industrialization in, 402
    occupation zones in, 615, 616*(m)*
    in Paris Peace Conference, 523
    Pietists, 99
    Protestant Reformation in, 30–31
    rebuilding after World War II, 615
    reparations by, 524
    reunification of, 731
    Tripartite Pact of, 586
    welfare spending in, 717
    after World War I, 540
    in World War I, 513–518
    in World War II, 584–586, 595, 597–599,
        601–602
Geronimo, 374, 385
Gettysburg, battle of (1863), 340, 341*(m)*
Gettysburg Address (Lincoln), 341
Ghettos, 456, 669
Ghost Dance, 385
Giants in the Earth (Rolvaag), 391
GI Bill (1944), 635, 636*(i)*
Gideon v. Wainwright, 672
Gilded Age, 414–420, 425
Gillespie, Dizzy, 645
Gilman, Charlotte Perkins, 479
Gingrich, Newt, 746
Ginsberg, Allen, 645
Glaciers, 3, 4*(m)*
Gladden, Washington, 476
Glasnost, 728, 730
Glass-Steagall Act (1933), 567, 572*(t)*
Glazer, Nathan, 709
Globalization, 729, 732–735, 739
    Clinton, Bill, on, 746

    the Great Recession and, 754
Global warming, 762
Glorious Revolution, 58, 85–86, 98
Glyphs, 17
Gold
    in Alaska, 447
    Aztec, 19
    in the Black Hills, 383
    Dutch trade in, 24
    from Africa, 11
    Incan, 19
    in Indian Territory, 385
    Mayan, 2
    Ponce de León's search for, 16
    Spanish exploration for, 15*(m)*, 19–21,
        22*(m)*, 23
Goldman, Emma, 437, 479, 531
Gold rush, California, 302–304, 304*(i)*
Gold standard, 446
Goldwater, Barry M., 672, 685–686, 709
Gompers, Samuel, 435, 509
Gonzalez, Alberto, 750
Goodluck, Tracy, 760
Gorbachev, Mikhail, 728, 731–732
Gordon, Kate, 480
Gore, Al, 749
Gorusch, Neil, 764
"Gospel of Wealth, The" (Carnegie), 412
Gossip, 91
Gould, Jay, 408
Government
    during the American Revolution, 149–153
    by commission, 519
    colonial era, 103–107
    economic growth fueled by, 223–225
    federal, 175–176
    laissez-faire and, 412
    progressivism on, 488–491
    promotion of the economy by in the
        twenties, 534–535
    reframing of, after the Revolution,
        171–178
    during World War I, 519
Grable, Betty, 592
Graft, 468, 470
Graham, Billy, 645, 710
Grand Alliance, 597
Grand Coulee Dam, 568
Grandfather clauses, 418, 483
Grand Old Party (GOP), 423
Grangers, 441–442, 449

Grant, Ulysses S., 327, 330
  Civil War policies of, 340, 343
  end of the war and, 345
  as president, 361
  in Reconstruction, 360
  reelection of, 367, 421
  scandals surrounding, 367
  Vicksburg and, 340, 341*(m)*
Grapes of Wrath, The (Steinbeck), 560
Grateful Dead, 679
Great Atlantic and Pacific Tea Company
    (A&P), 410
Great Awakening, 85, 99–100, 121
  communication and, 121–122
  Second, 255–256
Great Britain
  appeasement by, 584
  child care in, 590
  Civil War and, 333
  energy consumption per capita in, 699*(f)*
  frontier conflicts with, 181
  Great Depression in, 559
  Great Recession and, 754
  immigrants from, 248*(f)*
  industrialization in, 208
  investment in development of the West,
    376, 408
  in the Iraq War, 752
  Jay Treaty with, 179
  labor movement in, 435
  nuclear freeze movement in, 726–728
  in Paris Peace Conference, 523
  slavery abolished in, 310
  Suez Canal and, 628
  Thatcherism in, 717
  U.S. sovereignty undermined by, 171
  after World War I, 540
  in World War I, 514
  in World War II, 585, 590, 597–600
  World War II declared by, 585
Great Depression, 551–552, 555–579
  causes of, 551–552
  dust storms in, 560
  election of 1960 influenced by, 656
  ended by World War II, 582, 586
  families in, 562–563
  farm foreclosures in, 563, 564*(f)*
  Hoover's response to, 557–559
  Hoovervilles in, 559
  minorities during, 560–562
  New Deal and, 558*(f)*, 565–578
  organized protest in, 563–565
  soup kitchens in, 559*(i)*
  timeline of, 580
  worldwide effects of, 559
Great Lakes, the market revolution and, 247
Great migration, 532
Great Plains, 305*(m)*, 306, 376
  Dust Bowl in, 559
  farming on the, 389
  Indians of, 378–380, 379*(m)*
Great Railway Strike, 368
Great Recession, 754–755
Great Society programs, 661, 671–672, 673*(t)*,
    695
  Reagan on, 716
Greece
  civil war in, 612
  the Great Recession in, 754
  refugees in, 761
Greeley, Horace, 258, 368
Greenbacks, 443
Greene, Catherine, 208
Greene, Nathanael, 156
Greenham Common, England, 727
Greenhouse gases, 699*(f)*, 730, 762
Greenhow, Robert, 326
Greenhow, Rose O'Neal, 326, 333, 337, 346
Greenland, Norse settlements in, 14
Green Mountain Boys, 119, 138
Green Party, 749
Greensboro, North Carolina, sit-ins in, 650
Greenwich Village, 418, 645, 684
Gregg, William, 276
Grenada, 724
Grenville, George, 122–124
Grey, Philip, 353
Grey, Willie Ann, 352–353
Grimké, Angelina, 265
Grimké, Sarah, 265
Griswold, Roger, 184*(i)*
Griswold v. Connecticut, 672
Gross domestic product
  COVID-19 pandemic effects on, 766
  industrialization and, 402
  in World War II, 587
Gross national product (GNP), 637
Grosvenor, Leicester, 84
Grosvenor, Sarah, 84–85, 88, 91–92, 108
Grosvenor, Zerviah, 84
Group of Seven (G7), 732
Guadalcanal Island, 599

Guam, 16, 503, 508
Guantánamo Bay
  incarcerations at, 752–753
  naval base at, 509
Guatemala
  CIA covert action in, 628
  description of, 724
Guinn v. United States, 483
Guiteau, Charles, 421
Gulf of Tonkin Resolution (1964), 675, 693
Gulf War, 736, 752
Gunpowder, 11
Gun rights
  Brady Bill and, 746
  Bush, George H. W., on, 730
Guns, 13
  Indian conflicts and trade in, 63
  manufacturing of, 209
Gutenberg, Johannes, 16
Gutierrez, Carlos, 750
Guzman, Jacobo Arbenz, 628

Habermann, Franz Xavier, 105*(i)*
Hair (musical), 679
Haiti, U.S. intervention in, 503, 513
Haitian Revolution (1791–1799), 188, 213
Haldeman, H. R., 696
Hale, John, 310
Half Breeds, Republican, 423
Hall, G. Stanley, 417
Hallowell, John, 84
Hamer, Fannie Lou, 667
Hamilton, Alexander, 163, 185
  Adams' presidency and, 185
  in Annapolis convention, 171
  duties on imports recommended by, 164
  Federalist Papers by, 174
  foreign trade and, 178
  on governmental structure, 172
  as secretary of the treasury, 176
  on war debt, 167
  Whiskey Rebellion and, 180
Hamilton, Andrew, 107
Hammond, James Henry, 275, 285
Hampton, Anne, 273
Hampton Institute, 464*(i)*, 482
Handy, W. E., 440
"Hanging of the San Patricios," 295*(i)*
Hanna, Marcus Alonzo, 420, 422, 446
Harding, Warren G., 521, 534, 550*(m)*
Hard war strategy, 343–344

Hargis, Billy Joe, 685
Harlem Renaissance, 541–542
Harper, Frances Ellen Watkins, 362*(i)*, 363
Harpers Ferry, Virginia, raid on, 316–319, 323
Harris, Kamala, 768
Harrison, Benjamin, 421, 444
Harrison, William Henry, 219, 291
Harrison Narcotics Control Act (1914), 486,
  493*(t)*
Hartford Convention, 222
Hartford Wits, 193
Harvard College, 47, 99, 192
Hawaii, 226
  annexation of, 503–504, 507
  immigration to, 453
  martial law in, 595
  sugar plantations on, 504
Hawley-Smoot Act (1930), 558
Hawthorne, Nathaniel, 260
Hay, John, 511
Hayden, Tom, 678
Hayes, Rutherford B., 369, 370*(m)*, 401,
  421
Haymarket Square, 434–435
Hayne, Robert, 238
Hay-Pauncefote Treaty (1901), 511
Head Start, 671
Health care
  in Civil War, 334, 336–337
  Clinton, Bill, on, 746
  globalization and, 734
  Great Society programs in, 672
  for Indians, 546
  Obama on, 755–756
  women in, 336–337, 430
Health insurance
  American Plan on, 534
  Carter on, 701
  Obama on, 755–756
Hearst, William Randolph, 507
Hemingway, Ernest, 583
Henry, Patrick, 124, 126, 129, 131, 176
Henry IV (King of France), 33
Henry the Navigator, 10
Henry VIII (King of England), 31
Henson, Josiah, 312
Hepburn Act (1906), 492, 493*(t)*
Heritage Foundation, 710
Herkimer, Nicholas, 146
Herrara, Johnny, 655
Herrera, Juan Jose, 395

Hessian mercenaries, 145–146
Hetch Hetchy valley, 489, 491
Hewitt, Nancy, 452, 472
Heyrick, Elizabeth, 263
Hicks, Elias, 245
Hicks, Louise Day, 689–690, 704, 706
Hicksites, 245
Hidatsa Indians, 190
Higher education, after World War II, 636–637
Highways, after World War II, 639, 654, 657
Hill, Anita, 730
Hill, Elias, 367
Hirohito, 602
Hiroshima, atomic bomb dropped on, 602
Hispaniola, 17
Hiss, Alger, 621
History of the Revolution (Warren), 193
Hitler, Adolf, 584–585, 602
HIV (human immunodeficiency virus), 720
H1N1 virus, 522
Hoban, James, 197
Ho Chi Minh, 629, 674
Ho Chi Minh Trail, 693
Hohokam people, 6, 8*(m)*
Holder, Eric, 759
Holding, Susanna, 91
Holiday Inn, 637
Holloway, Houston H., 351
Hollywood, 563
Holmes, Oliver Wendell, 530
Holocaust, 597, 602–604, 603*(i)*
Homer, Winslow, 353*(i)*
Homes for Virtuous and Friendless Females, 259
Homestead, Pennsylvania, 427–428, 436–437, 459
Homestead Act (1862), 390
Homestead strike, 436–437
Homosexuals, 756
 "don't ask, don't tell" policy on, 746, 756
 gay liberation movement and, 661
 Gilded Age, 418
 in the Holocaust, 597, 603
 marriage for, 747, 757
 in the military, 746, 756
 Red scare and, 620
 in the 1950s, 645–646
 social conservatism and, 720
 in World War II, 589

Honda, 733
Honecker, Erich, 731
Honeymooners, The (TV show), 642
Honky tonks, 440
Hood, John B., 343
Hooker, Joseph, 340
Hoopas, 655
Hoover, Herbert, 519, 550, 656
 Bonus Army and, 564
 response to the Great Depression, 557–559
 unions weakened by, 534
Hoover, J. Edgar, 531, 624
Hoovervilles, 559–560
Hopewell people, 7, 8*(i)*, 8*(m)*
Hopkins, Harry, 568, 571
Horizontal integration, 408
Horses, 13
Horseshoe Bend, Battle of, 221, 240
Horticulture, 3–4
House of Burgesses, 39–41
House of Representatives
 Constitutional Convention on, 173
 first woman elected to, 516
 turnover in, 421
House Un-American Activities Committee (HUAC), 620–621, 624
Housework, in the 1950s, 644
Housing
 in black ghettos, 669
 discrimination in, 673*(t)*
 GI Bill and, 635
 Gilded Age, 414
 mail-order, 463
 public, in the 1960s, 662
 sales decline in the twenties, 539
 segregation in, 593, 640, 706
 settlement houses, 471
 in tenements, 466
 after World War II, 639–640
 in World War II, 593
 zoning and, 469
Howard Medical School, 529
Howard University, 593
Howe, Julia Ward, 479
Howe, William, 139, 145–146
Howl (Ginsberg), 645
How the Other Half Lives (Riis), 467
Hudson River, 119
Hudson River School, 258*(i)*, 259
Hughes, Charles Evans, 497, 515
Hughes, Langston, 560

Huguenots, 33
Hull House, 478
Human immunodeficiency virus (HIV), 720
Humanism, pragmatic, 565
Humanitarian reforms, 478
Human rights
    Carter on, 701
    under Reagan, 722–725
Humphrey, Hubert, 692, 692(m)
Hungarian immigrants, 429, 452
Hungary
    anti-Soviet revolution in, 624
    fall of the Soviet regime in, 730
    refugees in, 761
Hunkpapa Lakota, 380
Hunters and gatherers, 3, 7
Huron people, 34, 111
Hurricane Katrina, 753
Husband, Hermon, 128
    in Whiskey Rebellion, 180
Hussein, Saddam, 736
    capture of, 752
    as sponsor of terrorism, 752
Hutchinson, Anne, 29–30, 48–50
Hutchinson, Thomas, 125, 159
Hutchinson, William, 29–30
Hydrogen bomb, 615

Ickes, Harold, 568
Idaho
    miner riot in, 386
    mining in, 386
    Populists and, 447
    silver miner strike in, 438
Identity
    gay, 684
    Harlem Renaissance and, 542
    literature and culture in, 193–194
    national, 191–198
    development of, 191
    dilemmas of, 191–198
    new capital and, 197–198
    teenage, in the 1950s, 643
Illinois, presidents from, 423
Immigrants
    Americanization of, 546–547
    American Party on, 313
    anarchists, 434
    arrivals of 1960–2000, 720, 721(f)
    assimilation of, 453, 460–461
    bilingual education and, 684
    blamed for fallen women, 260

California gold rush and, 304, 304(i)
    in Civil War draft riots, 338
    colonial era, 76
    colonial era expansion and conflict among,
        96(m), 96–98
    communities of, 456–458
    Democratic Party and, 550
    departures vs. arrivals of, 456(t)
    dreamers, 758
    early twentieth century, 451–452
    economic incentives for, 455–456
    in the election of 1896, 446
    as farmers on the Great Plains, 391
    fear of communism and, 530
    generational conflicts among, 458
    hostility toward recent, 458–460
    industrialization and, 254, 429–432
    late twentieth to twenty-first century,
        745(f)
    in Mexican-American War, 295(i)
    in mining, 387
    narcotic use and, 486
    nativism and, 260–261, 460, 544–547
    in nineteenth century, 247–249, 248(f)
    political bosses and, 469
    Populists on, 443
    progressivism and, 476, 478, 487–488, 498
    quota system on, 545, 672
    radicalism and, 459
    radio shows for, 541
    religious revivals and, 245
    settlement patterns of, 455(m)
    social conservatives against, 720, 721(f)
    in social reform movements, 259
    suburb development and, 466
    Trump on, 763
    twenties attitudes toward, 544–547
    undocumented, under Reagan,
        720–721
    in the union movement, 433
    urban crowding and, 466–468
    urbanization and, 247, 249, 472
    urban life and, 247–249
    in the West, 393, 396–397
    women's suffrage and, 480
    after World War I, 537
Immigration Act (1924), 604
Immigration and Nationality Act (1965), 672,
    673(t)
Immigration and Naturalization Service, 655
Immigration Reform and Control Act (1986),
    720

Immigration Restriction League, 460
Imperialism, 501–526
  attitudes toward, 502
  awakening of, 503–506
  cultural justifications for, 504–505
  economics of, 503–504, 504(f)
  extension of, 511–513
  Philippine War and, 509–511
  Suez invasion and, 628
  under Roosevelt, 511–513
  war with Spain and, 506–511
  Wilson and, 513–518
  World War I and, 513–518
Imperial presidency, 614, 618–619
Implied powers clause, 203
Import duties, 123
Impressment, 105–106, 120–121
Incarceration rates, 746
Incas, 5–6, 18–19, 25
Income
  Chinese American, 653
  racial differences in, 706–707
  in the twenties, 536
  of women in World War II, 589, 592
  after World War II, 637, 638(f)
Income tax
  graduated, 495
  in the Great Depression, 558
  Populists on, 443
  progressivism on, 476, 495
  Wilson-Gorman Act on, 445
Indentured servants, 13
  abuse of, 42
  in colonial America, 55–56, 73–74
  diversity among, 95
  English, 37
  slavery and, 42, 73
  in tobacco cultivation, 39
  West Indies, 43
  women's status and, 88
India, 115(m)
  energy consumption in, 699(f)
  immigrants from, 744, 745(f)
  in Paris Climate Agreement, 762
Indian(s). See American Indians
Indiana
  Ku Klux Klan in, 548
  presidents from, 423
Indianapolis, 547
"Indian Burying Ground" (Freneau), 195
Indian Citizenship Act (1924), 546
Indian Removal Act (1830), 240, 287

Indian Reorganization Act (IRA), 576
Indian Territory, 240, 382–383
Indian Trade and Intercourse Act (1790), 181
Indian Wars (1754–1763), 112–114, 115(m),
    116–119
India trade, 11
Indigo, 57, 69, 79, 81
Individualism
  industrialization and, 425
  laissez-faire and, 413
  Lost Generation on, 541
  Modern Republicanism and, 654
  progressivism and, 476
Individualism, in early republic arts, 193
Indulgences, 31
Industrialization, 400–425
  cities and, 461–465
  Civil War, 333–336
  consolidation in, 406–408
  corporations in, 409–410
  cotton boom and, 226–228
  decline of craft work and, 253–254
  energy crisis and, 698–699, 700(m)
  environmentalism and, 475–476
  factories in World War II, 587
  factory towns and, 252–253
  gender roles and, 416–418
  immigrants and, 248
  imperialism and, 503–504, 504(f)
  labor movements and, 429–441
  laissez-faire and, 410–413
  leisure and, 438–441
  market revolution and, 247–252
  mechanization in, 254
  mid-nineteenth century, 252–255
  national politics and, 420–423
  in nineteenth century, 223–225
  panic of 1837 and, 254–255
  per capita energy consumption
    and, 699(f)
  politics and, 422
  railroads and, 403(f)
  second industrial revolution and, 536
  in the South, 335–336, 405–406,
    407(m)
  technology and, 208–209
  in the twenties, 535–536, 552
  wealth from, 432
  women in, 252
  workday length and, 253–254
  worker conditions in, 431–432
  in World War II, 587–588

Industrial revolution, 402–403
    second, 536
Industrial Workers of the World (IWW), 438,
        521, 531
Inflation
    in the 1970s, 695, 698–699
    after World War I, 530
Influence of Sea Power upon History, The
        (Mahan), 501
Influenza, 18*(m)*
    epidemic/pandemic of 1918, 522–523, 530
*Infortunate, the Voyage and Adventures of
        William Moraley, an Indentured Servant,
        The* (Moraley), 56
Infrastructure
    in 1837, 224*(m)*
    road and turnpikes, 206
    19th century, 223–225
    Works Progress Administration and, 571
    after World War II, 639–640
Inglis, Charles, 140
Inheritance taxes, 495
"Inner Light," 245
Inquisition, 10
Integration, economic, 406–408
Interchangeable parts, 209
Interest groups, 448
Intermediate Nuclear Forces Treaty, 728
Internal combustion engine, 404
Internal Revenue Service (IRS), 710
Internet, 744
Internment camps, Japanese American, 582,
        595–596, 653
    reparations for, 684
Interracial political coalitions, 364
Interstate commerce, Annapolis conference
        on, 171
Interstate Commerce Act (1887), 442
Interstate Commerce Commission (ICC), 442,
        492
Intolerable Acts (England), 129
Inuit people, 3
"Invisible Hand," 411
Iowa, statehood of, 292
Iran
    in axis of evil, 752
    CIA intervention in, 702–703
    Cold War intervention in, 628
    hostage crisis, 703, 725
    Islamic revolution in, 703
    nuclear program in, 762

    Reagan's backing of, 725
    repressive regime supported in, 694
Iran-Contra affair, 726
Iraq
    in axis of evil, 752
    Iraq War (2003–), 750–753
    Operation Desert Storm in, 736–737
    Reagan and, 725
    under Obama, 760
    U.S. invasion of, 729
Irish immigrants, 453
    Catholic church growth and, 257
    in Civil War draft riots, 338
    conflict of with African Americans,
        249–250
    Lease, 428
    in mining towns, 387
    nativists on, 260–261
    in New York City, 206
    political bosses and, 469
    in 1820s, 247, 248*(f)*
    temperance and, 261
    in textile mills, 254
Iron curtain, 611, 616*(m)*
Iron Man (film), 744
Iroquoian people, 8*(m)*, 34
    in American Revolution, 153
    fur trade, 51, 62
    land treaties with, 165
    Walking Purchase with, 97
    women's authority in, 63
    in World War II, 594
Iroquois, 33
Iroquois Confederacy, 65
    in American Revolution, 142
    British alliance with, 112
Irrigation, 6
Irving, Washington, 193
Isabella of Castile, 10, 15
ISIS, 760–761, 761*(m)*, 769
Islam
    Crusades against, 9
    slave culture and, 280
    slave trade and, 13
    Spanish reconquest and, 10
Islamic extremism
    Obama on, 760
    terrorism and, 731, 748
Islamic State of Iraq and Syria (ISIS),
        760–761, 761*(m)*, 769
Island-hopping, 599

Isolationism
    before World War II, 583–586
    Germany's challenges to, 585–586
    after Pearl Harbor, 595
Israel
    Camp David accords, 702
    Gaza Strip and West Bank and, 737
    Six-Day War, 694
    U.S. policies on, 726(m)
Italian immigrants
    Catholic Church influenced by, 457
    labor contracts with, 453
    in the Triangle Shirtwaist Company, 467
    in World War II, 595
Italy
    the Great Depression in, 559
    in the Group of Seven (G7), 732
    long-distance trade by, 25
    road to World War II in, 584
    Tripartite Pact of, 586
    war declared on, 585
    in World War I, 514
    in World War II, 584–585
Itinerant preachers, 101
Iwo Jima, battle of (1945), 599

Jackson, Andrew, 234–235, 378
    Cherokee removal under, 218
    election of 1828, 235–236
    Indian removal under, 240, 287–289
    in Indian wars, 225
    as president, 237–240
    on Texas, 285, 287
    in War of 1812, 220(m), 221(i), 222
Jackson, Gina, 760
Jackson, Helen Hunt, 383
Jackson, Mississippi, 336
Jackson, Rachel, 236
Jackson, Thomas "Stonewall," 328, 331,
    358(i)
Jamaica, slave markets in, 71
Jamarillo, Lucy, 715
James, Henry, 418
James, the Duke of York, 57
James I (King of England), 28, 37, 40, 49
James II (King of England), 58
Jamestown colony, 28–29, 37–38
Jane Crow, 690
Jansen, Eric, 262(i)
Japan
    atomic bombs dropped on, 582, 602

energy consumption per capita in, 699(f)
in the Group of Seven (G7), 732
invasions of China and Southeast Asia, 583
Pearl Harbor attack by, 582, 586
Russian invasion of Manchuria and, 512
trade with, 310
Tripartite Pact of, 586
war atrocities by, 604
in World War II, 599–600, 600(m), 602,
    604
Japanese American Citizens League, 684
Japanese Americans
    civil rights movement and, 653
    in the Great Depression, 562
    internment of, 582, 592, 595–596, 653,
        684
    reparations to internees, 684
Japanese immigrants, 454, 457, 487
Jaramillo, Juan, 25
Jay, John, 181
    in Continental Congress, 131
    in England, 179
    Federalist Papers by, 174
    in peace term negotiations, 157
Jay Treaty (1794), 179, 181
Jazz, 440, 542, 645
Jefferson, Thomas, 160
    agrarian vision of, 199, 376, 461
    on Alien and Sedition Acts, 185
    American system of manufacturing and,
        209
    on Bank of the United States, 177
    challenges facing, 199–200
    Declaration of Independence and, 141
    Dolley Madison and, 217
    economic growth and, 223
    election of 1800, 185–186
    Embargo Act and, 203
    on Hamilton's policies, 179
    on Judiciary Act, 201
    Louisiana Purchase and, 190, 200–201
    on national identity, 191
    on Neutrality Proclamation, 179
    Northwest Ordinance written by, 165
    reelection of, 201
    as secretary of state, 176
    as vice president, 183
    on Whiskey Rebellion, 181
Jefferson Airplane, 679
Jeffries, Jim, 486
Jehovah's Witnesses, 597

Jennings, Peter, 222
Jennings, Samuel, 194
Jesuits, 35, 61
Jews
    colonial era, 102(m)
    crimes committed by, 458
    generational conflicts among, 458
    Holocaust of, 597, 602–604, 603(i)
    immigrants, 257, 451–453, 544
    immigrants as white or not, 459
    international conspiracy of, 545
    Ku Klux Klan on, 548
    Oppenheimer and, 581
    prejudice against, 249
    religious practices of, 457
    in Rhode Island, 48
    in social reform, 257
    in South Carolina, 67–68
    in the Triangle Shirtwaist Company, 467
    in the twenties, 544–545
Jiang Jieshi, 615
Jihad, 748, 760
Jim Crow
    laws, 396, 418–420
    minstrel show character, 248
    white resistance to dismantling, 649
Jiménez, José Cha Cha, 683
Jingoists, 505, 507
Jobs, Steve, 743
Joel, Billy, 703
John Birch Society, 685
Johnny Got His Gun (Trumbo), 583
Johnson, Andrew, 350
    Congressional resistance to, 358–360
    impeachment of, 360, 420
    Reconstruction under, 356–358
    in state legislature, 368
Johnson, Guy, 142
Johnson, Jack, 486
Johnson, Lyndon B., 572
    black voter registration and, 668(f)
    in civil rights legislation, 654
    civil rights movement and, 666–668
    Freedom Summer killings and, 667
    Great Society programs, 661, 671–672,
        673(t)
    Kerner Commission and, 669
    Pentagon Papers on, 693
    reelection of, 671, 686, 692
    Vietnam War and, 674–676, 678
Johnson, Milly, 352

Johnson, Tom L., 489
Joint Chiefs of Staff, 614
Joint Electoral Commission, 369
Jones, Samuel "Golden Rule," 489
Jordan, Barbara, 704
Jordan, George, 382
Joseph, Chief, 381
Journalism
    muckrakers in, 477
    yellow, 507
Journey of Reconciliation, 661
Judicial review, 203
Judicial system
    Constitutional Convention on, 173–174
    in early republic, 201–203
    influence of business on, 422
    Puritan, 48
Judiciary Act (1801), 201
Juke joints, 440
Jungle, The (Sinclair), 492
Justice Department, 176
Juvenile delinquency, 486
    after World War II, 635

Kameny, Frank, 684
Kamikaze, 600
Kansas
    Bleeding Kansas, 314–316
    Exodusters in, 365
    prohibition in, 485
    temperance movements in, 392
    women homesteaders in, 393(i)
Kansas-Nebraska Act (1854), 312–314,
        314(m)
Kansas Workman (newspaper), 393(i)
Kant, Immanuel, 99, 193
Kaskaskia, 61
Katznelson, Ira, 575
Kavanaugh, Brett, 764
Kearney, Belle, 480
Keating-Owen Act (1916), 493(t), 497
Kelley, Abby, 267, 363
Kellogg-Briand Pact, 583
Kelly, Oliver H., 441
Kenjinkai, 457
Kennan, George, 608–611, 613, 630
Kennedy, John F., 655–656, 656(m)
    assassination of, 666
    black voter registration and, 668(f)
    civil rights movement and, 665–666
    Cold War and, 662(m), 662–664

Commission on the Status of Women, 680
Cuba and, 662(m), 662–664
New Frontier pledge of, 662
Pentagon Papers on, 693
Vietnam interventions by, 674
Kennedy, Robert, 665, 691
Kent State University, 693
Kentucky, statehood of, 206
Kenya, terrorism in, 748
Kerner, Otto, 669
Kerner Commission, 669
Kerosene, 404
Kerouac, Jack, 645
Kerry, John, 753, 760
Khomeini, Ayatollah Ruholla, 703
Khrushchev, Nikita, 626, 663–664
Kieft, William, 36
Kim II Sung, 616
King, Martin Luther, Jr., 648–649, 656
antiwar address by, 679
assassination of, 670, 691
Carter supported by, 698
Freedom Riders and, 665
"Letter from Birmingham Jail," 665
in March to Montgomery, 667
Rustin and, 661
King, Rufus, 225
King Philip's War, 50
King's College, 192
King's Mountain, Battle of, 156
King William's War, 62, 85
Kinsey, Alfred, 645–646
Kiowa Indians, 378
Kirkpatrick, Jeane, 722
Kissinger, Henry, 691–693
Kitchen Debate, 627
Klamath Indians, 306, 655
Klinghoffer, Leon, 725
Knights of Columbus, 415(t)
Knights of Labor, 433, 443
Knox, Henry, 139, 171, 176
Kohl, Helmut, 717
Korea
demilitarized zone in, 619(i)
immigrants from, 744, 745(f)
Korean War, 614, 619(i), 622, 630, 703
imperial presidency and, 618–619
Korematsu, Fred, 582–583, 595–596, 605
Kosciusko, Thaddeus, 148
Kosovo, 748
Kraus, Olaf, 262(i)

Kristol, Irving, 709
Ku Klux Klan, 366–367, 369
Birmingham church bombing by, 665
in Birth of a Nation, 498
civil rights movement and, 650
Democratic convention of 1924 on, 549
former Confederate officials in, 349
Freedom Rides and, 664
Freedom Summer and, 666–668
resurrection of in the twenties, 547–548, 552
in the twenties, 529
Kuwait, Iraqi invasion of, 736
Kyoto Protocol (1998), 734

La Alianza Federal de Mercedes (Federal Alliance of Land Grants), 682
Labor
during the Civil War, 338
colonial America, 55–56, 73–80, 88–89, 159
coping with economic distress by, 74–75
decline of craft work and, 253–254
deskilling of, 253
in families, 88–89
immigrants as competition for, 544
industrialization and, 252–255, 429–432
international division of, 178
middle class and, 250–252
shortages in Civil War, 335
skilled, 430
socialism and, 413
in spinning mills, 208
transient, 75
unskilled, 429
women's, 87–88, 250–252, 416
during World War I, 519
Labor Movement, The (Ely), 413
Labor movements
Civil War, 338
depression of 1893 and, 444
energy crisis and, 698
in the Great Depression, 562, 568
industrialization and, 429–432
in mining, 387
New Deal and, 568, 573
Solidarity, 730
Truman and, 619
after World War I, 531
after World War II, 635–636
Ladies Association of Philadelphia, 148

Lafayette, Marquis de, 156
La Follette, Robert M., 489, 516, 550(m), 551
Laissez-faire, 402, 410–413, 425
   the Great Depression and, 552
   progressivism on, 476
   in the 1960s, 685
   in the twenties, 534
Lake City, Florida, 353
Lakewood Church, 750
Lakota Sioux, 378, 382(i), 383
Lancaster Turnpike, 206
Land claims
   of freedpeople, 352, 356
   Indians and, 165, 384
   Northwest Ordinance on, 165–166
   sharecropping and, 365
   as solution to economic depression, 167
   westward migration and, 204–208
Landon, Alfred M., 576
Land riots, 119
Landscape, changes to from urbanization, 247
Land speculators, 105, 120
Laos, 758
La Raza Unida (The United Race), 683
La Salle, Sieur de, 60
Las Casas, Bartolome de, 24
Las Gorras Blancas (The White Caps), 395
Lassen Volcanic, 490(m)
Lassin, Beryl, 451–453, 457, 459, 472
Lassin, Lena, 451–452
Las Vegas, New Mexico, 395
Latchkey kids, 592
Lathrop, Julia, 479
Latin America, emerging democracies
   supported in, 665–666
Latinos/Latinas
   in feminism, 682
   in the Great Depression, 561–562
   immigration of, 757–758
   liberation movement of, 682
   in the 1930s, 556
Latrobe, Benjamin, 197
Latvia, 585, 613, 731
La Union Martí-Maceo, 457
Laurens, Henry, 77(i)
Law and order candidates, 692, 692(m)
Lawrence, Jacob, 571
Lawrence, Kansas, 315
Lawson, Steven F., 452, 472
Lazarus, Emma, 458

Lead mining, 387
League of Nations, 523, 525, 583
League of United Latin American Citizens
   (LULAC), 546, 594, 652
Lease, Charles L., 428
Lease, Mary Elizabeth, 428, 442–443, 447
Leave It to Beaver (TV show), 641
Lebanon, 725
Lecompton Constitution, 315
Lee, Richard Henry, 140–141
Lee, Robert E., 318, 328, 331
   at Antietam, 333
   in battle of Chancellorsville, 340
   on condition of his soldiers, 334
   end of the war and, 345
   Gettysburg, Vicksburg, and, 340, 341(m)
"Legend of Sleepy Hollow, The" (Irving), 193
Legislative branch
   big business and, 422
   Constitutional Convention on, 174
Leisure
   automobiles and, 536
   Gilded Age, 414–416
   middle class and, 248
   nineteenth century, 248
   working-class, 438–441
LeMay, Curtis, 599
Lend-Lease Act (1941), 585
Lenin, Vladimir, 564
Leningrad, battle of, 598(m)
Lenni-Lenape Indians, 58
"Letter from Birmingham Jail" (King), 665
Levellers, 119
Levitt, William, 639–640, 657
Levittown, Long Island, 639–640
Lewinsky, Monica, 747
Lewis, John, 666
Lewis, John L., 573
Lewis, Mercy, 87
Lewis, Meriwether, 201, 213
   route traveled by, 202(m)
   Sacagawea and, 190
Lewis, Sinclair, 541
Libel laws, colonial, 107
Liberalism
   challenges to the establishment in, 677–686
   civil rights movement and, 664–670
   conservatism's revival and, 684–686
   conservative backlash to, 689–713

counterculture and, 679–680
environmentalism and, 705–706
federal efforts toward social reform and, 671–673
liberation movements and, 680–684
New Frontier in, 662
the New Left and, 678–679
persistence of in the 1970s, 703–708
politics of, 661–664
timeline on, 688
Vietnam War and, 674–676
Warren court and, 672
Liberal Republicans, 368
Liberation movements, 680–684
Liberator (newspaper), 263
Liberty Displaying the Arts and Sciences (Jennings), 194
Liberty Party, 268, 292, 296
Libya, 725, 761(*m*)
Life expectancy, 90
Life (magazine), 643
Life of Riley, The (TV show), 642
Life of Washington (Weems), 193
Light bulbs, 405
Liliuokalani (Queen of Hawaii), 504
Limited liability, 409
Lincoln, Abraham, 323
    assassination of, 345
    Douglass and, 316, 326
    in election of 1860, 319
    on emancipation, 333
    Freedmen's Bureau created by, 352
    Gettysburg Address by, 341
    Grant and, 343
    inaugural address of, 356
    Johnson as vice president of, 350, 356
    Meade appointed by, 340
    Reconstruction for reunification by, 355–356
    reelection of, 342–343
    seamstresses' complaint to, 338
    Thirteenth Amendment and, 345
Listerine, 536
Literacy tests, voting and, 418, 419(*m*), 448, 667
Literature
    Beat, 645–646
    in early republic, 193–194
    in the 1950s, 645–646
    on slavery, 312
    in the twenties, 541

Lithuania, 585, 613, 731
Little Big Horn, Battle of the (1876), 382, 382(*i*)
Little Rock, Arkansas, desegregation in, 649–650
Little Rock Nine, 649
Little Turtle, 181
Livingston, Robert, 141
Living wage, 431
Locke, Gary, 758
Locke, John, 58, 99, 131, 141
Locomotives, 404
Lodge, Henry Cabot, 460, 524
Logan, James, 96–97
Loguen, Jermaine, 309
Lone Ranger, The (TV show), 641
Long, Huey Pierce, 570–571
Long, Jefferson Franklin, 349, 364, 370
Long, Thomas, 342
Long Drive, 388
Longstreet, James, 328, 331, 333, 364
Looking Backward, 413
Lopez, Ignacio Lutero, 594
Los Alamos Laboratories, 581
Los Angeles
    Brooklyn Dodgers moved to, 640
    foreign born population of, 720
    ghetto riots in, 669
    in the Great Depression, 561
    growth of in the twenties, 538, 538(*m*)
    Indian population in, 655
    population of, 461
    in World War II, 588
    zoot suit riots, 594
Lost Generation, 541
Louisiana, 35
    black majority in, 364
    ceded to Spain, 115
    civil rights movement investigation in, 624
    French settlers in, 61
    Hurricane Katrina, 753
    Long in, 570
    readmitted to the Union, 360
    secession of, 320
    slavery in, 212, 277, 278(*m*)
    statehood of, 212
Louisiana Purchase, 200–201, 206
Louisiana Territory, 200, 202(*m*)
    Lewis and Clark expedition and, 190, 201
Louis XIV (King of France), 35, 60, 68
Louis XVI (King of France), 151, 179

L'Ouverture, Toussaint, 199, 233
Love Canal, New York, 705
Lowell, James Russell, 257
Lowell, Massachusetts, 253
Loyalists, 142
Lucas, George, 56
Lujan, Manuel, Jr., 730
Lumber industry, 376, 387–388
  environmentalism and, 705
  itinerant musicians in, 440
  in the South, 406
  unions in, 438
Lumumba, Patrice, 629
Lunch counter sit-ins, 650, 651(m)
Lundberg, Ferdinand, 644
Lundy, Benjamin, 263
Luper, Clara M., 652
Lusitania, 515, 520(i)
Luther, Martin, 30–31
Luxembourg, in World War II, 585
Lynch, Loretta, 759
Lynchings, 419, 477, 482, 561
Lyon, Matthew, 184(i)

MacArthur, Douglas, 565, 599, 617–618
Maceo, Antonio, 506
Mackintosh, Ebenezer, 124, 131
Macune, Charles W., 442
Madison, Dolley, 216–217, 222, 226, 241
Madison, James, 216–217
  on Alien and Sedition Acts, 185
  amendments submitted by, 176
  in Annapolis convention, 171
  on Bank of the United States, 177
  conflicts facing, 218–219
  Federalist Papers by, 174
  on governmental structure, 172
  on Hamilton's policies, 178
  judge appointments and, 202
  papers of, 241
  plantation of, 226
  reelection of, 219
  on transportation projects, 223
  on Whiskey Rebellion, 181
Madonna del Carmine, 457
Mafia, 458
Magellan, Ferdinand, 15(m)
Mahan, Alfred Thayer, 501–502, 505, 511
Mailer, Norman, 645
Maine, 23, 49
  alcohol sales prohibited in, 261
  Bowdoin College community in, 189
  land claims of, 166(m)
  statehood of, 230
Maine, sinking of the, 507
Main Street (Lewis), 541
Maize, 4–5
"Make America Great Again," 763
Malaria, 18(m), 506
Malcolm X, 669
Malintzin, 1–2, 25
Mammoth Oil Company, 535
Mammoths, 3
Management, corporate, 402, 410
Manassas, battle of (1861), 328
Manchuria, Japanese invasion of, 586
Mandan people, 6, 8(m), 293
  epidemics among, 379
  Lewis and Clark and, 190
Mandela, Nelson, 737
Manhattan Project, 602, 620
Manifest destiny, 292, 297, 311
Man in the Gray Flannel Suit, The (Wilson),
  646
Mann, James R., 486
Mann Act (1910), 486
Manufacturers' Record, 405
Manufacturing, 206
  African Americans in, 463
  American system of, 209, 223–225
  assembly line in, 535, 552
  child workers in, 431
  Civil War, 333–336
  domestic, 209–210
  loss of jobs in, 757
  nineteenth-century, 226
  technology in, 208–209
  women in, 590
  after World War II, 637, 638(f)
Manumission, 283
Mao Zedong, 615
Mapmaking, 16–17
  Carta Marina, 2
  Universalis Cosmographia, 2, 16
Marbury, William, 202
Marbury v. Madison, 202
March on Washington for Jobs and Freedom
  (1963), 666
March to the Sea, 343
Marcy, William, 311
Marion, Francis, 156
Market revolution, 246–252

railroads and, 402–404
women in, 252
Marmaduke Multiply's Merry Method of Making Minor Mathematics, 192(i)
Marriage
   colonial era, 88–89
   companionate, 190, 210
   "complex," in Oneida community, 262
   cult of domesticity and, 250
   Gilded Age, 416
   interracial, 672
   as partnership, 88
   polygamy and, 257, 394–395
   progressivism on, 479
   same-sex, 747, 757
   under slavery, 353
   after World War II, 637–638
   in World War II, 592
Marshall, George, 613
Marshall, John, 202–203
Marshall, Thurgood, 648, 730
Marshall Plan, 613–614, 630
Martha Washington societies, 261
Marti, José, 502, 506, 509, 628
Martin, Trayvon, 742–743, 759
Martinez, Demetria, 715
Marx, Karl, 413, 438
Mary (Queen of England), 58
Maryland, 40–41
   colonial government of, 58
   Constitution ratified by, 175(t)
   English society and, 49
   slavery in, 78
M*A*S*H (film), 703
Mason, George, 141
Massachusetts
   arts and science in, 194
   charter of, 58
   committee of correspondence, 123
   Constitution ratified by, 175, 175(t)
   education for all children in, 169
   Fifty-fourth Colored Infantry, 332
   land claims by, 165, 166(m)
   Pilgrims in, 45–46
   public-accommodations law in, 345
   Puritan migration to, 45–46
   Shays's Rebellion in, 163, 171
   witchcraft trials in, 86–87
Massachusetts Bay, 29–30
Massachusetts Bay Company, 48
Massachusetts Indians, 45, 47

Massasoit, 46
Mass media
   globalization and, 733–734
   in the twenties, 541
Mass transit, 249, 463
Mather, Cotton, 85
Matrix, The (film), 744
Matroon, Ebenezer, 197
Mattachine Society, 645, 684
Maxwell House Hour, The (radio show), 541
May, Samuel J., 310
Mayans, 1–2, 5, 8(m)
   demographic disaster among, 17
   mapmaking, 17
Mayflower, 45
Mayflower Compact, 45
McCain, John, 754
McCarran, Pat, 622
McCarran-Walter Immigration Act (1952), 653
McCarthy, Joseph Raymond, 622–624
McCarthyism, 622–624
McClellan, George B., 331, 342
McCloy, John J., 604
McClure's (magazine), 477
McCormick, Cyrus, 505
McCoy, Elijah, 404
McCulloch v. Maryland, 203
McDonald's, 733
McFarlane, Robert, 725
McGirt v. Oklahoma, 760
McGovern, George, 696
McGuffey Readers, 411, 424
McKinley, William, 421–422
   Cuba under, 508
   in election of 1896, 446, 446(m), 449
   Hawaii annexation by, 507
   on intervention in Cuba, 507
   Open Door policy of, 512–513
   Philippine War and, 509–511
   Populists and, 447
   Roosevelt as vice president of, 491
McLuckie, John, 427–428, 436
Meade, George A., 340
Measles, 18(m), 305, 378
Meat Inspection Act, 492, 493(t)
Meatpacking industry, 410, 492
Mechanization, 429
Medicaid, 672, 718
Medical Care Act (1965), 673(t)
Medical education, 194

Medicare, 672, 718

Medicare Prescription Drug, Improvement, and Modernization Act (2003), 750

Mediterranean world, 9–10

Megachurches, 750

Mehaffry, J. W., 432

Mellon, Andrew, 534

Melting pot, 460

Melting-Pot, The (Zangwill), 460

Memphis, Tennessee
    lynching in, 483
    race riot in, 359

Mencken, Henry Louis (H. L.), 541

Mendez v. Westminster, 652

Menlo Park, New Jersey, 404–405

Menninger, William C., 635

Mennonites, 143

Mercantilism, 68–70, 72, 85

Meredith, James, 665

Mesa Verde, 490*(m)*

Metacom, 50

Metacom's War, 50

Metalious, Grace, 634–635, 646

Methodism, 99, 168
    abolitionism and, 266
    black churches, 355
    renewal in, 194
    Second Great Awakening and, 255

#MeToo movement, 764, 769

Metropolitan Opera House, 414

Mexica, 1–2

Mexican Americans, 389, 562
    Americanization of, 546
    Californios in the West, 395
    civil rights movement of, 652
    deportation of, 561, 655
    discrimination against, 708
    immigrants, 455
    women's suffrage and, 480*(m)*
    in World War II, 593–594

Mexican-American War, 293–295, 295*(i)*, 302, 307, 328, 395

Mexican immigrants
    arrivals of 1960–2000, 720, 721*(f)*
    labor contracts with, 453
    quota system on, 545
    1990s to twenty-first century, 744, 745*(f)*

Mexican revolution (1911), 513

Mexico
    battle for Texas and, 285–287

illegal immigration from, in the 1950s and 1960s, 655

Mexican-American War and, 293–295

NAFTA and, 747

World War I and, 516

Miami people, 113, 181

Michigan, 247, 548

Microsoft, 743

Middle Atlantic region, education in, 191

Middle class
    African Americans in, 464*(i)*
    the counterculture on, 679
    emergence of, 250–252
    growth of after World War II, 637, 638*(f)*
    industrialization and, 402
    leisure pursuits of, 415, 440
    progressivism and, 477
    in South, 284
    temperance and, 256
    under Reagan, 719

Middle East
    Carter and, 702–703
    early civilizations in, 9
    Reagan and, 725, 726*(m)*
    Six-Day War, 694
    terrorism and democratic uprisings in, 761*(m)*

Middle Passage, 70–71

Middleport, New York, 452

Midway Island, battle of (1942), 599

Midwest
    immigrants in, 247, 248*(f)*
    industrialization in, 402, 406
    swing states in, 423

Migrant workers, 562

Milano, Alyssa, 764

Military-industrial complex, 587, 625, 678

Military Reconstruction Acts (1867), 360

Militias, 105, 119
    in American Revolution, 140
    Civil War, 338

Miller, William, 257

Millerites, 256*(m)*, 257

Milosevic, Slobodan, 748

Milwaukee, Wisconsin, 455

Mimeograph machines, 404

Minguez, Juan, 61*(i)*

Minié balls, 334

Minimum wage laws
    New Deal, 574
    in the 1950s, 654

in the 1960s, 662
in the twenties, 534
Mining
    Californios in, 395
    child labor in, 431
    in the New South, 407(m)
    strikes, 438
    urbanization and, 462
    in the West, 376, 386–387
Minneapolis, Minnesota, 455
Minnesota, 319, 391
Minor, Virginia, 363
Minor v. Happersatt, 363
Minoso, Orestes "Minnie," 652
Minstrel shows, 248, 440
Miranda v. Arizona, 672
Misery index, 747
Miss America pageant protests, 681
Missionaries
    on gender roles, 170
    in Hawaii, 504
    Jesuit, 35
    praying towns and, 47
    Pueblo Revolt and, 60
    in schools for freedpeople, 354
    Spanish, 31–32, 32(i)
Missions, 61
Mission to Moscow (film), 591
Mississippi
    black majority in, 364
    civil rights movement in, 647
    desegregation resistance in, 665
    Freedom Summer in, 667
    secession of, 320
    slavery in, 212, 277, 278(m)
    statehood of, 212
Mississippian cultures, 7, 8(i), 8(m), 25
Mississippi Freedom Democratic Party
    (MFDP), 667
Mississippi River, 208
Missouri, 302, 339
    slavery in, 229–231
    statehood of, 218, 241
Missouri Compromise, 230(m), 230–231,
    308, 313, 314(m), 316
    Crittenden plan and, 320
Missouri Pacific Railroad, 434
Mitchell, John, 697
Mobile, Alabama, 336
Mobuto, Joseph, 629
Model Cities Act (1965), 671, 673(t)

Modernism, fundamentalism vs., 548–549
Modern Language Association, 415(t)
Modern Republicanism, 654–655
Modern Women: The Lost Sex (Lundberg and
    Farnham), 644
Mogollon people, 6, 8(m)
Mohawk Indians, 36, 50, 62, 112
    in American Revolution, 142
Mohegan Indians, 50
Molotov, Vyacheslav, 610
Mondale, Walter, 719
Money supply, Farmers' Alliance on, 443
Monitor vs. Merrimack (1862), 331(m)
Monopolies, 3
    railroad, farmers and, 442
    Sherman Antitrust Act and, 401,
        409–410
    telegraph, 408
    trusts and, 409
Monroe, James, 171, 200, 225
Monroe, Marilyn, 643
Monroe Doctrine, 225, 512, 524
Montana
    cattle ranching in, 389
    Indian reservations in, 381
    mining in, 387
Montezuma, 19–20
Montezuma, Carlos, 484
Montgomery, Alabama
    bus boycott, 648–649, 649(i)
    Freedom Rides in, 665
Montgomery, Richard, 139
Montgomery Improvement Association, 648
Montgomery Ward, 410
Montpelier, 226
Montreal, 34, 62–63, 139
Moondog, 633
Moonshiners, 544
Moorhead, Scipio, 144(i)
Moraley, William Jr., 55–56, 73, 80
Moraley, William Sr., 68
Morality
    baby boom and, 637–638
    progressivism and, 485–488
    wealth and, 412
Moral Majority, 710
Moral suasion, 248, 261, 268
Moral uplift, 484
Moravians, 98, 121, 143
Moreno, Luisa, 556, 562, 573, 578
Morgan, Daniel, 156

Morgan, John Pierpont, 405, 408, 414, 445, 492
Morgan, Lewis, 384
Morgan, Nancy Hart, 148
Mormons, 257, 302, 394–395
Mormon Trail, 305*(m)*
Morocco, in World War II, 597
Morris, Lewis, 106, 108
Morris, Lewis Jr., 107
Morrisites, 106
Morse, Samuel F. B., 260
Mortgages
    the Great Recession and, 754
    racial discrimination in, 640
    savings and loan collapse and, 719
    under Reagan, 719
    after World War II, 639
Morton, "Jelly Roll," 440, 542
Moses, Phoebe Ann, 373–374
Mossadegh, Mohammed, 628
Motel chains, 637
Mott, James, 267
Mott, Lucretia, 267
Mount Vernon, 110
Movimiento Estudiantil Chicano de Aztlán (MEChA), 708
Ms. (magazine), 681
Muckrakers, 477, 484
    on meatpacking, 492
Mueller, Robert, 765
Mueller Report, 765
Muir, John, 489
Mujahideen, 701–702, 702*(i)*, 726*(m)*, 731
Muller v. Oregon, 479
Multinational corporations, 733
Multiplier effect, 208
Munich Accord, 584
Municipal reforms, 488–489
Munn v. Illinois, 442
Murray, Anna, 325
Murray, Judith Sargent, 170
Murray, Pauli, 690, 704, 711
Murrow, Edward R., 623
Music
    the blues, 440
    counterculture and, 679
    itinerant musicians, 440
    rock 'n' roll, 633–634, 643
    in the 1950s, 645
    in teenage culture, 643
    in the twenties, 542

Musk oxen, 3
Mussolini, Benito, 584, 602
Mutual aid societies, 253
    African American, 464
    black, 350
    immigrant, 456, 458
Mutually assured destruction (MAD), 626
Myers, Daisy, 640
Myers, William, 640
My Lai massacre (1968), 675, 676*(i)*

Nader, Ralph, 749
Nagasaki, atomic bomb dropped on, 602
Nahuatl, 1–2
Napalm, 675
Naranjo, Joseph, 61*(i)*
Narragansett Indians, 50
Narrative of the Life of Frederick Douglass, as Told by Himself (Douglass), 266, 325
Narváez, Pánfilo de, 15*(m)*, 21, 22*(m)*
Nash, Diane, 665
Nashville, Tennessee, 463
Nasser, Gamal Abdel, 628
Natchez, Mississippi, 336
National Arts and Humanities Act (1965), 673*(t)*
National Association for the Advancement of Colored People (NAACP)
    black nationalism and, 543
    civil rights movement and, 593, 647
    Evers in, 666
    founding of, 483
    Freedom Summer and, 667
    integrationist strategy of, 540
    Sweet defended by, 529
National Association of Colored Women (NACW), 415, 415*(t)*, 420, 478, 481, 647
National Association of Manufacturers, 569
National Broadcasting Company (NBC), 641
National Cash Register Company, 488
National Committee on Influenza, 523
National Congress of American Indians, 655
National Council of Jewish Women, 415*(t)*
National Council of Women, 415*(t)*
National Defense Act (1916), 515
National Defense Education Act (1958), 654
National Endowment of the Arts, 673*(t)*
National Endowment of the Humanities, 673*(t)*
National Energy Act (1978), 699

National Farm Workers Association, 682
National Industrial Recovery Act (1933), 568, 572(t)
National Interstate and Defense Highway Act (1956), 654
National Labor Relations Act (1935), 573
National Labor Relations Board, 573
National League of Baseball, 415(t), 418
National Liberation Front (Vietcong), 630, 674
National Organization for Women (NOW), 680, 704
National Origins Act (1924), 545
National parks and forests, 490(m), 536, 705
National Recovery Administration (NRA), 568
National Republicans, 236–237
National Review (journal), 685
National Rifle Association, 746
National Road, 207
National Security Act (1947), 614
National Security Agency, 614, 761
National Security Council (NSC), 614–615, 723
National Socialism, 584
  Holocaust under, 603(i)
National Trades Union, 254
National War Labor Board (NWLB), 519, 589
National Woman's Party, 480
National Woman Suffrage Association, 479
National Women's Trade Union League (WTUL), 478
National Youth Administration, 571
Nation of Islam, 669
Native Americans. See American Indians and specific tribes
Nativism, 260, 460
  Ku Klux Klan resurrection and, 547
  Trump and, 763
  in the twenties, 544–547
Nativists, 260
Nat Turner's rebellion, 281–282
Naturalization Act (1798), 184
Natural law, 105
Natural resources, conservation and preservation of, 489–491
"Nature" (Emerson), 257
Nauvoo, Illinois, 257
Navajo people, 60
  civilization of, 378
  code talkers in World War II, 594
  forced onto reservation, 344

Indian Reorganization Act and, 576
Navigation Acts (England), 69, 122
Nebraska
  bicycles in, 417(i)
  immigrant farmers in, 391
  sod houses in, 391
Nebraska Territory, 312
Needlepoint samplers, 89(i)
Neoconservatives, 709
Neolin, 116
Netherlands
  colonies of, 35–36, 49
  English ties with, 33
  fur trade, 34
  gold trade by, 24
  slave trade, 13
  sugar industry, 43
  trade and, 11
  in World War II, 585
Neutrality Acts, 584, 586
Neutrality Proclamation (1793), 179
Nevada, 386–387
New Amsterdam, 36, 49
Newark, New Jersey, ghetto riots in, 669
New Bedford, Massachusetts, 249
New Bern, North Carolina, 354
Newburgh, New York, army officers encamped at, 164
New Deal, 558(f), 565–578
  critics of, 569–570
  decline of the, 576–578
  direct assistance and relief in, 568–569, 571
  liberalism in, 578–579
  major measures in, 572(t)
  minorities and, 574–576
  moves to the left in, 571–578
  New Frontier and, 662
  organized labor and, 574
  philosophy behind, 566
  Social Security in, 572–573
  steps toward recovery in, 566–568
  after World War II, 635–636
New England
  agricultural land in, 75
  colonization of, 28–29
  divorce in, 91
  education in, 191
  factories in, 247
  Metacom's War, 50
  settlement of, 45–51

New England (*Continued*)
    textile mills in, 252
    town meetings, 103
    transient workers in, 75
    War of 1812 and, 219, 221
    wars in, 49–51
    workday length in, 254
New England Courant, 72
Newfoundland, 23
New Freedom, 495–497, 496*(i)*
New Frontier, 662
New Guinea, in World War II, 599
New Hampshire
    Constitution ratified by, 175, 175*(t)*
    farmers' march in, 171
    land conflicts, 119
New Jersey, 58
    Constitution ratified by, 175, 175*(t)*
    free blacks in, 169
    presidents from, 423
    Revolution battles in, 146
    suburbs in, 640
New Jersey Plan, 172
New Left, 678–679
New Light clergy, 99, 101–102
New Look strategy, 625
New Mexico, 31–32, 32*(i)*
    atomic testing in, 581
    Compromise of 1850 on, 307
    immigrants in, 455
    native cultures in, 6
New Nationalism, 495, 497
New Negro, 542
New Orleans
    Battle of, 221*(i)*
    Civil War capture of, 332
    closed by Spain, 164, 167
    as commercial center, 206
    Hurricane Katrina, 753
    jazz in, 440
    slave market in, 212
    in War of 1812, 220*(m)*
Newport, Rhode Island, 414
Newport African Union Society, 196
New Republic (magazine), 603
    New Right, 709–710, 712, 716, 720–721
"New School" ministers, 244
New South, 405–406, 407*(m)*
Newspapers, 250
    abolitionist, 263, 266, 326
    for immigrants, 457
    on the Red scare, 531

    yellow journalism in, 507
Newton, Huey P., 670
New woman, 541
New York
    blacks in colonial, 74
    canals in, 246–247
    colonial government of, 58
    Constitution ratified by, 175, 175*(t)*
    ghetto riots in, 669
    land claims of, 165
    Love Canal in, 705
    population of, 247
    presidents from, 423
    revivals in, 245, 256, 256*(m)*
    young residents in, 248
New York City
    African American population of, 463
    American Revolution in, 147*(m)*, 151
    baseball teams lost by, 640
    Beats in, 645
    charter of, 106
    crime in, 468
    Democratic convention of 1924 in, 549
    draft riots in, 338
    electric lighting in, 405
    Erie Canal and, 224
    foreign born population of, 720
    free blacks in, 169
    gays and lesbians in, 418
    Gilded Age in, 414
    Harlem Renaissance, 542
    immigrant communities in, 455
    immigrants in, 452, 455
    industry in, 402
    labor activism in, 253
    nuclear freeze movement in, 727
    police killings in, 759
    political machine in, 470
    population density in, 467
    population of, 206, 461
    public transportation in, 249
    skyscrapers in, 404
    slave market in, 72
    slave revolts in, 79
    on slavery, 173
    Stonewall riots, 684
    tenements, 466
    time zone in, 403
    tongs in, 458
    Triangle Shirtwaist fire, 467
    women's suffrage movement in, 481*(i)*
New York Giants, 640

New York Herald Tribune (newspaper), 408
New York Journal (newspaper), 507
New York Times, 364, 693
New York Tribune, 258, 368
New York World (newspaper), 507
New Zealand, 453
    women's suffrage in, 482
    in World War II, 599
Nez Percé Indians, 305, 381
Ngo Dinh Diem, 629, 674
Niagara Movement, 483
Nicaragua
    filibusters to, 311
    repressive regime supported in, 694
    Sandinistas, 723, 737
    U.S. intervention in, 503, 513
Nickelodeons, 440
Nightclubs, 440
Nimitz, Chester, 599
9/11 attacks, 743, 750(i), 750–752, 768
Nineteenth Amendment, 481(i), 482, 493(t), 680
Nipmuck Indians, 50
Nixon, Richard M.
    Cold War and, 693–694
    conservatism and, 711
    in the election of 1960, 655–656, 656(m)
    in the election of 1968, 691–692, 692(m)
    in the election of 1972, 695–697
    foreign policy under, 701
    Hiss affair and, 621
    Kitchen Debate, 627
    Middle East crisis and, 694
    pragmatic conservatism of, 695
    reelection of, 695
    reputation of, 655
    Vietnamization and, 692–693
    Watergate scandal, 696–697
    wiretapping by, 696
Noble Order of the Knights of Labor, 433–434
Non-Intercourse Act (1809), 218
Nonviolence, 648–649, 669
Nonviolent direct action, 665
Noriega, Manuel, 735
Normandy, D Day at, 598(m), 599
North, Frederick, Lord, 151
North, Oliver, 726
North American Free Trade Agreement (NAFTA), 747
North Atlantic Treaty Organization (NATO), 615, 726–727, 748

North Carolina, 58
    black voters in, 364
    cigarette manufacturing in, 406
    Constitution ratified by, 175, 175(t)
    land claims of, 166(m)
    lumber industry in, 406
    readmitted to the Union, 360
    Regulators, 128
    sit-ins in, 650, 651(m)
    Tuscarora War, 65
North Carolina Life Insurance Company, 420
North Dakota
    cattle ranching in, 389
    gold in, 383
    Indian reservations in, 381
Northern Pacific Railroad, 368
Northern Securities Company, 492
North Korea, 614
    in axis of evil, 752
North Star (newspaper), 266, 326
Northup, Henry, 274
Northup, Solomon, 273–274, 277, 297
Northwestern Farmers' Alliance, 442–443
Northwest Ordinance, 165–166
Northwest Territory, 166, 166(m)
    conflict with Indians in, 218
    frontier conflicts and, 181, 182(m)
    slavery in, 173
Norway
    women's suffrage in, 482
    in World War II, 585
Nova Scotia, freed blacks in, 157
Noyes, John Humphrey, 262
NSC-68, 615–616, 628, 630
Nuclear arms race, 624–627
    Cuban missile crisis and, 662(m), 664
    de-escalation of, 728
    SALT I Treaty on, 694
    SALT II Treaty on, 701
    under Reagan, 721
Nuclear freeze movement, 726–728
Nuclear power, 705
Nuclear weapons
    bomb shelters and, 625(i)
    Cuban missile crisis and, 662(m), 664
    development of, 581–582
    in Iran, 762
    nuclear freeze movement and, 726–728
    protests against, 722
    the Rosenbergs and, 609
    in World War II, 602

Nullification, 238–239
Nye, Gerald, 583
Nye Committee, 584

Oakland, California, 537
Oakley, Annie, 373–374
Obama, Barack, 753–762, 769
    citizenship of, 763
    domestic policies of, 754–756
    election of, 754–756
    foreign policy of, 760–762
    Syrian refugees and, 761
    Trump on, 762
    war on terrorism and, 760–762
Obamacare, 755
Obergefell v. Hodges, 757
Oberlin College, 269
Occupational Safety and Health
        Administration (OSHA), 695
Occupy Wall Street movement, 757
O'Connor, Sandra Day, 719
Odd Fellows, 420
Odets, Clifford, 571
Office of Economic Opportunity, 695
Office of the Director of National Intelligence,
        750
Office of War Information, 590
Ohio
    abolitionism in, 265
    Ku Klux Klan in, 548
    market revolution and, 247
    presidents from, 423
    statehood of, 206
Ohio River valley, land conflicts in, 165, 167,
        181, 182*(m)*
Ohiyesa, 385
Oil embargo, 694
Okies, 560
Okinawa, battle of (1945), 599
Oklahoma, 381, 548
    Oklahoma Territory, 528
Old-Age Revolving Pensions Corporation, 570
Old Guard, Republican Party, 423
Old Light clergy, 99, 101–102
Oldsmobile, 536
Oliver, Andrew, 124–125
Olney, Richard, 437
Olympic Games, 701, 722
Oñate, Juan de, 32
O'Neal, John, 326
Oneida community, New York, 256*(m)*, 262

Oneida Indians, 62, 143
On the Origin of Species (Darwin), 412, 548
On the Road (Kerouac), 645
Opechancanough, 39–40
Open Door policy, 512–513, 583, 586
Open-hearth process of steel manufacturing,
        404
Operation Desert Storm, 736
Operation Just Cause, 735
Operation Rolling Thunder (1965), 675
Operation Warp Speed, 766
Operation Wetback, 655
Opium, 458, 486
Opium Wars (1839–1942), 396
Oppenheimer, J. Robert, 582, 584, 602, 605
    suspected of Communist affiliations, 623
Ordinance of Nullification, 239
Oregon, 292–293, 387, 547, 588
Oregon Territory, 225, 302
    statehood of, 319
Oregon Trail, 301–303, 305*(m)*
Organization of Petroleum Exporting
        Countries (OPEC), 694, 698
Organized crime, in prohibition, 544
Oriskany, Battle of (1777), 146
Ortiz, Juan, 21
Osage people, 292, 330, 546
Osceola, 287
Osteen, Joel, 750
Ostend Manifesto, 311
O'Sullivan, John L., 292
Oswald, Lee Harvey, 666
Ottoman empire, 24, 514
Our Country (Strong), 505
Overland trails, 302–303
Overseers of the Poor, 75
Owen, Robert Dale, 261

Pacifists, 143
Page, Patti, 643
Pahlavi, Mohammad Reza, 628, 703
Paine, Thomas, 135–136, 141, 160
Paiute Indians, 491
Pakenham, Edward, 221*(i)*
Palestine
    Camp David accords on, 702
    Gaza Strip and West Bank and, 737
    terrorism and, 725
Palestine Liberation Organization (PLO), 725,
        737
Palin, Sarah, 754

Palmer, A. Mitchell, 531
Palmer Memorial Institute, 484
Palmer raids, 531
Pamphlets, 135–136, 141
Panama, Noriega and, 735
Panama Canal, 503, 511, 628, 701
Pan-Arab nationalism, 629
Pandemics
    COVID-19, 766–767
    influenza (1918–1919), 522–523
Panic of 1819, 228–229
Panic of 1837, 252, 254–255, 269, 290, 302
Panic of 1873, 368
Paraffin, 404
Paris Climate Agreement (2015), 762, 765
Paris Peace Conference (1918), 523
Parker, Arthur C., 484
Parker, Charlie, 645
Parker, Ely, 330
Parks, Rosa, 648
Parris, Samuel, 86
Parrott arms factory, 338
Partial Nuclear Test Ban Treaty (1963),
    665–666
Partisanship, electoral participation and, 423
Partnerships, corporations compared with, 409
Partners in Health, 735
Patient Protection and Affordable Care Act
    (2010), 755, 764
Patriarchal family, 88, 90–93
Patriarchy, 681
Patriot Act (2001), 751, 761
Patrons of Husbandry, 441
Patterson, William, 172
Patton, George S., 565
Paul, Alice, 480–481
Paul, Thomas, 195
Paul II, Pope, 31
Pawnee Indians, 378
Paxton Boys, 117–118
Payola, 634
Pays d'en Haut, 60, 97
Peace Corps, 665–666, 671
Peace of Paris, 115, 118(i), 121, 157
Peace societies, 338–339
Peale, Charles Willson, 193–194
Peale, Norman Vincent, 645
Pearce, Charles H., 355
Pea Ridge, battle of (1862), 330, 331(m)
Pearl Harbor
    atomic bombs as retaliation for, 602

Japanese attack on, 582, 595
    naval base at, 504
Pearson, Isaac, 56
Peasants, 13
Pendleton Civil Service Reform Act (1883),
    471
Penn, William, 57–58, 95–96
Pennsylvania, 57–58
    constitution of, 150
    Constitution ratified by, 175, 175(t)
    emancipation of slaves in, 169
    expansion and conflict in, 94, 96, 96(m)
    German immigrants to, 76
    redemptioners in, 74
    road development in, 206
    sexual coercion cases in, 92(t)
    suburbs in, 640
    Three Mile Island, 705
    Whiskey Rebellion in, 170
Pennsylvania Gazette, 72, 99, 113(i)
Pennsylvania Magazine, 136
Pennsylvania Railroad Company, 400
Pension plans
    Townsend on, 570
    in the twenties, 534
Pentagon attack, 750, 768
Pentagon Papers, 693, 696
Pequot Indians, 49–50
Pequot War, 49
Perestroika, 728
Perez, Thomas, 758
Perkins, Frances, 567
Permanent Investigation Subcommittee
    of the Committee on Government
    Operations, 622
Perot, Ross, 737, 747
Perry, Jim, 389
Perry, Matthew C., 310
Perry, Oliver, 219
Pershing, John, 513, 516
Personal Responsibility and Work Opportunity
    Reconciliation Act (1996), 746
Peter, Hugh, 48
Petrified Forest, 490(m)
Petroleum industry
    Carter presidency and, 698
    cracking in, 404
    horizontal integration in, 408
    Iran intervention and, 628
    Mexican revolution and, 513
    the Middle East and, 726(m)

Petroleum industry (*Continued*)
  oil embargo of 1973 and, 694
  OPEC control of, 698
  Operation Desert Storm and, 736
  in the 1990s, 729
  trusts in, 409
Petticoat Affair, 238
Peyton Place (Metalious), 634, 646
Phalanxes, Fourierist, 256*(m)*, 262
Philadelphia
  African American population of, 463
  African Americans in, 249
  American Philosophical Society in, 194
  American Revolution in, 146, 147*(m)*, 148
  capital moved from, 191
  capital moved to, 177
  charitable organizations in, 254
  free blacks in, 169
  industry in, 226, 402
  nineteenth century, 206
  population of, 247
  racial violence in, 234
  transportation revolution in, 247
  yellow fever in, 178, 180
  young residents in, 248
Philadelphia and Reading Railroad
    bankruptcy, 444
Philadelphia Female Anti-Slavery Society, 265
Philanthropy, 401, 412, 484
Philip II (King of Spain), 23, 33, 35
Philippines
  annexation of, 503, 509
  immigrants from, 744, 745*(f)*
  independence of, 562
  Magellan in, 16
  occupation of, 508
  rebellion of, 510–511
  repressive regime supported in, 694
  war for, 509–511
  in World War II, 599, 600*(m)*
Phillips, Wendell, 363
Phips, William, 86
Phonographs, 535*(f)*
Pierce, Franklin, 307, 311–312, 315
Pietists, 99
Pike, Zebulon, 201, 202*(m)*
Pilgrims, 45–46
Pinchot, Gifford, 474–475, 477, 489, 494
Pinckney, Charles Cotesworth, 185
Pinckney, Eliza Lucas, 56–57, 81
Pinckney, Thomas, 182

Pinckney Treaty (1796), 182
Pingree, Hazen, 489
Pinkerton detectives, 437
Pinochet, Augusto, 737
Pirates, Barbary, 164, 199
Pitt, William, 114
Pittsburgh, 436*(m)*, 559
Pittsburgh Courier (newspaper), 464
Pizarro, Francisco, 20
Plane hijacking, 725
Plan of Union, 112
Plantation slavery, 42, 274–275
  domestic production in, 210
  Harpers Ferry raid and, 317
  tightened control of, 282–285
Platt, Orville, 509
Platt Amendment, 509
Pledge of allegiance, 644
Plessy v. Ferguson, 419, 484, 648
Plunkitt, George Washington, 470
Plyler v. Doe, 720
Plymouth colony, 45
Plymouth Plantation, 46
Pocahontas, 29
Podhoretz, Norman, 709
Poindexter, John, 726
Poland, 585, 610, 611, 613, 730
Police actions, 618
Police departments, 531
Polio, 555, 566*(i)*, 638
Political campaigns, 423, 424*(i)*, 641
Political cartoons
  on Alien and Sedition Acts, 184*(i)*
  first American, 113*(i)*
  on Wilson's New Freedom, 496*(i)*
Political machines, 469–472
  muckrakers on, 477
  progressivism on, 488
Political parties
  antislavery, 268–269
  campaigns as entertainment and, 424*(i)*
  in election of 1796, 183
  in election of 1800, 185–186
  first party system, 183–186
  labor and, 429
  Second Party System, 285
  in the twenties, 549–550
  workingmen's, 253
Politics
  big business and, 422
  colonial era, 103–107

farmer organizations and, 442–443
industrialization and, 420–423
in the twenties, 549–551
urbanization and, 468–472
Polk, James K., 268, 291–295, 297
Pollack v. Farmers Loan and Trust, 445
Poll taxes, 418, 419*(m)*, 448, 480, 667
Polygamy, 257, 394–395
Ponce de León, Juan, 15*(m)*, 16
Pontiac, 116–118
Poor Richard's Almanac, 99
Popé, 60
Popular Front, 570, 574
Popular Science (magazine), 643
Population growth
colonial era, 74, 95
in early republic, 206
European, 11
immigrants in, 745*(f)*
nineteenth-century, 223
in North vs. South, 328
after the Revolution, 165
in the twenties, 537–538, 538*(m)*
"undesirable" races and, 459
urban, 247
after World War II, 637–638, 639*(f)*
in World War II, 587
Populism, 476
Populist Party, 443–444
collapse of, 447–448
Coxey's army and, 445
decline of, 447–448
Lease in, 428
Pornography, 672
Port Hudson, battle of (1863), 340
Port Huron Statement, 678
Portland, Maine, Rum Riot, 261
Portland, Oregon
Hooverville in, 559
Ku Klux Klan in, 547
in World War II, 588
Portugal
American exploration by, 14–16
Enterprise of the Indies, 14
the Great Depression in, 559
long-distance trade by, 25
slave trade, 9, 14
trade of, 10–11
Post, Amy, 245, 256, 267, 269, 308
Post, Isaac, 245, 308
Post, Louis F., 531

Post Office, U.S., 410
Potosí, 20, 23
Potsdam Conference (1945), 610
Pottawatomie Massacre, 315, 317
Poverty
before the Great Depression, 556
in cities, 468
colonial era, 92–93
decline in after World War II, 637
in the Great Depression, 557, 577
Great Society programs on, 671, 673*(t)*
laissez-faire and, 413
morality and, 92, 260
NAFTA and, 747
of Native Americans, 575, 760
New Frontier on, 662
race and, 707
reform movements on, 260–261
in the twenties, 539
under Reagan, 719
Powderly, Terence V., 433
Powell, Colin, 750
Powell, John Wesley, 376
Power looms, 209
Power of Positive Thinking, The (Peale), 645
Powhatan, 28–29, 37
Powhatan Confederacy, 37, 40, 52
Pragmatic conservatism, 695
Pragmatic humanism, 565
Pragmatism, 476–477
Prague Spring, 691
Praying towns, 47
Prendergast, William, 119
Presbyterian Church, 84, 168
abolitionism and, 266
camp meetings in, 195
"New School" ministers in, 244
Second Great Awakening and, 256
Preservation, 475
Presidents
Constitutional Convention on election of, 173
election of 1924, 549
election of 1928, 550
elections of 1896, 446, 446*(m)*
industrialization and, 421
leadership role of, 579
progressivism under, 491–497
President's Committee on Civil Rights, 647
Presley, Elvis, 643
Preston, Thomas, 127

Price, Victoria, 561
Printing, 16
  American Revolution, 136, 141
  in colonial resistance to Britain, 126
  Enlightenment and, 99
Proclamation Line of 1763, 117*(m)*, 118–120, 142
Proclamation of Amnesty and Reconciliation (1863), 355
Professional organizations, Gilded Age, 415*(t)*
Progress, success linked with, 411–412
Progress and Poverty (George), 413
Progressive Era, 476
Progressive Party, 495, 498
  in the election of 1948, 636
  in the twenties, 550*(m)*, 551
  women in, 644
Progressivism, 474–498
  African Americans and, 482–483
  birth control and, 486–487
  conservation and, 705–706
  drug abuse and, 486
  environmentalism and, 475–476, 489–491, 705–706
  government and, 488–491
  in the Great Depression, 567
  immigration restriction and, 487–488
  imperialism and, 502, 509
  Indians and, 484
  juvenile delinquency and, 486
  legacy of, 497–498
  morality and social control in, 485–488
  muckrakers in, 477
  municipal and state reforms in, 488–489
  national legislation in, 493*(t)*
  origins of, 476–477
  presidential, 491–497
  prohibition and, 485
  prostitution and, 485–486
  roots of, 476–477
  social justice reform and, 477–484
  Square Deal and, 491–494
  Taft and, 494
  in the twenties, 551
  women in, 478
  on women's suffrage, 479–482, 480*(m)*, 481*(i)*
  World War I and, 521
Prohibition, 485, 521, 544
  Democrats and, 550
  ended, 567

Project Democracy, 723
Propaganda
  World War I, 520*(i)*, 520–521
  World War II, 591
Property rights
  of Californios, 395
  colonial era, 104–105, 119
  of freedpeople, 352
  Indians and, 155
  Mormons on, 394
  as personal liberty, 411
  squatters after the Revolution and, 165
  voting rights connected to, 169, 231
  of women, 170
Prophetstown, 219
Proposition 13, 709
Proprietary colonies, 58
Prostitution
  Chinese immigrants and, 396
  on the frontier, 387
  muckrakers on, 477
  progressivism and, 485–486
  in red-light districts, 440
  social reform movements against, 260
  tongs in, 458
Protestantism, 30–31
  cultural divisions and, 246
  immigrants and, 249
  in Netherlands, 35
  prohibition and, 486
  racial inferiority and, 459
  temperance and, 261
Protestant Reformation, 30–31, 33
Protocols of the Elders of Zion, 545
Providence, Rhode Island, 226
Pryor, Anne Beverley Whiting, 300
Psychoanalysis, 541
Ptolemy, 14
Public assistance
  colonial era, 75
  industrialization and, 254
Public health
  progressivism and, 485
  sanitation and, 468
Public transportation, 249, 465–466
  Freedom Rides and, 664–665
  Journey of Reconciliation and, 661
  Montgomery bus boycott of, 648–649
  segregation in, 648–649, 661
Public utilities, 469

Public Works Administration (PWA), 568, 572(t)
Public works projects, 558
Pueblo people, 6, 8(m), 378
 anthropologists on, 542
 civilization of, 378
 missionaries and, 31–32, 32(i)
Pueblo revolt, 32(i), 60, 61(i)
Puerto Ricans, 640, 683
Puerto Rico, 503, 508, 757
Pulaski, Casimir Count, 148
Pulitzer, Joseph, 507
Pullman, George, 433, 437
Pullman strike, 437–438, 445
Pure Food and Drug Act (1906), 492, 493(t)
Puritans, 45–49
 dissenters, 48
 Hutchinson and, 29–30
 religious anxieties and, 85–86
 wars with, 49–51
 worldview of, 47–48
Putin, Vladimir, 761, 763
Putnam, Thomas Jr., 87

Quakers, 102(m)
 in abolitionism, 169–170, 263
 on Fugitive Slave Act, 308
 Great Awakening and, 121
 growth of, 168, 256
 Harpers Ferry raid and, 318
 Hicksites, 245
 Indians and, 98
 neutrality of in American Revolution, 143
 in New York, 256(m)
 Pennsylvania as refuge for, 57–58
 Seneca removal and, 289
 women's authority in, 245
Quartering Act (England), 122–124
Quebec, 33
 battle of, 139, 147(m)
Queen Anne's War, 63
Queen's College, 192

Race and ethnicity
 and Americanization in the twenties, 546–547
 anthropology on, 541
 anti-immigrant fears and, 459
 in colonial America, 76(m)
 in the Great Depression, 560–562
 justifications for imperialism and, 505
 labor unions and, 254
 liberation movements and, 683
 national identity and, 191
 in the Philippines, 510–511
 stereotypes about, 459
 "superior" vs. "inferior," 459
 in the twenties, 540
 "whiteness" of immigrants and, 459
 World War I and, 521
Race music, 633
Race or Mongrel (Schultz), 460
Racism
 anticrime legislation and, 746
 election of 2016 and, 763
 in the Great Depression, 560–562
 Great Society programs on, 671–672, 673(t)
 in housing, 640
 immigrants and, 435
 immigration restriction and, 487–488
 industrialization and, 406, 429
 New Deal and, 574–576
 in the New South, 406
 Populism and, 448
 progressivism and, 476, 482–483, 487–488
 in railroads, 404
 systemic, 657, 759, 766
 in the twenties, 529, 540
 twenty-first century, 743
 upward mobility and, 414
 Wilson on, 497
 women's suffrage and, 480
Radiators, 465
Radicalism
 black power and, 669
 detention camps for, 622
 in feminism, 680
 Red scare and, 530–531
Radical Republicans, 357, 360–361
Radio, 541, 563
Radio receivers, 535(f)
"Rags to riches" stories, 411, 424
Railroad(s)
 bison slaughter by, 383
 British investment in, 377(i), 408
 Carnegie in, 401
 in Civil War, 335
 commercial ranching and, 390
 depression of 1893 and, 445
 freight rate regulations, 492
 government takeover of, 636

Railroad(s) (*Continued*)
  Grangers and, 442
  industrialization and, 402–403, 403(f)
  Kansas-Nebraska Act and, 313
  land grants to, 391
  locomotives, 404
  in the New South, 406, 407(m)
  in North vs. South, 328
  progressive reforms of, 492
  Pullman strike, 437–438, 445
  segregation in, 419
  in settlement of the West, 375(m),
     376–377
  in slave South, 276
  standardization of, 404
  steel rails in, 404
  strikes against, 433, 436(m), 437–438, 445
  telegraph and, 408
  transcontinental, 369, 376
  troop deployment against the Indians and,
     383
  urbanization and, 462
  U.S. advertised by, 455
  in westward migration, 391
  worker safety in, 431
Railroad Administration, 519
Raleigh, Walter, 23
Randolph, A. Philip, 543, 592, 649, 666
Randolph, Edmund, 176
Rankin, Jeanette P., 516
Rape
  colonial era, 91–92, 92(t). See also Sexual
     violence
  of slaves, 283
Rauschenbusch, Walter, 476
Ray, James Earl, 670
Reading Railroad, 491
Reagan, Ronald
  anti-Soviet rhetoric of, 716, 722, 728
  Contras and, 723
  election of, 716, 717(i), 717(m)
  Iran-Contra affair, 726
  Iran hostage release and, 703
  the New Right and, 712
  Noriega and, 735
  nuclear de-escalation under, 728
  nuclear freeze movement and, 726–728
  reelection of, 719, 728
  Shultz and, 715
  social conservatism and, 720–721
  terrorism fighting under, 725–726

Reagonomics, 717–719
Real estate speculation, 539
Reality shows, 733–734
Rebel Without a Cause (film), 642
Recession of 1937, 577
Reconstruction, 355–363
  black political participation and economic
     opportunity in, 364–366
  compromise of 1877 and, 369
  congressional, 360–361, 421
  congressional retreat from, 368
  economic scandals in, 366
  Grant and, 360
  Johnson, Andrew, in, 350
  judicial retreat from, 368–369
  legacies of, 370–371
  Lincoln's plans for reunification and,
     355–356
  military districts in, 360, 360(m)
  national, 355–363
  partisanship after, 423
  presidential, 356–358
  remaking the South in, 363–367
  unraveling of, 367–369
  white resistance to, 366–367
Reconstruction Finance Corporation (RFC),
     558
Redeemers, 366
Redemptioners, 74
Red-light districts, 440
Redlining, 575, 640
Red power movement, 683
Red scare, 530–531, 610
  second, 620–622
Redstockings, 681
Reformation, Protestant, 30–31, 33
Reform capitalism, 637, 662
Reform Judaism, 457
Reform movements, 269, 449
  humanitarian, 477
  mid-nineteenth-century, 259–262
  Progressive Era, 476
  temperance movement, 261
  urban, 471–472
Refrigerators, 535(f), 536
Refugees, 725, 761
Regulators, 128
Rehnquist, William, 720
Reign of Terror (France), 179
Religion
  abolitionism and, 266

anxieties over, 85–86
Aztec, 5
colonial era, 57, 59*(t)*, 98–103, 121–122
dissension in, 101–103
diversity in, 98
Great Awakening, 85
on homosexuality, 720
immigrants and, 249, 457
in imperialism, 505
Inca, 6
Mediterranean world, 9–10
megachurches, 750
middle class and, 250–252
modernism vs. fundamentalism, 548–549
music in, 440
New Deal and, 569
the New Right and, 710
"New School" ministers, 244–245
partisanship and, 423
Pilgrims, 45–46
Protestant Reformation, 30–31
renewal of in early republic, 194–195
in the 1950s, 644–645
Second Great Awakening, 255–256
separation of church and state, 168
slaves and, 98, 280–281
witchcraft and, 86–87
Religious toleration, 394–395
colonial era, 58, 101
in Maryland, 41
Remarque, Erich Maria, 583
Renaissance, 10
Reno, Marcus, 382*(i)*
Reno, Milo, 563
"Report on the Subject of Manufactures"
(Hamilton), 178
Representation
slavery and, 174
three-fifths compromise, 173
virtual, 124
Republican motherhood, 170
Republican Party
African Americans switching from, 575
after the Civil War, 370
congressional majority by, 421
conservatism's revival in the 1960s and,
684–686
constituents of, 423
Contract with America, 746
Douglass in, 326
Eisenhower and, 654–655
in election of 1856, 315
in election of 1860, 319
in election of 1896, 446, 446*(m)*
in election of 1912, 495
in election of 1928, 549–551
founding of, 314
Frémont and, 301
Modern Republicanism and, 654–655
Reconstruction under, 355–364
retreat from Reconstruction by, 368
Sherman in, 401
Stalwarts vs. Half Breeds, 423
Tea Party movement in, 756
Trump and, 762–768
in Wilmington, North Carolina massacre,
447*(i)*
Republican societies, 179
Restore Our Alienated Rights (ROAR), 690
Restrictive covenants, 640
Retail outlets, 410
Retirement
New Deal and, 570
Social Security and, 572–573
Revere, Paul, 137
Revivals, religious, 83–84
Great Awakening, 85, 99–100, 121
industrialization and, 253
music in, 440
in the 1950s, 644–645
Second Great Awakening, 255–256,
256*(m)*
temperance movement and, 261
Reykjavik, Iceland, summit in, 728
Reynolds v. United States, 394
Rhee, Syngman, 616
Rhineland, German occupation of the, 584
Rhode Island, 49
Constitution ratified by, 175, 175*(t)*
royal charter of, 57
Rice, Condoleezza, 750
Rice, slavery and, 78
Rice, Thomas, 248
Richards, Maria, 353
Richelieu, Cardinal, 33
Richmond, Virginia, 276
capture of, 345
as Confederate capital, 336
emancipation in, 351
"Rights of the Colonies" (Adams), 129
Riis, Jacob, 467
Ringmann, Mathias, 2

Ripley, George, 262
"Rip Van Winkle" (Irving), 193–194
Roads, 206
    to 1837, 224(m)
    automobiles and improvement of, 536
    in cities, 468
    transportation revolution and improvement
        in, 247
    after World War II, 639
Roanoke Island, 23
Robber barons, 402
Robertson, Pat, 710
Roberval, Sieur de, 23
Robinson, Harriet, 253
Robinson, Jackie, 647, 652
Rochambeau, Comte de, 156
Rochester, New York
    Douglass in, 326
    emergence of, 247
    growth of, 247
    immigrants in, 452
    revivals in, 245, 256
Rockefeller, John D., 408–409, 412
    income of, 432
    lavish home of, 414
Rockefeller, John D. Jr., 505
Rockefeller, Nelson A., 697
Rock Island, Illinois, 207(t)
Rock 'n' roll, 633–634, 643, 650
    counterculture and, 679
    in the 1970s, 703
Rock Springs massacre, 397
Roebling, Emily, 466
Roebling, John Augustus, 466
Roebling, Washington, 466
Roe v. Wade, 681, 704, 720, 763
Rolfe, John, 38
Rolling Stones, 679
Rolvaag, O. E., 391
Roman empire, 9
Romani, in the Holocaust, 597, 603
Romania, fall of the Soviet regime
    in, 731
Romanticism, 193–194
Romney, Mitt, 757
Rooming houses, 440
Roosevelt, Eleanor, 555–556, 565
    African Americans and, 574, 575(i)
    as go-between with Randolph, 592
    Perkins and, 567
    social welfare and, 579

Roosevelt, Franklin, 566(i)
    Atlantic Charter and, 586
    atomic bomb development under, 581
    Black Cabinet of, 574
    civil rights movement and, 592
    confidence instilled by, 565–566
    court-packing plan of, 577
    critics of, 569–570
    death of, 602
    election of, 565
    on entry into World War II, 585
    fireside chats of, 566
    the Holocaust and, 603–604
    House Un-American Activities Committee
        and, 620
    Japanese American internment under, 596,
        660
    labor and, 636
    migrant workers and, 562
    New Deal of, 558(f), 565–578
    on Pearl Harbor, 586
    polio of, 555, 566(i)
    reelection of, 576, 585, 599
    on the second front, 597
    wartime economy under, 587–590
    Yalta Agreement and, 600, 610
Roosevelt, James, 566(i)
Roosevelt, Theodore
    Big Stick diplomacy of, 511–513
    conservation and, 475
    in Cuba, 507
    in election of 1912, 494–495
    foreign policy of, 502, 511–513
    Japanese immigration restricted by, 488
    Mahan's influence on, 502, 511
    on the Maine, 507
    national parks created by, 490(m)
    Native Americans and, 494
    Open Door policy and, 512–513
    progressivism and, 476–477
    Roosevelt, Eleanor, and, 555
    Square Deal of, 491–494
    Taft and, 494–495
    on war and manhood, 505
    on World War I, 515
Roosevelt Corollary, 512
Rosenberg, Ethel, 609, 621–622
Rosenberg, Julius, 609, 621–622
Rosie the Riveter, 590
Ross, Betsy, 143
Ross, John, 217, 221, 240–241, 287, 330

Rough Riders, 507
Rowson, Susanna, 193–194
Royal African Company, 43, 70, 78
Royal Navy (England)
    Embargo Act and, 203
    impressment by, 105, 120
    U.S. neutrality ignored by, 179
Royall, Isaac and family, 74
Roybal, Edward, 652
Ruef, Abe, 469, 470*(i)*
Ruggles, David, 308
Rum, 57
Rum Riot (1855), 261
Rural Electrification Administration, 567
Rural free delivery (RFD), 410
Rural life
    colonial era, 75–77
    family labor in, 89, 89*(i)*
    in the Great Depression, 559, 562–563,
        564*(f)*
    in the twenties, 537, 538*(m)*
    urbanization vs, 462, 537, 538*(m)*
Rush, Benjamin, 170
Russia
    Bolshevik Revolution in, 530, 610
    election meddling by, 763
    in the Group of Seven (G7), 732
    Jewish immigrants from, 451, 453
    Manchuria invaded by, 512
    in World War I, 514
Russian Federation, 731
Russian Revolution, 516, 524, 620
Russo-Japanese War (1904–1905), 454
Rust Belt, 700*(m)*
Rustin, Bayard, 649, 661, 666, 684

Sacagawea, 190, 201, 204, 214
Sacco, Nicola, 545
Sacco and Vanzetti case, 545
Sadat, Anwar, 702
Salazar, Ken, 758
Salem witchcraft trials, 86–87
Salinger, J. D., 646
Salk, Jonas, 638
Saloons, 392
SALT II, 701
Salt Lake City, 394, 463, 537
Same-sex marriage, 746, 750, 757
Samoa, 226
Samoset, 45
Sampson, Deborah, 149
San Antonio School District v. Rodriguez, 708

Sanctuary Movement, 715
Sand Creek Massacre, 344, 380–381
San Diego, in World War II, 588
Sandinistas, 723, 737
San Esteban del Rey Mission, 32*(i)*
San Francisco
    Beats in, 645
    Chinatown, 432*(i)*, 456
    earthquake and fire, 467
    growth of in the twenties, 537, 538*(m)*
    Hetch Hetchy damn and, 489, 491
    immigrants in, 455
    New York Giants moved to, 640
    political bosses in, 469, 470*(i)*
    population of, 461
    railroad strike in, 436*(m)*
    tongs in, 458
    trolleys in, 465
    in World War II, 588
Sanger, Margaret, 486–487
San Salvador, 14
Santa Anna, Antonio López de, 286
Santa Clara County v. Southern Pacific Railroad
    Company, 409
Santa Fe, 378
Santa Fe Ring, 395
Santa Fe Trail, 223, 226, 305*(m)*, 306
Saratoga, Battle of (1777), 147*(m)*, 148
Savannah, Georgia, 227, 336
Savannah people, 64
Savings and loan institutions, 719
Scacki, Francisco, 221*(i)*
Scalawags, 364
Scandinavian immigrants
    as farmers, 391
    in the lumber industry, 387
    in mining towns, 387
    in 1820s, 247
    in utopian societies, 262*(i)*
Scarlet Letter, The (Hawthorne), 260
Schenck, Charles, 530
Schenck v. United States, 530
Schlafly, Phyllis, 704
School busing, 706
School prayer, 672
Schroeder, Patricia, 704
Schultz, Alfred P., 460
Schuyler, Elizabeth, 163
Scientific management, 410
Scots-Irish immigrants, 76, 95–96, 96*(m)*, 98
    education of, 192
    Whiskey Rebellion and, 180

Scott, Dred, 301, 306, 316, 321
Scott, Winfield, 288, 294, 310
Scottsboro Nine, 561, 564
Seale, Bobby, 670
Sears, Roebuck and Co., 410, 463
Seattle
    anti-Chinese assaults in, 397
    growth of in the twenties, 537
    Ku Klux Klan in, 547
    trolleys in, 465
    in World War II, 588
Second Bank of the United States, 203
    Jackson and, 239
    panic of 1819 and, 228–229
Second Continental Congress, 138
Second front, World War II, 597
Second Great Awakening, 255–256
Second industrial revolution, 536
Second Party System, 285
Second Seminole War, 287
Sectional crises, 311–316
    Bleeding Kansas and, 314–316
    Dred Scott decision and, 316
    John Brown's raid and, 318
    Kansas-Nebraska Act and, 312–314,
        314*(m)*
    secession of the South and, 319–322,
        321*(m)*
Securities and Exchange Commission (SEC),
    567, 572*(t)*
Sedition Act (1798), 184
Sedition Act (1918), 520–521
Segregation
    black nationalism and, 542–544
    declared unconstitutional, 623
    in Georgia, 350
    in government offices, 498
    Jim Crow laws, 396, 418–420
    Journey of Reconciliation and, 661
    of Latinos, 556, 561
    in the military, 521, 589, 593, 617*(i)*
    progressivism on, 476
    in public transportation, 345
    residential, 463
    in the South, 414
    in suburbs, 640
    urbanization and, 463
    Wilson on, 497
    in World War I, 521
    in World War II, 589, 593
Seixas, Eleanor Cohen, 343

Selective Service Act (1917), 516
Selective Service Act (1940), 585
Selma, Alabama, 336, 667–668
Seminole Indians, 225, 330
    Jackson and, 225
    removal of, 287
Senate
    continuity in, 421
    election by popular vote for, 489
Senate, Constitutional Convention on, 173
Senate Foreign Relations Committee, 623
Seneca Falls, Women's Encampment for a
        Future of Peace and Justice, 727
Seneca Falls convention, 267
Seneca Indians, 142
    in Civil War, 330
    Indian Reorganization Act and, 576
    removal of, 289
    on women's rights, 268
Separate Baptists, 121
Separate but equal, 419, 648, 657
Separate spheres, 250–251
Separation of church and state, 168, 750
Sepúlveda, Juan Gines de, 24
Servants
    Chinese immigrants as, 396
    domestic labor by, 210
    sexual abuse of female, 92
    women employed as, 249
Servicemen's Readjustment Act (1944), 635,
    636*(i)*
Sessions, Amasa, 84, 88
Settlement houses, 471, 478
Seven Days Battle (1862), 331
Seven Golden Cities, 21
Seventeenth Amendment, 489
Seventh-Day Adventist Church, 257
Seven Year Itch, The (film), 643
Sewage systems, 462, 468
Seward, William H., 307
Sewell, Samuel, 85–86
Sewing women, 335
Sexual Behavior in the Human Female
        (Kinsey), 646
Sexual coercion, 92, 92*(t)*
Sexuality
    change norms of after World War II,
        634–635
    changing norms of in the twenties, 536,
        540–541
    the Christian Right on, 710

colonial era, 84, 92
counterculture on, 679–680
double standard on, 679
Kinsey on, 646
in the 1970s, 703–704
in 1950s movies, 643
Sexual violence
against slaves, 283
MeToo movement and, 764, 769
myth of black men raping white women, 483
Scottsboro Nine and, 561
women's suffrage and, 481
Seymour, Horatio, 361
Shakers, 143
Sharecropping, 365
Communist Party and, 564
in the Great Depression, 560
industrialization and, 406
New Deal and, 575
in the twenties, 540
urbanization and, 463
in World War II, 588
Share Our Wealth, 570
Sharon Statement, 709
Shawnee Mission, Kansas, 315
Shawnee people, 96*(m)*
alliances of, 113
in American Revolution, 143
civilization of, 378
land treaties with, 165
Prophetstown and, 219
Shays, Daniel, 162–163
Shays's Rebellion (1787), 163, 171, 181, 193
Shelby v. Holder, 759
Shelley v. Kraemer, 640
Shepherd-Towner Act (1921), 479, 551
Sheridan, Philip, 343
Sherman, John, 401, 409, 420
Hanna and, 446
money supply under, 443
Sherman, Roger, 141
Sherman, William Tecumseh, 342–345, 381
Sherman Antitrust Act (1890), 401, 409
big business favored in implementation of, 442
Roosevelt's Square Deal and, 492
unions and, 437
Sherman Silver Purchase Act (1890), 443, 445
Shiloh, battle of (1862), 331*(m)*, 332
Shinseki, Eric, 758

Shoshone people, 60, 202*(m)*
displacement of, 204
Shultz, George, 714–716, 721
on the Iran-Contra affair, 726
on Nicaragua, 723
on Qaddafi, 725
Shuttlesworth, Fred, 665
Siberia, 3
Siemens, William, 404
Silent Spring (Carson), 705
Silver, 20
currency backed by, 445
Silverheels, Jay, 642
Silver mining, 387
Simmons, W. J., 547
Sinatra, Frank, 643
Sinclair, Harry F., 535
Sinclair, Upton, 492
Sioux Indians, 293
Battle of the Little Big Horn, 381–382, 382*(i)*
Wounded Knee massacre of, 385, 683
Sister Carrie (Dreiser), 463
Sit-down strikes, at General Motors, 574
Sit-ins, 593, 650, 651*(m)*, 656
at Berkeley, 678
Sitting Bull, 380, 385
Six Companies of San Francisco, 653
Six-Day War (1967), 694
Sixteenth Amendment, 493*(t)*, 495
Sketchbook (Irving), 193
Skilled workers, 430
Skyscrapers, 404, 465
Slater, Samuel, 208–209
Slaughter, Linda, 391
Slaughterhouse cases, 368
Slave laws, 78–79
Slave revolts, 79–80, 213, 281–282
in Haiti, 199, 213
Vesey, 233–234
Slavery, 12–13
abolished, 345, 356
after the American Revolution, 159
American Revolution and, 151
Aztec, 2, 5
building of Washington, D.C. and, 197–198
Carolinas, 58
Christianity and, 12
Civil War as war on, 329
Compromise of 1850 and, 307–308

Slavery (*Continued*)
  concentration of wealth and, 78
  Constitutional Convention on, 173
  cotton and, 210–213, 211(*i*), 278(*m*)
  Crittenden plan on, 320
  in domestic labor, 210
  Dred Scott case on, 301, 316
  Dunmore's Proclamation and, 140
  Emancipation Proclamation and, 326–327, 333
  emergence of, 41–42
  expansion of, 276–277, 278(*m*)
  family reunification after, 352–354
  fertility rates in, 90
  Fugitive Slave Act on, 308–310, 309(*i*)
  harsher treatment in, 282–283
  indentured servants and, 73–74
  intensification of debates over, 295–296
  justification of, 12, 285
  Kansas-Nebraska Act on, 312–314, 314(*m*)
  marriage under, 353
  Mexica, 1–2
  Missouri Compromise on, 230(*m*), 230–231
  of Native Americans, 65
  Northwest Ordinance on, 166
  planters in expansion of, 274–275
  religion and, 98, 213
  resistance to, 79–80, 281–282
  after the Revolution, 168–169
  society and culture under, 278–282
  in South, 77–79, 272–297
  tightening of control over, 282–285
  urban life and, 276
  in Virginia, 37, 39–42
  in West, 268, 272–297
  western expansion and, 302
  western settlement and, 307–311
  West Indies, 43, 44(*m*)
  white servants replaced by, 73
  white southerners without slaves on, 283–284
Slave trade, 70–71
  ads, 77(*i*)
  African, 9, 11–13
  Atlantic, 70–71
  Aztec, 5
  in Columbian exchange, 21
  Constitutional Convention on, 173
  England in, 63
  international, banning of, 212

Mayan, 1–2
  Middle Passage in, 70–71
  numbers in, 71(*f*)
  seaport cities and, 71–72
  slave rebellions in, 282
"Slave Wedding, A," 280(*i*)
Slidell, John, 293
Slovenia, 748, 749(*m*)
Slums, 468, 471
Smallpox, 17, 18(*m*), 306
  in American Revolution, 146
  Aztecs and, 20, 20(*i*)
  freedpeople killed by, 352
  Indians and, 293, 378
  Massachusetts Indians and, 47
  Plymouth and, 45
Smith, Adam, 178, 411
Smith, Alfred E., 549
Smith, Barbara, 704
Smith, Bessie, 542
Smith, Gerrit, 308, 309(*i*)
Smith, Jacob H., 510
Smith, John, 28–29, 37
Smith, Joseph, 257
Smith, Margaret Bayard, 237
Smith, Margaret Chase, 644
Smith Act (1940), 620
Smith-Connally Act (1943), 590
Smith v. Allwright, 593
Smuggling, 121, 123
Social activism
  against poverty, 260
  mid-nineteenth-century, 259–262, 269
  temperance movement, 261
Social Darwinism, 402, 412, 476
Social evolution, 411
Social gospel, 471, 476
Socialism, 413
  Bellamy on, 413
  income tax as, 445
  New Deal as, 569
  in Spain, 584
  unions and, 438
Socialist Party of America, 438, 495, 551
Social media
  Russian election meddling via, 763
Social Security, 572–573
  conservative opposition to, 685
  payroll tax for, 577
  raised in 1954, 654
  in the 1960s, 662

under Reagan, 718
Social Security Act (1935), 572, 572(t), 575, 577
Social Statics (Spencer), 411
Social structure
  Gilded Age, 414–420
  identity and classes in, 191
  laissez-faire and, 413
  middle class and, 250–252
  in mining towns, 387
  reform movements, 259–262
  technology and transformation of, 743–744
  in the twenties, 530–533, 537–538
Social welfare
  political machines and, 469
  progressivism and, 551
  in the 1960s, 684
  under Bush, George H. W., 729–730
  under Clinton, 747
  under Reagan, 717
  women's role in enacting, 579
Social workers, 478
Society of American Indians, 484
Sod houses, 391
Soil Conservation Service, 568
Soil Erosion Service, 568
Solar power, 699
Solidarity, 730
Solis, Hilda, 758
Somoza, Anastasio, 723
Sons of Liberty, 124, 127, 129, 137
Sons of Neptune, 124
Sorbonne protests, 691
Souls of Black Folk, The (Du Bois), 461, 483
Soup kitchens, 559(i)
South
  African American migration from, 463
  American Revolution in, 154(m), 155–157
  civil rights movement in, 646–653
  Civil War legacy in, 347
  cotton and slavery in, 210–213
  devotion to the "Lost Cause" in, 358(i)
  education in, 192
  food shortages in, 339
  the great migration from, 532
  immigrants in, 744
  industrialization in, 402, 405–406, 407(m)
  itinerant preachers in, 101
  Jim Crow laws, 396, 418–420
  New, 405–406, 407(m)

plantation society in, 274–275
political, economic, and social influence of, 716
Populist Party in, 448
Reconstruction in, 363–367
reemergence of the KKK in, 529
resistance to desegregation in, 650
rise of slavery in, 77–79
secession of, 319–322, 321(m)
segregation in, 414
slavery in after the Revolution, 169
small farmers vs. planters in, 206
union movement in, 435
urbanization in, 276
after World War II, 640
South Africa, 453
  apartheid in, 723, 737
  repressive regime supported in, 694
South Carolina, 59
  American Revolution in, 151
  black majority in, 364
  civil rights movement in, 647
  Constitution ratified by, 175, 175(t)
  cotton and slavery in, 212
  emancipated blacks in, 352
  Fort Sumter, 328
  immigrants to, 66
  indigo in, 69
  land claims of, 166(m)
  lumber industry in, 406
  nullification and, 239
  readmitted to the Union, 360
  Regulators, 128
  Sea Islands, 352, 356
  secession of, 320
  Sherman's March to the Sea through, 343
  slavery in, 151
  slave trade ports, 71–72
  Spanish exploration of, 21
  Stono rebellion, 79
  Tuscarora War, 65
South Carolina Exposition and Protest, The (Calhoun), 238
South Carolina State University, 691
South Dakota, 381, 391
Southern Christian Leadership Conference (SCLC), 649, 665, 667
Southern Democrats, 577
Southern Farmers' Alliance, 442–443
South Korea, 614, 758
  passenger airliner of shot down, 722

Soviet-Afghan War (1980–1989), 731
Soviet missile crisis, Cuba, 662(m), 662–664
Space exploration, 654
Space race, 654
Spain
    American exploration by, 14–16, 15(m)
    Aztecs and, 1–2
    Californios and, 395
    civil war in, 584
    colonies of, 44(m), 59–60, 64(m)
    in Columbian exchange, 17–18, 18(m)
    Columbus and, 15
    conquest of native empires by, 19–20
    Counter-Reformation in, 31
    Cuba and, 311
    Cuban War for Independence from, 506
    decline of global empire, 31–33
    end of empire in, 225
    English attacks on, 33
    English conflicts with, 66
    enslavement of Indians by, 66
    frontier conflicts with, 181–182
    global trade by, 25
    the Great Depression in, 559
    the Great Recession in, 754
    imperialist wars with, 506–511
    Indian civilizations and, 378
    Jackson and, 225
    lands ceded to the U.S, 225
    New Orleans closed by, 164, 167
    northern exploration by, 21–22, 22(m)
    Philippine war with, 509
    Pueblo Revolt and, 60, 61(i)
    reconquest of, 10
    slavery outlawed by, 284
    slave trade, 14
    territory of after the Revolution, 166(m)
    torture and enslavement by, 24
    trade and, 11
    U.S. sovereignty undermined by, 171
    U.S. war with, 507–508
    War of the Spanish Succession, 63
Spanish-American War (1898–1899),
    506–508, 510(m)
Spanish armada, 33
Spanish Loyalists, 584
Spanish Trail, 305(m)
Spaulding, Eliza, 302
Speaker of the House, 421
Spear, Fred, 520(i)
Special interests, liberalism and, 709

Spectral evidence, 87
Spencer, Herbert, 411–413, 476
Spies, August, 434
Spinning machines, 208
Spiritual Mobilization, 569
Spock, Benjamin, 644
Spoils system, 238, 241, 368
Sports
    baseball, 417–418, 440–441, 647, 652
    crisis of masculinity and, 417–418
    desegregation of, 647, 652
    Gilded Age, 415(t)
    leisure and, 440–441
    women in, 416, 417(i)
    working-class leisure and, 439
Springfield, Illinois, riot of 1908, 482
Springsteen, Bruce, 703
Sputnik, 654
Squanto, 45
Square Deal, 491–494
Squash, 4
Squatters, 165
SS *St. Louis*, 604
St. Augustine, Florida, 21
St. Clair, Arthur, 181
St. Louis
    industry in, 402
    Irish immigrants in, 247
    population of, 461
    railroad strike in, 436(m)
Stagflation, 699
Stalin, Joseph, 597
    Greek civil war and, 612
    Khrushchev on, 626
    on the Marshall Plan, 613
    nonaggression agreement with Hitler, 585
    purges by, 608
    Truman and, 610
    Yalta Agreement and, 600, 610
Stalingrad, battle of, 598(m)
Stalwarts, 423
Stamp Act Congress, 125, 131
Stamp Act (England, 1765), 123–126
Standard Oil Company, 408
    antitrust action against, 492
    muckrakers on, 477
Standard Oil Trust, 409
Standish, Miles, 46
Stanton, Edwin, 344, 360
Stanton, Elizabeth Cady, 267, 337, 362,
    362(i), 479

Starr, Ellen, 478
State Department, 176
States
    constitutionality of laws by, 202–203
    Constitution on powers of, 173
    constitutions of, 149–150
    currency laws of after the Revolution, 167
    land claims of, 155, 165, 166*(m)*
    Northwest Ordinance on, 165
    progressive reforms in, 488–489
    Revolutionary war debts of, 177
States' rights doctrine, 238
States' Rights Party, 636
Statue of Liberty, 458
Steam engines, 207–208
Steel industry
    in Birmingham, 406
    consolidation in, 408
    Homestead strike, 428, 436–437
    skyscrapers and, 404
    technological innovations in, 404
Steffens, Lincoln, 477
Stein, Gertrude, 541
Steinbeck, John, 560
Steinem, Gloria, 681
Stela, 17
Stem cell research, 750
Stephens, Alexander H., 357
Stephens, Uriah, 433
Stephenson, David Curtis, 528–530, 542
Stereotypes, 459
    gender, in World War II, 590
Stevens, Thaddeus, 357
Stevenson, Adlai, 424*(i)*
Stewart, Maria, 265
Still, William, 308
Stock market
    Black Tuesday, 551
    SEC regulation of, 567
    speculation in the twenties, 539
Stockton, California, 559
Stone, Lucy, 337, 479
Stone Mountain, Georgia, 547
Stonewall riots (1969), 684
Stono rebellion, 79
Stop ERA, 703
Story, Joseph, 237
Stowe, Harriet Beecher, 312
Strategic Arms Limitation Treaty (SALT I), 694
Strategic Arms Limitation Treaty (SALT II), 701

Strategic Arms Reduction Talks (START), 722
Stratton-Porter, Geneva, 475
Strauss, Levi, 304
Streetcars, 249, 465
Strong, Josiah, 505
Structural steel, 404, 465
Student Nonviolent Coordinating Committee (SNCC), 650, 651*(m)*
    black power and, 669
    Freedom Rides and, 665
    Freedom Summer and, 667
Students for a Democratic Society (SDS), 678
Subtreasury system, 442, 448
Suburbs, 466, 639, 657
Success, doctrines of, 411–412
Sudan, 748
Sudentenland, German annexation of, 584
Suez Canal, 597, 628
Suffragists, 479–480
Sugar, 43, 57
    Embargo Act and, 203
    Hawaii annexation and, 504
    Navigation Acts on, 69
    West Indies, 43
Sugar Act (England, 1764), 123
Sugar trust, 409
Sullivan, John, 153
Sumner, Charles, 315, 332, 357
Sumter, Thomas, 156
Sun Belt, migration to the, 640, 685, 700*(m)*
Superfund, 705
Supermarkets, 410
Supply-side economics, 709, 717
Supreme Court, 202–203
    Amistad mutiny and, 282
    on anti-Communism, 624
    antitrust cases, 492
    Bush, George H. W. nominations to, 730
    Constitutional Convention on, 173–174
    on contraception, 672
    court-packing plan on, 577
    on desegregation, 648–649
    on the 2000 election, 749
    on equal but separate, 419
    on gay marriage, 757
    on grandfather clauses, 483
    on income tax, 445
    Indian removal and, 287
    on Japanese American internment, 582, 596
    laissez-faire and, 411

Supreme Court (*Continued*)
  on the National Recovery Administration, 568
  on New Deal legislation, 577
  Nixon nominations to, 695
  Reagan nominees to, 719
  in the Red scare, 530
  on school desegregation, 649
  on school segregation, 624
  on the Scottsboro Nine, 561
  Second Bank of the United States and, 229
  on steel plants seizure, 619
  Trump nominations to, 764
  under Warren, 660–661, 671–672
  unions damaged by, 534
  on voter qualifications, 448
  on working conditions for women, 479
Supreme Court cases
  Abrams v. United States, 530
  Brown v. Board of Education of Topeka, Kansas, 648, 706
  Cherokee Nation v. Georgia, 287
  Dennis v. United States, 621
  Dred Scott, 301, 316, 321, 359
  Gideon v. Wainwright, 672
  Griswold v. Connecticut, 672
  Guinn v. United States, 483
  Marbury v. Madison, 202
  McCulloch v. Maryland, 203
  McGirt v. Oklahoma, 760
  Minor v. Happersatt, 363
  Miranda v. Arizona, 672
  Muller v. Oregon, 479
  Munn v. Illinois, 442
  Obergefell v. Hodges, 757
  Plessy v. Ferguson, 419, 484, 648
  Plyler v. Doe, 720
  Pollack v. Farmers Loan and Trust, 445
  Reynolds v. United States, 394
  Roe v. Wade, 681, 704, 720, 763
  Santa Clara County v. Southern Pacific Railroad Company, 409
  Schenck v. United States, 530
  Shelby v. Holder, 759
  Shelley v. Kraemer, 640
  Slaughterhouse cases, 368
  Smith v. Allwright, 593
  Swann v. Charlotte-Mecklenburg Board of Education, 706
  United States v. Cruikshank, 369
  United States v. E.C. Knight Company, 409

  Wabash v. Illinois, 442
  Williams v. Mississippi, 448
  Worcester v. Georgia, 287
  Yates v. United States, 624
Survival of the fittest, 476
Susquehannock people, 42
Sutter's Mill, 303
Swann v. Charlotte-Mecklenburg Board of Education, 706
Sweatshops, 467, 734
Sweden, energy consumption per capita in, 699(*f*)
Sweet, Ossian, 529–530, 532, 548
Swift, Gustavus, 410
Swing states, 423
Syphilis, 18(*m*)
Syria
  civil war in, 761, 761(*m*)
  Six-Day War, 694
Systemic racism, 657, 759, 766

Tacoma, Washington, anti-Chinese assaults in, 397
Taft, Robert A., 622
Taft, William Howard, 494, 511–512
Taft-Hartley Act (1947), 636
Taino people, 16–17
Takacs, Karoly, 452
Takacs, Maria Vik, 452–453
Talented Tenth, 483
Taliban, 701, 731, 751
Tallahassee, Florida, bus boycott in, 649
Tallmadge, James, Jr., 229
Tammany Hall, 470
Tammany societies, 195
Tammend, 195
Tampa, Florida, 457
  black troops attacked in, 507
  ghetto riots in, 669
Taney, Roger, 316
Tanzania, terrorism in, 748
Tarbell, Ida, 477
Tariff of Abominations, 238
Tariffs
  of 1828, 235, 238
  Billion Dollar Congress and, 422
  Farmers' Alliance on, 442
  imperialism and, 504(*f*)
  in the twenties, 534, 540
  under Hamilton, 178
  under Jackson, 238–239

Wilson-Gorman Act on, 445
Wilson on, 495
Tarleton, Banastre, 156
Task system, 279
Taxes
  Bush, George H. W., on, 729
  in the Great Depression, 557
  Populists on, 443
  revolt against in the 1970s, 709
  Social Security and, 573
  in the twenties, 534
  under Bush, George W., 750
  under Johnson, Lyndon, 671
Taylor, Breonna, 767(i), 767–768
Taylor, Elizabeth, 643
Taylor, Frederick W., 410
Taylor, Zachary, 269, 296, 307–308
  in Mexican-American War, 293
Tea Party movement, 756
Teapot Dome scandal, 534, 551
Technology
  industrialization and innovation in,
    404–405
  slavery and, 277
  twenties consumer goods production and,
    536, 537(i)
  urbanization and, 462
Tecumseh, 218–219
Teenage culture, 639(f), 643, 657
  movies and, 643
Tehran, U.S. Embassy hostages in, 703, 712,
  725
Tejas Indians, 60
Telegraphs, 404, 408
Telephone
  invention of, 404
  women operators for, 430, 432(i)
Television, 637
  the Christian Right and, 710
  Nixon-Kennedy debate on, 656, 656(m)
  reality shows, 733–734
  the rise of, 641–642
  in the 1970s, 703
Teller, Henry M., 507
Teller Amendment (1898), 508
Temperance movement, 250, 261
  on the frontier, 392
  prohibition and, 485, 521, 544
  Second Great Awakening and, 256
Tenements, 466
Tennent, Gilbert, 83–85, 101, 108

Tennent, William, 100
Tennessee
  Battle of Shiloh, 332
  statehood of, 206
Tennessee Valley Authority (TVA), 567, 572(t)
Tenochtitlán, 5, 19, 25
Ten Percent Plan, 356
Tenskwatawa, 218–219, 291
Tenure of Office Act (1867), 360
Terra Incognita, 2
Terrorism, 748
  al-Qaeda in, 731
  9/11 attacks, 743, 750–752
  Obama in the war against, 760–762
  Reagan and, 725–726
Tet Offensive, 675–676
Texas
  agricultural worker strikes in, 562
  battle for, 285–287
  black voters in, 364
  Compromise of 1850 on, 307
  immigrants in, 455
  internment camps in, 595
  Mexican-American War and, 293–295
  Mexican immigrants in, 453–454
  migration into, 293
  refugees in, 725
  secession of, 320
  Spanish claims to, 60
  statehood of, 304
  after World War II, 640
Textile manufacturing, 254
  child labor in, 431
  Civil War and, 335
  in the New South, 406, 407(m)
  in South, 335
  unions in, 438
  women workers in, 252
  working conditions in, 431–432
  in World War II, 587
Thatcher, Margaret, 717
Thatcherism, 717
Thayendanegea, 142
Theater, 248, 440
Third World Liberation Front, 684
Thirteenth Amendment, 345, 356–358
This Side of Paradise (Fitzgerald), 541
Thomas, Clarence, 730
Thoreau, Henry David, 258, 649
Three-fifths compromise, 173, 284
Three Mile Island nuclear power plant, 705

Thurmond, Strom, 636
Tiananmen Square massacre (1989), 735
Tibeats, John, 273
Tijerina, Reies, 682(i)
Tilden, Samuel J., 369, 370(m)
Till, Emmett, 650
Timber and Stone Act (1878), 394
Timbuktu, 11
Time-and-motion studies, 410
Time zones, 403
Tippecanoe, Battle of, 291
Title IX, 704
Tito, Marshall, 612
Tituba, 86
Tobacco, 38–39, 57
    antitrust action against, 492
    child labor in, 431
    cigarette manufacturing, 406
    Navigation Acts on, 69
    in the New South, 407(m)
    slavery and, 42, 77–78
Toledo, Ohio, 489
Tometi, Opal, 742
Tongs, 458
Topaz internment camp, 582
Topeka, Kansas, 566(i)
To Secure These Rights, 647
Totalitarianism, authoritarianism vs., 722
Town meetings, 103
Townsend, Francis, 570–571
Townsend Clubs, 570
Townshend, Charles, 126
Townshend Act (England, 1767), 126–127
Toynbee Hall, 477
Toyota, 733
Trade
    Aztec, 5
    Billion Dollar Congress and, 422
    colonial America, 56–57, 67–72
    Columbian exchange in, 17–18, 18(m)
    consumer culture and, 71–72
    Dutch, 35–36
    efforts to regulate after the Revolution, 164
    expansion of U.S., 311
    foreign, 178–179
    French, 35
    fur, 23, 33–36
    globalization of, 67–68
    imperialism and, 503–504, 504(f)
    infrastructure development and, 206
    international, 422

    Mediterranean world, 9–10
    mercantilism and, 68–69
    nineteenth century, 223–225
    Puritans in, 47
    after the Revolution, 167
    Roman empire, 9
    seaport cities in, 71–72
Trading posts, 207(t), 302
Trail of Tears, 289
Transcendentalism, 257–259
Transcontinental railroad, 369, 376
Transnational corporations, 733
Transportation
    to 1837, 224(m)
    in cities, 249
    industrialization and, 403(f)
    nineteenth century revolution in, 247
    regulation of during World War I, 519
    urbanization and, 247, 465
    in the West, 375(m), 376–377
Transported convicts, 74
Travels (Bartram), 194
Treasury bills, 335
Treasury Department, 176, 545
Treaty of Buffalo Creek, 289
Treaty of Fort Laramie, 380
Treaty of Fort Stanwix, 165
Treaty of Ghent, 222
Treaty of Greenville, 181, 205(m)
Treaty of Guadalupe Hidalgo, 295, 395
Treaty of Medicine Lodge, 380–381
Treaty of New Echota, 288
Treaty of Paris, 157
Treaty of Utrecht, 63
Treaty of Versailles, 524, 584
Tredegar Iron Works, 276, 336
Trench warfare, 516
Trenton, Battle of (1777), 146
Triangle Shirtwaist Company fire, 467
Triborough Bridge, 568
Trickle-down economics, 534
    Hoover and, 558
    Reaganomics, 717
Tripartite Pact, 586
Tripoli
    bombing of, 725
    capture of, 199
Trolley cars, 465
Truman, Harry S.
    atomic bombs dropped by, 602
    Berlin airlift and, 615

civil rights movement and, 647
containment policy of, 608–609, 630
the imperial presidency and, 619
Korean War and, 616–618
labor and, 636
the Marshall Plan and, 613
military desegregation by, 617(i)
New Deal coalition of, 635
NSC-68 and, 615–616
reelection of, 636–637
steel plants seized by, 619
the Truman Doctrine and, 612–613
U.S.-Soviet relations under, 610
as vice president, 599
Truman Doctrine, 612–613, 617, 630
Trumbo, Dalton, 583
Trumbull, Lyman, 357
Trump, Donald, 743, 762–768
    COVID-19 pandemic, 766–767
    election of 2016, 762–763, 769
    election of 2020, 768
    health care and, 765
    immigration policies of, 763–765
    impeachment of, 768
    "Make America Great Again" slogan, 763
    MeToo movement and, 764, 769
    Mueller Report, 765
    presidential policies of, 764–766
    Supreme Court appointments by, 764
Trumpism, 769
Trusts, 409
    Clayton Antitrust Act on, 496
    muckrakers on, 477
    Roosevelt and, 492
    World War II and, 588
Truth, Sojourner, 363
Tryon, William, 128
Tuberculosis, 468, 638
Tubman, Harriet, 308, 337
Tulsa Massacre, 533, 533(f)
Turkey, U.S. military bases in, 613, 645
Turner, Frederick Jackson, 461, 503
Turner, Nat, 281–282
Tuscarora War, 65
Tuskaloosa, 21
Tuskegee airmen, 589
Tuskegee Institute, 482
Twain, Mark, 386, 414, 509
Tweed, William Marcy, 470
Twelve Years a Slave (Northup), 297
Twenties (1920s), 528–553

challenges to social conventions in,
    540–544
consumer culture in, 535–536
culture wars in, 544–549
economic warning signs in, 539(f),
    539–540
the financial crash in, 551–552
government promotion of the economy in,
    534–535
politics in, 549–552
progressivism in, 550(m), 551
prosperity and consumption in, 533–540
racial violence in, 532
the Red scare in, 530–531
social turmoil in, 530–533
timeline of, 542
transitions in, 552
urbanization in, 537–538, 538(m)
Twenty-first Amendment, 567
Twenty-sixth Amendment, 695
Tydings, Millard, 623
Tydings-McDuffie Act (1934), 562
Tyler, John, 291
Typewriters, 404
Typhus, 18(m), 468
Tyranny, 174

U-boats, 514–516
Ukraine, 731
Uncle Tom's Cabin (Stowe), 312
Underground railroad, 264, 264(m), 309
Underhill, Amos, 89(i)
Underwood Act (1913), 493(t)
Unemployment
    Coxey's army and, 444
    in the Great Depression, 558(f), 561–563
    in the 1970s, 698
    in the twenties, 539
    under Clinton, 747–748
    under Obama, 756
    under Reagan, 717
    in World War II, 587
Unemployment benefits, 662
Union Brotherhood Lodge, 350
Union maids, 574
Union of Soviet Socialist Republics (USSR)
    Afghanistan and, 701, 702(i)
    Bay of Pigs and, 662(m), 662–663
    Berlin wall and, 615
    breakup of the, 730–732, 732(m)
    Cold War with, 608–632

Union of Soviet Socialist Republics (USSR)
    (*Continued*)
  creation of and the Red scare, 530–531
  détente with, 701
  Egypt and, 628–629
  energy consumption per capita in, 699(*f*)
  iron curtain and, 611, 616(*m*)
  Nixon and, 691, 694
  nonaggression agreement of with Germany,
    585
  nuclear de-escalation and, 728
  nuclear freeze movement and, 726–728
  Prague Spring and, 691
  Reagan on, 716
  rebuilding after World War II, 611
  Six-Day War and, 694
  Sputnik launched by, 654
  as "the evil empire," 722
  U.S. diplomatic recognition of, 583, 610
  U-2 spy plane shot down over, 627
  Vietnam and, 629
  in World War II, 595, 597–599, 601, 610
Union Pacific Railroad, 377, 408, 434
Unions, 253–254, 428
  clashes with owners and, 435–438,
    436(*m*)
  definition of, 433
  globalization and, 734
  membership rates in, 434(*f*)
  New Deal and, 573–574
  organization of, 433–435
  Pullman strike, 437–438, 444
  Roosevelt's Square Deal and, 491–492
  strikes by, 433–434
  under Reagan, 719
  unskilled workers and, 556
  weakened in the twenties, 534
  after World War I, 531
  during World War I, 519
  after World War II, 635, 638(*f*)
  in World War II, 587, 590
Unitarians, 257
United Auto Workers, 574
United Cannery, Agricultural, Packing,
    and Allied Workers of America
    (UCAPAWA), 556
United Fruit Company, 628
United Kingdom
  Brexit, 763
  in the Group of Seven (G7), 732
  industrialization in, 403

United Mine Workers, 573
United Nations, 722
  in the Korean War, 617, 619(*i*)
  Suez Canal crisis and, 628
United Service Organizations (USO), 591
United States Chamber of Commerce, 569
United States Steel, 408, 494
United States v. Cruikshank, 369
United States v. E.C. Knight Company, 409
United Steel Workers of America, 619
Unity Leagues, 594, 652
Universalis Cosmographia, 2, 16
Universal Negro Improvement Association,
    542–544, 543(*i*)
University of California, 678
University of Oklahoma, 648
University of Pennsylvania, 194
University of Texas Law School, 648
Unorganized Territory, 240
Unskilled workers, 429, 556
Upward mobility, 414
  for African Americans, 464, 464(*i*)
  industrialization and, 432
Urbanization
  Civil War, 335–336
  colonial politics and, 106–107
  colonial seaport cities, 71–72
  commerce and, 462
  disorder in, 249–250
  electric lighting and, 405
  industrialization and, 406
  market revolution and, 246–252
  nineteenth century, 206, 246–247
  politics and, 468–472
  poverty in, 468
  progressive reforms and, 488–489
  progressivism and, 476–477
  reformers and, 471
  rural migration and, 442
  in slave South, 276
  in South, 335–336
  in the South, 406
  technology in, 465–466
  in the twenties, 537–538, 538(*m*)
  upward and outward expansion of,
    465–466
  urban life and, 247–249
  wealth and, 108
  in World War II, 587
  worldwide, 462
Uruguay, repressive regime in, 701

U.S. Immigration and Customs Enforcement (ICE), 765
U.S. Court of Claims, 484
U.S. Military Academy, 501
U.S. Military Railroads, 335
U.S. Naval War College, 501
U.S. Navy, 506
    in World War I, 515
    in World War II, 599–600, 600(m)
U.S. Public Health Service, 523
U.S. Sanitary Commission, 334, 336
U.S. Treasury, gold deposits withdrawn from, 445
USS *Cole* bombing, 748
Utah
    Compromise of 1850 on, 307
    internment camps in, 595
    Japanese internment camps in, 582
    Mormon migration to, 257, 302, 394–395
    Pueblo people in, 6
    statehood of, 395
    women's suffrage in, 395
Ute people, 60
Utopianism, societies for, 256(m), 261, 262(i)
Utrecht, Treaty of, 63

Vallandigham, Clement L., 338
Valley Forge, 148
Van Buren, Martin, 231, 234–235, 268
    election of 1848, 296
    Indian removal and, 290
    panic of 1837 and, 290
    on Texas, 285
Vanderbilt, Cornelius, 433
Vanderbilt, William, 414, 433
Vanzetti, Bartolomeo, 545
Vaqueros, 389
Vaudeville, 440
Vélasquez, Diego de, 121
Vergennes, Comte de, 157
Verrazano, Giovanni da, 22
Vertical integration, 407
Vesey, Denmark, 233–234
Vespucci, Amerigo, 2, 15(m), 16
Veterans Administration, 639
Vicksburg
    battle of (1862), 331(m), 340
    siege of (1863), 340, 341(m)
Victorio, 381
Victory gardens, 591
Video games, 744

Vietcong, 630, 674
Vietnam, 619
    early intervention in, 629–630
    immigrants from, 744, 745(f)
Vietnamization, 692–693
Vietnam War (1961–1969), 661, 674–676
    antiwar protests against, 679, 693
    My Lai massacre in, 675, 676(i)
    neoconservatives on, 709
    Vietnamization and, 692–693
View of the Round-Top in Catskills Mountains (Cole), 258(i)
Vigilance committees, 309
Vik, Mary, 457, 472
Villa, Francisco "Pancho," 513
Villasur expedition, 61(i)
Virginia
    black voters in, 364
    colonies in, 23, 37–40, 51
    constitution of, 150
    Constitution ratified by, 175, 175(t)
    emergence of slavery in, 40–42
    land claims by, 165
    Nat Turner's rebellion in, 281–282
    Resolves on the Stamp Act, 124
    slave rebellions in, 200, 213
    slavery in, 76–77
    Statute of Religious Freedom, 168
    tobacco in, 38–39
Virginia and Kentucky Resolutions, 185
Virginia City, Nevada, 386–387
Virginia Company, 29, 37–40
Virginia Declaration of Rights, 141, 174
Virginia Plan, 172
Visit from the Old Mistress, A (Homer), 353(i)
Volstead Act (1919), 545
Voltaire, 99
Voluntarism, in the Great Depression, 557
Volunteers in Service to America (VISTA), 671
Von Steuben, Friedrich, 148
Voter registration
    of blacks in the South, 668(f)
    legislation on blocking, 654
Voting fraud
    the 2000 election and, 749
    political machines and, 469–470
Voting rights
    for African Americans, 357
    Constitution on, 173
    early state constitutions on, 150
    in Europe, 436

Voting rights (*Continued*)
  expansion of in 1820s, 231–233, 253
  of free blacks after the Revolution, 169
  Freedom Summer and, 667
  Jim Crow laws and, 418–420, 419*(m)*
  poll taxes and, 448
  for poor white men, 365
  racial restrictions on, 233–234
  struggle for universal, 361–363
  for women, 170, 267–268, 362*(i)*, 363,
    370, 392, 479–482, 480*(m)*, 481*(i)*
Voting Rights Act (1965), 668
  Chicanos and, 683
  electoral politics after, 706
  extension of, 695
Vox Populi, 124

Wabash v. Illinois, 442
Wagner, Robert F., Sr., 573
Wagner Act (1935), 572*(t)*, 573, 577
Wagon trains, 302, 377
Walden (Thoreau), 258
Waldseemüller, Martin, 2–3, 16, 25
Walesa, Lech, 730
Walker, David, 263, 315
Walker, Margaret, 571
Walker, Mary E., 336
Walker, Quock, 150
Walker, William, 311
Walking Purchase, 97
Wallace, George C., 666, 685–686
  in the election of 1968, 692, 692*(m)*
  in the election of 1972, 696
Wallace, Henry A., 599, 611–612, 636, 644
Wall Street (film), 718
Walmart, 733
Walsh, Thomas J., 551
Waltham, Massachusetts, 252
Wampanoag people, 45–46
  Metacom's War, 50
War, as test of masculinity, 505
War Brides Act (1945), 652
Ward, Lester Frank, 413
Ward, Samuel, 309
War Department, 176, 335, 342
War Industries Board (WIB), 519
Warner, Charles Dudley, 414
War of 1812, 217–222, 220*(m)*, 240–241
War of 1898, 507–508, 510*(m)*
War of the Spanish Succession, 63
War on Poverty, 671, 695

War Powers Act (1942), 588
War Powers Act (1973), 693
War Production Board, 588
Warren, Earl, 648, 660–661, 671–672
Warren, Mercy Otis, 174, 193
Warsaw Pact, 615, 730
Washington, Booker T., 482
  invited to the White House, 492
Washington, D.C.
  battle of, 331*(m)*
  Bonus Army in, 564
  building of, 197–198
  Coxey's army in, 444
  March on Washington for Jobs and
    Freedom, 666
  100,000-person march on, 592
  race riots of 1919 in, 532
  smallpox epidemic in, 352
  in War of 1812, 222
Washington, George, 110–112, 114
  Adams and, 183
  in American Revolution, 139, 145, 148,
    156
  on Bank of the United States, 177
  biographies of, 194
  on camp followers, 145
  French Revolution and, 179
  on frontier rebellions, 171
  land surveyed by, 165
  militant officers confronted by, 165
  on political parties, 183
  portraits of, 194
  as president, 175, 178
  spies for, 148, 153
  Wheatley poems sent to, 143
  Whiskey Rebellion and, 181
Washington, Lawrence, 110
Washingtonian societies, 261
Washington Post, 693
Washington (state)
  anti-Chinese assaults in, 397
  in World War II, 588
Watergate scandal, 696–697
Water Quality Act (1965), 673*(t)*
Watie, Stand, 330, 345
Watson, Tom, 447–448
Way, Amanda M., 392
Wayne, Anthony, 181, 218
Wealth
  colonial consumer culture and, 71–72
  colonial era, 105*(i)*, 108

early nineteenth century, 210
Gilded Age, 414–415
the Great Recession and, 754
industrialization and, 409, 432
laissez-faire and, 410–413
New Frontier on, 662
philanthropy and, 412
in plantation society, 274–275
slavery and, 78
voting rights and, 231–232
Wealth inequality, 108, 409, 432
    colonial era, 108
    in the Great Depression, 577
    in the twenties, 539, 539(f)
    in the twenty-first century, 755(f)
    under Bush, George W., 750
    under Clinton, 747
    under Obama, 757
    under Reaganomics, 718–719
Wealth of Nations, The (Smith), 411
Weathermen, 679
Weaver, James B., 444
Webb-Kenyon Act (1913), 485
Webster, Daniel, 237, 308
    on Harrison, 291
    on nullification, 238
Webster, Noah, 191, 192(i)
Weems, Mason, 193
Weetamoo, 50
Wells, Emmeline B., 395
Wells, Ida B., 477, 482–483
Wesley, John, 99
West, 373–393, 375(m)
    American Revolution in, 153, 154(m)
    cattle industry and commercial farming in, 388–394
    civil rights movement in, 652–653
    commercial farming in, 389–390
    cowboys in, 388–389
    diversity in, 394–397
    expansion to Oregon and Texas, 292–293
    federal Indian policy and, 380–381
    federal policy and foreign investment in, 376–377
    the Great Plains in, 376
    growth of in the twenties, 537–538, 538(m)
    Indian resistance to expansion in, 378–385
    the legacy of the, 397
    Mexican-American War and, 293–295
    mining and lumber industries in, 385–388

opening the, 375–377
    political, economic, and social influence of, 716
    slavery and, 295–296
    after World War II, 640
    in World War II, 588
West, Benjamin, 118(i)
West Bank, 737
Western Federation of Miners, 386, 438
Western Negro Press Association, 463
Western New York Anti-Slavery Society, 245
Western settlement, 204–208, 302–306
    Compromise of 1850 and, 307–308
    gold rush and, 303–304, 304(i)
    overland trails and, 302–303
    slavery and, 307–311
Western Union, 407
West Indies, 58
    English and Spanish conflict over, 66
    English colonies, 37, 43, 44(m), 63
    imperialist conflicts in, 115(m)
    slave rebellions in, 199
    slavery in, 78, 310
    U.S. trade with, 167, 179
Westo people, 64
Weyerhaeuser, Frederick, 387
Wheat, 540
Wheatley, Phillis, 143, 144(i)
Wheeling, West Virginia, McCarthy speech in, 622
Whig Party, 285
    debates over slavery, 295–296
    economic and reform agenda of, 297
    Harrison and, 291
    Van Buren and, 290
Whigs, 311
    abolitionism and, 268
    Compromise of 1850 and, 307
    election of 1852 and, 310
    on Kansas-Nebraska Act, 313–314
    workingmen's interests and, 253
Whiskey Rebellion (1794), 180, 186, 195
White Citizens' Council (WCC), 650
White-collar workers, 415
Whitefield, George, 83, 99
White House, 198, 217, 222
White House Tribal Nations conference, 760
Whiteness
    cultural justification for imperialism and, 505
White primaries, 489
White Slave Trade Act (1910), 486, 493(t)

White supremacy, 285
  civil rights movement against, 646–653
  in the Great Depression, 561
  nativism and, 545
  Populists and, 448
  progressivism and, 482, 486
  in South Africa, 723
  in the twenties, 547–548
  in Wilmington, North Carolina massacre,
    447(i)
  women's suffrage and, 481
Whitman, Marcus, 305
Whitman, Narcissa, 302, 305
Whitney, Eli, 208–209, 211(i)
Who, The, 679
Whoolly rhinoceros, 3
Whooping cough, 638
Wiesel, Elie, 603(i)
WikiLeaks, 763
Wilberforce University, 529
Wilbur, Charles Dana, 376
Wild One, The (film), 642
Wild West shows, 374, 385
Wiley, Harvey, 493
Wilkinson, Jemima, 194
Willard, Frances, 485
William and Mary, College of, 99, 192, 282
William of Orange, 58
Williams, Aubrey, 575(i)
Williams, John Sharp, 505
Williams, Roger, 48–49, 51
Williams v. Mississippi, 448
Willkie, Wendell, 585
Wilmington, North Carolina massacre, 447(i)
Wilmot, David, 295
Wilmot Proviso, 296
Wilson, Charles, 625
Wilson, Edith, 525
Wilson, Sloan, 646
Wilson, Woodrow, 422
  diplomacy and, 513–515
  in election of 1912, 495
  foreign policy of, 502, 513–518
  Fourteen Points by, 523
  New Freedom agenda of, 495–497, 496(i)
  progressivism and, 476
  reelection of, 515
  stroke suffered by, 524
  World War I and, 513–518
Wilson-Gorman Act (1894), 445
Wilson's Creek, battle of (1861), 328, 331(m)

Winchester, battle of (1862), 331(m)
Wind Cave, 490(m)
Wind power, 699
Winthrop, John, 46
Wisconsin
  progressivism in, 489
  statehood of, 292
Witchcraft, 86–87
Wobblies, 438
Wolfe, James, 114
Woman in Nineteenth Century (Fuller), 258
Woman's Christian Temperance Union, 392,
  485
Women
  in abolitionism, 263, 267–268
  affirmative action and, 673(t)
  authors, 193
  the baby boom and, 637–638
  in bread riots, 104
  California gold rush and, 304
  Chinese immigrants, 396
  in Civil War, 336–337, 346
  colonial era, 87–90
  in companionate marriage, 190, 209
  cult of domesticity and, 250
  divorce and, 91
  in domestic production, 209
  double standard and, 679
  education of, 192–193
  employment of, in nineteenth century, 249,
    430–431
  equal pay for, 433
  excluded from Social Security, 573
  in factories, 431
  factory workers, 252
  Finney on, 245
  gender roles and, 89–90
  in the Gilded Age, 415–418
  in the Great Depression, 555–557, 562–563
  as homesteaders, 392, 393(i)
  imperialism and, 505
  in Indian hunting, 380
  in the Ku Klux Klan, 547
  labor unions and, 254
  MeToo movement, 764, 769
  in mining towns, 387
  in movies of the 1950s, 643
  in New Deal programs, 571
  in plantation society, 274–275
  poverty and, 260
  in progressivism, 477–478

Quakers, 245–246
in religious renewal, 194
republican motherhood and, 170
after the Revolution, 170
in Revolution, 136–137, 143, 149
in the 1950s, 644
slaves, 281
in social reform movements, 259
social welfare legislation and, 579
as spies, 326, 337
temperance movement and, 261
in Townshend Act boycott, 127
in the twenties, 541
unions and, 433
in the West, 374–375
in western migration, 303
in the workforce, 644
working-class, leisure activities of, 440
working outside the home, 562–563
in World War I, 519, 520(i)
after World War II, 635
in World War II, 589, 605
Women Accepted for Voluntary Emergency
    Service (WAVES), 589
Women and Economics (Gilman), 479
"Women Drawing Water, Bishop Hill Colony"
    (Kraus), 262(i)
Women's Army Corps, 589
Women's clubs, 478
Women's Emergency Brigade, 574
Women's Encampment for a Future of Peace
    and Justice, 727
Women's International League for Peace and
    Freedom, 645
Women's liberation movement, 680–682
Women's movement, 704–705
Women's National Indian Association, 383
Women's National Loyal League, 337, 345
Women's Political Council, 648
Women's rights
    abolitionism and, 267–268
    crisis of masculinity and, 417
    Lease on, 428
    women pioneers and, 392
Women's suffrage, 268
    emancipation and, 362(i), 363, 370
    frontier women on, 392
    male identity and, 505
    Populists on, 443
    progressivism on, 477, 479–482, 480(m),
        481(i)

in Utah, 395
Woodard, Isaac, 647
Woodhull, Mary, 89(i)
Woodward, Bob, 696
Woolworth, Frank W., 410
Worcester v. Georgia, 287
Wordsworth, William, 193
Workday length, 253–254
    corporate personhood and, 409
    industrialization and, 431
    for railroad workers, 493(t)
    unions and, 433
    during World War I, 519
Workhouses, 75, 260
Working class, leisure and, 438–441
Working conditions
    globalization and, 734
    industrialization and, 431–432
    OSHA and, 695
    Triangle Shirtwaist fire and, 467
    unions and, 435–438
    for women, 478
    after World War II, 635–636
Workingmen's Party, 396
Workmen's Compensation Act (1916), 493(t)
Works Progress Administration (WPA), 571,
    572(t)
World Anti-Slavery Convention, 267
World Health Organization, 735
World's Columbian Exposition (1893), 440
World Series, 418
World Student Christian Federation, 505
World Trade Center attack, 743, 750(i),
    750–752, 768
World Trade Organization (WTO), 748
World War I (1914–1918), 513–518
    Bonus Army, 564
    casualties in, 583
    debts after, 540
    European alliances and, 517(m)
    fighting of at home, 518–525
    government commissions during, 519
    harsh peace terms after, 583
    isolationism after, 584–585
    making the world safe for democracy,
        515–518
    peace plan after, 523–524
    U-boats in, 514–515
    U.S. entry into, 515
    U.S. neutrality in, 514
    winning hearts and minds in, 520–522

World War II (1933–1945), 581–605
  casualties in, 597
  challenges to isolationism in,
    584–586
  crisis in Europe leading to, 583–584
  economic boom after, 635–636
  ending, 600–602
  in Europe, 597–599, 598(m)
  everyday life in, 590–592
  global war in, 597–604
  Great Depression ended by, 582, 586
  the Holocaust in, 602–604, 603(i)
  the home-front economy in, 587–592
  impact of, 605
  Japanese American internment in, 582,
    595–596
  the Marshall Plan after, 614
  mobilization for, 589
  in the Pacific, 599–600, 600(m)
  paying for, 589
  peacetime challenges after, 635
  race relations and, 592–596
  the road toward, 583–587
  timeline of, 606–607
  U.S. entry into, 586
  U.S. neutrality in, 585
  war declared in, 586–587
  wartime economy in, 587–592
  women in, 589, 605
World Wide Web, 744
Wounded Knee massacre (1890),
  385, 683
Wovoka, 385
Wright, Carroll D., 431
Wright, Frances, 261
Wright, Richard, 571
Wyandot Indians, 165
Wyoming
  cattle ranching in, 389
  Indian reservations in, 381
  internment camps in, 595
  Rock Springs massacre, 396
  Teapot Dome scandal and, 535

XIT Ranch, 389
XYZ affair, 184

Yale College, 192
Yalta Agreement, 600
Yamasee people, 65
Yamasee War, 65–66
Yates v. United States, 624
Ybor City, Florida, 457
Yellow fever, 178, 180, 468
  in Cuban War for Independence, 506
Yellow journalism, 507
Yellowstone National Park, 490(m)
Yeltsin, Boris, 731
Yeomen, 365
Yeomen farmers, 283
Yiddish theater, 440
York (slave), 201
Yorktown, battle of (1781), 154(m), 157
Yosemite National Park, 489, 491
Young, Brigham, 394
Young, Brigham, 257
"Young America" movement, 312
Young Americans for Freedom (YAF), 685
Young Communist League, 609, 661
Young Lords Party (YLP), 683
Young Men's Christian Association (YMCA),
  416
Young Women's Christian Association
  (YWCA), 416, 420, 644
Youth culture, 639(f), 643, 657
  movies and, 643
Yugoslavia, breakup of, 748, 749(m)

Zaharias, Bab "Mildred" Didrikson, 644
Zaire, 629
Zangwill, Israel, 460
Zenger, John Peter, 106–107
Zero option proposal, 722
Zhou Enlai, 615
Zimmermann, Arthur, 516
Zimmermann telegram, 516
Zinc mining, 387
Zion National Park, 490(m)
Zitkala-Sa, 484
Zoning laws, 469
Zoot suit riots, 594
Zoot suits, 594
Zuñi Indians, 21